T0183276

# Lecture Notes in Artificial Intelligence    9120

Subseries of Lecture Notes in Computer Science

More information about this series at http://www.springer.com/series/1244

Leszek Rutkowski · Marcin Korytkowski
Rafal Scherer · Ryszard Tadeusiewicz
Lotfi A. Zadeh · Jacek M. Zurada (Eds.)

# Artificial Intelligence and Soft Computing

14th International Conference, ICAISC 2015
Zakopane, Poland, June 14–18, 2015
Proceedings, Part II

Springer

*Editors*

Leszek Rutkowski
Częstochowa University of Technology
Częstochowa
Poland

Marcin Korytkowski
Częstochowa University of Technology
Częstochowa
Poland

Rafal Scherer
Częstochowa University of Technology
Częstochowa
Poland

Ryszard Tadeusiewicz
AGH University of Science and Technology
Krakow
Poland

Lotfi A. Zadeh
University of California
Berkeley, California
USA

Jacek M. Zurada
University of Louisville
Louisville, Kentucky
USA

ISSN 0302-9743          ISSN 1611-3349   (electronic)
Lecture Notes in Artificial Intelligence
ISBN 978-3-319-19368-7        ISBN 978-3-319-19369-4   (eBook)
DOI 10.1007/978-3-319-19369-4
Library of Congress Control Number: 2015939285

LNCS Sublibrary: SL7 – Artificial Intelligence

Springer Cham Heidelberg New York Dordrecht London

Springer International Publishing AG Switzerland is part of Springer Science+Business Media
(www.springer.com)

# Preface

This volume constitutes the proceedings of the 14th International Conference on Artificial Intelligence and Soft Computing, ICAISC 2015, held in Zakopane, Poland, during June 14–18, 2015. The conference was organized by the Polish Neural Network Society in cooperation with the University of Social Sciences in Łódź, the Institute of Computational Intelligence at the Częstochowa University of Technology, and the IEEE Computational Intelligence Society, Poland Chapter. Previous conferences took place in Kule (1994), Szczyrk (1996), Kule (1997), and Zakopane (1999, 2000, 2002, 2004, 2006, 2008, 2010, 2012, 2013, and 2014) and attracted a large number of papers and internationally recognized speakers: Lotfi A. Zadeh, Hojjat Adeli, Rafal Angryk, Igor Aizenberg, Shun-ichi Amari, Daniel Amit, Piero P. Bonissone, Jim Bezdek, Zdzisław Bubnicki, Andrzej Cichocki, Włodzisław Duch, Pablo A. Estévez, Jerzy Grzymala-Busse, Martin Hagan, Yoichi Hayashi, Akira Hirose, Kaoru Hirota, Hisao Ishibuchi, Er Meng Joo, Janusz Kacprzyk, Jim Keller, Laszlo T. Koczy, Adam Krzyzak, Soo-Young Lee, Derong Liu, Robert Marks, Evangelia Micheli-Tzanakou, Kaisa Miettinen, Henning Müller, Ngoc Thanh Nguyen, Erkki Oja, Witold Pedrycz, Marios M. Polycarpou, José C. Príncipe, Jagath C. Rajapakse, Šarunas Raudys, Enrique Ruspini, Jörg Siekmann, Roman Słowiński, Igor Spiridonov, Boris Stilman, Ponnuthurai Nagaratnam Suganthan, Ryszard Tadeusiewicz, Ah-Hwee Tan, Shiro Usui, Fei-Yue Wang, Jun Wang, Bogdan M. Wilamowski, Ronald Y. Yager, Syozo Yasui, Gary Yen, and Jacek Zurada. The aim of this conference is to build a bridge between traditional artificial intelligence techniques and so-called soft computing techniques. It was pointed out by Lotfi A. Zadeh that "soft computing (SC) is a coalition of methodologies which are oriented toward the conception and design of information/intelligent systems. The principal members of the coalition are: fuzzy logic (FL), neurocomputing (NC), evolutionary computing (EC), probabilistic computing (PC), chaotic computing (CC), and machine learning (ML). The constituent methodologies of SC are, for the most part, complementary and synergistic rather than competitive." These proceedings present both traditional artificial intelligence methods and soft computing techniques. Our goal is to bring together scientists representing both areas of research. This volume is divided into six parts:

- Data Mining,
- Bioinformatics, Biometrics and Medical Applications,
- Concurrent and Parallel Processing,
- Agent Systems, Robotics and Control,
- Artificial Intelligence in Modeling and Simulation,
- Various Problems of Artificial Intelligence.

The conference has attracted a total of 322 submissions from 39 countries and after the review process, 142 papers have been accepted for publication. The ICAISC 2015 hosted the Workshop: Large-Scale Visual Recognition and Machine Learning organized by

- Marcin Korytkowski, Częstochowa University of Technology, Poland,
- Rafał Scherer, Częstochowa University of Technology, Poland,
- Sviatoslav Voloshynovskiy, University of Geneva, Switzerland.

The Workshop was supported by the project "New Perspectives on Intelligent Multimedia Management With Applications in Medicine and Privacy Protecting Systems" cofinanced by a grant from Switzerland through the Swiss Contribution to the Enlarged European Union, and supported by the project "Innovative methods of retrieval and indexing multimedia data using computational intelligence techniques" funded by the National Science Centre. I would like to thank our participants, invited speakers, and reviewers of the papers for their scientific and personal contribution to the conference. The following reviewers were very helpful in reviewing the papers:

| | | |
|---|---|---|
| R. Adamczak | A. Dzieliński | J. Kacprzyk |
| H. Altrabalsi | P. Dziwiński | W. Kamiński |
| S. Amari | S. Ehteram | T. Kaplon |
| T. Babczyński | A. Fanea | A. Kasperski |
| M. Baczyński | B. Filipic | V. Kecman |
| A. Bari | I. Fister | E. Kerre |
| M. Białko | C. Frowd | P. Klęsk |
| L. Bobrowski | M. Gabryel | J. Kluska |
| L. Borzemski | A. Gawęda | L. Koczy |
| J. Botzheim | M. Giergiel | Z. Kokosinski |
| T. Burczyński | P. Głomb | A. Kołakowska |
| R. Burduk | Z. Gomółka | J. Konopacki |
| K. Cetnarowicz | M. Gorawski | J. Korbicz |
| L. Chmielewski | M. Gorzałczany | P. Korohoda |
| W. Cholewa | G. Gosztolya | J. Koronacki |
| M. Choraś | D. Grabowski | M. Korytkowski |
| K. Choros | E. Grabska | J. Kościelny |
| P. Cichosz | K. Grąbczewski | L. Kotulski |
| R. Cierniak | C. Grosan | Z. Kowalczuk |
| P. Ciskowski | M. Grzenda | M. Kraft |
| S. Concetto | J. Grzymala-Busse | M. Kretowski |
| B. Cyganek | J. Hähner | D. Krol |
| J. Cytowski | H. Haberdar | B. Kryzhanovsky |
| R. Czabański | R. Hampel | A. Krzyzak |
| I. Czarnowski | Z. Hendzel | A. Kubiak |
| J. de la Rosa | F. Hermann | E. Kucharska |
| K. Dembczynski | Z. Hippe | J. Kulikowski |
| J. Dembski | A. Horzyk | O. Kurasova |
| N. Derbel | M. Hrebień | V. Kurkova |
| G. Dobrowolski | E. Hrynkiewicz | M. Kurzyński |
| W. Duch | I. Imani | J. Kusiak |
| L. Dutkiewicz | D. Jakóbczak | N. Labroche |
| L. Dymowa | A. Janczak | J. Liao |

# Organization

ICAISC 2015 was organized by the Polish Neural Network Society in cooperation with the University of Social Sciences in Łódź, the Institute of Computational Intelligence at Częstochowa University of Technology, and the IEEE Computational Intelligence Society, Poland Chapter and with technical sponsorship of the IEEE Computational Intelligence Society.

## ICAISC Chairpersons

### Honorary chairmen

| | |
|---|---|
| Lotfi A. Zadeh | University of California, Berkeley, USA |
| Hojjat Adeli | The Ohio State University, USA |
| Jacek Żurada | University of Louisville, USA |

### General chairman

| | |
|---|---|
| Leszek Rutkowski | Częstochowa University of Technology, Poland |

### Co-chairmen

| | |
|---|---|
| Włodzisław Duch | Nicolaus Copernicus University, Poland |
| Janusz Kacprzyk | Polish Academy of Sciences, Poland |
| Józef Korbicz | University of Zielona Góra, Poland |
| Ryszard Tadeusiewicz | AGH University of Science and Technology, Poland |

## ICAISC Program Committee

| | |
|---|---|
| Rafał Adamczak, Poland | Bernadette Bouchon-Meunier, France |
| Cesare Alippi, Italy | Tadeusz Burczynski, Poland |
| Shun-ichi Amari, Japan | Andrzej Cader, Poland |
| Rafal A. Angryk, USA | Juan Luis Castro, Spain |
| Jarosław Arabas, Poland | Yen-Wei Chen, Japan |
| Robert Babuska, Netherlands | Wojciech Cholewa, Poland |
| Ildar Z. Batyrshin, Russia | Fahmida N. Chowdhury, USA |
| James C. Bezdek, Australia | Andrzej Cichocki, Japan |
| Marco Block-Berlitz, Germany | Paweł Cichosz, Poland |
| Leon Bobrowski, Poland | Krzysztof Cios, USA |
| Piero P. Bonissone, USA | Ian Cloete, Germany |

Erkki Oja, Finland
Stanisław Osowski, Poland
Nikhil R. Pal, India
Maciej Patan, Poland
Witold Pedrycz, Canada
Leonid Perlovsky, USA
Andrzej Pieczyński, Poland
Andrzej Piegat, Poland
Vincenzo Piuri, Italy
Lech Polkowski, Poland
Marios M. Polycarpou, Cyprus
Danil Prokhorov, USA
Anna Radzikowska, Poland
Ewaryst Rafajłowicz, Poland
Sarunas Raudys, Lithuania
Olga Rebrova, Russia
Vladimir Red'ko, Russia
Raúl Rojas, Germany
Imre J. Rudas, Hungary
Enrique H. Ruspini, USA
Khalid Saeed, Poland
Dominik Sankowski, Poland
Norihide Sano, Japan
Robert Schaefer, Poland
Rudy Setiono, Singapore
Pawel Sevastianow, Poland
Jennie Si, USA
Peter Sincak, Slovakia
Andrzej Skowron, Poland
Ewa Skubalska-Rafajłowicz, Poland
Roman Słowiński, Poland
Tomasz G. Smolinski, USA
Czesław Smutnicki, Poland
Pilar Sobrevilla, Spain
Janusz Starzyk, USA
Jerzy Stefanowski, Poland

Vitomir Štruc, Slovenia
Pawel Strumillo, Poland
Ron Sun, USA
Johan Suykens, Belgium
Piotr Szczepaniak, Poland
Eulalia J. Szmidt, Poland
Przemysław Śliwiński, Poland
Adam Słowik, Poland
Jerzy Świątek, Poland
Hideyuki Takagi, Japan
Yury Tiumentsev, Russia
Vicenç Torra, Spain
Burhan Turksen, Canada
Shiro Usui, Japan
Michael Wagenknecht, Germany
Tomasz Walkowiak, Poland
Deliang Wang, USA
Jun Wang, Hong Kong
Lipo Wang, Singapore
Zenon Waszczyszyn, Poland
Paul Werbos, USA
Slawo Wesolkowski, Canada
Sławomir Wiak, Poland
Bernard Widrow, USA
Kay C. Wiese, Canada
Bogdan M. Wilamowski, USA
Donald C. Wunsch, USA
Maciej Wygralak, Poland
Roman Wyrzykowski, Poland
Ronald R. Yager, USA
Xin-She Yang, United Kingdom
Gary Yen, USA
John Yen, USA
Sławomir Zadrożny, Poland
Ali M.S. Zalzala, United Arab Emirates

## ICAISC Organizing Committee

Rafał Scherer
Łukasz Bartczuk
Piotr Dziwiński
Marcin Gabryel
Marcin Korytkowski

Secretary
Organizing Committee Member
Organizing Committee Member
Finance Chair
Databases and Internet Submissions

# Contents – Part II

## Data Mining

## Bioinformatics, Biometrics and Medical Applications

## Concurrent Parallel Processing

## Agent Systems, Robotics and Control

## Artificial Intelligence in Modeling and Simulation

# Various Problems of Artificial Intelligence

# Contents – Part I

## Neural Networks and Their Applications

## Fuzzy Systems and Their Applications

# Evolutionary Algorithms and Their Applications

## Classification and Estimation

# Computer Vision, Image and Speech Analysis

## Workshop: Large-Scale Visual Recognition and Machine Learning

# Data Mining

# Improvement of the Multiple-View Learning Based on the Self-Organizing Maps

Tomasz Galkowski[✉], Artur Starczewski, and Xiuju Fu

Institute of Computational Intelligence, Częstochowa University of Technology,
Al. Armii Krajowej 36, 42-200 Częstochowa, Poland
{tomasz.galkowski,artur.starczewski}@iisi.pcz.pl
Institute of High Performance Computing,
1 Fusionopolis Way, # 16-16 Connexis North, Singapore 138632, Singapore
fuxj@ihpc.a-star.edu.sq

**Abstract.** Big data sets and variety of data types lead to new types of problems in modern intelligent data analysis. This requires the development of new techniques and models. One of the important subjects is to reveal and indicate heterogeneous of non-trivial features of a large database. Original techniques of modelling, data mining, pattern recognition, machine learning in such fields like commercial behaviour of Internet users, social networks analysis, management and investigation of various databases in static or dynamic states have been recently investigated. Many techniques discovering hidden structures in the data set like clustering and projection of data from high-dimensional spaces have been developed. In this paper we have proposed a model for multiple view unsupervised clustering based on Kohonen self-organizing-map method.

## 1   Introduction to the Issue

Lots of methods discovering hidden structures in the big data sets base on variations of correlation analysis, see e.g. [41], [40]. The curse of dimensionality has the unpleasant features in practice: the requirements for the memory space and CPUs time. Most known techniques accent the automation and efficiency of the data analysis systems, but omit the effectiveness of them. Therefore, techniques leading to reduction of dimensionality of data sets [21] or reduction of attributes in the rough sets [20] are applied by many researchers. Also Kohonen maps perform a low-dimensional visualization of high-dimensional data [25]. Big data sets with undiscovered structure are inherent e.g. in the following areas. In earth sciences, for example, the detailed information about the energy reflected or emitted by the different materials has been used in mineral and geological exploration, forest biomass estimation, urban monitoring, cultivation assessment, detection of areas with a relatively hot temperature (possible seismic activity) etc. [40]. Analysed images are composed of tens to thousands of variables. They represent the amount of solar energy reflected by the sensed objects at different wavelengths (hyperspectral images). During the analysis information is divided into narrowband pass channels ranging from visible to infrared frequencies.

© Springer International Publishing Switzerland 2015
L. Rutkowski et al. (Eds.): ICAISC 2015, Part II, LNAI 9120, pp. 3–12, 2015.
DOI: 10.1007/978-3-319-19369-4_1

In social sciences and marketing behavioral analysis of likes of potential customers lead to the precise commercial offer. The similar groups of web surfers probably should buy similar products in internet shops. Collected data on visited web pages, clicked links etc. could help in making the characteristics or profiles of such groups. The multiple view approach arises from the fact that the web pages have following multiple representations [7]:

- the term vector corresponding to words occurring in the pages themselves,
- the graph of hyper-links between the pages, and
- the term vectors corresponding to words contained in anchor text of links pointing to the pages.

Solving the problem of clustering of web-surfers leads to an appropriate offer for the possible customer expectation. As "views" we mean multiple representations in different spaces of the same multidimensional samples. The different representations often could have different statistical properties, then the question how to find a compatible pattern from multiple representations is a challenge. Note that the view in each space could have different measures. We are still looking for the answer of the question: does a prototype vector of patterns, trained basing on multiple representations is better, more accurate and robust than one based on a single view? Many researchers are inspired to work for satisfactory solutions relating tasks like multi-view clustering [7] and intelligent data analysis [43]. The space of interests with respect to initial knowledge could be pointed and developed as supervised, semi-supervised and unsupervised methods. The multiple-view learning using the co-training method (semi-supervised), was introduced and investigated in [6] by Blum and Mitchell. Next researchers (see e.g. [12], [8], [19], [24], [30]) extend the idea of co-training to explicitly measure the degree of agreement between the rules in different views. A few works on multiple view clustering [5], [35], [44] are focused on the simpler cases of two views with limiting assumptions. The spectral clustering algorithms using the minimizing-disagreement rule and the normalized cut from a single view to multiple views were investigated in [35] and [44] respectively. The authors also investigated related new methods like e.g. ensemble clustering [17], [39] which combines different clusters for a single view data or multi-type clustering [38] using attribute information for clustering process.

Similar algorithms derived from artificial intelligence methodology have been applied for variety of tasks (see e.g. [1], [2], [10], [13], [14], [15], [26], [27], [31], [33], [34], [36], [37]).

In this paper, we investigate the method of multiple-view unsupervised clustering derived from the Kohonen SOM (Self-Organizing-Map) algorithm. This approach leads to the dimensionality reduction and realise the initial grouping of the data set. In the classification phase for the clustering process we used in our previous work [18] the well known k-means method. In this article we present the results of implementation of the different approach: fuzzy c-means classifier. In Section 2 we describe the main scope of the article. In Section 3, the experimental results on artificial data sets are illustrated.

## 2 Main Overview of Work and Used Tools

This paper is a proposition of a distributed framework for unsupervised clustering methodology. We apply the Kohonen ([25]) Self Organizing Map (SOM) for initial grouping of the data. The SOM has the natural convenience to perform reduction of dimensionality of the data set, allows to discover the internal structure of the data and visualize the results in two dimensional space. The SOM algorithm is used in unsupervised mode. In the next phase of our framework the fuzzy c-means algorithm (see [42]) is used to find the optimal (in a certain sense) representation for the previously learnt classes. The final step uses Xie-Beni index as a validity measure of our fuzzy clustering.

Now we present a brief description of operation rules of algorithms. The Figure 1 shows the base structure of the Kohonen SOM network. The input vectors (feature space) are projected to the network at input layer and the classes are formed on the output layer basing of similarities and differences of inputs.

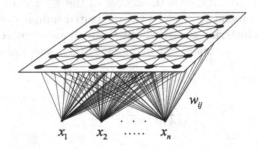

**Fig. 1.** The base structure of the Kohonen SOM network

Algorithm operates as follows:

1. Initialize weights of the map nodes (for instance: random or uniform)
2. Pass input vector to the input nodes
3. Calculate the Euclidean distance between input vector and all nodes, finding the smallest distance output node (so called: winner node).
4. Update weights of the winning node and its neighbour by the formulas:

$$w_{n+1}(k,j) = w_n(k,j) + \xi(n)[x(j) - w_n(k,j)] \tag{1}$$

for the input weights of winner node, and

$$w_{n+1}(m,j) = w_n(m,j) + d(m,n,k)\xi(n)[x(j) - w_n(k,j)] \tag{2}$$

for the neighbour nodes inside the area around the winner with radius defined by function $d(m,n,k)$ (decreasing function depending on the number of iteration);

where $n$ - number of iteration, $k$ - number of winning node, $j - j'th$ coordinate of the vector, $\xi(n)$ - decreasing function of modification weights depending on number of iteration, $x(j)$ input pattern vector $j'th$ coordinate.

5. Repeat above steps until a measure of convergence (e.g. recursive mean square error method RMS) reaches assumed limit level.

The self-organizing-map performs in natural manner human brain method of organizing information. The outcome of the algorithm is a low-dimensional representation of the input space of the training samples, called a map. SOM reduces the dimensionality of the input space preserving its topological properties.

The fuzzy c-algorithm was formulated by Dunn [16] and developed by Bezdek [4]. This method of clustering allows the elements of data to belong to more than one clusters. It is based on minimization of the following measure function:

$$J_m = \sum_{i=1}^{N} \sum_{j=1}^{C} u_{ij}^m \|x_i - c_j\|^2 \tag{3}$$

where $u_{ij}$ is the degree of membership of $x_i$ in the cluster $j$, $x_i$ is the $i-th$ of $d$-dimensional measured data, $c_j$ is the center of the $j-th$ cluster, and $\|\cdot\|$ is a norm expressing the similarity between the measured sample and the center, and $1 \leq m < \infty$. Fuzzy clustering is carried out through an iterative optimization of the function (3), with the update of membership $u_{ij}$ and the cluster center $c_j$ by:

$$u_{ij} = \left[ \left( \sum_{k=1}^{C} \frac{\|x_i - c_j\|}{\|x_i - c_k\|} \right)^{\frac{2}{m-1}} \right]^{-1} \tag{4}$$

and

$$c_j = \frac{\sum_{i=1}^{N} u_{ij}^m \cdot x_i}{\sum_{i=1}^{N} u_{ij}^m} \tag{5}$$

The iteration process stops when

$$\max_{ij} \left\{ \left| u_{ij}^{(k+1)} - u_{ij}^{(k)} \right| \right\} < \varepsilon \tag{6}$$

where $k$ is the number of iteration step, and $\varepsilon$ is a termination criterion constant. Algorithm operates as follows:

1. Initialize $\mathbf{U}^{(0)} = \left[ u_{ij}^{(0)} \right]$ matrix;
2. At $k-th$ step calculate the vector of centers $C^{(k)} = [c_j]$ with $\mathbf{U}^{(k)}$ using expression (5);
3. Update $\mathbf{U}^{(k)}$, $\mathbf{U}^{(k+1)}$ using (4);
4. Repeat above steps until (6) is fulfilled.

The fuzzy behaviour of this algorithm is caused by factors of matrix $\mathbf{U}^{(k)}$ which are the numbers between 0 and 1, and represent the degree of membership between data and centers of clusters. The last phase of our work is the test of validity of performed clustering. We applied the Xie-Beni index (see [42]) as a measure of compactness and intra-cluster diversity of obtained partitions. This index is a function of the data set and the centroids of the clusters. The Xie-Beni factor (for details see: [42]) is in the form:

$$
u_{XB}(U, V; X) = \frac{\sum\limits_{j=1}^{k} \sum\limits_{i=1}^{N} u_{ij}^2 \|x_i - c_j\|^2}{n \cdot \left( \min_{(j \neq l)} \|c_j - c_l\|^2 \right)} \tag{7}
$$

where $n$ is a whole number of objects in set. Its sense may be understood as a ratio of the total variation of the partition and the centroids and the separation of the centroids vectors.

# 3 Simulation Experiments Results

In simulation experiments we used the artificially generated sets, named View 1 and View 2, consisting of data with 30 attributes and 4 clusters each. Detailed information on sets is presented in Table 1 and Table 2.

**Table 1.** Detailed information of the data set View 1

| Cluster No. | Number of attributes | Standard deviation | Number of instances |
|---|---|---|---|
| 0 | 30 | 0.16 | 36 |
| 1 | 30 | 0.14 | 11 |
| 2 | 30 | 0.07 | 48 |
| 3 | 30 | 0.28 | 48 |

Total number of instances in View 1 is 143.

**Table 2.** Detailed information of the data set View 2

| Cluster No. | Number of attributes | Standard deviation | Number of instances |
|---|---|---|---|
| 0 | 30 | 0.10 | 53 |
| 1 | 30 | 0.10 | 22 |
| 2 | 30 | 0.07 | 68 |
| 3 | 30 | 0.14 | 67 |

Total number of instances in View 2 is 210.

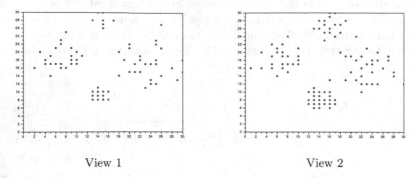

| View 1 | View 2 |

**Fig. 2.** Graphic representation of the classification of Views 1 and 2 by the Kohonen SOM

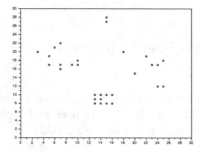

**Fig. 3.** The diagram of resulting patterns combined from two views

The Kohonen SOM - the net of 30x30 neurons - applied for testing sets, led to results presented in Figure 2. The final map of neurons is a logical multiplication of the matrices, which represent the activity of neurons in different views. Values of active neurons (visible on diagrams) are equal to one, the remaining values of neurons are zeros (not shown). The final map of the active neurons, which defines the prototype vector is shown in Figure 3.

Next we combined obtained views by the operation of logical multiplication. Figure 3 shows active neurons belonging to both previous views jointly. Then the active neurons weights were applied with the Fuzzy c-means clustering procedure as the input vectors. The Xie-Beni factor $u_{XB}$ was used for validation of obtained results - reaching its minimum value $u_{XB_{min}} = 0.0583558$. The resulting pattern consists of four clusters. The validated centers, representing optimal patterns of the tested data sets, are sixty-dimensional vectors - shown in Table 3.

**Table 3.** Detailed information of the validated centers

| Centre No. | Coordinates in D=60 |
|---|---|
| 0 | [1.970, 1.000, 1.070, 1.060, 0.978, 1.100, 0.980, 1.060, 1.040, 1.000, 0.997, 0.995, 1.030, 1.020, 0.981, 1.010, 0.990, 1.050, 1.020, 1.060, 0.966, 1.040, 0.948, 1.040, 1.050, 0.990, 1.050, 1.010, 1.020, 1.010, 1.200, 0.562, 0.654, 0.647, 0.610, 0.632, 0.644, 0.611, 0.644, 0.619, 0.651, 0.657, 0.617, 0.633, 0.604, 0.599, 0.624, 0.638, 0.631, 0.607, 0.613, 0.634, 0.612, 0.600, 0.618, 0.614, 0.640, 0.608, 0.621, 0.663] |
| 1 | [0.987, 1.010, 1.020, 1.060, 0.991, 1.020, 1.040, 0.990, 0.998, 1.020, 1.030, 1.030, 0.982, 0.992, 1.030, 0.998, 1.000, 1.050, 1.030, 1.030, 0.968, 1.020, 0.995, 1.010, 0.997, 1.020, 1.020, 1.010, 1.060, 1.050, 0.610, 0.608, 0.627, 0.633, 0.601, 0.627, 0.632, 0.623, 0.615, 0.623, 0.620, 0.619, 0.627, 0.611, 0.595, 0.601, 0.607, 0.65, 0.623, 0.623, 0.586, 0.618, 0.594, 0.625, 0.611, 0.618, 0.640, 0.610, 0.637, 0.636] |
| 2 | [1.980, 2.100, 1.050, 0.976, 1.050, 1.090, 0.989, 1.080, 1.080, 1.050, 1.030, 0.972, 1.020, 1.020, 0.931, 1.040, 1.010, 1.090, 0.989, 1.020, 1.020, 1.020, 0.968, 1.060, 1.070, 1.020, 1.080, 1.010, 1.030, 1.030, 1.210, 1.240, 0.638, 0.635, 0.615, 0.614, 0.613, 0.604, 0.625, 0.630, 0.644, 0.656, 0.608, 0.628, 0.595, 0.625, 0.600, 0.616, 0.604, 0.603, 0.639, 0.629, 0.654, 0.612, 0.607, 0.610, 0.614, 0.619, 0.607, 0.630] |
| 3 | [1.030, 2.030, 1.020, 1.000, 1.030, 1.020, 1.030, 1.010, 1.030, 1.030, 1.040, 1.020, 1.020, 1.020, 1.000, 1.020, 1.020, 1.050, 1.010, 1.000, 1.020, 1.020, 1.020, 1.010, 1.010, 1.030, 1.030, 1.010, 1.030, 1.040, 0.631, 1.220, 0.614, 0.604, 0.614, 0.624, 0.612, 0.618, 0.621, 0.632, 0.624, 0.614, 0.614, 0.619, 0.604, 0.636, 0.618, 0.631, 0.611, 0.621, 0.627, 0.619, 0.617, 0.622, 0.617, 0.623, 0.625, 0.620, 0.627, 0.619] |

## 4   Conclusions and Remarks

In this paper, we have proposed the distributed framework for multiple view classification task. Our method is based on Kohonen Self-Organizing-Map and fuzzy c-means clustering method. The evaluation of the numerical experiments for synthetic data sets is presented. The simulations show the effectiveness and great potential of the proposed approach. The framework could be applied to various types of multiple view data sets. Our methodology seems to be applicable to many data mining problems including stream data ([23], [32]). In the future research we plan to develop new algorithms for multiple view unsupervised learning.

# References

1. Aldahdooh, R.T., Ashour, W.: DSMK-Means Density-Based Split-and-Merge K-Means Clustering Algorithm. Journal of Artificial Intelligence and Soft Computing Research 3(1), 51–71 (2013)
2. Bazarganigilani, M.: Optimized Image Feature Selection Using Pairwise Classifiers. Journal of Artificial Intelligence and Soft Computing Research 1(2), 147–153 (2011)
3. Berkhin, P.: Survey of clustering data mining techniques. Technical report, Accrue Software, San Jose, CA (2002)
4. Bezdek, J.C.: Pattern Recognition with Fuzzy Objective Function Algoritms. Plenum Press, New York (1981)
5. Bickel, S., Scheffer, T.: Multi-view clustering. In: ICDM 2004, pp. 19–26 (2004)
6. Blum, A., Mitchell, T.: Combining labeled and unlabeled data with co-training. In: COLT 1998, pp. 92–100 (1998)
7. Long, B., Yu, P.S., Zhang, Z.: A General Model for Multiple View Unsupervised Learning. In: Proceedings of the 2008 SIAM International Conference on Data Mining, pp. 822–833 (2008)
8. Brefeld, U., Scheffer, T.: Co-em support vector learning. In: ICML 2004, p. 16 (2004)
9. Camps-Valls, G., Bruzzone, L.: Kernel-based methods for hyperspectral image classification. IEEE Trans. Geosci. Remote Sens. 43, 1351–1362 (2005)
10. Chang, Y., Wang, Y., Chen, C., Ricanek, K.: Improved Image-Based Automatic Gender Classification by Feature Selection. Journal of Artificial Intelligence and Soft Computing Research 1(3), 241–253 (2011)
11. Cierniak, R., Rutkowski, L.: On image compression by competitive neural networks and optimal linear predictors. Signal Processing: Image Communication - a Eurasip Journal 15(6), 559–565 (2000)
12. Collins, M., Singer, Y.: Unsupervised models for named entity classification (1999)
13. Cpałka, K., Rutkowski, L.: Flexible Takagi-Sugeno Fuzzy Systems. In: Proceedings of the International Joint Conference on Neural Networks 2005, Montreal, pp. 1764–1769 (2005)
14. Cpałka, K., Rutkowski, L.: A New Method for Designing and Reduction of Neuro-fuzzy Systems. In: Proceedings of the 2006 IEEE International Conference on Fuzzy Systems (IEEE World Congress on Computational Intelligence, WCCI 2006), Vancouver, BC, Canada, pp. 8510–8516 (2006)
15. Cpalka, K., Rebrova, O., Nowicki, R., et al.: On design of flexible neuro-fuzzy systems for nonlinear modelling. International Journal of General Systems 42(6, special issue si), 706–720 (2013)
16. Dunn, J.C.: A Fuzzy Relative of the ISODATA Process and Its Use in Detecting Compact Well-Separated Clusters. Journal of Cybernetics 3, 32–57 (1973)
17. Fern X.Z., Brodley C.E.: Solving cluster ensemble problems by bipartite graph partitioning. In ICML 2004 (2004)
18. Gałkowski, T., Starczewski, A.: An Application of the Self-Organizing Map to Multiple View Unsupervised Learning. In: Rutkowski, L., Korytkowski, M., Scherer, R., Tadeusiewicz, R., Zadeh, L.A., Zurada, J.M. (eds.) ICAISC 2012, Part II. LNCS, vol. 7268, pp. 181–187. Springer, Heidelberg (2012)
19. Ghani, R.: Combining labeled and unlabeled data for text classification with a large number of categories. In: ICDM 2001, pp. 597–598 (2001)
20. Hedar, A.R., Wang, J., Fukushima, M.: Tabu search for attribute reduction in rough set theory. Soft Computing 12, 909–918 (2008)

21. Herawan, T., Ghazali, R., Deris, M.M.: Soft Set Theoretic Approach for Dimensionality Reduction. International Journal of Database Theory and Application 3(2) (June 2010)
22. Jain, A.K., Murty, M.N., Flynn, P.J.: Data cluster-ing: a review. ACM Computing Surveys 31(3), 264–323 (1999)
23. Jaworski, M., Duda, P., Pietruczuk, L.: On fuzzy clustering of data streams with concept drift. In: Rutkowski, L., Korytkowski, M., Scherer, R., Tadeusiewicz, R., Zadeh, L.A., Zurada, J.M. (eds.) ICAISC 2012, Part II. LNCS, vol. 7268, pp. 82–91. Springer, Heidelberg (2012)
24. Karypis, G., Kumar, V.: A fast and high quality mul-tilevel scheme for partitioning irregular graphs. SIAM J. Sci. Comput. 20(1), 359–392 (1998)
25. Kohonen, T.: The Self-Organizing Map. Proceedings of the IEEE 78(9) (September 1990)
26. Korytkowski, M., Rutkowski, L., Scherer, R.: From ensemble of fuzzy classifiers to single fuzzy rule base classifier. In: Rutkowski, L., Tadeusiewicz, R., Zadeh, L.A., Zurada, J.M. (eds.) ICAISC 2008. LNCS (LNAI), vol. 5097, pp. 265–272. Springer, Heidelberg (2008)
27. Korytkowski, M., Nowicki, R., Rutkowski, L., Scherer, R.: AdaBoost Ensemble of DCOG Rough–Neuro–Fuzzy Systems. In: Jędrzejowicz, P., Nguyen, N.T., Hoang, K. (eds.) ICCCI 2011, Part I. LNCS, vol. 6922, pp. 62–71. Springer, Heidelberg (2011)
28. Long, B., Yu, P.S., Zhang, Z.: A General Model for Multiple View Unsupervised Learning. In: Proceedings of the 2008 SIAM International Conference on Data Mining, pp. 822–833 (2008)
29. MacQueen, J.B.: Some Methods for classification and Analysis of Multivariate Observations. In: Proceedings of 5th Berkeley Symposium on Mathematical Statistics and Probability, vol. 1, pp. 281–297. University of California Press, Berkeley (1967)
30. Nigam, K., Ghani, R.: Analyzing the effectiveness and applicability of co-training. In: CIKM 2000, pp. 86–93 (2000)
31. Nowicki, R.: Rough Neuro-Fuzzy Structures for Classification With Missing Data. IEEE Transactions on Systems Man and Cybernetics Part B-Cybernetics 39(6), 1334–1347 (2009)
32. Pietruczuk, L., Duda, P., Jaworski, M.: A new fuzzy classifier for data streams. In: Rutkowski, L., Korytkowski, M., Scherer, R., Tadeusiewicz, R., Zadeh, L.A., Zurada, J.M. (eds.) ICAISC 2012, Part I. LNCS, vol. 7267, pp. 318–324. Springer, Heidelberg (2012)
33. Romaszewski, M., Gawron, P., Opozda, S.: Dimensionality Reduction of Dynamic Mesh Animations Using HO-SVD. Journal of Artificial Intelligence and Soft Computing Research 3(3), 277–289 (2013)
34. Rutkowski, L., Przybył, A., Cpałka, K., Er, M.J.: Online Speed Profile Generation for Industrial Machine Tool Based on Neuro-fuzzy Approach. In: Rutkowski, L., Scherer, R., Tadeusiewicz, R., Zadeh, L.A., Zurada, J.M. (eds.) ICAISC 2010, Part II. LNCS (LNAI), vol. 6114, pp. 645–650. Springer, Heidelberg (2010)
35. Sa, V.R.: Spectral clustering with two views. In: ICML Workshop on Learning with Multiple Views (2005)
36. Starczewski, J.T., Scherer, R., Korytkowski, M., Nowicki, R.: Modular Type-2 Neuro-fuzzy Systems. In: Wyrzykowski, R., Dongarra, J., Karczewski, K., Wasniewski, J. (eds.) PPAM 2007. LNCS, vol. 4967, pp. 570–578. Springer, Heidelberg (2008)

37. Tambouratzis, T., Chernikova, D., Pzsit, I.: Pulse Shape Discrimination of Neurons and Gamma Rays Using Kohonen Artificial Neural Networks. Journal of Artificial Intelligence and Soft Computing Research 3(2), 77–88 (2013)
38. Taskar, B., Segal, E., Koller, D.: Probabilistic classification and clustering in relational data. In: Proceeding of IJCAI 2001 (2001)
39. Topchy, A., Jain, A.K., Punch, W.: Combining multiple weak clusterings. In: Proceedings of the Third IEEE International Conference on Data Mining, p. 331 (2003)
40. Volpi, M., Matasci, G., Kanevski, M., Tuia, D.: Semi-supervised multiview embedding for hyperspectral data classification. Neurocomputing 145, 427–437 (2014)
41. Wang, Y., Gongxuan, Z., Qian, J.-B.: ApproxCCA: An approximate correlation analysis algorithm for multidimensional data streams. Knowledge-Based Systems 24, 952–962 (2011)
42. Xie, L.X., Beni, G.: Validity measure for fuzzy clustering. IEEE Transactions on Pattern Analysis and Machine Intelligence 3(8), 841–847 (1991)
43. Chen, Y., Yao, Y.: A multiview approach for intelligent data analysis based on data operators. Information Sciences 178, 1–20 (2008)
44. Zhou, D., Burge, C.J.C.: Spectral clustering and transductive learning with multiple views. In: ICML 2007, pp. 1159–1166 (2007)

# Natural Language Processing Methods Used for Automatic Prediction Mechanism of Related Phenomenon

Krystian Horecki[1] and Jacek Mazurkiewicz[2(✉)]

[1] Nokia Networks, Technology Center Wroclaw, Poland
ul. Strzegomska 36, 53-611 Wroclaw, Poland
Krystian.Horecki@nokia.com
[2] Department of Computer Engineering, Wroclaw University of Technology
ul. Wybrzeze Wyspianskiego 27, 50-370 Wroclaw, Poland
Jacek.Mazurkiewicz@pwr.edu.pl

**Abstract.** The paper presents an idea to combine variety of Natural Language Processing techniques with different classification methods as a tool for automatic prediction mechanism of related phenomenon. Different types of preprocessing techniques are used and verified, in order to find the best set of them. It is assumed that such approach allows to recognize the phenomenon which is related to the text. Research uses the real input from the big data systems. The news website articles are the source of raw text data. The paper proposes the new, promising ways of automatic data and content mining methods for the big data systems. The presented accuracy results are much better than average classification for sentimental analysis done by the human.

## 1 Introduction

The number of web pages which are available on the Internet has grown from 10 million to more than 150 billion from 2001 to 2009. The enormous number of Internet users together with vastly increasing amount of web content push engineers to find new ways of automatic data and content mining methods for the big data systems. Content of this paper concerns topic of raw text data classification using multiple techniques and classifiers. The main aim of this paper was to show how our additional techniques could improve classification accuracy with different classifiers [1]. Studies were based on idea to check whether it is possible to categorize raw text by some particular phenomenon, which relates to it, using text mining, Natural Language Processing and multiple classification methods. Paper tries to answer the question if Natural Language Processing methods can be used as an input for automatic mechanism to predict related phenomena. Whole research was based on English language as it is the most popular language used in the web [16][20]. A human can recognize if given data concerns some particular phenomenon, e.g. war, disaster, or more general one e.g. being positive or negative. It is very hard to implement human-like detection

© Springer International Publishing Switzerland 2015
L. Rutkowski et al. (Eds.): ICAISC 2015, Part II, LNAI 9120, pp. 13–24, 2015.
DOI: 10.1007/978-3-319-19369-4_2

mechanism of relations, which could work with various text data types and give high classification accuracy. The assumption is that text which has some particular phenomenon should contain unique features for this phenomenon, which could be extracted using NLP [10].

The first area for which existing solutions should be shown is sentiment analysis. The topic has been covered by many approaches and implementations, where one of them is WordNet-Affect project created and described by Carlo Strapparava and Alessandro Valitutti [18]. It assumed a usage of WordNet text corpora as a base for affective categorization of particular words. As in case of regular WordNet corpora, here each word received at least one label describing this word in connection with such characteristics as emotion or mood. This kind of categorization is later useful for sentimental analysis.

A bit different approach was presented by Stefano Baccianella, Andrea Esuli, and Fabrizio Sebastiani [5], who created text corpora also based on WordNet but included categorization of words for particular sentiment. Each element in the net was categorized into three types: negative, positive and neutral. Authors created natural language processing base later used for text categorization and sentiment analysis. Complete solution and research in this area was presented by Bo Pang and Lillian Lee [15]. Authors created sentiment analysis solution, which was based on movie reviews which are tend to be sentimental oriented. During the research several machine learning techniques has been used in order to check best possible solution. Authors used IMDB reviews set for training purpose and results validation. The used text corpora allowed to base training on huge amount of text, which could express most language details regarding sentimental analysis. Second important part for this research of Natural Language Processing area is text simplification. Simplification of text was described by Beata Beigman Klebanov, Kevin Knight, and Daniel Marcu [9], who implemented the algorithm of automatic phrases simplification, which could be used for later processing of the text. R. Chandrasekar, B. Srinivas [2] also tried to cover the topic of text simplification and presented few approaches for it.

## 2  Natural Language Processing Techniques

Natural language processing is an approach which allow to find meaning of the free text [6]. The first technique which should be described for NLP is tokenization. It is cutting string into still useful linguistic units. Tokenization can be done using given regular expressions in order to reach more advanced text split, which allow to control a tokenization process. There are many approaches of tokenization, e.g. the most simple one is tokenization using whitespaces [8]. Another method is a tokenization with the usage of regular expressions. It gives much better control over the process and it can be extended with the usage of text corporas or even machine learning techniques such as regression, as it can give better results for more complicated text data [14]. Another NLP technique which was used during the research is a lemmatization, which is a transformation of word into base form. This kind of a base form is called lemma. The lemmatization matches words which basically have the same meaning but differ in form (e.g. plural or singular). The lemmatization is a normalization process which can be applied to text in order to get the as simple version of words as possible. It simplifies the processed text and it gives benefits during later text data usage such as text categorization [11]. Very useful concept which was extensively used during the research is WordNet. It is a lexical database of the English language. It groups words within synonymic groups which can be called synsets [13]. It is possible to get information about relation between words, such as hypernyms, antonyms,nouns related to adjectives, root adjectives [22]. WordNet is accessible with some libraries like NLTK framework and allows to find relations which are required during text mining.

Topic covered by the research is a sentimental analysis which is also within a scope of natural language processing. It is a categorization of a text into few given subjective groups e.g., emotions, opinion or mood. The sentimental analysis is usually applied for whole texts in order to get information about selected feature.

# 3 Research Design and Methodology

## 3.1 Source Data Processing Methods

The data used for research was taken from web pages containing news articles from different categories such as www.bbc.com, www.cnn.com, www.yahoo.com, in order to reach a maximal level of accuracy and to reflect real live usage. It was assumed that the data extracted from a collection of articles should contain a title, an author and an actual article text.

Raw texts which can be found in articles, books and web pages are full of elements which do not introduce any additional information and are useful mostly by humans [21][19]. Such elements could be useful only when text would be analyzed from the perspective of the human, not the machine which is a modern computer. It's not trivial to determine which exactly parts of the raw text should be removed in order to reduce noises crated by uninformative elements. Our idea was to divide text filtering process into three main parts called later levels of text filtering. Each level of the filtering uses additional techniques which should give better results than other once. It is a very important part of the categorization process because it determines categorization accuracy due to interrelation between information and noise amount, which could have great influence on results. Please find the description of levels below. *Level 1* - filtering is mostly focused on short words, stop words and punctuation marks removal, including also conversion to lowercase. It also uses lemmatisation [4] techniques. This level contains techniques which are commonly used in text processing and will be later used as a reference for results analysis. *Level 2* - filtering is based on semantic trees analysis and removal of similar words according to the neighborhood in the tree. It was our idea to combine such extensive related words merging with text categorization. Diagram of the 2nd filtering level was presented in the Figure 1. *Level 3* - filtering is connected with removal of adjectives and replacing them with corresponding nouns. The method should give accuracy enhancement in case of using words such as "Polish" and "Poland", so we could get the same word two times instead of having two different words. Our idea was to combine this method with text categorization to check if it gives satisfying results.

The result of input data processing was the list of the most frequent words extracted from the article for each filtering level. It was obligatory to perform tokenization of the raw text before any mechanism proceeding. As a result of the tokenization, the list of single words is obtained, on which allows frequency analysis is being based. This initial processing is included in the first level of the filtering and functions as a base for later activities. The first level was based on well-known and widely used techniques. The first level of filtering which was performed on raw tokens contained following elements: lemmatization, removal of stop words, removal of punctuation, removal of short words [12].

In case of the second and the third filtering levels it was our idea to use NLTK as a basis for filtering of related words, and to test them as a group with many different classifiers.

The lemmatization process was performed by the method from NLTK library [14]. It allows conversion of token to their simplified version. The second level of data filtering was focused on the extended lemmatization method which could match less similar words [19][21]. Whole concept was based on semantic trees which are available with NLTK Wordnet corpus [22]. Each token from the list is compared with each other to check if they are close enough in the semantic tree that they can be merged. As a result of merging token which is located closer to tree trunk is placed as an output token. Minimal similarity level and minimal distance between two words can be configured, so it is possible to check how such merging could impact later classification results. In case of the later research only one set of fixed values for both parameters was used. Minimal similarity was set to 85% and maximum semantic tree distance was set to 2. The third level of the filtering is based on transformation of adjectives into nouns. This operation is performed in order to get one word instead of two which have almost the same meaning but by the frequency distribution are counted as a separate word. First step of this process is to find synonyms that share a common meaning with the token. Later all lemmas that have a proper type are extracted, which means in this case that they have to be adjectives. After that, for each lemma we search for derivationally related forms. In the end, all related forms are put into result list. First element from the list is used later as transformed token. We planned that feature vector will contain $N$ features where each feature meaning would be the existence of particular word in examined text. The creation of the feature vector consisted in creating a separate frequency distribution for words from articles marked as positive and negative. This kind of approach makes it possible to have the most popular words which are used in each text category. Technique can be also applied for a categorization with more than two possible output categories. It can be done by creation of $M$ number of separate frequency distribution, where $M$ is a number of categories. After that $N$ most popular words could be taken as a feature vector. Important note here is that $N/3$ words should be taken from each frequency distribution, so each category would be represented by the same number of features. Due to the fact that the feature vector is a set of words it

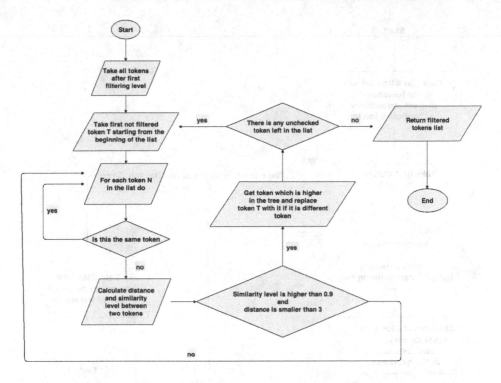

**Fig. 1.** Diagram presenting *Level* 2 filtering algorithm

is possible to have less words than it was planned. Most frequent pools of words for each category might overlap which cause a shrink of the final feature vector.

## 3.2   Natural Language Processing and Classification Mechanisms

According to the filtering levels the following NLP techniques were applied: dividing text into tokens - called also as tokenization, usage of ready-to-use semantic trees, usage of text dictionaries, frequency distribution analysis, lemmatization. It was expected that each of listed methods should give additional accuracy enhancement that should be examined by testing different filtering levels. Most of them were taken from the NLTK library but some required additional custom implementation. Important thing here was the usage of the ready-to-use dictionaries and corpuses which contain already collected data for different purposes. Two corpuses used during the implementation were a stop words dictionary and a wordnet dictionary. Wordnet corpus was the most important one because it allowed to analyze the relations between examined words. Having such large lexical database of English it was possible to match words having the same meaning but different form, which was extremely useful during research. This technique was mainly used by the us in order to implement the 2nd and the 3rd filtering level. NLTK library provides also many mechanisms for text processing such as

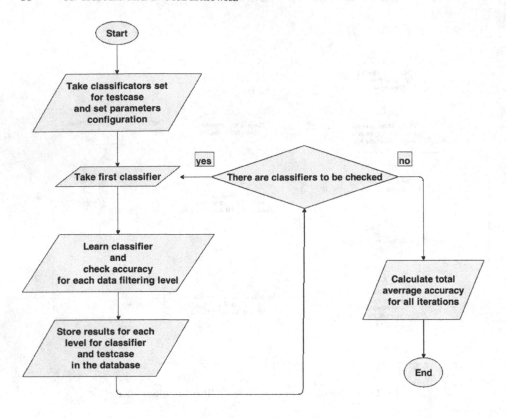

**Fig. 2.** Algorithm for different classifiers testing

frequency distribution and classifiers [14]. Each classifier has unified interface and can be used separately. The assumption was that interface should contain a learning method, a testing method and a classifying method. Learning method receive a training set and a train classifier object. Later classifier instance can be tested with the test method that receives test data set and returns an average accuracy for all test set elements. Additionally it is possible to classify one feature vector. Classifiers were used to test whether our additional techniques improved the classification. Comparison of classifiers wasn't the aim of this work.

The neural network classifier was implemented to let user create Multilayer Perceptron with custom parameters such as a number of hidden neurons, a number of hidden layers, a number of input and output neurons, a type of the network and types of the activation functions.

Some of the parameters were used to test classification accuracy by changing them. During the test also 3 other classifiers were used in order to verify if results can be reproduced with other classifier types.

Max Entropy classifier was used with improved Iterative Scaling algorithm without Gaussian prior. Second classifier was the Naive Bayes classification algorithm which due to simplicity and popularity could give good comparison point. The last classifier was based on decision tree with maximum depth of 100 and the use of a single n-way branch for each feature.

Research part concerning a testing of the classifiers was designed and implemented that each classifier could be tested with different parameters [17]. The core part of the test mechanism is a definition of test case where user can put data regarding the values of parameters which are later used by the classifiers. Such approach makes it possible to check how different classifiers behave against changing parameters. The testing is done by first shuffling dataset and later by splitting it into two parts. The classifier is trained with a training part of the data set and later is tested with the test data set. An average accuracy of classification is a result for the classifier testing - Figure 2. Important remark is that testing is done for each filtering level. Each classifier is tested many times with shuffled data set which removes chance of wrong results and let user calculate an average accuracy from those many iterations. Results of each test case, each classifier, each filtering level are stored in the database to make them easier for later results visualization and analysis.

For each case there was separate test description structure which contained the following element: a parameter name from configuration, a parameter values range, a parameter values step, a test case name, a test case description, classifiers which should be used during testing. Test cases examined the relation between a number of training epochs for Multilayer Perceptron Classifier and the classification accuracy. The reason why this test was executed is that possibly minimal number of training epochs can make learning time shorter and it means that training is more efficient. In the test, the number of training epochs was set as a range of values between 1 and 20. Number of features which were extracted from the data set was set to 100. Only 30 most informative features were selected using Naive Bayesian Classifier.

The test for each number of epochs was repeated 15 times in order to get average results. The test gave very important outcome which is information that any number of training epochs bigger than 3 can give proper classification results that made later tests much shorter. The conclusion is that neural networks does not have to be trained with big amount of learning epochs when the big amount of data is used for the training.

Test cases examined the relation between number of training epochs for Maxent Classifier and classification accuracy. In this case a number of iterations was examined in order to get information when a number of iterations is sufficient. In the test, number of training iterations was set as a range of values between 1 and 20. Number of features which were extracted from data set was set to 100. Only 20 most informative were selected using Naive Bayesian Classifier. The test for each number of epochs was repeated 15 times in order to get average results. It is possible to get a few important remarks. The first remark is that Maxent Classifier reaches relatively stable classification accuracy after the 9th iteration and was later used as a number of iterations. The second remark was that classification accuracy for the 3rd level of input data filtration was better during early training stages. It can be noticed that results in iterations between 10 and 20 are quite similar for all filtering levels.

The data set used for testing contained 1039 articles, where each article had at least 200 words. For the testing purposes the data set was divided into 2 parts, where one part was used for the training and the rest was used as a testing data set. The verification of the results was done by presenting randomly shuffled data set for the training and testing purposes to each classifier for more than 10 times. The test resulted in obtaining the accuracy of classification for classifier type and test parameters.

## 4　Results

In the first test all possible classifiers were used to check how size of features vector used as an input influence the ability to classify phenomenon. It was also important how classifiers behave using different filtering levels. The reason why this test was performed is importance of training speed and ability to reach really good results using as small number of features as it is possible. Usage of filtering most informative features was disabled during the test in order to check only relation between features number and accuracy. In the test, number of features in vector was set as a range of values between 1 and 20. In the second test, it was examined how different classifiers types behave using most informative features, which were selected from whole set of features using Naive Bayes Classifier. As previously feature vector was used as a input data for classification, the difference was that such vector contained only features with the biggest information gain. Both tests were executed in order to check if techniques used by us enhance the classification accuracy. The first thing which could be observed is the accuracy gain in case of Naive Bayes Classifier. As it was presented in the Figure 3 and Figure 4, it can be noticed that for both case accuracy enhance was reached for additional input data filtering levels. The result presented in the Figure 3 shows that the best results are reached using 3rd filtering level and they oscillate around 70% accuracy. For results presented in the Figure 4 it can be noticed that there is no significant difference in terms of accuracy for 2nd and 3rd filtering level, nevertheless both additional filtering techniques introduced by us gave accuracy gain comparing to 1st filtering level. There is also difference in the maximal accuracy for test where most informative features were used. Maximal accuracy reached in the test oscillated around 73%, which means that 3% accuracy gain was reached comparing to test where most frequent words were used.

Results presented in Figure 5 and 6 show that from different classifiers, when most frequent words are used as a input data, the best results are reached for Naive Bayes Classifier and Max Entropy Classifier. There is also no significant difference for different classifiers, when most informative words are used as a input, which shows that some classifiers are better in classification of data with information noise, as it takes place in case of most frequent words.

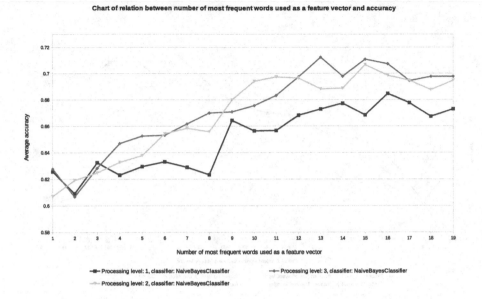

**Fig. 3.** Results of test for relation between classification accuracy and number of feature words in case of Naive Bayesian Classifier

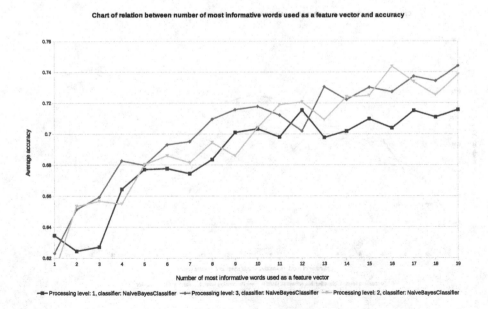

**Fig. 4.** Results of test for relation between classification accuracy and number of most informative feature words in case of Naive Bayesian Classifier

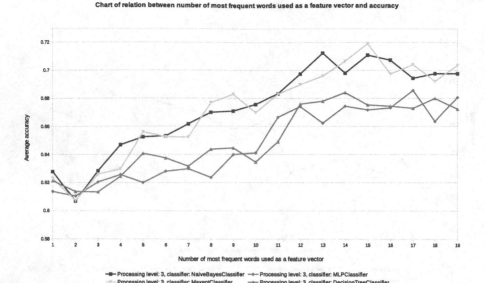

**Fig. 5.** Results of test for relation between classification accuracy and number of feature words in case *Level 3* of filtering and different classifiers

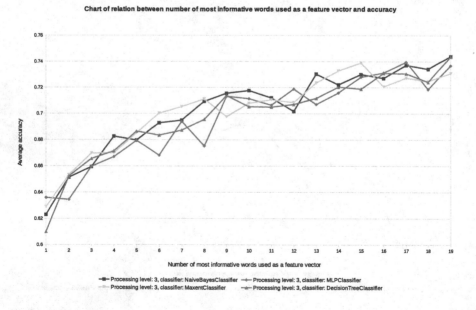

**Fig. 6.** Results of test for relation between classification accuracy and number of most informative feature words in case *Level 3* of filtering and different classifiers

# 5   Conclusion

Based on the research results we reached the conclusion that it is very important hot the raw data is prepared before providing it to a classifier. Some classifiers are less sensitive to information noises which are included in unfiltered data. Interesting information gives also test which showed that Naive Bayesian Classifier provides decent accuracy with the lowest training set size and training effort.

We got promising results when using Maxent Classifier since it proved to be not sensitive to noise as in case of Naive Bayesian model. The the usage of additional features filtering methods and big amount of features can possibly give very good results. It is clear that usage of Naive Bayesian Classifier with the 3rd input data filtering level and features filtering is probably the best method to be used for text data classification.

The aim of this research was to check if this is possible to recognize phenomenon related to the text. Sentiment which is used as phenomenon in this research, was successfully categorized on the bases of random articles which were found on the Internet. It was proved that it is possible to build a system that can be trained to recognize given phenomenon using Natural Language Processing and machine learning techniques. This phenomenon was divided into set of output categories.

We found additional techniques which helped us to improve classification accuracy using different classification models. Tests we performed proved that our additional techniques allowed to enhance accuracy of the classification for each type of the classification model.

We support the idea of some researchers [7] that the selection of most informative features of the text leads to improvement in accuracy. Our observation is that some classifiers are less sensitive to unfiltered features of an input data than than the others. The most useful and efficient classifier seems to be Naive Bayes, since it combines high training speed, ability to work with small data sets and high classification accuracy.

The results of our research correspond to the results which were observed by other researcher who used sentimental analysis data set containing movies reviews and much bigger features number [15]. It is promising that methods created by us proved to give accuracy gain. It is important that the accuracy results which were gained during automatic classification of articles are much better than average classification for sentimental analysis done by the human.

We conducted our research on one phenomenon, however it is theoretically possible to apply existing methodology and implementation to other phenomena. It would be very good to execute tests against other types of phenomena and check how classifiers and filtering methods behave within such conditions. The suggested future usage of Support Vector Machine Classifier could give promising results since this classifier is popular in sentimental analysis and proved to be the best in terms of categorization accuracy [3].

Further filtering algorithm enhancement is also possible. Filtering of raw text could be extended with additional procedures using additional linguistic elements such as adjectives and more sophisticated search of related words.

# References

1. Aggarwal, C.C., Zhai, C.X.: Mining Text Data, pp. 12–14. Springer US (2012)
2. Chandrasekar, R., Srinivas, B.: Automatic induction of rules for text simplification. University of Pennsylvania Institute for Research in Cognitive Science Technical Report No. IRCS-96-30 (1996)
3. Colas, F., Brazdil, P.: Comparison of svm and some older classification algorithms in text classification tasks. In: Bramer, M. (ed.) Artificial Intelligence in Theory and Practice. IFIP, vol. 217, pp. 169–178. Springer, Boston (2006)
4. Definition of word lammatize (2014), http://www.thefreedictionary.com/lemmatise
5. Esuli, A., Baccianella, S., Sebastiani, F.: Sentiwordnet3.0: An enhanced lexical resource for sentiment analysis and opinion mining (2010)
6. Frank, E., Witten, I.H., Hall, M.A.: Data Mining: Practical Machine Learning Tools and Techniques, 3rd edn. Morgan Kaufmann (2011)
7. Gabrilovich, E., Markovitch, S.: Text categorization with many redundant features: Using aggressive feature selection to make svms competitive with c4.5. In: ICML 2004, pp. 321–328 (2004)
8. Kao, A., Poteet, S.R.: Natural Language Processing and Text Mining, p. 12. Springer, London (2007)
9. Beigman Klebanov, B., Knight, K., Marcu, D.: Text simplification for information-seeking applications. In: Meersman, R., Tari, Z. (eds.) OTM 2004. LNCS, vol. 3290, pp. 735–747. Springer, Heidelberg (2004)
10. Konchady, M.: Text Mining Application Programming. Cengage Learning (2006)
11. Liu, H., Christiansen, T.: Biolemmatizer: A lemmatization tool for morphological processing of biomedical text. Journal of Biomedical Semantics 2012 (2012)
12. Martin, J., Jurafsky, D.: Speech and language processing: An introduction to natural language processing, computational linguistics and speech recognition, 2nd edn. Prentice Hall. (2008)
13. Miner, G.: Practical Text Mining and Statistical Analysis for Non-structured Text Data Applications, 1st edn. Academic Press (2012)
14. Nltk tokenization methods (2014), https://nltk.googlecode.com/svn/trunk/doc/howto/tokenize.html
15. Pang, B., Lee, L.: Thumbs up? sentiment classification using machine learning techniques. In: Proceedings of the ACL 2002 Conference on Empirical Methods in Natural Language Processing, vol. 10, pp. 79–86 (2002)
16. Pimienta, D., Prado, D., Blanco, A.: Twelve years of measuring linguistic diversity in the internet. UNESCO (2009)
17. Sober, M.M., Soria, O.E., Guerrero, J.D.M.: Information Science Reference. In: Handbook of Research on Machine Learning Applications and Trends: Algorithms, Methods, and Techniques, ch. 14, pp. 302–324 (2009)
18. Strapparava, C., Valitutti, A.: Wordnet-affect: an affective extension of wordnet. In: Proceedings of the 4th International Conference on Language Resources and Evaluation (2004)
19. Cha, S.-H., Ahmed, B., Charles, T.: Language identification from text using n-gram based cumulative frequency addition. Proceedings of Student/Faculty Research Day, CSIS, Pace University (2004)
20. Q-Success. Usage of content languages for websites (2014)
21. Vatanen, T., Vyrynen, J.J., Virpioja, S.: Language identification of short text segments with n-gram models. LREC (2010)
22. Wordnet (2014), http://wordnetweb.princeton.edu

# Visual Exploration of Data with Multithread MIC Computer Architectures

Piotr Pawliczek[1], Witold Dzwinel[2(✉)], and David A. Yuen[3,4,5]

[1] Department of Molecular and Human Genetics, Baylor College of Medicine,
Houston, TX 77030, USA
pppawliczek@gmail.com
[2] AGH University of Science and Technology, Institute of Computer Science,
Krakow, Poland
dzwinel@agh.edu.pl
[3] School of Environment Sciences, China University of Geosciences,
430074 Wuhan, China
daveyuen@gmail.com
[4] Department of Earth Sciences, University of Minnesota,
Minneapolis, MN 55455, USA
[5] Minnesota Supercomputing Institute, University of Minnesota,
Minneapolis, MN 55455, USA

**Abstract.** Knowledge mining from immense datasets requires fast, reliable and affordable tools for their visual and interactive exploration. Multidimensional scaling (MDS) is a good candidate for embedding of high-dimensional data into visually perceived 2-D and 3-D spaces. We focus here on the way to increase the computational performance of MDS in the context of interactive, hierarchical, visualization of big data. To this end we propose a parallel implementation of MDS on the modern *Intel Many Integrated Core Architecture* (MIC). We compare the timings obtained for MIC architecture to GPU and standard multi-core CPU implementations of MDS. We conclude that despite 30-40% lower computational performance comparing to GPU/CUDA tuned MDS codes, the MIC solution is still competitive due to dramatically shorter code production and tuning time. The integration of MIC with CPU will make this architecture very competitive with more volatile on technological changes GPU solutions.

**Keywords:** Interactive data visualization · Many integrated core architecture (MIC) · Multidimensional scaling · Method of particles

## 1 Introduction

Interactive data visualization is an important component of analytics in the age of big data. It allows an expert to be directly involved in the process of knowledge extraction. The possibility of manipulation on visualized data can radically accelerate this processes by:

© Springer International Publishing Switzerland 2015
L. Rutkowski et al. (Eds.): ICAISC 2015, Part II, LNAI 9120, pp. 25–35, 2015.
DOI: 10.1007/978-3-319-19369-4_3

- more precise selection of data mining tools,
- faster matching their parameters,
- formulation and instant verification of larger set of hypotheses.

Nowadays, multidimensional scaling (MDS) becomes one of the key component and data embedding technique used for big data analytics and visualization [1]. There are many overview papers describing plenty of algorithms realizing MDS concept in confrontation to other feature extraction techniques (see e.g. [1, 2]). In general, multidimensional scaling is defined as a non-linear mapping $F : \Omega \to \mathbf{X}$ of a "source" space of abstract items $\Omega = \{\mathbf{O_i}; i = 1, \dots, M\}$ (e.g. $N$-dimensional vectors $\{\mathbf{y}_i = (y_{i1}, \dots, y_{iN})\}_{i=1,\dots,M}$) into a "target" vector space $\Re^n \ni \mathbf{X} = \{\mathbf{x_i} = (x_{i1}, \dots, x_{in})\}_{i=1,\dots,M}$, where $dim\mathbf{X} = n << N$. It transforms a matrix of dissimilarities $\mathbf{\Delta} = [\delta_{ij}] = [\delta(\mathbf{O_i}, \mathbf{O_j})]$ between all the objects from $\Omega$ into a respective matrix $\mathbf{d} = [d_{ij}] = [d(\mathbf{x_i}, \mathbf{x_j})]$ of the Euclidean distances between corresponding vectors $\mathbf{x_i}$ from $\mathbf{X}$. The mapping $F$ can be realized by minimizing a cost (error) function $V(\mathbf{\Delta}, \mathbf{d})$. Its proper selection is crucial for the quality of data embedding [6].

In the classical MDS algorithms [1, 2] the error $V(||\mathbf{\Delta} - \mathbf{d}||)$ (called also the "stress") depends on the norm of difference between distance matrices from the "source" $\Omega$ and the "target" $\mathbf{X}$ spaces, respectively. For relatively low-dimensional data (i.e., $N$ is of order $10^1$) the MDS mapping is able to properly approximate the structure of original data in the visually perceived 2-D and 3-D Euclidean spaces. Visualization of data by using various forms of the "stress" allows to focus on many aspects of the original data such as its local or global properties.

However, for very high-dimensional data (i.e., $N$ is of order $10^{3+}$) the error functions based on direct $||\mathbf{\Delta} - \mathbf{d}||$ difference does not work properly due to the "curse of dimensionality" principle [3]. As shown in [3–5], the results of MDS mapping will improve dramatically when the cost function $V(\mathbf{\Delta}, \mathbf{d})$ is represented by the Kullback-Leibler (K-L) metrics. Instead of minimizing the error between $\mathbf{\Delta}$ and $\mathbf{d}$, the K-L divergence computes the distance between probability densities of the nearest-neighbors occurrence in $\Omega$ and $\mathbf{X}$ spaces, respectively. Nevertheless, the "stress" remains the function of $\Omega$ and $\mathbf{d}$. It can be minimized by using the same optimization procedures as those employed for the classical MDS formulation. Because, the error function can be extremely complex and multimodal, the heuristic optimization methods are often preferred over gradient base techniques in search for the global minimum of $V(\mathbf{\Delta}, \mathbf{d})$. In this paper we focus on the N-body (particle) solver, which belongs to one of the most efficient heuristics used for the "stress" minimization (e.g.[6, 7]).

The classical MDS implementations, which base on the definition presented above (including relatively novel and robust t-SNE algorithm based on the K-L metrics [3]), suffers at least $O(M^2)$ computational and memory complexity due to $M \times M$ sizes of both $\mathbf{\Delta}$ and $\mathbf{d}$ matrices. Currently, only $10^3$-$10^4$ data objects can be visualized interactively on a desktop computer. As shown in [4, 5], visualization of large data consisting of $10^5+$ of objects requires approximated versions of MDS. They can be developed by limiting the number of computed distances, e.g., via random sampling [8, 9], landmark particles [8], core points selection, hierarchical clustering and k-NN interpolation [10, 11], or by using more sophisticated thinning or approximation procedures such as: deep belief networks (DBN) [12], Barnes-Hut-SNE [4], Q-SNE [5] or LoCH [10]. There are also many parallel realization of approximated versions of MDS including such the solvers as SMACOF [13], GLIMMER [11] and SUBSET [8]. They were implemented in both multiprocessor architectures by using OpenMP interface (SMACOF, SUBSET) and GPU boards by employing both low level GPU instructions (GLIMMER) and CUDA environments (SUBSET).

However, the "brute force" particle-based MDS with $O(M^2)$ computational complexity remains still the core of the most of these approximations. Its strong point is both methodological and implementational simplicity with relatively high fidelity in embedding of low-dimensional (i.e. $N$ is of order 10) data [8, 11, 13]. Moreover, this method can be efficiently parallelized on the most of existing and emerging computer architectures. It is also very important, that its parallel implementation is relatively simple and does not involve sophisticated algorithms, long coding and testing time.

In this paper we show that the brute force MDS can be used as the engine for interactive exploration of large datasets. In this context we propose the *Intel Many Integrated Core* (MIC) architecture [14] as computational platform for its efficient implementation. We stress here the great advantage of the MIC solution over GPU competitors in much shorter code production time with a comparable performance.

## 2 Methodology

### 2.1 Particle-Based MDS

In particle-based multidimensional scaling [6, 7] the criterion function $V(\mathbf{\Delta}, \mathbf{d})$ is minimized by employing the N-body solver [6]. We assume that each data object $\mathbf{O_i}, i = 1, 2, \ldots, M$ from a feature ("source") space $\mathbf{\Omega}$ is represented by a corresponding "particle" $\mathbf{x_i}$ in 3-D $\mathbf{X}$ ("target") space. The particle-particle interactions are equal to 0 when the distance $d_{ij} = d(x_i, x_j)$ between particles in $\mathbf{X}$ is equal to the dissimilarity $\delta_{ij} = \delta(\mathbf{O_i}, \mathbf{O_j})$ in the source space. Otherwise, the particles repel ($d_{ij} < \delta_{ij}$) or attract ($d_{ij} > \delta_{ij}$) one another. The total potential energy of the particle system is equal to the value of the error function $V(\mathbf{\Delta}, \mathbf{d})$. The system of particles evolve in time according to the Newtonian dynamics. Apart of the particle interaction forces we assume that the kinetic energy is dissipated due to a friction force proportional to the particle velocity [6]. Resulting frozen configuration is the visual representation of $\mathbf{\Omega}$ in $\mathbf{X}$. This particle-based MDS is well-known and has already been described in many papers (e.g. [6–9, 11]).

As shown in the pseudocode from Listing 1, this N-body version of MDS, similar to all "brute-force" MDS algorithms including its clones such as t-SNE [3], suffers at least $O(M^2)$ memory and computational complexity. Therefore, the interactive visualization of larger data sets consisting of $M > 10^4$ items on up-to-the-date personal computers is impossible.

```
M ← number of particles;
Forces[0...(M − 1)] ← 0;
for i ← 0 to (M − 1) do
    for j ← 0 to (i − 1) do
        x_i ← Positions[i];
        x_j ← Positions[j];
        f_ij ← ComputeForce(x_i, x_j, Distances[i, j]);
        Forces[i] ← Forces[i] + f_ij;
        Forces[j] ← Forces[j] − f_ij;
    end
end
for i ← 0 to (M − 1) do
    F_i ← Forces[i];
    v_i ← ComputeVelocity(v_i, F_i);
    x_i ← Positions[i];
    Positions[i] ← ComputePosition(x_i, v_i);
end
```

**Listing 1:** The pseudo-code of the sequential version of particle-based MDS algorithm [9]

To find analytically the global minimum of criterion (1) a system of $n \times M$ nonlinear equations in $n$-dimensional target space should be solved. However, such the system is strongly overdetermined [8]. This means that only a subset of all distances from $\Delta$ is needed to reconstruct N-D data topology in 3(2) dimensions. We show in [8], that a proper choice of this subset, which preserve the topological structure of data, improves radically the computational efficiency of MDS. One can employ even more sophisticated approximations of inter-particle forces in $\mathbf{X}$. For example, the Burnes-Hut trees were used for approximation of forces from distant particles in t-SNE realizaton of MDS [4]. Another approximation is used in LoCH algorithm [10], which seeks to place each point $x_i$ close to the convex hull of its nearest neighbors in $\mathbf{X}$. All of these approximate methods have computational comlexity lower than $O(M^2)$ (e.g., $O(M \log M)$ for BH-SNE) and are really very efficient. They produce excellent results especially for very high-dimensional data, which give similar distances between feature vectors due to the "curse of dimensionality" principle. They allow indeed for visualization of $10^5$ data vectors in 2-D space in tens of minutes on a modern laptop [4]. However, it is still not enough for interactive data exploration of big data. We expect that by using highly parallelized $O(M^2)$ MDS codes for smaller $M$ resulting from a proper data coarse-graining we can do much better.

## 2.2 Particle-Based MDS in Interactive Data Visualization

Direct visualization of millions of data points, even on high-resolution screens, disables any type of generalization and obscures both the overall and local data structures. Therefore, to perceive the overall structure of big data set, approximation and thinning schemes are necessary to decrease the number of visualized data vectors (particles). Similarly, exploring finer scales we do not need the most of vectors lying outside of the region of interest (ROI). Otherwise, we waste the effort required for embedding all feature vectors in $\mathbf{X}$ and slowdown the process of visualization.

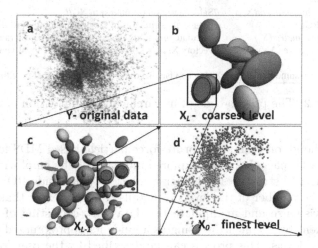

**Fig. 1.** The scheme demonstrating the concept of hierarchical decomposition and visualization of big data using brute-force formulation of MDS

Meanwhile, instead of the whole dataset, only its approximate representation can be visualized. In particular, the big dataset can be organized in a hierarchical way similar to that presented in Fig. 1. The hierarchical zoom-in of ROI and their mapping into $\mathbf{X}$ by the brute-force particle-based MDS allows to observe in 3-D (or 2-D) space both the global approximate view of $\Omega$ and its structures of higher resolution. This visualization scheme can be developed in many ways. For example, the original dataset in $\Omega$ can be pre-clustered using simple agglomerative clustering schemes or one can apply more sophisticated algorithms allowing for extraction of muti-resolution clusters. This procedure is of $O(M \log M)$ computational complexity and is performed only once at the beginning of MDS mapping. For really big data this step can be accomplished by using e.g. a Hadoop system. One can stop the agglomerative clustering when the number of clusters $K$ (and outliers) is small enough to be visualized interactively by the brute-force particle-based MDS. For example, $K \approx 10^4$ or even more by using an efficient parallel version of MDS implemented on new multi-core CPU or GPU architectures. After this pre-clustering, the cluster-cluster proximity matrix $\mathbf{\Delta}_K$ has to be computed and, if necessary, the representative core points (feature vectors) calculated. On the base of $\mathbf{\Delta}_K$, the brute-force particle-based MDS can be used for mapping, where the masses $m_i$ of particles $\mathbf{x}_i$ are proportional to the cardinality of clusters the respective particles represent.

As shown in Fig. 1 by zooming-in a selected ROI of this pre-clustered structure and complementing core points laying in this fragment of $\Omega$ with data from

```
Y = read_big_data (N,M)              //Y → M N-dimensional vectors from Ω //
Y₀ = agglomerative_clustering(Y)     //#Y₀<<K₀-threshold, Y₀-pre-clustered Y//
Δ_{K0} = proximity_matrix(Y₀)        //calculate proximity matrix Δ_{K0} between clusters//
X₀ = MDS_visualize(Δ_{K0})           //X₀ → vectors in 3-D → global view of Ω//
i=1;
while i ≠ stop do
    ROIᵢ = zoom_in_fragment(X_{i-1})  //Select a region of interest in X_{i-1}//
    Yᵢ = MDS⁻¹(ROIᵢ)                  //finer scale structures in Ω corresponding to ROIᵢ//
    Δ_{Ki} = proximity_matrix(Yᵢ)     //calculate proximity matrix Δ_{Ki} between clusters in Yᵢ//
    Xᵢ = MDS_visualize (Δ_{Ki})       //vectors Xi in X corresponding to Yᵢ → local view//
    i++
end            // we assume that X₀ and Xᵢ can be visualized interactively using MDS with dense Δ_{Ki}
```

**Listing 2:** The pseudo-code of hierarchical decomposition of data

their neighborhood, one can apply brute-force particle-based MDS for mapping this subset to 3-D space. It can be explored interactively by employing as particles the fine-grained structures of higher resolution lying inside ROI. For really big datasets, the number of the levels of details can be greater than two. This way one can visualize and manipulate big data sets (consisting of millions of objects) fragment by fragment by using as a guide its approximated views from lower resolution levels. This process can be described by the pseudo-code from Listing 2.

Summarizing, instead of approximated MDS procedures described in the previous section, we can use for interactive visualization the brute-force particle-base MDS in a hierarchical way. In this case it is not necessary to store both all the particles positions and distances in the operational memory. Currently, the limited number of particles $\#Y_i$, which can be visualized at the same time remains the main disadvantage of this approach. However, by using modern multi-core processors, such as MIC, this flaw can be mitigated.

## 3  Implementation and Tests

Unlike in classical N-body codes, the particle-particle interactions in **X** space (e.g. 3-D Euclidean space) depend not only on the distances **d** between particles in **X** but also on the proximity measure array **Δ** in **Ω**, which is computed only once at the beginning of simulation. This proximity measure matrix has to be kept in the memory and distributed among computational nodes. This is an important factor decreasing the computational efficiency of MDS parallel implementation comparing to N-body parallel codes (e.g. molecular dynamics codes). The large size of **Δ** with $O(M^2)$ memory complexity, poses a serious problem for efficient use of cache memory. Therefore, the approaches for MDS parallelization are very different than those used, e.g., for molecular dynamics. The effective MDS algorithm for multi-core CPU was published previously in [9]. However it did not allow for efficient utilization of SIMD instructions. Below we outline a new algorithm which is more computationally efficient on both multi-thread CPU and novel *Intel Many Integrated Core* MIC architectures. It allows to utilize efficiently multi-threading and vectorization mechanisms. The hyper-threading mechanism allows to run up to 244 threads on Xenon Phi processor. Moreover, SSE and AVX instructions available in Intel's processors enable operations on 128 bits and 256 bits registers, respectively. MIC devices offer analogical set of instructions called IMIC, basing on 512 bits registers. These two attributes can greatly enhance the performance of MIC.

As shown in Fig. 2, in our algorithm the matrix of distances $\Delta$ is organized in square blocks. Each block is split into vectors of variables corresponding to SIMD registers. The size of these SIMD vectors depends on the type of SIMD instructions employed. It equals to 4 single precision variables for SSE instructions, 8 single precision variables for AVX instructions' set and 16 single precision variables for MIC devices. The matrix is saved in the memory and is processed block by block in the order shown in Fig. 2. When more than one core is available, the following blocks are assigned to different threads to distribute the calculations between cores. This simple algorithm enables efficient and effective usage of processors' cache and minimizes the number of memory reads. The cache conflicts are avoided by assuming that each thread works on its own copy of the Forces[] array (see Listing 1). Before particle velocities are calculated we sum up all these arrays.

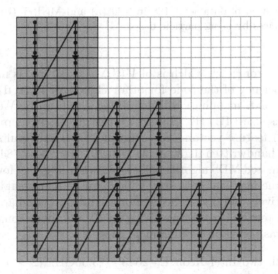

**Fig. 2.** The structure and organization of distances matrix $\Delta$ in the parallel code

Data topology does not noticeably influence the timings of a single MDS iteration (see Listing 1) albeit it may have the crucial effect on the quality of final mapping and the number of iterations necessary to obtain the optimal value of the "stress". Because we are focused here on the efficiency of a single iteration and on parallel implementation issues, we do not discuss the problem of mapping quality. The former depends on the hardware and software issues while the latter on a proper choice of heuristics and its parameters. This is the reason that we use here only one artificially generated dataset in which $O_i$ object corresponds to vectors with 40 dimensions. The vectors belong to two classes of the same size. The first 1-20 vector coordinates were generated randomly from $[-\frac{3}{2}, \frac{3}{2}]$ interval. For vectors belonging to the class 1 their 21-40 coordinates were generated randomly from $[-\frac{3}{2}, \frac{1}{2}]$ interval, while those from class 2 from $[-\frac{1}{2}, \frac{3}{2}]$ one. We assume additionally that $\Delta$ is the Euclidean matrix.

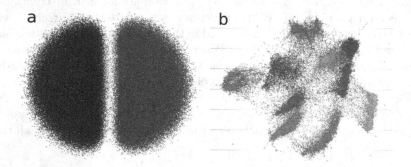

**Fig. 3.** The visualization of data set H128 in 3-D (a) and MNIST (b) dataset in 2-D target Euclidean spaces by using particle based MDS

The Sammon's error [1, 2], which is of $V(||\Delta - d||)$ type, is minimized. The computational efficiency of the code for other choices of $V(\Delta, d)$ (such as K-L cost function in t-SNE mapping) will not differ significantly. We can generate datasets of various sizes: H1, H2, H3 etc. consisting of 1024 up to $256 \times 1024$ ($M = 2.68 \times 10^5$) feature vectors. For example, the final results of H256 and MNIST datasets (handwritten digits $\rightarrow M = 0.70 \times 10^5$; $N = 784$) visualization using our approximated MDS algorithm [8] is shown in Fig. 3. However, to focus our attention on the maximal data size, which can be manageable by our code, visualized interactively and fits to the memory of all the tested architectures, we have selected H31 test bed consisting of $3.17 \times 10^4$ 40-dimensional vectors. Our MDS algorithm was tested on 2 different platforms:

1. a desktop with two Intel Xeon E5-2643 @ 3.30GHz (2 × 4 cores, Sandy-Bridge).
2. Intel Xeon Phi (SE 10P) Coprocessor card (61 cores, 1.1 GHz).

In all the tests, the codes were compiled by the Intel's compiler icpc 13.1.3 20130607. We used two floating point arithmetics: *ieee* - compatible with the standard IEEE-754 and *fast* - producing binaries based on simplified floating point instructions.

The speedups obtained for two Intel Xeon E5-2643 processors and Intel Xeon Phi SE 10P co-processor board are presented in Fig. 4. To check the scalability of the proposed parallel algorithm, we measured the average computational times of a single iteration for the various number of threads. The speedups refer to the average timings obtained for the serial single-thread code. In the tests we use AVX instructions sets.

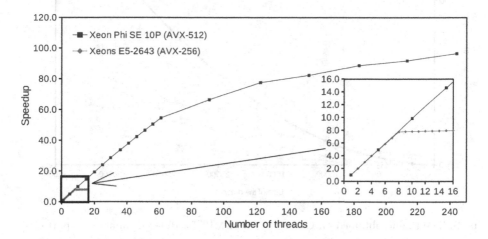

**Fig. 4.** The speedups obtained for two Intel Xeons E5-2643 @ 3.30GHz (AVX-256) and Intel Xeon Phi SE 10P (version with AVX-512 instructions set)

As shown in Fig. 4, the speedup obtained for 8 cores of the Intel Xeon E5-2643 CPU processor board is 7.8. We also showed that the influence of the hyper-threading technology on the speedup is insignificant. Similarly, the efficiency obtained for MIC platform is about 90% when the number of threads is equal to the number of cores. However, unlike in the previous architecture, the hyper-threading is meaningful for MIC. Though the efficiency dropped significantly when the number of threads exceeded 61 (the number of cores) the best speedup of 96.4 was obtained for as many as 244 threads.

The best timings obtained on three different platforms are compared in Fig. 5. In tests of multi-core CPU and MIC implementations, the AVX-256 and AVX-512 SIMD instruction sets were used, respectively. The results obtained for GPU (and the details concerning the efficient GPU algorithms) were presented earlier in [9]. For each platform two different binaries were tested. The first one ieee uses floating point arithmetics compliant to IEEE standard. The second, called fast, uses the fastest (unreliable) floating point operations available on a given platform.

The best computational performance was obtained for Nvidia Tesla M2090 GPU board. The timings measured for Intel Xeon Phi (MIC) board are only slightly worse taking into account ieee binaries and 30%-40% slower when using fast arithmetics. For the largest dataset tested, the board with two Intel Xeon E5-2643 processors was more than 2.5 times slower than MIC.

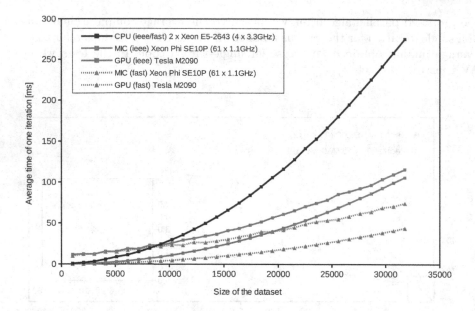

**Fig. 5.** The timing obtained on GPU, CPU and MIC for different number of particles

## 4 Concluding Remarks

We show that the multidimensional scaling based on N-body dynamics can be a viable and robust engine for interactive visualization of multidimensional data when implemented on the MIC multi-thread architecture. Even though direct MDS mapping of billion of data points into 3-D/2-D space is unrealistic, it can be used for visualization of big data in hierarchical way on various levels of details. We demonstrate also, that even though the GPU tuned MDS codes remain still at most 30%-40% faster (only for unreliable fast arithmetics) the dramatic difference between production time of CUDA (or OpenCL) codes over OpenMP based implementations definitely favors new MIC architectures. In particular, in our tests we used identical OpenMP code for both brute-force multi-core CPU boards with 2 × Xeon E5 processor and MIC Xeon Phi accelerator. Meanwhile, GPU implementations involve high programming skills and weeks spent for coding, implementation, tedious tuning and testing. Moreover, the optimal tuning parameters depend strongly on the type of GPU board used [9].

Summing up, we show that a novel MIC computer architecture is very competitive to both classical and GPU based solutions when applied for multidimensional scaling and interactive visualization of multidimensional data. Moreover, announced integration of MIC with CPU board (Knights Landing 72 cores 14nm Xeon Phi architecture) will make this architecture less volatile on changes in technology than GPU solutions.

**Acknowledgments.** This research is supported by the Polish National Center of Science (NCN) DEC-2013/09/B/ST6/01549. It has also been supported by CMG program of the U.S. National Science Foundation.

# References

1. van der Maaten, L., Postma, E., van den Herik, H.J.: Dimensionality reduction: A comparative review. Journal of Machine Learning Research 10, 66–71 (2009)
2. France, S.L., Carroll, J.: Two-Way Multidimensional Scaling: A Review. IEEE Transactions on Systems Man, and Cybernetics, Part C: Applications and Reviews 41, 644–661 (2011)
3. van der Maaten, L., Hinton, G.: Visualizing data using t-SNE. Journal of Machine Learning Research 9, 2579–2605 (2011)
4. van der Maaten, L.: Accelerating t-SNE using Tree-Based Algorithms. Journal of Machine Learning Research 15, 3221–3245 (2014)
5. Ingram, S., Munzner, T.: Dimensionality Reduction for Documents with Nearest Neighbor Queries. Neurocomputing (2014) (in press)
6. Dzwinel, W., Basiak, J.: Method of particles in visual clustering of multidimensional and large data sets. Future Generation Computer Systems 15, 365–379 (1999)
7. Andrecut, M.: Molecular dynamics multidimensional scaling. Physics Letters A 373(23/24), 2001–2006 (2009)
8. Pawliczek, P., Dzwinel, W.: Interactive data mining by using multidimensional scaling. Procedia Computer Science 18, 40–49 (2013)
9. Pawliczek, P., Dzwinel, W., Yuen, D.A.: Visual exploration of data by using multidimensional scaling on multi-core CPU, GPU and MPI cluster. Concurrency and Computation: Practice and Experience 26(3), 662–682 (2014)
10. Fadel, S.G., Fatore, F.M., Duarte, F.S., Paulovich, F.V.: LoCH: A neighborhood-based multidimensional projection technique for high-dimensional sparse spaces. Neurocomputing (2014) (in press)
11. Ingram, S., Munzner, T., Olano, M.: Glimmer: Multilevel MDS on the GPU. IEEE Transactions on Visualization and Computer Graphics 15, 249–261 (2009)
12. Sohn, K., Zhou, G., Lee, C., Lee, H.: Learning and Selecting Features Jointly with Pointwise Gated Boltzmann Machines. In: Proceedings of The 30th International Conference on Machine Learning, pp. 217–225 (2013)
13. De Leeuw, J., Mair, P.: Multidimensional scaling using majorization: SMACOF in R. Journal of Statistical Software 31, 1–30 (2009)
14. Reinders, J.R., et al. (eds.): Parallel Programming and Optimization with IntelR Xeon Phi Coprocessors 2013. Published by Colfax International, 750 Palomar Ave, Sunnyvale, CA 94085, USA, p. 495 (2013)

# Random Forests with Weighted Voting for Anomalous Query Access Detection in Relational Databases

Charissa Ann Ronao[(✉)] and Sung-Bae Cho[(✉)]

Department of Computer Science, Yonsei University,
50 Yonsei-ro, Seodaemun-gu, Seoul, South Korea
Pcvronao@sclab.yonsei.ac.kr, sbcho@cs.yonsei.ac.kr
http://sclab.yonsei.ac.kr

**Abstract.** Data has become more and more important to individuals, organizations, and companies, and therefore, safeguarding these sensitive data in relational databases has become a critical issue. However, despite traditional security mechanisms, attacks directed to databases still occur. Thus, an intrusion detection system (IDS) specifically for the database that can provide protection from all possible malicious users is necessary. In this paper, we present a random forests (RF) method with weighted voting for the task of anomaly detection. RF is a graph-based technique suitable for modeling SQL queries, and weighted voting enhances its capabilities by balancing the voting impact of each tree. Experiments show that RF with weighted voting exhibits a more superior performance consistency, as well as better error rates with increasing number of trees, compared to conventional RF. Moreover, it outperforms all other state-of-the-art data mining algorithms in terms of false positive rate (0.076) and false negative rate (0.0028).

**Keywords:** Intrusion detection · Anomaly detection · Database security · Data mining · Random forest · Weighted voting

## 1 Introduction

Big data, in the broadest sense, refer to a collection of information so large and multi-faceted that it becomes too difficult to process using traditional data management tools. With this, relational database management systems (RDBMS) have been widely developed for the purpose of organizing and safeguarding this kind of data. Most of these are sensitive information about individuals and organizations; any form of illegal access or modification on these data can lead to serious damages, lawsuits, and financial fraud [1]. Traditional database security mechanisms alone are not enough to provide protection against malicious attacks [2].

An intrusion detection system (IDS) is the embodiment of any strong security framework. Although much has been made in the field of network-based and host-based IDS, they have been found to be ineffective and unsuitable in detecting database-specific attacks [3]. These IDSs do not work at the application layer;

© Springer International Publishing Switzerland 2015
L. Rutkowski et al. (Eds.): ICAISC 2015, Part II, LNAI 9120, pp. 36–48, 2015.
DOI: 10.1007/978-3-319-19369-4_4

thus, they are not suited for intrusion detection at the information level because the semantics of the applications are not reflected in the low-level audit logs [4].

The most important part of an effective and reliable IDS is its core mechanism. A number of researchers have already investigated the use of data mining techniques for the task of database anomaly detection. However, most of the proposed systems failed to take into account all users of the database. A legitimate user with malicious intent is a more serious threat than a user with limited privileges [3]. Unlike outsider threats that can be mitigated with the use of defensive programming techniques or prepared statements, insider threats cannot be alleviated by these measures. Thus, a strong and effective IDS with a robust core mechanism especially for the database that can handle all possible malicious users is needed. In this paper, we present a random forest algorithm with weighted voting as the core IDS mechanism for the relational database. Weighted voting enables us to calculate the probabilistic decision for each unseen query sample based on the strength of each tree [5]. Not only is an ensemble graph-based method suitable in modeling SQL query access, but also weighted voting minimizes confusion between profiles, emphasizes trees in the forest that perform well over other trees, and effectively improves false positive and false negative rates.

The paper is organized as follows: Section II reviews the related work, while the system architecture and feature extraction, random forest, and the weighted voting scheme are discussed in Section III. Section IV presents the experimental results, and Section V closes the paper with a conclusion.

## 2  Related Work

Data mining techniques have garnered a lot of attention in mature IDS fields such as network-based and host-based, so it is not a surprise that database IDS researchers have ventured into incorporating them into their proposed frameworks, as seen in Table 1. One of the earliest works is an IDS that exploits hidden Markov models to detect changes in database behavior [6]. In addition to that, Hu et al. and Srivastava et al. developed an IDS on the concept of data dependency and association rules mining [7,8]. However, the former method had only experimented on a very small number of tables and is not very scalable to typical database sizes, while the latter method requires the user to manually assign attribute weights. Artificial neural networks were also proposed by Ramasubramanian and Pinzon in their separate works, with Pinzon combining multilayer perceptrons and support vector machines in their proposed IDS framework [4,9]. One of the simplest techniques, nave Bayes, were also tackled in [10]. Other methods such as Bayesian and tree kernel models have been proposed in [18] and [19]. These works, although comprehensive in terms of their framework, neither paid much attention to the core data mining mechanism, nor compared their proposed techniques to other alternatives. We believe that the latter points are very important in arguing that a proposed method is indeed a suitable one for the problem.

**Table 1.** Related Work on Database Intrusion Detection Using Data Mining Techniques

| Authors | Method | Description |
|---|---|---|
| Barbara et al. (2003),[6] | Hidden Markov Model | Creates an HMM for each cluster |
| Hu et al. (2004) [7], Srivastava et al. (2006) [8] | Association Rules | Mines dependencies among attributes |
| Valeur et al. (2005) [18] | Bayesian model | SQL grammar generalization |
| Ramasubramanian et al. (2006) [4] | Artificial Neural,Networks and Genetic Algorithm | Used GA to speed-up the training process of ANN |
| Kamra et al. (2008),[10] | Nave Bayes | Took into account,imbalanced SQL query access |
| Bockermann et al. (2009) [19] | Tree Kernels | Exploited the inherent,tree-structure of SQL queries |
| Pinzon et al. (2010) [9] | Support Vector Machines | Agent-based intrusion,detection |

We utilize the role based access control (RBAC) mechanism typically incorporated in databases today, in conjunction with the database IDS framework to be able to effectively reduce the number of profiles to maintain, as in [10]. By keeping track of profiles instead of monitoring the behavior of individual users, the resulting system can be easily scalable to a large user population (a typical scenario of a company). In this scheme, privileges are assigned to profiles and profiles are assigned to users. The same concept was presented in our previous work [11], where we found out that graph-based models are far more effective in discriminating between profiles than other techniques. Moreover, among the graph-based methods evaluated, random forests (RF) came out to be the best in terms of performance and time complexity. SVM and MLP, in combination with PCA, yielded comparable results with RF, but the time complexity is unsuitable for the field of database IDS, where timely detection is of utmost importance.

RF, being an ensemble model, can adopt several voting schemes other than the classic balanced voting. Instance similarity or distance metrics like dynamic integration have been used to assign weights and were found to effectively boost performance [12,13]. Another approach is by exploiting the internal out-of-bag (OOB) error metric in RF, which is a more practical and straightforward method to improve performance [14,15]. We adopt the latter approach and make use of the built-in OOB error to calculate the weights to be integrated during tree voting.

## 3   Random Forest with Weighted Voting

This section discusses a brief overview of the system architecture, followed by the concept of random forest ensemble learning, and finally, the proposed weighted voting scheme for improved anomaly detection performance.

### 3.1   System Architecture and Feature Extraction

Database anomaly detection, in conjunction with RBAC profiles, is considered as a standard classification problem. Figure 1 shows the training and detection

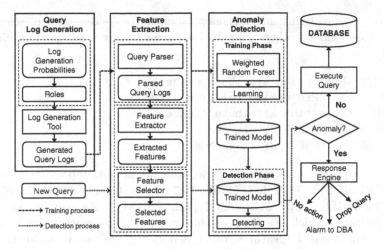

**Fig. 1.** Database intrusion detection system architecture

phases of the proposed IDS framework. During the training phase, query logs collected from the database, with their corresponding RBAC profile annotations, are fed to the query parser. Features are extracted from these parsed logs (as seen in Table 2), and these query logs in the form of features are then fitted to the RF model for training [11]. The final output of this phase is the RF trained model. During the detection phase, the RF trained model evaluates the new query (in the form of the same features as in the training phase). If it is an anomaly, an alarm is raised and it goes to the response engine. Otherwise, it directly goes to the database for processing.

**Table 2.** Query Features

| Vector field | Description | Feature elements |
|---|---|---|
| SQL-CMD[] | Command features | query mode, $c$<br>query length, $Q_L$ |
| PROJ-REL-DEC[] | Projection relation features | Number of projected relations, $P_R$<br>Position of projected relations, $P_{RID}$ |
| PROJ-ATTR-DEC[] | Projection attribute features | $(P_A, P_A[], P_{AID}[])$ [a] |
| SEL-ATTR-DEC[] | Selection attribute features | $(S_A, S_A[], S_{AID}[])^a$ |
| ORDBY-ATTR-DEC[] | ORDER BY clause features | $(O_A, O_A[], O_{AID}[])^a$ |
| GRPBY-ATTR-DEC[] | GROUP BY clause features | $(G_A, G_A[], G_{AID}[])^a$ |
| VALUE-CTR[] | Value counter features | Number of string values, $S_V$<br>Length of string values, $S_L$<br>Number of numeric values, $N_V$<br>Number of JOINs, $J$<br>Number of ANDs and ORs, $AO$ |

[a] Convention $(N_A, N_A[], N_{AID}[])$:
$N_A$ number of attributes in a particular clause
$N_A[]$ number of attributes in a particular clause counted per table
$N_{AID}[]$ position of the attributes present in a particular clause, represented in decimal

We parse queries so as query clauses (such as projection clause, selection attribute clause, among others), line-by-line, are separated, i.e., for the SELECT command:

```
SELECT    <Projection attribute clause>
FROM         <Projection relation clause>
WHERE     <Selection attribute clause>
ORDER BY    <ORDER BY clause>
GROUP BY    <GROUP BY clause>
```

From these parsed queries, we extract query features, represented by the vector: $Q$(SQL-CMD[], PROJ-REL-DEC[], PROJ-ATTR-DEC[], SEL-ATTR-DEC[], ORDBY-ATTR-DEC[], GRPBY-ATTR-DEC[], VALUE-CTR[]). As seen in Table 2, counting features, which are features that count the presence of an element in a query clause, and ID features, which denote the position of an element in the query clause, are extracted from a parsed query log. All features use the decimal encoding scheme for their final values, as with our previous work in [11]. Extending the feature extraction method to other SQL commands is pretty straightforward.

## 3.2 Random Forests

Random forests (RF) are an ensemble method composed of simple decision trees (DT). DTs are tree-structured models that perform decisions at each node using a certain feature $y \in Y$. At each node, the feature with the highest information gain (IG)

$$IG(Y) = I(S) - \sum_{m=1}^{M} \frac{|s_m|}{|s|} I(S_m)$$ (1)

is chosen, where $s$ is the total number of queries in data set $S$ with $K$ different profiles/roles, and $s_m$ is the number of queries in subset $m$ after the split using feature $Y$. I(S) in (1) is the entropy, characterized by

$$I(S) = -\sum_{k=1}^{K} \frac{|s_k|}{|s|} \log \frac{|s_k|}{|s|},$$ (2)

where $s_k$ is the number of queries in class $k$. For each feature chosen at each node, query instances $q \in S$ are split into leaves. At each leaf, a node is again constructed and feature picked through (1), and the process is repeated until all $q$s in the terminal nodes have the same class. Note that the DTs used in RF are not pruned. Random forest, as the term implies, is a combination of bagging and random feature selection. For every tree $t$ in the forest $F$, $m$ features are randomly selected and one third of data set $S$ are left out of the bootstrap sample. The rest of the sample, other than the ones left out, together with the $m$ random features, are used to construct tree $t$. The process is repeated for each tree $t$, until $n$ trees are produced, which will form the ensemble. The number of random features are usually set to $\log_2 M + 1$, where $M$ is the number of features in the data set, since the number of random features does not have a significant effect on performance [10]. Moreover, for each $t$, the left-out or out-of-bag (OOB) cases become test samples that are used to compute useful internal estimates like OOB error and variable importance [17]. In the conventional RF, detection is done by balanced tree voting, i.e., given a query $q$ and tree $t$ in the forest $F$, the predicted class $r^*$ is the one with the most votes from the trees,

$$r^*_{RF} = \arg\max_{r \in R} \sum_{t \in F} [h(q|t) = r]. \tag{3}$$

We incorporate a different kind of voting scheme to the conventional RF, which we will discuss in the next section.

## 3.3   Weighted Tree Voting

It is apparent that each tree in the forest contributes differently in the classification of unseen query samples. These trees have different classification accuracies, and thus, different strengths. To emphasize the strongest trees in the forest, we exploit the OOB error of each tree $t$ in $F$ to compute the weight of each tree to be used at detection time, i.e., we obtain the weights internally during training time. This enables us to weigh the voting impact of each tree by its local performance, which is the rate of how correctly it can classify its OOB cases [14]. The weight of tree $t$ given a test query $q$ instance of class $r$ is

$$w_{t,r} = \frac{\sum_{\text{OOB samples}} score_{t,r}(q)}{\text{no. of OOB samples}} \tag{4}$$

where

$$score_{t,r}(q) = \begin{cases} 1 \text{ if tree } t \text{ gives class } r \text{ for instance } q \\ 0 \qquad\qquad\qquad\qquad\qquad \text{otherwise} \end{cases}. \tag{5}$$

The weights are normalized so that they sum to one:

$$w_{t,r(norm)} = \frac{w_{t,r} - minw_r}{maxw_r - minw_r}. \tag{6}$$

This effectively creates a normalized matrix of weights during training time, which denotes the strength of each tree $t$ given a class $r$. These normalized weights are then embedded into the probabilistic classification process (as seen in Fig. 2), i.e.,

$$votes(q) = \sum_{t \in F} w_{t,r(norm)} \times p_r(q|t, leaf_t), \tag{7}$$

of which the class with the highest score will be predicted class:

$$r^*_{wRF} = \arg\max votes(q). \tag{8}$$

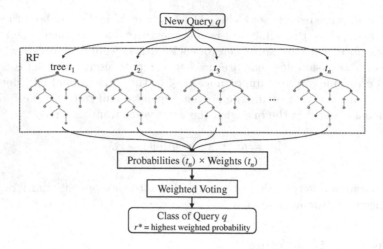

**Fig. 2.** Random forest with weighted voting

## 4   Experiment

We adopt the schema and standard transactions of the TPC-E benchmark database for all our experiments [16]. This benchmark is composed of 33 relations and a total of 191 attributes. 11 read-only and read/write transactions were treated as roles/profiles, as if it were obtained from an RBAC model. We note that several transactions can also be included in one profile, depending on the organizational structure or access pattern of the users.

### 4.1   Datasets

Normal queries for each role are generated according to the database footprint and pseudo-code found in [16]. For each role r, we set the tables $t \in T$ that it is allowed to access, the set of commands $c \in C$ that it is allowed to issue, and a set of probabilities based on $T$ and $C$, as seen in Table 3 [11]. We generate two data sets with different probability distributions: data set A uses a uniform probability distribution, while data set B follows the zipf probability distribution function (pdf), denoted by

$$zipf(X, N, s) = \frac{x^{-s}}{\sum\limits_{i=1}^{N} i^{-s}}, \tag{9}$$

**Table 3.** Role Probabilities

| Probability | Description |
|---|---|
| $p(c\|r)$ | the probability of using a command $c \in C$ given a role $r$ |
| $p(P_t\|c, r)$ | the probability of projecting a table $t \in T$ given a command $c$ and a role $r$ |
| $p(S_t\|P_T, c, r)$ | the probability of selecting a table $t$ given a set of projected tables $P_T$, command $c$, and role $r$ |
| $p(P_a\|P_t, c, r)$ | the probability of projecting an attribute $a \in A$ given a projected table $P_t$, command $c$, and role $r$ |
| $p(S_a\|S_t, c, r)$ | the probability of selecting an attribute $a$ given a selected table $S_t$, command $c$, and role $r$ |
| $p(v_{sn}\|c, r)$ | the probability of including a random string or numeric value $v \in V$ in the selection clause given a command $c$ and role $r$ |
| $p(J\|c, r)$ | the probability of including a JOIN $J$ given a command $c$ and role $r$ |
| $p(AO\|c, r)$ | the probability of including an AND or OR given a command $c$ and role $r$ |

where $x$ is the rank of a random variable, $N$ is the number of elements, and $s$ is the degree of skewness. We incorporate the zipf pdf to mimic non-uniform access in real-world databases. For example, the random variable $x$ can be represented by the relations in a given schema—for a schema with 10 relations ordered in a certain manner and a skewness degree of 1, each table will get a probability of being accessed that corresponds to a point in Fig. 3, $s = 1$. The value of $s$ is varied to make the access pattern more skewed, i.e., the access pattern becomes more skewed as $s$ increases.

For both data sets, we generate 1,000 normal queries for each role, with a total of 11,000 queries for each of our intrusion-free data sets. Since we have built the system with insider threats in mind, we generate anomalous queries with the same probability distribution as the normal ones, only with the role annotation negated [10]. That is, if the role of a normal query is role 1, we simply change it to any other role than role 1, effectively making it an anomalous query. We perform 10-fold cross validation in each run, and with each fold we transform 100 queries into anomalous queries.

## 4.2   Results

A total of 277 features were extracted given the TPC-E schema. Using data set A, we varied the number of trees and compared the results of the conventional RF, which we will call balance random forest (bRF), and RF with weighted voting (wRF) in terms of recall, as shown in Fig. 4(a). It is apparent that the performance of wRF is more consistent than bRF, and that there is also no significant change in performance (a mere 0.008 min-max difference in recall despite varying the number of trees from 10-5000). In addition to that, boxplots of true positive rate (TPR), true negative rate (TNR), false positive rate (FPR), and false negative rate (FNR) are shown in Fig. 4(b), which are results yielded from 10-fold cross validation runs of both bRF and wRF with the number of trees set to 5000. As seen in the figure, the results of different folds of wRF is more compact than those of BRF for all metrics. It goes to show that the integration of the weighted voting scheme makes the algorithm performance more consistent and with less spread-out.

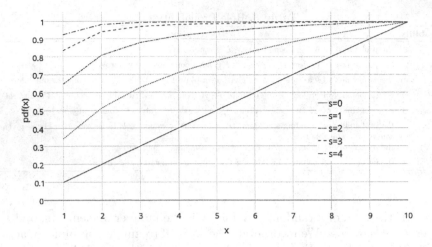

**Fig. 3.** An example of a zipf distribution (N=10)

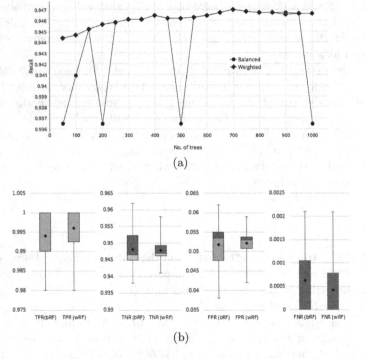

(a)

(b)

**Fig. 4.** Comparison of (a) recall and (b) 10-fold cross validation boxplots (*ntree*=5000) of RF with balanced and weighted voting

Fig. 5 shows the FPR and FNR comparison of bRF and wRF with increasing number of trees. The FPR of wRF is relatively lower than that of BRF in most of the tree configurations, while there is not much difference in the behavior of their FNR (the FNR value fluctuations are not that significant). With 700

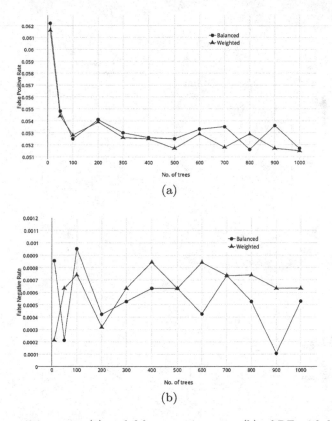

**Fig. 5.** False positive rates (a) and false negative rates (b) of RF with balanced and weighted voting

trees, wRF reached the highest recall at 94.7% and yielded a low FPR of 0.0518, compared to bRFs FPR of 0.0535.

With data set B, we obtained the FPR and FNR of bRF and wRF. Setting the number of trees to 700 and feature selection to PCA2 (obtained by applying PCA with parallel analysis method as in [10]), wRF yielded similar or better FPR as skewness is increased, as shown in Fig. 6. It can also be observed that spread-out of FNR results for wRF have noticeably been reduced compared to bRF.

Lastly, we compare the performance of the proposed method with six other state-of-the-art data mining algorithms, including the conventional RF. This time, 30% of the test set is transformed into anomalies in each fold. We use PCA2 as the feature selector configuration and set the number of trees to 700 for RF. As seen in Table 4, wRF outperforms all other classifiers in terms of both FPR and FNR. wRF is also one of the classifiers that produces more consistent results, in line with the other graph-based models such as J48 and BN.

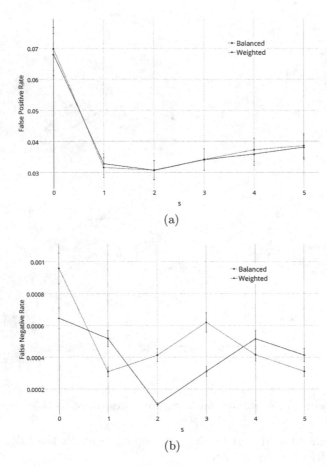

(a)

(b)

**Fig. 6.** False positive rates (a) and False negative rates (b) of balance and weighted RF with increasing $s$

**Table 4.** Comparison of False Positive and False Negative Rates of Different Classifiers

| Classifiers | FPR | FNR |
|---|---|---|
| NB | $0.248 \pm 0.013$ | $0.0121 \pm 0.004$ |
| KNN | $0.126 \pm 0.014$ | $0.0068 \pm 0.003$ |
| MLP | $0.082 \pm 0.010$ | $0.0035 \pm 0.002$ |
| SVM | $0.103 \pm 0.010$ | $0.0046 \pm 0.002$ |
| BN | $0.168 \pm 0.008$ | $0.0102 \pm 0.003$ |
| J48 | $0.118 \pm 0.009$ | $0.0056 \pm 0.001$ |
| bRF | $0.077 \pm 0.013$ | $0.0036 \pm 0.002$ |
| wRF | $\mathbf{0.076} \pm 0.009$ | $\mathbf{0.0028} \pm 0.002$ |

# 5    Conclusion

In this paper, we have presented a weighted voting scheme into RF. Experiments have shown that the proposed method exhibits a more consistent performance than that with balanced voting. The performance of the algorithm is still consistent even with highly skewed datasets. Moreover, the proposed wRF have outperformed other classifiers in terms of both false positive rate and false negative rate.

There are still a lot to be done when it comes to incorporating weights into RF. Future works will include comparison of the proposed weighted voting scheme with other alternative voting schemes. Balancing the performance among classes is another issue to explore.

# References

1. Lee, S.Y., Low, W.L., Wong, P.Y.: Learning Fingerprints for a Database Intrusion Detection System. In: Gollmann, D., Karjoth, G., Waidner, M. (eds.) ESORICS 2002. LNCS, vol. 2502, pp. 264–279. Springer, Heidelberg (2002)
2. Huynh, V.H., Le, A.N.T.: Process mining and security: Visualization in database intrusion detection. In: Chau, M., Wang, G.A., Yue, W.T., Chen, H. (eds.) PAISI 2012. LNCS, vol. 7299, pp. 81–95. Springer, Heidelberg (2012)
3. Jin, X., Osborn, S.L.: Architecture for Data Collection in Database Intrusion Detection Systems. In: Jonker, W., Petković, M. (eds.) SDM 2007. LNCS, vol. 4721, pp. 96–107. Springer, Heidelberg (2007)
4. Ramasubramanian, P., Kannan, A.: A Genetic Algorithm Based Neural Network Short-term Forecasting Framework for Database Intrusion Prediction System. Soft Computing 10(8), 699–714 (2006)
5. Yaqub, M., Javaid, M.K., Cooper, C., Noble, J.A.: Investigation of the Role of Feature Selection and Weighted Voting in Random Forests for 3-D Volumetric Segmentation. IEEE Transactions on Medical Imaging 33(2), 258–271 (2014)
6. Barbara, D., Goel, R., Jajodia, S.: Mining Malicious Corruption of Data with Hidden Markov Models. In: Gudes, E., Shenoi, S. (eds.) Research Directions in Data and Applications Security. IFIP, vol. 128, pp. 175–189. Springer, Boston (2003)
7. Hu, Y., Panda, B.: A Data Mining Approach for Database Intrusion Detection. In: ACM Symposium on Applied Computing, pp. 711–716 (2004)
8. Srivastava, A., Sural, S., Majumdar, A.K.: Database Intrusion Detection Using Weighted Sequence Mining. Journal of Computers 1(4), 8–17 (2006)
9. Pinzón, C., Herrero, Á., De Paz, J.F., Corchado, E., Bajo, J.: CBRid4SQL: A CBR intrusion detector for SQL injection attacks. In: Corchado, E., Graña Romay, M., Manhaes Savio, A. (eds.) HAIS 2010, Part II. LNCS, vol. 6077, pp. 510–519. Springer, Heidelberg (2010)
10. Kamra, A., Terzi, E., Bertino, E.: Detecting Anomalous Access Patterns in Relational Databases. The VLDB Journal 17(5), 1063–1077 (2008)
11. Ronao, C.A., Cho, S.-B.: A Comparison of Data Mining Techniques for Anomaly Detection in Relational Databases. In: Intl. Conf. on Digital Society (ICDS), pp. 11–16 (2015)
12. Robnik-Šikonja, M.: Improving Random Forests. In: Boulicaut, J.-F., Esposito, F., Giannotti, F., Pedreschi, D. (eds.) ECML 2004. LNCS (LNAI), vol. 3201, pp. 359–370. Springer, Heidelberg (2004)

13. Tsymbal, A., Pechenizkiy, M., Cunningham, P.: Dynamic Integration with Random Forests. In: Fürnkranz, J., Scheffer, T., Spiliopoulou, M. (eds.) ECML 2006. LNCS (LNAI), vol. 4212, pp. 801–808. Springer, Heidelberg (2006)
14. El Habib Daho, M., Settouti, N., El Amine Lazouni, M., El Amine Chikh, M.: Weighted Vote for Trees Aggregation in Random Forest. In: Intl Conf. on Multimedia Computing Systems (ICMCS), pp. 438–443 (2014)
15. Kulkarni, V.Y., Sinha, P.K.: Effective Learning and Classification using Random Forest Algorithm. Intl. Journal of Engg. and Innovative Technology (IJEIT) 3(11), 267–273 (2014)
16. Transaction Processing Performance Council (TPC): TPC Benchmark E, Standard Specification, Version 1.13.0 (2014)
17. Breiman, L.: Random Forests. Machine Learning 45(1), 5–32 (2001)
18. Valeur, F., Mutz, D., Vigna, G.: A Learning-Based Approach to the Detection of SQL Attacks. In: Julisch, K., Kruegel, C. (eds.) DIMVA 2005. LNCS, vol. 3548, pp. 123–140. Springer, Heidelberg (2005)
19. Bockermann, C., Apel, M., Meier, M.: Learning SQL for Database Intrusion Detection Using Context-Sensitive Modelling (Extended abstract). In: Flegel, U., Bruschi, D. (eds.) DIMVA 2009. LNCS, vol. 5587, pp. 196–205. Springer, Heidelberg (2009)

# Performance Evaluation of the Silhouette Index

Artur Starczewski[1]([✉]) and Adam Krzyżak[2]

[1] Institute of Computational Intelligence, Częstochowa University of Technology,
Al. Armii Krajowej 36, 42-200 Częstochowa, Poland
artur.starczewski@iisi.pcz.pl
[2] Department of Computer Science and Software Engineering,
Concordia University, Montreal, Canada
and Department of Electrical Engineering,
Westpomeranian University of Technology, 70-313 Szczecin, Poland
krzyzak@cs.concordia.ca

**Abstract.** This article provides the performance evaluation of the *Silhouette* index, which is based on the so called *silhouette width*. However, the index can be calculated in two ways, and so, the first approach uses the mean of the mean *silhouettes* through all the clusters. On the other hand, the second one is realized by averaging the *silhouettes* over the whole data set. These various approaches of the index have significant influence on indicating the proper number of clusters in a data set. To study the performance of the index, as the underlying clustering algorithms, two popular hierarchical methods were applied, that is, the *complete-linkage* and the *single-linkage* algorithm. These methods have been used for artificial and real-life data sets, and the results confirm very good performances of the index and they also allow to choose the best approach.

**Keywords:** Clustering · Validity index · Unsupervised classification

## 1 Introduction

The data clustering is important technique used to split the data elements into the homogeneous subsets (called clusters), inside which elements are more similar to each other, while they are more different in other groups. The clustering algorithms can be classified into some categories, for example; partitional, hierarchical or density-based clustering. Note that the partitional algorithms form, the so called, one-level partitioning of the data, whereas the hierarchical algorithms create multi-level ones. There are a lot of clustering algorithms described in the literature, for example, *k-means* is the popular and well-known partitional algorithm, which has many variations [5,10,15]. On the other hand, among hierarchical methods one can mention such as: *single-linkage*, *complete-linkage* or *average-linkage* [14,18,23]. Moreover, for the density-based methods, clusters are

---

A. Krzyżak carried out this research during his sabbatical leave from Concordia University.

L. Rutkowski et al. (Eds.): ICAISC 2015, Part II, LNAI 9120, pp. 49–58, 2015.
DOI: 10.1007/978-3-319-19369-4_5

defined as dense regions separated by low density ones and they are capable of finding arbitrary shaped clusters. A very important question that one should consider is how many clusters there are in a given data set. The right answer to this question has a significant influence on the optimal partitioning of data. For most algorithms, this parameter defining a number of clusters must be given *a priori*. Then, the cluster validity indices are used to indicate the perfect partitions of data. For this purpose, lots of various validity indices with clustering algorithms are employed. For example, the popular indices for the crisp clustering include *Dunn* [9], *Davies-Bouldin (DB)* [8] or *Silhouette* index [28]. Note that there are other indices used for the fuzzy clustering, e.g., *partition coefficient (PC)* [2], *Xie and Beni (XB)* [30] or *Fukuyama and Sugeno (FS)* [11] index.

In this paper the performance evaluation of two versions of the *Silhouette* index is described. The first is called $SILv1$-index, and the second $SILv2$-index. The paper is organized as follows. Section 2 describes these two versions of the *Silhouette* index. Sections 3 presents experimental results using artificial and real-life data sets. Finally, there are conclusions in Section 4.

## 2    Description of the *Silhouette* index

The *Silhouette* index is described in [28]. Let us denote a partition of a data set $X$ by $C = \{C_1, C, ..., C_K\}$, where $C_k$ indicates $k^{th}$ cluster in the data set, and $k = 1, .., K$. This index is based on the so called *silhouette width*, which can be expressed as follows:

$$S(\mathbf{x}) = \frac{b(\mathbf{x}) - a(\mathbf{x})}{max\,(a(\mathbf{x}), b(\mathbf{x}))} \qquad (1)$$

where $a(\mathbf{x})$ is the within-cluster mean distance defined as the average distance between $\mathbf{x}$ which belongs to $C_k$ and the rest of patterns $\mathbf{x}_k$ belonging to the same cluster, that is

$$a(\mathbf{x}) = \frac{1}{n_k - 1} \sum_{\mathbf{x}_k \in C_k} d\,(\mathbf{x}, \mathbf{x}_k) \qquad (2)$$

and $n_k$ is a number of patterns in $C_k$. On the other hand, $b(\mathbf{x})$ is the smallest of the mean distances of $\mathbf{x}$ to the patterns $\mathbf{x}_\iota$ belonging to the other clusters $C_\iota$, where $\iota = 1, ..., K$ and $\iota \neq k$. Thus, the smallest distance can be defined as:

$$b(\mathbf{x}) = \min_{\substack{\iota=1 \\ \iota \neq k}}^{K} \delta(\mathbf{x}, \mathbf{x}_\iota) \qquad (3)$$

where the mean distance for $C_\iota$ can be written as:

$$\delta(\mathbf{x}, \mathbf{x}_\iota) = \frac{1}{n_\iota} \sum_{\mathbf{x}_\iota \in C_\iota} d\,(\mathbf{x}, \mathbf{x}_\iota) \qquad (4)$$

and $n_\iota$ is a number of patterns in $C_\iota$. Consequently, the *silhouette width* for the given cluster $C_k$ can be expressed as:

$$S(C_k) = \frac{1}{n_k} \sum_{\mathbf{x} \in C_k} S(\mathbf{x}) \qquad (5)$$

Finally, this *Silhouette* index marked by $SILv1$ is defined as:

$$SILv1 = \frac{1}{K} \sum_{k=1}^{K} S(C_k) \tag{6}$$

The maximum of the $SILv1$-index indicates the best partitioning of the data set. Note, that unlike most of the validity indices, it can be applied to arbitrarily shaped clusters.

## 2.1  Another Version of the Index

It can be seen that the key issue in the *Silhouette* index is the calculation of the *silhouette width* for the pattern $\mathbf{x}$ (Eq.(1)). Then, these *silhouette* values of all patterns are summed for each cluster and finally the index is the mean of the mean *silhouettes* for all the clusters (Eq.(6)). This index can be calculated in another way, that is, by averaging *silhouettes* over the whole data set. So that, it can be expressed as follows:

$$SILv2 = \frac{1}{n} \sum_{\mathbf{x} \in X} \frac{b(\mathbf{x}) - a(\mathbf{x})}{\max(a(\mathbf{x}), b(\mathbf{x}))} \tag{7}$$

where $n$ is the number of patterns in the $X$ data set. Furthermore, this index can be represented by:

$$SILv2 = \frac{1}{n} \sum_{\mathbf{x} \in X} S(\mathbf{x}) \tag{8}$$

Like the previous version, the maximal value of the $SILv2$-index indicates the best partition scheme of a data set and, of course, it can be used for the arbitrarily shaped clusters. Note that most often, validity indices are a ratio of inter-cluster to intra-cluster distances, or vice versa and they can also be the sum of these distances. These distances are measures of two properties of clusters, i.e., separability and compactness. So, in the formula of $SILv1$-index (or $SILv2$-index) the factors $a(\mathbf{x})$ can be consider as a measure of the cluster compactness, and the difference $b(\mathbf{x})$ - $a(\mathbf{x})$ can be regarded as a measure of the cluster separation (see Eq.(2), Eq.(1)).

Of course, these two concepts of the index are equivalent if the number of patterns in particular clusters is identical. In the next section, the performance evaluation of these two concepts of the *Silhouette* index is presented for a various number of patterns in clusters. For this purpose, several experiments were carried out.

## 3  Experimental Results

The experiments presented in this section concern determining a number of cluster for artificial and real-life data sets. As the underlying clustering algorithms, two popular hierarchical methods were applied, that is, the *complete-linkage* and the *single-linkage* algorithm. The first experiments were carried out for artificial data sets, and to determine the optimal number of clusters the $SILv1$-index and the $SILv2$-index were used. In the subsequent experiments the same clustering methods in conjunction with these indices were used for real-life data sets. Note that the number of clusters $K$ varied from $K_{max} = \sqrt{n}$ to $K_{min} = 1$, where $n$ is number of elements in a given data set. This approach follows an accepted rule in literature [22].

## 3.1   Artificial Data Sets

The Fig.1 shows 2-dimensional and 3-dimensional data, and the detailed description of all artificial data sets is presented in Table 1.  It can be seen that the

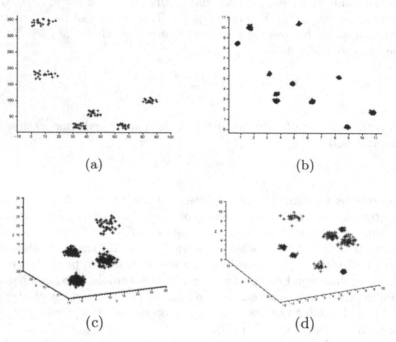

(a)                                    (b)

(c)                                    (d)

**Fig. 1.** Artificial data sets: (a) *Data* 1, (b) *Data* 2, (c) *Data* 3, (d) *Data* 4

number of instances and clusters is different in particular data sets. For example, the Data 1 and Data 2 are 2-dimensional and consist of 6 and 11 clusters, respectively. Moreover, clusters are located at various distances from each other, some of them are quite close. 3-dimensional data are presented in Figures 1c,d, which also have various sizes and a different number of patterns in clusters. On the other hand, the detailed description of the 5-dimensional and the 10-dimensional data sets is given in Table 1. As previously mentioned, two hierarchical algorithms, i.e., the *complete-linkage* and the *single-linkage*, were used for the partitioning of these data.

**Table 1.** Detailed information on artificial data sets

| Data sets | Number of attributes | Clusters | Total number of instances |
|-----------|----------------------|----------|---------------------------|
| Data 1 | 2 | 6 | 120 |
| Data 2 | 2 | 11 | 355 |
| Data 3 | 3 | 4 | 550 |
| Data 4 | 3 | 9 | 391 |
| Data 5 | 5 | 15 | 441 |
| Data 6 | 10 | 3 | 177 |

**Table 2.** Number of clusters obtained by means of the *complete-linkage* algorithm in conjunction with *SILv1*-index and *SILv2*-index

| Data set | Actual number of clusters | Number of clusters obtained | |
|----------|---------------------------|------------------|------------------|
| | | *SILv1-index* | *SILv2-index* |
| Data 1 | 6 | 5 | 6 |
| Data 2 | 11 | 10 | 11 |
| Data 3 | 4 | 4 | 4 |
| Data 4 | 9 | 7 | 9 |
| Data 5 | 15 | 14 | 15 |
| Data 6 | 3 | 2 | 3 |

## 3.2 Determination of the Number of Clusters for Artificial Data Sets

In the first experiments, the *complete-linkage* method in conjunction with the $SILv1$-index and the $SILv2$-index was applied. Table 2 shows a comparison of these two indices, taking into account the number of clusters obtained by the underlying clustering method. Note that the $SILv2$-index produces the right number of clusters for all artificial data sets. However, the $SILv1$-index fails to detect correctly the number of clusters for most cases. Furthermore, the Fig. 2 shows values of these validity indices with respect to the number of clusters for artificial data using the *complete-linkage* algorithm. It can be seen that the values of the $SILv2$-index drawn with solid line indicate the optimal number of clusters for all data sets. The next experiments are carried out with the use of the *single-linkage* algorithm. A comparison of these validity indices is presented in Table 3 with partitioning of the data realized by this algorithm. Here, it again can be noted, that the best results are obtained by using the $SILv2$-index. Finally, Fig. 3 shows the variation of these indices with respect to the number of clusters for the artificial data sets. As before, the solid line relates to the $SILv2$-index, and the other one to the $SILv1$-index. Note that although this clustering method has the chaining properties, the $SILv2$-index indicates the correct number of clusters for most data sets. The next experiments were carried out for real-life data sets.

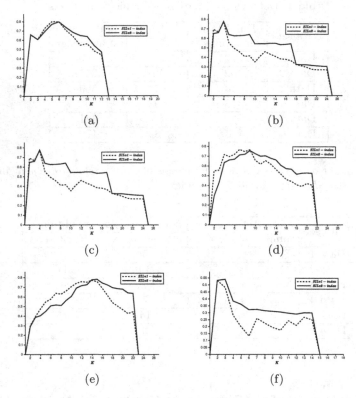

(a)          (b)

(c)          (d)

(e)          (f)

**Fig. 2.** Variation of the *SILv1*-index and the *SILv2*-index with respect to the number of clusters for artificial data sets using the *complete-linkage* algorithm: (a) *Data* 1, (b) *Data* 2, (c) *Data* 3, (d) *Data* 4, (e) *Data* 5, (f) *Data* 6

**Table 3.** Number of clusters obtained by means of the *single-linkage* algorithm in conjunction with *SILv1*-index and *SILv2*-index

| Data set | Actual number of clusters | Number of clusters obtained | |
|---|---|---|---|
| | | *SILv1-index* | *SILv2-index* |
| Data 1 | 6 | 5 | 6 |
| Data 2 | 11 | 10 | 11 |
| Data 3 | 4 | 22 | 4 |
| Data 4 | 9 | 21 | 9 |
| Data 5 | 15 | 11 | 14 |
| Data 6 | 3 | 14 | 2 |

## 3.3   Real-Life Data Sets

In these studies, two well-known real-life data sets, i.e., *Irys* and *Wine* [1] were used. The first data *Irys* is very popular and widely used in many experiments aiming at comparison of clustering methods. It has three classes *Setosa*,

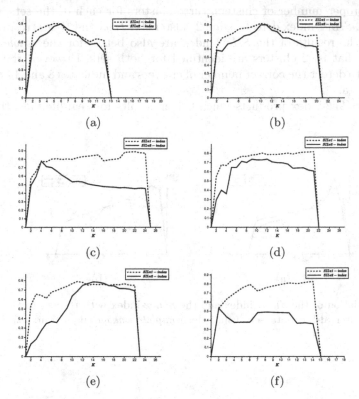

**Fig. 3.** Variation of the *SILv1*-index and the *SILv2*-index with respect to the number of clusters for artificial data sets using the *single-linkage* algorithm: (a) *Data 1*, (b) *Data 2*, (c) *Data 3*, (d) *Data 4*, (e) *Data 5*, (f) *Data 6*

*Virginica* and *Versicolor*, which contain 50 instances per class. Each pattern is represented by four features. Furthermore, two classes, *Virginia* and *Versicolor*, are overlapping each other, whereas the class *Setosa* is well separated from the other.

The next data set, called *Wine*, represents the results of a chemical analysis of 178 wines. Moreover, this set consist of three classes of wines with numbers of samples per class, that is, 59, 71 and 48, respectively. Each sample is represented by 13 features. Similarly to the previous examples, the two underlying clustering algorithms along with the validity indices were used for the partitioning of the data.

## 3.4 Determination of the Number of Clusters For Real-Life Data Sets

In the Fig. 4 and the Fig. 5 variations of the *SILv1*-index and the *SILv2*-index with respect to the number of clusters for real-life data sets are presented. It can be seen that when the *complete-linkage* algorithm is used, the *SILv2*-index indicates proper number of clusters, three clusters for each of the sets. On the other hand, *SILv1*-index detects 3 and 2 clusters for *Irys* and *Wine*, respectively. Moreover, the results of the *SILv2*-index are also better for the *single-linkage* algorithm, that is, 2 clusters are identified for both sets. However, the *SILv1*-index fails to detect the correct number of clusters and indicates 8 and 14 clusters for these data.

So, the *SILv2*-index products much better results for real-life data than the *SILv1*-index.

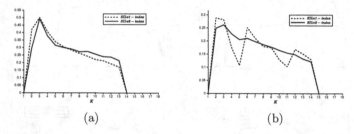

**Fig. 4.** Variation of the *SILv1*-index and the *SILv2*-index with respect to the number of clusters for real-life data sets using the *complete-linkage* algorithm: (a) *Irys*, (b) *Wine*

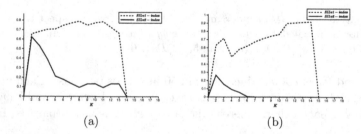

**Fig. 5.** Variation of the *SILv1*-index and the *SILv2*-index with respect to the number of clusters for real-life data sets using the *single-linkage* algorithm: (a) *Irys*, (b) *Wine*

## 4   Conclusions

In this paper, performance evaluation of two versions of the *Silhouette* index was carried out. For this purpose several artificial and real-life data were used. Note that these data sets contained various number of clusters of different sizes. Moreover, two popular hierachical algorithms, i.e., the *complete-linkage* and the *single-linkage* have been used as the underlying clustering methods. However, the properties of these algorithms also influence determination of the optimal number of clusters. For example, it is well-known that the *single-linkage* clustering has the tendency to form long chains that do not correspond to the compact clusters, and the *complete-linkage* is sensitive to the outliers. The results of the experiments proved the superiority of the *SILv2*-index (Section 2.1) compared to the previous version, i.e., the *SILv1*-index. To sum up, all the presented results confirm very good effectiveness of the *SILv2*-index, which found the right number of clusters in most cases, and it is applicable to arbitrarily shaped clusters. Our future research will be concerned with applications of clustering methods in conjuction with this index to designing neural networks [3,4,24,25], neuro-fuzzy systems [6,7,13,16,17,19,20,21,26,29] and creating some algorithms for recognition and identification of classes [12,27].

# References

1. Bache K., Lichman M.: UCI Machine Learning Repository. Irvine, CA: University of California, School of Information and Computer Science (2013), http://archive.ics.uci.edu/ml
2. Bezdek, J.C.: Numerical taxonomy with fuzzy sets. J.Match. Biol. 1, 57–71 (1974)
3. Bilski, J., Smolag, J.: Parallel Approach to Learning of the Recurrent Jordan Neural Network. In: Rutkowski, L., Korytkowski, M., Scherer, R., Tadeusiewicz, R., Zadeh, L.A., Zurada, J.M. (eds.) ICAISC 2013, Part I. LNCS (LNAI), vol. 7894, pp. 32–40. Springer, Heidelberg (2013)
4. Bilski, J., Smolag, J., Galushkin, A.I.: The Parallel Approach to the Conjugate Gradient Learning Algorithm for the Feedforward Neural Networks. In: Rutkowski, L., Korytkowski, M., Scherer, R., Tadeusiewicz, R., Zadeh, L.A., Zurada, J.M. (eds.) ICAISC 2014, Part I. LNCS, vol. 8467, pp. 12–21. Springer, Heidelberg (2014)
5. Bradley, P., Fayyad, U.: Refining initial points for k-means clustering. In: Proceedings of the Fifteenth International Conference on Knowledge Discovery and Data Mining, pp. 9–15. AAAI Press, New York (1998)
6. Chaibakhsh, A., Chaibakhsh, N., Abbasi, M., Norouzi, A.: Orthonormal basis function fuzzy systems for biological wastewater treatment processes modeling. Journal of Artificial Intelligence and Soft Computing Research 2(4), 343–356 (2012)
7. Cpałka, K., Rebrova, O., Nowicki, R., et al.: On design of flexible neuro-fuzzy systems for nonlinear modelling. International Journal of General Systems 42(6 special issue: sI), 706–720 (2013)
8. Davies, D.L., Bouldin, D.W.: A cluster separation measure. Trans. Pattern Analysis and Machine Intelligence 1(2), 224–227 (1979)
9. Dunn, J.C.: Well separated clusters and optimal fuzzy Partitions. Journal of Cybernetica 4, 95–104 (1974)
10. Faber, V.: Clustering and the continuous k-means algorithm. Los Alamos Science 22, 138–144 (1994)
11. Fukuyama, Y., Sugeno, M.: A new method of choosing the number of clusters for the fuzzy c-means method. In: Proceedings of the 5th Fuzzy Systems Symposium, Japan, pp. 247–250 (1989)
12. Gałkowski, T.: Kernel Estimation of Regression Functions in the Boundary Regions. In: Rutkowski, L., Korytkowski, M., Scherer, R., Tadeusiewicz, R., Zadeh, L.A., Zurada, J.M. (eds.) ICAISC 2013, Part II. LNCS (LNAI), vol. 7895, pp. 158–166. Springer, Heidelberg (2013)

13. Georgiou, D.A., Botsios, S., Mitropoulou, V., Papaioannou, M., Schizas, C., Tsoulouhas, G.: Learning style recognition based on an adjustable three-layer fuzzy cognitive map. Journal of Artificial Intelligence and Soft Computing Research 1(4), 333–347 (2011)
14. Jain, A., Dubes, R.: Algorithms for clustering data. Prentice-Hall, Englewood Cliffs (1988)
15. Jain, A.K., Murty, M.N., Flynn, P.J.: Data clustering: a review. ACM Comput. Surveys 31(3), 264–323 (1999)
16. Korytkowski, M., Rutkowski, L., Scherer, R.: From ensemble of fuzzy classifiers to single fuzzy rule base classifier. In: Rutkowski, L., Tadeusiewicz, R., Zadeh, L.A., Zurada, J.M. (eds.) ICAISC 2008. LNCS (LNAI), vol. 5097, pp. 265–272. Springer, Heidelberg (2008)
17. Kroll, A.: On choosing the fuzziness parameter for identifying ts models with multidimensional membership function. Journal of Artificial Intelligence and Soft Computing Research 1(4), 283–300 (2011)
18. Murtagh, F.: A survey of recent advantces in hierarchical clustering algorithms. The Computer Journal 26(4), 354–359 (1983)
19. Naim, S., Hagras, H.: A big-bang big-crunch optimized general type-2 fuzzy logic approach for multi-criteria group decision making. Journal of Artificial Intelligence and Soft Computing Research 3(2), 117–132 (2013)
20. Nowicki, R., Pokropińska, A.: Information criterions applied to neuro-fuzzy architectures design. In: Rutkowski, L., Siekmann, J.H., Tadeusiewicz, R., Zadeh, L.A. (eds.) ICAISC 2004. LNCS (LNAI), vol. 3070, pp. 332–337. Springer, Heidelberg (2004)
21. Nowicki, R., Scherer, R., Rutkowski, L.: A method for learning of hierarchical fuzzy systems. Frontiers in Artificial Intelligence and Applications 76, 124–129 (2002)
22. Pal, N.R., Bezdek, J.C.: On cluster validity for the fuzzy c-means model. IEEE Trans. Fuzzy Systems 3(3), 370–379 (1995)
23. Rohlf, F.: Single link clustering algorithms. In: Krishnaiah, P., Kanal, L. (eds.) Handbook of Statistics, pp. 267–284. North-Holland, Amsterdam (1982)
24. Rutkowski, L.: Generalized regression neural networks in time-varying environment. IEEE Transactions on Neural Networks 15(3), 576–596 (2004)
25. Rutkowski, L.: Adaptive probabilistic neural networks for pattern classification in time-varying environment. IEEE Transactions on Neural Networks 15(4), 811–827 (2004)
26. Rutkowski, L., Przybył, A., Cpałka, K., Er, M.J.: Online speed profile generation for industrial machine tool based on neuro-fuzzy approach. In: Rutkowski, L., Scherer, R., Tadeusiewicz, R., Zadeh, L.A., Zurada, J.M. (eds.) ICAISC 2010, Part II. LNCS (LNAI), vol. 6114, pp. 645–650. Springer, Heidelberg (2010)
27. Rutkowski, L., Jaworski, M., Pietruczuk, L., Duda, P.: Decision trees for mining data streams based on the gaussian approximation. IEEE Transactions on Knowledge and Data Engineering 26(1), 108–119 (2014)
28. Rousseeuw, P.J.: Silhouettes: A graphical aid to the interpretation and validation of cluster analysis. J. Comput. Appl. Math. 20, 53–65 (1987)
29. Theodoridis, D.C., Boutalis, Y.S., Christodoulou, M.A.: Robustifying analysis of the direct adaptive control of unknown multivariable nonlinear systems based on a new neuro-fuzzy method. Journal of Artificial Intelligence and Soft Computing Research 1(1), 59–79 (2011)
30. Xie, X.I., Beni, G.: A validity measure for fuzzy clustering. IEEE Trans. Pattern Anal. Mach. Intell. 13, 841–847 (1991)

# Convex Nonnegative Matrix Factorization with Rank-1 Update for Clustering

Rafał Zdunek[✉]

Department of Electronics, Wroclaw University of Technology,
Wybrzeze Wyspianskiego 27, 50-370 Wroclaw, Poland
rafal.zdunek@pwr.wroc.pl

**Abstract.** In convex nonnegative matrix factorization, the feature vectors are modeled by convex combinations of observation vectors. In the paper, we propose to express the factorization model in terms of the sum of rank-1 matrices. Then the sparse factors can be easily estimated by applying the concept of the Hierarchical Alternating Least Squares (HALS) algorithm which is still regarded as one of the most effective algorithms for solving many nonnegative matrix factorization problems. The proposed algorithm has been applied to find partially overlapping clusters in various datasets, including textual documents. The experiments demonstrate the high performance of the proposed approach.

**Keywords:** Nonnegative matrix factorization · Convex NMF · HALS algorithm · $\beta$-divergence · Partitional clustering

## 1 Introduction

Nonnegative Matrix Factorization (NMF) [1,2] is an unsupervised learning technique that is commonly used in machine learning and data analysis for feature extraction and dimensionality reduction of nonnegative data. The basic model for NMF assumes a decomposition of a nonnegative input matrix into two lower-rank nonnegative matrices. The one represents nonnegative feature or basis vectors, and the other, referred to as an encoding matrix, contains coefficients of nonnegative combinations of the feature vectors.

Convex NMF (CNMF) is a special case of the standard model in which the feature vectors are expressed by linear combinations of observation vectors. Hence, they lie in the space spanned by observation vectors, and may not be constrained to nonnegative values as in the standard NMF model. This model was first proposed by Ding *et al.* [3] for clustering of unsigned data. It is conceptually closely related to the k-means, however the experiments carried out in [3] demonstrated its superiority over the standard k-means with respect to clustering accuracy. Then, CNMF was further developed and improved.

Thurau *et al.* [4] proposed Convex-Hull NMF (CH-NMF) in which the clusters are restricted to be combinations of vertices of the convex hull formed by observation points. Due to distance preserving low-dimensional embeddings, the

© Springer International Publishing Switzerland 2015
L. Rutkowski et al. (Eds.): ICAISC 2015, Part II, LNAI 9120, pp. 59–68, 2015.
DOI: 10.1007/978-3-319-19369-4_6

vertices can be computed efficiently by formulating the CNMF on projected low-dimensional data. CH-NMF is thus scalable, and can be applied for clustering large-scale datasets. The convex model of NMF is also discussed by Esser *et al.* [5] in the context of endmember identification in hyperspectral unmixing.

The factors in CNMF [3] are updated with multiplicative rules, similarly as in the NMF models proposed by Lee and Seung [1]. The multiplicative algorithms are simple to implement and guarantee non-increasing minimization of the objective function. However, their convergence is terrible slow and unnecessarily towards to the minimum that is optimal according to the Karush-Kuhn-Tucker (KKT) optimality conditions. Hence, there is a need for searching more efficient algorithms for CNMF. Krishnamurthy *et al.* [6] extended CNMF by applying the Projected Gradient (PG) algorithm, which considerably improves the convergence properties. Despite this, the convergence is still linear and it might be a problem with satisfying the KKT optimality conditions in each iterative step.

To considerably improve the convergence properties of CNMF, we propose to apply the concept of the Hierarchical Alternating Least Squares (HALS) algorithm which was first used for NMF by Cichocki *et al.* [7]. In this method, the NMF model is expressed by the sum of rank-1 factors that are updated sequentially, subject to nonnegativity constraints. This approach can be also used for minimization of the $\alpha$- and $\beta$-divergence [2]. To significatively reduce its computational complexity, Cichocki and Phan [8] proposed the Fast HALS, which is a reformulated and considerably improved version of the original HALS. Many independent researches [9,10,11,12,13] confirm its high effectiveness for solving various NMF problems and its very fast convergence.

Motivated by the success of the HALS, we apply this concept to CNMF by expressing the factorization model by the sum of rank-1 factors, both for the standard Euclidean distance and the $\beta$-divergence. Then applying the similar transformations as in [8], the computational complexity of the proposed HALS-based algorithms for CNMF is considerably reduced.

The paper is organized as follows: Section 2 discusses the CNMF model. The optimization algorithms for estimating the factors in CNMF are presented in Section 3. The experiments carried out for clustering various datasets are described in Section 4. Finally, the conclusions are drawn in Section 5.

## 2   Convex NMF

The aim of NMF is to find such lower-rank nonnegative matrices $A = [a_{ij}] \in \mathbb{R}_+^{I \times J}$ and $X = [x_{jt}] \in \mathbb{R}_+^{J \times T}$ that $Y = [y_{it}] \cong AX \in \mathbb{R}_+^{I \times T}$, given the data matrix $Y$, the lower rank $J$, and possibly some prior knowledge on the matrices $A$ or $X$. The set of nonnegative real numbers is denoted by $\mathbb{R}_+$. When NMF is applied for model dimensionality reduction, we usually assume: $J << \frac{IT}{I+T}$ or at least: $J \leq \min\{I, T\}$.

Assuming each column vector of $Y = [y_1, \ldots, y_T]$ represents a single observation (a datum point in $\mathbb{R}^I$), and $J$ is *a priori* known number of clusters, we can interpret the feature vectors, i.e. the column vectors of $A = [a_1, \ldots, a_J]$, as the centroids (indicating the directions of central points of clusters in $\mathbb{R}^I$) and the entries in $\boldsymbol{X} = [x_{jt}]$ as indicators to the clusters. Normalizing each $\boldsymbol{x}_t$ to the unit $l_1$ norm, each $x_{jt}$ can be regarded as the probability of assigning the vector $\boldsymbol{y}_t$ to the $j$-th cluster. If the clusters are disjoint, $\boldsymbol{X}$ should be a binary matrix [14].

In CNMF, each feature vector $\boldsymbol{a}_j$ is assumed to be a convex combination of the data points, i.e. $\forall j : \boldsymbol{a}_j = \sum_{s=1}^{T} w_{sj}\boldsymbol{y}_s$, where $w_{sj} \in \mathbb{R}_+$ are weighting factors, and $\sum_{s=1}^{T} w_{sj} = 1$. Thus, the CNMF model has the form:

$$Y \cong YWX, \tag{1}$$

where $\boldsymbol{W} \in \mathbb{R}_+^{T \times J}$, $\boldsymbol{1}_T^T \boldsymbol{W} = \boldsymbol{1}_J^T$, and $\boldsymbol{1}_M = [1, \ldots, 1]^T \in \mathbb{R}^M$ is a $M$-dimensional vector of all ones.

Each centroid is therefore a weighted sum of observation vectors. If only a few vectors $\{\boldsymbol{y}_s\}$ affect the centroid $\boldsymbol{a}_j$, the vector $\boldsymbol{w}_j = [w_{sj}] \in \mathbb{R}_+^T$ is nonnegative and very sparse. If the clusters are only slightly overlapped, the matrix $\boldsymbol{X}$ is also nonnegative and very sparse. Hence, the nonnegativity and sparsity constraints are typically imposed on the factors $\boldsymbol{W}$ and $\boldsymbol{X}$ in CNMF.

If $\boldsymbol{X} = \boldsymbol{W}^T$ in (1), the model is known as the Cluster NMF [3], and it is suitable for clustering the columns in $\boldsymbol{Y}$. For clustering the rows, the nonlinear projective NMF [15] can be used. It is expressed by the model: $\boldsymbol{Y} = \boldsymbol{W}\boldsymbol{W}^T\boldsymbol{Y}$, where $\boldsymbol{W} = [w_{ij}] \in \mathbb{R}_+^{I \times J}$. If $w_{ij} = 1$ and $\forall m \neq i : w_{mj} = 0$, then $i$-th row of $\boldsymbol{Y}$ belongs to the $j$-th cluster.

## 3   Algorithms

The matrices $\boldsymbol{W}$ and $\boldsymbol{X}$ in (1) can be estimated by minimizing various objective functions. Assuming a normally distributed residual error, the objective function is expressed by the squared Euclidean distance:

$$\Psi(\boldsymbol{W}, \boldsymbol{X}) = \frac{1}{2}\|\boldsymbol{Y} - \boldsymbol{YWX}\|_F^2. \tag{2}$$

Let $\boldsymbol{Y}^T\boldsymbol{Y} = [\boldsymbol{Y}^T\boldsymbol{Y}]^+ - [\boldsymbol{Y}^T\boldsymbol{Y}]^-$, where $[b_{ij}]^+ = \max\{0, b_{ij}\}$ and $[b_{ij}]^- = \max\{0, -b_{ij}\}$. Applying the majorization-minimization approach, Ding *et al.* proposed the following multiplicative updating rules:

$$w_{tj}^{(k+1)} = w_{tj}^{(k)} \sqrt{\frac{\left[\left([\boldsymbol{Y}^T\boldsymbol{Y}]^+ + [\boldsymbol{Y}^T\boldsymbol{Y}]^-\boldsymbol{W}^{(k)}\boldsymbol{X}^{(k)}\right)(\boldsymbol{X}^{(k)})^T\right]_{tj}}{\left[\left([\boldsymbol{Y}^T\boldsymbol{Y}]^- + [\boldsymbol{Y}^T\boldsymbol{Y}]^+\boldsymbol{W}^{(k)}\boldsymbol{X}^{(k)}\right)(\boldsymbol{X}^{(k)})^T\right]_{tj}}}, \tag{3}$$

$$x_{jt}^{(k+1)} = x_{jt}^{(k)} \sqrt{\frac{\left[(\boldsymbol{W}^{(k+1)})^T\left([\boldsymbol{Y}^T\boldsymbol{Y}]^+ + [\boldsymbol{Y}^T\boldsymbol{Y}]^-\boldsymbol{W}^{(k+1)}\boldsymbol{X}^{(k)}\right)\right]_{jt}}{\left[(\boldsymbol{W}^{(k+1)})^T\left([\boldsymbol{Y}^T\boldsymbol{Y}]^- + [\boldsymbol{Y}^T\boldsymbol{Y}]^+\boldsymbol{W}^{(k+1)}\boldsymbol{X}^{(k)}\right)\right]_{jt}}}, \tag{4}$$

The computational complexity of the update rule (3) can be roughly estimated as $O(IT^2) + O(kJT^2)$, where the first term concerns the computation of the matrix $\boldsymbol{Y}^T\boldsymbol{Y}$, and $k$ is the number of alternating steps. The rule (4) has the similar cost.

## 3.1  HALS-Based CNMF

Let the model (1) be expressed by the sum of rank-1 matrices:

$$\boldsymbol{Y} = \sum_{t=1}^{T} \boldsymbol{y}_t \underline{\boldsymbol{w}}_t \boldsymbol{X} = \sum_{t=1}^{T} \boldsymbol{y}_t \underline{\boldsymbol{z}}_t, \tag{5}$$

where $\boldsymbol{y}_t \in \mathbb{R}^I$ is the $t$-th column vector of $\boldsymbol{Y}$, $\underline{\boldsymbol{w}}_t \in \mathbb{R}^{1 \times J}$ is the $t$-th row vector $\boldsymbol{W}$, and $\underline{\boldsymbol{z}}_t = \underline{\boldsymbol{w}}_t \boldsymbol{X} \in \mathbb{R}^{1 \times T}$. Note that $\forall t : \boldsymbol{y}_t \underline{\boldsymbol{z}}_t \in \mathbb{R}_+^{I \times T}$, $\mathrm{rank}(\boldsymbol{y}_t \underline{\boldsymbol{z}}_t) = 1$. Considering the model (5), the objective function in (2) can be rewritten as:

$$\Psi(\boldsymbol{W}, \boldsymbol{X}) = \frac{1}{2}||\boldsymbol{Y} - \sum_{r \neq t} \boldsymbol{y}_r \underline{\boldsymbol{w}}_r \boldsymbol{X} - \boldsymbol{y}_t \underline{\boldsymbol{w}}_t \boldsymbol{X}||_F^2 = \frac{1}{2}||\boldsymbol{Y}^{(t)} - \boldsymbol{y}_t \underline{\boldsymbol{w}}_t \boldsymbol{X}||_F^2, \tag{6}$$

where $\boldsymbol{Y}^{(t)} = \boldsymbol{Y} - \sum_{r \neq t} \boldsymbol{y}_r \underline{\boldsymbol{w}}_r \boldsymbol{X}$.

The stationary point of $\Psi(\boldsymbol{W}, \boldsymbol{X})$ with respect to $\underline{\boldsymbol{w}}_t$ can be obtained from the condition:

$$\nabla_{\underline{\boldsymbol{w}}_t} \Psi(\boldsymbol{W}, \boldsymbol{X}) = -\boldsymbol{y}_t^T \boldsymbol{Y}^{(t)} \boldsymbol{X}^T + \xi_t \underline{\boldsymbol{w}}_t \boldsymbol{X} \boldsymbol{X}^T \triangleq \boldsymbol{0}, \tag{7}$$

where $\xi_t = ||\boldsymbol{y}_t||_2^2$. The closed-form updating rule for $\underline{\boldsymbol{w}}_t$ has the form:

$$\underline{\boldsymbol{w}}_t = \xi_t^{-1} \boldsymbol{y}_t^T \boldsymbol{Y}^{(t)} \boldsymbol{X}^T (\boldsymbol{X}\boldsymbol{X}^T)^{-1}. \tag{8}$$

The computational complexity of the update rule in (8) depends on its implementation. Let the matrix $\boldsymbol{X}^T(\boldsymbol{X}\boldsymbol{X}^T)^{-1}$ and the vectors $\{\xi_t\}$ be precomputed with the approximative costs $O(J^3 + J^2T)$ and $O(IT)$, respectively. Then, the total cost of performing $k$ alternating steps with (8) is about $O(J^3 + J^2T + IT) + kO(IT^2 + JT^2)$. If $J << T$, we have $O(kIT^2)$. Thus the computational complexity is $I/J$-times higher than for the update rule (3). In practice, the implementation of (8) needs the sweeping over the index $t$, which involves a nested loop in Matlab but the rule (3) can be fully vectorized. Hence, there is a need to redefining the rule (8) in order to implement it more efficiently (especially in Matlab).

The matrix $\boldsymbol{Y}^{(t)}$ can be rewritten as:

$$\boldsymbol{Y}^{(t)} = \boldsymbol{Y} - \boldsymbol{Y}\boldsymbol{W}\boldsymbol{X} + \boldsymbol{y}_t \underline{\boldsymbol{w}}_t \boldsymbol{X}. \tag{9}$$

Inserting (9) to (8) and assuming $\boldsymbol{X}\boldsymbol{X}^T$ is a full rank matrix, we have:

$$\begin{aligned}
\underline{\boldsymbol{w}}_t &\leftarrow \xi_t^{-1} \boldsymbol{y}_t^T \left(\boldsymbol{Y} - \boldsymbol{Y}\boldsymbol{W}\boldsymbol{X} + \boldsymbol{y}_t \underline{\boldsymbol{w}}_t \boldsymbol{X}\right) \boldsymbol{X}^T (\boldsymbol{X}\boldsymbol{X}^T)^{-1} \\
&= \underline{\boldsymbol{w}}_t + \xi_t^{-1} \boldsymbol{y}_t^T \boldsymbol{Y} \left(\boldsymbol{X}^T(\boldsymbol{X}\boldsymbol{X}^T)^{-1} - \boldsymbol{W}\right).
\end{aligned} \tag{10}$$

The matrices $Y^T Y$ and $X^T(XX^T)^{-1}$ can be precomputed. Thus the overall computational complexity for $k$ iterations of (10) is $O(J^3 + J^2 T + I T^2) + O(kJT^2)$, which is at least $I/J$-times lower than for (8).

The rule (10) does not enforce nonnegativity of $W$. The standard approach to nonnegativity in the HALS is to apply the projection $[x]_+ = \max\{0, x\}$ onto the entries of $\underline{w}_t$ for each $t$. Thus we have: $\underline{w}_t^{(k+1)} = \left[\underline{w}_t^{(k)}\right]_+$, where $\underline{w}_t^{(k)}$ is calculated by (10). This simple projection used in the standard ALS algorithm does not ensure monotonic convergence. However, the projections in the HALS are nested and hierarchical. Note that the calculation of $\underline{w}_{t+1}^{(k+1)}$ involves $\underline{w}_t^{(k+1)}$, which is much more than only $\underline{w}_t^{(k)}$. Due to the nested and subsequent projections, the convergence of the HALS is monotonic and optimal according to the KKT optimality conditions [11].

After updating the whole matrix $W$, its columns are normalized to the unit $l_1$ norm.

Let $A^{(k+1)} = YW^{(k+1)}$. The factor $X$ can be estimated by solving the following regularized least squares problem with nonnegativity constraints:

$$\min_{X \geq 0} \frac{1}{2} \|Y - A^{(k+1)} X\|_F^2 + \lambda_X \Phi(X), \tag{11}$$

where $\Phi(X)$ is a penalty function to enforce sparsity in $X$, and $\lambda_X$ is a penalty parameter. If the clusters are disjoint, $X$ should be a binary matrix. For partially overlapping clusters, $X$ should still be quite sparse.

There are many ways to enforce the sparsity in the estimated factor. Here we assume one of the most efficient and simple approach that was nearly simultaneously proposed in [16] and [17]. Let $\Phi(X) = \mathrm{tr}\{X^T E_J X\}$, where $E_J \in \mathbb{R}_+^{J \times J}$ is a matrix of all ones. After reformulating the problem (11) according to [17], the solution $X$ can be obtained from:

$$\min_{X \geq 0} \left\| \begin{pmatrix} A^{(k+1)} \\ \sqrt{\lambda_X} \mathbf{1}_{1 \times J} \end{pmatrix} X - \begin{pmatrix} Y \\ \mathbf{0}_{1 \times T} \end{pmatrix} \right\|_F^2. \tag{12}$$

To solve the system (12), we used the Fast Combinatorial Nonnegative Least Squares (FC-NNLS) algorithm [18].

## 3.2   $\beta$-CNMF

The model (1) can be decomposed with respect to the entries of $W$ as:

$$Y = \sum_{r \neq t} y_r \underline{w}_r X + \sum_{s \neq j} y_t w_{ts} \underline{x}_s + w_{tj} y_t \underline{x}_j = \tilde{Y}^{(t,j)} + w_{tj} y_t \underline{x}_j. \tag{13}$$

Let $Y^{(t,j)} = Y - \tilde{Y}^{(t,j)}$ and $Q^{(t,j)} = w_{tj} y_t \underline{x}_j$, thus $y_{in}^{(t,j)} = [Y^{(t,j)}]_{in}$ and $q_{in}^{(t,j)} = [Q^{(t,j)}]_{in} = w_{tj} y_{it} x_{jn}$.

Assuming that the disimilarity between the observation $y_{in}^{(t,j)}$ and the model $q_{in}^{(t,j)}$ is expressed by the $\beta$-divergence [2], we have:

$$D^{(\beta)}(y_{in}^{(t,j)}||q_{in}^{(t,j)}) = \left(y_{in}^{(t,j)}\right)^{\beta+1} \psi\left(\frac{q_{in}^{(t,j)}}{y_{in}^{(t,j)}}\right), \tag{14}$$

where $\psi(z) = \frac{1}{\beta(1+\beta)}\left(1 - (\beta+1)z^\beta + \beta z^{\beta+1}\right)$. For $z \in \mathbb{R}_+$ and $\beta \in (0,1]$, $\psi(z)$ is strictly convex. The joint $\beta$-divergence has the form: $D^{(\beta)}(\boldsymbol{Y}^{(t,j)}||\boldsymbol{Q}^{(t,j)}) = \sum_{i=1}^I \sum_{n=1}^T D^{(\beta)}(y_{in}^{(t,j)}||q_{in}^{(t,j)})$.

From the stationarity condition $\nabla_{w_{tj}} D^{(\beta)}(\boldsymbol{Y}^{(t,j)}||\boldsymbol{Q}^{(t,j)}) \triangleq 0$, we have:

$$\nabla_{w_{tj}} D^{(\beta)}(\boldsymbol{Y}^{(t,j)}||\boldsymbol{Q}^{(t,j)}) = \sum_{i,n}\left(q_{in}^{(t,j)} - y_{in}^{(t,j)}\right)(q_{in}^{(t,j)})^{\beta-1} y_{it} x_{jn}$$

$$= \sum_{i,n}\left(w_{tj}^\beta y_{it}^{\beta+1} x_{jn}^{\beta+1} - y_{in}^{(t,j)} w_{tj}^{\beta-1} y_{it}^\beta x_{jn}^\beta\right) \triangleq 0. \tag{15}$$

After straightforward calculations, the update rule for $w_{tj}$ is derived from (15):

$$w_{tj} = \frac{\sum_{i,n} y_{in}^{(t,j)} y_{it}^\beta x_{jn}^\beta}{\sum_{i,n} y_{it}^{\beta+1} x_{jn}^{\beta+1}}. \tag{16}$$

Inserting $y_{in}^{(t,j)} = y_{in} - [\boldsymbol{YWX}]_{in} + w_{tj} y_{it} x_{jn}$ to (16), we obtain the simplified update rule for $w_{tj}$:

$$w_{tj} \leftarrow \frac{\sum_{i,n}\left(y_{in} - [\boldsymbol{YWX}]_{in} + w_{tj} y_{it} x_{jn}\right) y_{it}^\beta x_{jn}^\beta}{\sum_{i,n} y_{it}^{\beta+1} x_{jn}^{\beta+1}}$$

$$= \frac{\sum_{i,n} y_{in} y_{it}^\beta x_{jn}^\beta - \sum_{i,n}[\boldsymbol{YWX}]_{in} y_{it}^\beta x_{jn}^\beta + w_{tj} \sum_i y_{it}^{\beta+1} \sum_n x_{jn}^{\beta+1}}{\sum_{i,n} y_{it}^{\beta+1} x_{jn}^{\beta+1}}$$

$$= w_{tj} + \frac{[(\boldsymbol{Y}^\beta)^T \boldsymbol{Y}(\boldsymbol{X}^\beta)^T]_{tj} - [(\boldsymbol{Y}^\beta)^T \boldsymbol{YWX}(\boldsymbol{X}^\beta)^T]_{tj}}{(\mathbf{1}_I^T \boldsymbol{Y}^{\beta+1})_t (\boldsymbol{X}^{\beta+1} \mathbf{1}_T)_j}. \tag{17}$$

The operator $\boldsymbol{Z}^\beta = [z_{ij}^\beta]$ means element-wise raise to power $\beta$. The update rule (17) can be parallelized with respect to the index $t$ or $j$ (but not jointly). For $T \gg J$, higher efficiency can be obtained if only one loop **for** (sweeping through $t$) is used. Thus:

$$w_{t,*}^{(k+1)} = w_{t,*}^{(k)} + \frac{\left[(\boldsymbol{Y}^\beta)^T \boldsymbol{Y}(\boldsymbol{X}^\beta)^T\right]_{t,*} - \left[(\boldsymbol{Y}^\beta)^T \boldsymbol{Y}\right]_{t,*} \tilde{\boldsymbol{W}}^{(k)} \boldsymbol{X}(\boldsymbol{X}^\beta)^T}{(\mathbf{1}_I^T \boldsymbol{Y}^{\beta+1})_t (\boldsymbol{X}^{\beta+1} \mathbf{1}_T)_*}, \tag{18}$$

where $\tilde{\boldsymbol{W}}^{(k)} = [\boldsymbol{w}_1^{(k+1)}; \ldots; \boldsymbol{w}_{t-1}^{(k+1)}; \boldsymbol{w}_t^{(k)}; \ldots; \boldsymbol{w}_T^{(k)}] \in \mathbb{R}^{T \times J}$.

Neglecting the computational complexity for raising to power $\beta$, the matrices $(\boldsymbol{Y}^\beta)^T \boldsymbol{Y}$, $\boldsymbol{X}(\boldsymbol{X}^\beta)^T$ and $(\boldsymbol{Y}^\beta)^T \boldsymbol{Y}(\boldsymbol{X}^\beta)^T$ can be precomputed with the costs:

$O(IT^2)$, $O(TJ^2)$ and $O(JT^2) + O(IT^2)$, respectively. Hence the overall computational complexity for $k$ iterations with the update rule (18) can be roughly estimated as $O(IT^2 + JT^2 + TJ^2 + kT^2J^2)$. Assuming $J << \min\{I,T\}$, we have: $O(IT^2 + kT^2J^2)$. It is therefore $J$ higher than for the HALS-based CNMF.

If $T >> J$, i.e. the clusters are assumed to include many samples, the centroids do not have to be calculated using all samples. To accelerate the computations both for the HALS-CNMF and $\beta$-CNMF, the update rules in (10) and (18) may be applied to only the selected rows of $W$ in each iterative step. The selection can be random, and the number of the selected rows should depend on the rate $T/J$. In the experiments, we select only 10 percent of the rows in each iteration.

## 4  Experiments

The proposed algorithms were tested for solving partitional clustering problems using various datasets that are briefly characterized in Table 1.

**Table 1.** Details of the datasets

| Datasets | Variables ($I$) | Samples ($T$) | Classes ($J$) | Sparsity [%] |
|---|---|---|---|---|
| Gaussian mixture | 3 | 3000 | 3 | 0 |
| Hand-written digits | 64 | 5620 | 10 | 3.1 |
| TPD | 8190 | 888 | 6 | 98.45 |
| Reuters | 6191 | 2500 | 10 | 99.42 |

The samples in the *Gaussian mixture* dataset are generated randomly from a mixture of three 3D Gaussian distributions with the following parameters:

$$\boldsymbol{\mu}_1 = [40, 80, -30]^T, \quad \boldsymbol{\mu}_2 = [70, -40, 60]^T, \quad \boldsymbol{\mu}_3 = [20, 20, 30]^T,$$

$$\boldsymbol{\Sigma}_1 = \begin{bmatrix} 50 & -0.2 & 0.1 \\ -0.2 & 0.1 & 0.1 \\ 0.1 & 0.1 & 5 \end{bmatrix}, \quad \boldsymbol{\Sigma}_2 = \begin{bmatrix} 50 & -5 & -1 \\ -5 & 5 & -0.5 \\ -1 & 0.5 & 1 \end{bmatrix}, \quad \boldsymbol{\Sigma}_3 = \begin{bmatrix} 2 & 0 & 0 \\ 0 & 10 & 0 \\ 0 & 0 & 5 \end{bmatrix}.$$

Obviously, all the covariance matrices are positive-definite. From each distribution 500 samples are generated, hence $Y \in \mathbb{R}^{3 \times 1500}$.

The dataset entitled *Hand-written digits* is taken from the UCI Machine Learning Repository [19]. It contains hand-written digits used for optical recognition.

The datasets *TPD* and *Reuters* contain textual documents that should be grouped according to their semantic similarity. The documents in the first one come from the *TopicPlanet* document collection. We selected 888 documents classified into 6 topics: *air-travel, broadband, cruises, domain-names, investments, technologies*, which gives 8190 words after having been parsed. Thus $Y \in \mathbb{R}^{8190 \times 888}$ and $J = 6$. The documents in the *Reuters* database belong to the following topics: *acq, coffee, crude, eran, gold, interest, money-fx, ship, sugar, trade*. We selected 2500 documents that have 6191 distinctive and meaningful words; thus $Y \in \mathbb{R}^{6191 \times 2500}$ and $J = 10$. Both datasets are very sparse, since each document contains only a small portion of the words from the dictionary.

Several NMF algorithms are compared with respect to the efficiency for solving clustering problems. The proposed algorithms are referred to as the HALS-CNMF and $\beta$-CNMF. The other algorithms are listed as follows: HALS [8], UO-NMF(A) (Uni-orth. NMF with orthogonalization of the feature matrix) [20], UO-NMF(X) (Uni-orth. NMF with orthogonalization of the encoding matrix) [20], Bio-NMF (Bi-orthogonal NMF) [20], Cx-NMF (standard multiplicative convex NMF) [3], and k-means (standard Matlab implementation for minimization of the Euclidean distance). In the $\beta$-CNMF, we set $\beta = 5$.

All the tested algorithms were initialized by the same random initializer generated from an uniform distribution. To analyze the efficiency of the discussed methods, 100 Monte Carlo (MC) runs of each algorithm were carried out, each time the initial matrices were different. All the algorithms were implemented using the same computational strategy, i.e. the same stopping criteria are applied to all the algorithms, and the maximum number of inner iterations for updating the factor $A$, $W$ or $X$ is set to 10.

The quality of clustering is evaluated with the Purity measure [20] that reflects the accuracy of clustering. Fig. 1 shows the statistics of the Purity obtained from 100 MC runs of the tested algorithms. The average runtime is given in Table 2.

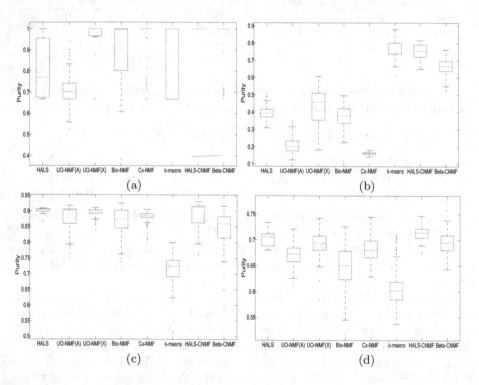

**Fig. 1.** Statistics of the purity measure for clustering the following datasets: (a) Gaussian mixture; (b) Hand-written digits; (c) TPD; (d) Reuters

**Table 2.** Average runtime [in seconds] of the tested algorithms: 1 – HALS, 2 – UO-NMF(A), 3 – UO-NMF(X), 4 – Bio-NMF, 5 – Cx-NMF, 6 – k-means, 7 – HALS-CNMF, 8 – $\beta$-CNMF

| Datasets | 1 | 2 | 3 | 4 | 5 | 6 | 7 | 8 |
|---|---|---|---|---|---|---|---|---|
| Gaussian mixture | 0.077 | 0.079 | 0.16 | 0.27 | 72.9 | 0.0053 | 2.76 | 4.66 |
| Hand-written digits | 1.02 | 0.71 | 1.1 | 2.26 | 39.3 | 0.53 | 25.8 | 24.5 |
| TPD | 3.85 | 2.26 | 4.34 | 6.07 | 14.1 | 36.53 | 7.0 | 11.37 |
| Reuters | 10.12 | 5.41 | 12.4 | 14.2 | 89.75 | 194.6 | 29.7 | 48.2 |

## 5   Conclusions

In this paper, we proposed two versions of CNMF for clustering mixed-sign and unnecessarily sparse data points. Both algorithms are more efficient with respect to the clustering accuracy and the computational time than the standard multiplicative CNMF. The results presented in Fig. 1 show that the HALS-CNMF gives the best clustering accuracy for the analyzed datasets. The $\beta$-CNMF can be tuned to the distribution of data points with the parameter $\beta$. If the number of variables in the dataset is much larger than the number of clusters, both proposed CNMF algorithms are faster than the k-means (see Table 2). When the number of samples is very large, the proposed algorithms provide high accuracy of clustering but at the cost of an increased computational cost.

Summing up, the proposed CNMF algorithms seem to be efficient for clustering mixed-signed data points. They can be also combined with the CH-NMF for clustering big data.

## References

1. Lee, D.D., Seung, H.S.: Learning the parts of objects by non-negative matrix factorization. Nature 401, 788–791 (1999)
2. Cichocki, A., Zdunek, R., Phan, A.H., Amari, S.I.: Nonnegative Matrix and Tensor Factorizations: Applications to Exploratory Multi-way Data Analysis and Blind Source Separation. Wiley and Sons (2009)
3. Ding, C., Li, T., Jordan, M.I.: Convex and semi-nonnegative matrix factorizations. IEEE Transactions on Pattern Analysis and Machine Intelligence 32(1), 45–55 (2010)
4. Thurau, C., Kersting, K., Bauckhage, C.: Convex non-negative matrix factorization in the wild. In: Proc. The 2009 Ninth IEEE International Conference on Data Mining, ICDM 2009, pp. 523–532. IEEE Computer Society, Washington, DC (2009)
5. Esser, E., Möller, M., Osher, S., Sapiro, G., Xin, J.: A convex model for nonnegative matrix factorization and dimensionality reduction on physical space. IEEE Transactions on Image Processing 21(7), 3239–3252 (2012)
6. Krishnamurthy, V., d'Aspremont, A.: Convex algorithms for nonnegative matrix factorization (2012), http://arxiv.org/abs/1207.0318
7. Cichocki, A., Zdunek, R., Amari, S.-I.: Hierarchical ALS algorithms for nonnegative matrix and 3D tensor factorization. In: Davies, M.E., James, C.J., Abdallah, S.A., Plumbley, M.D. (eds.) ICA 2007. LNCS, vol. 4666, pp. 169–176. Springer, Heidelberg (2007)

8. Cichocki, A., Phan, A.H.: Fast local algorithms for large scale nonnegative matrix and tensor factorizations. IEICE Transactions on Fundamentals of Electronics, Communications and Computer Sciences E92-A(3), 708–721 (2009)
9. Han, L., Neumann, M., Prasad, U.: Alternating projected Barzilai-Borwein methods for nonnegative matrix factorization. Electronic Transactions on Numerical Analysis 36, 54–82 (2009-2010)
10. Kim, J., Park, H.: Fast nonnegative matrix factorization: An active-set-like method and comparisons. SIAM J. Sci. Comput. 33(6), 3261–3281 (2011)
11. Gillis, N., Glineur, F.: Accelerated multiplicative updates and hierarchical ALS algorithms for nonnegative matrix factorization. Neural Comput. 24(4), 1085–1105 (2012)
12. Chen, W., Guillaume, M.: HALS-based NMF with flexible constraints for hyperspectral unmixing. EURASIP J. Adv. Sig. Proc. 54, 1–14 (2012)
13. Zdunek, R.: Nonnegative Matrix and Tensor Factorization: Applications to Classification and Signal Processing. Publishing House of Wroclaw University of Technology, Wroclaw (2014) (in Polish).
14. Zdunek, R.: Data clustering with semi-binary nonnegative matrix factorization. In: Rutkowski, L., Tadeusiewicz, R., Zadeh, L.A., Zurada, J.M. (eds.) ICAISC 2008. LNCS (LNAI), vol. 5097, pp. 705–716. Springer, Heidelberg (2008)
15. Yang, Z., Oja, E.: Linear and nonlinear projective nonnegative matrix factorization. IEEE Transactions Neural Networks 21(5), 734–749 (2010)
16. Zdunek, R., Cichocki, A.: Nonnegative matrix factorization with constrained second-order optimization. Signal Processing 87, 1904–1916 (2007)
17. Kim, H., Park, H.: Non-negative matrix factorization based on alternating nonnegativity constrained least squares and active set method. SIAM Journal in Matrix Analysis and Applications 30(2), 713–730 (2008)
18. Benthem, M.H.V., Keenan, M.R.: Fast algorithm for the solution of large-scale non-negativity-constrained least squares problems. Journal of Chemometrics 18, 441–450 (2004)
19. Bache, K., Lichman, M.: UCI machine learning repository (2013)
20. Ding, C., Li, T., Peng, W., Park, H.: Orthogonal nonnegative matrix trifactorizations for clustering. In: KDD 2006: Proc. of the 12th ACM SIGKDD International Conference on Knowledge Discovery and Data Mining, pp. 126–135. ACM Press, New York (2006)

# Bioinformatics, Biometrics
# and Medical Applications

# On the Convergence of Quantum and Distributed Computational Models of Consciousness

Susmit Bagchi[✉]

Department of Informatics, Gyeongsang National University,
Jinju, 660-701 South Korea
susmitbagchi@yahoo.co.uk

**Abstract.** The brain is a neurological device capable to carry out distributed computation and express cognition. The computational models of consciousness and cognition have potential applications in bio-inspired computing paradigm. This paper proposes a computational model of consciousness as a cognitive function following neurophysiology and elements of distributed computing. It is illustrated that the distributed computational model of consciousness has a basis in the quantum mechanical models in explaining the neurological cognitive functions. The transitions between the computing model and quantum basis are explained and analyzed considering different linear Hermitian operators.

**Keywords:** Cognition · Hermitian · Distributed computing · Quantum mechanics · Consciousness

## 1    Introduction

The brain is composed of billions of interconnected neurons capable of carrying out computation and providing cognition as well as consciousness. The inter-neuron communication involves gated signals generated by ion density gradient and threshold potential. Interestingly, the physical substrate of brain can explain working of individual neurons but it cannot explain the overall complex cognitive functions of brain. There are three main approaches to model cognitive functions of brain such as, (1) computational modeling, (2) physical modeling and, (3) quantum mechanical modeling. Conceptually, the conscious and abstract thinking are modeled by using the global workspace (GW) formalism [2, 3]. However, according to the physical modeling approach, the individual neurons implement computational mechanisms to achieve the overall cognitive functions in brain [19]. The computational models of artificial cognition and machine consciousness are developed by following artificial neural network theory incorporating probabilistic reasoning by employing Bayesian and hidden Markov models [20]. Researchers have proposed that, the modeling of cognitive actions and consciousness require the quantitative and algorithmic functions [1]. The neurological functioning of brain is a distributed computing mechanism where, specialized regions of brain process different environmental excitations [21]. However, it is proposed that the quantum mechanical and field theoretic models can

© Springer International Publishing Switzerland 2015
L. Rutkowski et al. (Eds.): ICAISC 2015, Part II, LNAI 9120, pp. 71–78, 2015.
DOI: 10.1007/978-3-319-19369-4_7

explain cognitive functions and consciousness of brain based on quantum tubulins [6, 10, 11]. This paper proposes that, a brain can be viewed as a hybrid distributed computing machine having a quantum mechanical basis of consciousness expression. There exists a bridge between distributed computing model of consciousness and the quantum mechanical processes. This paper proposes a novel bio-inspired distributed computational model of consciousness. Furthermore, it illustrates that the proposed model has a quantum mechanical basis depending upon linear Hermitian. The proposed model considers memory, where nodes evolve by storing information. The rest of the paper is organized as follows. Section 2 describes related work. Section 3 explains the construction of computational model of consciousness. Section 4 describes the quantum mechanical and field theoretic convergence of the model. Section 5 concludes the paper.

## 2    Related Work

The physical substrate of brain is a large collection of neurons having a highly complex network. The different regions of brain are specialized to perform different functions. Experimental evidences show that functions of brain require extended-assembly of neurons [7]. There are different approaches to explain brain functions and cognitive actions. In one approach, the brain functions are analyzed following the discrete stochastic pulse train model of a single neuron whereas, in second approach the brain functions are analyzed by employing spatially coherent phase-amplitude model [5]. These models consider mechanics and laws of classical physics, which are non-quantum in nature. Following a different approach, researchers have proposed that neuronal firing has quantum properties, where superimposed ion-states of firing and resting neurons decohere fast in time [10].

According to quantum theoretic model of brain, the brain-dynamics and functions obey quantum mechanical processes [6]. The quantum model of brain is proposed by employing Quantum Field Theory (QFT) of many-body physics [5, 8]. This model explains the functioning of memory and recalling in view of QFT, which is experimentally verified [5]. Furthermore, a combination of neural network and dissipative quantum model of brain is proposed [9]. According to this hybrid quantum model, the brain functions can be explained and analyzed following the mechanisms of quantum evolution [5, 9]. There is a relation between the microstructure of cerebral cortex of brain and consciousness where, the neuro-dynamics are controlled by quantum mechanical processes involving wave functions [12, 13, 14]. The model of neuro-dynamics and consciousness of brain is constructed as a composite wave function with differentiated quantum probabilities (probability amplitude) of excitations [12]. It is proposed that microstructure of neurons in brain contains microtubules where the cognitive functions are expressed due to quantum coherence as well as decoherence processes [15]. The Penrose-Hameroff model proposes that cognitive functions and consciousness of brain are achieved by quantum computation involving objective reduction (OR) within the microtubules of neurons [11]. The quantum mechanical forces acting in interior part of microtubules control the switching of conformational states. Researchers have indicated that, the relationship between quantum mechanical model and cognitive functions can be shown experimentally [14]. Thus, the quantum mechanical model plays a key role in understanding cognition and consciousness involving physical substrates.

On the other hand, the computational models of cognition and consciousness are formulated explaining determinism and indeterminism in neurological functions. The computational models of neurological cognitive actions are formulated by using finite state automation along with push-down stack [1, 16, 17]. According to this approach, a single neuron is modeled as the tree-shaped computing structure [1]. The tree-model tries to map the physiological structure and functions of neurons into the computational structure while explaining neurological cognitive functions. The model of consciousness based on artificial neural network (ANN) is proposed following global-workspace (GW) formulation in order to understand mechanisms of abstract thinking [18]. However, the questions about similarities and differences between quantum mechanical models and computational models of cognitive functions and consciousness remain unattended.

## 3    Computational Model of Consciousness

The consciousness is a neurobiological phenomenon in brain. The physical layer of consciousness is comprised of interactions of a living biological entity with the environment. The neurological network of brain receives inputs from environment through the sensors and the input signals are processed in brain to generate conscious outputs. Although cognition and consciousness mechanisms are often vaguely defined [4], however, these neurological functions of brain can be modeled by employing quantitative and theoretical frameworks bridging the neurobiological as well as algorithmic functions [1]. The neuro-computational modeling and experimentations have revealed that, the information processing in brain is inherently distributed in nature [1, 7, 19].

In general, the artificial neural network, Global-Workspace model and probabilistic reasoning are used to formulate computational models of cognition and consciousness [2, 3]. The specialized functional nodes (in brain) are connected by neuro-network and, the state of consciousness in brain is generated following distributed computing mechanism [3]. Let N be a set of specialized functional nodes in brain connected by neuro-network represented by graph $G = (N, L)$ where, $L \subset N^2$. Each node $n \in N$ of G has a set of output channels $(O_n)$ selected from the power-set $P(O_n)$, a boolean-valued message transmission function $(\gamma_t(.))$ and, a transformation function $(\sigma(.))$. Let $I_{\alpha n}$ be a set of inputs from environment or inter-nodal messages to a node $n \in N$ of G. The excitation at n is generated due to internalization of an input $x \in I_{\alpha n}$ through a fuzzy membership function $\mu_n(.) \in [0, 1]$ of a node $n \in N$ in the graph G. The specific excitation function of a node in brain is defined as, $\delta : I_{\alpha n} \to S$ where, $S \subset Z$. The value of local excitation at n due to an input is $\lambda_n \in [-u, v]$ where, the excitations are bounded in the domain $(u, v \in Z)$. The triplet function governing the overall functional dynamics in G is given by Equation (1) where, $\omega_{Gn}$ represents outputs of

$n \in N$ to environment, $f_n(.)$ is a selection function at n, $Y \subset P(O_n)$, $h \in f_n(.)$ and, $I_{nt}$ is set of inter-nodal signals/messages generated by $n \in N$ at time t:

$$\lambda_n = \sigma(\mu_n(\delta(I_{\alpha n})), \omega_{Gn})$$
$$f_n : (\delta(I_{\alpha n}), \lambda_n) \rightarrow Y \qquad (1)$$
$$\gamma_t : (I_{nt}, h) \rightarrow \{0, 1\}$$

Furthermore, let $g : \lambda_{\Sigma n} \rightarrow \mathbb{R}$ be a consciousness generating function depending upon the values in the row-matrix $\lambda_{\Sigma n} = (\lambda_n, \lambda_1, \lambda_2, \ldots\ldots, \lambda_m)$, $m = |f_n(.)|$ at a node n $\in N$ at any time t. The distributed computational model of consciousness considers the availability of memory embodied into $\omega_{Gn}$ at nodes by retaining history (log) of input-output pairs in time. The output at time $t + a$ $(a > 0)$ due to an excitation at time t from a conscious brain is computed by, $\beta_n|_{t+a} = g(\lambda_{\Sigma n}|_t)$ where, $\beta_n|_{t+a} \in [-r, r]$, r $\in \mathbb{Z}^+$. Let, an ordered pair $\psi_{n,t+i} = <I_{\alpha n}|_t, \beta_n|_{t+i}>$ represents memory in n for $i > 0$. Thus, the consciousness of a brain with merged memory (experiences) can be computed as a finite set, $\omega_G = \{\psi_{n,t} : n \in N, t \in \mathbb{Z}^+\}$ and, $\omega_{Gn} = \cup_{t \in z+} \psi_{n,t}$.

However, this algebraic computational model can be shown to be coherent to the quantum mechanical model of conscious brain if one considers $\lambda_n$ to be the real Eigen value $(\lambda_n \in \mathbb{Z} \subset \mathbb{R})$ generated at a node $n \in N$ of G due to an excitation.

# 4    Quantum Mechanical Convergence and Analysis

In the quantum mechanical model of consciousness, the brain is considered to be a graph $G = (N, L)$ as a physical substrate and the excitatory outputs of different nodes in G can have quantum superposition. Let a quantum state at time t of a functional node $n \in N$ be a $d$-dimensional $(d > 1)$ ket-vector represented as $|a_n\rangle$.

The set of all possible quantum states of G is $S(G|_t) = \{s_n = \mathbb{H}_{m+1} \bar{u}_{nm} : \forall n \in N\}$ such that, $m = |f_n(.)|$ and, $\mathbb{H}_{m+1} = (H_n, H_1, H_2, \ldots., H_m)$ is a row-matrix of Hermitian whereas, $\bar{u}_{nm} = (|a_n\rangle, |a_1\rangle, |a_2\rangle, \ldots., |a_m\rangle)^T$ is a transpose matrix of Eigen-vectors representing quantum states of the corresponding nodes. The quantum state of G at time t is ordered n-tuple $QS(G|_t) = <s_n : n = 1, 2, \ldots., |N|>$. The superposition of quantum states $s_n$ of a node n can be constructed considering different uniqueness properties of linear Hermitian in G.

## 4.1    States of Nodes with Identical Hermitian

If $\mathbb{H}_{m+1}$ is composed of identical linear Hermitian H and $\lambda_x$ is an Eigen-value of a node $x \in N$ then, $H|a_x\rangle = \lambda_x|a_x\rangle$. Thus, the quantum state of node n at time t is $s_n|_t = [\lambda_{\Sigma n} \bar{u}_{nm}]|_t$. Hence, $s_n$ is a quantum superposition of states at $n \in N$ due to an excitation in G following the input to node n. Let $g(\lambda_{\Sigma n}) \in \mathbb{R}_g$ be a permutation function with B $\leq$ $(m+1)!$ elements where, $\mathbb{R}_g = \cup_{j=1,\ldots B} \{D_j\}$ and, permutation $D_j \in \mathbb{Z} \subset \mathbb{R}$. The condition on B is that, $\exists \lambda_j \in \lambda_{\Sigma n}$ such that $\lambda_j < 0$ then, $B < (m+1)!$. Thus, the consciousness mappings are unique in the brain and, there exists a $g^{-1}$ in the system. This results in $s_n|_t = [g^{-1}(D_j)\bar{u}_{nm}]|_t$. Thus, the relation between quantum states in superposition at nodes and the consciousness mapping can be formulated as,

$$H\bar{u}_{nm} = g^{-1}(D_j)\bar{u}_{nm} \tag{2}$$

Let $\lambda_n = (m+1)g(\lambda_{\Sigma n}) - \Sigma_{i=1, m} \lambda_i$ considering the computation of output of $g(.)$ as global function. Thus, the quantum transformation $H|a_n\rangle = ((m+1)g(\lambda_{\Sigma n}) - \Sigma_{i=1,m} \lambda_i)|a_n\rangle$. Furthermore, $((m+1)g(\lambda_{\Sigma n}) - (\lambda_n + \Sigma_{i=1,m} \lambda_i) + \lambda_n)|a_n\rangle = \lambda_n|a_n\rangle$. This leads to following Equation where, $\lambda_{nm} = \lambda_n + \Sigma_{i=1,m} \lambda_i$,

$$(m+1)g(\lambda_{\Sigma n})|a_n\rangle = \lambda_{nm}|a_n\rangle \tag{3}$$

Hence, there exists a Hermitian $H_{nm}$ such that, $H_{nm}|a_n\rangle = \lambda_{nm}|a_n\rangle$. However, $k_{xn} = \lambda_x/\lambda_n$ is a ratio of (real) Eigen-values and, $\lambda_x|a_n\rangle = k_{xn}(H|a_n\rangle)$. This leads to the following Equation where, $(H|a_n\rangle \mathbf{1}_m)$ is $m$-dimensional row-matrix $(H|a_n\rangle, H|a_n\rangle, H|a_n\rangle, \ldots, H|a_n\rangle)$,

$$(m+1)g(\lambda_{\Sigma n})|a_n\rangle = (1, k_{1n}, k_{2n}, \ldots, k_{mn})(H|a_n\rangle \mathbf{1}_m)^T \tag{4}$$

Hence, $H_{nm}|a_n\rangle = (1, k_{1n}, k_{2n}, \ldots, k_{mn})(H|a_n\rangle \mathbf{1}_m)^T$.

## 4.2 States of Nodes with Non-Identical Hermitian

If the elements in linear Hermitian $\mathbb{H}_{m+1}$ are non-identical then, $s_n = (H_n, H_1, H_2, \ldots, H_m)\bar{u}_{nm}$. However, the transformation $H_x|a_x\rangle = \lambda_x|a_x\rangle$ can be further oriented as, $H_x|a_x\rangle = [\lambda_x/\lambda_1]\lambda_1|a_x\rangle$ because, $[\lambda_x/\lambda_1]$ is a ratio of real Eigen-values of two respective nodes. This results in $\lambda_1|a_x\rangle = H_{x1}|a_x\rangle$ where, Hermitian $H_{x1} = k_{1x}H_x$ and, $k_{1x} = [\lambda_1/\lambda_x]$. Hence, the quantum cross-superposition of states at node x due to m individual nodes can be stated as, $\lambda_1|a_x\rangle + \lambda_2|a_x\rangle + \ldots + \lambda_m|a_x\rangle = H_{x1}|a_x\rangle + H_{x2}|a_x\rangle + \ldots + H_{xm}|a_x\rangle$ which results in the following relation,

$$(\lambda_1, \lambda_2, \ldots, \lambda_m)(|a_x\rangle \mathbf{1}_m)^T = (H_{x1}, H_{x2}, \ldots, H_{xm})(|a_x\rangle \mathbf{1}_m)^T \tag{5}$$

However, at node $n \in N$, $\lambda_{\Sigma n}\bar{u}_{nm} = (H_{xn}, H_{x1}, H_{x2}, \ldots, H_{xm})\bar{u}_{nm}$ considering the m+1 functional nodes under excitation having quantum superposition of states. Thus, the relationship between superimposed quantum states at nodes under non-identical Hermitian and the consciousness mapping can be formulated as,

$$(H_{xn}, H_{x1}, H_{x2}, \ldots, H_{xm})\bar{u}_{nm} = g^{-1}(D_j)\bar{u}_{nm} \tag{6}$$

The quantum superposition of states due to excitation of $n \in N$ is given by, $(\lambda_n, \lambda_1, \lambda_2, \ldots, \lambda_m)\bar{u}_{nm} = H_n|a_n\rangle + H_1|a_1\rangle + \ldots + H_m|a_m\rangle$. However, $\lambda_1|a_n\rangle = k_{1n}H_n|a_n\rangle$ and, $H_n|a_n\rangle = ((m+1)g(\lambda_{\Sigma n}) - (\lambda_n + \Sigma_{i=1,m} \lambda_i) + \lambda_n)|a_n\rangle$.

Thus, the quantum superposition at n with respect to node 1 can be derived as $(\lambda_n, \lambda_1, \lambda_2, \ldots\ldots, \lambda_m)\bar{u}_{nm} = ([1/k_{1n}]H_{n1}, [1/k_{11}]H_{11}, [1/k_{12}]H_{21}, \ldots, [1/k_{1m}]H_{m1})\bar{u}_{nm}$. Furthermore, $k_{11} = 1$ and, $H_{11} = H_1$. Considering the Hermitian row-matrix $([1/k_{1n}]H_{n1}, [1/k_{11}]H_{11}, [1/k_{12}]H_{21}, \ldots, [1/k_{1m}]H_{m1}) = \mathbb{H}_{nm}$ the following relation can be concluded,

$$g^{-1}(D_j)\bar{u}_{nm} = \mathbb{H}_{nm}\bar{u}_{nm} \qquad (7)$$

The Eqs. (2) and (6) indicate that an invertible g(.) leads to the convergence of quantum basis and the algebraic functional mapping of models of consciousness. This leads to following lemma.

**Lemma:** Let $\lambda_D$ be a degenerate Eigen-value in G. If there exists $N_\lambda \subset N$ such that, $\forall n \in N_\lambda$, $H_n|a_n\rangle = \lambda_D|a_n\rangle$ then, an oriented consciousness is maintained by $N_\lambda$ in G.

**Proof:** Let there exists $N_\lambda \subset N$ such that, $|N_\lambda| \geq 0$. If the Hermitian operators are non-identical then, $\forall n \in N_\lambda$, $H_n|a_n\rangle = \lambda_D|a_n\rangle$ and, $\forall x \in N\backslash N_\lambda$, $H_x|a_x\rangle = \lambda_x|a_x\rangle$. Otherwise, in case of identical Hermitian, $\forall x \in N\backslash N_\lambda$, $H|a_x\rangle = \lambda|a_x\rangle$ and, $\forall n \in N_\lambda$, $H|a_n\rangle = \lambda_D|a_n\rangle$.

In any case, the relative weight in states of consciousness, denoted by orientation $\theta$, is represented as $\theta = (|N| - |N_\lambda| + 2)/(|N|+1)$ by considering set of nodes in $N_\lambda$ as a singular permutable element (having internal permutations) and *autapse*. The surface-map of orientation due to degenerate Eigen-values is illustrated in Fig. 1.

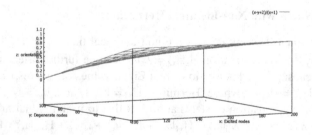

**Fig. 1.** Characteristic surface-map of orientation

However, if the condition $|N_\lambda| < |N|$ is relaxed further in G indicating the existence of permanent degenerate Eigen-values of nodes in G then, the permutation function g(.) generates the skew as, $\rho = (\|(|N| - |N_\lambda|)\| + 2)!/(|N|+1)!$. The surface-map of skew dynamics is illustrated in Fig. 2. It is evident that, the skew-zone is aggregated by the nodes having degenerate Eigen-values in G providing specific orientation.

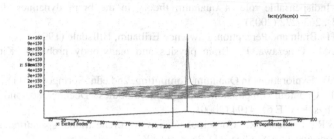

**Fig. 2.** Surface-map of skew dynamics in G with 100 nodes

Thus, the oriented consciousness is maintained by $N_\lambda$ in G.

# 5 Conclusion

The brain is a distributed computational device having neurons connected by neuro-network as a physical substrate. Generally, modeling of consciousness follows two diagonal approaches such as, computational modeling and quantum modeling. However, there is a transaction between the two approaches. This paper proposes a model of consciousness as an overall cognitive function of brain by using distributed computational elements and functional neurophysiology. However, the proposed computational model has a distinct basis in the quantum mechanical and field theory. The proposed model unifies the distributed computational model of consciousness to the quantum theoretic basis of the cognitive functions. According to the unified model, consciousness is a distributed neuro-computation having quantum superposition of states.

# References

1. Fitch, W.T.: Toward a Computational Framework for Cognitive Biology: Unifying approaches from cognitive neuroscience and comparative cognition. Physics of Life Reviews (2014), doi: 10.1016/j.plrev, 04.005
2. Reggia, J.A.: The rise of machine consciousness: Studying consciousness with computational models. Neural Networks 44, 112–131 (2013)
3. Lin, J., Yang, J.G.: Consciousness modeling: A neural computing approach. In: Proceedings of the Third International Conference on Machine Learning and Cybernetics, Shanghai. IEEE (2004)
4. Starzyk, J.A., Prasad, D.K.: A Computational model of machine consciousness. Int. J. Machine Consciousness 3(2) (2011)
5. Alfinito, E., Vitiello, G.: The dissipative quantum model of brain: how does memory localize in correlated neuronal domains. Information Sciences (Journal) 128(3-4), 217–229 (2000)

6. Kurita, Y.: Indispensable role of quantum theory in the brain dynamics. Biosystems Journal 80(3), 263–272 (2005)
7. Pribram, K.H.: Brain and Perception. Lawrence Erlbaum, Hillsdale (1991)
8. Ricciardi, L.M., Umezawa, H.: Brain physics and many-body problems. Kibernetik 4 (1967)
9. Williams, C.P.: Explorations in Quantum Computing, 2nd edn. Springer (2011)
10. Tegmark, M.: Quantum computation in brain microtubules? Decoherence and biological feasibility. Phys. Rev. E 61, 4194 (2000)
11. Hameroff, S.R., Penrose, R.: Conscious events as orchestrated spacetime selections. Journal of Consciousness Studies 3(1), 36–53 (1996)
12. Beck, F., Eccles, J.: Quantum aspects of brain activity and the role of consciousness. Proceedings of the National Academy of Sciences of the USA 89, 11357–11361 (1992)
13. Beck, F.: Quantum brain dynamics and consciousness. In: van Loocke, P. (ed.) The Physical Nature of Consciousness, pp. 83–116. Benjamins, Amsterdam (2001)
14. Conte, E., Todarello, O., Federici, A., Vitiello, F., Lopane, M., Khrennikov, A., Zbilut, J.P.: Some remarks on an experiment suggesting quantum-like behavior of cognitive entities and formulation of an abstract quantum mechanical formalism to describe cognitive entity and its dynamics. Journal of Chaos, Solitons and Fractals 31, 1076–1088 (2009)
15. Hagan, S., Hameroff, S.R., Tuszynski, J.A.: Quantum computation in brain microtubules: decoherence and biological feasibility, Phys. Rev. E 65(6), 061901 (2002)
16. Arbib, M.A., Caplan, D.: Neurolinguistics must be computational. Behavioral & Brain Sciences 2(3), 449–483 (1979)
17. Poeppel, D., Embick, D.: Defining the relation between linguistics and neuroscience. In: Cutler, A. (ed.) Twenty-First Century Psycholinguistics: Four Cornerstones, pp. 103–120. Lawrence Erlbaum, London (2005)
18. Sun, R., Franklin, S.: Computational models of consciousness. In: Zelazo, P., Moscovitch, M. (eds.) Cambridge Handbook of Consciousness, pp. 151–174. Cambridge University Press (2007)
19. Rees, G., Kreiman, G., Koch, C.: Neural correlates of consciousness in humans. Nature Reviews Neuroscience 3, 261–270 (2002)
20. Koch, C., Tononi, G.: Can machines be conscious? IEEE Spectrum, 55–59 (June 2008)
21. Fekete, T., Edelman, S.: Towards a computational theory of experience. Consciousness and Cognition 20, 807–827 (2011)

# Nature-Inspired Algorithms for Selecting EEG Sources for Motor Imagery Based BCI

Sebastián Basterrech[1(✉)], Pavel Bobrov[1,2], Alexander Frolov[2],
and Dušan Húsek[3]

[1] VŠB–Technical University of Ostrava
Ostrava, Czech Republic
`Sebastian.Basterrech.Tiscordio@vsb.cz`
[2] Institute of Higher Nervous Activity and Neurophysiologgy,
RAS, Moscow, Russia
`P-bobrov@yandex.ru, Aafrolov@mail.ru`
[3] Institute of Computer Science, Academy of Sciences of the Czech Republic
Prague, Czech Republic
`Dusan@cs.cas.cz`

**Abstract.** In this article we examine the performance of two well-known metaheuristic techniques (Genetic Algorithm and Simulating Annealing) for selecting the input features of a classifier in a BCI system. An important problem of the EEG-based BCI system consists in designing the EEG pattern classifier. The selection of the EEG channels used for building that learning predictor has impact in the classifier performance. We present results of both metaheuristic techniques on real data set when the classifier is a Bayesian predictor. We statistically compare that performances with a random selection of the EEG channels. According our empirical results our approach significantly increases the accuracy of the learning predictor.

**Keywords:** Brain computer interface · EEG pattern selection · Bayesian classifier · Genetic algorithms · Simulating annealing

## 1 Introduction

A *Brain Computer Interface (BCI)* is a functional interaction between the brain and an external device. It can be useful means for assisting and repairing human cognitive and sensory-motor functions. A BCI basically consists of three components: a brain signal acquisition system, an information processing device, and an external device. In respect of first component, there are several kinds of signals that have been used for BCI. The most widespread signal is the *Electroencephalography (EEG)* that presents good advantages in respect to the other ones, such as: good temporal resolution, portability, and low set-up cost. The second BCI provides a parametric mapping between the brain signals and the mental states. This tool is used for discriminating EEG patterns related to different mental states and includes supervised learning methods. The third component is an external device committed to receive commands from the classifier

© Springer International Publishing Switzerland 2015
L. Rutkowski et al. (Eds.): ICAISC 2015, Part II, LNAI 9120, pp. 79–90, 2015.
DOI: 10.1007/978-3-319-19369-4_8

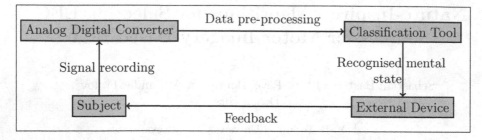

**Fig. 1.** General diagram of a signal based BCI system

and to provide feedbacks to the subject. Figure 1 is depicted a BCI architecture including information flows.

In the EEG-based BCI experiment the signals are recorded using $N$ electrodes. Then, we dispose of a high-dimensional time series data, which is most often affected by sources of noise. In order to improve the classification efficiency in the BCI, a pre-training step is performed. This consists among others in selecting a subset of the EEG signals from the all-channel time series data. The problem of finding the best configuration of the EEG signals via *brute-force search* has factorial algorithmic time. Instead, we propose an alternative approach to find a *good* configuration of EGG channels as relevant sources for BCI.

The goal of this article is to study the efficiency of two well-known nature-inspired metaheuristic techniques, *Genetic Algorithm (GA)* and *Simulating Annealing (SA)*, for selecting the input information of the EEG pattern classifier. The SA is a probabilistic metaheuristic for solving optimisation problems, that was inspired from the annealing process in thermodynamics. The original motivation of GA was to simulate the natural selection process. In this article, we consider a *Bayesian Predictor* as the EEG pattern classifier, due to well performances of this learning tool in our previous works [1]. Therefore, the learning process has two phases. The first one consists of performing the metaheuristic techniques for selecting the EEG channels. The second one consists in training a Bayesian classifier in order to generate a mapping between a set of EEG signals and mental tasks. The signals that are not selected in the first phase by the nature-inspired algorithms are omitted in the second learning phase. We compute the accuracy of that technique using the $\kappa$ function [2, 3].

A previous study of EEG feature selection using metaheuristic was presented in [4]. In this work, the authors use *Support Vector Machine (SVM)* as classification technique over a specific data set, and the EEG feature selection was done applying GA. In [5], the authors use GA and SVM to search the features on a EEG-based BCI. The main differences of our work with these articles are: we use our own BCI experimental data, we study the performance of two feature selection tools (GA and SA), and we use our own Bayesian learning classifier [6].

The article is organised as follows. Section 2 presents the experimental procedure used for collecting the data set. This section also contains a description of a Bayesian classifier, and it presents the criteria used for measuring its performance assesment. Section 3 introduces two nature-inspired techniques

(SA and GA) employed as feature selection. Besides, we present an algorithm that shows how to use the SA and GA in the BCI context. The experimental results are presented in Section 4. Next, we go for final conclusions and future work.

## 2   Methodology

In this Section, we specify the methodology and the protocol used during the experiments. In addition, a background about the Bayesian Classifier is introduced in subsection 2.2, and the definition of the performance assessment is presented in subsection 2.3.

### 2.1   Experimental Procedure

In this Section, we describe in brief the protocol used for collecting the data set. More details about the experiments can be seen in [2,7]. The data was collected during the experimental sessions with 5 right-handed and healthy subjects aged from 25 to 50. The subjects performed instructions displayed on a screen. There are four instructions: to *relax*, to imagine the movement of the *right hand*, to imagine the movement of the *left hand*, and to imagine the movement of the *feet*. The movement that they were asked to imagine was a handgrip or feet pressure. An experiment for each subject consists of training and testing sessions. The training session was performed in order to train the BCI classifier. During the testing session, in real time we provide to the subjects the output of the BCI classifier in orden to enhance the subject efforts to imagine a movement.

The subject was sitting in a comfortable chair located one meter from a 17" monitor. The subject was instructed to fix a gaze on a motionless circle of 1 cm in diameter, in the middle of the screen. Each 10 seconds, one command instruction was displayed in the screen. Four gray markers were placed around the circle. A marker changes the colour into green signalled to the subject that mental task must be performed. Each clue was preceded by a 4-second warning when the marker color changed into blue. Green color in the left and right markers indicates to *left and right hand movement imagining*, respectively. The top marker indicates *relaxation*. The lower marker corresponds to *feet movement imagining*. Four such instructions presented in random order constituted a block. The training session is composed by one block and the testing session has nine blocks as is illustrated in Figure 2. Each subject received 10 blocks of instructions at each experimental day. The structure of the block is presented in Figure 3. During the testing sessions, the result of the predictor classification was presented to the subject. This was done using green color in the central circle when the estimation of the classifier predictor coincides with the instruction. Besides, we increase the brightness of the central circle showing the augmenting of the classifying confidence. During the instruction to *relax* the subject does not receive feedbacks from the screen.

The EEG signals were recorded using 48 active electrodes and *g.USBamp* and *g.USBamp API* for MATLAB (g-tec, Graz, Austria). The sampling frequency employed was 256 Hz. The EEG signal were filtered by notch filter in order to suppress supply noise. The position of the electrodes were: Fz, F3, F4, Fcz, Fc3, Fc4, F7, F8, Fcz, Fc3, Fc4, Fc5, Fc6, Fc7, Fc8, Cz, C1, C2, C3, C4, C5, C6, T7, T8, Cpz, Cp1, Cp2, Cp3, Cp4, Cp5, Cp6, Tp7, Tp8, Pz, P1, P2, P3, P4, P5, P6, P7, P8, Pose, Po3, Po4, Po7, Po8, Oz, O1, O2. The central frontal electrode (Afz) was taken as reference. All codes of data processing were carry out with Matlab (Mathworks Inc. Natick, Ma, USA). The subjects have provided written a participation consent. The experimental procedure was approved by the *Board of Ethics at the Institute for Higher Nervous Activity and Neurophysiology of the Russian Academy of Sciences* [8].

| Daily experimental sessions | |
| --- | --- |
| Training | Testing |
| 1 block | 9 blocks |

**Fig. 2.** The sequence of sessions in the experimental protocol

| Block | | | | | | | |
| --- | --- | --- | --- | --- | --- | --- | --- |
| Relaxation | | Left hand MI | | Right hand MI | | Foot MI | |
| 4 | 10 | 4 | 10 | 4 | 10 | 4 | 10 |

**Fig. 3.** Structure of the experimental block. Each instruction was presented only once and using random selection. The light blue areas of the block represent time of the instruction for warnings. The rest of the blue areas of the block represent time of the instruction for performance.

## 2.2 Bayesian Classifier Description

In this article, the mental tasks were classified using a *Bayesian Classifier (BC)* [1, 6]. Let $L$ be the number of mental tasks to be classified and let $N$ be the number of active electrodes used for recording the EEG signals. We denote by $X_n(t)$ the EEG signal recorded by the electrode $n$ at time $t$. We assume that $X_n(t)$ has Gaussian distribution with zero mean for all $n$ and $t$. We denote by $C_i(t)$ the covariance matrix of the EEG signal corresponding to the $i$ task with $i = 1, \ldots, L$. Given a signal $X(t)$, for determining the class that the signal $X(t)$ is associated, we compute the values of $Prob(X(t) \mid i)$, for all $i$. We assign to $X(t)$ the class such that occurs the maximum value of $Prob(X(t) \mid i)$. Due to the distribution of $X(t)$ is Gaussian, the probability to obtain $X(t)$ under the condition that it corresponds to performing the mental tasks $i$ is given by

$$Prob(X(t) \mid i) \propto \exp\left(\frac{-V_i(t)}{2}\right), \tag{1}$$

where $V_i(t)$ is defined as $V_i(t) = X^T(t)C_i(t)X(t) + \ln(det(C_i(t)))$ and $det(\cdot)$ is the determinant function of a matrix. Note that, $C_i(t)$ must be a nonsingular matrix in order to compute the $\ln(det(C_i(t)))$.

The class that maximises the expression (1) is such that minimises the value $V_i(t)$. As a consequence, it is enough to find the minimal values of $V_i(t)$ at each time for all $i$. The value of $V_i(t)$ can be unstable in the time, therefore we split the signal in epochs. Let $u$ be an epoch of duration $\Delta t$. We compute the data covariance matrix at each epoch $u$ as

$$C(u) = \langle X(u)X^T(u) \rangle, \tag{2}$$

then we compute the average $V_i(u)$ by

$$\langle V_i(u) \rangle = \text{trace}(C(u)C_i^{-1}(u)) + \ln(\det(C_i(u))), \tag{3}$$

where $\text{trace}(\cdot)$ is the trace function of a matrix.

The training phase of the Bayesian predictor consists in computing the co-variance matrices $C_i$ for all $i$. The predictor was tested computing $C(u)$ and the $\langle V_i(u) \rangle$ values.

## 2.3   Accuracy of the Estimator

To evaluate the accuracy of the classifier and its generalisation capability we proceed as follows. We split the signals in epochs of a $\Delta t$ duration. We randomly divide the learning set in 10 blocks. We randomly chose 7 blocks of them for computing the covariance matrices $C_i$ for all mental tasks (training phase). The rest part of the learning set is used for testing the predictor. We repeat $M$ times these classification trials. Next, we generate a confusion matrix $P$ of dimensions $L \times L$ that contains the averages over all $M$ classification trials. The $P$ matrix has at the position $(i, j)$ the probability $p_{i,j}$, that is the probability to recognise the $i-$th mental state in case that the instruction $j-$th mental task is performed. Note that, the better learning predictor performs the $P$ is closer to the identity.

We chose the Cohen's $\kappa$ function as indice of classification efficiency. The $\kappa$ function is defined as follows:

$$\kappa = \frac{\dfrac{1}{L}\sum_{i=1}^{L} p_{i,i} - \dfrac{1}{L^2}\sum_{i=1}^{L}\sum_{j=1}^{L} p_{i,j}}{1 - \dfrac{1}{L^2}\sum_{i=1}^{L}\sum_{j=1}^{L} p_{i,j}}. \tag{4}$$

The value $\kappa$ belongs to the $[0, 1]$ interval, closer is $\kappa$ to 1 closer is the accuracy of the predictor, on the other hand a $\kappa$ value closes to 0 indicates a deficient classifier.

# 3   Nature-Inspired Algorithm Description

This section introduces our main contribution, that is the algorithm that uses metaheuristic techniques for doing the EEG channels selection on the context of BCI based on motor imagery experiments. The section starts with a description of the nature-inspired algorithms used in this article: the *Simulating Annealing (SA)* and the *Genetic Algorithm (GA)*. Next, we specify our approach that mixes the metaheuristic techniques and the bayesian classifier.

## 3.1   Simulating Annealing Description

The *Simulating Annealing (SA)* method is an optimisation technique particularly interesting for solving problems of large scale. It has been applied for solving both combinatorial and continuous optimisation problems. The technique is mainly useful when the goal is to find a global extremum that is hidden among several local ones [9]. The goal is to minimise/maximise an objective function that in the SA context is often referred as *energy function*. The algorithm tries random steps following some criteria that arises from physical phenomena. The method is an analogy with the thermodynamical process that liquids freeze and crystallise or metals cool and anneal. Following this analogy, the method has a parameter called *temperature* $(T)$, and a constant called *Boltzmann's constant* relates the temperature with the energy of the current system state. The technique is iterative, at each iteration we replace a current solution $\mathbf{s}^{\text{curr}}$ by a random *nearby solution* $\mathbf{s}^{\text{new}}$ that is chosen with a probability $p$. We consider a *nearby solution* such that its Hamming distance with the current solution is less than or equal to 1. In other words, the strings $\mathbf{s}^{\text{curr}}$ and $\mathbf{s}^{\text{new}}$ differ only in one bit. The temperature $T$ decreases at each iteration until is reached some arbitrary value $T^{\text{end}}$. The probability of selecting a new solution is given by

$$p = \min\{\exp\left(-(E(\mathbf{s}^{\text{new}}) - E(\mathbf{s}^{\text{curr}}))/kT\right), 1\}, \tag{5}$$

where $k$ is the Boltzmann's constant. The probability brings the capacity to jump from a local optimum to another part of the searching space. This exploration criteria usually takes a downhill step while sometimes takes an uphill step is popularly known under the name of *Metropolis Algorithm*. The algorithm starts from an initial solution with an initial temperature $T$, and a sequence of solutions are proposed, and the temperature decreases its value until it reaches a *frozen* condition.

## 3.2   Genetic Algorithm Description

The *Genetic Algorithm (GA)* family started in the 60's [10]. At the beginning, the technique was motivated by a biological analogy with the selective breeding of the plants and animals [10]. In the last 20 years, the GA trend has become increasingly popular for solving optimisation problems. A GA is an iterative procedure. At each iteration, points in the searching space are analysed as possible solutions, and they are combined according some rules. Following the biological analogy, the points collection is named *population*, each individual point is called *chromosome*, and the coordinates in a particular point are named *genes*. Each chromosome is evaluated by a fitness function $E(\cdot)$ that is the function to be optimised. The algorithm consists in modifying the population applying the following three evolutionary operations:

- Selection: there are several selection schema presented in the literature In this article, we study the selection following the *Baker's stochastic universal selection*, a single value is used for sample all of the solutions by choosing them at evenly spaced intervals.
- Crossover: It is a function that takes two chromosomes (often referred as *parents*) and generates two new ones (often referred as *offspring*). The operation replaces some genes of one parent by the corresponding genes of the other one. In general, the selection of which genes to replace is random. In this article, we follow the criteria of *one-point crossover*. Given two parents $A$ and $B$, this operation consists in random selecting a cutting-point, it means a random position in the chromosome. Next, to generate a new two chromosomes. One of them in its first part (until the cutting point) has genes from parent $A$ and the second part (from the cutting point till the end) has genes from the another parent $B$. Another chromosome has in its first part the genes from $B$ and in its second part has the genes from $A$.
- Mutation: In this operation a randomly selected group of genes is changed. In our problem, the genes are binaries, then the gene mutation is the binary complement operation.

### 3.3   Applying the Nature-Inspired Algorithms for Feature Selection

Without loss of generality we enumerate the EEG channels by $\{1, \ldots, N\}$, where $N$ is the number of electrodes sources of the EEG signals. The searching space of our problem is $\{0,1\}^N$. Possible solutions have the form $\mathbf{s} = [s_1, s_2, \ldots, s_N]$ where $s_i = 0$ represents that the signal captured by the electrode $i$ is omitted as source of the classification tool, and $s_i = 1$ represents that the signal measured by the electrode $i$ is an input of the classification tool. Besides, we consider as accuracy of our model the *kappa* function given by (4), that has domain in $[0,1]$. The problem is to find $\mathbf{s} \in \{0,1\}^N$ such that the kappa function is maximized when the BC is used for the mental class estimation. Note that a larger kappa value implies a better model accuracy. For this reason we have a maximisation problem instead of a minimisation one.

In the SA method, given a current solution $\mathbf{s}^{\mathrm{curr}}$ we must select a *nearby* solution of $\mathbf{s}^{\mathrm{curr}}$ that we denote by $\mathbf{s}^{\mathrm{new}}$. In this step, we randomly select a value $i$ in $[1, N]$. Next, we define the nearby solution as $s_j^{\mathrm{new}} = s_i^{\mathrm{curr}}$ for all $j \neq i$ and $s_j^{\mathrm{new}} = s_i^{\mathrm{curr}} + 1 \mod 2$, where $\mod$ is the module function. The procedure for generating the classification tool in the BCI using SA is presented in Algorithm (1). The algorithm has the following input parameters: an initial temperature $T^{(0)}$ and the stop condition $T^{\mathrm{end}}$. Besides, it must be defined the a cooling schedule for decreasing the temperature. Algorithm (2) presents the method for generating the feature selection using GA.

---

**Algorithm 1.** Procedure for generating the classification tool in the BCI using Simulated Annealing.

---

1  Define an initial population $\{s^{(1)}, \ldots s^{(K)}\}$;
2  **for** *(k = 1 to K)* **do**
3      Generate the time-series data with the electrodes channels that verifies $s_i^{(k)} = 1$;
4      Train the classification tool;
5      Compute the kappa function;
6  $T = T^{(0)}$;
7  $s^{\mathrm{curr}} = s^{(k)}$;
8  **while** *(T $\geq T^{\mathrm{end}}$)* **do**
9      Select a random nearby solution $s^{\mathrm{new}}$;
10     **if** $(kappa(s^{\mathrm{new}}) \leq kappa(s^{\mathrm{curr}}))$ **then**
11         $s^{\mathrm{curr}} = s^{\mathrm{new}}$;
12     **else**
13         Compute $p$ using expression (1);
14         **if** $(rand(0, 1) < p)$ **then**
15             $s^{\mathrm{curr}} = s^{\mathrm{new}}$;
16     $i = i + 1$;
17     Decrease temperature $T$;
18 Return $s^{\mathrm{curr}}$;

---

## 4  Experimental Results

We begin by specifying the notation. we use the following abbreviations: the Bayesian Classifier without using metaheuristic is denoted by BC, Bayesian Classifier with feature selection using Simulating Annealing is denoted by BC-SA, and Bayesian Classifier with feature selection using Genetic Algorithms is denoted by BC-GA. A tradeoff between time resolution and accuracy is presented in the expression (3), wherein must be defined the epoch length criteria. We follow the same criteria that in [1] where the authors used epochs of 1 second length. The setting of the GA method was done as follows. We perform 1500 generations, each generation has 100 chromosomes, we use the Baker selection for select the parent chromosomes, and the mutation factor is 1/48. In the SA technique the cooling schedule consists in decrease the temperature in one unit at each algorithm iteration. In order to compare performance between SA and GA, both algorithms are performed during the same time. In order to have reference values about the accuracy of the BC without the feature selection using the metaheuristics, we perform 50 times the BC using random selection of the EEG channels. Then, we compute the kappa value reached by the BC predictor for each one of the 50 trials.

Table 1 shows the accuracy obtained by the BC, BC-SA and the BC-GA procedures. First column shows an identificador of the studied subject. The columns

---

**Algorithm 2.** Procedure for generating the classification tool in the BCI using Genetic Algorithm.

---

1   Define an initial population $\{\mathbf{s}^{(1)}, \ldots \mathbf{s}^{(K)}\}$;

2   **for** *(k = 1 to K)* **do**

3      Generate the time-series data with the electrodes channels that verifies $s_i^{(k)} = 1$;

4      Train the classification tool;

5      Compute the kappa function;

6   **while** (cond is not satisfied) **do**

7      **repeat**

8         Select parent chromosomes;

9         Choose a cutting point;

10        Perform crossover;

11        Choose mutation points;

12        Perform mutation;

13        Evaluate fitness of the offspring;

14      **until** (New generation has enough offsprings);

15   Return the classification tool and the best combination of EEG channels;

---

**Table 1.** Classification accuracy using the kappa function. The first column presents the experiment identification. The second column presents the results when a Bayesian Classifier (BC) was performed using the all EEG channels. The third column shows the results of to use SA as feature selection and then to use BC. The last column shows the accuracy reached when GA is used for selecting the channels and BC is performed. 50 iteraciones

| Experiment Id | 50 random selections | | | | SA-BC | GA-BC |
|---|---|---|---|---|---|---|
| | Mean | Std | 95% | Max | | |
| A | 0.1424 | 0.0412 | 0.1538 | 0.2433 | 0.2522 | **0.2631** |
| B | 0.3398 | 0.0653 | 0.3579 | 0.4867 | 0.4836 | **0.4972** |
| C | 0.3076 | 0.1062 | 0.3370 | 0.4696 | 0.5360 | **0.5372** |
| D | 0.1152 | 0.0585 | 0.1314 | 0.2264 | 0.2478 | **0.2544** |
| E | 0.2028 | 0.0439 | 0.2150 | 0.2753 | **0.2922** | 0.2882 |

2 to 5 show results reached using the BC. In column 2, we can see the average value of kappa among the kappa values reached on the 50 trials. Column 3 presents the standard deviation of these set of kappa values, column 4 shows the upper endpoint of a 95% confidence interval, and the column 5 presents the maximum kappa value reached among the 50 trials. Column 6 shows the best kappa value reached by the BC-SA, and column 7 presents the best kappa value reached by the BC-GA. We can see that in all experiments the upper endpoint of the 95% confidence interval is lower than the kappa value reached used meta-heuristics. Even the maximum kappa value reached among the set of experiment

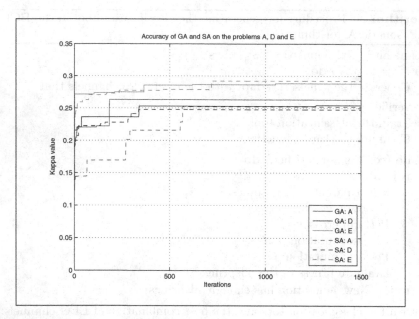

**Fig. 4.** Example of the evolution of the best kappa function for the experiments $A$, $D$ and $E$. The dashed lines correspond to values obtained using BC-SA and continuous lines refer to the values obtained withe BC-GA.

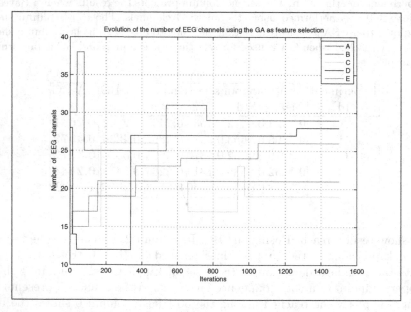

**Fig. 5.** Example of the evolution of the number of EEG channels used in the best solution when the BC-GA is applied

is less than the kappa value computed using BC-SA and BC-GA. In the 80% of the experiments the BC-GA reaches better kappa value than GA-SA. Figure 4 illustrates the evolution of the kappa value for the experiments $A$, $B$ and $C$ for both procedures BC-SA and BC-GA. Figure 5 presents an example of the evolution of the number of EEG channels used for computed the best kappa value at each generation of the BC-GA method. The figure has the evolution of number of electrodes used for the 5 experiments.

## 5   Conclusions and Future Work

An important task of a BCI system development consists in designing the EGG pattern classifier. The analysis based on EEG signals presents significant difficulties, due to the presence of noise. As a consequence, the selection of the EEG channels used for building a learning predictor can impact in the predictor performance. In general, in the EEG-based BCI experiments several EEG channels are used for collecting the data. For instance, in our experiments we are using 48 channels. Therefore, the selection of a best combination of EEG channels can not be done using a *brute-force* strategy.

In this article, we propose a solution for this problem that is based on two well-known metaheuristic techniques: *Simulating Annealing (SA) and Genetic Algorithms (GA)*. We analyse the performance of both techniques for selecting the EEG channels when we are using a Bayesian Classifier in the BCI system. We compare the performance of these techniques with a EEG random selection strategy. Besides, we present statistical results for that comparisons. We can affirm that the use of both metaheuristic procedures significantly improve the accuracy of the EEG pattern predictor. In particular, in the 80% of the experiments the higher accuracy is reached when the selection is done using the GA. As a for future work, we are interested in applying the same approach for EEG-based BCI visual imagery. Additionally, we have plans to compare the performance reached by SA and GA with other nature-inspired techniques.

**Acknowledgement.** This work was supported within the framework of the IT4Innovations Centre of Excellence project, reg. no. CZ.1.05/1.1.00/02.0070 supported by Operational Programme 'Research and Development for Innovations' funded by Structural Funds of the European Union and state budget of the Czech Republic and this article has been elaborated in the framework of the project New creative teams in priorities of scientific research, reg. no. CZ.1.07/2.3.00/30.0055. The authors also thank for their work support from the long-term strategic development financing budget of the Institute of Computer Science (RVO:67985807).

# References

1. Frolov, A.A., Husek, D., Bobrov, P.: Comparison of four classification methods for brain computer interface. Neural Network World 21(2), 101–115 (2011)
2. Frolov, A.A., Husek, D., Bobrov, P., Mokienko, O., Tintera, J.: Sources of electrical brain activity most relevant to performance of brain-computer interface based on motor imagery. In: Brain-Computer Interface Systems - Recent Progress and Future Prospects, pp. 175–193. InTech (2013)
3. Bobrov, P., Frolov, A.A., Cantor, C., Fedulova, I., Bakhnyan, M., Zhavoronkov, A.: Brain-computer interface based on generation of visual images. PLOS ONE 6(6), 1–12 (2011)
4. Schröder, M., Bogdan, M., Hinterberger, T., Birbaumer, N.: Automated EEG feature selection for brain computer interfaces. In: First International IEEE EMBS Conference on Neural Engineering, pp. 626–629 (March 2003)
5. Peterson, D.A., Knight, J.N., Kirby, M.J., Anderson, C.W., Thaut, M.H.: Feature selection and blind source separation in an EEG-based brain-computer interface. EURASIP J. Appl. Signal Process. 2005, 3128–3140 (2005)
6. Bobrov, P.D., Korshakov, A.V., Roshchin, V.I., Frolov, A.A.: Bayesian Classifier for Brain-computer Interface B]ased on Mental Representation of Movements. Zh Vyssh Nerv Deiat Im I P Pavlova 62(1), 89–99 (2012)
7. Frolov, A.A., Husek, D., Bobrov, P., Korshakov, A., Chernikova, L., Konovalov, R., Mokienko, O.: Sources of EEG activity most relevant to performance of brain-computer interface based on motor imagery. Neural Network World 22(1), 21–37 (2012)
8. Institute of Higher Nervous Activity and Neurophysiology of RAS (IHNA & NPh RAS), Moscow, Russia, http://www.ihna.ru/en/
9. Press, W.H., Teukolsky, S.A., Vetterling, W.T., Flannery, B.P.: Numerical Recipes in C++: The Art of Scientific Computing. Cambridge University Press (February 2002)
10. Reeves, C.R.: Genetic Algorithms for the Operations Research. INFORMS Journal of Computing 9(3), 231–250 (1997)

# PROCESS: Projection-Based Classification of Electroencephalograph Signals

Krisztian Buza[1(✉)], Júlia Koller[1], and Kristóf Marussy[1,2]

[1] BioIntelligence Lab, Institute of Genomic Medicine and Rare Disorders,
Semmelweis University, Budapest, Hungary
buza@biointelligence.hu, jkoller4@gmail.com
http://www.biointelligence.hu
[2] Budapest University of Technology and Economics, Budapest, Hungary
marussy@cs.bme.hu

**Abstract.** Classification of electroencephalograph (EEG) signals is the common denominator in EEG-based recognition systems that are relevant to many applications ranging from medical diagnosis to EEG-controlled devices such as web browsers or typing tools for paralyzed patients. Here, we propose a new method for the classification of EEG signals. One of its core components projects EEG signals into a vector space. We demonstrate that this projection may allow visual inspection and therefore exploratory analysis of large EEG datasets. Subsequently, we use logistic regression with our novel vector representation in order to classify EEG signals. Our experiments on a large, publicly available real-world dataset containing 11028 EEG signals show that our approach is robust and accurate, i.e., it outperforms state-of-the-art classifiers in various classification tasks, such as classification according to disease or stimulus. Furthermore, we point out that our approach requires only the calculation of a few DTW distances, therefore, our approach is fast compared to other DTW-based classifiers.

**Keywords:** Electroencephalography · Classification · Projection · Visualization · Dynamic time warping

## 1 Background

The growing interest in brain research is reflected by recent and still ongoing American and European large scale research projects that are dedicated to study the brain and its disorders. In particular, we mean the BRAIN Initiative announced by president Obama and the European Human Brain Project.[1] The expected impact of these projects may be compared to that of the celebrated Human Genome Project. Consequently, we expect an increased need for methods that allow exploratory analysis and predictions based on large datasets describing the dynamics of the brain.

---

[1] http://en.wikipedia.org/wiki/BRAIN_Initiative,
https://www.humanbrainproject.eu

© Springer International Publishing Switzerland 2015
L. Rutkowski et al. (Eds.): ICAISC 2015, Part II, LNAI 9120, pp. 91–100, 2015.
DOI: 10.1007/978-3-319-19369-4_9

There are various techniques that allow to capture the activity of the brain, such as electroencephalography (EEG), magnetoencephalography (MEG) and magnetic resonance imaging (MRI). While MEG captures the activity on much more channels than EEG, in case of MEG the noise is substantially higher than in case of EEG. MRI has an excellent spatial resolution, but its temporal resolution is limited, therefore, purely based on MRI, it may be difficult to study the dynamics of the brain. Taking these considerations into account, in this paper, we focus on EEG which is a well-established technique to study the activity of the brain. We note, however, that our ideas may simply be adapted to MEG and MRI data. The only requirement for that is the presence of an appropriate distance measure between the recordings.

EEG is widely used in research and clinical practice. For example, EEG is highly valuable for presurgical evaluation [12], diagnostic decision-making [2], assessment of chronic headaches [13] and diagnosis of particular diseases such as Alzheimers disease [9] or schizophrenia [19]. Paralyzed patients may benefit from EEG-controlled devices, such as spelling tools [4] or web browsers [3]. EEG was used to study sleepiness in long distance truck driving [11] and there were attempts to predict upcoming emergency braking based on EEG signals [10] which could result in reducing the braking distance of vehicles.

Continuous, long term EEG monitoring is required in case of various diseases, e.g. some forms of epilepsy [21], coma, cerebral ischemia, assessment of medications [20], sleep disorders, disorders of consciousness [14], psychiatric conditions and movement disorders [23]. Moreover, long term EEG monitoring is used during anesthesia and in neonatal intensive care units [15]. In these cases, EEG is recorded for hours or days resulting in gigabytes of multivariate time series data for each patient. The real-time evaluation of such huge amount of data is practically impossible without semi-automated techniques that assist human experts. A common feature of the aforementioned diagnostic problems and EEG-based tools is that they involve recognition tasks related to EEG signals. As EEG signals can be considered as multivariate time-series, these recognition tasks can be formulated as multivariate time-series classification tasks, for which state-of-the-art solutions are based on machine learning. A recognition model, called *classifier*, is constructed based on previously collected data and evidence (i.e., which signal was recorded under which conditions).

Various algorithms were developed for the classification of EEG signals in the last decades, see e.g. [5], [18], [22]. As EEG signals are time series, we consider the classification of EEG signals as a time-series classification problem, for which the $k$ nearest-neighbor ($k$-NN) method using dynamic time warping (DTW) as distance measure was reported to be competitive, if not superior, to many state-of-the-art time-series classifiers, such as neural networks or hidden Markov models, see e.g. [6], [8] and the references therein. Furthermore, in their recent work, Chen et al. [8] gave theoretical guarantees for the performance of nearest neighbor-like time-series classifiers. Meanwhile, considerable research effort was devoted to enhance DTW-based nearest neighbor classification of time series both in terms of accuracy and classification time. Here, we point out hubness-aware classifiers which represent one of the most promising research directions aiming to enhance nearest neighbor classification. Recent hubness-aware classifiers include hw-kNN, HFNN, NHBNN and HIKNN [17], [25], [26], [27]. These techniques were surveyed and extended to time series classification in [24]. In their extensions to time-series classification, all of these hubness-aware classifiers used DTW as distance measure.

In the light of the aforementioned results, we decided to base our approach on DTW. In contrast to the aforementioned direction of research which used DTW in nearest neighbor classifiers or their extensions, we use DTW in order to construct real-valued features which results in projecting multivariate time-series into a vector space. We demonstrate that this projection may allow visual inspection and therefore exploratory analysis of large EEG datasets. Furthermore, conventional classifiers developed for vector data may be used on the projected data. In particular, we use logistic regression [7] for classification. We call our approach PROCESS: Projection-based Classification of Electroencephalogram Signals. As we will show, PROCESS achieves significantly better accuracy than state-of-the-art classifiers. The most time-consuming step of the nearest neighbor classification using DTW is the calculation of the DTW-distances. In contrast, using PROCESS, we only need to calculate a few DTW-distances, therefore, our approach can quickly classify time-series. Additionally, we will show that PROCESS performs favorably even in cases when the test data is remarkably different from the training data which shows the robustness of our approach.

## 2   Our Approach: PROCESS

We begin this section by giving the basic notations. Subsequently, we describe our approach.

### 2.1   Basic Notations

We use $\mathcal{D}$ to denote the set of EEG signals used to construct the recognition model, called *classifier*. $\mathcal{D}$ is called *training data* and each signal in $\mathcal{D}$ belongs to one of the *classes*. The class of a signal is given by its *class label*. For example, a dataset may contain EEG signals that correspond to normal brain activity and some other signals that correspond to epileptic seizures. In this case, there are two classes, that may be called *normal* and *seizure* respectively. Therefore, the class label of each signal is either *normal* or *seizure*.

The class labels of the training data are known while constructing the classifier. The process of constructing the classifier is called *training*. Once the classifier is trained, it can be applied to new signals, i.e., the classifier can be used to predict the class labels of new signals. In order to evaluate our classifier we will use a second set of EEG signals $\mathcal{D}^{test}$, called *test data*. $\mathcal{D}^{test}$ is disjoint from $\mathcal{D}$ and the class labels of the signals in $\mathcal{D}^{test}$ are unknown to the classifier. We only use the class labels of the signals in $\mathcal{D}^{test}$ to quantitatively assess the performance of the classifier (by comparing the predicted and true class labels and calculating statistics regarding the performance).

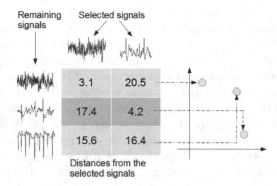

**Fig. 1.** Projection of signals into a vector space by PROCESS. In this example, the horizontal (vertical) axis of the coordinate system correspond to the distances from the first (second) selected signal.

## 2.2 Projecting EEG Signals into a Vector Space

First, we select a random subset of the training data. This random subset of $\mathcal{D}$ will contain $n$ EEG signals. Then, we calculate the distance of the *remaining* (i.e., non-selected) EEG signals from the selected ones using DTW. For the description of how to calculate DTW on multivariate time series we refer to [6]. Subsequently, the distances are used as real-valued features: the distance of the signal $x$ from the first selected signal will be the first feature of $x$, the distance of $x$ from the second selected signal will be the second feature of $x$, etc. Representing each signal as a vector of $n$ real-valued features allows to project the signals into an $n$-dimensional vector space.

The mapping into a vector space is illustrated in Fig. 1. In this example, the training data $\mathcal{D}$ contains five signals. Out of them, $n = 2$ were selected. We calculate the distances of the remaining $5 - 2 = 3$ signals from the selected ones. This results in a vector of length $n = 2$ for each non-selected signal, i.e., we projected the non-selected signals into a vector space of $n = 2$ dimensions.

Once the non-selected time series are projected into a vector space, we can train any conventional classifier working on vector data. In particular, we propose to use logistic regression [7].

In order to classify a new signal $x'$, we calculate the distance of $x'$ from the selected signals. Therefore, we project $x'$ into the aforementioned vector space. Then we use the previously trained classifier (logistic regression) to predict the class label of $x'$.

## 2.3 Example on EEG of Epileptic and Normal Brain Activity

In order to illustrate the projection produced by our approach we use the data [1] collected by Andrzejak et al. Similarly to [22], we consider EEG signals corresponding to normal brain activity with open eyes and "epileptic EEG signals

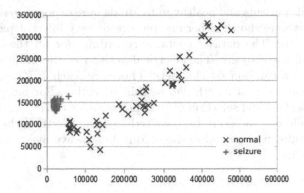

**Fig. 2.** The result of projecting the EEG signals into a two dimensional vector space. Signal either correspond to normal brain activity or epileptic seizures.

obtained from five different epileptic patients, recorded during the occurrence of epileptic seizures" [22]. We use half of the signals as training data and the other half of the signals as test data. The projection of the training data produced by our approach using $n = 2$ selected signals is shown in Fig. 2. As we can see, as the result of the projection, the two classes of signals are projected to well-separated regions. Note that this example also demonstrates that the proposed projection approach may be useful to map EEG signals into a low dimensional space in order to provide the user with an overview of the entire data set.

In fact, our approach achieves perfect classification of the test data which can be attributed to the fact that the original data was manually curated by human experts, in particular, only signals being free of artifacts were included in the data [1]. However, the labor-intensive process of revision of the data by human experts is only applicable to small or moderately-sized datasets, while in many applications we have to work with large sets of EEG data. Therefore, in the next section, we will evaluate our approach on EEG data recorded under real-world conditions *without* the labor-intensive revision by human-experts.

## 3   Experiments

In this section, we describe the data and the experimental protocol. This is followed by presenting and discussing our experimental results.

### 3.1   Data

In order to evaluate our approach, we used the publicly available EEG dataset[2] from the UCI machine learning repository [28]. This collection contains in total 11028 EEG signals recorded from 122 persons. Out of the 122 persons, 77 were alcoholic patients and 45 were healthy individuals.

---

[2] http://archive.ics.uci.edu/ml/datasets/EEG+Database

Both alcoholic patients and healthy individuals were exposed to three different stimuli: subjects were shown either one picture *or* two different pictures *or* the same picture twice. The dataset contains recordings for all these three types of stimuli for all the subjects. The electrical activity of the brain was captured at 256 Hz for 1 second on 64 channels. Therefore, each EEG signal is a 64-dimensional time series of length 256 in this collection. For more information about data collection and selection of patients we refer to [28]. In order to filter noise, as a simple preprocessing step, we reduced the length of the signals from 256 to 64 by binning with a window size of four, i.e., we averaged four consecutive values of the signal.

## 3.2   Baselines

We compared our approach, PROCESS, with $k$-NN using DTW and its hubness-aware extensions, i.e., hw-kNN, hFNN, NHBNN and HIKNN, as well as further state-of-the-art classifiers such as neural networks and SVMs. Both for $k$-NN and its hubness-based extensions, we tried all odd $k$ values in the range 1...10. For simplicity, we only report results for the best-performing variant of $k$-NN and its hubness-aware extensions. As further baselines, we used the logistic classifier, Support Vector Machines (SVMs) and neural networks from the Weka software package.[3] In logistic classifiers, neural networks and SVMs, we used the time series as 64-dimensional vectors. Neural networks were trained for 100 epochs. We tried five different neural networks: (i) simple perceptrons, multilayer perceptrons (MLPs) with one hidden layer containing (ii) 4, (iii) 16 and (iv) 64 nodes and (v) MLPs with two hidden layers containing 64 and 4 nodes. For brevity, we only report results for the best performing neural network in Table 1.

## 3.3   Experimental Protocol

We compared the accuracy of our approach and the baselines in three different contexts.

- In the *Disease* context the task is to recognize, based on the EEG signals, whether a person is affected by the disease (alcoholism) or not, i.e., the class label of an EEG-signal reflects whether this signal originates from an alcoholic patient or a healthy individual. In this context, both for our approach and the baselines, we make use of the information that we know which signals originate from the same person: we classify a person as healthy (or alcoholic, respectively) if majority of the signals originating from that person were classified as healthy (or alcoholic, respectively). While we do not claim that alcoholism should be diagnosed using EEG, with this context we aim to simulate scenarios in which EEG is used to asses the presence or the severity of a disease.

---

[3] Weka is available at http://www.cs.waikato.ac.nz/ml/weka/

– In the *Stimulus* context we classified signals according to the stimulus. Therefore, signals belong to one of three classes: (i) one picture was shown to the
person, (ii) the same picture was shown twice, (iii) two different pictures
were shown. We performed three experiments in this context: in the first one
(*Stimulus*) we used the entire dataset, in the second experiment (*Stim.H*)
only the signals originating from healthy individuals were used, while in the
third context (*Stim.A*) we only used the signals describing the electrical activity of the brain of alcoholic patients. This context simulates scenarios in
which patterns of different brain activities has to be distinguished, such as
in case of EEG-based spelling devices or web browsers.

– The *Application* context extends the Stimulus context: the goal is to recognize the stimulus again, however, we aim to simulate scenarios in which the
system is trained using a particular dataset, but the system is subsequently
applied to new data originating from a slightly different distribution. In the
*App.I* experiment we used only signals originating from healthy individuals
to train the classifier and we test the classifier on signals of alcoholic patients;
whereas in the *App.II* experiment we used signals of alcoholic patients to
train the classifier and we test it on signals of healthy individuals.

In all the aforementioned experiments, we used the $10 \times 10$-*fold crossvalidation*
protocol to evaluate our approach and the baselines. While splitting the data
for cross-validation, we pay attention that all the signals belonging to the same
person are assigned to the same split, and therefore each person either appears in
the training data or in the test data, but not in both. On the one hand, this allows
to simulate the real-world scenario in which the recognition system is applied to
new patients; on the other hand, EEG signals are known to be characteristic to
individuals, see e.g. person identification systems using EEG [16], therefore, if
the same person would appear in both the train and test data, this could lead
to overoptimistic results.

As performance measure we used accuracy, i.e., the number of correct classifications divided by the number of all the classifications.

While implementing PROCESS we used the publicly available implementation
of logistic regression [7] from the aforementioned Weka software package. We determined the number of selected signals $n$ using a validation subset of the training
data. In particular, we used one out of the 9 training splits as validation split and
we trained PROCESS on the remaining 8 splits with $n = 100, 200, 300, ..., 1000$
and evaluated its accuracy on the validation split. Finally, we set $n$ to the value
that resulted in the best performance on the validation split. Then we retrained
our classifier using the entire training data.

## 3.4 Experimental Results

We run the experiments on a computer with 6 CPU-cores, 16 GB RAM and 2TB
HDD. Table 1 summarizes the results of our experiments. We show accuracies
averaged over $10 \times 10$ folds for the previously described experiments. We show the
corresponding standard deviations on the right of the $\pm$ symbol. The symbol $\bullet/\circ$

**Table 1.** Accuracy ± standard deviation of PROCESS and its competitors averaged over 10 × 10 folds. Bold font denotes the best approach in each row. The symbol •/○ denotes if the difference between PROCESS and its competitor is statistically significant (•) or not (○) according to t-test at significance level of 0.01.

| Context | k-NN | best hubness-aware classifier | Logistic | best neural network | SVM | PROCESS (our approach) |
|---|---|---|---|---|---|---|
| Disease | 0.656±0.049• | 0.786±0.113○ | 0.791±0.110○ | 0.782±0.110○ | 0.798±0.089○ | **0.800±0.110** |
| Stimulus | 0.577±0.019• | 0.588±0.017• | 0.444±0.066• | 0.513±0.094• | 0.490±0.081• | **0.687±0.022** |
| Stim.H | 0.579±0.035• | 0.582±0.035• | 0.623±0.073• | 0.640±0.068○ | **0.666±0.076**○ | 0.645±0.040 |
| Stim.A | 0.573±0.028• | 0.588±0.026• | 0.435±0.064• | 0.497±0.096• | 0.488±0.081• | **0.673±0.031** |
| App.I | 0.550±0.022• | 0.557±0.024• | 0.572±0.053• | 0.602±0.056• | 0.611±0.049○ | **0.622±0.040** |
| App.II | 0.574±0.030• | 0.586±0.033• | 0.431±0.066• | 0.507±0.113• | 0.482±0.077• | **0.648±0.035** |

denotes if the difference between PROCESS and its competitor is statistically significant (•) or not (○) according to t-test at significance level of 0.01.

The results show that in the vast majority of the cases, our approach outperformed the baselines and the difference was statistically significant. An exception is the Stim.H experiment in which SVMs performed slightly better than our approach. However, the difference is statistically non-significant in this case.

In our experiments, the training time of PROCESS was close to the training time of SVMs and neural networks, while PROCESS was much faster to train then the best hubness-aware classifier. Regarding classification times, PROCESS was more than an order of magnitude quicker than k-NN and hubness-aware classifiers which may be attributed to the fact that PROCESS needs substantially less DTW calculations than these other classifiers. On the other hand, neural networks and SVMs were even quicker than PROCESS. Note, however, that in practical applications, PROCESS should be considered as an alternative even to SVMs or neural networks in cases where accuracy is more important than prediction time or if several CPU-cores are available in order to execute the DTW calculations of PROCESS in parallel.

## 4    Conclusions and Outlook

In this paper, we proposed a new approach for the analysis of electroencephalograph (EEG) signals. We demonstrated that the proposed projection approach may be useful to represent EEG signals of a real dataset in a low dimensional vector space and therefore it may allow exploratory analysis of the data by visual inspection. Our experiments on a publicly available real-world EEG dataset showed that our approach significantly outperforms the state-of-the-art in various EEG-related recognition tasks, including cases when the training and test data originate from slightly different distributions.

Our approach, PROCESS, maps multivariate time-series into a vector space. In order to do so, PROCESS calculates distances from randomly selected instances. As our experimental results show, this random selection leads to good results. However, in order to further increase classification performance, one may consider more advanced selection strategies.

In principle, the vector representation of the data constructed by PROCESS allows to use (almost) any vector classifiers including ensemble methods and semi-supervised classifiers. Furthermore, the projection might be useful for clustering or anomaly detection. Therefore, these applications are subject to future work. Additionally, we point out that PROCESS might be used for various classification tasks related to multivariate time-series, such as recognition tasks related to electrocardiograph (ECG) signals, gesture recognition or signature verification. From the point of view of medical diagnosis, classification of class-imbalanced data is of special interest, therefore, we aim at combining PROCESS with classifiers for class-imbalanced data in our future work.

**Acknowledgment.** This research was performed within the framework of the grant of the Hungarian Scientific Research Fund - OTKA 111710 PD. This paper was supported by the János Bolyai Research Scholarship of the Hungarian Academy of Sciences. We thank Henri Begleiter at the Neurodynamics Laboratory at the State University of New York Health Center at Brooklyn for making the EEG data used in Section 3 publicly available.

# References

1. Andrzejak, R.G., Lehnertz, K., Mormann, F., Rieke, C., David, P., Elger, C.E.: Indications of nonlinear deterministic and finite-dimensional structures in time series of brain electrical activity: Dependence on recording region and brain state. Physical Review E 64(6), 061907 (2001)
2. Askamp, J., van Putten, M.J.: Diagnostic decision-making after a first and recurrent seizure in adults. Seizure 22(7), 507–511 (2013)
3. Bensch, M., Karim, A.A., Mellinger, J., Hinterberger, T., Tangermann, M., Bogdan, M., Rosenstiel, W., Birbaumer, N.: Nessi: an EEG-controlled web browser for severely paralyzed patients. Computational Intelligence and Neuroscience (2007)
4. Birbaumer, N., Ghanayim, N., Hinterberger, T., Iversen, I., Kotchoubey, B., Kübler, A., Perelmouter, J., Taub, E., Flor, H.: A spelling device for the paralysed. Nature 398(6725), 297–298 (1999)
5. Boostani, R., Sadatnezhad, K., Sabeti, M.: An efficient classifier to diagnose of schizophrenia based on the EEG signals. Expert Systems with Applications 36(3, pt. 2), 6492 – 6499 (2009)
6. Buza, K.A.: Fusion Methods for Time-Series Classification. Peter Lang Verlag (2011)
7. le Cessie, S., van Houwelingen, J.: Ridge Estimators in Logistic Regression. Applied Statistics 41(1), 191–201 (1992)
8. Chen, G.H., Nikolov, S., Shah, D.: A latent source model for nonparametric time series classification. In: Advances in Neural Information Processing Systems 26, pp. 1088–1096 (2013)
9. Dauwels, J., Vialatte, F., Musha, T., Cichocki, A.: A comparative study of synchrony measures for the early diagnosis of alzheimer's disease based on eeg. NeuroImage 49(1), 668–693 (2010)
10. Haufe, S., Treder, M.S., Gugler, M.F., Sagebaum, M., Curio, G., Blankertz, B.: Eeg potentials predict upcoming emergency brakings during simulated driving. Journal of Neural Engineering 8(5), 056001 (2011)
11. Kecklund, G., Åkerstedt, T.: Sleepiness in long distance truck driving: an ambulatory eeg study of night driving. Ergonomics 36(9), 1007–1017 (1993)

12. Knake, S., Halgren, E., Shiraishi, H., Hara, K., Hamer, H., Grant, P., Carr, V., Foxe, D., Camposano, S., Busa, E., Witzel, T., Hinen, M., Ahlfors, S., Bromfield, E., Black, P., Bourgeois, B., Cole, A., Cosgrove, G., Dworetzky, B., Madsen, J., Larsson, P., Schomer, D., Thiele, E., Dale, A., Rosen, B., Stufflebeam, S.: The value of multichannel meg and eeg in the presurgical evaluation of 70 epilepsy patients. Epilepsy Research 69(1), 80–86 (2006)

13. Kramer, U., Nevo, Y., Neufeld, M.Y., Harel, S.: The value of eeg in children with chronic headaches. Brain and Development 16(4), 304 (1994)

14. Malinowska, U., Chatelle, C., Bruno, M.A., Noirhomme, Q., Laureys, S., Durka, P.J.: Electroencephalographic profiles for differentiation of disorders of consciousness. Biomedical Engineering Online 12(1), 109 (2013)

15. McCoy, B., Hahn, C.D.: Continuous EEG Monitoring in the Neonatal Intensive Care Unit. Journal of Clinical Neurophysiology 30(2), 106–114 (2013)

16. Poulos, M., Rangoussi, M., Alexandris, N., Evangelou, A.: Person identification from the eeg using nonlinear signal classification. Methods of Information in Medicine 41(1), 64–75 (2002)

17. Radovanović, M., Nanopoulos, A., Ivanović, M.: Time-Series Classification in Many Intrinsic Dimensions. In: Proceedings of the 10th SIAM International Conference on Data Mining (SDM), pp. 677–688 (2010)

18. Sabeti, M., Katebi, S., Boostani, R., Price, G.: A new approach for eeg signal classification of schizophrenic and control participants. Expert Systems with Applications 38(3), 2063–2071 (2011)

19. Sabeti, M., Katebi, S., Boostani, R.: Entropy and complexity measures for eeg signal classification of schizophrenic and control participants. Artificial Intelligence in Medicine 47(3), 263–274 (2009)

20. Scheuer, M.L.: Continuous EEG monitoring in the intensive care unit. Epilepsia 43(s3), 114–127 (2002)

21. Serafini, A., Rubboli, G., Gigli, G.L., Koutroumanidis, M., Gelisse, P.: Neurophysiology of juvenile myoclonic epilepsy. Epilepsy & Behavior 28(suppl. 1(0)), S30 – S39 (2013)

22. Srinivasan, V., Eswaran, C., Sriraam, N.: Artificial Neural Network Based Epileptic Detection Using Time-Domain and Frequency-Domain Features. Journal of Medical Systems 29(6), 647–660 (2005)

23. Tatum IV, W.O.: Long-term EEG monitoring: a clinical approach to electrophysiology. Journal of Clinical Neurophysiology 18(5), 442–455 (2001)

24. Tomašev, N., Buza, K., Marussy, K., Kis, P.B.: Hubness-aware classification, instance selection and feature construction: Survey and extensions to time-series. In: Stańczyk, U., Jain, L.C. (eds.) Feature Selection for Data and Pattern Recognition. SCI, vol. 584, pp. 231–262. Springer, Heidelberg (2015)

25. Tomašev, N., Mladenić, D.: Nearest neighbor voting in high dimensional data: Learning from past occurrences. Computer Science and Information Systems 9, 691–712 (2012)

26. Tomašev, N., Radovanović, M., Mladenić, D., Ivanovicć, M.: A probabilistic approach to nearest neighbor classification: Naive hubness Bayesian k-nearest neighbor. In: Proceeding of the CIKM Conference (2011)

27. Tomašev, N., Radovanović, M., Mladenić, D., Ivanović, M.: Hubness-based fuzzy measures for high-dimensional k-nearest neighbor classification. International Journal of Machine Learning and Cybernetics (2013)

28. Zhang, X.L., Begleiter, H., Porjesz, B., Wang, W., Litke, A.: Event related potentials during object recognition tasks. Brain Research Bulletin 38(6), 531–538 (1995)

# Feature Extraction of Palm Vein Patterns Based on Two-Dimensional Density Function

Mariusz Kubanek[1,2(✉)], Dorota Smorawa[1], and Taras Holotyak[3]

[1] Czestochowa University of Technology,
Institute of Computer and Information Science,
Dabrowskiego Street 73, 42-200 Czestochowa, Poland
{mariusz.kubanek,dorota.smorawa}@icis.pcz.pl
[2] European University of Information Technology,
and Economisc in Warsaw Department of Computer Science,
Bialostocka Street 22, 03-741 Warsaw, Poland
[3] University of Geneva Computer Science Department,
7 Route de Drize, Geneva, Switzerland
taras.holotyak@unige.ch

**Abstract.** The pattern of blood vessels of a hand to build a biometric system will be presented in the article. Being a unique feature this pattern is impossible to be forged. Acquisition of a given biometrics will be described. The method to improve contrast of the input image based on three stages: the image histogram equalization, a smoothing operation of the filter and image normalization will be presented. The feature extraction method based on the two-dimensional density function will be shown. The location of blood vessels method based on the nearest neighbour matching method will be discussed. This paper contains a comparison of available in the scientific literature common methods used in the process of creating the biometric system based on the distribution of blood vessels in the hand.

**Keywords:** Palm vein patterns · The contrast enhancement · Density function · Authentication

## 1 Introduction

Biometrics consists of the variety of methods for identification or verification by analyzing physical and behavioral characteristics of a man. Nowadays biometrics can replace the weaknesses of the available ways of identification or verification such as a PIN, access card or password. Various identification cards can be scanned and reproduced, passwords can be monitored or broken, and PIN codes can be forgotten or stolen. The system that uses biometric features is not burdened with these defects as an access card or PIN employ a unique biometric feature of a human being [1].

Some systems based on biometric patterns, however, also have drawbacks such as a given quality missing in all people. Another disadvantage is the inability to measure the biometrics [2]. Such systems include the ones based on the

© Springer International Publishing Switzerland 2015
L. Rutkowski et al. (Eds.): ICAISC 2015, Part II, LNAI 9120, pp. 101–111, 2015.
DOI: 10.1007/978-3-319-19369-4_10

distribution of fingerprint lines. Many cases of people suffering from a disorder called adermatoglyphia have been reported. Those affected by the disease lack a unique structure produced by the skin in the form of arching or looping ridges on the inner surface of the skin of hands and feet. Another example may be systems that use the iris pattern for identification or verification. To deceive such a system it is sufficient to have a printed image of an eye with a sufficient high resolution. The above-mentioned features are not only easy to be forged but the cost associated with the creation of a false pattern is also low.

A very interesting solution, largely resistant to these problems, is to use a pattern of blood vessels of the hand. The distribution of blood vessels in the hand being the only of its kind feature, even for identical twins, is also individual for the right or left hand. The biometric vein pattern is right under the skin so to get the image it is enough to use infrared light and a thermal imaging camera. The transmitted infrared light is partially absorbed by hemoglobin in the veins which finally results in the image of a natural contrast of veins. The infrared radiation causes no adverse effects in our bodies. There are no interferences from wrinkles, hand lines, hand roughness, dryness or other surface imperfections of the skin. In addition, the venous pattern does not change throughout life but the only parameter which undergoes changes is its size. The advantage of using the hand vascular biometric system is the inability to be forged or falsified. There have been no cases of forgery reported yet.

## 2   Related Work

The dynamic development of biometric systems makes applications do not have to remember a password or PIN. For this purpose we simply use biometric features individual for each person. An example of such a trait can be the above-mentioned pattern of blood vessels in the hand. This trait among all the other biometric features is distinguished by its stability, uniqueness and reliability. The pattern of blood vessels has gained interest among manufacturers of biometric systems as well as in research. The work [3] describes the structure of the verification system based on the pattern of blood vessels in the hand and presents various stages of the system with a description of the extraction methods based on Gaussian functions, and feature coding using a Hamming standardized distance.

The Gaussian function is often used in the process of feature extraction in blood vessels. Its application can be found also in the works by [4,5]. Apart from feature extraction the Gaussian function was applied to improve the image contrast as shown in [6] and [7]. The blood vessel pattern of the hand is extended enough to allow the use of different methods for extracting and coding features. In their research [8,6] suggested using the wavelet transform in the process of feature extraction.

To create biometric systems it is equally important to encode the pattern. The encoding method must be properly matched so that the process of verification or identification is accurate and quick. In the article by [9] the coding method based on minutiae can be found. This approach is used in the creation of biometric systems using fingerprints. In their research three characteristics of biometrics are referred to: ridge ending, bifurcation and ridge crossing. .

# 3    Description of the Test Stand and Photo Technique

The biometric vein pattern is located under the skin. To activate the image of the hand vascular system the infrared light and the active matrix infrared camera should be used. The near infrared light is partially absorbed by hemoglobin present in veins which creates a picture of the structure beneath the outer layer of the skin, presenting the natural contrast pattern of the blood vessels. The test stand consists of a CCTV active-matrix infrared camera, IR lamp, the tripod and a plate with five supportive wheels thanks to which during the acquisition the position of a hand is always the same, the picture is taken from the same distance. Our research considers the image of the palm section 256 x 256 pixels in size. Two bases of photos, the own one and CASIA MSPD [10] base have been used. Each of these contains data collected from 100 users, with 12 pictures of the left and right hand for each user.

# 4    Improving the Image Contrast

During the acquisition of the pattern of the hand blood vessels noise can be noticed. The blood vessels are not bulging enough which results in inaccurate feature extraction. To improve readability three operations to improve its quality are performed:

 – histogram equalization operation (1)
 – filter smoothing operation (2)
 – image normalization process (3).

The first step is to use a histogram equalization method (1) which magnifies the visibility of blood vessels by aligning the components of the image. The next step is to apply the smoothing filter (2), which removes the noise generated during the acquisition of images. The last step is to normalize (3) the image after the contrast enhancement, which means limiting the image into the range of 0 - 255. Sample contrast enhancement shown in Fig.1.

$$D_i = \frac{\sum_{k=1}^{i} h_i}{\sum_{k=1}^{N} h_i} \tag{1}$$

$$w(x,y) * F(x,y) = \sum_{i,j \in W} w(i,j)F(x-i,y-j) \tag{2}$$

$$Z(x,y) = F_\gamma(x,y) \tag{3}$$

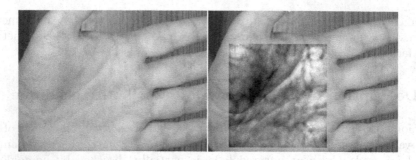

**Fig. 1.** Sample image of palm vein after using contrast enhancement

## 5    Extraction of Features

The pattern of palm blood vessels in the image looks like a dent, because the veins are darker than the surrounding area. Our method examines the entire profile of the hand, pixel by pixel, and finds its value over a specified threshold, in order to capture the curvature of the image. This method is based on a two-dimensional density function (4), which is presented below:

$$f(x) = \frac{1}{2\pi\delta^2} * exp\left(\frac{-(x_2 + y_2)}{2\delta^2}\right) \tag{4}$$

One of the first steps of our method is the initial location of curvature in the horizontal, vertical and both diagonal directions. For modeling the curvature localizing filter the first (5), (7), (9) and the second (6), (8) derivatives of the two-dimensional density function are used.

$$f'(x) = \left(\frac{-x}{\delta^2}\right) * f(x) \tag{5}$$

$$f''(x) = \frac{x^2 - \delta^2}{\delta^4} * f(x) \tag{6}$$

$$f'(y) = f'(x)' \tag{7}$$

$$f''(y) = f''(x)' \tag{8}$$

$$f'(x)(y) = \frac{x * y}{\delta^4} * f(x) \tag{9}$$

The filters are designed to locate all the existing curvature of the profile for the four directions. Filters for the horizontal direction (10), vertical (11) and two diagonal (12), (13) are described by the following formulas:

$$C(z) = \left(\frac{f''(x)}{(1 + f'(x)^2)^{\frac{3}{2}}}\right) \tag{10}$$

$$C(z) = \left( \frac{f''(x)'}{(1 + f'(x)^2)^{\frac{3}{2}}} \right) \tag{11}$$

$$C(z) = \left( \frac{0.5 * f''(x) + f'(x)(y) + 0.5 * f''(x)'}{(1 + ((0.5 * \sqrt{2}) * (f'(x) + f'(x)'))^2)^{\frac{3}{2}}} \right) \tag{12}$$

$$C(z) = \left( \frac{0.5 * f''(x) - f'(x)(y) + 0.5 * f''(x)'}{(1 + ((0.5 * \sqrt{2}) * (f'(x) - f'(x)'))^2)^{\frac{3}{2}}} \right) \tag{13}$$

The next step is to determine the local maximal points (14) along the cross-section of the input image for all 4 directions. These points indicate the central position of the veins. This operation can be defined as follows:

$$P(z_i) = C(z_i) \times N(i) \tag{14}$$

The variable N (i) is the width of the curvature area. At the same time the designated curvature maxima points are assigned to the plane V (x, y). The next step is to connect the designated vein centers. This is done basically by checking m pixels located to the right and left of (x, y). If the pixel (x, y) and the pixel value located on both sides is high (in terms of brightness), a horizontal line is drawn. But if the neighbouring pixel values are high, and the value of the pixel (x, y) is low, then it is treated as a gap between the veins. If the pixel value (x, y) is high and its neighbouring pixels have a low value, it is treated as an interference. This operation is used for all pixels designated in an earlier step. This action can be represented by the following formulas:

$$S_{d1} = min\{max(V(x + (m-1), y), V(x + m, y)) \\ + max(V(x - (m-1), y), V(x - m, y))\} \tag{15}$$

$$S_{d2} = min\{max(V(y + (m-1), x), V(y + m, x)) \\ + max(V(y - (m-1), x), V(y - m, x))\} \tag{16}$$

$$S_{d3} = min\{max(V(y - (m-1), x - (m-1)), V(y - m, x - m)) \\ + max(V(y + (m-1), x + (m-1)), V(y + m, x + m))\} \tag{17}$$

$$S_{d4} = min\{max(V(y + (m-1), x - (m-1)), V(y + m, x - m)) \\ + max(V(y - (m-1), x + (m-1)), V(y - m, x + m))\} \tag{18}$$

With so designated a vein line for all four directions considered, the final pattern of blood vessels is formed by means of the function (19).

$$F = max(S_{d1}, S_{d2}, S_{d3}, S_{d4}) \tag{19}$$

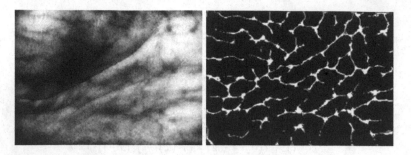

**Fig. 2.** The result of the detection method of palm vein pattern

The last step is to bring the early established pattern of blood vessels to binary function in order to reduce the amount of information contained therein. Binarization is performed by thresholding. The threshold value is determined by the mean value of all pixels within the image greater than 0. The result of these methods can be seen in Fig.2.

At this stage the resulting pattern of blood vessels has a lot of noise and redundant information for the feature encoding process. To eliminate unnecessary disruption and vein discontinuity four methods to improve the visibility of blood vessels have been applied. The first method is the dilatation (20), where the blood vessels are more protruded, which in time could result in a loss of relevant information about the position of the veins. The dilation function is as follows:

$$L'(m,n) = \max_{m_i,n_i \in B(m,n)} (L(m,n)) \qquad (20)$$

Then the thinning operation is performed (21). This operation reduces the size of the blood vessels to one pixel, making it easier to locate the veins fork. This method is as follows:

$$T(I,B) + I - T_{HOM}(I,B) \qquad (21)$$

After the dilation and thinning operations have been performed there are still some irregularities on the image and to smooth them out some operations are carried out which remove unnecessary forks and image noise. Fig.3 show the results of the dilation, thinng and nois reduction metgod.

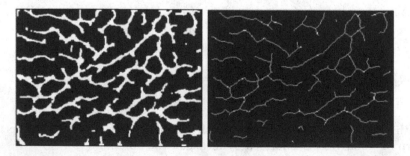

**Fig. 3.** The results of the dilation, thinning and noise reduction method

# 6    Encoding of Features and Matching

The studies included two ways of coding features [11]. The first method of coding features is to divide the image into sub-images of 8 x 8 pixels in size. Each of the sub-images is checked for the occurrence of the vein - white pixels. The feature vector equals one if in a given sub-picture there is one or a few fragments of veins. Otherwise the value equals 0. The following figure illustrates the way in which the feature vector was created. The feature vector consists of 1024 values of 0 or 1.

The second coding method is the division of the input image into sub-images of 8 x 8 pixels in size, the difference is that the sub-images are to check the number of white pixels. The sum of the pixels is assigned to each of the sub-images. The feature vector is of the same length as in the coding above. The difference consists in the values assigned to a given sub-picture. The feature vector being analyzed is compared with a vector in the database. The way in which the feature vector is created in this coding method is shown in the figure below.

# 7    Results of the Experiments

To carry out the experimental part two databases with images of blood vessels of a hand were used. As part of research a database with photos and widely available database CASIA MSPD were created. Each of them contains data collected from 100 users with 12 pictures of the left and right hand each. For the stage of studying 8 photos were used, and the remaining pictures were used in the tests. To check the level of security and accuracy of the systems two factors: the false rejection rate (FRR) and the false acceptance rate (FAR) were applied. The following table summarizes the results carried out for the left and right hand. The coefficients shown in the Table 1 were obtained in tests which take into account the second coding method.

**Table 1.** FAR and FRR results obtained by our method

| Base | Left Hand | | Right Hand | |
|---|---|---|---|---|
| | FAR [%] | FRR [%] | FAR [%] | FRR [%] |
| Our base | 0.14 | 2.37 | 0.18 | 3.19 |
| CASIA | 0.26 | 4.12 | 0.29 | 4.00 |

In order to assess the overall performance of the system the coefficient equal error rate (EER) was calculated. The following Table 2 and plot Fig.4 shows the obtained results.

**Table 2.** ERR results obtained by our method

| Base | Left Hand EER [%] | Right Hand EER [%] |
|---|---|---|
| Our base | 0.19 | 0.21 |
| CASIA | 0.38 | 0.25 |

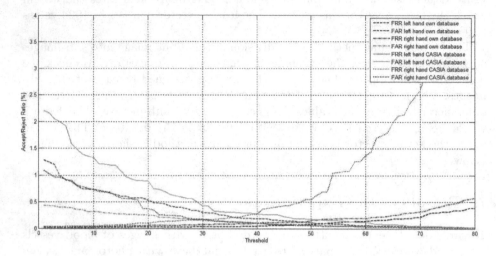

**Fig. 4.** Graph of comparing the FAR and FRR for the left and right palm

## Review and Comparison of Various Techniques Used in Biometric Systems Based on Blood Vessels in a Hand

Several selected methods used in the creation of biometric systems, based on the distribution of blood vessels in a hand, are presented in the Table 3. The study shows that the choice of a suitable method for the initial analysis of the blood vessels in the image is of utmost importance when the final outcome is considered. The work which applied the initial analysis method based on Gaussian function or the Wiener filter the FAR and FRR coefficients are very low. The research where the median filter was used on the image of a preliminary analysis of the veins, the final result is not satisfactory. The final result of the research described by the FAR and FRR coefficients is several times higher than the result of studies that used a more complicated method for the initial location of blood vessels. The review also shows that the final steps in the process of creating a system, such as the extraction of characteristic points or the choice of the method of matching patterns do not have a great impact on the final results without the use of complex methods to locate veins.

The FAR and FRR coefficients for the left hand obtained in our study were used in the above table. In some publications you can find information that the distribution of blood vessels of the left hand should be used for the right-handedpeople.

**Table 3.** The comparison of our method with other works

| Ref. | Thresh. | Bin. | Extraction of Veins Patterns | Minutiae extraction | Class. | Results [%] |
|---|---|---|---|---|---|---|
| [12] | Gaussian Low Pass and High Pass | Local Thresholding | Local Thresholding | - | - | FAR 0.01 |
| [13] | Median | Local Thresholding | Wavelet Transform | - | - | FRR 1.5 FAR 3.5 |
| [14] | Median | Local Thresholding | Local Thresholding | - | Hausdorff | FAR 0.4 |
| [15] | Median | Iterative Thresholding | Local Thresholding | - | Rigid | FAR 0.02 |
| [16] | Match Filter, Smoothing Filter | Seuillage Automatique | Quadratic Inference Function | - | Euclidean Distance | FAR 0.02 FRR 0.03 |
| [17] | Laplacian | Local Thresholding | OTSU | Crossing Number Distance | Euclidean Distance | FAR 1.14 |
| [18] | Match Filter, Wiener Threshold, Smoothing Filter | Automatic Tresholding | Cholesky Decomposition and Lancozos Algo | - | Euclidean Distance | FAR 0.5 |
| [19] | Gaussien | Local Thresholding | Local | - | Euclidean Distance | FRR 0.03 |
| [20] | Median | Histogram Equalization and Local Thresholding | OTSU | Crossing Number | - | - |
| Our method | Density Function | Local Thresholding | Local Thresholding | - | - | FAR 0.14 FRR 2.37 |

This assumption stems from the fact that the right hand is used more often than the left one. This hand is more exposed to scratches, scrapes, wounds or calluses. As a result, the image of the blood vessels can be hardly seen, which can result in a faulty verification or identification.

# 8  Conclusion

The pattern of blood vessels in a hand to build a biometric system was presented in the article. We have proposed a set of functions for analyzing images containing the distribution of blood vessels and the way of their acquisition. The work contains a description of the methods to improve the contrast of the image, the method of feature extraction based on two-dimensional density function. The method of locating veins based on the nearest neighbour matching. The research has been carried out on two bases: the own one and widely available on the internet CASIA. The results presented in the form of coefficients FAR, FRR and EER show that one of the important steps in the development of biometric systems based on the distribution of blood vessels in a hand is its acquisition.

# References

1. Bobulski, J.: Acces control system using face image. Control and Cybernetics 41(3), 691–703 (2012)
2. Bobulski J.: A hybrid method for face detection. Pomiary Automatyka Kontrola, 1498–1500 (December 2010)
3. Shyr Wu, K., Chun Lee, J., Ming Lo, T., Chin Chang, K., Ping Chang, C.: A Secure Vein Recognition System. The Journal of Systems and Software, 2870–2876 (2013)
4. Miura, N., Nagasaka, A., Miyatake, T.: Extraction of Finger Vein Patterns Usng Maxmum Curvature Points in Image Profiles. In: Conference on Machine Vision Applicationa (2005)
5. Zhou, Y., Liu, Y., Feng, Q., Yang, F., Huang, J., Nie, Y.: Palm-Vein Classification Based on Principal Orientation Features (2014)
6. Al-Juboori, A.M., Bu, W., Wu, X., Zhao, Q.: Palm Vein Verification Using Multiple Features and Locality Preserving Projections. The Scientific World Journal (2014)
7. Kang, W., Liu, Y., Wu, Q., Yue, X.: Contact-Free Palm-Vein Recognition Based on Local Invariant Features (2014)
8. Park, K.R.: Finger Vein Recognition by Combining Global and Local Features Based on SVM. Computing and Informatic 30, 295–309 (2011)
9. Wang, L., Graham, G., Cho, D.S.Y.: Minutiae feature Analysis for Infrared Hand Vein Pattern Biometrics. The Journal of The Pattern Recognition Society 41, 920–929 (2007)
10. http://biometrics.idealtest.org
11. Kubanek, M., Smorawa, D., Adrjanowicz, L.: Users Verification Based on Palm-Prints and Hand Geometry with Hidden Markov Models. In: Rutkowski, L., Korytkowski, M., Scherer, R., Tadeusiewicz, R., Zadeh, L.A., Zurada, J.M. (eds.) ICAISC 2013, Part II. LNCS (LNAI), vol. 7895, pp. 275–285. Springer, Heidelberg (2013)
12. Sony, M., Gupta, S., Rao, M.S., Gupta, P.: A New Vein Pattern-Based Verification System. International Journal of Computer Science and Information Security 8(11), 58–63 (2010)
13. Rajalakshmi, M., Rengaraj, R.: Biometric Authentification Using Near Infrared Images of Palms Dorsal Vein Patterns. International Journal of Advanced Engineering Technology 2(14), 384–389 (2011)

14. Kavitha, R., Flower, L.: Localization of Palm Dorsal Vein Pattern Using Image Processing for Automated Intra Venous Drug Needle Insertion. International Journal of Engieering Science and Technology 3(16), 4833–4838 (2011)
15. Pal, M.M., Jasutka, W.R.: Implementation of Hand Vein Structure Authentification Based System. Bioinfo Computer Engineering 2(11), 19–21 (2011)
16. Nandini, C., Ashwini, C., Aparna, M., Ramani, N., Kini, P., Sheeba, K.: Biometric Authentication by Dorsal Hand Vein Pattern. International Journal of Engineering and Technology 2(15), 837–840 (2012)
17. Rajankar, V.A.S.O.: Dorsal Hand Vein Biometry by Independent Component Analysis. International Journal on Computer Science and Engineering 4(17), 1338–1344 (2012)
18. Sathish, G., Saravanan, S., Narmadha, S., Maheswari, S.U.: Personal Authentication System Using Hand Vein Biometric. Computer Technology and Applications 3(11), 383–391 (2012)
19. Zhang, X.H.: Feature Extraction of Hand Vein Patterns Based on Ridgelet Transform and Local Interconnection Structure Neural Network. Intelligent Computing in Signal Processing and Pattern Recognition, 870–875 (2006)
20. Moffette, O.: Extraction des Informations Nutritionnelles D'une Etiquette Alimentaire Par Vision Artificielle, Ecole de Technologie Superieure (2011)

# Segmentation Based Feature Selection on Classifying Proteomic Spectral Data

Hsun-Chih Kuo[✉] and Sheng-Tzung Yeh

Department of Statistics, National Chengchi University, Taipei 11605, Taiwan
seankuo@nccu.edu.tw

**Abstract.** Feature selection has been an important issue for classification of proteomic mass spectra data since researchers are often interested in identifying potentially important biomarkers. In this study, a segmentation approach is adopted to locate the potential biomarker regions from the possible m/z range. Illustration is through real prostate cancer proteomic mass spectra data.

**Keywords:** AUC · Classification · Feature selection · SVM

## 1 Introduction

Early detection of diseases is very important in improving patient survival rate. To satisfy the growing need for effective screening and diagnosis, mass spectrometry (MS) based methods are studied intensively recently. In this study, the Surface-Enhanced Laser Desorption / Ionization (SELDI) spectra data [5] from serum samples of prostate cancer were obtained from the Virginia Prostate Center Tissue and Body Fluid Bank [2]. We adopted the idea of segmentations in mass-to-charge ratio (m/z) values to avoid problems caused by location shift and isotopes. The area under the Receiver-Operating Characteristic curve (AUC) is applied to split spectra data into segments and the support vector machine (SVM) is used for classification. A real prostate cancer spectra data shows the proposed method performs better than those in literatures.

## 2 Description of Data

A mass spectrum (MS) consists of a set of m/z values and their corresponding relative intensities. A candidate peptide biomarker in mass spectrum is an identified peptide that relates to a particular disease state. The goal of this study is to identify potentially useful protein biomarkers and to achieve high classification accuracy.

### 2.1 Samples

The prostate cancer data [2] consist of 327 surface enhanced laser desorption/ionization time-of-fight (SELDI-TOF) mass spectra of serum samples of 81 healthy men (NO), 78

© Springer International Publishing Switzerland 2015
L. Rutkowski et al. (Eds.): ICAISC 2015, Part II, LNAI 9120, pp. 112–119, 2015.
DOI: 10.1007/978-3-319-19369-4_11

benign prostatic hypertrophy (BPH) patients, 84 early cancer patients (CAB), and 84 late cancer patients (CCD).  Two spectra were duplicated from each serum sample. The spectra data were recorded and preprocessed from SELDI ProteinChip Reader and then summarized and examined by experts to remove any abnormality.

## 2.2   Data Preprocessing

The process of MS spectra generally introduces many sources of random noises. Hence, preprocessing steps are necessary in order to remove noises.  In general, preprocessing steps would include baseline subtraction, normalization, peak detection, and alignment.  The prostate cancer data in this study had been preprocessed before examined by field experts.

# 3   Methodology

Features selection and classification are important stages for finding biomarkers and building predictive model. There are several methods published to make the most accurate and reliable predictions. Adam, et al. [2] used the AUC to select informative peaks and then use a decision tree to classify normal samples from disease samples. They used nine peaks between 4 and 10k Dalton (Da) to generate a decision tree with 10 terminal nodes in their prostate cancer study. The classification result had a sensitivity of 83%, a specificity of 97%, a positive predictive value of 96%, and total 89 % accuracy on a single test set. Lilien et al. [6] also analyzed Adam's prostate cancer data and developed a probabilistic algorithm "Q5", that is combination of principal components analysis (PCA) and linear discriminant analysis (LDA). In 2003, Lilien et al. compared several cases using various training/test set sizes, and discovered that larger training/test proportion makes higher accuracy. When training/test proportion was larger than 75%, the average accuracy of 88% was achieved, while using only 50% of data for training, the performance only dropped to 86%.

Qu et al. [8] used discrete wavelet transform (DWT) for data reduction, and a linear discriminant function for classification for prostate cancer data, but they only classify the samples into two classes, namely, healthy and cancer samples. The classification has 97% of sensitivity and 100% of specificity. The classification results of the aforementioned three studies for the prostate cancer data are summarized in Table 1.

## 3.1   Area Under the Receiver-Operating Characteristic Curve (AUC)

The Receiver-Operating Characteristic (ROC) curve [3] is defined for two-class classification, and it usually plots the sensitivity (true positive rate) on the vertical axis against 1 minus specificity on the horizontal axis. By varying the decision threshold, different set of specificity and sensitivity is obtained. Different classifiers would produce different ROC curves. Generally, the larger the distance between two groups of samples measured by a classifier, the better the classifier is. The area under

**Table 1.** Sensitivity and specificity of the prostate cancer data in the literatures

|  | Adam et al. | Lilien et al. | Qu et al. |
|---|---|---|---|
| Method | AUC+ Tree | PCA+LDA | DWT+LDA |
| Comparison | Cancer / (NO, BPH) | Cancer / (NO, BPH) | Cancer / NO |
| Training : Validation | 5.4 : 1 (1 run) | 19:01 (1000 runs) | 5.5: 1 (1 run) |
| specificity | 97% | 93% | 100% |
| sensitivity | 83% | 91% | 97% |

an ROC curve (AUC) is a common measure of separation between two groups of samples. AUC is also widely used to measure the ranking quality of a classification algorithm.

Consider a binary classification problem with $m$ positive samples and $n$ negative samples. Let C denote a fixed classifier that outputs a strictly ordered list for these samples. In addition, let $x_1, \cdots, x_m$ be the output of C on the positive examples and $y_1, \cdots, y_n$ be the output on the negative examples. Then, the nonparametric estimation of AUC, A, associated to C can be written as:

$$A = \sum_{i=1}^{m} \sum_{j=1}^{n} f(x_i, y_j) \Big/ mn ,\tag{1}$$

where $f(x_i, y_j) = I(x_i > y_j) + 0.5 \cdot I(x_i = y_j)$ and $I(\cdot)$ is the indicator function.

This estimator of AUC turns out to be the famous Wilcoxon-Mann-Whitney statistic [4]. From equation (1), it can be seen that the AUC of a classifier is the proportion of time that a classifier would classify a randomly chosen positive example to be greater than a randomly chosen negative example.

### 3.2    Classification via SVM

SVM [9] has gained great importance in recent years. The basic idea of SVM is to map the input vectors into a higher-dimension feature space and an optimal separating hyperplane is constructed in this space. Thus, the binary classification of SVM constructs a hyperplane to separate the two classes so that the margin (distance between the hyperplane and the nearest "support vector" points from each class) is maximized. Hence, SVM is a maximal-margin classifier and it solves an optimization problem to find a separating hyperplane that optimizes a weighted combination of the misclassification rate and the distance of the decision boundary to a sample vector [10]. Let the data of two classes denote by $(x_1, y_1), \cdots, (x_m, y_m)$ , where $x_1, \cdots, x_m \in R^n$ are the data examples and $y_1, \cdots, y_m \in \{+1, -1\}$ define the

$$(\mathbf{w} \cdot \mathbf{x}) + b = 0 ,\tag{2}$$

where $\mathbf{w}$ is the normal vector of the hyperplane. Let $\|\mathbf{w}\|$ be the Euclidean norm of $\mathbf{w}$. Thus, $|b|/\|\mathbf{w}\|$ will be the distance perpendicular to the hyperplane from the origin. Since the optimal separating hyperplane is the hyperplane that maximizes the margin (i.e., the distance from the hyperplane to the closest points on either side), it is equivalent to minimize $\|\mathbf{w}\|$ subject to the set of constraints:

$$\begin{cases} (\mathbf{w} \cdot \mathbf{x}_i) + b \geq 1 \text{ if } y_i = 1 \\ (\mathbf{w} \cdot \mathbf{x}_i) + b \leq -1 \text{ if } y_i = -1 \end{cases} \tag{3}$$

The constraint equations (3) restrict the optimal separating hyperplane to classify each sample correctly according its membership. Alternatively, to find the optimal separating hyperplane is equivalent to solve the following constrained optimization problem:

$$\text{minize} \|\mathbf{w}\|^2 / 2$$
$$\text{subject to } y_i \cdot [(\mathbf{w} \cdot \mathbf{x}_i) + b] \geq 1 \tag{4}$$

# 4     Data Analysis Results

As described earlier, most of the analysis results reviewed in section 3 were based on the preprocessed data of the prostate cancer MS spectra administrated by Adam ea al. [2]. For comparison purpose, we mainly apply our proposed approach to the preprocessed data.

## 4.1     Selection of Training and Validation Data

As suggested by Lilien et al. [6], we also consider higher raining/test proportion. The 90% of samples were randomly selected for training data and the remaining 10% of samples were saved for validation data at each time of resampling. The resampling process was repeated for 100 times to prevent selection bias. The training data were used to rank segmentation of features (m/z values) for model building purpose and the validation data were used to evaluate the built model. In Adam et al's preprocessed data, the numbers of training samples for four spectra types (NO, BPH, CAB, and CCD) were 148, 139, 151, and 149, and the numbers of validation samples for four spectra types are16, 15, 17, and 17, respectively.

## 4.2     Segmentation of Features

Due to limitations of SELDI technology and existence of isotopes, we adopt the idea of splitting m/z values into segmentations because it is more reasonable to identify some segmentation regions than just a few single peaks where biomarkers could occur. We divide the range of m/z into several segmentations. The number of segmentation depends on the total number of peaks. In Adam et al's preprocessed data, there are original 779 peaks. Our first approach is to divide the whole m/z region into 78 segmentations with 10 peaks each.

## 4.3    Ranking Segments Based on AUCs

We compute the AUC value of linear SVM classification for each segment on the training samples. The AUC values were then applied to rank all segments. Since different training samples would usually produce different ranking of each segment at different resampling time, the averaged AUC values were used to rank all segments.

## 4.4    Pairwise Classification Based on Top Ranked Segments

In order to build the best predictive model, we first build SVM classification models sequentially based on the order of AUC ranked segments. For example, the first model consists of features in the best ranked segment as predictors and the second model would consist of features of the top two ranked segments. Following this fashion, the last model would contain all segments. Since there are four types of samples, namely, NO, BPH, CAB, and CCD, we conduct all six pairwise comparisons, NO vs. BPH, NO vs. CAB, NO vs. CCD, BPH vs. CAB, BPH vs. CCD, and CAB vs. CCD. The average accuracy (with standard deviation of accuracy in the parenthesis) resulted from classifying the validation samples at 100 resampling was shown in following tables. In Table 2, all pairwise classification attained more than 97% of accuracy except for CAB vs. CCD that still reached 87%.

To examine the classification results in Table 2 more closely, Table 3 shows the classification results using just the top ranked segment. In Table 3, all comparisons obtained more than 85% of accuracy except CAB vs. CCD even only using the top ranked segments that consists only 10 features.

**Table 2.** The accuracy for pairwise classification (last row indicates the number of segments)

| NO/ | NO/ | NO/ | BPH/ | BPH/ | CAB/ |
|---|---|---|---|---|---|
| BPH | CAB | CCD | CAB | CCD | CCD |
| 0.97 | 0.98 | 0.97 | 0.99 | 0.98 | 0.87 |
| (0.03) | (0.04) | (0.03) | (0.02) | (0.02) | (0.06) |
| 3 | 23 | 23 | 2 | 5 | 4 |

**Table 3.** The accuracy for pairwise classification using the best ranked segment

| NO/ | NO/ | NO/ | BPH/ | BPH/ | CAB/ |
|---|---|---|---|---|---|
| BPH | CAB | CCD | CAB | CCD | CCD |
| 0.96 | 0.9 | 0.86 | 0.94 | 0.86 | 0.74 |
| (0.03) | (0.05) | (0.05) | (0.05) | (0.05) | (0.10) |

## 4.5    Sensitivity and Specificity

In order to compare with the result in Adam et al.'s paper, we also combined the CAB and CCD into a category, called Prostate Cancer (PCA). The sensitivity and specificity of the classification on the new grouping are presented in Table 4 and Table 5 for Adam et al's paper [2] and for our proposed approach, respectively. It can be seen our proposed method performs better throughout all comparisons.

**Table 4.** Sensitivity and specificity of the classification results in Adam et al's paper

| Disease / non-disease | PCA / NO | PCA / BPH | PCA / (NO,BPH) | BPH / NO |
|---|---|---|---|---|
| Sensitivity | 83% | 83% | 83% | 93% |
| Specificity | 100% | 93% | 97% | 100% |

**Table 5.** Sensitivity and specificity of the our classification results

| Disease / non-disease | PCA / NO | PCA / BPH | PCA / (NO,BPH) | BPH / NO |
|---|---|---|---|---|
| Sensitivity | 91% | 91% | 91% | 97% |
| Specificity | 96% | 97% | 98% | 96% |

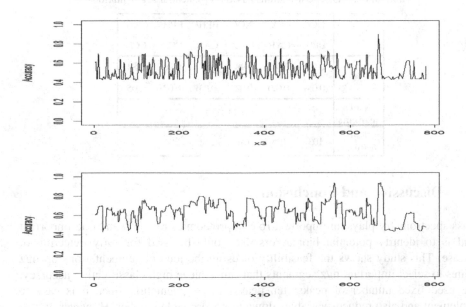

**Fig. 1.** Sequential plots of cumulative accuracy a in moving window of 3 features (top), 10 features (middle), and 20 features (bottom)

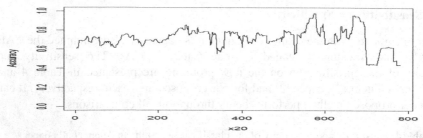

**Fig. 1.** *(Continued).*

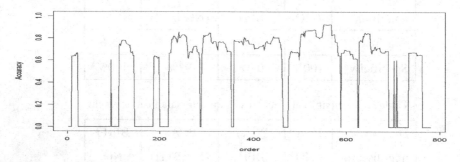

**Fig. 2.** The modified sequential plots of cumulative accuracy in a moving window of 10 features

**Table 6.** Pairwise classifications based on sequential segmentations

|  | NO/ BPH | NO/ CAB | NO/ CCD | BPH/ CAB | BPH/ CCD | CAB/ CCD |
|---|---|---|---|---|---|---|
|  | 0.96 | 0.98 | 0.98 | 0.96 | 0.96 | 0.84 |
|  | (0.03) | (0.02) | (0.02) | (0.03) | (0.02) | 0.05 |
| # of segments | 2 | 3 | 4 | 7 | 4 | 34 |
| # of features | 103 | 106 | 161 | 212 | 204 | 618 |

# 5  Discussion and Conclusion

Mass spectrometry plays an important role in proteomics research and one important goal is to identify potential biomarkers that could be used for early detection of disease. This study shows the feasibility of using the idea of segmentations on m/z values to select important m/z segments that can achieve high classification accuracy. We used fixed number of peaks (ten peaks) for segmentation since it is easy to implement and also reduces variables down to a reasonable number. However, it also makes sense to have larger size or dynamic size of segmentation in the higher range of m/z values. To answer that question, we also tried a type of sequential plot of cumulative accuracy a in moving window against the last feature in the moving window. For example, Fig. 1 shows the plots of cumulative accuracy of a moving window of 3 features, 10 features, and 20 features. It seems that a moving window of 3 features makes the cumulative accuracy plot too detailed, while a moving window of 20 features makes the plot too blurred. A good comprise would be to use 10 features as moving window. However, it still not quite clear how to segment the m/z values based on middle plot of Fig. 1. A solution to it would be to set all accuracy to 0 if it is less than 0.6. The resultant plot is shown in Fig. 2 and now it becomes clear that those valleys with 0 accuracy would indicate possible break points for segmentation. Based on this sequential type of segmentation, we have redone the classification as shown in Table 6. The classification shown in Table 6 did not show significant improvement over the segmentation approach with fixed number of features. This phenomenon will need further investigation in the future.

In this study, we chose to use linear kernel for SVM because the other kernels did not gain any significant improvement. Overall, this study adopts segmentations with fixed number of features to achieve better accuracy in the classification. It is simple and fast in computation. The other thing worth noticing is that the segmentation approach, in theory, should be able to solve problems due to location shift and isotopes so that it should be able to implement on raw spectra data directly without doing preprocessing steps such as peak detection and peak alignment.

# References

1. Aloaydin, E.: Introduction To Machine learning. The MIT Press (2004)
2. Adam, B.L., et al.: Serum Protein Fingerprinting Coupled with a Pattern-matching Algorithm Distinguishes Prostate Cancer from Benign Prostate Hyperplasia and Healthy Men. Cancer Research 62(13), 3609–3614 (2002)
3. Green, D.M., Swets, J.A.: Signal Detection Theory and Psychophysics. John Wiley, New York (1966)
4. Hanley, J.A., McNeil, B.J.: The meaning and use of the area under a receiver operating characteristic (ROC) curve. Radiology 143, 29–36 (1982)
5. Hutchens, T., Yip, T.: New desorption strategies for the mass spectrometric analysis of macromolecules. Rapid Communications in Mass Spectrometry 7, 576–580 (1993)
6. Lilien, R.H., Farid, H., Donald, B.R.: Probabilistic Disease Classification of Expression-Dependent Proteomic Data from Mass Spectrometry of Human Serum. Journal of Computational Biology 10(6), 925–946 (2003)
7. Kuo, H.C., Hunag, J.T., Hsueh, H.M.: On Feature Selection of High Dimensional Data - Application on Classifying Proteomic Spectra Data. Journal of Data Analysis 6(3), 67–80 (2011)
8. Qu, et al.: Data Reduction Using a Discrete Wavelet Transform in Discriminant Analysis of Very High Dimensionality Data. Biometrics 59, 143–151 (2003)
9. Vapnik, V.: The Nature of Statistical Learning Theory. Springer (1995)
10. Wagner, M., Naik, D.N., Pothen, A., Kasukurti, S., Devineni, R.R., Adam, B.L., Semmes, O.J., Wright Jr., G.L.: Computational protein biomarker prediction: a case study for prostate cancer. BMC Bioinformatics 5, 26 (2004)

# SOM vs FCM vs PCA in 3D Face Recognition

Sebastian Pabiasz[1](✉), Janusz T. Starczewski[1], and Antonino Marvuglia[2]

[1] Institute of Computational Intelligence,
Czestochowa University of Technology, Czestochowa, Poland
{sebastian.pabiasz,janusz.starczewski}@iisi.pcz.pl
[2] Public Research Centre Henri Tudor (CRPHT),
Resource Centre for Environmental Technologies (CRTE),
6A, avenue des Hauts-Fourneaux, L-4362 Esch-sur-Alzette, Luxembourg
antonino.marvuglia@tudor.lu

**Abstract.** The number of biometric solutions based on 3D face images has increased rapidly. Such solutions provide a much more accurate alternative to those using flat images; however, they are much more complex. In this paper, we present subsequent results of our research on a new representation of characteristic points for the 3D face. As a comparative methods SOM, FCM and PCA are applied. We discuss the usefulness of these methods with the new representation of characteristic points.

**Keywords:** Biometric · 3D face · Mesh · Depth map

## 1 Introduction

A pattern recognition system that determines the authenticity of an individual using physical or behavioral features is called a biometric system. The physical features include unique anatomical features such as fingerprint, DNA, etc. Behavioral features are related to the behavior of a person e.g. signature[3,4,33,34,7,8]. Biometric systems are divided into two groups. The first group is constituted by systems that require some user interaction, e.g. systems based on fingerprints. A biometric capture device must scan a fingerprint, hence a user intervention is required. The second group consists of systems based on the feature that is always and easily available such as faces.

Research on automatic face recognition has been carried out for more than half a century; however, a big step in this field was the development of the eigenface algorithm [15,32]. Currently, the mainstream focuses on the use of three-dimensional models of the face.

In our previous works, we have presented several approaches to determine three-dimensional facial landmarks [22] and early recognition results [21]. This work supplies two new comparative methods. The first method is based on self-organizing maps, and the second on the fuzzy c-means algorithm. We will discuss the usefulness of these methods with the new representation of characteristic points as well.

© Springer International Publishing Switzerland 2015
L. Rutkowski et al. (Eds.): ICAISC 2015, Part II, LNAI 9120, pp. 120–129, 2015.
DOI: 10.1007/978-3-319-19369-4_12

## 2    A New Three-Dimensional Facial Landmarks

In this section we present a new three-dimensional face representation which is based on recognition methods. In the beginning, the input set is organized in the form of a depth-map. Then, we have to examine the possibility of extracting face landmarks (new, with no relation to anthropometric points) on the basis of extremes. We assume that each row and each column is represented in function forms. Besides, each function can be classified as one of the four types of values:

**local minimum** of a function at a specified window size,
**local maximum** of a function at a specified window size,
**global minimum** of a function,
**global maximum** of a function.

Therefore, our method consists of two stages (Algorithm 1.1). The first stage extracts characteristic points from columns, and the second one does the same with rows. In each step, only points of the selected range are analyzed.

```
for x = 1 → COLUMNS do
   for y = 1 → WINDOWS_SIZE do
      find_Local_Minimum
      find_Local_Maximum
      if is_Global_Minimum_in_Range then
         save_Global_Minimum
      end if
      if is_Global_Maximum_in_Range then
         save_Global_Maximum
      end if
   end for
end for
for x = 1 → ROWS do
   for y = 1 → WINDOW_SIZE do
      find_Local_Minimum
      find_Local_Maximum
      if is_Global_Minimum_in_Range then
         save_Global_Minimum
      end if
      if is_Global_Maximum_in_Range then
         save_Global_Maximum
      end if
   end for
end for
```

**Algorithm 1.1.** The first state of landmark extraction

In our algorithm, the height of each point is the smallest distance from the straight line matching the function at the window borders (fig. 1).

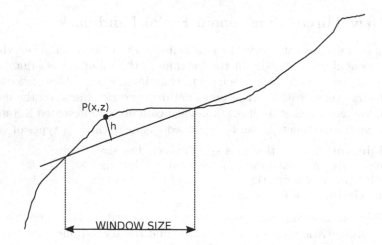

**Fig. 1.** Determination of the height of the point

## 3 Tests in Recognition

For the experiment, we firstly obtained characteristic points with the use of the previously described method. For each person face, the training set consisted of dozens of face shots. The extracted characteristic points were subsequently analyzed by the self-organizing maps (SOM), the fuzzy c-means (FCM) and the principal component (PCA) method to form the data base. During the testing phase, we made use of the image that was not present in the learning phase. A series of tests comparing different types of characteristic points with each other were performed.

### 3.1 3D Face Database

The comparative study was carried out on a set of biometric three-dimensional images *NDOff-2007*[10]. The collection of 6940 3D images (and corresponding 2D images) were gathered for 387 human faces. The advantage of this collection is that, for a single person, there are several variants of face orientation.

### 3.2 Results

In the study, we used thousand 3D images taken for sixty people. Individual features can be categorized as follows:

**all,** all local and global landmarks from columns and rows,
**col-l,** local landmarks from columns,
**col-g,** global landmarks from columns,
**glob,** global landmarks from columns and rows,
**row-l,** local landmarks from rows,
**row-g,** global landmarks from rows.

Tables 1, 2, 3 present results of the recognition process, in which the FAR (*False Acceptance Rate*) is given. In these cases, the FRR (*False Recognition Rate*) is equal 0. The gray background indicates a proper recognition of the reference image. In the first column, there are listed the landmark data used to recognize a pattern image, which are based on landmarks from the first row.

**Table 1.** A SOM based method recognition: results (FAR) with FRR = 0. The gray background indicates a proper recognition of the reference image.

| SOM | Template set | | | | | |
|---|---|---|---|---|---|---|
| | all | glob | row-l | row-g | col-l | col-g |
| all | 0.33% | 46.03% | 10.26% | 18.87% | 2.32% | 2.32% |
| glob | 13.25% | 0.99% | 0.99% | 3.97% | 3.64% | 14.90% |
| row-l | 2.98% | 14.24% | 4.64% | 11.59% | 20.86% | 12.58% |
| row-g | 3.31% | 19.54% | 0.99% | 8.61% | 10.26% | 7.28% |
| col-l | 31.13% | 9.27% | 28.15% | 18.21% | 4.64% | 25.50% |
| col-g | 0.66% | 26.16% | 7.95% | 16.89% | 5.30% | 1.32% |

The SOM based recognition method properly recognized all reference images with the same landmarks type. The accumulative error is equal to 409,93%, while the average error is 11,39%.

**Table 2.** FCM based method recognition: results (FAR) with FRR = 0. The gray background indicates a proper recognition of the reference image.

| FCM | Template set | | | | | |
|---|---|---|---|---|---|---|
| | all | glob | row-l | row-g | col-l | col-g |
| all | 13.91% | 13.91% | 3.31% | 0.00% | 4.97% | 26.82% |
| glob | 13.25% | 8.61% | 2.98% | 3.31% | 1.99% | 4.64% |
| row-l | 10.93% | 14.24% | 7.28% | 2.32% | 22.85% | 14.57% |
| row-g | 14.24% | 17.88% | 2.98% | 6.62% | 2.32% | 33.77% |
| col-l | 1.32% | 6.29% | 6.62% | 19.21% | 4.64% | 7.95% |
| col-g | 1.99% | 2.32% | 0.66% | 4.30% | 1.66% | 1.99% |

The FCM based recognition method properly recognized all reference images with the same landmarks type. The accumulative error is equal to 306,65%, while the average error is 8,52%.

The PCA based recognition method accurately recognized only two reference images with the same landmarks type, but with error equal to 0. This method correctly recognized four referenced images with different landmark type, which

**Table 3.** PCA based method: recognition results (FAR) with FRR=0. The gray background indicates a proper recognition of the reference image.

| PCA | Template set | | | | | |
|---|---|---|---|---|---|---|
| | all | glob | row-l | row-g | col-l | col-g |
| all | 0.00% | 1.62% | 0.00% | 1.03% | 0.00% | 0.30% |
| glob | 22.30% | 0.30% | 17.43% | 0.00% | 21.12% | 21.71% |
| row-l | 0.00% | 1.33% | 0.00% | 0.74% | 0.00% | 0.44% |
| row-g | 22.60% | 0.30% | 17.87% | 0.00% | 21.12% | 23.04% |
| col-l | 0.00% | 0.44% | 0.00% | 1.48% | 0.00% | 0.30% |
| col-g | 22.16% | 18.91% | 17.28% | 15.36% | 21.12% | 21.42% |

(Input set — row labels on the left)

was not the case of the previous methods. The accumulative error is equal to 291,72%, while the average error is 8,10%.

Figures 2, 3, 4 presents the ROC (*Receiver Operating Characteristic*) of the proposed methods.

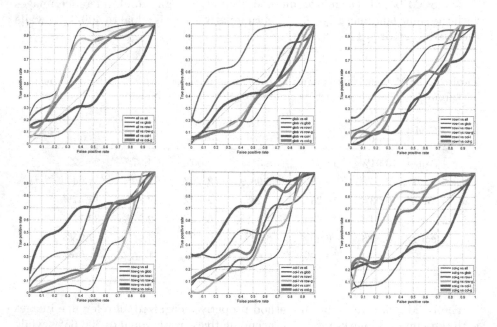

**Fig. 2.** Characteristic ROC for the method based on SOM

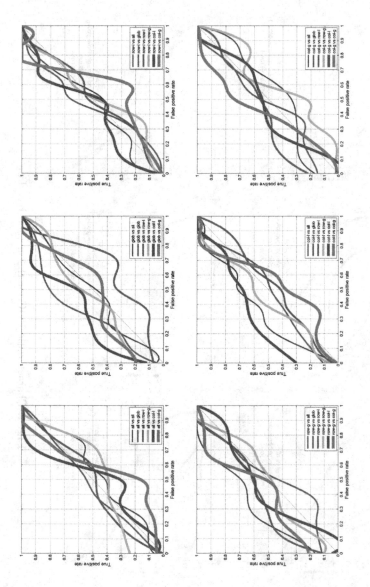

**Fig. 3.** Characteristic ROC for the method based on FCM

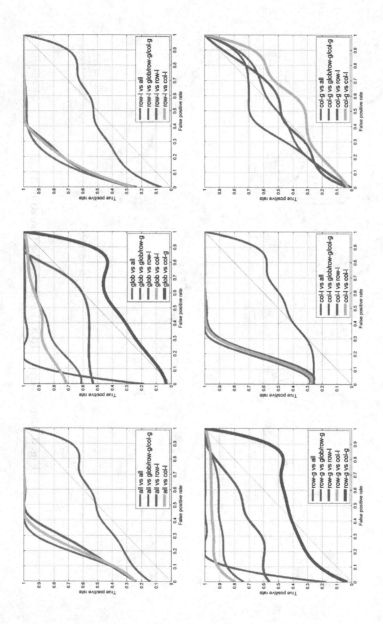

**Fig. 4.** Characteristic ROC for the method based on PCA

**Table 4.** Summary

|        | Accumulative error | Avg. error |
|--------|--------------------|------------|
| PCA:   | 291.72%            | 8.10%      |
| FCM:   | 306.65%            | 8.52%      |
| SOM:   | 409.93%            | 11.39%     |

Table 4 summarizes and averages errors for all presented methods.

## 4  Conclusion

In this contribution, the results of extraction of landmarks based on the new representation of 3D faces has been presented. In the comparison tests, the best result by PCA based method has been obtained, which can be regarded as a very promising for future works. FCM based method results are comparable, but this method recognized all reference images with the same landmark type.

In the future work, we want to focus on the further development of the representation of the face, in particular, on the methods for model interpretation, e.g. on fuzzy methods [6,12,19,20,23,30] or neuro-fuzzy methods [13,26,27,31,18,29,5] as well as combinations with methods of image understanding [2] and processing [1]. Some profits of non-parametric methods [9,11,14,16,17,24,25,28] can be exploited in our method as well.

## References

1. Bazarganigilani, M.: Optimized image feature selection using pairwise classifiers. Journal of Artificial Intelligence and Soft Computing Research 1(2), 147–153 (2011)
2. Chang, Y., Wang, Y., Chen, C., Ricanek, K.: Improved image-based automatic gender classification by feature selection. Journal of Artificial Intelligence and Soft Computing Research 1(3), 241–253 (2011)
3. Cpałka, K., Zalasiński, M.: A new method of on-line signature verification using a flexible fuzzy one-class classifier. In: Selected Topics in Computer Science Applications, pp. 38–53 (2011)
4. Zalasiński, M., Cpałka, K.: Novel algorithm for the on-line signature verification. In: Rutkowski, L., Korytkowski, M., Scherer, R., Tadeusiewicz, R., Zadeh, L.A., Zurada, J.M. (eds.) ICAISC 2012, Part II. LNCS, vol. 7268, pp. 362–367. Springer, Heidelberg (2012)
5. Cpałka, K., Rebrova, O., Nowicki, R., Rutkowski, L.: On designing of flexible neuro-fuzzy systems for nonlinear modelling. In: Kuznetsov, S.O., Ślęzak, D., Hepting, D.H., Mirkin, B.G. (eds.) RSFDGrC 2011. LNCS (LNAI), vol. 6743, pp. 147–154. Springer, Heidelberg (2011)
6. Cpałka, K., Rutkowski, L.: Flexible takagi Sugeno neuro-fuzzy structures for nonlinear approximation. WSEAS Transactions on Systems 4(9), 1450–1458 (2005)
7. Cpałka, K., Zalasiński, M.: On-line signature verification using vertical signature partitioning. Expert Systems with Applications 41(9), 4170–4180 (2014)

8. Cpałka, K., Zalasiński, M., Rutkowski, L.: New method for the on-line signature verification based on horizontal partitioning. Pattern Recognition 47(8), 2652–2661 (2014)

9. Duda, P., Jaworski, M., Pietruczuk, L., Scherer, R., Korytkowski, M., Gabryel, M.: On the application of fourier series density estimation for image classification based on feature description. In: Proceedings of the 8th International Conference on Knowledge, Information and Creativity Support Systems, Krakow, Poland, November 7-9, pp. 81–91 (2013)

10. Faltemier, T., Bowyer, K., Flynn, P.: Rotated profile signatures for robust 3d feature detection. In: 8th IEEE International Conference on Automatic Face Gesture Recognition, FG 2008, pp. 1–7 (September 2008)

11. Gabryel, M., Nowicki, R.K., Woźniak, M., Kempa, W.M.: Genetic cost optimization of the $gI/m/1/N$ finite-buffer queue with a single vacation policy. In: Rutkowski, L., Korytkowski, M., Scherer, R., Tadeusiewicz, R., Zadeh, L.A., Zurada, J.M. (eds.) ICAISC 2013, Part II. LNCS (LNAI), vol. 7895, pp. 12–23. Springer, Heidelberg (2013)

12. Gabryel, M., Rutkowski, L.: Evolutionary designing of logic-type fuzzy systems. In: Rutkowski, L., Scherer, R., Tadeusiewicz, R., Zadeh, L.A., Zurada, J.M. (eds.) ICAISC 2010, Part II. LNCS (LNAI), vol. 6114, pp. 143–148. Springer, Heidelberg (2010)

13. Greblicki, W., Rutkowski, L.: Density-free bayes risk consistency of nonparametric pattern recognition procedures. Proceedings of the IEEE 64(4), 482–483 (1981)

14. Greblicki, W., Rutkowska, D., Rutkowski, L.: An orthogonal series estimate of time-varying regression. Annals of the Institute of Statistical Mathematics 35(1), 215–228 (1983)

15. Kirby, M., Sirovich, L.: Application of the Karhunen-Loeve procedure for the characterization of human faces. IEEE Trans. Pattern Anal. Mach. Intell. 12(1), 103–108 (1990)

16. Korytkowski, M., Rutkowski, L., Scherer, R.: On combining backpropagation with boosting. In: International Joint Conference on Neural Networks, IJCNN 2006, 2006, pp. 1274–1277 (2006)

17. Korytkowski, M., Rutkowski, L., Scherer, R.: From ensemble of fuzzy classifiers to single fuzzy rule base classifier. In: Rutkowski, L., Tadeusiewicz, R., Zadeh, L.A., Zurada, J.M. (eds.) ICAISC 2008. LNCS (LNAI), vol. 5097, pp. 265–272. Springer, Heidelberg (2008)

18. Nowak, B.A., Nowicki, R.K., Mleczko, W.K.: A new method of improving classification accuracy of decision tree in case of incomplete samples. In: Rutkowski, L., Korytkowski, M., Scherer, R., Tadeusiewicz, R., Zadeh, L.A., Zurada, J.M. (eds.) ICAISC 2013, Part I. LNCS (LNAI), vol. 7894, pp. 448–458. Springer, Heidelberg (2013)

19. Nowicki, R.: Rough-neuro-fuzzy system with MICOG defuzzification. In: 2006 IEEE International Conference on Fuzzy Systems, pp. 1958–1965 (2006)

20. Nowicki, R.: On classification with missing data using rough-neuro-fuzzy systems. International Journal of Applied Mathematics and Computer Science 20(1), 55–67 (2010)

21. Pabiasz, S., Starczewski, J.T., Marvuglia, A.: A new three-dimensional facial landmarks in recognition. In: Rutkowski, L., Korytkowski, M., Scherer, R., Tadeusiewicz, R., Zadeh, L.A., Zurada, J.M. (eds.) ICAISC 2014, Part II. LNCS (LNAI), vol. 8468, pp. 179–186. Springer, Heidelberg (2014)

22. Pabiasz, S., Starczewski, J.T.: A new approach to determine three-dimensional facial landmarks. In: Rutkowski, L., Korytkowski, M., Scherer, R., Tadeusiewicz, R., Zadeh, L.A., Zurada, J.M. (eds.) ICAISC 2013, Part II. LNCS, vol. 7895, pp. 286–296. Springer, Heidelberg (2013)
23. Przybył, A., Cpałka, K.: A new method to construct of interpretable models of dynamic systems. In: Rutkowski, L., Korytkowski, M., Scherer, R., Tadeusiewicz, R., Zadeh, L.A., Zurada, J.M. (eds.) ICAISC 2012, Part II. LNCS (LNAI), vol. 7268, pp. 697–705. Springer, Heidelberg (2012)
24. Rutkowski, L.: A general approach for nonparametric fitting of functions and their derivatives with applications to linear circuits identification. IEEE Transactions on Circuits and Systems 33(8), 812–818 (1986)
25. Rutkowski, L., Przybył, A., Cpałka, K.: Novel online speed profile generation for industrial machine tool based on flexible neuro-fuzzy approximation. IEEE Transactions on Industrial Electronics 59(2), 1238–1247 (2012)
26. Rutkowski, L.: On bayes risk consistent pattern recognition procedures in a quasi-stationary environment. IEEE Transactions on Pattern Analysis and Machine Intelligence 4(1), 84–87 (1982)
27. Rutkowski, L.: Sequential pattern recognition procedures derived from multiple fourier series. Pattern Recognition Letters 8(4), 213–216 (1988)
28. Rutkowski, L.: Non-parametric learning algorithms in time-varying environments. Signal Processing 18(2), 129–137 (1989)
29. Rutkowski, L., Przybył, A., Cpałka, K., Er, M.: Online speed profile generation for industrial machine tool based on neuro-fuzzy approach. In: Rutkowski, L., Scherer, R., Tadeusiewicz, R., Zadeh, L.A., Zurada, J.M. (eds.) ICAISC 2010, Part II. LNCS (LNAI), vol. 6114, pp. 645–650. Springer, Heidelberg (2010)
30. Scherer, R., Rutkowski, L.: Connectionist fuzzy relational systems. In: Hagamuge, S., Wang, L.P. (eds.) Computational Intelligence for Modelling and Control. SCI, vol. 2, pp. 35–47. Springer, Heidelberg (2005)
31. Theodoridis, D., Boutalis, Y., Christodoulou, M.: Robustifying analysis of the direct adaptive control of unknown multivariable nonlinear systems based on a new neuro-fuzzy method. Journal of Artificial Intelligence and Soft Computing Research 1(1), 59–79 (2011)
32. Turk, M., Pentland, A.: Face recognition using eigenfaces. In: Proceedings of IEEE Computer Society Conference on Computer Vision and Pattern Recognition, CVPR 1991, pp. 586–591 (June 1991)
33. Zalasiński, M., Cpałka, K., Er, M.: New method for dynamic signature verification using hybrid partitioning. In: Rutkowski, L., Korytkowski, M., Scherer, R., Tadeusiewicz, R., Zadeh, L.A., Zurada, J.M. (eds.) ICAISC 2014, Part II. LNCS, vol. 8468, pp. 216–230. Springer, Heidelberg (2014)
34. Zalasiński, M., Cpałka, K., Hayashi, Y.: New method for dynamic signature verification based on global features. In: Rutkowski, L., Korytkowski, M., Scherer, R., Tadeusiewicz, R., Zadeh, L.A., Zurada, J.M. (eds.) ICAISC 2014, Part II. LNCS, vol. 8468, pp. 231–245. Springer, Heidelberg (2014)

# The Fuzzified Quasi-Perceptron in Decision Making Concerning Treatments in Necrotizing Fasciitis

Elisabeth Rakus-Andersson[1](✉), Janusz Frey[2], and Danuta Rutkowska[3]

[1] Blekinge Institute of Technology, Department of Mathematics and Science,
37179 Karlskrona, Sweden
Elisabeth.Andersson@bth.se
[2] Blekinge County Hospital, Department of Surgery and Urology,
371 85 Karlskrona, Sweden
Janusz.Frey@ltblekinge.se
[3] Institute of Computer and Information Sciences,
Częstochowa University of Technology, 42-201 Częstochowa, Poland
danuta.rutkowska@icis.pcz.pl

**Abstract.** In the current paper we mathematically try to support the decision concerning the treatment with hyperbaric oxygen for patients, suffering from necrotizing fasciitis. To accomplish the task, we involve the fuzzified model of a quasi-perceptron, which is our modification of the classical artificial simple neuron. By means of the fuzzification of input signals and output decision levels, we wish to distinguish between decisions "treatment without recommended hyperbaric oxygen" versus "treatment with hyperbaric oxygen". The number of decision levels can be arbitrary in order to extend the decision scale.

**Keywords:** Fuzzified quasi perceptron · Parametric membership functions · Necrotizing fasciitis · Treatment with hyperbaric oxygen

## 1    Introduction

Necrotizing fasciitis (NF) is a rare, but deadly soft tissue infection. The disease is known from Hippocratic times but has been newly rediscovered in modern times as an "infection with flesh eating bacteria" by Jones in 1871. More specifically, the illness was described in 1952 by Wilson, who also renamed these types of infections as necrotizing fasciitis. The NF group contains various types of infections, usually treated with antibiotics and surgery [2]. In some cases, the treatment with hyperbaric oxygen (HBO) is the adjunct of treatments, mentioned above [5]. Blekinge County City hospital in Karlskrona, Sweden, has the possibility of providing HBO; therefore we serve the treatment to patients from the south eastern part of Sweden, suffering from NF.

From the clinical point of view, it will be interesting to identify a group of patients that have a good prognosis of recovery without recommendations for the specialized treatment with HBO versus a group of patients that need the HBO supplement, provided in a specialized health center.

© Springer International Publishing Switzerland 2015
L. Rutkowski et al. (Eds.): ICAISC 2015, Part II, LNAI 9120, pp. 130–141, 2015.
DOI: 10.1007/978-3-319-19369-4_13

Nevertheless the number of patients is not so high and, due to the disease rarity, it is difficult to make decisions, which routinely can solve the problems of HBO dosing.

The decision, mainly concerning the HBO recommendation in conformity with the patient's health state, is often based on the physicians' experience. To support this choice, we have developed the mathematical model resembling a simple artificial neuron, called the perceptron. The fuzzified form of the perceptron, furnished with some extra complements created by the authors, is expected to constitute a good tool of the theoretical discrimination of the final decision in as many levels as we wish. In this version of the model, we extract only two levels in the practical application of HBO serving.

The decision objects are vectors consisting of values assigned to some essential quantitative and compound qualitative biological parameters. These values have been sampled during the patients' examinations, and their role is to inform of the disease severity.

The classical perceptron model, invented by Frank Rosenblatt [11], is built as an artificial neuron whose activation function is furnished with two integers [1] [11] [13]. The perceptron is a popular network applied to many engineering solutions. Even medical tasks such as diagnosing [14], predicting lung tumor motion [3], operation decision in stomach cancer [8] and others [6], have been handled by this uncomplicated unit. A neuro-fuzzy approach to medical applications has been considered, e.g., in [12].

The first trials of the introduction of fuzziness in the perceptron machinery were made in 1985 [4]. In our modification of the perceptron model proposed, the input data are constructed as membership degrees of patient values of biological markers, when assigning fuzzy sets to these markers. Instead to learn the perceptron to classify the output decisions by training randomly plucked initial weights, we state the importance weights of harmful effects of the biological markers as unchangeable entries following the input data. Last but not the least, the output is predicted as a collection of membership degrees of decision levels, also built as fuzzy sets. This allows determining the optimal decision level, characteristic of the highest degree.

Since the classical perceptron differs from our model, provided with new solutions inserted, then we will call it "the fuzzified quasi-perceptron".

We outline the fuzzified quasi-perceptron model in Section 2. Section 3 contains the descriptions of constructions of entry data, such as signals and weights. The structure of fuzzified output of the quasi-perceptron will be engineered in Section 4. The study, concerning the treatment with HBO, will be tested in Section 5. In the practical study case, we use the data concerning 13 patients (12 men and 1 woman), who were treated in the Blekinge County City Hospital in Karlskrona between 2006 and 2010. We will formulate some concluding remarks in Section 6.

## 2    The Fuzzified Quasi-Perceptron Model

Let us suppose that a disease is characterized by crucial biological markers $X_j, j = 1,\dots,n$. To these markers, we intend to assign fuzzy sets also named $X_j$. The set of patients contains $P_i$ objects, $i = 1,\dots,p$. If a marker value $x_{i,j}$ for symptom $X_j$ is registered for $P_i$, then the membership degree $\mu_{X_j}(x_{i,j})$ will be assigned to $x_{i,j}$. Let us name $\mu_{X_j}(x_{i,j})$ the input signals. The way of designing membership functions $\mu_{X_j}: X_j \to [0,1]$ will be evolved in Section 3.

Next, we introduce the importance weights $w_j$ of symptoms $X_j$ to emerge $X_j$'s harmful influence on the disease course. We suggest the placement of $X_j$ in the sequence $X_1 \succ \ldots \succ X_n$, where "$\succ$" stands for the statement "$X_j$ has more dangerous impact on the patient health state than $X_g$, $j$, $g = 1,\ldots,n$. By making this arrangement of symptoms, we deduce that $w_1 > \ldots > w_n$. We also desire that $\sum_{j=1}^{n} w_j = 1$.

The collected input signal $s_i$ for all $x_{i,j}$, characteristic of patient $P_i$, will be derived as

$$s_i = \sum_{j=1}^{n} \mu_{X_j}(x_{i,j}) \cdot w_j, \ i = 1, \ldots, p. \tag{1}$$

We note that $\min_{1 \le i \le n} s_i = 0$ since, for all minimal $\mu_{X_j}(x_{i,j}) = 0$, we obtain

$$s_i = \sum_{j=1}^{n} 0 \cdot w_j = 0, \ i = 1, \ldots, p. \tag{2}$$

The maximal value of $s_i$ will reach 1 if, for all maximal $\mu_{X_j}(x_{i,j}) = 1$,

$$s_i = \sum_{j=1}^{n} 1 \cdot w_j = 1 \cdot \sum_{j=1}^{n} w_j = 1 \cdot 1 = 1, \ i = 1, \ldots, p. \tag{3}$$

We formulate the equation of an activation function $f:\{s_1,\ldots,s_n\} \subset [0,1] \to [0,1]$ in the form of

$$f(s_i) = (\mu_{L_1}(s_i),\ldots,\mu_{L_m}(s_i)), i = 1,\ldots p, \tag{4}$$

where $L_l$, $l = 1,\ldots,m$, are fuzzy sets assisting decision levels. Sets $L_l$ are restricted over interval [0, 1] due to $f$'s domain. After comparing the membership degrees in (4), we determine the optimal decision level $L_l$ as the level $L^*$ fitted for $L^* = \max_{1 \le l \le m}(\mu_{L_l}(s_i))$.

Figure 1 shows the procedure of the fuzzified quasi-perceptron for two decision levels $L_1$ and $L_2$.

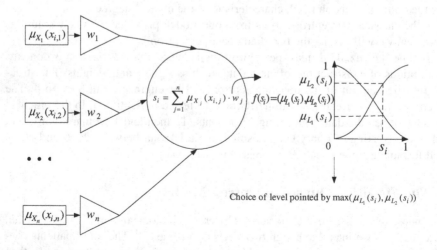

**Fig. 1.** The action of the quasi-perceptron for two decision levels concerning patient $P_i$

## 3    The Design of Input Data

Symptoms $X_j$ are recognized as quantitative and qualitative features. We assign fuzzy sets $X_j$, $j = 1,...,n$, to both types. As the rising order of symptom characteristics (real values or codes) is associated with the growing states of the disease threat then, as a consequence, the membership functions of $X_j$ will be constructed as ascending functions.

For the measurable symptoms $X_j$, taking values $x_{i,j}$ in interval $[\alpha_j, \gamma_j]$ continuously, we have prepared a parametric $s$-function $s(x_{i,j}, \alpha_j, \beta_j, \gamma_j)$ demonstrated by

$$\mu_{X_j}(x_{i,j}) = s(x_{i,j},\alpha_j,\beta_j,\gamma_j) = \begin{cases} 0 & \text{for } x_{i,j} \leq \alpha_j, \\ 2\left(\frac{x_{i,j}-\alpha_j}{\gamma_j-\alpha_j}\right)^2 & \text{for } \alpha_j < x_{i,j} \leq \beta_j, \\ 1-2\left(\frac{x_{i,j}-\gamma_j}{\gamma_j-\alpha_j}\right)^2 & \text{for } \beta_j < x_{i,j} \leq \gamma_j, \\ 1 & \text{for } x_{i,j} > \gamma_j, \end{cases} \tag{5}$$

where $\beta_j = \frac{\alpha_j+\gamma_j}{2}$, $j = 1,...,n$, $i = 1,...,p$.

**Example 1**
Symptom "*age*"$= X_2$ is a fuzzy set, constrained by the membership function $s(x_{i,2},$ 18, 59, 100). For, e.g., $x_{i,2} = 76$, we estimate $\mu_{X_2}(76) = 1-2\left(\frac{76-100}{100-18}\right)^2 = 0.828$ in accordance with the condition $59<76<100$.

By adopting the own procedure [7], we intend now to compute the membership degrees for compound qualitative symptoms $X_j$, characterized by codes $c_{j,0},...,c_{j,k},...,c_{j,z}$, where $c_{j,k+1}=c_{j,k}+1$, $k = 0,...,z-1$, and $c_{j,z}$ is an even integer. Let us first introduce a function $g(c_{j,k})$, which starts with $g(c_{j,0}) = -1$ and terminates with $g(c_{j,z}) = 1$. The length of each of $z-1$ subintervals $I = [c_{j,k}, c_{j,k+1}]$ of $X_j$, partitioning interval $[-1,1]$, is equal to $\frac{g(c_{j,z})-g(c_{j,0})}{z-1}$. After concluding that the end of each subinterval is tied to code $c_{j,k+1}$, we derive

$$g(c_{j,k+1}) = g(c_{j,k}) + \frac{g(c_{j,z})-g(c_{j,0})}{z-1} \tag{6}$$

for $k = 0,...,z-1$.

Interval $[-1, 1]$, containing discrete values $g(c_{j,k})$, constitutes a support of fuzzy set $X_j$ assisting the compound qualitative symptom. In order to estimate membership values of $g(c_{j,k})$, where $k = 0,...,z$ actually, we use an $s$ membership function

$$\mu_{X_j}(g(c_{j,k})) = s(g(c_{j,k}),-1,0,1). \tag{7}$$

When studying the properties of Eq. (7), we remark that: the lack of the symptom $g(c_{j,0}) = -1$ possesses membership 0, the critical value of the symptom $g(c_{j,z}) = 1$ is connected to membership 1, whereas the mean value $\frac{g(c_{j,0})+g(c_{j,z})}{2} = 0$ is furnished with membership 0.5. These features of (7) logically agree with the conditions demanded for symptoms coded.

**Example 2**

The states of symptom "*medical state*" = $S_1$ are coded as: "*comfortable*" = 0, "*satisfactory*" = 1, "*stable*" = 2, "*critical but stable*" = 3 and "*critical*" = 4. The length of each interval, placed between two adjacent codes, equals $\frac{1-(-1)}{5-1} = 0.5$. Hence, $g(0) = -1$, $g(1) = -1 + 0.5 = -0.5$, $g(2) = 0$, $g(3) = 0.5$ and $g(4) = 1$ due to (6). The degrees, found for $g(k)$, $k = 0,\ldots,4$, are, in accord with (7), numbers: $\mu_{X_1}(g(0)) = 0$, $\mu_{X_1}(g(1)) = 0.125$, $\mu_{X_1}(g(2)) = 0.5$, $\mu_{X_1}(g(3)) = 0.875$ and $\mu_{X_1}(g(4)) = 1$.

In the last part of Section 3, let us solve the problem of assigning the importance weights $w_j$ to symptoms $X_j$. By "importance" we mean the strength of $X_j$'s adverse and harmful power in the running process of the illness considered. We bring into light another own mathematical algorithm, allowing the estimation of weights [9].

Generally, if we consider $n$ symptoms $X_j$ to find importance weights for them, we wish to arrange them in the sequence $X_1 \succ \ldots \succ X_n$ in accordance with the expert's opinion. We want the sum of all weights $w_j$, joined to $Xj$, $j = 1,\ldots,n$, to be 1. Therefore,

$$n \cdot r + (n-1) \cdot r + \ldots + 2 \cdot r + 1 \cdot r = 1, \tag{8}$$

where $r$ is a quotient dependent on $n$.

Further,

$$w_j = (n - j + 1) \cdot r, \tag{9}$$

for $j = 1,\ldots,n$.

**Example 3**

The decisive symptoms for the recognition of necrotizing fasciitis are listed in the importance order, decided by a physician, as "*medical state*" = $X_1 \succ$ "*age*" = $X_2 \succ$ "*risk factors*" = $X_3 \succ$ "*crp*" = $X_4 \succ wbc = X_5 \succ$ "*temperature*" = $X_6$. It should be clarified that "*crp*" stands for C-reactive proteins and "*wbc*" means white blood cells. In conformity with (8), equation $6r+5r+4r+3r+2r+r = 1$ provides $r = 0,0476$. After employing (9), we receive, in turn for $j = 1,\ldots,6$, the weights $w_1 = (6-1+1)0.0476 = 0.2856$, $w_2 = 0.238$, $w_3 = 0.1904$, $w_4 = 0.1428$, $w_5 = 0.0952$, $w_6 = 0.0476$.

# 4     The Theoretical Construction of Fuzzified Output Levels

Due to Eq. (4), we should now generate a collection of output decision fuzzy levels $L_l$ stretched over interval $[0, 1]$, $l = 1,\ldots,m$, to calculate the membership degrees of signal $s_i$, $i = 1,\ldots,p$, in each $L_l$. The largest value $L^* = \max\limits_{1 \leq l \leq m} \mu_{L_l}(s_i)$ points out the optimal decision level assigned to $P_i$.

Theoretically, $m$ can be either an even or an odd positive arbitrary integer. An own procedure helps us to derive membership functions of $L_l$. These are dependent only on two parameters, namely, a number of levels and a length of the common set containing all supports of $L_l$. The proof of Theorem 1, edited by us for odd $m$ values, can be found in [10]. The formulas of $L_l$'s membership functions, containing an even $m$ quantity, have been brought forth for the sake of this paper.

**Theorem 1** [10]

Suppose that we want to find membership functions for fuzzy sets $L_1,\ldots,L_m$, where $m$ is an odd positive integer. We assume that supports of constraints $\mu_{L_l}(s_i)$, $l = 1,\ldots,m$, will cover parts of the reference set $L = [\min(L_1),\max(L_m)]$, $s_i \in L$. $E = |L|$ is the length of $L$.

We divide all $L_l$ in three groups, namely, a family of "*leftmost*" sets $L_1,\ldots, L_{\frac{m-1}{2}}$, the set $L_{\frac{m+1}{2}}$ "*in the middle*" and a collection of "*rightmost*" sets $L_{\frac{m+3}{2}},\ldots,L_m$. To design the membership functions of $L_l$, the $s$-class function $s(s_i, m, E)$ will be adopted.

The function of "*in the middle*" $= L_{\frac{m+1}{2}}$ is constructed as

$$\mu_{L_{\frac{m+1}{2}}}(s_i) = \begin{cases} 0 & \text{for } s_i \leq \frac{E(m-2)}{2m}, \\ 2\left(\frac{s_i - \frac{E(m-2)}{2m}}{\frac{E}{m}}\right)^2 & \text{for } \frac{E(m-2)}{2m} \leq s_i \leq \frac{E(m-1)}{2m}, \\ 1 - 2\left(\frac{s_i - \frac{E}{2}}{\frac{E}{m}}\right)^2 & \text{for } \frac{E(m-1)}{2m} \leq s_i \leq \frac{E}{2}, \\ 1 - 2\left(\frac{s_i - \frac{E}{2}}{\frac{E}{m}}\right)^2 & \text{for } \frac{E}{2} \leq s_i \leq \frac{E(m+1)}{2m}, \\ 2\left(\frac{s_i - \frac{E(m+2)}{2m}}{\frac{E}{m}}\right)^2 & \text{for } \frac{E(m+1)}{2m} \leq s_i \leq \frac{E(m+2)}{2m}, \\ 0 & \text{for } s_i \geq \frac{E(m+2)}{2m}. \end{cases} \quad (10)$$

All constraints, characteristic of the "*leftmost*" family of fuzzy sets, will be given by

$$\mu_{L_l}(s_i) = \begin{cases} 1 & \text{for } s_i \leq \frac{E(m-1)}{2(m+1)}\delta(t), \\ 1 - 2\left(\frac{s_i - \frac{E(m-1)}{2(m+1)}\delta(t)}{\frac{E(m-1)}{m(m+1)}\delta(t)}\right)^2 & \text{for } \frac{E(m-1)}{2(m+1)}\delta(t) \leq s_i \leq \frac{E(m-1)}{2m}\delta(t), \\ 2\left(\frac{s_i - \frac{E(m-1)(m+2)}{2m(m+1)}\delta(t)}{\frac{E(m-1)}{m(m+1)}\delta(t)}\right)^2 & \text{for } \frac{E(m-1)}{2m}\delta(t) \leq s_i \leq \frac{E(m-1)(m+2)}{2m(m+1)}\delta(t), \\ 0 & \text{for } s_i \geq \frac{E(m-1)(m+2)}{2m(m+1)}\delta(t). \end{cases} \quad (11)$$

where function $\delta(t) = \frac{2}{m-1}\cdot t$, $t = 1,\ldots, \frac{m-1}{2}$.

To generate the *"rightmost"* family of sets $L_{\frac{m+3}{2}},...,L_m$, we need to initiate a new function $\varepsilon(t)=1-\frac{2}{m-1}(t-1)$ , $t = 1,..., \frac{m-1}{2}$ . All right functions have a parametric equation

$$\mu_{L_{\frac{m+3}{2}+t-1}}(s_i)=$$

$$
\begin{cases}
0 & \text{for } s_i \leq E-\frac{E(m-1)(m+2)}{2m(m+1)}\varepsilon(t), \\[2mm]
2\left(\frac{s_i-\left(E-\frac{E(m-1)(m+2)}{2m(m+1)}\varepsilon(t)\right)}{\frac{E(m-1)}{m(m+1)}\varepsilon(t)}\right)^2 & \text{for } E-\frac{E(m-1)(m+2)}{2m(m+1)}\varepsilon(t) \leq s_i \leq E-\frac{E(m-1)}{2m}\varepsilon(t), \\[2mm]
1-2\left(\frac{s_i-\left(E-\frac{E(m-1)}{2(m+1)}\varepsilon(t)\right)}{\frac{E(m-1)}{m(m+1)}\varepsilon(t)}\right)^2 & \text{for } E-\frac{E(m-1)}{2m}\varepsilon(t) \leq s_i \leq E-\frac{E(m-1)}{2(m+1)}\varepsilon(t), \\[2mm]
1 & \text{for } s_i \geq E-\frac{E(m-1)}{2(m+1)}\varepsilon(t).
\end{cases}
\tag{12}
$$

Let us emphasize that we use only three equations in order to generate all membership functions of $L_l$, affected by $m$ and $E$. The mobile variable in Eqs (11) and (12) is an actual function number $t$. The procedure can be thus easily computerized.

**Theorem 2** (the proof will be provided in the extended version of the paper)
For an even $m$ value we remove the function *"in the middle"* from the model. The restrictions of the *"leftmost"* family of fuzzy sets $L_1,..., L_{\frac{m}{2}}$ will be thus recommended as

$$
\mu_{L_t}(s_i)=
\begin{cases}
1 & \text{for } s_i \leq \frac{E(m-2)}{2(m-1)}\delta(t), \\[2mm]
1-2\left(\frac{s_i-\frac{E(m-2)}{2(m-1)}\delta(t)}{\frac{E}{(m-1)}\delta(t)}\right)^2 & \text{for } \frac{E(m-2)}{2(m-1)}\delta(t) \leq s_i \leq \frac{E}{2}\delta(t), \\[2mm]
2\left(\frac{s_i-\frac{Em}{2(m-1)}\delta(t)}{\frac{E}{(m-1)}\delta(t)}\right)^2 & \text{for } \frac{E}{2}\delta(t) \leq s_i \leq \frac{Em}{2(m-1)}\delta(t), \\[2mm]
0 & \text{for } s_i \geq \frac{Em}{2(m-1)}\delta(t),
\end{cases}
\tag{13}
$$

where $\delta(t)=\frac{2}{m}\cdot t$ , $t=1,...,\frac{m}{2}$ .

The common equation of *"rightmost"* family of functions $L_{\frac{m}{2}+1},...,L_m$ is affected by the even $m$ value as

$$
\mu_{L_{\frac{m}{2}+t}}(s_i)=
\begin{cases}
0 & \text{for } s_i \leq E-\frac{Em}{2(m-1)}\varepsilon(t), \\[2mm]
2\left(\frac{s_i-\left(E-\frac{Em}{2(m-1)}\varepsilon(t)\right)}{\frac{E}{(m-1)}\varepsilon(t)}\right)^2 & \text{for } E-\frac{Em}{2(m-1)}\varepsilon(t) \leq s_i \leq E-\frac{E}{2}\varepsilon(t), \\[2mm]
1-2\left(\frac{s_i-\left(E-\frac{E(m-2)}{2(m-1)}\varepsilon(t)\right)}{\frac{E}{m-1}\varepsilon(t)}\right)^2 & \text{for } E-\frac{E}{2}\varepsilon(t) \leq s_i \leq E-\frac{E(m-2)}{2(m-1)}\varepsilon(t), \\[2mm]
1 & \text{for } s_i \geq E-\frac{E(m-2)}{2(m-1)}\varepsilon(t),
\end{cases}
\tag{14}
$$

for $\varepsilon(t)=1-\frac{2}{m}(t-1)$ , $t=1,...,\frac{m}{2}$ .

**Example 4**

We ascertain the propriety of Eqs (10)-(12) in Fig. 2(a) for $m = 3$ and $E = 1$, whereas the verification of Eqs (13)-(14) is accomplished in Fig. 2(b), when $m = 2$ and $E = 1$.

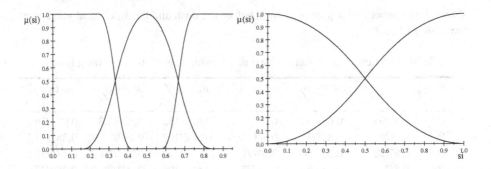

**Fig. 2. (a).** Functions of $L_1$, $L_2$, $L_3$, $m=3$          **Fig. 2(b).** Functions of $L_1$, $L_2$, $m=2$

## 5    The Decision Concerning the Treatment with HBO

It has already been mentioned in Section 1 that the mathematical apparatus, built in Sections 2-4, will be applied to verify (confirm or deny) a decision concerning the treatment with HBO of patients suffering from necrotizing fasciitis. The data, including the values of crucial clinical markers and the decisions made by physicians, have been sampled for 13 patients (12 men and 1 woman) treated in the Blekinge County City Hospital in Karlskrona, Sweden, between 2006 and 2010.

The clinical symptoms, essential in NF, have been introduced in Example 3. For quantitative symptoms we adapt Eq. (5) as follows:

$$\mu_{X_2 = "age"}(x_{i,2}) = s(x_{i,2}, 18, 59, 100) , \quad \mu_{X_4 = "crp"}(x_{i,4}) = s(x_{i,4}, 0, 250, 500) ,$$

$$\mu_{X_5 = "wbc"}(x_{i,5}) = s(x_{i,5}, 0, 15, 30) \quad \text{and} \quad \mu_{X_6 = "temp."}(x_{i,6}) = s(x_{i,6}, 36, 38.5, 41) .$$

In Example 2, we have already determined the membership degrees for the coded symptom $X_1$ = "*medical state*" as: $\mu_{X_1}(g(0)) = 0$, $\mu_{X_1}(g(1)) = 0.125$,

$\mu_{X_1}(g(2)) = 0.5$, $\mu_{X_1}(g(3)) = 0.875$ and $\mu_{X_1}(g(4)) = 1$.

We repeat the algorithm for symptom $X_3$ = "*risk factors*", coded between 0 and 6, where $g(0) = -1$, $g(1) = -0.666$, $g(2) = -0.333$, $g(3) = 0$, $g(4) = 0.333$, $g(5) = 0.666$ and $g(6) = 1$. When fixing $\mu_{X_3 = "risk factors"}(g(k)) = s(g(k), -1, 0, 1)$, $k = 0, \ldots, 6$, we list:

$\mu_{X_3}(g(0)) = 0$, $\mu_{X_3}(g(1)) = 0.056$, $\mu_{X_3}(g(2)) = 0.221$, $\mu_{X_3}(g(3)) = 0.5$,

$\mu_{X_3}(g(4)) = 0.779$, $\mu_{X_3}(g(5)) = 0.944$ and $\mu_{X_3}(g(6)) = 1$.

Table 1 contains the clinical data and assigned to them membership degrees, computed in compliance with the membership functions of $X_j$. The symbol $\mu_{X_j}(x_{i,j})/x_{i,j}$ shows the membership degree of $x_{i,j}$ in $X_j$ before the dash and the $x_{i,j}$ clinical value after the dash, $j = 1,\ldots,6$.

**Table 1.** Patient clinical data and their membership degrees in necrotizing fasciitis

| $P_i$ | $\mu_{X_1}(x_{i,1})/x_{i,1}$ | $\mu_{X_2}(x_{i,2})/x_{i,2}$ | $\mu_{X_3}(x_{i,3})/x_{i,3}$ | $\mu_{X_4}(x_{i,4})/x_{i,4}$ | $\mu_{X_5}(x_{i,5})/x_{i,5}$ | $\mu_{X_6}(x_{i,6})/x_{i,6}$ |
|---|---|---|---|---|---|---|
| $P_1$ | 0.125/1 | 0.058/32 | 0/0 | 0.825/352 | 0.52/15.3 | 0.003/36.2 |
| $P_2$ | 0.5/2 | 0.828/76 | 0.5/3 | 0.566/267 | 0.493/14.9 | 0.387/38.2 |
| $P_3$ | 0.875/3 | 0.304/50 | 0.056/1 | 0.43/232 | 0.222/10 | 0.135/37.3 |
| $P_4$ | 0.5/2 | 0.656/66 | 0.221/2 | 0.696/305 | 0.993/28.2 | 0.289/37.9 |
| $P_5$ | 0.875/3 | 0.749/71 | 0/0 | 0.286/189 | 0.989/27.8 | 0.135/37.3 |
| $P_6$ | 0.5/2 | 0.452/57 | 0/0 | 0.637/281 | 0.533/15.5 | 0.423/38.3 |
| $P_7$ | 1/4 | 0.285/49 | 0.056/1 | 0.849/363 | 0.755/19.5 | 0.028/36.6 |
| $P_8$ | 0.875/3 | 0.892/81 | 0.5/3 | 0.91/394 | 0.358/12.7 | 0.205/37.6 |
| $P_9$ | 1/4 | 0.475/58 | 1/6 | 0.939/413 | 0.68/18 | 0.32/38 |
| $P_{10}$ | 0.875/3 | 0.452/57 | 0.056/1 | 0.484/246 | 0.021/3.1 | 0/35.8 |
| $P_{11}$ | 0.5/2 | 0.524/60 | 0.221/2 | 0.058/85 | 0.619/16.9 | 0.289/36.5 |
| $P_{12}$ | 0.875/3 | 0.732/70 | 0.778/4 | 0.924/403 | 0.995/28.5 | 0.32/38 |
| $P_{13}$ | 1/4 | 0.881/80 | 0.221/2 | 0.046/76 | 0.726/18.9 | 0.98/40.5 |

As emerged in Eq. (1), the aggregation of membership degrees $\mu_{X_j}(x_{i,j})$ with weights $w_j$ evaluated in Example 3, $j = 1,\ldots,6$, will constitute a basis for the calculation of the cumulated entry signal $s_i$ for patient $P_i$.

**Example 5**

$s_1 = 0.125\cdot0.286+0.058\cdot0.238+0\cdot0.19+0.824\cdot0.1428+0.52\cdot0.095+0.003\cdot0.047 = 0.21676$ represents $P_1$.

In order to interpret two decision states by means of membership degrees in $L_1$ and $L_2$, we return to Eqs (13)-(14), for $m = 2$, $L = [0, 1]$ and $E = 1$ to derive functions $\mu_{L_1}(s_i) = 1 - s(s_i,0,0.5,1)$ and $\mu_{L_2}(s_i) = s(s_i,0,0.5,1)$. We identify $L_1$ with the decision about not recommending the treatment with HBO. On the contrary, $L_2$ confirms the decision about the HBO treatment. We choose the decision characterized by the largest membership degree out of $\mu_{L_1}(s_i)$ and $\mu_{L_2}(s_i)$.

Table 2 collects signals, their membership degrees and the physician's assertion already made.

We note that the fuzzy decisions converge to medical decisions in most of cases. In the future research, we plan to test the model with three decisions levels, where the middle level "wait and see", assigned to values about 0.5, will be often checked to study its tendencies.

**Table 2.** The comparison of fuzzy decisions (underlined) to decisions made by the physician

| $P_i$ | $s_i$ | $\mu_{L_1}(s_i)$ - without HBO | $\mu_{L_2}(s_i)$ - with HBO | Physician's decision about treating with HBO |
|-------|-------|-------------------------------|----------------------------|---------------------------------------------|
| $P_1$ | 0.217 | <u>0.906</u> | 0.094 | No |
| $P_2$ | 0.581 | 0.341 | <u>0.659</u> | Yes |
| $P_3$ | 0.422 | <u>0.643</u> | 0.357 | Yes |
| $P_4$ | 0.548 | 0.408 | <u>0.592</u> | Yes |
| $P_5$ | 0.569 | 0.371 | <u>0.629</u> | Yes |
| $P_6$ | 0.412 | <u>0.660</u> | 0.340 | No |
| $P_7$ | 0.559 | 0.390 | <u>0.610</u> | Yes |
| $P_8$ | 0.731 | 0.144 | <u>0.856</u> | Yes |
| $P_9$ | 0.802 | 0.078 | <u>0.922</u> | Yes |
| $P_{10}$ | 0.439 | <u>0.614</u> | 0.386 | No |
| $P_{11}$ | 0.390 | <u>0.695</u> | 0.305 | No |
| $P_{12}$ | 0.814 | 0.069 | <u>0.931</u> | Yes |
| $P_{13}$ | 0.659 | 0.232 | <u>0.768</u> | Yes |

# 6    Conclusions

By suggesting modifications in the classical perceptron, we have adapted it to make decisions concerning curation with hyperbaric oxygen, needed for patients afflicted by necrotizing fasciitis. We have proposed own parametric membership functions of fuzzy sets to be able to fuzzify the input data and output decision levels. We emphasize that the functions are affected only by a number of levels and the length of a set, common for all fuzzy constraints. The functions are derived in the way allowing to determine an arbitrary number of levels, which extends the decision scale of linguistic expressions without making changes in formulas.

The own procedures of estimating the importance weights of symptoms and approximating membership degrees of qualitative symptoms have been added as contributions in imprecise mathematics.

From the mathematical point of view, the results obtained seem to be logically correct.

Necrotizing fasciitis (NF) is a quite rare entity, and there is no widespread consensus regarding neither treatment nor grading. There were several attempts of using laboratory results only to facilitate diagnosis making and grading the disease's severity, but as far as we know, they are not used widely. The idea of combining analysis of numerical parameters, such as body temperature, white blood cell count, age etc. with the non-parametrical estimations, such as medical state etc. is very promising, because it will reflect the real decision making progress. The model, tested above, is based on retrospective analysis of data of patients treated with hyperbaric oxygen (HBO) at the hospital department in Karlskrona, Sweden.

We realize that the present model has weaknesses, mostly if the group used to check the model, has not been very numerous. In spite of this, it seems that we have been successful in selecting essential clinical and biochemical parameters, which has constituted the crucial decision for the correctness of the mathematical model. The results of the perceptron's analysis are not 100% concordant with the real medical decisions, but are quite near to the last ones. This reflects also the reliability of the mathematical technique, and we think that it is a promising beginning of our research work in this direction.

In the further research we will redefine the ordering of importance weights of symptoms more carefully to refine the results. The fuzzified quasi-perceptron can be used to more than two decisions, something, which makes it suitable for decision making in other diseases, characterized by more available treatment options.

To sum up, the authors think that the quasi-perceptron method has shown valuable decisions, when involving into them the commonly used parametric laboratory and clinical data.

# References

1. Engelbrecht, A.P.: Computational Intelligence. Wiley & Sons Ltd., Chichester (2007)
2. Hasham, S., Matteucci, P., Stanley, P.R., Hant, N.B.: Necrotizing Fasciitis. BMJ 330(7495), 830–833 (2005)
3. Isaksson, M., Jalden, J., Murphy, M.J.: On Using an Adaptive Neural Network to Predict Lung Tumor Motion During Respiration for Radiotherapy Applications, American Association of Physicists in Medicine (2005), doi: 10.1118/1.2134958
4. Keller, J.M., Hunt, D.J., Douglas, J.: Incorporating Fuzzy Membership Functions into the Perceptron Algorithm. IEEE Transactions on Pattern Analysis and Machine Intelligence 7(6), 693–699 (1985)
5. Mathieu, D., Favory, R., Cesari, J., Wattel, F.: Necrotizing Soft Tissue Infections. In: Handbook on Hyperbaric Medicine, pp. 263–298. Springer Netherlands (2006)
6. Miller, S., Blott, B.H., Hames, T.K.: Review of Neural Network Applications in Medical Imaging and Signal Processing. Medical and Biological Engineering and Computing 30(5), 449–464 (1992)
7. Rakus-Andersson, E.: Fuzzy and Rough Techniques in Medical Diagnosis and Medication. STUDFUZZ, vol. 212. Springer, Heidelberg (2007)
8. Rakus-Andersson, E.: The Parametric s-functions and the Perceptron in Gastric Cancer Surgery Decision Making. In: Essam, D., Sarker, R. (eds.) Proceedings of WCCI 2012 World Congress, pp. 1852–1859.IEEE Computational Intelligence Society (2012)
9. Rakus-Andersson, E., Frey, J.: The Choquet Integral Applied to Ranking Therapies in Radiation Cystitis. In: Filev, D., Jabłkowski, J., Kacprzyk, J., Krawczak, M., Popchev, I., Rutkowski, L., et al. (eds.) Intelligent Systems'2014. AISC, vol. 323, pp. 443–452. Springer, Heidelberg (2015)

10. Rakus-Andersson, E.: Complex Control Models with Parametric Families of Fuzzy Constrains in Evaluation of Resort Management System. Journal of Advanced Computational Intelligence and Intelligent Informatics 18(3), 271–279 (2014)
11. Rosenblatt, F.: Principles of Neurodynamics: Perceptrons and the Theory of Brain Mechanisms. Spartan Books, Washington, DC (1961)
12. Rutkowska, D.: Neuro-Fuzzy Architectures and Hybrid Learning. Springer, Heidelberg (2002)
13. Rutkowski, L.: Computational Intelligence: Methods and Techniques. Springer, Heidelberg (2008)
14. Yan, H., Jiang, Y., Zheng, J., Peng, C., Li, Q.: A Multilayer Perceptron-based Medical Decision Support System for Heart Disease Diagnosis. Expert Systems with Applications 30(2), 272–281 (2006)

# Mobile Fuzzy System for Detecting Loss of Consciousness and Epileptic Seizure

Paweł Staszewski[1(✉)], Piotr Woldan[1], and Sohrab Ferdowsi[2]

[1] Institute of Computational Intelligence, Częstochowa University of Technology,
Al. Armii Krajowej 36, 42-200 Częstochowa, Poland
p.staszewski90@gmail.com
http://iisi.pcz.pl
[2] University of Geneva, Computer Science Department,
7 Route de Drize, Geneva, Switzerland
http://sip.unige.ch

**Abstract.** A framework for detecting loss of consciousness and epilepsy attack based on a neuro-fuzzy system embedded in an accelerometer built-in mobile phone is presented. Additional filtering algorithms protect the system against excessive energy consumption. The system has the ability to monitor and control daily user behaviour as well as to react to situations that can be life or health threatening, with a self-learning mechanism that can adjust to motility of human movement. Moreover, an advantage of our system, is a function of quick contact with appropriate services or relatives, by sending health state and location data regarding the person, in case the user loses consciousness or has an epilepsy seizure.

**Keywords:** Mobile medical systems · Neuro-fuzzy system · Loss of consciousness detector · Faint detector · Epilepsy detector

## 1 Introduction

Every day many people face serious health problems associated with loss of consciousness. According to the World Health Organization statistics from 2012 [22], about 50 million people around the world have epilepsy and 75% of them are not treated at all. Epilepsy evinces itself by dangerous seizures. International Diabetes Federation shows that in 2014, 387 million people suffered from diabetes [4]. Unfortunately, this is a growing trend. IDF predicts [4] that in 2035 the number of people whose have diabetes will rise to 592 million. Patients afflicted with diabetes are vulnerable for losing consciousness. Mentioned problems might bring about life-threatening situations. Moreover, it might be a case when someone needs help and there is no one who can help him.

In the literature we can find a variety of systems which use accelerometer. It can be used in activity detection such as walking, sitting, standing, jogging and walking on stairs [10][13], in any mobile phone orientation and position [19]. There is also a possibility of detecting vibrations of keyboard keys to decode text which was typed [11] or developing gait authentication mobile system [2].

© Springer International Publishing Switzerland 2015
L. Rutkowski et al. (Eds.): ICAISC 2015, Part II, LNAI 9120, pp. 142–150, 2015.
DOI: 10.1007/978-3-319-19369-4_14

Triaxial accelerometer is very useful in epileptic seizure detection [7] in wrist-worn devices. It is also possible to build a fall recognition system [3][6].

This paper presents a mobile system that can recognise a loss of consciousness or epilepsy attack, developed by the authors. The motivation of the project was to help people living alone with large probability of occurrence of the above situations. The recognition is based on signals from an accelerometer built in a mobile device and a neuro-fuzzy module for epilepsy seizures detection. Soft computing [16] is often used for supporting healthcare, e.g. in medical imaging [1][5], orthopaedics [20][21] or rehabilitation [23]. Fuzzy systems [8][9][12][14][17][18] are very convenient machine learning systems as their parameters can be adjusted and, at the same time, the knowledge in the form of fuzzy rules is relatively easily interpretable for humans. The entire system proposed in the paper is embedded in a mobile phone, thus it can immediately contact appropriate people or services, e.g. by sending a text message.

## 2   Input Data

To calibrate the algorithm, a set of samples was generated, which approximated motor state for an average person as best as possible. Thanks to this, the system can recognize a loss of consciousness or epilepsy attack with high effectiveness from the beginning. With time, the application is more resistant to false alarms thanks to a self-learning procedure. The most serious problem in identifying an appropriate sample, is finding a common feature for a sector that will be a candidate to call an adequate event by a neuro-fuzzy system.

Built-in triaxial accelerometers output three values for x, y, z axis, respectively. These readings are collected in a determined period of time. In this case after every minute, the algorithm gathers 6000 samples (each sample defined by the axis: x, y, z). Unfortunately, these readings determine acceleration which is relative to the cell phone. To properly detect human fall, the authors developed an algorithm which returns values relative to the ground vector (denoted further as **RGV**). This vector is calculated based on readings from accelerometer. The most important feature of this algorithm is achieving direction of **RGV** as independent from the position or rotation of the smartphone. Each reading is generated in 10ms time intervals, which allows to determine precisely the position and orientation of the cell phone. An example candidate sector of samples is presented in Figure 1.

After calculating **RGV**, data are presented to filtering algorithm, which takes several parameters such as: $n$ – number of samples in the tested sector; $A$ – the threshold of the amplitude determined by the relative to ground vector (**RGV**); $r$ – number of samples from the fall sector calculated in the fall moment; $T$ – the threshold of the average mean of $r$ samples in the period of time until fall; $F$ – the threshold of the average mean of samples after the fall; $s$ – number of samples after fall. The system continuously captures the accelerometer data, and initially generates a vector of amplitude variations relative to the ground. These data are entered into the algorithm that checks the jump of value, and if this parameter

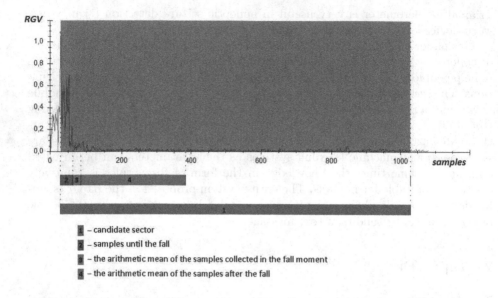

**Fig. 1.** The sector to check by the filtering algorithm

is above the threshold of the amplitude $A$, then the sector with the appropriate size (which was served based on the parameter $n$) is generated, and this range consists of all read values from the accelerometer relative to the time ratio $T$, from the moment of the amplitude jump. After creating a sector of appropriate size, it is tested if the sample is a suitable candidate to call an event in the neuro-fuzzy system. To define a sector as an adequate candidate, three values that reflects linguistic variables in the neuro-fuzzy network have to be specified: $A$ - amplitude jump above threshold, which was defined earlier; time since the jump of amplitude to fall; arithmetic mean of values from $s$ samples after the fall. First, the algorithm iterates next samples of sector from the first value, calculating arithmetic mean of consecutive $r$ - values, until the result of sum will be less than the value of fall threshold $F$ or until the last possible iteration exceeds the number of samples defined by formula $n(r+s)$. If appropriate result of the arithmetic mean is found, then the time from jump of amplitude to fall detected by the system is tested. The last value that is essential in the recognition of loss of consciousness or epilepsy attack is the arithmetic mean of next $s$ - samples after the fall. When all the above data are correctly found, this sector becomes a candidate, which can indicate loss of consciousness or epilepsy attack. The calculated values in the sector are served on the system in order to identify the corresponding event.

Thanks to the above method a significant number of samples, which can call false alarms is eliminated from the learning process. For calculations in neuro-fuzzy network, only these samples are passed that have a high probability of invoking loss of consciousness or epilepsy attack on the output.

# 3   System Architecture

The modular construction of the mobile system detecting loss of consciousness and epileptic seizures, allowed for programming universal elements, that can be modified on later phases of software evolution and can improve the testing process. Data obtained from the accelerometer is processed by a specialized

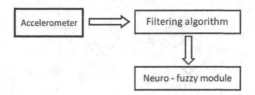

**Fig. 2.** Modules of the system

filtering algorithm. At this stage the system selects samples that correspond to the specified criteria, and the rest is discarded. This prevents excessive using computing power of the smartphone and, in consequence, to decrease battery consumption.

The important element of the system is the use of the neuro-fuzzy module for processing data, obtained after the filtration process. The first layer of module describes linguistic variables (amplitude, time after fall and average sum of amplitudes in time interval).

The inference block located in the second layer is based on 54 fuzzy rules, that were generated based on fuzzy sets. The parameters: $\alpha$ and $\beta$ that are determined for sharpening, are calculated in the third layer. The fourth layer calculates the output from neuro-fuzzy network as the centre of gravity method, which can be described by the following formula:

$$y = \frac{\alpha}{\beta} = \frac{\sum_{k=1}^{N} y^k \times \mu_{B^k}(y^k)}{\sum_{k=1}^{N} \times \mu_{B^k}(y^k)}. \tag{1}$$

Using of the neuro-fuzzy module allowed achieving learning ability of the system, according to presented input parameters. This is a very important factor, whereby learning module can adjust his reaction presented on the output and match his action to motility of the human movement. Correction of the membership function parameters for fuzzy sets (centres and widths of Gaussian functions), and centres of output sets that are represented as singletons, is realized [15] by the steepest descent optimization algorithm. Figure 3 reflects the neuro-fuzzy module which was implemented in the system. At the end of the system learning process, the correction of Gaussian functions parameters can be executed in case of invoking false alarm in the system. After displaying appropriate message, user can check the adequate option, and then correction will be done automatically by the system.

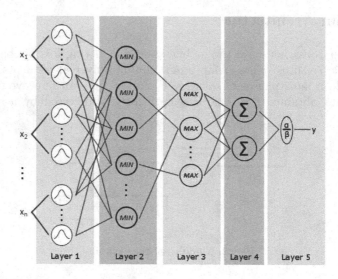

**Fig. 3.** Diagram of the neuro-fuzzy network implemented in the system

# 4  Algorithm Synchronization

The system is initialized with predefined data. Thanks to this, the device with installed application is ready to use and can detect loss of consciousness and epileptic attack with high probability . However, despite this, each person has a different movement dynamics, what makes the system a bit more or less susceptible to causing false alarms. Therefore, the system has the capability of self-correcting adequate parameters to adapt to the user and to accurately recognise loss of consciousness or epilepsy attack. When the alarm is triggered, the user has specified interval of time, in which he or she has the opportunity to cancel the alarm. In this case, the event is reported to be a false alarm, and the system corrects the corresponding values according to steepest descent optimization algorithm, which was implemented as the learning method for the neuro-fuzzy system. It is also possible a situation when no event is triggered but input data are close enough to invoke the alarm. It is then a certain tolerance threshold, presented in Figure 4, where the message is sent to inform the system that something is currently happening with the user, because the neuro-fuzzy module annotated behaviour that is close to „loss of consciousness" or „epileptic attack" event. In this case the system automatically detected nonconformity with parameters, and asks for giving additional information to correct them. User has a possibility to restore default settings, and then the entire database which contains initial parameters is recovered.

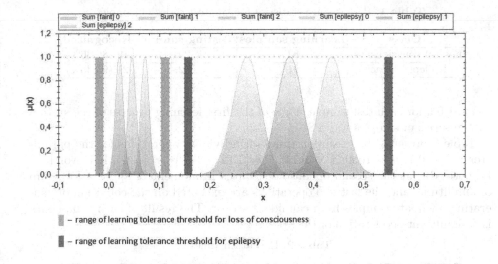

**Fig. 4.** Tolerance threshold of learning for the neuro-fuzzy system

# 5   System Capabilities

If one of events occurs and when the user did not cancel the alarm, a message with appropriate content can be sent to relatives, or to relevant services to inform about the circumstances. The mobile system can transfer information about the location of event thanks to the geolocalization function, as well as other important data e.g. age, blood group, medical history, etc. The software does not require any additional modules apart from a phone with built-in accelerometer. The application can be upgraded in many ways. Another advantage of the system is a very high detection rate of loss of consciousness and epilepsy attacks, presented in the next section. Minimization of energy consumption and self-learning mechanism significantly increases the comfort of using the application.

# 6   Research and Results

During the application development, numerous tests have been carried out, which allowed for solutions optimization. Series of samples was introduced on the system input and tested the effectiveness of the responses. The tests were performed on separate samples.

The neuro-fuzzy module was trained with filtered samples was accomplished with variable learning ratio, which is adjusted during the learning process and is equal 0.05 at the beginning. At this stage, it was assumed that learning continues, until the learning error reaches 0.01. The effectiveness of tests for a series of samples are presented in Table 1. Adjusting the neuro-fuzzy module by series of samples, allowed to establish the learning error level at $E = 0.00853$ after 375th epoch. Threshold activation level of output singletons was determined as

**Table 1.** Performance statistics for the test series of samples

| Class | Learning samples | Testing samples | Recognised |
|---|---|---|---|
| Loss of consciousness | 84 | 22 | 19 (86.36%) |
| Epilepsy attack | 91 | 22 | 21 (95.45%) |

at most 0.3 for each test sample. Time of the first learning process of the system by the series of samples was 8.81 s.

Table 2 presents the execution times of individual operations for the parameters: $A = 0.7$; $n = 1000$; $T = 0.14$; $F = 0.12$; $r = 20$; $s = 300$. It is worth to be noticed that the second operation executes in moment of appropriate jump of amplitude, and the last two operations are executed on the condition of generating adequate samples from candidate sector. The result of such complexity is a significant acceleration of the system.

**Table 2.** Execution times

| 1. Sampling fall amplitude | 100 samples/s |
|---|---|
| 2. Generating candidate sector | 0.0152s |
| 3. Calculating the response from neuro-fuzzy system | 0.00037s |
| 4. Parameters correction (self-learning) | 0.055s |

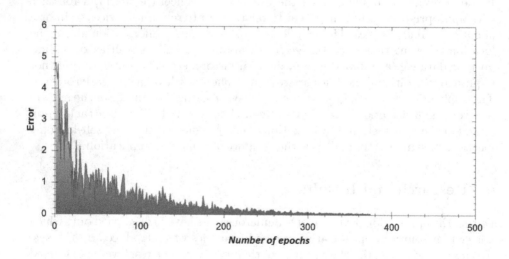

**Fig. 5.** The mean squared error in each epoch.

## 7    Conclusions

The results of simulations of the proposed mobile system for detecting loss of consciousness and epileptic attack allowed to optimize filtering algorithms and the neuro-fuzzy module. Time of executing critical system functions has been reduced. The use of filtering algorithms allowed to reduce the computational load and significantly increased the efficiency of the system. The modular design of the system allows for making improvements, without changing other existing component. Exhaustive tests demonstrated high efficiency of the implemented mechanisms. An advantage of this system, as well as the advanced mechanisms implemented by the authors, is the use of accelerometer built into a smartphone without any additional external sensors, which could reduce the quality of the user life.

Currently, the system is dedicated to the family of operating systems Microsoft Windows Phone 8. There is also ongoing work on developing this application for Android devices.

Constantly evolving technological level of modern smartphones favours adding new features and miniaturized internal sensors, with which the device can obtain information. Adding a feature for reading data from a heart rate monitor, available in many models of phones, can increase effectiveness of the application.

# References

1. Bruzdzinski, T., Krzyzak, A., Fevens, T., Jelen, Ł.: Web based framework for breast cancer classification. Journal of Artificial Intelligence and Soft Computing Research 4(2), 149–162 (2014)
2. Hoang, T., Choi, D., Nguyen, T.: Gait authentication on mobile phone using biometric cryptosystem and fuzzy commitment scheme. International Journal of Information Security, 1–12 (2015)
3. Huynh, Q.T., Nguyen, U.D., Tran, S.V., Nabili, A., Tran, B.Q.: Fall detection system using combination accelerometer and gyroscope. International Journal of Advancements in Electronics and Electrical Engineering 3(1), 15–19 (2014)
4. International Diabetes Federation: Idf diabetes atlas sixth edition poster update (2014) (accessed March 26, 2015)
5. Karimi, B., Krzyzak, A.: A novel approach for automatic detection and classification of suspicious lesions in breast ultrasound images. Journal of Artificial Intelligence and Soft Computing Research 3(4), 265–276 (2013)
6. Kazi, S.B., Sikander, S., Yousafzai, S., Mazhar, S.: Fall detection using single triaxial accelerometer. In: ASEE 2014 Zone I Conference (2014)
7. Klapuri, J.: Epileptic Seizure Detection Using a Wrist-Worn Triaxial Accelerometer. University of Helsinki (2013)
8. Korytkowski, M., Nowicki, R., Scherer, R.: Neuro-fuzzy rough classifier ensemble. In: Alippi, C., Polycarpou, M., Panayiotou, C., Ellinas, G. (eds.) ICANN 2009, Part I. LNCS, vol. 5768, pp. 817–823. Springer, Heidelberg (2009)
9. Koshiyama, A.S., Vellasco, M.M.B.R., Tanscheit, R.: Gpfis-control: A genetic fuzzy system for control tasks. Journal of Artificial Intelligence and Soft Computing Research 4(3), 167–179 (2014)
10. Kwapisz, J.R., Weiss, G.M., Moore, S.A.: Activity recognition using cell phone accelerometers. ACM SigKDD Explorations Newsletter 12(2), 74–82 (2011)
11. Marquardt, P., Verma, A., Carter, H., Traynor, P.: (sp) iphone: decoding vibrations from nearby keyboards using mobile phone accelerometers. In: Proceedings of the 18th ACM Conference on Computer and Communications Security, pp. 551–562. ACM (2011)

12. Nowicki, R., Rutkowska, D.: New neuro–fuzzy architectures. In: Proceedings of International Conference on Artificial and Computational Intelligence for Decision, Control and Automation in Engineering and Industrial Applications, AcIDcA 2000, Monastir, Tunisia, pp. 82–87 (March 2000)
13. Ravi, N., Dandekar, N., Mysore, P., Littman, M.L.: Activity recognition from accelerometer data. In: AAAI, vol. 5, pp. 1541–1546 (2005)
14. Rigatos, G.G., Siano, P.: Flatness-based adaptive fuzzy control of spark-ignited engines. Journal of Artificial Intelligence and Soft Computing Research 4(4), 231–242 (2014)
15. Rutkowska, D.: Neuro-fuzzy architectures and hybrid learning, vol. 85. Springer Science & Business Media (2002)
16. Rutkowski, L.: Computational Intelligence Methods and Techniques. Springer, Heidelberg (2008)
17. Scherer, R.: Neuro-fuzzy relational systems for nonlinear approximation and prediction. Nonlinear Analysis 71, e1420–e1425 (2009)
18. Scherer, R., Rutkowski, L.: Neuro-fuzzy relational classifiers. In: Rutkowski, L., Siekmann, J.H., Tadeusiewicz, R., Zadeh, L.A. (eds.) ICAISC 2004. LNCS (LNAI), vol. 3070, pp. 376–380. Springer, Heidelberg (2004)
19. Sun, L., Zhang, D., Li, B., Guo, B., Li, S.: Activity recognition on an accelerometer embedded mobile phone with varying positions and orientations. In: Yu, Z., Liscano, R., Chen, G., Zhang, D., Zhou, X. (eds.) UIC 2010. LNCS, vol. 6406, pp. 548–562. Springer, Heidelberg (2010)
20. Szarek, A., Korytkowski, M., Rutkowski, L., Scherer, R., Szyprowski, J.: Application of neural networks in assessing changes around implant after total hip arthroplasty. In: Rutkowski, L., Korytkowski, M., Scherer, R., Tadeusiewicz, R., Zadeh, L.A., Zurada, J.M. (eds.) ICAISC 2012, Part II. LNCS, vol. 7268, pp. 335–340. Springer, Heidelberg (2012)
21. Szarek, A., Korytkowski, M., Rutkowski, L., Scherer, R., Szyprowski, J.: Forecasting wear of head and acetabulum in hip joint implant. In: Rutkowski, L., Korytkowski, M., Scherer, R., Tadeusiewicz, R., Zadeh, L.A., Zurada, J.M. (eds.) ICAISC 2012, Part II. LNCS, vol. 7268, pp. 341–346. Springer, Heidelberg (2012)
22. World Health Organization: Media centre - epilepsy (2012) (accessed March 26, 2015)
23. Zhao, W., Lun, R., Espy, D.D., Reinthal, M.A.: Realtime motion assessment for rehabilitation exercises: Integration of kinematic modeling with fuzzy inference. Journal of Artificial Intelligence and Soft Computing Research 4(4), 267–285 (2014)

# Customization of Joint Articulations Using Soft Computing Methods

Arkadiusz Szarek[1], Marcin Korytkowski[2(✉)], Leszek Rutkowski[3],
Magdalena Scherer[4], Janusz Szyprowski[5], and Dimce Kostadinov[6]

[1] Institute of Mechanical Technology, Częstochowa University of Technology,
al. Armii Krajowej 21, 42-200 Częstochowa, Poland
szarek@iop.pcz.pl
http://www.itm.pcz.pl/
[2] Institute of Computational Intelligence, Częstochowa University of Technology,
al. Armii Krajowej 36, 42-200 Częstochowa, Poland
http://iisi.pcz.pl
[3] University of Social Sciences in Łódź, Sienkiewicza 9, 90-113 Łódź, Poland
http://www.san.edu.pl/
[4] Faculty of Management, Częstochowa University of Technology,
al. Armii Krajowej 19, 42-200 Częstochowa, Poland
[5] Orthopedics and Traumatic Surgery Department of NMP Voivodship Specialist
Hospital in Częstochowa. 42-200 Częstochowa, Bialska 104/118, Poland
[6] Computer Science Department, University of Geneva,
7 Route de Drize, Geneva, Switzerland
{marcin.korytkowski,leszek.rutkowski}@iisi.pcz.pl
http://sip.unige.ch

**Abstract.** The wear of artificial joints, which is one of the main causes of
re-implantation of the hip joint, can be minimized or entirely eliminated
through a precise adjustment of artificial biobearing to individual conditions of the patient. This is possible through utilization of modern engineering tools for support of doctors in multi-aspect selection of head elements
and acetabulum that work in the artificial joint. Despite a substantial number of materials used for the friction pair of both head and acetabulum,
there is no perfect and universal set of biomaterials that allow for recreation
of functionality of joints in all patients, while improperly selected joint articulation results in faster wear of components, migration of products of
wear to soft tissue and, consequently numerous complications and necessity of repeated surgical interventions. An innovative approach that allows
for customization of joint replacement, which is impossible to be achieved
using conventional methods, is to utilize machine learning systems to adjust friction pair to anthropometric and goniometric characteristics of a
patient. The internal elements which are used to train a fuzzy classifier ensemble are results of clinical, experimental and numerical studies that allow
for prediction of the functional cycle for a patient.

## 1 Introduction

Bone and joint diseases represent a very important social and economic problem
and, with development of civilization, the scale of problem is still increasing [9].

© Springer International Publishing Switzerland 2015
L. Rutkowski et al. (Eds.): ICAISC 2015, Part II, LNAI 9120, pp. 151–160, 2015.
DOI: 10.1007/978-3-319-19369-4_15

According to the most recent data, some 17% of Polish population suffer from degenerative joint disease, which causes that a substantial group of people are put at risk of becoming patients qualified for joint replacement [2]. Treatment of joint degeneration is a multifaceted problem, whereas a form of treatment depends on a number of factors, with particular focus on the type of joint and degree of pathology. Surgical intervention is usually considered a last resort. However, conservative treatment in the most of cases only extends (to various degree) function of the joint, with the last stage of treatment being typically joint replacement [14][23].

Hip joint is the joint that is exposed to the highest load, and, according to world reports, most surgical interventions on joints concern this location. Only in recent 5 years, over 260,000 prostheses were made in Poland, of which nearly 75% were hip joint prostheses [27]. Essentially, hip joint prosthesis is composed of the acetabulum part, fixed in the pelvic bone and the part that replaces the head of the femoral bone (stem) fixed in the medullary cavity of the bone, see Fig. 1. An element that forms the artificial joint is bone of prosthesis and acetabulum [24]. However, replacement of a natural with artificial joint does not

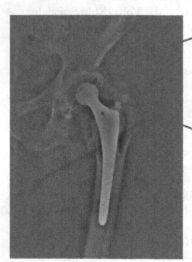

**Acetabula:**
- polyethylene components (XPLE)
- ceramic components
- metal components
- TiN layer components

**Ball head:**
- ceramic components
- metal components
- TiN layer components

**Fig. 1.** X-ray images of the bone with implanted hip endoprosthesis

solve the problem since mean life of hip joint prosthesis in human body is ca. 11 years. After this period, it is necessary in many cases to perform a revision treatment that consists in removing non-functional prosthesis and replacing it with a new one [26]. Among major causes of re-implantation are aseptic loosening and wear of components of the artificial biobearing leading to various complications. Fast civilization developments and introduction of modern biomaterials and medical technologies substantially improved opportunities for reconstruction of joints damaged through diseases or joint injuries. However, it did not eliminate wear of components of prostheses present in the artificial biobearing (see Fig. 2). Many combinations to match artificial joints that results from modern,

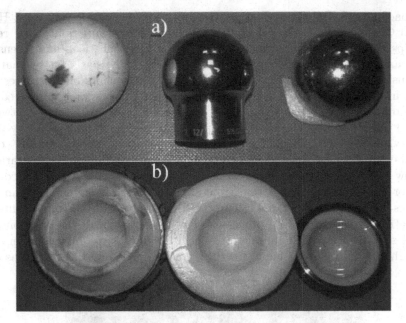

**Fig. 2.** Worn components of biobearing removed from human body. a) Acetabula, b) Ball head.

extremely different (in both mechanical and tribological terms) components and very high amount and a variety of prosthesis components available in the Polish market offer a wide range of opportunities to recreate biomechanical functions of joint and adjust friction and wear parameters of the friction pair to individual anthropometric and goniometric characteristics of the patient. Replacement of the damaged joint should ensure maximum comfort of its use and help regain full mobility of the joint and ensure its long and failure-free function. Intensity of wear of artificial joint depends on a number of factors, of which the most important are a type of biomaterials used in the artificial joint, load that results from human motor activity, intensity of using the joint and mobility in the joint and individual internal conditions [25]. The wear of components of prostheses has a chemical and mechanical character. Intensity of chemical wear depends on the type of biomaterial and changes in ion concentration inside human body, whereas the intensity of mechanical wear depends chiefly on body weight, intensity of use, range of motion in the artificial joint and precision of implantation of individual components of the prosthesis [22][24].

## 2    Material and Research Methods

The initial data for the classifier were obtained from clinical, experimental, numerical and empirical examinations performed using the components removed from human body due to wear. Based on these studies, intensity of wear was evaluated for individual components of prosthesis removed from patients of the

Orthopaedics and Traumatic Surgery Ward of the Voivodeship Specialist Hospital in Częstochowa. Empirical studies allowed for determination of the relationships between the type of materials of the friction pair, load and intensity of use and functional parameters of the prosthesis. The basis for evaluation of intensity of wear was microscopic analysis of components of prostheses removed from human body due to wear. These components were subjected to microscopic analysis, which allowed for determination of correlations between intensity of use (physical activity), patient's body weight, joint mobility and intensity of wear. Friction and wear examinations were carried out for commercial components of prostheses used with different tribological configurations to allow for determination of the values of friction forces and friction coefficient for the following articulations: metal-metal - XPLE, ceramics-ceramics, ceramics - XPLE, metal-ceramics, Tin - XPLE. Analysis of the components of articulation revealed that the processes of wear occur on all the components regardless of their strength parameters, which has only effect on wear intensity. The highest total wear was found for the elements made of XPLE, whereas the

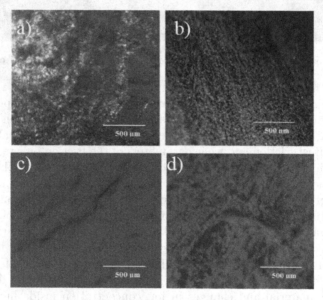

**Fig. 3.** Microstructure of the wear surface

least intensive wear was observed for the ceramic components. However, the size and number of products of wear and their migration to human body substantially affects both state of the joint and might significantly affect health or even life of the patient. Penetration of PE particles between the tissue and implant causes inflammatory reaction and development of granulation tissue, which leads to separation of the implant from the bone (Fig. 4). Further, the products of wear in metal-metal articulation are accumulated in soft tissues, causing inflammatory response and metallosis, which clinically is diagnosed as pseudotumors and qualifies prosthesis for re-implantation. Metallosis might have varied consequences: if a patient is allergic to any of the alloy elements, broad infections and complications might occur (Fig. 5). Fig. 4 presents separation of the acetabulum from the bone and Fig. 5 products of wear for XPLE (a) and metal (b).

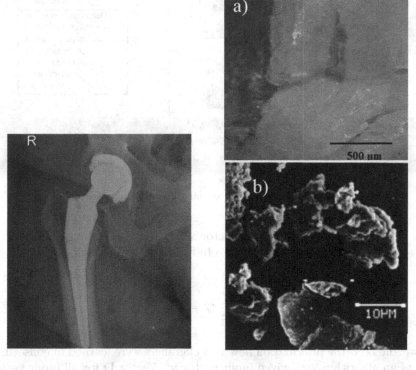

**Fig. 4.** Separation of the acetabulum from the bone

**Fig. 5.** Products of wear, a) XPLE, b) metal

The results obtained in the study allowed for training a classifier to select the type and material of the friction pair with regard for age and weight of the patient, intensity of use, joint mobility and individual anthropometric conditions of the patient.

## 3 Numerical Simulations

Computer science and soft computing are used extensively to support health care [1][5] [6][10][13]. Neural networks [3][4][12] and fuzzy systems [8][19][20][21] are common methods to assist medical science in various types of diagnosis. This section describes a system which was used for diagnosis support based on data acquired as in Fig. 6. We used the AdaBoost algorithm which is the most popular boosting meta learning method [17][18]. Let us denote the $l$-th learning vector by $\mathbf{z}^l = [x_1^l, ..., x_n^l, y^l]$ , $l = 1...L$ is the number of a vector in the learning

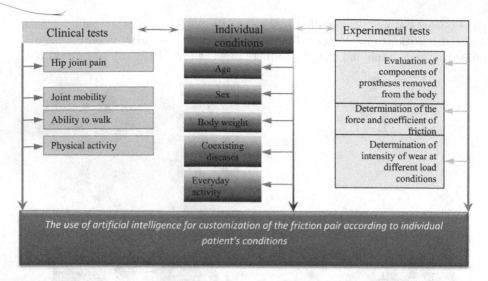

**Fig. 6.** Diagram of data acquisition

set, $n$ is the dimension of the input vector $\mathbf{x}^l$, and $y^l$ is the class label. Weights $D^l$ assigned to learning vectors, have to fulfill the following conditions

$$\text{(i) } 0 < D^l < 1,$$
$$\text{(ii) } \sum_{l=1}^{L} D^l = 1. \tag{1}$$

The weight $D^l$ is the information how well classifiers were learned in consecutive steps of an algorithm for a given input vector $\mathbf{x}^l$. Vector $\mathbf{D}$ for all input vectors is initialized according to the following equation

$$D_t^l = \frac{1}{L}, \quad \text{for } t = 0, ..., T, \tag{2}$$

where $t$ is the number of a boosting iteration (and a number of a classifier in the ensemble). Let $\{h_t(\mathbf{x}) : t = 1, ..., T\}$ denotes a set of hypotheses obtained in consecutive steps $t$ of the algorithm being described. For simplicity we limit our problem to a binary classification (dichotomy) i.e. $y \in \{-1, 1\}$ or $h_t(\mathbf{x}) = \pm 1$. Similarly to learning vectors weights, we assign a weight $c_t$ for every hypothesis, such that

$$\text{(i) } \sum_{t=1}^{T} c_t = 1,$$
$$\text{(ii) } c_t > 0. \tag{3}$$

Now in the AdaBoost algorithm we repeat steps 1-4 for $t = 1, ..., T$ :
1. Create hypothesis $h_t$ and train it with a data set with respect to a distribution $d_t$ for input vectors.

2. Compute the classification error $\varepsilon_t$ of a trained classifier $h_t$ according to the formula

$$\varepsilon_t = \sum_{l=1}^{m} D_t^l(\mathbf{z}^l) I(h_t(\mathbf{x}^l) \neq y^l) , \tag{4}$$

where $I$ is the indicator function

$$I(a \neq b) = \begin{cases} 1 \text{ if } a \neq b \\ 0 \text{ if } a = b \end{cases} . \tag{5}$$

If $\varepsilon_t = 0$ or $\varepsilon_t \geq 0.5$, stop the algorithm.
3. Compute the value

$$\alpha_t = 0.5 \ln \frac{1 - \varepsilon_t}{\varepsilon_t} . \tag{6}$$

4. Modify weights for learning vectors according to the formula

$$D_{t+1}(\mathbf{z}^l) = \frac{D_t(\mathbf{z}^l) \exp\{-\alpha_t \mathbf{I}(h_t(\mathbf{x}^l) = y^l)\}}{N_t} , \tag{7}$$

where $N_t$ is a constant such that $\sum_{l=1}^{m} D_{t+1}(\mathbf{z}^l) = 1$ . To compute the overall output of the ensemble of classifiers trained by AdaBoost algorithm, the following formula is used

$$f(\mathbf{x}) = \sum_{t=1}^{T} c_t h_t(\mathbf{x}) , \tag{8}$$

where

$$c_t = \frac{\alpha_t}{\sum_{t=1}^{T} \alpha_t} \tag{9}$$

is classifier importance for a given training set, $h_t(\mathbf{x})$ is the response of the hypothesis $t$ on the basis of feature vector $\mathbf{x} = [x_1, ..., x_n]$. The coefficient $c_t$ value is computed on the basis of the classifier error and can be interpreted as the measure of classification accuracy of the given classifier. Moreover, the assumption (1) should be met. As we see, the AdaBoost algorithm is a meta-learning algorithm and does not determine the way of learning for classifiers in the ensemble.

We used Mamdani-type neuro-fuzzy systems [7][11][15][16] as systems constituting the boosting ensemble. The output of the single, $t$th Mamdani neuro-fuzzy classifier, is defined

$$h_t = \frac{\sum_{r=1}^{N} \bar{y}^r \cdot \tau^r}{\sum_{r=1}^{N} \tau^r} , \tag{10}$$

where $\tau^r = \mathop{T}_{i=1}^{n} \left( \mu_{A_i^r}(\bar{x}_i) \right)$ is the activity level of the rule $r = 1, ..., N$, $T$ is a triangular norm operation (in our case product operation) and $\mu_{A_i^r}(x_i)$ is an input linguistic variable, described by the Gaussian membership function, that is

$$\mu_{A_i^r}(x_i) = \exp\left[-\left(\frac{x_i - \overline{x}_i^r}{\sigma_i^r}\right)^2\right],$$ (11)

and fuzzy rules are composed of input fuzzy set membership functions (11) and output fuzzy set singletons $\overline{y}^r$. The AdaBoost ensemble was made of five classifiers trained by the backpropagation gradient learning. The neuro–fuzzy system achieved 97.4% accuracy.

## 4    Summary and Conclusions

The choice of joint articulation according to individual patient's anthropometric and goniometric parameters is essential for patient's health, comfort of the use and life of artificial hip joint. Constructional and material solutions available on the Polish market allow for full customization and adjustment of the materials of the head and acetabulum for individual patient's needs. Improper choice of the friction pairs causes premature wear of components, while the products of wear that migrate to human joint and body cause changes in the near-bone tissue and get to other internal organs, e.g. liver or kidneys, thus causing serious changes or damages. The use of the ensemble of fuzzy classifiers for selection of the friction pair represents an innovative method to support doctors, allows for reduction of the costs of surgery and precise adjustment of the artificial joint to individual human conditions, which helps minimize the likelihood of premature wear of joint and necessity to replace it with a prosthesis. Application of machine learning systems allowed to reproduce doctor diagnosis by the ensemble of classifiers with relatively high accuracy.

**Acknowledgments.** This work was supported by the Foundation for Polish Science – TEAM project 2010-2014.

## References

1. Arabgol, S., Ko, H.S.: Application of artificial neural network and genetic algorithm to healthcare waste prediction. Journal of Artificial Intelligence and Soft Computing Research 34(4), 243–250 (2013)
2. Bedzinski, R.: Technical Mechanics XII, Biomechanics. IPPT PAN (2011)
3. Bilski, J., Smolag, J.: Parallel architectures for learning the rtrn and elman dynamic neural networks. IEEE Transactions on Parallel and Distributed Systems PP(99), 1–1 (2014)
4. Bilski, J., Smolag, J., Galushkin, A.I.: The parallel approach to the conjugate gradient learning algorithm for the feedforward neural networks. In: Rutkowski, L., Korytkowski, M., Scherer, R., Tadeusiewicz, R., Zadeh, L.A., Zurada, J.M. (eds.) ICAISC 2014, Part I. LNCS (LNAI), vol. 8467, pp. 12–21. Springer, Heidelberg (2014)

5. Biniaz, A., Abbasi, A.: Fast fcm with spatial neighborhood information for brain mr image segmentation. Journal of Artificial Intelligence and Soft Computing Research 3(1), 15–25 (2013)
6. Bruzdzinski, T., Krzyzak, A., Fevens, T., Jelen, Ł.: Ukasz Jelen: Web-based framework for breast cancer classification. Journal of Artificial Intelligence and Soft Computing Research 4(2), 149–162 (2014)
7. Cpałka, K.: A new method for design and reduction of neuro-fuzzy classification systems. IEEE Transactions on Neural Networks 20(4), 701–714 (2009)
8. Gaweda, A.E., Scherer, R.: Fuzzy number-based hierarchical fuzzy system. In: Rutkowski, L., Siekmann, J.H., Tadeusiewicz, R., Zadeh, L.A. (eds.) ICAISC 2004. LNCS (LNAI), vol. 3070, pp. 302–307. Springer, Heidelberg (2004)
9. Gzik, M.: Modelling and modern methods for engineering support of the locomotor system defects treatment. Publishing House of the Institute for Sustainable Technologies - PIB (2013)
10. Karimi, B., Krzyzak, A.: A novel approach for automatic detection and classification of suspicious lesions in breast ultrasound images. Journal of Artificial Intelligence and Soft Computing Research 3(4), 265–276 (2013)
11. Łapa, K., Przybył, A., Cpałka, K.: A new approach to designing interpretable models of dynamic systems. In: Rutkowski, L., Korytkowski, M., Scherer, R., Tadeusiewicz, R., Zadeh, L.A., Zurada, J.M. (eds.) ICAISC 2013, Part II. LNCS (LNAI), vol. 7895, pp. 523–534. Springer, Heidelberg (2013)
12. Laskowski, L.: A novel hybrid-maximum neural network in stereo-matching process. Neural Computing and Applications 23(7-8), 2435–2450 (2013)
13. Mallik, S., Mukhopadhyay, A., Maulik, U.: Integrated statistical and rule-mining techniques for dna methylation and gene expression data analysis. Journal of Artificial Intelligence and Soft Computing Research 3(2), 101–115 (2013)
14. Michnik, R.: Modeling and experimental study of human gait in terms of the rehabilitation process. Publishing House of the Institute for Sustainable Technologies - PIB (2013)
15. Nowicki, R.: Rough-neuro-fuzzy system with micog defuzzification. In: 2006 IEEE International Conference on Fuzzy Systems, pp. 1958–1965 (2006)
16. Rutkowski, L.: Computational Intelligence Methods and Techniques. Springer, Heidelberg (2008)
17. Schapire, R.E.: A brief introduction to boosting. In: Proceedings of the 16th International Joint Conference on Artificial Intelligence, IJCAI 1999, vol. 2, pp. 1401–1406. Morgan Kaufmann Publishers Inc., San Francisco (1999)
18. Scherer, R.: Boosting ensemble of relational neuro-fuzzy systems. In: Rutkowski, L., Tadeusiewicz, R., Zadeh, L.A., Żurada, J.M. (eds.) ICAISC 2006. LNCS (LNAI), vol. 4029, pp. 306–313. Springer, Heidelberg (2006)
19. Scherer, R.: Neuro-fuzzy relational systems for nonlinear approximation and prediction. Nonlinear Analysis 71, e1420–e1425 (2009)
20. Scherer, R.: An ensemble of logical-type neuro-fuzzy systems. Expert Systems With Applications (2011)
21. Scherer, R., Starczewski, J.T., Gawęda, A.: New methods for uncertainty representations in neuro-fuzzy systems. In: Wyrzykowski, R., Dongarra, J., Paprzycki, M., Waśniewski, J. (eds.) PPAM 2004. LNCS, vol. 3019, pp. 659–667. Springer, Heidelberg (2004)
22. Szarek, A.: Assessment of wear of metal heads in heap joint prosthesis removed from human body due to aseptic loosening. Engineering of Biomaterials 11, 6–10 (2008)

23. Szarek, A.: Hip Joint Replacement in Biomechanical and Clinical Approach. Belgorod, Rusnauckniga (2010)
24. Szarek, A.: Biomechanics and biomaterial determinants of aseptic loosening of human hip replacements. Czestochowa University of Technology Press (2015)
25. Szarek, A., Stradomski, G., Wlodarski, J.: The analysis of hip joint prosthesis head microstructure changes during variable stress state as a result of human motor activity. Materials Science Forum 706-709, 600–605 (2012)
26. Szyprowski, J.: Hip joint replacement in biomechanical and clinical approach. Oraldyn Fylym Zarsysy. Tehniceskie Nauki, Fizika, Sovremennye Informacionnye Tehnologii 36(9), 12–20 (2011)
27. The National Health Fund: The realization of benefits hip replacement in 2013. Technical report (2013)

# A New Method for the Dynamic Signature Verification Based on the Stable Partitions of the Signature

Marcin Zalasiński[1(✉)], Krzysztof Cpałka[1], and Meng Joo Er[2]

[1] Institute of Computational Intelligence,
Częstochowa University of Technology, Częstochowa, Poland
{marcin.zalasinski,krzysztof.cpalka}@iisi.pcz.pl
[2] Nanyang Technological University,
School of Electrical and Electronic Engineering, Singapore, Singapore
emjer@ntu.edu.sg

**Abstract.** Dynamic signature is a very interesting biometric attribute which is commonly socially acceptable. In this paper we propose a new method for the dynamic signature verification using stable partitions of the signature. This method assumes selection of two the most stable hybrid partitions individually for the signer. Hybrid partitions are formed by a combination of vertical and horizontal sections of the signature. The selected partitions are used during identity verification process. In the test of the proposed method we used BioSecure DS2 database, distributed by the BioSecure Association.

## 1 Introduction

A handwritten signature is a behavioural biometric attribute. It is very interesting because its acquisition is not controversial and it is commonly socially acceptable. There are two main approaches to the signature verification - static (off-line) which is based on the analysis of geometric features of the signature (see e.g. [13, 14, 35]) and dynamic (on-line) which is based on the analysis of the dynamics of signing process. Verification using on-line signature is much more effective than verification using off-line one.

In the literature one can find four main approaches to the dynamic signature analysis: (a) global feature based approach (see e.g. [21, 38, 41]), (b) function based approach (see e.g. [18, 32, 39]), (c) regional based approach (see e.g. [19, 20, 31], [61, 76, 77]), (d) hybrid approach (see e.g. [40, 42]). In this paper we present a new regional method for the dynamic signature verification. The proposed method is characterized by the following features: (a) It uses fuzzy sets and fuzzy systems theory in evaluation of the similarity of the test signatures to the reference signatures. (b) It allows to interpret the knowledge accumulated in the system used to the signature verification. (c) It creates partitions of the signature which have the following interpretation: high and low velocity in the initial, middle and final time of signing, high and low pressure in the initial,

© Springer International Publishing Switzerland 2015
L. Rutkowski et al. (Eds.): ICAISC 2015, Part II, LNAI 9120, pp. 161–174, 2015.
DOI: 10.1007/978-3-319-19369-4_16

middle and final time of signing. **(d)** It determines values of weights of importance for each partition. **(e)** In the classification process it uses two partitions (associated with the velocity and pressure signals) which are most characteristic for the signer. The main purpose of the proposed method is to reduce its the complexity and increase the interpretability of fuzzy rules of the one-class classifier used to evaluate the similarity of the test signatures to the reference ones. It is worth to note that many computational intelligence methods (see e.g. [1, 17, 23–26, 28, 48–50, 58, 62, 63, 65, 66]) are succesfully used in pattern recognition (see e.g. [27, 56, 57]), modelling (see e.g. [12, 54, 55, 64, 69, 70]) and optimization (see e.g. [72, 73]) issues. Simulations of the proposed method have been performed using BioSecure (BMDB) dynamic signatures database distributed by the BioSecure Association ([29]).

This paper is organized into 4 sections. Section 2 contains detailed description of the algorithm. Simulation results are presented in Section 3. Conclusions are drawn in Section 4.

## 2    Detailed Description of the Algorithm

The proposed algorithm for the dynamic signature verification works in two phases: training phase (Section 2.1) and test phase (Section 2.2). In both of them a pre-processing of the signatures using some standard methods should be realized (see e.g. [15, 16]).

### 2.1    Training Phase

During the training phase the algorithm performs hybrid partitioning and selects two the most stable partitions for the considered signer. Next, parameters of the classifier are determined using the reference signatures trajectories from selected partitions. A detailed description of each step of the training phase is described below.

**Creation of the Partitions.** Each reference signature $j$ ($j = 1, 2, \ldots, J$, where $J$ is a number of the reference signatures) of the user $i$ ($i = 1, 2, \ldots, I$, where $I$ is a number of the users) is represented by the following signals: **(a)** $\mathbf{x}_{i,j} = [x_{i,j,k=1}, x_{i,j,k=2}, \ldots, x_{i,j,k=K_i}]$ which describes the movement of the pen in the two-dimensional space along the $x$ axis, where $K_i$ is the number of signal samples. Thanks to the normalization of the signatures, all trajectories describing the signatures of the user $i$ have the same number of samples $K_i$. **(b)** $\mathbf{y}_{i,j} = [y_{i,j,k=1}, y_{i,j,k=2}, \ldots, y_{i,j,k=K_i}]$, which describes movement of the pen along the $y$ axis, **(c)** $\mathbf{v}_{i,j} = [v_{i,j,k=1}, v_{i,j,k=2}, \ldots, v_{i,j,k=K_i}]$ which describes velocity of the pen and **(d)** $\mathbf{z}_{i,j} = [z_{i,j,k=1}, z_{i,j,k=2}, \ldots, z_{i,j,k=K_i}]$ which describes the pen pressure on the surface of the graphic tablet. In order to simplify the description of the algorithm we used the same symbol $\mathbf{a}_{i,j} = [a_{i,j,k=1}, a_{i,j,k=2}, \ldots, a_{i,j,k=K_i}]$ to describe both shape signals ($a \in \{x, y\}$). We also used the same symbol $\mathbf{s}_{i,j} = [s_{i,j,k=1}, s_{i,j,k=2}, \ldots, s_{i,j,k=K_i}]$ to describe both dynamics signals ($s \in \{v, z\}$).

The purpose of the partitioning is to assign each point of the signal $\mathbf{v}_{i,jBase}$ and the signal $\mathbf{z}_{i,jBase}$ of the reference base signature to the single hybrid partition, resulting from a combination of the vertical and the horizontal section, where $jBase \in \{1,\ldots,J\}$ is an index of the base signature, selected during pre-processing (see [15, 16]).

At the beginning of the partitioning, the vertical sections of the signals $\mathbf{v}_{i,jBase}$ and $\mathbf{z}_{i,jBase}$ are created. Each of them represents different time moment of signing: (a) initial or final for the case $P^{\{s\}} = 2$, (b) initial, middle or final for the case $P^{\{s\}} = 3$, (c) initial, first middle, second middle or final for the case $P^{\{s\}} = 4$. The vertical sections are indicated by the elements of the vector $\mathbf{pv}_i^{\{s\}} = \left[pv_{i,k=1}^{\{s\}}, pv_{i,k=2}^{\{s\}}, \ldots, pv_{i,k=K_i}^{\{s\}}\right]$ determined as follows:

$$
pv_{i,k}^{\{s\}} = \begin{cases} 1 & \text{for} & 0 < k \leq \frac{K_i}{P^{\{s\}}} \\ 2 & \text{for} & \frac{K_i}{P^{\{s\}}} < k \leq \frac{2K_i}{P^{\{s\}}} \\ \vdots & & \\ P^{\{s\}} & \text{for} & \frac{(P^{\{s\}}-1)K_i}{P^{\{s\}}} < k \leq K_i \end{cases}, \tag{1}
$$

where $s \in \{v,z\}$ is the signal type used for determination of the partition (velocity $v$ or pressure $z$), $i$ is the user index ($i = 1,2,\ldots,I$), $j$ is the reference signature index ($j = 1,2,\ldots,J$), $K_i$ is a number of samples of normalized signals of the user $i$ (divisible by $P^{\{s\}}$), $k$ is an index of the signal sample ($k = 1,2,\ldots,K_i$) and $P^{\{s\}}$ is a number of the vertical signatures ($P^{\{s\}} \ll K_i$ and $P^{\{s\}} = P^{\{v\}} = P^{\{z\}}$). A number of the vertical sections can be arbitrary, but its increasing does not increase the interpretability and the accuracy of the method.

After creation of the vertical sections of the signals $\mathbf{v}_{i,jBase}$ and $\mathbf{z}_{i,jBase}$, horizontal sections are created. Each of them represents high and low velocity and high and low pressure in individual moments of signing. Horizontal sections indicated by the elements of the vector $\mathbf{ph}_i^{\{s\}} = \left[ph_{i,k=1}^{\{s\}}, ph_{i,k=2}^{\{s\}}, \ldots, ph_{i,k=K_i}^{\{s\}}\right]$ are determined as follows:

$$
ph_{i,k}^{\{s\}} = \begin{cases} 1 \text{ for } s_{i,j=jBase,k} < avgv_{i,p=pv_{i,k}^{\{s\}}}^{\{s\}} \\ 2 \text{ for } s_{i,j=jBase,k} \geq avgv_{i,p=pv_{i,k}^{\{s\}}}^{\{s\}} \end{cases}, \tag{2}
$$

where $jBase$ is the base signature index, $avgv_{i,p}^{\{s\}}$ is an average velocity (when $s = v$) or an average pressure (when $s = z$) in the section indicated by the index $p$ of the base signature $jBase$:

$$
avgv_{i,p}^{\{s\}} = \frac{1}{Kv_{i,p}} \sum_{k=\left(\frac{(p-1)\cdot K_i}{P^{\{s\}}}+1\right)}^{k=\left(\frac{p\cdot K_i}{P^{\{s\}}}\right)} s_{i,j=jBase,k}, \tag{3}
$$

where $Kv_{i,p}$ is a number of samples in the vertical section $p$, $s_{i,j=jBase,k}$ is the sample $k$ of the signal $s \in \{v,z\}$ describing dynamics of the signature.

As a result of partitioning, each sample $v_{i,jBase,k}$ of the signal $\mathbf{v}_{i,jBase}$ of the base signature $jBase$ and each sample $z_{i,jBase,k}$ of the signal $\mathbf{z}_{i,jBase}$ of the base signature $jBase$ is assigned to the vertical section (assignment information is stored in the vector $\mathbf{pv}_i^{\{s\}}$) and horizontal section (assignment information is stored in the vector $\mathbf{ph}_i^{\{s\}}$). The intersection of the sections is the partition. Fragments of the shape trajectories $\mathbf{x}_{i,j}$ and $\mathbf{y}_{i,j}$, created taking into account $\mathbf{pv}_i^{\{s\}}$ and $\mathbf{ph}_i^{\{s\}}$, will be denoted as $\mathbf{a}_{i,j,p,r}^{\{s\}} = \left[ a_{i,j,p,r,k=1}^{\{s\}}, a_{i,j,p,r,k=2}^{\{s\}}, \ldots, a_{i,j,p,r,k=Kc_{i,p,r}^{\{s,a\}}}^{\{s\}} \right]$. The number of samples belonging to the partition $(p, r)$ (created as an intersection of the vertical section $p$ and the horizontal section $r$, included in the trajectory $a_{i,j,p,r}^{\{s\}}$) of the user $i$ associated with the signal $a$ ($x$ or $y$) and created on the basis of the signal $s$ (velocity or pressure) will be denoted as $Kc_{i,p,r}^{\{s,a\}}$.

**Generation of the Templates.** The templates of the signatures are averaged fragments of the reference signatures represented by the shape trajectories $\mathbf{x}_{i,j}$ or $\mathbf{y}_{i,j}$. The partition contains two templates, so a number of the templates created for the user $i$ is equal to $4 \cdot P^{\{s\}}$. Each template $\mathbf{tc}_{i,p,r}^{\{s,a\}} = \left[ tc_{i,p,r,k=1}^{\{s,a\}}, tc_{i,p,r,k=2}^{\{s,a\}}, \ldots, tc_{i,p,r,k=Kc_{i,p,r}^{\{s,a\}}}^{\{s,a\}} \right]$ describes fragments of the reference signatures in the partition $(p, r)$ of the user $i$, associated with the signal $a$ ($x$ or $y$), created on the basis of the signal $s$ (velocity or pressure), where:

$$tc_{i,p,r,k}^{\{s,a\}} = \frac{1}{J} \sum_{j=1}^{J} a_{i,j,p,r,k}^{\{s\}}. \tag{4}$$

After determination of the templates $\mathbf{tc}_{i,p,r}^{\{s,a\}}$, weights of importance of the partitions are determined.

**Determination of the Weights of Importance and Selection of the Best Partitions.** Determination of the weights $w_{i,p,r}^{\{s,a\}}$ of the templates starts from determination of a dispersion of the reference signatures signals. The dispersion is represented by a standard deviation. Average standard deviation for all samples in the partition is determined as follows:

$$\bar{\sigma}_{i,p,r}^{\{s,a\}} = \frac{1}{Kc_{i,p,r}^{\{s,a\}}} \sum_{k=1}^{Kc_{i,p,r}^{\{s,a\}}} \sqrt{\frac{1}{J} \sum_{j=1}^{J} \left( a_{i,j,p,r,k}^{\{s\}} - tc_{i,p,r,k}^{\{s,a\}} \right)^2}. \tag{5}$$

Having average standard deviation $\bar{\sigma}_{i,p,r}^{\{s,a\}}$, normalized values of the templates weights are determined:

$$w_{i,p,r}^{\{s,a\}} = 1 - \frac{\bar{\sigma}_{i,p,r}^{\{s,a\}}}{\max\limits_{\substack{p=1,2,\ldots,P^{\{s\}} \\ r=1,2}} \left\{ \bar{\sigma}_{i,p,r}^{\{s,a\}} \right\}}. \tag{6}$$

Normalization of the weights adapt them for use in the one-class flexible fuzzy system used for evaluation of the similarity of the test signatures to the reference signatures. This evaluation is the basis for recognition of the signature authenticity.

Having weights of importance of the templates, the most characteristic partitions associated with the highest values of the weights are selected for the considered user. They are two partitions: **(a)** The partition $\left(p = pB^{\{v\}}, r = rB^{\{v\}}\right)$ associated with signal $v$. Indexes $pB^{\{v\}}$ and $rB^{\{v\}}$ are determined in such a way that a sum of the weights $w_{i,pB^{\{v\}},rB^{\{v\}}}^{\{v,x\}} + w_{i,pB^{\{v\}},rB^{\{v\}}}^{\{v,y\}}$ pointed by these indexes for the signal $v$ is the highest. **(b)** The partition $\left(p = pB^{\{z\}}, r = rB^{\{z\}}\right)$ associated with signal $z$. Indexes $pB^{\{z\}}$ and $rB^{\{z\}}$ are determined analogously as in the case of the partition $\left(p = pB^{\{v\}}, r = rB^{\{v\}}\right)$.

**Determination of the Parameters of the Fuzzy System.** The test signatures verification is based on the answers of the neuro-fuzzy system for evaluating the similarity of the test signatures to the reference signatures. Neuro-fuzzy systems (see e.g. [22, 33, 43–45, 53, 68]) combine the natural language description of fuzzy systems (see e.g. [2, 34, 46, 47]) and the learning properties of neural networks (see e.g. [3–11, 36, 37, 51, 52, 67, 71]). Parameters of the system have to be selected individually for each user from the database. In this paper we use a structure of the flexible neuro-fuzzy one-class classifier, whose parameters depend on the reference signatures descriptors. They are determined analytically (not in the process of supervised learning) and individually for the user (her/his reference signatures).

The first group of parameters of the proposed system are the parameters describing differences between the reference signatures and the templates in the partitions. They are used in the construction of fuzzy rules described later (see (9)) and determined as follows:

$$
\begin{aligned}
dmax_{i,pB^{\{s\}},rB^{\{s\}}}^{\{s,a\}} = \\
= \delta_i \cdot \max_{j=1,\ldots,J} \left\{ \frac{\sum\limits_{k=1}^{Kc_{i,pB^{\{s\}},rB^{\{s\}}}^{\{s,a\}}} \left| a_{i,j,pB^{\{s\}},rB^{\{s\}},k}^{\{s\}} - tc_{i,pB^{\{s\}},rB^{\{s\}},k}^{\{s,a\}} \right|}{Kc_{i,pB^{\{s\}},rB^{\{s\}}}^{\{s,a\}}} \right\}
\end{aligned}
\tag{7}
$$

where $\delta_i$ is a parameter which ensures matching of tolerance of the system for evaluating the similarity in the test phase.

The second group of parameters of the proposed system are weights of the templates determined in the previous step. A consequence of the large value of the weight is less tolerance of the system for similarity evaluation in the test phase.

## 2.2   Test Phase (Verification of the Signatures)

During the test phase the signer creates one test signature and claims her/his identity. This identity will be verified. Next, parameters of the considered user created during training phase are downloaded from the system database and the signature verification is performed. A detailed description of each step of the test phase is described below.

**Acquisition and Processing of the Test Signature.** The first step of the verification phase is acquisition of the test signature, which should be pre-processed. Normalized test signature is represented by two shape trajectories: $\mathbf{xtst}_i = [xtst_{i,k=1}, xtst_{i,k=2}, \ldots, xtst_{i,k=K_i}]$ and $\mathbf{ytst}_i = [ytst_{i,k=1}, ytst_{i,k=2}, \ldots, ytst_{i,k=K_i}]$.

Next, partitioning of the test signature is performed. As a result of partitioning of the shape trajectories $\mathbf{xtst}_i$ and $\mathbf{ytst}_i$ their fragments denoted as $\mathbf{atst}_{i,pB\{s\},rB\{s\}}^{\{s\}}$

$$= \left[ a_{i,pB\{s\},rB\{s\},k=1}^{\{s\}}, a_{i,pB\{s\},rB\{s\},k=2}^{\{s\}}, \ldots, a_{i,pB\{s\},rB\{s\},k=Kc_{i,pB\{s\},rB\{s\}}^{\{s,a\}}}^{\{s\}} \right] \quad \text{are}$$

obtained. During the partitioning the vectors $\mathbf{pv}_i^{\{s\}}$ and $\mathbf{ph}_i^{\{s\}}$ are used.

Next step of the test phase is determination of the similarity of fragments of the test signature shape trajectories $\mathbf{atst}_{i,pB\{s\},rB\{s\}}^{\{s\}}$ to the templates of the reference signatures $\mathbf{tc}_{i,pB\{s\},rB\{s\}}^{\{s,a\}}$ in the partition $\left(pB\{s\}, rB\{s\}\right)$ of the user $i$ associated with the signal $a$ ($x$ or $y$) created on the basis of the signal $s$ (velocity or pressure). It is determined as follows:

$$dtst_{i,pB\{s\},rB\{s\}}^{\{s,a\}} = \frac{\displaystyle\sum_{k=1}^{Kc_{i,pB\{s\},rB\{s\}}^{\{s,a\}}} \left| atst_{i,pB\{s\},rB\{s\},k}^{\{s\}} - tc_{i,pB\{s\},rB\{s\},k}^{\{s,a\}} \right|}{Kc_{i,pB\{s\},rB\{s\}}^{\{s,a\}}}. \tag{8}$$

After determination of the similarities $dtst_{i,pB\{s\},rB\{s\}}^{\{s,a\}}$, total similarity of the test signature to the reference signatures of the user $i$ is determined. Decision on the authenticity of the test signature is taken on the basis of this similarity.

**Evaluation of the Overall Similarity of the Test Signature to the Reference Signatures.** The system evaluating similarity of the test signature to the reference signatures works on the basis of the signals $dtst_{i,pB\{s\},rB\{s\}}^{\{s,a\}}$ and takes into account the weights $w_{i,pB\{s\},rB\{s\}}^{\{s,a\}}$. Its response is the basis for the evaluation of the signature reliability. The proposed system works on the basis of two fuzzy rules presented as follows:

$$\begin{cases} R^{(1)}: & \begin{bmatrix} \mathbf{IF}\left(dtst_{i,pB\{v\},rB\{v\}}^{\{v,x\}} \, \mathbf{is} A_{i,pB\{v\},rB\{v\}}^{1\{v,x\}}\right) \left|w_{i,pB\{v\},rB\{v\}}^{\{v,x\}} \, \mathbf{AND} \ldots \right. \\ \ldots \mathbf{AND}\left(dtst_{i,pB\{z\},rB\{z\}}^{\{z,y\}} \, \mathbf{is} A_{i,pB\{z\},rB\{z\}}^{1\{z,y\}}\right) \left|w_{i,pB\{z\},rB\{z\}}^{\{z,y\}} \right. \\ \mathbf{THEN} y_i \mathbf{is} B^1 \end{bmatrix} \\ R^{(2)}: & \begin{bmatrix} \mathbf{IF}\left(dtst_{i,pB\{v\},rB\{v\}}^{\{v,x\}} \, \mathbf{is} A_{i,pB\{v\},rB\{v\}}^{2\{v,x\}}\right) \left|w_{i,pB\{v\},rB\{v\}}^{\{v,x\}} \, \mathbf{AND} \ldots \right. \\ \ldots \mathbf{AND}\left(dtst_{i,pB\{z\},rB\{z\}}^{\{z,y\}} \, \mathbf{is} A_{i,pB\{z\},rB\{z\}}^{2\{z,y\}}\right) \left|w_{i,pB\{z\},rB\{z\}}^{\{z,y\}} \right. \\ \mathbf{THEN} y_i \mathbf{is} B^2 \end{bmatrix} \end{cases}, \tag{9}$$

where

- $dtst_{i,pB\{s\},rB\{s\}}^{\{s,a\}}$ $(i = 1, 2, \ldots, I, \ s \in \{v, z\}, \ a \in \{x, y\})$ are input linguistic variables. Values "high" and "low" taken by these variables are Gaussian fuzzy sets $A_{i,pB\{s\},rB\{s\}}^{1\{s,a\}}$ and $A_{i,pB\{s\},rB\{s\}}^{2\{s,a\}}$ (see Fig. 1).
- $y_i$ $(i = 1, \ldots, I)$ is output linguistic variable meaning "similarity of the test signature to the reference signatures of the user $i$". Value "high" of this variable is the fuzzy set $B^1$ of $\gamma$ type and value "low" is the fuzzy set $B^2$ of $L$ type (see Fig. 1).
- $w_{i,pB\{s\},rB\{s\}}^{\{s,a\}}$ are weights of the templates. Introducing of the weights of importance distinguishes the proposed flexible neuro-fuzzy system from typical fuzzy systems.

**Verification of the Test Signature.** In the proposed method the test signature is recognized as belonging to the user $i$ (genuine) if the assumption $\bar{y}_i > cth_i$ is satisfied, where $\bar{y}_i$ is the value of the output signal of neuro-fuzzy system described by the (9):

$$
\bar{y}_i \approx \frac{T^* \left\{ \begin{array}{l} \mu_{A_{i,pB\{v\},rB\{v\}}^{1\{v,x\}}} \left( dtst_{i,pB\{v\},rB\{v\}}^{\{v,x\}} \right), \ldots, \\ \mu_{A_{i,pB\{z\},rB\{z\}}^{1\{z,y\}}} \left( dtst_{i,pB\{z\},rB\{z\}}^{\{z,y\}} \right); \\ w_{i,pB\{v\},rB\{v\}}^{\{v,x\}}, \ldots, w_{i,pB\{z\},rB\{z\}}^{\{z,y\}} \end{array} \right\}}{\left( \begin{array}{l} T^* \left\{ \begin{array}{l} \mu_{A_{i,pB\{v\},rB\{v\}}^{1\{v,x\}}} \left( dtst_{i,pB\{v\},rB\{v\}}^{\{v,x\}} \right), \ldots, \\ \mu_{A_{i,pB\{z\},rB\{z\}}^{1\{z,y\}}} \left( dtst_{i,pB\{z\},rB\{z\}}^{\{z,y\}} \right); \\ w_{i,pB\{v\},rB\{v\}}^{\{v,x\}}, \ldots, w_{i,pB\{z\},rB\{z\}}^{\{z,y\}} \end{array} \right\} + \\ +T^* \left\{ \begin{array}{l} \mu_{A_{i,pB\{v\},rB\{v\}}^{2\{v,x\}}} \left( dtst_{i,pB\{v\},rB\{v\}}^{\{v,x\}} \right), \ldots, \\ \mu_{A_{i,pB\{z\},rB\{z\}}^{2\{z,y\}}} \left( dtst_{i,pB\{z\},rB\{z\}}^{\{z,y\}} \right); \\ w_{i,pB\{v\},rB\{v\}}^{\{v,x\}}, \ldots, w_{i,pB\{z\},rB\{z\}}^{\{z,y\}} \end{array} \right\} \end{array} \right)}, \tag{10}
$$

where $T^* \{\cdot\}$ is the weighted t-norm (see e.g. [59–61]) and $cth_i \in [0,1]$ is coefficient determined experimentally for each user to eliminate disproportion between FAR and FRR error (see e.g. [74]). The values of this coefficient are usually close to 0.5. Formula (10) was established by taking into account the following simplification, resulting from the spacing of the fuzzy sets shown in Fig. 1: $\mu_{B^1}(0) = 0$, $\mu_{B^1}(1) \approx 1$, $\mu_{B^2}(0) \approx 1$ and $\mu_{B^2}(1) = 0$.

## 3   Simulation Results

Simulations were performed in authorial test environment written in C# using commercial BioSecure DS2 Signature database which contains signatures of 210

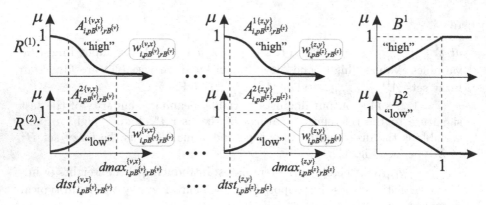

**Fig. 1.** Input and output fuzzy sets used in the rules (9) of the flexible neuro-fuzzy system for evaluation of similarity of the test signature to the reference signatures

users. The signatures were acquired in two sessions using the digitizing tablet. Each session contains 15 genuine signatures and 10 skilled forgeries per person. In the simulations we assumed that $P^{\{s\}} = 3$.

We repeated 5 times the verification procedure and the results obtained for all users have been averaged. In each of the five performed repetitions we used a different set of 5 training signatures. In the test phase we used 10 remaining genuine signatures and all 10 forged signatures. The described method is commonly used in evaluating the effectiveness of the methods for the dynamic signature verification, which corresponds to the standard crossvalidation procedure.

The results of the simulations are presented in Table 1. It contains information about values of the errors FAR (False Acceptance Rate) and FRR (False Rejection Rate) achieved by the considered method in comparison to the regional methods proposed by us earlier and the methods of other authors. Please note that the proposed method has the best accuracy in comparison to the methods presented in Table 1.

**Table 1.** Comparison of the accuracy of different methods for the signature verification for the BioSecure database

| Method | Average FAR | Average FRR | Average error |
|---|---|---|---|
| Methods of other authors ([30]) | - | - | 3.48 % - 30.13 % |
| Algorithm based on Horizontal Partitioning, AHP (Cpałka et al. (2014) [16]) | 2.94 % | 4.45 % | 3.70 % |
| Algorithm based on Vertical Partitioning, AVP (Cpałka, Zalasiński (2014) [15]) | 3.13 % | 4.15 % | 3.64 % |
| **Our method** | **3.43 %** | **3.30 %** | **3.37 %** |

## 4    Conclusions

In this paper we proposed the new algorithm for the dynamic signature verification based on stable partitions. Created partitions are associated with the areas of the signature characterized by: high and low pen velocity and high and low pen pressure at initial, middle and final moment of signing process. The algorithm selects two the most stable partitions individually for the considered signer. These partitions are used in the classification phase. The method assumes use of the classifier based on the Mamdani type neuro-fuzzy system which is characterized by very good accuracy and ease of interpretation of the collected knowledge. The achieved accuracy of signature verification in comparison with the other methods proves correctness of the assumptions.

**Acknowledgment.** The project was financed by the National Science Centre (Poland) on the basis of the decision number DEC-2012/05/B/ST7/02138.

## References

1. Bartczuk, Ł., Dziwiński, P., Starczewski, J.T.: New method for generationtype-2 fuzzy partition for FDT. In: Rutkowski, L., Scherer, R., Tadeusiewicz, R., Zadeh, L.A., Zurada, J.M. (eds.) ICAISC 2010, Part I. LNCS (LNAI), vol. 6113, pp. 275–280. Springer, Heidelberg (2010)
2. Bartczuk, Ł., Dziwiński, P., Starczewski, J.T.: A new method for dealing with unbalanced linguistic term set. In: Rutkowski, L., Korytkowski, M., Scherer, R., Tadeusiewicz, R., Zadeh, L.A., Zurada, J.M. (eds.) ICAISC 2012, Part I. LNCS, vol. 7267, pp. 207–212. Springer, Heidelberg (2012)
3. Bilski, J.: Momentum modification of the RLS algorithms. In: Rutkowski, L., Siekmann, J.H., Tadeusiewicz, R., Zadeh, L.A. (eds.) ICAISC 2004. LNCS (LNAI), vol. 3070, pp. 151–157. Springer, Heidelberg (2004)
4. Bilski, J., Rutkowski, L.: Numerically robust learning algorithms for feed forward neural networks. Advances in Soft Computing, pp. 149–154 (2003)
5. Bilski, J., Smolag, J.: Parallel realisation of the recurrent RTRN neural network learning. In: Rutkowski, L., Tadeusiewicz, R., Zadeh, L.A., Zurada, J.M. (eds.) ICAISC 2008. LNCS (LNAI), vol. 5097, pp. 11–16. Springer, Heidelberg (2008)
6. Bilski, J., Smolag, J.: Parallel Realisation of the Recurrent Elman Neural Network Learning. In: Rutkowski, L., Scherer, R., Tadeusiewicz, R., Zadeh, L.A., Zurada, J.M. (eds.) ICAISC 2010, Part II. LNCS (LNAI), vol. 6114, pp. 19–25. Springer, Heidelberg (2010)
7. Bilski, J., Smolag, J.: Parallel Realisation of the Recurrent Multi Layer Perceptron Learning. In: Rutkowski, L., Korytkowski, M., Scherer, R., Tadeusiewicz, R., Zadeh, L.A., Zurada, J.M. (eds.) ICAISC 2012, Part I. LNCS, vol. 7267, pp. 12–20. Springer, Heidelberg (2012)
8. Bilski, J., Smolag, J.: Parallel approach to learning of the recurrent jordan neural network. In: Rutkowski, L., Korytkowski, M., Scherer, R., Tadeusiewicz, R., Zadeh, L.A., Zurada, J.M. (eds.) ICAISC 2013, Part I. LNCS (LNAI), vol. 7894, pp. 32–40. Springer, Heidelberg (2013)
9. Bilski, J., Smolag, J.: Parallel architectures for learning the RTRN and Elman dynamic neural networks, IEEE Trans. Parallel and Distributed Systems PP(99) (2014)

10. Bilski, J., Smoląg, J., Galushkin, A.I.: The Parallel Approach to the Conjugate Gradient Learning Algorithm for the Feedforward Neural Networks. In: Rutkowski, L., Korytkowski, M., Scherer, R., Tadeusiewicz, R., Zadeh, L.A., Zurada, J.M. (eds.) ICAISC 2014, Part I. LNCS (LNAI), vol. 8467, pp. 12–21. Springer, Heidelberg (2014)

11. Bilski, J., Litwiński, S., Smoląg, J.: Parallel realisation of QR algorithm for neural networks learning. In: Rutkowski, L., Siekmann, J.H., Tadeusiewicz, R., Zadeh, L.A. (eds.) ICAISC 2004. LNCS (LNAI), vol. 3070, pp. 158–165. Springer, Heidelberg (2004)

12. Bartczuk, Ł., Przybył, A., Koprinkova-Hristova, P.: New method for nonlinear fuzzy correction modelling of dynamic objects. In: Rutkowski, L., Korytkowski, M., Scherer, R., Tadeusiewicz, R., Zadeh, L.A., Zurada, J.M. (eds.) ICAISC 2014, Part I. LNCS (LNAI), vol. 8467, pp. 169–180. Springer, Heidelberg (2014)

13. Batista, L., Granger, E., Sabourin, R.: Dynamic selection of generative discriminative ensembles for off-line signature verification. Pattern Recognition 45, 1326–1340 (2012)

14. Bhattacharya, I., Ghosh, P., Biswas, S.: Offline Signature Verification Using Pixel Matching Technique. Procedia Technology 10, 970–977 (2013)

15. Cpałka, K., Zalasiński, M.: On-line signature verification using vertical signature partitioning. Expert Systems with Applications 41, 4170–4180 (2014)

16. Cpałka, K., Zalasiński, M., Rutkowski, L.: New method for the on-line signature verification based on horizontal partitioning. Pattern Recognition 47, 2652–2661 (2014)

17. Dziwiński, P., Bartczuk, Ł., Przybył, A., Avedyan, E.D.: A New Algorithm for Identification of Significant Operating Points Using Swarm Intelligence. In: Rutkowski, L., Korytkowski, M., Scherer, R., Tadeusiewicz, R., Zadeh, L.A., Zurada, J.M. (eds.) ICAISC 2014, Part II. LNCS (LNAI), vol. 8468, pp. 349–362. Springer, Heidelberg (2014)

18. Faúndez-Zanuy, M.: On-line signature recognition based on VQ-DTW. Pattern Recognition 40, 981–992 (2007)

19. Faúndez-Zanuy, M., Pascual-Gaspar, J.M.: Efficient on-line signature recognition based on multi-section vector quantization. Formal Pattern Analysis & Applications 14, 37–45 (2011)

20. Fierrez, J., Ortega-Garcia, J., Ramos, D., Gonzalez-Rodriguez, J.: HMM–based on-line signature verification: Feature extraction and signature modeling. Pattern Recognition Letters 28, 2325–2334 (2007)

21. Fiérrez-Aguilar, J., Nanni, L., Lopez-Peñalba, J., Ortega-Garcia, J., Maltoni, D.: An On-Line Signature Verification System Based on Fusion of Local and Global Information. In: Kanade, T., Jain, A., Ratha, N.K. (eds.) AVBPA 2005. LNCS, vol. 3546, pp. 523–532. Springer, Heidelberg (2005)

22. Gabryel, M.: Cpałka K., Rutkowski L, Evolutionary strategies for learning of neuro-fuzzy systems. In: Proceedings of the I Workshop on Genetic Fuzzy Systems, Granada, pp. 119-123 (2005)

23. Gałkowski, T.: Kernel estimation of regression functions in the boundary regions. In: Rutkowski, L., Korytkowski, M., Scherer, R., Tadeusiewicz, R., Zadeh, L.A., Zurada, J.M. (eds.) ICAISC 2013, Part II. LNCS (LNAI), vol. 7895, pp. 158–166. Springer, Heidelberg (2013)

24. Galkowski, T., Pawlak, M.: Nonparametric function fitting in the presence of nonstationary noise. In: Rutkowski, L., Korytkowski, M., Scherer, R., Tadeusiewicz, R., Zadeh, L.A., Zurada, J.M. (eds.) ICAISC 2014, Part I. LNCS (LNAI), vol. 8467, pp. 531–538. Springer, Heidelberg (2014)

25. Gakowski, T., Rutkowski, L.: Nonparametric fitting of multivariate functions. IEEE Trans. Automatic Control AC-31(8), 785–787 (1986)
26. Greblicki, W., Rutkowska, D., Rutkowski, L.: An orthogonal series estimate of time-varying regression. Annals of the Institute of Statistical Mathematics 35(2), 215–228 (1983)
27. Greblicki, W., Rutkowski, L.: Density-free Bayes risk consistency of nonparametric pattern recognition procedures. Proc. of the IEEE 69(4), 482–483 (1981)
28. Greenfield, S., Chiclana, F.: Type-reduction of the discretized interval type-2 fuzzy set: approaching the continuous case through progressively finer discretization. Journal of Artificial Intelligence and Soft Computing Research 1(3), 183–193 (2011)
29. Homepage of Association BioSecure, http://biosecure.it-sudparis.eu (accessed: December 16, 2014)
30. Houmani, N., Garcia-Salicetti, S., Mayoue, A., Dorizzi, B.: BioSecure Signature Evaluation Campaign 2009 (BSEC 2009): Results (2009)
31. Ibrahim, M.T., Khan, M.A., Alimgeer, K.S., Khan, M.K., Taj, I.A., Guan, L.: Velocity and pressure-based partitions of horizontal and vertical trajectories for on-line signature verification. Pattern Recognition 43, 2817–2832 (2010)
32. Jeong, Y.S., Jeong, M.K., Omitaomu, O.A.: Weighted dynamic time warping for time series classification. Pattern Recognition 44, 2231–2240 (2011)
33. Korytkowski, M., Nowicki, R., Scherer, R.: Neuro-fuzzy rough classifier ensemble. In: Alippi, C., Polycarpou, M., Panayiotou, C., Ellinas, G. (eds.) ICANN 2009, Part I. LNCS, vol. 5768, pp. 817–823. Springer, Heidelberg (2009)
34. Kroll, A.: On choosing the fuzziness parameter for identifying TS models with multidimensional membership functions. Journal of Artificial Intelligence and Soft Computing Research 1(4), 283–300 (2011)
35. Kumar, R., Sharma, J.D., Chanda, B.: Writer-independent off-line signature verification using surroundedness feature. Pattern Recognition Letters 33, 301–308 (2012)
36. Laskowski, Ł.: A novel hybrid-maximum neural network in stereo-matching process. Neural Computing and Applications 23, 2435–2450 (2013)
37. Laskowski, Ł., Jelonkiewicz, J.: Self-correcting neural network for stereo-matching problem solving. Lecture Notes in Computer Science, vol. 138, pp. 1–26. Springer (2015)
38. Lumini, A., Nanni, L.: Ensemble of on-line signature matchers based on over-complete feature generation. Expert Systems with Applications 36, 5291–5296 (2009)
39. Maiorana, E.: Biometric cryptosystem using function based on-line signature recognition. Expert Systems with Applications 37, 3454–3461 (2010)
40. Moon, J.H., Lee, S.G., Cho, S.Y., Kim, Y.S.: A hybrid online signature verification system supporting multi-confidential levels defined by data mining techniques. International Journal of Intelligent Systems Technologies and Applications 9, 262–273 (2010)
41. Nanni, L., Lumini, A.: Advanced methods for two-class problem formulation for on-line signature verification. Neurocomputing 69, 854–857 (2006)
42. Nanni, L., Maiorana, E., Lumini, A., Campisi, P.: Combining local, regional and global matchers for a template protected on-line signature verification system. Expert Systems with Applications 37, 3676–3684 (2010)
43. Nowicki, R.: Rough-Neuro-Fuzzy System with MICOG Defuzzification. In: IEEE International Conference on Fuzzy Systems, IEEE World Congress on Computational Intelligence, Vancouver, BC, Canada, July 16-21, pp. 1958–1965 (2006)

44. Nowicki, R.: Rough-neuro-fuzzy structures for classification with missing data. IEEE Transactions on Systems, Man, and Cybernetics-Part B: Cybernetics 39(6), 1334–1347 (2009)
45. Nowicki, R., Pokropińska, A.: Information Criterions Applied to Neuro-Fuzzy Architectures Design. In: Rutkowski, L., Siekmann, J.H., Tadeusiewicz, R., Zadeh, L.A. (eds.) ICAISC 2004. LNCS (LNAI), vol. 3070, pp. 332–337. Springer, Heidelberg (2004)
46. Nowicki, R., Rutkowski, L., Scherer, R.: A method for learning of hierarchical fuzzy systems. In: Intelligent Technologies - Theory and Applications, pp. 124–129 (2002)
47. Nowicki, R., Scherer, R., Rutkowski, L.: A Method For Learning Of Hierarchical Fuzzy Systems. In: Sincak, P., et al. (eds.) Intelligent Technologies - Theory and Applications, pp. 124–129. IOS Press, Amsterdam (2002)
48. Pławiak, P., Tadeusiewicz, R.: Approximation of phenol concentration using novel hybrid computational intelligence methods. Applied Mathematics and Computer Science 24(1) (2014)
49. Pabiasz, S., Starczewski, J.T.: A new approach to determine three-dimensional facial landmarks. In: Rutkowski, L., Korytkowski, M., Scherer, R., Tadeusiewicz, R., Zadeh, L.A., Zurada, J.M. (eds.) ICAISC 2013, Part II. LNCS (LNAI), vol. 7895, pp. 286–296. Springer, Heidelberg (2013)
50. Pabiasz, S., Starczewski, J.T., Marvuglia, A.: A new three-dimensional facial landmarks in recognition. In: Rutkowski, L., Korytkowski, M., Scherer, R., Tadeusiewicz, R., Zadeh, L.A., Zurada, J.M. (eds.) ICAISC 2014, Part II. LNCS (LNAI), vol. 8468, pp. 179–186. Springer, Heidelberg (2014)
51. Patan, K., Patan, M.: Optimal Training strategies for locally recurrent neural networks. Journal of Artificial Intelligence and Soft Computing Research 1(2), 103–114 (2011)
52. Peteiro-Barral, D., Bardinas, B.G., Perez-Sanchez, B.: Learning from heterogeneously distributed data sets using artificial neural networks and genetic algorithms. Journal of Artificial Intelligence and Soft Computing Research 2(1), 5–20 (2012)
53. Przybył, A., Er, M.J.: The idea for the integration of neuro-fuzzy hardware emulators with real-time network. In: Rutkowski, L., Korytkowski, M., Scherer, R., Tadeusiewicz, R., Zadeh, L.A., Zurada, J.M. (eds.) ICAISC 2014, Part I. LNCS (LNAI), vol. 8467, pp. 279–294. Springer, Heidelberg (2014)
54. Przybył, A., Jelonkiewicz, J.: Genetic algorithm for observer parameters tuning in sensorless induction motor drive. In: Neural Networks and Soft Computing, pp. 376–381 (2003)
55. Przybył, A., Smoląg, J., Kimla, P.: Distributed control system based on real time ethernet for computer numerical controlled machine tool. Przegląd Elektrotechniczny 86(2), 342–346 (2010)
56. Rutkowski, L.: Nonparametric identification of quasi-stationary systems. Systems & Control Letters 6(1), 33–35 (1985)
57. Rutkowski, L.: Real-time identification of time-varying systems by non-parametric algorithms based on Parzen kernels. Int. Journal of Systems Science 16(9), 1123–1130 (1985)
58. Rutkowski, L.: A general-approach for nonparametric fitting of functions and their derivatives with applications to linear circuits identification. IEEE Trans. Circuits and Systems 33(8), 812–818 (1986)
59. Rutkowski, L.: Computational Intelligence. Springer, Heidelberg (2008)

60. Rutkowski, L., Cpałka, K.: Flexible structures of neuro-fuzzy systems. In: Sincak, P., Vascak, J. (eds.) Quo Vadis Computational Intelligence. STUDFUZZ, vol. 54, pp. 479–484. Springer, Heidelberg (2000)

61. Rutkowski, L., Cpałka, K.: Compromise approach to neuro-fuzzy systems. In: Sincak, P., Vascak, J., Kvasnicka, V., Pospichal, J. (eds.) Intelligent Technologies - Theory and Applications, vol. 76, pp. 85–90. IOS Press (2002)

62. Rutkowski, L., Jaworski, M., Pietruczuk, L., Duda, P.: Decision Trees for Mining Data Streams Based on the Gaussian Approximation. IEEE Transactions on Knowledge and Data Engineering 26, 108–119 (2014)

63. Rutkowski, L., Jaworski, M., Pietruczuk, L., Duda, P.: The CART decision tree for mining data streams. Information Sciences 266, 1–15 (2014)

64. Rutkowski, L., Przybył, A., Cpałka, K., Er, M.J.: Online speed profile generation for industrial machine tool based on neuro-fuzzy approach. In: Rutkowski, L., Scherer, R., Tadeusiewicz, R., Zadeh, L.A., Zurada, J.M. (eds.) ICAISC 2010, Part II. LNCS, vol. 6114, pp. 645–650. Springer, Heidelberg (2010)

65. Starczewski, J.T., Scherer, R., Korytkowski, M., Nowicki, R.: Modular type-2 neuro-fuzzy systems. In: Wyrzykowski, R., Dongarra, J., Karczewski, K., Wasniewski, J. (eds.) PPAM 2007. LNCS, vol. 4967, pp. 570–578. Springer, Heidelberg (2008)

66. Starczewski, J.T., Bartczuk, Ł., Dziwiński, P., Marvuglia, A.: Learning Methods for Type-2 FLS Based on FCM. In: Rutkowski, L., Scherer, R., Tadeusiewicz, R., Zadeh, L.A., Zurada, J.M. (eds.) ICAISC 2010, Part I. LNCS (LNAI), vol. 6113, pp. 224–231. Springer, Heidelberg (2010)

67. Szarek, A., Korytkowski, M., Rutkowski, L., Scherer, R., Szyprowski, J.: Application of Neural Networks in Assessing Changes around Implant after Total Hip Arthroplasty. In: Rutkowski, L., Korytkowski, M., Scherer, R., Tadeusiewicz, R., Zadeh, L.A., Zurada, J.M. (eds.) ICAISC 2012, Part II. LNCS, vol. 7268, pp. 335–340. Springer, Heidelberg (2012)

68. Szarek, A., Korytkowski, M., Rutkowski, L., Scherer, R., Szyprowski, J.: Forecasting wear of head and acetabulum in hip joint implant. In: Rutkowski, L., Korytkowski, M., Scherer, R., Tadeusiewicz, R., Zadeh, L.A., Zurada, J.M. (eds.) ICAISC 2012, Part II. LNCS, vol. 7268, pp. 341–346. Springer, Heidelberg (2012)

69. Szczypta, J., Przybył, A., Cpałka, K.: Some aspects of evolutionary designing optimal controllers. In: Rutkowski, L., Korytkowski, M., Scherer, R., Tadeusiewicz, R., Zadeh, L.A., Zurada, J.M. (eds.) ICAISC 2013, Part II. LNCS, vol. 7895, pp. 91–100. Springer, Heidelberg (2013)

70. Szczypta, J., Przybył, A., Wang, L.: Evolutionary approach with multiple quality criteria for controller design. In: Rutkowski, L., Korytkowski, M., Scherer, R., Tadeusiewicz, R., Zadeh, L.A., Zurada, J.M. (eds.) ICAISC 2014, Part I. LNCS (LNAI), vol. 8467, pp. 455–467. Springer, Heidelberg (2014)

71. Tadeusiewicz, R., Chaki, R., Chaki, N.: Exploring Neural Networks with C#. CRC Press, Taylor & Francis Group, Boca Raton (2014)

72. Woźniak, M., Kempa, W.M., Gabryel, M., Nowicki, R.: A finite-buffer queue with single vacation policy-analytical study with evolutionary positioning. Int. Journal of Applied Mathematics and Computer Science 24, 887–900 (2014)

73. Woźniak, M., Kempa, W.M., Gabryel, M., Nowicki, R.K., Shao, Z.: On applying evolutionary computation methods to optimization of vacation cycle costs in finite-buffer queue. In: Rutkowski, L., Korytkowski, M., Scherer, R., Tadeusiewicz, R., Zadeh, L.A., Zurada, J.M. (eds.) ICAISC 2014, Part I. LNCS (LNAI), vol. 8467, pp. 480–491. Springer, Heidelberg (2014)

74. Yeung, D.-Y., Chang, H., Xiong, Y., George, S., Kashi, R., Matsumoto, T., Rigoll, G.: SVC2004: First International Signature Verification Competition. In: Zhang, D., Jain, A.K. (eds.) ICBA 2004. LNCS, vol. 3072, pp. 16–22. Springer, Heidelberg (2004)
75. Zalasiński, M., Cpałka, K.: A new method of on-line signature verification using a flexible fuzzy one-class classifier, pp. 38–53. Academic Publishing House EXIT (2011)
76. Zalasiński, M., Cpałka, K.: New Approach for the On-Line Signature Verification Based on Method of Horizontal Partitioning. In: Rutkowski, L., Korytkowski, M., Scherer, R., Tadeusiewicz, R., Zadeh, L.A., Zurada, J.M. (eds.) ICAISC 2013, Part II. LNCS (LNAI), vol. 7895, pp. 342–350. Springer, Heidelberg (2013)
77. Zalasiński, M., Cpałka, K., Er, M.J.: New method for dynamic signature verification using hybrid partitioning. In: Rutkowski, L., Korytkowski, M., Scherer, R., Tadeusiewicz, R., Zadeh, L.A., Zurada, J.M. (eds.) ICAISC 2014, Part II. LNCS (LNAI), vol. 8468, pp. 216–230. Springer, Heidelberg (2014)

# New Fast Algorithm for the Dynamic Signature Verification Using Global Features Values

Marcin Zalasiński[1][✉], Krzysztof Cpałka[1], and Yoichi Hayashi[2]

[1] Institute of Computational Intelligence,
Częstochowa University of Technology, Częstochowa, Poland
{marcin.zalasinski,krzysztof.cpalka}@iisi.pcz.pl
[2] Department of Computer Science, Meiji University, Tokyo, Japan
hayashiy@cs.meiji.ac.jp

**Abstract.** Identity verification based on the dynamic signature is an important issue of biometrics. There are many effective methods to the signature verification which take into account the dynamic characteristics of the signature (e.g. velocity of the pen, the pen's pressure on the surface of the graphic tablet, etc.). Among these methods, the ones based on the so-called global features are very important. In our previous paper we have proposed new algorithm for evolutionary selection of the dynamic signature global features, which selects a subset of features individually for each user. Algorithm proposed in this paper is a faster version of the method proposed earlier. During development of the algorithm we resigned from using evolutionary selection of global features and standardized working of the classifier in the context of all users. The paper contains the simulation results for the BioSecure database of the dynamic signatures.

## 1 Introduction

Signature is a commonly used form of authentication. Its advantage is that the method of signature acquisition is not controversial, as in the case of certain biometric characteristics such as fingerprint or face image (see e.g. [47,48]).

In the literature there are two approaches to the signature verification. The first is based on the analysis of static features of the signature such as shape, size ratios, etc. (see e.g. [4,33]). The second approach is based on the analysis of the dynamics of signing process (see e.g. [12,28,39]). The dynamics of the signature is difficult to see and forge, so the use of the so-called dynamic signature brings much better results than the use of the so-called static signature. Moreover, the dynamic features of the signature are unique to the signer.

Approaches used to the dynamic signature verification can be divided into four main groups: **Global features based methods.** Some methods base on the global features which are extracted from signature and used during training and classification phase. Approach based on global features may be found in many research papers (see e.g. [14,37,39,79,75]). **Functions based methods.** Another approach commonly used in identity verification based on dynamic signature is functions-based approach. This approach bases on comparison of time

© Springer International Publishing Switzerland 2015
L. Rutkowski et al. (Eds.): ICAISC 2015, Part II, LNAI 9120, pp. 175–188, 2015.
DOI: 10.1007/978-3-319-19369-4_17

functions, which contains information about changes of signature features over time (see e.g. [12,27,29]). **Regional based methods.** The literature contains also approaches relying on segmentation of signature into some regions, which are used during training and verification phase (see e.g. [9,10,13,26,28,77,78]). **Hybrid methods.** In the literature one can also find the hybrid methods which are based on combination of the described approaches (see e.g. [38,40]).

In this paper we focus on the approach based on global features. We use a set of global features proposed in [14], which contains extended collection of features from three other papers: [36,41,42]. It should be noted that the proposed fast algorithm is not dependent on the initial feature set, especially it is not sensitive to the wrong choice of this set. Moreover, the feature set can be practically arbitrarily reduced or extended. This is very important from the point of view of the flexibility of the proposed method and the possibility of its easy adaptation to the hardware used for the acquisition of features. The following conditions have prompted us to develop a method proposed in this work: **The proposed method does not require complex calculations, in particular machine learning.** Its characteristic feature is that a typical set of features describing the dynamics of the signature is considered for each user, without the need for features selection. As a result, the proposed algorithm does not require machine learning. The two following facts are also worth to note: (a) proposed algorithm does not depend on the used set of features, (b) the set of features selected in the previous paper (i.e. [79]) could depend on the specificity of used databases. **The proposed method uses in the classification process a hierarchy of features individually for each user.** In particular, it allows to determine for each user weights of importance of each feature. Values of weights are related to the similarity of features values (specifying stability of the reference signatures creation), taking into account all signatures created by the user in the acquisition phase of genuine signatures (training phase). **The proposed method takes advantage of the theory of fuzzy sets and neuro-fuzzy systems.** Neuro-fuzzy systems (see e.g. [30,31,43,44,45,52,70]) combine the natural language description of fuzzy systems (see e.g. [2,15,32,46]) and the learning properties of neural networks (see e.g. [34,35,50,51,69,73]). For the purposes of the proposed method, we have developed a new neuro-fuzzy one-class classifier, proposed by us earlier (see e.g. [9,78]). The proposed classifier is characterized the following properties: (a) it does not require supervised learning (what is crucial in the context of the considered sphere of application), (b) it has a uniform structure for all users and it is based on values of descriptors of the signature's features, (c) it does not require forged signatures, so called skilled forgeries, to proper work (what not always distinguish methods of signature verification, so it is definitely a positive property), (d) it is distinguished by the interpretability of rules included in the base of rules (also semantic). It is worth to note that many computational intelligence methods (see e.g. [1,11,17,18,19,21,68,49,64,65]) are succesfully used in pattern recognition (see e.g. [20,22,23,55,56,57,58]) and modelling (see e.g. [3,54,66]) issues.

To test the proposed method we used the BioSecure Database (BMDB) distributed by the BioSecure Association (see [24]) which is admitted source of data used in this field.

This paper is organized into four sections. In Section 2 we present description of the new method for dynamic signature verification based on global features. In Section 3 simulation results are presented. Conclusions are drawn in Section 4.

## 2    Description of the New Method for Dynamic Signature Verification Based on Global Features

Idea of the proposed in this paper method can be summarized as follows: **(a)** It works on the basis of a set of features describing the dynamics of the signature which have been systematized, for example, in the paper [14] (in our simulations 78 features have been considered). As already mentioned, the proposed method does not depend on the base set of features. This set can be freely modified. We would like to emphasize that from the set of all features (i.e. 85) considered in the paper [14], we removed those which were not selected by the algorithm for automatic features selection proposed by us earlier (see e.g. [79]). **(b)** It uses (developed for the considered method) one-class classifier which is based on the capacities of the flexible fuzzy system (see e.g. [6,9,62,63,78]). It allows to take into account the weights of importance of individual features, selected individually for each user. **(c)** It works in two modes: learning and testing (operating mode). In the first mode descriptors of features and weights of importance of features are determined. They are needed for proper work of the classifier in the test phase. These parameters are stored in a database. In the second mode, mode of operation (verification of test signatures), the parameters stored for each user in the learning phase are downloaded from the database and then signature verification is realized on the basis of these parameters.

General description of the fast training phase for the user $i$ (procedure Training($i$)) can be described as follows: **Step 1.** Acquisition of $J$ training signatures of user $i$. **Step 2.** Determination of matrix $\mathbf{G}_i$ of all considered global features, describing dynamics of signatures, for all available $J$ training signatures of user $i$. **Step 3.** Determination of vector $\bar{\mathbf{g}}_i$ of average values for each global feature, determined in Step 2 for $J$ training signatures of user $i$. **Step 4.** Selection of classifier parameters used in the test phase (procedure Classifier Determination($i, \mathbf{G}_i, \bar{\mathbf{g}}_i$)). **Step 5.** Storing in a database the following information about user $i$: vector $\bar{\mathbf{g}}_i$, parameters of classifier $maxd_{i,n}$ and $w_{i,n}$ ($n = 1, \ldots, N$).

It is worth noting that for each user the procedure described above is independent, although the number of features $N$ for each user is the same. Later in this section steps 2 and 3 of the procedure Training($i$) have been described in details.

Matrix $\mathbf{G}_i$, which contains all considered global features of all $J$ training signatures of user $i$, has the following structure:

$$\mathbf{G}_i = \begin{bmatrix} g_{i,1,1} \ g_{i,2,1} \ \cdots \ g_{i,N,1} \\ g_{i,1,2} \ g_{i,2,2} \ \cdots \ g_{i,N,2} \\ \vdots \\ g_{i,1,J} \ g_{i,2,J} \ \cdots \ g_{i,N,J} \end{bmatrix} = \begin{bmatrix} \mathbf{g}_{i,1} \\ \mathbf{g}_{i,2} \\ \vdots \\ \mathbf{g}_{i,N} \end{bmatrix}^T, \tag{1}$$

where $\mathbf{g}_{i,n} = \begin{bmatrix} g_{i,n,1} \ g_{i,n,2} \ \cdots \ g_{i,n,J} \end{bmatrix}$, $g_{i,n,j}$ is a value of the global feature $n$, $n = 1, 2, \ldots, N$, determined for the signature $j$, $j = 1, 2, \ldots, J$, created by the user $i$, $i = 1, 2, \ldots, I$, $I$ is a number of the users, $J$ is a number of the signatures created by the user in the acquisition phase, $N$ is a number of the global features. As already mentioned, the detailed method of determining each of the considered features is described in [14].

Matrix $\mathbf{G}_i$ is used to determine value of the vector $\bar{\mathbf{g}}_i$ in the **Step 3**. Vector $\bar{\mathbf{g}}_i$ of average values of each global feature of all training signatures $J$ of user $i$ is described as follows:

$$\bar{\mathbf{g}}_i = [\bar{g}_{i,1}, \bar{g}_{i,2}, \ldots, \bar{g}_{i,N}], \tag{2}$$

where $\bar{g}_{i,n}$ is average value of $n$-th global feature of training signatures of user $i$, computed using the following formula:

$$\bar{g}_{i,n} = \frac{1}{J} \sum_{j=1}^{J} g_{i,n,j}. \tag{3}$$

## 2.1 Determination of Classifier

In the procedure described in this section all available global features of the dynamic signature are considered. It causes that matrix $\mathbf{G}_i$ and vector $\bar{\mathbf{g}}_i$ are taken into account during determination of classifier parameters. General form of the procedure Classifier Determination$(i, \mathbf{G}_i, \bar{\mathbf{g}}_i)$, which determines parameters of the our classifier, can be presented as follows: **Step 1.** Determination of Euclidean distances $d_{i,n,j}$ between each global feature $n$ and average value of the global feature for all $J$ signatures of user $i$. **Step 2.** Selection of maximum distance for each global feature $n$ from distances determined in Step 1. It should be emphasized that the maximum distance (labelled as $maxd_{i,n}$, $i = 1, 2, \ldots, I$, $n = 1, 2, \ldots, N$) are individual for each user $i$. They will be used in the classification phase of the signature (verification of the authenticity). Therefore, they must be stored in the database (in addition to vector $\bar{\mathbf{g}}_i$). **Step 3.** Computation of weights of importance $w_{i,n}$, $i = 1, 2, \ldots, I$, $n = 1, 2, \ldots, N$, associated with the feature number $n$ of the user $i$ and used in the classification phase. It should be emphasized that the weights also have individual character for the user $i$ and they will be used in the classification process of the signature. Therefore, they must be stored in the database (in addition to vector $\bar{\mathbf{g}}_i$ and distances

$maxd_{i,n}$). **Step 4.** Creation of parameters of the flexible neuro-fuzzy system (see e.g. [60,61,76] ) using values determined in Step 2 and Step 3.

In the **Step 1** distances $d_{i,n,j}$ between each global feature $n$ and average value of the global feature for all $J$ signatures of user $i$ is computed using the following formula:

$$d_{i,n,j} = |\bar{g}_{i,n} - g_{i,n,j}|. \tag{4}$$

Next, maximum distance for each global feature is selected (**Step 2**):

$$maxd_{i,n} = \max_{j=1,...,J} \{d_{i,n,j}\}. \tag{5}$$

Please note that distance $maxd_{i,n}$ is associated with the global feature $n$ of the user $i$ and determines instability of the signature in the context of the feature $n$. Value of the distance $maxd_{i,n}$ is also dependent on the variability of feature and it has an impact on the work of the signature classifier (see Fig. 1).

In the **Step 3** weights of importance of features $w_{i,n}$ for each global feature $n$ of user $i$ are determined. Weight of $n$-th global feature of the user $i$ is computed on the basis of standard deviation of $n$-th global feature of the user $i$ and average value of distances for $n$-th feature of the user $i$ (computed in the **Step 2**). This process is described by the following formula:

$$w_{i,n} = 1 - \frac{\sqrt{\frac{1}{J} \sum_{j=1}^{J} (\bar{g}_{i,n} - g_{i,n,j})^2}}{\frac{1}{J} \sum_{j=1}^{J} d_{i,n,j}}. \tag{6}$$

It should be noted that the larger value of the weight $w_{i,n}$, the corresponding feature is more important in the verification of the signature (as described in the next subsection).

Next, a classifier is created (**Step 4**). We use flexible neuro-fuzzy system of the Mamdani type (see e.g. [6,7,5,8]). This system is based on the rules in the form if-then. The fuzzy rules contain fuzzy sets which represent the values, e.g. "low" and "high", of the input and output linguistic variables. In our method the input linguistic variables are dependent on the similarity between the global features of test signature and average values of global features computed on the basis of training signatures. The system uses $N$ features. Output linguistic variables describe the reliability of the signature. In our method parameters of input fuzzy sets are individually selected for each user (**Step 2** of the procedure `Classifier Determination`$(i, \bar{\mathbf{g}}_i)$). Please note that if training signatures are more similar to each other, the tolerance of our classifier is lower ($maxd_{i,n}$ takes smaller values).

The flexibility of the classifier results from the possibility of using in the classification the importance of global features, which are selected individually for each user (**Step 3** of the procedure `Classifier Determination`$(i, \mathbf{G}_i, \bar{\mathbf{g}}_i)$).

Taking into account the weights of importance of the global features is possible thanks to the use of proposed by us earlier (see e.g. [7,62,67]) aggregation operators named the weighted triangular norms.

Our system for the signature verification works on the basis of two fuzzy rules presented as follows:

$$
\begin{cases}
R^{(1)}: & \begin{bmatrix} \text{IF } \left(dtst_{i,1}\text{is}A^1_{i,1}\right)\big|\,w_{i,1}\text{ANDIF } \left(dtst_{i,2}\text{is}A^1_{i,2}\right)\big|\,w_{i,2}\text{AND} \\ \vdots \\ \text{IF } \left(dtst_{i,N}\text{is}A^1_{i,N}\right)\big|\,w_{i,N}\text{THEN}y_i\text{is}B^1 \end{bmatrix} \\[4pt]
R^{(2)}: & \begin{bmatrix} \text{IF } \left(dtst_{i,1}\text{is}A^2_{i,1}\right)\big|\,w_{i,1}\text{ANDIF } \left(dtst_{i,2}\text{is}A^2_{i,2}\right)\big|\,w_{i,2}\text{AND} \\ \vdots \\ \text{IF } \left(dtst_{i,N}\text{is}A^2_{i,N}\right)\big|\,w_{i,N}\text{THEN}y_i\text{is}B^2 \end{bmatrix}
\end{cases}, \qquad (7)
$$

where: **(a)** $dtst_{i,n}$, $i = 1,2,\ldots,I$, $n = 1,2,\ldots,N$, $j = 1,2,\ldots,J$, are input linguistic variables in the system for the signature verification. **(b)** $A^1_{i,n}$, $A^2_{i,n}$, $i = 1,2,\ldots,I$, $n = 1,2,\ldots,N$, are input fuzzy sets related to the global feature number $n$ of the user $i$ represent values "high" assumed by input linguistic variables. Analogously, fuzzy sets $A^2_{i,1}, A^2_{i,2}, \ldots, A^2_{i,N}$ represent values "low" assumed by input linguistic variables. Thus, each rule contains $N$ antecedents. In the fuzzy classifier of the signature used in the simulations we applied a Gaussian membership function (see Fig. 1) for all input fuzzy sets. **(c)** $y_i$, $i = 1,2,\ldots,I$, is output linguistic variable interpreted as reliability of signature considered to be created by the $i$-th signer. **(d)** $B^1$, $B^2$ are output fuzzy sets shown in Fig. 1. Fuzzy set $B^1$ represents value "high" of output linguistic variable. Analogously, fuzzy set $B^2$ represents value "low" of output linguistic variable. In the fuzzy classifier of the signature used in the simulations we applied the membership function of type $\gamma$ (see e.g. [59]) in the rule 1 and the membership function of type $L$ (see e.g. [59]) in the rule 2. Please note that the membership function of fuzzy sets $B^1$ and $B^2$ are the same for all users (their parameters do not depend on the chosen global features of the dynamic signature and their values). **(e)** $maxd_{i,n}$, $i = 1,2,\ldots,I$, $n = 1,2,\ldots,N$, can be equated with the border values of features of individual users (see formula (5)). **(f)** $w_{i,n}$, $i = 1,2,\ldots,I$, $n = 1,2,\ldots,N$, are weights of importance related to the global feature number $n$ of the user $i$ (see formula (6)).

Please note that regardless of the set of features chosen individually for the user, the interpretation of the input and output fuzzy sets is uniform. Moreover, the way of the signature classification is interpretable (see [16])

## 2.2  Identity Verification Phase

Formal notation of the process of signature verification (`Signature Verification` $(i)$) is performed in the following way: **Step 1.** Acquisition of test signature of the user which is considered as user $i$. **Step 2.** Download of information about average values of global features of user $i$ computed during training phase ($\bar{g}_i$) and classifier

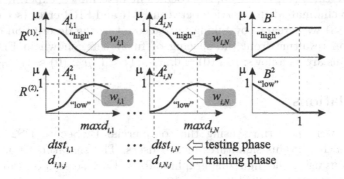

**Fig. 1.** Input and output fuzzy sets of the flexible neuro-fuzzy system of the Mamdani type for verification signature of user $i$

parameters of user $i$ from the database $(maxd_{i,n}, w_{i,n})$. **Step 3.** Determination of values of global features which have been selected as the most characteristic for user $i$ in training phase. **Step 4.** Verification of test signature using of one class flexible neuro-fuzzy classifier.

The purpose of the signature verification phase is therefore to determine whether the tested signature which belongs to the user claiming to be user $i$ in fact belongs to the user $i$. For such a signature values of global features are calculated. Next, they are put on the input of the classifier described by the rules (7). Parameters of the classifier are loaded from the database.

In the **Step 1** user which identity will be verified creates one test signature. In this step user claims his identity as $i$. Next, information about average values of global features of user $i$ computed during training phase ($\bar{g}_i$) and parameters of the classifier of user $i$ created during training phase ($maxd_{i,n}, w_{i,n}$) are downloaded from the database (**Step 2**). In the **Step 3** system determines global features of the test signature. Finally, verification is performed using flexible one-class neuro-fuzzy classifier of Mamdani type (**Step 4**). In the last step of the algorithm, the result of identity verification is presented. A signature is true if the following assumption is satisfied:

$$\bar{y}_i = \frac{T^* \left\{ \begin{array}{c} \mu_{A_{i,1}^1}(dtst_{i,1}), \ldots, \mu_{A_{i,N}^1}(dtst_{i,N}); \\ w_{i,1}, \ldots, w_{i,N} \end{array} \right\}}{\left( \begin{array}{c} T^* \left\{ \begin{array}{c} \mu_{A_{i,1}^1}(dtst_{i,1}), \ldots, \mu_{A_{i,N}^1}(dtst_{i,N}); \\ w_{i,1}, \ldots, w_{i,N} \end{array} \right\} + \\ T^* \left\{ \begin{array}{c} \mu_{A_{i,1}^2}(dtst_{i,1}), \ldots, \mu_{A_{i,N}^2}(dtst_{i,N}); \\ w_{i,1}, \ldots, w_{i,N} \end{array} \right\} \end{array} \right)} > cth_i, \qquad (8)$$

where $T^* \{\cdot\}$ is the algebraic weighted t-norm (see [7,62]), $\mu_A(\cdot)$ is a Gaussian membership function (see e.g. [59]), $\mu_{B^1}(\cdot)$ is a membership function of class $L$ (see e.g. [59]), $\mu_{B^2}(\cdot)$ is a membership function of class $\gamma$ (see e.g. [59]), $\bar{y}_i$, $i = 1, 2, \ldots, I$, is the value of the output signal of applied neuro-fuzzy system described by rules (7), $cth_i \in [0,1]$ - coefficient determined experimentally for each user to eliminate disproportion between FAR and FRR error (see e.g. [74]).

Formula (8) was created by taking into account in the description of system simplification resulting from the spacing of fuzzy sets, shown in Fig. 1. The simplifications are as follows: $\mu_{B^1}(0) = 0$, $\mu_{B^1}(1) \approx 1$, $\mu_{B^2}(0) \approx 1$, $\mu_{B^2}(1) = 0$.

## 3    Simulations

Simulations were performed using the commercial BioSecure DS2 Signature database which contains signatures of 210 users. The signatures was acquired in two sessions using the digitizing graphic tablet. Each session contains 15 genuine signatures and 10 skilled forgeries per person.

Test procedure proceeded as follows for signatures of each signer available in the database. During training phase we used 5 randomly selected genuine signatures of each signer. During test phase we used 10 remaining genuine signatures and all 10 skilled forgeries of each signer. The process was performed five times, and the results were averaged. The described method is commonly used in evaluating the effectiveness of methods for dynamic signature verification, which corresponds to the standard crossvalidation procedure. The test was performed using the authorial testing environment implemented in C# language.

### 3.1    Simulation Results

Table 1 contain a set of accuracies obtained using different methods in the field of the dynamic signature verification for the BioSecure database. The table contains values of FAR (False Acceptance Rate) and FRR (False Rejection Rate) errors which are commonly used in the literature to evaluate the effectiveness of identity verification methods (see e.g. [12,29]). Table 2 contains information on the computational complexity of the proposed method.

**Table 1.** Comparison of the results for the dynamic signature verification methods for the database BioSecure

| Method | Average FAR | Average FRR | Average error |
|---|---|---|---|
| Methods of other authors [25] | - | - | 3.48 % - 30.13 % |
| Horizontal partitioning [10] | 2.94 % | 4.45 % | 3.70 % |
| Vertical partitioning [9] | 3.13 % | 4.15 % | 3.64 % |
| Evolutionary selection with PCA [75] | 5.29 % | 6.01 % | 5.65 % |
| Evolutionary selection [79] | 2.32 % | 2.48 % | 2.40 % |
| **Our method** | **3.29 %** | **3.82 %** | **3.56 %** |

It may be seen that the proposed method works with a very good accuracy for the BioSecure database taking into account all methods considered in the Table 1. Moreover, it seems that the method proposed by us deserves attention

**Table 2.** The computational complexity of the proposed algorithm for dynamic signature verification based on global features

| | Step | | | | |
|---|---|---|---|---|---|
| **Procedure** | 1 | 2 | 3 | 4 | 5 |
| Training($i$) | $J$ | $J\sum\limits_{n=1}^{N} c_n$ | $JN$ | $4JN$ | $4N$ |
| Signature Verification($i$) | 1 | - | $\sum\limits_{n=1}^{N} c_n$ | $2N+1$ | - |

$c_n$ is computational complexity of feature $n$ determination, "-" means the reading or the writing to the database

both in the aspect of accuracy and additional advantages, such as taking into account a hierarchy of importance of global features in the classification process and interpretability of the fuzzy system rules used for the classification of signatures.

## 4   Conclusions

In this paper we propose a new method for the dynamic signature verification based on the so called global features. Proposed method works without access to the so-called skilled forged signatures, it implements individual (created individually for each user) hierarchy of features and it uses a dedicated flexible fuzzy one-class classifier. Efficiency of the proposed method has been tested with use of the BioSecure. The proposed algorithm worked with a very good accuracy. Moreover, our algorithm does not require high complexity computation (see Table 2). This is due to the fact that the algorithm does not use gradient or evolutionary (see e.g. [53,71,72]) machine learning. As a result, the proposed method can be used everywhere where speed of operation is crucial.

**Acknowledgment.** The project was financed by the National Science Centre (Poland) on the basis of the decision number DEC-2012/05/B/ST7/02138.

## References

1. Bartczuk, Ł., Dziwiński, P., Starczewski, J.T.: New method for generationtype-2 fuzzy partition for FDT. In: Rutkowski, L., Scherer, R., Tadeusiewicz, R., Zadeh, L.A., Zurada, J.M. (eds.) ICAISC 2010, Part I. LNCS (LNAI), vol. 6113, pp. 275–280. Springer, Heidelberg (2010)
2. Bartczuk, Ł., Dziwiński, P., Starczewski, J.T.: A new method for dealing with unbalanced linguistic term set. In: Rutkowski, L., Korytkowski, M., Scherer, R., Tadeusiewicz, R., Zadeh, L.A., Zurada, J.M. (eds.) ICAISC 2012, Part I. LNCS, vol. 7267, pp. 207–212. Springer, Heidelberg (2012)

3. Bartczuk, Ł., Przybył, A., Koprinkova-Hristova, P.: New method for nonlinear fuzzy correction modelling of dynamic objects. In: Rutkowski, L., Korytkowski, M., Scherer, R., Tadeusiewicz, R., Zadeh, L.A., Zurada, J.M. (eds.) ICAISC 2014, Part I. LNCS (LNAI), vol. 8467, pp. 169–180. Springer, Heidelberg (2014)
4. Bhattacharya, I., Ghosh, P., Biswas, S.: Offline Signature Verification Using Pixel Matching Technique. Procedia Technology 10, 970–977 (2013)
5. Cpałka, K., Łapa, K., Przybył, A., Zalasiński, M.: A new method for designing neuro-fuzzy systems for nonlinear modelling with interpretability aspects. Neurocomputing 135, 203–217 (2014)
6. Cpałka, K.: A New Method for Design and Reduction of Neuro-Fuzzy Classification Systems. IEEE Trans. on Neural Networks 20, 701–714 (2009)
7. Cpałka, K.: On evolutionary designing and learning of flexible neuro-fuzzy structures for nonlinear classification. Nonlinear Analysis Series A: Theory, Methods and Applications 71, 1659–1672 (2009)
8. Cpałka, K., Rebrova, O., Nowicki, R., Rutkowski, L.: On Design of Flexible Neuro-Fuzzy Systems for Nonlinear Modelling. International Journal of General Systems 42, 706–720 (2013)
9. Cpałka, K., Zalasiński, M.: On-line signature verification using vertical signature partitioning. Expert Systems with Applications 41, 4170–4180 (2014)
10. Cpałka, K., Zalasiński, M., Rutkowski, L.: New method for the on-line signature verification based on horizontal partitioning. Pattern Recognition 47, 2652–2661 (2014)
11. Dziwiński, P., Bartczuk, Ł., Przybył, A., Avedyan, E.D.: A New Algorithm for Identification of Significant Operating Points Using Swarm Intelligence. In: Rutkowski, L., Korytkowski, M., Scherer, R., Tadeusiewicz, R., Zadeh, L.A., Zurada, J.M. (eds.) ICAISC 2014, Part II. LNCS (LNAI), vol. 8468, pp. 349–362. Springer, Heidelberg (2014)
12. Faundez-Zanuy, M.: On-line signature recognition based on VQ-DTW. Pattern Recognition 40, 981–992 (2007)
13. Fierrez, J., Ortega-Garcia, J., Ramos, D., Gonzalez-Rodriguez, J.: HMM-based on-line signature verification: Feature extraction and signature modeling. Pattern Recognition Letters 28, 2325–2334 (2007)
14. Fiérrez-Aguilar, J., Nanni, L., Lopez-Peñalba, J., Ortega-Garcia, J., Maltoni, D.: An On-Line Signature Verification System Based on Fusion of Local and Global Information. In: Kanade, T., Jain, A., Ratha, N.K. (eds.) AVBPA 2005. LNCS, vol. 3546, pp. 523–532. Springer, Heidelberg (2005)
15. Gabryel, M., Korytkowski, M., Scherer, R., Rutkowski, L.: Object detection by simple fuzzy classifiers generated by boosting. In: Rutkowski, L., Korytkowski, M., Scherer, R., Tadeusiewicz, R., Zadeh, L.A., Zurada, J.M. (eds.) ICAISC 2013, Part I. LNCS (LNAI), vol. 7894, pp. 540–547. Springer, Heidelberg (2013)
16. Gacto, M.J., Alcala, R., Herrera, F.: Interpretability of linguistic fuzzy rule-based systems: An overview of interpretability measures. Information Sciences 181, 4340–4360 (2011)
17. Gałkowski, T.: Kernel Estimation of Regression Functions in the Boundary Regions. In: Rutkowski, L., Korytkowski, M., Scherer, R., Tadeusiewicz, R., Zadeh, L.A., Zurada, J.M. (eds.) ICAISC 2013, Part II. LNCS (LNAI), vol. 7895, pp. 158–166. Springer, Heidelberg (2013)
18. Galkowski, T., Pawlak, M.: Nonparametric function fitting in the presence of nonstationary noise. In: Rutkowski, L., Korytkowski, M., Scherer, R., Tadeusiewicz, R., Zadeh, L.A., Zurada, J.M. (eds.) ICAISC 2014, Part I. LNCS (LNAI), vol. 8467, pp. 531–538. Springer, Heidelberg (2014)

19. Galkowski, T., Rutkowski, L.: Nonparametric fitting of multivariate functions. IEEE Trans. Automatic Control AC-31(8), 785–787 (1986)
20. Greblicki, W., Rutkowski, L.: Density-free Bayes risk consistency of nonparametric pattern recognition procedures. Proc. of the IEEE 69(4), 482–483 (1981)
21. Greenfield, S., Chiclana, F.: Type-reduction of the discretized interval type-2 fuzzy set: approaching the continuous case through progressively finer discretization. Journal of Artificial Intelligence and Soft Computing Research 1(3), 183–193 (2011)
22. Grycuk, R., Gabryel, M., Korytkowski, M., Scherer, R.: Content-Based Image Indexing by Data Clustering and Inverse Document Frequency. In: Kozielski, S., Mrozek, D., Kasprowski, P., Małysiak-Mrozek, B. z. (eds.) BDAS 2014. CCIS, vol. 424, pp. 374–383. Springer, Heidelberg (2014)
23. Grycuk, R., Gabryel, M., Korytkowski, M., Scherer, R., Voloshynovskiy, S.: From single image to list of objects based on edge and blob detection. In: Rutkowski, L., Korytkowski, M., Scherer, R., Tadeusiewicz, R., Zadeh, L.A., Zurada, J.M. (eds.) ICAISC 2014, Part II. LNCS (LNAI), vol. 8468, pp. 605–615. Springer, Heidelberg (2014)
24. Homepage of Association BioSecure, http://biosecure.it-sudparis.eu (accessed: December 20, 2014)
25. Houmani, N., Garcia-Salicetti, S., Mayoue, A., Dorizzi, B.: BioSecure Signature Evaluation Campaign 2009 (BSEC 2009): Results (2009), http://biometrics.it-sudparis.eu/BSEC2009/downloads/BSEC2009_results.pdf (accessed: December 20, 2014)
26. Huang, K., Hong, Y.: Stability and style-variation modeling for on-line signature verification. Pattern Recognition 36, 2253–2270 (2003)
27. Jeong, Y.S., Jeong, M.K., Omitaomu, O.A.: Weighted dynamic time warping for time series classification. Pattern Recognition 44, 2231–2240 (2011)
28. Khan, M.A.U., Khan, M.K., Khan, M.A.: Velocity-image model for online signature verification. IEEE Trans. on Image Process. 15, 3540–3549 (2006)
29. Kholmatov, A., Yanikoglu, B.: Identity authentication using improved online signature verification method. Pattern Recognition Letters 26, 2400–2408 (2005)
30. Korytkowski, M., Nowicki, R., Rutkowski, L., Scherer, R.: AdaBoost Ensemble of DCOG Rough–Neuro–Fuzzy Systems. In: Jędrzejowicz, P., Nguyen, N.T., Hoang, K. (eds.) ICCCI 2011, Part I. LNCS, vol. 6922, pp. 62–71. Springer, Heidelberg (2011)
31. Korytkowski, M., Nowicki, R., Scherer, R.: Neuro-fuzzy rough classifier ensemble. In: Alippi, C., Polycarpou, M., Panayiotou, C., Ellinas, G. (eds.) ICANN 2009, Part I. LNCS, vol. 5768, pp. 817–823. Springer, Heidelberg (2009)
32. Korytkowski, M., Rutkowski, L., Scherer, R.: From ensemble of fuzzy classifiers to single fuzzy rule base classifier. In: Rutkowski, L., Tadeusiewicz, R., Zadeh, L.A., Zurada, J.M. (eds.) ICAISC 2008. LNCS (LNAI), vol. 5097, pp. 265–272. Springer, Heidelberg (2008)
33. Kumar, R., Sharma, J.D., Chanda, B.: Writer-independent off-line signature verification using surroundedness feature. Pattern Recognition Letters 33, 301–308 (2012)
34. Laskowski, Ł.: Hybrid-maximum neural network for depth analysis from stereo-image. In: Rutkowski, L., Scherer, R., Tadeusiewicz, R., Zadeh, L.A., Zurada, J.M. (eds.) ICAISC 2010, Part II. LNCS (LNAI), vol. 6114, pp. 47–55. Springer, Heidelberg (2010)

35. Laskowski, Ł.: Objects auto-selection from stereo-images realised by self-correcting neural network. In: Rutkowski, L., Korytkowski, M., Scherer, R., Tadeusiewicz, R., Zadeh, L.A., Zurada, J.M. (eds.) ICAISC 2012, Part I. LNCS, vol. 7267, pp. 119–125. Springer, Heidelberg (2012)

36. Lee, L.L., Berger, T., Aviczer, E.: Reliable on-line human signature verification systems. IEEE Trans. on Pattern Anal. and Machine Intell. 18, 643–647 (1996)

37. Lumini, A., Nanni, L.: Ensemble of on-line signature matchers based on overcomplete feature generation. Expert Systems with Applications 36, 5291–5296 (2009)

38. Moon, J.H., Lee, S.G., Cho, S.Y., Kim, Y.S.: A hybrid online signature verification system supporting multi-confidential levels defined by data mining techniques. International Journal of Intelligent Systems Technologies and Applications 9, 262–273 (2010)

39. Nanni, L., Lumini, A.: Ensemble of Parzen window classifiers for on-line signature verification. Neurocomputing 68, 217–224 (2005)

40. Nanni, L., Maiorana, E., Lumini, A., Campisi, P.: Combining local, regional and global matchers for a template protected on-line signature verification system. Expert Systems with Applications 37, 3676–3684 (2010)

41. Nelson, W., Kishon, E.: Use of dynamic features for signature verification. In: Proc. of the IEEE Intl. Conf. on Systems, Man, and Cyber., vol. 1, pp. 201–205 (1991)

42. Nelson, W., Turin, W., Hastie, T.: Statistical methods for on-line signature verification. Intl. Journal of Pattern Recognition and Artificial Intell. 8, 749–770 (1994)

43. Nowicki, R.: Rough-Neuro-Fuzzy System with MICOG Defuzzification. In: IEEE International Conference on Fuzzy Systems, IEEE World Congress on Computational Intelligence, Vancouver, BC, Canada, July 16-21, pp. 1958–1965 (2006)

44. Nowicki, R.: Rough-neuro-fuzzy structures for classification with missing data. IEEE Transactions on Systems, Man, and Cybernetics-Part B: Cybernetics 39(6), 1334–1347 (2009)

45. Nowicki, R., Pokropińska, A.: Information Criterions Applied to Neuro-Fuzzy Architectures Design. In: Rutkowski, L., Siekmann, J.H., Tadeusiewicz, R., Zadeh, L.A. (eds.) ICAISC 2004. LNCS (LNAI), vol. 3070, pp. 332–337. Springer, Heidelberg (2004)

46. Nowicki, R., Scherer, R., Rutkowski, L.: A Method For Learning Of Hierarchical Fuzzy Systems. In: Sincak, P., et al. (eds.) Intelligent Technologies - Theory and Applications, pp. 124–129. IOS Press, Amsterdam (2002)

47. Pabiasz, S., Starczewski, J.: Face reconstruction for 3d systems. In: Rutkowska, D., Cader, A., Przybyszewski, K. (eds.) Selected Topics in Computer Science Applications,, pp. 54–63. Academic Publishing House EXIT (2011)

48. Pabiasz, S., Starczewski, J.T.: Meshes vs. Depth maps in face recognition systems. In: Rutkowski, L., Korytkowski, M., Scherer, R., Tadeusiewicz, R., Zadeh, L.A., Zurada, J.M. (eds.) ICAISC 2012, Part I. LNCS, vol. 7267, pp. 567–573. Springer, Heidelberg (2012)

49. Pławiak, P., Tadeusiewicz, R.: Approximation of phenol concentration using novel hybrid computational intelligence methods. Applied Mathematics and Computer Science 24(1) (2014)

50. Patan, K., Patan, M.: Optimal Training strategies for locally recurrent neural networks. Journal of Artificial Intelligence and Soft Computing Research 1(2), 103–114 (2011)

51. Peteiro-Barral, D., Bardinas, B.G., Perez-Sanchez, B.: Learning from heterogeneously distributed data sets using artificial neural networks and genetic algorithms. Journal of Artificial Intelligence and Soft Computing Research 2(1), 5–20 (2012)
52. Przybył, A., Er, M.J.: The idea for the integration of neuro-fuzzy hardware emulators with real-time network. In: Rutkowski, L., Korytkowski, M., Scherer, R., Tadeusiewicz, R., Zadeh, L.A., Zurada, J.M. (eds.) ICAISC 2014, Part I. LNCS (LNAI), vol. 8467, pp. 279–294. Springer, Heidelberg (2014)
53. Przybył, A., Jelonkiewicz, J.: Genetic algorithm for observer parameters tuning in sensorless induction motor drive. In: Neural Networks and Soft Computing, pp. 376–381 (2003)
54. Przybył, A., Smoląg, J., Kimla, P.: Distributed control system based on real time ethernet for computer numerical controlled machine tool (in Polish). Przegląd Elektrotechniczny 86(2), 342–346 (2010)
55. Rutkowski, L.: Sequential estimates of probability densities by orthogonal series and their application in pattern-classification. IEEE Trans. Systems Man and Cybernetics 10(12), 918–920 (1980)
56. Rutkowski, L.: Sequential pattern-recognition procedures derived from multiple Fourier-series. Pattern Recognition Letters 8(4), 213–216 (1988)
57. Rutkowski, L.: Application of multiple Fourier-series to identification of multivariable non-stationary systems. Int. Journal of Systems Science 20(10), 1993–2002 (1989)
58. Rutkowski, L.: Identification of miso nonlinear regressions in the presence of a wide class of disturbances. IEEE Trans. Information Theory 37(1), 214–216 (1991)
59. Rutkowski, L.: Computational intelligence. Springer (2008)
60. Rutkowski, L., Cpałka, K.: Flexible structures of neuro-fuzzy systems. In: Sincak, P., Vascak, J. (eds.) Quo Vadis Computational Intelligence. STUDFUZZ, vol. 54, pp. 479–484. Springer, Heidelberg (2000)
61. Rutkowski, L., Cpałka, K.: Compromise approach to neuro-fuzzy systems. In: Sincak, J., Vascak, V., Kvasnicka, J. (eds.) Intelligent Technologies - Theory and Applications, vol. 76, pp. 85–90. IOS Press (2002)
62. Rutkowski, L., Cpałka, K.: Flexible neuro-fuzzy systems. IEEE Trans. on Neural Networks 14, 554–574 (2003)
63. Rutkowski, L., Cpałka, K.: Designing and learning of adjustable quasi triangular norms with applications to neuro-fuzzy systems. IEEE Trans. on Fuzzy Systems 13, 140–151 (2005)
64. Rutkowski, L., Jaworski, M., Pietruczuk, L., Duda, P.: Decision Trees for Mining Data Streams Based on the Gaussian Approximation. IEEE Transactions on Knowledge and Data Engineering 26, 108–119 (2014)
65. Rutkowski, L., Jaworski, M., Pietruczuk, L., Duda, P.: The CART decision tree for mining data streams. Information Sciences 266, 1–15 (2014)
66. Rutkowski, L., Przybył, A., Cpałka, K., Er, M.J.: Online speed profile generation for industrial machine tool based on neuro-fuzzy approach. In: Rutkowski, L., Scherer, R., Tadeusiewicz, R., Zadeh, L.A., Zurada, J.M. (eds.) ICAISC 2010, Part II. LNCS (LNAI), vol. 6114, pp. 645–650. Springer, Heidelberg (2010)
67. Rutkowski, L., Przybył, A., Cpałka, K.: Novel Online Speed Profile Generation for Industrial Machine Tool Based on Flexible Neuro-Fuzzy Approximation. IEEE Trans. on Industrial Electronics 59, 1238–1247 (2012)

68. Starczewski, J.T., Bartczuk, Ł., Dziwiński, P., Marvuglia, A.: Learning methods for type-2 FLS based on FCM. In: Rutkowski, L., Scherer, R., Tadeusiewicz, R., Zadeh, L.A., Zurada, J.M. (eds.) ICAISC 2010, Part I. LNCS (LNAI), vol. 6113, pp. 224–231. Springer, Heidelberg (2010)
69. Szarek, A., Korytkowski, M., Rutkowski, L., Scherer, R., Szyprowski, J.: Application of neural networks in assessing changes around implant after total hip arthroplasty. In: Rutkowski, L., Korytkowski, M., Scherer, R., Tadeusiewicz, R., Zadeh, L.A., Zurada, J.M. (eds.) ICAISC 2012, Part II. LNCS, vol. 7268, pp. 335–340. Springer, Heidelberg (2012)
70. Szarek, A., Korytkowski, M., Rutkowski, L., Scherer, R., Szyprowski, J.: Forecasting wear of head and acetabulum in hip joint implant. In: Rutkowski, L., Korytkowski, M., Scherer, R., Tadeusiewicz, R., Zadeh, L.A., Zurada, J.M. (eds.) ICAISC 2012, Part II. LNCS, vol. 7268, pp. 341–346. Springer, Heidelberg (2012)
71. Szczypta, J., Przybył, A., Cpałka, K.: Some aspects of evolutionary designing optimal controllers. In: Rutkowski, L., Korytkowski, M., Scherer, R., Tadeusiewicz, R., Zadeh, L.A., Zurada, J.M. (eds.) ICAISC 2013, Part II. LNCS, vol. 7895, pp. 91–100. Springer, Heidelberg (2013)
72. Szczypta, J., Przybył, A., Wang, L.: Evolutionary approach with multiple quality criteria for controller design. In: Rutkowski, L., Korytkowski, M., Scherer, R., Tadeusiewicz, R., Zadeh, L.A., Zurada, J.M. (eds.) ICAISC 2014, Part I. LNCS, vol. 8467, pp. 455–467. Springer, Heidelberg (2014)
73. Tadeusiewicz, R., Chaki, R., Chaki, N.: Exploring Neural Networks with C#. CRC Press, Taylor & Francis Group, Boca Raton (2014)
74. Yeung, D.-Y., Chang, H., Xiong, Y., George, S.E., Kashi, R.S., Matsumoto, T., Rigoll, G.: SVC2004: First International Signature Verification Competition. In: Zhang, D., Jain, A.K. (eds.) ICBA 2004. LNCS, vol. 3072, pp. 16–22. Springer, Heidelberg (2004)
75. Zalasiński, M., Łapa, K., Cpałka, K.: New Algorithm for Evolutionary Selection of the Dynamic Signature Global Features. In: Rutkowski, L., Korytkowski, M., Scherer, R., Tadeusiewicz, R., Zadeh, L.A., Zurada, J.M. (eds.) ICAISC 2013, Part II. LNCS (LNAI), vol. 7895, pp. 113–121. Springer, Heidelberg (2013)
76. Zalasiński, M., Cpałka, K.: A new method of on-line signature verification using a flexible fuzzy one-class classifier, pp. 38–53. Academic Publishing House EXIT (2011)
77. Zalasiński, M., Cpałka, K.: Novel algorithm for the on-line signature verification. In: Rutkowski, L., Korytkowski, M., Scherer, R., Tadeusiewicz, R., Zadeh, L.A., Zurada, J.M. (eds.) ICAISC 2012, Part II. LNCS, vol. 7268, pp. 362–367. Springer, Heidelberg (2012)
78. Zalasiński, M., Cpałka, K.: New Approach for the On-Line Signature Verification Based on Method of Horizontal Partitioning. In: Rutkowski, L., Korytkowski, M., Scherer, R., Tadeusiewicz, R., Zadeh, L.A., Zurada, J.M. (eds.) ICAISC 2013, Part II. LNCS (LNAI), vol. 7895, pp. 342–350. Springer, Heidelberg (2013)
79. Zalasiński, M., Cpałka, K., Hayashi, Y.: New method for dynamic signature verification based on global features. In: Rutkowski, L., Korytkowski, M., Scherer, R., Tadeusiewicz, R., Zadeh, L.A., Zurada, J.M. (eds.) ICAISC 2014, Part II. LNCS (LNAI), vol. 8468, pp. 231–245. Springer, Heidelberg (2014)

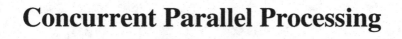
# Concurrent Parallel Processing

# Parallelization of a Block Cipher Based on Chaotic Neural Networks

Dariusz Burak[✉]

Faculty of Computer Science and Information Technology,
West Pomeranian University of Technology, 49 Żołnierska St.,
71-210 Szczecin, Poland
dburak@wi.zut.edu.pl

**Abstract.** In this paper the results of parallelizing a block cipher based on chaotic neural networks are presented. A data dependence analysis of loops is applied in order to parallelize the algorithm. The parallelism of the algorithm is demonstrated in accordance with the OpenMP standard. As a result of this study, it is stated that the most time-consuming loops of the algorithm are suitable for parallelization. The efficiency measurements of a parallel algorithm working in standard modes of operation are shown.

**Keywords:** Neural network · Chaos · Encryption algorithm · Parallelization · OpenMP

## 1 Introduction

One of the very important functional features of cryptographic algorithms is cipher speed. This feature is significant in case of block ciphers since they usually work on large data sets. Thus even not much differences of speed may cause the choice of the faster cipher by the user. Therefore, it is all-important to parallelize encryption algorithms in order to achieve faster processing using multi-core processors or multiprocessing systems. In recent years many chaos-based ciphers were proposed. Futhermore neural networks are often introduced to design encryption algorithms considering the complicated and time-varying nature of the structures. Chaotic neural networks (CNNs) are particulary suitable for data protection. Nowadays, there are many descriptions of various ciphers based on chaotic neural networks, for instance [1–10]. The critical issue in such ciphers is program implementation.

Unlike parallel implementations of classical block ciphers, for instance AES [11], IDEA [12], there are only a few parallel implementations of block ciphers based on chaotic neural networks, for example [13]. Being seemingly a research gap it is absolutely fundamental to show real functional advantages and disadvantages of the encryption algorithm using software or hardware implementation.

The main contribution of the study is developing a parallel algorithm in accordance with OpenMP standard of the cipher designed by Lian and presented in [8] based on transformations of a source code written in the C language representing the sequential algorithm.

© Springer International Publishing Switzerland 2015
L. Rutkowski et al. (Eds.): ICAISC 2015, Part II, LNAI 9120, pp. 191–201, 2015.
DOI: 10.1007/978-3-319-19369-4_18

This paper is organized as follows. The next section describes the block cipher based on chaotic neural networks. In Section 3, parallelization process is fully characterized. In Section 4, the experimental results obtained for developed parallel algorithm are presented. Finally, concluding remarks are given in Section 5.

## 2    Description of the Block Cipher Based on Chaotic Neural Networks

The block cipher based on chaotic neural networks [8] is composed of diffusion process and confusion process. The diffusion process is implemented by a chaotic neuron layer, and the confusion process is implemented by a linear neuron layer. Both of them are repeated for $t$ times to improve the encryption strength.

The encryption process is composed of a chaotic neuron layer and a linear neuron layer, and is described as:

$$\begin{cases} C_i = g(W_{ci}M_i + B_{ci}) = g(W_{ci}f(W_{di}P_i + B_{di}, A_i)) \\ P_i = C_{i-1} \end{cases}, \qquad (1)$$

where:

$P_i$, $K_i$ and $C_i$ are the $t$-th plaintext, key and ciphertext in the $i$-th iteration, respectively.

$W_{di}$, $B_{di}$, $f$ and $A_i$ are the chaotic neuron layer's weight, bias, transfer function and chaotic parameter, respectively.

$W_{ci}$, $B_{ci}$ and $g$ are the linear neuron layer's weight, bias and transfer function, respectively.

The chaotic neuron layer is defined as:

$$M_i = f(W_{di}P_i + B_{di}, A_i))$$

$$= f\left(\begin{bmatrix} w_{0,0}^{di} & w_{0,1}^{di} & \cdots & w_{0,n-1}^{di} \\ w_{1,0}^{di} & w_{0,1}^{di} & \cdots & w_{1,n-1}^{di} \\ \vdots & \vdots & \ddots & \vdots \\ w_{n-1,0}^{di} & w_{n-1,1}^{di} & \cdots & w_{n-1,n-1}^{di} \end{bmatrix} \begin{bmatrix} p_{i,0} \\ p_{i,1} \\ \vdots \\ p_{i,n-1} \end{bmatrix} + \begin{bmatrix} b_{i,0}^d \\ b_{i,1}^d \\ \vdots \\ b_{i,n-1}^d \end{bmatrix}, A_i\right), \qquad (2)$$

$$= f\left(\begin{bmatrix} m'_{i,0} \\ m'_{i,1} \\ \vdots \\ m'_{i,n-1} \end{bmatrix}, A_i\right) = \begin{bmatrix} f_{Tent}^z(a_{i,0}, m'_{i,0}) \\ f_{Tent}^z(a_{i,1}, m'_{i,1}) \\ \vdots \\ f_{Tent}^z(a_{i,n-1}, m'_{i,n-1}) \end{bmatrix} = \begin{bmatrix} m_{i,0} \\ m_{i,1} \\ \vdots \\ m_{i,n-1} \end{bmatrix}$$

where:

$P_i = [p_{i,0}, p_{i,1}, ..., p_{i,n-1}]^T \, (i = 0, 1, ..., t - 1)$ is the plaintext, $0 \le p_{i,j} < S$ ($S$ is a positive integer, and $j = 0, 1, ..., n - 1$), $n$ is the plaintext's length, $W_{di}$ and $B_{di} = [b_{i,0}, b_{i,1}, ..., b_{i,n-1}]^T \, (0 \le b_{i,j} < S, \, j = 0, 1, ..., n - 1)$ are the weight and bias of the neuron layer, $f$ is an reversible chaotic dynamic function, and

$A_i = [a_{i,0}, a_{i,1}, ..., a_{i,n-1}]$ $(1 \leq a_{i,j} \leq S, j = 0, 1, ..., n-1)$ is the control parameter of the chaotic map $f$. The $f$ function is composed of $z$ ($z \geq 10$) times of iteration of discrete tent map [14].

The discrete tent map is described as:

$$f_{Tent}(a, x) = \begin{cases} \left\lceil \dfrac{S}{a} x \right\rceil, 1 \leq x \leq a \\ \left\lfloor \dfrac{S}{S-a}(S-x) \right\rfloor + 1, a < x \leq S \end{cases} , \qquad (3)$$

where:

$a$ ($a \in [1, S]$ is an integer determined by user key $K$, and $\lceil x \rceil$ and $\lfloor x \rfloor$ denote ceiling and floor of $x$, respectively.

The linear neuron layer is defined as:

$$
\begin{aligned}
C_i &= g(W_{ci}M_i + B_{ci}) \\
&= g\left( \begin{bmatrix} w_{0,0}^{ci} & w_{0,1}^{ci} & \cdots & w_{0,n-1}^{ci} \\ w_{1,0}^{ci} & w_{0,1}^{ci} & \cdots & w_{1,n-1}^{ci} \\ \vdots & \vdots & \ddots & \vdots \\ w_{n-1,0}^{ci} & w_{n-1,1}^{ci} & \cdots & w_{n-1,n-1}^{ci} \end{bmatrix} \begin{bmatrix} m_{i,0} \\ m_{i,1} \\ \vdots \\ m_{i,n-1} \end{bmatrix} + \begin{bmatrix} b_{i,0}^{c} \\ b_{i,1}^{c} \\ \vdots \\ b_{i,n-1}^{c} \end{bmatrix} \right), \\
&= \begin{bmatrix} c_{i,0} \\ c_{i,1} \\ \vdots \\ c_{i,n-1} \end{bmatrix}
\end{aligned}
\qquad (4)
$$

where:

$B_{ci} = [0, 0, ..., 0]^T$, $g(x) = x$ and $W_{ci}$ satisfies:

$$W_{ci} = \begin{bmatrix} 0 & 1 & 0 & \cdots \\ 0 & \cdots & 1 & 1 \\ \vdots & \ddots & \ddots & \vdots \\ 1 & 0 & \cdots & 0 \end{bmatrix}. \qquad (5)$$

The decryption process is symmetric to encryption one, and is described as:

$$\begin{cases} P_i = W_{di}^{-1}(f^{-1}(M_i, A_i) - B_{di}) \\ P_i = W_{di}^{-1}(f^{-1}(W_{ci}^{-1}(g^{-1}(C_i) - B_{ci}), A_i) - B_{di}) \\ C_i = P_{i-1} \end{cases} , \qquad (6)$$

where:

$C_0 = P_{-1} = C$, $P = P_t$, $W_{di}^{-1}$ is the inverse matrix of $W_{di}$, $W_{ci}^{-1}$ is the inverse matrix of $W_{ci}$, $f^{-1}$ is the inverse function of $f$, $g^{-1}$ is the inverse function of $g$ and the other parameters are similar to the ones defined in encryption process.

The linear neuron layer is defined as:

$$M_i = W_{ci}^{-1}(g^{-1}(C_i) - B_{ci})$$

$$= \begin{bmatrix} w_{0,0}^{ci} & w_{0,1}^{ci} & \cdots & w_{0,n-1}^{ci} \\ w_{1,0}^{ci} & w_{0,1}^{ci} & \cdots & w_{1,n-1}^{ci} \\ \vdots & \vdots & \ddots & \vdots \\ w_{n-1,0}^{ci} & w_{n-1,1}^{ci} & \cdots & w_{n-1,n-1}^{ci} \end{bmatrix}^{-1} \left( \begin{bmatrix} g^{-1}(c_{i,0}) \\ g^{-1}(c_{i,1}) \\ \vdots \\ g^{-1}(c_{i,n-1}) \end{bmatrix} - \begin{bmatrix} b_{i,0}^{c} \\ b_{i,1}^{c} \\ \vdots \\ b_{i,n-1}^{c} \end{bmatrix} \right). \quad (7)$$

$$= \begin{bmatrix} m_{i,0} \\ m_{i,1} \\ \vdots \\ m_{i,n-1} \end{bmatrix}$$

The chaotic neuron layer is defined as:

$$P_i = W_{di}^{-1}(f^{-1}(M_i, A_i) - B_{di})$$

$$= \begin{bmatrix} w_{0,0}^{di} & w_{0,1}^{di} & \cdots & w_{0,n-1}^{di} \\ w_{1,0}^{di} & w_{0,1}^{di} & \cdots & w_{1,n-1}^{di} \\ \vdots & \vdots & \ddots & \vdots \\ w_{n-1,0}^{di} & w_{n-1,1}^{di} & \cdots & w_{n-1,n-1}^{di} \end{bmatrix}^{-1}$$

$$\times \left( \begin{bmatrix} f_{Tent}^{-z}(a_{i,0}, m_{i,0}) \\ f_{Tent}^{-z}(a_{i,1}, m_{i,1}) \\ \vdots \\ f_{Tent}^{-z}(a_{i,n-1}, m_{i,n-1}) \end{bmatrix} - \begin{bmatrix} b_{i,0}^{d} \\ b_{i,1}^{d} \\ \vdots \\ b_{i,n-1}^{d} \end{bmatrix} \right), \quad (8)$$

$$= \begin{bmatrix} m_{i,0} \\ m_{i,1} \\ \vdots \\ m_{i,n-1} \end{bmatrix}$$

where: $z$ is the iteration time, $f_{Tent}^{-1}(a, y)$ is composed of $z$ times of inverse tent map [14] defined as:

$$f_{Tent}^{-1}(a, y) = \begin{cases} \lfloor ay/S \rfloor, & \lfloor ay/S \rfloor - \lceil ay/S \rceil + 1 = 0, \\ & \dfrac{\lfloor ay/S \rfloor}{a} > \dfrac{-\lceil (a/S - 1)y \rceil}{S - a}, \\ \lceil (a/S - 1)y + S \rceil, & \lfloor ay/S \rfloor - \lceil ay/S \rceil + 1 = 0, \\ & \dfrac{\lfloor ay/S \rfloor}{a} \leq \dfrac{-\lceil (a/S - 1)y \rceil}{S - a}, \\ \lfloor ay/S \rfloor, & \lfloor ay/S \rfloor - \lceil ay/S \rceil = 0. \end{cases} \quad (9)$$

The neuron layers parameters ($W_{di}$, $B_{di}$, $A_i$ and $W_{ci}$) are generated under the control of symmetric key $K$ and $t \geq 10$. All the encryption parameters can be initialized by $4n$ pseudo-random numbers.

More detailed description of cipher designed by Lian is given in [8].

# 3   Parallelization Process of Encryption Algorithm

Given the fact that proposed algorithm can work in block manner it is necessary to prepare a C source code representing the sequential encryption algorithm working in Electronic Codebook (ECB), Cipher Block Chaining (CBC), Cipher Feedback (CFB), Output Feedback (OFB) and Counter (CTR) modes of operation. The source code of the encryption algorithm in the essential ECB mode contains twenty four *for* loops. Sixteen of them include no I/O functions. Some of these loops are time-consuming. Thus their parallelization is critical for reducing the total time of the parallel algorithm execution.

In order to find dependencies in program a research tool for analyzing array data dependencies called Petit was applied. Petit was developed at the University of Maryland under the Omega Project and is freely available for both DOS and UNIX systems [15].

The OpenMP standard was used to present parallelized loops. The OpenMP Application Program Interface (API) [16, 17] supports multi-platform shared memory parallel programming in C/C++ and Fortran on all architectures including Unix and Windows platforms. OpenMP is a collection of compiler directives, library routines and environment variables which could be used to specify shared memory parallelism. OpenMP directives extend a sequential programming language with Single Program Multiple Data (SPMD) constructs, work-sharing constructs, synchronization constructs and help to operate on both shared data and private data. An OpenMP program begins execution as a single task (called a master thread). When a parallel construct is encountered, the master thread creates a team of threads. The statements within the parallel construct are executed in parallel by each thread in a team. At the end of the parallel construct, the threads of the team are synchronized. Then only the master thread continues execution until the next parallel construct will be encountered. To build a valid parallel code, it is necessary to preserve all dependencies, data conflicts and requirements regarding parallelism of a program [16, 17].

The process of the encryption algorithm parallelization can be divided into the following stages:

- carrying out the dependence analysis of a sequential source code in order to detect parallelizable loops;
- selecting parallelization methods based on source code transformations;
- constructing parallel forms of program loops in accordance with the OpenMP standard.

There are the following basic types of the data dependencies that occur in *for* loops: a Data Flow Dependence, a Data Anti-dependence and an Output Dependence [18, 19]. Additionally, control dependence determines the ordering of an instruction $i$, with respect to a branch instruction so that instruction $i$ is executed in a correct program order.

To find the most time-consuming loops of the algorithm, experiments were carried out for an about 9 megabytes input file.

It appeared that the algorithm has two computational bottlenecks: the first is enclosed in the function lian_enc() and the second is enclosed in the function lian_dec(). The lian_enc() function enables enciphering of the whichever number of data blocks and the lian_dec() one does the same for deciphering process (analogically to similar functions of the classic block ciphers like DES- the des_enc(), the des_dec(), LOKI91- the loki_enc(), the loki_dec or IDEA- the idea_enc(), the idea_dec() presented in [20]). Thus the parallelization of *for* loops included in these functions has a unique meaning.

The bodies of the lian_enc() and the lian_dec() functions are as follows:

```
void lian_enc(lian_context *ctx,UINT8 *input,UINT8 *output,
              int input_length){
   for (int i = 0; i<NBLOCKS; i++) {
       Encryption(ctx, input, output);
       input+= BLOCKSIZE;
       output+= BLOCKSIZE;
   }
}.
```

```
void lian_dec(lian_context *ctx,UINT8 *input,UINT8 *output,
              int input_length){
   for (int i = 0; i<NBLOCKS; i++) {
       Decryption(ctx, input, output);
       input+= BLOCKSIZE;
       output+= BLOCKSIZE;
   }
}.
```

Taking into account the strong similarity of the above functions only the first one is examined. Subsequently this analysis is valid in the case of the second one.

In order to apply the data dependencies analysis of the loop included in lian_enc() function the body of the Encryption() function should be put in this loop.

Definitions of the tentMap(), multiplyTables(), addTables() and linearMap() functions included in the body of the Encryption() function are the following:

```
void tentMap(double param,double initial,int iter) {
for (int z = 0; z < NITERATIONS; z++) {
    for (int i=0;i<iter;i++) {
        if ((initial>=0) && (initial<param))
                initial=initial/param;
        else
                initial=((1-initial)/(1-param));
        }
    }
}.
```

```
void multiplyTables(double* multiplier,double* result,
                    int maxNumber) {
for (int i = 0; i < MAXLENGTH; i++) {
    if (multiplier[i] * result[i] > maxNumber)
        result[i] = (multiplier[i] * result[i]) %
                    (maxNumber + 1);
    else
        result[i] = multiplier[i] * result[i];
    }
}.

void addTables(double* result,double* addedTable,int maxNumber) {
for (int i = 0; i < MAXLENGTH; i++) {
    if (addedTable[i] + result[i] > maxNumber)
        result[i] = (addedTable[i] + result[i]) %
                    (maxNumber + 1) + 1;
    else
        result[i] = addedTable[i] + result[i];
    }
}.

void linearMap(double x,double y) {
    y = x
}.
```

The actual parallelization process of the loop included in the lian_enc() function consists of the six following stages:

- separation of the Parameter Generation from the Chaotic Neuron Layer and from the Linear Neuron Layer; all calculations placed in Parameter Generation have to be executed before starting the processing for the two next layers;
- removal of multiplications from Chaotic Neuron Layer and from the Linear Neuron Layer; multiplications have to be calculated immediately after all calculations placed in Parameter Generation are completed;
- insertion in the beginning of the loop body the following statements:
  plaintext = &input[BLOCKSIZE*i];
  ciphertext=&output[BLOCKSIZE*i];
- removal from the end of the loop body the following statements:
  input+= BLOCKSIZE;
  output+= BLOCKSIZE;
- suitable variables privatization (i, ii, plaintext, ciphertext, z, wdi, bdi, ai, wci, bci, x) using OpenMP (based on the results of data dependence analysis) for the loop indexing by i;
- adding appropriate OpenMP directive and clauses (#pragma omp parallel for private() shared()) for the loop indexing by i.

The steps above result in the following parallel form of the loop include in the lian_enc() function in accordance with the OpenMP standard:

```
#pragma omp parallel private (i,ii,plaintext,ciphertext,z,wdi,bdi,
                              ai,wci,bci,x)
#pragma omp for
for (i=0; i<nblocks; i++) {
    plaintext=&input[BLOCKSIZE*i];
    ciphertext = &output[BLOCKSIZE*i];
    for(ii=0; ii<t; ii++) {
        addTables(ciphertext,bdi,S);
        tentMap(ciphertext,ai,S);
        addTables(ciphertext,bci,S);
        linearMap(x,ciphertext);
    }
}.
```

## 4  Experimental Results

In order to study the efficiency of the presented encryption algorithm eight Quad-Core Intel Xeon Processors 7310 Series - 1.60 GHz and the Intel C++ Compiler (version 13.1.1 20130313 that supports the OpenMP 4.0) were used. The results received for an about 9 megabytes input file (8 bit per pixel image) using two, four, eight, sixteen and thirty-two cores versus the only one have been shown in Table 1 and Table 2. The number of threads is equal to the number of processors.

The total running time of the presented encryption algorithm consists of the following operations: data receiving from an input file, data encryption,data decryption and data writing to an output file.

Thus the total speed-up of the parallel encryption algorithm depends heavily on the following seven factors:

- the degree of parallelization of the loop included in the lian_enc() function;
- the degree of parallelization of the loop included in the lian_dec() function;
- the method of reading data from an input file;
- the method of writing data to an output file;
- the block size of encryption algorithm;
- the number of iterations of discrete tent map;
- the number of iterations of inverse tent map.

The results confirm that the loops included both the lian_enc() and the lian_dec() functions are parallelizable with high speed-up (see Table 1).

The block method of reading data from an input file and writing data to an output file was used. The following C language functions and block sizes was applied: fread(), 2048-bytes blocks for data reading and fwrite(), 256-bytes blocks for data writing.

**Table 1.** Speed-up of the parallel Lian encryption algorithm in the ECB mode of operation

| Number of threads | Speed-up of the encryption process | Speed-up of the decryption process | Speed-up of the whole algorithm |
|---|---|---|---|
| 1 | 1.00 | 1.00 | 1.00 |
| 2 | 1.92 | 1.99 | 1.44 |
| 4 | 3.75 | 3.92 | 1.90 |
| 8 | 6.01 | 6.28 | 2.26 |
| 16 | 6.18 | 6.35 | 2.45 |
| 32 | 5.98 | 6.07 | 2.20 |

**Table 2.** Speed-ups of the parallel Lian encryption algorithms in the CTR, CBC and CFB mode of operation

| Number of threads | Operation | Speed-up of the CTR mode of operation | Speed-up of the CBC mode of operation | Speed-up of the CFB mode of operation |
|---|---|---|---|---|
| 1 | Encryption | 1.00 | 1.00 | 1.00 |
| 1 | Decryption | 1.00 | 1.00 | 1.00 |
| 2 | Encryption | 1.90 | 1.00 | 1.00 |
| 2 | Decryption | 1.95 | 1.95 | 1.95 |
| 4 | Encryption | 3.50 | 1.00 | 1.00 |
| 4 | Decryption | 3.70 | 3.70 | 3.70 |
| 8 | Encryption | 5.90 | 1.00 | 1.00 |
| 8 | Decryption | 6.20 | 6.20 | 6.20 |
| 16 | Encryption | 6.10 | 1.00 | 1.00 |
| 16 | Decryption | 6.30 | 6.30 | 6.30 |
| 32 | Encryption | 5.90 | 1.00 | 1.00 |
| 32 | Decryption | 6.00 | 6.00 | 6.00 |

During experiments the block size of encryption algorithm equal to 16 bytes was chosen. Additional tests showed that this size of block gives a good result for encryption/decryption speed.

To minimize time of encryption/decryption process the number of iterations of discrete tent map and inverse tent map was limited to 10.

In accordance with Amdahl's Law the maximum speed-up of the encryption algorithm is limited to 4.817, because the fraction of the code that cannot be parallelized is 0.2076.

The encryption algorithm was also parallelized in the following standard modes of operation (CTR, CBC and CFB). The results are presented in Table 2.

When the encryption algorithm operates in the ECB and CTR modes of operation, both the encryption and decryption processes are parallelizable and speed-ups of the whole algorithm are similar (see details- Table 2). For the

CBC and CFB modes only the decryption process is parallelized so the values of speed-up are lower than for the ECB and CTR modes of operation (see Table 2).

## 5    Conclusions

In this paper, the parallelization process of the Lian designed encryption algorithm has been shown. The time-consuming $for$ loops included in the functions responsible for the encryption and decryption processes are parallelizable. The experiments have shown that the application of the parallel encryption algorithm for multiprocessor and multi-core computers would considerably boost the time of the data encryption and decryption. The speed-ups received for these operations can be admitted as satisfactory. Moreover, the developed parallel encryption algorithm can be also helpful for hardware implementations

## References

1. Guo, D., Cheng, L., Cheng, L.: A New Symmetric Probabilistic Encryption Scheme based on chaotic attractors of neural networks. Applied Intelligence 10(1), 71–84 (1999)
2. Chan, C., Cheng, L.: The Convergence Properties of a Clipped Hopfield Network and its Application in the Design of Keystream Generator. IEEE Transactions on Neural Networks 12(2), 340–348 (2001)
3. Rachel, M., Einat, K., Wolfgang, K.: Public Channel Cryptography by Synchronization of Neural Networks and Chaotic Maps. Physical Review Letters 91(11), 118701/1–118701/4 (2003)
4. Karras, D., Zorkadis, V.: On Neural Network Techniques in the Secure Management of Communication Systems through Improving and Quality Assessing Pseudorandom stream Generators. Neural Netwtworks 16(5-6), 899–905 (2003)
5. Lian, S., Chen, G., Cheung, A., Wang, Z.: A Chaotic-Neural-Network-Based Encryption Algorithm for JPEG2000 Encoded Images. In: Yin, F.-L., Wang, J., Guo, C. (eds.) ISNN 2004. LNCS, vol. 3174, pp. 627–632. Springer, Heidelberg (2004)
6. Xiao, D., Liao, X.: A Combined Hash and Encryption Scheme by Chaotic Neural Network. In: Yin, F.-L., Wang, J., Guo, C. (eds.) ISNN 2004. LNCS, vol. 3174, pp. 633–638. Springer, Heidelberg (2004)
7. Yu, W., Cao, J.: Cryptography Based on Delayed Chaotic Neural Networks. Physics Letters A 356(4-5), 333–338 (2006)
8. Lian, S.: A Block Bipher Based on Chaotic Neural Networks. Neurocomputing 72, 1296–1301 (2009)
9. Lian, S., Chen, X.: Traceable Content Protection Based on Chaos and Neural Networks. Applied Soft Computing 11(7), 4293–4301 (2011)
10. Fadil, T.A., Yaakob, S.N., Ahmad, R.B., Yahya, A.: A Chaotic Neural Network-Based Encryption Algorithm for MPEG-2 Encoded Video Signal. International Journal of Artificial Intelligence and Soft Computing 3(4), 360–371 (2013)
11. Bielecki, W., Burak, D.: Exploiting Loop-Level Parallelism in the AES Algorithm. WSEAS Transactions on Computers 5(1), 125–133 (2006)

12. Beletskyy, V., Burak, D.: Parallelization of the IDEA Algorithm. In: Bubak, M., van Albada, G.D., Sloot, P.M.A., Dongarra, J. (eds.) ICCS 2004. LNCS, vol. 3036, pp. 635–638. Springer, Heidelberg (2004)
13. Burak, D.: Parallelization of Encryption Algorithm Based on Chaos System and Neural Networks. In: Wyrzykowski, R., Dongarra, J., Karczewski, K., Waśniewski, J. (eds.) PPAM 2013, Part II. LNCS, vol. 8385, pp. 364–373. Springer, Heidelberg (2014)
14. Masuda, N., Aihara, K.: Cryptosystems with Discretized Chaotic Maps. IEEE Transactionson Circuits and Systems I: Fundamental Theory and Applications 49(1), 28–40 (2002)
15. Kelly, W., Maslov, V., Pugh, W., Rosser, E., Shpeisman, T., Wonnacott, D.: New User Interface for Petit and Other Extensions. User Guide (1996)
16. Chapman, B., Jost, G., van der Pas, R.: Using OpenMP - Portable Shared Memory Parallel Programming. MIT Press (2007)
17. OpenMP Application Program Interface. Version 4.0 (July 2013)
18. Allen, R., Kennedy, K.: Optimizing compilers for modern architectures: A Dependencebased Approach. Morgan Kaufmann Publishers, Inc. (2001)
19. Aho, A., Lam, M., Sethi, R., Ullman, J.: Compilers: Principles, Techniques, and Tools, 2nd edn. Prentice-Hall (2006)
20. Schneier, B.: Applied Cryptography: Protocols, Algorithms, and Source Code in C, 2nd edn. John Wiley & Sons (1995)

# Acceleration of Neighborhood Evaluation for a Multi-objective Vehicle Routing

Szymon Jagiełło, Jarosław Rudy[✉], and Dominik Żelazny

Institute of Computer Engineering, Control and Robotics,
Wrocław University of Technology,
Janiszewskiego 11-17, 50-372 Wrocław, Poland
{szymon.jagiello,jaroslaw.rudy,dominik.zelazny}@pwr.edu.pl

**Abstract.** In this paper a multi-objective vehicle routing problem (MOVRP) with the criteria being the total distance and the utilization of the vehicle space is considered. Two methods were developed to decrease the execution time of the main part of the algorithm – the neighborhood search procedure. First method, an accelerator, is defined in order to reduce the computational complexity of the algorithm from $O(n^3)$ to $O(n^2)$. The second method utilizes multiple threads of execution to speedup the neighborhood search. Both methods were applied to tabu search metaheuristic and tested against the basic version of the algorithm. In result, we concluded that the enhanced version allows for significant reduction of execution time (2500 times for 5000 clients) that scales well with the number of clients. Moreover, this allows the enhanced algorithm to find significantly better approximations of the Pareto front in the same time as the original algorithm.

**Keywords:** Vehicle routing problem · Acceleration scheme · Multi-objective

## 1   Introduction

The Vehicle routing problem (VRP) has significant applications in both in transport and logistics as efficient methods of optimization allow to improve performance for a wide range of services and production systems. Reducing the time of deliveries, increasing the efficiency of the production or reducing costs are prime examples and can affect the positions of companies on the market.

Over the last years, researchers have studied routing problems with more than one criterion considered, called multi-objective vehicle routing problem (MOVRPs). In the following subsection, some approaches concerning MOVRPs and speeding up of VRP are briefly reviewed.

The swap operation is one of the most basic operations used in local optimization. Computational effort required to check a single new solution obtained by this operation is dependent on the size of the problem. In this paper we describe a method which can be used to check single new solutions in fixed time.

© Springer International Publishing Switzerland 2015
L. Rutkowski et al. (Eds.): ICAISC 2015, Part II, LNAI 9120, pp. 202–213, 2015.
DOI: 10.1007/978-3-319-19369-4_19

## 1.1   Literature Overview

In paper [11], Moura proposed an implementation of Genetic Algorithm (GA) for MOVRP with time windows and loading. Three optimization criteria were considered, namely the number of vehicles, the total travel distance and volume utilization. Results were compared with other heuristic approaches developed by Moura.

Wang *et al.* [12] studied a MOVRP that simultaneously considers the depot desires and clients expectations, which can better expound the real logistics operations than a single objective VRP. Objective function minimizes the total delivering path distance, while maximizing client satisfaction by fulfilling time-window requirements. The study proposed a hybrid algorithm based in GA and some greedy techniques. Moreover, military application was employed in order to confirm practical values of the proposed model and algorithm.

In paper [9], Guerriero *et al.* proposed an approach to unmanned aerial vehicle routing. Authors presented a distributed system of autonomous Unmanned Aerial Vehicles (UAVs) that are able to self-coordinate and cooperate. Considered criteria included the total distances, customer satisfaction and the number of UAVs. Case study was introduced as an application scenario.

Garcia-Najera *et al.* [6] considered solving MOVRP with time windows using evolutionary algorithm. Proposed heuristic incorporated methods for measuring the similarity of solutions and was tested using standard benchmark problems. Analysis showed that the proposed algorithm provided more diverse solutions of higher quality than standard evolutionary algorithm.

In paper [8], Grandinetti *et al.* considered Multi-objective Undirected Capacitated Arc Routing Problem. Objectives included minimizing the total transportation cost, the longest route cost (makespan) and the number of vehicles. An approximation of the optimal Pareto front is determined through an optimization-based heuristic procedure. Performance was tested and analyzed on benchmark instances known from literature.

Baños *et al.* [1] considered Capacited VRP with Time Windows with objectives of minimum distance and workload imbalance. Proposed algorithm combined evolutionary computations and simulated annealing. Authors used benchmark instances known from literature and tests confirmed good performance of proposed hybrid approach.

In paper [7], Ghoseiri *et al.* considered another VRP with Time Windows problem. Authors used goal programming and genetic algorithm. Additionally, aspiration levels and their deviations are specified by decision maker. Considered objectives include number of vehicles and total distance. Algorithm was tested using Solomon's benchmark instances and results show that the approach is effective and provided solutions are competitive with those known from literature.

Concerning speeding up for vehicle routing problems Bożejko *et al.* [2] studied a memetic algorithm for CVRP in parallel computing environment. The study included theoretical analysis using PRAM model and practical research on multi-GPU with the use of CUDA platform.

Żelazny *et al.* proposed another concept of parallel solving DVRP in [10]. Proposed MOTS algorithm was implemented in CUDA architecture and tested using new benchmark instances and outperformed classic MOTS in terms of speed and quality of solutions.

Ant Colony Optimization (ACO) is an example of metaheuristic based on many seperate agents and is thus well-suited for parallel computation. Such parallel ACO approach with the use of GPU for the VRP was proposed by Diego *et al.* [5].

As a final note, readers interested in more information about several methods and approaches to parallel VRP should refer to the review by Crainic [4].

## 2  Problem Description

The problem can be formulated by using the following symbols: $c_{nr}$ (number of clients), $v_{nr}$ (number of vehicles), 0 (the base), $C = \{0, c_1, c_2, ..., c_{c_{nr}}\}$ (sequence that includes all clients and the base), $V = \{v_1, v_2, ..., v_{v_{nr}}\}$ (vehicles sequence), $\Xi = \{\xi_1, \xi_2, ..., \xi_{c_{nr}}\}$ (clients demands sequence), $max_\Xi$ such that $\bigvee_{\xi \in \Xi} max_\Xi \geq d$ (the capacity of a single vehicle), $max_\Theta$ (maximum track cost), $\Theta M \subseteq (c_{nr} + 1) \times (c_{nr} + 1)$ (travel cost matrix between elements form the $C$ sequence).

Let $V_{v_i}$, where $1 \leq v_i \leq v_{nr}$ denote the vehicle with the number $v_i$ and $S_{v_i}$ denote the track of the vehicle $V_{v_i}$. Moreover, let $\Theta[S_{v_i}]$ denote a function returning the cost of traveling the track $S_{v_i}$, $\Xi[S_{v_i}]$ denote a function returning the total clients demands of the track $S_{v_i}$. Let $C_{c_i}$, where $1 \leq c_i \leq c_{nr}$ denote the client with the number $c_i$ and $\Xi[C_{c_i}]$ denote the demand of the client $C_{c_i}$.

The optimal solution of our vehicle routing problem is a sequence of $v_{nr}$ tracks $S^* = \{S_1, ..., S_{v_{nr}}\}$ that minimizes the given cost function $f$:

$$f(S^*) = \min_{s \in S_{feas}} f(s), \tag{1}$$

where $S_{feas}$ is the set of all feasible solutions. A solution is feasible if: each client $C_{c_i} \in C$ is visited exactly once, each track $S_{v_i} \in S$ begins and ends in 0, $\bigvee_{1 \leq v_i \leq v_{nr}} \Theta[S_{v_i}] \leq max_\Theta$ and $\bigvee_{1 \leq v_i \leq v_{nr}} \Xi[S_{v_i}] \leq max_\Xi$. The exact cost function used in our case is mentioned in subsection 2.3.

### 2.1  Representation

The Giant Track Representation (GTR) is a method which provides an easy way for storing solutions inside computer memory and manipulating them. Let $Sg$ be a sequence and $Sg_{v_i} \in Sg$ be the track of vehicle $v_i$ where: $\bigvee_{1 \leq v_i \leq v_{nr}} Sg_{v_i}$ does not contain the 0 signifying the return to the base (it is default) and additionally track $Sg_1$ does not contain the 0 signifying the departure from the base (it is default). Then the sequence $Sg = \{Sg_1, ..., Sg_{v_{nr}}\}$ is called the giant track. For 9 clients (1 to 9) and 3 vehicles the giant track can look as follows:

$$4, 1, 6, 0, 3, 7, 0, 2, 9, 8, 5$$

and represents tracks: $0 \to 4 \to 1 \to 6 \to 0$ , $0 \to 3 \to 7 \to 0$ and $0 \to 2 \to 9 \to 8 \to 5 \to 0$. The number of elements of a GTR equals $|Sg| = c_{nr} + v_{nr} - 1$.

## 2.2 Swap Neighborhood

Let $N$ be a swap neighborhood for GTR solution $Sg$. Checking such neighborhood involves generating all solutions $Sg'$ that can be obtained by switching two elements (from positions $p_1$ and $p_2$) of the solution $Sg$ and calculating the values of the $\Theta[Sg']$, $Max_\Theta[Sg']$, $Min_\Xi[Sg]$ and $Min_\Xi[Sg']$ functions. The size of the neighborhood (the number of possible different $Sg'$ solutions) is:

$$|N| = \frac{|Sg|^2 - |Sg|}{2}. \tag{2}$$

Thus, the computational complexity of generating all $Sg'$ solutions without calculating the function values is $O(n^2)$.

## 2.3 Cost Function

The bi-criteria cost function considers the cost (distance) of visiting all clients:

$$\Theta[Sg] = \sum_{v_i=1}^{v_{nr}} \Theta[Sg_{v_i}] \tag{3}$$

and the maximum wasted space of all vehicles/tracks. It is computed by subtracting the minimum demand of all vehicles $Min_\Xi[Sg]$ from the capacity of a single vehicle:

$$Max_\Delta[Sg] = max_\Xi - Min_\Xi[Sg], \tag{4}$$

$$Min_\Xi[Sg] = \min_{S_{v_i} \in Sg} \Xi[Sg_{v_i}] \tag{5}$$

Now our cost function $f$ is constructed as a normalized sum of both criteria:

$$f[Sg] = \frac{\Theta[Sg]}{\Theta^W} + \frac{Max_\Delta[Sg]}{Max_\Delta^W}, \tag{6}$$

where $\Theta^W$ and $Max_\Delta^W$ are the worst (highest) total track distance and vehicle space waste (utilization) respectively. These values are updated during the course of the optimization algorithm. The algorithm also needs the values of $Max_\Theta[Sg]$ and $Max_\Xi[Sg]$ (the maximum distance and maximum demand of all tracks in $Sg$), in order to test the feasibility of a given solution.

As stated before, we aim to minimize the cost function $f[Sg]$. The computational complexity of a brute-force approach to this kind of DCVRP is $O(n!)$.

# 3   Acceleration

Acceleration is used to speedup the evaluation of solutions $Sg'$ from the swap neighborhood by quickly computing values $\Theta[Sg']$, $Max_\Theta[Sg']$, $Min_\Xi[Sg']$ and $Max_\Xi[Sg']$. The method utilizes additional data and specific properties of the $DCVRP$ problem. It has been designed for parallel computing with the primary focus on minimizing the maximal number of necessary memory operations as memory access takes tens to hundreds times longer than a single processor cycle.

## 3.1   Assumptions and Symbols

Data with size depending on the problem instance are kept as arrays in memory:

- standard DCVRP data: $Sg$, $\Theta M$, $\Xi$,
- support data: $v_A$ (array assigning the positions in the solution to indexes of vehicles), $v_P$ (array assigning vehicle/track indexes to positions in a solution), $p_\Theta$ (array of cumulated costs for the consecutive elements of the sequence $Sg$), $p_\Xi$ (array of cumulated demands for the consecutive members of the sequence $Sg$).

The rest of the data is kept in registers of the processor:

- standard DCVRP data: values of cost functions ($\Theta[Sg]$, $Max_\Theta[Sg]$, $Max_\Xi[Sg]$ and $Min_\Xi[Sg]$), other ($c_{nr}$ and $v_{nr}$),
- standard swap move data: swap positions ($p_1$, $p_2$),
- support data (for accelerator): second, third, and forth biggest cost values (denoted by $Max_{\Theta 2}[Sg]$, $Max_{\Theta 3}[Sg]$, $Max_{\Theta 4}[Sg]$), biggest demand values ($Max_{\Xi 2}[Sg]$, $Max_{\Xi 3}[Sg]$, $Max_{\Xi 4}[Sg]$) and smallest demand values ($Min_{\Xi 2}[Sg]$, $Min_{\Xi 3}[Sg]$, $Min_{\Xi 4}[Sg]$) for a given solution $Sg$.

All temporary variables are also kept in registers.

## 3.2   Basic Operations

The idea of the accelerator relies on several basic operations (some descriptions might seem obvious but they are essential for understanding the algorithm). Here we will describe a few of them in detail, while other cases will be described briefly for the sake of brevity. Before we start, let $P_i$ be the value of element on position $p_i$ in solution $Sg$. Moreover, let $bP_i$ and $aP_i$ be the values of elements on positions $p_i - 1$ and $p_1 + 1$ respectively. The basic operations are as follows:

1. Read the value of one of the following elements: $P_1$, $P_2$, $bP_1$, $bP_2$, $aP_1$ or $aP_2$. The operation reads the value from $Sg$ from the position $p_1$, $p_2$, $p_1 - 1$, $p_2 - 1$, $p_1 + 1$ or $p_2 + 1$. It involves *one* read from memory for each operation but:
   (a) if $p_1 = p_2 - 1$ then $aP_1 = P_2$, $bP_2 = P_1$ so we can save up to *two* reads from memory,

(b) if $p_1 = 0$ then $bP_1$ equals 0 by default so we can save up to *one* read from memory,

(c) if $p_2 = |Sg| - 1$ then $aP_2$ equals 0 by default so we can save up to *one* read from memory.

2. Find the index $v_i$ of the vehicle/track which is handling the $Sg$ element from position $e_i$. The operation reads the value from $v_A$ from the position $e_i$. It involves *one* read from memory.

3. Find the beginning of the $v_i$ track. The operation reads the value from $v_P$ from the position $v_i$. It involves *one* read from memory.

4. Find the beginning of the track which includes the element from the specified position $e_i$. The operation includes execution of operation 2 and 3, which involves *two* reads from memory but:

   (a) if $e_i = p_1$ and $P_1 = 0$ or $P_1! = 0$ and $bP_1 = 0$ then the first track element is placed on position $p_1$ or $bP_1$ respectively so we can save up to *two* reads from memory,

   (b) if $e_i = p_2$ and $P_2 = 0$ or $P_2! = 0$ and $bP_2 = 0$ then the first track element is placed on position $p_2$ or $bP_2$ respectively so we can save up to *two* reads from memory,

   (c) the end of the track $Sg_{v_i-1}$ is also the beginning of the track $Sg_{v_i}$ so if it is known we can save up to *one* read from memory.

5. Find the end of the track which includes the element from the specified position $e_i$. Similarly to operation 4, this operation includes execution of operation 2 and 3 which involves *two* reads from memory. Similar conditions as for operation 4 allows as to save up *one* or *two* reads from memory.

6. Read the travel cost between two clients or the base ($c_1$ and $c_2$). The operation reads the value from $\Theta M$ from the position $[c_1, c_2]$. It involves *one* read from memory. $\Theta M[c_1, c_2]$ denotes this operation.

7. Read the demand of the element $E_i$ from the solution $Sg$. The operation reads the value from $\Xi$ from the position $E_i$. It involves *one* read from memory.

8. Calculate the travel cost between two $Sg$ elements placed on positions $e_1$ and $e_2$. The operation includes calculating the difference of two values from $p_\Theta$ placed on positions $e_2$ and $e_1$ and involves *two* reads from memory but:

   (a) if $e_1 < 0$ then the value from the position $e_1$ is set to 0 by default so we can save up to *one* read from memory,

   (b) if a value from $p_\Theta$ has been read already it is not read again so we can save up to *two* reads from memory,

   (c) if $e_1 >= e_2$ then the travel cost is set to 0 so we can save up to *two* reads from memory,

   (d) if $e_1 = e_2 - 1$ and $E_1 = 0$ and $E_2 = 0$ then then the travel cost is set to 0 so we can save up to *two* reads from memory.

   $ACC\_Dist[e_1, e_2]$ denotes this operation. Executing with a track as the argument means executing it for the beginning and end of the track .Using standard procedure would require a number of memory reads equal to the length of the track + 1.

9. Calculate the total demand between two $Sg$ elements placed on positions $e_1$ and $e_2$ ($e_1 \leq e_2$). The operation includes calculating the difference of two values from $p_\Xi$ placed on positions $e_2$ and $e_1 - 1$ and involves *two* reads. Similarly to operation 8, four specific cases can be listed that nace save us up to *one* or *two* reads from memory.

   $ACC\_Dem[e_1, e_2]$ denotes this operation. Executing with a track as the argument means executing it for the beginning and end of the track. Using standard procedure would require a number of memory reads equal to the length of the track + 1.

Above operations are based on detailed analysis of the specific properties of the $DCVRP$ problem. All operations might be used for neighborhood checking for the $CVRP$ problem. For the $DVRP$ problem operations 1–6 and 8 will suffice. Thus, all benefits of using the accelerator will be preserved in those subproblems as well.

### 3.3   Initialization Step

The initialization step has to be executed before the neighborhood check of the solution $Sg$ can proceed. It is used to set the values of $v_A$, $v_P$, $p_\Theta$, $p_\Xi$, $\Theta[Sg]$, $Max_\Theta[Sg]$, $Max_{\Theta_2}[Sg]$, $Max_{\Theta_3}[Sg]$, $Max_{\Theta_4}[Sg]$, $Max_\Xi[Sg]$, $Max_{\Xi_2}[Sg]$, $Max_{\Xi_3}[Sg]$, $Max_{\Xi_4}[Sg]$, $Min_\Xi[Sg]$, $Min_{\Xi_2}[Sg]$, $Min_{\Xi_3}[Sg]$ and $Min_{\Xi_4}[Sg]$.

The computational complexity of this step is $O(n)$ for the sequential version as it requires a single passage through all members of the solution. Minimum computational complexity for the parallel version is $O(\log_2 n)$. It is the only part of the accelerator that is dependent on the problem instance size.

### 3.4   New Maximum and Minimum

During a swap move on the $Sg$ soluion up to three tracks can change. This is one of the most important observations used for calculating the values of $Max_\Theta[Sg']$, $Max_\Xi[Sg']$ and $Min_\Xi[Sg']$ for the $Sg'$ solutions. Let $Sg_{v_i}$, $Sg_{v_j}$, $Sg_{v_k}$ be those 3 tracks. The values of $\Theta[Sg'_{v_i}]$, $\Theta[Sg'_{v_j}]$ and $\Theta[Sg'_{v_k}]$ are compared only with four values ($Max_\Theta[Sg]$, $Max_{\Theta_2}[Sg]$, $Max_{\Theta_3}[Sg]$, $Max_{\Theta_4}[Sg]$) which were set during the initialization step. It is required to compare them with $v_{nr}$ values when using the standard method. Similar methods are used to quickly calculate $Max_\Xi[Sg']$ and $Min_\Xi[Sg']$.

### 3.5   Algorithm

In order to test the proposed accelerator we decided to implement a TS algorithm. Our algorithm was based on the implementation proposed in [3]. Some changes to the original algorithm were made.

**Tabu Search.** The algorithm stopped at a local minimum very fast when using the $max_\Theta$ and $max_\Xi$ values from the beginning. This problem was resolved by utilizing the following method:

- let $cMax_\Theta$ denote the current maximum distance and $cMax_\Xi$ the current maximum total demand of a single track. Also let IS denote the initial solution for the tabu search agorithm,
- before the optimization $cMax_\Theta = Max_\Theta[IS]$, $cMax_\Xi = Max_\Xi[IS]$,
- let $TABU[Sg]$ denote a function that returns the best solution obtained after a single tabu iteration executed on the solution $Sg$,
- after each iteration:
    - if $Max_\Theta[TABU[Sg]] > cMax_\Theta$ then $cMax_\Theta = Max_\Theta[TABU[Sg]]$ else if $cMax_\Theta > max_\Theta$ then $cMax_\Theta = cMax_\Theta - (cMax_\Theta - Max_\Theta[TABU[Sg]])/2$,
    - if $Max_\Xi[TABU[Sg]] > cMax_\Xi$ then $cMax_\Xi = Max_\Xi[TABU[Sg]]$ else if $cMax_\Xi > max_\Xi$ then $cMax_\Xi = Max_\Xi - (Max_\Xi - Max_\Xi[TABU[Sg]])/2$,
    - if $cMax_\Theta - max_\Theta \leq 1$ then $cMax_\Theta = max_\Theta$,
    - if $cMax_\Xi - max_\Xi \leq 1$ then $cMax_\Xi = max_\Xi$.

Each iteration the tabu search algorithm chooses the best solution from all possible $Sg'$ solutions from the swap neighborhood of the current solution. If there exits a $Sg'$ solution for which $Max_\Theta[Sg'] \leq cMax_\Theta$ and $Max_\Xi[Sg'] \leq cMax_\Xi$ then the iterations best solution will be the solution with the lowest bi-criteria function value. Otherwise the solution with the lowest $Err[Sg']$ function value will be chosen:

- set the return value to 0 ($ret = 0$),
- if $(Max_\Theta[Sg'] - cMax_\Theta)/cMax_\Theta > 0$ then $ret = Max_\Theta[Sg'] - cMax_\Theta)/cMax_\Theta$,
- if $(cMax_\Xi[Sg'] - cMax_\Xi)/cMax_\Xi > 0$ then $ret = ret + Max_\Xi[Sg'] - cMax_\Xi)/cMax_\Xi$,
- return the $ret$ value.

Choosing the best solution from all iterations is being done the same way.

## 4 Computer Experiment

In order to test the theoretical properties of the proposed speedup methods – both the accelerator and the parallel approach – in practice, we run a series of tests on Intel i7 X980 (6 cores, 12 concurrent threads) machine running Ubuntu (kernel 3.2.0-70-generic). All C/C++ programs were compiled with gcc 4.6.3. The tests were performed by running the tabu search metaheuristic with various neighborhood search methods (standard/accelerated, sequential/parallel) in order to compare them.

In our tests we focused on two aspects: a) the speedup obtained using the developed methods and b) the quality of the obtained solutions. We start with the former.

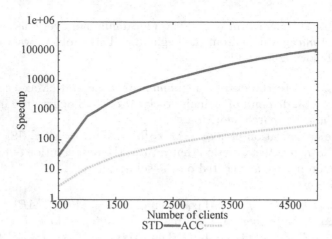

**Fig. 1.** Comparison of standard (STD) and accelarated (ACC) method for different number of clients (12 threads, log scale)

The relation between accelerated and standard version of the algorithm can be observed in Fig. 1. We have used logarithmic scale for clarity. We observe that accelerated version performs from approximately 10 to 350 times faster, depending on the number of clients.

Moreover, Tab. 1 can be consulted for the speedups of both accelerated and standard version when parallelization with multiple threads is used. All numbers were computed by dividing the execution time by the execution time of the sequential version (STD or ACC respectively). We observe that up to 6 threads

**Table 1.** Speedup for standard (STD) and accelerated (ACC) methods with different number of concurrent threads for 5000 clients

| Method | 1 thread | 6 threads | 12 threads |
|--------|----------|-----------|------------|
| STD    | 1        | 5.66      | 6.31       |
| ACC    | 1        | 5.41      | 7.02       |

(number of available physical cores) both algorithms can be sped up rather well, providing speedups of approximately 5.5. Further increase of the number of threads yielded much less increase in speedup (12 virtual cores available), however we can conclude that it is possible to speedup both versions of the method to comparable extent.

As a final test concerning the speedup aspect of our research, we decided to compare the slowest method (standard, only 1 concurrent thread) with the fastest (accelerated, 12 concurrent threads). The results, depending on the number of clients, are shown in Fig. 2. We observe that for as little as 500 clients we get a speedup of nearly 100. For 5 000 clients the speedup increases over 2 500 times compared to the original method. Moreover, the speedup increase is approximately linear in the function of the number of clients. We conclude that the

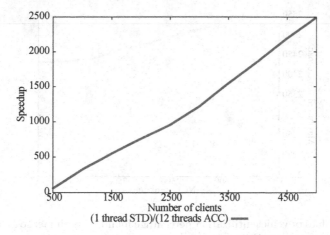

**Fig. 2.** Speedup of accelerated method (running 12 threads) over the standard method (running 1 thread)

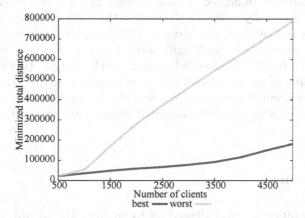

**Fig. 3.** Best values of total distance found by both methods for different number of clients (lesser is better)

improved method offers considerable speedup that scales well with the number of clients.

For the second aspect, the quality of obtained solutions, we simply decided to compare the best values of each criterion for different versions of the algorithm. For the sake of brevity we focused on two versions: "worst" (standard method, 1 thread) and "best" (accelerated method, 12 threads). In both cases the number of iterations of the tabu algorithm was adjusted so both algorithms would run for 1200 seconds. The results are shown in Fig. 3 (total distance, smaller is better) and Fig. 4 (vehicle utilization, greater is better).

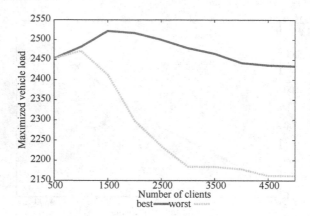

**Fig. 4.** Best values of vehicle utilization percentage found by both methods for different number of clients (greater is better)

It is clear that the improved version yielded much better results on both criteria. This is especially visible in the case of the total distance: the improved version yields even 4 times shorter distance (400% improvement over the original method). In the case of the vehicle utilization the improvement is much smaller, in the range of 5% to 15%. Those results are caused by the fact that the improved method is capable of running hundreds or thousands as many iterations in the same time as the original method, thus being able to check much more solutions. The greater speedup for greater number of clients only serves to amplify this effect.

# 5    Conclusions

Proposed acceleration scheme allowed us to speedup the algorithm up to 400 times over the classic one, independently from the the number of threads. Also, the accelerated version running on 12 threads was nearly 2500 times faster than classic algorithm running on single thread. Moreover, when comparing the quality of solutions, we observed that accelerated algorithm provided solutions with better values of both criteria. Hence, the proposed method allows to find better solutions to multi-criteria at the same time as the classic algorithm. This has a significant impact on solving multi- criteria problems of transport and logistics.

In the future research, an implementation of GPU version will be considered and tested using real-world data and order sets. Furthermore, some properties of multi-criteria problems and solutions evaluation will be considered in algorithm development, in order to further speed-up solving of MOVRPs.

**Acknowledgements.** The work was partially supported by the OPUS grant DEC-2012/05/B/ST7/00102 of Polish National Centre of Science and by the *Młoda Kadra*, grant no. B40129.

# References

1. Baños, R., Ortega, J., Gil, C., Márquez, A.L., de Toro, F.: A hybrid meta-heuristic for multi-objective vehicle routing problems with time windows. Computers & Industrial Engineering (65), 286–296 (2013)
2. Wodecki, M., Bożejko, W., Karpiński, M., Pacut, M.: Multi-GPU parallel memetic algorithm for capacitated Vehicle Routing Problem. In: Wyrzykowski, R., Dongarra, J., Karczewski, K., Waśniewski, J. (eds.) PPAM 2013, Part II. LNCS, vol. 8385, pp. 207–214. Springer, Heidelberg (2014)
3. Bożejko, W., Pempera, J., Smutnicki, C.: Parallel tabu search algorithm for the hybrid flow shop problem. Computers & Industrial Engineering (65), 466–474 (2013)
4. Crainic, T.G.: Parallel Solution Methods for Vehicle Routing Problems, The Vehicle Routing Problem: Latest Advances and New Challenges. Operations Research/Computer Science Interfaces (43), 171–198 (2008)
5. Diego, F.J., Gómez, E.M., Ortega-Mier, M., García-Sánchez, A.: Parallel CUDA Architecture for Solving de VRP with ACO. Industrial Engineering: Innovative Networks, 385–393 (2012)
6. Garcia-Najera, A., Bullinaria, J.A.: An improved multi-objective evolutionary algorithm for the vehicle routing problem with time windows. Computers & Operations Research (38), 287–300 (2011)
7. Ghoseiri, K., Ghannadpour, S.F.: Multi-objective vehicle routing problem with time windows using goal programming and genetic algorithm. Applied Soft Computing (10), 1096–1107 (2010)
8. Grandinetti, L., Guerriero, F., Laganá, D., Pisacane, O.: An optimization-based heuristic for the multi-objective undirected capacitated arc routing problem. Computers & Operations Research (39), 2300–2309 (2012)
9. Guerriero, F., Surace, R., Loscrí, V., Natalizio, E.: A multi-objective approach for unmanned aerial vehicle routing problem with soft time windows constraints. Applied Mathematical Modelling (38), 839–852 (2014)
10. Jagiełło, S., Żelazny, D.: Solving Multi-criteria Vehicle Routing Problem by Parallel Tabu Search on GPU. Procedia Computer Science (18), 2529–2532 (2013)
11. Moura, A.: A Multi-Objective Genetic Algorithm for the Vehicle Routing with Time Windows and Loading Problem. Intelligent Decision Support, 187–201 (2008)
12. Wang, C.-H., Li, C.-H.: Optimization of an established multi-objective delivering problem by an improved hybrid algorithm. Expert Systems with Applications (38), 4361–4367 (2011)

# A Concurrent Inconsistency Reduction Algorithm for the Pairwise Comparisons Method

Konrad Kułakowski[✉], Radosław Juszczyk, and Sebastian Ernst

Department of Applied Computer Science,
AGH University of Science and Technology,
Al. Mickiewicza 30, 30-059 Cracow, Poland
{kkulak,ernst}@agh.edu.pl, veriane16869@gmail.com

**Abstract.** This paper presents a concurrent algorithm for computing a consistent approximation to a generalized pairwise comparisons matrix (i.e. it is assumed that the reciprocity property is not required). Like its sequential counterpart, it is based on the iterative strategy *"find the worst case and fix it"*. The conducted experiments confirmed that a significant increase in speed between the sequential and concurrent approach is achieved. Our results may be particularly important for the large decision support systems where the number of pairs considered is large and the sequential approach may not be fast enough.

**Keywords:** Decision support systems · Pairwise comparisons · AHP · Concurrent algorithms

## 1 Introduction

Evaluating entities in pairs is more natural and easier than trying to arrange them according to certain quantifiable criteria [18]. This is especially apparent in difficult, complicated domains. However, a consistent ranking is usually the desired form of output; thus, the need arises to integrate the partial assessments and assign them easily comparable values. This is the primary goal of the pairwise comparisons *(PC)* method.

Comparing alternatives in pairs is used to solve various practical problems [17]. It is also an inspiring field of research in the field of the social welfare theory [16], fuzzy preference modeling [6], feature based classification of objects [4], public procurements handling [14] or ranking methods [8].

There are several different approaches as to how many different paired comparisons can be synthesized into one consistent result. One of the most popular is the eigenvalue approach proposed by *Saaty* [15]. Other methods include the logarithmic least squares (also called the geometric mean method [2]), the least squares method [5], or the heuristic rating estimation methods [11–13] useful when a ranking of some alternatives (references) is known in advance. A more comprehensive list of pairwise comparison methods can be found in [1, 3].

Another approach to the weight derivation problem is presented in [9]. Instead of explicitly introducing a new algorithm to calculate weights, Koczkodaj et al.

© Springer International Publishing Switzerland 2015
L. Rutkowski et al. (Eds.): ICAISC 2015, Part II, LNAI 9120, pp. 214–222, 2015.
DOI: 10.1007/978-3-319-19369-4_20

focus on inconsistency minimization in such a way that the result matrix is consistent and closest to the original matrix. The overall strategy adopted by Koczkodaj et al. can be summarized as *"find the worst case and fix it"*, since in every iteration of the algorithm, the triad with the highest inconsistency is found first, and then it is replaced by its consistent counterpart [9]. An interesting algorithm for computing a consistent replacement for the most inconsistent triad was proposed by Xu [19].

The presented solution is an attempt to parallelize the algorithm that can be found [9] and developed later in [10, 19]. For the purpose of implementation, Xu's version of the algorithm [19] has been selected. The prototype implementation has been tested using the *Monte Carlo* method, where the random pairwise comparisons *(PC)* matrices have been generated with some (but not too high) levels of inconsistency. Tests carried out were successful and indicated a great potential of the method.

## 2    Basics of the Pairwise Comparisons Method

The input and central point of the *PC* method is a matrix $A$, containing comparison results of pairs of entities:

$$A = [a_{ij}] \tag{1}$$

where $a_{ij} = \lambda_i / \lambda_j$.

Ideally, this matrix should be reciprocal (i.e. $a_{ij} = \frac{1}{a_{ji}}$) since the $i$-to-$j$ evaluation is expected to be the reciprocal of the $j$-to-$i$ evaluation. In addition it should have 1 on its main diagonal as $a_{ii}$ means entity $i$ is being compared with itself. In practice, even this condition is not always guaranteed [9].

Inconsistency of a matrix can be measured according to one of several metrics, including the eigenvector method [15] and *Koczkodaj's* distance-based inconsistency index [7].

The eigenvalue-based inconsistency index of a $n \times n$ matrix $A$ is equal to

$$\mathscr{S}(A) = \frac{\lambda_{max} - n}{n - 1} \tag{2}$$

where $\lambda_{max}$ is the principal eigenvalue of $A$.

Koczkodaj's distance-based inconsistency index $\mathscr{K}$ of a $n \times n$ matrix $A$ (for $n > 2$) is equal to

$$\mathscr{K}(A) = \max \left\{ \min \left\{ \left| 1 - \frac{a_{ij}}{a_{ik}a_{kj}} \right|, \left| 1 - \frac{a_{ik}a_{kj}}{a_{ij}} \right| \right\} \right\} \tag{3}$$

where $i, j, k = 1, \ldots, n$ and $i \neq j \wedge j \neq k \wedge i \neq k$.

Since in an ideally-reciprocal matrix, the equation

$$\forall i, j, k \in \{1, \ldots, n\} : m_{ij} \cdot m_{jk} \cdot m_{ki} = 1 \tag{4}$$

holds, Koczkodaj's index finds the worst triad, i.e. one that's furthest away from the ideal triad and adopts this distance as the inconsistency index of $A$.

The $PC$ method yields a ranking as its result. The ranking function assigns positive real numbers to the objects under evaluation, thus allowing for comparison of any two objects in a consistent way.

# 3    A Sequential Inconsistency Reduction Algorithm

The iterative inconsistency reduction algorithm, as can be found in [9], finds the most questionable triad and makes it consistent in each iteration step. The algorithm exits when the inconsistency index (3) reaches an appropriately low value (in [9], $\mathscr{K}(M)$ is set to $1/3$ for most practical applications as the acceptable threshold of inconsistency). Following $Xu$'s implementation [19], let us assume that $(a_{ik}, a_{kj}, a_{ij})$ is the most inconsistent triad in the $i$-th iteration step. Consistency can be restored by adding to (or subtracting from) the elements of the triad the following three values $\Delta_{ik}$, $\Delta_{kj}$ and $\Delta_{ij}$. Let us consider two possible cases:

Case 1     $a_{ik} * a_{kj} < a_{ij}$ then:

$$(a_{ik} + \Delta_{ik}) * (a_{kj} + \Delta_{kj}) = (a_{ij} - \Delta_{ij}) \qquad (5)$$

Case 2     $a_{ik} * a_{kj} > a_{ij}$ then:

$$(a_{ik} - \Delta_{ik}) * (a_{kj} - \Delta_{kj}) = (a_{ij} + \Delta_{ij}) \qquad (6)$$

where $\Delta_{ik} > 0$, $\Delta_{kj} > 0$ and $\Delta_{ij} > 0$.

To find suitable $\Delta_{ik}$, $\Delta_{kj}$ and $\Delta_{ij}$ $Xu$ [19] proposes to adopt:

$$\Delta_{ik} \overset{df}{=} \frac{a_{ik}c}{a_{ik} + a_{kj} + a_{ij}}, \Delta_{kj} \overset{df}{=} \frac{a_{kj}c}{a_{ik} + a_{kj} + a_{ij}}, \Delta_{ij} \overset{df}{=} \frac{a_{ij}c}{a_{ik} + a_{kj} + a_{ij}} \qquad (7)$$

where $c$ is a constant which can be calculated by combining (5, 6) and (7). Thanks to this, we can get the following equations:

Case 1     $a_{ik} * a_{kj} < a_{ij}$

$$\frac{a_{ik} * a_{kj}}{(a_{ik} + a_{kj} + a_{ij})^2}c^2 + \frac{a_{ij} + 2 * a_{ik} * a_{kj}}{a_{ik} + a_{kj} + a_{ij}}c + a_{ik} * a_{kj} - a_{ij} = 0 \quad (8)$$

Case 2     $a_{ik} * a_{kj} > a_{ij}$

$$\frac{a_{ik} * a_{kj}}{(a_{ik} + a_{kj} + a_{ij})^2}c^2 - \frac{a_{ij} + 2 * a_{ik} * a_{kj}}{a_{ik} + a_{kj} + a_{ij}}c + a_{ik} * a_{kj} - a_{ij} = 0 \quad (9)$$

By solving the above equations, $c$ can be obtained and then all values for $\Delta_{ik}$, $\Delta_{kj}$, $\Delta_{ij}$ can be determined. Since they are quadratic equations, they can have at most two solutions $c_1$ and $c_2$. At this point of processing, the algorithm may take the following three decisions:

1. Immediately go to the next step, ignoring this triad in the future, if both $c_1$ and $c_2$ are negative. In such a case, due to the nature of the problem, there is no solution for this triad.
2. Make the triad consistent using $\max\{c_1, c_2\}$ as $c$, if $\max\{c_1, c_2\} > 0$ and $\min\{c_1, c_2\} \leq 0$.
3. Make the triad consistent using $\min\{c_1, c_2\}$ as $c$, if both $\max\{c_1, c_2\} > 0$ and $\min\{c_1, c_2\} > 0$.

After restoring consistency in the triad $(a_{ik}, a_{kj}, a_{ij})$, iteration is repeated. Proof of convergence of this procedure can be found in [9].

## 4    A Concurrent Inconsistency Reduction Algorithm

Considering the computational complexity of particular parts of the algorithm, what we notice is that the most processor-intensive part is searching for the least consistent triad. For this reason, we focused on optimizing this particular part of the algorithm. Searching through all the triads of the $n \times n$ matrix requires checking all their combinations, which results in a running time of $O\left(n^3\right)$. In contrary, making the triad consistent always requires the same amount of time. The implemented parallel procedure splits the set of triads into $M$ disjoint subsets, then finds (in parallel) the worst triad in every subset and makes that triad consistent.

### 4.1    Dividing the Problem

The division of tasks among threads requires assigning a different starting point $(i_o, j_o, k_o)$ to each thread. To determine the value $i_o$ for the $x$-th consecutive triad, the largest possible $i$ needs to be found, for which the sum $S_i$ of the first $i$ combinations without repetitions[1] $C_{n-1}^2$ is not greater than $x$.

In the next step, the value $j_0$ is determined. For this purpose, the largest $j$ for which the sum $S'_j$ of the first $j$ combinations $C_{N-2}^1$ is not greater than $x - S_{i_0} - 1$ needs to be determined. Then, the assignment $j_0 \leftarrow i_0 + j$ is made. Finally, $k_0$ is determined as $j_0 + X - S_{i_0} - 1 - S'_{j_0} - 1$. The logic for calculating the starting point $(i_o, j_o, k_o)$ has been implemented in $Start.getStart(N, X)$ (Listing 1). The division of the problem has been implemented in the $divideProblem()$ method (Listing 1). The method takes two parameters: $n$ – the size of the $PC$ matrix, and $parts$ – the number of parts (jobs) to be processed concurrently. On its output, the method returns a list of instances of the $Start$ class. Every instance holds the start point $(i_o, j_o, k_o)$ and the variable $iters\_to\_do$ denoting the number of triads to be traversed.

---

[1] It is assumed that $C_n^k \overset{df}{=} \frac{n!}{(n-k)!k!}$.

**Code Listing 1.** Dividing the problem

```
1 class Start
2   method divideProblem(int n, int parts)
3     List starts
4     size ← getSize(n)
5     for i ← 0, i < parts, i ← i + 1 do
6       x ← i * floor(size/parts)
7       start ← Start.getStart(n, x)
8       iters_to_do ← floor((i+1)*size/parts) - start
9       start.iter ← iters_to_do
10      starts. add(start)
11    end method
12    return starts
13  end method
```

## 4.2  Shared Resources

After the tasks are assigned to the appropriate threads, each thread processes its sub-problem. As a result, it determines the most locally inconsistent triad. Although the subsets of triads are disjoint, the entries of the matrix $M$ that form these triads belong to different triads, thus they can be accessed from different threads at the same time. The problem is the situation in which one thread wants to read some entry, while the other wants to modify it (in order to make a triad consistent). Thus, the access to the entries needs to be synchronized. An adequate synchronization mechanisms has been implemented as the *BlockedTriad* class (Listing 2).

**Code Listing 2.** BlockedTriads synchronization mechanism

```
14 class BlockedTriads
15   List blockedPoints
16   method checkAndAdd(Triad triad)
17     synchronized(this)
18       if  blockedPoints.contains(triad. i) ||
19           blockedPoints.contains(triad. j) ||
20           blockedPoints.contains(triad. k) then
21         blockedPoints.add(triad. i)
22         blockedPoints.add(triad. j)
23         blockedPoints.add(triad. k)
24       end if
25     end synchronized
26   end method
27 end class
```

## 4.3  The Worker Algorithm and Class

The overall scheme of the algorithm in shown in (Listing 3). At the very beginning, the problem is divided and a list of problem markers is prepared (Listing 3, Line: 28).

---

**Code Listing 3.** BlockedTriads synchronization mechanism

```
28    Start startList ← divideProblem(no_processing_threads)
29    while (inconsistency is higher than ε)
30      foreach s in startList
31        execute Worker(s)
32      end foreach
33      wait until workers are done
34    end while
```

---

**Code Listing 4.** The Worker class

```
35 class Worker
36    PairwiseComparisonsMatrix matrix
37    int threadIdx
38    BlockedThreads blockedThreads
39    Start start
40    List worsts
41    method run()
42      maxInconsistency←0
43      for i ← 0, i < n, i←i+1 do
44        for j ←(first_j ? j0 : i+1), j < n, j←j+1 do
45          for k ←(first_k ? k0 : j+1, k < n, k←k+1 do
46            first_j←false
47            first_k←false
48            iter←iter + 1
49            inconsistency ←matrix.getInconsistencyOfaTriad(i,j,k)
50            if inconsistency > maxInconsistency do
51              maxInconsistency ← inconsistency
52            end if
53            if iter = iters_to_do do
54              worsts.set(threadIdx, maxInconsistency)
55              if blockedTriads.checkAndAdd( Triad(i,j,k) ) do
56                matrix.consistTriad( Triad(i,j,k) )
57              end if
58              return;
59            end if
60          end for
61        end for
62      end for
63    end method
64 end class
```

Then, iteratively, the workers are executed until the value of the inconsistency index $\mathscr{K}(M)$ drops below a predefined threshold (Listing 3, Lines: 29 - 34). The worker class is responsible for traversing the assigned scopes. For this reason, it executes three nested loops corresponding to the three indices of triad elements (Listing 4). Every loop starts from its starting point determined in *divideProblem()* (Listing 1). At the beginning of each iteration, the Worker class gets the inconsistency of the current triad (Listing 4, Line: 49), then updates the reference to the triad with the maximal local inconsistency (Listing 4, Line: 51). When the work is done, i.e. the end condition is true (Listing 4, Line: 53), the worst-case triad is made consistent (Listing 4, Line: 56). The function *consistTriad()* called from (Listing 4, Line: 56) implements the algorithm described in (Sec. 3), hence it is not discussed here in more detail.

## 5    Experimental Results

The algorithm has been implemented and tested using the *Java Runtime Environment*. The performance tests were carried out on a computer equipped with a quad-core *Intel Pentium i7-2600K* processor and 8 GB of RAM. The concurrent parts of the algorithm were implemented using the `Runnable` interface and the `ExecutorService` object available in the `java.util.concurrent` *Java* package.

When performing tests using an artificially-generated $n \times n$, $n = 100$ matrix and an acceptance threshold of $\epsilon = 0.01$ (highly consistent matrices), for $M = 2$ threads the obtained speed gain has been greater than the ideal speedup $Sp = M$, which can be seen in Fig. 2. It is also worth noting that such speedup occurs until the number of threads reaches *8*, which means that the system actually makes use of all *8* available virtual processors. Therefore, we have superlinear speedup, larger than $M$ for $M$ processors; this is due to the fact that the algorithm is not only parallelized but also modified so that each processor improves the matrix independently. Thanks to this, it is not only the worst triad that is being found and made consistent – as many as $M$ triads can be made consistent simultaneously. Tests (Fig. 1) have shown that results for multiple processors are not significantly different than those obtained using a sequential algorithm.

The distance between the matrices calculated using $dist = \sqrt{\sum_{i,j}(a_{ij} - o_{ij})^2}$, where $A$ is the starting matrix and $OUT = [o_{ij}]$ is the result matrix, is adopted as the divergence index. The difference between the original matrix and the one processed by *64* threads is only slightly higher than for a single thread, which provides additional confirmation of the correctness of the adopted solution (Fig. 1).

## 6    Summary

The $PC$ matrices are usually the result of the work of experts. Therefore, generally they are not large. Most of the cases considered in the literature are not greater than $7 \times 7$; however, there are exceptions. An example of a pairwise comparisons based algorithm that uses grater matrices is the official procedure of

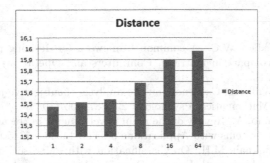

**Fig. 1.** Euclidean distance (change) of output matrix from initial, by number of threads

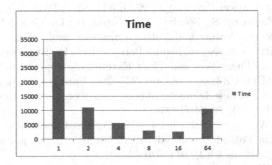

**Fig. 2.** Time taken by execution of algorithm, by number of threads

research entity evaluation in Poland [8]. In that algorithm, the results of paired comparisons do not come directly from human experts. Instead, they are generated according to an appropriate procedure. With the increasing popularity of agent systems, the situations where paired comparisons are made by an appropriate algorithm (possibly non-homogeneous, autonomous agents), may be more frequent. Hence, the need for efficient processing of large $PC$ matrices will increase.

The article presents an efficient concurrent version of the inconsistency reduction algorithm for the $PC$ matrix. Due to the nature of the problem and its susceptibility to parallelization, the obtained results are very promising. Despite this, it seems that many improvements are possible. Therefore, further optimizations of this algorithm and its applications will be the subject of further research.

**Acknowledgment.** This research is financed by AGH University of Science and Technology, contract no.: 11.11.120.859.

# References

1. Choo, E.U., Wedley, W.C.: A common framework for deriving preference values from pairwise comparison matrices. Computers and Operations Research 31(6), 893–908 (2004)
2. Crawford, R., Williams, C.: A note on the analysis of subjective judgement matrices. Journal of Mathematical Psychology 29, 387–405 (1985)
3. Ishizaka, A., Labib, A.: Review of the main developments in the analytic hierarchy process. Expert Systems with Applications 38(11), 14336–14345 (2011)
4. Janicki, R., Soudkhah, M.H.: On Classification with Pairwise Comparisons, Support Vector Machines and Feature Domain Overlapping. Computer Journal, bxu085 (September 2014)
5. Jensen, R.E.: An alternative scaling method for priorities in hierarchical structures. Journal of Mathematical Psychology 28(3), 317–332 (1984)
6. Kacprzyk, J., Zadrozny, S., Fedrizzi, M., Nurmi, H.: On Group Decision Making, Consensus Reaching, Voting and Voting Paradoxes under Fuzzy Preferences and a Fuzzy Majority: A Survey and some Perspectives. In: Bustince, H., Herrera, F., Montero, J. (eds.) Fuzzy Sets and Their Extensions: Representation, Aggregation and Models. STUDFUZZ, vol. 220, pp. 263–295. Springer, Heidelberg (2008)
7. Koczkodaj, W.W.: A new definition of consistency of pairwise comparisons. Math. Comput. Model. 18(7), 79–84 (1993)
8. Koczkodaj, W.W., Kułakowski, K., Ligęza, A.: On the quality evaluation of scientific entities in Poland supported by consistency-driven pairwise comparisons method. Scientometrics 99(3), 911–926 (2014)
9. Koczkodaj, W.W., Szarek, S.J.: On distance-based inconsistency reduction algorithms for pairwise comparisons. Logic Journal of the IGPL 18(6), 859–869 (2010)
10. Koczkodaj, W.W., Szybowski, J., Kosiek, M., Xu, D.: Fast Convergence of Distance-based Inconsistency in Pairwise Comparisons. Fundamenta Informaticae, 1–13 (January 2015)
11. Kułakowski, K.: Heuristic Rating Estimation Approach to The Pairwise Comparisons Method. Fundamenta Informaticae 133, 367–386 (2014)
12. Kułakowski, K.: A heuristic rating estimation algorithm for the pairwise comparisons method. Central European Journal of Operations Research 23(1), 187–203 (2015)
13. Kułakowski, K., Grobler-Dębska, K., Wąs, J.: Heuristic rating estimation: geometric approach. Journal of Global Optimization (2014)
14. Kułakowski, K., Szybowski, J., Tadeusiewicz, R.: Tender with Success The Pairwise Comparisons Approach. Procedia Computer Science 35, 1122–1131 (2014)
15. Saaty, T.L.: A scaling method for priorities in hierarchical structures. Journal of Mathematical Psychology 15(3), 234–281 (1977)
16. Saaty, T.L., Vargas, L.G.: The possibility of group choice: pairwise comparisons and merging functions. Social Choice and Welfare 38(3), 481–496 (2011)
17. Subramanian, N., Ramanathan, R.: A review of applications of Analytic Hierarchy Process in operations management. International Journal of Production Economics 138(2), 215–241 (2012)
18. Thurstone, L.L.: A law of comparative judgment, reprint of an original work published in 1927. Psychological Review 101, 266–270 (1994)
19. Xu, D.: Improving the reduction of distance-based inconsistency of pairwise comparisons matrix. Master's thesis, Laurentian University, Sudbury, Ontario (2013)

# OpenCL Implementation of PSO Algorithm for the Quadratic Assignment Problem

Piotr Szwed$^{(\boxtimes)}$, Wojciech Chmiel, and Piotr Kadłuczka

AGH University of Science and Technology, Karkow, Poland
{pszwed,wch,pkad}@agh.edu.pl

**Abstract.** This paper presents a Particle Swarm Optimization (PSO) algorithm for the Quadratic Assignment Problem (QAP) implemented on OpenCL platform. Motivations to our work were twofold: firstly we wanted to develop a dedicated algorithm to solve the QAP showing both time and optimization performance, secondly we planned to check, if the capabilities offered by popular GPUs can be exploited to accelerate hard optimization tasks requiring high computational power. We were specifically targeting low-cost popular devices, with limited capabilities. The paper discusses the algorithm and its parallel implementation, as well as reports results of tests.

**Keywords:** QAP · PSO · OpenCL · GPU calculation · Particle swarm optimization · Discrete optimization

## 1 Introduction

Quadratic Assignment Problem (QAP) is considered one of the most fundamental optimization problems, as it generalizes a large number of theoretical issues, including graph partitioning, finding maximal clique or linear arrangement. The QAP can be used to model several practical problems, such as balancing of jet turbines, less-than-truckload (*LTL*), very-large-scale integration (*VLSI*), backboard wiring problem and molecular fitting.

The basic QAP formulation is the following: given a set of $n$ *facilities* and $n$ *locations*, the goal is to find an assignment of facilities to locations that minimizes the goal function, which is calculated as a sum of flows between facilities multiplied by distances between locations. A there are $n!$ possible assignments, the QAP is one of the most difficult combinatorial problems belonging to the *NP-hard* class. Therefore, only approximation algorithms can be used for the case, where the $n$ is bigger than 30 ([2], [4], [5]).

Particle Swarm Optimization (PSO) is an optimization method inspired by an observation of social behavior. It attempts to find an optimal problem solution by moving a population of particles in a search space. Each particle is characterized by two features its position and velocity. Depending on a method variation, particles may exchange information on their positions and reached values of goal functions [7]. PSO is a metaheuristics, that can be mapped on various domains. Although the method was intended for continuous domains, its applications to

© Springer International Publishing Switzerland 2015
L. Rutkowski et al. (Eds.): ICAISC 2015, Part II, LNAI 9120, pp. 223–234, 2015.
DOI: 10.1007/978-3-319-19369-4_21

discrete problems, including the Traveling Salesman Problem (TSP) and the QAP were discussed in [6,15,13].

In this paper we present an implementation of PSO algorithm for the QAP problem on OpenCL platform. OpenCL is a solution allowing developers to accelerate applications by using computational power of multicore graphic cards and processors. OpenCL enabled devices are quite widespread, even if often their users don't fully realize it. They include popular components (graphic cards and CPUs) from AMD, Nvidia and Intel companies.

A motivation to our work was to check, if the capabilities offered by popular GPUs can be exploited to accelerate hard optimization tasks requiring high computational power. In this paper we make the following two contributions: firstly we present a developed PSO algorithm for the QAP problem, secondly we discuss its parallel implementation on OpenCL platform.

The paper is organized as follows: next Section 2 gives the definition of QAP. It is followed by Section 3, which discusses the application of PSO to the QAP, as well as its parallel implementation with OpenCL. Experiments performed and their results are presented in Section 4. Section 5 provides concluding remarks.

## 2    Quadratic AssignmentProblem

Quadratic Assignment Problem was introduced by Koopmans and Beckman in 1957 as a mathematical model of assigning a set of economic activities to a set of locations.

For the given set $N = \{1, ..., n\}$ we define two $n \times n$ non-negative matrices $F = [f_{i,k}]$, $D = [d_{j,l}]$. In the terminology of facilities-location the set $N$ is a set of facilities indexes and $\pi(i) \in N, i = 1, ..., n$ defines locations, to which the facilities are assigned. Matrix $D$ defines distances between locations, whereas matrix $F$ defines flows between pairs of facilities. Matrix $B$ describes a linear part of the assignment cost and in most cases is omitted. A solution of QAP (also denoted as $QAP(F, D)$) can be defined as a permutation $\pi = (\pi(1), ..., \pi(n))$ from the set of $n$ facilities. In the Koopman-Beckman's [12] model the goal is to find the permutation $\pi^*$ which minimizes the objective function:

$$f(\pi^*) = min_{\pi \in \Pi} \sum_{i=1}^{n} \sum_{j=1}^{n} f_{ij} d_{\pi(i),\pi(j)} + \sum_{i=1}^{n} b_{i,\pi(i)} \qquad (1)$$

The objective function $f(\pi), \pi \in \Pi$ describes the global cost of system realization and exploitation. $\Pi$ is a set of permutations of the set of natural numbers $1, ..., n$. In most cases matrix $D$ and $F$ are symmetric: distances $d_{i,j}$ and $d_{j,i}$ between two locations $i$ and $j$ are equal, the same applies to flows: $f_{i,j}$ and $f_{j,i}$.

QAP models found application in various areas including transportation [1], scheduling, electronics (wiring problem), distributed computing, statistical data analysis (reconstruction of destroyed soundtracks), balancing of turbine running [14], chemistry [20], genetics [16], creating the control panels and manufacturing [9].

In 1976 Sahni and Gonzalez proved that the QAP is strongly $\mathcal{NP}$-*hard* [17,8], by showing that a hypothetical existence of a polynomial time algorithm for solving the QAP would imply an existence of a polynomial time algorithm for an $\mathcal{NP}$-*complete* decision problem - the Hamiltonian cycle.

In many cases finding an optimal solution for the QAP by applying local search is very hard. The neighborhood definition often used in algorithms solving the QAP is the structure *2-opt* (based on a pair exchange in a permutation). Fig. 1 shows an example of landscape for the problem instance *Lipa60b*. As it could be seen, this landscape (*QAP, 2-opt*) is multimodal. The neighborhood solutions are characterized by weak autocorrelation, hence, this instance of QAP (and many others) is difficult to optimize. Several approximation algorithms for the QAP use procedures based on local search, but on the basis the above considerations, it can be proven that in a general case this approach does not guarantee finding a good solution.

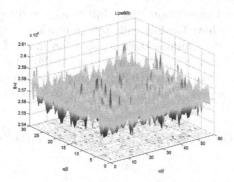

**Fig. 1.** An example of the landscape for the QAP problem (Lipa60) for *2-opt* neighborhood structure

## 3   Methods

The classical PSO algorithm [7] is an optimization method defined for continuous domain. During the optimization process a number of particles move through a search space and update their states and values of goal function at discrete time steps $t = 1, 2, 3, \ldots$ Each particle is characterized by its position $x(t)$ and velocity $v(t)$. A particle remembers its best position reached so far $p^L(t)$, as well as it can use information about the best solution found by the swarm $p^G(t)$.

The state equation for a particle is given by formula (2). Coefficients $c_1, c_2, c_3 \in [0, 1]$ are called respectively *inertia*, *cognition* (or *self recognition*) and *social* factors.

$$\left.\begin{array}{l} v(t+1) = c_1 \cdot v(t) + c_2 \cdot (p^L(t) - x(t)) + c_3 \cdot (p^G(t) - x(t)) \\ x(t+1) = x(t) + v(t) \end{array}\right\} \quad (2)$$

An adaptation of the PSO method to a discrete domain necessities in giving interpretation to the velocity concept, as well as defining equivalents of scalar multiplication, subtraction and addition for arguments being solutions and velocities. Examples of such interpretations can be found in [6] for the TSP and [15] for the QAP.

In the rest of this section we describe an adaptation of the Particle Swarm Optimization (PSO) method to the QAP problem. Some solutions, especially the interpretation of the velocity, are based ideas presented in [13].

## 3.1   PSO Adaptation for the QAP Problem

A state of a particle is a pair $(X, V)$. For the QAP problem both are $n \times n$ matrices, where $n$ is the problem size. The matrix $X = [x_{ij}]$ encodes an assignment of facilities to locations. Its elements $x_{ij}$ are equal to 1, if $j$-th facility is assigned to $i$-th location, and take value 0 otherwise.

A particle moves in the solution space following the direction given by the velocity $V$. Elements $v_{ij}$ have the following interpretation: if $v_{ij}$ has high positive value, then a procedure determining the next solution should favor an assignment $x_{ij} = 1$. On the other hand, if $v_{ij} \leq 0$, then $x_{ij} = 0$ should be preferred.

The state of a particle reached in $t$-th iteration will be denoted by $(X(t), V(t))$. In each iteration a state of a particle is updated according to formulas (3) and (4).

$$V(t+1) = S_v(c_1 \cdot V(t) + c_2 \cdot r_2(t) \cdot (P^L(t) - X(t)) + c_2 \cdot r_3(t) \cdot (P^G(t) - X(t))) \quad (3)$$

$$X(t+1) = S_x(X(t) + V(t)) \quad (4)$$

Coefficients $r_2$ and $r_3$ are random numbers from $[0, 1]$ generated for each particle and iteration. They are introduced to model a random choice between movements in the previous direction (according to $c_1$ – inertia), the best local solution (self recognition) or the global best solution (social behavior).

All operators appearing in (3) and (4) are standard operators from linear algebra. Instead of redefining them for a particular problem, see e.g. [6], we propose to use aggregation functions $S_v$ and $S_x$ that allow to adapt the algorithm to particular needs of a discrete problem.

The function $S_v$ is used to assure that particle velocity have reasonable values. Initially, we thought that unconstrained growth of velocity can be a problem, therefore we have implemented a function, which restricts the elements of $V$ to an interval $[-v_{max}, v_{max}]$. This function is referred as *raw* in Table 2. However, the experiments conducted shown, that in case of small inertia factor, e.g. $c_1 = 0.5$, after a few iterations all velocities tend to 0 and in consequence all particles converge to the best solution encountered earlier by the swarm. To avoid such effect another function was applied, which additionally performs column normalization. For each column $j$ a sum of absolute values of the elements $n_j = \sum_{i=1}^{n} |v_{ij}|$ is calculated and then the following assignment is made: $v_{ij} \leftarrow v_{ij}/n_j$.

According to formula (4) a new particle position $X(t+1)$ is obtained by aggregating the previous state components: $X(t)$ and $V(t)$. As elements of a matrix $X(t) + V(t)$ may take values from $[-v_{max}, v_{max}+1]$, the $S_x$ function is responsible for converting it into a valid assignment matrix having exactly one 1 in each row and column. Actually, $S_v$ is rather a procedure, than a function, as it incorporates some elements of random choice.

Three variants of $S_x$ procedures were implemented:

1. $GlobalMax(X)$ – iteratively searches for $x_{rc}$, a maximum element in a matrix $X$, sets it to 1 and clears other elements in the row $r$ and $c$.
2. $PickColumn(X)$ – picks a column $c$ from $X$, selects a maximum element $x_{rc}$, replaces it by 1 and clears other elements in $r$ and $c$.
3. $SecondTarget(X)$ – similar to $GlobalMax(X)$, discussed in detail in section 3.2.

Due to limited space we present only the algorithm for $GlobalMax$ (Algorithm 1). In a **while** loop, executed exactly $n$ times, it calculates $M$, the set of maximum elements in the input matrix $X(t) + V(t)$, whose row and column indices belong to the sets $R$ and $C$ respectively. Then, it picks an element $x_{rc}$ from $M$ (if it has more then one elements), clears elements in the row $r$ and the column $c$ and sets $x_{rc}$ to 1. Hence, the selected assignment represents the best choice, considering previous decisions (which in some cases can be random). Initially, $R$ and $C$ contain all indices $1, \ldots, n$. In each iteration exactly one ($r$ or $c$) is removed from both sets, hence the procedure stops after $n$ iterations.

---

**Algorithm 1.** Aggregation procedure $GlobalMax$)

---

1: **procedure** GLOBALMAX($X$)
2:    $R \leftarrow \{1, \ldots, n\}$
3:    $C \leftarrow \{1, \ldots, n\}$
4:    **while** $R \neq \emptyset \wedge C \neq \emptyset$ **do**
5:       $M \leftarrow \{(r,c) \colon \forall_{i \in R, j \in C}(x_{rc} \geq x_{ij})\}$    ▷ Calculate set of maximum elements
6:       Randomly select $(r,c)$ from $M$
7:       $R \leftarrow R \setminus \{r\}$    ▷ Update the sets $R$ and $C$
8:       $C \leftarrow C \setminus \{c\}$
9:       **for** $i$ in $[1,n]$ **do**
10:          $x_{ri} \leftarrow 0$    ▷ Clear $r$-th row
11:          $x_{ic} \leftarrow 0$    ▷ Clear $c$-th column
12:       **end for**
13:       $x_{rc} \leftarrow 1$    ▷ Assign for 1 for a maximum value
14:    **end while**
15:    **return** $X$
16: **end procedure**

---

## 3.2  Second Target Aggregation Procedure

In several experiments, where which $GlobalMax$ aggregation procedure was used, particles seemed to get stuck, even if their velocities were far from zero. We reproduce this effect on a small $3 \times 3$ example:

$$X = \begin{bmatrix} 1 & 0 & 0 \\ 0 & 0 & 1 \\ 0 & 1 & 0 \end{bmatrix} V = \begin{bmatrix} 7 & 1 & 3 \\ 0 & 4 & 5 \\ 2 & 3 & 2 \end{bmatrix} X+V = \begin{bmatrix} 8 & 1 & 3 \\ 0 & 4 & 6 \\ 2 & 4 & 2 \end{bmatrix} S_x(X+V) = \begin{bmatrix} 1 & 0 & 0 \\ 0 & 0 & 1 \\ 0 & 1 & 0 \end{bmatrix}$$

For the described case in subsequent iterations it will hold $X(t+1) = X(t)$, until another particle is capable of changing $(P^G(t) - X(t)))$ component of formula (3) for velocity calculation. A solution for this problem can be to move a particle to a secondary direction, by ignoring $k < n$ elements that are in the solution $X(t)$ already set to 1. This, depending on $k$, gives an opportunity to reach other solutions with a smaller goal function value (see Fig. 2). If they are maximum elements in the remaining matrix denoted here as $X \oslash_k V$, they are still reasonable movement directions. Formula (5) shows $X \oslash_k V$ matrix for $k = 3$ in the discussed example. Elements of a new solution are marked with circles.

$$X \oslash_{k=3} V = \begin{bmatrix} 0 & 1 & ③ \\ 0 & ④ & 0 \\ ② & 0 & 2 \end{bmatrix} \tag{5}$$

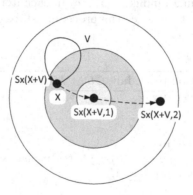

**Fig. 2.** An idea of the *second target* aggregation function

## 3.3  OpenCL Platform

OpenCL [11] is a standard providing a common language, programming interfaces and hardware abstraction for heterogeneous platforms including GPU, multicore CPU, DSP and FPGA [18]. It allows to accelerate computations by decomposing them into a set of parallel tasks (work items) operating on separate data.

A program on OpenCL platform is decomposed into two parts: sequential executed by the CPU *host* and parallel executed by multicore *devices*. Functions executed on devices are called *kernels*. They are written in a language being a variant of C with some restrictions related to keywords and datatypes. When first time loaded, the kernels are automatically translated into a target device instruction set. The whole process takes about 500ms.

OpenCL supports 1D, 2D or 3D organization of data (arrays, matrices and volumes). Each data element is identified by 1 to 3 indices, e.g. $d[i][j]$ for two-dimensional arrays. A *work item* is a scheduled kernel instance, which obtain a combination of data indices within the data range. To give an example, a 2D array of data of $n \times m$ size should be processed by $n \cdot m$ kernel instances, which are assigned with a pair of indices $(i, j)$, $i < n$ and $j < m$. Those indices are used to identify data items assigned to kernels.

Additionally, kernels can be organized into workgroups, e.g. corresponding to parts of a matrix, and synchronize their operations within a group using so called *local barrier* mechanism. However, workgroups suffer from several platform restrictions related to number of work items and amount of accessible memory.

OpenCL uses three types of memory: global (that is exchanged between the host and the device), local for a work group and private for a work item.

### 3.4  OpenCL Algorithm Implementation

In our implementation we used *aparapi* platform [10] that allows to write OpenCL programs directly in Java language. The platform comprises two parts: an API and a runtime capable of converting Java bytecodes into OpenCL workloads. Hence, the host part of the program is executed on a Java virtual machine, and originally written in Java kernels are executed on an OpenCL enabled device.

The basic functional blocks of the algorithm are presented in Fig. 3. Implemented kernels are marked with gray color. The code responsible for generation of random particles is executed by the host. We have also decided to leave the code for updating best solutions at the host side. Actually, it comprises a number of native `System.arraycopy()` calls.

Each particle is represented by a number of matrices (see Fig. 4): $X$ and $X_{new}$ – solutions, $P^L$ – local best particle solution and $V$ – velocity. Moreover, particles share read-only global best solution – $P^G$ and generated by the host arrays of random numbers (there is no `rand()` equivalent on OpenCL platform). The amount of the memory used can be high. It can be estimated, that for the biggest test case reported in Table 1: 10000 particles using $60 \times 60$ matrices, the global memory GPU consumption ranged at 550MB.

An important decision related to OpenCL program design is related to data ranges selection. The memory layout in Fig. 4 suggests 3D range, whose dimensions are: row, column and particle number. This can be applied for relatively simple velocity or goal function calculation. However, the proposed algorithms for $S_x$, see Algorithm 1, are far too complicated to be implemented as a simple parallel work item. In consequence, we decided to use only one dimension representing a particle number, what implicates that parallel work items process

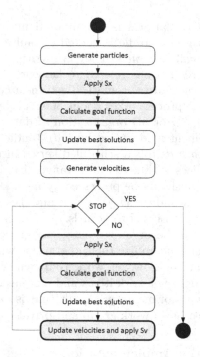

**Fig. 3.** Functional blocks of OpenCL based algorithm implementation

whole particles. To give an example, $X$ components being $60 \times 60$ matrices of all 100 particles are represented by a single array of 360000 floats with a range $i = 0, \ldots, 99$.

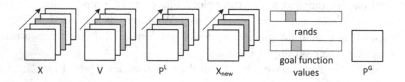

**Fig. 4.** Global variables used in the algorithm implementation

## 4    Experiments and Results

We have conducted two types of experiments. The first aimed at evaluating the time performance of GPU based implementation for various setups of PSO algoritms (varying numbers of particles and numbers of iterations). The goal of the second group of test cases was to establish the influence of parameters controlling the implemented PSO algorithm on its optimization efficiency. All tests were performed on instances defined in QAPLIB problem library [3].

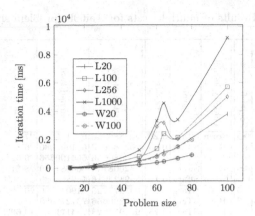

**Fig. 5.** Time spent in one iteration for various problem sizes. L20, L100, L256 and L1000: 20, 100, 256 and 1000 particles (laptop), W20 and W100: 20 and 100 particles (workstation)

**Table 1.** Comparison of iteration times for parallel and sequential implementations. All times (PAR and SEQ) expressed in ms.

| Problem size | Particles | Iterations | Time PAR [ms] | Sx | Goal | Best | Velocity | Time SEQ [ms] | Gain: SEQ/PAR |
|---|---|---|---|---|---|---|---|---|---|
| 12 | 20 | 100 | 1.42 | 63.53% | 17.40% | 0.19% | 18.89% | 0.07 | 0.05 |
| 26 | 20 | 100 | 4.75 | 69.98% | 19.62% | 0.47% | 9.93% | 0.55 | 0.12 |
| 50 | 20 | 100 | 25.40 | 76.90% | 19.57% | 0.31% | 3.23% | 3.61 | 0.14 |
| 60 | 20 | 100 | 43.46 | 76.37% | 21.10% | 0.06% | 2.46% | 5.16 | 0.12 |
| 64 | 20 | 100 | 56.80 | 57.70% | 38.33% | 0.02% | 3.94% | 5.57 | 0.10 |
| 72 | 20 | 100 | 73.35 | 76.23% | 21.60% | 0.20% | 1.97% | 6.21 | 0.08 |
| 100 | 20 | 100 | 189.29 | 75.92% | 22.60% | 0.16% | 1.32% | 9.84 | 0.05 |
| 12 | 100 | 100 | 0.38 | 63.53% | 17.40% | 0.19% | 18.89% | 0.11 | 0.30 |
| 26 | 100 | 100 | 1.38 | 69.98% | 19.62% | 0.47% | 9.93% | 0.79 | 0.57 |
| 50 | 100 | 100 | 8.15 | 76.90% | 19.57% | 0.31% | 3.23% | 4.69 | 0.58 |
| 60 | 100 | 100 | 13.59 | 76.37% | 21.10% | 0.06% | 2.46% | 6.76 | 0.50 |
| 64 | 100 | 100 | 24.08 | 57.70% | 38.33% | 0.02% | 3.94% | 9.64 | 0.40 |
| 72 | 100 | 100 | 21.54 | 76.23% | 21.60% | 0.20% | 1.97% | 8.15 | 0.38 |
| 100 | 100 | 100 | 57.06 | 75.92% | 22.60% | 0.16% | 1.32% | 12.96 | 0.23 |
| 12 | 1000 | 10 | 0.07 | 47.42% | 23.90% | 0.44% | 28.24% | 0.15 | 2.12 |
| 26 | 1000 | 10 | 0.23 | 53.33% | 27.41% | 2.76% | 16.50% | 1.04 | 4.56 |
| 50 | 1000 | 10 | 1.27 | 53.75% | 37.92% | 1.51% | 6.82% | 6.71 | 5.29 |
| 60 | 1000 | 10 | 3.31 | 72.54% | 23.12% | 0.56% | 3.78% | 7.12 | 2.15 |
| 64 | 1000 | 10 | 4.56 | 44.95% | 41.54% | 0.30% | 13.20% | 12.38 | 2.72 |
| 72 | 1000 | 10 | 3.39 | 57.58% | 36.68% | 1.02% | 4.72% | 10.79 | 3.18 |
| 100 | 1000 | 10 | 9.19 | 56.17% | 40.36% | 0.38% | 3.09% | 17.51 | 1.91 |
| 60 | 10000 | 100 | 1.61 | 42.38% | 47.74% | 0.02% | 9.86% | 12.18 | 7.56 |

## 4.1  Time Performance

The OpencCL implementation was tested on two platforms, referred as *laptop* (AMD Radeon HD 6750M card, i7-2657QM, 2.2Ghz processor, Windows 7) and *workstation* (NVIDIA GeForce GT 430, i7-4860HQ processor, 3.60GHz, Windows 7)). In both cases Java 8 runtime was used for host operations.

**Table 2.** Results of multiple tests for Tai60b (problem size: 60)

| Particles | Iterations | Inertia $c_1$ | Self recognition $c_2$ | Social factor $c_3$ | Velocity kernel | Sx kernel | STarg depth | First goal | Reached goal | Gain | Iteration | Gap |
|---|---|---|---|---|---|---|---|---|---|---|---|---|
| 100 | 3000 | 0.5 | 0.5 | 0.5 | Norm | STarg | 0.25 | 903886656 | 659155648 | 27.08% | 2840 | 7.73% |
| 100 | 6000 | 0.5 | 0.5 | 0.5 | Raw | STarg | 0.25 | 903886656 | 661662080 | 26.80% | 5852 | 8.08% |
| 100 | 3000 | 0.9 | 0.3 | 0.3 | Norm | STarg | 0.75 | 903886656 | 664190656 | 26.52% | 2715 | 8.43% |
| 50 | 1000 | 0.5 | 0.5 | 0.5 | Raw | STarg | 0.25 | 932608128 | 666681280 | 28.51% | 904 | 8.77% |
| 1000 | 6000 | 0.5 | 0.5 | 0.5 | Norm | STarg | 0.25 | 899822016 | 669809536 | 25.56% | 5755 | 9.20% |
| 500 | 100 | 0.5 | 0.5 | 0.5 | Raw | STarg | 0.5 | 901977728 | 719012736 | 20.28% | 50 | 15.41% |
| 200 | 250 | 0.9 | 0.3 | 0.3 | Raw | STarg | 0.5 | 903886656 | 731279680 | 19.10% | 176 | 16.83% |
| 500 | 100 | 0.3 | 0.9 | 0.3 | Raw | STarg | 0.75 | 901977728 | 734171136 | 18.60% | 99 | 17.16% |
| 200 | 250 | 0.9 | 0.3 | 0.3 | Raw | PCol | N/A | 902798080 | 736113152 | 18.46% | 67 | 17.37% |
| 500 | 100 | 0.5 | 0.5 | 0.5 | Raw | STarg | 0.5 | 901977728 | 741909632 | 17.75% | 100 | 18.02% |
| 50 | 1000 | 0.5 | 0.5 | 0.5 | Raw | GMx | N/A | 902798080 | 858625408 | 4.89% | 11 | 29.16% |
| 500 | 100 | 0.9 | 0.3 | 0.3 | Raw | GMx | N/A | 901977728 | 871849536 | 3.34% | 72 | 30.24% |
| 500 | 100 | 0.5 | 0.5 | 0.5 | Raw | GMx | N/A | 901977728 | 877890624 | 2.67% | 83 | 30.72% |
| 500 | 100 | 0.3 | 0.9 | 0.3 | Raw | PCol | N/A | 890460224 | 879615744 | 1.22% | 3 | 30.85% |
| 50 | 1000 | 0.3 | 0.9 | 0.3 | Raw | PCol | N/A | 902798080 | 902798080 | 0.00% | 0 | 32.63% |
| 200 | 250 | 0.3 | 0.9 | 0.3 | Raw | PCol | N/A | 902798080 | 902798080 | 0.00% | 0 | 32.63% |

Fig. 5 gives the average times spent in one iteration for various numbers of particles. It should be noted, that at the workstation platform it was not possible to run tests for the problem size 100.

Detailed results of tests related to execution time are given in Table 1. It can be observed, that the tested parallel implementation is inferior to the sequential, if the number of particles is relatively small. For 20 or even 100 particles the overhead related to data transfer between the host and the GPU prevails potential benefits.

A real speedup can be observed for 200 or more particles being simultaneously processed. This is visible in last eight table rows giving results for 1000 and 10000 particles. The results suggest quite different algorithm design, e.g. to exploit the platform capabilities sequential algorithm runs for 20 particles should be transformed into independent 500 parallel runs.

It should be noted, however, that all tests were not performed on a dedicated GPU hardware, but on popular graphic cards installed in mid-range laptops or workstations.

## 4.2   Optimization Performance

The second group of tests aimed at establishing the optimization performance of the algorithm for various combinations of parameters (including kernels used). The tests were performed a randomly generated problem *Tai60b* from the QAPLIB collection [3]. The best known goal function value (608215054) for *Tai60b* was established with a robust Tabu search algorithm [19]. We consider it a reference in the comparisons.

Table 2 gives selected results of tests, which yielded the bests, average and the worst results. It can be observed that the best solutions were obtained for large numbers of iterations (the reference value for *Tai60b* was also obtained the number of iterations in order of 100000 [19]). In most cases *raw* $S_v$ function (without normalization) returned worse results than *Norm*. For $S_x$ aggregation function, results of applying global maximum (*GMax*) and pick column (*PCol*) are comparable. The kernel implementing the second target (*STarget*) gave the best results. Good results were reported for equal values of $c_1$, $c_2$ and $c_3$ coefficients. It may be stated that $c_2$ (self recognition) should not dominate other factors, whereas high inertia $c_1$ is acceptable.

## 5  Conclusions

In this paper we describe a PSO algorithm designed for solving the QAP problem, as well as its parallel implementation on the OpenCL platform. Several mechanisms applied in the algorithm were inspired by Liu at al. work [13], however, they were refined to provide better performance.

Another contribution of this work is a parallel implementation of the discussed algorithm on the OpenCL platform. We developed a Java program that uses *aparapi* library to deliver computational tasks to an OpenCL enabled device. We were specifically targeting low-cost popular devices, e.g. 200$ graphics cards, with limited capabilities.

We report results of tests aiming at evaluating the implementation in terms of execution times and optimization capability. The tests targeting time performance revealed that benefits of GPU calculations can be observed, if the number of particles processed in parallel is big. The optimization performance, here presented on a selected large QAP instance ($n = 60$), showed that the algorithm behaves differently, depending on values of control parameters. However, the proposed *second target* method for updating particle position yielded better results, than the others.

## References

1. Bermudez, R., Cole, M.H.: A genetic algorithm approach to door assignments in breakbulk terminals. Tech. Rep. MBTC-1102, Mack-Blackwell Transportation Center, University of Arkansas, Fayetteville, Arkansas (2001)
2. Burkard, R., Karisch, S., Rendl, F.: Qaplib-a quadratic assignment problem library. Journal of Global Optimization 10(4), 391–403 (1997)
3. Burkard, R., Karisch, S., Rendl, F.: QAPLIB a Quadratic Assignment Problem library. Journal of Global Optimization 10(4), 391–403 (1997)
4. Chmiel, W.: Evolution Algorithms for optimisation of task assignment problem with quadratic cost function. Ph.D. thesis, AGH Technology University, Poland (2004)
5. Chmiel, W., Kadłuczka, P., Packanik, G.: Performance of swarm algorithms for permutation problems. Automatyka 15(2), 117–126 (2009)

6. Clerc, M.: Discrete particle swarm optimization, illustrated by the traveling sales-man problem. In: Onwubolu, G.C., Babu, B.V. (eds.) New Optimization Techniques in Engineering. STUDFUZZ, vol. 141, pp. 219–239. Springer, Heidelberg (2004)

7. Eberhart, R., Kennedy, J.: A new optimizer using particle swarm theory. In: Proceedings of the Sixth International Symposium on Micro Machine and Human Science, MHS 1995, pp. 39–43 (October 1995)

8. Garey, M.R., Johnson, D.S.: Computers and Intractability: A Guide to the Theory of NP-Completeness. W. H. Freeman & Co., New York (1979)

9. Grötschel, M.: Discrete mathematics in manufacturing. In: Malley, R.E.O. (ed.) ICIAM 1991: Proceedings of the Second International Conference on Industrial and Applied Mathematics, pp. 119–145. SIAM (1991)

10. Howes, L., Munshi, A.: Aparapi - AMD, http://developer.amd.com/tools-and-sdks/opencl-zone/aparapi/ (last accessed: January 2015)

11. Howes, L., Munshi, A.: The OpenCL specification, https://www.khronos.org/registry/cl/specs/opencl-2.0.pdf (last accessed: January 2015)

12. Koopmans, T.C., Beckmann, M.J.: Assignment problems and the location of economic activities. Econometrica 25, 53–76 (1957)

13. Liu, H., Abraham, A., Zhang, J.: A particle swarm approach to quadratic assignment problems. In: Saad, A., Dahal, K., Sarfraz, M., Roy, R. (eds.) Soft Computing in Industrial Applications. ASC, vol. 39, pp. 213–222. Springer, Heidelberg (2007)

14. Mason, A., Rönnqvist, M.: Solution methods for the balancing of jet turbines. Computers & OR 24(2), 153–167 (1997)

15. Onwubolu, G.C., Sharma, A.: Particle swarm optimization for the assignment of facilities to locations. In: Onwubolu, G.C., Babu, B.V. (eds.) New Optimization Techniques in Engineering. STUDFUZZ, vol. 141, pp. 567–584. Springer, Heidelberg (2004)

16. Phillips, A.T., Rosen, J.B.: A quadratic assignment formulation of the molecular conformation problem. Journal of Global Optimization 4, 229–241 (1994)

17. Sahni, S., Gonzalez, T.: P-complete approximation problems. J. ACM 23(3), 555–565 (1976)

18. Stone, J.E., Gohara, D., Shi, G.: Opencl: A parallel programming standard for heterogeneous computing systems. Computing in Science & Engineering 12(3), 66 (2010)

19. Taillard, E.D.: Comparison of iterative searches for the quadratic assignment problem. Location Science 3(2), 87–105 (1995)

20. Ugi, I., Bauer, J., Brandt, J., Friedrich, J., Gasteiger, J., Jochum, C., Schubert, W.: Neue anwendungsgebiete fur computer in der chemie. Angewandte Chemie 91(2), 99–111 (1979)

# Agent Systems, Robotics and Control

# Towards a Better Understanding and Behavior Recognition of Inhabitants in Smart Cities. A Public Transport Case

Radosław Klimek[✉] and Leszek Kotulski

AGH University of Science and Technology,
Al. Mickiewicza 30, 30-059 Kraków, Poland
{rklimek,kotulski}@agh.edu.pl

**Abstract.** The idea of modern urban systems and smart cities requires monitoring and careful analysis of different signals. Such signals can originate from different sources and one of the most promising is the BTS, i.e. base transceiver station, an element of mobile carrier networks. This paper presents the fundamental problems of elicitation, classification and understanding of such signals so as to develop context-aware and pro-active systems in urban areas. These systems are characterized by the omnipresence of computing which is strongly focused on providing on-line support to users/inhabitants of smart cities. A method of analyzing selected elements of mobile phone datasets through understanding inhabitants' behavioral fingerprints to obtain smart scenarios for public transport is proposed. Some scenarios are outlined. A multi-agent system is proposed. A formalism based on graphs that allows reasoning about inhabitant behaviors is also proposed.

**Keywords:** Smart city · Cell phone network · Base transceiver station · Call detail record · Behaviour recognition · Pervasive computing · Context-awareness · Pro-active system · Multi agent system

## 1 Introduction

We face today an unprecedented interest for the idea of smart cities. This idea requires smart analysis of many signals and information bits which are generated in urban areas, as well as the use of network facilities and interaction of citizens through new technologies. Thus, new and innovative ways of analyzing behaviors in cities through understanding the data they generate are needed. New ways to analyze and classify this data, as well as further reasoning, in order to better understand and plan pro-active support offered by systems to inhabitants are a crucial necessity. Pervasive computing is an idea which assumes the omnipresence of computer systems to give strong support for inhabitants in smart cities. These systems must be characterized by context-awareness, basing on different urban signals, to provide pro-active assistance for inhabitants.

Widespread availability and use of mobile phones, as well as their growing ubiquity, is based on BTS wireless networks which guarantee basic communication in the system. Wireless networks have great potential to provide information

© Springer International Publishing Switzerland 2015
L. Rutkowski et al. (Eds.): ICAISC 2015, Part II, LNAI 9120, pp. 237–246, 2015.
DOI: 10.1007/978-3-319-19369-4_22

to identify activities of people. People keep a phone with them most of the time. Inhabitant movements and locations are being recorded in many different ways. BTSs are responsible for communicating with mobile phones within the network. They record many important and useful events, stored in the CDR format, for example about the presence of a phone device, which gives an indication of the geographic location of the user. Thus, it allows to identify places of inhabitants' lives using mobile networks. Being able to identify users' movements is crucial for smart decisions as well as to work fast and get results in a short time.

We show that analyzing selected information generated by BTS devices can indeed identify inhabitants' behaviors, help understand human mobility and social patterns and implement smart scenarios for software systems. A classification of sensed behaviors for applications that operate in a smart city is proposed. Outlines of smart scenarios are provided. A multi agent system is proposed. A formalism which allows reasoning about inhabitant behaviors in the BTS network is proposed.

The topic of sensing and monitoring urban activities basing on mobile phone datasets seems hot and relatively new. In work by Calabresse et al. [1] a real time monitoring system is described. Buses and taxis, as well as pedestrians movements, are positioned providing urban mobility. In work by Gonzalez et al. [3] trajectories of anonymized mobile phone owners are discussed. Human trajectories are characterized by a high degree of both temporal and spatial regularity. Work by Isaacman et al. [5] proposes clustering and regression-oriented techniques supporting identification semantically-meaningful locations (home, work). Work by Reades et al. [12] offers a new way of looking at the city as a holistic and dynamic system. Some experiments in explorations in urban data collection are discussed.

## 2 Technical Preliminaries

Systems for mobile communications (e.g. GSM or UMTS) are now well established. There are many works introducing in the world of data communication procedures, e.g. work [4]. Selected technical aspects of such system are briefly outlined below.

The most obvious part of the cellular/mobile phone network is a base station. A *base transceiver station* (BTS) is a piece of equipment that enables wireless communication between the user and the network. Every BTS performs immediate communication with mobile phones. Nowadays, cities and regions are covered with a relatively dense network of BTSs, see for example Figure 1. Although outside the cities networks are less dense, in each case they gather and store important and interesting information about users' activities. Broadly speaking, the entire network system consists of many elements that operate together but an ordinary user is not aware of the different entities within the system.

A *call detail record* (CDR) is contains data recorded and produced by telecommunications equipment. The purpose is to store information about current system usage; however, CDR is rather retrospective. It contains data that is specific

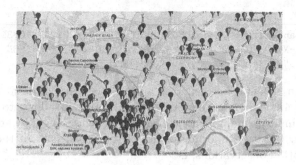

**Fig. 1.** A sample BTS city network (source: http://btsearch.pl/)

to a single instance of a phone call or other communication transaction. The structure of CDR is relatively complex, and its format varies among providers. In some situations CDR can also be configured by a user. There is an entry done for each call, at the start of a call and at the end of the call. The management system is usually configured to update the CDRs periodically. The CDR contains variables, e.g. the called number. Variables might be grouped into: variables used for identifying calls, timestamps, information related to signaling, information related to media, statistics, information related to routing, and others. Records are very detailed and contain much information, e.g. point of origin (sources), points of destination (endpoints), the phone number of the calling party, the phone number of the party being called, duration of each call, the amount billed for each call, the route for a call entering the exchange, the route for a call leaving the exchange, call type (voice, SMS, etc.), etc. Some data depends on the service provider and even in a case of timestamps there are over a dozen of different fields.

CDRs, as collections of information, have a special format [2]. Below is a sample fragment of a CDR text decoded from the binary format. The first row must contain a header row which includes the field names:

```
Call Type,Call Cause,Customer Identifier,Telephone Number Dialled,
Call Date,Call Time,Duration,Bytes Transmitted,Bytes Received,
Description,Chargecode,Time Band,Salesprice,
Salesprice (pre-bundle), Extension,DDI,Grouping ID,Call Class,
Carrier,Recording,VAT,Country of Origin,Network,
Retail tariff code,Remote Network,APN,Diverted Number,
Ring time,RecordID,Currency
```

The meaning of the columns is not analyzed here since they are intuitive and the detailed discussion is outside the scope of the paper. Below is a sample decoded text:

```
"V","0","+441999887000","+441999878333","28/01/2012","10:37:23",
"233","","","Hampton","UK Local","Peak","0.8","0.8","654",
"+441999887654","","UKL","Talk Talk","","S","","","","","","",
"","778789","GBP"
```

```
"VOIP","0","Brianb@M1.com","+442086019080","28/01/2012","10:39:23",
"345","","","On-Net","On-Net","Peak","0.0","0.0","","","","ON" ,
"Talk Talk","1","S","","","","","","","",8011229,"GBP"
```

There are many events that generate a CDR record, e.g. data services, such as SMS and Internet access. The gathered information allows to obtain BTS locations according to a mobile phone activity, i.e. changing a location from one BTS to another. Location information is extracted as part of the interaction data. These location observations, i.e.

- the moment of the phone's/object's entry into the area of a station (log in), and
- the moment of they leave that area (log out),

are of fundamental importance to the considerations given in the following sections of the paper.

## 3    Behaviour Recognition and Classification

This work discusses the possibility of analyzing data generated and obtained from BTS devices/stations. Such stations constitute a rich source of information for smart and context-aware systems. This information is related to many aspects of users'/inhabitants' behaviors and base on relatively raw data. From all the information generated by a BTS, the most important for these considerations are events describing the presence/location (login/logout) of the phone in the BTS area.

Information, or events, obtained from the BTS network can be used to provide the following classification of user behaviors:

1. **Static behavior**, that is without moving outside the BTS area. Some scenarios which are appropriate for such behavior are proposed. The aim of such scenarios is to increase the user's/inhabitant's comfort of staying in a particular area. Appropriate algorithms can take the behaviors registered in the past into account which can build a suitable preference model [9,6]. For example, providing information about local customer services, shops or special offers. If preferences (behavior in the past) also also taken into account, then support for users/inhabitants staying in the area becomes more mature and valuable. For example, people working in local offices, when approaching the habitual and observed time for their lunch, are notified about current opportunities in their neighborhood, and table bookings in restaurants are suggested, offering personalized ads, etc. In other words, these actions are performed after gaining a deep understanding of the inhabitants' needs.
   The algorithm to identify home/residential or work/office locations might be based on the tracking the entire mobile activity during the selected days of a week and selected time of a day. In other words, home is defined when

the mobile phone location is registered after a certain time at night during certain days.

Another example of such support might be the situation when two people are informed about the possibility of their meeting as a result of being in the same geographic location, if such a meeting has been "ordered" before (e.g.: when I am in the same area as the person X, please notify and make an appointment).

2. **Dynamic, or mobile, behavior**, that is related to the movement of both individual users or groups of inhabitants, between neighboring BTS points. It seems that dynamic behaviors, as understood here, give a great number of possibilities to introduce pro-active scenarios. Such scenarios are especially important for the ideas of pervasive computing and smart cities. The desired effect is particularly evident when applying some additional, and free, technologies related to the geographical location and maps, e.g. *OpenStreetMap* OSM [1], or maps of existing urban infrastructure networks, e.g. public transport lines, c.f. Fig. 2. Dynamic behaviors, due to their great potential for interesting uses, are to be discussed separately.

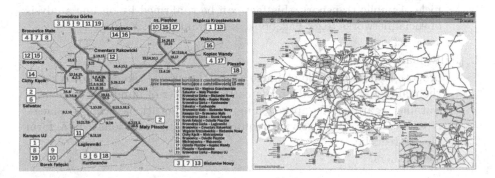

**Fig. 2.** A sample city tram/bus network (source: http://www.mpk.krakow.pl/pl/mapki-komunikacyjne/ )

Scenarios related to dynamic behaviors are of fundamental importance in the paper. Further considerations are focused on the classification of different types of travel in the urban area. The purpose of this classification is to distinguish two kinds of situations which relate to the observed quick move:

1. a group of people traveling by public transport, i.e. simultaneously traveling groups of persons (phones) after finding that this is not a solitary case of traveling by private cars – confirmation of this case is a result of the following observations: the comparison to a similar behavior in the past, quick change of BTS areas, i.e. switching between BTSs, and comparison of the current travel route with public transport lines, c.f. Fig. 2;

---

[1] OSM is a project to create a free editable map of the world.

2. people traveling by private cars – evidence of this case might be a result of the following observations: a greater speed of a travel comparing groups traveling by public transport, traveling outside the area of public transport lines, etc.

When the above basic classification is done, the following support for inhabitants is considered as a result of a performance of the context-aware and pro-active system:

1. (group) trip by public transport
   - finding convenient transfers for travelers if transfers are expected;
   - in the case of transfers with a long wait for a new connection: finding bar/cafeteria facilities in the area in advance to make a reservation;
   - propose to notify people at home (destination) about the arrival time, or notifying of the planned arrival in advance a certain number of minutes before;
   - finding alternative connections and transfers, if there are traffic jams which slow down a trip or make it difficult;
   - notification of friends/colleagues about a common trip in the same vehicle of public transport, this fact can be confirmed by on-line analysis of social networks (e.g.: Facebook, Instagram, etc.);
   - some others;
2. (individual) trip by a car
   - propose to notify people at home about the arrival time, or notifying of the planned arrival in advance a certain number of minutes before;
   - warning regarding the approaching a critical locations, schools, places, crossroads, etc., this service requires gathering additional data form OpenStreetMap;
   - some others.

## 4   System Architecture

In this section we introduce the agent system structure that supports the IoT services mentioned in the previous sections. Let us consider the structure of a system supporting the simple task of determination of the way in which the owner of a mobile phone travels, that is whether travel is done via public transportation or via private car.

The outline of the proposed agent system is shown in Fig. 3. The basic types of agents are:

- a *personal agent* PA, that maintains the trace of the current route of a mobile phone in the entire city among BTS areas, as well as its stored characteristic, taking into account some historical information about previous behaviors; every mobile phone owner has its personal agent PA (informally, a guardian angel PA);

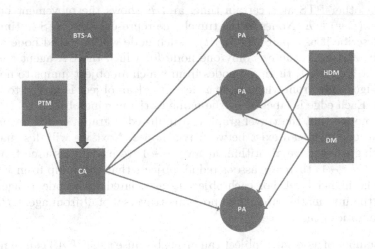

**Fig. 3.** A sample agent system for a public transportation system

- a *BTS agent* BTS-A for every base transceiver station BTS, that, for every personal agent PA that came into the BTS area at the same time slot, creates a temporary *coordination agent* CA which stamps the time of the entry to an area and try to characterize every PA's behaviour in the following way:
  1. if jump among (at least three) regions is slow, then walking,
  2. if jump among (at least three) regions is medium, then private car or public transportation,
  3. if jump among (at least three) regions is fast, then private car;
  the speed (slow, medium, fast) is determined taking into account speeds observed in the considered area; every agent CA is removed/killed when its reasoning process, initiated by an agent BTS-A for a list of jumping PA agents passed to CA is finished;
- a *public transportation manager agent* PTM[2] that tries to recognize and represent the group of personal agents PAs that move in the same line.

The following are rules for the CA agent creation algorithm:

- for every pair of neighboring BTS regions the BTS generates a list of PA agents which passed/jumped between two regions in a given time slot;
- the CA agent is created and the list of jumping agents PAs constitute its input; CA gathers information about the trace of previous travel and creates a *travel graph* for all PA agents considered by CA.

Let us consider a graph $G = \langle V, E \rangle$, c.f. [11], where vertices $V$ are parts of the BTS state which maintains the collection of PA agents that jump to this

---

[2] That can be associated with some buses, if such buses are identified in the network, or of it represents a virtual bus - a group of personal agents that move together in the same destination.

BTS from other BTS at a certain time, and $E$ shows the movement between nodes, i.e. $(v, w) \in E$. Nodes in the travel tree represents the BTS in time $t$, so we will describe it as a pair $(BTS_{ID}, t)$ – such node will be called node at level $t$. Initially, at time $t$, there is only one node for which the CA agent has been created. At level $t - 1$, there are nodes from which an object jumps to nodes at level $t$. Edges show from which node at level $t - 1$ an object is moved to a node at level $t$. Each edge is labelled by the name of the moving object.

Let us notice that the travel graph is a multi-edge graph, which means that more than one edge can exist between two nodes. Next we will designate the object using a recursive algorithm; at level $t - 1$ we initially assume that with node $x = (id, t - 1)$ there are associated all objects that will jump from $x$ to any node at the higher level. For each object $Q$ associated with node $x$, agent CA retrieves the information about the previous traversal of $Q$ from agent $PA_Q$; It should be noticed that:

- the number of associated object can grow, because agent $PA_Q$ can remember that at time $t - 1$, $Q$ was in $id_{BTS}$ with other objects;
- this travel enriches the travel graph at levels lower then $t - 1$.

When we gather all the information about the route of the object from level $t - 1$, we will update the information about the nodes at level $t - 2$ and the following ones. Time is an attribute of the edge. The following rules should be fulfilled in the travel graph:

- $\forall v, w \in V : (w, PA_Q) \in E \Rightarrow time(v) + 1 = time(w)$;
- $y_v = x_w$;
- and agent $PA_Q$ moves from $w$ to $v$.

The travel graph is a multi-graph, which means that more than one edge can exist between the same two graphs nodes. They are differentiated by a label that identifies the PA agent. This graph might constitute a base for reasoning.

The decision made by the CA agent is supported by the information from the PTM agent that can verify if the route traveled by a PA agent can be covered using public transportation. Let us note that we still have a problem with differentiation of two situations:

1. traveling by a bus,
2. traveling in a column of a few/column cars.

In such case, historical data is used to make a decision with the most probability. Let us note that in next steps we can determine the type of transportation because either it is not possible to find a bus travel in this destination or the column of cars has been split. A sample travel graph is shown in Figure 4, where two arrows from one node to another (if any) symbolize that more than one edge exists between two nodes, (i.e. there are two or more edges). Analysis of the graph shows that agents from 51 to 71 are traveling together using the public transport system. Agent 14 travels by car.

The agent system can be extended by two more types of agents:

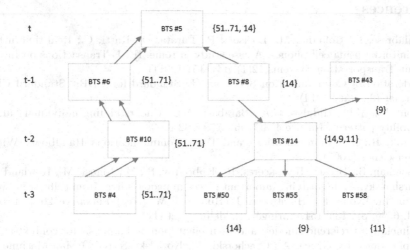

**Fig. 4.** A screen shot of a sample travel graph

- a *historical data maintainer agent* HDM, i.e. an agent that maintains the historical data of personal agents;
- a *data mining agent* DM, that takes the trace of route traveled by a personal agent and processes it into some interesting historical behavior; for example:
  - routes that are covered by walking, via public or private transportation,
  - public agents which usually travel together,
  - a schedule of routes that are executed periodically.

A personal agent PA returns the information to the DM agent (after finishing the travel) and takes it from HDM before starting a new travel.

Historical data maintained by some agents open an interesting issue that supplements the approach presented here. The historical behaviors are encoded into logical specifications, and can be later analyzed for satisfiability, c.f. works [9] or [7,8,10], supporting the current reasoning process and behavior recognition.

## 5    Conclusions

In this paper, the problem of sensing inhabitant behaviors in a smart city are considered. The classification of behaviors observed using the BTS networks is proposed. A public transportation case is discussed, and a multi-agent system is proposed. This work opens a research area which is of crucial importance for the idea of smart cities.

Future works may include the implementation of the reasoning engine. It should result in a CASE software, which could be a first step involved in creating industrial-proof tools.

# References

1. Calabrese, F., Colonna, M., Lovisolo, P., Parata, D., Ratti, C.: Real-time urban monitoring using cell phones: A case study in rome. IEEE Transactions on Intelligent Transportation Systems 12(1), 141–151 (2011)
2. Federation of Communication Services: UK Standard for CDRs. Standard CDR Format (January 2014)
3. Gonzalez, M.C., Hidalgo, C.A., Barabasi, A.L.: Understanding individual human mobility patterns. Nature 453(7196), 779–782 (2008)
4. Horak, R.: Telecommunications and Data Communications Handbook. Wiley-Interscience (2007)
5. Isaacman, S., Becker, R., Cáceres, R., Kobourov, S., Martonosi, M., Rowland, J., Varshavsky, A.: Identifying important places in people's lives from cellular network data. In: Lyons, K., Hightower, J., Huang, E.M. (eds.) Pervasive 2011. LNCS, vol. 6696, pp. 133–151. Springer, Heidelberg (2011)
6. Klimek, R.: Preference models and their elicitation and analysis for context-aware applications. In: Gruca, A., Czachórski, T., Kozielski, S. (eds.) Man-Machine Interactions 3. AISC, vol. 242, pp. 357–364. Springer, Heidelberg (2014)
7. Klimek, R.: A system for deduction-based formal verification of workflow-oriented software models. International Journal of Applied Mathematics and Computer Science 24(4), 941–956 (2014),
http://www.amcs.uz.zgora.pl/?action=paper\&paper=802
8. Klimek, R., Faber, Ł., Kisiel-Dorohinicki, M.: Verifying data integration agents with deduction-based models. In: Proceedings of Federated Conference on Computer Science and Information Systems (FedCSIS 2013), Kraków, Poland, September 8-11, pp. 1049–1055. IEEE Xplore Digital Library (2013)
9. Klimek, R., Kotulski, L.: Proposal of a multiagent-based smart environment for the iot. In: Augusto, J.C., Zhang, T. (eds.) Workshop Proceedings of the 10th International Conference on Intelligent Environments. Ambient Intelligence and Smart Environments, Shanghai, China, June 30-July 1, vol. 18, pp. 37–44. IOS Press (2014)
10. Klimek, R., Rogus, G.: Modeling context-aware and agent-ready systems for the outdoor smart lighting. In: Rutkowski, L., Korytkowski, M., Scherer, R., Tadeusiewicz, R., Zadeh, L.A., Zurada, J.M. (eds.) ICAISC 2014, Part II. LNCS(LNAI), vol. 8468, pp. 257–268. Springer, Heidelberg (2014)
11. Kotulski, L.: Gradis – multi-agent environment suppporting distributed graph transformations. In: Bubak, M., van Albada, G.D., Dongarra, J., Sloot, P.M.A. (eds.) ICCS 2008, Part III. LNCS, vol. 5103, pp. 644–653. Springer, Heidelberg (2008)
12. Reades, J., Calabrese, F., Sevtsuk, A., Ratti, C.: Cellular census: Explorations in urban data collection. IEEE Pervasive Computing 6(3), 30–38 (2007)

# Aspects of Structure and Parameters Selection of Control Systems Using Selected Multi-Population Algorithms

Krystian Łapa[1](✉), Jacek Szczypta[1], and Rajasekar Venkatesan[2]

[1] Institute of Computational Intelligence,
Częstochowa University of Technology, Częstochowa, Poland
{krystian.lapa,jacek.szczypta}@iisi.pcz.pl
[2] School of Electrical and Electronic Engineering,
Nanyang Technological University, Singapore, Singapore
raja0046@e.ntu.edu.sg

**Abstract.** In this paper a new approach for automatic design of control systems is presented. It is based on multi-population algorithms and allows to select not only parameters of control systems, but also its structure. Proposed approach was tested on a problem of stabilization of double spring-mass-damp object.

## 1 Introduction

The problem of selecting the structure and parameters of control systems is a typical optimization problem (see e.g. [37, 52, 53]). In the literature are many approaches to automatization of this process can be found. However, they are based mostly on selecting parameters of control systems with structures experimentally selected by experts (see e.g. [23]). These approaches are often based on computational intelligence methods such as: neural networks (see e.g. [13, 42]), neuro-fuzzy systems (see e.g. [7, 9–12, 26]) and population algorithms (see e.g. [15, 16, 33]). In this paper we present a new method for automatic selection of both the control system structure and structure parameters. Proposed method bases on a PID correction terms (Proportional-Integral-Derivative controller). PID controllers respond to the needs of most of automation systems (see e.g. [28]) and they are used most often in practice (see e.g. [32]).

In our previous paper the problem of automatic selection of both the control system structure and structure parameters based on PID correction terms was considered (see [49]). In this process we used an accurate model of an object and selected population-based algorithms (i.e. firefly algorithm, gravitational search algorithm). We took into account and tested different variety of criteria, which allowed us obtain satisfactory results. In current paper we propose an approach using multi-population algorithms (instead of using population-based algorithms) which can be also called subpopulation algorithms or island algorithms (see e.g. [4, 30, 31]). The idea of these algorithms is based on splitting population into subpopulations (islands) in which an evolution process

© Springer International Publishing Switzerland 2015
L. Rutkowski et al. (Eds.): ICAISC 2015, Part II, LNAI 9120, pp. 247–260, 2015.
DOI: 10.1007/978-3-319-19369-4_23

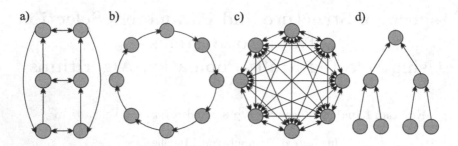

**Fig. 1.** Typical topologies between subpopulations in multi-population algorithms (migration directions was marked by arrow heads): (a) ladder-type topology (see e.g. [5]), (b) one direction circle topology (see e.g. [4]), (c) peer to peer topology (see e.g. [4]), (d) hierarchical topology (see e.g. [31])

(see e.g. [24, 25, 51]) takes place independently (in most parts of the algorithm). It allows to obtain a diversity of population which make a possibility to find different extremes of fitness function. It results in a convergence. This effectively prevents premature convergence of the algorithm (see e.g. [47]). The additional characteristics of multi-population algorithms are: i.e. (a) different topologies of subpopulations (see e.g. [4, 5]), (b) cooperations and competitions between subpopulations and (c) migration of individuals between subpopulations. Typical topologies of multi-population algorithms can be seen on Fig. 1. The topologies determine a communication between subpopulations (islands) and directions of migrations between subpopulations. The competitions and cooperations between subpopulations (which are not used in some multi-population algorithms) usually consist of determining the ranking of subpopulations (using additional fitness function) and they result usually in making changes in subpopulations (i.e. changing tuning parameters, determining individuals and their amounts for migrations, changing size of subpopulations, etc.). We have chosen two typical algorithms from this group: golden ball algorithm ([31]) and multi-swarm cooperative particle swarm optimizer ([30]). Considered algorithm was modified for our structure and structure parameters selection of the control systems.

Please note that the proposed method can be successfully applied to all optimization problems which require not only parameters selection but also structure selection, e.g. structure selection of fuzzy systems (see e.g. [3]), neuro-fuzzy systems (see e.g. [21, 35, 43–46]), type-2 fuzzy systems (see e.g. [1, 14, 48]). Proposed algorithm may be also used in some modelling (see e.g. [2, 6, 8, 27, 34]) and pattern recognition issues ([40, 41, 55–58]).

This paper is organized into four sections. Section 2 presents a detailed description of the proposed approach to designing controllers. In Section 3 simulation results are drawn. Conclusions are presented in Section 4.

## 2 Proposed Approach to Designing Controllers

Key remarks regarding approaches presented in the paper can be stated as follows: **(a)** Fig. 2 presents the controller structure which is initial point for execution of our algorithm. Controller structure is a result of generalization of typical controllers used in practice: PID controller, cascaded PID controller with feedforward signals and state-feedback controller. It is important to remark that in generalization any controller can be taken into consideration. **(b)** In Fig. 2 the connections that can be generated during evolution were marked with dashed line. This remark applies to control system structure (see Fig. 2.a) and its basic block (CB). Basic block (CB) consists of proportional term ($P$), integral term ($I$) and derivative term ($D$) (see Fig. 2.b). Signal $fb_n$, $n$=1, ..., $N$, denotes feedback signal, signal $ff_m$, $m = 1, ..., M$, denotes feed-forward signal. **(c)** Selection of the control system structure is performed using genetic algorithm (see e.g. [4, 5, 36, 54, 59]). Selection of the control system parameters is performed using one of the chosen multi-population algorithm. Selection of the control system structure and parameters is performed concurrently during evolution process. The evolution is performed on the basis of the knowledge about controlled object and properly defined fitness function. It is important that proposed approach eliminates a need of trial and error selection of the control system. Usage of controlled object model, despite the advantage like elimination of the controlled object damage risk, has also disadvantages. Primary disadvantage is a need of knowledge about controlled object. Models of the controlled object have to be not only precise enough and have the knowledge about typical operational conditions of the controlled object (representing engine run under load or idle state), but it also have to take into account an unusual operating conditions (e.g. engine short circuit, engine state as a result of surge or overload in supply circuit). It is important that when it is a need to design the control system using classic methods (basing on the designer experience), only typical operating conditions are taken into consideration. Moreover, development of precise model of the controlled object is not currently a big problem (see e.g. [22, 38]).

### 2.1 Coding of the Structure and Parameters

In proposed method full controller (with its structure and parameters) is encoded in a single chromosome $\mathbf{X}_{ch}$. The chromosome $\mathbf{X}_{ch}$ (further called individual) is described as follows:

$$\mathbf{X}_{ch} = \left\{ \mathbf{X}_{ch}^{\mathrm{par}}, \mathbf{X}_{ch}^{\mathrm{red}} \right\}, \tag{1}$$

where $\mathbf{X}_{ch}^{\mathrm{par}}$ is a chromosome encoding correction term parameters, $\mathbf{X}_{ch}^{\mathrm{red}}$ is a chromosome encoding connection in general (proposed) structure of the control system presented in Fig. 2. The chromosome $\mathbf{X}_{ch}^{\mathrm{par}}$ is described as follows:

$$\mathbf{X}_{ch}^{\mathrm{par}} = (P_1, I_1, D_1, P_2, I_2, D_2, \ldots) = \left( X_{ch,1}^{\mathrm{par}}, X_{ch,2}^{\mathrm{par}}, \ldots, X_{ch,L^{\mathrm{par}}}^{\mathrm{par}} \right), \tag{2}$$

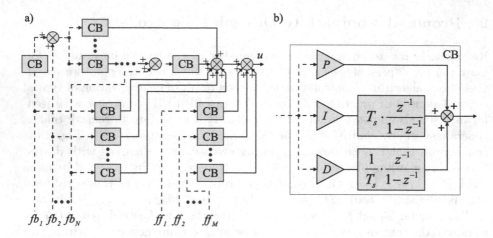

**Fig. 2.** Initial discrete controller structure (connections that can be obtained in evolution process are marked with continuous line): a) considered, generalized control system, b) CB definition idea ($T_s$ stands for discretization constant in time domain)

where $P_1$, $I_1$, $D_1$, $P_2$, $I_2$, $D_2$,... denote control system parameters values, $ch = 1, .., Ch$ denotes index of the chromosome in the population, $Ch$ denotes a number of chromosomes in the population, $L^{\mathrm{par}}$ denotes length of the chromosome $\mathbf{X}_{ch}^{\mathrm{par}}$. The chromosome $\mathbf{X}_{ch}^{\mathrm{red}}$ is described as follows:

$$\mathbf{X}_{ch}^{\mathrm{red}} = \left( X_{ch,1}^{\mathrm{red}}, X_{ch,2}^{\mathrm{red}}, \ldots, X_{ch,L^{\mathrm{red}}}^{\mathrm{red}} \right), \tag{3}$$

where every gene $X_{ch,g}^{\mathrm{red}} \in \{0,1\}$, $ch = 1, .., Ch$, $g = 1, .., L^{\mathrm{red}}$ decides if relevant part of the control system occurs in control process (relevant gene $X_{ch,g}^{\mathrm{red}} = 1$), $L^{\mathrm{red}}$ denotes length of the chromosome $\mathbf{X}_{ch}^{\mathrm{red}}$.

## 2.2  Evolution Process

The proposed approach for selection of the system structure and parameters is based on a fusion between genetic algorithm and multi-population algorithm. It determines evolution process, in which the following algorithm steps are taken:

- **Step 1.** Initialization of population $\mathbf{P}$ by creating $N$ individuals.
- **Step 2.** Evaluation of population $\mathbf{P}$ with defined fitness function.
- **Step 3.** Division of population $\mathbf{P}$ into $G$ subpopulations: $\mathbf{R}_i$, $i = 1, ..., G$. It is worth to mention that steps 3-7 depend on multi-population algorithm.
- **Step 4.** Modification of structures (3) of individuals in $\mathbf{R}_i$, $i = 1, ..., G$ by mutation operator from genetic algorithm (see e.g. [42, 49]).
- **Step 5.** Tuning of parameters (2) of individuals in $\mathbf{R}_i$, $i = 1, ..., G$ by multi-population algorithm (subpopulation $\mathbf{R}_i$ tuning).
- **Step 6.** Cooperation and competition between subpopulations $\mathbf{R}_i$, $i = 1, ..., G$. Each subpopulation can be evaluated separately or with other subpopulations. Results from this step may determine the next step.

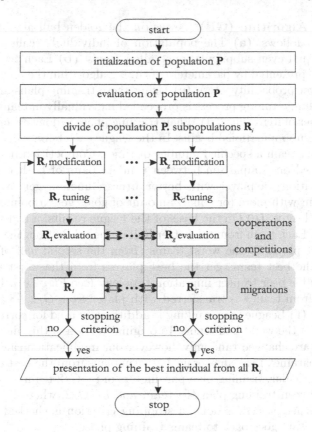

**Fig. 3.** Main schema of proposed hybrid multi-population algorithms

- **Step 7.** Migrations between subpopulations $\mathbf{R}_i$, $i = 1, ..., G$. Migrations are based on topologies defined by multi-population algorithm and on fitness value of individuals and subpopulations.
- **Step 8.** Checking stopping criterion, which is mostly based on checking iteration number of the algorithm. If the criterion is not achieved, algorithm goes back to Step 4.
- **Step 9.** Presentation of the best chromosome from all populations $\mathbf{R}_i$.

Genetic algorithm is a well-known method (see e.g. [18, 26, 29, 42]). In our simulations it processes solely chromosomes (3) for selection of the control system structure. On the other hand, multi-population algorithm fused with genetic algorithm processes exclusively the parameters of the control system encoded in the chromosome (2).

In the literature many different multi-population algorithms can be found. In our simulations we used two of them: **(a)** golden ball algorithm (GB) (see [31]) and **(b)** multi-swarm cooperative particle swarm optimizer (MCPSO, in short MC) (see [30]).

**Golden Ball Algorithm (GB).** Notes on the golden ball algorithm can be summarized as follows: **(a)** The population of individuals (called *players*) is divided into equal even subpopulations called *teams*. **(b)** Each team gets own *training plan* represented by parameters of tuning algorithm (i.e. mutation probability, crossover probability, etc.). **(c)** Using these training plans and standard genetic algorithm, a tuning process is proceeded individually in teams. It takes a specified number of iterations. **(d)** When training phase is done a *league* (competition between subpopulations) begins. In the league each team *plays* (competes) with every other team a specified number of times. Competition between teams (*match*) is based on comparison between random pairs of both teams players (without repetition), a player with better fitness function gets a *goal* for its team. The team with more (or equal) amount of goals gets a point in the team ranking in the league. **(e)** On the basis of the league results, a transfer between teams is made. Each team from the better half of the table (from the best teams) gives the worst player to the worst teams (from the second half of the table). In exchange, the best teams get the best players from the worst teams. This process stands for peer to peer migration topology (see Fig. 1.c)). In case of $G$ teams, player from team $i$ is transferred with player from $G/2 + i$ team, where $i = 1, ..., G/2$). **(f)** League team ranking is additionally used for correction of the training plans of the worst half teams. In original version of this algorithm those training plans are changed randomly, however our modification calculate a new training plan parameters as an average between plans from the best teams in the ranking. In particular, training plan parameters of $i - G/2$ team is calculated as an average between training plan of $i$ team and $i - G/2$, where $i = G/2, ..., G$. **(g)** When transfer process is done, a stopping criterion is checked. If it is not achieved, algorithm goes back to teams training phase.

**Multi-Swarm Cooperative Particle Swarm Optimizer (MC).** Notes on the multi-swarm cooperative particle swarm optimizer can be summarized as follows: **(a)** The idea of algorithm is to divide population into subpopulations with equal number of individuals. One of these subpopulations is chosen randomly as a parent subpopulation. **(b)** In the tuning process, all subpopulations (beside parent subpopulation) are tuned by standard particle swarm optimization (PSO, see e.g. [20, 39]) method for a period of one iteration. Those subpopulations are not competing with each other. **(c)** However, each of them sends a specified (by algorithm parameter) number of copies of the best individuals into the parent subpopulation. This migration process uses a hierarchical topology many-to-one, which can be seen on Fig. 1.d). **(d)** When migration process is finished, parent subpopulation is also tuned by standard PSO algorithm and next the excess of individuals in parent subpopulation is reduced (individuals with worse fitness function values are removed) to standard size. **(e)** When reduction process is done, a stopping criterion is checked. If it is not achieved, algorithm goes back to tuning phase.

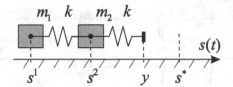

**Fig. 4.** Simulated spring-mass-damp object

## 2.3   Individuals Evaluation

The way of defining fitness function in most of the control systems does not depend from algorithm but from considering problem. In case of selecting structure and parameters of control system, fitness function can consist of the following elements: RMSE error, oscillations of the controller output signal, controller complexity and overshoot of the control signal. High number of the controller output signal oscillations is a negative phenomenon, because it tends to induce an excessive use of mechanical control parts and may cause often a huge changes of the controller output signal value. This is a very important issue, because the overshoot of the control signal is not acceptable in many industrial applications. The chromosome evaluation function is described as follows:

$$ff\left(\mathbf{X}_{ch}\right) = \frac{1}{RMSE_{ch} + c_{ch} \cdot w_c + os_{ch} \cdot w_{os} + ov_{ch} \cdot w_{ov}}, \tag{4}$$

where $c_{ch} > 0$ denotes the complexity of the controller structure and it is calculated by the formula:

$$c_{ch} = \sum_{g=1}^{L} \mathbf{X}_{ch,g}^{\text{red}}, \tag{5}$$

$w_c \in [0, 1]$ denotes a weight factor for the complexity of the controller structure, $os_{ch} \geq 0$ denotes oscillation count of controller output signal (in simulations its value is calculated automatically), $w_{os} \in [0, 1]$ denotes a weight for the oscillations factor, $ov_{ch} \geq 0$ denotes value of the greatest overshoot of the controlled $s^1$ signal and finally $w_{ov} \in [0, 1]$ denotes a weight for the overshoot factor. RMSE error function of the chromosome $ch$ is described by the following formula:

$$RMSE_{ch} = \sqrt{\frac{1}{N} \sum_{i=1}^{N} \varepsilon_{ch,i}{}^2} = \sqrt{\frac{1}{N} \sum_{i=1}^{N} \left(s_{ch,i}^* - s_{ch,i}^1\right)^2}, \tag{6}$$

where $i = 1, \ldots, N$, denotes sample index, $N$ denotes the number of samples, $\varepsilon_{ch,i}$ denotes controller tracking error for the sample $i$, $s_{ch,i}^*$ denotes the value of the reference signal of the controlled value for the sample $i$, $s_{ch,i}^1$ denotes its current value for the sample $i$. In our method we maximize the function described by formula (4).

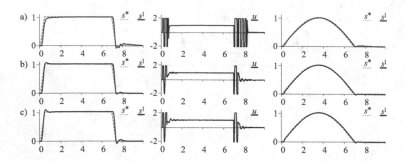

**Fig. 5.** Signal values $s^1$, $s^*$ and output signal of the controller $y$ in case of fusion between genetic algorithm with: a) evolutionary algorithm (GA+EA) used for a comparison, b) golden ball algorithm (GA+GB), c) multi-swarm cooperative particle swarm
optimizer (GA+MC)

## 3    Simulations Results

In our simulations a problem of designing controller structure and tuning parameters for double spring-mass-damp object was considered (see Fig. 4). More
details about this model can be found in our previous paper [50]).

Remarks about considering model can be summarized as follows: **(a)** Object
parameters values were set as follows: spring constant $k$ was set to 10 N/m,
coefficient of friction $\mu = 0.5$, masses $m_1 = m_2 = 0.2$ kg. Initial values of: $s^1$, $v^1$,
$s^2$ i $v^2$ were set to zero. **(b)** Simulation length was set to 10 s, a shape of the
reference signal $s^*$ (trapezoid) is presented in Fig. 5, a shape of test signal $s^*$
(sinuous) is presented in Fig. 5. **(c)** Search range for genes encoding controller
parameters were set as follows: $P = [0,20]$, $I = [0,50]$, $D = [0,5]$. **(d)** Output
signal of the controller was limited to the range $y \in (-2, +2)$. **(e)** Quantization
resolution for the output signal $y$ of the controller as well as for the position
sensor for $s^1$ and $s^2$ was set to 10 bit. **(f)** Time step in the simulation was equal
to $T = 0.1$ ms, while interval between subsequent controller activations were set
to twenty simulation steps.

The authorial environment (implemented in C# language) was used for simulations. Parameters of the algorithms for the simulations were determined as
follows: **(a)** Genetic algorithm: the number of chromosomes in the population
was set to 100, the algorithm performs 2 000 steps (generations), the crossover
probability was set as $p_c = 0.8$, the mutation probability was set as $p_m = 0.3$.
**(b)** For both considered multi population-based algorithms: the number of individuals in subpopulations was set to 16, number of subpopulations was set to
16. **(c)** For GB algorithm training time of subpopulations was set to 50 iterations, for MC algorithm a standard PSO parameters were used: learning factors
$c_1 = c_2 = 2$.

Observations obtained from results of the simulations can be summarized as
follows: **(a)** Signal values $s^1$, $s^*$ and output signal of the control $y$ are highly
acceptable (see Fig. 5). The smallest oscillations of the signals were obtained by

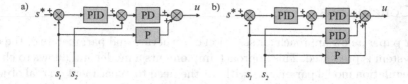

**Fig. 6.** Structure of the controller obtained in the evolution process in case of fusion between genetic algorithm with: a) golden ball algorithm (GA+GB), b) multi-swarm cooperative particle swarm optimizer (GA+MC)

**Table 1.** Number of correction terms obtained in evolution process

| name | number of the correction terms | | | | | |
|------|------|------|------|------|------|------|
| | our results | | previous results (see [49]) | | | |
| | GA+GB | GA+MC | GA+EA | GA+FA | GA+GA | GA+BA |
| $P$ | 3 | 4 | 2 | 3 | 3 | 5 |
| $I$ | 1 | 3 | 1 | 1 | 1 | 2 |
| $D$ | 2 | 3 | 3 | 2 | 3 | 2 |
| All | 6 | 10 | 6 | 6 | 7 | 9 |

**Table 2.** Values of the components of the fitness function (4) obtained in evolution process. Assumed weights of the fitness function are set to: $w_c = 0.001$, $w_z = 0.01$, $w_{ov} = 0.0001$

| name | parameters of the control systems | | | | | |
|------|------|------|------|------|------|------|
| | our results | | previous results (see [49]) | | | |
| | GA+GB | GA+MC | GA+EA | GA+FA | GA+GA | GA+BA |
| $RMSE$ | **0.0502** | **0.0511** | 0.0625 | 0.1276 | 0.1790 | 0.0901 |
| $c_{ch} \cdot w_c$ | 0.0060 | 0.0100 | 0.0060 | 0.0060 | 0.0070 | 0.0090 |
| $z_{ch} \cdot w_z$ | 0.0153 | 0.0123 | 0.0350 | 0.0170 | 0.0170 | 0.0299 |
| $ov_{ch} \cdot w_{ov}$ | 0.0004 | 0.0005 | 0.0001 | 0.0002 | 0.0005 | 0.0014 |
| $ff$ | **13.9082** | **13.5317** | 9.6525 | 6.6312 | 4.9140 | 7.6687 |

the golden ball algorithm (see Fig. 5). **(b)** The simplest structure of the system was achieved using the golden ball algorithm (see e.g. [16–19]). It is worth to mention that in every case presented in Fig. 6 the system structure is quite simple (see Table 1) and it does not affect requirements of the fitness function (4) (see Table 2). Obtaining a similarly simple structures using classic algorithms of the selection of control systems would be difficult and time consuming. **(c)** The structures and parameters of the control system obtained in the learning process, which was performed on the trapezoid shape of the signal (see Fig. 6), were tested additionally on the sinusoidal shape of the signal (see Fig. 6) and resulted with good performance (generalization). **(d)** Obtained results are characterized by better parameters (including most important RMSE and fitness function value defining quality of whole solution) than results achieved in our previous paper (see [49]) with use of the single population-based algorithms.

# 4    Conclusions

In our paper a new approach for selection of structure and parameters of the control system is presented. This approach implements a model and allows to choose safe regulation model parameters without the need to experiment on real objects. Our method uses a fusion between genetic algorithm (for selecting the structure of the control system) and possibilities of specified multi population-based algorithms (based on different migration topologies): golden ball and multi-swarm cooperative particle swarm optimizer (for selecting the parameters of the control system). Obtained (according to fitness function components) simulation results allows us to achieve non-complex control systems characterized by good accuracy with acceptable infinitesimal oscillations. The results are significantly better than the ones obtained using single population-based methods.

**Acknowledgment.** The project was financed by the National Science Centre (Poland) on the basis of the decision number DEC-2012/05/B/ST7/02138.

# References

1. Bartczuk, Ł., Dziwiński, P., Starczewski, J.T.: New method for generation type-2 fuzzy partition for FDT. In: Rutkowski, L., Scherer, R., Tadeusiewicz, R., Zadeh, L.A., Zurada, J.M. (eds.) ICAISC 2010, Part I. LNCS(LNAI), vol. 6113, pp. 275–280. Springer, Heidelberg (2010)
2. Bartczuk, Ł., Przybył, A., Koprinkova-Hristova, P.: New method for nonlinear fuzzy correction modelling of dynamic objects. In: Rutkowski, L., Korytkowski, M., Scherer, R., Tadeusiewicz, R., Zadeh, L.A., Zurada, J.M. (eds.) ICAISC 2014, Part I. LNCS(LNAI), vol. 8467, pp. 169–180. Springer, Heidelberg (2014)
3. Bartczuk, Ł., Dziwiński, P., Starczewski, J.T.: A new method for dealing with unbalanced linguistic term set. In: Rutkowski, L., Korytkowski, M., Scherer, R., Tadeusiewicz, R., Zadeh, L.A., Zurada, J.M. (eds.) ICAISC 2012, Part I. LNCS, vol. 7267, pp. 207–212. Springer, Heidelberg (2012)
4. Borovska, P., Lazarova, M.: Migration policies for island genetic models on multicomputer platform. In: Intelligent Data Acquisition and Advanced Computing Systems: Technology and Applications, pp. 143–148 (2007)
5. Cantu-Paz, E.: Topologies, migration rates, and multi-population parallel genetic algorithms (1999)
6. Cpałka, K., Łapa, K., Przybył, A., Zalasiński, M.: A new method for designing neuro-fuzzy systems for nonlinear modelling with interpretability aspects. Neurocomputing 135, 203–217 (2014)
7. Cpałka, K.: On evolutionary designing and learning of flexible neuro-fuzzy structures for nonlinear classification. Nonlinear Analysis Series A: Theory, Methods and Applications 71, 1659–1672 (2009)
8. Cpałka, K., Rebrova, O., Nowicki, R., Rutkowski, L.: On design of flexible neuro-fuzzy systems for nonlinear modelling. Int. Journal of General Systems 42(6), 706–720 (2013)
9. Cpałka, K., Rutkowski, L.: Flexible Takagi-Sugeno Fuzzy Systems. In: Proceedings of the International Joint Conference on Neural Networks 2005, Montreal, pp. 1764–1769 (2005)

10. Cpałka, K., Rutkowski, L.: A New Method for Designing and Reduction of Neuro-fuzzy Systems. In: Proceedings of the 2006 IEEE International Conference on Fuzzy Systems (IEEE World Congress on Computational Intelligence, WCCI 2006), Vancouver, BC, Canada (2006), pp. 8510–8516 (2006)
11. Cpałka, K., Zalasiński, M.: On-line signature verification using vertical signature partitioning. Expert Systems with Applications 41, 4170–4180 (2014)
12. Cpałka, K., Zalasiński, M., Rutkowski, L.: New method for the on-line signature verification based on horizontal partitioning. Pattern Recognition 47, 2652–2661 (2014)
13. Dziwiński, P., Bartczuk, Ł., Starczewski, J.T.: Fully controllable ant colony system for text data clustering. In: Rutkowski, L., Korytkowski, M., Scherer, R., Tadeusiewicz, R., Zadeh, L.A., Zurada, J.M. (eds.) SIDE 2012 and EC 2012. LNCS, vol. 7269, pp. 199–205. Springer, Heidelberg (2012)
14. Dziwiński, P., Starczewski, J.T., Bartczuk, Ł.: New linguistic hedges in construction of interval type-2 fls. In: Rutkowski, L., Scherer, R., Tadeusiewicz, R., Zadeh, L.A., Zurada, J.M. (eds.) ICAISC 2010, Part II. LNCS(LNAI), vol. 6114, pp. 445–450. Springer, Heidelberg (2010)
15. Dziwiński, P., Bartczuk, Ł., Przybył, A., Avedyan, E.D.: A New Algorithm for Identification of Significant Operating Points Using Swarm Intelligence. In: Rutkowski, L., Korytkowski, M., Scherer, R., Tadeusiewicz, R., Zadeh, L.A., Zurada, J.M. (eds.) ICAISC 2014, Part II. LNCS(LNAI), vol. 8468, pp. 349–362. Springer, Heidelberg (2014)
16. El-Abd, M.: On the hybridization on the artificial bee colony and particle swarm optimization algorithms. Journal of Artificial Intelligence and Soft Computing Research 2(2), 147–155 (2012)
17. Fogel, D.B.: Evolutionary Computation: Toward a New Philosophy of Machine Intelligence, 3rd edn. IEEE Press, Piscataway (2006)
18. Gabryel, M., Cpałka, K., Rutkowski, L.: Evolutionary strategies for learning of neuro-fuzzy systems. In: I Workshop on Genetic Fuzzy Systems, Granada, pp. 119–123 (2005)
19. Gabryel, M., Woźniak, M., K. Nowicki, R.: Creating Learning Sets for Control Systems Using an Evolutionary Method. In: Rutkowski, L., Korytkowski, M., Scherer, R., Tadeusiewicz, R., Zadeh, L.A., Zurada, J.M. (eds.) SIDE 2012 and EC 2012. LNCS, vol. 7269, pp. 206–213. Springer, Heidelberg (2012)
20. Kennedy, J., Eberhart, R.C.: Particle swarm optimization. In: Proc. IEEE Int'l Conf. on Neural Networks, vol. IV, pp. 1942–1948 (1995)
21. Korytkowski, M., Rutkowski, L., Scherer, R.: From ensemble of fuzzy classifiers to single fuzzy rule base classifier. In: Rutkowski, L., Tadeusiewicz, R., Zadeh, L.A., Zurada, J.M. (eds.) ICAISC 2008. LNCS (LNAI), vol. 5097, pp. 265–272. Springer, Heidelberg (2008)
22. Leva, A., Papadopoulos, A.V.: Tuning of event-based industrial controllers with simple stability guarantees. Journal of Process Control 23, 1251–1260 (2013)
23. Li, W.: Design of PID Controller Based on an Expert System. International Journal of Computer, Consumer and Control (IJ3C) 3(1), 31–40 (2014)
24. Lobato, F.S., Steffen Jr., V.: A new multi-objective optimization algorithm based on differential evolution and neighborhood exploring evolution strategy. Journal of Artificial Intelligence and Soft Computing Research 1(4), 259–267 (2011)
25. Lobato, F.S., Steffen Jr., V., Silva Neto, A.J.: Solution of singular optimal control problems using the improved differential evolution algorithm. Journal of Artificial Intelligence and Soft Computing Research 1(3), 195–206 (2011)

26. Łapa, K., Przybył, A., Cpałka, K.: A new approach to designing interpretable models of dynamic systems. In: Rutkowski, L., Korytkowski, M., Scherer, R., Tadeusiewicz, R., Zadeh, L.A., Zurada, J.M. (eds.) ICAISC 2013, Part II. LNCS(LNAI), vol. 7895, pp. 523–534. Springer, Heidelberg (2013)

27. Łapa, K., Zalasiński, M., Cpałka, K.: A new method for designing and complexity reduction of neuro-fuzzy systems for nonlinear modelling. In: Rutkowski, L., Korytkowski, M., Scherer, R., Tadeusiewicz, R., Zadeh, L.A., Zurada, J.M. (eds.) ICAISC 2013, Part I. LNCS(LNAI), vol. 7894, pp. 329–344. Springer, Heidelberg (2013)

28. Malhotra, R., Sodh, R.: Boiler Flow Control Using PID and Fuzzy Logic Controller. IJCSET 1(6), 315–331 (2011)

29. Michalewicz, Z.: Genetic Algorithms + Data Structures = Evolution Programs. Springer (1999)

30. Niu, B., Zhu, Y., He, X., Wu, H.: MCPSO: A multi-swarm cooperative particle swarm optimizer. Applied Mathematics and Computation 185(2,15), 1050–1062 (2007)

31. Osaba, E., Diaz, F., Onieva, E.: Golden ball: a novel metaheuristic to solve combinatorial optimization problems based on soccer concepts. Applied Intelligence 41(1), 145–166 (2014)

32. Perng, J.-W., Chen, G.-Y., Hsieh, S.-C.: Optimal PID Controller Design Based on PSO-RBFNN for Wind Turbine Systems. Energies 7, 191–209 (2014)

33. Prampero, P.S., Attux, R.: Magnetic particle swarm optimization. Journal of Artificial Intelligence and Soft Computing Research 2(1), 59–72 (2012)

34. Przybył, A., Cpałka, K.: A new method to construct of interpretable models of dynamic systems. In: Rutkowski, L., Korytkowski, M., Scherer, R., Tadeusiewicz, R., Zadeh, L.A., Zurada, J.M. (eds.) ICAISC 2012, Part II. LNCS, vol. 7268, pp. 697–705. Springer, Heidelberg (2012)

35. Przybył, A., Er, M.J.: The idea for the integration of neuro-fuzzy hardware emulators with real-time network. In: Rutkowski, L., Korytkowski, M., Scherer, R., Tadeusiewicz, R., Zadeh, L.A., Zurada, J.M. (eds.) ICAISC 2014, Part I. LNCS(LNAI), vol. 8467, pp. 279–294. Springer, Heidelberg (2014)

36. Przybył, A., Jelonkiewicz, J.: Genetic algorithm for observer parameters tuning in sensorless induction motor drive. Neural Networks and Soft Computing, pp. 376–381 (2003)

37. Przybył, A., Smołąg, J., Kimla, P.: Distributed control system based on real time ethernet for computer numerical controlled machine tool. Przegląd Elektrotechniczny 86(2), 342–346 (2010) (in Polish)

38. Rasoanarivo, I., Brechet, S., Battiston, A., Nahid-Mobarakeh, B.: Behavioral Analysis of a Boost Converter with High Performance Source Filter and a Fractional-Order PID Controller. In: IEEE Industry Applications Society Annual Meeting (IAS), pp. 1–6 (2012)

39. Rini, D.P., Shamsuddin, S.M., Yuhaniz, S.S.: Particle Swarm Optimization: Technique, System and Challenges. International Journal of Computer Applications (0975-8887) 14(1), 19–27 (2011)

40. Rutkowski, L.: Sequential estimates of probability densities by orthogonal series and their application in pattern-classification. IEEE Trans. Systems Man and Cybernetics 10(2), 918–920 (1980)

41. Rutkowski, L.: Multiple Fourier-series procedures for extraction of nonlinear regressions from noisy data. IEEE Trans. Signal Processing 41(10), 3062–3065 (1993)

42. Rutkowski, L.: Computational Intelligence. Springer (2008)

43. Rutkowski, L., Cpałka, K.: A neuro-fuzzy controller with a compromise fuzzy reasoning. Control and Cybernetics 31(2), 297–308 (2002)
44. Rutkowski, L., Cpałka, K.: Compromise approach to neuro-fuzzy systems. In: Sincak, P., Vascak, J., Kvasnicka, V., Pospichal, J. (eds.) Intelligent Technologies - Theory and Applications, vol. 76, pp. 85–90. IOS Press (2002)
45. Rutkowski, L., Cpałka, K.: Neuro-fuzzy systems derived from quasi-triangular norms. In: Proceedings of the IEEE International Conference on Fuzzy Systems, Budapest, July 26-29, vol. 2, pp. 1031–1036 (2004)
46. Rutkowski, L., Przybył, A., Cpałka, K., Er, M.J.: Online speed profile generation for industrial machine tool based on neuro-fuzzy approach. In: Rutkowski, L., Scherer, R., Tadeusiewicz, R., Zadeh, L.A., Zurada, J.M. (eds.) ICAISC 2010, Part II. LNCS(LNAI), vol. 6114, pp. 645–650. Springer, Heidelberg (2010)
47. Skolicki, Z., De Jong, K.: The influence of migration sizes and intervals on island models. In: GECCO 2005: Proceedings of the 2005 Conference on Genetic and Evolutionary Computation, pp. 1295–1302 (2005)
48. Starczewski, J.T., Bartczuk, Ł., Dziwiński, P., Marvuglia, A.: Learning methods for type-2 FLS based on FCM. In: Rutkowski, L., Scherer, R., Tadeusiewicz, R., Zadeh, L.A., Zurada, J.M. (eds.) ICAISC 2010, Part I. LNCS(LNAI), vol. 6113, pp. 224–231. Springer, Heidelberg (2010)
49. Szczypta, J., Łapa, K., Shao, Z.: Aspects of the Selection of the Structure and Parameters of Controllers Using Selected Population Based Algorithms. In: Rutkowski, L., Korytkowski, M., Scherer, R., Tadeusiewicz, R., Zadeh, L.A., Zurada, J.M. (eds.) ICAISC 2014, Part I. LNCS(LNAI), vol. 8467, pp. 440–454. Springer, Heidelberg (2014)
50. Szczypta, J., Przybył, A., Cpałka, K.: Some aspects of evolutionary designing optimal controllers. In: Rutkowski, L., Korytkowski, M., Scherer, R., Tadeusiewicz, R., Zadeh, L.A., Zurada, J.M. (eds.) ICAISC 2013, Part II. LNCS(LNAI), vol. 7895, pp. 91–100. Springer, Heidelberg (2013)
51. Szczypta, J., Przybył, A., Wang, L.: Evolutionary approach with multiple quality criteria for controller design. In: Rutkowski, L., Korytkowski, M., Scherer, R., Tadeusiewicz, R., Zadeh, L.A., Zurada, J.M. (eds.) ICAISC 2014, Part I. LNCS(LNAI), vol. 8467, pp. 455–467. Springer, Heidelberg (2014)
52. Theodoridis, D.C., Boutalis, Y.S., Christodoulou, M.A.: Robustifying analysis of the direct adaptive control of unknown multivariable nonlinear systems based on a new neuro-fuzzy method. Journal of Artificial Intelligence and Soft Computing Research 1(1), 59–79 (2011)
53. Tran, V.N., Brdys, M.A.: Optimizing control by robustly feasible model predictive control and application to drinking water distribution systems. Journal of Artificial Intelligence and Soft Computing Research 1(1), 43–57 (2011)
54. Zalasiński, M., Łapa, K., Cpałka, K.: New Algorithm for Evolutionary Selection of the Dynamic Signature Global Features. In: Rutkowski, L., Korytkowski, M., Scherer, R., Tadeusiewicz, R., Zadeh, L.A., Zurada, J.M. (eds.) ICAISC 2013, Part II. LNCS(LNAI), vol. 7895, pp. 113–121. Springer, Heidelberg (2013)
55. Zalasiński, M., Cpałka, K.: Novel algorithm for the on-line signature verification. In: Rutkowski, L., Korytkowski, M., Scherer, R., Tadeusiewicz, R., Zadeh, L.A., Zurada, J.M. (eds.) ICAISC 2012, Part II. LNCS, vol. 7268, pp. 362–367. Springer, Heidelberg (2012)
56. Zalasiński, M., Cpałka, K.: New approach for the on-line signature verification based on method of horizontal partitioning. In: Rutkowski, L., Korytkowski, M., Scherer, R., Tadeusiewicz, R., Zadeh, L.A., Zurada, J.M. (eds.) ICAISC 2013, Part II. LNCS(LNAI), vol. 7895, pp. 342–350. Springer, Heidelberg (2013)

57. Zalasiński, M., Cpałka, K.: Novel Algorithm for the On-Line Signature Verification Using Selected Discretization Points Groups. In: Rutkowski, L., Korytkowski, M., Scherer, R., Tadeusiewicz, R., Zadeh, L.A., Zurada, J.M. (eds.) ICAISC 2013, Part I. LNCS(LNAI), vol. 7894, pp. 493–502. Springer, Heidelberg (2013)
58. Zalasiński, M., Cpałka, K., Er, M.J.: New Method for Dynamic Signature Verification Using Hybrid Partitioning. In: Rutkowski, L., Korytkowski, M., Scherer, R., Tadeusiewicz, R., Zadeh, L.A., Zurada, J.M. (eds.) ICAISC 2014, Part II. LNCS(LNAI), vol. 8468, pp. 216–230. Springer, Heidelberg (2014)
59. Zalasiński, M., Cpałka, K., Hayashi, Y.: New Method for Dynamic Signature Verification Based on Global Features. In: Rutkowski, L., Korytkowski, M., Scherer, R., Tadeusiewicz, R., Zadeh, L.A., Zurada, J.M. (eds.) ICAISC 2014, Part II. LNCS(LNAI), vol. 8468, pp. 231–245. Springer, Heidelberg (2014)

# Optimization of Controller Structure
# Using Evolutionary Algorithm

Andrzej Przybył[1(✉)], Jacek Szczypta[1], and Lipo Wang[2]

[1] Institute of Computational Intelligence,
Częstochowa University of Technology, Częstochowa, Poland
{andrzej.przybyl,jacek.szczypta}@iisi.pcz.pl
[2] School of Electrical and Electronic Engineering,
Nanyang Technological University, Singapore, Singapore
elpwang@ntu.edu.sg

**Abstract.** PID-based controller structures are typically used in industrial control systems. However, in different areas the controller structures are slightly different. The differences are due to the modifications introduced by the expert. Expert, based on his experience and on trial-and-error method, adjusts the initial controller structure in order to obtain a better quality of control. In this paper a method based on an evolutionary algorithm is proposed. Usage of the proposed method makes this difficult and time consuming task easier and faster.

## 1 Introduction

In the literature there are presented various approaches to design of control system. Typically the following approaches are considered: controllers based on the combination of linear correction terms [37], e.g. PID controllers [29] (optionally with gain scheduling algorithm, with feed-forward path or with additional low-pass filters [35]), state feedback controllers [42], nonlinear controllers based on computational intelligence and hybrid controllers which combine approaches from other groups. However, in practice PID controllers (see e.g. [4]) are most commonly used. It results from a general knowledge of how they work and their relatively simple implementation in a microprocessor-based control system.

During controller design, engineer can modify PID parameters (i.e. tune controller) and he performs it if the need arises. It is important to point out that controller tuning is a difficult and time consuming process. Moreover, engineer based on his experience can modify the controller structure by means of trial-and-error method in order to obtain a better quality of control. Modification of controller structure causes the process of controller design much more difficult. Exemplary PID-based controller structures which affected by this modification are shown in Fig. 1. The presented controllers, despite the differences in the structure, are used to perform the same control task, i.e. follow-up position control in the CNC machine tool [29], [41].

How we can see, the presented structures are slightly different. This is because there is no common and proved knowledge regarding which structure is superior and should be applied rather than others.

© Springer International Publishing Switzerland 2015
L. Rutkowski et al. (Eds.): ICAISC 2015, Part II, LNAI 9120, pp. 261–271, 2015.
DOI: 10.1007/978-3-319-19369-4_24

Despite the fact that knowledge regarding control theory is widespread and well developed, the analytically obtained controller structures do not sufficiently take into account the impact of various disturbances (measurement, process, control, etc.) which are common in the real world. As a result, the common rule is that the human expert basing on his experience and applying the trial-and-error method have to improve the initial controller in order to obtain the satisfactory quality of control. In this paper it is proposed a method which allow to do this difficult and time consuming task automatically using an evolutionary algorithm (see e.g. [17,23,24,25,33,34,56,60]). In the literature thera are also many other nature-inspired algorithms, e.g. swarm algorithms (see [2,18,20,21,39]), however in this case classic evolutionary algorithm performs very well.

In our previous work [53] we dealt with the evolutionary selection (see e.g. [36,38,51]) of the structure and parameters of the control system (Fig. 2). The results encouraged us to develop a new approach. In this paper we propose a method for constructing more complex control systems. In this new approach we use first order infinite impulse response (IIR) input filters and extra feedforward paths (Fig. 3) in addition to standard PID blocks, which are typically used in a complex controller structure.

Please note that the proposed method can be successfully applied to all optimization problems which require not only parameters selection but also structure selection, e.g. structure selection of fuzzy systems (see e.g. [6,7,30]), neuro-fuzzy systems (see e.g. [11,14,16,15,47,49,50]), type-2 fuzzy systems (see e.g. [5,19,27,52]). Proposed algorithm may be also used in modelling (see e.g. [8,10,12,13,22,26,40,44,48]) and pattern recognition issues (see e.g. [43,45,55,57,58,59]).

This paper is organized into 4 sections. Section 2 contains an idea of using evolutionary method for optimization of the controller structure. Simulation results are presented in Section 3. Conclusions are drawn in Section 4.

## 2   Evolutionary Method for Designing the New Representation of the Controller Structure

In proposed method full controller (with its structure and parameters) is encoded in a single chromosome $\mathbf{X}_{ch}$. Chromosome $\mathbf{X}_{ch}$ is described as follows:

$$\mathbf{X}_{ch} = \left\{ \mathbf{X}_{ch}^{\text{par}}, \mathbf{X}_{ch}^{\text{red}} \right\}, \tag{1}$$

where $\mathbf{X}_{ch}^{\text{par}}$ is a chromosome encoding correction term parameters, $\mathbf{X}_{ch}^{\text{red}}$ is a chromosome encoding CB connection. Chromosome $\mathbf{X}_{ch}^{\text{par}}$ is described as follows:

$$\begin{aligned} \mathbf{X}_{ch}^{\text{par}} &= \left( a^1, K_P^1, T_I^1, T_D^1, a^2, K_P^2, T_I^2, T_D^2, \ldots, ff^1, \ldots, ff^4 \right) \\ &= \left( X_{ch,1}^{\text{par}}, X_{ch,2}^{\text{par}}, \ldots, X_{ch,L}^{\text{par}} \right), \end{aligned} \tag{2}$$

where $a^1, K_P^1, T_I^1, T_D^1, \ldots, ff^1 \ldots$, denotes control system parameter values, $ch = 1, .., Ch$, denotes index of the chromosome in the population, $Ch$ denotes a number of chromosomes in the population, $L$ denotes length of the chromosome $\mathbf{X}_{ch}^{\text{par}}$. Chromosome $\mathbf{X}_{ch}^{\text{red}}$ is described as follows:

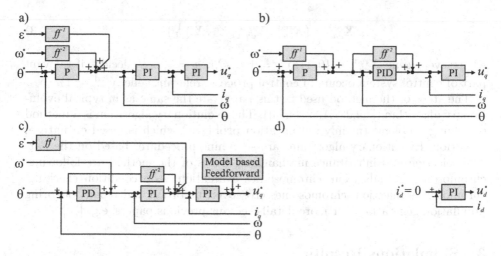

**Fig. 1.** Different controller structures a), b), c) used in industrial systems and d) common part of the PMSM servo-drive controller structure

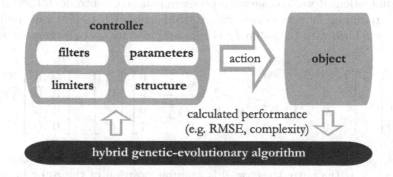

**Fig. 2.** Proposed idea of optimizing the controller using the evolutionary algorithm

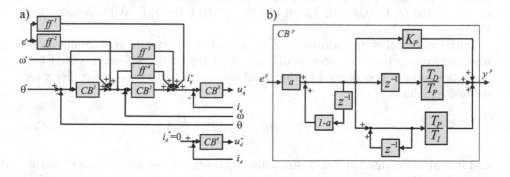

**Fig. 3.** The initial controller definition for the evolutionary algorithm

$$\mathbf{X}_{ch}^{\mathrm{red}} = \left( X_{ch,1}^{\mathrm{red}}, X_{ch,2}^{\mathrm{red}}, \ldots, X_{ch,L}^{\mathrm{red}} \right), \tag{3}$$

where every gene $X_{ch,g}^{\mathrm{red}} \in \{0,1\}$, $ch = 1, .., Ch$, $g = 1, .., L$, decides if relevant part of control system occurs in control process (relevant gene $X_{ch,g}^{\mathrm{red}} = 1$).

The steps of the method used in this paper are the same as in typical evolutionary algorithm ([3,9,28,31,32,46,54]). The evolutionary algorithm is a method of solving problems (mainly optimization problems) which is based on natural evolution. Evolutionary algorithms are searching procedures based on the natural selection and inheritance mechanisms. Steps of the method are following: chromosomes initialization, chromosomes evaluation, stop condition checking, chromosomes selection, chromosomes crossover, mutation and repair, offspring population generation. For more details see our previous papers, e.g. [53].

## 3    Simulations Results

### 3.1    Controlled Object

In our simulations it was considered a problem of design controller structure and parameters tuning for servo-drive with PMSM motor [1]. PMSM was modelled in a discrete form with time step $T_s=10~\mu s$ and in state space representation as follows:

$$\begin{bmatrix} i_d^{k+1} \\ i_q^{k+1} \\ \omega^{k+1} \\ \theta^{k+1} \end{bmatrix} = \begin{bmatrix} 1 - T_s\frac{R}{L} & 0 & i_q T_s & 0 \\ 0 & 1 - T_s\frac{R}{L} & -T_s(i_d + \frac{\lambda_m}{L}) & 0 \\ 0 & 1.5 T_s P^2 \frac{\lambda_m}{J} & 1 - T_s\frac{F}{J} & 0 \\ 0 & 0 & T_s & 1 \end{bmatrix} \begin{bmatrix} i_d^k \\ i_q^k \\ \omega^k \\ \theta^k \end{bmatrix} + \begin{bmatrix} \frac{T_s}{L} & 0 \\ 0 & \frac{T_s}{L} \\ 0 & 0 \\ 0 & 0 \end{bmatrix} \begin{bmatrix} u_d^k \\ u_q^k \end{bmatrix}, \tag{4}$$

where $i_d$, $i_q$, $\omega$ and $\theta$ are PMSM motor state variables, $u_d$, $u_q$ is the input vector, $i_d$, $i_q$ is the output vector. $\theta$ is angular position of the rotor flux, $\omega$ is its angular velocity. The $i_d$, $i_q$ are direct and quadrature components (in a rotor reference frame) of electrical currents in the motor windings, while $u_d$, $u_q$ are electrical voltages applied to the motor terminals. The motor model parameters are: R=1.456 $\Omega$, L=0.008 H, $\lambda_m$=0.175 V·s, J=0.06 kg·m, F=0.001 N·m·s, and P=3.

Initial values of state variables ( $i_d$, $i_q$, $\omega$ and $\theta$) were set to zero. Simulation was carried out for time interval of 1.5s. A shape of the reference signal for the follow-up position control in the simulation with servo-drive controller was defined as follows

$$\theta^* = 100 \cdot \left( 1 + sin\left( \frac{t}{1.5} \cdot \Pi - \frac{\Pi}{2} \right) \right), \tag{5}$$

and it is also presented in Fig. 4. According to practical reasons (i.e. the physical limitation of the actuators) output signal of each CB was limited. Output of $CB^1$, $CB^2$, $CB^3$ and $CB^4$ was limited to values 100 rad/s, 20 A, 350 V and 350 V

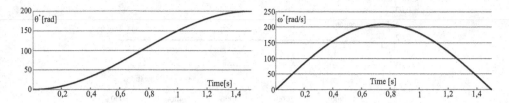

**Fig. 4.** Angular position ($\theta$) and velocity ($\omega$) reference values

respectively. Moreover, limited resolution of position and motor current sensors was the cause of quantization for the input signals ( $\theta$, $\omega$, $i_d$ and $i_q$) to values $0.628 \cdot 10^{-3} rad$ (10000 pulse per rev.), $0.314 \, rad/s$, $0.01$ A and $0.01$ A (4096 ADC voltage levels) respectively. Quantization resolution for the output signal ( $u_d^*$ and $u_q^*$) was set to value $0.07V$ (5000 levels) because of the limited resolution of the pulse width modulation (PWM) module. Time interval between subsequent controller activations was set to 100 $\mu s$ which is a reasonable value for today microprocessor systems.

### 3.2  Controller Design

Initial controller definition is presented in Fig. 3. Search range for parameters contained inside each CB block ($a, K_P, T_I, T_D$) and for feedforward gain ($ff$) was set experimentally. Search ranges were set as follows: $K_P = <0,300>$, $T_I = <10^{-6}, 1>$, $T_D = <0, 10^{-3}>$, $a = <0.1, 1>$ and $ff = <0, 200>$. On the basis of the assumption of the vector control algorithm symmetry, the values of the $CB^4$ block parameter were copied from the values obtained for block $CB^3$ and therefore they were not tuned separately.

### 3.3  Hybrid Evolutionary Algorithm

Controller structure definition and parameter tuning were performed using hybrid evolutionary algorithm. Algorithm was executed with following settings: the number of chromosomes in the population was set to 50, the algorithm performs 5000 steps (generations), the crossover probability was set as 0.99, the mutation probability was set as 0.3, the mutation intensity was set as 0.3. the fitness function with weights was defined as follows:

$$\text{ff}(\mathbf{X}_{ch}) = \left( \frac{MSE_{ch}^1 \cdot w_1 + MSE_{ch}^2 \cdot w_2 + MSE_{ch}^3 \cdot w_3 + MSE_{ch}^4 \cdot w_4 +}{os_{ch}^{u_q} \cdot w_{os}} \right). \quad (6)$$

$MSE_{ch}^1$ error function of the $ch$ chromosome is described by the following formula:

$$MSE_{ch}^p = \frac{1}{N} \cdot \sum_{j=1}^{N} (e_{ch,j}^p)^2, \quad (7)$$

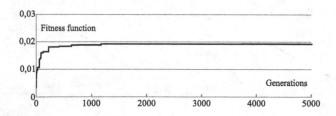

**Fig. 5.** The process of controller structure search by means of the evolutionary algorithm

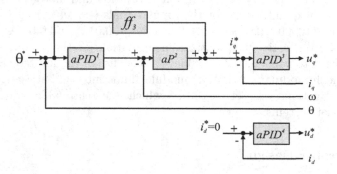

**Fig. 6.** Controller structure obtained by means of hybrid evolutionary algorithm

**Table 1.** Parameter values of CB terms obtained by means of hybrid evolutionary algorithm

| $K_P^1$ | $T_I^1$ | $T_D^1$ | $a^1$ | $K_P^2$ | $a^2$ |
|---------|---------|---------|-------|---------|-------|
| 38.48 | $175.4 \cdot 10^{-6}$ | $623.0 \cdot 10^{-6}$ | 0.6015 | 29.80 | 0.0796 |
| $K_P^3$ | $T_I^3$ | $T_D^3$ | $a^3$ | $ff^3$ | |
| 48.77 | $29.59 \cdot 10^{-6}$ | $735.4 \cdot 10^{-6}$ | 0.6891 | 1.977 | |

where $e^p$ denotes error value on $CB^p$ input, $j = 1, \ldots, N$, denotes sample index, $N$ denotes the number of samples, $p = 1 \ldots, 4$ denotes CB-index, and $e_{ch,j}^1$ is defined as follows:

$$e_{ch,j}^1 = \theta_j^* - \theta_{ch,j}, \tag{8}$$

while $e_{ch,j}^2$, $e_{ch,j}^3$, $e_{ch,j}^4$ are defined as it is shown in Fig. 3. Value of the $os_{ch,j}^{u_q}$ is defined as a number of oscillations of the signal $u_q$, which is feed to the actuator. Existence of large number of oscillation with amplitude higher than experimentally chosen value can cause negative increase of the noise level generated by the PMSM motor. The number of oscillations should be reduced.

The fitness function weights were set as follows: $w_1 = 194.4$, $w_2 = 33.43$, $w_3 = 1229$, $w_4 = 62518$ and $w_{os} = 4.383 \cdot 10^{-4}$. Process of controller structure search is presented in Fig. 5.

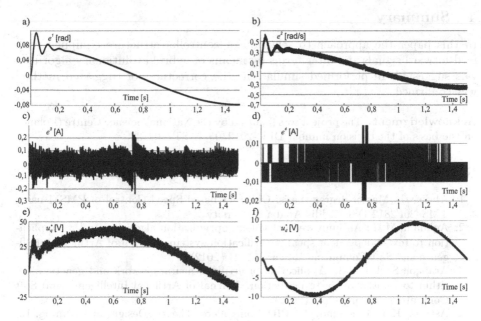

**Fig. 7.** Values on the input of: a) position, b) velocity, c) current $i_d$, b) current $i_q$ controller. Values of the : e) voltage $u_q$, f) voltage $u_d$ signal

## 3.4  Search Results

Controller structure obtained by means of hybrid evolutionary algorithm is presented in Fig. 6. Parameters of structure obtained by means of hybrid evolutionary algorithm are presented in Table 1, while its performance is presented in Fig. 7.

Control problem presented in this paper confirms application of one $(ff^3)$ feed-forward path, as presented in controller structure in Fig. 3. Values of parameters $a^1$, $a^2$ and $a^3$ lower than one confirm application of first order IIR filter.

As we can see in Fig. 7.a, the position error $(e^1)$ is relatively high, i.e. about 0.1 rad. In some applications it can be an unacceptable value. However, it was confirmed by the experiment that it is possible to reduce the position controller error to level as low as 0.002 rad. This can be obtained by proper setting of fitness function weight $(w_1, \ldots, w_5)$, although it causes an negative increase of the noise level generated by the PMSM motor. Setting of mentioned weights relies on the human designer of the control system.

Simulation results can be summarized as follows: quality of evolutionary designed controller structure as presented in Fig. 7 is acceptable. Obtaining and tuning of similar controller structure by means of typical methods would be daunting.

## 4  Summary

In this paper the approach to selection of controller structure equipped with feed-forward signals and filter terms by means of hybrid evolutionary algorithm was suggested. In performed simulations the correctness of suggested method was confirmed.

**Acknowledgment.** The project was financed by the National Science Centre (Poland) on the basis of the decision number DEC-2012/05/B/ST7/02138.

## References

1. Abdie, H.: Master degree thesis: Observer based Speed Control of PMSM using TMS320F2812 DSP. Addis Ababa University
2. Aghdam, M.H.: An improved ant colony optimization algorithm and its application to text-independent speaker verification system. Journal of Artificial Intelligence and Soft Computing Research 2(4) (2012)
3. Arabgol, S., Ko, H.S.: Application of artificial neural network and genetic algorithm to healthcare waste prediction. Journal of Artificial Intelligence and Soft Computing Research 2(4) (2012)
4. Astrom, K.J., Hagglund, T.: PID Controllers: Theory, Design, and Tuning. Instrument Society of America: Research Triangle Park (1995)
5. Bartczak, Ł., Dziwiński, P., Starczewski, J.T.: New Method for Generation Type-2 Fuzzy Partition for FDT. In: Rutkowski, L., Scherer, R., Tadeusiewicz, R., Zadeh, L.A., Zurada, J.M. (eds.) ICAISC 2010, Part I. LNCS(LNAI), vol. 6113, pp. 275–280. Springer, Heidelberg (2010)
6. Bartczuk, Ł., Przybył, A., Dziwiński, P.: Hybrid State Variables-Fuzzy Logic Modelling of Nonlinear Objects. In: Rutkowski, L., Korytkowski, M., Scherer, R., Tadeusiewicz, R., Zadeh, L.A., Zurada, J.M. (eds.) ICAISC 2013, Part I. LNCS(LNAI), vol. 7894, pp. 227–234. Springer, Heidelberg (2013)
7. Bartczuk, Ł., Dziwiński, P., Starczewski, J.T.: A new method for dealing with unbalanced linguistic term set. In: Rutkowski, L., Korytkowski, M., Scherer, R., Tadeusiewicz, R., Zadeh, L.A., Zurada, J.M. (eds.) ICAISC 2012, Part I. LNCS, vol. 7267, pp. 207–212. Springer, Heidelberg (2012)
8. Bartczuk, Ł., Przybył, A., Koprinkova-Hristova, P.: New method for nonlinear fuzzy correction modelling of dynamic objects. In: Rutkowski, L., Korytkowski, M., Scherer, R., Tadeusiewicz, R., Zadeh, L.A., Zurada, J.M. (eds.) ICAISC 2014, Part I. LNCS(LNAI), vol. 8467, pp. 169–180. Springer, Heidelberg (2014)
9. Chen, M., Simone, A., Ludwig, S.A.: Particle swarm optimization based fuzzy clustering approach to identify optimal number of clusters. Journal of Artificial Intelligence and Soft Computing Research 4(1) (2014)
10. Cpałka, K., Łapa, K., Przybył A., Zalasiński, M.: A new method for designing neuro-fuzzy systems for nonlinear modelling with interpretability aspects. Neurocomputing 135, pp. 203–217 (2014)
11. Cpałka, K.: On evolutionary designing and learning of flexible neuro-fuzzy structures for nonlinear classification. In: Nonlinear Analysis Series A: Theory, Methods and Applications, vol. 71, pp. 1659–1672. Elsevier (2009)
12. Cpałka, K., Rebrova, O., Nowicki, R., Rutkowski, L.: On design of flexible neuro-fuzzy systems for nonlinear modelling. Int. Journal of General Systems 42(6), 706–720 (2013)

13. Cpałka, K., Rutkowski, L.: Flexible Takagi-Sugeno Fuzzy Systems. In: Proceedings of the International Joint Conference on Neural Networks 2005, Montreal, pp. 1764–1769 (2005)
14. Cpałka, K., Rutkowski, L.: A New Method for Designing and Reduction of Neuro-fuzzy Systems. In: Proceedings of the 2006 IEEE International Conference on Fuzzy Systems (IEEE World Congress on Computational Intelligence, WCCI 2006), Vancouver, BC, Canada, pp. 8510–8516 (2006)
15. Cpałka, K., Zalasiński, M.: On-line signature verification using vertical signature partitioning. Expert Systems with Applications 41, 4170–4180 (2014)
16. Cpałka, K., Zalasiński, M., Rutkowski, L.: New method for the on-line signature verification based on horizontal partitioning. Pattern Recognition 47, 2652–2661 (2014)
17. Fogel, D.B.: Evolutionary Computation: Toward a New Philosophy of Machine Intelligence, 3rd edn. IEEE Press, Piscataway (2006)
18. Dziwiński, P., Bartczuk, Ł., Starczewski, J.T.: Fully controllable ant colony system for text data clustering. In: Rutkowski, L., Korytkowski, M., Scherer, R., Tadeusiewicz, R., Zadeh, L.A., Zurada, J.M. (eds.) SIDE 2012 and EC 2012. LNCS, vol. 7269, pp. 199–205. Springer, Heidelberg (2012)
19. Dziwiński, P., Starczewski, J.T., Bartczuk, Ł.: New linguistic hedges in construction of interval type-2 fls. In: Rutkowski, L., Scherer, R., Tadeusiewicz, R., Zadeh, L.A., Zurada, J.M. (eds.) ICAISC 2010, Part II. LNCS(LNAI), vol. 6114, pp. 445–450. Springer, Heidelberg (2010)
20. Dziwiński, P., Bartczuk, Ł., Przybył, A., Avedyan, E.D.: A New Algorithm for Identification of Significant Operating Points Using Swarm Intelligence. In: Rutkowski, L., Korytkowski, M., Scherer, R., Tadeusiewicz, R., Zadeh, L.A., Zurada, J.M. (eds.) ICAISC 2014, Part II. LNCS(LNAI), vol. 8468, pp. 349–362. Springer, Heidelberg (2014)
21. El-Abd, M.: On the hybridization on the artificial bee colony and particle swarm optimization algorithms. Journal of Artificial Intelligence and Soft Computing Research 2(2), 147–155 (2012)
22. Gałkowski, T., Rutkowski, L.: Nonparametric fitting of multivariate functions. IEEE Trans. Automatic Control 31(8), 785–787 (1986)
23. Gabryel, M., Cpałka, K., Rutkowski L.: Evolutionary strategies for learning of neuro-fuzzy systems. In: I Workshop on Genetic Fuzzy Systems, Granada, pp. 119–123 (2005)
24. Gabryel, M., Rutkowski, L.: Evolutionary Learning of Mamdani-Type Neuro-fuzzy Systems. In: Rutkowski, L., Tadeusiewicz, R., Zadeh, L.A., Żurada, J.M. (eds.) ICAISC 2006. LNCS (LNAI), vol. 4029, pp. 354–359. Springer, Heidelberg (2006)
25. Gabryel, M., Rutkowski, L.: Evolutionary methods for designing neuro-fuzzy modular systems combined by bagging algorithm. In: Rutkowski, L., Tadeusiewicz, R., Zadeh, L.A., Zurada, J.M. (eds.) ICAISC 2008. LNCS (LNAI), vol. 5097, pp. 398–404. Springer, Heidelberg (2008)
26. Greblicki, W., Rutkowska, D., Rutkowski, L.: An orthogonal series estimate of time-varying regression. Annals of The Institute of Statistical Mathematics 35(2), 215–228 (1983)
27. Greenfield, S., Chiclana, F.: Type-reduction of the discretized interval type-2 fuzzy set: approaching the continuous case through progressively finer discretization. Journal of Artificial Intelligence and Soft Computing Research 1(3), 183–193 (2011)
28. Guderian, F., Schaffer, R., Fettweis, G.: Administration- and communication-aware ip core mapping in scalable multiprocessor system-on-chips via evolutionary computing. Journal of Artificial Intelligence and Soft Computing Research 2(2) (2012)

29. iTNC 530, The Versatile Contouring Control for Milling, Drilling, Boring Machines and Machining Centers, Information for the Machine Tool Builder
30. Kroll, A.: On choosing the fuzziness parameter for identifying TS models with multidimensional membership functions. Journal of Artificial Intelligence and Soft Computing Research 1(4), 283–300 (2011)
31. Lobato, F.S., Steffen Jr., V.: A new multi-objective optimization algorithm based on differential evolution and neighborhood exploring evolution strategy. Journal of Artificial Intelligence and Soft Computing Research 1(4), 259–267 (2011)
32. Lobato, F.S., Valder Jr., J.S., Silva Neto, A.: Solution of singular optimal control problems using the improved differential evolutionary algorithm. Journal of Artificial Intelligence and Soft Computing Research 1(3), 195–206 (2011)
33. Łapa, K., Przybył, A., Cpałka, K.: A new approach to designing interpretable models of dynamic systems. In: Rutkowski, L., Korytkowski, M., Scherer, R., Tadeusiewicz, R., Zadeh, L.A., Zurada, J.M. (eds.) ICAISC 2013, Part II. LNCS(LNAI), vol. 7895, pp. 523–534. Springer, Heidelberg (2013)
34. Łapa, K., Zalasiński, M., Cpałka, K.: A new method for designing and complexity reduction of neuro-fuzzy systems for nonlinear modelling. In: Rutkowski, L., Korytkowski, M., Scherer, R., Tadeusiewicz, R., Zadeh, L.A., Zurada, J.M. (eds.) ICAISC 2013, Part I. LNCS(LNAI), vol. 7894, pp. 329–344. Springer, Heidelberg (2013)
35. Maggio, M., Bonvini, M., Leva, A.: The PID + p controller structure and its contextual autotuning, Journal of Process Control, vol. Journal of Process Control 22, 1237–1245 (2012)
36. Michalewicz, Z.: Genetic Algorithms + Data Structures = Evolution Programs. Springer (1999)
37. Ogata, K.: Modern Control Engineering. Prentice Hall (2001)
38. Peteiro-Barral, D., Guijarro-Berdinas, B., Perez-Sanchez, B.: Learning from heterogeneously distributed data sets using artificial neural networks and genetic algorithms. Journal of Artificial Intelligence and Soft Computing Research 2(1) (2012)
39. Prampero, P.S., Attux, R.: Magnetic particle swarm optimization. Journal of Artificial Intelligence and Soft Computing Research 2(1) (2012)
40. Przybył, A., Cpałka, K.: A new method to construct of interpretable models of dynamic systems. In: Rutkowski, L., Korytkowski, M., Scherer, R., Tadeusiewicz, R., Zadeh, L.A., Zurada, J.M. (eds.) ICAISC 2012, Part II. LNCS, vol. 7268, pp. 697–705. Springer, Heidelberg (2012)
41. Przybył, A., Smoląg, J., Kimla, P.: Distributed Control System Based on Real Time Ethernet for Computer Numerical Controlled Machine Tool. Przeglad Elektrotechniczny 86(2), 342–346 (2010) (in Polish)
42. Przybył, A., Jelonkiewicz, J.: State feedback-based control of an induction motor in a single fixed-point DSP. In: Proceedings of the EPE-PEMC 11th International Power Electronics and Motion Control Conference, vol. 4, pp. 260–267 (2004)
43. Rutkowski, L.: Sequential pattern-recognition procedures derived from multiple Fourier-series. Pattern Recognition Letters 8(4), 213–216 (1988)
44. Rutkowski, L.: Application of multiple Fourier-series to identification of multivariable non-stationary systems. Int. Journal of Systems Science 20(10), 1993–2002 (1989)
45. Rutkowski, L.: Identification of miso nonlinear regressions in the presence of a wide class of disturbances. IEEE Trans. Information Theory 37(1), 214–216 (1991)
46. Rutkowski, L.: Computational Intelligence. Springer (2008)

47. Rutkowski, L., Cpałka, K.: Compromise approach to neuro-fuzzy systems. In: Sincak, P., Vascak, J., Kvasnicka, V., Pospichal, J., (eds.) Intelligent Technologies - Theory and Applications, vol. 76, pp. 85–90. IOS Press (2002)
48. Rutkowski, L., Cpałka, K.: Neuro-fuzzy systems derived from quasi-triangular norms. In: Proceedings of the IEEE International Conference on Fuzzy Systems, Budapest, July 26-29, vol. 2, pp. 1031–1036 (2004)
49. Rutkowski, L., Przybył, A., Cpałka, K., Er, M.J.: Online speed profile generation for industrial machine tool based on neuro-fuzzy approach. In: Rutkowski, L., Scherer, R., Tadeusiewicz, R., Zadeh, L.A., Zurada, J.M. (eds.) ICAISC 2010, Part II. LNCS(LNAI), vol. 6114, pp. 645–650. Springer, Heidelberg (2010)
50. Rutkowski, L., Przybył, A., Cpałka, K.: Novel Online Speed Profile Generation for Industrial Machine Tool Based on Flexible Neuro-Fuzzy Approximation. IEEE Transactions on Industrial Electronics 59(2), 1238–1247 (2012)
51. Santucci, V., Milani, A., Vella, F.: A study on the synchronization behaviour of differential evolution and a self-adaptive extension. Journal of Artificial Intelligence and Soft Computing Research 2(4) (2012)
52. Starczewski, J.T., Bartczuk, Ł., Dziwiński, P., Marvuglia, A.: Learning methods for type-2 FLS based on FCM. In: Rutkowski, L., Scherer, R., Tadeusiewicz, R., Zadeh, L.A., Zurada, J.M. (eds.) ICAISC 2010, Part I. LNCS(LNAI), vol. 6113, pp. 224–231. Springer, Heidelberg (2010)
53. Szczypta, J., Przybył, A., Cpałka, K.: Some aspects of evolutionary designing optimal controllers. In: Rutkowski, L., Korytkowski, M., Scherer, R., Tadeusiewicz, R., Zadeh, L.A., Zurada, J.M. (eds.) ICAISC 2013, Part II. LNCS(LNAI), vol. 7895, pp. 91–100. Springer, Heidelberg (2013)
54. Vivekanandan, P., Nedunchezhian, R.: Mining rules of concept drift using genetic algorithm. Journal of Artificial Intelligence and Soft Computing Research 1(2) (2011)
55. Zalasiński, M., Cpałka, K.: Novel algorithm for the on-line signature verification. In: Rutkowski, L., Korytkowski, M., Scherer, R., Tadeusiewicz, R., Zadeh, L.A., Zurada, J.M. (eds.) ICAISC 2012, Part II. LNCS, vol. 7268, pp. 362–367. Springer, Heidelberg (2012)
56. Zalasiński, M., Cpałka, K.: Novel Algorithm for the On-Line Signature Verification Using Selected Discretization Points Groups. In: Rutkowski, L., Korytkowski, M., Scherer, R., Tadeusiewicz, R., Zadeh, L.A., Zurada, J.M. (eds.) ICAISC 2013, Part I. LNCS(LNAI), vol. 7894, pp. 493–502. Springer, Heidelberg (2013)
57. Zalasiński, M., Cpałka, K.: New approach for the on-line signature verification based on method of horizontal partitioning. In: Rutkowski, L., Korytkowski, M., Scherer, R., Tadeusiewicz, R., Zadeh, L.A., Zurada, J.M. (eds.) ICAISC 2013, Part II. LNCS(LNAI), vol. 7895, pp. 342–350. Springer, Heidelberg (2013)
58. Zalasiński, M., Cpałka, K., Er, M.J.: New Method for Dynamic Signature Verification Using Hybrid Partitioning. In: Rutkowski, L., Korytkowski, M., Scherer, R., Tadeusiewicz, R., Zadeh, L.A., Zurada, J.M. (eds.) ICAISC 2014, Part II. LNCS(LNAI), vol. 8468, pp. 216–230. Springer, Heidelberg (2014)
59. Zalasiński, M., Cpałka, K., Hayashi, Y.: New Method for Dynamic Signature Verification Based on Global Features. In: Rutkowski, L., Korytkowski, M., Scherer, R., Tadeusiewicz, R., Zadeh, L.A., Zurada, J.M. (eds.) ICAISC 2014, Part II. LNCS(LNAI), vol. 8468, pp. 231–245. Springer, Heidelberg (2014)
60. Zalasiński, M., Łapa, K., Cpałka, K.: New Algorithm for Evolutionary Selection of the Dynamic Signature Global Features. In: Rutkowski, L., Korytkowski, M., Scherer, R., Tadeusiewicz, R., Zadeh, L.A., Zurada, J.M. (eds.) ICAISC 2013, Part II. LNCS(LNAI), vol. 7895, pp. 113–121. Springer, Heidelberg (2013)

# Multi-Criteria Fuel Distribution: A Case Study

Jarosław Rudy[1] and Dominik Żelazny[1(✉)]

Department of Control Systems and Mechatronics,
Wrocław University of Technology,
Janiszewskiego 11-17, 50-372 Wrocław, Poland
{jaroslaw.rudy,dominik.zelazny}@pwr.edu.pl

**Abstract.** In this paper a multi-criteria fuel distribution problem similar to the common CVRP is considered with the real-life coordinates of gas stations obtained from a certain petrol company. The optimized criteria are the total distance of all tours and the number of tours. A certain method of solution representation, which ensures a feasible solution was used along a decoding scheme. A simulated annealing (SA) metaheuristic algorithm was implemented in order to obtain the approximations of the Pareto set for a number of instances with varying number of gas stations and demands for each station. The results show 17–18% improvement over the starting solution in all cases for both criteria. Moreover, the number of found solutions per instance increases with the number of gas stations. The improvements can be translated directly into profit, which was shown as well.

**Keywords:** Fuel distribution · CVRP · Simulated annealing · Multi-criteria optimization · Case study

## 1 Introduction

Vehicle routing problems (VRP), which aim at servicing demands of a given set of customers with a fleet of vehicles are one of the more common and more complex problems in combinatorial optimization and have great practical applications in the field of transportation and logistics. Moreover, they are characterized by their significant complexity, in particular many variants of they VRP are consider NP-complete/NP-hard and for VRP the problem sizes considered solvable are two orders of magnitude lower than compared to the less general Travelling Salesman Problem (TSP) as estimated by Ralphs *et. al* [11].

VRP problems often include additional constraints like limited capacity for vehicles (CVRP), limited distance per vehicle/tour (DVRP) or dedicated time windows when the client can be serviced (VRP-TW). Mixed variants (DCVRP, CVRP-TW *etc.*) also exist. The goal for common single-criteria VRP is the minimization of such criteria like the total distance, the maximum distance or the maximization of the vehicle utilization (*i.e.* average or minimal loading volume used). Bi- and multi-criteria approaches to VRP are less common.

Fuel distribution is one example of the vehicle routing problems encountered in practice, which has considerable impact on the various aspect of daily life

© Springer International Publishing Switzerland 2015
L. Rutkowski et al. (Eds.): ICAISC 2015, Part II, LNAI 9120, pp. 272–281, 2015.
DOI: 10.1007/978-3-319-19369-4_25

**Fig. 1.** Gas stations and refinery for considered fuel distribution problem

around the globe, as access to fuels determines developments of many sectors of the economy. In this paper we focus our efforts on a specific instance of the fuel distribution problem. Namely, we consider a real-life petrol company with a network of 424 gas stations and one refinery acting as a depot, similarly to the usual VRP. Fig. 1 shows locations of the refinery and all gas stations, taken from real-world data. The distances between each pair of locations were computed using Google Maps API, resulting in distance matrix numbering $425^2$ (or over 180625) edges. Let us also take note that the depot is located off the center of the map. Moreover, the analysis of some edges shows that the graph is directed *i.e.* distance from location $A$ to $B$ is not necessarily the same as distance from $B$ to $A$. According to aforementioned estimate, VRP with 425 nodes is as difficult to solve as TSP with 42 500 nodes.

In this paper we decided to use multi-criteria approach to the fuel distribution problem, as we consider it more practical and closer to the real-life needs of such companies. The chosen criteria are the total distance of all tours and the number of tours (the latter can be translated into the numbers of tankers). The remainder of the paper is organized as follows. In Section 2 we present a brief literature overview concerning the multi-criteria vehicle routing problems. Section 3 contains the definition of the problem, while in section 4 we describe the chosen solution representation and problem solving method. Section 5 shows the results of the computer experiment and, finally, section 7 offers the conclusions.

## 2  Literature Overview

Over the last decade multi-criteria transportation problems have received some interest. Albeit, most of the multi-criteria VRP approaches were based on evolutionary algorithms (EA), while only some researchers of local search methods like simulated annealing (SA) or tabu search (TS). We will mention a few of all those approaches in the following section.

Bowerman *et al.* proposed one of the promising scalar techniques in [1]. In the evaluation, they used five different sets of weights chosen by a decision-maker. Proposed algorithm first groups the nodes into clusters that can be served by a vehicle, and then determines a tour. It's an allocation-routing-location strategy. Lee and Ueng proposed insertion algorithm in [7]. In each iteration, using a saving criterion, it adds one node to the vehicle with the shortest path. Other insertion heuristic was proposed by Zografos and Androutsopoulos in [15]. The selection of the customers to be inserted allows both routed and unrouted demand points to be inserted.

In [8] Pacheco and Marti optimize the makespan objective for every possible value of the second objective and then use a TS algorithm to solve each problem. Their approach uses a scalar method, called the $\epsilon$-constraint. Similar strategy was used by Corberan *et al.* [3], albeit authors used scatter search approach instead of TS.

The Pareto concept was frequently used within an evolutionary multi-objective framework. A modification of NSGA-II algorithm was proposed in [12]. Proposed algorithm uses local search method in each iteration, in order to further improve the Pareto frontier approximation. Pareto dominance has also been used by Ulungu *et al.* in a SA technique called Multi-Objective Simulated Annealing (MOSA) [14]. Paquete et al. [9] have called upon Pareto Local Search techniques. These techniques are based on the principle that the next current solution is chosen from the non-dominated solutions of the neighborhood. Rudy and Żelazny proposed a new hybrid of genetic algorithm and ant colony optimization in [13]. Tests shown it performed well in multi-objective job shop scheduling problem.

Some studies employ neither scalar nor Pareto methods to solve multi-objective routing problems. These non-scalar and non-Pareto methods are based on lexicographic strategies or specific heuristics. Aforementioned VEGA algorithm might be included, as an example of this specific heuristics. While lexicographic strategy was used in works of Keller and Goodchild [5,6]. Their approach was such, that the objectives are each assigned a priority value, and the problems are solved in order of decreasing priority. When one objective has been optimized, its value cannot be changed and it becomes a new constraint for the problem.

Moreover, Żelazny *et al.* proposed a new concept of solving VRP in [4]. New approach to GPU implementation of TS algorithm was proposed and significant speed-ups, as well as an improvement of the approximation of the Pareto front were observed.

# 3   Problem Description

The problem is defined as a modification of the basic CVRP problem, which is considered NP-hard. There is given a directed graph $G = (N, E)$ with $|N| - 1$ vertices representing filling stations and one vertex $B$ representing the depot (in our case the oil refinery). There is an edge between each pair of vertices $n_1, n_2 \in N$, thus the number of edges is $|N|^2 - |N|$. The directed edge $e(n_1, n_2)$ from vertex $n_1$ to $n_2$ represents the driving distance from gas station $v_1$ to $n_2$. In general $(n_1, n_2) \neq (n_2, n_1)$. Moreover, each station has a demand for two fuel types: diesel fuel (henceforth called diesel) and petrol, both expressed in the number of liters. The demands are met by a set of tank trucks (henceforth called tankers), with each tanker outfitted with four separate fuel compartment. We assume that compartment can contain the fuel of only one type (either diesel or gasoline) or be empty. Thus, each tanker has a limited capacity $C = V \times K$, where $V$ is the volume of a single compartment and $K$ is the number of compartments per tanker (we assume that compartments are identical).

The goal is to find a solution that minimizes our bi-criteria goal function. The considered criteria are: 1) the total number of routes $R$ and 2) the total distance of all routes $D$ given as:

$$D = \sum_{i=1}^{R} \sum_{n \in N_i} w(n), \tag{1}$$

where $R$ is the total number of routes, $N_i$ is the set of edges in route $i$ and $w(n)$ is the weight of edge $n$.

$$s^* = \min_{s \in \mathbb{S}_{\text{feas}}} f(D_s, R_s), \tag{2}$$

where $D_s$ ($R_s$) is the total distance (number of routes) for the solution $s$, $f$ is our goal function and $\mathbb{S}_{\text{feas}}$ is the set of feasible solutions. A solution is feasible if:

– the demands for all gas stations are met,
– all routes begin and end in the depot $B$,
– the sum of fuel transported on any single route does not exceed $C$.

# 4   Model and Solving Method

In this chapter we will present the solution representation as well as decoding method used to calculate the values of the goal function. We will also describe the chosen metaheuristic algorithm.

## 4.1   Representation

Let us assume $N$ gas stations and $K$ identical compartments per tanker. For every station $i$ we are given two numbers $d_i$ and $p_i$ indicating diesel and petrol demands respectively. The required number of compartments $Z_i$ for station $i$ is then calculated as:

$$Z_i = \left\lceil \frac{d_i}{V} \right\rceil + \left\lceil \frac{p_i}{V} \right\rceil, \tag{3}$$

where $V$ is the volume of a single compartment. In the next step a sequence of numbers is created. For each city $i$ its number is written $Z_i$ times. For example, for 3 cities with $d_1 = 4000$, $d_2 = 1500$, $d_3 = 2100$, $p_1 = 2200$, $p_2 = 3800$, $p_3 = 4700$ and $V = 5000$ (all in liters) we have:

$$Z_1 = 4 + 3 = 7, \tag{4}$$

$$Z_2 = 2 + 4 = 6, \tag{5}$$

$$Z_3 = 3 + 5 = 8, \tag{6}$$

and the resulting sequence is:

$$1\,1\,1\,1\,1\,1\,1\,2\,2\,2\,2\,2\,2\,3\,3\,3\,3\,3\,3\,3\,3. \tag{7}$$

Next each station is filled with zeroes to the nearest multiple of $K$ (if $Z_i$ is divisible by $K$ then no zeroes are added). In our example (we assume $K = 4$) we have:

$$|1\,1\,1\,1|1\,1\,1\,0|2\,2\,2\,2|2\,2\,0\,0|3\,3\,3\,3|3\,3\,3\,3|. \tag{8}$$

We thus obtained a representation of 6 "tours" by placing additional zeroes. Let us call this an extended representation. This representation will be further modified due to the neighborhood search during the course of our metaheuristic algorithm. For example, the above representation can be modified into the following:

$$|1\,1\,2\,3|2\,3\,3\,3|1\,2\,3\,2|1\,0\,3\,3|1\,3\,0\,0|1\,1\,2\,2|. \tag{9}$$

However, before the metaheuristic algorithm starts we add one more step. Let us consider all tours consisting of only one station $e.g.$ $|2\,2\,2\,2|$. Those tours mean that tanker leaves from the refinery (location 0), then delivers fuel (all its four compartments) to specific station (2 in this example) and then goes back to the refinery. Such tours are removed from the representation. However, they still affect the values of the goal function. In our example from representation (8) four tours are removed and we get the following representation:

$$|1\,1\,1\,0|2\,2\,0\,0|. \tag{10}$$

The next essential part of the algorithm is the decoding procedure responsible for transforming a given representation into an actual tour and calculating the value of the goal function. Let us consider the following representation ($K = 4$):

$$|1\,2\,3\,3|5\,6\,7\,0|. \tag{11}$$

The decoding procedure works by employing the nearest neighbor method. In our example the first tour consists of stations 1, 2 and 3. Thus, we first visit the station with the shortest distance from the current location (*i.e.* from refinery at location 0). Let us assume this is station 2. Next, we repeat the reasoning, searching for the closest station to the current location (station 2). Let it be station 3. The last station to visit is station 1 and then we go back to the refinery. The second tour consists of stations 5, 6 and 7 (0 means empty compartment). We use the nearest neighbor method again to chose the order of stations to visit. In result, both tours might look as follows:

$$0 \rightarrow 2 \rightarrow 3 \rightarrow 3 \rightarrow 1 \rightarrow 0 \tag{12}$$

$$0 \rightarrow 6 \rightarrow 7 \rightarrow 5 \rightarrow 0 \tag{13}$$

Now that we know the number of tours we can compute the value of the goal function. Let us also note that tours consisting of only zeroes (*i.e.* $|0\,0\,0\,0|$) are considered empty and do not affect the value of the goal function.

Let us also note some of the properties of the given representation. First, the lower bound for the number of resulting tours is given as:

$$\frac{\sum_{i=1}^{N} Z_i}{K}, \tag{14}$$

while the upper bound is given as $\frac{Z^*}{K}$, where $Z^*$ is the number of compartments (including empty ones) in the extended representation. Moreover, the solutions resulting from the chosen representation are always feasible, as the number of compartments for each station is always the same as the demand of the given station and no tour has a load exceeding the assumed capacity $C$.

## 4.2   Simulated Annealing

Classic SA was formulated for the case of optimization of a single objective function $f(x)$. Proposed algorithm, although similar to original version, was adapted to solving multi-objective problems. Moreover, we have added an auto-tuning phase, in which parameters of the algorithm are set.

In each iteration, from the neighborhood $N(x)$ of current solution $x$, a neighbor $x'$ is selected. The neighbor is chosen randomly, assuming uniform distribution of probability. First, we use Pareto-optimality concept to determine whether solution $x'$ dominates current solution $x$ and replaces it in next iteration of the algorithm. In other case, when solution $x'$ is dominated by $x$ or neither solution dominates the other, we evaluate the objective difference $\Delta = \sqrt{\sum_{i=1}^{q} (f_i(x') - f_i(x))^2}$. The value $\Delta$ is no less than $\max_{1 \le i \le q}\{f_i(x') - f_i(x)\}$ and each difference $f_i(x') - f_i(x)$, $i = 1, ..., q$ influence this value i.e. increase it. Solution $x'$ is accepted as the new solution for the next iteration with probability $p = exp(-\Delta/T)$, where $T$ is parameter called temperature. Starting from the initial temperature $T_0$, the temperature is reduced slowly with each iteration using cooling scheme. Higher values of temperature $T$ give a higher probability of acceptance. The influence of quality of solution (measured by $\Delta$) on acceptance probability is opposite. We used a geometric cooling scheme, in which the temperature during $s$-th iteration is $T_s = \lambda T_0$, where $\lambda$ is a parameter.

Similar algorithm has been successfully used in [10]. A parallel SA algorithm was proposed in [2]. Super linear speed-up was obtained when using representative-based neighborhood.

## 5   Computer Experiment

Proposed algorithm was implemented in C++ programming language and compiled with Embarcadero C++Builder XE7 Professional. The program was tested on Intel Core i7-3770 3400MHz, 8GB RAM and running Windows 7 64-bit.

We have tested our SA algorithm using real-world data obtained from a certain petrol company and accordingly generated orders. For each test instance and for each run of algorithms, we collected the following values:

- $\delta F1$ – improvement of first optimization criteria over initial solution,
- $\delta F2$ – improvement of second optimization criteria over initial solution,
- $|P|$ – average number of non-dominated solutions in Pareto front.

Tab. 1 shows summary of results obtained for all problem instances considered in this paper. The mean improvement was over 18% for the first criterion, and over 17% for the second. Moreover, the average number of non-dominated solutions increased with the size of the problem. It is important to note that the number of nodes indicates only the number of gas stations (*e.g.* the size of the distance matrix), while the true problem size depends on the size of the demands for each station.

**Table 1.** The evaluation of the solutions – summary

| Nodes | $\delta F1$ [%] | $\delta F2$ [%] | $|P|$ |
|---|---|---|---|
| 25 | 18.07 | 15.83 | 1.1 |
| 50 | 18.66 | 17.02 | 1.8 |
| 75 | 18.33 | 17.19 | 2.1 |
| 100 | 18.57 | 17.25 | 1.8 |
| 150 | 18.45 | 17.52 | 2.7 |
| 200 | 18.13 | 17.50 | 2.6 |
| 275 | 18.35 | 17.40 | 3.7 |
| 350 | 18.33 | 17.45 | 3.6 |
| 425 | 18.27 | 17.65 | 5.0 |
| Average | 18.35 | 17.20 | 2.71 |

Proposed SA has improved the initial solution significantly. It is worth mentioning, that proposed method was extremely fast. Biggest instances were computed in less than 5 minutes, while smallest took around 1 second. In comparison, using other decoding scheme took over 30 minutes to compute instances with 425 nodes and provided worse solutions.

**Table 2.** The evaluation of biggest instances

| Nodes | Instance No. | $\delta F1$ [%] | $\delta F2$ [%] | $|P|$ | Nodes | Instance No. | $\delta F1$ [%] | $\delta F2$ [%] | $|P|$ |
|---|---|---|---|---|---|---|---|---|---|
| 200 | 1 | 17.74 | 17.29 | 4 | 350 | 1 | 18.03 | 17.65 | 2 |
| | 2 | 19.75 | 19.60 | 3 | | 2 | 18.94 | 17.97 | 4 |
| | 3 | 19.03 | 17.78 | 1 | | 3 | 17.34 | 16.29 | 6 |
| | 4 | 18.71 | 18.83 | 2 | | 4 | 19.53 | 18.43 | 3 |
| | 5 | 17.75 | 16.84 | 4 | | 5 | 18.90 | 18.43 | 2 |
| | 6 | 17.06 | 16.45 | 4 | | 6 | 17.54 | 16.42 | 1 |
| | 7 | 17.85 | 17.36 | 2 | | 7 | 19.28 | 18.12 | 3 |
| | 8 | 17.79 | 16.12 | 4 | | 8 | 18.82 | 17.88 | 4 |
| | 9 | 17.99 | 16.98 | 1 | | 9 | 17.67 | 16.80 | 6 |
| | 10 | 17.66 | 17.72 | 1 | | 10 | 17.24 | 16.49 | 5 |
| 275 | 1 | 18.65 | 17.02 | 3 | 424 | 1 | 18.03 | 17.36 | 4 |
| | 2 | 18.75 | 17.93 | 3 | | 2 | 19.33 | 18.53 | 1 |
| | 3 | 18.44 | 16.72 | 4 | | 3 | 17.76 | 17.36 | 4 |
| | 4 | 18.71 | 18.32 | 3 | | 4 | 17.47 | 16.78 | 9 |
| | 5 | 18.25 | 16.76 | 2 | | 5 | 17.39 | 17.54 | 7 |
| | 6 | 18.21 | 17.19 | 4 | | 6 | 18.20 | 17.83 | 4 |
| | 7 | 18.25 | 17.84 | 4 | | 7 | 17.37 | 16.50 | 3 |
| | 8 | 17.92 | 17.61 | 6 | | 8 | 19.77 | 18.47 | 5 |
| | 9 | 16.91 | 15.89 | 6 | | 9 | 19.15 | 18.30 | 7 |
| | 10 | 19.36 | 18.71 | 2 | | 10 | 18.24 | 17.80 | 6 |

We also provided, in Tab. 2, more detailed results for the 4 largest instance sizes: 200, 275, 350 and 424 gas stations respectively (instances of smaller size were omitted for the sake of brevity). The results serve to show that improvement rates for all considered instances remain close to the 17% on both criteria. In fact, all improvement values from Tab. 2 range between 15.89% and 19.57%.

Let us also note the practical significance of such optimization. For example, SA algorithm for one of the instances for 424 stations (depot is not considered a gas station) managed to reduce the total distance (in km) from 694194 to 568694. Assuming that a tanker consumes 30 liters of fuel per 100 kilometers (real values are even higher if driving style is taken into account) and that liter of fuel costs around 1.2 € (European countries), then the total fuel costs of such distribution operation can be reduced by around 45000 € or over 55000 $.

## 6   Conclusions

In this paper we considered a multi-criteria fuel distribution problem similar to the common CVRP. The chosen criteria were the total distance of all tours and the number of all tours, without explicitly stating the available number of tankers. The distance matrix was created based on the real-life data of a certain petrol company with refinery acting as a depot.

90 instances of the problem (*i.e.* fuel demands for stations) were defined and combined into group of ten, depending on the number of stations. We employed a simple solution representation method, which provides only feasible solutions and then applied it to the SA metaheuristic algorithm to obtain the approximation of the Pareto set. Our research yielded good results (consistent 17–18% improvement of starting solution for both criteria) in reasonable time (5 minutes for largest instances with 424 stations).

Further research include consideration of other criteria (especially use of 3 criteria at once) and development of a Decision Support System (DSS) for the presented fuel distribution problem.

**Acknowledgements.** This work is co-financed by the European Union as part of the European Social Fund.

## References

1. Bowerman, R., Hall, B., Calamai, P.: A multi-objective optimization approach to urban school bus routing: Formulation and solution method. Transportation Research (29), pp. 107–123 (1995)
2. Bożejko, W., Pempera, J., Smutnicki, C.: Parallel Simulated Annealing for the Job Shop Scheduling Problem. In: Allen, G., Nabrzyski, J., Seidel, E., van Albada, G.D., Dongarra, J., Sloot, P.M.A. (eds.) ICCS 2009, Part I. LNCS, vol. 5544, pp. 631–640. Springer, Heidelberg (2009)

3. Corberan, A., Fernandez, E., Laguna, M., Marti, R.: Heuristic solutions to the problem of routing school buses with multiple objectives. Journal of Operational Research Society (53), 427–435 (2002)
4. Jagiełło, S., Żelazny, D.: Solving Multi-criteria Vehicle Routing Problem by Parallel Tabu Search on GPU. Procedia Computer Science (18), 2529–2532 (2013)
5. Keller, C.: Multiobjective routing through space and time: The MVP and TDVRP problems, Ph.D. thesis, University of Western Ontario (1985)
6. Keller, C., Goodchild, M.: The multiobjective vending problem: A generalization of the traveling salesman problem. Environment and Planning B: Planning and Design (15), 447–460 (1988)
7. Lee, T.-R., Ueng, J.-H.: A study of vehicle routing problem with load balancing, International Journal of Physical Distribution and Logistics Management (29), 646–657 (1998)
8. Pacheco, J., Marti, R.: Tabu search for a multi-objective routing problem. Journal of Operational Research Society (57), 29–37 (2006)
9. Paquete, T.S.L., Chiarandini, L.: Pareto local optimum sets in the bi-objective traveling salesman problem: An experimental study. In: Lecture Notes in Economics and Mathematical Systems, pp. 177–200 (2004)
10. Pempera, J., Smutnicki, C., Żelazny, D.: Optimizing bicriteria flow shop scheduling problem by simulated annealing algorithm. Procedia Computer Science (18), 936–945 (2013)
11. Ralphs, T.K., Kopman, L., Pulleyblank, W.R., Trotter Jr., L.E.: On the Capacitated Vehicle Routing Problem. Mathematical Programming (94), 343–359 (2003)
12. Rudy, J., Żelazny, D.: Memetic algorithm approach for multi-criteria network scheduling. In: Proceeding of the International Conference on ICT Management for Global Competitiveness and Economic Growth in Emerging Economies (ICTM 2012), pp. 247–261 (2012)
13. Rudy, J., Żelazny, D.: GACO: A parallel evolutionary approach to multi-objective scheduling. In: Gaspar-Cunha, A., Henggeler Antunes, C., Coello, C.C. (eds.) EMO 2015, Part I. LNCS, vol. 9018, pp. 307–320. Springer, Heidelberg (2015)
14. Ulungu, E., Teghem, J., Fortemps, P., Tuyttens, D.: Mosa method: A tool for solving moco problems. Journal of Multi-Criteria Decision Analysis (8), 221–236 (1999)
15. Zografos, K., Androustsopoulos, K.: A heuristic algorithm for solving hazardous material distribution problems. European Journal of Operational Research (152), 507–519 (2004)

# A Robust Heuristic for the Multidimensional A-star/Wavefront Hybrid Planning Algorithm

Igor Wojnicki, Sebastian Ernst[✉], and Wojciech Turek

AGH University of Science and Technology,
Al. Mickiewicza 30, 30-059 Kraków, Poland
ernst@agh.edu.pl

**Abstract** Automated planning using heuristic search or gradient algorithms is a feasible method for solving many planning problems. However, if planning is performed for several (possibly colliding) entities, the size of the state space increases dramatically. If these entities have limited predictability, observability or controllability, a single plan can no longer suffice, and robust multi-variant planning is no longer feasible due to scale. This paper presents the A-star/Wavefront hybrid planning algorithm and proposes a new heuristic for selection of its deviation zones.

## 1 Introduction

Domain-independent planning algorithms have received enormous attention over the last decades. New methods for solving various real-life planning problems are still needed by different branches of industry, where even minor improvements can result in significant savings. Particular applications of planning have their specific requirements, regarding the state space features, solution quality or response time. This makes AI planning a very interesting and important research area.

The class of problems considered in this work assumes the existence of a group of autonomous beings, operating in a common space. The beings, or entities, have their own, individual goals to achieve. The entities may or may not expect to receive orders from a global planner – the level of autonomy may differ between the entities. Certain rules define unacceptable situations in the environment.

Thy dynamics of changes of the entities' states may lead to an unacceptable situation within a very short time, compared to the time needed to calculate a plan for the entities. This situation creates new requirements for the planning method used. A solution cannot be limited to a singe plan of actions for each entity. It must also provide solutions for possible alternative plan execution scenarios.

Real-life problems which may need such planning method include mobile robot motion coordination [1] and urban traffic optimization [2]. The solutions must guarantee safety of physical manoeuvres. Virtual entities, like computational

This work is supported by the Polish National Science Centre (NCN) grant 2011/01/D/ST6/06146.

L. Rutkowski et al. (Eds.): ICAISC 2015, Part II, LNAI 9120, pp. 282–291, 2015.
DOI: 10.1007/978-3-319-19369-4_26

tasks scheduled for execution on a HPC systems, also may require methods for robust resource assignment.

The algorithm presented in this paper provides robust, multi-variant plans for groups of coexisting entities. It solves the planning problem using two different algorithms, A-star and Wavefront. A novel heuristic is proposed for determining the situations where multiple variants must be computed. Experimental results prove the usefulness of the proposed approach.

## 2  State-of-the-Art and Important Assumptions

The problem of planning is concerned with determining the necessary steps, which lead to a certain goal. Planning can be performed *a priori* or when the actions are being performed; planning is the *reasoning part of acting* [3]. A common conceptual model for planning is a *state-transition system*, also called a *discrete-event system*. It can be defined as a 4-tuple $\Sigma = (S, A, E, \gamma)$ [3,4], where:

- $S = \{s_1, s_2, \ldots\}$ is a set of *states*,
- $A = \{a_1, a_2, \ldots\}$ is a set of *actions*,
- $E = \{e_1, e_2, \ldots\}$ is a set of *events*,
- $\gamma : S \times A \times E \rightarrow 2^S$ is a state-transition function.

This definition is often used together with a graph model, where states $s \in S$ are nodes, and state transitions (given as pairs $(a, e), a \in A, e \in E$) are directed edges. If the graph formalism is used, finding a plan consists in finding a path in that graph, which leads from the node representing the initial state to the node representing the goal state. The path can then be reconstructed into a sequence of actions, which in turn can be executed by an entity (such as a robot).

The state space can be traversed using well-known graph search algorithms: they are either "blind" methods (which do not try to direct the search towards the goal) [4] or heuristic methods, which take the characteristics of the search space into account. The latter are especially useful for large state spaces [5]. Heuristic functions aim to estimate the "goodness" of a certain state, which refers to how close it is to the goal.

If a certain planning problem consists in actually moving within a certain (physical) space, and the planning is performed for one entity, the states often represent locations within the physical space, and transitions represent traveling from one location to another. In this case, one of the most often-used heuristics is the *straight-line distance* function; however, it isn't the most optimal if the structure of the space is irregular, as is the case with a city divided by a river with sparse bridges.

The "direct" representation of physical spaces in a state-space is very intuitive, but for more sophisticated problems, the states are often *encodings* of certain parameters. For instance, planning of paths for multiple entities in a common space may utilise a heuristic which is a sum of the straight-line distances of all entities to their respective goals.

Section 3 presents the possibility of using one of the most popular heuristic search algorithms, A-star, in a multi-entity setting, by preparing a multi-dimensional state space.

In the considered setting, the entities may be characterised by different levels of the following features:

- *controllability* – the extent to which the supervisor may influence the entities; inversely proportional to the entities' *autonomy*,
- *predictability* – certainty that the entity will act according to the prediction, either due to its intents or its abilities to fulfil the orders,
- *observability* – the ability of the supervisor to observe the actions of an entity, whether autonomous or performed to fulfil an order.

Therefore, even a set of non-conflicting plans computed for several entities may not guarantee the required level of robustness in case any of the entities fails in exact execution of its plan. Therefore, the plan needs to provide multiple (suboptimal) means of achieving the goal for each entity.

This characteristic is fulfilled by the wavefront algorithm, also described in Section 3. However, this algorithm, used to determine paths in a multi-dimensional state space, has an overwhelmingly large complexity.

Therefore, a hybrid algorithm has been proposed: the paths for entities are calculated using the A-star algorithm, but detected collision- or deviation-prone spots are used to define deviation zones, where multi-variant plans using the Wavefront algorithm are computed. This hybrid algorithm is presented in Section 4.

Determination of the deviation zones is a difficult task, as it needs to balance the performance of computations and robustness. Therefore, one has to define a heuristic function, used to determine the scope of the Wavefront-based phase.

The main contribution of this paper is proposal of a new heuristic, which has been described in detail in the further part of Section 4. The applicability and characteristics of the proposed heuristic are discussed in Section 5.

## 3    A-star and Wavefront Algorithms for Multi-Entity Planning

Planning actions for a single entity in a given search space can be solved using general-purpose algorithms, such as the ones described in Section 2. If multiple entities coexist in the same search space, simply performing the calculations for each entity separately does not guarantee lack of collisions. Therefore, planning should be performed in a multi-dimensional search space, which represents the state of all individual entities at any given time.

Together with the number of considered entities, the number of state space dimensions increases, while the number of acceptable state transitions slightly decreases assuming that no two entities can occupy the same location.

Let us consider a simple example of a 2-dimensional $7 \times 7$ grid with a single entity. There are $7 \times 7 = 49$ states, which are locations the entity occupies, being its coordinates $(x, y)$. Let us assume that the entity can move in four directions: north, south, east and west. Having two entities in the same grid yields a 4-dimensional state space. A single state is expressed as a quadruple: $(x_1, y_1, x_2, y_2)$, where $(x_1, y_1)$ and $(x_2, y_2)$ are the locations of individual entities. A state of that form will be called a *collective state*, whereas its components are referred to as *entity states*. There is an occupation constraint introduced: no two or more entities can occupy the same location in the grid. It reduces the number of transitions in the state space by applying $(x_1, y_1) \neq (x_2, y_2)$. Assuming that the plane is a $7 \times 7$ grid, there are $(7 \times 7) \times (7 \times 7) = 2,401$ states. However, compensating for the occupation constraint it is actually reduced to: $(7 \times 7) \times (7 \times 7 - 1) = 2,352$. There are some efforts carried out regarding further state space reduction e.g. using preferences [6].

Regardless of the state space size, the algorithms remain basically unchanged. The following two subsections present two algorithms and provide some estimates with regard to their complexity in a multi-dimensional setting.

### 3.1   A-star

The A-star algorithm [7] is a heuristic search algorithm which finds the optimal path from the start state to the goal state. The path should be understood as a sequence of state transitions.

Let us assume a state space, containing a finite set of $n$ states. As outlined in Section 2, collective states will be used for planning purposes. Therefore, while the basic concept of A-star remains unchanged, the number of states grows significantly, as each consists of a much larger number of dimensions.

The state space can be viewed as a directed, weighted graph $G$. Put formally, a graph $G$ is a tuple $G = (V, E, c)$ where $V$ is a set of vertices, $E$ is a set of edges ($e_i = (v_i, v_j)$ indicates that there is an edge from vertex $v_i$ to vertex $v_j$), and $c : E \rightarrow \mathbb{R}^+ \cup \{0\}$ is the cost function.

Mapping this formalism to state spaces, vertices represent states and edges represent actions.

The A-star algorithm begins from the start vertex and expands it, adding all reachable vertices to the so-called *fringe*. At each subsequent step, a vertex to be expanded is selected from the fringe. The basis for selection is the value of the evaluation function $f(v)$:

$$f(v) = g(v) + h(v)$$

where $g(v)$ is the known cost of achieving vertex $v$ from the start vertex, and $h(v)$ is the estimated cost of achieving the goal state. Function $h(v)$, called the heuristic, must give an optimistic estimate of the remaining cost, as outlined in Section 2.

For the A-star algorithm to be complete and optimal, the heuristic function $h$ must be *admissible* and *consistent* [8], which means that it must not overestimate the remaining cost of getting to the goal, and that for two subsequent vertices $v'$ and $v''$, $h(v') \leq c(v', v'') + h(v'')$.

With a good heuristic, A-star search is significantly quicker than blind search (which expands nodes without considering their relation to the goal node). However, if some of the characteristics outlined in Section 2 (e.g. controllability or predictability) are not perfect, the initial plan would become useless, requiring re-planning, which often cannot be performed in real time.

Therefore, in the ideal situation, it is desirable to have multi-variant plans, which cover the situations of detours from the original plan during execution. Such algorithm is presented in Section 3.2.

## 3.2   Wavefront

As mentioned in Section 3.1, the A-star algorithm lacks robustness: the plans assume that the entities follow them exactly and in a timely manner. On the other hand, the Wavefront algorithm, well known in the field of robotics, can provide a multi-variant plan.

The Wavefront algorithm finds the shortest (*cheapest*) path in a graph from any starting point to a given goal and consists of two phases:

1. vertex labeling,
2. selecting a path.

Let us assume a search space given by a graph, which is invariant to multi-dimensional or collective issues mentioned earlier:

$$S = (V, E, c, g)$$

where the additional component, $g$, is a labeling function: $g : V \rightarrow \mathbb{N}$. The initial labeling is $\forall x \in V : g(x) = 0$. The first step is to re-label the vertices, starting with the goal vertex $g$ which is relabeled $g(g) = 1$. A breadth-first search algorithm is then used to find the vertices which have not been labeled with a positive value yet. At the first step $p = g$, $C$ becomes a set of subsequent vertices to label:

$$C = \{k : (k, p) \in E, g(k) = 0\}$$

then the labeling is carried out:

$$g(k) = g(p) + c((k, p)) : \forall k \in C$$

where $c((k, p))$ is a transition cost assigned to the edge corresponding to an activity. The process is repeated for each element in $C$.

The second step of the algorithm selects a path from any start vertex $s$ to $g$ by descending values of function $g$.

As the Wavefront algorithm provides a gradient map from any vertex to $g$, the shortest path from any state can be found by simply descending the gradient. However, for multi-dimensional planning, the algorithm suffers from combinatorial explosion and cannot be applied to large spaces.

Therefore, Section 4 presents a hybrid approach, which combines the performance of A-star with the robustness of Wavefront-generated gradients, and proposes a new heuristic for determination of deviation zones.

# 4    The Hybrid A-star/Wavefront Algorithm

Planning for multiple agents is not different than planning for a single agent, except that the number of dimensions in the search space increases. Also, some possible side effects need to be taken into consideration. The ones considered here regard collisions between agents and deviations from the plan due to uncertainty[1].

The wavefront-based approach seems to be the most suitable for such multi-agent planning with uncertainty, but its time complexity sometimes renders it hardly applicable. On the other hand, the A-star algorithm, with better time complexity, does not provide alternatives in case the aforementioned side effects occur.

The proposed hybrid approach tries to combine better time complexity of A-star with robustness of Wavefront. It assumes that:

- there is a global plan provided by the A-star algorithm,
- deviation-prone sub-spaces of the search space are identified; they are called *deviation sub-spaces*,
- for deviation sub-spaces, the wavefront algorithm is used to compute the optimal path to exit the sub-space, thus to return to the original A-star based path.

Let us have a plan $\mathcal{P}_V = (v_1, \ldots, v_n)$, generated by the A-star algorithm over a state space given as $G = (E, V, c)$, where $v_i \in V$. A single vertex represents the locations of all agents for which the plan is being computed, while an edge represents a possible transition to another state, thus an allowed move of an agent.

There is a possibility-of-deviation detection function $cd$ such that:

$$cd : N \to S$$

where $N$ is a neighbourhood of states such as $N = (v_{i+1}, \ldots, v_{i+m})$ such that $N \subset \mathcal{P}_V$ and $S = (V_S, E_S, c_S, g_S)$, being a deviation sub-space, is a state sub-space for the wavefront algorithm subdivided from $G$ in such a way that $V_S \subset V, E_S \subset E, c_S \subset c$. In this case, the goal for Wavefront is $v_{i+m}$, which is the last state in the neighborhood of states. There can be a set of sub-spaces $SS = \{S_1, \ldots, S_o\}$ for a given $\mathcal{P}_V$ identified.

As a result, if an agent deviates from the original plan and a deviation occurs in any of the previously identified areas covered by any $S$, a wavefront-generated path is used to return to the original plan as quickly as possible.

Therefore, the function $cd$ is a heuristic, used to determine the scope of application of Wavefront, thus balancing performance and robustness in the proposed approach. It should consider domain-specific properties of the agents which reflects the likelihood of collision. Increasing the cardinality of $S$ requires more calculations but, at the same time, makes the plan more robust.

---

[1] There might also be different reasons for deviations, such as limited controllability, predictability and observability.

The number of states, or transitions, if there are any unreachable states, is the core factor of computational complexity, regardless of the planning algorithm used. Two factors influence the computational complexity of the proposed algorithm:

1. the number of neighbourhoods ($N$) which might result in deviations, either due to collisions between agents or obstacles, or general deviations from the plan: $d_c$,
2. the size of the deviation sub-space ($S$): $r_c$.

More neighbourhoods make the solution more robust and takes more uncertainty into account. With larger deviation sub-spaces, more significant deviations can be covered. However, increase of both the number of neighbourhoods and their size makes it necessary to perform more computations to synthesise the plan.

A deviation neighbourhood can be heuristically defined as a sequence in the plan, for which particular agents get close to each other at a distance smaller than some given $d_c$. A particular $d_c$ value should take the properties of the world being modelled into consideration; these include the likelihood of slipping, the uncertainty of agents' behaviour, their controllability, observability, autonomy, etc.

The deviation sub-space size $r_c$ should take physical aspects of the agents into consideration. These include their maximum and minimum speed, acceleration, mass, etc.

## 5    Experimental Results

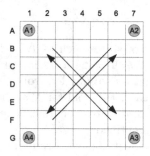

**Fig. 1.** Initial state of the proposed world

Let us assume that the world being considered is a two-dimensional space, based on a $7 \times 7$ grid. The agents, denoted as $A_n$, can move from one location to another only orthogonally, in accordance with the von Neumann neighbourhood: they can move north, south, east and west, which defines their activity functions. A single location is allowed to be occupied by no more than one agent at a time. There are four agents initially located in the corners (see Fig. 1). Each agent's goal it to get to the diagonally opposite corner; $A_1$ to $(G, 7)$, $A_2$ to $(G, 1)$, $A_3$ to $(A, 1)$, $A_4$ to $(A, 7)$. The global goal is to guide all the agents to their goals corners.

Assuming the above, a state consists of the information about agent locations, thus it is a tuple: $s = (x_1, y_1, x_2, y_2, x_3, y_3, x_4, y_4)$ where $(x_1, y_1)$, $(x_2, y_2)$, $(x_3, y_3)$, $(x_4, y_4)$ correspond to locations of agents $A_1$, $A_2$, $A_3$, $A_4$ respectively.

A good indication of the complexity of A-star-based search is the number of states that have to be considered before the goal is reached, i.e. the number of heuristic function computations for candidate states. For the given example, assuming a von Neumann neighbourhood and a straight-line distance heuristic, the number of these operations is

$$O_A = 5,432.$$

The A-star approach does not provide robustness and cannot handle uncertainty.

Assuming that each agent can be at any location, having a $7 \times 7$ grid and applying the Wavefront algorithm, the computational complexity is proportional to the state space cardinality. It is given as: $|S_T| = (7*7)^4 = 5,764,801$. Applying the world constraints (no two agents sharing the same location) reduces number of states slightly, having a product of arithmetic progression: $|S_W| = (7*7) * (7*7-1)*(7*7-2)*(7*7-3) = 5,085,024$. It renders such fully robust plan unfeasible to calculate.

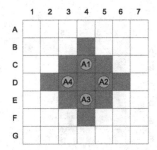

**Fig. 2.** Possible deviation subspace, representing collisions among agents

Let us assume a single deviation neighbourhood with $d_c = 2$. It indicates that if an agent comes within a distance of 2 of any other agent, that is identified as a possible collision. The path of the four agents calculated using the A-star algorithm results in a possible collision of all agents at $N = (4, C, 5, D, 4, E, 3, D)$. Assuming the deviation sub-space size $r_c = 2$, the actual sub-space $S$ is given as a gray area in Fig. 2. The number of operations $O_S$ is equal to the sub-space cardinality and it is expressed as:

$$O_S = |S_S| = 13 * (13 - 1) * (13 - 2) * (13 - 3) = 17,160$$

The total number of operations to establish a robust plan is proportional to:

$$O_H = O_A + O_S = 22,592.$$

Comparing with $S_W$, it makes the problem over 225 times smaller. As a result, there is a plan in a multidimensional space providing optimal paths for multiple agents. The plan is multi-variant to a certain degree. During execution, if there is any deviation from the plan within a previously identified deviation sub-space, there are means to return to the previously optimal path without any additional computations. However, it does not imply that in such a case the plan is still optimal.

If a deviation takes place outside the deviation sub-space there are no means to compensate, thus proper identification of these sub-spaces and their sizes is crucial. Some heuristics can be used in such a case. A simple one would direct an agent back to the planned path using just a proper direction (assuming euclidean distance). Another solution, presented below, is to provide a set of deviation sub-spaces at each agents' trajectories. It would allow the agent to return to the original trajectory as fast as possible. Such a set of deviation sub-spaces for the agent $A_1$ is presented in Fig. 3. They are indicated as four hatched areas which are: $S_{A_11} = (A,1),(A,2),(B,1),(B,2)$, $S_{A_12} = (B,2),(B,3),(C,2),(C,3)$, $S_{A_13} = (E,5),(E,6),(F,5),(F,6)$, $S_{A_14} = (F,6),(F,7),(G,6),(G,7)$. It needs to be pointed out that the above sub-spaces are just two-dimensional, while $S$ is has eight dimensions. Thus, Wavefront calculations performed in these sub-spaces are far less intensive. The number of planning operations is equal to the sub-space cardinality, which in each case is 4. $|S_{A_11}| = |S_{A_12}| = |S_{A_13}| = |S_{A_14}|$. Similarly for $A_2$, $A_3$, $A_4$.

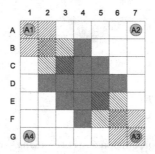

**Fig. 3.** A set of deviation sub-spaces for $A_1$

A complete deviation sub-space is given as 8-dimensional $S$ and 2-dimensional sub-spaces, for each of the agents: $S_{A_11}$, $S_{A_12}$, $S_{A_13}$, $S_{A_14}$, $S_{A_21}$, $S_{A_22}$, $S_{A_23}$, $S_{A_24}$, $S_{A_31}$, $S_{A_32}$, $S_{A_33}$, $S_{A_34}$, $S_{A_41}$, $S_{A_42}$, $S_{A_43}$, $S_{A_44}$. The sum of cardinalities, thus the number of operations to be performed is:

$$O'_S = 17,160 + 4^3 = 17,224$$

The total number of operations to establish a robust plan, taking into considerations deviations of individual agents is given as:

$$O'_H = O_A + O'_S = 22,656$$

The difference between $O'_H$ and $O_H$ being 64 is almost insignificant, still allowing to establish a plan 224 times faster than establishing a fully robust one using a pure Wavefront algorithm. It leads to the conclusion that creating more deviation sub-spaces to compensate for agent observability or predictability does not significantly increase the number of operations needed to calculate such a robust plan.

## 6 Conclusions and Future Work

Planning for multiple entities causes an explosion of the number of states in the state space. Variations of agent controllability, observability and predictability add to the problem by introducing belief states and states which would not otherwise be considered by the supervisor.

The presented hybrid A-star/Wavefront planning algorithm maintains reasonably good performance when searching multi-entity or multi-dimensional state spaces, and provides the necessary robustness in the crucial (deviation- or conflict-prone) areas, called deviation zones. This paper proposes a new heuristic for determination of deviation zones an presents some performance estimations based on a simple grid-world example.

Further work includes investigation of real-world multi-entity planning problems to tune the deviation zone determination heuristics, as well as large-scale simulations to further assess the feasibility of the proposed hybrid approach.

## References

1. Turek, W., Cetnarowicz, K., Zaborowski, W.: Software agent systems for improving performance of multi-robot groups. Fundam. Inf. 112(1), 103–117 (2011)
2. Blaszczyk, P., Turek, W., Cetnarowicz, K.: Formal model for micro-scale traffic simulation and control. In: 2013 18th International Conference on Methods and Models in Automation and Robotics (MMAR), pp. 305–310 (August 2013)
3. Ghallab, M., Nau, D., Traverso, P.: Automated Planning: Theory & Practice. Morgan Kaufmann Publishers Inc., San Francisco (2004)
4. Russell, S.J., Norvig, P.: Artificial Intelligence: A Modern Approach, 3rd edn. Pearson Education (2010)
5. Bonet, B.: Planning as heuristic search. Artificial Intelligence 129(1-2), 5–33 (2001)
6. Klimek, R., Wojnicki, I., Ernst, S.: State-space reduction through preference modeling. In: Rutkowski, L., Korytkowski, M., Scherer, R., Tadeusiewicz, R., Zadeh, L.A., Zurada, J.M. (eds.) ICAISC 2013, Part II. LNCS (LNAI), vol. 7895, pp. 363–374. Springer, Heidelberg (2013)
7. Hart, P., Nilsson, N., Raphael, B.: A formal basis for the heuristic determination of minimum cost paths. IEEE Transactions on Systems Science and Cybernetics 4(2), 100–107 (1968)
8. Dechter, R., Pearl, J.: Generalized best-first search strategies and the optimality of A*. J. ACM 32(3), 505–536 (1985)

# Human-Agent Interaction Design
# for Decreasing Indebtedness

Saori Yamamoto and Yugo Takeuchi[✉]

Graduate School of Informatics, Shizuoka University,
3-5-1, Johoku, Naka-ku, Hamamatsu-shi, Shizuoka, 432-8011 Japan
gs13044@s.inf.shizuoka.ac.jp
takeuchi@inf.shizuoka.ac.jp

**Abstract.** People experience feelings of indebtedness when receiving
help from an agent. This feeling of indebtedness has a potentially negative impact on the human attitude. However, few experimental analyses
this evaluating effect of the help an agent are available. The aim of this
study is to design an agent that can assist people without making them
feel indebted to that agent. The present research proposed a help method
where the agent helps people to achieve their goal using a different approach from the recipient and verified its effectiveness by experiment.
It was established that an agent can assist recipients without adverse
effects if the help method is different.

**Keywords:** Media equation · Indebtedness · Help · Agent · Perception
of self and others · Social interaction

## 1 Introduction

The goal of an information system is to provide support to people. Some information systems provide support flexibly through behavior activity and autonomy.
It was defined such an information system as an 'agent' in the present paper. In
general, people suppose that they are not indebted to such information systems
for any assistance they receive because they understand that systems do not
having conscious intentions. However, people have a cognitive tendency to treat
an artifact as a person, and attribute humanness unconsciously[1]. People have
potential to treat an agent as a helper when they are helped by an agent. Therefore, it is theorized that people feel unconsciously indebted to the agent. Previous
studies reveal the recipient's reaction when receiving help from an agent. It has
been suggested that people behave according to the social norms of reciprocity[2].
This reciprocity norm generates recipient's feelings of indebtedness, such as, "I
have a duty to repay something," from the concept of reciprocity[3]. People are
conditioned to feel indebted from positive motivation, such as gratitude toward
the helper and the joy of association. On the other hand, it appears that indebtedness, also develops from negative motivation, such as feeling repayment is
required to 'prevent deteriorating relations with a helper,' 'eliminate feelings of
guilt,' or to 'recover self-esteem.' People's feelings of indebtedness have serious

© Springer International Publishing Switzerland 2015
L. Rutkowski et al. (Eds.): ICAISC 2015, Part II, LNAI 9120, pp. 292–302, 2015.
DOI: 10.1007/978-3-319-19369-4_27

negative implications, such as increased stress and hindrance in achieving their goal. For example, people with a negative impression to receive the help has tendencies that reluctant to ask for help[4]. In addition, the negative experience of help-seeking produces feelings of distrust towards the helper, further decreasing their self-esteem[5][6]. This issue is a concern not only in Human-Human Interaction, but also in Human-Agent Interaction. The reason is that people have also tended to respond politely unconsciously to computers[7]. It revealed that it is possible for people to feel indebted when they are helped by an agent. However, few experimental analyses evaluating effects of the help an agent is available to date. Therefore, how to design of agent's help methods in consideration of recipient's indebtedness feelings has become a problem to be solved. The purpose of the present study is to design a method in which an agent can provide help without giving rise to feeling of indebtedness on the part of recipients. Toward this goal, we investigated design to decrease recipient indebtedness. The uniqueness of this study is to try the decreasing indebtedness by design of agents' behavior without the change of a recipient's behavior. Thus, this study is expected to contribute to social life of human in Human-computer interaction.

## 2  Theoretical Background

### 2.1  The Media Equation

People are considered to feel indebted to an agent. In previous study, people showed the tendency to regard information media as a communication with the real world, and respond politely to the computer[8]. This theory was defined as the 'Media Equation.' In addition, people showed the tendency to react kindly to computers that help them[9]. Therefore, people have potential to recognize an agent as a helper when they receive a benefit and thus sense indebtedness to their helper. This reaction makes it likely that participants who are adversely affected psychologically by such help will continue to feel indebted. Therefore, it was explored that a method by which an agent can help people without generating feelings of indebtedness.

### 2.2  Cognitive Factor Relating to Decreasing Indebtedness Feeling of Recipients

It is expected that recipients are able to receive the help of an agent without feeling indebtedness, when they do not recognize an agent's intention to help. Recipients want to give back in order to decrease their indebtedness. This is because that recipients who regard indebtedness as a burden believe indebtedness will lead to deteriorating relations, a sense of guilt, feelings of shame, and low self-esteem. For those reasons, the recipient's sense of duty to give back is dependent on the magnitude of indebtedness they feel(Fig. 1). It is considered that recipients estimate the amount of their indebtedness to the helper by comparing the benefit and the cost of the help action[8]. This cost includes non-material resources, such as time and effort. If the cost of the recipient and the benefit of the helper is enough for small, the extent of indebtedness is represented by the following formula:

$Indebtednessofrecipient = Costtothehelper + Benefittotherecipient$ The cost of the helper on above equation is able to resolve into components as next formula:

$Costtothehelper = Costtothehelper(orotherperson) + Costfortherecipient$

These equations show that recipients will generate a less indebtedness feeling when the helper's behavior has no relationship with them. Therefore, It is expected that the indebtedness feeling of recipients becomes decrease if the helper's cost to help recipients is enough small from the recipient's view. It was explored that the design of help method which disguising the goal of an agent's behavior, in order to decrease the cost of an agent to help recipients on the recipient's view.

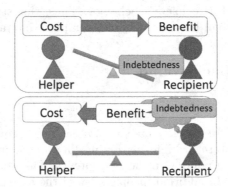

**Fig. 1.** The amount that a recipient gives back to a helper is correlated with the amount of indebtedness they feel

## 2.3  Help Method Model without Impression of the Agent's Intention to Help

It was speculated that recipients will decrease indebtedness feeling when they receive the agent's help by different behavior from them. People attribute a purpose to the others by imagining a situation from the others behavior[10]. Therefore, the recipient is predicted to try to guess the agent's intention by observing its behavior when the purpose of an agent is unknown. In the present research, it was proposed that the model which a recipient estimates the purpose of the agent who helped based on the cognitive processing model of Norman[11]. It is supposed that the people in this workspace will try to guess the agent's intention by observing its behavior. If the agent's action matches an act the person's planning, that person can easily guess the relationship between the agent's behavior and their goal. Therefore, that person will estimate that the purpose of agent is help them and feel indebted. Conversely, If an agent helps a person by using the different behavior from this person, they are estimated that cannot recognize the relationship between them and the agent's behavior, and not feels indebted to the agent. Therefore, the present research proposed the agent's help method to use the different behavior of the recipient's, due to decrease indebtedness. It was conducted that the following experiment to test the effectiveness of the proposed method.

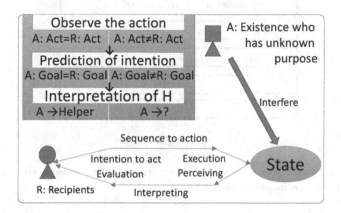

**Fig. 2.** Model of interpretation of an agent who has an unknown propose in extended Norman cognitive processing models

# 3   Experiment

**Purpose.** The purpose of the present experiment was to investigate whether the agent's help method by using different behavior from the recipient can decrease recipient's indebtedness than the other method or not.

**Hypotensis.** Recipients are hard to feel an indebtedness when they don't recognize the purpose of the agent as help them less than when they were helped by using another method.

## 3.1   Experimental Design

This experiment consisted of two distinct tasks in order to measure the amount of each participants' feeling of indebtedness. The first task was the Object Erase Task (OET), in which the participants experience help from an agent. The second task was the Color Perception Task (CPT). The purpose of this task was to investigate whether participants felt indebted to the agent by observing the participant's attitude when they attempted the task. It was observed how many times the participants tried the CPT and compared the perceived amount of indebtedness between each condition. A flowchart of the entire task procedure is shown in Fig. 3.

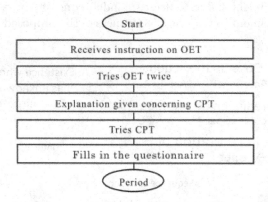

**Fig. 3.** Object Erase Task: Participants were tasked with erasing the black circle-shaped objects with a mouse in each trial

30 students acted as participants. Each had been using a computer on a daily basis and did not have any color vision defect.

## 3.2 Procedure

**Object Erase Task (OET).** The purpose of OET was to give participants an impression that the help agent's behavior give benefit for them. OET task requires participants to erase objects on the display using the mouse(Fig. 4). The goal of the participants was to erase the specied number of black circles-shaped objects from the display as possible before the time ran out. These objects were defined as 'targets' in this experiment. Participants were able to catch a target by holding down the left key of the mouse. They then moved the targets in order from the left upper side of the display, one by one, using drag and drop, and erased them by releasing the left key over a box set in the center of the display. The agent provided help to recipients by erasing the twenty-fifth target. This agent was defined as the 'help agent.' The recipients' mouse pointer was displayed as a yellow stick man. The help agent was also displayed as a blue stick man.

The aim of the OET was to make participants recognize that the action of the help agent was to help them reach their goal. Therefore, this task was performed twice.

In the first OET trial, the help agent did not appear and did not help the participant. This trial finished automatically when the time was up. It was almost impossible for the participants reach their goal in the first trial of the OET. Therefore, the participants recognized that it was difficult to succeed alone. In

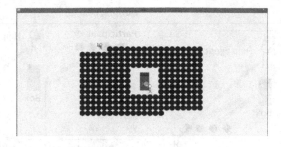

**Fig. 4.** Object Erase Task: Participants were tasked with erasing the black circle-shaped objects with a mouse in each trial

the second OET trial, the help agent did not appeared on the display when participants erased the third target. The help agent erased the twenty–fifth target in order from the right. Therefore, the participants were able to successfully accomplish their goal on the second trial thanks to the help of the agent. In the present experiment, the factor defined as the help method factor was expressed via two different conditions as the between-participants factors. One procedure was the procedure of the same method, in which participants received assistance from a help agent using the same approach as the participants. The other procedure was the procedure of the different method, in which the help agent helped using a different approach from that of the participants.

**Same Method Procedure(Fig. 5, Left Figure)**
  The help agent erased targets using the same approach as the participants. They repeated carrying the targets to the box at the center of the display.
**Different Method Procedure(Fig. 5, Right Figure)**
  The help agent erased targets using a different approach from that of the participants. They repeated carrying targets to a disposal point outside of the display according to the procedure described below. The distance between each target and the disposal point was equal to that between each target and the center box.

**Color Perception Task (CPT).** The purpose of CPT was to give recipients a chance that they can return benefit for the help agent. The CPT required participants to assign a number to each of three cards based on the brightness of the color displayed on the card(Fig. 6). Participants compared the cards arrayed on the display and ranked them according to which they thought brighter. After the OET, the participants were asked to undertake the CPT via a message on the display. The system then displayed a picture of the help agent with the following message: "The aim of the CPT is to enhance the yellow stick person." Thus, the participants understood that the task was designed to benefit the help agent. Each trial consisted of ranking a set of cards and pressing a decision button. Three cards were set for each color randomly, but their level of brightness

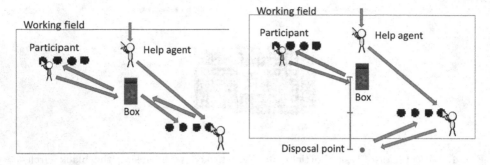

**Fig. 5.** The left figure represents the action of the help agent using the same method procedure. The right figure represents the action of the help agent in the different method procedure.

was equal. The participants undertook at least five trials. After the fifth trial, the participants were given the choice of whether to continue the CPT or exit the task. Therefore, it was regarded as return the help agent's favors that the recipient decides to continue the task of OPT.

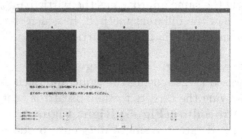

**Fig. 6.** The working field of the CPT. Participants were asked to assign a number to each card using radio buttons in order of brightness.

### 3.3 Measure

In the present research, the number of CPT trials was used as a measurement of the degree of participant indebtedness toward the help agent. Through the number of trials, it was observed how the participants positively tackled the task to assist the help agent, which provided evidence of the participant's desire to reciprocate for the assistance the help agent provided in the OET task. After each task, the participants completed a post test questionnaire concerning their impressions of the agent and the task. Regarding the OET, the participants were asked whether they thought that the help agent benefited them and whether they thought that the help agent wanted to help them. For the CPT, the participants were asked whether they were aware of any benefit they received from the help agent while tackling the CPT and whether they successfully performed the CPT or not.

It was predicted that the number of attempts at the CPT with the same method procedure would be less than with the different method procedure. The amount of benefit provided by the agent between each condition was equal because the help agent erased the same number of targets. Therefore, the participants decide whether to reciprocate based on the action of the help agent. It was predicted that the participants would undertake the CPT more seriously in proportion to their feeling that the agent was trying to help them. With the procedure of the same method, the help agent erased targets using the same approach as the participants. Thus, it would be apparent to the participants that the help agent was working toward the same goal in the OET. Participants could, therefore, be expected to recognize the help agent as a helper. With the procedure of the different method, the help agent erased targets using a different approach from that of the participants. Thus, the relationship between the participants' goal and the help agent's action would not be readily apparent to the participants. Therefore, it was predicted that participants would not recognize the help agent as their helper with this procedure. Based on this reasoning, the relationship between the number of trials could be expected to be as follows:

$$SameMethodProcedure > DifferentMethodProcedure$$

## 4   Results

Support was found the hypothesis that recipients a few feel an indebtedness when helped by an agent using a help method where as does not appear that the agent's intention as compared when an agent using another method. Of the 30 participants, 16 were in the different method procedure group, while 14 were in the same method procedure group.

**Behavior Observation in CPT.** The results of CPT provide evidence consistent with the number of trials predictions(Fig. 7). Comparison of the mean number of CPT trials by analysis of variance (ANOVA) yielded significant differences for the help method factor manipulation: $F(1,29) = 4.26, p < .05$. According to this data, the same method procedure participants reported significantly lower CPT trials per person. This result concurs with our predictions. In addition, it was compared that the average time (seconds) for each trial for each participant between the two groups in order to evaluate politeness during the CPT trial par once (Fig. 8). This comparison found no significant differences in the mean levels of the time per trial between the same method procedure group and the different method procedure group($F(1,29) = 0.47, n.s.$)

**Post Test Questionnaire.** Participants were asked their estimate what the purpose of the yellow stick man (the help agent) in the OET. This result indicates that the same method participants were more aware of the benefits of the agent than the different method participants. For the procedure of the same method,

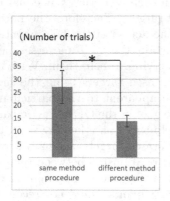

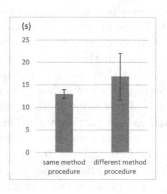

**Fig. 7.** The mean number of CPT trials per person. Abscissae(See the figure on the left): Experimental condition. Ordinate: The average number of trials per person. $*p < .05$.

**Fig. 8.** The mean number of CPT trials per person. Abscissae(See the figure on the right): experimental condition. Ordinate: The average time of trials per person (seconds). $Bars = astandarderror.n.s. = nonsignificant.$

the participants answer what they thought were the intentions of the help agent, in particular whether the agent was trying to help or trying to sabotage them. In contrast, the participants in the different method procedure were seemed that the answer were not related to their task. Participants was asked a further question what the meaning that they tries many trial of CPT. The most common answer for the same method participants indicated that they were conscious that their behavior would contribute a benefit to the help agent. In contrast, the answers of the different method participants were more varied. Participants were asked a further question what the meaning that they try many trials of CPT. The most common answer for the same method participants indicated that they were conscious that their behavior would contribute a benefit to the help agent. In contrast, the answers of the different method participants were more varied.

Additionally, participants evaluated the behavior of the help agent on a scale of 0 to 6. Participants answered the question whether the yellow stick man helped them to achieve their goal in the second OET trial. It was conducted that an ANOVA of scores between each condition, but there were no significant differences between the two groups ($F(1, 29) = 0.14, n.s.$). Participants also answered the question whether the existence of the yellow stick man was necessary to achieve their goal in the second OET trial. There was no significant difference between the results of the scores of the two groups ($F(1, 29) = 0.40, n.s.$).

# 5 Discussion

Taking these results into consideration, it appears that, if an agent uses a different approach than the participants, the participants are able to benefit without feeling the mental burden of indebtedness. According to the questionnaire, there were no significant differences in the degree of impression of benefit based on the behavior of the help agent between the same method group and the different method group. However, the results for the CPT show that participants assigned to the different method procedure were less motivated to reciprocate for the agent the benefit than the other group. In addition, participants assigned to the different method procedure were indifferent to the motives of the agent as compared to the other participants.

# 6 Conclusion

The purpose of the present study is to design a method in which an agent can provide help without giving rise to feelings of indebtedness on the part of recipients. The present research proposed a help method where the agent helps the user to achieve their goal using a different approach from the recipient and verified its effectiveness by experiment. It was established that an agent can assist recipients without adverse effects if the help method is different.

In future, it is believed that agents will provide more and more assistance in our society. This will enhance the opportunities for people to feel indebted to an agent. However, few experimental analyses have evaluated the negative effect of help. The present research focused on the need to reciprocate for the help provided by an agent and explored how to decrease that debt. The present study will assist in advancing the design behavior of a useful agent for Human-Agent Interaction. Potential applications include making a nursing care agent look more businesslike and less intimate. In addition, to further decrease the impression of intimacy between the nursing care agent and the recipient, the agent can be designed to behave as though it serves an unspecified, large number of people, rather than the one recipient. These designs should allow an agent to help the user achieve their goal without causing stress. One question worthy of future research is how to improve the help agent's performance.

# References

1. Reeves, B., Nass, C.: The Media Equation: How People Treat Computers, Television, and New Media Like Real People and Places. Cambridge University Press, California (1996)
2. Gouldner, A.W.: The Norm of Reciprocity: A Preliminary Statement. American Sociological Review 25(2), 161–178 (1960)
3. Greenberg, M.S., Westcott, D.R.: Indebtedness as a Mediator of Reactions to Aid. In: Fisher, J.D., Nadler, A., DePaulo, B.M. (eds.) New Directions in Helping: Recipient Reaction and Aid, vol. 1, pp. 85–112. Elsevier (1983)

4. Yablon, Y.B.: Social goals and willingness to seek help for school violence. International Journal of Educational Research 53, 192–200 (2012)
5. Bohns, V.K., Flynn, F.J.: "Why didn't you just ask?" Underestimating the discomfort of help-seeking. Journal of Experimental Social Psychology 46(2), 402–409 (2010)
6. Yap, M.B.H., Reavley, N., Jorm, A.F.: Where would young people seek help for mental disorders and what stops them? Findings from an Australian national survey. Journal of Affective Disorders 147(1–3), 255–261 (2013)
7. Takeuchi, Y., Katagiri, Y.: Establishing Affinity Relationships toward Agents: Effects of Sympathetic Agent Behaviors toward Human Responses. In: Proceedings of WETICE 1999, pp. 253–258 (1999)
8. Greenberg, M.S.: A Theory of Indebtedness. In: Gergen, K.J., Greenberg, M.S., Willis, R.H. (eds.) Social Exchange. Advances in Theory and Research, pp. 3–26. Springer, New York (1980)
9. Takeuchi, Y., Katagiri, Y., Nass, C., Fogg, B.J.: Social Response and Cultural Dependency in Interaction. In: Proceedings of the Pacific Rim International Human-Computer Conference on Artificial Intelligence 1998, pp. 114–123 (1998)
10. Gallese, V., Goldman, A.: Mirror Neurons and the Simulation Theory of Mind-reading. Trends in Cognitive Sciences 2(12) (1998)
11. Norman, D.A.: User Centered Systems Design: New Perspectives on Human-Computer Interaction. In: Norman, D.A., Draper, S.W. (eds.) Cognitive Engineering, Hillsdale, pp. 31–61 (1986)

# Artificial Intelligence in Modeling and Simulation

# Fuzzy Xor Classes from Quantum Computing

Anderson Ávila[1], Murilo Schmalfuss[1], Renata Reiser[1(✉)],
and Vladik Kreinovich[2]

[1] CDTEC/PPGC/UFPEL, Federal University of Pelotas, Pelotas, Brazil
{abdavila,mfschmalfuss,reiser}@inf.ufpel.edu.br
[2] CSD/UTEP, University of Texas at El Paso, El Paso, TX 79968, USA
vladik@utep.edu

**Abstract.** By making use of quantum parallelism, quantum processes provide parallel modelling for fuzzy connectives and the corresponding computations of quantum states can be simultaneously performed, based on the superposition of membership degrees of an element with respect to the different fuzzy sets. Such description and modelling is mainly focussed on representable fuzzy Xor connectives and their dual constructions. So, via quantum computing not only the interpretation based on traditional quantum circuit is considered, but also the notion of quantum process in the qGM model is applied, proving an evaluation of a corresponding simulation by considering graphical interfaces of the VPE-qGM programming environment. The quantum interpretations come from measurement operations performed on the corresponding quantum states.

## 1 Introduction

Fuzzy logic (FL) and quantum computing (CQ) are relevant research areas consolidating the analysis and the search for new solutions for difficult problems faster than the classical logical approach or conventional computing. Similarities between these areas in the representation and modelling of uncertainty have been explored in [1],[2], [3], [4] and [5].

The former expresses the uncertainty of human being's reasoning by making use of the Fuzzy Sets Theory (FST), as a mathematical model inheriting the imprecision of natural language and determining the membership degree of an element in a fuzzy set. Based on such theory, fuzzy techniques will help physicists and mathematicians to transform their imprecise ideas into new computational programs [6]. The latter approach models the uncertainty of the real world by making use of properties (superposition and entanglement) of quantum mechanics, suggesting an improvement in the efficiency regarding complex tasks. Thus, simulations using classical computers allow the development and validation of basic quantum algorithms (QAs), anticipating the knowledge related to their

This work is supported by the Brazilian funding agencies CNPq (Ed. Universal and PQ, under the process numbers 448766/2014-0 and 309533/2013-9) and FAPERGS (Ed. 02/2014 - PqG, under the process number 11/1520-1).

© Springer International Publishing Switzerland 2015
L. Rutkowski et al. (Eds.): ICAISC 2015, Part II, LNAI 9120, pp. 305–317, 2015.
DOI: 10.1007/978-3-319-19369-4_28

behaviors when executed in a quantum hardware. In this scenario, the *VPE-qGM* (Visual Programming Environment for the Quantum Geometric Machine Model), previously described in [7] and [8], is a quantum simulator that adds the following advantages: the visual modelling and the parallel or distributed simulation of QAs. Additionally, it is possible to show the application and evolution of quantum states through integrated graphical interfaces [9].

So, it would be interesting to investigate new methods dealing with quantum fuzzy applications. Extending previous works in [10] and [11], the aim of this work is mainly related to: (i) the description via $QC$ of representable fuzzy Xor connectives and dual constructions, by using the traditional quantum circuits (qCs); (ii) the modelling of fuzzy X(N)or connectives based on quantum processes in the qGM model and corresponding simulation, by considering graphical interfaces of the VPE-qGM.

The class of exclusive or is actively used in commonsense and expert reasoning, justifying a practical need for a fuzzy version. Additionally, the novelty and interest of the discussion and new results about the fuzzy Xor can also be applied in computer design and in quantum computing algorithms.

In this context, this paper considers the uncertainty described by such connectives which can be modelled by quantum transformations and related computations, by quantum states. Thus, it contributes to develop quantum algorithms representing fuzzy X(N)or operations.

This paper is organized as follows: Sect. 2 presents the fundamental concepts of fuzzy logic. $FSs$ can be obtained by fuzzy X(N)or operators as presented in Section 2. Moreover, Section 3 brings the main concepts of $QC$ connected with FSs resulting from X(N)or-connectives. In Section 4, the approach for describing $FSs$ using the $QC$ is depicted. Sect. 5 presents the operations on $FSs$ modelled from quantum transformations, considering the fuzzy X(N)operations. Finally, conclusions and further studies are discussed in Section 7.

## 2    Preliminary on Fuzzy Logic

Fuzzy sets ($FSs$) aim to overcome the limitations when the transitions from one class to another are carried out smoothly. Properties and operations of FSs are obtained from the generalization of the classical approach.. A **membership function** $f_A(x) : \mathcal{X} \to [0,1]$ determines the membership degree ($MD$) of the element $x \in \mathcal{X}$ to the set $A$, such that $0 \leq f_A(x) \leq 1$. Thus, a **fuzzy set A** related to a set $\mathcal{X} \neq \emptyset$ is given by the expression: $A = \{(x, f_A(x)) : x \in \mathcal{X}\}$.

A function $N : [0,1] \to [0,1]$ is a **fuzzy negation** (FN) when the following conditions hold:

N1  $N(0) = 1$ and $N(1) = 0$;
N2  If $x \leq y$ then $N(x) \geq N(y)$, for all $x, y \in [0,1]$;
N3  $N(N(x)) = x$, for all $x \in [0,1]$.

Fuzzy negations verifying the involutive property in N3 are called strong fuzzy negations. See the standard negation: $N_S(x) = 1 - x$.

When $N$ is a FN, the $N$-*dual function* of $f : [0,1]^n \to [0,1]$ is given by

$$f_N(x_1, \ldots, x_n) = N(f(N(x_1), \ldots, N(x_n))). \tag{1}$$

If $N$ is involutive, $(f_N)_N = f$, that is the $N$-dual function of $f_N$ coincides with $f$. In addition, if $f = f_N$ then it is clear that $f$ is a self-dual function.

Fuzzy connectives can be represented by aggregation functions. Herein, we consider triangular norms (t-norms) and triangular conorms (t-conorms).

**Definition 1.** *A **triangular (co)norm** is an operation $(S)T : [0,1]^2 \to [0,1]$ such that, for all $x, y, z \in [0,1]$, the following properties hold:*

*T1*: $T(x,y) = T(y,x)$;      *S1*: $S(x,y) = S(y,x)$;
*T2*: $T(T(x,y),z) = T(x,T(y,z))$;    *S2*: $S(S(x,y),z) = S(x,S(y,z))$;
*T3*: *if* $x \leq z$ *then* $T(x,y) \leq T(z,y)$; *S3*: *if* $x \leq z$ *then* $S(x,y) \leq S(z,y)$;
*T4*: $T(x,0) = 0$ *and* $T(x,1) = x$;    *S4*: $S(x,1) = 1$ *and* $S(x,0) = x$

Among different definitions of t-norms and t-conorms [12], in this work we consider the *Algebraic Product* and *Algebraic Sum*, respectively given as:

$$T_P(x,y) = x \cdot y; \quad \text{and} \quad S_P(x,y) = x + y - x \cdot y, \ \forall x, y \in [0,1]. \tag{2}$$

In the following, a fuzzy eXclusive or (Xor) operator $E : [0,1]^2 \to [0,1]$ and its dual construction, a fuzzy eXclusive Not or (XNor) connective $E : [0,1]^2 \to [0,1]$ are both defined via axiomatization:

A function $E(D) : [0,1]^2 \to [0,1]$ is a **fuzzy exclusive (not) or**, called X(N)or, if it satisfies the following properties, for all $x, y \in [0,1]$:

**E0**: $E(1,1) = E(0,0) = 0$ and $E(1,0) = 1$;   **D0**: $D(1,1) = D(0,0)=1$ and $D(0,1)=0$;
**E1**: $E(x,y) = E(y,x)$;                 **D1**: $D(x,y) = D(y,x)$;
**E2**: If $x \leq y$ then $E(0,x) \leq E(0,y)$;    **D2**: If $x \leq y$ then $D(0,x) \geq D(0,y)$;
     If $x \leq y$ then $E(1,x) \geq E(1,y)$.       If $x \leq y$ then $D(1,x) \leq D(y,1)$.

This paper considers the class of representable fuzzy X(N)or connectives meaning that they can be obtained by compositions performed over aggregation functions (t-norms and t-conorms) and fuzzy negations. In particular, a fuzzy X(N)or operator obtained via a defining standard over the Algebraic Product and Algebraic Sum, respectively given by Eq.(2)a and Eq.(2)b, together with standard fuzzy negation is defined in the following.

## 2.1 Operations over Fuzzy Sets

Let $A, B$ be *FSs* based on the complement, intersection and union operations.

**Definition 2.** *Let $N$ be a fuzzy negation. The **complement of** $A$ with respect to $\mathcal{X}$, is a FS $A' = \{(x, f_{A'}) : x \in \mathcal{X}\}$, whose MF $f_{A'} : \mathcal{X} \to [0,1]$ is given by $f_{A'}(x) = N(f_A(x))$, for all $x \in \mathcal{X}$.*

So, a membership degree related to $A'$ is given by the following expression $f_{A'}(x) = N_S(f_A(x)) = 1 - f_A(x)$, for all $x \in \mathcal{X}$.

**Definition 3.** *Let $T, S : [0,1]^2 \to [0,1]$ be a t-norm and a t-conorm. The **intersection** and **union** between the FSs $A$ and $B$, both defined with respect to $X$, results in the corresponding fuzzy sets*

$$A \cap B = \{(x, f_{A \cap B}(x)) : x \in \mathcal{X} \text{ and } f_{A \cap B}(x) = T(f_A(x), f_B(x))\}; \qquad (3)$$

$$A \cup B = \{(x, f_{A \cup B}(x)) : x \in \mathcal{X} \text{ and } f_{A \cup B}(x) = S(f_A(x), f_B(x))\}. \qquad (4)$$

In this paper, the MFs related to an intersection $A \cap B$ and an union $A \cup B$ are obtained by applying the product t-norm, the algebraic sum and standard negation to the MDs $f_A(x)$ and $f_B(x)$ respectively given as:

$$f_{A \cap B}(x) = f_A(x) \cdot f_B(x), \forall x \in \mathcal{X}; \qquad (5)$$

$$f_{A \cup B}(x) = f_A(x) + f_B(x) - f_A(x) \cdot f_B(x), \forall x \in \mathcal{X}. \qquad (6)$$

## 3    FSs Resulting from X(N)or-connectives

The representable class of fuzzy Xor connective obtained by aggregation functions $T, S$ and a FN $N$, denoted as $\mathsf{E}_{S,T,N} \colon [0,1]^2 \to [0,1]$, is based on the classical logical equivalence $\alpha \bigcirc \beta \equiv (\neg \alpha \wedge \beta) \vee \neg(\alpha \wedge \neg \beta)$.

**Definition 4.** *Let $S$ be a t-conorm, $T$ be a t-norm and $N$ be a strong FN, $A$ and $B$ be FS related to $\mathcal{X}$, a non- empty set. The fuzzy X(N)or operator $\mathsf{E}_{S,T,N}(\mathsf{D}_{T,S,N}) \colon [0,1]^2 \to [0,1]$ results in a FS*

$$A \bigcirc B = \{(x, f_{A \bigcirc B}(x)) : x \in \mathcal{X}\} \quad and \quad A \square B = \{(x, f_{A \square B}(x)) : x \in \mathcal{X}\}$$

*whose corresponding membership function $f_{A \bigcirc B}, (f_{A \square B}) \colon \chi \to [0,1]$ is given as*

$$f_{A \bigcirc B}(x) = \mathsf{E}(f_A(x), f_B(x)) \quad and \quad f_{A \square B}(x) = \mathsf{D}(f_A(x), f_B(x)). \qquad (7)$$

Representable fuzzy X(N)ors obtained by compositions performed on the product t-norm $T_P$, the probabilistic sum $S_P$ and the standard negation $N_S$ are expressed as:

$$\mathsf{E}_\oplus \equiv \mathsf{E}_{S_P,T_P,N_S} \qquad \qquad \mathsf{D}_\boxplus \equiv \mathsf{D}_{T_P,S_P,N_S}$$

**Proposition 1.** *Let $S_P$ be the probabilistic sum t-conorm, $T_P$ be the product t-norm, $N_S$ be the standard fuzzy negation and the related $\mathsf{E}_\oplus$ ($\mathsf{D}_\boxplus$) fuzzy X(N)or. Consider $A$ and $B$ as FS related to $\mathcal{X} \neq \emptyset$.*

(i) *The FS **obtained by the fuzzy Xor operator** $\mathsf{E}_\oplus$, denoted by $A \oplus B$ and whose MF $f_{A \oplus B} \colon \chi \to [0,1]$ provides, for all $x \in \chi$, a MD given as*

$$f_{A \oplus B}(x) = (f_B(x) + f_A(x) - f_A(x)f_B(x))(1 - f_A(x)f_B(x)) - 2f_A(x)f_B(x). \qquad (8)$$

(ii) *The FS **obtained by the fuzzy XNor operator** $\mathsf{E}_\boxplus$, denoted by $A \boxplus B$ and whose MF $f_{A \boxplus B} \colon \chi \to [0,1]$ provides, for all $x \in \chi$, a MD given as*

$$f_{A \boxplus B}(x) = 1 - (1 - f_A(x)f_B(x))(f_A(x) + f_B(x) - f_A(x)f_B(x)). \qquad (9)$$

In a dual construction, we have the following:

**Definition 5.** *Let $S$ be a t-conorm, $T$ be a t-norm and $N$ be a strong fuzzy negation, $A$ and $B$ be FS related to $\mathcal{X}$. The dual construction of a fuzzy X(N)or operator* $\mathsf{E}(\mathsf{D})\colon [0,1]^2 \to [0,1]$ *results in a FS*

$$(A\bigcirc B)_N = \{(x, f_{(A\bigcirc B)_N}(x))\colon x \in \mathcal{X}\} \text{ and } (A\square B)_N = \{(x, f_{(A\square B)_N}(x))\colon x \in \mathcal{X}\}.$$

**Proposition 2.** *The MFs* $(f_{A\bigcirc B})_N, (f_{A\square B})_N \colon \chi \to [0,1]$ *in Def. 5 are given as*

$$(f_{A\bigcirc B})_N(x) = (f_{A\bigcirc_N B})(x) = f_{A\square B}(x); \quad (f_{A\square B})_N(x) = (f_{A\square_N B})(x) = f_{A\bigcirc B}(x)(10)$$

*Proof.* Based on Eq. (7) in Definition 4, for all $x \in \chi$, it holds that:

$$(f_{A\bigcirc B})_N(x) = N\left(\mathsf{E}(N(f_A(x)), N(f_B(x)))\right) = \mathsf{D}(f_A(x), f_B(x)) = f_{A\square B}(x);$$
$$(f_{A\square B})_N(x) = N\left(\mathsf{D}(N(f_A(x)), N(f_B(x)))\right) = \mathsf{E}(f_A(x), f_B(x)) = f_{A\bigcirc B}(x).$$

**Theorem 1.** *Let* $(\mathsf{E}_\oplus, \mathsf{D}_\boxplus)$ *be a pair of mutual $N_S$-dual fuzzy Xor-connectives. Then* $(f_{A\oplus B}, f_{A\boxplus B})$ *is also a pair of mutual $N_S$-dual MFs.*

*Proof.* It follows from Eq. (10) and the expressions below:

$$\begin{aligned}
(f_{A\oplus B})_{N_S}(x) \\
&= \mathsf{E}_{\oplus N_S}(f_A(x), f_B(x)) \quad \text{by Eq. (7)} \\
&= N_S\left(\mathsf{E}_\oplus(N_S(f_A(x)), N_S(f_B(x)))\right) \quad \text{by Eq. (1)} \\
&= 1 - ((1 - f_B(x) + 1 - f_A(x) - (1 - f_A(x))(1 - f_B(x))) \\
&\quad (1 - (1 - f_A(x))(1 - f_B(x))) - 2(1 - f_A(x))(1 - f_B(x))\text{by Eq.(8)} \\
&= 1 - (1 - f_A(x)f_B(x))(f_A(x) + f_B(x) - f_A(x)f_B(x)) = f_{A\boxtimes B}(x)\text{by Eq. (9)}.
\end{aligned}$$

## 4    Modelling Fuzzy Sets through Quantum Computing

In $QC$, the qubit is the basic information unit, being the simplest quantum system, defined by a unitary and bi-dimensional state vector. Qubits are generally described, in Dirac's notation [13], by $|\psi\rangle = \alpha|0\rangle + \beta|1\rangle$.

The coefficients $\alpha$ and $\beta$ are complex numbers for the amplitudes of the corresponding states in the computational basis (state space), respecting the condition $|\alpha|^2 + |\beta|^2 = 1$, which guarantees the unitarity of the state vectors of the quantum system, represented by $(\alpha, \beta)^t$.

The state space of a quantum system with multiple *qubits* is obtained by the tensor product of the space states of its subsystems. Considering a quantum system with two *qubits*, $|\psi\rangle = \alpha|0\rangle + \beta|1\rangle$ and $|\varphi\rangle = \gamma|0\rangle + \delta|1\rangle$, the state space comprehends the tensor product $|\psi\rangle \otimes |\varphi\rangle = \alpha\cdot\gamma|00\rangle + \alpha\cdot\delta|01\rangle + \beta\cdot\gamma|10\rangle + \beta\cdot\delta|11\rangle$.

The state transition of a quantum system is performed by controlled and unitary transformations associated with orthogonal matrices of order $2^N$, with $N$ being the number of *qubits* within the system, preserving norms, and thus, probability amplitudes.

For instance, the definition of the *Pauly X* transformation and its application over a one-dimensional and two-dimensional quantum systems are presented in the Fig. 1. Furthermore, a Toffoli transformation is also shown in order to describe a controlled operation for a 3 *qubits* system. In this case, the *NOT* operator (*Pauly X*) is applied to the *qubit* $|\sigma\rangle$ when the current states of the first two *qubits* $|\psi\rangle$ and $|\varphi\rangle$ are both $|1\rangle$.

| 1 and 2-qubit Pauly X transformations | Toffoli transformation |
|---|---|
| $X\|\psi\rangle = \begin{pmatrix} 0 & 1 \\ 1 & 0 \end{pmatrix} \cdot \begin{pmatrix} \alpha \\ \beta \end{pmatrix} = \begin{pmatrix} \beta \\ \alpha \end{pmatrix}$ $X^{\otimes 2}\|\Pi\rangle = \begin{pmatrix} 0 & 1 \\ 1 & 0 \end{pmatrix} \otimes \begin{pmatrix} 0 & 1 \\ 1 & 0 \end{pmatrix} = \begin{pmatrix} 0 & 0 & 0 & 1 \\ 0 & 0 & 1 & 0 \\ 0 & 1 & 0 & 0 \\ 1 & 0 & 0 & 0 \end{pmatrix} \cdot \begin{pmatrix} \alpha \\ \beta \\ \gamma \\ \delta \end{pmatrix} = \begin{pmatrix} \delta \\ \gamma \\ \beta \\ \alpha \end{pmatrix}$ | $T = \begin{pmatrix} Id & 0 & 0 & 0 \\ 0 & Id & 0 & 0 \\ 0 & 0 & Id & 0 \\ 0 & 0 & 0 & X \end{pmatrix}$ |

**Fig. 1.** Examples of quantum transformations

In order to obtain information from a quantum system, it is necessary to apply measurement operators, defined by a set of linear operators $M_m$, called projections. The index $M$ refers to the possible measurement results. If the state of a quantum system is $|\psi\rangle$ immediately before the measurement, the probability of an outcome occurrence is given by $p(|\psi\rangle) = \frac{M_m|\psi\rangle}{\sqrt{\langle\psi|M_m^\dagger M_m|\psi\rangle}}$.

When measuring a *qubit* $|\psi\rangle$ with $\alpha, \beta \neq 0$, the probability of observing $|0\rangle$ and $|1\rangle$ are, respectively, given by the following expressions:

$$p(0) = \langle\phi|M_0^\dagger M_0|\phi\rangle = \langle\phi|M_0|\phi\rangle = |\alpha|^2 \text{ and } p(1) = \langle\phi|M_1^\dagger M_1|\phi\rangle = \langle\phi|M_1|\phi\rangle = |\beta|^2.$$

After the measuring process, the quantum state $|\psi\rangle$ has $|\alpha|^2$ as the probability to be in the state $|0\rangle$ and $|\beta|^2$ as the probability to be in the state $|1\rangle$.

### 4.1  Describing Fuzzy Sets through Quantum States

The description of $FSs$ from the $QC$ viewpoint considers a $FS$ $A$, which is given by the membership function $f_A(x)$. Without losing generality, let $\mathcal{X}$ be a finite subset with cardinality $N$ ($|\mathcal{X}| = N$). Thus, the definitions can be extended to infinite sets, by considering a quantum computer with an infinite quantum register [13].

As stated in [14], consider $\mathcal{X} \neq \emptyset, |\mathcal{X}| = N, i \in \mathbb{N}_N = \{1, 2, ..., N\}$ and a membership function, $f_A : \mathcal{X} \rightarrow [0, 1]$. A **classical fuzzy state**(CFS) of N-*qubits* is an $N$-dimensional quantum state, given by

$$|s_f\rangle = \bigotimes_{1 \leq i \leq N} [\sqrt{1 - f_A(x_i)}|0\rangle + \sqrt{f_A(x_i)}|1\rangle]. \tag{11}$$

When $f(1) = a$, $f(2) = b$ and $a, b \in ]0, 1[$, superpositions of quantum states corresponding to $FSs$ are obtained and expressed as

$$|s_f\rangle = (\sqrt{a}|1\rangle + \sqrt{1-a}|0\rangle) \otimes (\sqrt{b}|1\rangle + \sqrt{1-b}|0\rangle)$$
$$= \sqrt{(1-a)(1-b)}|00\rangle + \sqrt{b(1-a)}|01\rangle + \sqrt{a(1-b)}|10\rangle + \sqrt{ab}|11\rangle. \tag{12}$$

As it can be seen, the application of a membership function $f$ to each element in the image-set $f[\mathcal{X}]$ defines a quantum state. In other words, a canonical orthonormal basis in $\otimes^N \mathcal{C}$ denotes a classical quantum register of $N$-qubits. Thus, one can describe the classical state of the register $|1100\ldots0\rangle$ of $N$ qubits when $f(1) = f(2) = 1$ and $f(i) = 0$ when $i \in \{\mathbb{N}_N - \{1,2\}\}$.

The generalized expression, described in [14], states a CFS of $N-qubits$ as:

$$|s_f\rangle = (1 - f(1))^{\frac{1}{2}}(1 - f(2))^{\frac{1}{2}}\ldots(1 - f(n))^{\frac{1}{2}}|00\ldots00\rangle + f(1)^{\frac{1}{2}}(1 - f(2))^{\frac{1}{2}}\ldots$$
$$(1 - f(n))^{\frac{1}{2}}|10\ldots00\rangle + f(1)^{\frac{1}{2}}f(2)^{\frac{1}{2}}\ldots f(n)^{\frac{1}{2}}|11\ldots11\rangle. \tag{13}$$

From the perspective of QC, a $FS$ is a superposition of crisp sets. Each $|s_f\rangle$ is a quantum state described as a superposition of crisp sets and generated by the tensor product of non-entangled quantum registers [13].

A linear combination of membership functions representing the fuzzy classical states formalizes the notion of a fuzzy quantum state [14]. So, a **quantum fuzzy set** (QFS) is conceived as quantum superposition of $FSs$, simultaneously.

In Eq (13), a quantum state $|s_f\rangle$ in $\mathcal{C}^{2^N}$ is characterized as a N-dimensional orthonormal set in $\mathcal{C}^{2^N}$, see more details in [13] and [15].

**Definition 6.** *Consider $f_i : X \to [0,1]$, $i \in \{1, ..., k\}$, as a collection of MFs generating fuzzy subsets $A_i$ and $\{|s_{f_1}\rangle, \ldots, |s_{f_k}\rangle\} \subseteq [CFS]$, such that their components are two by two orthonormal vectors. When $\{c_1, \ldots, c_k\} \subseteq \mathcal{C}$, the linear combination $|s\rangle = c_1|s_{f_1}\rangle + \ldots + c_k|s_{f_k}\rangle$ defines a **quantum FS (QFS)**.*

By Def. 6, an $N$-dimensional quantum fuzzy state can be entangled or not, depending on the family of classical fuzzy states.

# 5  $FS$ Operations from Quantum Transformations

According to [14], $FSs$ can be obtained by quantum superposition of CFSs associated with a quantum state. Additionally, interpretations for fuzzy operations such as complement, intersection and union are obtained from the $NOT$, $AND$ and $OR$ quantum transformations.

Let $f, g : \mathcal{X} \to [0,1]$ be MFs related to $FSs$ $A$ and $B$. For $x \in \mathcal{X}$, the corresponding pair $(|s_{f(x)}\rangle, |s_{g(x)}\rangle)$ of CFSs is given as:

$$|S_f(x)\rangle = \sqrt{f(x)}|1\rangle + \sqrt{1 - f(x)}|0\rangle \text{ and } |S_g(x)\rangle = \sqrt{g(x)}|1\rangle + \sqrt{1 - g(x)}|0\rangle \tag{14}$$

In order to simplify the paper notation, the $MD$ defined by $f_A(x)$, which is related to an element $x \in \mathcal{X}$ in the $FS$ $A$, will be denoted by $f_A$.

## 5.1  Fuzzy Complement Operator

The complement of a $FS$ is performed by the standard negation, which is obtained by the $NOT$ operator, defined as

$$NOT(|S_{f_A}\rangle) = \sqrt{1 - f_A}|1\rangle + \sqrt{f_A}|0\rangle \tag{15}$$

The complement operator $NOT^N$ can be applied to the state $|s_f\rangle = \otimes_{1 \leq i \leq N} |s_{f_i}\rangle$, resulting in an $N$-dimensional quantum superposition of 1-*qubit* states, described as $\mathcal{C}^{2^N}$ in the computational basis, represented by $NOT^N|s_f\rangle$ and expressed as

$$NOT^N(|S_{f_A}\rangle) = NOT(\otimes_{1 \leq i \leq N}(f_A(i)^{\frac{1}{2}}|1\rangle(1 - f_A(i))^{\frac{1}{2}}|0\rangle)) \tag{16}$$

Now, Eqs. (17) and (18) describe other applications related to the $NOT$ transformation used to describe other fuzzy Xor operators, which act on the 2nd e 3rd-*qubits* of a quantum system, respectively:

$$NOT_2(|S_{f_1}\rangle|s_{f_2}\rangle) = |S_{f_1}\rangle \otimes NOT|s_{f_2}\rangle \tag{17}$$

$$NOT_{2,3}(|S_{f_1}\rangle|S_{f_2}\rangle|s_{f_3}\rangle) = |s_{f_1}\rangle \otimes NOT|s_{f_2}\rangle \otimes NOT|s_{f_3}\rangle. \tag{18}$$

## 5.2   Modelling of Fuzzy Intersection and Union Operators

The fuzzy intersection operator is modelled by the **AND operator** expressed through the *Toffoli* quantum transformation as

$$AND(|s_{f_i}\rangle, |s_{g_i}\rangle) = T(|s_{f_i}\rangle, |s_{g_i}\rangle, |0\rangle). \tag{19}$$

So, we obtain the quantum state $|S_2\rangle$ given by the following expression:

$$|S_2\rangle = \sqrt{f_A f_B}|111\rangle + \sqrt{f_A(1-f_B)}|100\rangle + \sqrt{(1-f_A)f_B}|010\rangle + \sqrt{(1-f_A)(1-f_B)}|000\rangle. \tag{20}$$

Thus, a measurement performed over the third *qubit* ($|1\rangle$) in the quantum state expressed by Eq. (20), provides the following output:

- $|S_{f_0}\rangle = |111\rangle$, with probability $p(1) = f_A \cdot f_B$.

Then, for all $x \in X$, let $f_A(x)$ and $f_B(x)$ be the MD of $x \in \mathcal{X}$ in the $FS$ defined by MF $f_A(x) : \mathcal{X} \to U$ and $g_A(x) : \mathcal{X} \to U$, respectively. Then, $f_A(x) \cdot f_B(x)$ indicates the MD of $x$ in the intersection of such $FSs$ $A, B$. Analogously, a measurement of third *qubit* ($|0\rangle$) in Eq. (20), returns an output state given as:

- $|S_{f_1}\rangle = \dfrac{1}{\sqrt{(1-f_A)f_B}}(\sqrt{f_A(1-f_B)}|100\rangle + \sqrt{(1-f_A)f_B}|010\rangle + \sqrt{(1-f_A)(1-f_B)}|000\rangle)$,

with probability $p(0) = 1 - f_A(x) \cdot f_B(x)$. In this case, an expression of the complement of the intersection between $FSs$ $A$ and $B$ is given by $1 - p(0) = f_A(x) \cdot f_B(x)$. This probability indicates the non-$MD$ of $x$ is in the $FS$ $A \cap B$. We also conclude that, by Eq. (20), it corresponds to the standard negation of product t-norm [12].

Let $|s_{f_i}\rangle$ and $|s_{g_i}\rangle$ be quantum states given by Eqs. (14)a and (14)b, respectively. The union of $FSs$ is modelled by the **OR operator** as the complement of $AND$ operator, and therefore it is given as:

$$OR(|S_f\rangle, |S_g\rangle) = NOT^3(T(NOT|S_f\rangle, NOT|S_g\rangle, |0\rangle)). \tag{21}$$

In the following, by applying the $NOT^3$ and Toffoli operators we have that:

$$|S_4\rangle = \sqrt{(1-f_A)(1-f_B)}|000\rangle + \sqrt{(1-f_A)f_B}|011\rangle + \sqrt{f_A(1-f_B)}|101\rangle + \sqrt{f_A f_B}|111\rangle. \tag{22}$$

Observe that, a measure performed on third *qubit* ($|1\rangle$) of quantum state in Eq. (22) results in the final state:

- $|S_{f_1}\rangle = \dfrac{1}{\sqrt{f_B(1-f_A)+f_A}}(\sqrt{(1-f_A)f_B}|011\rangle+ \sqrt{f_A(1-f_B)}|101\rangle+\sqrt{f_Af_B}|111\rangle)$,

with corresponding probability $p = f_A + f_B - f_A \cdot f_B$ of $x_i \in \mathcal{X}$ is in both $FSs$ $A$ e $B$. The $OR$ operator, expressed by Eq. (22), is therefore defined by the t-conorm product [12]. Additionally, a measure also performed in the third *qubit* (but related to state $|0\rangle$) returns

- $|S_{f_0}\rangle = |000\rangle$, with probability $p(0) = (1 - f_A) \cdot (1 - f_B)$,

indicating that $x \in \mathcal{X}$ does not belong to $A \cup B$ (neither $A$ nor $B$).

# 6   Modelling and Simulation of a Fuzzy Xor Connective$\mathsf{E}_\oplus$

A representable fuzzy X(N)or can be obtained by a composition of quantum operations ($NOT, T, CNOT, \ldots$) and other controlled ones ($AND, OR, NOT_N$) previously discussed in Sections 5.1 and 5.2. Extending this approach, this section introduces the expressions modelling the quantum operators of fuzzy X(N)or and simulating them in the VPE-qGM based on Eqs. (23)a and (23)b, respectively given as

$$|S_f\rangle = \frac{\sqrt{2}}{2}|1\rangle + \frac{\sqrt{2}}{2}|0\rangle \quad \text{and} \quad |S_g\rangle = \frac{\sqrt{3}}{3}|1\rangle + \frac{\sqrt{6}}{3}|0\rangle. \tag{23}$$

Let $|s_{f_i}\rangle$ and $|s_{g_i}\rangle$ be quantum states in Eqs. (14)a and (14)b, respectively. The fuzzy Xor $\mathsf{E}_\oplus$ is modelled by the **quantum operator** $XOR_\oplus$ given by:

$$XOR_\oplus(|S_f\rangle,|S_g\rangle) = OR(AND(NOT|S_f\rangle,|S_g\rangle), AND(|S_f\rangle, NOT|S_g\rangle)) \tag{24}$$

By applying the $NOT_6$ and $AND$ operators, we obtain the quantum state

$$|S_5\rangle = NOT_7(T_{3,6,7}(NOT_3(T_{1,2,3}(|S_f\rangle,|S_g\rangle),|0\rangle), NOT_6(T_{4,5,6}(NOT|S_f\rangle, NOT|S_g\rangle),|0\rangle),|0\rangle)))$$

The initial state $|s_0\rangle = (|f_A\rangle \otimes |f_B\rangle \otimes |0\rangle)^2 \otimes |0\rangle$ graphically presented in the quantum circuit of Figure 2(a) is extended in Eq. (25) below,

$$|s_0\rangle = (((\sqrt{1 - f_A}|0\rangle + \sqrt{f_A}|1\rangle) \otimes (\sqrt{1 - f_B}|0\rangle + \sqrt{f_B}|1\rangle) \otimes |0\rangle)) \otimes$$
$$((\sqrt{1 - f_A}|0\rangle + \sqrt{f_A}|1\rangle) \otimes (\sqrt{1 - f_B}|0\rangle + \sqrt{f_B}|1\rangle) \otimes |0\rangle))) \otimes |0\rangle. \tag{25}$$

Thus, according with column 5 related to Table 1, presenting the non zero coefficients of quantum states in a temporal evolution of computations related to the fuzzy Xor $E_\oplus$, we obtain the quantum state in the following Eq.(26):

$$|S_5\rangle_{\mathsf{E}_\oplus} = \sqrt{f_Af_B(1 - f_A)(1 - f_B)}|0010010\rangle + (1 - f_B)\sqrt{f_A(1 - f_A)}|0010110\rangle +$$
$$f_A\sqrt{f_B(1 - f_B)}|0011010\rangle + f_B\sqrt{f_A(1 - f_A)}|0110010\rangle +$$
$$\sqrt{f_Af_B(1 - f_A)(1 - f_B)}|0110110\rangle + f_Af_B|0111010\rangle +$$
$$(1 - f_A)\sqrt{f_B(1 - f_B)}|1010010\rangle + (1 - f_A)(1 - f_B)|1010110\rangle+$$

**Table 1.** Temporal evolution related to computation of the fuzzy Xor $E_\oplus$

| | T0 | T1 | T2 | T3 | T4 | T5 |
|---|---|---|---|---|---|---|
| $(1 - f_A)(1 - f_B)$ | 0000000 | 1000100 | 1000100 | 1010110 | 1010111 | 1010110 |
| $(1 - f_A)\sqrt{f_B(1 - f_B)}$ | 0000100 | 1000000 | 1000000 | 1010010 | 1010011 | 1010010 |
| $(1 - f_B)\sqrt{f_A(1 - f_A)}$ | 0001000 | 1001100 | 1001110 | 1011100 | 1011100 | 1011101 |
| $\sqrt{f_A f_B(1 - f_A)(1 - f_B)}$ | 0001100 | 1001000 | 1001000 | 1011010 | 1011011 | 1011010 |
| $(1 - f_A)\sqrt{f_B(1 - f_B)}$ | 0100000 | 1100100 | 1110100 | 1100110 | 1100110 | 1100111 |
| $f_B(1 - f_A)$ | 0100100 | 1100000 | 1110000 | 1100010 | 1100010 | 1100011 |
| $\sqrt{f_A f_B(1 - f_A)(1 - f_B)}$ | 0101000 | 1101100 | 1111110 | 1101100 | 1101100 | 1101101 |
| $f_B\sqrt{f_A(1 - f_A)}$ | 0101100 | 1101000 | 1111000 | 1101010 | 1101010 | 1101011 |
| $(1 - f_B)\sqrt{f_A(1 - f_A)}$ | 1000000 | 0000100 | 0000100 | 0010110 | 0010111 | 0010110 |
| $\sqrt{f_A f_B(1 - f_A)(1 - f_B)}$ | 1000100 | 0000000 | 0000000 | 0010010 | 0010011 | 0010010 |
| $f_A(1 - f_B)$ | 1001000 | 0001100 | 0001110 | 0011100 | 0011100 | 0011101 |
| $f_A\sqrt{f_B(1 - f_B)}$ | 1001100 | 0001000 | 0001000 | 0011010 | 0011011 | 0011010 |
| $\sqrt{f_A f_B(1 - f_A)(1 - f_B)}$ | 1100000 | 0100100 | 0100100 | 0110110 | 0110111 | 0110110 |
| $f_B\sqrt{f_A(1 - f_A)}$ | 1100100 | 0100000 | 0100000 | 0110010 | 0110011 | 0110010 |
| $f_A\sqrt{f_B(1 - f_B)}$ | 1101000 | 0101100 | 0101110 | 0110000 | 0110000 | 0110001 |
| $f_A f_B$ | 1101100 | 0101000 | 0101000 | 0111010 | 0111011 | 0111010 |

$$\sqrt{f_A f_B(1 - f_A)(1 - f_B)}|1011010\rangle + f_A(1 - f_B)|0011101\rangle +$$
$$f_A\sqrt{f_B(1 - f_B)}|0110001\rangle + (1 - f_B)\sqrt{f_A(1 - f_A)}|1011101\rangle +$$
$$f_B(1 - f_A)|1100011\rangle + (1 - f_A)\sqrt{f_B(1 - f_B)}|1100111\rangle +$$
$$f_B\sqrt{f_A(1 - f_A)}|1101011\rangle + \sqrt{f_A f_B(1 - f_A)(1 - f_B)}|1101101\rangle \qquad (26)$$

Additionally, a measure performed on the 7th *qubit* of quantum state described by Eq. (26) results in the final state:

$$\bullet|S'_{f_0}\rangle = \frac{1}{\sqrt{f_A + f_B - 3f_A f_B + f_A f_B^2 + f_A^2 f_B - f_A^2 f_B^2}}(f_A(1 - f_B)|0011101\rangle +$$
$$f_A\sqrt{f_B(1 - f_B)}|0110001\rangle + (1 - f_B)\sqrt{f_A(1 - f_A)}|1011101\rangle +$$
$$f_B(1 - f_A)|1100011\rangle + (1 - f_A)\sqrt{f_B(1 - f_B)}|1100111\rangle$$
$$+f_B\sqrt{f_A(1 - f_A)}|1101011\rangle + \sqrt{f_A f_B(1 - f_A)(1 - f_B)}|1101101\rangle).$$

with corresponding probability $p(1) = f_A + f_B - 3f_A f_B + f_A f_B^2 + f_A^2 f_B - f_A^2 f_B^2$ indicating the MD of an element $x \in \mathcal{X}$ in the *FS* $A \oplus B$ obtained by applying the fuzzy Xor connective $E_\oplus$ and taking $f_A(x), f_B(x)$ as the arguments of the related MF. So, a measure also performed in the 7th *qubit* (but related to state $|0\rangle$) returns

$$\bullet|S_{f_1}\rangle = \frac{1}{\sqrt{1 - (f_A + f_B - 3f_A f_B + f_A f_B^2 + f_A^2 f_B - f_A^2 f_B^2)}}$$
$$(\sqrt{f_A f_B(1 - f_A)(1 - f_B)}|0010010\rangle + (1 - f_B)\sqrt{f_A(1 - f_A)}|0010110\rangle$$
$$+f_A\sqrt{f_B(1 - f_B)}|0011010\rangle + f_B\sqrt{f_A(1 - f_A)}|0110010\rangle$$

$$+\sqrt{f_A f_B (1 - f_A)(1 - f_B)}|0110110\rangle + f_A f_B|0111010\rangle +$$
$$(1 - f_A)\sqrt{f_B(1 - f_B)}|1010010\rangle + (1 - f_A)(1 - f_B)|1010110\rangle +$$
$$\sqrt{f_A f_B (1 - f_A)(1 - f_B)}|1011010\rangle),$$

with $p(0) = 1 - (f_A + f_B - 3f_A f_B + f_A f_B^2 + f_A^2 f_B - f_A^2 f_B^2)$.

See in Figure 2(b) that the simulation in *VPE-qGM* is consistent with Eq. (26) by taking initial states of Eq. (23)a and Eq. (23)b. After a measurement, one of the following states is reached:

$- \ |S_5'\rangle \ = \ \frac{\sqrt{324}}{\sqrt{144}}(\frac{1}{3}|0011101\rangle + \frac{\sqrt{18}}{18}|0110001\rangle + \frac{1}{9}|1011101\rangle + \frac{1}{6}|1100011\rangle$
$+ \frac{\sqrt{18}}{18}|1100111\rangle + \frac{1}{6}|1101011\rangle + \frac{\sqrt{18}}{18}|1101101\rangle)$, with probability $p(1) = 44\%$

$- \ |S_5''\rangle \ = \ \frac{\sqrt{324}}{\sqrt{180}}(\frac{\sqrt{18}}{18}|0010010\rangle + \frac{1}{3}|0010110\rangle + \frac{\sqrt{18}}{18}|0011010\rangle + \frac{1}{6}|0110010\rangle +$
$\frac{\sqrt{18}}{18}|0110110\rangle + \frac{1}{6}|0111010\rangle + \frac{\sqrt{18}}{18}|1010010\rangle + \frac{1}{3}|1010110\rangle + \frac{\sqrt{18}}{18}|1011010\rangle)$,
with probability $p(0) = 56\%$

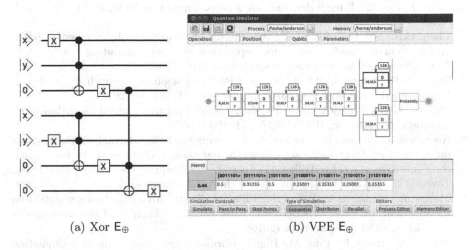

(a) Xor $\mathsf{E}_\oplus$          (b) VPE $\mathsf{E}_\oplus$

**Fig. 2.** Modelling and simulating fuzzy Xor $\mathsf{E}_\oplus$ operator in the VPE-qGM

Analogously, in order to model and simulate the fuzzy XNor $\mathsf{D}_\boxplus$, consider the quantum operator $XNOR_\boxplus$ given as:

$$XNOR_\boxplus(|s_{f_i}\rangle, |s_{g_i}\rangle) = AND(OR(NOT|s_{f_i}\rangle, |s_{g_i}\rangle), OR(|s_{f_i}\rangle, NOT|s_{g_i}\rangle)) \qquad (27)$$

Therefore, based on the *AND*, *OR* and *NOT* transformation, we obtain that

$$|S_5\rangle = T_{3,6,7}(NOT_3(T_{1,2,3}(|s_{f_i}\rangle, NOT|s_{g_i}\rangle, |0\rangle)), NOT_6(T_{4,5,6}(NOT|s_{f_i}\rangle, |s_{g_i}\rangle, |0\rangle)), |0\rangle)$$

Analogously, it can be developed for simulation in the *VPE-qGM* of Eq. (27).

# 7 Conclusion and Final Remarks

The visual approach of the VPE-qGM environment enables the implementation and validation of fuzzy X(N)or operations using $QC$. The description of these operations is based on compositions of controlled and unitary quantum transformations, and the corresponding interpretation of fuzzy operations is obtained by applying operators of projective measurements.

Further work aims to consolidate this specification including not only other fuzzy connectives, constructors (e.i. automorphisms and reductions) and the corresponding extension of (de)fuzzyfication methodology from formal structures provided by $QC$. Finally, it may also contribute to designing new algorithms based on considering the abstractions provided by quantum $FSs$ and related interpretation of fuzzy logic concepts.

# References

1. Herrera, F.: Applicability of the fuzzy operators in the design of fuzzy logic controllers. Technical report (1995)
2. Melnichenko, G.: Energy discriminant analysis, quantum logic, and fuzzy sets. J. Multivariate Analysis 101(1) (2010)
3. Chen, C.H., Lin, C.J., Lin, C.-T.: An efficient quantum neurofuzzy classifier based on fuzzy entropy and compensatory operation. Softing Computing - A fusion of foundations, methodologies and applications 12(6) (2008)
4. Nikam, S.R., Nikumbh, P.J., Kulkarni, S.P.: Fuzzy logic and neuro-fuzzy modeling. International Journal of Computer Applications (4), 22–31 (2012)
5. Rigatos, G.G., Tzafestas, S.G.: Parallelization of a fuzzy control algorithm using quantum computation. IEEE-FS 10, 451–460 (2002)
6. Kosheleva, O., Reiser, R., Kreinovich, V.: Formalizing the informal, precisiating the imprecise: How fuzzy logic can help mathematicians and physicists by formalizing their intuitive ideas. In: Trillas, E., Seising, R., Kacprycz, J. (eds.) Fuzzy Logic: Towards the Future. LNCS. Springer Netherlands (to appear)
7. Maron, A., Pinheiro, A., Reiser, R., Pilla, M.: Distributed quantum simulation on the vpe-qgm. In: Proc. WSCAD-SSC 2010, pp. 128–135. IEEE Computer Society - Conference Publising Services (2010)
8. Maron, A., Reiser, R., Pilla, M.: High performance quantum computing simulation for the quantum geometric machine model. In: Proc. of IEEE ACM Intl. Conference on Cluster, Cloud and Grid Computing, CCGRID 2013, pp. 1–8. IEEE Computer Science Press, USA (2013)
9. Avila, A., Maron, A., Reiser, R., Pilla, M., Yamin, A.: GPU-aware distributed quantum simulation. In: Proceedings of the 29th Annual ACM Symposium on Applied Computing, SAC 2014, pp. 860–865 (2014)
10. Visintin, L., Maron, A., Reiser, R., Abeijon, A., Kreinovich, V.: Relation between polling and likert–scale approaches to eliciting membership degrees clarified by quantum computing. In: 2013 IEEE International Conference on Fuzzy Systems, FUZZ–IEEE 2013, pp. 1–6 (2013)
11. Maron, A., Visintin, L., Reiser, R., Abeijon, A., Kreinovich, V.: Aggregation operations from quantum computing. In: 2013 IEEE International Conference on Fuzzy Systems, FUZZ–IEEE 2013, pp. 1–6. IEEE (2013)

12. Klir, G.J., Yuan, B.: Fuzzy Sets and Fuzzy Logic; Theory and Applications. Prentice Hall, Upper Saddle River (1995)
13. Nielsen, M.A., Chuang, I.L.: Quantum Computation and Quantum Information, Cambridge (2003)
14. Mannucci, M.A.: Quantum fuzzy sets: Blending fuzzy set theory and quantum computation. CoRR abs/cs/0604064 (2006)
15. Imre, S., Balazs, F.: Quantum Computing and Communications - an Engineering Approach. John Wiley & Sons, NJ (2005)

# New Method for Non-linear Correction Modelling of Dynamic Objects with Genetic Programming

Łukasz Bartczuk[1]([⊠]), Andrzej Przybył[1], Petia Koprinkova-Hristova[2]

[1] Institute of Computational Intelligence,
Częstochowa University of Technology, Częstochowa, Poland
{lukasz.bartczuk,andrzej.przybyl}@iisi.pcz.pl
[2] Institute of Information and Communication Technologies,
Bulgarian Academy of Sciences, Sofia, Bulgaria
pkoprinkova@bas.bg

**Abstract.** In the paper a method to adapt the equivalent linearization technique of the non-linear state equation is proposed. This algorithm uses correction matrices. It also uses arrays amendments which elements are determined for each new point. These elements are generated by a formula created automatically using genetic programming.

## 1 Introduction

Models of real objects are important from scientific and practical point of view. They make it possible to better understand and simulate behaviour of the modelled object, which allows us to develop more accurate control and fault detection systems. Such models describe the relationship linking the input signals with the response of the object and they are created from observation of a real object behaviour. In the literature we can find many different approaches to perform this task. Some of them are based on analytical methods (see e.g. [1], [32], [33]) and the others are based on computational methods (see e.g. [43–46, 50, 51]). Most commonly used computational methods are neural networks (see e.g. [6–14, 31, 39, 40]), fuzzy systems (see e.g. [2, 16, 17, 19–21, 25, 34, 37, 38, 42, 47–49, 52–54, 56, 58]), neuro-fuzzy systems (see e.g. [5, 18, 22, 23, 35, 57, 59–61]), population based algorithms (see e.g. [24, 26, 30, 41, 55]). In the real world relationship linking the input signals with the response of the object is usually non-linear but in practice it is approximated by linear models. This allows us to use well-established method of control theory but it can affect the accuracy of the real object mapping. Let's consider the non-linear state equation:

$$\frac{dx}{dt} = f(\mathbf{x}, \mathbf{u}) = \mathbf{A}\mathbf{x} + \mathbf{B}\mathbf{u} + \eta g(\mathbf{x}, \mathbf{u}),　\tag{1}$$

where: $\mathbf{x}$, $\mathbf{u}$ are vectors of state variables and input signals, $\mathbf{A}$, $\mathbf{B}$ are system and input matrices respectively, $g(\mathbf{x}, \mathbf{u})$ is a separate non-linear part of the system and $\eta$ is the influence factor of the whole system non-linarites. If we assume that $\eta$ is small and the system is weakly non-linear, then the linear approximation about

© Springer International Publishing Switzerland 2015
L. Rutkowski et al. (Eds.): ICAISC 2015, Part II, LNAI 9120, pp. 318–329, 2015.
DOI: 10.1007/978-3-319-19369-4_29

the equilibrium point will be useful in some strictly defined range. However, it should be noted that if the actual operating point goes beyond the defined range, the accuracy of this model significantly decreases.

In papers [3, 4] we proposed the solution to increase accuracy of the method described above by the method based on equivalent linearization technique [15]. In such a case the state equation (1) can be shown as follows:

$$\frac{dx}{dt} = f(\mathbf{x}, \mathbf{u}) = \mathbf{A_{eq}}\mathbf{x} + \mathbf{B_{eq}}\mathbf{u} + e(\mathbf{x}, \mathbf{u}), \tag{2}$$

where: $\mathbf{A_{eq}} = \mathbf{A} + \mathbf{P_A}$, $\mathbf{B_{eq}} = \mathbf{B} + \mathbf{P_B}$ and $e(\mathbf{x}, \mathbf{u})$ is an error term. Separation of the system matrices $\mathbf{A}$ and $\mathbf{B}$ into two parts allows us to use some linear model of the same or very similar phenomena (which we assume to be known). The purpose of correction matrices is non-linear modelling of the relationship between the known linear model and unknown model that is constructed. The coefficients of correction matrices $\mathbf{P_A}, \mathbf{P_B}$ are estimated for current operating point. When we analyse a small area around current operating point and the error term is small (i.e. it can be neglected), then the state equation (2) can be treated as linear. To solve an accuracy decreasing problem when operating point is changing, in the paper it is proposed to calculate the new values of the correction matrices $\mathbf{P_A}, \mathbf{P_B}$ for each new point of work. In our earlier works [3, 4] the coefficients of correction matrices were generated by the fuzzy rules for each new point of work. In this paper we use genetic programming paradigm to discover functional dependency that allows us to generate an adequate values of correction matrices $\mathbf{P_A}, \mathbf{P_B}$.

## 2    Genetic Programming in Nonlinear Modelling of Dynamic Objects

Evolutionary algorithms (see e.g. [36]) are inspired by biological evolution methods that allow to solve optimization problems. They allow for simultaneous analysis of multiple solutions represented by the individuals whose parameters are stored in the form of linear chromosomes.

Genetic programming is an extension of this concept, allowing for automatic creation of computer programs that solve the considered problem. This idea is also used for non-linear modelling. In such case the aim of the genetic programming is to generate a mathematical formula which will reconstruct the analysed phenomenon in the best way possible.

In genetic programming methods, individuals represent programs which are usually described in the form of a tree composed of non-terminal symbols (functions) and terminal symbols (constants and inputs parameters). Set of possible functions consists of arithmetic operators, mathematical and logic functions. It should be selected carefully, according to the domain of the problem being solved. One of the varieties of genetic programming is a technique Gene Expression Programming (GEP). In this technique programs are represented in the form of linear chromosomes, which require adequate conversion procedure

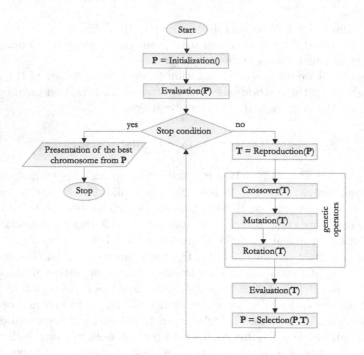

**Fig. 1.** Flowchart of basic GEP algorithm

(from the form of a tree to linear one). It makes possible to use standard genetic operators. In original algorithm proposed by Ferreira [27–29] the population contains $\mu$ individuals. Each of them encodes one function. A chromosome $\mathbf{C}_{ch}$, $ch = 1, \ldots, \mu$ of each individual is composed of three parts:

$$\mathbf{C}_{ch} = \{\mathbf{C}_{ch}^{\text{head}}, \mathbf{C}_{ch}^{\text{tail}}, \mathbf{C}_{ch}^{\text{constants}}\}, \tag{3}$$

where: $\mathbf{C}_{ch}^{\text{head}}$ can contain information about non-terminals and terminals symbols and its length $|\mathbf{C}_{ch}^{\text{head}}|$ is arbitrary, $\mathbf{C}_{ch}^{\text{tail}}$ can contain information about non-terminals only and its length can be computed using the following formula:

$$|\mathbf{C}_{ch}^{\text{tail}}| = |\mathbf{C}_{ch}^{\text{head}}| * (f_{\max} - 1) + 1, \tag{4}$$

where: $f_{\max}$ is a maximum arity of a non-terminal symbol. Part $\mathbf{C}_{ch}^{\text{constant}}$ contains numerical constants and its length is arbitrary too.

The flowchart of GEP algorithm is presented in Fig. 1. Thanks to such representation of chromosome, it is possible to apply standard genetic operators used in evolutionary algorithms. In addition, some special operators like e.g. rotation can be used too.

In our implementation of GEP algorithm we assume that:

- Chromosome is composed from $m$ such 3-tuples, each of them encodes one of $m$ equations required by model:

$$\mathbf{C}_{ch} = \bigcup_{j=1}^{m}\{\mathbf{C}_{ch,j}^{head}, \mathbf{C}_{ch,j}^{tail}\} \cup \bigcup_{j=1}^{m}\{\mathbf{C}_{ch,j}^{constants}\}. \tag{5}$$

- Fitness function is a dependency determining the difference between output signals $\hat{x}_j$, $j = 1, \ldots, m$ generated by the created model at step $k + 1$ and corresponding to reference $x_j$ values:

$$fAcc(\mathbf{X}) = \sqrt{\frac{1}{m \cdot K} \sum_{j=1}^{m} \sum_{k=1}^{K} (x_j(k+1) - \hat{x}_j(k+1))^2}. \tag{6}$$

- We use simple one point crossover with replacement genes as a crossover operation. This operation is carried out separately for part of a chromosome describing the structure of the corrections functions and for parts that contain numeric constants.
- We use multigene mutation as a mutation operation. Similarly to the crossover, this operation is performed separately for part of a chromosome describing the structure of the corrections functions and for parts that contain numeric constants.
- We use elitist selection mechanism, so the best individual from parental population is carrying over to the next population unaltered.

## 3  Simulation Results

To examine the effectiveness of applying Gene Expression Programming algorithm to non-linear correction modelling of dynamic objects we considered two problems (1) well-known harmonic oscillator and (2) the non-linear electrical circuit with solar generator and DC drive system. The harmonic oscillator can be defined using the following formula:

$$\frac{d^2x}{dt^2} + 2\zeta\frac{dx}{dt} + \omega^2 x = 0, \tag{7}$$

where $\zeta$, $\omega$ are oscillator parameters and $x(t)$ is a reference value of the modelled process as function of time. We used the following state variables $x_1(t) = dx(t)/dt$ and $x_2(t) = x(t)$. In such a case the system matrix $\mathbf{A}$ and the matrix of corrections coefficients $\mathbf{P_A}$ is described as follows:

$$\mathbf{A} = \begin{bmatrix} 0 & \omega \\ -\omega & 0 \end{bmatrix} \qquad \mathbf{P_A} = \begin{bmatrix} 0 & p_{12}(\mathbf{x}) \\ p_{21}(\mathbf{x}) & 0 \end{bmatrix}.$$

In our experiments the parameter $\omega$ was modified in simulation according with a formula:

$$\omega(x) = 2\pi - \frac{\pi}{(1 + |2 \cdot x|^6)}. \tag{8}$$

In the second experiment the nonlinear electrical circuit with solar generator and DC drive system was modelled. In this case the following state variables were used: $x_1(k) = -\frac{I_s}{C}e^{-au(k)} - \frac{1}{C}i(k) + \frac{I_s + I_0}{C}$, $x_2(k) = \frac{1}{L}i(k) - \frac{R_m}{L}u(k) - \frac{K_x}{L}\Omega(k)$, $x_3(k) = \frac{K_x}{L}u(k) - \frac{K_r}{J}\Omega(k)$, where: $u(k)$ is the generator voltage, $i(k)$ is the rotor current, $\Omega(k)$ is DC motor rotational speed. Parameters of the circuit were chosen as in [32] and they had the following values: $R_m = 12.045\Omega$, $L = 0.1H$, $C = 500\mu F$, $K_x = 0.5Vs$, $K_r = 0.1Vs^2$, $J = 10^{-3}Ws^3$, $I_0 = 2A$, $I_s = 1.28 \cdot 10^{-5}A$, $a = 0.54V^{-1}$. In this experiment we also assumed that the system matrix $\mathbf{A}$ and correction matrix $\mathbf{P_A}$ have values:

$$\mathbf{A} = \begin{bmatrix} -2163.86 & 2000.00 & 0.00 \\ 10.00 & -120.45 & -5.00 \\ 0.00 & 500.00 & -100.00 \end{bmatrix} \quad \mathbf{P_A} = \begin{bmatrix} p_{11}(\mathbf{x}) & 0 & 0 \\ 0 & 0 & 0 \\ 0 & 0 & 0 \end{bmatrix}.$$

The values of the matrix $\mathbf{A}$ were determined with Taylor's series expansion linearization method [33] in point $[22.15, 0, 0]$. In out method we assume that the system matrix $\mathbf{A}$ is known, so the goal of the modelling was to recreate the unknown coefficient of the correction matrix $\mathbf{P_A}$ in such a way that the model reproduces the reference data as accurately as possible.

For both problems the correction matrix $\mathbf{P_B}$ was not considered and its coefficients were equal to 0.0.

The parameters of evolutionary process that we use in the simulations are shown in table 1.

**Table 1.** Parameters of Gene Expression Programming algorithm used in simulations

| | Harmonic oscillator | Non-linear electric circuit |
|---|---|---|
| functions set $F$ | $\{+, -, \cdot, /, \text{abs}, \text{pow}\}$ | $\{+, -, \cdot, /, \text{pow}, \exp, \log\}$ |
| head size $|\mathbf{C}_{ch}^{head}|$ | 10 | 10 |
| number of constants $|\mathbf{C}_{ch}^{constants}|$ | 5 | 5 |
| constants range | $[-5, 5]$ | $[-100, 100]$ |
| number of epochs | 3000 | 5000 |
| population size $\mu$ | 50 | 50 |
| probability of crossover $p_c$ | 0.7 | 0.7 |
| probability of mutation $p_m$ | 0.3 | 0.1 |

Simulation results are shown in the Fig. 2 and Fig. 3 and they can be summarized as follows:

– Three best models discovered by GEP algorithm for harmonic oscillator problem, after some arithmetical simplification, can be written as follows:

$$\text{Model 1:} \quad \begin{cases} p_{12}(\mathbf{x}) &= -3.8889 + 4.7520 \cdot \text{abs}(x_0) \\ p_{21}(\mathbf{x}) &= 1.7517 \cdot x_1 \cdot x_1, \end{cases} \tag{9}$$

Model 2: $\begin{cases} p_{12}(\mathbf{x}) & = -3.8633 + 4.5824 \cdot abs(x_0) \\ p_{21}(\mathbf{x}) & = \frac{5.7960 \cdot x_1 \cdot x_1 + x_1}{3.5266 + x_1}, \end{cases}$ (10)

and

Model 3: $\begin{cases} p_{12}(\mathbf{x}) & = -4.0430 + 5.2284 \cdot abs(x_0) \\ p_{21}(\mathbf{x}) & = abs(x1). \end{cases}$ (11)

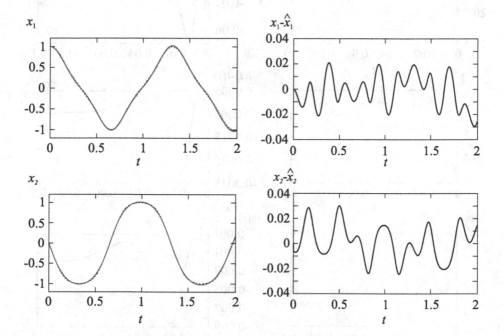

**Fig. 2.** Flowchart of basic GEP algorithm

– Three best models discovered by GEP algorithm for harmonic oscillator problem, after some arithmetical simplification, can be written as follows:

Model 1: $\left\{ p_{11}(\mathbf{x}) = x_1 - 59.8450 \cdot \left( x_0 + x_1 + \exp\left( \frac{x_1}{x_0} - 2.0 \cdot x_2 \right) - 56.4505 \right), \right.$ (12)

Model 2: $\left\{ p_{11}(\mathbf{x}) = 56.9699 \cdot \left( \frac{x_2}{x_2 + \exp(x_2)} + 56.9699 - x_0 \right) - x_2, \right.$ (13)

and

$$\text{Model 3: } \left\{ p_{11}(\mathbf{x}) = 56.9079 \cdot \left( \frac{x_2}{\exp(x_2)} - x_0 + 56.9079 \right). \right. \tag{14}$$

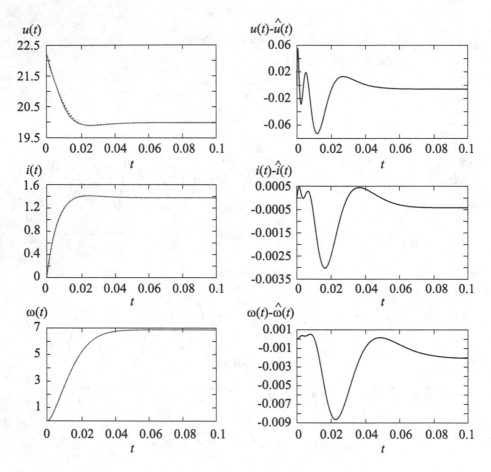

**Fig. 3.** Flowchart of basic GEP algorithm

- The accuracy of non-linear modelling obtained in our simulations are depicted in Fig. 2 and 3, and in Table 2.
- In our previous work, where we used neural-fuzzy systems to determine values of correction matrices coefficients, obtained error values were 0.007655 for the harmonic oscillator modelling problem and 0.007616 for the non-linear electrical circuit with solar generator and DC drive system modelling problem. It should be noted that these values are relatively slightly lower than the ones obtained in this work, but now resulting models are characterized by a lower computational costs.

**Table 2.** Root mean square error values obtained during simulations

|          | Harmonic oscillator | Non-linear electric circuit |
|----------|---------------------|-----------------------------|
| Model 1  | 0.0128              | 0.0116                      |
| Model 2  | 0.0135              | 0.0128                      |
| Model 3  | 0.0169              | 0.0134                      |

# 4 Conclusions

In this paper the method to create the linear model of the non-linear dynamic system was proposed. This method assumes that the linear model of analysed phenomena is known. In order to improve its accuracy, the correction matrices were introduced and their values are generated for all operating points. Formulas that allow to compute values of these coefficient in current operating point are determined automatically by Gene Expression Programming algorithm. The presented experimental results proved the validity of the proposed method.

**Acknowledgment.** The project was financed by the National Science Center on the basis of the decision number DEC-2012/05/B/ST7/02138.

# References

1. Barland, M., et al.: Commende optimal d'un systeme generateur photovoltaique converisseur statique - receptur. Revue Phys. Appl. 19, 905–915 (1984)
2. Bartczuk, Ł., Dziwiński, P., Starczewski, J.T.: New Method for Generation Type-2 Fuzzy Partition for FDT. In: Rutkowski, L., Scherer, R., Tadeusiewicz, R., Zadeh, L.A., Zurada, J.M. (eds.) ICAISC 2010, Part I. LNCS, vol. 6113, pp. 275–280. Springer, Heidelberg (2010)
3. Bartczuk, Ł., Przybył, A., Koprinkova-Hristova, P.: New Method for Non-linear Fuzzy Correction Modelling of Dynamic Objects. In: Rutkowski, L., Korytkowski, M., Scherer, R., Tadeusiewicz, R., Zadeh, L.A., Zurada, J.M. (eds.) ICAISC 2014, Part I. LNCS (LNAI), vol. 8467, pp. 169–180. Springer, Heidelberg (2014)
4. Bartczuk, Ł., Przybył, A., Dziwiński, P.: Hybrid State Variables - Fuzzy Logic Modelling of Nonlinear Objects. In: Rutkowski, L., Korytkowski, M., Scherer, R., Tadeusiewicz, R., Zadeh, L.A., Zurada, J.M. (eds.) ICAISC 2013, Part I. LNCS (LNAI), vol. 7894, pp. 227–234. Springer, Heidelberg (2013)
5. Bartczuk, Ł., Dziwiński, P., Starczewski, J.T.: A new method for dealing with unbalanced linguistic term set. In: Rutkowski, L., Korytkowski, M., Scherer, R., Tadeusiewicz, R., Zadeh, L.A., Zurada, J.M. (eds.) ICAISC 2012, Part I. LNCS, vol. 7267, pp. 207–212. Springer, Heidelberg (2012)
6. Bilski, J.: Momentum modification of the RLS algorithms. In: Rutkowski, L., Siekmann, J.H., Tadeusiewicz, R., Zadeh, L.A. (eds.) ICAISC 2004. LNCS (LNAI), vol. 3070, pp. 151–157. Springer, Heidelberg (2004)
7. Bilski, J., Rutkowski, L.: Numerically robust learning algorithms for feed forward neural networks. Advances in Soft Computing, pp. 149–154 (2003)

8. Bilski, J., Smoląg, J.: Parallel realisation of the recurrent RTRN neural network learning. In: Rutkowski, L., Tadeusiewicz, R., Zadeh, L.A., Zurada, J.M. (eds.) ICAISC 2008. LNCS (LNAI), vol. 5097, pp. 11–16. Springer, Heidelberg (2008)

9. Bilski, J., Smoląg, J.: Parallel Realisation of the Recurrent Elman Neural Network Learning. In: Rutkowski, L., Scherer, R., Tadeusiewicz, R., Zadeh, L.A., Zurada, J.M. (eds.) ICAISC 2010, Part II. LNCS (LNAI), vol. 6114, pp. 19–25. Springer, Heidelberg (2010)

10. Bilski, J., Smoląg, J.: Parallel Realisation of the Recurrent Multi Layer Perceptron Learning. In: Rutkowski, L., Korytkowski, M., Scherer, R., Tadeusiewicz, R., Zadeh, L.A., Zurada, J.M. (eds.) ICAISC 2012, Part I. LNCS, vol. 7267, pp. 12–20. Springer, Heidelberg (2012)

11. Bilski, J., Smoląg, J.: Parallel approach to learning of the recurrent jordan neural network. In: Rutkowski, L., Korytkowski, M., Scherer, R., Tadeusiewicz, R., Zadeh, L.A., Zurada, J.M. (eds.) ICAISC 2013, Part I. LNCS (LNAI), vol. 7894, pp. 32–40. Springer, Heidelberg (2013)

12. Bilski, J., Smoląg, J.: Parallel architectures for learning the RTRN and Elman dynamic neural networks. IEEE Trans. Parallel and Distributed Systems PP(99) (2014)

13. Bilski, J., Smoląg, J., Galushkin, A.I.: The Parallel Approach to the Conjugate Gradient Learning Algorithm for the Feedforward Neural Networks. In: Rutkowski, L., Korytkowski, M., Scherer, R., Tadeusiewicz, R., Zadeh, L.A., Zurada, J.M. (eds.) ICAISC 2014, Part I. LNCS, vol. 8467, pp. 12–21. Springer, Heidelberg (2014)

14. Bilski, J., Litwiński, S., Smoląg, J.: Parallel realisation of QR algorithm for neural networks learning. In: Rutkowski, L., Siekmann, J.H., Tadeusiewicz, R., Zadeh, L.A. (eds.) ICAISC 2004. LNCS (LNAI), vol. 3070, pp. 158–165. Springer, Heidelberg (2004)

15. Caughey, T.K.: Equivalent Linearization Techniques. The Journal of the Acoustical Society of America 35(11), 1706–1711 (1963)

16. Chaibakhsh, A., Chaibakhsh, N., Abbasi, M., Norouzi, A.: Orthonormal Basis Function Fuzzy Systems for Biological Wastewater Treatment Processes Modeling. Journal of Artificial Intelligence and Soft Computing Research 2(4), 343–356

17. Cpałka, K., Łapa, K., Przybył, A., Zalasiński, M.: A new method for designing neuro-fuzzy systems for nonlinear modelling with interpretability aspects. Neurocomputing 135, 203–217 (2014)

18. Cpałka, K., Łapa, K., Przybył, A., Zalasiński, M., Rutkowski, L.: A new method for designing neuro-fuzzy systems for nonlinear modelling with interpretability aspects. Neurocomputing 135, 203–217 (2014)

19. Cpałka, K.: On evolutionary designing and learning of flexible neuro-fuzzy structures for nonlinear classification. Nonlinear Analysis Series A: Theory, Methods and Applications 71, 1659–1672 (2009)

20. Cpałka, K., Rutkowski, L.: Flexible Takagi-Sugeno Fuzzy Systems. In: Proceedings of the International Joint Conference on Neural Networks 2005, Montreal, pp. 1764–1769 (2005)

21. Cpałka, K., Rutkowski, L.: A New Method for Designing and Reduction of Neuro-fuzzy Systems. In: Proceedings of the, IEEE International Conference on Fuzzy Systems (IEEE World Congress on Computational Intelligence, WCCI 2006), Vancouver, BC, Canada, pp. 8510–8516 (2006)

22. Cpałka, K., Zalasiński, M.: Online signature verification using vertical signature partitioning. Expert Systems with Applications 41, 4170–4180 (2014)

23. Cpałka, K., Zalasiński, M., Rutkowski, L.: New method for the on-line signature verification based on horizontal partitioning. Pattern Recognition 47, 2652–2661 (2014)
24. Dziwiński, P., Bartczuk, Ł., Starczewski, J.T.: Fully controllable ant colony system for text data clustering. In: Rutkowski, L., Korytkowski, M., Scherer, R., Tadeusiewicz, R., Zadeh, L.A., Zurada, J.M. (eds.) EC 2012 and SIDE 2012. LNCS, vol. 7269, pp. 199–205. Springer, Heidelberg (2012)
25. Dziwiński, P., Starczewski, J.T., Bartczuk, Ł.: New linguistic hedges in construction of interval type-2 FLS. In: Rutkowski, L., Scherer, R., Tadeusiewicz, R., Zadeh, L.A., Zurada, J.M. (eds.) ICAISC 2010, Part II. LNCS (LNAI), vol. 6114, pp. 445–450. Springer, Heidelberg (2010)
26. Dziwiński, P., Bartczuk, Ł., Przybył, A., Avedyan, E.D.: A New Algorithm for Identification of Significant Operating Points Using Swarm Intelligence. In: Rutkowski, L., Korytkowski, M., Scherer, R., Tadeusiewicz, R., Zadeh, L.A., Zurada, J.M. (eds.) ICAISC 2014, Part II. LNCS, vol. 8468, pp. 349–362. Springer, Heidelberg (2014)
27. Ferreira, C.: Gene expression programming: a new algorithm for solving problems. Complex Systems 13(2), 87–129 (2001)
28. Ferreira, C.: Gene expression programming in problem solving. In: Soft Computing and Industry, pp. 635–653. Springer London (2002)
29. Ferreira, C.: Gene Expression Programming: Mathematical Modeling by an Artificial Intelligence, 2nd edn. Springer, Germany (2006)
30. Folly, K.: Parallel Pbil Applied to Power System Controller Design. Journal of Artificial Intelligence and Soft Computing Research, 3(3), 215–223 (2013)
31. Ismail, S., Pashilkar, A.A., Ayyagari, R., Sundararajan, N.: Neural-Sliding Mode Augmented Robust Controller for Autolanding of Fixed Wing Aircraft. Journal of Artificial Intelligence and Soft Computing Research 2(4), 317–330 (2012)
32. Jordan, A.J.: Linearization of non-linear state equation. Bulletin of the Polish Academy of Science. Technical Science 54(1), 63–73 (2006)
33. Kaczorek, T., Dzieliński, A., Dąbrowski, L., Łopatka, R.: The Basis of Control Theory. WNT, Warsaw (2006) (in Polish)
34. Kamyar, M.: Takagi-Sugeno Fuzzy Modeling for Process Control Industrial Automation, Robotics and Artificial Intelligence (EEE8005), vol. 8 (2008) School of Electrical, Electronic and Computer Engineering
35. Koprinkova-Hristova, P.: Backpropagation through time training of a neuro-fuzzy controller. International Journal of Neural Systems 20(5), 421–428 (2010)
36. Lobato, F.S., Steffen Jr., V., Silva Neto, A.J.: Solution of singular optimal control problems using the improved differential evolution algorithm. Journal of Artificial Intelligence and Soft Computing Research 1(3), 195–206 (2011)
37. Łapa, K., Przybył, A., Cpałka, K.: A new approach to designing interpretable models of dynamic systems. In: Rutkowski, L., Korytkowski, M., Scherer, R., Tadeusiewicz, R., Zadeh, L.A., Zurada, J.M. (eds.) ICAISC 2013, Part II. LNCS (LNAI), vol. 7895, pp. 523–534. Springer, Heidelberg (2013)
38. Łapa, K., Zalasiński, M., Cpałka, K.: A new method for designing and complexity reduction of neuro-fuzzy systems for nonlinear modelling. In: Rutkowski, L., Korytkowski, M., Scherer, R., Tadeusiewicz, R., Zadeh, L.A., Zurada, J.M. (eds.) ICAISC 2013, Part I. LNCS (LNAI), vol. 7894, pp. 329–344. Springer, Heidelberg (2013)
39. Patan, K., Patan, M.: Optimal Training strategies for locally recurrent neural networks. Journal of Artificial Intelligence and Soft Computing Research 1(2), 103–114 (2011)

40. Peteiro-Barral, D., Bardinas, B.G., Perez-Sanchez, B.: Learning from heterogeneously distributed data sets using artificial neural networks and genetic algorithms. Journal of Artificial Intelligence and Soft Computing Research 2(1), 5–20 (2012)

41. Prampero, P.S., Attux, R.: Magnetic particle swarm optimization. Journal of Artificial Intelligence and Soft Computing Research 2(1), 59–72 (2012)

42. Przybył, A., Cpałka, K.: A new method to construct of interpretable models of dynamic systems. In: Rutkowski, L., Korytkowski, M., Scherer, R., Tadeusiewicz, R., Zadeh, L.A., Zurada, J.M. (eds.) ICAISC 2012, Part II. LNCS, vol. 7268, pp. 697–705. Springer, Heidelberg (2012)

43. Rutkowski, L.: On Bayes risk consistent pattern-recognition procedures in a quasi-stationary environment. IEEE Trans. Pattern Analysis and Machine Intelligence 4(1), 84–87 (1982)

44. Rutkowski, L.: Online Identification Of Time-Varying Systems by Nonparametric Techniques. IEEE Trans. Automatic Control 27(1), 228–230 (1982)

45. Rutkowski, L.: On nonparametric identification with prediction of time-varying systems. IEEE Trans. Automatic Control 29(1), 58–60 (1984)

46. Rutkowski, L.: Multiple Fourier-series procedures for extraction of nonlinear regressions from noisy data. IEEE Trans. Signal Processing 41(10), 3062–3065 (1993)

47. Rutkowski, L., Cpałka, K.: A neuro-fuzzy controller with a compromise fuzzy reasoning. Control and Cybernetics 31(2), 297–308 (2002)

48. Rutkowski, L., Cpałka, K.: Compromise approach to neuro-fuzzy systems. In: Sincak, P., Vascak, J., Kvasnicka, V., Pospichal, J. (eds.) Intelligent Technologies - Theory and Applications, vol. 76, pp. 85–90. IOS Press (2002)

49. Rutkowski, L., Cpałka, K.: Neuro-fuzzy systems derived from quasi-triangular norms. In: Proceedings of the IEEE International Conference on Fuzzy Systems, Budapest, July 26-29, vol. 2, pp. 1031–1036 (2004)

50. Rutkowski, L., Jaworski, M., Pietruczuk, L., Duda, P.: Decision Trees for Mining Data Streams Based on the Gaussian Approximation. IEEE Transactions on Knowledge and Data Engineering 26, 108–119 (2014)

51. Rutkowski, L., Jaworski, M., Pietruczuk, L., Duda, P.: The CART decision tree for mining data streams. Information Sciences 266, 1–15 (2014)

52. Rutkowski, L., Przybył, A., Cpałka, K.: Novel on-line speed profile generation for industrial machine tool based on flexible neuro-fuzzy approximation. IEEE Transactions on Industrial Electronics 59, 1238–1247 (2012)

53. Rutkowski, L., Przybył, A., Cpałka, K., Er, M.J.: Online speed profile generation for industrial machine tool based on neuro-fuzzy approach. In: Rutkowski, L., Scherer, R., Tadeusiewicz, R., Zadeh, L.A., Zurada, J.M. (eds.) ICAISC 2010, Part II. LNCS (LNAI), vol. 6114, pp. 645–650. Springer, Heidelberg (2010)

54. Theodoridis, D.C., Boutalis, Y.S., Christodoulou, M.A.: Robustifying analysis of the direct adaptive control of unknown multivariable nonlinear systems based on a new neuro-fuzzy method. Journal of Artificial Intelligence and Soft Computing Research 1(1), 59–79 (2011)

55. Tran, V.N., Brdys, M.A.: Optimizing control by robustly feasible model predictive control and application to drinking water distribution systems. Journal of Artificial Intelligence and Soft Computing Research 1(1), 43–57 (2011)

56. Zalasiński, M., Cpałka, K.: Novel algorithm for the on-line signature verification. In: Rutkowski, L., Korytkowski, M., Scherer, R., Tadeusiewicz, R., Zadeh, L.A., Zurada, J.M. (eds.) ICAISC 2012, Part II. LNCS, vol. 7268, pp. 362–367. Springer, Heidelberg (2012)

57. Zalasiński, M., Cpałka, K.: Novel algorithm for the on-line signature verification using selected discretization points groups. In: Rutkowski, L., Korytkowski, M., Scherer, R., Tadeusiewicz, R., Zadeh, L.A., Zurada, J.M. (eds.) ICAISC 2013, Part I. LNCS (LNAI), vol. 7894, pp. 493–502. Springer, Heidelberg (2013)
58. Zalasiński, M., Cpałka, K.: New approach for the on-line signature verification based on method of horizontal partitioning. In: Rutkowski, L., Korytkowski, M., Scherer, R., Tadeusiewicz, R., Zadeh, L.A., Zurada, J.M. (eds.) ICAISC 2013, Part II. LNCS (LNAI), vol. 7895, pp. 342–350. Springer, Heidelberg (2013)
59. Zalasiński, M., Cpałka, K., Er, M.J.: New Method for Dynamic Signature Verification Using Hybrid Partitioning. In: Rutkowski, L., Korytkowski, M., Scherer, R., Tadeusiewicz, R., Zadeh, L.A., Zurada, J.M. (eds.) ICAISC 2014, Part II. LNCS (LNAI), vol. 8468, pp. 216–230. Springer, Heidelberg (2014)
60. Zalasiński, M., Cpałka, K., Hayashi, Y.: New Method for Dynamic Signature Verification Based on Global Features. In: Rutkowski, L., Korytkowski, M., Scherer, R., Tadeusiewicz, R., Zadeh, L.A., Zurada, J.M. (eds.) ICAISC 2014, Part II. LNCS (LNAI), vol. 8468, pp. 231–245. Springer, Heidelberg (2014)
61. Zalasiński, M., Łapa, K., Cpałka, K.: New Algorithm for Evolutionary Selection of the Dynamic Signature Global Features. In: Rutkowski, L., Korytkowski, M., Scherer, R., Tadeusiewicz, R., Zadeh, L.A., Zurada, J.M. (eds.) ICAISC 2013, Part II. LNCS (LNAI), vol. 7895, pp. 113–121. Springer, Heidelberg (2013)

# Clustering Algorithm Based on Molecular Dynamics with Nose-Hoover Thermostat. Application to Japanese Candlesticks

Leszek J. Chmielewski[✉], Maciej Janowicz, and Arkadiusz Orłowski

Faculty of Applied Informatics and Mathematics (WZIM),
Warsaw University of Life Sciences (SGGW),
ul. Nowoursynowska 159, 02-775 Warsaw, Poland
{leszek_chmielewski,maciej_janowicz,arkadiusz_orlowski}@sggw.pl
http://www.wzim.sggw.pl

**Abstract.** A hybrid pattern clustering algorithm connecting Particle Swarm Optimization with Simulated Annealing is proposed. The swarm particles are directly associated with the centroids of each cluster. They are assumed to move in the phase space associated under the influence of a potential generated by each pattern to be partitioned and interacting with each other. Thus, the problem of partitioning acquires a direct physical interpretation. The motion of swarm particles is simulated with the help of a thermal bath represented by one additional dynamical variable within the Nose-Hoover formalism. The temperature is decreased at each step in the dynamics of the swarm providing the resemblance to the Simulated Annealing. Clustering of the Japanese candlesticks which appear in the dynamics of assets in the Warsaw stock market is used as an example.

**Keywords:** Clustering · Molecular dynamics · Japanese candlesticks

## 1 Introduction

Clustering denotes the partitioning of a set of data into groups of similar objects. Each group, called a *cluster*, consists of objects that are similar between themselves and dissimilar to objects of other groups. In the past few decades, cluster analysis has played an important role in a broad range of scientific disciplines including engineering, computer science, life and medical sciences, social sciences, and economics, as documented, e.g., in [1,2,3,4,5,6].

Even though human brains are well-known to have excellent abilities in clustering of various types of objects, this becomes rather problematic if the data set to be partitioned is large and the number of features according to which the cluster analysis has to be performed is larger than, say, three. Under such circumstances, the use of computers with implementation of some efficient algorithms appears to be necessary. As a matter of fact, the task of computerized data clustering has been approached from diverse domains of knowledge like graph

© Springer International Publishing Switzerland 2015
L. Rutkowski et al. (Eds.): ICAISC 2015, Part II, LNAI 9120, pp. 330–340, 2015.
DOI: 10.1007/978-3-319-19369-4_30

theory, statistical multivariate analysis, artificial neural networks, fuzzy set theory, etc. [7,8,9,10,11,12,13,14,15,16,17]. One of the most popular approaches in this direction has been the formulation of clustering as an optimization problem. That is, the best partitioning of a given dataset is obtained by minimizing or maximizing one or more objective functions. As a result, a variety of methods and techniques known from the optimization domain can be applied to the partitioning problem provided that a useful objective function to be optimized is found. Among the efficient optimization methods the so-called swarm intelligence algorithms have recently attracted considerable attention. Two examples of particularly successful research directions in swarm intelligence are Ant Colony Optimization (ACO) [18,19] and Particle Swarm Optimization (PSO) [20]. In the context of cluster analysis, the PSO-based method was first introduced by Omran, Salman, and Engelbrecht in [21]. The results of Omran et al. [21,22] suggest that PSO-based method can outperform $k$-means, fuzzy $c$-means (FCM), and a few other state-of-the-art clustering algorithms. A very useful survey of the application of PSO to the cluster analysis has been given (together with original results) in [23].

In this work we attempt to develop a clustering algorithm which is very much in the spirit of PSO, but still similar to the Simulated Annealing techniques in that the concept of temperature and its lowering during simulation is introduced. The swarm particles are to represent the centroids of each cluster. Each particle is subject to a force field generated by objects which should be partitioned. In addition, the particles repel each other. Since the particles should visit a sufficiently large subset of the configuration space, their interaction with a thermal bath is introduced. This bath, however, is modelled deterministically with the help of an additional dynamical variable as described by Nose [24] and Hoover [25].

We have found that a related approach to the optimization problems has been developed earlier by Fukuda [26], who, however, has used temperature-dependent potential function and sampling under finite temperature rather than annealing.

Our simulations have one feature very unusual from the point of view of PSO: the elements of the swarm are single particles rather than the whole bunch of particles. The only reason for that is our wish to make the simulations very similar to the standard molecular dynamics ones.

As a non-trivial application of our PSO-like procedure, we have chosen clustering of the Japanese candlesticks having in mind their possible use in the field of technical analysis of assets in the stock market. It is often claimed by the technical analysts (see, e.g., [27]) that some particular sequences of candlesticks with a given shape (which is obviously a fuzzy concept) can be used to predict, e.g., the breaking or continuation of a trend. Now, clusterization of candlesticks for a given asset allows one to ascribe labels to candlesticks. This, in turn, makes it possible to investigate how their sequences with given labels have performed in the past and what is the predictive power (if any) of sequences with particular labels.

The main body of this work is organized as follows. In Section 2 we recall the definition of the Japanese candlesticks which form our working example. In Section 3 we present our hybrid algorithm in some detail. Section 4 contains the results of our variant of PSO simulation. Finally, Section 5 comprises some concluding remarks.

## 2    Japanese Candlesticks as a Representation of Value of Assets in Stock Market

The Japanese candlestick is a sequence of four numbers $(O(a,t), X(a,t), N(a,t), C(a,t))$, where $O$ denotes the opening value of the asset $a$ on the trading day $t$, $X$ is the maximum value (*high*) reached during the trading session, $N$ is the minimum (*low*), and $C$ is the closing value. There exist a well-known graphical representation of the candlestick [28] often considered important in the so-called technical analysis of stock markets.

In what follows below we employ a sequence of five elements $(O, X, N, C, V)$ which we call an *augmented Japanese candlestick* where $V$ represents the transaction volume associated with the asset and the trading day. An augmented candlestick of the asset $a$ on the day $t$ can be denoted as a 5-tuple

$$\mathbf{y}(a;t) = (O(a,t), X(a,t), N(a,t), C(a,t), V(a,t)) \ . \tag{1}$$

In the following we shall call it simply a candlestick. The time series of $n+1$ candlesticks, called otherwise a sequence, can be written down as

$$S_n(a;t) = (\mathbf{y}(a;t), \mathbf{y}(a;t+1), ..., \mathbf{y}(a;t+n)) \ . \tag{2}$$

Each sequence has its own starting time $t$ and ending time $t+n$.

We define the (non-Euclidean) distance between two candlesticks as

$$d(\mathbf{y}_1, \mathbf{y}_2) = 1 - \exp\left[-\sum_{A_1,A_2} (A_1 - A_2)^2 / (2b)\right] , \tag{3}$$

where $A_1$ and $A_2$ are corresponding components of $\mathbf{y}_1$ and $\mathbf{y}_2$ respectively, i.e., they run through the elements of appropriate sets $\{O, X, N, C, V\}$, and $b$ is a constant. In order to consider this formula meaningful, the values of the asset and the transaction volume must be comparable. To achieve this, we normalize all time series by subtracting the closing values from the opening ones as well as from the maxima and minima, and dividing $O$, $X$, $N$, and $C$ by the standard deviation of $C$. Similarly, the volume is also divided by its standard deviation. This way, the standard deviations of renormalized $C$ and $V$ are exactly 1. All candlesticks analysed further are normalized in the above sense.

The reason for introduction of the above non-Euclidean metric is that in the following we use the notion of potential energy, and we want that potential energy to be expressed simply as a *sum* of the distances (up to an additive constant). Such a formulation allows one to keep the physical analogy of the cluster centroids as "particles" and the vectors to be clusterized as "centers of potential". Indeed, the potential energy should become zero or a constant in the worst case when the "particle" is very far away from the "centers of potential". There would be, of course, nothing wrong in writing the potential energy as a more complicated function of Euclidean distances.

## 3 Molecular Dynamics-based Variant of the Particle Swarm Optimization

Let us denote by $\mathbf{y}_n$, $n = 1, 2, ..., N$ the objects to be partitioned into the clusters. Each object possesses a number of features; it is assumed that the features can be quantified and labelled with the help of a real number. All objects are assumed to have the same number $d$ of the features. Thus, the whole dataset is characterized by $N \cdot d$ real numbers. Let us assume that we need to partition the data into $L_k$ number of clusters. For a time being we assume that $L_k$ is fixed (specified by the user of the algorithm). The goal is to partition the $N$ objects in such a way that the following requirements are met:

- The distance between the objects and their centroid within the cluster is minimized. This can accomplished by requirement that a centroid is attracted by the objects to which it is similar while its interaction with dissimilar objects is negligible.
- The distance between different clusters (represented by their centroids) is maximized. This can result from the requirement that the centroids repel each other.

From these requirements it follows that we have to optimize the following function (cf. [21]):

$$f(X, Y) \equiv \mathcal{U}_Y(X) = w_1 \mathcal{U}_1 + w_2 \mathcal{U}_2 , \tag{4}$$

where

$$\mathcal{U}_1 = \sum_{i=1}^{L_k} \sum_{n_i \in C_i} d(\mathbf{y}_{n_i}, \mathbf{x}_i) , \tag{5}$$

$$\mathcal{U}_2 = Z - \sum_{i,j=1}^{L_k} d(\mathbf{x}_i, \mathbf{x}_j) . \tag{6}$$

In the above equations the centroids are represented with the help of $d$-dimensional vectors $\mathbf{x}_i$, $i = 1, 2, ..., L_k$; $X$ denotes the whole set of those vectors, $Y$ denotes the set of vectors representing the to-be-partitioned objects, and $Z$ is a constant chosen such to make $\mathcal{U}_2$ non-negative. The symbol $C_i$ represents the $i$th cluster and $n_i$ enumerates the vectors belonging to that cluster. The parameters $w_1$ and $w_2$ are relative weights assigned to the attraction of centroids to the candles (i.e. sources of potential) vs. repulsion among the centroids themselves. The skill-full choice of these weights can sometimes lead to the improvement of the results of optimization. However, in our simulations we have not seen any particular influence of those weights (unless one of them has been very close to zero). The fitness function $f(X, Y)$ defines a multi-objective optimization problem, which minimizes the intra-cluster distances and maximizes inter-cluster separation.

In order to solve the above optimization problem, we propose to apply the following dynamical scheme. Let the centroids be represented with the help of both $\mathbf{x}_i$ (called coordinates of the centroids) and associated momenta $\mathbf{p}_i$, $i = 1, 2, ..., L_k$. The coordinates and momenta exhibit dynamics in *continuous* pseudo-time $\tau$ generated by the Hamiltonian:

$$H = \sum_{i=1}^{L_k} \frac{\mathbf{p}_i^2}{2ms^2} + \mathcal{U}_Y(X) + \frac{P_s^2}{2M} + gk_B T \ln(s) \ , \tag{7}$$

where g is a constant which may be the number of independent momentum de-grees of freedom of the system ($L_k$ in our case), $k_B$ is a constant that is an analog of the Boltzmann constant, $T$ is the temperature, $s$ is an additional dynamical variable to represent the influence of the thermal bath on the system of centroids, $P_s$ is the associated momentum, and $m$ and $M$ are constants (called "masses"). Let us notice here that all the quantities which appear in the Hamiltonian above are dimensionless, and that the product $gk_B$ can be included into the dimen-sionless temperature. The time evolution of the above variables is given by the Hamilton equations of motion:

$$\frac{d}{d\tau}\mathbf{x}_i = \frac{\partial H}{\partial \mathbf{p}_i} \ , \tag{8}$$

$$\frac{d}{d\tau}\mathbf{p}_i = -\frac{\partial H}{\partial \mathbf{x}_i} \ , \tag{9}$$

$$\frac{d}{d\tau}s = \frac{\partial H}{\partial P_s} \ , \tag{10}$$

$$\frac{d}{d\tau}P_s = -\frac{\partial H}{\partial s} \ . \tag{11}$$

Let us now define the velocities $\mathbf{v}_i$ and $V_s$ as:

$$\mathbf{v}_i = \frac{\mathbf{p}_i}{ms^2} \ , \tag{12}$$

$$V_s = \frac{P_s}{M} \ . \tag{13}$$

Then the Hamilton equations take the form:

$$\frac{d}{d\tau}\mathbf{x}_i = \mathbf{v}_i \ , \tag{14}$$

$$\frac{d}{d\tau}\mathbf{v}_i = -\frac{1}{ms^2}\frac{\partial \mathcal{U}_Y}{\partial \mathbf{x}_i} - \frac{2\mathbf{v}_i V_s}{s} \ , \tag{15}$$

$$\frac{d}{d\tau}s = V_s \ , \tag{16}$$

$$\frac{d}{d\tau}V_s = \frac{ms}{M}\sum_i \mathbf{v}_i^2 + \frac{gk_B T}{Ms} \ . \tag{17}$$

The temperature measures the mean kinetic energy of the system (given by the second term in the Hamiltonian). If the temperature approaches zero, the dynamics of the system variables gradually becomes frozen, and the coordinates of the centroids approach a minimum of the potential function $\mathcal{U}_Y$. Obviously, this characteristic of the algorithm resembles the Simulated Annealing (SA). It is to be noted, however, that there are significant conceptual differences since SA is clearly associated with Monte Carlo simulations and no time is involved. Here, it is the Molecular Dynamics which is at the root of the algorithm, and time (or pseudo-time) evolution is essential.

Needless to say, there is no guarantee that that minimum is global. However, since the system can be kicked off by thermal fluctuations from a shallow local minimum, one might hope that at least a deep local minimum is achieved as the temperature goes to zero. Let us notice that the specific values of $g$ and $k_B$ are irrelevant here as the temperature enters the dynamics only via the product $gk_B T$ so that we always deal with a scaled temperature.

There are at least two very difficult questions related to the above procedure. Firstly, one has to specify the parameters $w_i$ of the potential function $\mathcal{U}_Y$, the masses $m$ and $M$ (more precisely, only their ratio $m/M$ is important), and the parameter $b$. The second question is what is the best starting temperature and how it should be made lower. We are at the moment not able to offer any recommendation except of the trail-and-error procedure which has been used by us in this work.

Let us also briefly mention the problem of choice of the number of clusters $L_k$. Actually, every reasonable clustering analysis method should provide some means to find the proper $L_k$. Here, we propose the following "soft" rule to obtain $L_k$. One has to start with a quite large number and look whether the centroids tend to coalesce as the pseudo-time grows and the temperature is lower. If the final distance between two or more centroids is smaller than some prescribed value (being, for instance, a fraction of the maximal distance between the objects), one should launch a new simulation with a smaller value of $L_k$.

## 4  Clustering of Candlesticks: Results

To illustrate our clustering algorithm, we have used the augmented Japanese candlesticks as they arise in the dynamics of the stocks registered in Warsaw stock market (GPW). Thus, the set of objects which is to be partitioned is the

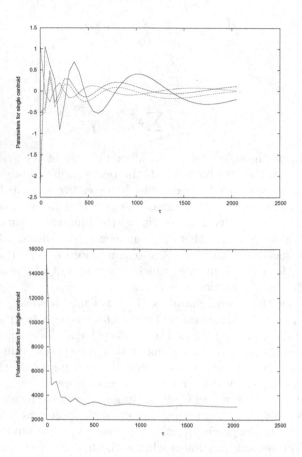

**Fig. 1.** Evolution of (a) parameters and (b) potential function of a single centroid in pseudo-time $\tau$. (a) the solid line: $x_1(1)$, dashed line: $x_1(2)$, dot-dashed line: $x_1(3)$, dotted line: $x_1(4)$; (b) the solid line: $\mathcal{U}(X)$.

set of vectors representing the candlesticks, and each vector has five components. To evolve the system in time, a modified version of the velocity Verlet algorithm [29,30] has been used. Given that we know the coordinates and velocities $\mathbf{x}$ and $\mathbf{v}$ at the pseudo-time $\tau$, they can be computed at the time $\tau + \varDelta t$ in the following steps:

1. Using $\mathbf{x}_i(\tau)$, the forces $\mathbf{F}_i(\tau)$ have to be computed as

$$\mathbf{F}_i(\tau) = -\frac{1}{s^2}\frac{\partial \mathcal{U}_Y}{\partial \mathbf{x}_i}. \tag{18}$$

Also, the force $F_s$ is computed according to:

$$F_s(\tau) = ms\sum_i \mathbf{v}_i^2 + \frac{gk_BT}{s} . \tag{19}$$

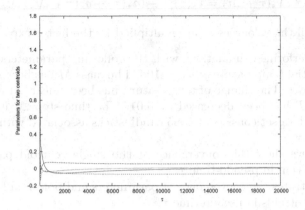

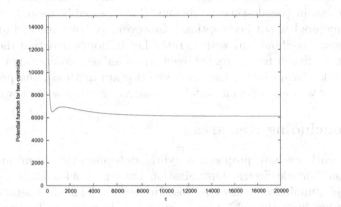

**Fig. 2.** Evolution of (a) components (parameters) and (b) potential function for two centroids in pseudo-time $\tau$. (a) the solid line: $x_1(1)$, dashed line: $x_1(2)$, dot-dashed line: $x_1(3)$, dotted line: $x_1(4)$; (b) the solid line: $\mathcal{U}(X)$.

Then, the accelerations $\mathbf{a}_i(\tau)$ are obtained as $\mathbf{F}_i(\tau)/m$ and $a_s(\tau) = F_s(\tau)/M$. New coordinates are then computed from the equations:

$$\mathbf{x}_i(\tau + \Delta t) = \mathbf{x}_i(\tau) + \mathbf{v}_i(\tau)\,\Delta t + \frac{1}{2}\,\mathbf{a}_i(\tau)\,\Delta t^2 \ , \qquad (20)$$

$$s(\tau + \Delta t) = s(\tau) + V_s(\tau)\,\Delta t + \frac{1}{2}\,a_s(\tau)\,\Delta t^2 \ . \qquad (21)$$

2. Using $\mathbf{x}_i(\tau + \Delta t)$ and $s(\tau + \Delta t)$ we get new forces $\mathbf{F}_i(\tau + \Delta t)$ and $F_s(\tau + \Delta \tau)$ as well as new accelerations $\mathbf{a}_i(\tau + \Delta t) = \mathbf{F}_i(\tau + \Delta t)/m$ and $a_s(\tau + \Delta \tau) = F_s(\tau + \Delta \tau)/M$.

3. New velocities are obtained according to the formulas:

$$\mathbf{v}_i(\tau + \Delta t) = \mathbf{v}_i(\tau) + \frac{1}{2}\,(\mathbf{a}_i(\tau) + \mathbf{a}_i(\tau + \Delta t))\,\Delta t \ , \qquad (22)$$

$$V_s(\tau + \Delta t) = V_s(\tau) + \frac{1}{2}\left(a_s(\tau) + a_s(\tau + \Delta t)\right)\Delta t \ . \tag{23}$$

4. Finally, all the velocities $\mathbf{v}_i$ are multiplied by the factor $\exp(-2V_s\,\Delta t/s)$.

We have performed simulations with the following parameters: $b = 5$, $w_1 = w_2 = 1/2$, initial temperature $gk_BT = 100$. The mass $M$ has been equal to 1000, the mass $m$ to 1. The change of temperature has been linear. At each time step temperature $T$ has been decreased by 0.01. The time step $\Delta t$ has been equal to 0.01. The data set consists of 5095 candlesticks associated with the BZWBK stocks of GPW.

In Fig. 1 we show the convergence of the single centroid parameters and potential function in pseudo-time $\tau$.

Fig. 2 illustrates the convergence of parameters and potential function in the case of two centroids in pseudo-time $\tau$.

It is clear that the convergence has been rather slow, and the presence of fluctuations in pseudo-time is obvious. This probably means that our choice of parameters has not been optimal. However, we have not had any issues with convergence itself but only with its ratio. Let us notice here that the optimization problem for five or ten degrees of freedom under very complicated (multi-center) potential landscape is by no means trivial (for any method). Our procedure works reasonably well and offers a useful alternative to other well-known approaches.

## 5   Concluding Remarks

In this work we have proposed a hybrid deterministic optimization algorithm based on Particle Swarm Optimization combined with ideas from Molecular Dynamics simulations using the Nose-Hoover model of the thermostat. That algorithm has been applied for the purposes of clustering of Japanese candlesticks which commonly appear in the technical analysis of stock market assets. The optimization problem enjoys the feature of having almost a direct physical interpretation. Every *particle* in the swarm represents the centroid of a cluster and moves in the force field generated by each pattern to be classified. In addition, the centroids repel each other. The Nose-Hoover model of the thermostat provides the necessary amount of stochastic interaction by simulating the energy exchange between the swarm and its thermal bath. Lowering the temperature allows the system to find a deep local minimum of the objective function thus making the algorithm similar to the Simulated Annealing.

We have performed some preliminary comparison of our precedure with the standard $k$-means approach. It has turned out that our technique is slower than $k$-means but there is still some room for improvement. Moreover, in several cases we could see improvement in the accuracy of our optimization. We have yet to find the proper ways to suggest a proper value of the critical parameter, namely the mass $M$ of the Nose-Hoover pseudo-particle. So far, our experimentation has not lead to any specific recommendation.

Finally, we would like to mention that the Nose-Hoover formalism can be supplemented by adding the Langevin (stochastic) forces to the right-hand sides of the equations of motion in order to improve the ergodicity. However, this is somewhat against the very spirit of Nose-Hoover approach and we have not attempted to use any such forces.

# References

1. Evangelou, I.E., Hadjimitsis, D.G., Lazakidou, A.A., Clayton, C.: Data Mining and Knowledge Discovery in Complex Image Data using Artificial Neural Networks. In: Workshop on Complex Reasoning on Geographical Data, Cyprus (2001)
2. Lillesand, T., Keifer, R.: Remote Sensing and Image Interpretation. John Wiley and Sons, New York (1994)
3. Rao, M.R.: Cluster Analysis and Mathematical Programming. J. Am. Stat. Assoc. 22, 622 (1994)
4. Duda, R.O., Hart, P.E.: Pattern Classification and Scene Analysis. John Wiley and Sons, New York (1973)
5. Everitt, B.S.: Cluster Analysis. Halsted Press (1993)
6. Xu, R., Wunsch, D.: Clustering. IEEE Press Series on Computational Intelligence (2008)
7. Forgy, E.W.: Cluster analysis of multivariate data: efficiency versus interpretability of classification. Biometrics 21, 768 (1965)
8. Zahn, C.T.: Graph-theoretical methods for detecting and describing gestalt clusters. IEEE Transactions on Computers C-20, 6886 (1971)
9. Mitchell, T.: Machine Learning. McGraw-Hill, New York (1997)
10. Mao, J., Jain, A.K.: Artificial neural networks for feature extraction and multivariate data projection. IEEE Trans. Neural Networks 6, 296 (1995)
11. Pal, N.R., Bezdek, J.C., Tsao, E.C.K.: Generalized clustering networks and Kohonen's self-organizing scheme. IEEE Trans. Neural Networks 4, 549 (1993)
12. Kohonen, T.: Self-Organizing Maps. Series in Information Sciences, vol. 30. Springer, Berlin (1995)
13. Falkenauer, E.: Genetic Algorithms and Grouping Problems. John Wiley and Sons, New York (1998)
14. Paterlini, S., Minerva, T.: Evolutionary Approaches for Cluster Analysis. In: Bonarini, A., Masulli, F., Pasi, G. (eds.) Soft Computing Applications, pp. 167–178. Springer, Berlin (2003)
15. Xu, R., Wunsch, D.: Survey of clustering algorithms. IEEE Transactions on Neural Networks 16(3), 645 (2005)
16. Rokach, L., Maimon, O.: Clustering Methods. In: Data Mining and Knowledge Discovery Handbook, pp. 321–352. Springer, Berlin (2005)
17. Mitra, S., Pal, S.K., Mitra, P.: Data mining in soft computing framework: A survey. IEEE Transactions on Neural Networks 13(3) (2002)
18. Dorigo, M., Maniezzo, V., Colorni, A.: The ant system: Optimization by a colony of cooperating agents. IEEE Trans. Systems Man and Cybernetics, Part B: Cybernetics 26, 21 (1996)
19. Dorigo, M., Gambardella, L.M.: Ant colony system: A cooperative learning approach to the traveling salesman problem. IEEE Trans. Evolutionary Computing 1, 5366 (1997)
20. Kennedy, J., Eberhart, R.: Particle swarm optimization. In: Proc. IEEE International Conference on Neural Networks, pp. 1942–1948 (1995)

21. Omran, M., Salman, A., Engelbrecht, A.P.: Image Classification using Particle Swarm Optimization. In: Proc. Conference on Simulated Evolution and Learning, vol. 1, pp. 370–374 (2002)
22. Omran, M., Engelbrecht, A.P., Salman, A.: Particle Swarm Optimization Method for Image Clustering. International Journal of Pattern Recognition and Artificial Intelligence 19, 297 (2005)
23. Das, S., Abraham, A.: Pattern Clustering Using a Swarm Intelligence Approach. In: Maimon, O., Rokach, L. (eds.) Data Mining and Knowledge Discovery Handbook, pp. 469–504. Springer, Berlin (2010)
24. Nose, S.: A unified formulation of the constant temperature molecular-dynamics methods. J. Chem. Phys. 81, 511 (1984)
25. Hoover, W.G.: Canonical dynamics: Equilibrium phase-space distributions. Phys. Rev. A 31, 1695 (1985)
26. Fukuda, I.: Application of the Nose-Hoover method to optimization problems. Phys. Rev. E 64(1), 16203 (2001)
27. Murphy, J.: Technical Analysis of Financial Markets. New York Institute of Finance (1999)
28. Wikipedia. Candlestick chart – Wikipedia, the free encyclopedia (2014), http://en.wikipedia.org/w/index.php?title=Candlestick_chart (accessed December 19, 2014)
29. Verlet, L.: Computer "Experiments" on classical fluids. I. Thermodynamical properties of Lennard Jones molecules. Phys. Rev. 159(1), 98 (1967)
30. Swope, W.C., Andersen, H.C., Berens, P.H., Wilson, K.R.: A computer simulation method for the calculation of equilibrium constants for the formation of physical clusters of molecules: Application to small water clusters. J. Chem. Phys. 76, 648 (1982)

# Improving the Analysis of Context-Aware Information via Marker-Based Stigmergy and Differential Evolution

Mario G.C.A. Cimino$^{(\boxtimes)}$, Alessandro Lazzeri, and Gigliola Vaglini

Department of Information Engineering, University of Pisa, Pisa, Italy
{mario.cimino,gigliola.vaglini}@unipi.it,
alessandro.lazzeri@for.unipi.it

**Abstract.** We use the marker-based stigmergy, a mechanism that mediates animal-animal interactions, to perform context-aware information aggregation. In contrast with conventional knowledge-based models of aggregation, our model is data-driven and based on self-organization of information. This means that a functional structure called track appears and stays spontaneous at runtime when local dynamism in data occurs. The track is then processed by using similarity between current and reference tracks. Subsequently, the similarity value is handled by domain-dependent analytics, to discover meaningful events. Given the changeability of human-centered scenarios, the overall process is also adaptive, thanks to parametric optimization performed via differential evolution. The paper illustrates the proposed approach and discusses its characteristics through two real-world case studies.

**Keywords:** Context-aware information · Marker-based stigmergy · Optimization · Differential evolution

## 1 Introduction and Motivation

Context-awareness is a computing paradigm by which software systems can sense the user's context in order to provide personalized services. This paradigm relies on the *context*, that is, all information helping to understand what is happening in the user's physical or logical environment. Context-aware information can be supplied through different channels: data repositories, web applications, mobile applications, embedded systems, and so on [1]. To properly support service personalization, context-aware information should be adequately aggregated so as to detect human-centric events in a number of domains: financial transactions, health care needs, traffic jam, territorial emergency, and so on [2].

In the literature of context-awareness, at the core of aggregation of human-centric data is the construction of two possible types of model: (i) knowledge-based models, explicitly designed at the business level in terms of logical or mathematical rules, determined by a domain expert; (ii) data-driven models, i.e., systems that can learn from prototypical data via machine learning or statistical algorithm. Nevertheless, modeling and reusing application contexts remains a

© Springer International Publishing Switzerland 2015
L. Rutkowski et al. (Eds.): ICAISC 2015, Part II, LNAI 9120, pp. 341–352, 2015.
DOI: 10.1007/978-3-319-19369-4_31

difficult task. An important lesson learned is that the algorithms performing the parametric data aggregation must use a limited number of states, be highly adaptable and handle variability [3,4].

Generally speaking, knowledge-based models belong to the *cognitivist* paradigm [5]. In this paradigm, the system is a descriptive product of a human designer, whose knowledge has to be explicitly formulated for a representational system of symbolic information processing. It is well known that knowledge-based systems are highly context-dependent, neither scalable nor manageable. With respect to knowledge-based models, data-driven models are more robust in the face of noisy and unexpected inputs, allowing broader coverage and being more adaptive. The data-driven approach discussed in this paper takes inspiration from the *emergent* paradigm [5], in which context information is augmented with locally encapsulated structure and behavior. Emergent paradigms are based on the principle of self-organization of data, which means that a functional structure appears and stays spontaneous at runtime when local dynamism in data occurs [6].

In this paper we propose to use the principles of the marker-based stigmergy to perform context-aware information aggregation. In biology, stigmergy is a class of mechanisms that mediate animal-animal interactions. It consists of indirect communication between individuals of an insect society by local modifications induced by these insects on their environment. Social insect colonies employ chemical markers (pheromones) that the insects deposit on the ground in specific situations. Pheromone concentrations in the environment disperse in space and evaporate over time, because pheromones are highly volatile substances. Multiple deposits at the same location aggregate in strength. Members of the colony who perceive pheromones of a particular flavor may change their behavior.

In computer science, marker-based stigmergy occurs when marks are left in an environment to enable self-coordination [7]. Marker-based stigmergy can be employed as a powerful computing paradigm exploiting both spatial and temporal dynamics, because it intrinsically embodies the time domain. Moreover, the mapping provided is not explicitly modeled at design-time and then not directly interpretable. This provides a kind of information blurring of the human data, and can be exploited to solve privacy issues.

In this work the main goal of data aggregation is to distinguish different spatio-temporal patterns occurring over time. For this purpose, we use stigmergic tracks for assessing similarity between context-aware data. Similarity is computed between a reference and a current track, and over different time periods, in order to measure the differences. Since context-data source is application-dependent, we have included an adaptive scheme on the marking and detection sub-processes. The setting of different applications consisting in different parameterizations can be automatically performed via a biologically-inspired optimization algorithm.

More specifically, the system architecture proposed in this paper is made of four subsystems: (i) the *marking* subsystem takes context information samples and releases marks in a computational environment; here, marks interact with each other at micro level generating a collective mark distribution. Collective mark can be considered as a short-term and a short-size memory which abstracts the complexity and the variability in the information sources; (ii) the *perception* subsystem compares the collective mark with a reference mark by similarity function; (iii) the *detection* subsystem connects similarity to specific application domain analytics; (iv) finally, the *adaptation* subsystem consists in the parametric optimization of the other subsystems. We used differential evolution among the other optimization methods [8].

The paper is structured as follows. Section 2 details on the first three subsystems, whereas Section 3 covers the adaptation subsystem. Both sections are based on two real-world pilot case studies. Finally, Section 4 draws some conclusions.

## 2    Processing with Stigmergy: A Three-Level Architecture

This section is focused on the marking, perception, and detection subsystems, described by considering a pilot real-world case study in the field of *ambient assisted living* (AAL): to monitor elderly people living alone in their own homes with the purpose of detecting possible disease situations. In the pilot case study, the context-aware input information is the $x, y$ position of the elderly at home, periodically sampled, whereas the binary output is the detection of unusual behavior, with respect to a reference behavior sampled in a healthy period. The case study of the vendor rating is also presented.

### 2.1    The Marking Subsystem

The marking subsystem periodically takes as an input the position of the user at home and releases a mark in a computer-simulated spatial environment, thus allowing the accumulation of marks. A mark has four attributes: position $(x, y)$, maximum intensity $I_{MAX}$, width $\varepsilon$, and evaporation $\theta$. Fig. 1a-d shows some mark sample of the pilot scenario. The position of the elderly is represented by a dot, in Fig. 1a and Fig. 1c.

The levels of mark intensity are represented by different gray gradations: the darker the gradation is, the higher the intensity of the mark. In Fig. 1a the highest intensity of the mark $I_{MAX}$ is in the middle, which corresponds to the position of the person where the mark is left. Mark intensity proportionally decreases with the number of squares from the position of the person, reaching its minimum at distance $\varepsilon$. Further, mark intensity has a temporal decay, i.e., a percentage $\theta$ of decrease after a step of time (tick). Hence, an isolated mark after a certain time tends to disappear, as shown in Fig. 1b sampled after a tick with respect to Fig. 1a. The time that a mark takes to disappear is longer than the period used by the marking subsystem to release a new mark. Hence, if the user is still in a specific position, new marks at the end of each period will superimpose on the old marks, thus increasing the intensity up to a stationary level. If the person moves to other locations, consecutive marks will be partially superimposed and intensities will decrease with the passage of time without being reinforced. Fig. 1c shows two consecutive and overlapping marks, and Fig. 1d shows the same track after a step of evaporation. The stigmergic track can then be considered as a short-term and a short-size action memory. The marking subsystem allows capturing a coarse spatiotemporal structure in the domain space, which hides the complexity and the variability in data.

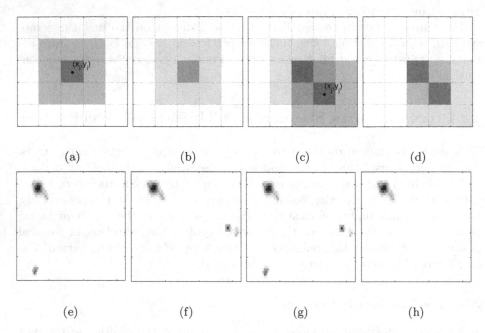

**Fig. 1.** (a) example of a two-dimensional mark; (b) the mark after a step of evaporation; (c), the aggregation of two consecutive marks; (d) the aggregated marks after a step of evaporation; (e) aggregated mark generated by an elderly moving in his apartment on a Friday at 19:20; (f) aggregated mark on the next Friday at 19:20; (g) the union of the marks of Fig. 1e and Fig. 1f; (h) the intersection of the marks of Fig. 1e and Fig. 1f.

## 2.2   The Perception Subsystem

At the second level there is the perception subsystem, consisting in the sensing of the track accumulated in the environment at the macro-level. Here, we take advantage of stigmergy (computed at the first level) as a means of information aggregation of the spatiotemporal tracks. Indeed, the process of information aggregation is a vehicle of abstraction, leading to the emergence of high-level behavior. The perception subsystem performs a comparison, called similarity, which aims at sensing the variation of the current behavior with respect to what was judged a normal behavior.

More specifically, given an accumulated mark, i.e., a track, the perception subsystem performs a similarity computation between the current track, $T_i$, and a reference track, $T_i^{REF}$, at the $i$-th step. A reference track is generated offline, by averaging the marks collected during healthy periods. Indeed in the case study the objective is to detect unusual behavior, and reference tracks were created when the elderly was healthy, for each day of week. Thus, the similarity with the current track and the reference track, $S(T_i, T_i^{REF})$, in the same day of a week provides information about unusual behavior.

Fig. 1e shows a two-dimensional representation of the track generated by an elderly moving in his apartment on a Friday at 19:20. Fig. 1f shows the track on the next Friday at 19:20. Fig. 1g shows the union of the tracks of Fig. 1e and Fig. 1f, whereas Fig. 1h shows the intersection of the same tracks. In general, given two marks, their similarity is a real value calculated as the volume covered by their intersection divided by the total volume (the union of them). The lowest similarity is zero (tracks with no intersection), whereas the highest is one (identical tracks).

## 2.3   The Detection Subsystem

The detection subsystem enhances and discovers relevant variation of the current distribution through sharpening and domain-dependent analytics. For this purpose, to achieve a better distinction of the critical phenomena, the $s$-shaped activation function is applied to the similarity output. As an effect, at each tick values lower than a lower threshold $\alpha$ are further decreased, whereas values higher than an upper threshold $\beta$ are further amplified, to evidence major dissimilarity.

Fig. 2a shows the similarity values between current and reference track, in a sampling period of 14 hours and 35 minutes (175 total ticks, 1 tick corresponding to 5 minutes). A similarity value close to 1 means that there are no behavior differences, while a similarity close to 0 means that there are significant modification in behavior. Here, two horizontal dotted lines are also shown, representing sample values of the lower ($\alpha$=0.4) and the upper ($\beta$=0.8) thresholds of the $s$-shape. In Fig. 2b, the thick line represents the s-shaped similarity, whereas the thin line represents actual behavioral changes, annotated by a human observer who analyzed video tracks of the elderly. From Fig. 2a and Fig. 2b it is apparent that three actual behavioral changes occurred, but only the third one is detected by the system. To improve the system quality, the system parameters can be better adjusted. In Fig. 2c a quality indicator is shown, by using the third event of Fig. 2b. More specifically, let $\ddot{t} = [\underline{t}, \overline{t}]$ be the duration of an actual event, and $\ddot{\tau} = [\underline{\tau}, \overline{\tau}] = [\min\{i | S(T_i, T_i^{REF}) = 0\}, \max\{i | S(T_i, T_i^{REF}) = 0\}]$ be the duration of an event detected by the system. To assess the error between the actual and the detected event we compute the one-dimensional similarity between the two time intervals: $S(\ddot{t}, \ddot{\tau}) = (\ddot{t} \cap \ddot{\tau})/(\ddot{t} \cup \ddot{\tau})$. From the interval arithmetic: $S(\ddot{t}, \ddot{\tau}) = \max\{0, \min(\overline{\tau}, \overline{t}) - \max(\underline{\tau}, \underline{t})\}/\{\max(\overline{\tau}, \overline{t}) - \min(\underline{\tau}, \underline{t})\} = (\overline{t} - \underline{\tau})/(\overline{\tau} - \underline{t})$. To assess the global error, the average similarity is calculated considering each $j$-th event.

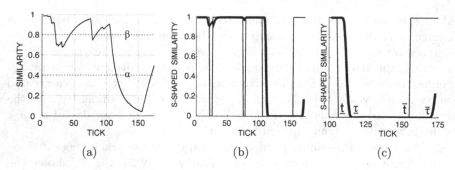

**Fig. 2.** (a) Similarity between current and reference tracks, in a sampling period of 14 hours and 35 minutes; (b) $s$-shaped similarity (thick line) with $\alpha=0.4$ and $\beta=0.8$, against actual behavioral changes of the elderly (thin line); (c) start and end of an actual (thin line) and a detected (thick line) behavioral event

In order to show the generality of the approach, in the next section we briefly present a second real-world case study, concerning a vendor rating problem.

## 2.4 Application of the Approach to Another Case Study: Vendor Rating

Let us consider four manufacturing competitor firms, with the role of buyers with respect to a community of vendors. Context-aware information is provided by a community system for supplier relationship management, to carry out a *vendor rating* (VR). An important problem in the field is that, usually, a buyer is not willing to share the performance of his vendors, to keep a competitive advantage over its rivals. However, without information sharing each buyer can analyze only his subset of vendors. A solution to this problem is to use marker-based stigmergy for analyzing vendors context-aware information, so as to maximize its usability without violating its market value. Indeed, stigmergy preserves privacy since it controls the level of *perturbation* of information, which means that information is scrambled to be partially hidden but up to preserve its utility. Stigmergy allows masking plain information by replacing it with a mark, as a surrogate keeping some piece of the original information. The perturbation level can be controlled via mark's structural parameters. More specifically to increase the mark's width $\varepsilon$ implies a higher uncertainty, whereas to decrease the evaporation $\theta$ implies a higher merging of past and new marks. A very large width ($\varepsilon \to \infty$) and a very small evaporation rate ($\theta \to 0$) may cause growing collective marks with no stationary level, because of a too expansive and long-term memory effect. A very small width ($\varepsilon \to 0$) and a very small evaporation rate ($\theta \to 0$) may cause the plain real values to appear for long time.

Fig. 3a-c shows three stigmergic perturbation levels applied to vendors' productivity values, calculated as output divided by labor, with increasing values of $\varepsilon$. We used information of publicly available dataset [9]. More specifically, in the marking subsystem, each $k$-th buyer locally produces a track $T_k$ (represented as

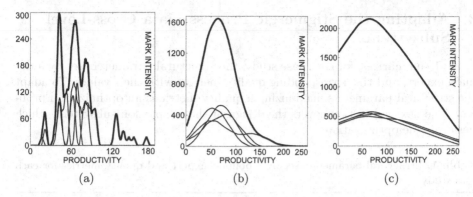

**Fig. 3.** Different stigmergic perturbation levels, in a community of four buyers, represented by individual track (thin line) and aggregated track (thick line). (a) low perturbation with $\varepsilon$=5: comparable but interpretable performance; (b) medium perturbation with $\varepsilon$=60: comparable and non-interpretable performance; (c) high perturbation with $\varepsilon$=200: non-comparable and non-interpretable performance.

a thin line in figure) by aggregating marks on the productivity of his vendors. In the perception subsystem, the tracks of the four buyers are aggregated and averaged online to create a reference track, $T^{REF}$ (represented as a thick line in the figure), together with its average level, $\overline{T^{REF}}$, both shared between the buyers. The similarity value $S_k$ between $T_k$ and $T^{REF}$ is then calculated. In the detection subsystem, such similarity is used as a performance indicator, to compare the buyer track with respect to the reference track. Moreover, to assess the utility of the information against its privacy, a quality indicator has been also defined as the product between $(\overline{T^{REF}})$ and the variance of $S_k$, to take into account two factors:

(a) *low perturbation* ($\varepsilon = 5$): a high variance of $S_k$ and a low $(\overline{T^{REF}})$ makes the individual tracks easily interpretable from the aggregated track; as an example, Fig. 3a shows a bad scenario where an individual track in the interval [120,180] is not overlapped to other individual tracks and then it is transparent to the other buyers;

(b) *average perturbation* ($\varepsilon = 60$): an average variance of $S_k$ and an average $(\overline{T^{REF}})$ makes the individual tracks totally overlapped, as shown in the good scenario of Fig. 3b;

(c) *high perturbation* ($\varepsilon = 200$): a low variance of $S_k$ and a high $(\overline{T^{REF}})$ makes the buyers performance non-comparable, as shown in the bad scenario of Fig. 3c. In addition to $\varepsilon$, other structural parameters may also affect the perturbation level. As shown for both scenarios presented in this paper, to choose the parameters corresponding to the best quality of the performance indicators is crucial in the proposed approach. The next section is devoted to the adaptation subsystem, which traverses all levels of processing since it may affect all parameters to find the best setting.

## 3　Adapting the Stigmergic Process via a Cross-Level Subsystem

Table 1 summarizes, for each case study, the structural parameters set by a domain expert, and the corresponding quality metrics with their values. To adapt the structural parameters maximizing a quality metric is an optimization problem. The next subsection covers the design of the adaptation subsystem, which performs the optimization.

**Table 1.** Structural parameters set by a domain expert and quality metrics for each case study

| Case | width $(\varepsilon)$ | evap.$(\theta)$ | thr.$(\alpha, \beta)$ | Quality metric |
|------|------|------|------|------|
| AAL | 10 | 0.9 | 0.4, 0.4 | $Q = avg\{S(\ddot{t}_j, \ddot{r}_j)\}$=0.63 |
| VR | 60 | 0.9 | 0.0, 1.0 | $Q = var\{S(T_k, T^{REF})\} \cdot avg\{T^{REF}\}$=4.57 |

### 3.1　The Adaptation Subsystem

Many optimization problems may be solved by *search* methods, i.e., procedures that look for a solution by trying out many attempts until a satisfactory result is obtained. Biologically inspired algorithms (BIAs) implement search mechanisms applicable to problems that cannot be efficiently solved using exact and analytical techniques [8]. Indeed, it is apparent from Table 1 that each case employs a different quality metrics. Then, an optimization method using a "black box" approach, i.e., which is not based on formal properties of the quality function, may be effective. Due to their random nature, BIAs can find near-optimal solutions rather the optimal solution.

BIAs optimize a problem by iteratively trying to improve a population of candidate solutions with regard to a given measure of quality, or *fitness*. Solutions are improved by means of stochastic transformation mechanisms inspired by biology, such as reproduction, mutation, recombination, selection, survival, swarm, movement, in an environment whose dynamics are represented by the quality measure.

Since the mid-sixties many BIAs have been proposed, and many efforts have also been devoted to compare them. In the last decade, most notably the following three classes of methods attracted attention: Genetic Algorithm (GA), Differential Evolution (DE), and Particle Swarm Optimization (PSO) [8]. A quantitative comparison of GA, DE, and PSO is beyond the scope of this paper. For the sake of brevity, an excerpt of their qualitative properties is summarized in Table 2 [8]. The interested reader is referred to the specialized literature for further details. It is apparent from Table 2 that DE is a simple and efficient adaptive scheme for global optimization. For this reason, it was selected to design the adaptation subsystem. Next subsection is devoted to DE and its different variants.

**Table 2.** An excerpt of the properties of the algorithms GA, PSO, and DE [8]

| Property | GA | PSO | DE |
|---|---|---|---|
| Require ranking of solution | Yes | No | No |
| Influence of population size on solution time | Exponential | Linear | Linear |
| Influence of best solution on population | Medium | Most | Less |
| Average fitness cannot get worse | False | False | True |
| Tendency for premature convergence | Medium | High | Low |
| Density of search space | Less | More | More |
| Ability to reach good solution without local search | Less | More | More |

### 3.2   The Differential Evolution

In DE algorithm, a solution is represented by a real $D$-dimensional vector, where $D$ is the number of parameters to tune. DE starts with a population of $N$ candidate solutions, injected or randomly generated. At each iteration and for each member (target) of the population, a mutant vector is created by mutation of randomly selected members and then a trial vector is created by crossover of mutant and target. Finally, the best fitting among trial and target replaces the target. More formally:

**DifferentialEvolution()**
  $P(0) \leftarrow$ InitializePopulation()
  $f \leftarrow$ ComputeFitness($P(0)$)
  $t \leftarrow 0$
  **while** !$stopCondition$ {
    **for each** $p(t) \in P(t)$ {
      $p' \leftarrow$ GenerateMutant($P(t), p(t)$)
      $q \leftarrow$ Crossover($p(t), p'$)
      **if** $f(q) < f(p(t))$
      **then** $p(t+1) \leftarrow q$
      **else** $p(t+1) \leftarrow p(t)$
    }
    $t \leftarrow t+1$
    $f \leftarrow ComputeFitness(P(t))$
  }

In the literature, many variants of the DE algorithm have been designed, by combining different structure and parameterization of mutation and crossover operators [10]. Mutant vector is usually generated by combining three randomly selected vectors from the population excluding the target vector. More formally:

**GenerateMutant($P, p$)**
  $p_1, p_2, p_3 \leftarrow$ randomExtraction($P - p$)
  **return** $p_1 + F \cdot (p_2 - p_3)$

The scaling factor $F \in [0, 2]$ is a parameter of the DE algorithm. We used a commonly set value, i.e., $F = 0.8$.

There are different crossover methods. Results show that a competitive approach can be based on binomial crossover [11]. With binomial crossover, a component of the offspring is taken with probability $CR$ from the mutant vector and with probability $1 - CR$ from the target vector. More formally:

**BinomialCrossover**$(p, q)$
   $k \leftarrow$ randomInteger$(1, n)$
   **for** $i = 1$ **to** $n$ {
     **if** randomReal$(0,1) < CR$ **or** $i = k$
     **then** $z_i \leftarrow p_i$
     **else** $z_i \leftarrow q_i$
   }
   **return** $z$

A small crossover probability leads to a vector that is more similar to the target vector while the opposite favors the mutant vector. We used a commonly set value, i.e., $CR = 0.7$, with the population size $N$ equals to 15.

### 3.3  Experimental Studies

The aim of this section is to illustrate the possibilities offered by our approach, rather than to focus on a systematic optimization spectrum. For this purpose, we experimented the optimization offered by DE on both AAL and VR case studies. We used the parameters values found by domain experts as an initial (injected) solution, and the quality metrics already summarized in Table 1.

Fig. 4 shows the fitness versus number of generations for both cases. Here, it is apparent that the parametric optimization sensibly improved the initial setting, after a small number of generations (about 10) and with a very fast convergence: the quality metric has been highly improved, up to 44% and 62%, for AAL and VR, respectively. The parameters and the quality metrics (fitness) values

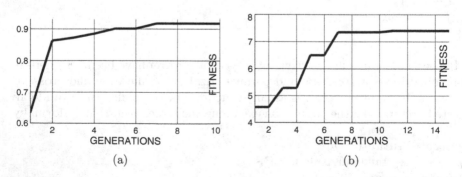

(a)

(b)

**Fig. 4.** Fitness versus number of generations for two case studies: (a) AAL; (b) VR

**Table 3.** Best solution provided by the adaptation module for each case study

| Case | width ($\varepsilon$) | evap.($\theta$) | thr.($\alpha, \beta$) | Quality metric |
|------|-----------------------|-----------------|-----------------------|----------------|
| AAL  | 37                    | 0.51            | 0.52, 0.52            | 0.91           |
| VR   | 42                    | 0.94            | 0.00, 1.00            | 7.40           |

provided at the end of the optimization processes are summarized in Table 3, to be easily compared with the values set by domain experts (Table 1). In the AAL case $\varepsilon$ has been sensibly increased and $\theta$ has been considerably reduced, whereas in the VR case $\varepsilon$ has been strongly reduced keeping $\theta$ about constant. To focus the analysis on the marking structure, $\alpha$ and $\beta$ were constrained to be equal (AAL) or fixed to constant values (VR).

## 4 Conclusions

We have presented a novel approach to analyze context-aware information. The approach is based on representing the context datum as a mark, to enable self-organization between data. An architecture exploiting the mechanisms of the marker-based stigmergy have been designed and discussed on two real-world domains. An adaptation subsystem based on differential evolution has been also designed and experimented to enable a self-parameterization of the architecture. Experimental results show the effectiveness of the approach. However, to ensure high-quality design, the system should be cross-validated against more dynamic context data series. Indeed, one of the problems to solve when optimizing parameters is that optimization encompasses all available scenarios at once and may include different contexts, spread across the entire search space. This global tuning leads to increasing difficulties from the practical perspective, due to fitting different scaled spatiotemporal data. An alternative is local modeling, which requires an architecture based on sub-models that focus predominantly on some selected regions of the entire domain. An overall model is then formed by combining such local models. This modular layer may provide a topology offering a considerable level of flexibility, as the resulting sub-models can be highly diversified according to the distribution of the local data. For this reason, future work will be focused on using more dynamic context data series, to assess the fitting properties of the current system and to enable the design of a composite architecture.

## References

1. Cimino, M.G.C.A., Lazzerini, B., Marcelloni, F., Ciaramella, A.: An Adaptive Rule-Based Approach for Managing Situation-Awareness. Expert Systems With Applications 39(12), 10796–10811 (2012)
2. Feng, L., Apers, P.M.G., Jonker, W.: Towards context-aware data management for ambient intelligence. In: Galindo, F., Takizawa, M., Traunmüller, R. (eds.) DEXA 2004. LNCS, vol. 3180, pp. 422–431. Springer, Heidelberg (2004)

3. Ciaramella, A., Cimino, M.G.C.A., Marcelloni, F., Straccia, U.: Combining Fuzzy Logic and Semantic Web to Enable Situation-Awareness in Service Recommendation. In: Bringas, P.G., Hameurlain, A., Quirchmayr, G. (eds.) DEXA 2010, Part I. LNCS, vol. 6261, pp. 31–45. Springer, Heidelberg (2010)

4. Ciaramella, A., Cimino, M.G.C.A., Lazzerini, B., Marcelloni, F.: A Situation-Aware Resource Recommender Based on Fuzzy and Semantic Web Rules. International Journal of Uncertainty, Fuzziness and Knowledge-Based Systems (IJUFKS) 18(4), 411–430 (2010)

5. Vernon, D., Giorgio, M., Giulio, S.: A survey of artificial cognitive systems: Implications for the autonomous development of mental capabilities in computational agents. IEEE Transactions on Evolutionary Computation 11(2), 151–180 (2007)

6. Avvenuti, M., Daniel, C., Cimino, M.G.C.A.: MARS, a Multi-Agent System for Assessing Rowers' Coordination via Motion-Based Stigmergy. Sensors 13(9), 12218–12243 (2013)

7. Van Dyke Parunak, H.: A survey of environments and mechanisms for human-human stigmergy. In: Weyns, D., Van Dyke Parunak, H., Michel, F. (eds.) E4MAS 2005. LNCS (LNAI), vol. 3830, pp. 163–186. Springer, Heidelberg (2006)

8. Kachitvichyanukul, V.: Comparison of three evolutionary algorithms: GA, PSO, and DE. Industrial Engineering & Management Systems 11(3), 215–223 (2012)

9. Bache, K., Lichman, M.: UCI Machine Learning Repository. Irvine, CA: University of California, School of Information and Computer Science(2013), http://archive.ics.uci.edu/ml

10. Mezura-Montes, E., Velázquez-Reyes, J., Coello Coello, A.: A comparative study of differential evolution variants for global optimization. In: Proceedings of the 8th Annual Conference on Genetic and Evolutionary Computation (GECCO), pp. 485–492. ACM (2006)

11. Zaharie, D.: A comparative analysis of crossover variants in differential evolution. In: Proceedings of IMCSIT 2007, pp. 171–181 (2007)

# Modeling Manufacturing Processes with Disturbances - A New Method Based on Algebraic-Logical Meta-Models

Ewa Dudek-Dyduch[✉]

Department of Automatics and Biomedical Engineering,
AGH University of Science and Technology, Kraków, Poland
edd@agh.edu.pl

**Abstract.** The paper discusses modeling and control of discrete manufacturing processes (DMP) with disturbances of various types: machine failures, quality defects, unexpected additional orders etc. A novel formal modeling method is presented for DMP with disturbances. The method is based on formal description of DMP given by the algebraic logical meta model (ALMM). It is called two stage AL model transformation method (2SALMT method). Method application is shown herein for IT systems managing manufacturing on both operational and tactical levels. The paper also shows how 2SALMT method can be applied for modeling scheduling problems with disturbances such as machine failure.

**Keywords:** Discrete manufacturing processes · Discrete manufacturing processes with disturbances · Algebraic-logical meta-model · Two stage AL model transformation method · 2SALMT method · ALMM of DMP · Multistage decision process · Failure modes · Manufacturing defects · Switching algebraic-logical models

## 1 Introduction

The paper refers to modeling and control of discrete manufacturing processes (DMP) encountering disturbances of various types. The notion of a disturbance is understood in a broad sense here, unlike the definition encountered in the classical control theory. Such disturbances can take forms of unexpected events with a specific details ranging from an unexpected machine breakdown, a new incoming order to be realized, a detection of quality defect that requires repeat performance of certain operations or others.

Even though issues related to DMP with disturbances have been raised in multiple research papers [1,2,10,11,15,12] no satisfactory solutions have been offered so far. The first step towards such a solution is to provide a formal method to model processes with disturbances (belonging to various classes). This is necessary as a basis for further development of control methods and algorithms realized both offline and online.

The main aim of this work is to present a new, unified modeling method for manu-facturing processes with disturbances to be implemented in IT systems used for discrete manufacturing process control.

© Springer International Publishing Switzerland 2015
L. Rutkowski et al. (Eds.): ICAISC 2015, Part II, LNAI 9120, pp. 353–363, 2015.
DOI: 10.1007/978-3-319-19369-4_32

The method presented is based on Algebraic-Logical Meta-Model of Multistage decision process (ALMM of MDP) as well as the theoretical background established based on, the said ALMM theory, both created and developed by the author heretofore [3,4].

Using the ALMM of MDP it is possible to develop so-called algebraic logical (AL) models for a large class of discrete optimization problems including control problems of various manufacturing processes, logistics problems, project management problems and others [3,4,5,12,14]. The paper shows that although AL models are deterministic, they can also be used to model processes with disturbances (partially non-deterministic) as long as the disturbances occur infrequently.

The modeling method for discrete manufacturing processes with disturbances proposed herein is called a two-stage AL model transformation method (2SALMT method). The method allows the determination (calculation) of optimized control decisions in case of emergence of various disturbances even though timing of such emergence is not known in advance.

To date two papers have been published with regard to DMP with disturbances that involve AL models. In [10] ALMM based approach was presented for scheduling DMP in a failure mode. [12] presents a preliminary idea of modeling manufacturing process with a disturbance consisting in manufacturing defects. The idea was developed for a flow shop system and was referred to as "switching algebraic-logical models". The method presented in this article is different and more developed in comparison with [12]. Moreover it is suitable for disturbances of many different classes and can be applied for many different manufacturing processes.

Control of discrete manufacturing processes with disturbances is a current hot topic. In particular, control in failure modes as well as diagnostics of pre-failure states are of significance [1,2,10,11,15].

Therefore, for illustrative purposes a simple manufacturing process is presented here just with machine failure as a disturbance. The AL model for scheduling process on parallel machines is shown as well as the AL model for the disturbed process obtained by means of the 2SALMT method.

## 2    Algebraic-Logical Meta-Model of Multistage Decision Process

The notion of a multistage decision process is understandable on an intuitive level and has been used for long. Most commonly, a multistage process graph model is applied in form of a decision tree. Such graph model, though, is not capable of including all kinds of information regarding the problem to be solved, in particular the information defining the state, decision, algorithm used to generate consecutive states and various temporal relationships of the process. Furthermore, the graph model is only appropriate for problem instances, not for a problem understood as a set of instances. That is why it was necessary to establish a formal model for the multistage decision processes, or a meta-model of the multistage decision process to be more specific, that would allow the inclusion of more information. The meta-model concept was developed by the author [3,4] and put to use in multiple cases [5,6,7,8,9].

The meta-model name has been changed as different aspects of the meta-model was stressed. The current most general name is the algebraic-logical meta-model of multistage decision process (ALMM of MDP) or an algebraic-logical meta-model (ALMM) for an abbreviated name. In [3,4] author has provided two base classes of multistage decision processes: a common process, denoted here as cMDP (or AL-cMDP to emphasize the algebraic-logical description) and a dynamic process, denoted as MDDP (or AL-MDDP) [11].

Below a formal definition of ALMM of MDDP is given. With its use, models can be established for many discrete optimization problems, hence the name "meta-model". The definition refers to dynamic decision processes, i.e. processes wherein both the constraints and the transition function (and in particular the possible decision sets) depend on time. Therefore, the concept of the so-called "generalized state" has been introduced, defined as a pair containing both the state and the time instant.

*Definition 1.* The algebraic logical model of multistage dynamic decision process is a knowledge representation paradigm that specifies any AL-MDDP by the sextuple $(U, S, s_0, f, S_N, S_G)$ where $U$ is a set of decisions, $S = X \times T$ is a set named a set of generalized states, $X$ is a set of proper states, $T \subset \Re + \cup \{0\}$ is a subset of non negative real numbers representing the time instants, $f : U \times S \rightarrow S$ is a partial function called a transition function, (it does not have to be determined for all elements of the set $U \times S$), $s_0 = (x_0, t_0)$, $S_N \subset S$, $S_G \subset S$ are respectively: an initial generalized state, a set of not admissible generalized states, and a set of goal generalized states, i.e. the states in which we want the process to take place at the end. Obviously, $S_G \cap S_N = \varnothing$.

The transition function is defined by means of two functions, $f = (f_x, f_t)$ where $f_x : U \times X \times T \rightarrow X$ determines the next state, $f_t : U \times X \times T \rightarrow T$ determines the next time instant. It is assumed that the difference $\Delta t = f_t(u, x, t) - t$ has a value that is both finite and positive.

Thus, as a result of the decision u that is taken or realized at the proper state $x$ and the moment $t$, the state of the process changes for $x' = f_x(u, x, t)$ that is observed at the moment $t' = f_t(u, x, t) = t + \Delta t$.

Because not all decisions defined formally make sense in certain situations, the transition function $f$ is defined as a partial one. As a result, all limitations concerning the decisions in a given state $s$ can be defined in a convenient way by means of so-called sets of possible decisions $U_p(s)$, and defined as: $U_p(s) = \{u \in U : (u, s) \in Dom f\}$.

In the most general case, sets $U$ and $X$ may be presented as a Cartesian product $U = U^1 \times U^2 \times ... \times U^m$, $X = X^1 \times X^2 \times ... \times X^n$ i.e. $u = (u^1, u^2, ..., u^m)$, $x = (x^1, x^2, ..., x^n)$. Particular $u^i$, $i = 1, 2..m$ represent separate decisions that must or may be taken at the same time and relate to particular objects. There are no limitations imposed on the sets; in particular they do not have to be numerical. Thus values of particular co-ordinates of a state or a decision may be names of elements (symbols) as well as some objects (e.g. finite set, sequence etc.). The sets $S_N$, $S_G$ and $U_p$ are formally defined with the use of logical formulae, **hence the algebraic-logic model descriptor**.

Based on the meta-model given herein, algebraic-logical models (AL models) may be created for individual problems consisting in seeking admissible or optimal solutions. In case of admissible solution, AL model is equivalent to suitable multistage decision process, hence is denoted as process $\boldsymbol{P}$. If an **optimization** problem is encountered, it requires a further definition of an optimization criterion $\boldsymbol{Q}$, and then it is denoted as a $(\boldsymbol{P},\ \boldsymbol{Q})$ pair.

The key point for two stage AL model transformation method is the proper definition of the problem and its instance [3]. A problem definition requires a prior dataset definition as well as definition of the six components of the process $\boldsymbol{P}$. This way all the information and constraints defining the problem of seeking an admissible solution are split into 6 basic components: the definition of a state, and in particular the information structure defining the state, the definition of a decision (and its structure), an algorithm that defines the transition function and the definition of goal states and non-admissible states.

For specific data (provided overtly) a problem instance $(P,Q)$ is a result, with $P$ standing for a so-called individual process and $Q$ for a criterion calculated for the instance of problem.

At the same time, an individual process represents a set of its trajectories that starts from the initial state $s_0$. It is assumed that no state of a trajectory, apart from the last one, may belong to the set $S_N$ or has an empty set of possible decisions. Only a trajectory that ends in the set of goal states is admissible. The task of optimization lies in the fact of finding such an admissible decision sequence $\tilde{u}$ that determines an admissible trajectory and minimizes a certain criterion $Q$.

A defined optimization **problem** is a set of optimization tasks that have a commonly determined data set (the same type of data fulfilling the commonly determined properties), common (parametric) definition of individual process set and common (parametric) definition of criterion functions. A set of individual processes determined as above will also be referred to as a problem process denoted as a $\boldsymbol{P}$, while an individual process is denoted as $P$.

The common definition of an individual process set includes common (identical) definitions of process specification components, that is the definitions of state set, decision set, transition function (including $U_p(s)$ sets), initial state as well as goal state set and non-admissible state set.

## 3    Algebraic-Logical Model of Discrete Manufacturing Process

Control of DMP lies in determining a manner of performing some set of jobs under restrictions referring to machines/devices, resources, energy, time, transportation possibilities, order of operation performing and others. Let us notice, that control of DMP is understood in a broad sense than scheduling.

The meta-model presented herein can be applied quite simply in modeling a whole host of discrete manufacturing processes. To achieve AL model of some DMP all sorts of technological and organizational constraints need to be reflected in the definition of process $P$ i.e. included in the definition of state set, decision set, possible decision sets $U_p(s)$, transition function algorithm $f(s)$ as well as the non-admissible state set w $S_N$ and the goal state set $S_G$.

Any AL model of DMP includes the following properties of a real manufacturing process:

- influence on the process (process control) and its observable state change both occur at strictly determined temporal instances, with the instances not necessarily equidistant; in a general case, the next time instance depends on the state, decision and current time; control can be achieved both by physical signals and by decisions; thus no limitations are imposed as to the structure of the control and state (it does not have to be determined in a numerical space),
- manufacturing technology specifics determine decisions that are possible in given situations (e.g. in terms of sequential constraints), on the other hand not all formally defined decisions would make sense in certain situations; this is taken into account when determining the possible decisions set $U_p(s)$, thus a calculation of the transition function is a two-step process - first the decision is checked for its presence in the $U_p(s)$ set and then the next state is determined,
- there are additional constraints within the process regarding both time and the proper state (deadlines, raw material constraints); these are taken into account through definition of the inadmissible states $S_N$.

## 3.1 Exemplary AL Model for a Manufacturing Process

This section presents an AL model of parallel identical machine processes as a sample model for a simple manufacturing process. The model given herein expands the model presented in [3].

*Example 1.*

A finite set of jobs is given, represented by natural numbers $J = \{1, 2...n\}$ and a function $p : J \to R^+$ that determines the processing times. The jobs are to be performed using $m$ parallel identical machines. Preemptions of jobs is not allowed. We have to find an assigning jobs to the machines and order of the job performance so that any regular performance index is at minimum (e.g. the weighted sum of the particular jobs completion times is at minimum). For notation convenience we introduce a job number 0 with processing time of $p(0) = 0$ to represent no job assigned to a machine. For all other jobs the processing time is positive. The job set plus the zero job will be denoted as $J^*$, hence $J^* = J \cup 0$.

Let us define the elements specifying the process $P = (U, S, s_0, f, S_N, S_G)$ and provide their interpretation. The proper state $x$ is determined by the set of completed jobs and the states of particular machines. The decision consists in determining the next jobs to be performed by the particular machines.

Thus, the decision values are the names (numbers) of the chosen jobs. Formally:
The set of a proper states $X = X^0 \times X^1 \times X^2 \times ... \times X^m$, a proper state is
a $m$-touple $x = (x^0, x^1, x^2...x^m)$ where:

$x^0 \subset 2^J$ - a set of completed jobs,

$x^k = (\beta^k, \tau^k)$, $k = 1, 2..m$ - the $k$-th machine states where: $\beta^k \in J^* - x^0$,
$k = 1, 2..m$ - denotes the number of a job that is currently performed by $k$-th
machine, $\tau^k \in \mathbb{R}$, $k = 1, 2..m$ - time remaining to complete the performed job
(if $\tau^k \geq 0$); time $\tau^k \leq 0$ denotes that the performed job is completed and the
machine is free;

The initial state $s_0 = (x_0, t_0)$ where $t_0 = 0$ and $x_0 = (\varnothing, (0, 0), (0, 0), ...(0, 0))$.
It denotes that no job is assigned to any machine to perform and no job has
been completed jet.

The set of non-admissible states $S_N = \varnothing$.

The set of goal states $S_G = \{(x, t) : x^0 = J\}$ - it denotes that the process is
in a goal state if all the jobs are completed.

The set of decisions $U \subset J^* \times J^* \times .. \times J^*$; $u = (u^1, u^2..u^m)$, with the $u^k$
coordinate denoting job number assigned to the $k$-th machine as a result of the
decision.

To define a possible decision set $U_p(s)$ let us introduce the notion of a decision
state of a machine and define a set of jobs processed by machines in a state $s$ (that
is the currently processed jobs) $J_M(s)$,

$$J_M(s) = \bigcup_{k=1}^{m} \beta_k \setminus \{0\}$$

We say that a state $s = (x, t)$ is a decision state for the $k$-the machine if for the
state occures $\tau^k \leq 0$, that is if a job processed by the $k$-th machine is completed
while no new is assigned yet. Then, for a correctly developed model, $\beta^k = 0$.
The decision state set for machine $k$ will be denoted as $S_d(k)$.

Sets of possible decisions $U_p(s) = U_p^1(s) \times U_p^2(s) \times ..U_p^m(s)$, with the following
properties:

(a) sets $U_p^k(s) \subset \{(J \setminus x^0 \setminus J_M(s)) \cup \{0\}\}$ for $k = 1, 2..m$ (only jobs that have
    not been completed yet and are not currently processed can be assigned for
    processing),
(b) $u = (0, 0, ..0) \notin U_p(x)$ (it is necessary to assign at least one job for processing
    in a state that is not a goal state),
(c) $u^l = u^k \Leftrightarrow u^l = 0 \wedge u^k = 0$ for $k, l = 1, 2, ..m$, $k \neq l$ (the same job cannot
    be assigned simultaneously to two different machines; this property will be
    satisfied as long as $U_p(s)$ and the transition function are defined properly),
(d) if a given state $s = (x, t)$ is not a decision state for the $k$-th machine, that
    is $\tau^k > 0$, then $U_p(s) = \{\beta^k\}$.

Let us determine the transition function $f(u_i, x_i, t_i) = (x_{i+1}, t_{i+1})$.

We need to bear in mind that the transition function is defined as a pair of
$f = (f_x, f_t)$, $f_x(u_i, x_i, t_i) = x_{i+1}$, $f_t(u_i, x_i, t_i) = t_{i+1}$.

Let $u_i = (u_i^1, ..., u_i^m)$, $x = (x_i^0, x_i^1, ...x_i^m)$, $f_t(u_i, x_i, t_i) = t_{i+1} = t_i + \Delta t_i$ while $\Delta t_i = min^+\{p(u_i^1), p(u_i^2), ...p(u_i^m), \tau_i^1, \tau_i^2...\tau_i^m\}$ where $min^+$ denotes minimization only for elements of positive values.

Let us define the $f_x$ function.

For the process contemplated here, a transition function can be expressed as a vector of the $f_x = (f_x^0, f_x^1, ...f_x^m)^T$ function. Algorithms for functions: $f_x^0(u_i, s_i) = x_{i+1}^0$ and $f_x^k(u_i, s_i) = x_{i+1}^k$ for $k = 1, 2..m$ differ.

In order to be able to provide an algorithm for the $f_x^0$ function, let us define a set of jobs (job indices) completed in state $s_{i+1} = (x_{i+1}, t_{i+1})$ as a result of a decision $u_i$ taken in a state $x_i$ denoted as $J_{cmp}(u_i, x_i, t_i)$. Such a set is a sum of two subsets: a subset of jobs started earlier (being processed) $J_{cmp}(x_i)$, with completion time of $\Delta t_i$, and a subset $J_{cmp}(u_i)$, containing jobs assigned under decision $u_i$, with processing time of $\Delta t_i$.

$J_{cmp}(x_i) = \{x_i^k : \tau_i^k = \Delta t_i, \ k \in M\}$

$J_{cmp}(u_i) = \{u_i^k : p(u_i^k) = \Delta t_i, \ k \in M\}$

$J_{cmp}(u_i, x_i, t_i) = J_{cmp}(u_i) \cup J_{cmp}(x_i)$

$x_{i+1}^0 = x_i^0 \cup J_{cmp}(u_i, x_i, t_i)$

Algorithm for function $f_x^k(u_i, s_i) = x_{i+1}^k = (\beta_{i+1}^k, \ \tau_{i+1}^k)$ for $k = 1, 2..m$:

(a) if state $s_i$ is not a decision state for the $k$-th machine, $s_i \notin S_d(k)$, then:
$U_p^k(s_i) = \{\beta_i^k\}$, $\beta_{i+1}^k = \beta_i^k$ and $\tau_{i+1}^k = \tau_i^k - \Delta t_i$,

(b) if state $s_i$ is a decision state for the $k$-th machine, that is $s_i \in S_d(k)$, then:
$\beta_{i+1}^k = u_i^k, ... \tau_{i+1}^k = p(u_i^k)$.

The same in an abbreviated form:

$$x_{i+1}^k = \begin{cases} (\beta_i^k, \tau_i^k - \Delta t_i) \text{ for } s_i \notin S_d(k) \\ (u_i^k, p(u_i^k)) \text{ for } s_i \in S_d(k) \end{cases}$$

# 4  Two Stage AL Model Transformation Method for Processes with Disturbances

Manufacturing disturbances can be grouped into several typical classes, such as machine and/or transportation failures, unexpected raw material shortages (or poor quality), detection of quality defects, unexpected orders and others. Obviously, within each of these classes denoted as $E_k$ $k = 1, 2, ..$ production managers differentiate certain disturbance types $e_i$ $i = 1, 2..$ that are not uniform (e.g. breakdown of various pieces of machinery, different types of quality defects). It is also significant that the disturbances in question occur only rarely, hence theory of stochastic processes is not applicable here.

This chapter shows how a modeling technology based on ALMM of MDDP can be used to develop a uniform way of modeling manufacturing processes, both in a regular mode and obstructed by unforeseen disturbances. What is more, the modeling methodology presented is suitable for all the disturbance classes mentioned above.

## 4.1  Base Process and Process with Disturbance

It is known that every manufacturing process has its characteristic structure
determined by machinery and logistics resources as well as other organizational
constraints. All these contribute towards the regular AL model structure where
the process is referred to as the base process $P_B$ as given by definitions of state
and decision structures, transition function algorithm, definitions of $U_p(s)$ sets,
definitions of $S_N$ and $S_G$ subsets and definition of the $s_0$ state.

In the most general case a disturbance causes changes to the AL model i.e.
the base process $P_B$. Such changes consist in modifications to definitions of
one or many elements of the following: $X$, $U$, $f$, $S_N$, $S_G$. Finally, AL model of
a disturbed process, denoted as $P_D$ is defined by $X_D$, $U_D$, $f_D$, $S_{ND}$, $S_{GD}$. The
modifications are performed at the first stage of transformation in the two-stage
modeling method.

If a specific set of jobs and all parameter values are given (processing times,
due dates, etc.), we are dealing with a specific base process instance i.e. the
individual base process $P_B$. Such process proceeds in line with a pre-determined
decision sequence $\tilde{u}$ and as such corresponds to the trajectory $\tilde{s}$.

A disturbance $e_k$ occurs at a certain state of the trajectory $s_D = (x_D, t_D)$
that is not known in advance. To enable process control that would minimize
the impact of such disturbance a new individual process $P_D$ (a disturbed process)
needs to be determined. The algorithm based on a two-stage AL model transformation method yields that very modified individual process $P_D$ that requires
new controls to be determined.

The two-stage transformation algorithm depends on the type of DMP and
its AL model, the class of the $E_i$ disturbance (machine failure, manufacturing
defect, additional orders, other), the specific disturbance $e_k$ belonging to class
$E_i$, the process state at which the disturbance occurred (or was noticed) and the
availability of additional information such as disturbance duration and remedial
procedure.

**The first stage** of transformation consists in modification of the AL model
of the regular DMP i.e. modification of the base process $P_B$ resulting in development of an AL model of disturbed DMP i.e. process $P_D$. For a given type of
disturbance ek the transformation is performed using one or more transformation
rules that modify appropriate elements of the base process. The first stage transformations denoted as TRANS1 $(P_B, e_k)$ for $k = 1, 2$, yield processes $P_D(e_k)$ for
all types of disturbances included. These models are stored in a knowledge base
of the IT system together with a model of the base process. They are used as
a basis for simulation software of manufacturing processes (normal and disturbed
mode) and for control algorithms.

**The second stage** takes the state and time of disturbance occurrence into
account. The second stage of transformation consists of determination of an individual process $P_D(e_k)$ for a disturbance $e_k$ noticed at state $s_D = (x_D, t_D)$. The
second stage transformation TRANS2 $(P_B, e_k, s_D)$ takes an individual process
$P_B$ and converts it into an appropriate individual process
$P_D = (U_D, S_D, s_{0D}, f_D, S_{ND}, S_{GD})$. The $s_D$ state is transformed into an initial

state $s_{0D}$ of the $P_D$ process. If the state structure for process $\boldsymbol{P_D}$ (obtained under the first stage) is the same as the state structure for the base process $\boldsymbol{P_B}$, the $s_D$ state simply becomes the initial state for process $P_D$.

When disturbance $e_k$ occurs, the process model $\boldsymbol{P_B}$ is automatically switched to model $\boldsymbol{P_D}(e_k)$ and its individual process $P_D$ is generated with new controls calculated for it.

## 4.2   AL. Model Including a Machine Failure

In order to illustrate the 2SALMT method let us consider a failure disturbance consisting in full inoperability of a single $k$-th machine. Let us present an AL model for disturbed DMP i.e.the $\boldsymbol{P_D}$ process developed by means of transformation of the AL model presented in example 1.

*Example 2.*

Let us assume for the sake of simplicity that the state when the machine failure occurred $s_D = (x_D, t_D)$ is a decision state. Repair time depends on failure type and can be estimated. Let the time of repair be trep meaning that the machine is broken (unavailable) in the range $[t_D, t_{rep})$.

AL model for the $P_D$ process can be presented in various ways. Here it will be shown so that right after the failure resolution it will automatically return to the base process model. At the first stage only the definition of $U_p(s)$ is transformed. The set of possible decisions $U_{pD}(s)$ for the $P_D$ process:

$U_{pD}(s) = U^1_{pD}(s) \times U^2_{pD}(s) \times ..U^m_{pD}(s)$

with only the $U^k_{pD}(s)$ changing and now dependent on parameters $t_D$ and $t_{rep}$
$U^k_{pD}(x,t) = \{0\}$ for $t_D \leq t < t_{rep}$ and $U^k_{pD}(x,t) = U^k_p(x,t)$ for $t \geq t_{rep}$. For $t_D \leq t < t_{rep}$, conditions a) - d) from example 1 only refer to sets $U^i_{pD}(s)$ $i = 1, 2, ..m$ but $i \neq k$.

As the $P_D$ process state structure remains unchanged, the second stage transformation assign state $s_D$ to the initial state $s_{0D}$ of the $P_D$ process.

Note that the definition of process $P_D$ as non-stationary enables automatic return to the regular base manufacturing process once the disturbance cases.

The total AL model for the process stored in the IT system consists of a combination of two models, provided in example 1 and example 2.

# 5   Conclusion

The paper presents a new, formal modeling method of manufacturing processes including occurrence of various types of disturbances that may emerge relatively infrequently. The method referred to as Two-Stage AL Model Transformation method utilizes an algebraic-logical meta-model of multistage dynamic decision process (ALMM of MDDP). The meta-model can be used as a basis for development of AL models for a broad class of discrete manufacturing processes, especially AL models for discrete manufacturing processes both in the regular and disturbed modes.

The method is innovative in that it enables the modeling of manufacturing processes with disturbances occurring with unpredictable timing through appropriate switching of deterministic AL models.

The method presented herein is to be implemented in IT systems managing manufacturing processes on the operational level, in particular in MES class systems.

# References

1. Albers, S., Schmidt, G.: Scheduling with unexpected machine breakdowns. Discrete Applied Mathematics 110, 85–99 (2001)
2. Miora, M.: Business Continuity Planning. In: Bosworth, S., Kabay, M.E., Whyne, E. (eds.) Computer Security Handbook, ch.58, 5th edn. John Wiley & Sons (2009)
3. Dudek-Dyduch, E.: Formalization and Analysis of Problems of Discrete Manufacturing Processes, vol. 54. Scientific Bulletin of AGH University, Automatyka (1990) (in Polish)
4. Dudek-Dyduch, E.: Computer Systems for manufacturing management. Wyd. Poldex, Cracow (2002) (in Polish)
5. Dudek-Dyduch, E.: Learning based algorithm in scheduling. Journal of Intelligent Manufacturing (JIM) 11(2), 135–143 (2000)
6. Dudek-Dyduch, E., Dyduch, T.: Learning Algorithms for Scheduling Using Knowledge Based Model. In: Rutkowski, L., Tadeusiewicz, R., Zadeh, L.A., Żurada, J.M. (eds.) ICAISC 2006. LNCS (LNAI), vol. 4029, pp. 1091–1100. Springer, Heidelberg (2006)
7. Dudek-Dyduch, E., Kucharska, E.: Learning Method for Co-operation. In: Jędrzejowicz, P., Nguyen, N.T., Hoang, K. (eds.) ICCCI 2011, Part II. LNCS, vol. 6923, pp. 290–300. Springer, Heidelberg (2011)
8. Dudek-Dyduch, E., Kucharska, E.: Optimization learning method for discrete process control. In: Proceedings of the 8th International Conference on Informatics in Control, Automation and Robotics, ICINCO 2011, Noordwijkerhout, The Netherlands, 2831, vol. 1, p. 2433 (2011) ISBN 978-989-8425-74-4
9. Dudek-Dyduch, E., Dutkiewicz, L.: Substitution Tasks Method for Discrete Optimization. In: Rutkowski, L., Korytkowski, M., Scherer, R., Tadeusiewicz, R., Zadeh, L.A., Zurada, J.M. (eds.) ICAISC 2013, Part II. LNCS (LNAI), vol. 7895, pp. 419–430. Springer, Heidelberg (2013)
10. Sękowski, H., Dudek-Dyduch, E.: Knowledge Based Model for Scheduling in Failure Modes. In: Rutkowski, L., Korytkowski, M., Scherer, R., Tadeusiewicz, R., Zadeh, L.A., Zurada, J.M. (eds.) ICAISC 2012, Part II. LNCS, vol. 7268, pp. 591–599. Springer, Heidelberg (2012)
11. Glowacz, A.: Diagnostics of DC and Induction Motors Based on the Analysis of Acoustic Signals, pp. 257–262 (2014)
12. Grobler-Debska, K., Kucharska, E., Dudek-Dyduch, E.: Idea of switching algebraic-logicalmodels in flow-shop scheduling problem with defects. In: The 18th International Conference on Methods and Models in Automation and Robotics, MMAR Proceedings, pp. 532–537 (2013)
13. Joseph, O. A., Sridharan, R.: Evaluation of routing flexibility of a flexible manufacturing system using simulation modelling and analysis. Int. J. Adv. Manuf. Technol. (2011), doi 10.1007/s00170-011-3153-5

14. Kucharska, E., Dutkiewicz, L., Grobler-Dbska, K., Rczka, K.: ALMM approach for optimization of the supply routes for multi-location companies problem. In: Advances in Decision Sciences and Future Studies - Proceedings of the 8-th International Conference on Knowledge, Information and Creativity Support Systems, Krakw, vol. 2, pp. 321–332 (2013)
15. McDermott, R., Mikulak, R., Beauregard, M.: The Basics of FMEA, 2nd edn. Productivity Press (2009) ISBN:9781563273773

# A New Approach to Nonlinear Modeling Based on Significant Operating Points Detection

Piotr Dziwiński[1](✉) and Eduard D. Avedyan[2]

[1] Institute of Computational Intelligence,
Częstochowa University of Technology, Częstochowa, Poland
piotr.dziwinski@iisi.pcz.pl
[2] Moscow Institute of Physics and Technology, Moscow, Russia
eavedian@mail.ru

**Abstract.** The paper presents a new approach to nonlinear modeling based on significant operating points detection from non-invasive identification of nonlinear dynamic system. The swarm intelligence supported by the genetic algorithm is used in the proposed approach to identify the unknown parameters of the nonlinear dynamic system in different significant operating points. The parameters of the membership functions of the fuzzy rules and the parameters of the linear models are simultaneously identified. The new approach was tested on the nonlinear electrical circuit, which was replaced by the approximate linear model. The obtained results prove efficiency of the new approach based on the significant operating points detection.

**Keywords:** Nonlinear modeling · Non-invasive identification · Significant operating point · Particle swarm optimization · Genetic algorithm · Electrical circuit · Takagi-Sugeno neuro-fuzzy system

## 1 Introduction

Non-invasive identification of nonlinear dynamic system is the art of the discovery of the mathematic model allowing the reproduction of the reference values obtained from the non-invasive measurement of the nonlinear dynamic system with sufficient precision. Determination of the enough sufficient precise mathematic model, which reproduces nonlinear dynamic system, in many situations is very hard to obtain or impossible.

In practice, the mathematical models of the nonlinear dynamic systems are the approximate models and cannot describe some unpredictable dynamics or another phenomena. A large number of mathematical models, which describe the nonlinear systems in universal way have been proposed in the literature, among others, neural networks [21], [24], [26] treated as black box models, Fuzzy Inference Systems (FIS) [20], [54], neuro-fuzzy systems [4–8], [27], [32–34], [44–46], flexible neuro-fuzzy systems [53, 55, 56, 58, 59] and Takagi-Sugeno models (TS) [9], [10], [19]. Particular attention should be given to the latter mentioned. They give the possibility of obtaining much better results for the identification or classification. Moreover, defuzzification is not necessary in the TS model.

L. Rutkowski et al. (Eds.): ICAISC 2015, Part II, LNAI 9120, pp. 364–378, 2015.
DOI: 10.1007/978-3-319-19369-4_33

A large number of researchers conducted study on the identification of the nonlinear dynamic systems [2], [22], [23], [29], [35–43], [50], [51], Eftekhari [14] used substractive clustering algorithm [3], [12] to discover potential areas of applying local linear models which have been identified subsequently. The structure obtained in this way has been learned by using ant colony optimization for continuous space [13]. Optimization was used to increase interpretability of the obtained fuzzy rules describing the local linear models. Rudenko [31] used evolutionary computation for determining the topology of the neural network and its parameters in order to identify nonlinear non-stationary systems. Imam [47] proposed quasi-arx neural network. The weights of the neural network and the parameters of the fuzzy adaptive controller were estimated using Lyapunov algorithm.

The main objective of this paper is nonlinear dynamic system identification described by using approximate linear models, in which some dependencies were not included in mathematical model. These models are activate in significant operating points [11] described by the fuzzy rules of the Takagi-Sugeno model.

The remainder of this paper is organized as follows. In section 2, modeling of nonlinear dynamic system using linear combination of the algebraic equations and based on the state variable technique, is described. Section 3 deals with fuzzy modeling of the significant operating points using Takagi-Sugeno model. In section 4 overall assumptions of the PSO-GA algorithm used for determining the parameters of the fuzzy rules and local linear model are outlined. A new approach to significant operating points detection is discussed in section 5. Section 6 presents the nonlinear electrical circuit and the placeholder circuit. Finally section 7 shows simulation results, proves effectiveness of the new approach to nonlinear modeling based on significant operating points detection.

## 2   Nonlinear Dynamic System Identification

Let us consider the nonlinear dynamic system described by the algebraic equations and based on the state variable technique

$$\frac{dx}{dt} = f(x, u) = \mathbf{A}\mathbf{x} + \mathbf{B}\mathbf{u} + \eta g(\mathbf{x}, \mathbf{u}), \tag{1}$$

$$\mathbf{y} = \mathbf{C} \cdot \mathbf{x}, \tag{2}$$

where $g(x, u)$ is the separate nonlinear part of the system and $\eta$ is the influence factor of nonlinearities of the whole system, $\mathbf{A}$, $\mathbf{B}$ are the system input and output matrices, $x$, $y$ is input and output signals respectively, $\mathbf{u}$ is the vector of the state variables.

Assuming that $\eta$ is small and system is weakly nonlinear then linear approximation about an equilibrium point may give good results in a certain region. However, overall accuracy of such model may be too low for many practical applications.

In this paper we propose extension of the algorithm studied in [11] to increase the accuracy of that algorithm by identifying the parameters affecting the behavior of the linear models in selected regions. Selected regions, called the operating points, are described by the fuzzy rules of the Takagi-Sugeno neurofuzzy system [9], [10], [12], [19]. In that structure, the local linear model can be identified by using the reference values obtained from measurements or acquired from the internal state of the nonlinear dynamic system. The local linear model is described by the algebraic equations and based on state variables technique, which does not contain nonlinear part:

$$f_l(x, u) = \mathbf{A}^r \mathbf{x} + \mathbf{B}^r \mathbf{u}, \tag{3}$$

where: $r = 1, \ldots, n$, $n$ - the number of the local linear models.

The entire model can be described by the linear combination of the local linear models, which are activated in the specific regions called significant operating points.

The model is defined as follows:

$$f_g(x, u) = \sum_{r=1}^{n} \zeta_r(x, u)(\mathbf{A}^r \mathbf{x} + \mathbf{B}^r \mathbf{u}), \tag{4}$$

where $\zeta_r(x, u)$ is the function specifying the activity level of the local linear model in particular states described by using a vector of the state variables $\mathbf{u}$ for a specific input values $x$. The local linear model in the significant operating point $r$ is defined by the set of parameters $\Theta_r = \{\mathbf{A}^r, \mathbf{B}^r, \mathbf{u}\}$. The function of the activation $\zeta_r$, if depends on output values of the modeled nonlinear dynamic system, can be in the form $\zeta_r(x, y, u)$.

The change of the states of the nonlinear dynamic system usually does not occur rapidly, but in a smooth manner, which is difficult to describe by using the mathematical model. Linear models existing in operating points pass fluently among themselves and overlap.

Neuro-fuzzy systems described in the next section are perfect to model the activation level of the local linear models with the specified parameters.

## 3   Fuzzy Modeling of the Significant Operating Points

The construction of the most neuro-fuzzy structures [4], [5], [8], [9], [27], [32], [33], [44], [54], [57], is based on the Mamdani reasoning type described by using t-norm, for example product or minimum. They require defuzzification of the output values, thus they cannot be applied easily for modeling of the activation level of the local linear models, such as Takagi-Sugeno model [9], [10], [12], [19], [34]. These systems include dependences between a premise and a consequent of the rule in the form

$$R^{(r)} : \text{ IF } \bar{\mathbf{x}} \text{ is } \mathbf{D}^r \text{ THEN } y^r = f^{(r)}(\bar{\mathbf{x}}) \tag{5}$$

where: $\bar{\mathbf{x}}=[\bar{x}_1, \bar{x}_2, \ldots, \bar{x}_N] \in \mathbf{X}, y \in \mathbf{Y}, \mathbf{D}^r = D_1^r \times D_2^r \times \ldots \times D_N^r, D_1^r, D_2^r, \ldots, D_N^r,$ are the fuzzy sets described by the membership functions $\mu_{D_i^r}(\bar{x}_i)$, $i = 1, \ldots, N$, $r = 1, \ldots, n$, $n$ is the number of the rules and $N$ is the number of the inputs of the neuro-fuzzy system.

The aggregation in the Takagi-Sugeno model is described by the formula

$$y = f(\bar{\mathbf{x}}) = \frac{\sum_{r=1}^{n} f^{(r)}(\bar{\mathbf{x}}) \cdot \mu_{\mathbf{D}^r}(\bar{\mathbf{x}})}{\sum_{r=1}^{n} \mu_{\mathbf{D}^r}(\bar{\mathbf{x}})} \tag{6}$$

The following form of the Takagi-Sugeno model is obtained through replacing the function $f^{(r)}(\bar{\mathbf{x}})$ in consequent of the rule by the local linear model (3)

$$R^{(r)} : \text{ IF } \bar{\mathbf{x}} \text{ is } \mathbf{D}^r \text{ THEN } \mathbf{y}^r = \mathbf{A}^r \mathbf{x} + \mathbf{B}^r \mathbf{u} \tag{7}$$

By using the aggregation (6), we obtain the output of the Takagi-Sugeno model containing the local linear models in the consequents

$$\mathbf{y} = f(\mathbf{x}, \bar{\mathbf{x}}) = \frac{\sum_{r=1}^{n} (\mathbf{A}^r \mathbf{x} + \mathbf{B}^r \mathbf{u}) \cdot \mu_{\mathbf{D}^r}(\bar{\mathbf{x}})}{\sum_{r=1}^{n} \mu_{\mathbf{D}^r}(\bar{\mathbf{x}})} \tag{8}$$

where $\mu_{\mathbf{D}^r}(\bar{\mathbf{x}}) = \mathrm{T}_{i=1}^{N} \{\mu_{\mathbf{D}_i^r}(\bar{x}_i)\}$, T is t-norm.

The state vector $\mathbf{u}$ describing the internal state of the local linear models is shared for all models in all work points. The parameters of the local linear models encoded inside input matrix $\mathbf{A}^r$ and output matrix $\mathbf{B}^r$ are changing. Thus, the complete model is defined through the set of the parameters $\Theta_r' = \{\mathbf{A}^r, \mathbf{B}^r, \mathbf{u}, \mathbf{D}^r\}$. Assuming the initial state $\mathbf{u}$ of the entire model is known, only $\mathbf{A}^r, \mathbf{B}^r, \mathbf{D}^r$ parameters will be identified.

## 4 PSO-GA Algorithm

Juang [19] proposed a hybrid algorithm HGAPSO in 2004. He used HGAPSO for determination of the parameters of the Takagi-Sugeno recurrent neuro-fuzzy network for controlling plant growth. The author significantly improved the convergence of the Genetic Algorithm (GA) by introducing the cooperation between the chromosomes taken from the Particle Swarm Optimization (PSO) algorithm. Szczypta [48], [49] used evolutionary algorithm to design optimal controllers. The hybridization of the evolutionary algorithms, usually gives good results and has been used in many papers [1], [13], [15], [17], [18], [25], [31].

In this paper a PSO-GA algorithm is used for identification of the parameters of the linear model in the specified significant operating point $r$. Parameters are stored in the input matrix $\mathbf{A}^r$ and an output matrix $\mathbf{B}^r$. The significant operating points are described by the membership functions of the fuzzy sets $\mathbf{D}^r$ in the

Takagi-Sugeno neuro-fuzzy system [9], [10], [12], [19]. The PSO-GA algorithm is obtained by using the Particle Swarm Optimization (PSO) algorithm and a crossover and mutation operators taken from the Genetic Algorithm (GA) [11], [15], [17], [30].

In the PSO-GA algorithm, just as in PSO algorithm, each particle $p_i \in N^t_{PSO}, i = 1, 2, \ldots |N^t_{PSO}|$, is in a specific location $\mathbf{x}^t_i$, $\mathbf{x}^t_i \in \mathbf{R}^N$, $\mathbf{R}^N$ - search space, $t = 1, 2, \ldots, T$, $T$ - the maximum number of the epochs. It moves with the velocity $\mathbf{v}^t_i$ (9) in continuous search space. When moving according to (9) and (10), they are looking for high quality solutions. They are using the best solutions, which have been found so far $\mathbf{xp}^t_i$ and the best solution, which has been found by all particles of the colony $\mathbf{xg}^t$. The global best solution $\mathbf{xg}^t$ is some type of the shared memory for all the particles of the colony in subsequent generations

$$\mathbf{v}^{t+1}_i = w^t \cdot \mathbf{v}^t_i + \mathbf{U}(0, \psi_1)^t \cdot (\mathbf{xp}^t_i - \mathbf{x}^t_i) + \mathbf{U}(0, \psi_2)^t \cdot (\mathbf{xg}^t - \mathbf{x}^t_i), \qquad (9)$$

$$\mathbf{x}^{t+1}_i = \mathbf{x}^t_i + \mathbf{v}^{t+1}_i, \qquad (10)$$

where $\omega^t$, $\omega^t \in (0, 1)$ is the factor specifying the velocity $\mathbf{v}^t_i$ influence on velocity $\mathbf{v}^{(t+1)}_i$. For small value of the $\omega^t$, the velocity of the particles rapidly decreases. As a result, the algorithm is fast convergent, it can easily stop in local optima. For $\omega^t > 1$, the movement velocity of the particles permanently increases - the algorithm becomes divergent. $\psi_1, \psi_2$ are the factors specifying influence of the best solution of particle $\mathbf{xp}^t_i$ and the best solution of the entire colony $\mathbf{xp}^t_i$ on the velocity value in the next iteration $(t + 1)$, respectively. Values of the factors $\psi_1$ and $\psi_2$ specify cognitive and social abilities of the particles, respectively. The $\mathbf{U}(0, \psi_k)$ is a vector of random numbers which are uniformly distributed in the range $[0, \psi_k]$, $k \in 1, 2$.

The mutation and crossover genetic operators are used for the best elite particles, selected according to the roulette wheel principle [52], from the population of the solutions $\mathbf{x}^t_i$, according to probability $P^t_{GA}$ (11).

$$P^t_{GA} = \begin{cases} P_{GA_{min}} + \beta & \text{if } (t \leq T_{stop}) \\ P_{GA_{min}} & \text{otherwise} \end{cases}, \qquad (11)$$

$$\beta = \frac{(P_{GA_{max}} - P_{GA_{min}}) \cdot (T_{stop} - t)}{T_{stop}}, \qquad (12)$$

where $T_{stop}$ is the number of epochs, for which the probability of using of the genetic operators decreases to the value $P_{GA_{min}}$, $T_{STOP} < T$.

The real coding is used in the PSO-GA algorithm. It is much more effective than boolean coding in case of the complex multidimensional problems [16]. It was confirmed by many researches. The following decomposition of the parameters in chromosome illustrated in Fig. 1 is used for real coding of the solutions.

The number of the individual parameters in the matrices $\mathbf{A}^r$ and $\mathbf{B}^r$, depends on the modeled nonlinear dynamic system. The number of the parameters for

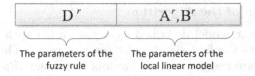

**Fig. 1.** Coding of the parameters in chromosome

the fuzzy sets depends on the membership functions, the input and output of the nonlinear dynamic system, which are used for detection of the operating points.

A new population is created $N_a^t = N_{PSO}^t \cup N_{GA}^t$ as a result of moving of the participles (9)(10) and executing of the genetic operators. The best elite participles $|N_{PSO}^t|$ remain out of the all participles of the colony $N_a^t$. They become a new population of particles $N_{PSO}^{t+1}$ in a new epoch of the algorithm.

Finally, for the participles $N_{PSO}^{t+1}$, the best solution $\mathbf{xp}_i^{t+1}$ for every particle and the best global solution $\mathbf{xg}^{t+1}$ is refreshed according to equations (13) and (14), respectively

$$\mathbf{xp}_i^{t+1} = \begin{cases} \mathbf{x}_i^t & \text{when } f(\mathbf{x}_i^t) < f(\mathbf{xp}_i^t) \\ \mathbf{xp}_i^t & \text{in other case} \end{cases}, \tag{13}$$

$$\mathbf{xg}^{t+1} = \arg \min_{i=1,\dots,|\mathbf{N}_{PSO}^{t+1}|} (\mathbf{xp}_i^{t+1}). \tag{14}$$

Algorithm stops, when it reaches the maximum number of the epochs or the minimum value of the Root Mean Square Error (RMSE).

## 5 Identification of the Significant Operating Points

Nonlinear dynamic system identification in the entire measurement area is very hard or even impossible if it is not known precise enough mathematical model, which contains linear and nonlinear part (1). The nonlinear part of the system is frequently hard for modeling with using algebraic equations. In that case the system can be described by using a linear combination of the local linear models (4), for which mathematical model is defined precisely enough in some regions.

Eftekhari [14] used substractive clustering algorithm to discover regions of the measurements, which can be potential candidates for operating points. Dziwiński [11] proposed algorithm for identification of significant operating points. In the algorithm he expands measurement region, until the identified local linear model was able to reproduce reference values.

In this work the identification of the parameters of the local linear model and significant operating points described by fuzzy rules of the Takagi-Sugeno neuro-fuzzy system is proposed. The PSO-GA algorithm determines the parameters of the fuzzy sets which activate local linear model in the significant operating point and parameters of the local linear model at the same time.

The significant operating points detection algorithm is described in subsequent sections.

## 5.1    Initialization of the Algorithm

Initially a local linear model described by equation (8) with one fuzzy rule is created and becomes the first significant operating point. The reference values from time interval are assigned on the basis of the range of parameters change used for detecting an operating point. The values of the parameters change can be determined based on expert knowledge about the modeled nonlinear dynamic system.

## 5.2    The Parameters Determination for the Local Linear Model

PSO-GA is used with solution coded according to Fig. 1. The parameters of the membership function and parameters of the local linear model are determined for the assigned part of the reference values.

If identification of the parameters is ineffective - reference data reproduction error by the model $RMSE > RMSE_{end}$ does not decrease, then the time interval for the operating point is decreased until meeting the criterion $\epsilon < \epsilon_{MIN}$; $\epsilon$ - error at the end of the assigned time interval; next a new significant operating point is added in accordance with subsection 5.4.

## 5.3    Extending the Time Interval for the Reference Data

When identifying parameters of the local linear model described according to equation (8), the time interval of the reference data is extended until it satisfies the error criterion $\epsilon < \epsilon_{stop}$ in each iteration step of the algorithm. The selected initial parameters of the fuzzy sets are determined as a result of extending of the time interval.

## 5.4    Adding a New Significant Operating Point

If the process of extending of the time interval for the reference data is inefficient, then time interval for the reference data is limited until it satisfies the error criterion $\epsilon < \epsilon_{MIN}$. This means, that the identified significant operating point/points are no longer able to reproduce a new reference data sufficiently precisely using a local linear models with a fixed value of the parameters. There are phenomena, that are not possible to model by using identified significant operating points. A new significant operating point together with a new local linear model described by a new fuzzy rule is added. The new reference data is assigned from the time interval for the new significant operating point according to subsection 5.1.

As a result of adding the new significant operating point, the participles and corresponding chromosomes are extended according to Fig. 2.

## 5.5    Ending of the Algorithm

The algorithm works until it does not reproduce the all reference data with the acceptable accuracy $RMSE_{end}$, or does not reach a predetermined number of epochs for the PSO-GA algorithm.

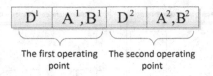

The first operating
point                The second operating
point

**Fig. 2.** The coding of the parameters in chromosome for two significant operating points

# 6  Nonlinear Model

The simulations were performed for the created electrical circuit with the nonlinear element for which measurements data have been collected. The approximate local linear model with the replacement resistance for the diode $R_{zd}$, has been designed for the electrical circuit. The electrical circuit is shown in Fig. 3

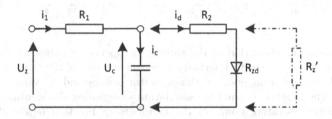

**Fig. 3.** The electrical circuit with the diode and the replacement resistance for the diode

In the electrical circuit, the internal state of the model is described by the value of the voltage $U_c$ on capacitor with the capacitance $c = 10\mu F$ described by equation (15).

$$U_c = \frac{1}{c}\int i_c dt \rightarrow \frac{dU_c}{dt} = \frac{1}{c}i_c \qquad (15)$$

where

$$i_c = i_1 - i_d = \frac{U_z - U_c}{R_1} - \frac{Uc}{R_2 + R_{zd}} \qquad (16)$$

Introducing replacement resistance for the branch with diode $R'_z = R_2 + R_{zd}$, substituting a designated value of the current (16) to equation (15), using rectangular integration method, the approximate mathematical model of real nonlinear object is obtained in discrete form and shown in equation (17)

$$U_c(k+1) = U_c(k) + \left(\frac{1}{C} \cdot \left(-\frac{1}{R_1} - \frac{1}{R'_z}\right) \cdot U_c(k) + \frac{1}{C \cdot R_1} \cdot U_z\right) \cdot \Delta t \qquad (17)$$

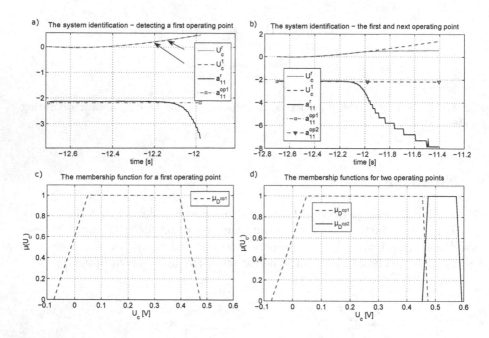

**Fig. 4.** The initial identification of the significant operating point; a) the capacitor voltage and the value of identified parameters in the function of the time simulation for the first significant operating point; b) the capacitor voltage and the values of identified parameters in the function of the time simulation - beginning the identification of the second significant operating point; c) the membership function $\mu_{D^{op1}}$ of the fuzzy set for the first significant operating point; d) the membership functions $\mu_{D^{op1}}$ and $\mu_{D^{op2}}$ of the fuzzy sets for the first and second significant operating point, respectively, $U_c^r, U_c^1$ - the reference voltage values and obtained voltage values on the capacitor $C$, respectively, $a_{11}^r$ - the reference value of the identified parameter , $a_{11}^{op1}$, $a_{11}^{op2}$ - the values of the identified parameters for the first and the second significant operating point, respectively, where $a_{11} = \frac{1}{C} \cdot \left( -\frac{1}{R_1} - \frac{1}{R_{z'}} \right)$

where: $U_c(k), U_c(k+1)$ - voltage of the capacitor C in integration step $k$, $k+1$, respectively, $i_1$ - value of the current, $U_z$ - input voltage, $R_1$ - input resistance $(4,7\ k\Omega)$, $U_c$ - capacitor voltage, $i_c$ - current of the capacitor $C$, $i_d$ - current in branch with nonlinear diode, $R_2$ - resistance in branch with diode $(980\Omega)$, $R_{zd}$ - unknown replacement resistance of the diode.

## 7 Experimental Results

Experiments were done for the identification of the nonlinear electrical circuit, replaced by the approximate linear model with replacement resistance. Obtained results are presented in Fig. 6a and Fig. 6b and prove the effectiveness of the proposed method. The 100 times better results have been obtained by using

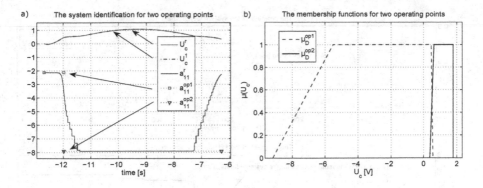

**Fig. 5.** The complete identification of the significant operating points; a) the capacitor voltage and values of the identified parameters in function of the simulation time; b) the membership functions for the fuzzy sets for the detected significant operating points

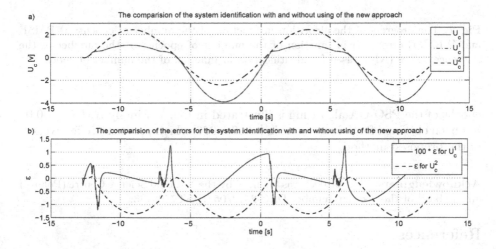

**Fig. 6.** The comparison of the efficiency of the identification nonlinear electrical circuit; a) the capacitor voltage in function of the simulation time; $U_c^r$ - the reference voltage; $U_c^1$, $U_c^2$ - the obtained capacitor voltage with using and without using of the significant operating points detection, respectively; b) the comparison of the error results with using (it was obtained approximately 100 times smaller result error) and without using of the significant operating points detection, respectively

the new approach to nonlinear modeling based on significant operating points detection. The initial stage of the parameters identification is shown in Fig. 4. Fig. 5 contains results obtained for the fully identified parameters of the local linear models and parameters of the membership functions for two significant operating points. The progress of the algorithm in function of the number of

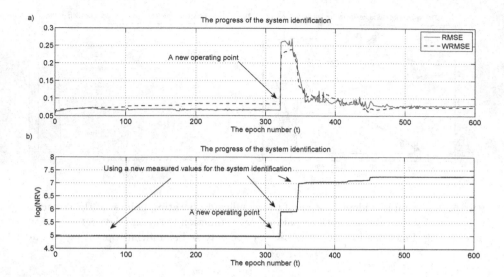

**Fig. 7.** The progress of the algorithm in function of the number of epochs; a) RMSE and WRMSE error [11] in function of the number of epochs; b) the number of the reference values (NRV) used for identification in function of the number of epoch

epochs of the PSO-GA algorithm is illustrated in Fig. 7. Finally $RMSE = 0.08$ has been obtained for voltage value in [-3.99,1.076] which proves the effectiveness of the proposed method.

**Acknowledgment.** The project was financed by the National Science Centre (Poland) on the basis of the decision number DEC-2012/05/B/ST7/02138.

# References

1. Alsumait, J., Sykulski, J., Al-Othman, A.: A hybrid ga–ps–sqp method to solve power system valve-point economic dispatch problems. Applied Energy 87, 1773–1781 (2010)
2. Bartczuk, Ł., Przybył, A., Koprinkova-Hristova, P.: New method for nonlinear fuzzy correction modelling of dynamic objects. In: Rutkowski, L., Korytkowski, M., Scherer, R., Tadeusiewicz, R., Zadeh, L.A., Zurada, J.M. (eds.) ICAISC 2014, Part I. LNCS (LNAI), vol. 8467, pp. 169–180. Springer, Heidelberg (2014)
3. Chiu, S.: Fuzzy model identification based on cluster estimation. J. Intell. Fuzzy Systems 2(3) 2, 267–278 (1994)
4. Cpalka, K.: A method for designing flexible neuro-fuzzy systems. In: Rutkowski, L., Tadeusiewicz, R., Zadeh, L.A., Żurada, J.M. (eds.) ICAISC 2006. LNCS (LNAI), vol. 4029, pp. 212–219. Springer, Heidelberg (2006)
5. Cpałka, K.: On evolutionary designing and learning of flexible neuro-fuzzy structures for nonlinear classification. Nonlinear Analysis Series A: Theory, Methods and Applications 71, 1659–1672 (2009)

6. Cpałka, K., Łapa, K., Przybył, A., Zalasiński, M.: A new method for designing neuro-fuzzy systems for nonlinear modelling with interpretability aspects. Neuro-computing 135, 203–217 (2014)
7. Cpałka, K., Rebrova, O., Nowicki, R., Rutkowski, L.: On design of flexible neuro-fuzzy systems for nonlinear modelling. Int. Journal of General Systems 42(6), 706–720 (2013)
8. Cpałka, K., Rutkowski, L.: A New Method for Designing and Reduction of Neuro-fuzzy Systems. In: Proceedings of the 2006 IEEE International Conference on Fuzzy Systems (IEEE World Congress on Computational Intelligence, WCCI 2006), Vancouver, BC, Canada, pp. 8510–8516 (2006)
9. Cpałka, K., Rutkowski, L.: Flexible Takagi-Sugeno Fuzzy Systems. In: Proceedings of the International Joint Conference on Neural Networks, Montreal, pp. 1764–1769 (2005)
10. Cpałka, K., Rutkowski, L.: Flexible Takagi-Sugeno neuro-fuzzy structures for nonlinear approximation. WSEAS Transactions on Systems 9(4), 1450–1458 (2005)
11. Dziwiński, P., Bartczuk, Ł., Przybył, A., Avedyan, E.D.: A new algorithm for identification of significant operating points using swarm intelligence. In: Rutkowski, L., Korytkowski, M., Scherer, R., Tadeusiewicz, R., Zadeh, L.A., Zurada, J.M. (eds.) ICAISC 2014, Part II. LNCS (LNAI), vol. 8468, pp. 349–362. Springer, Heidelberg (2014)
12. Dziwiński, P., Rutkowska, D.: Algorithm for generating fuzzy rules for WWW document classification. In: Rutkowski, L., Tadeusiewicz, R., Zadeh, L.A., Żurada, J.M. (eds.) ICAISC 2006. LNCS (LNAI), vol. 4029, pp. 1111–1119. Springer, Heidelberg (2006)
13. Eftekhari, M., Deai, B., Katebi, S.: Gradient-based ant colony optimization for continuous spaces. Esteghlal Journal of Eng. 25, 33–45 (2006)
14. Eftekhari, M., Zeinalkhani, M.: Extracting interpretable fuzzy models for nonlinear systems using gradient-based continuous ant colony optimization. Fuzzy Information and Engineering 5, 255–277 (2013)
15. El-Abd, M.: On the hybridization on the artificial bee colony and particle swarm optimization algorithms. Journal of Artificial Intelligence and Soft Computing Research 2(2), 145–155 (2012)
16. Fang, N., Zhou, J., Zhang, R., Liu, Y., Zhang, Y.: A hybrid of real coded genetic algorithm and artificial fish swarm algorithm for short-term optimal hydrothermal scheduling. International Journal of Electrical Power & Energy Systems 62, 617–629 (2014)
17. Gandomi, A.H., Yun, Y.G.J., Yang, X.S., Talatahari, S.: Chaos-enhanced accelerated particle swarm optimization. Communications in Nonlinear Science and Numerical Simulation 18, 327–340 (2013)
18. He, D.K., Wang, F.L., Mao, Z.Z.: Hybrid genetic algorithm for economic dispatch with valve-point effect. Electric Power Systems Research 78, 626–633 (2008)
19. Juang, C.F.: A hybrid of genetic algorithm and particle swarm optimization for recurrent network design. IEEE Transactions on Systems, MAN, AND Cybernetics - Part B: Cybernetics 34(2), 997–1006 (2004)
20. Korytkowski, M., Rutkowski, L., Scherer, R.: From ensemble of fuzzy classifiers to single fuzzy rule base classifier. In: Rutkowski, L., Tadeusiewicz, R., Zadeh, L.A., Zurada, J.M. (eds.) ICAISC 2008. LNCS (LNAI), vol. 5097, pp. 265–272. Springer, Heidelberg (2008)
21. Liu, X., Jiang, M., Jike, G.: A method research on nonlinear system identification based on neural network. Lecture Notes in Electrical Engineering, vol. 154(1), pp. 234–240. Springer (2012)

22. Łapa, K., Przybył, A., Cpałka, K.: A new approach to designing interpretable models of dynamic systems. In: Rutkowski, L., Korytkowski, M., Scherer, R., Tadeusiewicz, R., Zadeh, L.A., Zurada, J.M. (eds.) ICAISC 2013, Part II. LNCS (LNAI), vol. 7895, pp. 523–534. Springer, Heidelberg (2013)

23. Łapa, K., Zalasiński, M., Cpałka, K.: A new method for designing and complexity reduction of neuro-fuzzy systems for nonlinear modelling. In: Rutkowski, L., Korytkowski, M., Scherer, R., Tadeusiewicz, R., Zadeh, L.A., Zurada, J.M. (eds.) ICAISC 2013, Part I. LNCS (LNAI), vol. 7894, pp. 329–344. Springer, Heidelberg (2013)

24. Arain, M.A., Hultmann Ayala, H.V., Ansari, M.A.: Nonlinear system identification using neural network. In: Chowdhry, B.S., Shaikh, F.K., Hussain, D.M.A., Uqaili, M.A. (eds.) IMTIC 2012. CCIS, vol. 281, pp. 122–131. Springer, Heidelberg (2012)

25. Niknam, T.: A new fuzzy adaptive hybrid particle swarm optimization algorithm for non-linear, non-smooth and non-convex economic dispatch problem. Applied Energy 87, 327–339 (2010)

26. Peteiro-Barral, D., Bardinas, B.G., Perez-Sanchez, B.: Learning from heterogeneously distributed data sets using artificial neural networks and genetic algorithms. Journal of Artificial Intelligence and Soft Computing Research 2(1), 5–20 (2012)

27. Przybył, A., Er, M.J.: The idea for the integration of neuro-fuzzy hardware emulators with real-time network. In: Rutkowski, L., Korytkowski, M., Scherer, R., Tadeusiewicz, R., Zadeh, L.A., Zurada, J.M. (eds.) ICAISC 2014, Part I. LNCS (LNAI), vol. 8467, pp. 279–294. Springer, Heidelberg (2014)

28. Przybył, A., Jelonkiewicz, J.: Genetic algorithm for observer parameters tuning in sensorless induction motor drive. In: Neural Networks and Soft Computing, pp. 376-381 (2003)

29. Przybył, A., Smoląg, J., Kimla, P.: Distributed control system based on real time ethernet for computer numerical controlled machine tool. Przegląd Elektrotechniczny 86(2), 342–346 (2010) (in Polish)

30. Prampero, P.S., Attux, R.: Magnetic particle swarm optimization. Journal of Artificial Intelligence and Soft Computing Research 2(1), 59–72 (2012)

31. Rudenko, O., Bezsonov, O.: Robust neuroevolutionary identification of nonlinear nonstationary objects. Cybernetics and Systems Analysis 50(1), 17–30 (2014)

32. Rutkowski, L., Cpałka, K.: Neuro-fuzzy systems derived from quasi-triangular norms. In: Proceedings of the IEEE International Conference on Fuzzy Systems, Budapest, July 26-29, vol. 2, pp. 1031–1036 (2004)

33. Rutkowski, L., Cpałka, K.: Compromise approach to neuro-fuzzy systems. In: Sincak, P., Vascak, J., Kvasnicka, V., Pospichal, J. (eds.) Intelligent Technologies - Theory and Applications, vol. 76, pp. 85–90. IOS Press (2002)

34. Rutkowski, L., Przybył, A., Cpałka, K., Er, M.J.: Online speed profile generation for industrial machine tool based on neuro-fuzzy approach. In: Rutkowski, L., Scherer, R., Tadeusiewicz, R., Zadeh, L.A., Zurada, J.M. (eds.) ICAISC 2010, Part II. LNCS (LNAI), vol. 6114, pp. 645–650. Springer, Heidelberg (2010)

35. Rutkowski, L.: Online Identification Of Time-Varying Systems by Nonparametric Techniques. IEEE Trans. Automatic Control 27(1), 228–230 (1982)

36. Rutkowski, L.: On nonparametric identification with prediction of time-varying systems. IEEE Trans. Automatic Control 29(1), 58–60 (1984)

37. Rutkowski, L.: Nonparametric identification of quasi-stationary systems. Systems & Control Letters 6(1), 33–35 (1985)

38. Rutkowski, L.: Real-time identification of time-varying systems by non-parametric algorithms based on Parzen kernels. Int. Journal of Systems Science 16(9), 1123–1130 (1985)

39. Rutkowski, L.: A general-approach for nonparametric fitting of functions and their derivatives with applications to linear circuits identification. IEEE Trans. Circuits and Systems 33(8), 812–818 (1986)

40. Rutkowski, L., Rafajłowicz, E.: On optimal global rate of convergence of some nonparametric identification procedures. IEEE Trans. Automatic Control 34(10), 1089–1091 (1989)

41. Rutkowski, L.: Application of multiple Fourier-series to identification of multivariable non-stationary systems. Int. Journal of Systems Science 20(10), 1993–2002 (1989)

42. Rutkowski, L.: Identification of miso nonlinear regressions in the presence of a wide class of disturbances. IEEE Trans. Information Theory 37(1), 214–216 (1991)

43. Rutkowski, L.: Multiple Fourier-series procedures for extraction of nonlinear regressions from noisy data. IEEE Trans. Signal Processing 41(10), 3062–3065 (1993)

44. Rutkowski, L., Cpałka, K.: A neuro-fuzzy controller with a compromise fuzzy reasoning. Control and Cybernetics 31(2), 297–308 (2002)

45. Starczewski, J.T., Rutkowski, L.: Connectionist Structures of Type 2 Fuzzy Inference Systems. In: Wyrzykowski, R., Dongarra, J., Paprzycki, M., Waśniewski, J. (eds.) PPAM 2001. LNCS, vol. 2328, pp. 634–642. Springer, Heidelberg (2002)

46. Starczewski, J., Rutkowski, L.: Interval type 2 neuro-fuzzy systems based on interval consequents. Advances in Soft Computing, pp. 570–577 (2003)

47. Sutrisno, I., Mohammad, A.J., Jinglu, H.: Modified fuzzy adaptive controller applied to nonlinear systems modeled under quasi-arx neural network. Artificial Life and Robotics 19, 22–26 (2014)

48. Szczypta, J., Przybył, A., Cpałka, K.: Some aspects of evolutionary designing optimal controllers. In: Rutkowski, L., Korytkowski, M., Scherer, R., Tadeusiewicz, R., Zadeh, L.A., Zurada, J.M. (eds.) ICAISC 2013, Part II. LNCS (LNAI), vol. 7895, pp. 91–100. Springer, Heidelberg (2013)

49. Szczypta, J., Przybył, A., Wang, L.: Evolutionary approach with multiple quality criteria for controller design. In: Rutkowski, L., Korytkowski, M., Scherer, R., Tadeusiewicz, R., Zadeh, L.A., Zurada, J.M. (eds.) ICAISC 2014, Part I. LNCS (LNAI), vol. 8467, pp. 455–467. Springer, Heidelberg (2014)

50. Theodoridis, D.C., Boutalis, Y.S., Christodoulou, M.A.: Robustifying analysis of the direct adaptive control of unknown multivariable nonlinear systems based on a new neuro-fuzzy method. Journal of Artificial Intelligence and Soft Computing Research 1(1), 59–79 (2011)

51. Tran, V.N., Brdys, M.A.: Optimizing control by robustly feasible model predictive control and application to drinking water distribution systems. Journal of Artificial Intelligence and Soft Computing Research 1(1), 43–57 (2011)

52. Wang, F., Qiu, Y.: A modified particle swarm optimizer with roulette selection operator. In: Natural Language Processing and Knowledge Engineering, IEEE NLP-KE 2005, pp. 765–768 (2005)

53. Zalasiński, M., Cpałka, K.: New approach for the on-line signature verification based on method of horizontal partitioning. In: Rutkowski, L., Korytkowski, M., Scherer, R., Tadeusiewicz, R., Zadeh, L.A., Zurada, J.M. (eds.) ICAISC 2013, Part II. LNCS (LNAI), vol. 7895, pp. 342–350. Springer, Heidelberg (2013)

54. Zalasiński, M., Cpałka, K.: Novel algorithm for the on-line signature verification. In: Rutkowski, L., Korytkowski, M., Scherer, R., Tadeusiewicz, R., Zadeh, L.A., Zurada, J.M. (eds.) ICAISC 2012, Part II. LNCS, vol. 7268, pp. 362–367. Springer, Heidelberg (2012)

55. Cpałka, K., Zalasiński, M.: On-line signature verification using vertical signature partitioning. Expert Systems with Applications 41, 4170–4180 (2014)

56. Cpałka, K., Zalasiński, M., Rutkowski, L.: New method for the on-line signature verification based on horizontal partitioning. Pattern Recognition 47, 2652–2661 (2014)

57. Zalasiński, M., Cpałka, K.: New approach for the on-line signature verification based on method of horizontal partitioning. In: Rutkowski, L., Korytkowski, M., Scherer, R., Tadeusiewicz, R., Zadeh, L.A., Zurada, J.M. (eds.) ICAISC 2013, Part II. LNCS (LNAI), vol. 7895, pp. 342–350. Springer, Heidelberg (2013)

58. Zalasiński, M., Cpałka, K., Er, M.J.: New method for dynamic signature verification using hybrid partitioning. In: Rutkowski, L., Korytkowski, M., Scherer, R., Tadeusiewicz, R., Zadeh, L.A., Zurada, J.M. (eds.) ICAISC 2014, Part II. LNCS (LNAI), vol. 8468, pp. 216–230. Springer, Heidelberg (2014)

59. Zalasiński, M., Cpałka, K., Hayashi, Y.: New Method for Dynamic Signature Verification Based on Global Features. In: Rutkowski, L., Korytkowski, M., Scherer, R., Tadeusiewicz, R., Zadeh, L.A., Zurada, J.M. (eds.) ICAISC 2014, Part II. LNCS (LNAI), vol. 8468, pp. 231–245. Springer, Heidelberg (2014)

# An Application of Differential Evolution to Positioning Queueing Systems

Marcin Gabryel[1], Marcin Woźniak[2(✉)], and Robertas Damaševičius[3]

[1] Institute of Computational Intelligence, Czestochowa University of Technology,
Al. Armii Krajowej 36, 42-200 Czestochowa, Poland
Marcin.Gabryel@iisi.pcz.pl
[2] Institute of Mathematics, Silesian University of Technology,
Kaszubska 23, 44-101 Gliwice, Poland
Marcin.Wozniak@polsl.pl
[3] Software Engineering Department, Kaunas University of Technology,
Studentu 50, Kaunas, Lithuania
Robertas.Damasevicius@ktu.lt

**Abstract.** In this paper, we present positioning of the queueing system by the use of Differential Evolution algorithm. Positioned system is a $H_3/GI/M/1/N$-type queueing model with exponentially distributed service and vacation. In the following sections of this article we discuss the possibility of positioning of the selected system in various common scenarios of operation, which are modeled with the independent 3-order hyper exponential input stream of packets and exponential service time distribution. The research results on positioning are presented and discussed to show potential benefits of applied optimization method.

**Keywords:** Differential evolution · Queueing system · Mass service model positioning

## 1 Introduction

In modern world the devices very often must operate on big data. This happens in financial services, various analytics, information applied in technology processes, cloud computing and so on. Moreover in mass service systems (MSS) we need to operate on many requests and serve various clients at the best possible time, costs and efficacy to optimize the system performance and assist workflow executions [1]. Therefore we need to position these Queuing Systems (QS) for the best Quality of Service (QoS). QS model is a proper tool for operation analysis of various MSS, which can be mathematically modeled and then positioned by the application of some specialized methods or sophisticated tools. QS models are used in positioning of:

- IP routers,
- database servers (in common and also in NoSQL mode),
- video streaming devices,
- voice/music streaming devices,

© Springer International Publishing Switzerland 2015
L. Rutkowski et al. (Eds.): ICAISC 2015, Part II, LNAI 9120, pp. 379–390, 2015.
DOI: 10.1007/978-3-319-19369-4_34

- network interface controllers,
- smoke/fire/danger detection systems,
- manufacturing management,
- transport optimization, etc.

Operation of all these MSSs can be mathematically modeled and then positioned by the application of selected Evolutionary Computation method.

In a typical QS system we must model not only the income and the service, but also disturbances of incoming requests (like burstiness). For this task we can fit one of non-recurrent MAP-type processes describing input stream (MMPP-Markov Modified Poisson Process or BMAP-Batch Markovian Arrival Process). The other possibility is to divide observation horizon of the MSS operation on relatively short time intervals. In these the arrival process can be recurrent with different distributions of inter-arrival times. This conclusion was a motivation for transient analysis of finite-buffer queue with general independent $(GI)$ input flow of packets. Mathematical representation for joint transform of the first busy period, first idle time and number of packets completely served during first busy period in $GI/G/1$-type QSs with batch arrivals and exponential single server vacation was given in [8] and [10]. Transient characteristics of QSs with single vacations with compound Poisson arrivals, generally distributed service times and infinite buffers can be found in [9] and [11]. In [12] non-stationary behavior of waiting time distribution in a finite-buffer queue with single server vacations is investigated. In the paper we discuss application of Differential Evolution (DE) for positioning a transient finite-buffer QS model with hyper exponential independent input stream of packets and exponential service times. In the positioned system a hyper exponentially distributed server vacation is being initialized immediately after the system becomes empty. During server vacation all the arriving packets are buffered in the queue. After vacation, transmission of packets begins normally. The results presented in this paper are continuation of the research on efficient positioning of various QSs presented in [5], [24], [29], [28], [26] and [1]. Where positioning of service cost in $GI/M/1/N$ QS was presented in [5] by the use of Evolutionary Strategy (ES) and in [24] by the use of Cuckoo Search Algorithm (CSA). The detailed mathematical model of the applied finite-buffer queue with a single vacation policy was presented and discussed in [28]. As presented in the cited articles, traffic in the MSS and the most efficient service at the lowest possible cost of work can be optimized and positioned by the use of various EC methods. In each of MSS operation model is based on applied QS model defined in a particular way.

**Definition 1.** *Queueing System model is a process, that gives a mathematical description of the requests arrivals from remote clients to be served by the MSS. Each of them leaves the system after being served. However after arrival, some of them are buffered in a queue to wait for the service.*

This sample definition gives a description of the purpose of mathematical modeling of the service in a dedicated QS applied to optimize operation cost and increase QoS of MSS. In all the mathematical OSs modeling presented in [5],

[24], [29], [28] or [26] the situation was modeled for $T_{service}$-average time of service for each request, $T_{income}$-average time of incoming requests and $T_{vacation}$-average time in which the system takes break. All these times are totally independent random variables, where the symbols used in QS description in time $t$ are:

- $\tau_1$ — the first busy period of the system (starting at $t = 0$);
- $\delta_1$ — the first idle time of the system (consisting of the first vacation time $v_1$ and the first server standby time $q_1$);
- $h(\tau_1)$ — the number of packets completely served during $\tau_1$;
- $X(t)$ — the number of packets present in the system at time $t$.

QS model presents the amount of the request arrivals and response departures at the certain time. Mainly in the cited research we were trying to give the optional positioning for QS, where at the time there is only one request arrival and one response departure. Sample operation schema in this MSS type pictures Fig. 1.

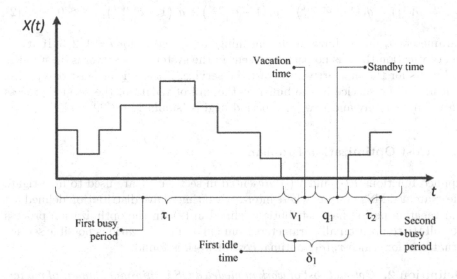

**Fig. 1.** Sample queue process where one request arrives or one departures

## 2    Queueing Model

Similar attempt to model and position QSs by dividing observation horizon on relatively short time intervals in which arrival process is recurrent with different distributions in different interval times is presented in [5], [24], [29], [28], [26] or [27]. Here to model MSS operation was applied a finite-buffer $H_3/M/1/N$-type QS. Let us also present a brief description of the QS model, just to help in understanding positioning and simulation problem using Definition 1, a full analytical model is presented in details in [28].

## 2.1   Applied Inter-Arrival and Vacation Distribution Functions

In modeled MSS are used inter-arrival times of 3-order, hyper exponentially distributed random variables with distribution function:

$$F(t) = p_1\left(1 - e^{-\lambda_1 t}\right) + p_2\left(1 - e^{-\lambda_2 t}\right) + p_3\left(1 - e^{-\lambda_3 t}\right), \quad t > 0, \qquad (1)$$

where $\lambda_i > 0$ for $i = 1, 2, 3$ and $p_1, p_2, p_3 \geq 0$. Distribution of inter-arrival times is mixture of exponential distributions with parameters $\lambda_1$, $\lambda_2$ and $\lambda_3$ which are being "chosen" with probabilities $p_1$, $p_2$ and $p_3$ respectively. In the system, there are $(N - 1)$ places in the queue and one for packet in the service. System starts working at $t = 0$ with at least one packet present, where the MSS process goes schematically as pictured in Fig. 1. After busy period the server begins compulsory single vacation in the service which is modeled with 3-order hyper exponentially distributed random variable with distribution function:

$$V(t) = q_1\left(1 - e^{-\alpha_1 t}\right) + q_2\left(1 - e^{-\alpha_2 t}\right) + q_3\left(1 - e^{-\alpha_3 t}\right), \quad t > 0. \qquad (2)$$

Parameters $\alpha_i$ and $q_i$ have similar meanings to $\lambda_i$ and $p_i$ for $i = 1, 2, 3$. If at the end of vacation there is no packet present in the system, the server is on standby and waits for the first arrival to start the service. If there is at least one packet waiting for the service in the buffer at the end of vacation, the service process starts immediately and new busy period begins (similarly to [29] and [27]).

## 2.2   Cost Optimization Problem

Applied functions $F(\cdot)$ and $V(\cdot)$ presented in section 2.1 are used to investigate the examined MSS system, where inter-arrival times have distribution defined (1) and vacation period has distribution defined in (2). In the optimization process we will try to position all parameters from (1) and (2) in various possible service situations, for which $r_n(c_1)$-optimal cost of work is found.

**Definition 2.** *Optimal cost of work in modeled QS is minimal amount of money, energy or any other resources that the system may need to perform all operations.*

Define in Definition 2 optimal cost of work has a form of equation applicable in optimization process:

$$r_n(c_1) = \frac{Q_n(c_1)}{\mathbf{E}_n(c_1)} = \frac{r(\tau_1)\mathbf{E}_n\tau_1 + r(\delta_1)\mathbf{E}_n\delta_1}{\mathbf{E}_n\tau_1 + \mathbf{E}_n\delta_1}, \qquad (3)$$

where the notations are: $r(\tau_1)$–fixed unit operation costs during busy period $\tau_1$, $r(\delta_1)$–fixed unit operation costs during idle time $\delta_1$, $\mathbf{E}_n\tau_1$–mean of busy period $\tau_1$ and $\mathbf{E}_n\delta_1$–mean of idle time $\delta_1$ on condition that system starts with $n$ packets present. The explicit formula with detailed information and description for conditional joint characteristic functions of $\tau_1$, $\delta_1$ and $h(\tau_1)$ is presented in [28]. Here let us briefly remind the modeling. General equation to calculate this values is

$$B_n(s, \varrho, z) = \mathbf{E}\{e^{-s\tau_1 - \varrho\delta_1} z^{h(\tau_1)} \,|\, X(0) = n\} =$$

$$= \frac{D(s, \varrho, z) - G(s, \varrho, z)}{H(s, z)} R_{n-1}(s, z) + \sum_{k=2}^{n} R_{n-k}(s, z)\Psi_k(s, \varrho, z), \quad 2 \le n \le N. \tag{4}$$

where $s \ge 0$, $\varrho \ge 0$ and $|z| \le 1$, $n \ge 1$. Moreover $a_n(s, z)$, $\Psi_n(s, \varrho, z)$, $D(s, \varrho, z)$, $G(s, \varrho, z)$ and $H(s, z)$ are defined in (5), (6), (9), (10) and (11) respectively.

$$a_n(s, z) = \int_0^\infty \frac{(z\mu t)^n}{n!} e^{-(\mu+s)t} dF(t), \quad n \ge 0, \tag{5}$$

$$\Psi_n(s, \varrho, z) = -\frac{(z\mu)^n}{(n-1)!} \left[ \int_0^\infty dF(t) \int_0^t x^{n-1} e^{-(\mu+s)x} \right.$$

$$\times \left( e^{-\varrho(t-x)} V(t-x) + \int_{t-x}^\infty e^{-\varrho y} dV(y) \right) dx \right]. \tag{6}$$

Moreover, sequence $(a_n(s, z))$ in (5) helps to recursively define

$$R_0(s, z) = 0, \quad R_1(s, z) = a_0^{-1}(s, z),$$

$$R_{n+1}(s, z) = R_1(s, z)(R_n(s, z) - \sum_{k=0}^{n} a_{k+1}(s, z) R_{n-k}(s, z)). \tag{7}$$

With introduced following function

$$f(s) = \int_0^\infty e^{-st} dF(t), \quad s > 0 \tag{8}$$

we finally have components of $r_n(c_1)$ operation costs defined in (3):

$$D(s, \varrho, z) = \sum_{k=1}^{N-1} a_k(s, z) \sum_{i=2}^{N-k+1} R_{N-k+1-i}(s, z)\Psi_i(s, \varrho, z), \tag{9}$$

$$G(s, \varrho, z) = \Psi_N(s, \varrho, z) + \left(1 - f(\mu+s)\right) \sum_{k=2}^{N} R_{N-k}(s, z)\Psi_k(s, \varrho, z) \tag{10}$$

and

$$H(s, z) = \left(1 - f(\mu+s)\right) R_{N-1}(s, z) - \sum_{k=1}^{N-1} a_k(s, z) R_{N-k}(s, z). \tag{11}$$

Indeed, since:

$$\mathbf{E}_n e^{-s\tau_1} = \mathbf{E}\{e^{-s\tau_1} \,|\, X(0) = n\} = B_n(s, 0, 1), \tag{12}$$

then

$$\mathbf{E}_n \tau_1 = -\frac{\partial}{\partial s} B_n(s, 0, 1)\Big|_{s=0} \tag{13}$$

and

$$\mathbf{E}_n \delta_1 = -\frac{\partial}{\partial \varrho} B_n(0, \varrho, 1)\Big|_{\varrho=0}. \tag{14}$$

The QS model presented above was solved using Wolfram Mathematica 9.0 to prepare analytical form of total cost equation in (3). QS mathematical models are complicated differential and integral equations, which are not easy to solve. Therefore application of EC method is very helpful. In [5], [24], [29], [28], [26], [27] or [32], [23], [14] we were using selected EC methods. Here let us describe another possibility.

## 3   Differential Evolution Algorithm

Differential Evolution (DE) was introduced by Storn and Price in [20]. DE is a heuristic approach for minimizing possibly nonlinear and non-differentiable continuous space functions. This method belongs to the class of evolutionary algorithms.

The DE algorithm is very simple, however works surprisingly effectively. It requires three parameters:

- $NP$ - population size,
- $F$ - a parameter to control the mutation,
- $CR$ - crossover probability.

DE operates on a population $\mathcal{X}$ of individuals $\mathbf{x_i}$, where $i = 1, ..., NP$ and $\mathbf{x_i} = [x_{1i}, x_{2i}, ..., x_{Di}]^T$. Firstly we create at random population $\mathbf{x_i}^G$, where $G = 1$ is the number of the individuals in the population. In the algorithm, all the individuals are $D$-dimensional vectors of the real numbers, where the phenotype is identical to the genotype.

Mutation in this method is based on random permutation of each vector $\mathbf{x_i}$ by differencing two other vectors from the population $\mathcal{X}$ multiplying them by a constant value. For each vector $\mathbf{x_i}^G$ we generate the mutant vector $\mathbf{v_i}^G$ according to:

$$\mathbf{v_i}^{G+1} = \mathbf{x_{r1}}^G + F \cdot (\mathbf{x_{r2}}^G - \mathbf{x_{r3}}^G), \tag{15}$$

with random indexes $r1, r2, r3 \in \{1, 2, ..., NP\}$ and $r1 \neq r2 \neq r3 \neq i$ and $F \in [0, 2]$ is a real and constant factor.

Crossover operator is introduced to mix random elements of parent vector $\mathbf{x_i}^G$ and elements of the vector $\mathbf{v_i}^{G+1}$ after mutation, where as the output is received trial vector:

$$u_{ji}^{G+1} = \begin{cases} v_{ji}^{G+1} & \text{if } rnd_j < CR \text{ or } j = d_i \\ x_{ji}^G & \text{if } rnd_j > CR \text{ and } j \neq d_i \end{cases}, j = 1, ..., D, \tag{16}$$

where $CR \in [0,1]$ is the crossover constant, $rnd_j$ is a uniform random number generator with outcome $\in [0,1]$ and $d_i \in 1,2,\ldots,D$ is a randomly chosen index. The crossover operation refers to optimization process. If $f(u_i^{G+1}) < f(x_i^G)$ then $x_i^{G+1} = u_i^{G+1}$, where $f(\cdot)$ is a fitness function. In other case $x_i^{G+1} = x_i^G$. Description in pseudo-code of applied DE is presented in Algorithm 1.

Start,
Define all coefficients: $NP$ - population size, $F$ - a parameter to control the mutation, $CR$- crossover probability,
Define fitness function $f(\cdot)$ for the algorithm using (3),
Create a random population $x_i^G$ in QS solution space,
$t = 0$,
**while** $t \le generation$ **do**
    **foreach** *vector* $x_i^G$ *from population* $\mathcal{X}$ **do**
        Generate mutant vector $v_i^G$ according to (15),
        Crossover vectors within the population according to (16),
        **if** $f(u_i^{G+1}) < f(x_i^G)$ **then**
          | $x_i^{G+1} = u_i^{G+1}$–change the values,
        **end**
        **else**
          | $x_i^{G+1} = x_i^G$–leave them unchanged,
        **end**
    **end**
    Next generation $t = t + 1$,
**end**
Values from last population with best fitness are optimal solution,
Stop.
**Algorithm 1.** Differential Evolution algorithm to position defined QS

## 4 Optimal Positioning Problem

In the research we have preformed calculations to position QS for lowest response time and service cost. DE simulations were performed for $r(\tau_1) = 0.5$ and $r(\delta_1) = 0.5$, what means that according to Definition 2, QS service and vacation uses 0.5 energy unit each, which costs differ depending on the local energy billing rate. These values may be changed in (3), what makes presented model flexible and easily applicable. Presented results are averaged values of 100 samplings for DE in 200 generations with $NP = 200$, $F = 0.5$, $CR = 0.1$, where:

- Average service time: $T_{service} = \frac{1}{\mu}$,
- Average packages income time: $T_{income} = \frac{p_1}{\lambda_1} + \frac{p_2}{\lambda_2} + \frac{p_3}{\lambda_3}$,
- Average system vacation time: $T_{vacation} = \frac{q_1}{\alpha_1} + \frac{q_2}{\alpha_2} + \frac{q_3}{\alpha_3}$,
- Examined system size: $N =$ buffer size $+1$.

## Scenario 1.

DE was performed to find set of parameters for lowest cost of work and best QoS. In Table 1 are optimum values.

**Table 1.** Parameters $\mu$, $\lambda_i$, $\alpha_i$, $p_i$, $q_i$ for $i = 1, 2, 3$ and lowest value of (3)

| $\lambda_1$ | $\lambda_2$ | $\lambda_3$ | $\alpha_1$ | $\alpha_2$ | $\alpha_3$ | $p_1$ | $p_2$ | $p_3$ | $q_1$ | $q_2$ | $q_3$ |
|---|---|---|---|---|---|---|---|---|---|---|---|
| 2.67 | 1.79 | 2.02 | 2.69 | 2.88 | 2.34 | 1.92 | 2.53 | 1.78 | 1.71 | 1.31 | 0.9 |

| $\mu$ 0.38 | | $r_n(c_1)$ 1.79 |
|---|---|---|
| | $T_{service}$ | $T_{income}$ | $T_{vacation}$ |
| [sec] | 2.65 | 3.02 | 3.66 |

DE was also arranged to position QS in various scenarios. The system parameters represent possible traffic situation.

## Scenario 2.

NoSQL $T_{service} = 1[sec]$, what means that request service takes about $1[sec]$. Modeling results are shown in Table 2.

**Table 2.** Parameters $\mu$, $\lambda_i$, $\alpha_i$, $p_i$, $q_i$ for $i = 1, 2, 3$ and lowest value of (3)

| $\lambda_1$ | $\lambda_2$ | $\lambda_3$ | $\alpha_1$ | $\alpha_2$ | $\alpha_3$ | $p_1$ | $p_2$ | $p_3$ | $q_1$ | $q_2$ | $q_3$ |
|---|---|---|---|---|---|---|---|---|---|---|---|
| 3.22 | 1.42 | 1.44 | 2.6 | 2.95 | 3.07 | 1.73 | 2.44 | 2.44 | 1.19 | 1.33 | 0.4 |

| $\mu$ 1 | | $r_n(c_1)$ 2.37 |
|---|---|---|
| | $T_{service}$ | $T_{income}$ | $T_{vacation}$ |
| [sec] | 1 | 3.08 | 2.14 |

## Scenario 3.

$T_{service} = 0.5[sec]$, what represents extensively used QS with heavy traffic. Modeling results with system positioning are shown in Table 3. We can also position

**Table 3.** Parameters $\mu$, $\lambda_i$, $\alpha_i$, $p_i$, $q_i$ for $i = 1, 2, 3$ and lowest value of (3)

| $\lambda_1$ | $\lambda_2$ | $\lambda_3$ | $\alpha_1$ | $\alpha_2$ | $\alpha_3$ | $p_1$ | $p_2$ | $p_3$ | $q_1$ | $q_2$ | $q_3$ |
|---|---|---|---|---|---|---|---|---|---|---|---|
| 10.6 | 3.91 | 5.86 | 11.04 | 13.31 | 0.00 | 4.84 | 4.75 | 0.67 | 4.54 | 4.39 | 0.00 |

| $\mu$ 0.5 | | $r_n(c_1)$ 0.06 |
|---|---|---|
| | $T_{service}$ | $T_{income}$ | $T_{vacation}$ |
| [sec] | 0.5 | 1.21 | 1.26 |

QS for given $T_{income}$, which corresponds to incoming situations.

## Scenario 4.

$T_{income}$ was given as $1[sec]$, research results are shown in Table 4.

**Table 4.** Parameters $\mu$, $\lambda_i$, $\alpha_i$, $p_i$, $q_i$ for $i = 1, 2, 3$ and lowest value of (3)

| $\lambda_1$ | $\lambda_2$ | $\lambda_3$ | $\alpha_1$ | $\alpha_2$ | $\alpha_3$ | $p_1$ | $p_2$ | $p_3$ | $q_1$ | $q_2$ | $q_3$ |
|---|---|---|---|---|---|---|---|---|---|---|---|
| 4.60 | 4.04 | 3.13 | 3.64 | 5.43 | 1.55 | 8.0 | 1.05 | 0.00 | 2.98 | 2.97 | 1.19 |
| $\mu$ 0.58 | | | | | | $r_n(c_1)$ 0.28 | | | | | |

| | $T_{service}$ | $T_{income}$ | $T_{vacation}$ |
|---|---|---|---|
| $[sec]$ | 1.70 | 1.0 | 2.85 |

## Scenario 5.

$T_{income}$ was given as $0.5[sec]$, what means that requests are incoming to the server twice in every second. Modeling results are shown in Table 5.

**Table 5.** Parameters $\mu$, $\lambda_i$, $\alpha_i$, $p_i$, $q_i$ for $i = 1, 2, 3$ and lowest value of (3)

| $\lambda_1$ | $\lambda_2$ | $\lambda_3$ | $\alpha_1$ | $\alpha_2$ | $\alpha_3$ | $p_1$ | $p_2$ | $p_3$ | $q_1$ | $q_2$ | $q_3$ |
|---|---|---|---|---|---|---|---|---|---|---|---|
| 6.44 | 6.29 | 2.16 | 3.79 | 6.84 | 0.48 | 20.10 | 1.43 | 0.00 | 3.46 | 3.44 | 0.56 |
| $\mu$ 0.59 | | | | | | $r_n(c_1)$ 0.003 | | | | | |

| | $T_{service}$ | $T_{income}$ | $T_{vacation}$ |
|---|---|---|---|
| $[sec]$ | 1.67 | 0.5 | 2.27 |

## Scenario 6.

$T_{vacation}$ was given as $1[sec]$, what means that after busy period the system has a compulsory break. Modeling results are shown in Table 6.

**Table 6.** Parameters $\mu$, $\lambda_i$, $\alpha_i$, $p_i$, $q_i$ for $i = 1, 2, 3$ and lowest value of (3)

| $\lambda_1$ | $\lambda_2$ | $\lambda_3$ | $\alpha_1$ | $\alpha_2$ | $\alpha_3$ | $p_1$ | $p_2$ | $p_3$ | $q_1$ | $q_2$ | $q_3$ |
|---|---|---|---|---|---|---|---|---|---|---|---|
| 6.06 | 2.82 | 2.25 | 2.42 | 6.56 | 2.96 | 3.16 | 3.25 | 2.36 | 2.72 | 1.9 | 0.32 |
| $\mu$ 0.71 | | | | | | $r_n(c_1)$ -3.32 | | | | | |

| | $T_{service}$ | $T_{income}$ | $T_{vacation}$ |
|---|---|---|---|
| $[sec]$ | 1.4 | 2.72 | 1.0 |

**Scenario 7.**

$T_{vacation}$ was given as $2[sec]$. Modeling results are shown in Table 7.

**Table 7.** Parameters $\mu$, $\lambda_i$, $\alpha_i$, $p_i$, $q_i$ for $i = 1, 2, 3$ and lowest value of (3)

| $\lambda_1$ | $\lambda_2$ | $\lambda_3$ | $\alpha_1$ | $\alpha_2$ | $\alpha_3$ | $p_1$ | $p_2$ | $p_3$ | $q_1$ | $q_2$ | $q_3$ |
|------|------|------|------|------|------|------|------|------|------|------|------|
| 3.14 | 2.18 | 2.15 | 2.97 | 3.97 | 1.84 | 1.88 | 2.59 | 1.47 | 5.49 | 1.44 | 0.79 |

| $\mu$ 0.65 | | | $r_n(c_1)$ -0.87 | | |
|---|---|---|---|---|---|

| | $T_{service}$ | $T_{income}$ | $T_{vacation}$ |
|---|---|---|---|
| [sec] | 1.52 | 2.47 | 2.0 |

## 5    Conclusions

EC methods are useful in simulation or positioning of various types of objects. They help to collect representative samples, which can be used by AI decision support systems [6]. EC methods help to position various objects [3], [13], [22], [21], [25], [31], [30] and position dynamic systems [18], [17]. The free design makes calculations possible even in discontinuous spaces [2], [4] [7], [19], .

Positioned QS model was simulated in situations with predefined time of service or income, which reflect common or heavy traffic in the system. Conducted experiments confirm efficiency in simulation of examined object in many possible scenarios representing common situations in reality.

Further work should be carried out to reduce time consuming operations, tentatively by using some knowledge prior to generate initial population. Moreover, modeled system could be non-stationary and parameters could change during work due to e.g. wear (expenditure) of elements (battery, voltage, etc.) or environment changes (temperature, air composition etc.). So, in future research it is important to take into account this aspects by e.g. fuzzyfication of the system parameters [16], [15].

**Acknowledgements.** The project was financed by the National Science Centre (Poland) on the basis of the decision number DEC-2012/05/B/ST7/02138.

## References

1. Borowik, G., Woźniak, M., Fornaia, A., Giunta, R., Napoli, C., Pappalardo, G., Tramontana, E.: A software architecture assisting workflow executions on cloud resources. International Journal of Electronics and Telecommunications 61(1), 17–23 (2015)

2. Cpałka, K.: On evolutionary designing and learning of flexible neuro-fuzzy structures for nonlinear classification. Nonlinear Analysis: Theory, Methods & Applications 71(12), e1659–e1672 (2009)

3. Cpalka, K., Rutkowski, L.: Flexible takagi-sugeno fuzzy systems. In: Proceedings of 2005 IEEE International Joint Conference on Neural Networks, IJCNN 2005, vol. 3, pp. 1764–1769 (2005)
4. Damasevicius, R.: Generation of combinatorial circuit meta-programs from truth table specifications using evolutionary design techniques. In: Proc. of 15th Conference on Information and Software Technologies, Kaunas, Lithuania, April 23-24, pp. 109–116 (2009)
5. Gabryel, M., Nowicki, R.K., Woźniak, M., Kempa, W.M.: Genetic cost optimization of the $GI/M/1/N$ finite-buffer queue with a single vacation policy. In: Rutkowski, L., Korytkowski, M., Scherer, R., Tadeusiewicz, R., Zadeh, L.A., Zurada, J.M. (eds.) ICAISC 2013, Part II. LNCS, vol. 7895, pp. 12–23. Springer, Heidelberg (2013)
6. Gabryel, M., Woźniak, M., Nowicki, R.K.: Creating learning sets for control systems using an evolutionary method. In: Rutkowski, L., Korytkowski, M., Scherer, R., Tadeusiewicz, R., Zadeh, L.A., Zurada, J.M. (eds.) EC 2012 and SIDE 2012. LNCS, vol. 7269, pp. 206–213. Springer, Heidelberg (2012)
7. Hetmaniok, E., Nowak, I., Słota, D., Zielonka, A.: Determination of optimal parameters for the immune algorithm used for solving inverse heat conduction problems with and without a phase change. Numer. Heat Transfer B 62, 462–478 (2012)
8. Kempa, W.M.: $GI/G/1/\infty$ batch arrival queuing system with a single exponential vacation. Mathematical Methods of Operations Research 1(69), 81–97 (2009)
9. Kempa, W.M.: Some new results for departure process in the $M^X/G/1$ queuing system with a single vacation and exhaustive service. Stochastic Analysis and Applications 1(28), 26–43 (2009)
10. Kempa, W.M.: Characteristics of vacation cycle in the batch arrival queuing system with single vacations and exhaustive service. International Journal of Applied Mathematics 4(23), 747–758 (2010)
11. Kempa, W.M.: On departure process in the batch arrival queue with single vacation and setup time. Annales UMCS Informatica 1(10), 93–102 (2010)
12. Kempa, W.M.: The virtual waiting time in a finite-buffer queue with a single vacation policy. In: Al-Begain, K., Fiems, D., Vincent, J.-M. (eds.) ASMTA 2012. LNCS, vol. 7314, pp. 47–60. Springer, Heidelberg (2012)
13. Łapa, K., Przybył, A., Cpałka, K.: A new approach to designing interpretable models of dynamic systems. In: Rutkowski, L., Korytkowski, M., Scherer, R., Tadeusiewicz, R., Zadeh, L.A., Zurada, J.M. (eds.) ICAISC 2013, Part II. LNCS, vol. 7895, pp. 523–534. Springer, Heidelberg (2013)
14. Ludwig, S.: Repulsive self-adaptive acceleration particle swarm optimization approach. Journal of Artificial Intelligence and Soft Computing Research 4(3), 189–204 (2014)
15. Niewiadomski, A.: A Type-2 Fuzzy Approach to Linguistic Summarization of Data. IEEE Transactions on Fuzzy Systems 16(1), 198–212 (2008)
16. Niewiadomski, A.: On Finity, Countability, Cardinalities, And Cylindric Extensions of Type-2 Fuzzy Sets in Linguistic Summarization of Databases. IEEE Transactions on Fuzzy Systems 18(3), 532–545 (2010)
17. Nowak, A., Woźniak, M.: Analysis of the active module mechatronical systems. In: Proceedings of Mechanika 2008 - ICM 2008, Kaunas, Lietuva, pp. 371–376. Kaunas University of Technology Press (2008)
18. Nowak, A., Woźniak, M.: Multiresolution derives analysis of module mechatronical systems. Mechanika 6(74), 45–51 (2008)
19. Słota, D.: Reconstruction of the boundary condition in the problem of the binary alloy solidification. Arch. Metall. Mater. 56, 279–285 (2011)

20. Storn, R., Price, K.: Differential evolution – a simple and efficient heuristic for global optimization over continuous spaces. Journal of Global Optimization 11(4), 341–359 (1997)
21. Swiechowski, M., Mandziuk, J.: Self-adaptation of playing strategies in general game playing. IEEE Trans. Comput. Intellig. and AI in Games 6(4), 367–381 (2014)
22. Waledzik, K., Mandziuk, J.: An automatically generated evaluation function in general game playing. IEEE Trans. Comput. Intellig. and AI in Games 6(3), 258–270 (2014)
23. Wang, X., Liu, X., Japkowicz, N., Matwin, S.: Automated approach to classification of mine-like objects using multiple-aspect sonar images. Journal of Artificial Intelligence and Soft Computing Research 4(2), 133–148 (2015)
24. Woźniak, M.: On applying cuckoo search algorithm to positioning GI/M/1/N finite-buffer queue with a single vacation policy. In: Proceedings of the 12th Mexican International Conference on Artificial Intelligence, MICAI 2013, Mexico City, Mexico, November 24-30, pp. 59–64. IEEE (2013)
25. Woźniak, M.: Fitness function for evolutionary computation applied in dynamic object simulation and positioning. In: Proceedings of the IEEE Symposium Series on Computational Intelligence, SSCI 2014: 2014 IEEE Symposium on Computational Intelligence in Vehicles and Transportation Systems, CIVTS 2014, Orlando, Florida, USA, December 9-12, pp. 108–114. IEEE (2014)
26. Woźniak, M.: On positioning traffic in nosql database systems by the use of particle swarm algorithm. In: Proceedings of XV Workshop DAGLI OGGETTI AGLI AGENTI - WOA 2014, Catania, Italy, September 25-26. CEUR Workshop Proceedings (CEUR-WS.org), RWTH Aachen University, paper 5 (2014)
27. Woźniak, M., Gabryel, M., Nowicki, R.K., Nowak, B.: A novel approach to position traffic in nosql database systems by the use of firefly algorithm. In: Papadopoulos, G.A. (ed.) Proceedings of the 9th International Conference on Knowledge, Information and Creativity Support Systems, November 6-8, pp. 208–218. University of Cyprus Press, Limassol (2014)
28. Woźniak, M., Kempa, W.M., Gabryel, M., Nowicki, R.K.: A finite-buffer queue with single vacation policy - analytical study with evolutionary positioning. International Journal of Applied Mathematics and Computer Science 24(4), 887–900 (2014)
29. Woźniak, M., Kempa, W.M., Gabryel, M., Nowicki, R.K., Shao, Z.: On applying evolutionary computation methods to optimization of vacation cycle costs in finite-buffer queue. In: Rutkowski, L., Korytkowski, M., Scherer, R., Tadeusiewicz, R., Zadeh, L.A., Zurada, J.M. (eds.) ICAISC 2014, Part I. LNCS (LNAI), vol. 8467, pp. 480–491. Springer, Heidelberg (2014)
30. Woźniak, M., Marszałek, Z.: An idea to apply firefly algorithm in 2D image key-points search. In: Dregvaite, G., Damasevicius, R. (eds.) ICIST 2014. CCIS, vol. 465, pp. 312–323. Springer, Heidelberg (2014)
31. Woźniak, M., Połap, D.: Basic concept of cuckoo search algorithm for 2D images processing with some research results. In: Proceedings of the 11th International Conference on Signal Processing and Multimedia Applications, SIGMAP 2014, Vienna, Austria, August 28-30, pp. 164–173. SciTePress - INSTICC (2014)
32. Woźniak, M., Połap, D.: On some aspects of genetic and evolutionary methods for optimization purposes. International Journal of Electronics and Telecommunications 61(1), 7–16 (2015)

# Experimental Evaluation of Selected Approaches to Covariance Matrix Regularization

Przemysław Głomb and Michał Cholewa[✉]

Institute of Theoretical and Applied Informatics,
Polish Academy of Sciences, Bałtycka 5, 44-100 Gliwice, Poland
mcholewa@iitis.pl

**Abstract.** Our objective is to asses the performance of covariance matrix regularization methods on real world data, to provide points of reference for future applications. We analyse the following estimators: OAS, Rao-Blackwell-Ledoit-Wolf, Ledoit-Wolf in two versions, and Thresholding on data from several publicly available datasets (K9, Isolet, Slice, Gistette, S1 ADL1). We investigate through several norms the error of estimation from reduced data.

## 1   Introduction

Many practical problems require an estimation of covariance matrix of high dimensional data. Example such fields are EEG signal analysis, DNA microarrays processing, clustering of text documents, or models in financial economics. A typical approach of estimation of covariance matrix from $n$ observations $\{X_1, \ldots, X_n\}$ of $X \in \mathbb{R}^p$ is by using the sample (or empirical) covariance matrix estimator, $\hat{\Sigma} = \frac{1}{n} \sum_{i=1}^{n} (X_i - \bar{X})(X_i - \bar{X})^\top$ which is known to be unbiased and does not require assumptions about the distribution of $X$. It is well known, however, that this estimator performs poorly if the ratio of dimension $p$ to number of samples $n$, $\theta = \frac{p}{n}$ is small (see e.g. [13,19,1]). The problem is so widespread, that some popular function libraries[1] by default use a regularization of covariance matrix in the estimation process.

A number of approaches have been developed to address this problem, including: the regularization (or shrinkage) approach, which mixes the sample covariance with identity matrix [13,3], thresholding small elements [1], constraining matrix structure for ordered data [2], and others. The related problem of estimation of concentration matrix (inverse of covariance) in high dimensional setting is approached by e.g. by using penalized normal likelihood approach [20] or Moore–Penrose pseudoinverse.

The objective of this article is to study actual performance of selected covariance matrix estimations on several publicly available, real data sets. This paper is organized as follows: we first review the related work and state the basic problem, then present a number of estimators that will be compared, then present experiments results with dataset discussion and conclusions.

---

[1] For example the scikit-learn Machine Learing package.

© Springer International Publishing Switzerland 2015
L. Rutkowski et al. (Eds.): ICAISC 2015, Part II, LNAI 9120, pp. 391–401, 2015.
DOI: 10.1007/978-3-319-19369-4_35

## 2   Related Work

Estimating the large covariance matrix methods have to deal with two main problems. First, the number of unknown elements in the matrix grows quadratically with the dimension. Second, there is a constraint on the results to be positive definite. The problem of positive-definiteness was approached Leonard and Hsu in [14] as well as Chiu et al. in [4] by modelling the matrix logarithm of a covariance matrix. Different research was conducted by Pourahmadi [15,16], who considered generalised linear models for covariances with the use of components of modified Cholesky decomposition of the concentration matrix.

Current methods to solve this problem are usually associated with one of two approaches: first one that relies on natural ordering of the variables, assuming that correlation between variables close in the ordering is stronger than those far apart and second one that is invariant to permutation of the variables, not constraining the variable correlation.

The estimators from the first type often include regularization of covariance matrix by banding or tapering. They often use the lasso and ridge penalties [12], or the nested lasso penalty [20], methods designed for the ordered variables situation. There were also propositions for banding of the Cholesky factor (see e.g. [2] and [17]).

The permutation-invariant estimators include early proposed shrinkage estimators [6,11]. More recent work of Ledoit and Wolf in [13] focuses on a shrinkage estimator where the optimal amount of shrinkage is estimated from given data. This approach is very useful in the analysis of graphical models, where zero partial correlations imply a sparse graph structure.

## 3   Problem Statement

Suppose we observe $n$ i.i.d. $p$-dimensional observations $X_1, \ldots, X_n$ distributed according to distribution $F$, with expected value $E(X) = 0$ and let $\Sigma = E(XX^T)$ be the covariance matrix. Let *sample covariance matrix* be defined as

$$\hat{\Sigma} = \frac{1}{n} \sum_{k=1}^{n} (X_k - \bar{X})(X_k - \bar{X})^T \tag{1}$$

with $\bar{X} = \frac{1}{n} \sum_{k=1}^{n} X_k$ and where $\hat{\Sigma} = [\hat{\sigma}_{ij}]_{p \times p}$

Sample covariance matrix is most commonly used estimator of covariance matrix. It has, however tendency to lose precision with decreasing $\theta = \frac{p}{n}$. Since use of multidimensional data has become common, new methods for estimation have been developed.

For measuring error we will be using several widely used norms for $M \in \mathbb{R}^{p \times p}$ such as

- Frobenius norm (following [2,1]) $\|\cdot\|_F$ defined as $\|M\|_F = \sqrt{\frac{\mathrm{Tr}(MM^T)}{p}}$
- Operator norm $\|\cdot\|$ for positively defined matrices (following [7] and [21]), defined as $\|M\| = \max_{1 \le j \le p} \lambda_j(M)$ where $\lambda_j(M)$ is $j$-th eigenvalue of covariance matrix $M$.
- Matrix 1-norm (as is in [22]), $\|M\|_1 = \sum_{i,j=1}^{p} |m_{ij}|$.
- Maximum difference between real and estimated eigenvalues (following [1]), $e_{\max}(\Sigma) = \left|\max_i \lambda_i(\Sigma) - \max_i \lambda_i(\hat{\Sigma})\right| = \left|\|\Sigma\| - \|\hat{\Sigma}\|\right|$.

## 4  Materials and Methods

This section reviews in detail the two elements of our experiments: used estimators and datasets.

### Estimators

In this section we review selected approached for high dimensional covariance matrix estimation. We focus on non-ordered case, or permutation-invariant estimators.

**Ledoit-Wolf Method.** Ledoit-Wolf is one of estimators that try to approximate Oracle estimator in achieving the optimal balance between scaled $I$ and $\hat{\Sigma}$.

This estimator was introduced in [13] and can be defined as follows:

**Definition 1.** *Let* $m_n = \langle \hat{\Sigma}_n, I_n \rangle_n$, $\bar{b}_n^2 = \frac{1}{n^2} \sum_{i=1}^{n} \|X_i^n(X_i^n)^t - \hat{\Sigma}_n\|_{F(n)}^2$, $d_n^2 = \|\hat{\Sigma}_n - m_n I_n\|_{F(n)}^2$, $b_n^2 = \min(\bar{b}_n^2, d_n^2)$ *and* $a_n^2 = d_n^2 - b_n^2$. *We can define*

$$\Sigma_{LW,n} = \frac{b_n^2}{d_n^2} m_n I_n + \frac{a_n^2}{d_n^2} \hat{\Sigma}_n \tag{2}$$

Ledoit and Wolf then proved in [13], that $\Sigma_{LW,n}$ is asymptomatically optimal linear shrinkage estimator.

**Rao-Blackwell Ledoit-Wolf.** Rao-Blackwell Ledoit-Wolf (RBLW) is an improvement of Ledoit- Wolf estimator optimized for Gaussian distributions of $X_1, \ldots, X_n$. It is defined as

$$\Sigma_{RBLW} = E[\Sigma_{LW}|\hat{\Sigma}] = (1 - \rho_{RBLW})\hat{\Sigma} + \rho_{RBLW}\hat{A} \tag{3}$$

Under assumption of Gaussian distribution of $X_1, \ldots, X_n$, for every $\Sigma$ it yields better results than original Lediot-Wolf scheme.

**Oracle Approximation Shrinkage (OAS) Estimator.** The OAS estimator follows different premise tan both LW and RBLW estimators, that asymptotically approximate Oracle estimator results. However, this approach fails when dealing with small $n$. Given $n = 1$ both LW and RBLW give $\rho_{LW} = \rho_{RBLW} = 1$, which puts entire weight of the estimators on sample covariance matrix $\hat{\Sigma}$. Intuitively, however, if the single sample is available it seems more valid to put more confidence into parsimonious $\hat{A} = \frac{\text{Tr}(\hat{\Sigma})}{p}I$, than $\hat{\Sigma}$.

The OAS estimator is designed to cope with low values of $n$. The idea behind the OAS is to approximate oracle through iterative procedure. Iterations are initialized with arbitrary guess and with each step refine it towards Oracle. The sole constraint on the initial guess is to be symmetric positive semidefinite estimator. The iteration process is continued until convergence. The limit, denoted as $\Sigma_{OAS}$, is the OAS solution. The OAS iteration proceeds as follows

$$\Sigma_j = \rho_j \hat{A} + (1 - \rho_j)\hat{\Sigma} \tag{4}$$

$$\rho_{j+1} = \frac{\left(1 - \frac{2}{p}\right)\text{Tr}(\Sigma_j\hat{\Sigma}) + \text{Tr}(\Sigma_j)^2}{\left(n + 1 - \frac{2}{p}\right)\text{Tr}(\Sigma_j\hat{\Sigma}) + (1 - \frac{n}{p})\text{Tr}(\Sigma_j)^2} \tag{5}$$

The above iterative process converges to the OAS estimator as stated in [3].

**Thresholding.** Thresholding is a method of permutation–invariant covariance matrix estimation based on setting a threshold on sample covariance matrix elements. We will understand *thresholding with threshold $s$* as an operator $T_s(M) = [t^s(m_{ij})]$, where $t^s(m_{ij}) = m_{ij}1_{m_{ij} \geq s}$. It has been proven by Bickel and Levina in [1], that for a class of covariance matrices invariant under permutation

$$\mathcal{U}_t(q, c_0(p), m) = \left\{ \Sigma : \sigma_{ii} < m, \forall_i \sum_{j=1}^{p} \sigma_{i,j}^q < c_0(p) \right\}, \tag{6}$$

where $q, c_0(p), m \in \mathbb{R}, 0 \leq q < 1$, thresholding allows the covariance matrix estimate to be close to approximated matrix in terms of Frobenius norm $\|\cdot\|_F^2$.

For finding appropriate value of threshold within bounds, authors of [1] propose minimization of

$$\hat{R}(s) = \frac{1}{N}\sum_{v=1}^{N}\|T_s(\hat{\Sigma}_{1,v}) - \hat{\Sigma}_{2,v}\|_F^2 \tag{7}$$

Where $N$ is number of test divisions $v$ so that $r(\hat{\Sigma}_{1,v}) = n_1$, $r(\hat{\Sigma}_{2,v}) = n_2$ and $n_1 + n_2 = n$.

## Datasets

For our experiments we have used the following datasets:

*K9 dataset.* Full descriptions of the dataset can be found in [5]–the dataset is composed of calculations performed on in silico models of the mutant *p53* structures. Biophysical models of mutant *p53* proteins yield features which can be used to predict *p53* transcriptional activity.

There are a total of 5409 attributes per data record. Attributes 1-4826 represent 2D electrostatic and surface based features. Attributes 4827-5408 represent 3D distance based features.

- $K9_{3300-3800}$ – 500 feature vectors from 2D features
- $K9_{4827-5407}$ – 580 feature vectors representing 3D based features.

*Isolet.* Full description of this database can be found in [8]–'Isolated Letter' is data set of digitized letter names spoken by 150 subjects. These data were then digitally processed, results of which was 617 features such as the number of zero crossings of the waveform and peak-to-peak amplitudes in each 10 ms window, 256-point DFT or amplitudes after low-pass filtering. We have used 530 (the ones with complete data vectors across the dataset) of those 617 features to build our dataset for experiment.

*Slice.* This dataset contains 386 features and its full description may be found in [9]–it is a dataset of relative location of Computer Tomography slices on axial axis. The data was retrieved from a set of 53500 CT images from 74 different patients (43 male, 31 female).

*Gisette.* This dataset is described in [10]–GISETTE is a handwritten digit recognition problem. The digits have been size-normalized and centered in a fixed-size image of dimension 28x28. A number of distracting features called 'probes' having no predictive power was added. The order of the features and patterns were randomized. Each record describes 5000 features of which we selected 530.

*S1 ADL1.* The dataset is described in [18]–it is an element of Opportunity dataset; The 'OPPORTUNITY Dataset for Human Activity Recognition from Wearable, Object, and Ambient Sensors' is a dataset for benchmarking various classes of activity recognition algorithms. The data contains the readings of motion sensors (body worn, object sensors, ambient sensors) recorded while users executed typical daily activities. From this extensive set of 24 datasets we have selected one and focused on 120 readings from body sensors.

## 5   Results

The experiment has been designed to evaluate various covariance matrix estimators by comparing their results to result of sample covariance matrix estimator. Its goal is to determine how much is gained (in terms of assumed error measure or the ability to inverse, measured by condition matrix), when using specific estimator instead of just calculating sample covariance.

**Table 1.** Norms of covariance matrices for experimental datasets

| Data | $\theta$ | $\|\cdot\|_F^2$ | Operator | $\|\cdot\|_1$ | $\log(c)$ |
|---|---|---|---|---|---|
| $K9_{3300-3800}$ | 2.0 | 2819.2587 | 2556.8826 | 6306.2055 | 16.9547 |
| $K9_{4827-5407}$ | 4.31 | 0.0834 | 0.0775 | 0.2293 | 5.6060 |
| Isolet | 1.89 | 30.9218 | 26.8428 | 52.9168 | 6.1044 |
| Slice | 7.77 | 98.6281 | 98.2522 | 413.9503 | 23.0527 |
| Gistette | 5.66 | $3.8115 \cdot 10^6$ | $2.0503 \cdot 10^6$ | $4.6781 \cdot 10^6$ | 19.7457 |
| S1 ADL1 | 50.0 | $3.3361 \cdot 10^9$ | $3.3361 \cdot 10^9$ | $3.9160 \cdot 10^9$ | 37.4736 |

**Table 2.** Absolute error for sample covariance matrix estimator

| Data | $\theta$ | $\|\cdot\|_F^2$ | $e_{\max}$ | Operator | $\|\cdot\|_1$ |
|---|---|---|---|---|---|
| | | N= | 300 | | |
| $K9_{3300-3800}$ | 0.6000 | 0.9981 | 1.0458 | 1.0089 | 0.9918 |
| $K9_{4827-5407}$ | 0.5172 | 0.0299 | 0.0039 | 0.0164 | 0.0689 |
| Isolet | 0.5660 | 4.7342 | 0.8115 | 2.6742 | 8.4289 |
| Slice | 0.7792 | 8.5288 | 6.1507 | 7.9491 | 51.2996 |
| Gistette | 0.5660 | $3.6422 \cdot 10^6$ | $5.8791 \cdot 10^5$ | $1.3083 \cdot 10^6$ | $4.8151 \cdot 10^6$ |
| S1 ADL1 | 2.500 | $1.2476 \cdot 10^8$ | $1.2262 \cdot 10^8$ | $1.2452 \cdot 10^8$ | $2.1368 \cdot 10^8$ |
| | | N= | 50 | | |
| $K9_{3300-3800}$ | 0.1000 | 1163.1437 | 343.1393 | 897.7430 | 3283.8147 |
| $K9_{4827-5407}$ | 0.0862 | 0.0726 | 0.0149 | 0.04775 | 0.2164 |
| Isolet | 0.0943 | 13.1286 | 2.7340 | 7.5098 | 22.9198 |
| Slice | 0.1299 | 21.6575 | 15.2617 | 20.1110 | 130.8658 |
| Gistette | 0.0943 | $5.1250 \cdot 10^6$ | $9.7884 \cdot 10^5$ | $1.8934 \cdot 10^6$ | $6.6799 \cdot 10^6$ |
| S1 ADL1 | 0.4167 | $3.4051 \cdot 10^8$ | $3.3597 \cdot 10^8$ | $3.3990 \cdot 10^8$ | $5.3824 \cdot 10^8$ |
| | | N= | 5 | | |
| $K9_{3300-3800}$ | 0.0100 | 3351.7081 | 1924.0746 | 2867.8142 | 9551.8432 |
| $K9_{4827-5407}$ | 0.0086 | 0.1566 | 0.086871 | 0.135176 | 0.6501 |
| Isolet | 0.0094 | 39.0063 | 10.1110 | 25.8013 | 73.4532 |
| Slice | 0.0130 | 67.8143 | 47.8704 | 63.5922 | 387.3427 |
| Gistette | 0.0094 | $1.4410 \cdot 10^7$ | $7.5875 \cdot 10^6$ | $9.1364 \cdot 10^6$ | $1.8458 \cdot 10^7$ |
| S1 ADL1 | 0.0417 | $1.3280 \cdot 10^9$ | $1.3181 \cdot 10^9$ | $1.3276 \cdot 10^9$ | $1.9297 \cdot 10^9$ |

## The Experiment

The experiment has been designed to evaluate various covariance matrix estimators calculating their relative error to sample covariance. Its goal is to determine how much is gained in terms of error when using specific estimator instead of just calculating sample covariance.

**Table 3.** Error relative to sample covariance estimator error. $N = 100,300$

| Data | Estimator | $\|\cdot\|_F^2$ | $e_{\max}$ | Operator | $\|\cdot\|_1$ | $\|\cdot\|_F^2$ | $e_{\max}$ | Operator | $\|\cdot\|_1$ |
|---|---|---|---|---|---|---|---|---|---|
| | | | N= | 300 | | | N= | 100 | |
| $K9_{3300-3800}$ | OAS | 0.998 | 1.046 | 1.009 | 0.992 | 0.955 | 0.922 | 0.936 | 0.947 |
| (1000) | RBLW | 0.997 | 1.031 | 1.009 | 0.993 | 0.963 | 0.941 | 0.948 | 0.957 |
| | LW - 2 | 0.999 | 1.002 | 1.001 | 0.999 | 0.997 | 0.995 | 0.996 | 0.996 |
| | LW - 1 | 1.015 | 1.222 | 1.046 | 0.989 | 0.942 | 0.989 | 0.926 | 0.906 |
| | T | 1.002 | 0.999 | 1.000 | 1.006 | 1.008 | 1.024 | 0.994 | 0.989 |
| $K9_{4827-5407}$ | OAS | 0.973 | 1.346 | 0.979 | 0.958 | 0.922 | 0.936 | 0.920 | 0.9053 |
| (1-2500) | RBLW | 0.974 | 1.293 | 0.979 | 0.960 | 0.929 | 0.931 | 0.927 | 0.915 |
| | LW - 2 | 2.756 | 19.633 | 4.698 | 3.322 | 1.555 | 6.510 | 2.4170 | 1.646 |
| | LW - 1 | 0.967 | 2.984 | 1.0268 | 0.911 | 0.842 | 1.763 | 0.9154 | 0.770 |
| | T | 1.000 | 1.000 | 1.000 | 1.000 | 1.019 | 1.557 | 1.073 | 0.999 |
| Isolet | OAS | 1.013 | 1.635 | 1.120 | 0.991 | 0.978 | 1.612 | 1.112 | 0.933 |
| (1-1000) | RBLW | 1.009 | 1.550 | 1.103 | 0.990 | 0.974 | 1.495 | 1.086 | 0.935 |
| | LW - 2 | 1.499 | 6.297 | 2.180 | 1.395 | 1.8297 | 8.041 | 2.799 | 1.757 |
| | LW - 1 | 1.010 | 1.550 | 1.103 | 0.990 | 0.7035 | 1.997 | 1.052 | 0.773 |
| | T | 1.000 | 1.0000 | 1.000 | 1.000 | 1.000 | 1.000 | 1.000 | 1.000 |
| Slice | OAS | 1.005 | 1.020 | 1.009 | 0.997 | 1.0123 | 1.015 | 1.009 | 0.992 |
| (1-3000) | RBLW | 1.002 | 1.013 | 1.006 | 0.998 | 1.0073 | 1.011 | 1.005 | 0.994 |
| | LW - 2 | 1.026 | 1.061 | 1.034 | 1.003 | 1.0684 | 1.098 | 1.070 | 1.007 |
| | LW - 1 | 1.002 | 1.016 | 1.006 | 0.997 | 1.000 | 0.991 | 0.994 | 0.990 |
| | T | 1.000 | 1.000 | 1.000 | 1.000 | 10000 | 1.000 | 1.000 | 1.000 |
| Gistette | OAS | 0.867 | 3.731 | 1.247 | 0.946 | 0.703 | 1.9461 | 1.043 | 0.772 |
| (1-3000) | RBLW | 0.866 | 3.651 | 1.237 | 0.943 | 0.703 | 1.857 | 1.027 | 0.772 |
| | LW - 2 | 1.000 | 1.000 | 1.000 | 1.000 | 1.000 | 1.000 | 1.000 | 1.000 |
| | LW - 1 | 0.867 | 3.850 | 1.262 | 0.949 | 0.703 | 1.997 | 1.052 | 0.773 |
| | T | 1.000 | 1.000 | 1.000 | 1.000 | 1.000 | 1.000 | 1.000 | 1.000 |
| S1 ADL1 | OAS | 1.014 | 1.013 | 1.014 | 1.005 | 1.108 | 1.109 | 1.107 | 1.062 |
| (24600-30600) | RBLW | 1.005 | 1.002 | 1.004 | 1.001 | 1.047 | 1.048 | 1.047 | 1.027 |
| | LW - 2 | 1.000 | 1.000 | 1.000 | 1.000 | 1.000 | 1.000 | 10000 | 1.000 |
| | LW - 1 | 1.006 | 1.005 | 1.006 | 1.002 | 1.046 | 1.047 | 1.046 | 1.027 |
| | T | 1.000 | 1.000 | 1.000 | 1.000 | 1.000 | 1.000 | 1.000 | 1.000 |

It is performed in following way: for a set of datasets $\{D_1, D_2, \ldots, D_K\}$, a sample covariance matrices $\{\hat{\Sigma}(D_k)\}_{k=1}^K$ are calculated as reference points. Then $N$ vectors are randomly selected from each dataset. For each dataset then we estimate covariance matrix using estimators $E_1, E_2, \ldots, E_L$ obtaining estimations $\Sigma_{k,l}^N$. We also use sample covariance for $N$ samples to get $\hat{\Sigma}_k^N$ – sample covariance matrix for given dataset $D_k$ and $N$ data vectors.

We now use set of measures $\mu_1, \ldots, \mu_J$ to obtain error of each $\Sigma_{k,l}^N$ and $\hat{\Sigma}_k^N$ compared to $\hat{\Sigma}(D_k)$ – sample covariance matrix calculated from full dataset $D_k$.

We then calculate relative error results using as reference errors of $\hat{\Sigma}_k^N$ for each measure $\mu_j$. We formulate it as a function

$$\phi(k, l, N, j) = \frac{\mu_j(\Sigma_{k,l}^N)}{\mu_j(\hat{\Sigma}_k^N)}, \tag{8}$$

**Table 4.** Error relative to sample covariance estimator error. $N = 50,\ 10$

| Data | Estimator | $\|\cdot\|_F^2$ | $e_{max}$ | Operator | $\|\cdot\|_1$ | $\|\cdot\|_F^2$ | $e_{max}$ | Operator | $\|\cdot\|_1$ |
|---|---|---|---|---|---|---|---|---|---|
| $K9_{3300-3800}$ | OAS | 0.968 | 1.163 | 0.956 | 0.922 | 0.836 | 0.769 | 0.792 | 0.767 |
| (1000) | RBLW | 0.972 | 1.106 | 0.960 | 0.939 | 0.884 | 0.808 | 0.860 | 0.841 |
|  | LW - 2 | 0.997 | 1.008 | 0.995 | 0.994 | 0.989 | 0.989 | 0.988 | 0.985 |
|  | LW - 1 | 1.001 | 1.757 | 1.029 | 0.881 | 0.817 | 0.957 | 0.792 | 0.704 |
|  | T | 1.011 | 1.119 | 1.019 | 1.000 | 1.022 | 1.233 | 1.043 | 0.905 |
| $K9_{4827-5407}$ | OAS | 0.877 | 0.942 | 0.851 | 0.848 | 0.732 | 0.611 | 0.703 | 0.682 |
| (1-2500) | RBLW | 0.892 | 0.917 | 0.868 | 0.869 | 0.812 | 0.715 | 0.793 | 0.782 |
|  | LW - 2 | 1.138 | 5.177 | 1.612 | 1.057 | 0.603 | 1.133 | 0.674 | 0.438 |
|  | LW - 1 | 0.752 | 2.077 | 0.838 | 0.642 | 0.817 | 0.957 | 0.792 | 0.704 |
|  | T | 0.961 | 3.285 | 1.203 | 0.882 | 0.599 | 1.095 | 0.662 | 0.433 |
| Isolet | OAS | 0.962 | 1.866 | 1.156 | 0.915 | 0.756 | 1.524 | 0.937 | 0.703 |
| (1-1000) | RBLW | 0.956 | 1.684 | 1.116 | 0.912 | 0.762 | 1.089 | 0.863 | 0.714 |
|  | LW - 2 | 2.187 | 9.077 | 3.319 | 2.148 | 1.045 | 3.581 | 1.453 | 0.996 |
|  | LW - 1 | 0.959 | 1.721 | 1.125 | 0.916 | 0.764 | 1.195 | 0.884 | 0.719 |
|  | T | 1.000 | 1.000 | 1.000 | 1.000 | 1.056 | 3.568 | 1.465 | 1.004 |
| Slice | OAS | 1.054 | 1.130 | 1.071 | 0.991 | 0.981 | 1.088 | 1.006 | 0.898 |
| (1-3000) | RBLW | 1.032 | 1.081 | 1.043 | 0.991 | 0.985 | 1.058 | 1.004 | 0.934 |
|  | LW - 2 | 1.195 | 1.402 | 1.240 | 1.031 | 1.331 | 1.655 | 1.387 | 1.066 |
|  | LW - 1 | 1.039 | 1.102 | 1.054 | 0.992 | 0.958 | 1.028 | 0.977 | 0.918 |
|  | T | 1.000 | 1.000 | 1.000 | 1.000 | 1.000 | 1.000 | 1.000 | 1.000 |
| Gistette | OAS | 0.563 | 1.015 | 0.757 | 0.613 | 0.317 | 0.238 | 0.325 | 0.349 |
| (1-3000) | RBLW | 0.566 | 0.915 | 0.736 | 0.617 | 0.392 | 0.079 | 0.327 | 0.420 |
|  | LW - 2 | 1.000 | 1.000 | 1.000 | 1.000 | 1.000 | 1.000 | 1.000 | 1.000 |
|  | LW - 1 | 0.563 | 1.035 | 0.761 | 0.613 | 0.353 | 0.116 | 0.317 | 0.385 |
|  | T | 1.000 | 1.000 | 1.000 | 1.000 | 1.000 | 1.000 | 1.000 | 1.000 |
| S1 ADL1 | OAS | 1.042 | 1.044 | 1.042 | 1.020 | 1.216 | 1.220 | 1.213 | 1.093 |
| (24600-30600) | RBLW | 1.011 | 1.015 | 1.012 | 1.004 | 1.051 | 1.052 | 1.050 | 1.009 |
|  | LW - 2 | 1.000 | 1.000 | 1.000 | 1.000 | 1.000 | 1.000 | 1.000 | 1.000 |
|  | LW - 1 | 1.024 | 1.028 | 1.025 | 1.014 | 1.138 | 1.142 | 1.137 | 1.067 |
|  | T | 1.000 | 1.000 | 1.000 | 1.000 | 1.000 | 1.000 | 1.000 | 1.000 |

where $\mu_j(\cdot)$ is value of error measure $\mu_j$. The results are presented in Tables 1-5.

## The Discussion

We follow with discussion of observed behaviors of individual estimators.

The LW-1 estimator is very stable, giving consistently the results close to the references (but with better-conditioned matrices) with only slightly worse result in $e_{max}$ norm for Gistette dataset for high $N$, which seems to be a common result for all shrinkage-based estimators (apart from LW-2).

The similar, albeit slightly better results are given by RBLW and OAS estimators, which seems to yield very similar results, with RBLW being slightly better for higher $N$s and OAS for lower $N$s. That would suggest that prefer-

**Table 5.** Error relative to sample covariance estimator error. $N = 5$

| Data | Estimator | $\|\cdot\|_F^2$ | $e_{max}$ | Operator | $\|\cdot\|_1$ |
|---|---|---|---|---|---|
| $K9_{3300-3800}$ | OAS | 0.739 | 0.649 | 0.669 | 0.662 |
| (1000) | RBLW | 0.836 | 0.772 | 0.775 | 0.811 |
| | LW - 2 | 0.983 | 0.994 | 0.985 | 0.982 |
| | LW - 1 | 0.771 | 0.690 | 0.672 | 0.701 |
| | T | 0.927 | 1.071 | 0.930 | 0.826 |
| $K9_{4827-5407}$ | OAS | 0.622 | 0.486 | 0.593 | 0.540 |
| (1-2500) | RBLW | 0.768 | 0.634 | 0.743 | 0.735 |
| | LW - 2 | 0.528 | 0.887 | 0.570 | 0.352 |
| | LW - 1 | 0.631 | 0.448 | 0.591 | 0.559 |
| | T | 0.528 | 0.882 | 0.568 | 0.349 |
| Isolet | OAS | 0.676 | 1.462 | 0.831 | 0.597 |
| (1-1000) | RBLW | 0.723 | 0.834 | 0.778 | 0.637 |
| | LW - 2 | 0.785 | 2.640 | 1.034 | 0.718 |
| | LW - 1 | 0.714 | 0.967 | 0.794 | 0.628 |
| | T | 0.792 | 2.654 | 1.040 | 0.720 |
| Slice | OAS | 1.017 | 1.260 | 1.067 | 0.852 |
| (1-3000) | RBLW | 0.989 | 1.114 | 1.018 | 0.901 |
| | LW - 2 | 1.370 | 1.903 | 1.452 | 1.029 |
| | LW - 1 | 0.985 | 1.127 | 1.015 | 0.888 |
| | T | 0.972 | 1.151 | 1.001 | 1.000 |
| Gistette | OAS | 0.289 | 0.057 | 0.217 | 0.315 |
| (1-3000) | RBLW | 0.486 | 0.317 | 0.438 | 0.504 |
| | LW - 2 | 1.000 | 1.000 | 1.000 | 1.000 |
| | LW - 1 | 0.454 | 0.271 | 0.400 | 0.474 |
| | T | 1.000 | 1.000 | 1.000 | 1.000 |
| S1 ADL1 | OAS | 1.198 | 1.194 | 1.190 | 1.072 |
| (24600-30600) | RBLW | 1.023 | 1.022 | 1.022 | 0.983 |
| | LW - 2 | 1.000 | 1.000 | 1.000 | 1.000 |
| | LW - 1 | 1.089 | 1.088 | 1.087 | 1.033 |
| | T | 1.000 | 1.000 | 1.000 | 1.000 |

able estimator among these two would be OAS, since we usually use estimators having low number of sample vectors.

Thresholding estimator, as it is basically sample covariance with some of the values zeroed out, yields very similar results as sample covariance; it improves as $N \to 0$. Problem of this estimator, however, lies in the fact that resulting matrix may not be well-conditioned, thus concentration matrix derived from thresholding estimation could be encumbered with high error.

The LW-2 estimator seems to be not well-adjusted. It often generates relatively high error in comparison not only to other estimators, but also to reference sample covariance; this can be seen in $K9_{4827-5407}$ and Isolet datasets for $N > 5$, two datasets with the lowest norms of true covariance matrices. Also, it it sometimes puts whole weight on sample covariance element (which leads to identical covariance matrix as sample, and therefore the same error), which can be observed on Gistette and S1 ADL1 datasets, which have the highest norms of true covariance matrices.

What we can notice is that structure of the results actually give us some knowledge of the data itself–for Gistette for example we can notice that most shrinkage estimators yield very low error comparing to reference, which means that the diagonal element of the true covariance matrix is high compared to non-diagonal data. Contrary to that we can assume that S1 ADL1 has the values equally distributed on the covariance matrix–in context of error sample covariance seems to be the best choice.

Overall scores show that if nothing is known about the data to be analyzed, the on average best estimators are OAS, RBLW and LW-1. They work well with low number of samples and with any tested dataset. That choice however is not obvious. The rest of estimators do not perform significantly worse when it comes to arbitrary datasets, but have their peak performances in specific problems. LW-2, for instance, easily outperform other estimators when analyzed datasets have small norms of covariance matrix and has far worse results in opposite case. Thresholding is not designed for optimizing inversability of resulting matrix, so condition number of its estimation is very similar to sample covariance.

## 6  Conclusions

Usability of covariance matrix estimators to a degree varies depending of analyzed dataset. While it is possible to determine estimators which behave stable and well in most cases, sometimes they are not the optimal choice. There is, therefore no surefire way to select a covariance matrix estimator when no information is known on the data. If, however, the choice must be done without any additional information, the safest one seems to be either OAS or LW-1. The former outperforms slightly other estimators though it comes at a price of higher computational cost; the latter is stable and gives consistently well-conditioned results, with error similar or better than the reference sample covariance matrix.

**Acknowledgements.** This work has been partially supported by the project 'Representation of dynamic 3D scenes using the Atomic Shapes Network model' financed by National Science Centre, decision DEC-2011/03/D/ST6/03753. The authors would like to thank Z. Puchała and P. Gawron for remarks on initial version of the paper.

## References

1. Bickel, P.J., Levina, E.: Covariance regularization by thresholding. The Annals of Statistics 36(6), 2577–2604 (2008)
2. Bickel, P.J., Levina, E.: Regularized estimation of large covariance matrices. The Annals of Statistics 36(1), 199–227 (2008)

3. Chen, Y., Wiesel, A., Eldar, Y.C., Hero, A.O.: Shrinkage algorithms for MMSE covariance estimation. IEEE Transactions on Signal Processing 58(10), 5016–5029 (2010)
4. Chiu, T.Y.M., Leonard, T., Tsui, K.W.: The matrix-logarithm covariance model. Journal of American Statistics Assocciation 91, 198–210 (1996)
5. Danziger, S.A., Baronio, R., Ho, L., Hall, L., Salmon, K., Hatfield, G.W., Kaiser, P., Lathrop, R.H.: Predicting positive p53 cancer rescue regions using most informative positive (MIP) active learning. PLOS Computational Biology 5(9), 1000498 (2009)
6. Dey, D.K., Srinivasan, C.: Estimation of a covariance matrix under Stein's loss. Annals of Statistics 13, 1581–1591 (1985)
7. El Karoui, N.: Operator norm consistent estimation of large dimensional sparse covariance matrices. Annals of Statistics 36(6), 2717–2756 (2008)
8. Fanty, M., Cole, R.: Spoken letter recognition. Advances in Neural Information Processing Systems 3, 220–226 (1991)
9. Graf, F., Kriegel, H.-P., Schubert, M., Pölsterl, S., Cavallaro, A.: 2D image registration in CT images using radial image descriptors. In: Fichtinger, G., Martel, A., Peters, T. (eds.) MICCAI 2011, Part II. LNCS, vol. 6892, pp. 607–614. Springer, Heidelberg (2011)
10. Guyon, I., Gunn, R., Ben-Hur, S.A., Dror, G.: Result analysis of the NIPS 2003 feature selection challenge. Neural Information Processing Systems (2004)
11. Haff, L.R.: Empirical Bayes estimation of the multivariate normal covariance matrix. Annals of Statistics 8, 586–597 (1980)
12. Huang, J.Z., Liu, N., Pourahmadi, M., Liu, L.: Covariance selection and estimation via penalised normal likelihood. Biometrika 93(1), 85–98 (2006)
13. Ledoit, O., Wolf, M.: A well-conditioned estimator for large-dimensional covariance matrices. Journal of Multivariate Analysis 88(2), 365–411 (2004)
14. Leonard, T., Hsu, J.S.J.: Bayesian inference for a covariance matrix. The Annals of Statistics 36, 1669–1696 (1992)
15. Pourahmadi, M.: Joint mean-covariance models with applications to longitudinal data: unconstrained parameterisation. Biometrika 86, 677–690 (1999)
16. Pourahmadi, M.: Maximum likelihood estimation of generalized linear models for multivariate normal covariance matrix. Biometrika 87, 425–435 (2000)
17. Pourahmadi, M., Wu, W.B.: Nonparametric estimation of large covariance matrices of longitudinal data. Biometrika 90, 831–844 (2003)
18. Roggen, D., Calatroni, A., Rossi, M., Holleczek, T., Förster, G., Lukowicz, P., Pirkl, G., Bannach, D., Ferscha, A., Doppler, J., Holzmann, C., Kurz, M., Holl, G., Chavarriaga, R., Sagha, H., Bayati, H., del R. Millán, J.: Collecting complex activity data sets in highly rich networked sensor environments. In: Seventh International Conference on Networked Sensing Systems, INSS 2010 (2010)
19. Rothman, A.J., Bickel, P.J., Levina, E., Zhu, J.: Sparse permutation invariant covariance estimation. Electronic Journal of Statistics 2, 494–515 (2008)
20. Rothman, A.J., Levina, E., Zhu, J.: Sparse estimation of large covariance matrices via nested Lasso penalty. The Annals of Applied Statistics 2, 245–263 (2008)
21. Tony Cai, T., Zhang, C.H., Zhou, H.H.: Optimal rates of convergence for covariance matrix estimation. Annals of Statistics 38(4), 2118–2144 (2010)
22. Tony Cai, T., Zhou, H.H.: Minimax estimation of large covariance matrices under l1-norm. Statistica Sinica 22, 1319–1378 (2012)

# A New Approach to Security Games

Jan Karwowski[✉] and Jacek Mańdziuk

Faculty of Mathematics and Information Science, Warsaw University of Technology,
Koszykowa 75, 00-662 Warsaw, Poland
{jan.karwowski,j.mandziuk}@mini.pw.edu.pl

**Abstract.** The paper proposes a new approach to finding Defender's strategy in Security Games. The method is based on a modification to the Upper Confidence bound applied to Trees (UCT) algorithm that allows to address the imperfect information games. The key advantage of our approach compared to the ones proposed hitherto in the literature lies in high flexibility of our method which can be applied, without any modifications, to a large variety of security games models. Furthermore, due to simulation-based nature of the proposed solution, various Attacker's profiles (e.g. non-completely rational behavior) can be easily tested, as opposed to the methods rooted in the game-theoretic framework.

**Keywords:** Machine learning · UCT · Security games · Imperfect information · Bounded rationality

## 1 Introduction

Terrorism threats in 21st century raised many concerns in security of crowded public places like airports or trains stations. Governments are spending large amounts of financial resources on creating better technology for scanning, surveillance, weapon production as well as on increasing number of security officers. Even vast amount of all those resources is still insufficient to protect all vulnerable targets all the time. Hence, tactical planning remains a crucial aspect of national security and one way of its addressing is by means of Security Games (SG). The goal of SG is to provide optimal Defender strategy for protecting several targets. In such games it is usually assumed that Defender's resources are insufficient to protect all targets all the time (e.g. the number of security patrols is lower than the number of buildings to protect).

Many real life security problems are modeled via SG. The list of problems includes: securing airports and plane flights [4,8], US Coast Guard patrol planning [11], protecting forests from illegal cut [5] or protecting ferries on sea [3]. The first two works were deployed into real life and are used in LAX airport and Boston Coast, resp. The authors of the above listed papers use Stackelberg Game model to express SG problem. This is a simple non-zero-sum finite matrix game. Defender's moves represent targets to be protected and Attacker's moves represent the targets to be attacked. The game lasts only one round and the Defender seeks Stackelberg Equilibrium [12] to define their optimal strategy.

© Springer International Publishing Switzerland 2015
L. Rutkowski et al. (Eds.): ICAISC 2015, Part II, LNAI 9120, pp. 402–411, 2015.
DOI: 10.1007/978-3-319-19369-4_36

There are three main assumptions made with respect to the game model: (1) all rounds are independent (e.g. Defender's moves do not affect Attacker's tactics); (2) Attacker knows Defender's strategy; (3) Attacker makes perfectly rational decisions.

Moreover finding Stackelberg Equilibrium requires solving Mixed Integer Linear Programming (MILP) problem, which is in general NP-hard. All presented papers propose polynomial time solution for some subset of the problem or approximate solution.

Another, more flexible, model used for SG is Pursuer-Evader game of a graph. We are given a graph, where some vertices are targets. Attacker and Defender move their units between vertices connected with an edge. Attackers goal is to reach target vertex and not get caught. Defender's goal is to prevent Attacker from reaching the targets. When the Defender and the Attacker are in the same vertex at the same time, the Attacker is caught and loses the game. The game is divided into discrete time steps. In each step players can move each of their units to any vertex that is adjacent to the current unit's position. This game model is considered in the paper.

The remainder of the paper is structured as follows: Section 2 provides a detailed description of a game model and Section 3 gives a brief overview of the UCT method, which is the main SG playing engine proposed in this paper. Experimental setup, results and conclusions are presented in the last two sections.

## 2  Game Definition

Two players, Defender and Attacker, are taking part in the game. Let $G = (V, E)$ be a directed simple graph. $V$ is a vertex set and $E$ is an edge (arc) set. Let $T \subset V$ be a set of targets (resources that the Defender has to protect), $S \subset V$ be a set of spawns (vertices where the Attacker can enter the graph). Let $b \in V$ be a base (vertex where Defender units are in the first round). Let $D$ be set of Defender units (patrols). Defender has a fixed number of units, no Defender's unit can be added or removed during the game. Let $A_\sigma$ be a set of Attacker units being present in given a game state $\sigma$. The number of Attacker's units changes during the game as Attacker can introduce new unit in each round as well as some units can get caught. Game is divided into rounds (time steps). In each round players make decisions about new positions of their units in the next round.

### 2.1  Game State

Current positions of all units in game optionally accompanied by some variant-specific information form a game state. Let $\Sigma$ be a set of all possible game states. We will usually use $\sigma \in \Sigma$ to denote some game state. Besides $A_\sigma$ introduced earlier, each game state has information about units' positions. Let $P_\sigma : A_\sigma \cup D \to V$ be a function describing positions.

In the initial game state $\sigma_0$, there are no Attacker units and all Defender's are in the base: $A_{\sigma_0} = \emptyset$, $(\forall d \in D) P_{\sigma_0}(d) = b$.

The game does not provide perfect information to the players. Defender knows only his own units' positions. Attacker knows his units' positions and can see Defender units if they are in the targets.

## 2.2 Movement

A Defender move consists of decisions on each Defender unit position in the next round. A new unit's positions must be either the same vertex (unit is not moved) or be a vertex adjacent to the current position.

Attacker moves are more complex. Besides making analogous move decision to all Attacker units in the game, Attacker can also introduce a new unit, which will be available since the beginning of the next round. If Attacker decides to introduce a unit he must also set its initial position $s$, choosing it from the spawns set: $s \in S$.

The players make their decisions simultaneously, not knowing the opponent's plans. When decisions are made, units are moved and new positions are checked for *Attack and Defense Situations*. A **Defense Situation** is when at least one Attacker and one Defender unit are in the same vertex. In such a case all Attacker units in this vertex are caught (removed from a game) and players are given appropriate pay-offs. An **Attack Situation** is when Attacker is in a target vertex $t \in T$ (and no Defender's units are present in that vertex). This Situation is considered a successful attack - players are given appropriate pay-offs and Attacker unit is removed from the game.

The order of checking Situations is important. Defense Situations are checked in the first place (so Defender can catch Attacker in a target). After checking and possibly removing some Attackers a new state with units' positions is set. The transition is discrete and no intermediate positions on edges are considered. In particular when $a, b$ are adjacent vertices, Defender moves from $a$ to $b$, and Attacker moves from $b$ to $a$, they will not meet and Attacker will not be caught.

## 2.3 Pay-Offs

At the end of each round after all requested units have been moved and all Defense and Attacks situations have been evaluated each player is given some pay-off according to encountered Situations. For each Attacker Situation, Attacker is rewarded according to $R_A : T \to \mathbb{Z}^+$ reward function and Defender gets penalty $P_D : T \to \mathbb{Z}^-$. In case of Defense Situations we have similarly: $R_D : V \to \mathbb{Z}^+$ to describe Defender's reward and $P_A : V \to \mathbb{Z}^-$ for Attacker's penalty. Each round pay-off is a sum of rewards and penalties for all Situations that happened during that round. The reward/penalty functions are game parameters.

# 3    UCT Applied to Security Games

Upper Confidence Bounds (UCB) was introduced in [2] to optimize a long-term pay-off from playing a number of Single-Armed Bandit (Slot) Machines in a casino. It is assumed that each machine has some unknown stationary probability distribution of pay-offs. UCB starts with random sampling the machines. Once some initial information is gathered the algorithm tries arms with higher average pay-off more frequently while still sampling the rest of arms from time to time. The algorithm was proven to converge to the optimal playing policy (maximal expected pay-off in the long run) [2].

Upper Confidence Bounds applied to Trees (UCT) [6], is an extension of UCB approach applied to games, whose states are represented in the form of a (game) tree. In the current game state (root of a tree) UCT performs massive simulations traversing the game tree until the leaf nodes. In each such simulation (playout), in each game state, the algorithm performs, similar to UCB, sampling of the child nodes, chooses one of them, moves to this node, etc. Once the simulation is completed (reaches the terminal state) the game outcome is propagated back from that node all the way to the root node, updating the quality statistics of all nodes on a path that was traversed in this playout. After finalizing the simulation phase, a move with the highest average reward (game outcome) is selected in the actual play (in our case the SG). A pseudocode of the UCT method is presented in Algorithm 1. It is worth mentioning that UCT converges to min-max strategy when the number of samples increases to infinity [6]. For the sake of space limits we are not able to go into more details. For a detailed description of the UCT method please consult, for instance, [6,13,15].

UCT method was successfully applied to various problems, in particular: Go game [17], combinatorial optimization expressed as a game [9,10], General Game Playing [13,14,15], project scheduling [16], dynamic vehicle routing [7] or problems which involve MILP [1].

### 3.1 Imperfect Information Games

The UCT algorithm cannot be straightforwardly applied to imperfect information games. The problem lies in line 4 of the Algorithm 1 where multiple simulations from a given state are performed. In imperfect information games, this state

---

**Algorithm 1.** The UCT algorithm

---

1 State ← InitialState // `Starting state of game`
2 while *not* *IsTerminal(State)* do
   | // `Game is not over`
3 | for $i \leftarrow 1 \ldots simCount$ do
   | | // `Number of times each node on path is evaluated - alogrithm`
   | | `parameter`
4 | | SingleRun(State) // `Performs a game simulation from given state`
   | |    `and updates payoff statistics for all moves after` *State*
5 | Best ← UCTBestMove(State) // `Choose best move from State`
   |    `according to pay-off statistics gathered in simulations`
6 | MakeMove(State, Best)

---

is not fully observable (only the Defender's units' locations are available - for Defender). The information about Attacker's positions constitutes an unknown context of a given state (UCT tree node). Therefore we propose a modification of Algorithm 1, which is presented in Algorithm 2. The baseline idea is to evaluate the $n$-th move in a game which may lead to different game states when invisible information is included. In addition the modified algorithm introduces the move limit of SG (variable $maxDepth$).

---

**Algorithm 2.** UCT variant for SG (imperfect information games)

1 **for** $depth \leftarrow 1 \cdots maxDepth$ **do**
　　// Limit depth (number of rounds) of evaluation (game is now finite)
2 　　**for** $i \leftarrow 1 \ldots simCount$ **do**
　　　　// simCount - the same parameter as in Algorithm 1
3 　　　　State $\leftarrow$ InitialState
4 　　　　**for** $d \leftarrow 1 \cdots depth - 1$ **do**
　　　　　　// Play given number of steps, so we will be evaluating $depth$-th move in game
5 　　　　　　Best $\leftarrow$ UCTBestMove(State)
6 　　　　　　MakeMove(State, Best)
7 　　　　SingleRun(State)// State may be different at each simulation now

---

### 3.2 Game Model Implementation

Two variants of states and move modeling were proposed and compared in this paper. Both of them implement a model defined in Section 2 and strategy defined on one of them can be transformed the equivalent strategy on the other one.

In the first variant, the game state is encoded as a vector of length $k = |D|$, where each element describes state of one Defender's unit. The state maintains one of two kinds of values: $\bullet v$ – the unit is in vertex $v$, $\rightarrow v$ – the unit was requested to go to $v$, i.e. it was sent to $v$ in one of the previous moves and is on his way to $v$ (information about current position is discarded). In a given round Defender can move any number of his $\bullet u$ units to any of their adjacent nodes (reachable by a single directed edge of a graph). All units $\rightarrow v$ move one step forward towards their destination vertex.

The second variant implements a more straightforward idea. Defender's state is represented as a numerical vector in which the $i$-th element denotes the vertex number of the current location of the $i$-th unit. A Defender's move is a vector of the requested unit's positions in the next round, resp. Again, the requested position of a unit can only be either its current position (no movement) or a vertex adjacent to this position.

The game ends after a pre-defined number of rounds.

## 3.3    Attacker Implementation

UCT simulation phase requires simulating an opponent (Attacker) to play against. In our implementation the opponent choose target to attack based on the expected pay-off in that vertex.

Please recall, that due to a game definition Attacker can see positions of Defender's units when they are located in any of the targets. The Attacker player, therefore, gathers statistics of Defender visits in each target and calculates the expected pay-off for each target vertex using formula (1), where: $c_v$ is the number of times vertex $v$ was covered by Defender, $t$ is the number of rounds in which the statistics were collected.

$$EP(v) = \frac{c_v P_A(v) + (t - c_v) R_A(v)}{t} \tag{1}$$

Furthermore, Attacker decides to start an attack with probability 0.2 (see Algorithm 3).

---

**Algorithm 3.** Single Attacker move

---

1  **if** $UniformRandom(0, 1) < 0.2$ **then**
    // decided to start an attack
2      Start ← UniformRandom($S$)            // Random starting vertex
3      Destination ← Roulette($T$, $EP$)    // Destination from distribution
    where probability is proportional to value of $EP$ function
4      ScheduleAttack(Start,Destination)// This function puts new Attacker
        unit on $Start$ vertex and makes that during consequent rounds
        it moves to $Destination$ using the shortest path

---

# 4    Experimental Design

The algorithm was tested on a few different games with several parameter sets. For each pair $(game, parameterset)$21 repetitions of the training process followed by a game playing phase were performed. In the game playing phase payoffs and Situation counts from 40 games each of length 10 000 rounds were used. The UCT configuration used in the experiments is presented in Table 1.

## 4.1    Test Games

For each of the graphs presented in Graphs 1.1,1.2,1.3 one game was defined. In all test games a winning strategy that allows protection of all the targets all the time exists for the Defender. In all graphs, the targets (elements of $T$) are denoted as green diamonds, and spawns (elements of $S$) as red triangles.

The results of experiments are presented in Table 2 as average values of 21 experiment runs. All experiments were computed on Intel Core i7-2600 3.4GHz CPU. A single experiment lasted approximately 14 minutes regardless of the

**Table 1.** UCT parameters for the experiments

| Parameter | Value |
|---|---|
| Depth of full evaluation (*maxDepth* in Algorithm 2) | 20 |
| Number of evaluation of each level (*simCount*) | 6000 |
| Number of rounds after which each simulation is stopped | 20 |
| Expansion coefficient ($C$ in UCT formula) | See Table 2 |
| Number of rounds each pay-off is back-propagated | See Table 2 |
| Repetitions of the whole training phase before evaluation | 20 |

**Graph 1.1.** A graph with single central vertex to protect. In a game the Defender had one unit at his disposal. The optimal strategy is to stay in node 6.

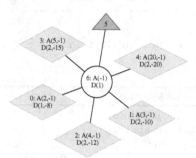

**Graph 1.2.** Graph based on cycle with two path to protect. In a game the Defender had 2 units at his disposal. The optimal strategy is to patrol the section of nodes 3, 9, 10 (one unit) and the one of the nodes 5, 6, 7 (the other unit).

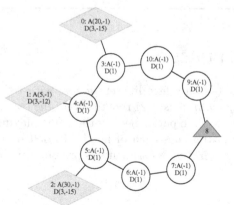

game being played and the configuration set used. Please note the restriction imposed in the length of he path along which the results of simulations are back-propagated. Such a limited, local impact of simulation result introduces a significant difference compared to "typical" UCT implementation, in which the result would be back-propagated along the whole path, however, our preliminary tests proved the advantage of proposed implementation over the "regular" one.

**Graph 1.3.** More complex graph with two vertices to protect. In a game the Defender had 2 units at his disposal. Please note that in this game the timing is crucial since Defender's units (located in node 0) and Attacker's units (located in nodes 16 and 17) have the same distance to the targets.

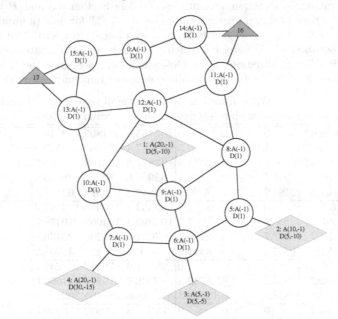

## 5    Results and Discussion

On a general note, the results show that our modified-UCT algorithm was able to repeatedly find a winning strategy for all games tested. In many of the cases the Attacker did not make even a single attempt to attack, in many other the median value of Attacker Situations is equal to 0 which means a visible win of Defender. Also a comparison with random-walk strategy proves a clear upper-hand of proposed method.

An important difference between our algorithm and existing approaches is flexibility. Our game model can be easily extended without making any changes to training algorithm since the base of the UCT method is an abstract model of states and moves which can reflect virtually any Attacker profile. Replacing the current Attacker strategy with any other, e.g. game theory-based solutions, randomly or systematically biased, or the one based on bounded rationality, is straightforward and does not require any changes in Defender algorithm.

The detailed conclusions include the observation that depending on a particular game different values for expansion coefficient $C$ were more suitable than the others. The investigation of the quasi-formal rule for $C$ parameter selection for a given game is one of our current targets. Furthermore, we plan to test our method in the cases when Defender resources are insufficient to secure all targets all the time.

**Table 2.** Number of Attack Situations and pay-offs in test games with different UCT configurations. The exploration coefficient $(C)$ was equal to $4, 7, 12, 15$ or $20$ and the the length of back-propagation of results $len$ was one of $2, 3$ or $4$. Game variant $A$ denotes the first implementation variant described in Section 3.2 and $B$ means the second one. $Configset$ column presents values of $C$ in UCT formula (a number placed after $ex$) and back-propagation length (a number placed after $len$). The results for those $(game, parameterset))$ pairs for which there were no attack attempts in all 21 tests are omitted. Such situations favor Defender's behavior since the reluctance to attack may often stem from efficient patrolling schedule implemented by Defender.

| Game | Config set | Attacker Situations mean | median | stddev | Overall pay-off mean | median | stddev | Random player avg pay-off |
|---|---|---|---|---|---|---|---|---|
| Graph2A | ex20-len2 | 0 | 0 | 0 | 102455.8 | 101805 | 2218.7 | -547124 |
| Graph2A | ex15-len2 | 1 | 0 | 2.9 | 104847.4 | 101552 | 6519.9 | -547124 |
| Graph2A | ex12-len4 | 0.8 | 0 | 1.5 | 107871.6 | 103169 | 12187 | -547124 |
| Graph2A | ex7-len2 | 908.7 | 0 | 2863.4 | 82902.6 | 80123 | 48089.9 | -547124 |
| Graph2A | ex4-len3 | 2486.2 | 5 | 4569 | 52859.1 | 79923 | 62337.1 | -547124 |
| Graph2B | ex15-len2 | 0 | 0 | 0 | 102553.3 | 100966 | 3197.3 | -544089 |
| Graph2B | ex12-len4 | 0.2 | 0 | 1.1 | 106392.3 | 104069 | 10478.7 | -544089 |
| Graph2B | ex7-len2 | 557.7 | 4 | 2536.1 | 107031.5 | 103290 | 22436.9 | -544089 |
| Graph2B | ex4-len3 | 1052.5 | 4 | 3311.9 | 75123 | 80126 | 45902.9 | -544089 |
| Graph1A | ex12-len4 | 0 | 0 | 0 | 79981.9 | 79987 | 241.7 | -674773 |
| Graph1A | ex7-len2 | 1907.2 | 0 | 8739.8 | 51276 | 79944 | 131656.6 | -674773 |
| Graph1A | ex4-len3 | 3806.5 | 0 | 12022.3 | 19356 | 80125 | 192247.8 | -674773 |
| Graph1B | ex7-len2 | 0 | 0 | 0 | 79950.3 | 79942 | 239.5 | -674925.6 |
| Graph1B | ex4-len3 | 3829.9 | 0 | 12096 | 19511.1 | 79862 | 190970.3 | -674925.6 |
| Grap3A | ex20-len2 | 0.8 | 0 | 1.9 | 80010.1 | 80064 | 218.9 | -522846.5 |
| Grap3A | ex15-len2 | 1.2 | 0 | 2.1 | 80062 | 80118 | 274.5 | -522846.5 |
| Grap3A | ex12-len4 | 356.6 | 4 | 1618.9 | 76033 | 79885 | 17669.8 | -522846.5 |
| Grap3A | ex7-len2 | 1928 | 0 | 5852.2 | 59649.7 | 79951 | 60579.8 | -522846.5 |
| Grap3A | ex4-len3 | 9084.2 | 12 | 11624.6 | -20358.3 | 79538 | 125375 | -522846.5 |
| Grap3B | ex20-len2 | 2089.6 | 4 | 6617.7 | 83586.1 | 79908 | 13466 | -522190.5 |
| Grap3B | ex15-len2 | 2 | 0 | 3.1 | 79936.9 | 79948 | 194 | -522190.5 |
| Grap3B | ex12-len4 | 1169 | 2 | 5341.7 | 81385.2 | 79980 | 6734.9 | -522190.5 |
| Grap3B | ex7-len2 | 1041.3 | 6 | 2596.7 | 68444.9 | 79836 | 28531.5 | -522190.5 |
| Grap3B | ex4-len3 | 8270.5 | 21 | 10791.5 | -10813 | 79423 | 118137.9 | -522190.5 |

**Acknowledgment.** The research was financed by the National Science Centre in Poland, grant number DEC-2012/07/B/ST6/01527.

# References

1. Ahmadizadeh, K., Gomes, C.P., Sabharwal, A.: Game playing techniques for optimization under uncertainty (2010)
2. Auer, P., Cesa-Bianchi, N., Fischer, P.: Finite-time analysis of the multiarmed bandit problem. Machine Learning 47(2-3), 235–256 (2002)

3. Fang, F., Jiang, A.X., Tambe, M.: Optimal patrol strategy for protecting moving targets with multiple mobile resources. In: Proceedings of the 2013 International Conference on Autonomous Agents and Multi-agent Systems, pp. 957–964. International Foundation for Autonomous Agents and Multiagent Systems (2013)
4. Jain, M., Tsai, J., Pita, J., Kiekintveld, C., Rathi, S., Tambe, M., Ordóñez, F.: Software assistants for randomized patrol planning for the lax airport police and the federal air marshal service. Interfaces 40(4), 267–290 (2010)
5. Johnson, M.P., Fang, F., Tambe, M.: Patrol strategies to maximize pristine forest area. In: AAAI (2012)
6. Kocsis, L., Szepesvári, C.: Bandit based monte-carlo planning. In: Fürnkranz, J., Scheffer, T., Spiliopoulou, M. (eds.) ECML 2006. LNCS (LNAI), vol. 4212, pp. 282–293. Springer, Heidelberg (2006)
7. Mańdziuk, J., Świechowski, M.: UCT application to Dynamic Vehicle Routing Problem with Heavy Traffic Jams (submitted) (2015)
8. Pita, J., John, R., Maheswaran, R., Tambe, M., Yang, R., Kraus, S.: A robust approach to addressing human adversaries in security games. In: Proceedings of the 11th International Conference on Autonomous Agents and Multiagent Systems, vol. 3, pp. 1297–1298. International Foundation for Autonomous Agents and Multiagent Systems (2012)
9. Rimmel, A., Teytaud, F., Cazenave, T.: Optimization of the nested monte-carlo algorithm on the traveling salesman problem with time windows. In: Di Chio, C., et al. (eds.) EvoApplications 2011, Part II. LNCS, vol. 6625, pp. 501–510. Springer, Heidelberg (2011)
10. Sabharwal, A., Samulowitz, H., Reddy, C.: Guiding combinatorial optimization with UCT. In: Beldiceanu, N., Jussien, N., Pinson, É. (eds.) CPAIOR 2012. LNCS, vol. 7298, pp. 356–361. Springer, Heidelberg (2012)
11. Shieh, E., An, B., Yang, R., Tambe, M., Baldwin, C., DiRenzo, J., Maule, B., Meyer, G.: Protect: A deployed game theoretic system to protect the ports of the united states. In: Proceedings of the 11th International Conference on Autonomous Agents and Multiagent Systems, vol. 1, pp. 13–20. International Foundation for Autonomous Agents and Multiagent Systems (2012)
12. Stackelberg, H.V.: Marktform und gleichgewicht. Springer, Vienna (1934)
13. Świechowski, M., Mańdziuk, J.: Self-adaptation of playing strategies in general game playing. IEEE Transactions on Computational Intelligence and AI in Games 6(4), 367–381 (2014)
14. Walędzik, K., Mańdziuk, J.: Multigame playing by means of UCT enhanced with automatically generated evaluation functions. In: Schmidhuber, J., Thórisson, K.R., Looks, M. (eds.) AGI 2011. LNCS(LNAI), vol. 6830, pp. 327–332. Springer, Heidelberg (2011)
15. Walędzik, K., Mańdziuk, J.: An automatically-generated evaluation function in general game playing. IEEE Transactions on Computational Intelligence and AI in Games 6(3), 258–270 (2014)
16. Walędzik, K., Mańdziuk, J., Zadrożny, S.: Proactive and reactive risk-aware project scheduling. In: 2nd IEEE Symposium on Computational Intelligence for Human-like Intelligence (CIHLI 2014), pp. 94–101. IEEE Press (2014)
17. Wang, Y., Gelly, S.: Modifications of uct and sequence-like simulations for monte-carlo go. CIG 7, 175–182 (2007)

# Proposal of a Context-Aware Smart Home Ecosystem

Radosław Klimek[✉] and Grzegorz Rogus

AGH University of Science and Technology,
Al. Mickiewicza 30, 30-059 Kraków, Poland
{rklimek,rogus}@agh.edu.pl

**Abstract.** Smart homes are more and more popular since they are regarded as synonyms of an ideal and friendly environment. Novel aspects like context awareness and pro-activity are fundamental requirements for development of such systems. Smart scenarios enable switching devices in a desired way when a certain user activity considered as a trigger involves a system activity. Some smart scenarios are proposed. Context modeling and reasoning for smart homes is widely considered. A software architecture including web services is introduced and discussed.

**Keywords:** Smart home · Ecosystem · Context-awareness · Smart scenario · Context modeling · Context reasoning · Architecture for smart homes · Web service · SOA · Pervasive computing

## 1 Introduction

A smart home is a house that uses information technology to monitor the environment, control the electric appliances and communicate with the outer world. Smart homes sometimes mean automated homes. Automation systems have been developed to automatically achieve some activities performed frequently in daily life, to obtain a more comfortable and easier living environment. There are many different systems classified as smart home systems. On one hand, a simple system using only the remote controls of electrical devices such as lighting, heating, air conditioning, audio and video entertainment systems and security is considered as a synonym of the smart home. On the other hand, contrary to the above approach, there are complex systems which are able to make their own decisions basing on the expected behavior of users. Some use cases are as follows: "Children usually go to sleep at 8.00 PM; The system automatically turns on air condition at 7.30 PM to decrease the temperature in the children's room (if the temperature is too high), when children leave the living room and enter bedrooms, then lights in bedrooms are still on, and the brightness is decreased, the TV set is muted. How much the TV volume is lowered also depends on the individual preferences of the viewer. Information about the preferences of users were collected automatically by the system basing on historical data".

Such systems can be classified as context-aware systems. One of the main goal of context-aware applications is to make inhabitants feel more comfortable and

© Springer International Publishing Switzerland 2015
L. Rutkowski et al. (Eds.): ICAISC 2015, Part II, LNAI 9120, pp. 412–423, 2015.
DOI: 10.1007/978-3-319-19369-4_37

safe. To achieve this goal, ubiquitous computing is brought into our living space. By collecting sensor data and extracting specific information from datasets we can develop many kinds of context-aware applications which would improve our quality of life.

In this paper we propose some scenarios as well as a novel architecture to create an intelligent, automated home and a context-aware smart home ecosystem to control and manage all sensors and devices used in such scenarios. These aspects constitute the main findings of the paper. The proposed system covers the following features. The dynamic nature of a context-aware application requires a system allowing on-line reconfigurations. Adding or removing sensors or devices, as well defining new features, requires applications that dynamically (reactively and pro-actively) adapt their behaviors. Scenarios are considered as skeleton scenarios which are context-sensitive and filled with actions when necessary.

## 2    Related Works

Research in context-aware computing has recognized the need for building infrastructures to support context-awareness activities [12,26]. The authors of works [1,24,11] have conducted surveys in the context-awareness domain, whereas the work documented in [22,19] describes middleware approaches for this area of research.

Paper [13] presents a survey distinguishing different solutions for context aware engineering proposed by different researchers and developers. The approaches can be divided into the following categories: middleware solutions and dedicated service platforms; use of ontologies; rule-based reasoning; source code level programming/language extensions; model-driven approaches; essage interception. There are, however, generic cases where several paradigms or patterns are used together in the same approach. However, the above approaches are not completely disjoint and a potential developer may opt for a combination of several techniques.

Although there are a lot of frameworks and middlewares developed for context-aware systems, they are usually limited to a specific domain and designed. Examples include CoBrA [5] and SOUPA [6] for building smart meeting rooms, GAIA [9] for active spaces; ezContext [18] is a framework that provides automatic context life cycle management. The authors of [20] present a framework bridging the communication between heterogeneous devices, whereas [2] presents a system capable for integrating heterogeneous devices dynamically enabling interoperability between those.

Paper [21] presents a survey distinguishing different architectural styles used in context-aware systems. These are as follows:

1. Component-based architecture, where the entire solution is based on loosely coupled major components, interacting with each other. For example, the Context Toolkit [10] builds a framework for interfacing with devices and software entities which provide contextual information. There are three major components which perform the most critical functionalities of the system.

A set of abstractions, namely, context widgets, context interpreters and context aggregators can be used by application developers to prototype new context-aware applications. Widgets abstract sensor-originated information and make that information available to applications.

2. Distributed architecture enables peer-to-peer interaction in a distributed fashion, such as in Solar [4].
3. Service-based architecture, where the entire solution consists of several services working together.
4. Node-based architecture allows deployment of pieces of software with similar or different capabilities; these communicate and collectively process data in sensor networks [23].
5. Centralized architecture which acts as a complete stack (e.g. middleware) and provides applications to be developed on the top of that, but provides no communication between different instances of the solution.
6. Client-server architecture separates sensing and processing, as shown in CaSP [7].
7. Agent-oriented paradigm [3] with agent-oriented computing, autonomous entities in the system which individually manage specific tasks and cooperate among themselves with standardized protocols to achieve a greater goal. An example of using that style is ACAI [14].

## 3   Smart Scenarios

Scenarios for smart homes are descriptions of all relevant elements including aims and context to provide context-aware automation. Scenarios are focused on functionalities and resources and how they can improve the quality of life. Smart functionalities help in easing everyday life tasks. Both normal and abnormal behaviors for smart homes are identified and considered. Smart behaviors are usually specified using use cases and their scenarios. Applying these tools is ubiquitous in software engineering, since they relatively precisely describe the desired interactions. Recognizing interactions and services enables reasoning to provide smart reactions based on context awareness.

The scenario expressed in Tab. 1 for a use case is a scenario for normal behavior. It might also refer to some social networks, for example Facebook, Instagram, or others, where some data identifying the inhabitants might be stored. That data, e.g. photos, might be used in a smart home system.

Some abnormal behaviors for smart homes are presented in work [25]. Let us consider some of them in a more general form and more formally. The scenario expressed in Tab. 3 deals with everyday activity which is taking a shower or bath. The cloud, rather than a local database, allows to analyze profile/preferences no matter where a person takes a shower.

Some other use cases and their scenarios proposed here refer to a security system enabling to detect intrusion in a smart home. The system is switched on manually using a wall-mounted panel. The night alarm is an option of the security system and enables activating the system in the entire zone, excluding

**Table 1.** The use case scenario for a guest recognition

| UC name: "Guest recognition when the door bell rings" |
| --- |
| Precondition: Access to the local database and social networks |
| Scenario:<br>1. A person appears in the front door and presses the entrance button;<br>2. The guest is scanned by the entrance camera;<br>3. The identification data is compared with local data base;<br>4. If there is a negative result, the identification data is compared with data and profiles available in social networks searching their family and friends;<br>5. Depending on the search result, the sound of a door bell is divided into three categories:<br>  (a) family,<br>  (b) friends,<br>  (c) others. |
| Postcondition: The bell at the front door rings. |

**Table 2.** Use case scenario for the night option of the security system (turn on) (top). Use case scenario for the temporary turn off the security system (middle). Use case scenario for the night option of the security system (turn off) (bottom)

| UC name: "The security system automatically turns on for a night" |
| --- |
| Precondition: Everything works normal |
| Scenario:<br>1. If it is night time (say from 11 p.m. to 6 a.m.) then skip to the next step else finish scenario;<br>2. If residents are upstairs and their activity has stopped for a half hour, then turn on automatically the night option for the system. |
| Postcondition: The night option for the security system is on, if necessary |
| UC name: "The security system is (temporarily) switched off" |
| Precondition: The night option for the security system is on. |
| Scenario:<br>1. If it is night (say, from 11 p.m. to 6 a.m.) then skip to the next step, else finish scenario;<br>2. If a resident begins to go downstairs, then the security system is turned off automatically. |
| Postcondition: The night option for the security system is off. |
| UC name: "The security system is automatically switched off after the night" |
| Precondition: The night option for the security system is on. |
| Scenario:<br>1. If the night (say, from 11 p.m. to 6 a.m.) is over, then skip to the next step, else finish scenario;<br>2. If any resident begins to go downstairs, then turn off the security system. |
| Postcondition: The security system is off, if necessary |

**Table 3.** The use case scenario for a too long showering

| |
|---|
| UC name: "Too long shower or bath" |
| Precondition: Access to a local/cloud database |
| Scenario:<br>1. A person/resident starts taking a shower;<br>2. The person is scanned and identified by the system;<br>3. The shower/bath timer starts;<br>4. The profile in a local/cloud database is searched for the longest shower/bath time of a given person, taking into account different circumstances, e.g. summer, winter, morning, evening, etc.<br>5. If the shower/bath time exceeds the profiled value, then other family members are notified. |
| Postcondition: Generating a warning to other residents, if necessary. |

bedrooms upstairs. On the other hand, the night option could be activated by a system itself, i.e. automatically, in other words without direct action of inhabitants, when some general circumstances are satisfied, see Tab. 2, as well as other scenarios.

# 4   Understanding of Context

Context awareness is a kind of intelligent computing behavior. For computing systems, context awareness is the capability to provide relevant services and information to the users based on their situational conditions. Formally, according to [8], "A system is context-aware if it uses context to provide relevant information and/or services to the user, where relevancy depends on the user's task."

In this section, we discuss the basic concepts underlying the fundamentals of context-aware systems. There are many definitions of *context*. One of the most popular is a definition presented in [8]: "Context is any information that can be used to characterise the situation of an entity. An entity is a person, place, or object that is considered relevant to the interaction between a user and an application, including the user and applications themselves." According to that definition, context is a result of data interpretation. The source of data in context-aware systems are sensor networks.

Context is represented in context models. Those are data structures, which are populated by abstracting and representing contextual information for further processing. Context can be represented in various formats ranging from simple key-value models to graphical representations [24]. Out of those, current research indicates that ontologies are the most expressive context representation models [11,24]. Ontologies provide a powerful paradigm for context modeling, which offers rich expressiveness and supports the dynamic aspects of context awareness. Ontologies represent concepts and relationships between them. An ontology is used to define different entities like objects, services, sensor data and relations between concept and situation. With the existing ontology from different sources, the context models can be used for modeling user behaviors and surrounding situations. These will be useful for a smart home system to make suitable choices for users. Ontology reasoning is needed to guide the smart home system to provide suitable services to the users. It uses the environment entities and information.

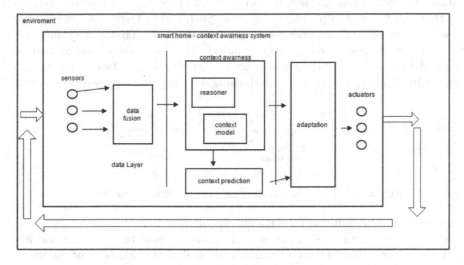

**Fig. 1.** Context processing in a smart home

Figure 1 provides an overview of how the context is processed and how the smart home system actions emerge from context processing efforts. On Figure 1 the context processing is viewed from the aspects of algorithms and information flows. For simplicity the aspects like hardware, physical communications, interaction protocols are intentionally left out in Figure 1.

Context-aware applications differ from traditional applications since they use sensed information to adapt the service provisioning to the current context of the user. In order to achieve that, context-aware applications, in general, should be capable of:

- sensing context from the environment;
- observing, collecting and composing context information from various sensors;
- autonomously detecting relevant changes in the context;
- reacting to these changes, by either adapting their behaviour or by invoking appropriate services;
- interoperating with output service providers.

The data gathered by sensors needs to be evaluated and processed in order to provide useful information. Raw context data can be collected either from a single sensor node, or by aggregating context data available from multiple sensor nodes. The collected context data need to be stored for further processing. The raw context tends to be noisy and inconsistent, which calls for proper context

pre-processing, inconsistency detection and resolution mechanisms. After processing, context is represented using particular pattern or design descriptions,
called context models. In addition, if the data is organized as low level information toward concepts, then it may not be usable when domains change. Thus,
organizing the data into a higher level concept it is necessary to give users understandable definitions, as well as building up knowledge concerning general
rules that will be used in providing services. Such higher level concept will also
be useful in transferring experiences to different domains. That is why data collected directly from sensor have to computed. That secondary context can be
computed by using sensor data fusion or data retrieval operations such as web
service calls. Figure 2 presents approach using data layer to represent raw sensor

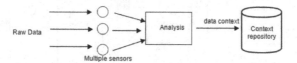

**Fig. 2.** From raw data to context information – data layer

readings in a format suitable for data classification.

Sensors collect data, and many sets of data are used to construct the abstract concept to describe the environment, as well as the attribute of the users.
For situation, the semantics of high-level behaviours and services are processed
together to provide extra information that will benefit the system to make decisions. During such processes, the output of sensors is categorized and matched
with the ontology built for application domain.

External devices generate very large amounts of data. Often, these are data
that can not be directly used in the model context. An example of such data
are data generated by the camera in in scenario expressed in Tab. 1. The data
streaming transmitted by a camera from a point of view of the context model
does not seem interesting. Interesting is the information about the user id identified by image analysis. We need data that uniquely identifies a person calling to
the door. The streaming data from camera are compared to digital images from
a local database or in a case then we obtain the negative comparison result, the
service is called to link and search images from Facebook profile. That external
service identify the person by searching a list of friends' profiles. The result of
the activities are context data that classify person to one of the group: family,
friend, alien.

## 5    Proposal of a System Architecture

In this section we present our concept of the overall architecture for context-
aware applications in smart homes. The proposed system is based on a service-
oriented architecture with active use of certain architectural patterns. Based
on [18], we the adopted the following design principles related to context-aware
management frameworks:

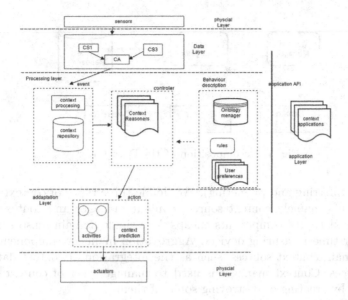

**Fig. 3.** Overview architecture for smart homes

- the functionalities need to be divided into layers and components in a meaningful manner,
- multi-model reasoning,
- monitoring and event detection: Events play a significant role in smart home systems, which is complemented by monitoring. Detecting an event triggers an action autonomously.

The system architecture, see Figure 3, is divided into the physical layer, the data layer, the processing layer, the adaptation layer and the application layer. They are responsible for sensor operation, data processing, behavior recognition, evolution of the evaluation process and interaction with the user's work. The application API provides access to the context-awareness system for user applications (for example mobile). It represents the architectural cut between context management and context utilization. The application API has direct access to the context repository, ontology model, user preferences and set of defined rules. It reads the current context and commits user updates into the context. The inference engine may also notify user applications through the application API, if that is required to infer new context. Processing of context information is a challenging task. Deducing rich information from basic sensor samples may require complex computation. The system should provide mechanisms to distribute context processing activities among multiple components. That way we propose to use the context sources and the managers hierarchy architectural pattern aimed at providing a structural schema to enable the distribution and composition of context information processing components.

This approach, see Figure 4, enables encapsulation, is more efficient and enables flexible and decoupled distribution of context processing activities (sensing,

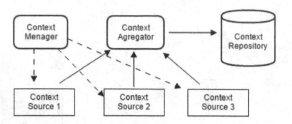

**Fig. 4.** Decomposition of the Data Layer

aggregating, inferring and predicting). We define three types of context processor components, namely context source, context manager and context aggregation. Context source components encapsulate single domain sensors, such as movement or time measuring devices. Aggregation manager components cover multiple domain context sources, such as the integration of context data from context sources. Context manager is used to manage a set of context sources dynamically by creating or destroying some of them.

The second architecture pattern used in our approach is the schema of Event-Condition-Action (ECA). Figure 5 provides an overview of how the context is processed and how the pervasive computing system actions emerge from context processing efforts. The entire system consists of three components.

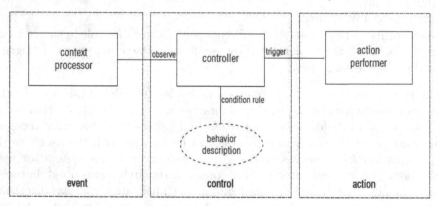

**Fig. 5.** Processing and matching schema: Event – Control – Action

1. Context processor gathers information about all events that occur in the smart home.
2. Controller analyses incoming events regarding some patterns of behavior descriptions, i.e. it matches incoming events to patterns stored as a behavior description.
3. Action performer produces smart actions switching devices in a desired way.

By using pattern decomposition and ECA, we model advanced context processing as it is seen in Figure 7. For example, in scenario "Security System",

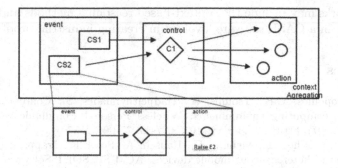

**Fig. 6.** Sample processing of events for the ECA schema

see Tab. 2, the event (*IsNight* and *ResidentgoDown*) is a compound event observed on the following components: (i) a context source component (CS1 in Figure 6) that detects an *Night* event (E1) and (ii) a context source component (CS2 in Figure 6) that detects when a resident go down on stairs (E2). Within the security system detector context Agregator (CA), the following condition rule2 is described in controller C1, characterizing the recursive nature of the event-control-action pattern. As we said before, one of the important foundations for modern context awareness is parallelization of reasoning. There are many independent events which smart home systems have to analyze. We propose some extend pattern ECA by using the publish/subscribe pattern to define the connection between controller and set of event, see Figure 7. The historical behaviors might be encoded into logical specifications, and can be later analyzed for satisfiability, c.f. works [16,15,17], supporting the current reasoning process and behavior recognition.

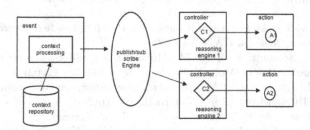

**Fig. 7.** Distributed Context Reasoning

# 6   Conclusions

In this paper we propose some solutions that refer a novel software architecture smart homes. The findings include a new approach for context modeling and reasoning for smart homes. This work opens some research areas which are of crucial importance for the idea of smart homes.

Future works may include the context-based reasoning methods and tools. It should result in a CASE software involved in creating industrial-proof tools.

# References

1. Anagnostopoulos, C.B., Tsounis, A., Hadjiefthymiades, S.: Context awareness in mobile computing environments. Wireless Personal Communications 42(3), 445–464 (2007), http://dx.doi.org/10.1007/s11277-006-9187-6
2. Bartelt, C., Fischer, T., Niebuhr, D., Rausch, A., Seidl, F., Trapp, M.: Dynamic integration of heterogeneous mobile devices. ACM SIGSOFT Software Engineering Notes 30(4), 1–7 (2005), http://dblp.uni-trier.de/db/journals/sigsoft/sigsoft30.html#BarteltFNRST05
3. Bradshaw, J.M.: Software Agents. MIT Press, Cambridge (1997)
4. Chen, G., Li, M., Kotz, D.: Data-centric middleware for context-aware pervasive computing. Pervasive Mob. Comput. 4(2), 216–253 (2008)
5. Chen, H., Finin, T., Joshi, A.: Semantic web in the context broker architecture. In: Proceedings of Percom 2004, pp. 277–286 (2004)
6. Chen, H., Perich, F., Finin, T.W., Joshi, A.: Soupa: Standard ontology for ubiquitous and pervasive applications. In: MobiQuitous, pp. 258–267. IEEE Computer Society (2004)
7. Devaraju, A., Hoh, S., Hartley, M.: A context gathering framework for context-aware mobile solutions. In: Chong, P.H.J., Cheok, A.D. (eds.) Mobility Conference, pp. 39–46 (2007)
8. Dey, A.K., Abowd, G.D.: Towards a better understanding of context and context-awareness. In: Workshop on The What, Who, Where, When, and How of Context-Awareness (CHI 2000) (April 2000), http://www.cc.gatech.edu/fce/contexttoolkit/
9. Dey, A.K., Abowd, G.D., Salber, D.: A context-based infrastructure for smart environments, tech. report of georgia institute of technology (1999), http://www.cc.gatech.edu/fce/contexttoolkit/pubs/MANSE99.pdf
10. Dey, A.K.: Providing Architectural Support for Building Context-aware Applications. Ph.D. thesis, Atlanta, GA, USA (2000)
11. Gellersen, H.W., Schmidt, A., Beigl, M.: Multi-sensor context-awareness in mobile devices and smart artifacts. Mob. Netw. Appl. 7(5), 341–351 (2002)
12. Hong, J.I., Landay, J.A.: An infrastructure approach to context-aware computing. Human-Computer Interaction 16(2-4), 287–303 (2001), http://dblp.uni-trier.de/db/journals/hhci/hhci16.html#HongL01
13. Kapitsaki, G.M., Prezerakos, G.N., Tselikas, N.D., Venieris, I.S.: Context-aware service engineering: A survey. J. Syst. Softw. 82(8), 1285–1297 (2009), http://dx.doi.org/10.1016/j.jss.2009.02.026
14. Khedr, M., Karmouch, A.: Acai: agent-based context-aware infrastructure for spontaneous applications. J. Network and Computer Applications 28(1), 19–44 (2005)
15. Klimek, R.: Preference models and their elicitation and analysis for context-aware applications. In: Gruca, A., Czachórski, T., Kozielski, S. (eds.) Man-Machine Interactions 3. AISC, vol. 242, pp. 353–360. Springer, Heidelberg (2014)
16. Klimek, R.: A system for deduction-based formal verification of workflow-oriented software models. International Journal of Applied Mathematics and Computer Science 24(4), 941–956 (2014), http://www.amcs.uz.zgora.pl/?action=paper\&paper=802

17. Klimek, R., Faber, Ł., Kisiel-Dorohinicki, M.: Verifying data integration agents with deduction-based models. In: Proceedings of Federated Conference on Computer Science and Information Systems (FedCSIS 2013), Kraków, Poland, September 8-11, pp. 1049–1055. IEEE Xplore Digital Library (2013)
18. Martin, D., Lamsfus, C., Alzua, A.: Automatic context data life cycle management framework. In: 2010 5th International Conference on Pervasive Computing and Applications (ICPCA), pp. 330–335 (2010)
19. Modahl, M., Bagrak, I., Wolenetz, M., Hutto, P., Ramachandran, U.: Mediabroker: An architecture for pervasive computing. In: Proc. of the 2nd IEEE International Conference on Pervasive Computing and Communications, pp. 253–262 (2004)
20. Nakazawa, J., Tokuda, H., Edwards, W.K., Ramachandran, U.: A bridging framework for universal interoperability in pervasive systems. In: ICDCS. IEEE Computer Society (2006)
21. Perera, C., Zaslavsky, A.B., Christen, P., Georgakopoulos, D.: Context aware computing for the internet of things: A survey. IEEE Communications Surveys and Tutorials, 414–454 (2014)
22. da Rocha, R.C.A., Endler, M.: Evolutionary and efficient context management in heterogeneous environments. In: Proceedings of the 3rd International Workshop on Middleware for Pervasive and Ad-hoc Computing, MPAC 2005, pp. 1–7. ACM (2005)
23. Sanchez, L., Lanza, J., Olsen, R., Bauer, M., Girod-Genet, M.: A generic context management framework for personal networking environments. In: 2006 Third Annual International Conference on Mobile and Ubiquitous Systems: Networking Services, pp. 1–8 (July 2006)
24. Strang, T., Linnhoff-Popien, C.: A context modeling survey. In: UbiComp 1st International Workshop on Advanced Context Modelling, Reasoning and Management, pp. 31–41 (2004)
25. Tran, A.C., Marsland, S., Dietrich, J., Guesgen, H.W., Lyons, P.: Use cases for abnormal behaviour detection in smart homes. In: Lee, Y., et al. (eds.) ICOST 2010. LNCS, vol. 6159, pp. 144–151. Springer, Heidelberg (2010)
26. Yau, S.S., Karim, F., Wang, Y., Wang, B., Gupta, S.K.S.: Reconfigurable context-sensitive middleware for pervasive computing. IEEE Pervasive Computing 1(3), 33–40 (2002), http://dx.doi.org/10.1109/MPRV.2002.1037720

# Computational Models of Immediate and Expected Emotions for Emotional BDI Agents

Hanen Lejmi-Riahi[✉], Fahem Kebair, and Lamjed Ben Said

Higher Institute of Management of Tunis,
Optimization Strategies and Intelligent Information Engineering Laboratory,
41, Rue de la Liberté 2000 Le Bardo, Tunisia
{hanene.lejmi,kebairf}@gmail.com lamjed.bensaid@isg.rnu.tn

**Abstract.** In line with the multi-disciplinary growing interest in emotions and the scientific proof of their usefulness for taking decisions, scholars, in agent-oriented systems, start to account for emotions when building upon intelligence and realism in rational agents. As a result, several computational models of emotions were developed and new architectures for emotional artificial agents were proposed, in particular the Emotional Belief Desire Intention (EBDI) agents. In this paper, we provide a comprehensive description of two computational models which are used to generate immediate and expected emotions. These models will be incorporated within an EBDI agent architecture that takes into consideration these two types of emotions. ...

**Keywords:** Emotional agents · Belief desire intention architecture · Immediate emotions · Expected emotions · Computational model of emotions

## 1 Introduction

In recent years, several studies were conducted to develop computational models of emotions due to their role to improve researches in different scientific areas such as psychology, AI (Artificial Intelligence) and Human Computer Interaction [12,9]. In the current research, we deal with the issue of developing a new computational model of emotions in the context of the AI field. In particular, we aim to enrich the Belief Desire Intention (BDI) agent architecture, which encapsulates concepts and processes of thinking and deciding for rational agents, with emotional mechanism [17]. In fact, almost of works that elaborate on this type of architecture propose models of rational agents in which the agent decision is determined by its mental states without considering emotions. Moreover, by incorporating emotions, we intend to enhance the decision- making of the artificial agents especially under uncertainty, time pressure and resources constraints. Thus, we provide in the current work a modeling of the emotion-related influences on the decision-making process. The originality of this work stems from the distinction between two types of emotions, which are immediate and

© Springer International Publishing Switzerland 2015
L. Rutkowski et al. (Eds.): ICAISC 2015, Part II, LNAI 9120, pp. 424–435, 2015.
DOI: 10.1007/978-3-319-19369-4_38

expected, within emotional BDI agents. This distinction springs from the idea proposed in [11]. This work has been influential in psychology, decision theory and management but not sufficiently in agent-oriented systems researches. It addresses the issue of developing a theoretical framework that serves to explain the way in which immediate and expected emotions influence decision-making. The authors define the expected emotions as the predictions about the emotional experience if ever the decision option takes place and the associated outcomes occur [11]. They also present immediate emotions as emotions felt at the time of the decision-making. They arise either due to the anticipations made about the decision outcomes and their emotional consequences or they can simply be experienced in relation to some situational stimuli unrelated to the decision process itself [11]. In this context, our work proposes two computational models of immediate and expected emotions. For each type of emotion, the associated model provides a detailed description of the emotion generation mechanism and its intensity calculation. This work is built upon a new E-BDI agent architecture model based on immediate and expected emotions that we have proposed in [10]. It explains the interplay among the immediate emotions, the expected emotions and the decision-making of artificial agents. By adopting this new approach of modeling, we intend to build agents that operate as faithful as possible to the human reasoning pattern. We mention that our work will be later applied within organizational settings on which we focus our attention, this explains the choice of the examples that we cite throughout this paper.

## 2   Theoretical Framework

### 2.1   Cognitive Appraisal Theory and Immediate Emotions Generation

Theories in emotions have investigated the emotion elicitation process and have described the different steps whereby stimuli lead to specific emotions. In particular, we find the "cognitive appraisal theory" which is the most influential theory of emotions within computational systems [12]. It assumes that emotions arise from a cognitive evaluation of stimuli, events or situations. The evaluation is performed depending on certain criteria (i.e. appraisal variables) that describe the individual significance attributed to these stimuli. In this context, the OCC (Ortony Clore Collins) model is one of the proposed emotion-derivation models which are based on the cognitive appraisal theory [14]. It has been widely used through the computational models of emotions. It defines twenty two emotion types and it suggests that emotions represent a valenced reaction to either the consequence of events, the actions of an agent, or the aspects of objects. This valenced reaction is done regarding to the goals, standards, and attitudes of the agent [14]. The OCC model addresses also the issue of emotion intensity; it suggests using some global and local appraisal variables. While, the global variables, such as sense of reality and unexpectedness, are related to the overall emotion types, local variables, such as desirability and likelihood of an event, are linked to specific types of emotions. In the current work, in order to define the immediate emotion-derivation process, we intend to use the OCC model which is characterized by its clarity, its computation-oriented nature and its wide use to synthesize emotions in artificial agents.

## 2.2   Somatic Marker Hypothesis and Expected Emotions Generation

The somatic marker hypothesis argues that when an individual is facing an uncertain decision problem and he has to choose one option among others, a somatic marker can help the decision maker and guide his deliberation process. Damasio defines the somatic markers as special feelings and emotions which have been connected by learning from past experiences to predicted future outcomes of certain circumstances [3]. In this manner, the process behind this hypothesis starts from a decision problem that leads to a deliberation about the available options. Then, anticipations in relation to the possible outcomes of the different options generate emotion-related mental markers. These latter are retrieved from an emotional memory and are constructed based upon past positive or negative emotions elicited in earlier similar decisions. In the way indicated, somatic markers provide feedback to the decision maker by marking each option as advantageous or harmful. By reference to the presentation of somatic markers cited above, expected emotions can match the role played by somatic markers. In that regard, they can be used by the decision makers as indicators to be oriented toward or against specific options. Moreover, they are learned according to past experienced emotions felt at previous similar scenarios.

## 2.3   Emotional BDI Architecture and Computational Models of Emotions (CME)

The BDI architecture is a widely accepted approach to model rational agents. The significant popularity of this model is due mainly to its foundation on folk psychology. According to this architecture, agents behave along the lines of the human practical reasoning which includes first a process of deliberation followed then by a process of means-end reasoning [1]. More recently, scholars in the agent community started to pay attention to a new form of BDI agent architecture in which artificial emotions have been incorporated. Subsequently, several models of emotional BDI agents have been proposed particularly [15], [8] and [16]. In [15], an emotional state manager is used to control the agent resources and its capabilities. In [8], a special emphasis is given to the influence of both primary and secondary emotions on the agent decision-making process. The work in [16] was inspired by [15] and [8] to propose a domain-independent EBDI agent architecture. While these aforementioned works have brought new contributions to the agent community by incorporating emotions next to the classical BDI agent architecture components, they present some limitations. In fact, they don't provide details about the emotional components namely specific emotions generation rules and intensities calculations. They claim that such details can be left to the models designers. Another interesting architecture is proposed in [13]. In this work, affective states are used to generate emotionally driven responses.

This work provides a CME named EMotion and Adaptation (EMA) in order to explain for each type of emotions the generation rule as well as the intensity valuation. However, this emotional model is not based on the OCC model but, instead, on the work of Smith and Lazarus [18] which is commonly argued as a complex appraisal theory of emotions. In addition, the model takes into consideration a limited number of emotions (only six emotions). In this context, other CMEs based on the OCC model can be presented in particular [9], [5] and [2]; and, by which, we have been inspired to develop the proposed CME. The main similarities and differences with these works are discussed later.

## 3  Immediate and Expected Emotions in Agent Architectures: Previous Work and Adopted approach

In Sect. 2.3, we have presented some related work in relation to the EBDI agent architecture as well as the computational models of emotions. In this section, we put the focus, particularly, on the existing agent-based models that address the distinction between expected and immediate emotions and that incorporate their influences on the agent decision-making process. However, there is only two works from literature where an attempt has so far been carried out in this direction. The first work, which has been reported by [19], represents an emotion-based cognitive framework of an agent decision-making in which the influences of both immediate and expected emotions are included. This model differs to our proposed model in three important ways. First, in spite of its integration into cognitive agent architecture, the decision-making process proposed in [19] does not represent explicitly the mental states of the agents (i.e. beliefs, desires and intentions). Second, contrarily to their assertion to follow the interaction among expected emotions, immediate emotions and decision as it was presented by [11], the model of Xu and Wang [19] has ignored different components dynamics such as the anticipatory influence of expected emotions on the immediate ones. Third, as it is commonly known, most of the computational models of emotions are based on the appraisal theory according to which emotions are the result of a cognitive evaluation of a situation [13]. Nevertheless, in the aforementioned model, immediate emotions can only be triggered by a direct impact of stimulus. They are then considered as the result of a reactive behavior that doesn't require any deliberation. The second work has been proposed in [7]. It presents a computational architecture for emotional synthetic agents. This work differs to our work in two relevant aspects. First, it is concerned with shaping the outline between the agent emotions and its behavior in general; it doesn't emphasize the relationship between emotions and decision-making. Second, their work uses the "causal interpretation" component in order to deal with the agent mental states and its relation with its environment. However, such as the work of [19], this component is presented as a black box that doesn't provide any information about its internal structure or the mechanism that draws the dynamics among the agent beliefs, desires, intentions and the reasoning process components.

In this work, the agent model is built upon a new EBDI architecture that has been proposed in a previous work [10]. The agent architecture comprises two main parts. First, the first part deals with the agent practical reasoning (i.e. deliberation and means-end reasoning). It is built upon the practical reasoning model of [16] which represents a general domain-independent EBDI architecture (see Sect. 2.3). Second, the second part is concerned with the emotional component and it corresponds to our contribution. In this agent architecture the influence of both immediate and expected emotions on the agent decision-making process is incorporated. A full description of this architecture can be found in [10]. In fact, we introduce its different components and its interaction mechanism by presenting the sequence of the execution process, in a control loop mode. We also explain the information flow among these different components.

## 4    Computational Model of Emotions

The proposed EBDI agent architecture described in [10] provides insights about the mechanism according to which immediate and expected emotions are generated. It also explains how these emotions affect the agent reasoning process (i.e. deliberation and means-end reasoning). However, a further description is required to make this conceptual model effectively computational (i.e. implemented in a machine). In the current paper, we mainly focus our interest in the emotion generation process in relation to both immediate and expected emotions. For the emotional effect on the agent decision, it is the intent of future work.

### 4.1    Immediate Emotions Model

The specification of a computational model of immediate emotions generation is twofold. First, it is required to define the emotion-derivation model according to which immediate emotions are elicited given the occurrence of a specific situation. Second, it is also necessary to determine how emotions intensities will be formalized and computed. In this regard, we have adopted the OCC model [14] in order to deal with these twofold issues. In fact, we have used the OCC model description of emotions to define a set of emotion-elicitation rules that evaluate events and agent actions by respect to the list of the agent goals and standards. To this end, a list of emotion-elicitation variables has been used by the I-Emotion elicitation component. Moreover, a subset of the appraisal variables, as proposed in the OCC model, has been employed by the I-Emotion intensity component to calculate the emotions intensities. We mention that, actually, we take into consideration 20 over 22 emotions of the OCC model. We leave the specification of love and hate emotions for future work.

**I-Emotion Elicitation Component.** In order to define the elicitation rules of the immediate emotions along the line of the OCC model, the I-Emotion elicitation component uses a set of seven variables. These include *desirability(event, actor)*, *actualState(event)*, *pastState(event)*, *friendship(self, other)*, *actor(action)* and *praiseworthiness(action)*. According to the *actualState(event)* and *pastState(event)* variables, they represent the actual state of an event and its previous state. Their values can be unconfirmed, confirmed or disconfirmed to correspond respectively to an event which is not yet confirmed, already confirmed and disconfirmed after a possible occurrence. For the remaining variables, they are also used as appraisal variables for the emotions intensities calculation. Thus, a further description and methods of their evaluation are provided below.

Depending on the values of these emotions elicitation variables cited above, the appropriate rules are elected and immediate emotions are generated. These rules are formalized using IF-THEN statements and they are evaluated as shown in Table 1. We mention that compound emotions (i.e. gratification, remorse, gratitude and anger) are triggered if the elicitation conditions of well-being and attribution emotions are simultaneously satisfied. For instance, anger is elicited if both of distress and reproach emotions are triggered.

**Table 1.** Immediate emotions generation conditions based on the OCC model

| Immediate emotions elicitation variables | Well-being | | Prospect-based | | | | | | Fortunes-of-others | | | | Attribution | | | |
|---|---|---|---|---|---|---|---|---|---|---|---|---|---|---|---|---|
| | Joy | Distress | Hope | Fear | Satisfaction | Fear-confirmed | Relief | Disappointment | Happy-for | Sorry-for | Resentment | Gloating | Pride | Shame | Admiration | Reproach |
| *desirability(event,self)* | + | - | + | - | + | - | - | + | + | - | - | + | | | | |
| *desirability(event,other)* | | | | | | | | | + | - | + | - | | | | |
| *actualState(event)* | C | C | UNC | UNC | C | C | DISC | DISC | | | | | | | | |
| *pastState(event)* | | | | | UNC | UNC | UNC | UNC | | | | | | | | |
| *friendship(self,other)* | | | | | | | | | + | + | - | - | | | | |
| *actor(action)* | | | | | | | | | | | | | self | self | other | other |
| *praiseworthiness(action)* | | | | | | | | | | | | | + | - | + | - |

*Note.* ***C*** *refers to confirmed,* ***UNC*** *refers to unconfirmed and* ***DISC*** *refers to disconfirmed events.*

**I-Emotion Intensity Component.** Throughout this subsection, we follow the OCC model classification of emotions which is mainly based on their elicitation conditions. We provide for each group of emotions, the method according to which appraisal variables are evaluated and emotions intensities are calculated. To do so, we were inspired by FLAME, ParleE and GEmA which are domain-independent computational models of emotions which are based on the OCC model and conducted respectively in [5], [2] and [9]. We also, illustrate by citing examples from the organizational context.

*Well-Being Emotions.* These emotions are about the outcomes of events which can be desirable or undesirable for the agent itself. An event is desirable if it facilitates the achievement of the agent goal(s); otherwise, it is considered as undesirable. Accordingly, the *desirability(event,self)* is the main appraisal variable which is used to evaluate well-being emotions. Almost models of emotions computes the desirability of an event to the agent itself on the basis of its impact on the agent goals, denoted as *Impact(event, goal)*, weighted by the importance of each goal, denoted as *Importance(goal)*, as follows:

$$desirability(e_i, self) = \sum\nolimits_{g_j \in G} Importance(g_j) * Impact(e_i, g_j) \quad (1)$$

where $G$ is the set of the agent goals. Models of desirability assign generally pre-determined values to the $Importance(goal)$ variable. However, the difference among them resides essentially in the method according to which the $Impact(event, goal)$ is calculated. For instance, in [2], the difference between the probabilities of achieving a goal after and before the occurrence of the event is used to evaluate the $Impact(event, goal)$; where these probabilities are retrieved from a planning algorithm. Moreover, in [9], a goal attainment method has been used. In this method, goals are defined in a tree structure from the abstract goals (top goals) to the immediate goals (sub-goals). The attainment of top goals is computed on the basis of the attainment of its relative sub-goals (set as events) as well as the links degree among them. In the current work, our approach for evaluating the impact of an event on the agent goals relies on Fuzzy Cognitive Map (FCM). We propose to use this technique as a means for modeling the cause-effect relationship that links events occurring in the agent environment to its goals and to measure the strength of the impact among them. The FCM is a direct graph which is composed of nodes, called as concepts, and edges among these concepts. Each concept in the agent domain can be either a cause or/and an effect variable and it refers generally to events, actions, values, moods, trends, or goals [4]. Concepts have numeric fuzzy values traditionally located in the interval [0,1]; where 0 corresponds to a full absence of the concept, 1 to its full presence and the fractional value to its partially presence. In other words, if the concepts correspond to events, the values of the FCM concepts refer to fuzzy events that have occurred to some degree. The edges of the FCM are signed and weighted arcs and are used to interconnect concepts, to model the influences among them and to define with which degree these influences are exerted. The edges weights have fuzzy values in the range between [-1,1]. If the weight is positive, it indicates that an increase (resp. a decrease) in the cause node value implies also an increase (resp. a decrease) in the effect node value; otherwise, the values of the cause and the effect nodes are related in an inversely proportional relationship. To illustrate, Fig. 1 shows a FCM related to the organizational context. The cause nodes stand for the events that can occur in the agent environment and they influence the agent goals which represent the effect nodes. According to this example, if the FCM takes as input the employee reception of an extremely "good reward" with a degree of presence of 0.89, the effect of this reward increase affects positively the "employee motivation" goal with a strength of 0.9. Consequently, the global impact of the event "good reward" on the goal "employee motivation" is equal to 0.89 * 0.9 = 0.801. Generally speaking, using FCM, the impact of an event (cause concept $C_i$) on an agent goal (effect concept $C_j$) is formalized as:

$$Impact(e_i, g_j) = C_i * w_{ij} \qquad (2)$$

where $C_i$ is a fuzzy degree of the presence of an event $e_i$ and $w_{ij}$ is the fuzzy strength of causality linking $C_i$ to $C_j$ (or $e_i$ to $g_j$).

The $Unexpectedness$ is another appraisal variable that impacts the well-being emotions intensities and that refers to how surprised one is by the situation [14]. This variable is claimed as influencing for the intensities of several emotions.

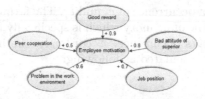

**Fig. 1.** Example of FCM from the organizational context

This explains the reason behind considering unexpectedness as a global variable in the OCC model. In this work, unexpectedness takes a value in the range [0,1]; it's related to the occurrence of an event or an action of agent and it's formalized as $unexpectedness(e) = 1 - expectedness(e)$ where expectedness presents the prediction made about the occurrence of an event (or an action) given past knowledge. Following FLAME [5] and GEmA [9] , the expectedness can be learnt dynamically and is built upon past experienced patterns of events. More specifically, conditional probabilities can be computed based on the frequency of the occurrence of an event given a sequence of other items (i.e. events or agent actions) occurrence (e.g. $P(e_1/e_2, a_3, e_1)$ where $e_1$ and $e_2$ are events and $a_3$ is an agent action ). Using these two appraisal variables (i.e. $desirability(e_i, self)$ and $unexpectedness(e_i)$), the I-Emotion intensity component computes the intensity of well-being emotions (i.e. joy and distress) as follows:

$$I_{WB} = |desirability(e_i, self)| * unexpectedness(e_i) \ . \tag{3}$$

*Prospect-Based Emotions.* This cluster of emotions is about prospective outcomes of events [14]. According to hope and fear, to calculate their intensities, two main approaches from the literature have been proposed. The first approach, such as in [2], claims that hope and fear are related respectively to the belief that goals are going to succeed or to fail. Hence, these two emotions are not associated to a particular event that has occurred but they focus rather on the overall goals attainment state. In this approach, the intensity of hope and fear is calculated based on the importance of the agent goals and the probabilities of their achievement. The second approach, such as in [9], argues that hope and fear are related to events (desirable or undesirable) which are not yet confirmed (i.e. unconfirmed). Their intensities are evaluated using the desirability of the event and its likelihood of occurrence. In the current work, we adopt a hybrid method which combines the two aforementioned approaches. In fact, we use the product of the two variables desirability and likelihood of events but we take also into consideration the influence of the overall goals attainment state. As such, we ensure that the hope/fear intensity model is as faithful as possible to the real-world human emotions. Assuming that the *likelihood* of an event corresponds to how likely is an event occurrence, this appraisal variable is measured using the frequency of the event $e_i$ occurrence as well as the occurrence of its opposite $e_i^c$. Examples of $e_i$ and $e_i^c$ could be respectively "promotion acceptance" and "promotion reject". The *likelihood* takes a value in the range [-1,1] and it is calculated as follows:

$$likelihood(e_i) = \frac{COUNT(e_i) - COUNT(e_i^c)}{n} \tag{4}$$

where $n$ is the number of occurrence of $e_i$ and $e_i^c$. The formula parameters values can be derived from a type of memory which is specifically used to preserve trace of past-experienced events occurrence. Accordingly, the intensity of hope and fear, denoted as $I_{HF}$, is calculated as following:

$$I_{HF} = |desirability(e_i, self) * likelihood(e_i)| * \frac{\sum_{g_j \in G} C_j}{n} \qquad (5)$$

where $G$ is the set of the agent goals and $n$ corresponds to their number. Moreover, $C_j$ is a concept from the agent FCM described above; it is related to an agent goal and it takes a fuzzy value that determines the degree of a goal achievement. The average of these fuzzy concepts, which are related to goals, is used in order to highlight the impact of the overall goals attainment state on hope and fear intensities calculation.

According to satisfaction and fear-confirmed, these emotions arise if the prospective outcomes of events have been realized; otherwise, disappointment or relief emotions are generated. Their intensities are usually evaluated on the basis of the intensities of the hope or the fear emotions which have been previously experienced [2] [5] [9]. Consequently, the intensities of satisfaction and disappointment, denoted as $I_{SD}$, and, fear-confirmed and relief, denoted as $I_{FcR}$, are computed as follows:

$$I_{SD} = previous(I_H) \qquad (6) \qquad\qquad I_{FcR} = previous(I_F) \qquad (7)$$

where $I_H$ and $I_F$ represent respectively the intensities of hope and fear.

*Fortunes of Others Emotions.* These emotions (i.e. happy-for, resentment, gloating and pity) are about events which can be desirable or undesirable for another agent [14]. Among the few attempts that have been conducted in order to measure these emotions intensities, we cite the model proposed in ParleE [2]. According to this work, the liking level towards another agent and the degree of happiness of this other agent are used to determine the intensity of fortune-of-others emotions [2]. In our reproach, we use two appraisal variables which are the *desirability( event, other)* and the *friendship(self,other)*. For the *desirability(event, other)* is evaluated in the same way the *desirability(event, self)* is assessed (see (1)). Nevertheless, parameters values are derived from the model of the other agent which is in form of a FCM. In fact, we assume that the agent has a partial knowledge about the other agents models including their goals and the events occurrences. These data constitute the other agents FCM models and they are continuously updated via the agent perception and his communication with other agents. According to the *friendship(self,other)* appraisal variable, it describes the quality of relation linking an agent to another. Following the model proposed in ParleE [2], it takes a value in the interval [-1,1] and it's initially set to 0. Moreover, its value is updated based on the other agents actions which can be desirable if they affect positively the agent goals or undesirable otherwise. Using the two aforementioned appraisal variables, the intensity of fortune-of-others emotions, denoted as $I_{FO}$, is computed using the following formula:

$$I_{FO} = |friendship(self, other) * desirability(e_i, other)| . \tag{8}$$

*Attribution Emotions.* According to the OCC model, these emotions arise from a cognitive appraisal of the agent actions by respect to its standards. If the actions are conducted by the agent itself, they can be appraised as praiseworthy or blameworthy and they generate pride or shame emotions. Otherwise, admiration and reproach emotions are elicited. Similarly to the way the desirability of events is assessed regarding the list of the agent goals, the praiseworthiness of the agent actions is also evaluated by respect to the list of its standards based on FCM. This allows the representation of cause-effect relationship relating actions of agents to its standards using fuzzy values. Two appraisal variables are considered in this model, which are the *praiseworthiness(action)* and the *unexpectedness(action)*, in order to compute the intensities of attribution emotions, denoted as $I_A$. The latter is evaluated using the following formula:

$$I_A = |praiseworthiness(action)| * unexpectedness(action) \tag{9}$$

*Compound Emotions.* As already mentioned in the I-Emotion elicitation component and by respect to the OCC model, compound emotions (i.e. gratification, remorse, gratitude and anger) combine well-being and attribution emotions. Consequently, their intensities, denoted as $I_C$, are evaluated using the product of their compounding emotions intensities as following:

$$I_C = I_{WB} * I_A \tag{10}$$

## 4.2   Expected Emotions Model

According to the specification of the proposed EBDI architecture [10], when a decision problem takes place, after generating and filtering options, the agent is committed to one option $o_i$ (i.e. its current intention). Due to the architecture closed-loop design, the consequences of the option $o_i$ execution in the environment are perceived by the agent as events or actions that are evaluated by the incidental stimulus appraisal (*isa*) to generate immediate emotion. This latter represents emotion felt at the time of the decision-making and it is defined by its label $ie_j$ (e.g. joy) and its intensity $I_{ie_j/o_i}$. In this context, an Emotional Memory (EM) is used in order to keep trace accordingly. In fact, each time a new option is generated and a decision is made, the associated immediate emotional experience is saved in this EM. This information will serve to generate the expected emotions which represent the forecast of possible emotions if ever the decision option takes place and the associated outcomes occur. As a result, to generate expected emotions, the agent selects unconsciously the immediate emotion which maximizes the product: $F(ie_j/o_i) * AVG(I_{ie_j/o_i})$. Where $F(ie_j/o_i)$ represents the frequency of experiencing the immediate emotion $ie_j$ when the option $o_i$ is selected ; it is defined as:

$$F(ie_j/o_i) = \frac{COUNT(o_i, ie_j)}{\sum_k COUNT(o_i, ie_k)} \tag{11}$$

given that $COUNT$ is a function used to enumerate the number of occurrence of an element and $k$ is the number of all different emotions which are associated to option $o_i$ in the EM. Moreover $AVG(I_{ie_j/o_i})$ is the average intensities of $ie_j$ when the option $o_i$ is selected; it is calculated as:

$$AVG(I_{ie_j/o_i}) = \frac{\sum_n I_{ie_j/o_i}}{n} \quad \text{where} \quad n = COUNT(o_i, ie_j). \tag{12}$$

Consequently, the expected emotion $ee$ at time $t$ for option $o_i$ is formalized as:

$$ee_{t,o_i} = argmax_{ie_j}(F(ie_j/o_i) * AVG(I_{ie_j/o_i})) \tag{13}$$

As it was aforementioned, expected emotions can play the role of somatic markers in the sense that they are learned from past experienced emotions felt at previous similar decision statements. In addition, they can be used by the decision makers to favor one option over another. Hence, it is possible to employ the generated expected emotion by the *filter* component in the proposed EBDI architecture [10] in order to select the option that the agent will be committed to. For instance, at time t, if A has to choose between $o_1$ and $o_2$. If by respect to the EM, the expected emotion for $o_1$ is $ie_2$ and for $o_2$ is $ie_1$. If $ie_1$ and $ie_2$ represent respectively the joy and distress emotions, the decision maker favors the option which is associated to the emotion with positive valence. In this case, the agent selects $o_2$ because it's associated to joy.

## 5   Conclusion and Future Work

In this paper, we developed two computational models of immediate and expected emotions which are incorporated within a new EBDI agent architecture. The immediate emotions model is based on the OCC model and it provides a new domain-independent approach to compute the appraisal variables. In particular, we used the FCM technique which is able to represent the fuzzy causal reasoning among the agent events, actions, goals and standards. According to the expected emotions, their model is based on past experienced emotions felt during decisions statements and it serves to guide decision makers on line with the somatic markers hypothesis. For the future work, it consists in setting the focus on complementary aspects about the models of emotions such as the decay function which represents the fade phenomenon of the emotional intensity. Moreover, a comprehensive model of the emotional influences on the decision-making is needed. Finally, and in relation to implementations and tests, we are actually developing a new agent-based simulator of an organization in which employees are endowed with emotions. The implementation is conducting using Madkit [6] which is java-based multi-agent development platform, based on an organizational model with no predefined agent architecture. The employee agent model is based on the EBDI architecture that we have developed and uses the proposed CME in order to simulate the emotional experiences of employees. To this date, such simulator can't be found in literature. Moreover, this type of simulator can be very useful when used by managers and employees as a software-based human resources development tool. For example, it can help employees to identify which emotions can be triggered in a given situation and to assume the impact of their emotions on their decisions; it can also provide what-if analysis to support new organizational practices assessment.

# References

1. Bratman, M.E., Israel, D.J., Pollack, M.E.: Plans and resource-bounded practical reasoning. Computational Intelligence 4(3), 349–355 (1988)
2. Bui, T.D., Heylen, D., Poel, M., Nijholt, A.: Parlee: An adaptive plan based event appraisal model of emotions. In: Jarke, M., Koehler, J., Lakemeyer, G. (eds.) KI 2002. LNCS (LNAI), vol. 2479, p. 129. Springer, Heidelberg (2002)
3. Damasio, A.: Descartes' Error: Emotion, Reason, and the Human Brain (2005)
4. Dickerson, J.A., Kosko, B.: Virtual worlds as fuzzy cognitive maps. In: Virtual Reality Annual International Symposium, pp. 471–477. IEEE (1993)
5. El-Nasr, M.S., Yen, J., Ioerger, T.R.: Flame–zzy logic adaptive model of emotions. Autonomous Agents and Multi-agent Systems 3(3), 219–257 (2000)
6. Gutknecht, O., Ferber, J.: The MADKIT agent platform architecture. In: Wagner, T., Rana, O.F. (eds.) Infrastructure for Agents 2000. LNCS (LNAI), vol. 1887, pp. 48–55. Springer, Heidelberg (2001)
7. Hu, J.W., Feng, L., Yin, Q.J., Deng, H.J.: A computational architecture for modeling emotional behavior in synthetic agent. In: Computer Modeling and Simulation, vol. 1, pp. 394–398. IEEE (2010)
8. Jiang, H., Vidal, J.M., Huhns, M.N.: Ebdi: an architecture for emotional agents. In: Proceedings of the 6th International Joint Conference on AAMAS, p. 11 (2007)
9. Kazemifard, M., Ghasem-Aghaee, N., Ören, T.I.: Design and implementation of gema: A generic emotional agent. Expert Systems with Applications 38(3) (2011)
10. Lejmi-Riahi, H., Kebair, F., Ben Said, L.: Agent decision-making under uncertainty: Towards a new e-bdi agent architecture based on immediate and expected emotions. International Journal of Computer Theory & Engineering 6(3) (2014)
11. Loewenstein, G., Lerner, J.S.: The role of affect in decision making. Handbook of Affective Science 619(642), 3 (2003)
12. Marsella, S., Gratch, J., Petta, P.: Computational models of emotion. A Blueprint for Affective Computing-A Sourcebook and Manual, 21–46 (2010)
13. Marsella, S.C., Gratch, J.: Ema: A process model of appraisal dynamics. Cognitive Systems Research 10(1), 70–90 (2009)
14. Ortony, A., Clore, G.L., Collins, A.: The cognitive structure of emotions (1988)
15. Pereira, D., Oliveira, E., Moreira, N., Sarmento, L.: Towards an architecture for emotional bdi agents (2005)
16. Puică, M.A., Florea, A.M.: Emotional belief-desire-intention agent model: Previous work and proposed architecture. IJARAI 2(2), 1–8 (2013)
17. Reisenzein, R., Hudlicka, E., Dastani, M., Gratch, J., Hindriks, K., Lorini, E., Meyer, J.J.: Computational modeling of emotion: Toward improving the inter-and intradisciplinary exchange. IEEE Transactions on Affective Computing (2013)
18. Smith, C.A., Lazarus, R.S.: Emotion and adaptation (1990)
19. Xu, P., Wang, T.: Emotion in decision making under uncertainty and cognitive control: a computational framework. In: Natural Computation, pp. 149–154 (2007)

# A Graph Grammar Tool for Generating Computational Grid Structures

Wojciech Palacz[✉], Iwona Ryszka, and Ewa Grabska

Faculty of Physics, Astronomy and Applied Computer Science,
Jagiellonian University, Kraków, Poland
wojciech.palacz@uj.edu.pl

**Abstract.** This paper deals with the implementation of the graph based model for generating structures of computing grids. The GraphTool system proposed supports graph modeling with the use of computer tools for graph transformations. The model of computing grids is an extension of the standard graph model by adding a new level of elements called layers. In GraphTool application, the user specifies layers during creating a new project. This paper presents an example of a layered graph to simulate generation and operations in a grid that realizes the concept of distributed computing.

## 1 Introduction

Grid computing is related to distributed computing with coordinated resource sharing and problem solving in dynamic, multi-institutional virtual organizations [5]. It is used for many applications in the area of science, engineering, industry and commerce [9]. As it has been considered in [14], [7] and [12] the concept of grid needs a heterogeneous, changing model of its structure based on clusters distributed on different geographical locations. Graph transformations are useful for specification, modeling and prototyping of the structure of information processing tasks, for example these entities can be described by directed weighted graphs [8]. The hierarchical graph structure with layers has been proposed in [7]. This flexible and powerful representation has been used to implement the graph grammar tool called the GraphTool and applied for generating computational grid structures.

In general, GraphTool is implemented to support conceptual design and modeling with graphs. It is a What You See Is What You Get (WYSIWYG) editor. The tool offers building graph transformations named graph grammars by defining graph rules and a control diagram. Additionally, the process of graph derivation can be simulated and controlled by the user.

In this paper GraphTool is used to model the grid environment and verify its correctness after some operations. Many projects based on Grid environments have been developed and the descriptions of some well known projects are presented in [3].

© Springer International Publishing Switzerland 2015
L. Rutkowski et al. (Eds.): ICAISC 2015, Part II, LNAI 9120, pp. 436–447, 2015.
DOI: 10.1007/978-3-319-19369-4_39

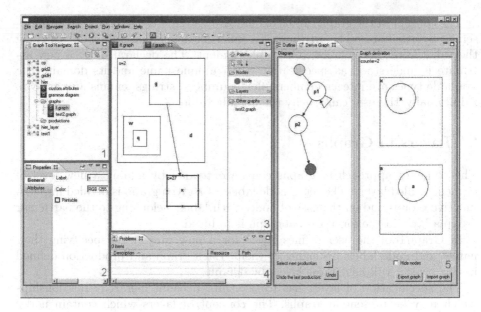

**Fig. 1.** A screenshot of GraphTool

## 2   GraphTool Overview

The motivation for work on GraphTool – a new tool for graphs was to propose an unified environment that offers the possibility not only to create a structure of graphs with semantic layers, but to generate new graphs in an automatic manner as well [13]. GraphTool uses Java SDK 7.0 environment. It is based on Eclipse Rich Client Application graphical editor for modeling and generating graphs [4]. The base perspective GraphTool application is shown in Fig. 1. It is divided into several working areas.

The view is used to present the current content of the workspace. Within the workspace the user can define own projects. In each project a set of graph transformation rules, a control diagram for these rules and a collection of initial graphs for transformations are specified.

A graph rule called a production is defined by two graphs, left-hand side and right-hand side graphs. The production application to a graph results in its transformation to a new graph by replacing a subgraph being a copy of left side to the graph with the copy of right side of the production. The entity can have associated predicate that is a logical statement describing a condition when the rule can be applied. Within the tool transformation rules can be built from scratch or on the top of existing ones. The same rules as in case of graph definition apply to productions.

Transformation rules can be grouped and then the order of their application is determined by the control diagram. It is a directed graph with highlighted start and stop node. The other nodes represent the productions. The diagram is valid when at least one path exists from the start to the end node.

The concept of the graph can be extended by adding the semantic layer represented by attributes. The attribute is a function defined on a domain assigning the value from this domain to a graph element. The declaration of a new attribute is understood as specification of an unique name and its domain (the available types are integer numbers, float numbers, strings, enums and arrays). Additionally, the user can specify the default value.

## 3    Layers in Graphs

The standard approach to graphs can be extended by adding a new level of elements called layers. The set of node labels of a given graph is divided into disjunctive groups and on the base of nodes with labels belonging to the particular group a layer in the form of a subgraph is induced.

In GraphTool the user defines layers for a new project by specifying their names and node labels belonging to them. Each graph and production defined in this project will have these layers by default.

The specification of layers has to take into account hierarchy relationships which may be present in graphs. The concept of layers which contain nodes is very similar to the concept of hierarchical nodes which contain other nodes. Obviously, if a layer contains a node then it also should contain all children of this node. This means that if the node's label belongs to a specific layer, then the children's labels should also belong to this layer.

This requirement has not been considered in the previous paper on GraphTool [12]. Therefore this paper proposes a new definition of layers.

**Definition 1 (hierarchical graph).** *Let $\Sigma$ be a fixed set of labels. A hierarchical graph $G$ is a 6-tuple $(V, E, s, t, lab, ch)$, where*
- *$V$ and $E$ are finite sets, whose elements are called nodes and edges, respectively,*
- *$s : E \to V$ and $t : E \to V$ are mappings assigning to edges their source and target nodes, respectively,*
- *$lab : V \to \Sigma$ is a node labeling function,*
- *$ch : V \to 2^V$ is known as a child nesting function, and assigns to every node a (possibly empty) set of its children,*

*such that*
- *$V$ and $E$ are disjoint,*
- *$\forall v \in V : v \notin ch^+(v)$, which means that a node cannot be its own descendant,*
- *$\forall v, w \in V : v \neq w \Rightarrow ch(v) \cap ch(w) = \emptyset$, i.e. a node cannot have two parents.*

**Definition 2 (induced hierarchical subgraph).** *Let $G = (V_G, E_G, s_G, t_G, lab_G, ch_G)$ be a hierarchical graph, and let $S$ be a subset of its nodes $(S \subseteq V_G)$. Let us define a 6-tuple $H = (V_H, E_H, s_H, t_H, lab_H, ch_H)$ such that*
- *$V_H = S \cup ch_G^+(S)$ ,*
- *$E_H = \{e \in E_G : s_G(e) \in V_H \wedge t_G(e) \in V_H\}$ ,*
- *$s_H = s_G|_{E_H}$ ,*
- *$t_H = t_G|_{E_H}$ ,*

$-\ lab_H = lab_G|_{V_H}$ ,
$-\ ch_H = ch_G|_{V_H}$ .
$H$ is a hierarchical graph, known as the subgraph induced by $S$.

**Definition 3 (attributes).** Let null be a fixed value. An attribute $a$ is a function $a : O_a \to D_a \cup \{null\}$, where $O_a$ is a finite set. $D_a$ is known as the domain of attribute $a$.

The domain of an attribute can be finite or infinite (e.g. English names for months or integer numbers). null is used to represent missing knowledge.

**Definition 4 (attributed hierarchical graph).** Let $G$ be a hierarchical graph. Let $A$ be a set of attributes defined over $G$ and $G$'s nodes, i.e. $\forall a \in A : \{G\} \in O_a$ and $V_G \subset O_a$. An attributed graph is a triple $G_A = (G, att_\Sigma, att_G)$, where
 $-\ att_\Sigma : \Sigma \to 2^A$ is a function which determines attributes assigned to nodes with specific labels,
 $-\ att_G \subset 2^A$ is a set of attributes assigned to the whole graph.

**Definition 5 (hierarchical graph with values).** Let $G_A$ be an attributed hierarchical graph. It has values if its attributes have non-null values, that is if
 $-\ \forall a \in att_G : a(\{G\}) \in D_a$ ,
 $-\ \forall v \in V_G : \forall a \in att_\Sigma(lab_G(v)) : a(v) \in D_a$ .

Attributed graphs and graphs with values are defined as extensions of hierarchical graphs. Because of this, the notion of induced subgraphs (def. 2) can be easily generalized to all three graph types. Likewise, the following definition of layers also can be applied to any of three types of graphs defined above.

**Definition 6 (graph layers).** Let $L = \{L_1, L_2, \dots L_n\}$ be a partition of $\Sigma$. If, for a given graph $G$, the condition $\forall v \in V : lab(v) \in L_i \Rightarrow lab(ch^+(v)) \subseteq L_i$ is true, then $G$ can be split into a family of subgraphs $\{G_1, \dots G_n\}$ such that every $G_i$ is induced by $\{v \in V : lab(v) \in L_i\}$, and every node from $G$ belongs to exactly one subgraph. Members of this family are called layers of $G$.

The layers are denoted by numbers, but to make reading easier they can be given informal names, like "the resource layer" or "the jobs layer", and denoted by $G_{jobs}$ or simply *Jobs*.

GraphTool ensures that graphs created by the user fulfill the condition from def. 6.

## 3.1 Advantages of Layers

The most important advantage of layers introduction into graph is the increase of readability of the graph structure. The issue of drawing graph nodes on a 2D plane is commonly discussed and different approaches have been suggested [1]. The layout techniques can cover trees, arc diagrams, circular drawings or force-based layouts. There is also a group of algorithms designed for directed graphs like Coffman–Graham algorithm [2]. The layout approach can depend on different sets of quality factors defining required aesthetics and readability level.

The layer extension to the graph can be regarded as a support for node layout. The visualization of the layer as a rectangle allows to group nodes within it and this subset can be drawn using a suitable algorithm.

The design of GraphTool follows a rule that layers are the additional hierarchy level in the graph. Such an approach and a paradigm that the layers are defined by nodes labels can leverage the process of nodes searching in the graph. The definition of layers implies the subsets of nodes based on their labels therefore the searching can be limited to a given set of subsets.

## 4    Graph Transformation Rules

As it has been considered, a transformation rule is defined by two graphs known as the left- and the right-hand side. Usually they are denoted by $L$ and $R$.

A rule can be applied to a graph $G$ only if a part of $G$ is the same as $L$. Formally, there exists an isomorphism between $L$ and a subgraph of $G$.

**Definition 7 (graph morphism).** *Let $G$ and $H$ be attributed hierarchical graphs over the set of labels $\Sigma$ and the set of attributes $A$. A graph morphism $f$ is a pair of functions, $f_V : V_G \to V_H$ and $f_E : E_G \to E_H$, such that*
- $\forall e \in E_G : f_V(s_G(e)) = s_H(f_E(e))$ *and* $\forall e \in E_G : f_V(t_G(e)) = t_H(f_E(e))$,
- $\forall v \in V_G : lab_G(v) = lab_H(f_V(v))$,
- $\forall v \in V_G : f_V(ch_G(v)) = ch_H(f_V(v))$,
- $att_{\Sigma G} = att_{\Sigma H}$,
- $att_G = att_H$.

Let $L$ and $R$ be the left- and the right-hand side of a rule, respectively. Let $G$ be a graph to be transformed. Let $m : L \to G$ be an injective morphism that has been found and fixed. Graph $G$ can then be split into two subgraphs, the first one induced by $m(V_L)$, the second one induced by $V_G - m(V_L)$. In other words, $G$ is split into an image of $L$ (which will be removed and replaced by $R$) and the remainder.

In most cases there are edges connecting these two parts of $G$. They would be left dangling after the image of $L$ is removed, thus they also must be removed. In their place some new edges can be created, which will connect the remainder of $G$ with an added copy of $R$. This process is described by an embedding transformation, defined as follows:

**Definition 8 (embedding transformation).** *Let $L$, $R$ be two sides of a transformation rule. Embedding transformation $T = (TIN, TOUT)$ is a pair of functions $TIN, TOUT : \Sigma \times V_L \to 2^{V_R}$.*

For example, if $TIN(v_1, \alpha) = \{v_4, v_7\}$, then all nodes from the remainder that had edges going to the image of $v_1$ and are labeled $\alpha$ should now be connected with copies of $v_4$ and $v_7$.

The previous definitions usually used pushout rules with node gluing [11]. Change to rules with label-controlled embedding transformation was motivated by ease of use. Rules which can reroute specific edges, but do not require them to be present in the graph are convenient in grid simulations.

$L$ and $R$ do not have values assigned to their attributes, but $G$ does. So, a rule must have a way to calculate attribute values for the added nodes. It also needs to be able to change values of attributes assigned to the graph as a whole.

Additionally, the attribute values in the image of $L$ can be checked to decide if the rule can be applied. This mechanism is known as the application predicate.

Let us denote by $\mathcal{G}$ a class of all hierarchical graphs with values, and by $\mathcal{M}_L$ a class of all graph morphisms which match the left-hand side $L$ to some graph from $\mathcal{G}$.

**Definition 9 (application predicate).** *For a rule with left-hand side $L$, an application predicate is a function $\Pi : \mathcal{G} \times \mathcal{M}_L \to \{true, false\}$.*

**Definition 10 (direct derivation).** *Let $G$ and $H$ be attributed hierarchical graphs with values. Let $p = (L, R, T, \Pi, FV, FG)$ be a transformation rule. Graph $H$ is a direct derivation from $G$ by $p$ (denoted as $G \overset{p}{\Rightarrow} H$) if and only if:*
- *there exists an isomorphism $m : L \to G'$ where $G'$ is a subgraph of $G$,*
- *there exists an isomorphism $n : R \to H'$ where $H'$ is a subgraph of $H$,*
- *$\Pi(G', m) = true$,*
- *$G - G' = H - H'$,*
- *let $IN_G = \{e \in E_G : s_G(e) \notin G' \land t_G(e) \in G'\}$,*
- *let $IN_H = \{e \in E_H : s_H(e) \notin H' \land t_H(e) \in H'\}$,*
- *$\forall\, e_1 \in IN_G\ \forall\, r \in TIN(lab_G(s_G(e_1)), m^{-1}(t_G(e_1)))$ there exists $e_2 \in IN_H$ such that $s_H(e_2) = s_G(e_1)$ and $t_H(e_2) = n(r)$,*
- *$\forall\, e_2 \in IN_H$ there exists $e_1 \in IN_G$ such that $s_H(e_2) = s_G(e_1)$ and $n^{-1}(t_H(e_2)) \in TIN(lab_G(s_G(e_1)), m^{-1}(t_G(e_1)))$,*
- *let $OUT_G = \{e \in E_G : s_G(e) \in G' \land t_G(e) \notin G'\}$,*
- *let $OUT_H = \{e \in E_H : s_H(e) \in H' \land t_H(e) \notin H'\}$,*
- *$\forall\, e_1 \in OUT_G\ \forall\, r \in TOUT(lab_G(t_G(e_1)), m^{-1}(s_G(e_1)))$ there exists $e_2 \in OUT_H$ such that $t_H(e_2) = t_G(e_1)$ and $s_H(e_2) = n(r)$,*
- *$\forall\, e_2 \in OUT_H$ there exists $e_1 \in OUT_G$ such that $t_H(e_2) = t_G(e_1)$ and $n^{-1}(s_H(e_2)) \in TOUT(lab_G(t_G(e_1)), m^{-1}(s_G(e_1)))$,*
- *$\forall\, v \in V_{H'} : \forall\, a \in att_{\Sigma H}(lab_H(v)) : a(v) = FV(a, n^{-1}(v), G', m)$,*
- *$\forall\, a \in att_G : a(H) = FG(a, G', m)$.*

GraphTool generates a result in the form of a graph by applying a sequence of direct derivations to an initial graph. Rules are selected from the set specified by the user.

## 5 An Example – Modeling the Grid

The idea of layers in graphs can be presented by means of modeling the Grid environment and simulation of this infrastructure processes changing. The Grid describes the computing environment belonging to the distributed computing paradigm [5]. It provides the controlled resource sharing and the coordinated usage of them enables the members of the community to achieve their computational goals. The most important feature of this environment is its flexibility and the possibility to create on-demand powerful computing systems transparently for the end user. The idea of control of distributed resources covers the requirement for building a high-availability and fault-tolerant system.

The structure of the Grid allows to distinguish a set of group elements basing on their functionality and group them into layers. The method of such a distinction was proposed in [7]. The attention was put to formal aspects of layers in graphs and it was shown that a graph based representation enables to use graph grammars as a tool to generate a Grid environment structure.

In this paper the extended version of the graph presenting the Grid structure is described. By means of GraphTool application a new graph grammar system will be presented. The purpose of this grammar is a verification that the modeled structure of the Grid is fault-tolerant and the environment is able to process jobs after a sequence of events that have caused changes in the Grid structure.

The Grid paradigm enables to introduce multiple components of given type with the hierarchical structure (for example several instances of GRIS elements) to realize the requirement of the high availability system. Therefore, the usage of hierarchical directed graphs to model Grid structure will be beneficial here.

In the beginning, the computational resource layer in the Grid can be extracted. It can contain computers, storage systems or data sources that are used for the execution of Grid jobs. These objects can be grouped in order to create an entity called a computing element. The layer will be denoted as Resources and node labels associated with it are as follows C, ST, CE.

Additionally two layers related to a job execution can be described. The layer containing jobs schedulers available in the Grid is one of them. The label for this layer will be Schedulers and contain nodes with JS label. Another called Jobs holds entities describing the Grid jobs marked with J label. Executing jobs can require their specific sequence and it can be modeled using edges between a given subset of jobs.

The next layer contains the elements that are responsible for the management of resources and this group will be called Management. The following entities according to general Grid concept can be extracted:

- Grid Resource Information Service (labeled GRIS) – the tool collecting data information about available resources. This component can be hierarchical and interpreted as a given GRIS node merges information from all its children nodes.
- Grid Resource Allocation Manager (labeled GRAM) – the controller responsible for monitoring the computational resource during a job execution.

By means of attributes Grid elements can have attached some additional properties. Attributes in this paper are only specified for low-level nodes in the hierarchical graph. The attributes for the grouping nodes are calculated on the basis of the children attributes. Let define the attribute space to nodes with label C, which assign integer values interpreted as a currently available space for jobs. To the jobs node a RAM attribute will be assigned that specifies an integer value describing needed space for executing this job. For the nodes with JS label the attribute max_load and load are specified. Both of them are defined in integer domain, the former specify the maximal number of jobs that can currently scheduled and the latter shows the number of being scheduled in a given moment.

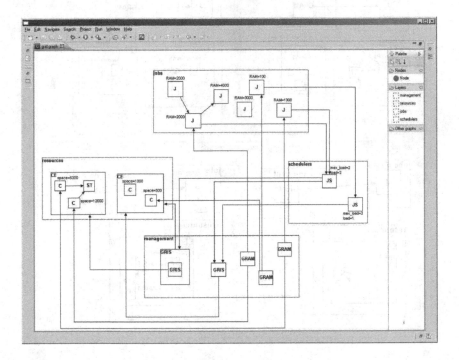

**Fig. 2.** The example of the Grid environment

The graph shown in Fig. 2 presents an example of the current stage of the Grid.

There are edges between nodes from different layers. The edges between nodes J and JS determinate which job scheduler is responsible for dispatching a given job. These edges can be calculated in an optimize way using an external mechanism (in GraphTool an option to export/import the graph during the derivation can be useful here). CE nodes are connected with GRIS nodes to inform about their availability through the given GRIS node. The next group of edges link JS nodes with GRIS nodes to model the possibility of allocation a job scheduled by the job scheduler on a computing element registered with the GRIS. Finally, the edges between J nodes, C nodes and GRAM node can be extracted and they can be interpreted as the allocation of the job on the specific computing resource for the execution and the association is stored in the GRAM node.

## 5.1   Transformation Rules for Grid

Let define a set of productions that describe some possible changes in the Grid structure. It is worth to notice that introduction of nodes categorization into layers leverages the process of defining the transformation rules.

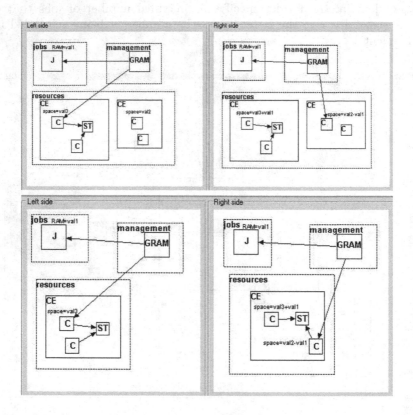

**Fig. 3.** Rules responsible for reattaching job execution (productions p1, p2)

Deleting a computer system from a computing element is associated with reattaching currently running jobs to different entities. This process is presented in Fig. 3a and 3b. For each of these production a predicate has to be fulfilled: val2 > val1.

Finally, the rule removing the computer system can be presented (see Fig. 4).

A transformation rule can be also used to describe adding a new computing element (see Fig. 5). Such a procedure requires registering it within a GRIS object.

The group of rules showing the job assignment can be prepared. An example of such a rule is shown in Fig. 6, for the production the following predicate has to be true: val2 > val1 && val4 + 1 <= val3.

In a similar way a production to mark a job completion can be created (see Fig. 7). This production does not require any predicate.

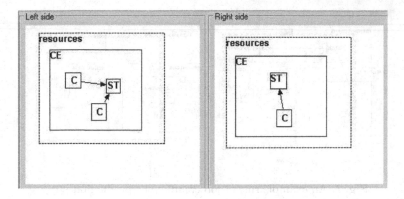

**Fig. 4.** An example of rule for deleting a node with C label (production p3)

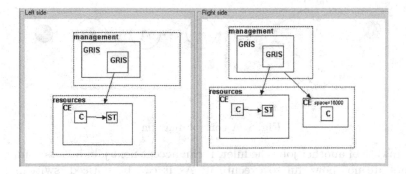

**Fig. 5.** Adding a new computing element (production p4)

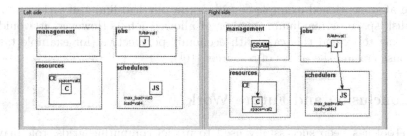

**Fig. 6.** An example rule of job assignment (production p5)

With this set of transformation rules the following control diagram can be proposed (see Fig. 8).

The choice of the path *p2*, *p3*, *p4*, *p5* and *p6* during the graph derivation will lead to deadlock. After applying the production *p4*, the predicate for production *p5* is not fulfilled. The job scheduler with attributed $max\_load=2$ and $load=2$ is too overloaded to manage one more job, thus it has an access to a computing element that offer enough space to handle a job with the requirement for 3000

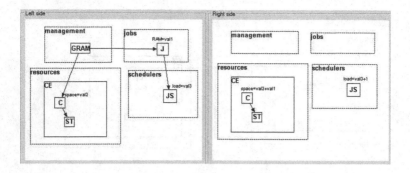

**Fig. 7.** An example rule of job completion (production p6)

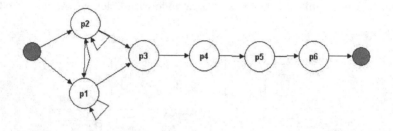

**Fig. 8.** A control diagram

RAM. In case of another job scheduler, it can accept next job, but its computing elements are not powerful to execute it. As it can be noticed, switching the production *p5* and *p6* will solve the issue, as then the first job scheduler can handle this outstanding job.

The aforementioned example considers the physical limits of Grid resources (like disk space or maximum number of allowed jobs). However, it would be interesting to extend this case with economic perspective (for example taking into consideration the prices of resources [10]).

# 6   Conclusion and Future Work

GraphTool has been successfully used to model computing grids, role-playing games, and FEM meshes. The example shows the benefits of layers in the process simulation. In future it will probably be applied in additional areas.

Integrating GraphTool with knowledge-based design support systems is a future project which seems worth investigating. As a first step we will investigate ways in which GraphTool can be integrated with a system developed to support architects [6].

# References

1. Di Battista, G., Eades, P., Tamassia, R., Tollisd, I.: Algorithms for drawing graphs: an annotated bibliography. Computational Geometry 4(5), 235–282 (1994)
2. Di Battista, G., Eades, P., Tamassia, R., Tollis, I.: Layered Drawings of Digraphs. In: Graph Drawing: Algorithms for the Visualization of Graphs, pp. 265–302. Prentice-Hall (1998)
3. Bubak, M., Nowakowski, P., Pajak, R.: An Overview of European Grid Projects. In: Fernández Rivera, F., Bubak, M., Gómez Tato, A., Doallo, R. (eds.) Across Grids 2003. LNCS, vol. 2970, pp. 299–308. Springer, Heidelberg (2004)
4. Eclipse Rich Client Platform (2014), http://wiki.eclipse.org/index.php/Rich_Client_Platform
5. Foster, I., Kesselman, C., Tuecke, S.: The Anatomy of the Grid: Enabling Scalable Virtual Organizations. International Journal of High Performance Computing Applications 15(3), 200–220 (2001)
6. Grabska, E., Łachwa, A., Ślusarczyk, G.: New visual languages supporting design of multi-storey buildings. Advanced Engineering Informatics 66(4), 681–690 (2012)
7. Grabska, E., Palacz, W., Strug, B., Ślusarczyk, G.: A Graph-Based Generation of Virtual Grids. In: Wyrzykowski, R., Dongarra, J., Karczewski, K., Waśniewski, J. (eds.) PPAM 2011, Part I. LNCS, vol. 7203, pp. 451–460. Springer, Heidelberg (2012)
8. Kulikowski, J.L.: Synthesis of Distributed Information Processing Systems (IPS) Based on PST-Networks. In: Bazewicz, M. (ed.) Information Systems Architecture and Technologies ISAT 1991, pp. 189–206 (1991)
9. Lu, D., Dinda, P.A.: GridG: Generating Realistic Computational Grids. ACM SIGMETRICS Performance Evaluation Review 30(4), 33–40 (2003)
10. Moreno, R., Alonso-Conde, A.B.: Job Scheduling and Resource Management Techniques in Economic Grid Environments. In: Fernández Rivera, F., Bubak, M., Gómez Tato, A., Doallo, R. (eds.) Across Grids 2003. LNCS, vol. 2970, pp. 25–32. Springer, Heidelberg (2004)
11. Palacz, W.: Algebraic Hierarchical Graph Transformation. Journal of Computer and System Sciences 68(3), 497–520 (2004)
12. Palacz, W., Ryszka, I., Grabska, E.: Graphs with layers – a visual tool for conceptual design and graph generation. In: 21st International Workshop: Intelligent Computing in Engineering (EG-ICE 2014) (2014)
13. Ryszka, I., Grabska, E.: GraphTool – a new system of graph generation. In: 2nd International Conference on Data Analytics, Porto, Portugal (2013)
14. Strug, B., Ryszka, I., Grabska, E., Ślusarczyk, G.: Generating a Virtual Computational Grid by Graph Transformations. In: Davoli, F., et al. (eds.) Remote Instrumentation for eScience and Related Aspects, pp. 209–226 (2012)

# Assessment of Fertilizer Nitrogen Requirement of Sugar Beetroot Using Info-Gap Theory

Andrzej Piegat[✉] and Karina Tomaszewska

West Pomeranian University of Technology, Zolnierska 49, 71-210 Szczecin, Poland
{apiegat,mtomaszewska}@wi.zut.edu.pl

**Abstract.** The aim of this paper is to present an interesting application of one of the decision-making methods used in problems with lack of knowledge. This method is called Info-Gap Theory and can be applied to describe the phenomenon where no classic uncertainty description in form of probability density or possibility distribution is at disposal. A general outline of Info-Gap Theory is presented and its functions (robustness and opportuneness) are shown. The numerical example of fertilizer nitrogen requirement is given to illustrate the efficiency of the proposed method to practical issues.

**Keywords:** Uncertainty · Info-Gap theory · Opportuneness · Robustness · Fertilizer

## 1    Introduction

The real-world problems are often complex in nature and have a high degree of uncertainty. The term uncertainty has got many different meanings, but in the context of practical applications in decision analysis, the most appropriate is given by Zimmermann [22]: 'Uncertainty implies that in a certain situation a person does not possess the information which quantitatively is appropriate to describe, prescribe or predict numerically a system, its behavior or other characteristics.' In this paper we concentrate on problem where external uncertainty appears. This kind of uncertainty represents concern about issues outside the control of the decision maker.  External uncertainty can be assessed through two ways. A distributional mode based on some distribution or range of chance and a probability or singular mode based on an assessed chance of an event happening. Where uncertainties are of sufficient magnitude and importance to be modeled, however the modeling approaches for external (but also internal) uncertainties may often become qualitatively difficult in nature. Decision Theory applies different methods to predict future events, physical measurements which are already unknown. Among these methods some of the following references should be mentioned: Fuzzy set approaches [16,19,21], Rough set approaches [7,14], Interval arithmetic [2,13], Grey Systems [6], Granular Computing [15]. As F. Knight [10] said: 'We cannot be certain about uncertainty', that is why scientists are still looking for new solutions, introducing modifications of these methods or trying to find new one. All of the methods used in decision- making theory under uncertainty have its own interpretation and modeling of uncertainty and they are used to different problems. For example, Fuzzy sets use membership functions as

© Springer International Publishing Switzerland 2015
L. Rutkowski et al. (Eds.): ICAISC 2015, Part II, LNAI 9120, pp. 448–459, 2015.
DOI: 10.1007/978-3-319-19369-4_40

possibility density distributions and do operations (the generalization of crisp set operations) on them; Interval arithmetic bases on interval representation of uncertain variable giving its lower and upper limit and in many cases it uses Moore's arithmetic or other types of this arithmetic [18]. Fig.1. shows representations of an uncertain variable in some of the mentioned methods.

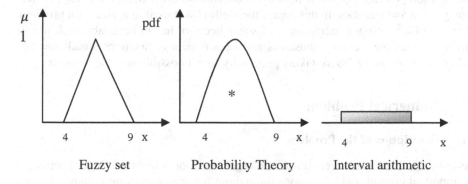

Fuzzy set             Probability Theory        Interval arithmetic

**Fig. 1.** The representation of an uncertain variable in different methods

Each of these methods has its supporters but also opponents and it is important that there is no scientific method, which can compare and verify all these approaches on the same level. In this paper, an application of the method which is capable to deal with uncertain information is presented. It is called Info-Gap Theory and was introduced by Ben-Haim Yakov [3]. This method supports decision making problems in situations when any probability distributions of uncertain variables or membership functions are at disposal and represents a new way of modeling uncertainty. In Info-Gap Theory the first step in the decision process is to establish the info-gap model - an unbounded family of nested sets that share a common structure. The structure strictly dependents on the prior information and its uncertainty. Because uncertainty can be not only pernicious but propitious as well, there are two functions introduced to this method. The first one is called robustness function and it expresses the greatest level of uncertainty (parameter $\alpha$) at which failure cannot occur:

$$\hat{\alpha}(q) = \max\{\alpha : \text{min requirements are always satisfied}\}$$

$$\hat{\alpha}(q) = \max_{\alpha \geq 0}\{\alpha : \forall u \in U(\alpha, \tilde{u})\} \tag{1}$$

Here, q denotes a vector of decision variables such as parameters or operational options. $\hat{\alpha}(q)$ expresses robustness — the degree of immunity against errors or deviations from ones' assumptions — so a large value of $\hat{\alpha}(q)$ is desirable [3]. The second function is opportuneness function, which can be expressed as the lowest horizon of uncertainty that is necessary for better than anticipated outcomes to be possible:

$$\hat{\beta}(q) = \min\{\alpha : \text{sweeping success is possible}\}$$

$$\hat{\beta}(q) = \min_{\alpha \geq 0}\{\alpha : \forall u \in U(\alpha, \tilde{u})\} \tag{2}$$

A small value of $\hat{\beta}(q)$ reflects the opportune situation that great reward is possible even in the presence of little ambient uncertainty. Both these functions are complementary and are defined in an anti-symmetric sense. Thus "bigger is better" for $\hat{\alpha}(q)$ while "big is bad" for $\hat{\beta}(q)$. Info-gap theory has been applied in a range of applications from different science areas including engineering [8,9,17], biological conservation [11,12], theoretical biology, homeland security, economics [1,4], project management and statistics. In this paper, the method was used to agricultural problem, where fertilizer nitrogen requirement of sugar beetroot has to be established. In this numerical example we use robustness and opportuneness functions simultaneously and add decision maker's risk-taking propensity to get possibly suitable solution.

## 2     Numerical Problem

### 2.1     Description of the Problem

Described problem has a great impact on sugar beetroot cultivation. Sugar beetroot is an important crop of arable rotations throughout the major growing regions of many countries. Commonly grown in conjunction with wheat, barley or pulses, sugar beetroot provides a valuable break crop returning organic matter to the soil and preventing the build up of disease. The root of the beet has a sugar content of around 17% and in Poland provides over half of the sugar we use. The profit from Polish sugar beetroot cultivation starts at yield $\in$ [350; 400] [q/ha]. Using appropriate agrotechnic factors, some of the growers receive yield $\in$ [600; 700] [q/ha]. Adequate soil fertility is one of the requirements for profitable sugar beet production. Nitrogen (N) is the most yield-limiting nutrient, and N management is critical to obtain optimum sugar beet yield and quality. The most common response curve for nitrogen fertilization is presented in Fig.2.   Phosphorus (P) is the next most limiting nutrient, while levels of available potassium (K), sulfur (S), and micronutrients are adequate for sugar beet production in most soils [20]. The value of a soil test to predict nutrient availability during the growing season directly relates to how well the sample collected represents the area sampled. We should remember that these samples affect only a small area and could not exactly model the whole field.

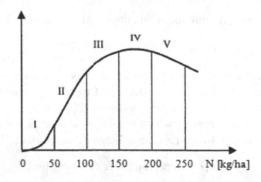

**Fig. 2.** The most common response curve for nitrogen fertilization

The curve shown in Fig.2. has several specific episodes. The first episode is a very rare situation, taking place in the case where a plant is grown on a poor quality soil. The third section is most commonly observed in the fertilizer trials. The last episode shows a decrease in yield because of excessive amount of the nutrient which causing mineral imbalance of nutrition. Looking at this curve, it is easy to be observed how a major role plays appropriate amount of nitrogen to achieve satisfied yield. The aim of the investigations described in the next section is to improve fertilizer nitrogen recommendations in such a way that high crop yields of a good quality can be obtained while detrimental effects of fertilizer nitrogen application on the environment are minimized. Yield response curves of numerous fertilizer nitrogen trials with sugar beet could be described by a modified equation. Fertilizer recommendations are usually based on results from experimental, academic field trials in which crop response to various rates of fertilizer application has been determined in course of many years. In this case, we have no information about precise coefficients of equation modeling the entire field, we know only the results from the trial. This lack of knowledge forces us to use Info-Gap Theory to solve the problem and decide what amount of the fertilizer should we apply on a given field.

## 2.2    Solution Using Info-Gap Theory

The problem concerns the relationship between the yield of sugar beetroot and the nitrogen fertilizer. The function (3) parameters were determined on the basis of many year trials on an academic experimental field. Let the yield of sugar beetroot $\tilde{p}\,(d)$ expressed in [q/ha] will be described in the following equation:

$$\tilde{p} = a_2 d^2 + a_1 d + a_0 = -0.003 d^2 + 1.3 d + 300 \tag{3}$$

This function can be called nominal yield model. The Fig.3. shows the samples obtained from trials and the curve of nominal yield $\tilde{p}\,(d)$.

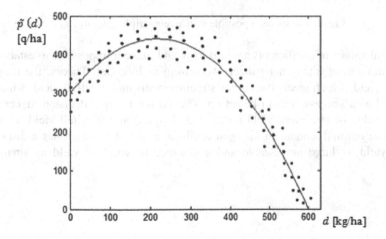

**Fig. 3.** The samples of sugar beetroot yield in relation to nitrogen fertilizer

Equation (3) gives only a rough indication of yield because there are many environmental factors that affect determination of sugar beet growing processes. Some of them are unknown and difficult to predict during the whole growing season. Among these factors temperature, precipitation, insolation and soil moisture can be mentioned. The meanings of each of quadratic function coefficients are following:

$a_0 = 300 \quad \rightarrow$ the nominal yield without fertilization process (d = 0) [q/ha];

$a_1 = 1.3 \rightarrow$ the increase of the yield due to fertilization of 1 [kg/ha] of nitrogen;

$a_2 = -0.003 \rightarrow$ reducing the impact of each kilogram of fertilizer due to saturation of the soil.

The possible changes in coefficients are presented in Fig. 4.

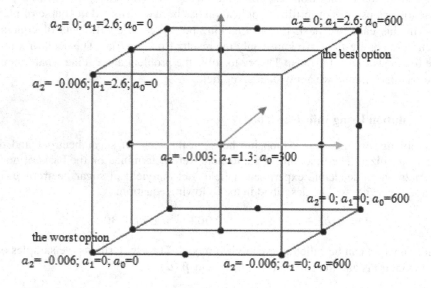

**Fig. 4.** The space of possible coefficients triples $\{a_2, a_1, a_0\}$

The real values of coefficients are info-gaps and make it impossible to establish the optimal amount of nitrogen fertilizer. According to Info-Gap Theory, the minimum (critical) yield, which meets the farmer's requirements and windfall yield, which will be treated as a success, should be set up. The farmer being a decision maker determined a value of minimum yield on $p_c = 330$ [q/ha] and windfall yield $p_w = 500$ [q/ha]. The optimal amount of nitrogen fertilizer is that one which has a distance to critical yield as large as possible and a distance to windfall yield as small as it could be.

## The Robustness Function

Let assume that environmental factors (a quality of soil, weather conditions) unfavorably affect the field, and make adverse deviations of the coefficients $a_0, a_1, a_2$ of the model (3) with the following forms:

$a_0 < 300$  (yield ratio without fertilization)

$a_1 < 1.3$ (a growth rate of the first kilogram of fertilizer)

$a_2 < -0.003$ (a rate of inhibiting the growth yield)

A variable $\alpha$ is introduced as a negative impact of nature resulting in unfavorable changes in the model. The meaning of this coefficient is illustrated in Fig. 5.

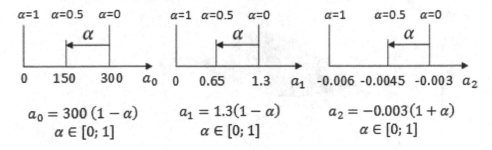

$$a_0 = 300\,(1 - \alpha) \qquad a_1 = 1.3(1 - \alpha) \qquad a_2 = -0.003(1 + \alpha)$$
$$\alpha \in [0; 1] \qquad\qquad \alpha \in [0; 1] \qquad\qquad \alpha \in [0; 1]$$

**Fig. 5.** The forms of uncertain coefficients $a_0, a_1, a_2$ using variable $\alpha$

Taking into consideration a variable $\alpha$, the equation (3) takes the following form:

$$p(d, \alpha) = 300(1 - \alpha) + 1.3(1 - \alpha)d - 0.003(1 + \alpha)d^2, \alpha \in [0; 1] \qquad (4)$$

It should be noted that the equation $p(d, \alpha)$ is in 3D space. In contrast, the equation of the nominal $\tilde{p}(d)$ exists in the lower 2D space. It means that the uncertainty of the coefficients increases the dimensionality of the model. The notation of the robustness function $\hat{\alpha}(d)$ should be introduced.

$$\hat{\alpha}(d, p_c) = \max\{\alpha: \min p\,(d, \alpha) \geq p_c\} \qquad (5)$$

Including the value of minimum yield $p_c = 330$ [q/ha] the formula (5) can be written in a form:

$$\hat{\alpha}(d, 330) = \max\{\alpha: \min\,[300(1 - \alpha) + 1.3(1 - \alpha)d - 0.003(1 + \alpha)d^2] \geq 330\} \quad (6)$$

The robustness $\hat{\alpha}(d, 330)$ informs us how strong adverse impact of variable $\alpha$ could be, despite the yield still will be higher than $p_c$. It is some kind of safety stock, the higher alpha - the greater guarantee to obtain yield above 330 [q/ha]. Depending on how differ from the nominal field will be the conditions of the field defined by $\alpha$, the model (3) can take different forms. Table 1. shows the yield model (3) for various values of $\alpha$.

**Table 1.** The function of the yield for different values of α

| Parameter $\alpha$ | Function of the yield | Max d | Max p |
|---|---|---|---|
| $\alpha = 0$ | $p(d,0) = 300 + 1.3d - 0.003d^2$ | $d_{max} = 216{,}7$ | $p_{max} = 440{,}83$ |
| $\alpha = 0.25$ | $p(d,0.25) = 225 + 0.975d - 0.00375d^2$ | $d_{max} = 130{,}0$ | $p_{max} = 288{,}37$ |
| $\alpha = 0.50$ | $p(d,0.50) = 150 + 0.650d - 0.0045d^2$ | $d_{max} = 72{,}2$ | $p_{max} = 173{,}47$ |
| $\alpha = 0.75$ | $p(d,0.75) = 75 + 0.3250d - 0.00525d^2$ | $d_{max} = 30{,}9$ | $p_{max} = 80{,}03$ |

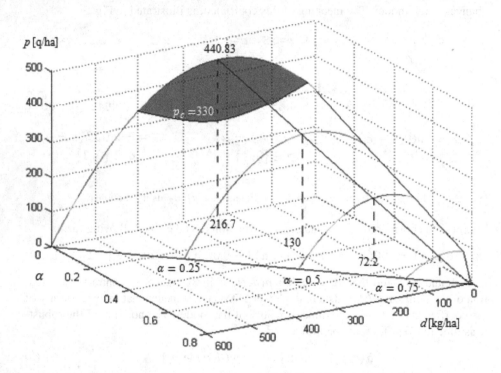

**Fig. 6.** The surface of uncertain model (3) for different values of α

In Fig. 6. the minimum yield $p_c = 330$ was marked as a border of grey zone. The values of robustness $\hat{\alpha}(d)$ corresponding to different possible values of fertilization can be calculated in the following way:

$$p_c(d, \hat{\alpha}) = 330 = 300(1 - \alpha) + 1.3(1 - \alpha)d - 0.003(1 + \alpha)d^2, \ \alpha \in [0; 1]$$

$$\hat{\alpha} = \frac{-0.003d^2 + 1.3d - 30}{0.003d^2 + 1.3d + 300} \tag{7}$$

Fig.7. shows a plot of $\hat{\alpha}(d)$ where the minimum yield $p_c = 330$ [q/ha] is ensured. It is a projection of the border of grey zone $p_c = 330$ [q/ha] visible in Fig. 6. The robustness $\hat{\alpha}$ can only assume positive values. The amount of nitrogen fertilizer d < 24.5 and d > 408.8 have a lack of robustness to error of the model $p(d)$.

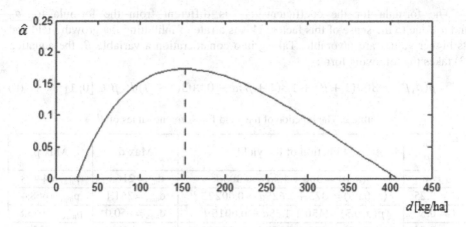

**Fig. 7.** A plot of $\hat{\alpha}(d,330)$

As shown in Fig. 7., due to a single criterion to obtain yield, which exceed the minimum established by decision maker, the optimal amount of nitrogen fertilizer is $d = 152.6$ [kg/ha]. It guarantees the maximum distance from the border of unacceptably low yield. Even when the field conditions will be differ by $\hat{\alpha} = 0{,}173$ from the nominal field, a farmer still receives yield $p_c = 330$ [q/ha].

## The Opportuneness Function

Not only adverse environmental conditions which affect the field are possible, but the beneficial as well. In this case, the deviations of the coefficients $a_0, a_1, a_2$ of the model (3) will take the following forms: $a_0 > 300$, $a_1 > 1.3$, $a_2 > -0.003$. A variable $\beta$ is called opportuneness and it is introduced as a windfall impact of nature (positive changes in the model). The meaning of this coefficient is illustrated in Fig.8.

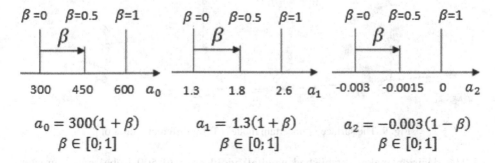

**Fig. 8.** The forms of uncertain coefficients $a_0, a_1, a_2$ using variable $\beta$

`The formula for the coefficient $a_2$ is different from the formula for $a_0$ and $a_1$, due to the sense of this factor. This is a rate of inhibiting the growth yield and its higher values are favorable. Taking into consideration a variable $\beta$, the equation (3) takes the following form:

$$p(d,\beta) = 300(1 + \beta) + 1.3(1 + \beta)d - 0.003(1 - \beta)d^2, \beta \in [0; 1] \qquad (8)$$

**Table 2.** The function of the yield for different values of $\beta$

| Parameter $\beta$ | Function of the yield | Max d | Max p |
|---|---|---|---|
| $\beta = 0$ | $p(d,0) = 300 + 1.3d - 0.003d^2$ | $d_{max} = 216{,}7$ | $p_{max} = 440{,}8$ |
| $\beta = 0.25$ | $p(d,0.25) = 375 + 1.625d - 0.00225d^2$ | $d_{max} = 361{,}1$ | $p_{max} = 668{,}4$ |
| $\beta = 0.50$ | $p(d,0.5) = 450 + 1.95d - 0.0015d^2$ | $d_{max} = 650{,}0$ | $p_{max} = 1083{,}8$ |
| $\beta = 0.75$ | $p(d,0.75) = 525 + 2.275d - 0.00075d^2$ | $d_{max} = 1516{,}7$ | $p_{max} = 2250{,}0$ |

The analysis of Table 2. shows that the positive displacement $\beta$ greater than 0.3 in Polish conditions is impossible. The maximum yield of sugar beetroot in Poland is from 500 to 700 [q/ha]. The maximum yield for $\beta = 0.3$ is above 700 [q/ha] (730 [q/ha]).

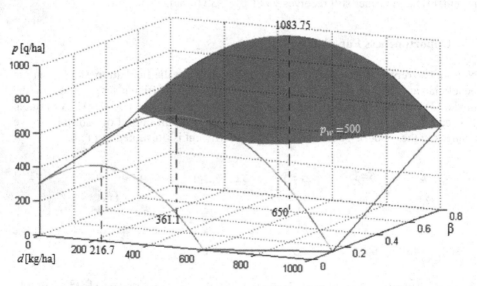

**Fig. 9.** The surface of uncertain model (3) for different values of $\beta$

The decision maker established windfall yield ($p_w$) to 500 [q/ha] and a greater achieved yield would be for him a success. The question is, how great deviation of variable $\beta$ relative to nominal model should be to get the yield higher than $p_w$. The notation of the opportuneness function $\hat{\beta}(d, p_w)$ should be determined.

$$\hat{\beta}(d, p_w) = \min \{ \beta : (\max p(d, \beta) \geq p_w\} \tag{9}$$

Including the value of windfall yield $p_w$ = 500 [q/ha] the formula (9) can be written in a form:

$$\hat{\beta}(d, p_w) = \min\{\alpha : \max [300(1 - \alpha) + 1.3(1 - \alpha)d - 0.003(1 + \alpha)d^2] \geq 500\} \tag{10}$$

The values of opportuneness $\hat{\beta}(d, p_w)$ corresponding to different possible values of fertilization can be calculated in the following way:

$$p_w(d, \hat{\beta}) = 500 = 300(1 + \beta) + 1.3(1 + \beta)d - 0.003(1 - \beta)d^2, \ \beta \in [0; 1]$$

$$\hat{\beta} = \frac{0.003d^2 - 1.3d + 200}{0.003d^2 + 1.3d + 300} \tag{11}$$

Visualization of the opportuneness $\hat{\beta}(d, 500)$ is presented in Fig. 10. It shows that the most beneficial amount of fertilizer is d = 252.8 [q/ha], which offers the easiest success border crossing $p_w$= 500 [q/ha].

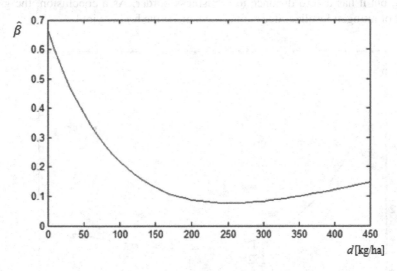

**Fig. 10.** A plot of $\hat{\beta}(d, 500)$

## 2.3    Results

The presented problem has uncertain variables and we could not apply the classical optimization methods to calculate the optimal nitrogen fertilizer requirement. The real model $p = f(d)$ can be any of 3D-surfaces shown in Fig.6. and Fig.9. Under these conditions, it is necessary to change the criterion: the criterion of maximum yield is replaced by two sub-criteria. The optimal amount of fertilizer is that value, which also ensures optimal (according to the decision maker) distance $\alpha(d)$to minimum yield 330 [q/ha] and to opportuneness border $\beta(d)$ equals 500 [q/ha]. Both functions are shown in Fig.11.To determine the optimal decision, a criterion including risk-taking propensity [5] of the decision maker should be developed. The proposed criterion has the following equation:

$K(d)$ = robustness $(1 -$ risk-taking propensity$) -$ opportuneness (risk-taking propensity)

$$K(d) = (1 - r)\hat{\alpha}(d) - r\hat{\beta}(d) \tag{12}$$

Assume that risk-taking propensity in this problem is low and it is $r = 0.2$, where $r \in [0;1]$:

$$K(d) = 0.8\hat{\alpha}(d) - 0.2\hat{\beta}(d) \tag{13}$$

It means that a farmer, who is a decision maker, prefers to have a guarantee to achieve the minimum required yield than expects higher yield. With these assumptions, we get the result. The analysis shows that the optimal amount of nitrogen fertilizer for a decision maker is d = 172 [kg/ha]. This result has almost maximum distance to the robustness border and minimum distance to the windfall border. It is interesting that a large d = 408.8 does not guarantee a short distance to the border of success, but it has a zero distance to robustness border. As a conclusion, the greater amount of nitrogen fertilizer does not always mean the higher yield.

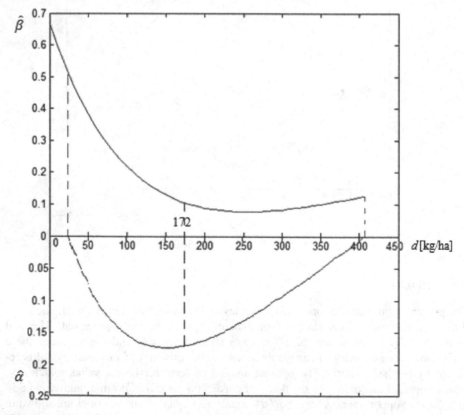

**Fig. 11.** Visualization of both functions $p = f(d, \alpha)$ and $p = f(d, \beta)$

# 3    Conclusions

Decision making under uncertainty is an inherent part of many science areas. Info-Gap Theory is a method for supporting problems in situation when no distributions are at disposal. The paper presents the general outline of this method and an example of the application. The numerical problem of fertilizer nitrogen requirement with uncertain variables is analyzed. The solved problem shows how to use robustness and opportuneness functions simultaneously and how important is decision maker's risk-taking propensity to make a final decision.

# References

1. Akram, F., Ben-Haim, Y., Řyvinde, E.: Managing uncertainty through robust satisficing monetary policy, Working Paper, Oslo (2006)
2. Bandemer, H.: Mathematics of uncertainty. Springer, New York (2005)
3. Ben-Haim, Y.: Info-Gap decision theory, 2nd edn. Elsevier (2006)
4. Ben-Haim, Y.: Info-Gap economics. Palgrave Macmillan, New York (2010)
5. Brockhaus, R.H.: Risk-taking propensity of entrepreneurs. Academy of Management Journal 23 (1980)
6. Deng, J.L.: Introduction to grey system theory, The Journal of Grey System (1989)
7. Greco, S., Matarazzo, B., Słowiński, R.: Rough sets theory for multicriteria decision analysis. European Journal of Operational Research (2001)
8. Hipel, K., Ben-Haim, Y.: Decision making in an uncertain world: Information-gap modelling in water resources management. IEEE Trans. Systems, Man and Cybernetics (1999)
9. Kanno, Y., Takewaki, I.: Robustness analysis of trusses with separable load and structural uncertainties. International Journal of Solids and Structures (2006)
10. Knight, F.: Risk, Uncertainty and Profit, Hart, Schaffner, and Marx Prize Essays, No. 31. Houghton Mifflin, Boston (1921)
11. Levy, J.K., Hipel, K., Kilgour, M.: Using environmental indicators to quantify the robustness of policy alternatives to uncertainty. Ecological Modelling (2000)
12. Moilanen, A., Wintle, B.A.: Uncertainty analysis favours selection of spatially aggregated reserve structures. Biological Conservation (2006)
13. Moore, R.E.: Interval analysis. Prentice Hall, Englewood Cliffs (1966)
14. Pawlak, Z.: Rough Sets. Int. J. of Information and Computer Science 11 (1982)
15. Pedrycz, W., Skowron, A., Kreinovich, V.: Handbook of Granular Computing. Wiley, England (2008)
16. Piegat, A.: Fuzzy modeling and control. Physica Verlag, Heidelberg (2001)
17. Piegat, A., Tomaszewska, K.: New approach to the decision analysis in conditions of uncertainty – Info-Gap Theory. Journal of Theoretical and Applied Computer Science 6(1) (2012)
18. Piegat, A., Tomaszewska, K.: Decision-Making under uncertainty using Info-Gap Theory and a new multi-dimensional RDM interval arithmetic. Electrotechnical Review 8 (2013)
19. Romaniuk, M., Nowak, P.: A fuzzy approach to option pricing in a levy process setting. Int. Journal of Applied Mathematics and Computer Science 23(3), 613–622 (2013)
20. Tinker, P.B.H.: The effects of nitrogen, potassium and sodium fertilizers on sugar beet. Journal of Agricultural Science 65 (1965)
21. Zadeh, L.A.: Fuzzy sets. Information and Control 8 (1965)
22. Zimmermann, H.: An application-oriented view of modeling uncertainty. European Journal of Operational Research (2000)

# Geometric Approach in Local Modeling: Learning of Mini-models Based on n-Dimensional Simplex

Marcin Pietrzykowski[✉] and Andrzej Piegat

Faculty of Computer Science and Information Technology,
West Pomeranian University of Technology,
Żołnierska 49, 71-210 Szczecin, Poland
{mpietrzykowski,apiegat}@wi.zut.edu.pl

**Abstract.** The paper presents the mini-models' method (MM-method) based on n-dimensional simplex. Its learning algorithm is in some respects similar to the method of k-nearest neighbors. Both methods use samples only from the local neighborhood of the query point. In the mini-model method, group of points which are used in the model-learning process is constrained by a polytope (n-simplex) area. The MM-method can on a defined local area use any approximation algorithm to determine the mini-model and to compute its answer for the query point. The article describes a learning technique for the MM-method and presents experiment results that show effectiveness of mini-models.

**Keywords:** Mini-model · Local self-learning · Function approximation · K-nearest neighbor

## 1 Introduction

The concept of mini-models method was developed by A. Piegat [1,2]. However, the learning method applied and investigated in first mini-models was rather inappropriate for higher space dimensions. In this paper a learning method will be presented which is more effective for high-dimensional problems. Because the mini-model idea is new, further on it will be shortly explained. In contrast to most well-known methods of modeling which approximate functions in the entire domain (such as neural networks, neuro-fuzzy networks, polynomial approximation end etc.), the MM-method does not create a global model when it is not necessary. A mini-model operates only on data from the local neighborhood of a query. Generally in the learning process of a MM one tries to identify a mathematical function which describes the dependency between input and output variables. However, very often we are only interested in an answer to a specific query, such as "How large will be fuel consumption in miles per gallon when a car accelerates from zero to 100 km/h in 10 seconds, number of cylinders amounts to 4 and horsepower amounts to 130 hp" and not in full model. To answer this question identification of the full function over a great input domain of the problem is not necessary.

© Springer International Publishing Switzerland 2015
L. Rutkowski et al. (Eds.): ICAISC 2015, Part II, LNAI 9120, pp. 460–470, 2015.
DOI: 10.1007/978-3-319-19369-4_41

In the general case the query point is a set of values of independent variables. Value of the dependent variable should be determined. Mini-models based on polytopes in 2D- and 3D-space were described in publications [1,2,3,4,5,6]. The aim of this paper is to present the MM-method based on $n$-dimensional simplex. The method uses geometric approach to the modeling task. The set of points which is used in the learning process of a MM is contained in a basic polytope, which creates the *mini-model area* and is defined only in the input space of the problem. In $n$-dimensional space the mini-model area has character of a $n$-$1$-dimensional convex polytope, which is a line segment in a 2D-space, polygon in 3D-space (triangle, quadrilateral, etc.), polyhedron in 4D-space (simplex, hexahedron, etc.). The MM-area could also have hyper-ellipsoidal shape [7,8].

## 2 Comparison Between Mini-Models and $k$-Nearest Neighbors Method

The $k$-nearest neighbors ($k$-NN) method [9,10,11] can be considered as the main competitor of the MM-method. Both algorithms are partly similar, both realize local modeling and use data samples only from the local neighborhood of the query point. Local approach is free from the time consuming process of determining the global model. The answer to the query point is calculated on the basis of actually possessed data points. When new data points come the previous MM can be corrected. If someone is interested in the global model then set of local MMs can be used for its determining.

The $k$-NN method is simple and uses only $k$ nearest samples. The classic version of this method uses Euclidean metric to identify nearest samples. The $k$-NN model-answer is calculated as the mean value of a target function values or as the weighted mean value. The $k$-NN method is very effective [12,13,14,15] and some of scientists are of the opinion that other methods are not necessary [16].

The $k$-NN method can be considered as a special case of a mini-model method. In the MM-method learning points can be encircled by any polygon in 3D-space, by any polyhedron in 4D-space and by any $n$-$1$-polytope in $n$-dimensional space. Mini-models can also be based on sphere. In $k$-NN method, $k$ nearest points are encircled by circle in 3D-space, by sphere in 4D-space and by $n$-$1$-sphere in $n$-dimensional space. Both methods differ in number of samples which are taken into account. In mini-models the number of samples is not constant, but usually it is contained in a specified range. In the $k$-NN method the points number $k$ is assumed *a priori*. Hence, $k$-NN method has only one "mini-model area", whilst the mini-model method exmaines many possible local neighborhoods to find the optimal one. The difference between both methods in input space (2D in the example) is presented in Fig. 1. To calculate the model answer $k$-NN method, in its classic version, uses the mean value eventually the weighted mean value. In contrast, the mini-model method for determining the MM can use any method of mathematical modeling, also the mean value as $k$-NN method does. The idea of mini-model is more wider and includes also $k$-NN method. The differences between methods in the full space (3D in the presented example) is shown in Fig. 2.

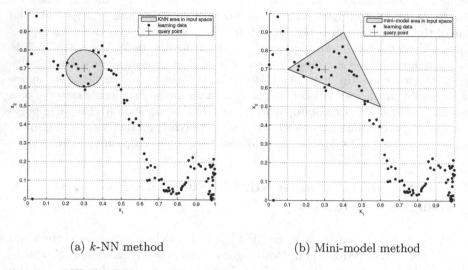

(a) $k$-NN method  (b) Mini-model method

**Fig. 1.** Comparison of $k$-NN and MM-method in input space

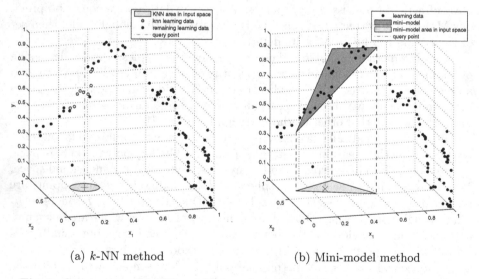

(a) $k$-NN method  (b) Mini-model method

**Fig. 2.** Comparison of $k$-NN and MM-method in the full space (inputs/output)

## 3    Mini-Model Method: Algorithms

The method consists of two groups of algorithms: algorithms for defining the local neighborhood of the query point (learning part of the algorithm) and algorithms for mathematical modeling of the mini-model area (learning and operating parts of the algorithm).

## 3.1   Algorithms for Defining Local Neighborhood of The Query Point

If one wants to manipulate the geometric figure the first idea could be moving the figure vertices. However, this approach in the space grater 3D-one is difficult, because manipulation of a single point requires also manipulation of other points belonging to the same face in order to maintain vertices co-planarity. Another problem is the task of including or excluding data points within or from the MM area. In this article authors present an approach of face manipulation instead of vertices manipulation [6].

The first part of the algorithm is the data points' conversion from Cartesian coordinate system into spherical coordinate system [17,18,19]. The transformation occurs only in the input space. The output variable remains untouched. It will be used in the process of the mathematical model output-calculation. It means that 3-dimensional data points are converted into polar coordinate system, 4D data points into spherical coordinate system, and in the general case, $n+1$-dimensional data point are converted into coordinate system based on $n$-sphere. The query point $Q = x_{Q1}, x_{Q2}, \ldots, x_{Qn}, y_Q$ is assumed to be the coordinate system center. Values of input variables $x_{Q1}, x_{Q2}, \ldots, x_{Qn}$ are known, but the value of output variable $y_Q$ is to be calculated. All data points $p_i$ are transformed into spherical coordinate system where they are defined by radius $r \in [0, \infty)$ (distance from the center) and angles $\varphi_{i1}, \varphi_{i2}, \ldots, \varphi_{i(n-2)} \in [0; \pi), \varphi_{i(n-1)} \in [0; 2\pi)$. The set of points $P$ can be denoted as:

$$\begin{aligned} P &= \{p_1, p_2, \ldots, p_i, \ldots, p_I\} \\ p_i &= (x_{i1}, \ldots, x_{in}, y_i) = (r_i, \varphi_{i1}, \ldots, \varphi_{i(n-1)}, y_i). \end{aligned} \tag{1}$$

The conversion method between 2D (3D) Cartesian coordinate system and polar (spherical) coordinate system is quite obvious and can be found in any mathematical handbook. In higher dimensional spaces, conversion equations are more complicated. They are defined as follows:

$$\begin{aligned} x_1 &= r\cos(\varphi_1) \\ x_2 &= r\sin(\varphi_1)\cos(\varphi_2) \\ x_3 &= r\sin(\varphi_1)\sin(\varphi_2)\cos(\varphi_3) \\ &\ \vdots \\ x_{n-1} &= r\sin(\varphi_1)\cdots\sin(\varphi_{n-2})\cos(\varphi_{n-1}) \\ x_n &= r\sin(\varphi_1)\cdots\sin(\varphi_{n-2})\sin(\varphi_{n-1}). \end{aligned} \tag{2}$$

The inverse transformation is unique, except special cases described below:

$$r = \sqrt{x_1^2 + x_2^2 + \cdots + x_n^2}$$

$$\varphi_1 = \operatorname{arccot} \frac{x_1}{\sqrt{x_2^2 + x_3^2 + \cdots + x_n^2}}$$

$$\varphi_2 = \operatorname{arccot} \frac{x_2}{\sqrt{x_3^2 + x_4^2 + \cdots + x_n^2}}$$

$$\vdots$$ (3)

$$\varphi_{n-2} = \operatorname{arccot} \frac{x_{n-2}}{\sqrt{x_{n-1}^2 + x_n^2}}$$

$$\varphi_{n-1} = 2\operatorname{arccot} \frac{x_{n-1} + \sqrt{x_{n-1}^2 + x_n^2}}{x_n}$$

if $x_k > 0$ for some $k$ but all of $x_{k+1}, \ldots, x_n$ are equal to zero, then $\varphi_k = 0$, if $x_k < 0$ then $\varphi_k = \pi$. When $x_k, \ldots, x_n$ are equal to zero, then transformation is not unique. In this case $\varphi_k$ may be chosen to be zero.

The mini-model area, in the general case is a polytope and contains $J$ faces (for simplex $J = n + 1$, for cube $J = 2n$, for octahedron $J = 2^n$, where $n$ is dimensionality of the space). A particular polyhedron face $j$ is a part of a plane $F_j$. In further considerations the whole plane $F_j$ will be called *face*. The face is defined by point $G_j$, which will be called *face generation point*. It was assumed that the plane is orthogonal to the vector $\overrightarrow{QG_j}$. Each face is defined as:

$$F_j = \left\{ G_j, p_i : \varphi_{ij} < \frac{\pi}{2} \wedge r_i = \frac{r_j}{\cos \varphi_{ij}} \right\}$$ (4)

where $\varphi_{ij}$ is the angle value between vectors $\overrightarrow{QG_j}$, $\overrightarrow{Qp_i}$. The angle value can be computed using the dot product, which for Cartesian coordinates is given by (5).

$$\varphi_{ij} = \arccos \frac{x_{i1}x_{j1} + \cdots + x_{in}x_{jn}}{\sqrt{x_{i1}^2 + \cdots + x_{in}^2}\sqrt{x_{j1}^2 + \cdots + x_{jn}^2}}$$ (5)

After substitution from (3) and after simplifications formula (6) was obtained.

$$\varphi_{ij} = \arccos( \cos \varphi_{i1} \cos \varphi_{j1} + \sin \varphi_{i1} \sin \varphi_{j1}($$
$$\cos \varphi_{i2} \cos \varphi_{j2} + \sin \varphi_{i2} \sin \varphi_{j2}($$
$$\cdots$$ (6)
$$\cos \varphi_{i(n-2)} \cos \varphi_{j(n-2)} + \sin \varphi_{i(n-2)} \sin \varphi_{j(n-2)}($$
$$\cos(\varphi_{i(n-1)} - \varphi_{j(n-1)}))\cdots))).$$

The face in fact divides all the space into two half-spaces. The first half-space consists of data points which may be included into the area of a mini-model.

The set of points which may be included in face $F_j$ is defined by (7).

$$I_j = \left\{ p_i : \varphi_{ij} \geq \frac{\pi}{2} \cup \left( \varphi_{ij} < \frac{\pi}{2} \wedge r_i \leq \frac{r_j}{\cos \varphi_{ij}} \right) \right\}. \tag{7}$$

The second half-space consists of data points which are certainly excluded from the figure area. This set of points $E_j$ is defined by (8).

$$E_j = \left\{ p_i : \varphi_{ij} < \frac{\pi}{2} \wedge r_i > \frac{r_j}{\cos \varphi_{ij}} \right\}. \tag{8}$$

Every face divides the space in the way described above. Intersections of half-spaces (which include data points) of all faces contain points which are included into the polyhedron area. Set of points $Z$ included in the polyhedron is given by (9).

$$Z = I_1 \cap I_2 \cap \ldots I_J. \tag{9}$$

The way how a face divides 3D space into two half-spaces is presented in Fig. 3. Data points marked by triangles are certainly excluded from the mini-model area whilst points marked by squares are possibly included into the area. Whether the point will be included in the mini-model area or not also depends on its position in relation to other faces. Only points included by all faces will be included in the mini-model area. For the mini-model area defined in this way any method of mathematical modeling can be used. In the process of the mini-model learning the model-area rotation is of great importance. It can be realized by multiplying coordinates of faces "generation points" by appropriate rotation matrix. In Euclidean space there exist a single base rotation matrix given by (10).

$$R = \begin{pmatrix} \cos \phi & -\sin \phi \\ \sin \phi & \cos \phi \end{pmatrix} \tag{10}$$

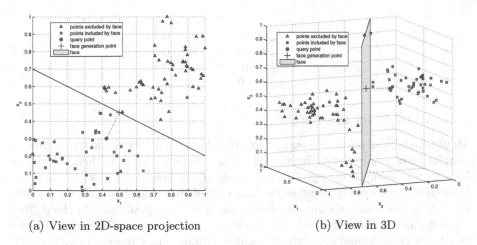

(a) View in 2D-space projection                    (b) View in 3D

**Fig. 3.** Example of space partition by a face

where $\phi$ is rotation angle. In 3D space three three rotation matrix given by (11) are used.

$$R_{x_1} = \begin{pmatrix} 1 & 0 & 0 \\ 0 & \cos\phi & -\sin\phi \\ 0 & \sin\phi & \cos\phi \end{pmatrix}$$

$$R_{x_2} = \begin{pmatrix} \cos\phi & 0 & -\sin\phi \\ 0 & 1 & 0 \\ \sin\phi & 0 & \cos\phi \end{pmatrix} \tag{11}$$

$$R_{x_3} = \begin{pmatrix} \cos\phi & -\sin\phi & 0 \\ \sin\phi & \cos\phi & 0 \\ 0 & 0 & 1 \end{pmatrix}.$$

Realization of rotation in higher dimensions [20] is difficult to imagine. The first idea is to use the rotation around an axis. Such rotation is an idea which comes from modeling experiences in 3D-space. Rotations in 3D-space should be thought of as rotations not around an axis, but rather as rotations parallel to a 2D plane. We can mathematically formulate them as $R_{x_1} = R_{x_2 x_3} = \ldots, R_{x_2} = R_{x_1 x_3} = \ldots, R_{x_3} = R_{x_1 x_2} = \ldots$. This way of rotation understanding is consistent with 2D-space where only one plane exists. In 4D-space there are 6, in 5D-space there are 10 rotation matrices, and in $n$-dimensional space the number of matrices is equal to $\binom{n}{2}$. If we rotate point around the $(x_2, x_4)$ plane in 4D space the rotation matrix is given by (12).

$$R_{x_2 x_4} = \begin{pmatrix} 1 & 0 & 0 & 0 \\ 0 & \cos\phi & 0 & -\sin\phi \\ 0 & 0 & 1 & 0 \\ 0 & \sin\phi & 0 & \cos\phi \end{pmatrix} \tag{12}$$

For 5D-space the rotation matrix is given by (13).

$$R_{x_2 x_4} = \begin{pmatrix} 1 & 0 & 0 & 0 & 0 \\ 0 & \cos\phi & 0 & -\sin\phi & 0 \\ 0 & 0 & 1 & 0 & 0 \\ 0 & \sin\phi & 0 & \cos\phi & 0 \\ 0 & 0 & 0 & 0 & 1 \end{pmatrix} \tag{13}$$

### 3.2   Mini-Model Learning

Manipulating the polytope size and location by faces makes the learning process simpler than manipulating by vertices. The learning process is then reduced to location changing of face generation points $(G_j)$. The manipulation procedure is heuristic and usually involves random way of changing the location of points $G_j$. There are numerous mini-models' areas which are available. On the defined mini-model area, any method of mathematical modeling can be use e.g.: linear regression, polynomial approximation, mean value, fuzzy reasoning, neural network, etc. After defining the local neighborhood, a mini-model uses data points which are inside of the mini-model area. These points are used to calculate the error of the model on learning data. Then the mini-model calculates numeric answer for the query point. In the next step the MM-algorithm tries to find another mini-model area, calculates new error, the mini-model answer etc. The model which makes the smallest error is chosen as the optimal one. Not every mini-model area is valid. The area has to satisfy following initial MM-properties:

- minimal number of points inside the mini-model area,
- maximal number of points inside the mini-model area,
- ratio between the minimal and the maximal lengths of vectors $\overrightarrow{QG_j}$,
- query point should not be extrapolated by learning points (it is not always possible and sometimes is not required or necessary).

There is no simple rule how to choose initial values of the properties. The minimal and the maximal number of points inside the mini-model area depends on learning data. The lower boundary has to be greater than dimensionality of the problem space. Sometimes for certain query point, there exist no valid mini-model area which fulfills initial constraints. In such situation the mini-model is unable to return a reliable numeric answer.

In the experiments authors used many times the learning procedure which included the whole figure rotation and changing radiuses of faces generation points. Rotation angle, rotation direction and radius-delta were taken at random. The ratio between the minimal and the maximal radii values has to be greater than 0.5 in order to prevent the figure over-stretching. A single face cannot change their angles coordinates, thus the angles between faces are constant. Results of preliminary numerical experiments have shown that mini-models very often were over-fitted when faces of polytopes were changed in the completely random way.

## 4    Result of Experiments

The MM-method was compared with $k$-NN method. Both methods work on points from local neighborhood. They can be compared with use of leave-one-out cross validation method. $K$-NN method performs very well if it is optimally tuned. Additionally, both methods were compared with a General Regression Neural Network (GRNN) [21,22,23,24] which is a global modeling. The method was tested with use of the 10-fold cross validation. The experiments were conducted on six datasets from UCI Machine Learning [25]:

- Boston Housing - ($x_3$ - proportion of non-retail business acres per town, $x_5$ - nitric oxides concentration (parts per 10 million), $x_6$ - average number of rooms per dwelling, $x_7$ - proportion of owner-occupied units built prior to 1940, $x_{10}$ - full-value property-tax rate per \$ 10,000, $x_{11}$ - pupil-teacher ratio by town, $x_{13}$ - % lower status of the population) (506 instances),
- Concrete Compressive Strength - (all available input attributes) (1029 instances),

- Auto MPG - (all available input attribute except: $x_8$ - origin, $x_9$ - car name) (391 instances),
- Concrete Slump Test - (all available input attribute, output attribute: 28-day Compressive Strength) (102 instances),
- Yacht Hydrodynamics - (all available input attribute) (307 instances),
- Servo - (all available input attributes) (166 instances)

Results of experiments is presented in Table 1. Experiments were performed with the optimal values of all parameters for all tested methods. Mini-models were based on $n$-simplexes, and used the linear regression to calculate the model answer. The dimension of the polytope was appropriate to the dimension of input space. The method discarded the result for particular query point if it was unable to find a valid mini-model area. Results of experiments have shown that in this situation usually the mean square error was very high.

**Table 1.** Comparison of effectiveness of tested methods

| dataset | $k$-NN error | $k$ | MM-method error | samples | GRNN error | spread |
|---------|------|-----|------|---------|------|--------|
| Housing | 0.0567 | 4 | 0.0551 | 25 - 40 | 0.0545 | 0.1 |
| Concrete | 0.0722 | 1 | 0.0483 | 20 - 40 | 0.0699 | 0.03 |
| Auto MPG | 0.0531 | 3 | 0.0529 | 20 - 60 | 0.0502 | 0.08 |
| Slump Test | 0.0600 | 2 | 0.0500 | 8 - 20 | 0.0621 | 0.1 |
| Yacht | 0.0371 | 2 | 0.0167 | 12 - 25 | 0.0385 | 0.07 |
| Servo | 0.0437 | 3 | 0.0493 | 10 - 25 | 0.0381 | 0.05 |

# 5    Conclusion

Results of experiments proved that accuracy of mini-models is good. The proposed version of mini-models is able to model multidimensional problems. The presented variant is rather simple. It is based on simplexes and uses the linear regression for computing numeric answers. In multidimensional space, volume of the $n$-simplex is smaller than e.g. volume of $n$-cube and the model area is more constrained than in case of figures with higher number of faces. Mini-models also have very advantageous extrapolation properties. It results from the fact, that they take into account the tendency existing in the neighborhood of the query point. The $k$-NN method does it not. Using information about this tendency allows for better modeling in places with information gaps. Another advantage of mini-models is the ability of detection of situations in which the mini-model cannot satisfy its initial criteria and thus it is unable to return a reliable numeric answer. Certain weakness of mini-models in comparison with the $k$-NN method is the necessity of using greater number of points for learning process. It is caused by greater number of model parameters that have to be tuned according to the principle "no free lunch". The MM-method is of partially heuristic nature and its accuracy sometimes may slightly vary. In the article only one variant of the method was tested. In the next research authors plan to check more complex variants of this method.

# References

1. Piegat, A., Wasikowska, B., Korzeń, M.: Application of the self-learning, 3-point mini-model for modelling of unemployment rate in. Studia Informatica, vol. 27, pp. 59–69. University of Szczecin (2010) (in Polish)
2. Piegat, A., Wasikowska, B., Korzeń, M.: Differences between the method of mini-models and the k-nearest neighbors an example of modeling unemployment rate in Poland. In: Information Systems in Management IX-Business Intelligence and Knowledge Management, pp. 34–43. WULS Press, Warsaw (2011)
3. Pietrzykowski, M.: Comparison of effectiveness of linear mini-models with some methods of modelling. Młodzi Naukowcy dla Polskiej Nauki. CREATIVETIME, Kraków, pp. 113–123 (2011)
4. Pietrzykowski, M.: The use of linear and nonlinear mini-models in process of data modeling in a 2D-space. Nowe trendy w Naukach Inzynieryjnych. CREATIVE-TIME, Kraków, pp. 100–108 (2011)
5. Pietrzykowski, M.: Effectiveness of mini-models method when data modelling within a 2D-space in an information deficiency situation. Journal of Theoretical and Applied Computer Science 6(3), 21–27 (2012)
6. Pietrzykowski, M.: Mini-models working in 3D space based on polar coordinate system. Nowe trendy w Naukach Inzynieryjnych 4. Tom II, CREATIVETIME, Kraków, pp. 117–125 (2013)
7. Pluciński, M.: Mini-models - Local Regression Models for the Function Approximation Learning. In: Rutkowski, L., Korytkowski, M., Scherer, R., Tadeusiewicz, R., Zadeh, L.A., Zurada, J.M. (eds.) ICAISC 2012, Part II. LNCS, vol. 7268, pp. 160–167. Springer, Heidelberg (2012)
8. Pluciński, M.: Nonlinear ellipsoidal mini-models - application for the function approximation task. Przeglad Elektrotechniczny (Electrical Review), R. 88 NR 10b, 247–251 (2012)
9. Fix, E., Hodges, J.L.: Discriminatory analysis, nonparametric discrimination: Consistency properties, pp. 1–21. Randolph Field, Texas (1951)
10. Fukunaga, K., Narendra, P.: Branch and bound algorithm for computing k-nearest neighbors. IEEE Transactions on Computers 24(7), 750–753 (1975)
11. Beis, J., Low, D.: Shape indexing using approximate nearest-neighbour search in high-dimensional space. In: Proceedings of the IEEE Computer Society Conference on Computer Vision and Pattern Recognition, pp. 1000–1006 (1997)
12. Yakowitz, S.: Nearest-neighbour methods for time series analysis. Journal of Time Series Analysis 8(2), 235–247 (1987)
13. Bottou, L., Vapnik, V.: Local Learning Algorithms. Neural Computation 4(6), 888–900 (1992)
14. Ma, L., Crawford, M., Tian, J.: Local manifold learning-based k-nearest-neighbor for hyperspectral image classification. IEEE Transaction on Geoscience and Remote Sensing 48(11), 4096–4109 (2010)
15. Lee, S., Kang, P., Cho, S.: Probabilistic local reconstruction for k-NN regression and its application to virtual metrology in semiconductor manufacturing. Neurocomputing 131, 427–439 (2014)

16. Kordos, M., Blachnik, M., Strzempa, D.: Do We Need Whatever More than k-NN? In: Proceedings of 10th International Conference on Artificial Intelligence and Soft Computing, Zakopane (2010)
17. Bronshtein, I., Semendyayev, K., Musiol, G., Muhlig, H.: Handbook of Mathematics. Springer (2007) ISBN 9783540721215
18. Polyanin, A., Manzhirov, A.: Handbook of Mathematics for Engineers and Scientists. Taylor & Francis (2010) ISBN 9781584885023
19. Moon, P., Spencer, D.: Field theory handbook: including coordinate systems, differential equations, and their solutions. Springer (1988) ISBN 9780387027326
20. Hollash, S.: R.: Four Space Visualization of 4D Objects. Arizona State Univeristy (1991)
21. Specht, D.: A General Regression Neural Network. IEEE Transactions on Neural Networks 2(6), 568–576 (1991)
22. Celikoglu, H.: Application of radial basis function and generalized regression neural networks in non-linear utility function specification for travel mode choice modelling. Mathematical and Computer Modelling 44(7-8), 640–658 (2006)
23. Kisi, O.: River flow forecasting and estimation using different artificial neural network techniques. Hydrology Research 39(1), 27–40 (2008)
24. Jeyamkondan, S., Jayas, D., Holley, R.: Microbial growth modelling with artificial neural networks. International Journal of Food Microbiology 64(3), 343–354 (2001)
25. UCI Machine Learning Repository, http://archive.ics.uci.edu/ml/

# Immune Optimal Design of 2-D and 3-D Structures

Arkadiusz Poteralski[1]([✉]), Mirosław Szczepanik[1], and Tadeusz Burczyński[2]

[1] Faculty of Mechanical Engineering,
Institute of Computational and Mechanical Engineering,
Silesian University of Technology, ul. Konarskiego 18a, 44-100 Gliwice, Poland
arkadiusz.poteralski@polsl.pl
[2] Institute of Fundamental Technological Research, Polish Academy of Sciences,
Warsaw, Poland
tburczynski@ippt.pan.pl

**Abstract.** The paper deals with an application of the artificial immune system (AIS) to the optimization of shape, topology and material properties of 2-D and 3-D structures. Structures considered in this work are analyzed by the finite element method (FEM). Optimization criteria that are taken into account concern minimize mass of the structure. Numerical examples demonstrate that the method based on soft computing is a very effective technique for solving computer aided optimal design.

**Keywords:** Artificial immune system (AIS) · Optimization · Finite element method (FEM) · Computational intelligence · Shape and topology optimization

## 1 Introduction

Optimal properties of spatial structures can be provided by using the computer aided optimization techniques. For example, an appropriate strength of structures can be established by changing their shape, topology and material properties. The choice of optimal shape and topology are the key elements defining the effectiveness of structures, and thus finding them is the problem of great practical interest. Shape and topology structural optimization is a very active research area. Several competing approaches for topology optimization exist [3][8][25]. More recently, intelligent optimal design techniques based on bio-inspired methods [21] like the evolutionary algorithm (EA) [11], the particle swarm optimizer (PSO) [9][10][20] and artificial immune system (AIS) [7][16][19] have found applications to structural optimization problems. The evolutionary methods are based on the theory of evolution. The main feature of those methods is to simulate biological processes based on heredity principles (genetics) and the natural selection (the theory of evolution) to create optimal individuals (solutions) presented by single chromosomes. The swarm algorithms are based on the models of the social behavior of animals: moving and living in groups. PSO algorithm

© Springer International Publishing Switzerland 2015
L. Rutkowski et al. (Eds.): ICAISC 2015, Part II, LNAI 9120, pp. 471–482, 2015.
DOI: 10.1007/978-3-319-19369-4_42

realizes directed motion of the particles in n-dimensional space to search for solution for n-variable optimization problem [22][23]. The information about artificial immune system [17] is described in the chapter 2. The main advantage of the mentioned bio-inspired methods is the fact that these approaches do not need any information about the gradient of the fitness function and give a strong probability of finding the global optimum. The main drawback of these approaches is the long calculation times. In the present paper the bio-inspired method (AIS) is applied to optimize shape, topology and material properties of 2-D and 3-D structures [4][5][18] modeled by the FEM [27]. The proposed approach can be considered as the kind of the level set-based structural optimization method where the idea is to parameterize the level set surface by a set of control points defining a B-cell receptor. The considered structures are optimized using the mass dependent optimization criterion. Numerical examples demonstrate that the method based on the soft computing is an effective technique for solving computer aided optimal design problems. The effectiveness of this method has been tested and compared with evolutionary algorithm and particle swarm optimizer for many mechanical systems for example: topology optimization of 2D and 3D structures [4][5], identification of room acoustic properties [22], identification of material constants in piezoelectrics [16], in optimization of composite structures [18] and in optimization of thermomechanical structures [21].

## 2    Artificial Immune Systems

The artificial immune systems (AIS) are developed on the basis of a mechanism discovered in biological immune systems [2][15][19]. An immune system is a complex system which contains distributed groups of specialized cells and organs. The main purpose of the immune system is to recognize and destroy pathogens - funguses, viruses, bacteria and improper functioning cells. The lymphocytes cells play a very important role in the immune system. The lymphocytes are divided into several groups of cells. There are two main groups B and T cells, both contains some subgroups (like B-T dependent or B-T independent). The AIS [7][24] take only a few elements from the biological immune systems. The most frequently used are the mutation of the B cells, proliferation, memory cells, and recognition by using the B and T cells. The AIS have been used to optimization problems in classification and also computer viruses recognition. The cloning algorithm presented by de Castro [7] uses some mechanisms similar to biological immune systems to global optimization problems. The unknown global optimum is the searched pathogen. The memory cells contain design variables and proliferate during the optimization process. The B cells created from memory cells undergo mutation. The B cells evaluate and better ones exchange memory cells. In Wierzchoń [24] version of Clonalg the crowding mechanism is used - the diverse between memory cells is forced. A new memory cell is randomly created and substitutes the old one, if two memory cells have similar design variables.

The crowding mechanism allows finding not only the global optimum but also other local ones. The presented approach is based on the Wierzchoń algorithm [24], but the mutation operator is changed. The Gaussian mutation is

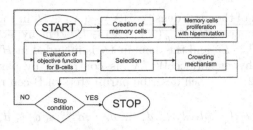

**Fig. 1.** An artificial immune system

used instead of the nonuniform mutation in the presented approach [17]. The Fig. 1 presents the flowchart of an artificial immune system. The memory cells are created randomly. They proliferate and mutate creating B cells. The number of clones created by each memory cell is determined by the memory cells objective function value. The objective functions for B cells are evaluated. The selection process exchanges some memory cells for better B cells. The selection is performed on the basis of the geometrical distance between each memory cell and B cells (measured by using design variables). The crowding mechanism removes similar memory cells. The similarity is also determined as the geometrical distance between memory cells. The process is iteratively repeated until the stop condition is fulfilled (maximum number of iterations). The unknown global optimum is represented by the searched pathogen. The memory cells contain design variables and proliferate during the optimization process.

## 3   Optimization Method

Consider a structure which, at the beginning of an optimization process, occupies a domain $\Omega_0$ $(in\ E^d, d = 2\ or\ 3)$, bounded by a boundary $\Gamma_0$. The domain $\Omega_0$ is filled by elastic homogeneous and isotropic material of a Youngs modulus $E_0$, mass density $\rho_0$ and a Poissons ratio $\nu$. The structures are considered in the framework of the linear theory of elasticity. During the optimization process the domain $\Omega_t$, its boundary $\Gamma_t$ and the field of mass densities $\rho(X) = \rho_t$, $(X) \in \Omega_t$ (or thickness $g(X) = g_t$, $(X) \in \Omega_t$ can change for each iteration $t$ (for t=0, $\rho_0$=const). The optimization process proceeds in the environment in which the structure fitness is described as minimization of the mass of the structure

$$J = \int_{\Omega} \rho d\Omega \tag{1}$$

with constraints imposed on equivalent stresses $\sigma_{eq}$ and displacements $u$ of the structure

$$\sigma_{eq}(x, y, z) \leqslant \sigma^{ad}, \ (x, y, z) \in \Omega \tag{2}$$

$$|u(x, y, z)| \leqslant u^{ad}, \ (x, y, z) \in \Omega \tag{3}$$

The distribution of the mass density $\rho(X)$, $(X) \in \Omega_t$ in the spatial structure is described by a hyper surface $W_\rho(X)$, $(X) \in H^3$. The hyper surface $W_\rho(X)$ is stretched under $H^3 \subset E^3$ and the domain $\Omega_t$ is included in $H^3$, i.e. $(\Omega_t \subseteq H^3)$. The shape of the hyper surface $W_\rho(X)$ is controlled by parameters of B-cell receptor $d_j, j = 1, 2, , G$, which describe parameters of B-cell receptor

$$B - cell = \langle d_1, d_2, ..., d_j, ..., d_G \rangle, d_j^{\min} \leqslant d_j \leqslant d_j^{\max} \tag{4}$$

where: $d_j^{\min}$, $d_j^{\max}$ - are minimum and maximum values of the parameters of B-cell receptor. The parameters of B-cell receptor are the values of the function $W_\rho(X)$ in the control points $(X)_j$ of the hyper surface, i.e. $d_j = W_\rho \left[ (X)_j \right], j = 0, 1, 2, ..., G$. The finite element method [26] is applied in analysis of the structure. The domain $\Omega$ of the structure is discretized using the finite elements, $\Omega = \bigcup_{e=1}^{E} \Omega_e$. The assignation of the mass density to each finite element $\Omega_e$, $e = 1, 2, ..., E$ is adequately performed by the mappings $\rho_e = W_\rho[(X)_e]$, $(X)_e \in \Omega_e$, $e = 1, 2, ..., E$. It means that each finite element can have the different mass density. When the value of the mass density for the e-th finite element is included in the interval $0 \leqslant \rho_e < \rho_{\min}$, the finite element is eliminated and the void is created and when in the interval $\rho_{\min} \leqslant \rho_e < \rho_{\max}$, the finite element remains. The illustration of the idea of immune optimization for a 2-D structure is presented in the Fig. 2. In the next step the Youngs modulus for the e-th finite element is evaluated using the following equation

$$E_e = E_{\max} \left( \frac{\rho_e}{\rho_{\max}} \right)^r \tag{5}$$

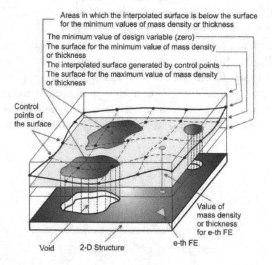

**Fig. 2.** The illustration of the idea of topology optimization for a 2-D structure

where: $E_{max}$, $\rho_{max}$ - Youngs modulus and mass density for the same material, respectively, r parameter which can change from 1 to 9. The dependence between the Youngs modulus and the mass density in topology optimization was proposed for the first time by Bendsoe [3]. The proposed approach can be considered as the kind of the level set-based structural optimization method. The idea is to parameterize the level set surface by a set of control points defining a B-cell receptor. In this method, the level set function represents a boundary between the material and void domains. The boundary is expressed by means of the level set function $\varphi(X)$

$$\begin{cases} \varphi(X) > \rho_{min}, \forall X \in \Omega \backslash \Gamma \\ \varphi(X) = \rho_{min}, \forall X \in \Gamma \\ \varphi(X) < \rho_{min}, \forall X \in H^d \backslash \Omega \end{cases} \tag{6}$$

In the level set-based methods, the changes of boundaries are defined by solving the Hamilton-Jacobi partial differential equation [14]. Allarie et al [1] discussed that, the optimal solutions obtained in this way are strongly dependent on the initial configurations. To overcome this problem Yamada et al [26] proposed the level set model incorporating a fictitious interface energy derived from the phase field concept. Our idea, to overcome this problem, is based on the application of the bio-inspired algorithm, which works on the population of memory cells (potential solutions). Then changes of the boundaries are realized by an intelligent evolution of the individuals during the immune process (without necessity to solve the Hamilton-Jacobi partial differential equation). In order to improve optimization results two different additional procedures (explained in the next subsections) have been introduced [6]: the additional procedure aiding the topology optimization and the smoothing procedure. Using the described method, one can change material properties of finite elements during the immune optimization process and some elements are eliminated. As a result, the optimal shape, topology and material of structure are obtained. Parameterization is the key stage in structural optimization. The great number of design variables causes that the optimization process is not effective. A connection between design variables (parameters of B-cell receptor) and the number of finite elements leads to poor results. The better results can be obtained when the surface (or hyper surface) of the mass density (or thickness) distribution is interpolated by suitable number of values given in control points $(X)_j$. This number, on the one hand, should provide the good interpolation, and on the other hand, the number of design variables should be small.

The interpolation procedure works in an iterative way:

$$I^{k+1} = f(I^k), \quad k = 0, 1, 2, ..., K \tag{7}$$

where the approximations of the interpolation vector in the following steps $k$ are given by the expression

$$I^k = [p_1^k, p_2^k, ..., p_i^k, ..., p_N^k], \quad i = 1, 2, ..., N, \quad k = 0, 1, 2, ..., K \tag{8}$$

and the interpolation parameters $p_i^k$ are the values of the function $W_\rho^k$ in the interpolation nodes $(X)_i$ (nodes of the finite element mesh):

$$p_i^k = W_\rho^k\,[(X)_i]\,,\ \mathrm{i} = 1,2,...,\mathrm{N},\ k = 0,1,2,...,K \qquad (9)$$

The number and the arrangement of the control points of the interpolation function $W_\rho^k$ are the input data to the optimization program. The control points are located in selected nodes of the finite element mesh and the inequality $G \leqslant N$ is satisfied. The number of the control points is equal to the number of design variables. The number and the locations of the control points are arbitrary declared by the user of the optimization program, who simultaneously introduces value 1 in the additional vector $T_i, i = 1,2,...,N$ in the position which corresponds with the number of the chosen node. In order to distinguish the nodes which play the role of control points, the additional vector $T_i, i = 1,2,...,N$ is introduced. If $T_i = 1$ then $p_i^k = d_j$, j = 1,2,...,G - node plays the role of the control point. In the other way $T_i = 0$ and interpolation parameters are calculated by equation

$$p_i^{k+1} = \frac{1}{2}[\max(p_l^k) + \min(p_l^k)],\ l = 1,2,...,M \qquad (10)$$

where:

$M$ - the number of neighbors, $S_l,\ l = 1,2,...,M$ for i-th node $R_i,\ i = 1,2,...,N$,

$p_i^{k+1}$ - the value of the interpolation parameter for i-th node, in step k+1,

$p_l^k$ - the value of the interpolation parameter for l-th node which is a neighbor for node i-th, in step k-th,

$\max(p_l^k)$ - the maximal value of the interpolation parameter for nodes which are neighbors for node i-th, in step k-th,

$\min(p_l^k)$ - the minimal value of the interpolation parameter for nodes which are neighbors for node i-th, in step k-th.

The step of the iteration procedure depends on the density of finite element mesh and of the number and arrangement of the control points. The value of optimization parameter for each finite element is computed on the base of the values in its nodes. The interpolation procedure is presented in Table 1. The immune algorithm works on the population of the B-cell receptors. The operations described above are performed for a single B-cell receptor from the immune population and lead to the evaluation of the fitness function value (Fig. 3).

In order to calculate the fitness function value for a single B-cell receptor, the boundary value problem for a structure has to be solved. To solve the boundary value problem the professional FEM program MSC Nastran is applied. Coupling of the immune optimization program and the finite element method is based on data transfer between both programs. First, the file containing input data to the optimization program (the mesh, the thickness of 2-D structure, boundary conditions, material data ) is built. This file has a special structure, which can be read by MSC Nastran and is the basis on which the boundary value problem is solved. After the computations the MSC Nastran returns the result file from which the result data, necessary for the calculation of the fitness function value (stresses, strains, displacements) are taken.

**Table 1.** Interpolation procedure in the optimization of spatial structures

Load nodes i=1,2,...,N and elements e=1,2,,E
For i=1,2,...,N, load the initial vector of interpolation parameters
For k=0,1,2,...,K, $k$ is a step of iteration
(
For i=1,2,...,N, for all the nodes
(
If $T_i$=0, i-th node does not contain a control point
(
For l=1,2,...,M, for all neighboring nodes of i-th node
Calculate $\max(p_l^k)$ and $\min(p_l^k)$
Calculate pik+1=1/2[$\max(p_l^k)$+ $\min(p_l^k)$]
)
If $T_i$=1 $(p_i^{k+1})$= $dj$, j=j+1, i-th node contains a control point
)
)

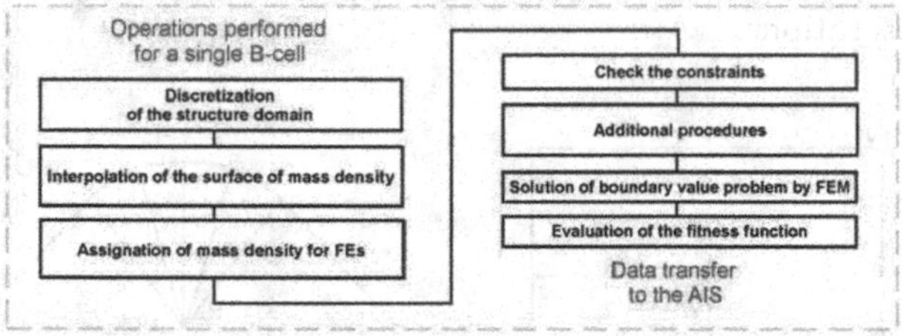

**Fig. 3.** Operation scheme performed for a single B-cell receptor

# 4 Immune Optimization Examples

Two numerical examples of design optimization by minimization of the mass of the structure are presented. To perform a comparative study two benchmark problems have been carried out. First example concerns minimization of the mass of Michell type structure. In the case of this optimization task the influences of the most important optimization parameters have been tested. At the end, additional example of the mass minimization of a solid structure is presented. The structure is considered in the framework of the theory of elasticity. The structure was discretized into cubic finite elements. The optimization problems have been solved by means of immune optimizer. The parameters of algorithms are included in Tables 2. The optimization processes were stopped if there was no fitness function improvement through the declared number of iterations.

**Table 2.** Parameters of the AIS

| the number of memory cells | the number of the clones | crowding factor | Gaussian mutation |
|---|---|---|---|
| 6 | 30 | 0.25 | 0.25 |

## 4.1   Example 1 (benchmark)   The Optimization of Michell Type Structure

A rectangular 2-D structure (plane stress) loaded with the concentrated force F in the center of the lower boundary and fixed on the bottom corners is considered (Fig. 4a). This task has been analytically solved as a typical structural layout optimization problem by Hemp [8]. The optimum topology consist of two 45° arms extending from the supports toward an approximately 90° center fan section which extends upwards from the point of application of the force (Fig. 4b). In order to obtain the symmetrical results a half of the structure has been analyzed. The input data to the optimization program and the parameters of immune algorithm are included in Tables 2 and 3, respectively. In the case of the mass minimization problem of Michell type structure, the influences of the most important optimization parameters have been tested. Figure 5 shows the effects of the optimization process with the different numbers and locations of the control points of the interpolation surface, with and without the application of the additional procedure aiding the topology optimization and after the same number of 10 iterations.

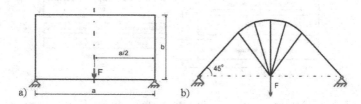

**Fig. 4.** The Michell type structure (Example 1): a) the geometry and boundary conditions, b) analytical solution obtained by Hemp

**Table 3.** The input data to optimization task of Michell type structure (Example 1)

| axb | thickness | $\sigma_{min}$, c | F | range of $\rho_e$ [g/cm3] |
| --- | --- | --- | --- | --- |
| [mm] | [mm] | [MPa] | [N] | existence or elimination of the finite element |
| 200x100 | 4.0 | 8.0 ; 1.0 | 4000 | $7.3 \leqslant \rho_e < 7.5$ elimination |
| | | | | $7.5 \leqslant \rho_e \leqslant 7.86$ existence |

Therefore the control points should be arranged in the whole structure domain (both inside and on the structure boundary). Such an arrangement guarantees good control of the interpolation surface and mass densities distribution in all sub-domains of the structure. The application of the appropriate control points number is also important. Bigger number of the control points, on the one hand, should provide better control of the interpolation surface, and on the other hand decreases the effectiveness of the optimization process (bigger number of design variables). The structures obtained after 10 iterations without application of the additional procedure, in the case of application of 13 and 25 control points, are better. However the optimization algorithm needs much more iteration to obtain

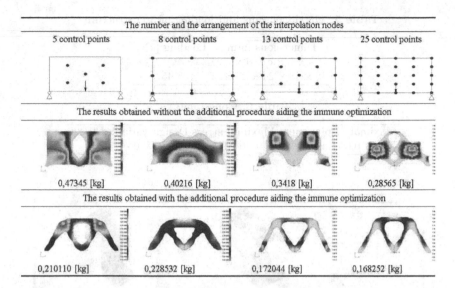

**Fig. 5.** The influence of the number and the arrangement of the interpolation nodes. All the results are obtained in $10^{th}$ iteration of the optimization process; number of the finite elements of the initial structure equals 1600, $\sigma_{MAX} = 85$ MPa

the optimal shapes - the optimization process should continue. The results are best when the additional procedure aiding the topology optimization is used. Then, all the results have similar shapes independently on the number and arrangement of the control points and they agree well with the Hemp [8] solution (Fig. 5). However, appropriate arrangement and number of the control points can increase the effectiveness of the optimization procedure.

### 4.2    Example 2   The Optimization of the Shape, the Topology and Material of the L 3-D Structure

In the next example a L structure (Fig. 6a) is optimized. The criterion of optimization is the minimization of the mass. Computational results obtained after 62 iterations are presented in the form of a map distribution of mass density (Fig. 6 b, c). The structure after smooth is presented in Fig. 7. The Tab. 4 contains input data. The dimensions, loading of 3-D structure and constraint are included in Tab. 5 and 6.

**Table 4.** Input data

| Minimal mass density | Step of iteration in smooth procedure |
|---|---|
| 0.4 x 7.85 g/cm3 | 25 |

**Table 5.** The dimensions and loading of 3-D structure

| Dimensions [mm] | Loading [kN] |
|---|---|
| a x b x c x d x e | Q |
| 48 x 48 x 24 x 24 x24 | 8.45 |

**Table 6.** Constraints

| Maximal displacement | Maximal stress | Design variables 1 - 27 |
|---|---|---|
| 0.08 mm | 600 MPa | 0 - 1 |

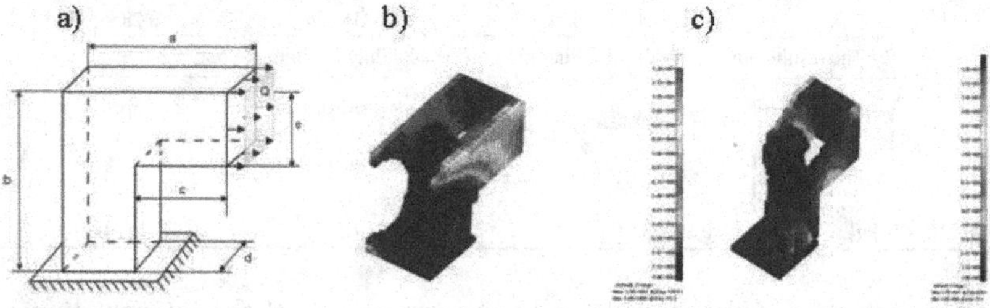

a)                         b)                         c)

**Fig. 6.** L structure: a) the scheme of loading, b) distribution of mass density after first generation, c) distribution of mass density after optimization

**Fig. 7.** Structure after smooth

## 5    Conclusions

The effective intelligent approaches for topology optimization of 2-D and 3-D structures based on immune computing are presented and discussed. By using the proposed approaches, the optimal topology of spatial structures can be found. In particular, the application of the bio-inspired algorithm gives a strong probability of finding globally optimal solutions. Described approach is free from limitations connected with classic gradient-based optimization methods, requiring to the continuity of the objective function, the gradient or the objective function Hessian and the substantial probability of converging only to a local optimum. By coupling the finite element method and the proposed immune algorithm, results with an effective and efficient alternative optimization tool, capable of solving a large class of optimization problems of mechanical structures. The main

feature of the proposed topology optimization method is the immunology distribution of the material in the construction changing its material properties. This
process leads to the elimination of the part of material from the structure and
as a result a new shape and the topology of the structure emerges. The use of
the interpolation surface (hyper surface) reduces the number of design variables
and significantly reduces the computational time requirement. The application
of the additional procedure aiding topology optimization facilitates finding the
optimal topologies and improves the effectiveness of the proposed method. Coupling the proposed approach with the finite element method and a commercial
computer codes, such as MSC NASTRAN, enables to tackle the optimization of
quite complex mechanical systems. The influence of the immune parameters and
mechanical constraints on the final solutions using this method are presented in
the paper [17]. Efficiency of presented approaches and comparison with evolutionary algorithms is presented in the paper [22][16]. There are possibilities of
further efficiency improvement of the proposed method, e.g. by the application
of adjoint variable method in the sensitivity analysis. Also, the application of
another hybridized global optimization algorithms, like hybrid artificial immune
system, would be interesting. Moreover, the use of fuzzy approach in the optimization process, like the one presented in works by Mrozek et al. [12][13] may
bring some improvements when working with uncertainties.

# References

1. Allaire, G., Jouve, F., Toader, A.M.: Structural optimization using sensitivity analysis and a level-set method. J. Comput. Phys. 194, 363–393 (2004)
2. Balthrop, J., Esponda, F., Forrest, S., Glickman, M.: Coverage and generalization
   in an artificial immune system. In: Proceedings of the Genetic and Evolutionary
   Computation Conference GECCO 2002, pp. 3–10. Morgan Kaufmann, NY (2002)
3. Bendsoe, M.: Optimal shape design as a material distribution problem. Struct.
   Optim. (1989)
4. Burczyński, T., Długosz, A., Kus, W., Orantek, P., Poteralski, A., Szczepanik, M.:
   Intelligent computing in evolutionary optimal shaping of solids. In: Proceedings of
   3rd International Conference on Computing, Communications and Control Technologies, vol. 3, pp. 294–298 (2005)
5. Burczyński, T., Kuś, W., Długosz, A., Poteralski, A., Szczepanik, M.: Sequential and Distributed Evolutionary Computations in Structural Optimization. In:
   Rutkowski, L., Siekmann, J.H., Tadeusiewicz, R., Zadeh, L.A. (eds.) ICAISC 2004.
   LNCS (LNAI), vol. 3070, pp. 1069–1074. Springer, Heidelberg (2004)
6. Burczyński, T., Szczepanik, M.: Intelligent optimal design of spatial structures.
   Computer and Structures (2013)
7. de Castro, L.N., Timmis, J.: Artificial immune systems as a novel soft computing
   paradigm. Soft Computing 7(8), 526–544 (2003)
8. Hemp, W.S.: Michells structural continua. Optimum Structures, ch. 4. Clarendon
   Press, Oxford (1973)
9. Heppner, F., Grenander, U.: A stochastic nonlinear model for coordinated bird
   flocks. In: Krasner, S. (ed.) The Ubiquity of Chaos. AAAS Publ., Washington, DC
   (1990)

10. Kennedy, J., Eberhart, R.C.: Particle Swarm Optimisation. In: Proceedings of IEEE Int. Conf. on Neural Networks, Piscataway, NJ, pp. 1942–1948 (1995)
11. Michalewicz, Z.: Genetic Algorithms + Data Structures = Evolutionary Programs. Springer, Berlin (1992)
12. Mrozek, D., Małysiak, B., Kozielski, S.: An optimal alignment of proteins energy characteristics with crisp and fuzzy similarity awards. In: 2007 IEEE International Conference on Fuzzy Systems, FUZZ-IEEE 2007, England, pp. 1513–1518 (2007)
13. Mrozek, D., Maysiak, B., Kozielski, S.: Alignment of Protein Structure Energy Patterns Represented as Sequences of Fuzzy Numbers. In: 2009 Annual Meeting of the North-American-Fuzzy-Information-Processing-Society, NAFIPS 2009, Cincinnati, OH, USA, pp. 35–40 (2009)
14. Osher, S., Sethian, J.A.: Front propagating with curvature dependent speed: algorithms based on the Hamilton Jacobi-formulations. J. Comp. Phys. 78, 12–49 (1988)
15. Poteralski, A., Szczepanik, M., Ptaszny, J., Kuś, W., Burczyński, T.: Hybrid artificial immune system in identification of room acoustic properties Inverse Problems in Science and Engineering. Taylor and Francis (2013)
16. Poteralski, A., Szczepanik, M., Dziatkiewicz, G., Kuś, W., Burczyński, T.: Comparison between PSO and AIS on the basis of identification of material constants in piezoelectrics. In: Rutkowski, L., Korytkowski, M., Scherer, R., Tadeusiewicz, R., Zadeh, L.A., Zurada, J.M. (eds.) ICAISC 2013, Part II. LNCS(LNAI), vol. 7895, pp. 569–581. Springer, Heidelberg (2013)
17. Poteralski, A.: Optimization of mechanical structures using artificial immune algorithm. In: Kozielski, S., Mrozek, D., Kasprowski, P., Małysiak-Mrozek, B.z. (eds.) BDAS 2014. CCIS, vol. 424, pp. 280–289. Springer, Heidelberg (2014)
18. Poteralski, A., Szczepanik, M., Beluch, W., Burczyński, T.: Optimization of composite structures using bio-inspired methods. In: Rutkowski, L., Korytkowski, M., Scherer, R., Tadeusiewicz, R., Zadeh, L.A., Zurada, J.M. (eds.) ICAISC 2014, Part II. LNCS(LNAI), vol. 8468, pp. 385–395. Springer, Heidelberg (2014)
19. Ptak, M., Ptak, W.: Basics of Immunology. Jagiell. Univ. Press (2000) (in Polish)
20. Reynolds, C.W.: Flocks, herds, and schools, A distributed behavioral model. Computer Graphics 21, 25–34 (1987)
21. Szczepanik, M., Poteralski, A., Długosz, A., Kuś, W., Burczyński, T.: Bio-inspired optimization of thermomechanical structures. In: Rutkowski, L., Korytkowski, M., Scherer, R., Tadeusiewicz, R., Zadeh, L.A., Zurada, J.M. (eds.) ICAISC 2013, Part II. LNCS, vol. 7895, pp. 79–90. Springer, Heidelberg (2013)
22. Szczepanik, M., Poteralski, A., Ptaszny, J., Burczyński, T.: Hybrid Particle Swarm Optimizer and its Application in Identification of Room Acoustic Properties. In: Rutkowski, L., Korytkowski, M., Scherer, R., Tadeusiewicz, R., Zadeh, L.A., Zurada, J.M. (eds.) SIDE 2012 and EC 2012. LNCS, vol. 7269, pp. 386–394. Springer, Heidelberg (2012)
23. Szczepanik, M., Burczyński, T.: Swarm optimization of stiffeners locations in 2-D structures. Bulletin of the Polish Academy of Sciences, Technical Sciences 60(2), 241–246 (2012)
24. Wierzchoń, S.T.: Artificial Immune Systems, Theory and Application (2001) (in Polish)
25. Xie, Y.M., Steven, G.P.: Evolutionary Structural Optimization. Springer (1997)
26. Yamada, T., et al.: A topology optimization method based on the level set method in-corporating a fictitious interface energy. Comput. Meth. Appl. Mech. Eng. (2010)
27. Zienkiewicz, O.C., Taylor, R.L.: The finite element method, vol. I, II. McGraw Hill (1989)

# Swarm and Immune Computing of Dynamically Loaded Reinforced Structures

Arkadiusz Poteralski[1]([✉]), Mirosław Szczepanik[1], Radosław Górski[1], and Tadeusz Burczyński[2]

[1] Institute of Computational and Mechanical Engineering,
Faculty of Mechanical Engineering,
Silesian University of Technology, ul. Konarskiego 18a, 44-100 Gliwice, Poland
arkadiusz.poteralski@polsl.pl
[2] Institute of Fundamental Technological Research, Polish Academy of Sciences,
Warsaw, Poland
tburczynski@ippt.pan.pl

**Abstract.** In the paper an application of the particle swarm optimizer (PSO) and artificial immune system (AIS) to optimization problems is presented. Reinfored structures considered in this work are dynamically loaded and analyzed by the coupled boundary and finite element method (BEM/FEM). The metod is applied to optimize location of stiffeners in plates using criteria depended on displacements. The main advantage of the particle swarm optimizer, contrary to gradient methods of optimization, is the fact that it does not need any information about the gradient of fitness function. A comparison of the PSO, artificial immune system and evolutionary algorithm (EA) is also shown and it proves the efficiency of the former over other artificial intelligence methods of optimization. The coupled BEM/FEM, which is used to analyse structures, is very accu-rate in analysis and attractive in optimization tasks. It is because of problem dimensionality reduction in comparison with more frequently used domain methods, like for instance the FEM. Numerical examples demonstrate that the combination of the PSO with the BEM/FEM is an effective technique for solving computer aided optimal design problems, both with respect to accuracy and computational resources.

**Keywords:** Particle swarm optimization · Immune optimization · Boundary element method · Finite element method · Dynamics

## 1 Introduction

Reinforced structures, which are characterized by high resistance, stiffeness, stability and low weight, are often used in practice for instance in an aircraft industry. Many aircraft elements are made as thin panels reinforced by stiffeners. Reinforced structures or their elements are frequently subjected to dynamic loads and gaining an information about their transient dynamic response is of practical importance. If the response is not satisfactory, it may be improved in the

© Springer International Publishing Switzerland 2015
L. Rutkowski et al. (Eds.): ICAISC 2015, Part II, LNAI 9120, pp. 483–494, 2015.
DOI: 10.1007/978-3-319-19369-4_43

optimization process in order to satisfy the requirements. The optimal choice of a number, properties and locations of stiffeners in a structure decides about the effectiveness of the reinforcement. In the present paper, the coupled BEM/FEM and the particle swarm or immune method in optimization of dynamically loaded reinforced structures is presented. Such a combination is advantageous in comparison with other approaches presented in the literature because it utilizes three very effective methods, i.e. the BEM/FEM for the simulation and the PSO or AIS for the optimization. The former is very effective in optimization problems because it reduces the problem dimensionality by one in comparison with more commonly used the FEM. The mesh generation and modification required in optimization tasks is thus much easier. The method is also attractive in dynamic problems and it is very accurate, especially in problems with high concentrations of stresses. They are present for instance in reinforced structures which are usually made of different materials. The efficiency comparison presented in the paper between the PSO [9][10] and the AIS [1][22] and other artificial intelligence methods, i.e. the evolutionary algorithms (EAs) [3][4][11] shows, that the former usually requires smaller number of fitness function evaluations for the same problem. The advantages each of the method and especially their combination, i.e. high accuracy and low computational resources like memory and time, make the presented approach a powerful computer aided optimization tool. The method is formulated and then applied in several numerical examples. The optimal locations of stiffeners in two-dimensional dynamically loaded plates is searched in order to maximize their stiffness.

## 2    The Particle Swarm Optimiser

The particle swarm algorithms [9][10][19], similarly to the evolutionary and immune algorithms, are developed on the basis of the mechanisms discovered in the nature. The swarm algorithms are based on the models of the animals social behaviours: moving and living in the groups. The animals relocate in the three-dimensional space in order to change their stay place, the feeding ground, to find the good place for reproduction or to evading predators. We can distinguish many species of the insects living in swarms, fishes swimming in the shoals, birds flying in flocks or animals living in herds. The flowchart of the particle swarm optimiser is presented in Fig. 1. At the beginning of the algorithm the particle swarm of assumed size is created randomly. Starting positions and velocities of the particles are created randomly. In the next step the objective function values are evaluated for each particle. The data necessary for calculation of the objective function are obtained in consequance of solving the boundary value problem by means of the coupled BEM/FEM (described in the next section). After obtaining information about fitness of all the particles, the best positions of the particles are updated and the swarm leader is chosen. Then the particles velocities and particles positions are modified. The process is iteratively repeated until the stop condition is fulfilled. The stop condition is typically expressed as the maximum number of iterations. The general effect is that each particle oscillates in the search space between its previous best position (position with the best fitness function value) and the best position of its best neighbour (relatively swarm leader), hopefully finding new best positions (solutions) on its trajectory, what in whole swarm sense leads to the optimal solution [5][22].

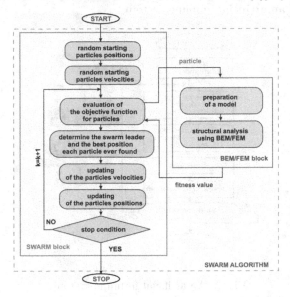

**Fig. 1.** The flowchart of the swarm algorithm

## 3   Artificial Immune Systems

The artificial immune systems (AIS) are developed on the basis of a mechanism discovered in biological immune systems [17]. An immune system is a complex system which contains distributed groups of specialized cells and organs. The main purpose of the immune system is to recognize and destroy pathogens - funguses, viruses, bacteria and improper functioning cells. The artificial immune systems [15][14] take only a few elements from the biological immune systems. The most frequently used are the mutation of the B cells, proliferation, memory cells, and recognition by using the B and T cells. The artificial immune systems have been used to optimization problems in classification and also computer viruses recognition. The cloning algorithm presented by von Zuben and de Castro [6] uses some mechanisms similar to biological immune systems to global optimization problems. The unknown global optimum is the searched pathogen. The memory cells contain design variables and proliferate during the optimization process. The B cells created from memory cells undergo mutation. The B cells evaluate and better ones exchange memory cells. In Wierzchoń S. T. [22] version of Clonalg the crowding mechanism is used - the diverse between memory cells is forced. A new memory cell is randomly created and substitutes the old one, if two memory cells have similar design variables. The crowding mechanism allows finding not only the global optimum but also other local ones.

The presented approach is based on the Wierzchoń S. T. algorithm [22], but the mutation operator is changed. The Gaussian mutation is used instead of the nonuniform mutation in the presented approach [ **??** ]. The Figure 2 presents the flowchart of an artificial immune system.

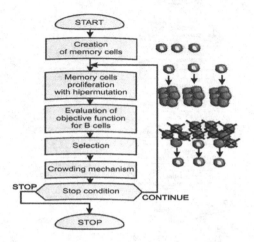

**Fig. 2.** An artificial immune system

The memory cells are created randomly. They proliferate and mutate creating B cells. The number of clones created by each memory cell is determined by the memory cells objective function value. The objective functions for B cells are evaluated. The selection process ex-changes some memory cells for better B cells. The selection is performed on the basis of the geometrical distance between each memory cell and B cells (measured by using design variables). The crowding mechanism removes similar memory cells. The similarity is also determined as the geometrical distance between memory cells. The process is iteratively repeated until the stop condition is fulfilled. The stop condition can be expressed as the maximum number of iterations. The unknown global optimum is represented by the searched pathogen. The memory cells contain design variables and proliferate during the optimization process [15].

## 4    The Coupled BEM/FEM in Analysis of Dynamically Loaded Reinforced Structures

A two-dimensional, homogenous, isotropic and linear elastic deformable body with the boundary $\Gamma^1$, occupying the domain $\Omega^1$ is considered. The body is supported and subjected to the dynamic tractions $t(\mathbf{x}, \tau)$, applied at the boundary and the body forces $b(\mathbf{x}, \tau)$, distributed in the domain $\Omega^2$. The displacement and traction fields should satisfy the following boundary conditions:

$$u_i(x,\tau) = \bar{u}_i(x,\tau) \ on \ \Gamma^u t_i(x,\tau) = \sigma_{ij}(x,\tau)n_j = \bar{t}_i(x,\tau) \ on \ \Gamma^t \qquad (1)$$

and initial conditions:

$$u_i(x,0) = u_i^o(x) \; and \; \dot{u}_i(x,0) = v_i^o(x) \; in \; \Omega^1 \tag{2}$$

where: $u_i$ is the component of displacement, $t_i$ is the component of traction, $\bar{u}_i$ and $\bar{t}_i$ denote the prescribed boundary conditions, $\sigma_{ij}$ is the stress tensor, $n_j$ is the component of the outward normal versor at the boundary, $\Gamma^u$ and $\Gamma^t$ are parts of the boundary $\Gamma^1$ ($\Gamma^u \cup \Gamma^t = \Gamma^1$), $u_i^o$ and $v_i^o$ are the prescribed initial conditions, x are coordinates of a point, $\tau$ is time. Repeated indices denote the summation convention and overdots indicate time derivatives; the indices for the two-dimensional problem are $i,j = 1,2$. Zero initial conditions are considered in this work. The mechanical fields satisfy the following integral equation [7]:

$$c_{ij}(x')u_j(x',\tau) = \int_{\Gamma_1} U_{ij}(x',x)t_j(x,\tau)d\Gamma(x) - \int_{\Gamma_1} T_{ij}(x',x)u_j(x,\tau)d\Gamma(x)$$

$$- \rho \int_{\Omega_1} U_{ij}(x',X)\ddot{u}_j(X,\tau)d\Omega(X) + \rho \int_{\Omega_2} U_{ij}(x',X)b_j(X)d\Omega(X) \tag{3}$$

where: $c_{ij}$ is a constant, which depends on the position of a point, $\rho$ is mass density, $U_{ij}$ and $T_{ij}$ are fundamental solutions of elastostatics, $x'$ is a collocation point, $x$ is a boundary point and $X$ is a domain point. In order to transform the inertial domain integral in (5) into the boundary integrals, the dual reciprocity method (DRM) proposed by Brebbia and Nardini [2] is used (see also Dominguez [7]). In this method, it is assumed that the accelerations can be interpolated using the equation

$$\ddot{u}_i(x,\tau) = \ddot{\alpha}_i^n(\tau)f^n(x^*,x) \tag{4}$$

where: $\ddot{\alpha}_i^n$ is a time-dependent function and $f^n$ is a coordinate function. In the present work, the following function is chosen

$$f^n(x^*,x) = r - C \tag{5}$$

where: $r$ is the distance between a defining point $x^*$ and a boundary point $x$, and $C$ is a constant (maximal dimension of the body). The defining point can be a boundary or a domain point. Taking into account the transformation, the inertial domain term (Eqn 5) has the form:

$$\rho \int_{\Omega_1} U_{ij}(x',X)\ddot{u}_j(X,\tau)d\Omega(X) = \rho[c_{ij}(x')\hat{u}_{jl}^n(x^*,x')$$

$$- \int_{\Gamma_1} U_{ij}(x',x)\hat{t}_{jl}^n(x^*,x)d\Gamma(x) + \int_{\Gamma_1} T_{ij}(x',x)\hat{u}_{jl}^n(x^*,x)d\Gamma(x)]\ddot{\alpha}_l^n(\tau) \tag{6}$$

where: $\hat{u}_{jl}^n$ and $\hat{t}_{jl}^n$ are respectively fictitious displacements and tractions [7], corresponding to the fictitious body force f n defined by Eqn (7).

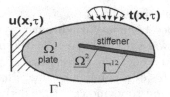

**Fig. 3.** Plate reinforced by a stiffener

For the plate reinforced by the stiffener and shown in Fig.3, the deformed stiffener acts on the plate along the line of the attachment. In this case, the body forces $b_j$ are unknown interaction forces between the plate and the stiffener, i.e. tractions $t_j$, and they are distributed along the interface $\Gamma^{12}$. Therefore, the integral equation (5) has the form:

$$c_{ij}(x')u_j(x',\tau) = \int_{\Gamma_1} U_{ij}(x',x)t_j(x,\tau)d\Gamma(x) - \int_{\Gamma_1} T_{ij}(x',x)u_j(x,\tau)d\Gamma(x)$$

$$- \rho[c_{ij}(x')\hat{u}_{jl}^n(x^*,x') - \int_{\Gamma_1} U_{ij}(x',x)\hat{t}_{jl}^n(x^*,x)d\Gamma(x) \qquad (7)$$

$$+ \int_{\Gamma_1} T_{ij}(x',x)\hat{u}_{jl}^n(x^*,x)d\Gamma(x)]\ddot{a}_l^n(\tau) + \rho\int_{\Gamma_{12}} U_{ij}(x',X)t_j(X)d\Gamma(X)$$

Equation (9) demonstrates that the DRM allows the expression of the equation of motion for the reinforced plate in the boundary integral form. The structures considered in the paper are analyzed by the coupled BEM/FEM using the subregion method [8]. The method consists in treating the finite element region as an equivalent boundary element region. The BE and FE matrix equations for all regions are coupled by transforming the FE matrices into the equivalent BE matrices. The relationship between the FE nodal forces and the BE tractions is expressed by a special transformation matrix. Matrix equations of motion for the plate, the stiffener and the coupled equations are given in this section. The boundary of the plate and the interface, where the stiffener is attached, are divided into the quadratic boundary elements. The boundary integral equations are applied for collocation points, which are nodes along the boundary and the interface. The variations of boundary coordinates, displacements, tractions and interface tractions are interpolated using quadratic shape functions. A set of algebraic equations for the plate has the following form:

$$\begin{bmatrix} M^1 \ M^{12} \end{bmatrix} \begin{Bmatrix} \ddot{u}^1 \\ \ddot{u}^{12} \end{Bmatrix} + \begin{bmatrix} H^1 \ H^{12} \end{bmatrix} \begin{Bmatrix} u^1 \\ u^{12} \end{Bmatrix} = \begin{bmatrix} G^1 \ G^{12} \end{bmatrix} \begin{Bmatrix} t^1 \\ t^{12} \end{Bmatrix} \qquad (8)$$

where: $\mathbf{M}$ is the mass matrix, $\mathbf{H}$ and $\mathbf{G}$ are the BEM coefficient matrices, $\mathbf{u}$ and $\ddot{u}$ are displacement and acceleration vectors, respectively, $\mathbf{t}$ is a vector of tractions applied at the outer boundary or the interface. The superscripts denote the matrices, which correspond to the outer boundary or the interface. The equation of motion for the stiffener in a matrix form is:

$$M^{21}\ddot{u}^{21} + K^{21}u^{21} = T^{21}t^{21} \qquad (9)$$

where: $\mathbf{K}$ is the FEM stiffness matrix, $\mathbf{T}$ is the matrix, which expresses the relationship between the FE nodal forces and the BE tractions. The latter matrix allows treatment the finite element region as an equivalent boundary element region. If the structure is subjected to time dependent boundary conditions, the dynamic interaction forces between the plate and the stiffener act along the interface. These tractions are treated as body forces distributed along the attachment line and they are unknowns of the problem. The displacement compatibility conditions and the traction equilibrium conditions at the nodes along the interface are:

$$u^{12} = u^{21}; t^{12} = -t^{21} \qquad (10)$$

If the above conditions are taken into account in equations for the plate (10) and stiffener (11), the following system of equations for the whole structure is obtained:

$$\begin{bmatrix} M^1 & M^{12} \\ 0 & M^{21} \end{bmatrix} \begin{Bmatrix} \ddot{u}^1 \\ \ddot{u}^{12} \end{Bmatrix} + \begin{bmatrix} H^1 & H^{12} & -G^{12} \\ 0 & K^{21} & T^{21} \end{bmatrix} \begin{Bmatrix} u^1 \\ u^{12} \\ t^{12} \end{Bmatrix} = G^1 t^1 \qquad (11)$$

The unknowns are displacements and tractions on the external boundary and at the interface in each time step.

## 5   Numerical Examples

Optimization of a reinforced rectangular plate (Fig.3) is performed by means of the AIS, PSO and EA. The plate is dynamically loaded and it is reinforced by the frame-like structure composed of straight beams. The plate and the stiffeners are modeled by the boundary elements and frame finite elements, respectively. Different kinds of load and support are considered. The structure before optimization (the reference plate) is shown in Fig. 4.

The length and the height of the plate is L=10 cm and H=5 cm, respectively. The thickness of the plate is g=0.25 cm, the dimensions of beams cross-section are 2a=0.5 cm and b=0.5 cm. The material of the plate and frame is aluminum and the mechanical properties are: modulus of elasticity E=70 GPa, Poissons ratio $\nu$=0.34 and density $\rho$=2700 kg/m3. The material is homogeneous, isotropic

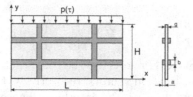

**Fig. 4.** Reinforced rectangular plate

and linear elastic and the plane stress is assumed. The uniformly distributed load is applied at the upper edge of the plate. Two kinds of time dependent loads are considered (see Fig. 5): a) the sinusoidal load $p(\tau) = p_0 sin(2\pi\tau/T)$ with the period of time $T = 20\pi$ $\mu s$ and b) the Heaviside load $p(\tau) = p_0 H(\tau)$. The value of the load in both cases is $p_o$=10 MPa. The time of analysis is 600 $\mu s$ and the time step $\Delta t = 2\mu s$.

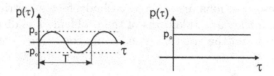

**Fig. 5.** Dynamic loadings: a) sinusoidal, b) Heaviside

Three different supports are considered (see Fig.6):
a) support A  the plate is fixed on the left and right edge,
b) support B  the plate is supported at two segments, each of 0.5 cm long,
c) support C  the plate is fixed at the bottom edge.

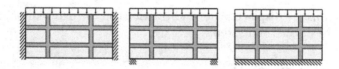

**Fig. 6.** Types of supports: a) support A, b) support B, c) support C

The optimal positions of stiffeners are searched in order to maximize stiffness of the plate. The maximal dynamic vertical displacement on the loaded edge is minimized. Because of symmetry of the structure and boundary conditions, only a half of the structure is considered. The number of design variables defining the position of the frame is 4: X1, X2, Y1 and Y2 (see Fig.7). The longer beams are parallel to the x axis. The end points of beams can move along the edges of the plate within the constraints, as shown in Fig.19. The constraints on design variables are imposed: X1 and X2 variables are within the range from 0.5 to 4.75 cm, Y1 from 0.5 to 2.25 cm and Y2 from 2.75 to 4.5 cm. The parameters of AIS are: the number of memory cells and the clones is 6, the crowding factor and the

Gaussian mutation is 0.5. The parameters of EA are: the number of chromosomes is 20, the probability of the Gaussian mutation is 0.5, the probability of a simple and arithmetic crossover is 0.05. The parameters of PSO are: numbers of particles is 20, inertia weight is 0.73 and two acceleration coefficients are 1.47.

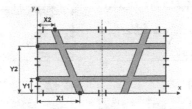

**Fig. 7.** Design variables and constraints

The total number of boundary and finite elements in the BEM/FEM analysis is 120 and 120, respectively (each horizontal and vertical beam is discretized into 40 and 20 finite elements, respectively). The number of boundary and finite elements during the optimization is constant. The values of design variables obtained by AIS, PSO and EA for the plate subjected to the sinusoidal load, the Heaviside load and for three kinds of supports, are presented in Table 1. The results obtained by three different methods are the same. The values of $J_0$ and J (where: $J_0$ and J is the objective function for the reference and the optimal plate, respectively) and the reduction $R = (J_o - J)/J_o \cdot 100\%$, are also presented. A significant reduction R, resulting in the improvement of dynamic re-sponse of the optimal plates in comparison with the initial designs, can be observed. The optimal structures for different kinds of supports and for the sinusoidal and the Heaviside loads are shown in Fig.8a and Fig.8b, respectively. It can be seen that in the present example most of constraints are active. Efficiency comparison of the particle swarm optimizer, artificial immune system (AIS) and evolutionary algorithms (EA), presented in the Table 2, proves the efficiency of the optimization methods based on the PSO.

**Table 1.** Values of design variables, J and R

| Support | X1 | X2 | Y1 | Y2 | $J_0$ | J | R |
|---|---|---|---|---|---|---|---|
| Design variables [cm] | | | | | | | |
| AIS, PSO and EA for Sinusoidal load | | | | | | | |
| A | 4.75 | 2.86 | 0.88 | 2.75 | 89 | 76 | 15 |
| B | 4.75 | 1.81 | 0.57 | 2.75 | 92 | 73 | 21 |
| C | 1.20 | 1.82 | 0.50 | 2.75 | 82 | 62 | 24 |
| AIS, PSO and EA for Heaviside load | | | | | | | |
| A | 0.50 | 4.75 | 0.50 | 4.50 | 112 | 91 | 19 |
| B | 4.75 | 1.41 | 0.50 | 4.50 | 211 | 149 | 29 |
| C | 0.50 | 2.20 | 1.70 | 2.80 | 49 | 42 | 14 |

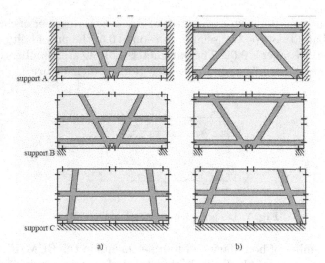

**Fig. 8.** Optimal plates subjected to dynamic loads: a) sinusoidal, b) Heaviside

**Table 2.** Efficiency of bio-inspired methods

| Support | EA | AIS | PSO |
|---------|-----|-----|-----|
| | fitness function evaluations for Sinusoidal load | | |
| A | 2515 | 588 | 360 |
| B | 3705 | 714 | 440 |
| C | 1952 | 756 | 520 |
| | fitness function evaluations for Heaviside load | | |
| A | 303 | 483 | 60 |
| B | 1526 | 441 | 120 |
| C | 2797 | 924 | 580 |

## 6    Conclusions

An effective tool of swarm and immune optimization of 2-D structures stiffened by ribs is presented. Using this approach the optimal arrangement of the stiffeners in geometry of 2-D structures can be found. Implementing of the bioinspired algorithms to this approach gives a strong probability of finding the global optimal solutions. Described approach is free from limitations connected with classic gradient optimization methods referring to the continuity of the objective function, the gradient or hessian of the objective function and the substantial probability of getting a local optimum. Besides in the case of using gradient methods finding the global solution depends on the starting point. The bio-inspired algorithms [16][19][20] perform multidirectional optimum searching by exchanging information between particles (PSO) or B-cell recptor (AIS) and finding better results. Numerical examples demonstrate that the methods based on the particle swarm and immune optimizer is an effective technique for solv-ing computer aided optimal design problems. Comparison between PSO, AIS and EA proves good effectiveness of particle swarm and immune optimization method. There are possibilities of further efficiency improvement of the proposed method, e.g. by the application of adjoint variable method in the sensitivity analysis. Also, the application of another hybridized global optimization algorithms, like hybrid particle swarm optimizer or hybrid artificial immune system, would be interesting. Moreover, the use of fuzzy approach in the optimization process, like the one presented in works by Mrozek et al. [12][13] may bring some improvements when working with uncertainties. Using this approach the multi-objective optimization is also possible to use with artificial immune system.

# References

1. Balthrop, J., Esponda, F., Forrest, S., Glickman, M.: Coverage and generalization in an artificial immune system. In: Proceedings of the Genetic and Evolutionary Computation Conference, GECCO 2002, pp. 3–10. Morgan Kaufmann, New York (2002)
2. Brebbia, C.A., Nardini, D.: Dynamic analysis in solid mechanics by an alternative boundary element procedure. Solid Dynamics and Earthquake Engineering 2(4), 228–233 (1983)
3. Burczyński, T., Długosz, A., Kus, W., Orantek, P., Poteralski, A., Szczepanik, M.: Intelligent computing in evolutionary optimal shaping of solids. In: Proceedings of 3rd International Conference on Computing, Communications and Control Technologies, vol. 3, pp. 294–298 (2005)
4. Burczyński, T., Kuś, W., Długosz, A., Poteralski, A., Szczepanik, M.: Sequential and Distributed Evolutionary Computations in Structural Optimization. In: Rutkowski, L., Siekmann, J.H., Tadeusiewicz, R., Zadeh, L.A. (eds.) ICAISC 2004. LNCS (LNAI), vol. 3070, pp. 1069–1074. Springer, Heidelberg (2004)
5. Burczyński, T., Szczepanik, M.: Intelligent optimal design of spatial structures. Computer and Structures (2013)
6. de Castro, L.N., Timmis, J.: Artificial immune systems as a novel soft computing paradigm. Soft Computing 7(8), 526–544 (2003)
7. Dominguez, J.: Boundary elements in dynamics, Computational Mechanics Publications. Elsevier Applied Science, Southampton-Boston (1993)
8. Fedeliński, P., Górski, R.: Analysis and optimization of dynamically loaded reinforced plates by the coupled boundary and finite element method. Computer Modeling in Engineering and Sciences 15(1), 31–40 (2006)
9. Heppner, F., Grenander, U.: A stochastic nonlinear model for coordinated bird flocks. In: Krasner, S. (ed.) The Ubiquity of Chaos. AAAS Publications, Washington, DC (1990)
10. Kennedy, J., Eberhart, R.: Particle Swarm Optimisation. In: Proceedings of IEEE Int. Conf. on Neural Networks, Piscataway, NJ, pp. 1942–1948 (1995)
11. Michalewicz, Z.: Genetic Algorithms + Data Structures = Evolutionary Programs. Springer, Berlin (1992)
12. Mrozek, D., Małysiak-Mrozek, B.: An Improved Method for Protein Similarity Searching by Alignment of Fuzzy Energy Signatures. International Journal of Computational Intelligence Systems 4(1), 75–88 (2011)
13. Poteralski, A., Szczepanik, M., Ptaszny, J., Kus, W., Burczynski, T.: Hybrid artificial immune system in identification of room acoustic properties. In: Inverse Problems in Science and Engineering. Taylor and Francis (2013)

14. Poteralski, A., Szczepanik, M., Dziatkiewicz, G., Kuś, W., Burczyński, T.: Comparison between PSO and AIS on the basis of identification of material constants in piezoelectrics. In: Rutkowski, L., Korytkowski, M., Scherer, R., Tadeusiewicz, R., Zadeh, L.A., Zurada, J.M. (eds.) ICAISC 2013, Part II. LNCS(LNAI), vol. 7895, pp. 569–581. Springer, Heidelberg (2013)
15. Poteralski, A.: Optimization of mechanical structures using artificial immune algorithm. In: Kozielski, S., Mrozek, D., Kasprowski, P., Małysiak-Mrozek, B.z. (eds.) BDAS 2014. CCIS, vol. 424, pp. 280–289. Springer, Heidelberg (2014)
16. Poteralski, A., Szczepanik, M., Beluch, W., Burczyński, T.: Optimization of composite structures using bio-inspired methods. In: Rutkowski, L., Korytkowski, M., Scherer, R., Tadeusiewicz, R., Zadeh, L.A., Zurada, J.M. (eds.) ICAISC 2014, Part II. LNCS(LNAI), vol. 8468, pp. 385–395. Springer, Heidelberg (2014)
17. Ptak, M., Ptak, W.: Basics of Immunology. Jagiellonian University Press, Cracow (2000) (in Polish)
18. Reynolds, C.W.: Flocks, herds, and schools, A distributed behavioral model. Computer Graphics 21, 25–34 (1987)
19. Szczepanik, M., Poteralski, A., Długosz, A., Kuś, W., Burczyński, T.: Bio-inspired optimization of thermomechanical structures. In: Rutkowski, L., Korytkowski, M., Scherer, R., Tadeusiewicz, R., Zadeh, L.A., Zurada, J.M. (eds.) ICAISC 2013, Part II. LNCS(LNAI), vol. 7895, pp. 79–90. Springer, Heidelberg (2013)
20. Szczepanik, M., Poteralski, A., Ptaszny, J., Burczyński, T.: Hybrid Particle Swarm Optimizer and its Application in Identification of Room Acoustic Properties. In: Rutkowski, L., Korytkowski, M., Scherer, R., Tadeusiewicz, R., Zadeh, L.A., Zurada, J.M. (eds.) SIDE 2012 and EC 2012 . LNCS, vol. 7269, pp. 386–394. Springer, Heidelberg (2012)
21. Szczepanik, M., Burczyński, T.: Swarm optimization of stiffeners locations in 2-D structures. Bulletin of the Polish Academy of Sciences, Technical Sciences 60(2), 241–246 (2012)
22. Wierzchoń, S.T.: Artificial Immune Systems, Theory and Applications, EXIT, Warsaw (2001) (in Polish)

# The Setup Method of the Order with the Help of the Rough Sets Convention

Aleksandra Ptak[1], Henryk Piech[1(✉)], and Nina Zhou[2]

[1] Czestochowa University of Technology, Czestochowa, Poland
hpiech@adm.pcz.czest.pl, olaptak@gmail.com
[2] Institute for Infocomm Research ($I^2R$)
1 Fusionopolis Way #21-01 Connexis, Singapore 138632, Singapore
zhoun@i2r.a-star.edu.sg

**Abstract.** Configuration of the order is related to the determination of the range of goods (raw materials) and their size. Using a policy of continuous suppllies and constant periods, we are dealing with a simplified analysis, but also often far from optimal supplies efficiency [10]. By using the monitoring, we can get closer to the optimal solutions. Monitoring should be supported by a simple expert system, usually based on the inference mechanism, which is the set of rules [15]. All of these have to take into account the limitations and all the additional costs. These costs are related to, inter alia, the storage, transportation, giving out storage, capital binding, insurance, etc. It is difficult to consider them separately and also difficult to aggregate them in the same way. Grouping together costs, according to the specificity of merger costs (delivery, order, the manner of storage, etc.) we can observe the typical management and inventory planning policy operations [8]. Specific features of such policy can be described as both deterministic and linguistic. Methodical apparatus for analysis of similar data is proposed in rough set theory of Pawlak and the theory of Dampster Shaffer [15]. These theories give the possibility to reduce the rules and simplify the inference method on decision-making under conditions of dynamic changes in the data structure.In the paper rough set theory of Pawlak is being used.

**Keywords:** Cost analysis · Delivery plan · Rough set theory

## 1 Introduction

The combination of cost analysis, optimization of the structure and the size of the delivery [4] with the convention of rough sets [11] aims to develop a reduced number of rules [5] making decisions about the organization of supplies. Rules can take an estimate, approximate and linguistic form [7]. Separation of supplies for different types of materials does not meet the expectations of suitability as practical measures are complex, and this in turn requires the aggregation of partial results, which is even more complex problem [14]. The main criteria is of course the global cost of purchase and deliveries realization [16]. Supporting criteria include the degree of risk while postponing the term of supplies. Such

© Springer International Publishing Switzerland 2015
L. Rutkowski et al. (Eds.): ICAISC 2015, Part II, LNAI 9120, pp. 495–503, 2015.
DOI: 10.1007/978-3-319-19369-4_44

offsets can also affect changes in the cost of storage (which is not always taken into account [6,8]). The degree of risk can be estimated as exceeding the threshold of inventories or deviation from the optimal value of the contract (the policy $(s, Q)$ (variable time between deliveries) [3]). It can also be regarded as extending the time between deliveries in the implementation of policy $(T, S)$ (variable supplies). Generally, the optimal size (value) of the delivery [4] is associated with the corresponding optimal time between deliveries. Scheduling of supplies may be associated with permanent monitoring of stocks. The strategy proposed in the rough set theory is based on the selection of conditional and decision-making attributes. The proposed procedures allow to evaluate the degree of certainty of each decision and degrees of coverage of these decisions by individual attributes [13]. On the basis of these parameters, sets of decision rules are generated and then reduced. This is of course part of the mechanism of inference, which is the main component of the expert system [15].

## 2    The Economic Basis for Planning the Size and Delivery Time

Economic order quantity depends on the cost of order processing, storage costs and costs of raw materials [3]:

$$Cd = Cs + c * D + Cm = cd * (D/Q) + c * D + cm * (Q/2), \tag{1}$$

where
$Cs$ -the cost of orders service,
$c$ - the unitary purchase price,
$D$ - the purchase volume (total supply),
$Cm$ - the cost of storage of purchased raw materials,
$Q$ - the quantity of delivery,
$cd$ - the coefficient of storage costs for a single delivery,
$cm$ - the coefficient of the cost of the inventory maintaining.
Optimizing the order quantity, we compare derivative of the variable $Q$ to zero:
$\frac{d(Cd)}{dQ} = -\frac{D}{Q^2} + \frac{cm}{2} = 0,$
hence
$Qopt = \sqrt{\frac{2*D*cd}{cm}},$
with the optimal size of the delivery, the corresponding optimal time is related:

$$Topt = \frac{Qopt}{D} = \sqrt{\frac{2 * cd}{D * cm}} \quad (part\ of\ the\ year) \tag{2}$$

In practice, the economic size of the optimal order can not always be used as an accurate deterministic parameter directly related to the decisions made. It comes to the assumption of the stability of the demand for raw materials. Furthermore, we can not always assume that the coefficients $cd$ and $cm$ are constant. In real situations, very often, one has to deal with mergers of several types of raw materials in one delivery. In the paper [13] the possibility of correcting the size and assortment of supply on the basis of supply in preceding periods has been considered. In this approach, one proposed the transition from the quantitative to the valuable estimation of the size of supplies:

$Dv = D * c$ or $Dv = \sum_{i=1}^{la} D_i * c_i$ where

$la$ - the assortment of the delivery or the number of types of raw materials,

$D_i$ - the sum of $i$-th raw material supply,

$c_i$- the unitary price of $i$-th raw material.

It is easy to see that the introduction of the parameter $Dv$ to formula (1) is a simplification which one can not always afford (the cost of order processing and storage do not need to be comparable). Therefore often, one has to define the optimal size of the supply for each type of raw material or its grouped sets separatly. $Q_1, Q_2, ..., Q_{la}$. As one can see from the formula (2) we can use the raw materials grouping when $\sqrt{cd_i/cm_i} \approx const$. Then we can write:

$$Qopt_i = \sqrt{D_i}\sqrt{2 * cds/cms} = \sqrt{D_i} * cg, \tag{3}$$

where $cds$, $cdm$ - the average values of the coefficients of the delivery and storage handling,

$cg$ - the grouping coefficient,

and

$n_i = \sqrt{D_i}/cg,$

where $n_i$ - the number of deliveries of $i$-th raw material.

We can go as far as to estimate the $cg$ value by considering all the raw materials together:

$$\sum_{i=1}^{la} n_i * cg = \sum_{i=1}^{la} \sqrt{D_i}, . \tag{4}$$

Therefore

$$cg = \frac{\sum_{i=1}^{la} \sqrt{D_i}}{\sum_{i=1}^{la} n_i}.$$

We can now determine the estimated value of the cost $cd$. Separate consideration of transport service leads to a modification of the (1) [11]:

$$Cd = Cs + Ct + c * D + Cm = cd * (D/Q) + ct * (D/Q) + c * D + cm * (Q/2), \tag{5}$$

where $ct$ - the unitary cost of the transportation.

In [12] different sets of vehicles and the cheapest configuration for each delivery were considered. Then one calculated the global cost of purchasing raw materials for each variant size (value) of the delivery $Q$ and determined the cheapest one. Such an approach is deterministic but does not guarantee the optimal strategy.

## 3   The Strategy of Using Rough Sets

In this strategy, one creates configuration of types of raw materials or configuration of vehicles used for transportation. The configuration sets are treated as

objects endowed with certain attributes. Depending on the policy and strategy of supplies such attributes may be, for example:
- the change in the overall costs of the $i$-th raw material order with respect to the optimal estimation,
- the change in the size (value) of the $t$-th raw material supply in relation to the optimal value,
- the relative size of the risk associated with combining the supply of selected raw materials,
- the variance of the levels of risk in relation to different types of raw materials,
- the change in the value of order, depending on the configuration of vehicles,
- the change in the time of delivery for the $i$-th type of raw material.
As a decision-making parameter (attribute) the entirety of the costs in relation to all raw materials in the scale of the settlement period (e.g. annual) can be used. One can also use the total number of transportations and the transportations time. Defining the delivery assortment one can provide various configurations of the vehicles that can be used for delivery. The characteristics of such delivery can be defined with the help of a similar structure as shown in Figure 1. In one

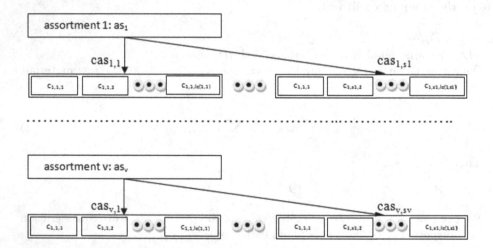

**Fig. 1.** The structure of conditional attributes of supplies configuration, $as_i$ - $i$-th configuration of supply of raw materials, $casi_{i,j}$ - $j$-th vehicle configuration for the $i$-th configuration of raw materials, $c_{i,j,k}$ - the code of the $k$-th vehicle $j$-th configuration of vehicles and $i$-th configuration of raw materials

variant, one can evaluate the increases of the size of the supply. For the selected assortment in terms of delivery we assess the optimal size of each raw material and the corresponding time between deliveries. Then we calculate the size of the partial costs for the defined moment of total supply and their changes in relation to the size of the corresponding optimal strategy:

$$dQ = \sum_{i \in asQ_i > Qupt} (Q_i - Qopt_i) \tag{6}$$

for the supply policy assuming variability in supply,

$$dT = \sum_{i \in as} (T_i - Topt_i) \tag{7}$$

for the supply policy assuming variability of time distance between deliveries,
where
$dQ$ - the change in the value of delivery of a set consisting of different types of
raw materials,
$c$ - the commodity code from the defined assortment delivery,
$as$ - the defined assortment of the delivery,
$Qc$ - the real size of the supply of the $c$-th raw material (after adjusted time of
the delivery),
$Tc$ - the real distance between the previous and the current supply of the c-th
raw material.
The decision on the choice of the supply policy does not correspond to the most
of real situations, because while monitoring the stocks using up at the time,
we make a decision on the configuration of the current supply which involves a
change in both time and size (value) of the transported raw materials. Increasing
the size (value) of supply increases the calculation time between deliveries. This
in turn may affect the reduction in the number of deliveries for certain raw
materials. At the same time it causes an increase in storage costs. The risk
of loss of inventory of raw materials can be taken into account with the help
of temporal parameters as exceeding the time point indicated theoretically as
an optimal, taking into account the offset for the previous delivery of the raw
material.

$$R = \sum_{i \in as} |T_i - Topt_i| / \sum_{i \in as} Topt_i \tag{8}$$

The [14] presents an algorithm showing the ability to configure a set of means of
transportation. Depending on the configuration, the size (value) of transported
material is formed, but it oscillates (with the defined acceptable percentage
threshold) around the value determined by the calculation range of the particular configuration of delivery. The overall strategy of the analysis based on rough
sets is to create data structures in the form presented as the structure on table
in fig.2. Sample data for the implementation of the monitored supply strategy
are presented on table in fig.3. In the Convention of rough sets it is convenient
to use linguistic or character encoding attribute values for each configuration. It
allows to create simple decision rules.
   To assess the strength of a decision, we conduct the normalization of complements of the relative risk estimated from the formula (8) and stated in the last
column of table in fig.3.:
$Str(k) = (1 - R_k) / \sum_{i=1}^{lk} (1 - R_j)$,
where
$R_k$ - the degree of risk for $k$ -th supply configuration,
$lk$ - the number of supply configurations.

| configuration | $dQ_1$ | $dQ_2$ | ...... | $dQ_{1a}$ | $dT_1$ | $dT_2$ | ...... | $dT_{1a}$ | R |
|---|---|---|---|---|---|---|---|---|---|
| 1.1 | | | | | | | | | |
| 1.2 | | | | | | | | | |
| ...... | | -/L/M/H | | | | | | | |
| 1.s1 | | | | | | | | | |
| 2.1 | | | | | | | | | |
| 2.2 | | | | | | | | | |
| ...... | | | | | | | | | |
| 2.s2 | | | | | | | | | |
| ...... | | | | | | | | | |
| v.1 | | | | | | | | | |
| v.2 | | | | | | | —/+++ | | |
| ...... | | | | | | | | | |
| v.sv | | | | | | | | | |

**Fig. 2.** The data structure prepared for analysis using the convention of rough sets, the configuration $i, j$ means $i$-th variant of the size (value) for raw materials and $j$ - th variant for a set of vehicles. The linguistic encoding "-" means no correction in relation to the calculated optimum size, L - low correction level , M - medium correction level, H - high correction level. The character encoding "-" ("+") - small correction negative (positive), "—" ("+++") - large correction negative (positive)

| configuration | $dQ_1$ | $dQ_2$ | $dQ_3$ | $dQ_4$ | $dT_1$ | $dT_2$ | $dT_3$ | $dT_4$ | R |
|---|---|---|---|---|---|---|---|---|---|
| 1.1 | L | M | L | L | + | + | + | + | 0,18 |
| 1.2 | M | - | M | L | ++ | - | + | + | 0,22 |
| 1.3 | L | L | M | M | + | + | ++ | ++ | 0,28 |
| 2.1 | H | M | - | - | ++ | + | - | -- | 0,44 |
| 2.2 | - | M | - | H | - | ++ | -- | +++ | 0,37 |
| 3.1 | L | H | L | L | - | ++ | + | -- | 0,34 |
| 3.2 | L | L | H | - | + | + | +++ | -- | 0,43 |
| 3.3 | L | L | L | H | + | -- | ++ | ++ | 0,45 |
| 3.4 | M | L | L | - | ++ | - | - | - | 0,19 |

**Fig. 3.** Data prepared for analysis using the convention of rough sets

The decision $Dec(k)$ is the result of the analysis of the strength including the decision thresholds:
$thl = 0, 25 * RR$; $thbl = 0, 5 * RR$; $thbu = 0, 75 * RR$, where $thl$ - the lower threshold of the negative decision, $thbl$ - the lower threshold of the limit of uncertainty , $thbu$ - the upper threshold of the limit of uncertainty, $RR$ - range of risks. Another table called the table of decision rules arises [11] (fig.4). The degree of certainty $Cer(k)$ has been calculated by separating the probabilities in the area of uncertainty [11,12].

The complementation of these data is the information concerning the degree of coverage of the attributes of $Cev(k)$ for each decision (fig.5). The choice of the delivery configuration is caused by:

| configuration | k | Str(k) | Cer(k) | Dec(k) |
|---|---|---|---|---|
| 1.1 | 1 | 0,13 | 1 | yes |
| 1.2 | 2 | 0,13 | 1 | yes |
| 1.3 | 3 | 0,12 | 0,36 | yes/no |
| 2.1 | 4 | 0,09 | 0 | no |
| 2.2 | 5 | 0,10 | 0,31 | no/yes |
| 3.1 | 6 | 0,11 | 0,33 | no/yes |
| 3.2 | 7 | 0,09 | 0 | no |
| 3.3 | 8 | 0,09 | 0 | no |
| 3.4 | 9 | 0,13 | 1 | yes |

**Fig. 4.** Table of data for decision-making rules

| configuration | k | Cov(k){yes} | Cov(k){no} | Dec(k) |
|---|---|---|---|---|
| 1.1 | 1 | 0,26 | | yes |
| 1.2 | 2 | 0,25 | | yes |
| 1.3 | 3 | 0,23 | | yes/no |
| 2.1 | 4 | | 0,19 | no |
| 2.2 | 5 | | 0,21 | no/yes |
| 3.1 | 6 | | 0,22 | no/yes |
| 3.2 | 7 | | 0,19 | no |
| 3.3 | 8 | | 0,19 | no |
| 3.4 | 9 | 0,26 | | yes |

**Fig. 5.** Table of data on the decision coverage

- the high value of the confidence coefficient ($\geq 0,75$),
- the low and zero-value of the changes level of the constituent raw material in relation to the optimal value,
- the low time correction value with respect to the optimal value.
The decision on the rejection of the delivery configuration is caused by:
- the low value of the confidence coefficient ($< 0,25$),
- the high value of the changes level of the constituent raw material in relation to the optimal value,
- the high time correction value with respect to the optimal value.
Uncertain decision-making area is defined by:
- the average value of the confidence coefficient ($\geq 0,25$ or $< 0,75$),
- the low and zero-value of the changes level of the constituent raw material in relation to the optimal value,
- the low time correction value with respect to the optimal value.

Let us create a set of decision rules

1)if $\neg\exists(dQ(i)_{i=1,2,3} = H)\wedge(dQ(4) = L)\wedge\forall_i(dT(i) = ("+"))$ then $Dec(k) = Yes$
with certainty $Cer(k) = 1,$

2)if $\neg\exists(dQ(i)_{i=1,2,3} = H) \wedge (dQ(4) = L) \wedge \forall_i(dT(i) < ("+++"))$ then $Dec(k) = Yes$ with certainty $Cer(k) = 1$,

3)if $\neg\exists(dQ(i)_{i=1,2,...,la} = H) \wedge (dQ(4) = M) \wedge \forall_i(dT(i) = ("++"))$ then $Dec(k) = Yes$ with certainty $Cer(k) = 0, 36$,

4)if $dQ(1) = H) \wedge \forall_i(dT(i) < ("+++"))$ then $Dec(k) = No$ with certainty $Cer(k) = 1$,

5)if $dQ(4) = H) \wedge \forall_i(dT(i) < ("+++"))$ then $Dec(k) = No$ with certainty $Cer(k) = 0, 31$,

6)if $dQ(2) = H) \wedge \forall_i(dT(i) \leq ("+++"))$ then $Dec(k) = No$ with certainty $Cer(k) = 0, 33$,

7)if $dQ(3) = H) \wedge \forall_i(dT(i) < ("+++"))$ then $Dec(k) = No$ with certainty $Cer(k) = 1$,

8)if $dQ(1) = H) \wedge \forall_i(dT(i) \leq ("+++"))$ then $Dec(k) = Yes$ with certainty $Cer(k) = 1$,

9)if $\neg\exists(dQ(i)_{i=1,2,...,la} = H) \wedge (dQ(4) = " -") \wedge \forall_i(dT(i) = ("+++"))$ then $Dec(k) = Yes$ with certainty $Cer(k) = 1$.

A set of the inverse decision rules has the form:

1)if $Dec(i) = Yes$ then $\neg\exists(dQ(i)_{i=1,2,3} = H) \wedge (dQ(4) = L) \wedge \forall_i(dT(i) = ("+"))$ with coverage $Cov = 0, 26$,

2)if $Dec(i) = Yes$ then $\neg\exists(dQ(i)_{i=1,2,3} = H) \wedge (dQ(4) = L) \wedge \forall_i(dT(i) = ("+++"))$ with coverage $Cov = 0, 25$,

3)if $Dec(i) = Yes$ then $\neg\exists(dQ(i)_{i=1,2,...,la} = H) \wedge (dQ(4) = M) \wedge \forall_i(dT(i) = ("+"))$ with coverage $Cov = 0, 23$,

4)if $Dec(i) = No$ then $dQ(1) = H) \wedge \forall_i(dT(i) < ("+++"))$ with coverage $Cov = 0, 19$,

5)if $Dec(i) = No$ then $dQ(4) = H) \wedge \forall_i(dT(i) < ("+++"))$ with coverage $Cov = 0, 21$,

6)if $Dec(i) = No$ then $dQ(2) = H) \wedge \forall_i(dT(i) \leq ("+++"))$ with coverage $Cov = 0, 22$,

7)if $Dec(i) = No$ then $dQ(3) = H) \wedge \forall_i(dT(i) < ("+++"))$ with coverage $Cov = 0, 19$,

8)if $Dec(i) = No$ then $dQ(1) = H) \wedge \forall_i(dT(i) < ("+++"))$ with coverage $Cov = 0, 19$,

9)if $Dec(i) = Yes$ then $\neg\exists(dQ(i)_{i=1,2,...,la} = H) \wedge (dQ(4) = " -") \wedge \forall_i(dT(i) = ("+++"))$ with coverage $Cov = 0, 26$.

From the inverse rules, we can determine the most reliable characteristics for selected and rejected decisions.

## 4 Conclusions

The proposed method for creating decision rules can be implemented in expert systems for the supplies organization both in the "off" and "on" line. This method is enriched by the analysis of the configuration in terms of the assortment selection and creates a set of vehicles for the transport of supplies. The advantage of this method is the fact that it is based on the classic formula for determining the optimal value and the delivery of the raw materials. To determine the criteria characteristics, one used the corrected deviations from the optimal parameters of supplies.

# References

1. Baumgarten, H.: Logistik-Management. Technische Universitaet Berlin 12 (2004)
2. Blackstock, T.: Keynote Speech, International Association of Food Industry Suppliers, San Francisco, CA (March 11, 2005), Gattorna, J.: Supply Chains Are the Business. Supply Chain Management Review 10(6), 42–49 (2005)
3. Chen, I.J., Paulraj, A., Lado, A.: Strategic purchasing, supply management, and firm performance. Journal of Operations Management 22(5), 505–523 (2004)
4. Christopher, M.: Logistics and Supply Chain Management, p. 288. Pearson, UK (2013)
5. Douglas, M.L.: Supply Chain Management: Processes. Supply Chain Management Institute, Sarasota (2008)
6. Fawcett, S.E., Ellram, L.M., Ogden, J.A.: Supply chain management; from vision to implementation, p. 520. Pearson (2014)
7. Douglas, M., Lambert, S.J., Garca-Dastugue, K.L.: Croxton, An evaluation of process-oriented supply chain management frameworks. Journal of Business Logistics 26(1), 25–51 (2005)
8. Lambert, D.M.: Supply Chain Management: Processes, Partnerships, Performance. Supply Chain Management Institute, Sarasota (2008)
9. Gattorna, J.: Supply Chains Are the Business. Supply Chain Management Review 10(6), 42–49 (2006)
10. Hugos, M.H.: Essentials of Supply Chain Management, p. 288. John Wiley and Sons (2011)
11. Pawlak, Z., Sugeno, M.: Decision Rules Bayes, Rule and Rough, New Decisions in Rough Sets. Springer, Berlin (1999)
12. Simchi-Levy, D., Kaminski, P., Simchi-Levy, E.: Designing and Managing the Supply Chain: Concepts, Strategies, and Case Studies. Irwin/McGraw Hill, Boston (2000)
13. Simchi-Levi, D., Xin, C., Bramel, J.: The Logic of Logistics: Theory, Algorithms, and Applications for Logistics Management. Springer Science and Business Media, 467 (2013)
14. Straka, M., Malindzak, D.: Distribution logistics. Express Publicity, Kosice (2008)
15. Tadeusiewicz, R.: Place and role of Intelligence Systems in Computer Science. Computer Methodsin Material Science 10(4), 193–206 (2010)
16. Wisner, J.D., Keong Leong, G., Tan, K.-C.: Keah-Choon Tan, Supply Chain Management: A Balanced Approach. Thomson South-Western, Mason (2004)

# ALMM Solver: The Idea and the Architecture

Krzysztof Rączka[✉], Ewa Dudek-Dyduch, Edyta Kucharska,
and Lidia Dutkiewicz

Department of Automatics and Biomedical Engineering,
AGH University of Science and Technology,
30 Mickiewicza Av, 30-059 Krakow, Poland,
{kjr,edd,edyta,lidia}@agh.edu.pl

**Abstract.** The ALMM Solver is a software tool which aim is generating
solutions for discrete optimization problems, in particular for NP-hard
problems. The idea of the solver is based on Algebraic Logical Meta-
Model of Multistage Decision Process (ALMM of MDP). The aim of
the paper is to present the architecture of the ALMM Solver and to
describe requirements regarding the solver, in particular non-functional
ones. SimOpt, the core module of the solver, is described in detail. The
practices, design patterns and principles, that was used to ensure the
best quality of the solver software, are mentioned in the paper.

**Keywords:** Solver · Optimizer · Algebraic-logical meta-model (ALMM) ·
Scheduling problem · Simulation tool · Software architecture · Design
patterns · Framework

## 1 Introduction

Difficult optimization problems arise in many different areas. There is, therefore,
a need to develop theoretical solutions and to create tools that help people solve
such problems, in particular NP-hard problems [2], [43], [42]. For this purpose,
we create a tool which we call the ALMM Solver. It is based on Algebraic Logical
Meta-Model (ALMM) methodology, which is dedicated to complex discrete optimization problems, including dynamic problems. This paper is a continuation
of the work presented in [16].

The idea of an ALMM paradigm was proposed and developed by Dudek-
Dyduch E. [4], [5], [6], [9], [8], [12]. According to this theory, a problem is modeled as a multistage decision process (DMP) together with optimization criterion.
DPM is defined as a sextuple which elements are: a set of decisions, a set of generalized states, an initial generalized state, a partial function called a transition
function, a set of not admissible generalized states, a set of goal generalized
states.

With the use of a model, a sequence of consecutive process states is generated.
In this sequence, each state depends on the previous state and the decision made
at this state. The decision is chosen from different decisions one can make at the
given state. Generation of the state sequence is terminated if the new state is a

© Springer International Publishing Switzerland 2015
L. Rutkowski et al. (Eds.): ICAISC 2015, Part II, LNAI 9120, pp. 504–514, 2015.
DOI: 10.1007/978-3-319-19369-4_45

goal state (state we want the process to be at the end), a non-admissible state, or state with an empty set of possible decisions. The sequence of consecutive process states from a given initial state to a final state (goal or non-admissible) form a process trajectory.

Our tool, ALMM Solver, allows one to solve discrete optimization problems by finding optimal or suboptimal solutions (trajectories). The solver can also be used to solve those problems, in which it suffices to find an admissible solution only.

The aim of the paper is to present the architecture of the ALMM Solver and to describe requirements regarding the solver, in particular non-functional ones. The presented research is based on the previous works [4], [6], [7], [9], [5] that lays the groundwork for the basic ALMM theory and later papers [11], [15], [17], [38] and [25].

## 2   The Idea of the ALMM Solver

The goal of the ALMM Solver is to compute solutions for different optimization problems using ALMM methodology. Thus, it provides following features:

- representation of problems in accordance with the ALMM methodology,
- searching for solutions to the problems (by building process trajectories),
- implementation of algorithms used in computations,
- collection of algorithms in the internal repository,
- collection, analysis and interpretation of results.

The idea of the ALMM Solver, including functional requirements, is described in [16]. Figure 1 presents the proposed modular structure of the ALMM Solver. The solver consist of four basic functional modules:

- The ALM Modeler, which allows one to define the model of the problem in ALMM methodology,
- The Algorithm Module, which provides a collection of already implemented methods and algorithms, and allows one to design new ones,
- SimOpt, which solves given problems (by generating trajectories) on the basis of the ALMM methodology,
- The Results Interpreter, which identifies the final solution of the given problem in the data (generated trajectories) stored in the solver database.

The core of the ALMM Solver is SimOpt together with the Algorithm Module. Apart from its main role (searching solutions to the problems), SimOpt has to provide following features:

- writing output data in a database,
- logging run-time information to output stream,
- obtaining algorithms from Algorithm Module,
- cooperating with an additional software layer that corresponds to implementation of individual features for different classes of problems

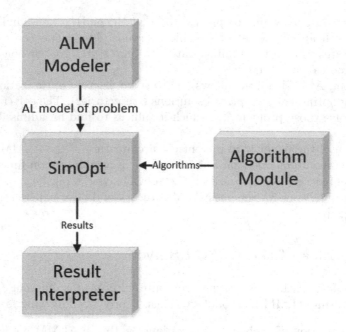

**Fig. 1.** Modules of the ALMM Solver [16]

These requirements entail building SimOpt as an abstract module. We decided to use a framework design. The SimOpt module is implemented partly in a way open for extensions and partly in a way closed for modifications. Modules related to building trajectories within the ALMM methodology are closed, and modules connected with modeling of the given problem are open.

The ALM Modeler module allows one to create a model of a problem. It has to be saved in a form understandable for the SimOpt module. In the current version of the solver, the algebraic-logical models of the problems are implemented using a programming language. The ALM Modeler is constantly developed. It is intended to provide models of problems that belong to classes known by the solver. Thus, the ALM Modeler will have a repository of models for various optimization problems. The SimOpt module will obtain models from this knowledge base.

The Algorithm Module, which closely cooperates with SimOpt, provides a collection of already implemented methods and algorithms, and allows one to design new algorithms. It consists of two parts: the Algorithm Repository and the Algorithms Designer. Algorithm Repository stores methods and algorithms both in the database and as software libraries. These algorithms come from the Algorithm Designer. SimOpt and the Algorithm Module share common interface. The SimOpt module constitutes a frame for generating process trajectories within the ALMM methodology. It provides interfaces for all the algorithms, but their actual implementation is provided by Algorithm Module.

The Results Interpreter cooperates and communicates with the SimOpt module. It reads and analyses data uploaded by SimOpt to the database.

# 3  Non-Functional Requirements

Non-functional requirements describes how the use of application has an effect on user satisfaction and constitutes a software quality model. For over 60% of system architects, non-functional requirements are at the basis of software system architecture and technological choices [1]. Full model of software quality consists of following non-functional requirements:

- Functional suitability - the degree to which the software product provides functions that meet stated and implied needs (functional requirements).
- Reliability - the degree to which the software product: can maintain a specified level of performance, is available when required for use, recover the data directly affected in the case of a failure.
- Performance efficiency - the degree to which the software product provides appropriate performance, relative to the amount of resources used, under stated conditions.
- Operability - The degree to which the software product can be understood, learned, used and attractive to the user, when used under specified conditions.
- Security - the degree to which the software product provides protection from unauthorized disclosure of data or information, accidental or deliberate.
- Compatibility - the degree to which the software product can co-exist with other independent software and can be used in place of another specified software product for the same purpose in the same environment.
- Maintainability - the degree to which a system or computer program is composed of discrete components such that a change to one component has minimal impact on other components. Furthermore, its ability to reusing one asset in more than one software system, or in building other assets.
- Transferability - the degree to which the software product can be transferred from one environment to another [39].

We have set the non-functional requirements and created a model of software quality for the ALMM Solver. We were guided by the need to develop a platform that is easy to extend with new functionalities. Another important feature of the solver is its ability to integrate with other systems. The created quality model meets the following non-functional requirements: functional suitability, reliability, operability, compatibility, maintainability. These are the characteristics of the quality model for the solver:

- Functional suitability - our solver satisfies non-functional requirements necessary at the current stage of development (which are described in [16]). Applied data structures allow to implement any model of the problem prepared according to the ALMM methodology. Architecture of the solver standardizes building ALM models of problems through designed data structures. We also developed common rigorous language (Ubiquitous Language [20], [41]) for the ALMM methodology. This created language improves understanding of the problem and communication between the development team and domain experts. We did not introduce restrictions on the calculation accuracy.

Thus the ALMM Solver allows one to perform calculations with an accuracy resulting from hardware limitations.

- Reliability - the SimOpt module is designed using the component architecture [32], [29], [28], [33], [37]. This allowed us to reduce the software regression [36] during the development of the framework. One can choose the way of storing the data generated during calculations: as either storing the data in a database, or in-memory. Both methods have advantages and disadvantages. The database can store huge amount of data generated during the computation, but is much slower than in-memory storage. In-memory storage, however, does not guarantee restoring all the processing data after an unexpected interruption.

- Operability - There are two kinds of solver users. Users of the first type simply run the solver in order to perform calculations for a given problem. Users of the second type design models, algorithm and methods. The solver is started by a special launching application which requires input information: instance data and simulation parameters (methods, algorithm, etc). Also, some external application can start the solver. In order to facilitate designing models and algorithms, there is a need to fit up ALM Modeler and Algorithm Designer with specially developed meta language. This language should eliminate the need of using programming languages and thus allow more users to make use of these modules.

- Compatibility - designing the solver as a framework allows one to use it as an external module in other systems. The SimOpt framework is a standardized set of rules for building trajectories in order to find a solution to a problem. The SimOpt module can be started by means of either dedicated or external software application and supports a real-time analysis of the results. Specially designed API is provided, which enables integration of the solver with external applications.

- Maintainability - the solver architecture is open for extensions. In places where it is intended, additional functionality may be included due to development of the ALMM methodology. The other hand, the components (or their parts) that constitute the core of the ALMM methodology are closed for modifications. Application of good design patterns and high code coverage (unit tests) decreases the risk of regression bugs after modifications [36]. Individual parts of the solver can thus be modified and developed almost without any influence on the other modules and components. Each algorithm, once applied in calculations, is stored in the Algorithm Repository, which allows using it also in other problems. There is also an advanced module for logging run-time information (errors, warnings, infos) to a variety of output streams. It allows for real-time monitoring of the simulation (calculations).

## 4    Architecture of the ALMM Solver

ALMM Solver meets the functional and non-functional requirements. The solver architecture supports construction of extensions and integration with other

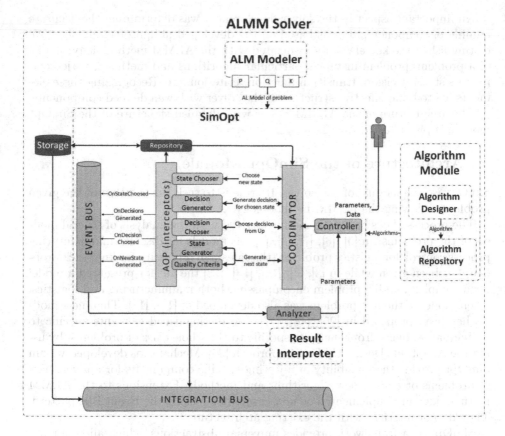

**Fig. 2.** Structure of ALMM Solver

systems. As proper system architecture is the foundation of good quality software, we have designed the solver in accordance with the best practices, design patterns and principles. This has required both strategic and tactical decisions during the design process [19].

Our strategic decisions were: use the Domain-Driven Design approach [20], [41], develop the main module of the solver as a framework, use the Event-Driven Architecture [41] and aspect oriented programming [30].

Our tactical decisions, which are solutions of specific implementation problems and have a lesser impact on a software architecture, were associated with using Creational Patterns, Structural Patterns, Behavioral Patterns [24], the repository pattern [20], [41], event bus, the plug-in pattern [22]. We also used SOLID principles developed by Robert C. Martin to help keeping a software product as simple for maintain and as easy to extend as possible [35].

ALMM Solver is a very complex tool. Depending on the given problem, it requires different data structures and algorithms. There was a high risk of creating a system that is a "Big Ball of Mud" [21] or have a code smell symptom [23]. This risk was minimized by creating SimOpt as a framework, by proper requirements analysis, and by using relevant design patterns and principles.

An important aspect in the solver development was determining the accurate naming of components. It was based on the developed ubiquitous language. We distinguished the key elements associated with the ALMM methodology: model of a problem, problem instance, particular algorithms and methods, trajectory, process state, decision, transition function, criterion, etc. Recognizing these elements led to build effective structure of the solver with well defined components.

The architecture of the ALMM Solver with detailed structure of the SimOpt module is presented in Fig. 2.

# 5    Architecture of the SimOpt Module

SimOpt is core module of the solver. Its role is to seek the solution of the given problem, following the ALMM methodology.

The process of designing the module started with the analysis of several models of the problems. In [9], [6], [7], [4], [5] AL models for discrete manufacturing process control, for logistics problems (the salesman problem), for knapsack problem, has been given while in [8], [3], [14], [13], [18] the author presented a model for a complex real-life problem encompassing both manufacturing and logistics. Then model of the last problem was also developed in [15], [11]. Then new models has been proposed in [25], [10], [17]. We distinguished elements specific to individual problems from elements specific to the whole class of problems, by using the Adaptable Design Up Front approach [34]. Mechanisms developed within SimOpt provide the possibility of injecting specific components for a given class of problems or adding new algorithms and methods. Extensions to the ALMM methodology are implemented as new components using the Event Bus pattern. They do not interfere with the existing architecture.

SimOpt as a framework provides universal abstractions, which allow for implementing any given model. It is built according to the component-based development. Components are loosely-coupled and perform a separate responsibilities [40] related to the ALMM methodology. They are implemented using the Inversion of Control Paradigm. SimOpt consists of several components: State Chooser, Decision Generator, Decision Chooser, State Generator, Quality Criteria and Coordynator, which coordinates the whole procedure of building a trajectory. Each of the components can be developed independently. They are loosely coupled. In effect, the risk of regression during their modification is low.

SimOpt is the core subdomain [20], [41] of solver. SimOpt acts as a Shared Kernel [20], [41], i.e., it is a common part for all classes of problems. Cooperation of the SimOpt module with the ALM Modeler and the Algorithm Module (which belong to other Bounded Contexts) is implemented using the Anticorruption Layer approach [20], [41]. This approach defines the principles on which cooperation of modules from different Bounded Contexts is implemented. Integration of SimOpt and the Algorithm Module is implemented in accordance with the plug-in pattern. This combination allows for extensions of the algorithms repository without recompiling the whole solver source code. The SimOpt module and the Result Interpreter module are mutually independent. The Result Interpreter module simply uses the data stored in the database by SimOpt.

SimOpt is designed according to the KISS rule [31] that recommends avoiding of complications in the implemented systems. Thus it realizes the basic pattern of the ALMM methodology, but has the infrastructure that allows for injections of additional components. It is done with the use of the event bus pattern, which is used in all places where domain events [41] occur as potential places for extensions.

SimOpt can use problem models created in two ways:

– designed by the ALM Modeler module. ALM Modeler will have a user interface enabling users to create a model of a given problem without knowing any programming language.
– implemented using a programming language in accordance with the interfaces provided by SimOpt. This option is for problems that do not belong to the classes known by the solver and, thus, cannot be designed within the ALM Modeler.

## 6    Solution Generation within the ALMM Solver

The process of finding a solution with the use of the ALMM Solver is as follows. In the launching application, a user selects an appropriate model of the problem, chooses methods and algorithms along with its parameters and uploads the instance data. These settings are stored in the Controller component, which than decides what actions individual component take. According to the Inversion Of Control paradigm, Controller is injected to all components of the SimOpt module: State Chooser, Decision Generator, Decision Chooser, State Generator, Quality Criteria.

After the initialization, the Coordinator component starts to operate, i.e., to execute the solution finding process. It is done by executing in a cycle appropriate components of the SimOpt module. Launch of each component is connected with executing of the relevant cross-cutting concerns (according to aspect oriented programming), e.g., recording the results of the component actions to the database. Writing to the database is performed using the repository design pattern. Launch of each component also launch relevant event which allow extending the procedure of generation of trajectories by the solver with additional elements.

In each cycle managed by Coordinator the next node (corresponding to a state) of the state tree is generated. Each cycle begins with the selection (by StateChooser) of the state for which the next state will be generated, according to chosen search strategy. For this state, DecisionGenerator generates a whole or a part of a set of possible decisions. From this set, DecisionChooser selects one decision, in accordance to a particular procedure specified in Controller. Controller decides which algorithms from the repository is to use in computations. Selected one is transferred to the SimOpt module using the Inversion Of Control paradigm and is injected to the appropriate component.

The decision selected by DecisionChooser, and the current state selected by StateChooser are sent to StateGenerator, where a new state is calculated, and to the QualityCriteria component, where the criterion value is calculated for this state. The state is verified whether it belongs to the set of non-admissible or goal states. A new node is created in the state tree. The node corresponds to the newly generated state. All the information connected with it is stored in the database. After generation of the node, a related event, to which the Analyzer component is subscribed, is generated. Analyzer performs the analysis of the new state and changes the parameters stored in Controller due to information gained during generation of the trajectory.

## 7    Conclusions

The paper presents results of the new research concerning the ALMM Solver, the tool for solving various discrete problems, especially NP-hard in particular dynamic problems. The idea of the solver based on ALMM paradigm and the initial architecture comes from Dudek-Dyduch E. and is developed by her research team.

The paper describes the architecture of the ALMM Solver and requirements regarding the solver, that includes funtional and non-functional requirements (functional suitability, reliability, operability, compatibility, maintainability). The solver architecture supports construction of extensions and integration with other systems. As proper system architecture is the foundation of good quality software, we have designed the solver in accordance with the best practices, design patterns and principles. The SimOpt module, the core of the ALMM Solver, is designed as a framework and it is implemented partly in a way open for extensions and partly in a way closed for modifications. Modules related to building trajectories within the ALMM methodology are closed, and modules connected with modeling of the given problem are open.

Further work will focus on developing the solver by adding new elements or improving old ones. At the same time new problems, methods and algorithms will be implemented.

## References

1. Ameller, D., Franch, X.: How Do Software Architects Consider Non-Functional Requirements: A Survey. In: Wieringa, R., Persson, A. (eds.) REFSQ 2010. LNCS, vol. 6182, pp. 276–277. Springer, Heidelberg (2010)
2. Barbucha, D., Czarnowski, I., Jędrzejowicz, P., Ratajczak-Ropel, E., Wierzbowska, I.: JABAT Middleware as a Tool for Solving Optimization Problems. T. Computational Collective Intelligence 2, 181–195 (2010)
3. Dudek-Dyduch, E.: Simulation of some class of discrete manufacturing processes. In: Proc. of European Congress on Simulation, Praha (1987)
4. Dudek-Dyduch, E.: Formalization and Analysis of Problems of Discrete Manufacturing Processes. Scientific Bulletin of AGH University, Automatyka 54 (1990) (in Polish)

5. Dudek-Dyduch, E.: Control of discrete event processes - branch and bound method. In: Proc. of IFAC/Ifors/Imacs Symposium Large Scale Systems: Theory and Applications, Chinese Association of Automation, vol. 2, pp. 573–578 (1992)
6. Dudek-Dyduch, E.: Discrete determinable processes - compact knowledge-based model, Notas de Matematica No 137, Universidad de Los Andes, Merida, Venezuela (1993)
7. Dudek-Dyduch, E.: Heuristic algorithms - formal approach based on compact knowledge-based model, Notas de Matematica No 138, Universidad de Los Andes, Merida, Venezuela (1993)
8. Dudek-Dyduch, E.: Learning based algorithm in scheduling. Journal of Intelligent Manufacturing 11(2), 135–143 (2000)
9. Dudek-Dyduch, E.: Information systems for production management (in Polish) Wyd. Poldex, Krakow (2002)
10. Dudek-Dyduch, E.: Modeling Manufacturing Processes with Disturbances - A New Method Based on Algebraic-Logical Meta-Models. In: Rutkowski, L., Korytkowski, M., Scherer, R., Tadeusiewicz, R., Zadeh, L.A., Zurada, J.M. (eds.) ICAISC 2015. LNCS, vol. 9120, pp. 350–360. Springer, Heidelberg (2015)
11. Dudek-Dyduch, E., Dutkiewicz, L.: Substitution Tasks Method for Discrete Optimization. In: Rutkowski, L., Korytkowski, M., Scherer, R., Tadeusiewicz, R., Zadeh, L.A., Zurada, J.M. (eds.) ICAISC 2013, Part II. LNCS, vol. 7895, pp. 419–430. Springer, Heidelberg (2013)
12. Dudek-Dyduch, E., Dyduch, T.: Scheduling some class of discrete processes. Proc.of 12th IMACS World Congress, Paris (1988)
13. Dudek-Dyduch, E., Dyduch, T.: Formal approach to optimization of discrete manufacturing processes. In: Hamza M.H (ed) Proc. of the Twelfth IASTED Int. Conference Modelling, Identification and Control. Acta Press Zurich (1993)
14. Dudek-Dyduch, E., Dyduch, T.: Learning algorithms for scheduling using knowledge based model. In: Rutkowski, L., Tadeusiewicz, R., Zadeh, L.A., Żurada, J.M. (eds.) ICAISC 2006. LNCS (LNAI), vol. 4029, pp. 1091–1100. Springer, Heidelberg (2006)
15. Dudek-Dyduch, E., Kucharska, E.: Learning method for co-operation. In: Jędrzejowicz, P., Nguyen, N.T., Hoang, K. (eds.) ICCCI 2011, Part II. LNCS, vol. 6923, pp. 290–300. Springer, Heidelberg (2011)
16. Dudek-Dyduch, E., Kucharska, E., Dutkiewicz, L., Rączka, K.: ALMM solver - A tool for optimization problems. In: Rutkowski, L., Korytkowski, M., Scherer, R., Tadeusiewicz, R., Zadeh, L.A., Zurada, J.M. (eds.) ICAISC 2014, Part II. LNCS, vol. 8468, pp. 328–338. Springer, Heidelberg (2014)
17. Dutkiewicz L., Kucharska E., Rączka K., Grobler-Dębska K.: ST Method Based Algorithm for the Supply Routes for Multi-location Companies Problem. In: Kacprzyk J. (ed.) Advances in Intelligent Systems and Computing (to appear) ISSN 2194-5357
18. Dyduch, T., Dudek-Dyduch, E.: Learning based algorithm in sheduling. In: Proc of Int. Conf. on Industrial Engineering and Production Management, Lyon, vol. 1, pp. 119–128 (1997)
19. Eden, A.H.: Strategic Versus Tactical Design. In: Proceedings of the 38th Annual Hawaii International Conference on System Sciences, HICSS 2005 (2005)
20. Evans, E.: Domain-Driven Design: Tackling Complexity in the Heart of Software. Prentice-Hall (2003)
21. Foote, B., Yoder, J.: Big Ball of Mud. In: Fourth Conference on Patterns Languages of Programs (1999)

22. Fowler, M.: Patterns of Enterprise Application Architecture (2002)
23. Fowler, M.: Refactoring. Improving the Design of Existing Code. Addison-Wesley (1999)
24. Gamma, E., Helm, R., Johnson, R., Vlissides, J.: Design Patterns: Elements of Reusable Object-Oriented Software. s.l.: Addison-Wesley (1994)
25. Grobler-Dębska, K., Kucharska, E., Dudek-Dyduch, E.: Idea of switching algebraic-logical models in flow-shop scheduling problem with defects. In: The 18th International Conference on Methods and Models in Automation and Robotics, MMAR Proceedings, pp. 532–537 (2013)
26. Harrison, N., Avgeriou, P.: Pattern-Driven Architectural Partitioning: Balancing Functional and Non-functional Requirements. In: Second International Conference on Digital Telecommunications, ICDT 2007 (2007)
27. Johnson, R.E., Foote, B.: Designing Reuseable Classes (1988)
28. Jurgens, D.: Survey on software engineering for scientific applications - reuseable software, grid computing and application. Informatikbericht 2009?02, Institut fur Wissenschaftliches Rechnen, Technische Universitat Braunschweig, Braunschweig (2009)
29. Kaur, A.: Kulvinder Singh Mann. Component based software engineering. International Journal of Computer Applications 2(1), 105–108 (2010)
30. Kiczales, G.: Aspect-Oriented Programming. In: Akşit, M., Matsuoka, S. (eds.) ECOOP 1997. LNCS, vol. 1241, pp. 220–242. Springer, Heidelberg (1997)
31. KISS Principle, http://people.apache.org/~fhanik/kiss.html
32. Krosche, M.: A Generic Component-Based Software Architecture for the Simulation of Probabilistic Models, Dissertation (2013)
33. Lau, K., Wang, Z.: Software componentmodels. IEEE Transactions on Software Engineering 33(10), 709–724 (2007)
34. Makabee, H.: http://effectivesoftwaredesign.com/adaptable-design-up-front/
35. Martin, C.R.: http://butunclebob.com/ArticleS.UncleBob.PrinciplesOfOod
36. Osherove, R.: The Art of Unit Testing: With Examples in.Net. Manning Publications Co. (2013)
37. Ravichandran, T., Rothenberger, M.A.: Software reuse strategies and component markets. Communications of the ACM 46(8), 109–114 (2003)
38. Sękowski, H., Dudek-Dyduch, E.: Knowledge based model for scheduling in failure modes. In: Rutkowski, L., Korytkowski, M., Scherer, R., Tadeusiewicz, R., Zadeh, L.A., Zurada, J.M. (eds.) ICAISC 2012, Part II. LNCS, vol. 7268, pp. 591–599. Springer, Heidelberg (2012)
39. Software engineering - Software product Quality Requirements and Evaluation (SQuaRE) - Software and quality in use models, ISO/IEC 25010:2008
40. Wirfs-Brock, R., McKean, A.: Object Design: Roles, Responsibilities, and Collaborations. Addison Wesley (2002)
41. Vernon, V.: Implementing Domain-Driven Design. s.l.: Addison-Wesley Professional (2013)
42. http://www.jacop.eu/
43. http://www.solver.com

# Graph-Based Optimization of Energy Efficiency of Street Lighting

Adam Sędziwy[(✉)] and Leszek Kotulski

Department of Applied Computer Science, AGH University of Science
and Technology, al. Mickiewicza 30, 30-059 Kraków, Poland
{sedziwy,kotulski}@agh.edu.pl

**Abstract.** Designing energy efficient street lighting got an emerging domain due to technological potential of LED light sources. To profit those
solutions however one has to use effective computational methods enabling low-energy-solution finding. In this article we focus particularly
on the problem of discovering and removing over-illuminated areas being the side-effect of using typical lighting design methods, especially in
the case of non-regular areas. We propose the approach which combines
hypergraph-based modeling of objects, the concept of *slashed graphs* and
heuristics addressing optimal lighting issue. The synergy of those three
parts creates practically usable methodology for time and energy efficient
outdoor lighting design.

**Keywords:** Slashed graphs · Street lighting · Agent systems · Bulk
computations

## 1 Introduction

The emergence of advanced, LED-based technologies on the outdoor lighting
market opened new perspectives on creating energy efficient and well suited
lighting infrastructures [18]. Two most important drivers staying behind are:
luminous flux dimming capability (which was rudimentarily present for high-
intensity discharge lamps, abbrev. HID) and possibility of *shaping* a photometric
solid of a fixture [6,9]. In particular, the former property is not reachable in other
technologies: dimming HID or metal halide lamps is not feasible in the full range
(i.e., 0-100%) and reduces the source's lifetime. Besides that, the onset time
of typical light sources is significantly higher than for LEDs, and makes those
sources unsuitable for an adaptive street lighting.

A lot of commercial photometric software profiting of those properties are
available on the market. Their common feature however is ability of making
computations for a single scene only. Thus, if one aims at computing photometry for some region consisting of several blocks and including a couple of streets
then he needs to set up manually a sequence of separate scenes corresponding
to particular lighting situations. Another problem arising in this context is computing photometry and optimizing street lighting configuration for non-typical
(contrary to straight, uniform street sections) road situations like cross roads,

© Springer International Publishing Switzerland 2015
L. Rutkowski et al. (Eds.): ICAISC 2015, Part II, LNAI 9120, pp. 515–526, 2015.
DOI: 10.1007/978-3-319-19369-4_46

conflict areas and so on. The typical approach to photometric design results in producing over-illuminated scenes and thus increased energy usage (see [2]).

Summarizing the issues mentioned above: there is no tool enabling time efficient and scalable photometric computing, especially for non-standard scenes. To illustrate the problem of a time efficient solution finding in lighting design tasks let us consider the trivial example of a row of ten LED lamps[1], being designed along some motor road. Since the considered installation is made from scratch the following parameters may be varied to find the best solution:

1. fixture model/photometric solid (500 – variants),
2. fixture mounting angle (from $0°$ to $20°$ with step $1°$ – 21 variants),
3. pole height (from $6m$ to $12m$ with step $0.1m$ – 61 variants),
4. lamp spacing (from $20m$ to $40m$ with step $0.1m$ – 201 variants),
5. arm length (from $0m$ to $2m$ with step $0.1m$ – 21 variants),
6. dimming level (from $0\%$ to $99\%$ with step $1\%$ – 100 variants).

The resultant total number of variants to be checked is $N \approx 2.7 \times 10^{11}$.

The computing time for a single variant takes about $0.1\ s$, so the total time of the calculation (for all variants) takes over 14 years on a single 4-core processor. What is worse, in real life cases we design photometric scenes containing thousands of lamps (e.g., about 7,000 lamps in SOWA Project carried out in Cracow, Poland). We suggest to solve the above problem twofold: by applying AI methods to finding an optimal variants and by parallelization of computations.

In this paper the representation of slashed graphs [21] as a formal background for this purpose is proposed. It offers a flexible and scalable formal framework for scene modeling, allowing parallelizing and distributing the photometric computations. It enables defining a set of computational tasks ascribed to subsequent lighting situations covering the entire considered area. The proposed methodology is based on a problem's graph representation which is a broadly used in various domains [15,17,14,7,8,11,19]. Such a graph model constitutes an environment for a multi-agent system. Particular agents are ascribed to subtasks performed in parallel and an agent's knowledge is sewn in a graph structure [16,12,13].

The key property of this methodology is processing a given area not "as is" i.e., with some assigned set of luminaires but analyzing all lamps available in its neighborhood, selecting those among them which influence a scene and, in the sequel, dividing logically a scene into subareas having different levels of illumination. The objective is to equalize those levels, reducing power usage overhead and stay aligned with mandatory lighting standards. Such an approach allows for more accurate adjustment of lamp work parameters (dimming, photometric solid) and thus minimizing the power consumption.

Although a single task (i.e., made on one scene) seems to be a low complexity operation, from the perspective of an entire considered urban space however we face the scalability related issue. To overcome this problem we use *slashed*

---

[1] Computing time may be regarded as constant wrt the number of poles.

*graphs* model introduced in [21] This formalism was introduce to support parallel distributed computations.

The structure of the article is organized as follows. In the next section the problem formulation will be introduced. Sections 3 and 4 contain formal basics of used graph models: the short overview of the used hypergraph representation of complex solids and the slashed graphs model mentioned above. The way of formulating a computational task is presented in Section 5 while an overall computation process will be discussed in Section 6. The final conclusion may be found in Section 7.

## 2    Problem Formulation

The main objective of the outdoor lighting design is preparing infrastructure which fulfills mandatory standards ([3,4,10]) related to lamps performance. Those norms are expressed quantitatively by threshold values of certain photometric quantities which have to be ensured by a lighting system. Among those quantities are: average illuminance – $E_{avg}$, average luminance – $L_{avg}$, longitudinal and overall uniformity – $U_l$ and $U_o$ respectively, threshold increment – $TI$, surround ratio – $SR$ and others. Values of those parameters for each a road must not cross the established thresholds defined by a standard. The sample set of norms given for street lighting is shown in Table 1.

**Table 1.** ME lighting classes according to DIN EN 13201-2

| class | $L_{avg} [cd/m^2]$ [min. value] | $U_o$ [min. value] | $U_l$ [min. value] | $TI [\%]$ [max. value] | $SR$ [min. value] |
|---|---|---|---|---|---|
| ME1 | 2.0 | 0.4 | 0.7 | 10 | 0.5 |
| ME2 | 1.5 | 0.4 | 0.7 | 10 | 0.5 |
| ME3a | 1.0 | 0.4 | 0.7 | 15 | 0.5 |
| ME3b | 1.0 | 0.4 | 0.6 | 15 | 0.5 |
| ME3c | 1.0 | 0.4 | 0.5 | 15 | 0.5 |
| ME4a | 0.75 | 0.4 | 0.6 | 15 | 0.5 |
| ME4b | 0.75 | 0.4 | 0.5 | 15 | 0.5 |
| ME5 | 0.5 | 0.35 | 0.4 | 15 | 0.5 |
| ME6 | 0.3 | 0.35 | 0.4 | 15 | - |

When designing lighting for a zone consisting of numerous streets and pedestrian routes one has to perform computations for multiple lighting situation ($LS$) assigned to particular areas. Each $LS$ is defined for a single area $A$ which may be either homogeneous in terms of geometric properties (number of lanes, width, surface type) and street lamps locations (arrangement, spacing, setback, overhang) or non-regular e.g., for some types of road junctions (see Fig.1). Applying the results reusing approach in the former case [22] may reduce significantly the computing time. Another factor which has to be taken into account while considering an $LS$, is the presence of objects (buildings) dropping shadows on it.

In those circumstances some luminaires may be excluded from computations as not affecting a scene.

Figure 1 shows the trivial example of a scene: the cross road (area $A_1$) with three incoming streets (areas $A_2, A_3, A_4$) and adjacent sidewalks. Luminaires are marked with diamonds. Moreover, circles indicating light ranges are shown for selected lamps[2]. A particular lighting situation, delimited with a dashed line, consists of a relevant area and luminaires located on it. It should be stressed that a given area may be affected by luminaires belonging to foreign $LS$'s, for example lamps 2 and 3 standing on $A_2$ influence illuminance on $A_1$.

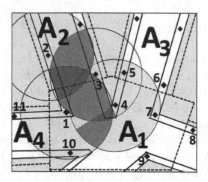

**Fig. 1.** The sample crossroad. The diamond marks denote luminaires and gray areas - buildings. For the better readability the figure illustrates an impact of four lamps only (numbered $1 \ldots 4$) and the lamps are denoted with indices only (instead of $F_i$). A circle delimits a range of a single luminaire while colors are related to overlapping of particular ranges: *red* – 3 lamps, *orange* – 2 lamps, *yellow* – single luminaire

The complete input for photometric computations performed for a given $LS$, is a compound of road related data $(\mathbf{R}_d)$ and luminaires related data $(\mathbf{L}_d)$. The latter ones include a set of fixtures which luminous flux affects a given area. This set will be denoted as $\mathrm{Aff}(A)$ where $A$ is an area underlying $LS$. For Figure 1 we have: $\mathrm{Aff}(A_1) = \{F_1, F_2, \ldots F_{11}\}$. The impact of other fixtures is neglectable due to actual distances.

## 3    Graph Model of Urban Space

To enable the efficient analysis and modeling of large-scale or complex systems, their description needs to be formalized. Such a formalization is required prior to computer aided problem solving. In the paper [20] the 3D-compliant hypergraph model of an urban space was introduced. Hypergraph formalism is broadly accepted and used in the 3D modeling [5,1,24]. In this model both buildings and areas (e.g. streets, sidewalks, squares, lawns) are represented by hypergraphs[3]

---

[2] Note that a circle is valid only for a photometric solid having radial symmetry. We make here such a simplifying assumption for more clarity.

[3] In the case of surfaces a given area is assigned with an infinitesimal height to obtain 3D object which, in the sequel, may be described by a hypergraph.

with fixtures (luminaires) as their vertices (or more precisely, vertices of a certain type).

Besides hypergraphs, we will also use the typical graph model (see Section 4) as it will be obtained as a result of hypergraphs *aggregation*. The basics of the hypergraph approach and its transition to the regular graphs presented below.

**Hypergraphs.** Let $T$ will be a polyhedron consisting of $n$ faces $(f_1, f_2, \ldots f_n)$, $k$ edges $(a_1, a_2, \ldots a_k)$ and $m$ vertices $(h_1, h_2, \ldots h_m)$. Hypergraph $H_T$ representing the polyhedron $T$ is a tuple $H_T = (V, A, H)$, where $V = \{f_1, f_2, \ldots f_n\}$ is a set of hypergraph nodes (representing physical faces), $H = \{h_1, h_2, \ldots h_m\}$ is a set of hypergraph hyperedges (representing physical vertices), and $HA = \{a_1, a_2, \ldots a_k\}$ is a set of hypergraph edges (representing physical edges).

Figure 2 presents the hypergraph model of a cuboid. For the case of two adhering polyhedrons, we introduce the additional, logical type of edge (referred to as an *external edge*), which denotes adherence of two faces.

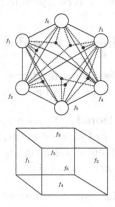

**Fig. 2.** A hypergraph representation of a cuboid

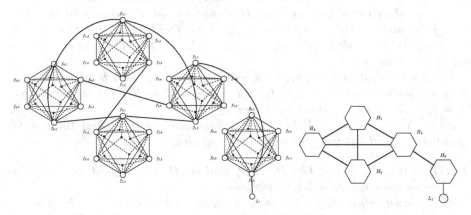

**Fig. 3.** A hypergraph model of adhering polyhedrons (left) and its aggregated form (right)

In some cases, one requires general information about an overall object structure rather than its detailed properties. In such circumstances, it is sufficient to get information about relations among particular components of a considered scene. To accomplish that, we transform (*collapse*) hypergraphs to vertices using *aggregating transformation*. Such an operation, also referred to as *synthesis*, is described in [23]. All data describing how external edges (i.e. edges connecting two adjacent solids) were attached to the collapsed hypergraph are stored as values of supplementary attributes of those edges. Thanks to that the inverse operation, namely *analysis*, may be executed [23].

Figure 3 (left) presents a hypergraph model of five adhering cuboidal objects (external edges are represented as thick lines). Additionally, one of them has a point object attached (which may represents fixture/luminaire). In Figure 3, the aggregated form of this composite object is presented: hexagonal nodes $(H_1, \ldots, H_5)$ correspond to *collapsed* hypergraphs.

## 4    Slashed Graphs

In this section a brief overview of a distributed graph representation will be presented. This model is crucial for parallel execution of photometric computations.

**Definition 1.** $(\mathcal{L}, \mathcal{A})$-*graph is a digraph* $G = (V, E)$, *where* $V$ *is nonempty, finite set of indexed nodes*, $E \subseteq V \times (\mathcal{L} \times \mathcal{A}) \times V$ *is a set of arcs and* $\mathcal{L}, \mathcal{A}$ *denote respectively a set of labels and attributes of edges. The family of* $(\mathcal{L}, \mathcal{A})$-*graphs will be denoted as* $\mathcal{G}$.

In the sequel we introduce the notion of *slashed form* of a graph, being fundamental for $(\mathcal{L}, \mathcal{A})$-graph decomposition considered further.

**Definition 2.** *Let* $G = (V, E) \in \mathcal{G}$. *We define a set* $\{G_i\}_{i \in I}$ *of graphs in the following manner: (i)* $G_i = (V_i, E_i) \in \mathcal{G}$ *and* $V_i = C_i \cup D_i$, $C_i \cap D_i = \emptyset$, *where* $C_i$ *is a set of* **internal vertices** *and* $D_i$ *denotes a set of* **dummy nodes**, *(ii)* $V = \bigcup_i C_i$, *where* $C_i \cap C_j = \emptyset$ *for* $i \neq j$, *(iii)* $\forall v \in D_i \exists! v' \in D_j (i \neq j)$ *such that* $v'$ *is a replica of a node* $v$; $\forall v \in D_i : d_{G_i^*}(v) = 1^4$, *(iv)* $\forall e \in E_i : e$ *is incident to at last one dummy node.*

An edge incident to a dummy node will be referred to as a **border edge**. A set of all border edges in a graph $G_i$ will be denoted as $E_i^b$. On the other side $E_i^c = E_i - E_i^b$ is a set of **internal edges** of $G_i$.

Let us denote $M = \mathcal{L} \times \mathcal{A}$ then $\{G_i\}$ defined above is a **slashed form** of $G$ (denoted as $\mathcal{G}$) iff following conditions are satisfied:

1. $\forall G_i^c = (C_i, E_i^c), \exists H_i \subset G : H_i \overset{\alpha}{\simeq} G_i^c$ *and* $H_i, H_j$ *are disjoint for* $i \neq j$ $(\overset{\alpha}{\simeq}$ *denotes isomorphism* $\alpha$ *between graphs).*
2. *There exists bijection* $f : M^2 \to M$ *such that for* $(e, e') \in E_i^b \times E_j^b (i \neq j)$, *where* $e = (x_c, m, v) \in C_i \times M \times D_i$, $e' = (v', m', y_c) \in D_j \times M \times C_j$ *and* $v'$ *is a replica of a node* $v$, *there exists exactly one edge* $e_{ij} = (x, m_e, y) \in E$ *such that* $x_c = \alpha(x), y_c = \alpha(y)$ *and* $f(m, m') = m_e$. $e_{ij}$ *is referred to as a* **slashed edge** *associated with dummy nodes* $v, v'$.
3. $\forall e = (x, m, y) \in E : (i) \exists! e_c \in E_i^c$ *for some* $i$, *such that* $e_c = \alpha(e)$ *or (ii)* $\exists! (v, v') \in D_i \times D_j$ *for some* $i, j$, *such that* $e$ *is a slashed edge associated with dummy nodes* $v, v'$.

$G_i \in \mathcal{G}$ *is referred to as a* **slashed component** *of a graph* $G$.

---

[4] For a given digraph $G$, $G^*$ denotes an underlying undirected graph.

Having the formal definition of a graph's slashed form we may introduce two complementary mappings. $\Delta : \mathcal{G} \rightarrow \mathcal{G} \times \mathcal{G}$ decomposes $X \in \mathcal{G}$ into slashed components $X_1, X_2 \in \mathcal{G}$ and $\Psi : \mathcal{G} \times \mathcal{G} \rightarrow \mathcal{G}$ merges two slashed components and removes all relevant dummy nodes shared by both of them.

In Figure 4 the centralized and slashed form of a certain graph $G$ are shown. Internal nodes are denotes as circles ($\bigcirc$), and dummy ones as squares ($\square$). Moreover the following indexing convention is applied (see Figure 4b).

– An index of an internal node has the form $(i, k)$, where $i$ is an unique identifier of a slashed component $G_i \in \mathcal{G}$ and $k$ is an unique (in $G_i$) node index.
– A dummy node index has the form $(-1, k)_r$, where $k$ is a globally unambiguous identifier of a pair of dummy nodes and $r$ is a reference of a slashed component containing the complementary replica of a given dummy node. Using reference $r$ enables instant retrieving of a dummy node's replica.

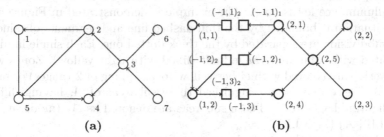

**Fig. 4.** (a) Graph $G$ (b) $\mathcal{G}$ representation

The above definition of a slashed representation may be too complicated for practical use. For that reason two transformations, namely Split and Merge, enabling migration between centralized and distributed graph model were introduced in [21]. The complexity of both operations is $\mathcal{O}(|E|)$ which means that it is linear wrt a number of dummy node pairs. The detailed discussion on their complexity in a distributed environment may be found in the mentioned article.

## 5   Defining Computational Tasks

Before the algorithm of $LS$'s generation will be introduced let us define the following auxiliary notation.

1. $V_{com}$ denotes a set of nodes corresponding to computational areas like streets with sidewalks, cross sections, conflict areas and so on.
2. $N(x \in V_{agg})$ is a set of aggregated nodes (i.e., representing some hypergraphs) being the neighbors of $x$.
3. $L_x$ for $x \in V_{agg}$ is a set of nodes labeled by $F$ (i.e., representing fixtures) which are neighbors of $x$.
4. $B(u, v) = \{x : lab(x) = B \wedge x \in N(u) \cap N(v)\}$ for $(u, v) \in V_{agg} \times V_{agg}$ denotes a set of vertices representing buildings (labeled with $B$) which are adjacent to areas represented by $u$ and $v$.

5. $B(u) = \bigcup_{v \in N(u)} B(u,v)$ is a set of all buildings adjacent to area $u$ and to some area neighboring $u$.

Suppose that an area $A$ represented by $v_A \in V_{com}$ is given. To perform photometric computations on $A$ one has to collect all luminaires affecting it i.e., $\text{Aff}(A)$. To accomplish that a neighborhood $N(v_A)$ has to be determined by using some search algorithm, e.g., BFS. Next, the influence of buildings adjacent to $A$ on its illumination has to be investigated: for each $v \in N(v_A)$ we compute a set $L_v^- = \{x : lab(x) = F \wedge B(v_A) \text{ blocks the influence of } F \text{ on } A\}$. Finally we get $\text{Aff}(A) = \bigcup_{v \in N(v_A)} (L_v - L_v^-)$.

An important phase of computations leading to definition of an $LS$ is related to evaluating the expression $B(v_A)$ *blocks the influence of* $F$ *on* $A$, present in the definition of $L_v^-$. This evaluation is accomplished by geometric analysis of an overlapping of physical objects and photometric solids.

Next step is subdividing an $LS$'s underlying area, $A$, into segments on the basis of illuminance levels on $A$. The example is demonstrated in Figure 5: the lighting situation is bounded by the thin dashed line and segments obtained by an area subdivision are separated by the thick dotted one. Each single luminaire is associated with a circular range limit (filled with light yellow). Zones where ranges overlap are colored with either yellow (overlapping of 2 ranges) or orange (3 ranges). There may be distinguished three subareas of $A$, having different average lighting levels (LL). Those subareas are denoted as $A_1$ (moderate LL), $A_2$ (low LL), $A_3$ (high LL).

*Remark.* Let us note that boundaries separating subareas are set in an arbitrary manner. In particular, to avoid too high granularity some lower limit for a subarea's size should be established.

The important property of the proposed approach is that lighting levels are tuned separately (for $A_1, A_2, A_3$) rather than for the entire area $A$. Thanks to this over-illuminating and related energy costs may be avoided. Prior to that $\text{Aff}(A_i)$ sets have to be determined:

- $\text{Aff}(A_1) = \{F_4, F_5, F_6, F_{11}\}$, $A_7 \notin \text{Aff}(A_1)$ because $A_1$ is shaded by $B_1$,
- $\text{Aff}(A_2) = \{F_1, F_4, F_6, F_7\}$,
- $\text{Aff}(A_3) = \{F_1, F_2, F_3, F_4, F_8, F_9, F_{10}\}$.

Note that complexity of determining $\text{Aff}(A_i)$ is polynomial with respect to both a number of luminaires and a number of streets incoming to $A$.

Finally we obtain:

$$LS_i = \{\mathbf{R}_d^{(i)}, \mathbf{L}_d^{(i)}\}, \text{ where } \mathbf{R}_d^{(i)} = A_i, \mathbf{L}_d^{(i)} = \text{Aff}(A_i).$$

Tuning of a luminaire relies on adjusting its luminous flux. This operation does not change a radius of a range circle itself (or in the real-life cases – a shape and size of a range area) because photometric solid may be alternated by modifying a fixture's optics only [6,9]. One can decrease however intensity (by dimming) and thereby practically minimize an illuminated zone. Assuming that $A_1$ illuminance is compliant with a standard, fluxes from $F_1, F_4$ and $F_7$ should be increased while fixtures $F_2, F_3, F_{10}$ have to be dimmed.

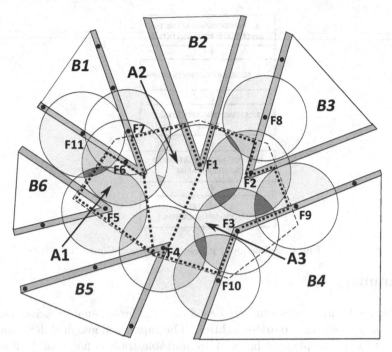

**Fig. 5.** The sample crossroad. Bolded points denote lamps and gray strips - sidewalks. Buildings are denoted with $B_1 \ldots B_6$ and considered luminaires with $F_1 \ldots F_{10}$. A circle delimits a range of a single luminaire while colors are related to overlapping of particular ranges: *orange* – 3 lamps overlapping, *yellow* – 2 lamps overlapping, *light yellow* – single luminaire range

# 6   Computations

Computational tasks introduced in the previous section are preformed on all aggregated nodes (see Fig.2) representing roads, sidewalks and other similar areas. Additionally, nodes representing buildings and other massive objects may be applicable during computations (see points 4 and 5 in Section 5). From the global perspective computations are made on a *normal* graph (i.e., not on a hypergraph) and they are node-oriented which means that almost all input data are located in aggregated vertices. For that reason a natural environment for their execution are slashed graphs introduced in Section 4.

From the local (aggregated node) perspective which covers blocks 3–5 in Figure 6, task execution may be either centralized (for simple, homogeneous lighting situations) or recursively distributed when a given area is partitioned (Section 2). For the latter case a slashed graph representation is used again: subsequent subareas are assigned with aggregated nodes hosting particular sub-calculations.

Regarding the polynomial complexities of subsequent phases of computations, the overall complexity is polynomial as well.

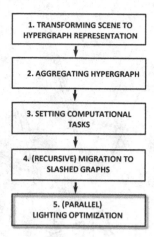

**Fig. 6.** Subsequent phases of computations

# 7    Summary

Well designed lighting infrastructure based on LED lamps enables achieving important energy savings in outdoor lighting. The rapid technological development in this field is not supported however by suitable tools capable of performing bulk computations, required in large scale retrofit projects (e.g., in cities) covering a huge number of streets, squares and so on. In previous articles (e.g., see [22]) the main effort was put into facilitating massive outdoor lighting optimization made on typical regular road situations. In this paper we fill this gap by introducing the enhancement to graph-based photometric computations, which enables optimizing lighting parameters for non-standard areas (e.g. non-regular crossroads). This goal is achieved by fine-grained analysis of a considered area and finding a balance between energy efficiency and requirements imposed by mandatory lighting standards.

The complexity of computations performed in the proposed methodology is polynomial but their execution in a distributed environment of slashed graphs reduces the computation time substantially. Computations performed in the SOWA project (7,000 lamps with altered parameters: pole height, arm length, fixture model, dimming) were completed in 6 hours.

# References

1. Ansaldi, S., De Floriani, L., Falcidieno, B.: Geometric modeling of solid objects by using a face adjacency graph representation. SIGGRAPH Comput. Graph. 19(3), 131–139 (1985), http://doi.acm.org/10.1145/325165.325218
2. Boyce, P., Hunter, C., Vasconez, S.: An evaluation of three types of gas station canopy lighting. Tech. rep., Lighting Research Center, Rensselaer Polytechnic Institute, Troy, NY 12180-3352 (December 2001)
3. British Standards Institution (BSI): Road lighting. performance requirements, bs en 13201-2:2003, London: BSI (2003)

4. Commission Internationale de l'Eclairage: Lighting of Roads for Motor and Pedestrian Traffic, CIE 115:2010, Vienna: CIE (2010)
5. De Floriani, L., Falcidieno, B.: A hierarchical boundary model for solid object representation. ACM Trans. Graph. 7(1), 42–60 (1988), http://doi.acm.org/10.1145/42188.46164
6. Doskolovich, L.L., Dmitriev, A.Y., Bezus, E.A., Moiseev, M.A.: Analytical design of freeform optical elements generating an arbitrary-shape curve. Appl. Opt. 52(12), 2521–2526 (2013), http://ao.osa.org/abstract.cfm?URI=ao-52-12-2521
7. Ehrig, H., Heckel, R., Korff, M., Löwe, M., Ribeiro, L., Wagner, A., Corradini, A.: Algebraic approaches to graph transformation II: Single pushout approach and comparison with double pushout approach. In: Rozenberg, G. (ed.) The Handbook of Graph Grammars and Computing by Graph Transformation. Foundations, vol. 1. World Scientific (1997)
8. Engelfriet, J., Rozenberg, G.: Node replacement graph grammars. In: Rozenberg, G. (ed.) Handbook of Graph Grammars and Computing by Graph Transformation, vol. I, ch. 1, pp. 1–94. World Scientific (1997)
9. Feng, Z., Luo, Y., Han, Y.: Design of led freeform optical system for road lighting with high luminance/illuminance ratio. Opt. Express 18(21), 22020–22031 (2010), http://www.opticsexpress.org/abstract.cfm?URI=oe-18-21-22020
10. Illuminating Engineering Society of North America (IESNA): American National Standard Practice For Roadway Lighting, RP-8-00, New York: IESNA (2000)
11. Dasso, J.: w., Păun, G., Rozenberg, G.: Grammar systems. In: Salomaa, A., Rozenberg, G. (eds.) Handbook of Formal Languages, vol. 2, ch. 4, pp. 155–213. Springer, Heidelberg (1997)
12. Kotulski, L.: Distributed graphs transformed by multiagent system. In: Rutkowski, L., Tadeusiewicz, R., Zadeh, L.A., Zurada, J.M. (eds.) ICAISC 2008. LNCS (LNAI), vol. 5097, pp. 1234–1242. Springer, Heidelberg (2008)
13. Kotulski, L.: GRADIS – Multiagent Environment Supporting Distributed Graph Transformations. In: Bubak, M., van Albada, G.D., Dongarra, J., Sloot, P.M.A. (eds.) ICCS 2008, Part III. LNCS, vol. 5103, pp. 644–653. Springer, Heidelberg (2008)
14. Kotulski, L., Strug, B.: Multi-agent system for distributed adaptive design. Key Engineering Materials 486, 217–220 (2011)
15. Kotulski, L., Sędziwy, A., Strug, B.: Heterogeneous graph grammars synchronization in {CAD} systems supported by hypergraph representations of buildings. Expert Systems with Applications 41(4, pt. 1), 990 – 998 (2014), http://www.sciencedirect.com/science/article/pii/S0957417413005307
16. Kotulski, L., Sędziwy, A.: GRADIS - The multiagent environment supported by graph transformations. Simulation Modelling Practice and Theory 18(10), 1515–1525 (2010)
17. Kotulski, L., Strug, B.: Distributed adaptive design with hierarchical autonomous graph transformation systems. In: Shi, Y., van Albada, G.D., Dongarra, J., Sloot, P.M.A. (eds.) ICCS 2007, Part II. LNCS, vol. 4488, pp. 880–887. Springer, Heidelberg (2007)
18. Ramadhani, F., Bakar, K., Shafer, M.: Optimization of standalone street light system with consideration of lighting control. In: 2013 International Conference on Technological Advances in Electrical, Electronics and Computer Engineering (TAEECE), pp. 583–588 (May 2013)
19. Rozenberg, G., Ehrig, H., et al. (eds.): Handbook on Graph Grammars and Computing by Graph Transformation 3 (Concurrency). World Scientific, Singapore (1999)

20. Sędziwy, A.: Representation of objects in agent-based lighting design problem. In: Zamojski, W., Mazurkiewicz, J., Sugier, J., Walkowiak, T., Kacprzyk, J. (eds.) Complex Systems and Dependability. AISC, vol. 170, pp. 209–223. Springer, Heidelberg (2012)
21. Sędziwy, A.: Effective graph representation for agent-based distributed computing. In: Jezic, G., Kusek, M., Nguyen, N.-T., Howlett, R.J., Jain, L.C. (eds.) KES-AMSTA 2012. LNCS, vol. 7327, pp. 638–647. Springer, Heidelberg (2012)
22. Sędziwy, A.: On acceleration of multi-agent system performance in large scale photometric computations. In: Barbucha, D., Le, M.T., Howlett, R.J., Jain, L.C. (eds.) KES-AMSTA. Frontiers in Artificial Intelligence and Applications, vol. 252, pp. 58–67. IOS Press (2013)
23. Sędziwy, A.: Graph-Based Computing Environment For Parallel Computations And Its Application To Lighting Design Problem. Wydawnictwo AGH (2015) (in press)
24. Strug, B., Grabska, E., Ślusarczyk, G.: Supporting the design process with hypergraph genetic operators. Advanced Engineering Informatics 28(1), 11–27 (2014), http://www.sciencedirect.com/science/article/pii/S1474034613000785

# Extended AMUSE Algorithm and Novel Randomness Approach for BSS Model Aggregation with Methodology Remarks

Ryszard Szupiluk[1,2], Tomasz Ząbkowski[3(✉)], Krzysztof Gajowniczek[3,4]

[1] T-Mobile Polska S.A, Marynarska 12, 02-674 Warsaw, Poland
[2] Warsaw School of Economics, Al. Niepodleglosci 162, 02-554 Warsaw, Poland
[3] Warsaw University of Life Sciences, Nowoursynowska 159, 02-787 Warsaw, Poland
[4] Systems Research Institute, Polish Acad. of Sciences, Newelska 6, 01-447 Warsaw, Poland
rszupi@sgh.waw.pl,
{tomasz_zabkowski,krzysztof_gajowniczek}@sggw.pl

**Abstract.** In this paper we propose application of extended AMUSE blind signal separation method to improve a model prediction. In our approach we assume, that results generated by any regression model usually include both constructive and destructive components. In case of a few models, some of the components can be common to all of them. Our aim is to find the basis elements via AMUSE algorithm and distinguish the components with the constructive influence on the modelling quality from the destructive ones. We extend the standard AMUSE algorithm for cases with strong noises. The crucial question is to determine number of delays used in separation process and define criterion for destructive components identification. We propose novel method of randomness analysis to solve above problems. Due to complexity of the whole BSS aggregation method we include some methodological remarks as the framework for proposed approach.

**Keywords:** Blind signal separation · Models aggregation · AMUSE algorithm

## 1    Introduction

In this paper we develop model aggregation concept based on multivariate decompositions via AMUSE algorithm taken form blind signal/source separation (BSS). The AMUSE algorithm is one of most popular second order statistics approach in BSS [4, 16, 18]. We utilize it in our aggregation/ensemble method. Having a few prediction models we treat their results as multivariate variable with interesting latent components [15]. Some of those basic latent components can be destructive so their identification and elimination should improve final prediction. In such methodology applying BSS methods with separation and again mixing stage can be treated as specific filtration processes [19]. Since the standard separation methods are addressed for the linear model of signals mixing then for the aggregation we use a stage with nonlinear transformation based on

© Springer International Publishing Switzerland 2015
L. Rutkowski et al. (Eds.): ICAISC 2015, Part II, LNAI 9120, pp. 527–537, 2015.
DOI: 10.1007/978-3-319-19369-4_47

neural network, to be able to imitate complex and more realistic relationships between the signals.

The BSS aggregation tasks set out a number of specific research problems related to both, the process of blind source separation and aggregation issues. These key issues include, inter alia, parameters determination of the separation algorithm and identification of destructive components. In general these issues can treated separately [17]. However, in case of AMUSE algorithm for which the key factor is the number of time delays, we show that there are such criteria that can solve two problems: the choice of number of delays and destructive components identification. For this reason we will propose a method for randomness analysis which is inspired by widely known R/S analysis [9,13]. The authors' contribution is variability measure which is addressed to the data with the temporal structure that directly describes the shape of the signal. The proposed method seems to be much more accurate and unambiguous than the R/S analysis.

To demonstrate the effectiveness of the proposed method, we will perform computer simulation using benchmark Friedman functions [7]. In this experiment, we will also compare the proposed method to the bagging. However, it should be noted, that although comparison of the final result is always possible, BSS aggregation differs from the typical aggregation methods like bagging or boosting [2,5,20]. These aspects are discussed in the section devoted to methodological issues and compared with other aggregation methods.

## 2    BSS and Model Aggregation Statement

Blind signal/source separation methods aim to find latent source signals hidden in their mixture [4,10]. The standard model for BSS is described as

$$\mathbf{x}(t) = \mathbf{A}\mathbf{s}(t) \,, \tag{1}$$

where $\mathbf{x} = [x_1,...,x_n]^T$ are observed signals, $\mathbf{s} = [s_1,...,s_m]^T$ are hidden (unknown) source signals, and $\mathbf{A} \in \Re^{n \times m}$ is unknown nonsingular matrix representing the mixing system. In our case for simplicity we assume $n=m$. The purpose of the BSS is proper separation (reconstruction, estimation) of the observed signals $\mathbf{x}$ into source signals $\mathbf{s}$, accepting the ambiguity according to the scale and permutation of source signals. To find the solution we need such matrix $\mathbf{W}$ that for

$$\mathbf{y}(t) = \mathbf{W}\mathbf{x}(t) = \mathbf{W}\mathbf{A}\mathbf{x}(t) = \mathbf{P}\mathbf{D}\mathbf{s}(t) \,, \tag{2}$$

where $\mathbf{P}$ is permutation matrix to define the order of estimated signals and $\mathbf{D}$ is a diagonal scaling matrix [4].

The basic BSS method can be applied for filtration approach what in prediction context can be treated as some kind of ensemble method [14]. Let's assume that observed signals $x_1,...,x_n$ are the prediction results of different modeling techniques. Assume further that the results are the combination of hidden components (source signals). Some of these components are constructive, associated with the actual value and the others are destructive in its nature, associated with incomplete data or imprecise recognition system (model).

Under assumption that the source signal vector **s** contains certain constructive components $\hat{s}_j$, for $j = 1,...,p$ and noises $\tilde{s}_l$, for $l = 1,...,q$ then we can write:

$$\mathbf{s}(t) = [s_1(t),..., s_n(t)]^T = [\hat{s}_1(t),..., \hat{s}_p(t), \tilde{s}_{p+1}(t)...., \tilde{s}_{p+q}(t)]^T . \tag{3}$$

After separation of latent components we reject the destructive ones (replacing them with zero $\tilde{s}_l = 0$) to obtain improved version $\hat{\mathbf{x}}$ of observed signals **x**:

$$\hat{\mathbf{x}}(t) = \mathbf{A}[\hat{s}_1(t),..., \hat{s}_p(t), 0_{p+1}(t)...., 0_n(t)]^T . \tag{4}$$

Let's note that term $\mathbf{A}\hat{s}(k)$ is equivalent with $\hat{\mathbf{A}}s(k)$ where $\hat{\mathbf{A}} = [a_1, a_2,..., a_n, \mathbf{0}, \mathbf{0},..., \mathbf{0}]$ is matrix created as a result of replacement a certain columns corresponding to destructive signals with zero vectors. The improved prediction, due to the elimination of noise can be written as a linear combination of the initial result as

$$\hat{\mathbf{x}}(t) = \hat{\mathbf{A}}\mathbf{W}\mathbf{x}(t) . \tag{5}$$

Thus, noise filtration with BSS methods can be treated as a form of aggregation.

Note that the components can be not pure constructive or destructive so their impact should have weight other than 0. It means that there could be a better mixing system than described by $\hat{\mathbf{A}}$ and it can be formulated even more general than the simple linear. The wide range of nonlinear mixing can be modelled as neural networks systems [8]. In our case we can take MLP neural network as the mixing system:

$$\hat{\mathbf{x}} = \mathbf{g}_2(\mathbf{B}_2[\mathbf{g}_1(\mathbf{B}_1\mathbf{s} + \mathbf{b}_1)] + \mathbf{b}_2) , \tag{6}$$

where $\mathbf{g}_i(.)$ is a vector of nonlinearities, $\mathbf{B}_i$ is a weight matrix and $\mathbf{b}_i$ is a bias vector respectively for $i$-th layer, $i = 1, 2$. If $\mathbf{B}_1 = \hat{\mathbf{A}}$ the first weight layer produces results related to (1), but we can expect that the weights in consecutive layers and applied nonlinearities can improve result in the learning process. In other words, in the learning process we search for better mixing then system starting from system described by $\hat{\mathbf{A}}$ (the initial weights are $\mathbf{B}_1(0) = \hat{\mathbf{A}}$).

The proposed process has the following steps:

1. Building the models and collecting their results in one multivariate variable.
2. Decomposition results into basis components by BSS methods.
3. Identification and elimination of destructive components from basis signals.
4. Returning from cleaned basis signals to "cleaned" prediction results, in simplest case by transformation inverse to decomposition.
5. Choice of the best results from "cleaned" prediction results.

## 3    AMUSE Algorithm for BSS Aggregation

To solve BSS problem in aggregation context we choose AMUSE algorithm. It is second order statistics type algorithm which adequate for data with temporal structure. The basic AMUSE type algorithm can be described as follow [4,16,18].

1. Let $\mathbf{z}(t) = \mathbf{x}(t)$, $p=0$, $\mathbf{W} = \mathbf{I}$;
2. Estimate the time delay correlation matrix [11] of observed signals with delay $p$

$$\mathbf{R}_z(p) = E\left[\mathbf{z}(t)\mathbf{z}^T(t-p)\right];\tag{7}$$

3. Perform the symetrization of $\mathbf{R}_z(p)$ by

$$\mathbf{R}_{zz}(p) = \frac{1}{2}\left[\mathbf{R}_z(p) + \mathbf{R}_z(p)^T\right];\tag{8}$$

4. Find matrix orthogonal matrix $\mathbf{Q}_p$ (eg. from SVD) which diagonalize the $\mathbf{R}_{zz}$;
5. Perform decorrelation for given delay

$$\mathbf{y}(t) = \mathbf{Q}_p\mathbf{z}(t);\tag{9}$$

6. Let $\mathbf{W} \leftarrow \mathbf{Q}_p\mathbf{W}$, $\mathbf{z}(t) \leftarrow \mathbf{y}(t)$, $p \leftarrow p+1$ and go to step 2 until chosen stop criterion is fulfilled;
7. The separation matrix is $\mathbf{W}$.

After AMUSE algorithm we have decorrelated time delay matrices $\mathbf{R}_{zz}(0) = \mathbf{I}$ and $\mathbf{R}_{zz}^T(1) = \mathbf{I}$. The basic version of the AMUSE algorithm assumes double iteration with p=0 and p=1 time delays. This ensures effective separation in a variety of cases and has a theoretical justification from the theorem 1, please refer to [3,4]. However, it should be noted that the AMUSE algorithm in its basic two-step version is effective only for the model described by (1). The presence of even small additive noise, what typically for other standard BSS algorithms can be neglected and allows to take model (1) and obtain satisfied separation quality, for AMUSE algorithm can result in lack of effective separation. Similarly, even in the standard mixing model where the source signals are highly affected by random noises, the problems with the correct separation may occur.

The solution to this problem is to take more delays and/or the exploration of a more general form of the correlation matrix to replace the standard (7). So the proposal is

$$\mathbf{R}_{G(z)}(p) = aE\left[\mathbf{z}(t)\tilde{\mathbf{z}}^T(t)\right] + bE\left[\mathbf{f}(\mathbf{z}(t))\mathbf{g}^T(\tilde{\mathbf{z}}(t))\right],\tag{10}$$

where $\tilde{\mathbf{z}}(t)$ stands for filtered version of the signals, $\mathbf{z}(t)$, $\mathbf{f}()$ and $\mathbf{g}()$ are the vectors of some chosen nonlinearities.

Note that depending on the values of the parameters $a$ and $b$ in (10) we obtain the weighted effect of the second order statistics or higher order statistics on the separation process. In case of (10) entered in the algorithm (7) – (9) for non-zero values of $b$, it will be typical for ICA (independent component analysis) algorithms.

The use of filtered matrix allows for a more effective separation if the noise is present, for both cases: the additive noises and the high noises in source signals.

## 4    Randomness Analysis for Parameters Estimation

The proposed aggregation technique with AMUSE algorithm requires solving two major problems. Firstly, we need to perform a proper separation and that means that we need to determine the number of iterations (the number of time delays). Secondly, we need to determine which components are destructive and which ones are these constructive. Basically, these are separate tasks, however, in the case of AMUSE algorithm they can be considered with common criterion to assesses both, the number of time delays and destructive components. For this purpose we will use a criterion based on which we will assess the randomness of the signal. To measure the randomness level will use two approaches. The first one is R/S analysis and Hurst exponent [6, 9,11,14]. The second one is inspired by the author's analysis of the R/S which is based on new volatility measure.

*R/S analysis.* In this method the fractal dimension is calculated using Hurst exponent $H$ [9]. To estimate the $H$ value the signal observations are divided into sequence of $n$-element subseries. For each subseries standard deviation $\sigma$ and $R$ range on cumulated subseries $y$ are calculated and from regression $\ln E \left( R / \sigma \right)_n = \ln c + H \ln n$ we find $H$. In practice, the determination of the H exponent from this basic formula is rather difficult and often ambiguous, since it should include linear portion of dependence taking into account the deterministic components characteristics. However, it requires some a priori knowledge as to the form of deterministic and random components which is in fact unattainable in case of blind source separation and BSS aggregation.

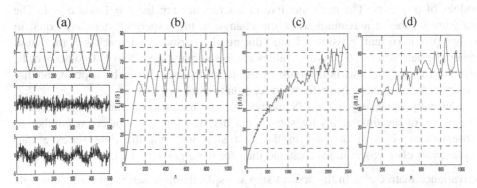

**Fig. 1.** Signals and their R/S characteristics: a) Signals used in the experiment: sinusoid, random noise N(0,1) and mixture of sinusoid and noise N(0,1) having SNR=-3dB; b) R/S characteristic of sinusoid; c) R/S characteristic of noise N(0,1); d) R/S characteristic of the mixture

Please refer to Fig. 1 to see the complexity of the R/S characteristics and possible problem to determine unambiguous regression relationship.

Therefore, in practice Hurst exponent can determined using other methods like variogram function or roughness length [1]. Variogram function which is a function $2\gamma(p)$ describing the degree of spatial dependence of stochastic process $z(t)$ It is defined as the expected squared increment of the values between locations $t$ and $t+p$ as $2\gamma(p) = E\left\{(z(t) - z(t+p))^2\right\}$. For small values of $p$ we can compute $H$ from $2\gamma(p) = p^{2H}$. Roughness length method computes root-mean-square roughness of the data in widows of size $p$. The standard deviation measured in widow of size p grows with widow length as $\sigma(p) = p^H$.

R/S analysis have gained popularity due to number of advantages in comparison to analysis based on the autocorrelation function [13]. However, as indicated above, in practice, the R/S analysis requires some detailed inspection of the signal what makes it difficult to use in algorithmic manner.

For this reason we propose new approach which is consistent to R/S analysis using variation analysis in intervals of different length but based on a new variability measure which is given as:

$$c_q(y) = E\left\{\| y(k) - y(k-q) \|_p \right\} \rho^{-1}(R) \approx \frac{1}{N-q} \sum_{t=q+1}^{N} \| y(t) - y(t-q) \|_p \rho^{-1}(R) \tag{11}$$

where $R = \max(y) - \min(y)\rho(u)$, $\rho(u)$ is zero indicator (unimodal Kronecker function), $\|.\|p$ is p-norm.

Depending on the parameters p and q, we get different characteristics that describe the average signal variation at selected time windows in relation to the total variability. Variability itself designates as a direct difference between successive values of p q units. The most intuitive characteristics are for p = 1 and q = 1. The measure reaches a maximum when the change in the respective steps are equal to range (the maximum possible change during the period), and reaches a minimum when the data is fixed. Therefore, values are in the range from 0 to 1. In other words, we can assume that this is the ratio of the total distance driven by a point moving along with signal shape (waveform) in relation to total range.

Currently, in analogy to the R/S analysis we are interested in relationships between fragments of the time series for subsequent division into parts of equal number of observations. This means that in the first step we split the time series $z$ into $k_1$ intervals of $n_1$ observations each and then for these parts $z_i$, $i = 1,...,k_1$ we calculate covariance matrix $c^{n_1}$. In the second step we split the time series $z$ into $k_2$ intervals of $n_2$ observations each and then for these parts $z_i$, $i = 1,...,k_2$ we calculate covariance matrix $c^{n_2}$. In subsequent stages we proceed similarly with all possible $n_i$, $k_i$ and finally we get a set of $M$ covariance matrices $c^n$.

The final aggregated information is determined as the following noise index:

$$C = \frac{1}{M} \sum_{i=1}^{M} c^{n_i}.$$  (12)

In Fig. 2 we present characteristics of the coefficient of variation C and H exponent at different levels of noise being present in deterministic signal. It can be noted that the precision of C index is much higher than the H exponent.

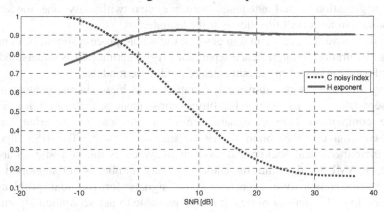

**Fig. 2.** Characteristics of the coefficient of variation C and H exponent at different levels of noise present in deterministic signal

The application of C index in the aggregation process can finally determine two issues: the choice of number of delays and destructive components identification. These include in particular:

1. Stop criterion to determine the number of delays used in the AMUSE algorithm which can be written as:

$$K = \min \sum_{i=1}^{n} C(y_i).$$  (13)

2. Identification of destructive components as these having the highest level of noise.

## 5   Methodological Discussion on BSS Aggregation

With proposed aggregation approach a question about the similarity to the other ensemble methods may arise. First of all, we underline that the aim of the method is prediction improvement which is the result of destructive component elimination. It is possible to benefit the prediction improvement since there are many effective separation methods applicable for multidimensional case, in which we assume many source signals and many observed signals formed as a mixture of signals. In proposed case, some of these observed mixed signals are considered as destructive. To separate them, we use separation algorithms defined for the multidimensional case, what can be presented as linear (or nonlinear) combination of observed signals.

In case of prediction task (such as electricity load prediction) the observed signals are simply the models outcomes (predicted values). Therefore, the proposed approach can be classified to the broad class of aggregation method. However, the combination of models is apparent from the technical aspect of separation algorithms. In our case, the proposed concept and its formal description is well established even for one model. Then in the model (1), the matrix A has dimension $1xn$. For this example, the term models aggregation is not adequate since we deal with only one model being decomposed but term BSS filtration is still adequate.

From the above we can see that in general, the whole process should be considered in terms of filtration or interference separation. Aggregation part is understood as the use of information nested in the outcomes of predictive models.

Taking into account the above, the formulated problem (in the context of blind source separation) and its solution has further consequences. First of all, it is assumed that the components (source signals) are of a physical nature what has been established as a result of blind source separation methods. The BSS algorithms despite their theoretical background have in many cases the heuristic nature. For instance, in AMUSE algorithm the choice of delay number is not supported by any formal argumentation. We expect that the signals for the real problems will correspond to real signals or noises. It is also possible to use separation algorithms as interpretable mathematical decomposition methods.

As a result, we have a number of fundamental differences in relation to conventional aggregation methods like boosting and bagging. The following main properties of the proposed approach can be distinguished:

(1) The elimination of the noise component of the physical nature (real noise/interference) should result in improved prediction on all criteria. The method don't assume optimization of one selected criterion, e.g. MSE, MAD or MAPE.

(2) The prediction improvement (after noise elimination) can be achieved taking into account small number of models (prediction results), and in extreme cases, having only one model.

(3) Since we decompose / separate the components of the physical nature, the form of predictive models is free of any assumptions. In other words, we can aggregate models (more specifically, the results of their prediction) regardless to specific modeling technique and the learning criterion.

Additionally, it should be noted that although the effect of aggregation appears here by the way, due to the properties (1) – (3) it fits into the basic idea of aggregation since it combines different results in the wider extent than just typical ensemble methods. In particular, it should be emphasized the lack of restrictive assumptions to the form of aggregated models, what causes that in many conventional methods, the process of aggregation is limited to different forms of averaging, performed for the same model (of the same architecture) but trained on the different subsets of data.

# 6    Practical Experiment

In this section we present the effectiveness of the presented aggregation method when it is used for: (a) aggregation using the AMUSE algorithm (referred to as *statistical aggregation*); (b) neural re-composition (referred to as *neural aggregation*). The results are then compared to the results obtained using bagging technique. The numerical experiments were conducted using Friedman's benchmark function [7] of the following form:

$$f(x) = 10 \cdot \sin(\pi \cdot x_1 \cdot x_2) + 20 \cdot (x_3 - \tfrac{1}{2})^2 + 10 \cdot x_4 + 5 \cdot x_5 + \sum_{i=6}^{10} 0 \cdot x_i \,, \tag{14}$$

$$y = f(x) + e \,,$$

where $x_i \sim U([0,1])$, $i = 1, \ldots, 10$ ( $x_6 \div x_{10}$ are surpluses), and noise $e \sim N(0,1)$.

We have created 25 MLP models with different architectures and activation functions. The training was performed on 2480 cases (permutations with repetitions out of 4000) with Levenberg-Marquard optimization algorithm. Although the training pairs are $\{x_1, \ldots, x_{10}, y\}$ and the estimated response value is $\hat{y}$, we measure the MSE for $f(x)$, because we expect the model to be robust for $e$. Then we have compared our method with one of the ensemble method – bagging.

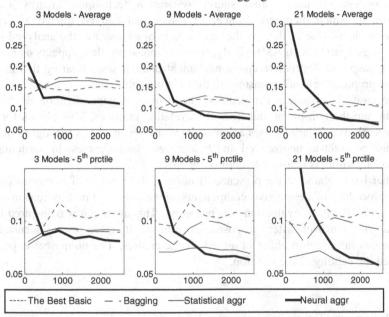

**Fig. 3.** The quality of aggregation for different number of aggregated models (3, 9, 21) and different combining procedures (bagging, statistical aggregation and neural aggregation)

As the number of observations can influence the precision of the decomposition matrix estimation and also the quality of neural aggregation, therefore we have analyzed the testing sets with different number of observations, for N = 100, 500, 900,

1300, 1700, 2100, 2500. For the initial decomposition matrix estimation and for the noise selection we have chosen N cases in the dataset, while for the final decomposition matrix – 2N cases (including test set). For neural aggregation we have used training and validation data sets of N cases.

For each N one hundred simulations were performed. In each simulation 3, 9 and 21 randomly chosen models (out of 25) were combined using bagging, statistical aggregation and neural aggregation. The results of the numerical experiments are presented in Fig. 3.

The experiment revealed that both, statistical aggregation using AMUSE algorithm and neural network re-composition improves the initial (base) models if the number of models is greater than 3 and performs better than bagging, taking into account the average error and also the values in the 5$^{th}$ percentile. Another observation is that the neural aggregation performs better than other combining procedures, especially for 3 models being considered, but it usually requires a greater number of cases and it grows with the complexity of the network.

# 7    Conclusions

Models aggregation using blind source separation techniques creates a broad framework in which there are number of issues that can be treated as separate research problems. One of them is the randomness assessment of the analyzed signal. In case of aggregation with AMUSE algorithm the noise problem appears on both, the separation step and destructive component identification step. Bearing this in mind, this paper proposed several extensions to the existing solutions.

In the case of separation problem, we have made a generalization of AMUSE algorithm into the non-linear and filtered correlation matrices. This allows for more effective separation if large noises are present. Moreover, it makes the algorithm more robust and resistant to unobserved and hidden real dependencies. In particular, the separation algorithm is resistant to additive noises.

Another issue related to the presence of noise is the number of iterations (delays) and the procedure of destructive components identification. For this reason, a new measure of randomness evaluation was proposed. This approach was inspired by the R/S analysis, however after proposed extensions, it gives more accurate and unambiguous information about observed characteristics. The numerical experiment confirmed the validity of the solution.

**Acknowledgements.** The study is cofounded by the European Union from resources of the European Social Fund. Project PO KL „Information technologies: Research and their interdisciplinary applications", Agreement UDA-POKL.04.01.01-00-051/10-00.

# References

1. Benoit, http://www.trusoft.netmegs.com; Seffens, W.: Science 285(5431), 1228 (1999)
2. Breiman, L.: Bagging predictors. Machine Learning 24, 123-140 (1996)
3. Choi, S., Cichocki, A., Belouchrani A.: Second order nonstationary source separation. Journal of VLSI Signal Processing 32 (1-2), 93-104 (2002)
4. Cichocki, A., Amari, S.: Adaptive Blind Signal and Image Processing. John Wiley, Chichester (2002)
5. Clements, R.T.: Combining forecasts: A review and annotated bibliography. International Journal of Forecasting 5, 559–581 (1989)
6. Feder, J.: Fractals, Plenum Press, New York (1988)
7. Friedman, J.H.: Multivariate Adaptive Regression Splines. Annuals of Statistics 19, 1-141 (1991)
8. Haykin, S.: Neural networks: a comprehensive foundation. Macmillan, New York (1994)
9. Hurst, H.E.: Long term storage capacity of reservoirs. Trans. Am. Soc. Civil Engineers 116 (1951)
10. Hyvärinen, A., Karhunen, J., Oja, E.: Independent Component Analysis. John Wiley, (2001)
11. Mandelnbrot, B.: Multifractals and 1/f noise. Springer-Verlag, Berlin-Heidelberg (1997)
12. Molgedey, L., Schuster, H.: Separation of a mixture of independent signals using time delayed correlations. Phisical Review Letters 72(23), 3634-3637 (1994)
13. Peters, E.: Fractal market analysis, John Wiley and Son, Chichester (1996)
14. Samorodnitskij, G., Taqqu, M.: Stable non-Gaussian random processes: stochastic models with infinitive variance. Chapman and Hall, New York, (1994)
15. Szupiluk, R., Wojewnik, P., Zabkowski, T.: Model Improvement by the Statistical Decomposition. Artificial Intelligence and Soft Computing Proceedings. LNCS, Springer-Verlag Heidelberg 2004, 1199-1204.
16. Szupiluk, R., Cichocki, A.: Blind signal separation using second order statistics. Proc. of SPETO 2001, 485-488 (2001)
17. Szupiluk, R., Wojewnik, P., Ząbkowski, T.: The Noise Identification Method Based on Divergence Analysis in Ensemble Methods Context. Lecture Notes in Computer Science 6594, 206-214 (2011)
18. Tong, L., Liu, R., Huang, Y.-F.: Indeteminacy and Identifiability of Blind Identification. IEEE Trans. on Circuits and Systems 38(5), 499-509 (1991)
19. Vialatte1, F., Cichocki, A. Dreyfus, G., Musha, T., Shishkin, S., Gervais, R.: Early Detection of Alzheimer's Disease by Blind Source Separation. Time Frequency Representation, and Bump Modeling of EEG Signals, Lecture Notes in Computer Science 3696, 683 – 692 (2005)
20. Yang, Y.: Adaptive regression by mixing. Journal of American Statistical Association 96 (2001)

# Various Problems
# of Artificial Intelligence

# Constraint Optimization Production Planning Problem. A Note on Theory, Selected Approaches and Computational Experiments

Weronika T. Adrian[1,2(✉)], Nicola Leone[1], Antoni Ligęza[2],
Marco Manna[1], and Mateusz Ślażyński[2]

[1] University of Calabria, via Pietro Bucci,
Arcavacata di Rende 87036 Cosenza, Italy
{w.adrian,leone,manna}@mat.unical.it
[2] AGH University of Science and Technology,
al. A.Mickiewicza 30, 30-059 Krakow, Poland
{ligeza,mslaz}@agh.edu.pl

**Abstract.** This paper presents an interesting discrete optimization problem which was stated as a challenge at the 2014 Bologna Summer School of Constraint Programming. The problem is given in two versions: a tractable one of a small size, for training, and a large one for the competition. A formalization of the problem is proposed, and its theoretical properties are analyzed. Several approaches for solving the problem are presented in detail. Namely, formalizations in Answer Set Programming, Prolog, and Julia are presented, and the obtained results are discussed and compared. The experiments show that different tools allow to handle different aspects of constraint programming.

**Keywords:** Discrete optimization · Constraint programming · Declarative programming · Constraint solving · Answer set programming · Programming in logic

## 1 Introduction

Over recent decades, deep theoretical studies in Discrete Constraint Programming in general, and Discrete Constraint Optimization, have been carried out, and a number of techniques and tools have been developed [2,4]. A state-of-the-art research is summarized in [9]. Unfortunately, the tackled problems are not only computationally intractable; they are also diversified w.r.t. their internal structure and formalization possibility. Some methods working well for small scale problems e.g. [7] do not scale well.

In this paper we present an interesting discrete optimization problem. It was defined by Alessio Bonetti, Michele Lombardi and Pierre Schaus and presented as a challenge at the 2014 Constraint Programming Summer School in Bologna, Italy.[1] The problem has a small, training case of the size 15 variables, and a hard, realistic instance of the size 150 variables.

---

[1] See http://school.a4cp.org/summer2014/competition.

© Springer International Publishing Switzerland 2015
L. Rutkowski et al. (Eds.): ICAISC 2015, Part II, LNAI 9120, pp. 541–553, 2015.
DOI: 10.1007/978-3-319-19369-4_48

The goal of the paper is to present and analyze several approaches to solving such irregular, discrete optimization problems. More precisely, the motivation of the paper is as follows:

- to present to a wider Audience a realistic, challenging problem, being a matter of competition at the Bologna CP Summer School,
- to define it formally and conduct a complexity analysis,
- to present and analyze some tools and techniques applied for the problem, as well as to point out some of their limitations, and finally,
- to show diversity of computational model-building ways and tools.

The structure of the paper is as follows: in Section 2 we present the problem and undertake a formal analysis of it. We start with a proposal of a formal definition, and follow with the complexity analysis. Then, in Sections 3, 4 and 5, we demonstrate selected approaches to represent and solve the problem. We summarize our experiments and outline future directions in Section 6. For space limitations, we omit full proofs which are available in the extended version of this paper.[2]

## 2    Problem Description

The considered problem, entitled "A Production Planning Problem", has been presented at ACP Summer School 2014 for an Optimization Competition. Below, we cite its description.

### 2.1    A Production Problem

In this problem, a single machine can produce at each time slot at most one item to satisfy input orders. If the production time of a corresponding order is before its actual due-date, an inventory cost, which is the same for every item, must be paid (per each time slot before the due-date). Backlogging is not allowed so each due-date is a hard constraint. There are several types of items to produce. A change-over cost must be paid to configure the machine from one type to another. The objective is to minimize the sum of the total change-over costs plus the total inventory cost (see Figure 1).

### 2.2    Formal Definition of the Problem

An instance of the Production Planning Problem (PPP) is a tuple of the following form: $I = \langle O, T, \tau, \delta, c, \gamma \rangle$ where: i) $O = \{o_1, \ldots, o_n\}$ are *items* to be produced. ii) $T = \{t_1, \ldots, t_m\}$ are *types* of items. iii) $\tau : O \to T$ is a *typing* function associating a type to each item. iv) $\delta : O \to \mathbb{N}^+$ is a *due-date* function with the following meaning: for each $o \in O$, $\delta(o)$ is the strict deadline for $o$. v) $c \in \mathbb{N}^+$ is an *inventory cost* which says how much must be paid if an item $o$ is produced before its due-date $\delta(o)$. More precisely, assuming $o$ is produced at time $t \leqslant \delta(o)$,

---

[2] See http://home.agh.edu.pl/wta/papers/icaisc2015main-fullversion.pdf.

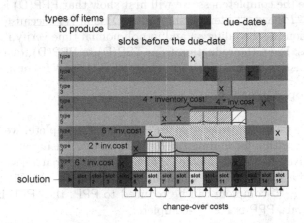

**Fig. 1.** An exemplary scheduling for the production planning problem of a size 15

the total inventory cost for $o$ is $(\delta(o) - t) \cdot c$. (Of course, if $t = \delta(o)$, the total inventory cost for $o$ is zero.) vi) $\gamma : T \times T \to \mathbb{N}$ is a *change-over cost* function which says how much has to be paid if, after producing an item of type $t$, we produce an item of type $t' \neq t$ (and no item in the between). In particular, for each $t \in T$, $\gamma(t,t) = 0$.

A solution for $I$, called a *scheduling*, is some (total) injective function $\sigma : O \to \mathbb{N}^+$ such that, for each $o \in O$, $\sigma(o) \leqslant \delta(o)$. Intuitively, given $o$, $\sigma(o)$ is a timeslot in which the item $o$ will be produced. $\Sigma(I)$ is the set of all the solutions for $I$.

Since $\sigma$ is injective, then $\sigma$ induces a total order over $O$, denoted by $\preceq_\sigma$. Let $min(O, \sigma)$ denote the minimum element in the totally ordered set $(O, \preceq_\sigma)$, and $\hat{O} = O \setminus \{min(O, \sigma)\}$ Hence, for every $o \in \hat{O}$, the item that precedes $o$ in the scheduling is denoted by $prec(o, \sigma)$.

The *overall cost* of a scheduling $\sigma \in \Sigma(I)$ is defined as follows:

$$cost(\sigma) = \left( c \cdot \sum_{o \in O} (\delta(o) - \sigma(o)) \right) + \left( \sum_{o \in \hat{O}} \gamma(\tau(prec(o, \sigma)), \tau(o)) \right)$$

An optimal solution of an instance $I$ of PPP is any scheduling $\sigma$ that minimizes the overall cost $cost(\sigma)$.

### 2.3  Complexity Analysis

Let us now formulate the decision version of the PPP problem: PPP(D) = $\{\langle I, k \rangle \mid I \in$ PPP $\wedge k \in \mathbb{N}^+ \wedge \exists \sigma \in \Sigma(I)$ s.t. $cost(\sigma) \leq k\}$ We will show that PPP is $FP^{NP}$-complete, and PPP(D) is $NP$-complete, using a reduction from the *Travelling Salesman Problem* (TSP), and its decision verion TSP(D).[3]

**Theorem 1** PPP(D) *is* $NP$-*complete.*

---

[3] See the full reduction in the extended version of the paper.

*Proof.* To prove the completeness, we will first show that PPP(D) is in $NP$, and then that it is $NP$-hard. 1) Membership: PPP(D) is in $NP$ because it is possible to guess a solution (a scheduling $\sigma$) and in polynomial time verify if $cost(\sigma) \leq k$. 2) $NP$-hardness: From the reduction from TSP(D) to PPP(D), one can see that PPP(D) is at least as hard as TSP(D). Thus, PPP(D) is $NP$-complete.

**Theorem 2** PPP *is* $FP^{NP}$-*complete.*

*Proof.* 1) Membership: To prove that PPP is $FP^{NP}$-complete, we first use the binary search algorithm for finding the optimal cost $C^*$ (using an $NP$-oracle for answering if a given cost is attainable). Then, by guessing partial schedulings, we iteratively build a solution (total scheduling) of the found cost $C^*$. 2) Hardness: TSP which is $FP^{NP}$-complete can be reduced to PPP, thus PPP is at least as hard as TSP. Thus, PPP is $FP^{NP}$-complete.

# 3    Declarative Encoding Using Answer Set Programming

In this section, we present a declarative approach for representing and solving the PPP. To this end, we have used Answer Set Programming (ASP) – a powerful knowledge representation and reasoning paradigm that is able to express problems up to the second level of complexity in the polynomial hierarchy.

## 3.1    Preliminaries

Answer Set Programming is a declarative programming paradigm based on the stable model semantics. The syntax of ASP follows the logic programming style, and the stable models of the program constitute the solutions of the original problem. The inference uses SAT-based approach for calculating minimal stable models. In this work, we present our experiments with the DLV [6] system, in which the basic ASP language is extended with aggregates an weak constraints.

## 3.2    Knowledge Representation

We have encoded the problem using the *Guess-Check-Optimize* (GCO) methodology. We have divided the representation of the problem into three parts:

1. *Guess:* Definition of the search space with regular rules,
2. *Check:* Checking the admissibility of solutions with hard constraints, and
3. *Optimize:* Optimization with weak constraints.

The encoding is compact and readable (in total it comprises of only 14 lines of code, except for the encoding of input). The guessing part consists of a single assignment:

```
{ schedule(O, S) } :- item(O), slot(S), delta(O, Ddl), S <= Ddl.
```

where `item` predicate denotes the objects to be produced, `slot` – time slots, and `delta` – the due-dates for each item. With this rule, we want to obtain a subset of a Cartesian product of the set of items and set of time slots, such as the due-dates are respected. Then, there are several constraints, represented as:

```
% 1: every item must be produced
produced(O) :- schedule(O, _).
:- item(O), not produced(O).
```

```
% 2: each item is produced only once
:- schedule(O,S1), schedule(O,S2), S1<S2.
```

```
% 3: no more than 1 item in the same timeslot
:- schedule(O1,S), schedule(O2, S), O1<O2.
```

Finally, we have two optimization criteria: minimization of the sum of inventory costs, and minimization of the sum of change-over costs. Let us assume that predicate `iCost` for each item and each time slot gives the inventory cost calculated for them. Also, let `typeInSlot` define which type of item is produced at a given time slot, `nextSlot` predicate fix the order of slots, and all the change-over costs are stored with the `changeOver` predicate. Then, it is possible to express the optimization easily with weak constraints as follows:

```
% Sum of the inventory costs must be minimal
:~ schedule(O, S), iCost(O,S,Cost). [Cost@1,O]
```

```
% Sum of the transition costs must be minimal
:~ typeInSlot(T1,S1), typeInSlot(T2,S2), nextSlot(S1, S2),
   changeOver(T1,T2,TCost), TCost > 0. [TCost@1, S1,S2]
```

The weak constraints can be intuitively read as: if it is not possible to satisfy (all) the constraints, minimize the total sum of costs assigned to the violated ones. The cost of a weak constraint is given by its weight and priority in the first argument of the `[weight@priority, identifiers]` expression. In our problem, the weight is given by the inventory and change-over costs, and the priorities are equal. Instances of weak constraints are distinguished by the identifiers given as the second argument of the above mentioned expression. In our example, the first weak constraint is computed for each item (identified by variable `O`), and the second one – for each pair (`S1`, `S2`) of consecutive time slots.

## 3.3 Challenges and Used Techniques

The biggest problem when using ASP systems or SAT-solvers is constituted by the large search space (when using a straightforward, naive encoding, we reached hundreds of millions of clauses in the ground program). To minimize this effect, we have added some auxiliary rules and constraints to our encoding:

```
% removing symmetric solutions to minimize the search space
:-schedule(O1,S1),schedule(O2,S2),S2>S1,O1>O2,typeOf(O1,T),typeOf(O2,T).
```

```
% precomputing the inventory cost for all the items and time slots
iCost(O,S,IC) :- delta(O,D), slot(S), invCost(C), S<=D, IC=X*C, X=D-S.

% computing which type follows which in production, ignoring empty slots
hasItem(S) :- schedule(O,S), item(O).
empty(S) :- slot(S), not hasItem(S).

nextSlot(S1,S2) :- slot(S1), slot(S2), S2 = S1+1.
typeInSlot(T,S) :- schedule(O,S), typeOf(O,T).
typeInSlot(T,S2) :- typeInSlot(T,S1), empty(S2), nextSlot(S1,S2).
```

### 3.4  Experiments and Results

Reasoning in ASP employs bottom-up approach and is divided into two stages: grounding, when all the variables are replaced with possible constants of the program, and solving, when the rules and constraints are applied.

For our experiments, we have used WASP 2 [3] solver that uses gringo4[4] as a grounder. WASP 2 is an award-winning ASP solver that is memory efficient and employs several algorithms and heuristics. For our problem, it has been experimentally shown that the best results are obtained with the oll algorithm, first introduced in [1] for unclasp solver, and applied to MaxSAT problem in [8].

For the instance of size 15, WASP 2 run on a PC machine[5] reached the optimum in 10 minutes. For the hard instance of a size 150, the grounder gringo4 produces about 3 millions clauses and WASP finds the first sub-optimal solutions of a cost around 40 thousands in seconds. Specifically, after 17 seconds, it founds the solution of a cost 42050, but unfortunately, no improvements are found in reasonable time (hours).

## 4  Prolog Encoding

This section is devoted to the presentation of experiment with PROLOG applied as a tool for solving the optimization problem. Both instances are taken into consideration, a training one of the size 15 and the hard instance of the size 150. A powerful implementation of PROLOG was used, namely the SWI PROLOG[6]. It provides extremely fast search engine for Depth-First Search with backtracking. The approach, encoding ideas and results are reported below.

### 4.1  Preliminaries

The main idea of the applied approach was based on two-stage search concept:

- find a first, admissible solution, allocated in the search space so that the inventory cost is heuristically minimized — the ordered items are placed as close to the due dates as possible,

---

[4] See http://sourceforge.net/projects/potassco/files/gringo/.
[5] IntelCore 2 Duo T6600, 2.2GHz, 800MHz FSB, 4GB DDR3 Ram.
[6] http://www.swi-prolog.org/

– taking the cost of the current solution as a reference point, try to improve it in a simple find_new_solution -- fail loop.

Since the main constraint is of the type *all-different*, the generation of new solutions is based on removing the day (time slot) variable value from a predefined domain (in fact a list of the form [1,2, ... 15] for the training case and [1,2, ... 150] for the hard instance.

Since the calculation of the final cost is a bit complicated (it depends on the total inventory cost and the sum of the change-over cost), a double representation of a solution was applied to speed-up the cost calculation. The first representation of the current solution is a list of the form:

```
[p(7, [12, 8]), p(6, [4]), p(5, [15, 9]), p(4, [11, 10]),
 p(3, [14]), p(2, [3]), p(1, [7,6]), p(0, [5])].
```

where each predicate p(N,[D1,D2, ... Dk]) denotes the fact that product of a type N is scheduled for days D1,D2, ... Dk; this representation is fine for fast determining the inventory cost for product N, and, in consequence, the total inventory cost being the sum of costs over products. The other representation, being a linear list of product identifiers with order corresponding to delivery dates, is used for calculation of the transition costs. Most important, selected encoding details are presented below.

## 4.2 Encoding and Basic Reasoning Algorithm

The definition of the problem is as follows:

```
delivery(0,[9]). delivery(1,[13,10]). delivery(2,[11]).
delivery(3,[14]). delivery(4,[11,10]). delivery(5,[15,11]).
delivery(6,[7]). delivery(7,[12,10]).

d([15,14,13,12,11,10,9,8,7,6,5,4,3,2,1]).
```

The delivery/2 predicate specifies the constraints: the first argument is the product type number, and the second one — the list of due days. The domain of admissible delivery days is defined in the last line.

The main loop employing build-in DFS strategy is encoded as:

```
run:- retractall(pp(_)),retractall(pl(_)),retractall(pc(_)),
      assert(pp(start)),assert(pl(start)),assert(pc(100000)),
      find_new_solution.
find_new_solution :- findall(p(P,LD), delivery(P,LD),LS), d(Domain),
      reload(LS,[],LR, Domain,_), trans(LR,LV), cost(LR,LV,C),
      pc(CC), C < CC,
      retractall(pp(_)),retractall(pl(_)),retractall(pc(_)),
      assert(pp(LR)),assert(pl(LV)),assert(pc(C)),
      write(C),nl,
      fail.
```

The run command simply initializes the search; it cleans the current solution, and asserts some starting point, where the pp/1 predicate keeps the product-list-of-days representation, the pl/1 keeps the linear list of products and the pc/1 predicate keeps the solution total cost.

The find_new_solution gathers all the product-delivery day list constraints into a single list LS, and transforms the constraints in an admissible solution LR with the reload/5 predicate; its working is explained in Section 4.3 below. The LR representation is transformed into the linear representation — the LV list of the trans/2 predicate — and the current cost is calculated. In case there is an improvement over the best-so-far cost CC, the new solution and cost replace the current one in the memory, and the final fail enforces backtracking search. At the end of search, the best results are kept in memory.

## 4.3  Employed Techniques

Several techniques and tricks were employed and examined in different versions of the PROLOG code. First, the backtracking search with the main loop directly employing the built-in search engine. Then, the first solution generation, based on the reload/5 iterative loops with accumulator, which works as follows:

```
reload([],LR,LR,_,_):- !.
reload([H|T],A,LR, Domain,Rest):- make(H,HR,Domain,DomainH),
    reload(T,[HR|A],LR,DomainH,Rest).
% make an admissible element p(D,LD)
make(p(P,[D]),p(P,[R]),DD,DDR):- select(R,DD,DDR), R =< D.
make(p(P,LD),p(P,LR),DD,DDN):- change(LD,LR,DD,DDN).
change([],[],DD,DD):- !.
change([D|LD],[R|LR],DD,DDN):- select(R,DD,DDR), R =< D,
    change(LD,LR,DDR,DDN).
```

Consider the following shortcuts: D — delivery due day, R — delivery realization day, LD/LR — a list of such days, respectively. Now, the reload/5 predicates takes the product delivery constraints and reloads them as a delivery proposal (realization), satisfying the constraints; the delivery days are removed from the domain. The make/2 predicate exchanges a single-predicate constraint into a single-fact delivery specification; for a single due day, only a selection of an admissible day is necessary. For a list of due days, the change/4 predicate is called, which performs such reloading day-by-day for all the days in the constraint specifying list. An optimizing trick is that the domain list given by d/1 is placed in a reversed order; hence, the possible latest days are selected first to satisfy the constraint, and potentially minimizing the inventory cost.

## 4.4  Experiments and Results

The proposed solution used advantages and built-in PROLOG mechanism in a straightforward way. The code is simple; the whole program is encoded within less than 50 PROLOG clauses (practically: lines of code), without the data specification and some comments. The code is relatively readable.

Since the program uses systematic search, the results are repeatable, and the final solution, if found, is sure to be the global minimum. The global minimum for the small instance equals 784[7]. Depending on the computer (several simple PC/laptops with Linux/Ubuntu were tried) and some simplifications of the code, it takes minutes to hours to find the global minimum. The fastest solution is obtained after reducing the domain to 13 days (not all 15 days are necessary). The initial, first-choice admissible solution (1287) is obtained immediately (less than one second). A good estimate (960) is also found in reasonable time (a few minutes). Unfortunately, generation of the next, improved solutions slows down, as the criteria solution reference is lowered.

As for the hard problem, the main encoding is practically the same; only problem specification takes a bit more space. The first admissible solution (equal to 34808) is again obtained immediately. Unfortunately, in reasonable time (hours) no significant improvements are found. As an optimization task, this problem is really hard for simple systematic backtracking search.

## 5 Simulated Annealing

As we have shown in earlier sections, the presented problem belongs to the group of problems with difficult computational features. In fact, the search space is simply too vast to be searched in the systematic way, at least not without a way to cut off the unpromising branches of computation. In this section, we present the results obtained using the Simulated Annealing algorithm, presented by Kirkpatrick in [5], which is one of the most popular generic methods in the combinatorial optimization field.

### 5.1 Preliminaries

The Simulated Annealing algorithm belongs to the group of the so called local search optimization methods. The process of optimization starts with the generation of an initial solution — it can be a random solution, not even complying to the problem's constraints. In our case, we have used the greedy approach: the initial solution consists of items sorted according to their due dates — an item with the earliest due date appears first on the list. Despite the obvious shortcomings of such a naive approach, it has one desirable feature – it is an admissible solution; it can be easily shown that whenever this greedy approach produces a non-admissible solution, there is no solution to the problem's instance.

In the basic version of the algorithm, every next step of the search process starts with the currently best solution (initial at beginning) and then tries to improve it with the set of simple (and fast to compute) transformations. The new state is called neighbor of the state, and whenever it appears to be better (has

---

[7] As the search is systematic, the computation – when finished – can be considered as a proof; for the 15 variables case, after reduction of the domain to 13 days, a simple PC performed obtaining the following parameters on an example run: 8,237,939,613 inferences, 1273.917 CPU in 1905.941 seconds (67% CPU, 6466623 Lips).

a lower cost), it is selected as the next state to start from. The neighborhood of the planning problem can be defined as a set of all the solutions which differ only in positions of the maximally three items and no such place swap can break the due dates constraints. The two important features of this choice are that the search process using this neighborhood is closed under the admissibility property, and that the every admissible solution (including the global minimum) can be reached from an arbitrary selected admissible solution. Combining this with the admissibility of the initial solution, we can be sure that the global solution is at least reachable.

In order to avoid the local minimums, Simulated Annealing provides a meta-heuristic used to decide whether the search should move to the neighboring state. The algorithm should change state with probability defined as 1 when $cost(current) > cost(neighbor)$ and $exp((cost(current) - cost(neighbor)/t)$ in other case, where $t$ is a "temperature", a parameter which directly impacts only this threshold. We are setting the temperature according to the standard cooling scheme, where the value of the temperature in the $i$ step of computation, written as $t_i$, can be calculated according to the equality $t_i = t_0 \cdot n^i$, where initial temperature $t_0$ and cooling factor $n$ are experimentally selected constants. In our case, we have found that the best values of these constants lie in ranges $10 \le t_0 \le 20$ and $0.99999 \le n < 1$.

Furthermore, in case the algorithm has stuck in a local minimum (the state has not changed for a relatively long time), the algorithm can be enriched with the other meta-heuristics. In our case, we have used three simple techniques which are tried in the following order:

1. try to "reheat" the search; change the value of $t$ to the value closer to the initial one;
2. perform large amount of steps without taking costs into account (change the state in every step); this way the search can move easily to the distant part of the search space;
3. reset temperature to $t_0$ and start from the best found state.

## 5.2   Implementation

We have implemented the algorithm in Julia, a high-level programming language for numerical and technical computing[8]. The resulting code was nearly 500 lines long. Due to the efficiency reasons, state was encoded in a dual form, both as: i) an array of ordered items where the value in the array represents a time slot, when the item is going to be produced; and ii) an array of time slots where the value in the array represents the item produced in this slot (0 if there is no item produced). As a local search needs only the two states in memory at the same time, there is no memory penalty in this dual approach.

The neighborhood described in earlier section was implemented in a brute force manner. Firstly, the three time slots are randomly chosen. Then, if they

---

[8] http://julialang.org/

conform to the requirements (they can not share the same item and their swapping should create an admissible solution), they are swapped. In other case, as long as it is necessary, the other three time slots are chosen randomly again. The process is guaranteed to stop and produce a valid neighbor state.

## 5.3   Results and Limitations

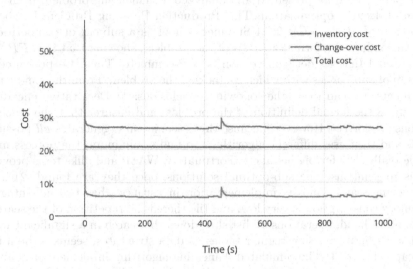

**Fig. 2.** Costs of the solutions produced by Simulated Annealing during the first 1000 seconds. Initial temp $t_0$ was equal 20 and the cooling factor $n$ had value 0.999999. The algorithm was executed on the Mac OSX notebook with 2,4 GHz Intel Core i5 processor and 8 GB 1600 MHz DDR3 ram memory.

The results of the first 1000 seconds of algorithm's work on the hard instance of the problem can be observed in Figure 2. While the initial solution generated with the greedy approach has a total cost near the value 60 000 (exactly 56042), after only a second it decreases to 29015. Then the progress slows, the best solution found in this period of time was 26454. It is instructive to see that the inventory cost stays on the same level while all the fluctuations are occurring only due to the change-over costs. The bigger jump near the 450 second is an effect of the reheating.

As the results suggest, the stochastic search easily outperforms systematic search, but this improvement comes with the price:

1. Because of its not exhaustive nature, it cannot proof the optimality of the result; in fact there is no clear rule when to stop the algorithm.
2. The cooling schedule has a large impact on the performance — the parameters had to be chosen experimentally;.
3. Problem representation is not declarative, therefore hard to grasp and modify for the non-technical user.

The last limitation can be overcome with the hybrid approach; exploiting the declarative description of problem to generate a proper local search routine. This approach was most famously implemented in Comet programming language [10].

## 6   Summary and Outlook

In this paper, we have presented and analyzed a challenging problem from the domain of discrete optimization. This Production Planning Problem has been first presented at the ACP 2014 Summer School as a subject of competition. We have conducted a formal analysis of the problem, showing that it is $FP^{NP}$-complete and that its decision version is $NP$-complete. Then, we presented a spectrum of approaches with which we tackled the problem. From the conducted experiments, we can draw the following conclusions: 1) Declarative encoding best mimics the formal definition of the problem and ensures that the reached solutions are correct. However, because the reasoning first generates *all* possible models and then uses different algorithms to find a minimum, the process may become really slow for big instances. Fortunately, WASP and alike tools provide options to print also the sub-optimal solutions, once they are found. 2) The backtracking search, and its implementation in PROLOG, has two advantages: (i) memory consumption is very low, and (ii) there is no repetition of the search. On the other hand, operations on list slow down the search in a significant way, and thus PROLOG, missing regular tables as data structures, seems to be a bit handicapped here. 3) The Simulated Annealing algorithm implemented in Julia programming language, being a stochastic method, easily copes with the large combinatorial search spaces and finds a decent solution within a short period of time. Despite its excellent results, it has an inherent disadvantage — it is not able to tell whether the found solution is globally optimal.

For future work, we will further improve the logic-based encodings, and compare the results with the ones obtained by an evolutionary optimization algorithm. Moreover, we plan to work on a hybrid representation for such problems that would enable to use the advantages of both logic-based approaches and stochastic methods.

## References

1. Andres, B., Kaufmann, B., Matheis, O., Schaub, T.: Unsatisfiability-based optimization in clasp. In: Dovier, A., Costa, V.S. (eds.) Technical Communications of the 28th International Conference on Logic Programming, ICLP 2012, Budapest, Hungary, September 4-8. LIPIcs, vol. 17, pp. 211–221. Schloss Dagstuhl - Leibniz-Zentrum fuer Informatik (2012)
2. Dechter, R.: Constraint Processing. Morgan Kaufmann Publishers, San Francisco (2003)
3. Dodaro, C.: Engineering an efficient native ASP solver. TPLP 13(4-5-Online-Supplement) (2013)
4. Van Hentenryck, P., Michel, L.: Constraint-Based Local Search. MIT Press, Cambridge (2005)

5. Kirkpatrick, S., Gelatt, C.D., Vecchi, M.P.: Optimization by simulated annealing. Science 220(4598), 671–680 (1983)
6. Leone, N., Pfeifer, G., Faber, W., Eiter, T., Gottlob, G., Perri, S., Scarcello, F.: The dlv system for knowledge representation and reasoning. ACM Trans. Comput. Logic 7(3), 499–562 (2006)
7. Ligęza, A.: Models and tools for improving efficiency in constraint logic programming. Decision Making in Manufacturing and Services 5(1-2), 69–78 (2011)
8. Morgado, A., Dodaro, C., Marques-Silva, J.: Core-guided maxSAT with soft cardinality constraints. In: O'Sullivan, B. (ed.) CP 2014. LNCS, vol. 8656, pp. 564–573. Springer, Heidelberg (2014)
9. Rossi, F., van Beek, P., Walsh, T. (eds.): Handbook of Constraint Programming. Elsevier (2006)
10. Van Hentenryck, P., Michel, L.: Constraint-Based Local Search. The MIT Press, Cambridge (2005)

# Investigating the Mapping between Default Logic and Inconsistency-Tolerant Semantics

Abdallah Arioua[1,2(✉)], Nouredine Tamani[3], Madalina Croitoru[1],
Jérôme Fortin[1], and Patrice Buche[2]

[1] University Montpellier, France
[2] IATE, INRA, Montpellier, France
[3] INRIA Sophia Antipolis, France

**Abstract.** In this paper we propose a mapping between inconsistent ontological knowledge bases and semi-monotonic, prerequisite-free closed normal default theories. As a proof of concept of the new results obtained by the proposed mapping we introduce an any-time algorithm for query answering that starts off by a small set of facts and incrementally adds to this set.

## 1 Introduction

The ONTOLOGY-BASED DATA ACCESS (ODBA) problem [18] investigates querying multiple data sources defined over the same ontology [13]. We distinguish ourselves from other approaches in the OBDA community by considering a rule based language that gains more and more interest from a practical point of view [4]. We consider existential variables in the head of the rules as well as n-ary predicates and conflicts (and generalise certain subsets of Description Logics (e.g. DL-Lite) [1,5]). The tractability conditions of the considered rule based language rely on different saturation (chase) methods [15]. For algorithmic considerations here we will restrict ourselves to a tractable fragment (such as weakly-acyclic rule sets) [4].

The hypothesis made by OBDA setting is that each data source is assumed to be self-consistent along with the ontology, whereas the integration of homogeneous factual information from all data sources might be no longer consistent [12]. A common solution is to construct a maximal (with respect to set inclusion) consistent subsets of the knowledge base called repair. Once repairs computed, different semantics can be used for query answering over the knowledge base. In this paper we focus on **All R**epairs semantics (*AR*-semantics) and *Brave*-semantics [2,3,12].

Much research has been undertaken in the field of Default Logics and several tools and frameworks have been developed (GaDeL [16], X-Ray [21], DeReS[6]). Moreover, there was an increasing interest in relating Reiter's Default Logic to other non-monotonic formalism such as Minimal Temporal Epistemic Logic [8], Autoepistemic Logics [11,9], Circumscription [10], Argumentation [7] and the modal logic S4F [22]. Any attempt to find a relation between inconsistency handling in OBDA and Reiter's Default Logic would benefit from such well-established tools and equivalent formalisms. To the best of our knowledge, there

L. Rutkowski et al. (Eds.): ICAISC 2015, Part II, LNAI 9120, pp. 554–564, 2015.
DOI: 10.1007/978-3-319-19369-4_49

is no work on relating both inconsistent ontological knowledge bases semantics and Reiter's Default Logic considering (1) the expressive setting of existential rules [4] and (2) assuming that the inconsistency comes from the set of facts. Our work differs from existing work in the literature considering a similar intuition but only focusing on the propositional case.

**The contribution** of the paper lies in the following points. We propose an efficient (with respect to time and space complexity) mapping between inconsistent ontological knowledge bases (expressed in a general rule-based language) and a class of default theories (semi-monotonic, precisely *prerequisite-free closed normal default theories*). We formally prove the equivalence between the *inconsistency-tolerant semantics (AR and Brave)* in OBDA and inference in Default Logic *(sceptical and credulous)* in the aforementioned class of default theories. We also formally prove the property of semi-monotonicity for inconsistency-tolerant semantics. This property will serve as a basis for an *anytime algorithm* for query answering.

We show that the non-ontological information (that is information contained in the data sources, also called facts in the remainder of the paper) can be viewed as closed normal defaults. Defaults along with the ontological rules will form a closed normal default theory. We show then the link between default extensions and maximal consistent subsets of facts (called repairs). Based on this link we obtain equivalences between the inconsistency-tolerant semantics *(AR and Brave)* and inference in Default Logic *(sceptical and credulous)*.

From an engineering perspective, our work paves the way for an inconsistency handling hybrid system that incorporates different formalisms at distinct levels. While the algorithm presented in the paper constitutes a proof of concept of the benefit of our mapping, it could be the case that clever application of algorithms for default logic could improve the state of art in OBDA. For example, by bridging the gap between the two fields we can make use of the relation between Reiter's Default Logic and Answer Set Programming [14] for an efficient query answering engine.

## 2   Preliminaries

Let us briefly recall the basics of the rule-based language used in this paper (equivalent to Datalog± [4]), namely, existential rules, negative constraints, facts and knowledge base as well as inconsistency-tolerant semantics.

### 2.1   Rule-Based Language

We consider *The positive existential* conjunctive fragment of first-order logic, which is composed of formulas built with the connectives $\{\wedge, \rightarrow\}$ and the quantifiers $\{\exists, \forall\}$. We consider first-order vocabularies with constants but no other function symbol. A term $t$ is a constant or a variable, different constants represent different values (unique name assumption), an atomic formula (or atom) is of the form $p(t_1, ..., t_n)$ where $p$ is an n-ary predicate, and $t_1, ..., t_n$ are terms. A *ground* atom is an atom with no variables. Given an atom or a set of atoms $A$, $vars(A)$, $consts(A)$ and $terms(A)$ denote its set of variables, constants and terms.

An *existential rule* (rule) is a first-order formula of the form $R = \forall \vec{x} \forall \vec{y} (H \rightarrow \exists \vec{w} C)$ where $H$ (resp. $C$) is a conjunction of atoms called the *hypothesis* (resp. *conclusion*) of $R$. The variables in the hypothesis (resp. conclusion) are denoted as $vars(H) = \vec{x} \cup \vec{y}$ (resp. $vars(C) = \vec{w}$). Note that, the notation $\vec{x}$ represents a sequence of variables. We omit quantifiers and we use $R = (H, C)$ as a contracted form of a rule $R$. An existential rule with an empty hypothesis is called a *fact*. A fact is an existentially closed (with no free variable) conjunction of atoms. i.e. $\exists x(teacher(x) \wedge employee(x))$. This fact allows to assert an unknown individual which is an essential aspect in open-domain perspectives where it cannot be assumed that all individuals are known in advance. A boolean conjunctive query has the same form as a fact. A *negative constraint* is a rule with a conclusion equals to the truth constant false "$\perp$". $N = \forall x, y, z \, (supervises(x, y) \wedge work\_in(x, z) \wedge directs(y, z)) \rightarrow \perp$ means it is impossible for $x$ to supervise $y$ if $x$ works in department $z$ and $y$ directs $z$.

Given a conjunction of atoms $A_1$ and $A_2$, a homomorphism $\pi$ from $A_1$ to $A_2$ is a substitution of $vars(A_1)$ by $terms(A_2)$ such that $\pi(A_1) \subseteq A_2$.

A rule $R = (H, C)$ is *applicable* to a set of atoms $A$ if and only if there exists $A' \subseteq A$ such that there is a homomorphism $\pi$ from $H$ to the conjunction of elements of $A'$. For example, the rule $\forall x(teacher(x) \rightarrow employee(x))$ is applicable to the set $\{teacher(Tom), cute(Tom)\}$, since there is a homomorphism from $teacher(x)$ to $teacher(Tom)$. If a rule $R$ is applicable to a set $A$, the application of $R$ to $A$ according to $\pi$ produces a set $A \cup \{\pi(C)\}$. In our example, the produced set is $\{teacher(Tom), employee(Tom), cute(Tom)\}$. We then say that the new set (which includes the old one and adds the new information to it) is an *immediate derivation* of $A$ by $R$. This new set is denoted by $R(A)$. Since facts are conjunction of atoms, given two facts $f$ and $f'$, $f \models f'$ iff there is a homomorphism from $f'$ to $f$.

Let $F$ be a set of facts and $\mathcal{R}$ be a set of rules. An $\mathcal{R}$-derivation of $F$ is a finite sequence $\langle F_0, ..., F_n \rangle$ s.t $F_0 = F$, and for all $0 \leq i < n$, there is a rule $R_i = (H_i, C_i) \in \mathcal{R}$ and a homomorphism $\pi_i$ from $H_i$ to $F_i$ s.t $F_{i+1} = F_i \cup \{\pi(C_i)\}$. For a set of facts $\mathcal{F}$ and a query $Q$ and a set of rules $\mathcal{R}$, we say $\mathcal{F}, \mathcal{R} \models Q$ iff there exists an $\mathcal{R}$-derivation $\langle (F_0 = F), ..., F_n \rangle$ such that $F_n \models Q$ [15]. Given a set of facts $\{f_0, ..., f_k\}$ and a set of rules $\mathcal{R}$, the closure of $\{f_0, ..., f_k\}$ with respect to $\mathcal{R}$, denoted by $\mathrm{Cl}_{\mathcal{R}}(\{f_0, ..., f_k\})$, is defined as the smallest set (with respect to $\subseteq$) which contains $\{f_0, ..., f_k\}$, and is closed under $\mathcal{R}$-derivation (that is, for every $\mathcal{R}$-derivation $D_i = \langle (F'_1 = \{f_i\}), ..., F'_m \rangle$ of $f_i \in \{f_0, ..., f_k\}$ s.t $i \in \{0, ..., k\}$, we have $F'_m \subseteq \mathrm{Cl}_{\mathcal{R}}(\{f_0, ..., f_k\})$ and $m \in \mathbb{N}$. Finally, we say that a set of facts $\mathcal{F}$ and a set of rules $\mathcal{R}$ *entail* a fact $G$ (and we write $\mathcal{F}, \mathcal{R} \models G$) iff the closure of the facts by all the rules entails $G$ (i.e. if $\mathrm{Cl}_{\mathcal{R}}(\mathcal{F}) \models G$).

A *knowledge base* $\mathcal{K} = (\mathcal{F}, \mathcal{R}, \mathcal{N})$ is composed of finite set of facts $\mathcal{F}$, finite set of existential rules $\mathcal{R}$ and a finite set of negative constrains $\mathcal{N}$. Given a knowledge base, one can ask if a boolean conjunctive query $Q$ holds or not. The answer to the query $Q$ is *yes* if and only if $\mathcal{F}, \mathcal{R} \models Q$. In this paper we refer to a *boolean conjunctive query* as *query*.

Given a knowledge base $\mathcal{K} = (\mathcal{F}, \mathcal{R}, \mathcal{N})$, a set $\{f_1, \ldots, f_k\} \subseteq \mathcal{F}$ is said to be *inconsistent* if and only if there exists a constraint $N \in \mathcal{N}$ such that $\{f_1, \ldots, f_k\} \models H_N$, where $H_N$ denotes the hypothesis of the constraint $N$. A set of facts is consistent if and only if it is not inconsistent. A set $\{f_1, \ldots, f_k\} \subseteq \mathcal{F}$ is $\mathcal{R}$-*inconsistent* if and only if there exists a constraint $N \in \mathcal{N}$ such that $\mathtt{Cl}_\mathcal{R}(\{f_1, \ldots, f_k\}) \models H_N$, where $H_N$ is the hypothesis of the constraint $N$. A set of facts is said to be $\mathcal{R}$-*consistent* if and only if it is not $\mathcal{R}$-inconsistent. A knowledge base $(\mathcal{F}, \mathcal{R}, \mathcal{N})$ is said to be *inconsistent* iff $\mathcal{F}$ is $\mathcal{R}$-inconsistent.

*Example 1.* Let us consider the following knowledge base $\mathcal{K} = (\mathcal{F}, \mathcal{R}, \mathcal{N})$, with: $\mathcal{F} = \{teacher(Tom), student(Tom)\}$, $\mathcal{R} = \{\forall x(teacher(x) \rightarrow university\_member(x)), \forall x(student(x) \rightarrow university\_member(x))\}$, $\mathcal{N} = \{\forall x(student(x) \wedge teacher(x) \rightarrow \bot)\}$. It is obvious that $\mathcal{K}$ directly violates the constraint $\mathcal{N}$ ($\mathcal{F}$ is $\mathcal{R}$-inconsistent since $\mathtt{Cl}_\mathcal{R}(\mathcal{F})$ entails the hypothesis of the negative constraint). Consequently, $\mathcal{K}$ is inconsistent.

## 2.2   Inconsistency-Tolerant Semantics

Notice that (like in classical logic), if a knowledge base $\mathcal{K} = (\mathcal{F}, \mathcal{R}, \mathcal{N})$ is inconsistent then everything can be entailed from it. A common solution [2,12] is to construct maximal (with respect to set inclusion) consistent subsets of $\mathcal{K}$. These repairs represent different ways of regaining consistency while maintaining as much information as possible from the original knowledge base. Such subsets are called *repairs*.

**Definition 1 (Repair).** *Let* $\mathcal{K} = (\mathcal{F}, \mathcal{R}, \mathcal{N})$ *be a knowledge base. A repair* $\mathcal{A}$ *of* $\mathcal{K}$ *is an inclusion-maximal subset of* $\mathcal{F}$ *such that (i)* $\mathcal{A}$ *is* $\mathcal{R}$-*consistent, (ii) there exist no* $\mathcal{A}'$ *such that* $\mathcal{A} \subset \mathcal{A}'$ *and* $\mathcal{A}'$ *is* $\mathcal{R}$-*consistent. The set of all repairs of* $\mathcal{K}$ *is denoted by* $Repair(\mathcal{K})$.

Once the repairs are calculated, different semantics can be used for query answering over the knowledge base[1]. For example, we may want to accept a query if it is entailed by *all repairs* (AR-semantics), another possibility is to accept the query if it is entailed by at least some repairs (Brave-semantics). The definitions of the previous semantics are introduced by [2,12] and adapted for the rule-based language:

**Definition 2 (AR-Semantics).** *Let* $\mathcal{K} = (\mathcal{F}, \mathcal{R}, \mathcal{N})$ *be a knowledge base and let* $\alpha$ *be a query. Then* $\alpha$ *is AR-entailed from* $\mathcal{K}$, *written* $\mathcal{K} \models_{AR} \alpha$ *iff for every repair* $\mathcal{A}' \in Repair(\mathcal{K})$, *it holds that* $\mathtt{Cl}_\mathcal{R}(\mathcal{A}') \models \alpha$.

**Definition 3 (Brave-Semantics).** *Let* $\mathcal{K} = (\mathcal{F}, \mathcal{R}, \mathcal{N})$ *be a knowledge base and let* $\alpha$ *be a query. Then* $\alpha$ *is* **brave-entailed** *from* $\mathcal{K}$, *written* $\mathcal{K} \models_{Brave} \alpha$ *iff* $\mathtt{Cl}_\mathcal{R}(\mathcal{A}') \models \alpha$ *for at least one* $\mathcal{A}' \in Repair(\mathcal{K})$.

---

[1] These semantics are called inconsistency-tolerant semantics.

*Example 2 (Example 1 Cont.).* $Repair(\mathcal{K})=\{\mathcal{A}_1, \mathcal{A}_2\}$ with $\mathcal{A}_1=\{teacher(Tom)\}$ and $\mathcal{A}_2 = \{student(Tom)\}\}$. $Cl_\mathcal{R}(\mathcal{A}_1) = \{teacher(Tom), university\_member(Tom)\}$, $Cl_\mathcal{R}(\mathcal{A}_2) = \{student(Tom), university\_member(Tom)\}$. For example, we get $\mathcal{K} \models_{AR} university\_member(Tom)$, $\mathcal{K} \models_{brave} teacher(Tom)$ and $\mathcal{K} \models_{brave} student(Tom)$.

## 2.3   Reiter's Default Logic

We presume a basic familiarity with Default Logic [19] and only recall basic notions. In Default Logic, we represent certain facts about the world in a background theory $W$, whereas we represent certain rules that express normally and generally in a set $D$, these rules are called defaults. A default theory $\Delta = (W, D)$ is a pair composed of a background theory $W$ and a set of defaults $D$ expressed in a logical language (we consider first-order logic). A default takes the form of $\delta = A : B/C$, where $A$, $B$ and $C$ are first-order logic (FOL) formulae (possibly, with free variables) denoted by $pre(\delta), just(\delta)$ and $cons(\delta)$ respectively and standing for **prerequisite, justification** and **conclusion** respectively. The default is interpreted as "If it is the case that $A$ and it is consistent to assume $B$ then deduce $C$". A default $\delta$ where $just(\delta) = cons(\delta)$ is called a normal default, if $\delta$ has no free variables then it is closed. Moreover, if $pre(\delta) = \emptyset$ we call the default $\delta$ prerequisite-free. A default theory is said to be a closed normal default theory if and only if all its defaults are closed and normal. A default theory may induce zero, one, or multiple *extensions*:

**Definition 4 (Reiter's Extension [19]).** *Let $\Delta = (D, W)$ be a default theory. The operator $\Gamma$ assigns to every set $S$ of formulae the smallest set $U$ of formulae such that: (i) $W \subseteq U$, (ii) $\mathcal{T}h(U)=U$, (iii) If $(A : B/C) \in D$ , $U \models A$, $S \nvDash \neg B$, then $C \in U$. A set $E$ of formulae is an extension of $\Delta$ if and only if $E = \Gamma(E)$, that is, $E$ is a fixed point of $\Gamma$.*

Notice that, $\mathcal{T}h(U)$ is the deductive closure of U ( i.e. the set of logical consequences of a set of formulae U).

Any extension represents a set of acceptable beliefs that can be deduced from an incomplete description of the world described in $W$. Furthermore, for a given extension $E$ and a set of defaults $D$, the set of *generating defaults* for E with respect to $\Delta$ is $GD(D, E) = \{\delta \in D | E \models pre(\delta) \text{ and } E \nvDash \neg just(\delta)\}$. For a set of defaults $D' \subseteq D$ we denote by $\mathrm{Con}(D')$ the set of the conclusions of all defaults in $D'$, Namely, $\mathrm{Con}(D')=\{cons(\delta) \mid \delta \in D'\}$. Note that if $\mathcal{G}$ is the set of generating defaults for an extension $E$ then $E=\mathcal{T}h(W \cup \mathrm{Con}(\mathcal{G}))$[19].

Reiter defined some inference problems in Default Logic as follows. For a given default theory $\Delta = (W, D)$ a well-formed formula $\alpha$ is *sceptically entailed* from $\Delta$ iff $\alpha$ belongs to all extensions of $\Delta$. Whereas it is *credulously entailed* from $\Delta$ iff it belongs to at least one extension of $\Delta$.

In this paper we are interested in *closed normal default theories*. This type of default theories is a subset of the so called semi-monotonic default theories that have gained an increasing interest for it desirable properties (it admits local proof procedures as mentioned in [20,19] and it is implemented in many systems such as X-Ray [17]).

**Theorem 1.** *[19] Let $\Delta = (W, D)$ be a closed normal default theory, let $E$ and $F$ be two extensions of $\Delta$ and let $D, D'$ be set of closed normal defaults s.t $D' \subseteq D$. Then, $\Delta$ enjoys the following properties:*

1. *Minimality: if $F \subseteq E$, then $E = F$.*
2. *Orthogonality: If $F$ and $E$ are distinct then $F \cup E$ is inconsistent.*
3. *Semi-monotonicity: if $E'$ is an extension of $\Delta' = (W, D')$ then $\Delta = (W, D)$ has an extension $E$ s.t $E' \subseteq E$ and $GD(D', E') \subseteq GD(D, E)$.*

**Theorem 2.** *[19] Let $\Delta = (W, D)$ be a closed normal default theory such that $D' \subseteq D$. Suppose that $E'_1$ and $E'_2$ are distinct extensions of $(W, D')$. Then $\Delta$ has distinct extensions $E_1$ and $E_2$ such that $E'_1 \subseteq E_1$ and $E'_2 \subseteq E_2$.*

The property of *semi-monotonicity* in Theorem 1 stipulates that a closed normal default theory is *monotone* with respect to the addition of new defaults. Theorem 2 implies that the addition of new closed normal defaults to a closed normal default theory can never lead to a default theory with fewer extensions than the original.

## 3   A Default Logic Interpretation of Inconsistent Knowledge Base

In the OBDA setting we consider the set of facts as the source of inconsistency. Let $\mathcal{K} = (\mathcal{F}, \mathcal{R}, \mathcal{N})$ be a knowledge base, the intuition underlying the mapping is that we handle all the facts according to the principle "every fact in $\mathcal{K}$ is consistent with the rest unless proven inconsistent". That is, we transform each fact in $\mathcal{F}$ into a default while maintaining the set $\mathcal{R}$ and $\mathcal{N}$ since they are assumed to be consistent. Specifically, if we have a fact $\alpha$ in our knowledge base $\mathcal{K}$ we consider it as "generally consistent" until we prove the other way around by developing our initial knowledge in $W$ using defaults. This leads to the following:

**Definition 5 (Mapping $\tau$).** *Let $\mathcal{K} = (\mathcal{F}, \mathcal{R}, \mathcal{N})$ be an inconsistent knowledge base and $\Delta_{\mathcal{K}} = (W, D)$ be a closed normal default theory. Furthermore, Let $\mathcal{S}$ be the set of all possible inconsistent knowledge bases and $\mathcal{D}$ be the set of all possible closed normal default theories. The mapping $\tau$ is defined from $\mathcal{S}$ to $\mathcal{D}$ such that $\tau(\mathcal{K}) = \Delta_{\mathcal{K}}$ as follows:*

(a) *The mapping $\tau$ associates for every fact $f_i \in \mathcal{F}$ its default $\delta_{f_i} =: f_i/f_i$ in $D$. Notice that $\delta_{f_i}$ is a prerequisite-free, closed normal default since facts in $\mathcal{K}$ are either ground atoms or existentially closed conjunction of atoms (see Section 2.1).*

(b) *The mapping $\tau$ associates for every rule $R_i \in \mathcal{R}$ ($N_i \in \mathcal{N}$, resp.) the same $\mathcal{R}_i$ ($N_i$, resp.) in $W$.*

One major implication of the mapping is that every inconsistent knowledge base can be efficiently (w.r.t time and space) mapped to a closed normal default theory. The benefit of such mapping is that we can handle inconsistency issues with a theoretically and practically well-established framework (i.e. Default Logic). In what follows, we present the application of mapping on Example 1.

*Example 3.* Consider $\mathcal{K} = (\mathcal{F}, \mathcal{R}, \mathcal{N})$ of example 1, the corresponding default theory $\tau(\mathcal{K}) = \Delta_{\mathcal{K}} = (D, W)$ is a closed normal default theory with a background knowledge:

$W = \{\forall x(teacher(x) {\rightarrow} university\_member(x)), \forall x(student(x) {\rightarrow} university\_member(x)), \forall x(teacher(x) \land student(x) \rightarrow \perp)\}$.
And a set of defaults:

- $D = \{: teacher(Tom)/teacher(Tom), : student(Tom)/student(Tom)\}$.

With a set of extensions $Ext(\Delta_{\mathcal{K}}) = \{E_1, E_2\}$ such that:

- $E_1 = Th(W \cup \{teacher(Tom)\}) = Th(\{teacher(Tom), university\_member(Tom)\})$.
- $E_2 = Th(W \cup \{student(Tom)\}) = Th(\{student(Tom), university\_member(Tom)\})$.

The set of generating defaults for $E_1$ (resp. $E_2$) is the singleton $GD(D, E_1) = \{: teacher(Tom)/teacher(Tom)\}$ (resp. $GD(D, E_2) = \{: student(Tom)/student(Tom)\}$).

## 4    Equivalences and New Results

As stated above, the previous mapping establishes a relation between inconsistent knowledge bases and closed normal default theories. We show how this relation also holds for repairs and extensions; consequently between inconsistency-tolerant semantics and inference in Default Logic.

Let $\mathcal{K} = (\mathcal{F}, \mathcal{R}, \mathcal{N})$ be an inconsistent knowledge base and $\Delta_{\mathcal{K}} = (D, W)$ the corresponding default theory using the mapping $\tau$. Let $Ext(\Delta_{\mathcal{K}})$ be the set of all extensions of $\Delta_{\mathcal{K}}$ and $\mathcal{R}epair(\mathcal{K})$ the set of all repairs of $\mathcal{K}$.

**Proposition 1.** *For every extension $E_i \in Ext(\Delta_{\mathcal{K}})$ it holds that the set $Con(GD(D, E_i)) \in \mathcal{R}epair(\mathcal{K})$.*

**Proof 1** *First, notice that the set $Con(D)=\mathcal{F}$, since every fact in $\mathcal{F}$ has been mapped to a default.*

*Let us first prove that the for every $E_i \in Ext(\Delta_{\mathcal{K}})$ the set $Con(GD(D,E_i))$ is consistent (contradiction free). On the one hand, we have $Con(GD(D,E_i)) \subset E_i$. On the other hand, since $E_i$ is an extension then it has to be consistent ($E_i \nvDash \perp$). Hence, $Con(GD(D,E_i))$ has to be consistent. By means of contradiction we prove now that for every $E_i \in Con(GD(D,E_i))$ is maximally (w.r.t $\subseteq$) consistent subset of $\mathcal{F}$. Let us suppose the contrary, i.e. $Con(GD(D,E))$ is not maximally* *consistent. Then there exists another extension $E'$ for which $Con(GD(D,E_i))$ $\subseteq Con(GD(D,E'))$ such that $GD(D,E')$ is the set of generating defaults of $E'$. Consequently, $Th(W \cup Con(GD(D,E_i))) \subseteq Cn(W \cup Con(GD(D,E')))$. In other words, $E_i \subseteq E'$ is in contradiction with Theorem 1 (minimality).*

*Example 4 (Example 3 cont.).* Consider $\Delta_{\mathcal{K}}$, we have $Con(GD(D,E_1)) = \{teacher(Tom)\}$ and $Con(GD(D,E_2)) = \{student(Tom)\}$, it is obvious that $Con(GD(D,E_1)) \in \mathcal{R}epair(\mathcal{K})$ and $Con(GD(D,E_2)) \in \mathcal{R}epair(\mathcal{K})$.

On one hand, extensions in $\Delta_{\mathcal{K}}$ represent a maximal set of beliefs that can be together. On the other hand, repairs also represent a maximal non-conflicting set of facts. Thus there is a relation between extensions and repairs.

**Proposition 2.** *Every extension $E$ contains one and only one repair $\mathcal{A} \in \mathcal{R}epair(\mathcal{K})$.*

**Proposition 3.** *Every repair $\mathcal{A} \in \mathcal{R}epair(\mathcal{K})$ is contained in one and only one extension $E \in Ext(\Delta_{\mathcal{K}})$.*

**Proof 2** *First, we prove that every repair is contained in at least one extension. Next, we prove that every repair is contained in only one extension.*

1. *On one hand we have $\mathcal{A} \subseteq \mathcal{F}$ thus $R \subseteq Con(D)$ (there exists a set of defaults $D' \subseteq D$ such that $\mathcal{A} = Con(D')$). On other hand, since $\mathcal{A}$ is maximally consistent (w.r.t $\subseteq$), by definition we get $\forall f_i \in \mathcal{F} - \mathcal{A}$, $\text{Cl}_{\mathcal{R}}(\mathcal{A} \cup f_i)$ is $\mathcal{R}$-inconsistent, similarly, $\forall d_i \in D - D'$ the set $Th(W \cup \mathcal{A} \cup cons(d_i)) \vDash \bot$. Therefore we conclude that; (1) $E = Th(W \cup \mathcal{A})$ is closed under $D'$ (there is no default that can be applied), (2) $W \subseteq E$; (3) $Th(E) = E$. Consequently, $E$ is an extension (according to Definition 4) such that $\mathcal{A} \in E$.*

2. *Now let us prove that $E$ is the only extension that contains $\mathcal{A}$. Suppose that $E$ and $E'$ are two extensions and $\mathcal{A} \in E$ and $\mathcal{A} \in E'$, from (1) we have $E = Th(W \cup \mathcal{A})$ and $E' = Th(W \cup \mathcal{A})$, it is not hard to see that $E$ and $E'$ are not orthogonal which contradicts Theorem 1.*

*From 1 and 2 we conclude that a repair $\mathcal{A}$ is contained in one and only one extension.*

In the following example we show the relation between extensions and repairs.

*Example 5 (Example 3 count.).* Consider the repairs $\mathcal{A}_1$ and $\mathcal{A}_2$ of example 2 and the extensions $E_1$ and $E_2$ of the corresponding default theory $\Delta_{\mathcal{K}}$. One can clearly see that $E_1 = Th(\{teacher(Tom), university\_member(Tom)\}) \supset \mathcal{A}_1 = \{teacher(Tom)\}$ and $E_2 = Th(\{student(Tom), university\_member(Tom)\}) \supset \mathcal{A}_1 = \{student(Tom)\}$.

Previous propositions in this section show that the mapping $\tau$ induces a link between *repairs* and *extensions*. We use this link to prove the relation between *AR-semantics* and *sceptical* inference and also between the *Brave-semantics* and *credulous inference* in closed normal default theories.

**Theorem 3.** *Let $\mathcal{K} = (\mathcal{F}, \mathcal{R}, \mathcal{N})$ be an inconsistent knowledge base, $\Delta_{\mathcal{K}}=(W, D)$ be the corresponding closed normal default theory obtained by the mapping $\tau$ and let $\alpha$ be a query. Then:*

1. *$\mathcal{K} \vDash_{\mathtt{AR}} \alpha$ iff $\alpha$ is sceptically entailed by $\Delta_{\mathcal{K}}$.*
2. *$\mathcal{K} \vDash_{\mathtt{brave}} \alpha$ iff $\alpha$ is credulously entailed by $\Delta_{\mathcal{K}}$.*

In Example 2, we mentioned that the query $\alpha = university\_member(Tom)$ is $AR$-entailed by the knowledge base $\mathcal{K}$ ($\mathcal{K} \vDash_{\mathtt{AR}} \alpha$). In the next example we show that $\alpha$ is sceptically entailed by $\Delta_K$.

*Example 6 (Example 3 count.).* Consider the extensions $E_1$ and $E_2$ and let $\alpha_1 = university\_member(tom)$ and $\alpha_2 = teacher(tom)$. It is clear that $\alpha_1 \in E_1$ and $\alpha_1 \in E_2$, thus $\alpha$ is sceptically entailed by $\Delta_{\mathcal{K}}$. Whereas $\alpha_1$ belongs only to $E_1$ thus $\alpha_1$ is credulously entailed by $\Delta_{\mathcal{K}}$.

Note that a closed normal default theory always has an extension, and if it has more than one extension then the extensions are inconsistent together (orthogonal). Based on this we can observe that if the corresponding default theory $\Delta_{\mathcal{K}}$ has more than one extension then $\mathcal{K}$ is inconsistent.

By virtue of the equivalences provided in this section, we can prove interesting properties about inconsistency-tolerant semantics. In Section 2 we have shown that closed normal default theories enjoy the property of semi-monotonicity which states that the extensions of the original theory are always preserved within the extension of the new theory (with the addition of new closed normal defaults). We show how this property holds in inconsistency-tolerant semantics.

**Theorem 4 (Semi-monotonicity).** *Let $\mathcal{K} = (\mathcal{F}, \mathcal{R}, \mathcal{N})$ and $\mathcal{K}' = (\mathcal{F}', \mathcal{R}, \mathcal{N})$ be two inconsistent knowledge bases such that $\mathcal{F}' \subseteq \mathcal{F}$ and let $\mathcal{A}'$ be a repair of $\mathcal{K}'$. Then, $\mathcal{K}$ has a repair $\mathcal{A} \in Repair(\mathcal{K})$ such that $\mathcal{A}' \subseteq \mathcal{A}$.*

*Proof.* Let us suppose the following, $\mathcal{K}' = (\mathcal{F}', \mathcal{R}, \mathcal{N})$ and $\mathcal{K} = (\mathcal{F}, \mathcal{R}, \mathcal{N})$ such that $\mathcal{F} = \mathcal{F}' \cup \{f\}$ (we get $\mathcal{K}$ by adding a new fact to $\mathcal{F}'$), suppose further that $\mathcal{A}_1 \in Repair(\mathcal{K})$ and $\mathcal{A}'_1 \in Repair(\mathcal{K}')$, then either (1) $\mathcal{A}_1 = \mathcal{A}'_1 \cup \{f\}$ is consistent, then $\mathcal{A}_1$ is a repair of $\mathcal{K}$ such that $\mathcal{A}'_1 \subset \mathcal{A}_1$; or (2) $\mathcal{A}_1 = \mathcal{A}'_1 \cup \{f\}$ is inconsistent, thus $\{f\}$ will form a new repair $\mathcal{A}_2$ such that $\{f\} \in \mathcal{A}_2$. In two cases there exists always a repair $\mathcal{A}_1$ such that $\mathcal{A}'_1 \subseteq \mathcal{A}$.

The next corollary then follows.

**Corollary 1.** *Let $\mathcal{K} = (\mathcal{F}, \mathcal{R}, \mathcal{N})$ and $\mathcal{K}' = (\mathcal{F}', \mathcal{R}, \mathcal{N})$ be two inconsistent knowledge bases such that $\mathcal{F}' \subseteq \mathcal{F}$ and let $\mathcal{A}'_1$ and $\mathcal{A}'_2$ be two repairs of $\mathcal{K}'$. Then $\mathcal{K} = (\mathcal{F}, \mathcal{R}, \mathcal{N})$ has two repairs $\mathcal{A}_1$ and $\mathcal{A}_2$ such that $\mathcal{A}'_1 \subseteq \mathcal{A}_1$ and $\mathcal{A}'_2 \subseteq \mathcal{A}_1$.*

This stipulates that for an inconsistent knowledge base $\mathcal{K}$, $\mathcal{K}$ is monotone with respect the addition of new facts. That means the repairs of a knowledge base with fewer facts from the original knowledge base are always preserved within the repairs of the original knowledge base. Notice that, $\mathcal{K}$ is non-monotone with respect to the addition of new constraints, because the added constraints can alter its repairs.

In what follows we show the result of Corollary 1 and Theorem 4 on AR and Brave semantics.

**Proposition 4.** *Let* $\mathcal{K}' = (\mathcal{F}', \mathcal{R}, \mathcal{N})$ *and* $\mathcal{K} = (\mathcal{F}, \mathcal{R}, \mathcal{N})$ *be two inconsistent knowledge bases such that* $\mathcal{F}' \subseteq \mathcal{F}$ *and let* $\alpha$ *be a query. Then, (i) if* $\mathcal{K}' \vDash_{\mathsf{brave}} \alpha$ *then* $\mathcal{K} \vDash_{\mathsf{brave}} \alpha$; *(ii) if* $\mathcal{K}' \vDash_{\mathsf{AR}} \alpha$ *then* $\mathcal{K} \vDash_{\mathsf{brave}} \alpha$.

## 5 Conclusion

We have studied the relation between Default Logic and inconsistent ontological knowledge bases within a rule-based language in the OBDA setting and shown that every inconsistent knowledge base can be efficiently represented as a closed normal default theory. This gives the possibility to bridge two different formalisms. We proved that inconsistency-tolerant semantics enjoys the same property of a closed normal default theory, namely semi-monotonicity. In addition, this work shows the expressiveness of Default Logic as a powerful nonmonotonic formalism that is capable of handling different problems. A further study on the equivalences with another variants of Default Logic (constrained, justified, rational, etc) will be a matter of interest; as well as the relation with Answer Set Programming given its computational efficiency.

## References

1. Baader, F., Brandt, S., Lutz, C.: Pushing the el envelope. In: Proc. of IJCAI 2005 (2005)
2. Bienvenu, M.: On the complexity of consistent query answering in the presence of simple ontologies. In: Proc. of AAAI (2012)
3. Bienvenu, M., Rosati, R.: Tractable approximations of consistent query answering for robust ontology-based data access. In: Proceedings of the Twenty-Third International Joint Conference on Artificial Intelligence, pp. 775–781. AAAI Press (2013)
4. Calì, A., Gottlob, G., Lukasiewicz, T.: A general datalog-based framework for tractable query answering over ontologies. Web Semantics: Science, Services and Agents on the World Wide Web 14, 57–83 (2012)
5. Calvanese, D., De Giacomo, G., Lembo, D., Lenzerini, M., Rosati, R.: Tractable reasoning and efficient query answering in description logics: The dl-lite family. J. Autom. Reasoning 39(3), 385–429 (2007)
6. Cholewiski, P., Marek, V.W., Truszczyski, M., Mikitiuk, A.: Computing with default logic. Artificial Intelligence 112(1-2), 105–146 (1999)
7. Dung, P.M.: On the acceptability of arguments and its fundamental role in nonmonotonic reasoning, logic programming and n-persons games. Artificial Intelligence 77(2), 321–357 (1995)
8. Engelfriet, J., Treur, J.: An interpretation of default logic in minimal temporal epistemic logic. J. of Logic, Lang. and Inf. 7(3), 369–388 (1998)

9. Gottlob, G.: Translating default logic into standard autoepistemic logic. J. ACM 42(4), 711–740 (1995)
10. Imielinski, T.: Results on translating defaults to circumscription. Artif. Intell. 32(1), 131–146 (1987)
11. Konolige, K.: On the Relation Between Default and Autoepistemic Logic. In: Readings in Nonmonotonic Reasoning, pp. 195–226. Morgan Kaufmann Publishers Inc. (1987)
12. Lembo, D., Lenzerini, M., Rosati, R., Ruzzi, M., Savo, D.F.: Inconsistency-tolerant semantics for description logics. In: Hitzler, P., Lukasiewicz, T. (eds.) RR 2010. LNCS, vol. 6333, pp. 103–117. Springer, Heidelberg (2010)
13. Lenzerini, M.: Data integration: A theoretical perspective. In: Proc. of PODS 2002 (2002)
14. Marek, W., Truszczynski, M.: Stable semantics for logic programs and default theories. In: NACLP, pp. 243–256 (1989)
15. Mugnier, M.-L.: Ontological query answering with existential rules. In: Rudolph, S., Gutierrez, C. (eds.) RR 2011. LNCS, vol. 6902, pp. 2–23. Springer, Heidelberg (2011)
16. Nicolas, P., Saubion, F., Stéphan, I.: Gadel: a genetic algorithm to compute default logic extensions. In: ECAI, pp. 484–490 (2000)
17. Nicolas, P., Schaub, T.: The xray system: An implementation platform for local query-answering in default logics. In: Hunter, A., Parsons, S. (eds.) Applications of Uncertainty Formalisms. LNCS (LNAI), vol. 1455, pp. 354–378. Springer, Heidelberg (1998)
18. Poggi, A., Lembo, D., Calvanese, D., De Giacomo, G., Lenzerini, M., Rosati, R.: Linking data to ontologies. In: Spaccapietra, S. (ed.) Journal on Data Semantics X. LNCS, vol. 4900, pp. 133–173. Springer, Heidelberg (2008)
19. Reiter, R.: A logic for default reasoning. Artificial Intelligence 13 (1980)
20. Schaub, T., Brüning, S.: Prolog technology for default reasoning: proof theory and compilation techniques. Artificial Intelligence 106(1), 1–75 (1998)
21. Schaub, T., Nicolas, P.: An implementation platform for query-answering in default logics: The xray system, its implementation and evaluation. In: Fuhrbach, U., Dix, J., Nerode, A. (eds.) LPNMR 1997. LNCS, vol. 1265, pp. 441–452. Springer, Heidelberg (1997)
22. Truszczynski, M.: The modal logic s4f, the default logic, and the logic here-and-there. In: AAAI, pp. 508–514. AAAI Press (2007)

# Automated Discovery of Mobile Users Locations with Improved K-means Clustering

Szymon Bobek[✉], Grzegorz J. Nalepa, and Olgierd Grodzki

AGH University of Science and Technology,
al. Mickiewicza 30, 30-059 Krakow, Poland
{szymon.bobek,gjn}@agh.edu.pl

**Abstract.** Location is one of the most commonly used contextual information in mobile context-aware systems. It can be considered on many different levels of granularity, varying from geolocation that is based on GPS systems, up to microlocation that uses Bluetooth Low Energy devices and WiFi access points for locating users inside buildings. Most common use of location is navigation, however recently it is more often considered also as an important component of the user profile. One of the biggest challenges in location-based context-aware systems is the discovery of patterns in user transportation traces and extraction of the most often visited places. In this paper we presented and evaluated a method that allows for automatic extraction of clusters from user location traces. These clusters represents user points of interest like home, work, favourite restaurants, but also transportation routines. The original contribution of this work is a proposal of an approach based on the K-means clustering algorithm equipped with a module for automatic discovery of number of clusters and density-based cluster merging. This method allows for online, adaptable discovery of user points of interests, and transportation routines in mobile systems.

**Keywords:** Context-awareness · Mobile devices · Clustering · Localisation

## 1 Introduction

Due to the rapid development of personal mobile devices, context-aware systems gained a huge popularity in recent years. Nowadays smartphones and tablets are equipped with a variety of sensors that can provide valuable information about user context. However, efficient collecting, modelling and processing of large amount of information streaming from such sensors is still a challenge for mobile systems developers [19,3]. Due to this fact, in practical applications of mobile context-aware systems only the location context is used, as there was a lot of research devoted to the problem of geolocation and positioning [25]. Although localization is relatively mature area of research there is still a lot of challenges

This work was funded by the National Science Centre, Poland as a part of the KnowMe project (reference number 2014/13/N/ST6/01786).

© Springer International Publishing Switzerland 2015
L. Rutkowski et al. (Eds.): ICAISC 2015, Part II, LNAI 9120, pp. 565–577, 2015.
DOI: 10.1007/978-3-319-19369-4_50

in terms of modelling and processing locational data for automatic discovery of user profiles.

Two different classes of information can be extracted from user location traces, which forms the locational user profile. These are:

- Transportation routines – describing routes which are most often used by a user to travel between points of interests.
- Usual locations, or points of interests (POIs) – places which are special for the user in some way. This can be home, work, favourite shopping centre or restaurant, etc.

These two types of information can be used for example by the mobile context-aware navigation system to suggest different routes from work to home when the usual route is slow. On the other hand, the user favourite locations may be used by the mobile context-aware tourist application to suggest POIs that fit best the user preferences. In the area of ambient assisted living, discovery of both: transportation routines and user POIs, can be used for monitoring user behaviour and detecting anomalies in daily routines, as well as helping the user in reaching important places like home, pharmacy, etc.

One of the major challenges in such systems is the discovery and recognition of position clusters from user location traces. Although there was a lot of research done in a field of automatic clustering of data, there is still need to investigate methods for clustering and labeling data in highly dynamic environments. In mobile context-aware systems number of clusters is unknown a priori. Moreover, clusters are of different densities and nature (work, shops, etc.) and they are evolving, as the learning data streams constantly from the device sensors. What is more, semantics of such clusters is also not known, and has to be inferred or labelled by the user in a process of mediation [5].

In this paper we proposed a solution that allows for an automatic discovery of clusters from user GPS traces. These clusters can represent both POIs and transportation routines. Number of clusters is discovered automatically by the algorithm that is based on the modified K-means with analysis of distortion function and cluster merging module. Discovered clusters can later be labelled by the user or inferred from other contextual information or data embedded on the maps.

Rest of the paper is organised as follows. In Section 2 related work was presented and a motivation for our work was given. Detailed description of the algorithm used in our approach is described in Section 3, while the practical evaluation was presented in Section 4. Section 5 contains summary and remarks on the challenges and future work.

## 2   Related Work and Motivation

In [2] authors used K-means algorithm for clustering user GPS traces into locations. They performed offline clustering of data gathered by the mobile users, and manually estimated number of clusters, by analysing the cost function curve for different $K$ values. The solution presented in this approach uses standard version of

K-means. In such, every execution of the algorithm goes through the entire data set iteratively until convergence. In the case of location data, the data set is updated roughly every minute or even more often. Because of this, running the standard K-means algorithm for every updated data set would introduce significant computational overhead. As a solution to this problem, using a *streaming* modification of the K-means algorithm is proposed [22]. It aims to resolve a problem associated with large growth in data and proposes a streaming model, where the algorithm can make one or very few passes through the data, reducing the computational overhead. The most important advantage of the K-means algorithm is that it allows for efficient clustering of high-dimensional data. This allows performing an automated sensor-fusion without any special adjustment of the algorithm. On the other hand the standard version of K-means requires knowledge of the number of clusters into which the data has to be divided, which is not always available.

---

**Algorithm 1.** k-means clustering

    **input**: data $D \in \mathbb{R}^d$; number of clusters $K \in \mathbb{N}$
    **output**: K cluster means $\mu_1, ..., \mu_K \in \mathbb{R}^d$
1  randomly initialize $K$ vectors $\mu_1, ..., \mu_K \in \mathbb{R}^d$;
2  **repeat**
3     assign each $x \in D$ to $\arg\min\limits_{j} d(x, \mu_j)$;
4     **for** $j = 1$ **to** $K$ **do**
5         $D_j \leftarrow \{x \in D \mid x \text{ assigned to cluster } j\}$;
6         $\mu_j = \frac{1}{|D_j|} \sum_{x \in D_j} x$;
7  **until** *no change in* $\mu_1, ..., \mu_K$;
8  **return** $\mu_1, ..., \mu_K$;

---

**Fig. 1.** Basic K-Means formulation [8]

To solve the problem of the unknown number of clusters in dataset an algorithm called DBSCAN [6] was developed. It is a density-based clustering algorithm that was designed to efficiently partition two-dimensional data. The knowledge of the number of clusters in not required as the algorithm uses density threshold to label high-density areas as clusters and discard all the remaining low-density areas as noise. DBSCAN and its variations like SMoT [1] and CB-SMoT [20] are most often used for discovery of stops and moves in user locational data. Simillar goals can be achieved with X-means [21] and G-means [10] algorithms which are modified versions of standard K-means. They allow for automated discovery of number of clusters by performing statistical analysis on the generated sets to determine these which should be splitteed. However, such methods tend to discover too many clusters, as they do not provide any merging mechanism [4].

Among standard solutions like these mentioned previously, there is also a lot of hybrid approaches that optimize some of the bottlenecks of the clustering task. To avoid clustering the large trajectory dataset a co-clustering method called CADC was proposed [13]. It enhances clustering process by discovering similar objects in dataset and allows for efficient incremental clustering in response to new GPS trajectory data.

In [17] two levels of clustering are used to obtain places of interest. First, user location points are grouped using a time-based clustering technique which discovers stay points while dealing with missing location data. The second level performs clustering on the stay points to obtain stay regions. Time based clustering was proposed in [12]. It eliminates the intermediate locations between important places, and determines the number of clusters (important places) autonomously. Also, it is also efficient enough to run on a mobile device as a background task.

Although there is a lot of work devoted to the problem of discovery of user POIs and transportation routines, there is none that tackles all the following issues in terms of mobile context-aware systems:

1. In such systems the number of clusters is unknown a priori and may change over time, so clusters may evolve.
2. The problem of clusters discovery is therefore a continuous process that should be based on streaming data.
3. Clustering two-dimensional location data can be significantly improved by other sensor information. This turns the problem into high-dimensionality clustering task which can be difficult to handle for most DBSCAN-based clustering approaches.

Therefore, the motivation for the work described in this paper was to provide a solution that combines strengths of DBSCAN which allows for automatic discovery of clusters without knowledge of their number, and efficiency of K-means for high dimensional cases and streaming data. For this purpose the modified version of K-means algorithm was proposed. The following section describes in details the approach.

## 3    Automated Clustering with K-means

The automated clustering algorithm presented in this paper consist of three steps that can be briefly defined as follows:

1. Discover number of clusters $K$ with a distortion function approach (*jump method*).
2. Cluster data using the K-means algorithm.
3. Perform cluster merging to combine several low-density clusters into one.

Steps 1 and 3 that correspond to the original contribution of the paper were discussed in details in the following section. As our research demonstrated, the discovery of $K$ should be preceded by the filtering of data to eliminate peaks and false readings. However, the complete analysis of the different filtering algorithms – although extremely important – is beyond the scope of this paper and therefore, only a two different approaches were evaluated and presented in Section 4.

## 3.1   Distortion Function Approach

The standard K-means clustering algorithms requires providing the number of clusters as a parameter. In other words, it can only divide the data set into a given number of parts and have no way of choosing that number. Therefore, the automated clustering problem can be reduced to finding the number of clusters $K$. There is a number of methods for finding $K$ [24]. The one that has been implemented in this paper is called the *jump method* [23]. The procedure is based on distortion, which is a measure of cluster dispersion. The minimum achievable distortion associated with fitting K centres to the data is given as follows:

$$d_K = \frac{1}{p} \min_{c_1,...,c_K} E\left[(\mathbf{X} - \mathbf{c_X})^T \mathbf{\Gamma}^{-1}(\mathbf{X} - \mathbf{c_X})\right] \tag{1}$$

where:

- $\mathbf{X}$ – $p$-dimensional random variable having a mixture distribution of G components, each with covariance $\mathbf{\Gamma}$
- $\mathbf{\Gamma}$ – covariance matrix
- $\mathbf{c}_1,..., \mathbf{c}_K$ – a set of $K$ candidate cluster centres
- $\mathbf{c_X}$ – cluster centre closest to $\mathbf{X}$
- $E$ – expected value

The formula above represents the average Mahalanobis distance[1] per dimension, between $\mathbf{X}$ and $\mathbf{c_X}$. In the case where $\mathbf{\Gamma}$ is the identity matrix distortion is simply mean squared error. In practice one generally estimates $d_K$ using $\hat{d}_K$, the minimum distortion obtained by applying the K-means clustering algorithm [23].

Plotting $d_K$ versus $K$ results in a *distortion curve* in which all the requisite information for choosing the correct number of clusters are contained. It is also shown, both theoretically and empirically, that for a large class of distributions the distortion curve, when transformed to an appropriate negative power, will exhibit a sharp jump at the true number of clusters. The *jump method* is based on this and can be represented as a follows [23]:

---

**Algorithm 2.** Jump method

---

1   Run the k-means algorithm for different numbers of clusters, $K$, and calculate the corresponding distortions, $\hat{d}_K$
2   Select a transformation power, $Y > 0$ (A typical value is $\frac{p}{2}$)
3   Calculate the *jumps* in transformed distortion, $J_K = \hat{d}_K^{-Y} - \hat{d}_{K-1}^{-Y}$
4   Estimate the number of clusters in the data set by $K^* = \arg\max_K J_K$, the value of $K$ associated with the largest jump.

---

The method has advantages: makes limited parametric assumptions, can be theoretically motivated using ideas from the field of rate distortion theory, is both simple to understand and compute, and is highly effective on a wide range of problems [23].

---

[1] It is a measure of the distance between a point P and a distribution D [16].

## 3.2    Clusters Merging Approach

During the preliminary evaluation of the method (standard K-means clustering with the jump method) the quality of the automated clustering was assessed as unsatisfactory. The analysed location data was collected by driving from home to the university and back. The automatically discovered number of clusters turned out to be higher than expected, e.g. 9 instead of 3, which was the desirable result (3 clusters corresponding to *home, road* and *university*).

The analysis of clustered data revealed an expected cluster size difference between two main clusters: POIs and routes. Much bigger clusters were constructed in the endpoints representing *home* and *university*, and much smaller were constructed in between representing transportation trace. Although clustering data at endpoints was desired, splitting transportation route into several tiny clusters was considered as a fault. Two main reasons for this behaviour were observed. The first reason comes from the changes in location data at these places – either only a slight change (at the university) or even a lack of change (at home), which causes the collected location data to be closer. The second reason comes from the time spent in these locations – generally, more time is spent at routine places than in any place on the road between them, which causes the location data collected at these places to be more dense.

Based on these observations, a *clusters merging* approach was proposed. In this approach the smaller clusters were merged into one, based on the density threshold value. Assuming one location data reading per minute, this variable directly corresponds to how much time spent at a location would classify it as a cluster. The cluster merging approach can be represented by the following algorithm:

---

**Algorithm 3.** Clusters merging

---

    **input**: set of clusters $C$ calculated by standard K-means with $k$
              calculated by the jump method; density threshold value $d$
    **output**: set of big clusters $C_b$
1  initialize empty set $C_s$ representing small clusters
2  initialize empty set $C_b$ representing big clusters
3  **foreach** $c \in C$ **do**
4     **if** *number of points assigned to* $c < d$ **then**
5        add $c$ to $C_s$
6     **else**
7        add $c$ to $C_b$
8  initialize empty cluster $c_m$
9  **foreach** $c_s \in C_s$ **do**
10    **if** $c_m$ *is empty* **then**
11       set $c_m$ cluster center to $c_s$ cluster center
12    **else**
13       set $c_m$ cluster center to average of $c_m$ center and $c_s$ center
14    assign all points from $c_s$ to $c_m$
15  add $c_m$ to $C_b$
16  **return** $C_b$

---

It is worth noting that this approach allows to cluster data that characterised by different densities compared to the DBSCAN algorithm, which would either classify the entire data as one big cluster, or discover only high density clusters treating all the other data as noise.

# 4  Practical Evaluation in a Mobile System

Evaluation of the proposed method was performed by developing two mobile applications. The first one was created only as a proof of concept. The second one was created as a more practical solution. Both of them were developed for Android 4.3 system, and were evaluated on the Samsung Galaxy SII device.

## 4.1  Proof of Concept Application

The proof of concept application was developed as a standalone Android application. Besides implementing the automated clustering method described in Section 3, the application also focused on collecting data. That meant considering which data to collect, how to ensure its quality, and how to construct machine learning features from it.

The most important and obvious data to collect was geolocation data – longitude and latitude. The Android API provides two sources of this data (*providers*): the GPS module and network location data. The two providers differ greatly in terms of quality, with the GPS module providing much more accurate location data, but also battery life – keeping the GPS module turned on would have a heavy impact on battery life, while network provider is less energy consuming.

The basic feature set for the clustering algorithm was constructed from longitude, latitude and speed. It was later extended by introducing feature "weighting", which in this case meant constructing two new features by raising longitude and latitude to a power of 2, thus giving the geolocation data a greater "weight".

Data collection was performed by running the proof of concept application. The following experiment was conducted for the sake of evaluation:

1. began collecting at a starting point, in this case home, spent some time there,
2. left the starting point and travelled to a destination, in this case the university,
3. spent some time at the destination,
4. travelled back to the starting point, spent some time there, stopped collecting.

Time between turning on the GPS module was set to one minute and the time window to ensure a location fix was set to 30 seconds. The collected data analysis confirmed the difference in data quality between the two providers, and hence the data from the GPS provider was chosen as a better estimate almost every time the provider was available. Because of the unavailability of the GPS provide indoor, the location data collected inside buildings came almost exclusively from the network provider, which turned out to be significantly distorted.

To overcome this problem, data filtering was introduced. Two filters were compared – a low-pass filter and a Kalman filter. Figure 2 shows unfiltered location data collected at the starting point of the described data collection sequence. As mentioned before, presented data was collected almost exclusively from the network provider due to the unavailability of the GPS provider indoors. Figure 3 shows the comparison of unfiltered data and data filtered with both filters (blue colour represents low-pass filter and green for Kalman filter).

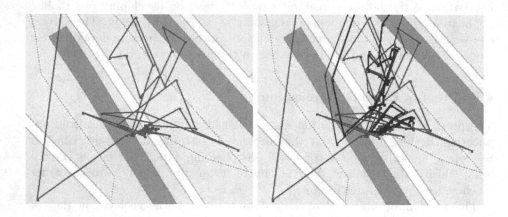

**Fig. 2.** Unfiltered location data        **Fig. 3.** Location data filtered with Kalman filter (green) and low-pass filter (blue)

The second module of the proof of concept application was the automated clustering module. The module implemented the jump method described in section 3.1. The implementation of the K-means algorithm was taken from the WEKA API [2]. Clustering experiments began with the simplest case – only longitude and latitude were used as features and clustered data was unfiltered. A sample result is shown in Figure 4. The algorithm divided the data set into 9 clusters, which was not the desired result, these results were also described in Section 3.2.

As a next step in improving the method, experiments with the feature set began. The feature set was extended by additional data, such as speed, and clustering was repeated. The experiments were unsuccessful as the clustering quality decreased – clusters began to be inconsistent on the Cartesian plane. As a countermeasure, feature ”weighting”, described in earlier in this section, was introduced, unfortunately the quality was not improved enough. Further experiments involved introducing data filtering, Figure 5 shows the result of clustering filtered data. Introducing filtering improved the quality of clustering with a feature set extended by speed with feature ”weighting”, but the number of clusters was still too large.

---

[2] Weka is a powerful, yet easy to use tool for machine learning and data mining offering API in Java, see https://weka.waikato.ac.nz.

Further experiments involved introducing clusters merging, Figure 6 shows the result of clustering unfiltered data with clusters merging. The threshold value between small and large cluster was 15. The number of clusters was greatly improved, the algorithm reached the desired number of 3, but the overall quality was still unsatisfactory, with clusters again being inconsistent. Fortunately, combining clusters merging with data filtering helped to solve this problem, Figure 7 shows this solution, which is also the best solution achieved.

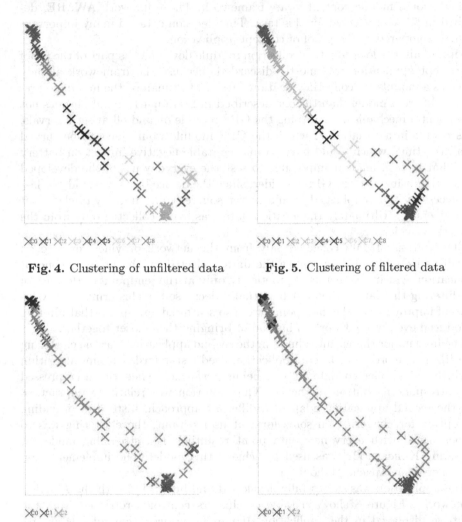

**Fig. 4.** Clustering of unfiltered data      **Fig. 5.** Clustering of filtered data

**Fig. 6.** Clustering of unfiltered data with   **Fig. 7.** Clustering of filtered data with
clusters merging                                 clusters merging

## 4.2  Mobile Context-Aware Framework Integration Application

The proof of concept application worked relatively well in simulated conditions, that is clustering data collected during a specified sequence. The limited practical applications of such a solution and the need for practical evaluation of the general method were the main motivation for developing the second application. It represents a more practical approach, which was achieved by designing it as a plugin for a mobile context-aware framework. The framework AWARE, described in [7], was selected for this task. This decision entailed many important changes compared to the proof of concept application.

First of all, the location data collection module developed as part of the proof of concept application was mostly discarded, because the framework already provides a module for collecting location data. Unfortunately, the module represents a different model than the one described in Section 4.1, mainly it does not implement a mechanism for turning the GPS module on and off at set intervals. This results in a situation in which the GPS module would have to be turned on all the time, which would have an unacceptable negative impact on battery life. That in turn made it impossible to test the everyday use of the developed application using also the GPS provider, since the device battery would not last the necessary time unplugged from a power source (e.g. a full day of classes at the university). Ultimately the location data was being collected only from the network provider.

The analysis of data collected only from the network provider revealed an overall bad quality of data, unlike the data collected by the proof of concept application, which was distorted practically only at the "endpoints". Because of this filtering the data turned out to actually decrease the clustering quality instead of improving it. The data points were so scattered and sparse that filtering introduced even more distortion instead of bringing then closer together.

The final major change introduced in the second application was the clustering algorithm. The proof of concept application used a standard K-means algorithm to cluster the collected data, it was being performed when the user pressed the corresponding button in the UI. That solution was relatively impractical and the second application adapted a different approach. Instead of providing the option for clustering on some form of user's input, the clustering was to be performed with every new data point resulting in a streaming model. A streaming K-means [22] was used to achieve this model. The implementation was taken from Apache Mahout [9].

The application was successfully developed and integrated with the AWARE framework[3]. Figure 8 shows a table of clusters centroids retrieved from the database displayed in the application. It can be noticed that all IDs are repeated four times, which corresponds to 4 clusters centroids calculated for every new data point. The most recent data in the table represents current cluster centroids assignment. Remaining data corresponds to cluster centroids calculated for the past data. This can be used to observe the evolution of cluster centroids

---

[3] See http://www.awareframework.com

over time. Figure 9 shows the collected data assigned to the most recent clusters from the database.

| ID | Longitude | Latitude | Timestamp |
|---|---|---|---|
| 1538 | ,0592 | ,9300 | 2014-06-06 21:33:20.173 |
| 1538 | ,9703 | ,0127 | 2014-06-06 21:33:20.173 |
| 1538 | ,0127 | ,9702 | 2014-06-06 21:33:20.173 |
| 1538 | ,0289 | ,9046 | 2014-06-06 21:33:20.173 |
| 1537 | ,0660 | ,9214 | 2014-06-06 21:28:19.653 |
| 1537 | ,9703 | ,0127 | 2014-06-06 21:28:19.653 |
| 1537 | ,0127 | ,9702 | 2014-06-06 21:28:19.653 |
| 1537 | ,0524 | ,9386 | 2014-06-06 21:28:19.653 |
| 1536 | ,0660 | ,9214 | 2014-06-06 21:23:20.123 |
| 1536 | ,9702 | ,0127 | 2014-06-06 21:23:20.123 |
| 1536 | ,0127 | ,9702 | 2014-06-06 21:23:20.123 |
| 1536 | ,0524 | ,9386 | 2014-06-06 21:23:20.123 |
| 1535 | ,0524 | ,9386 | 2014-06-06 21:18:19.939 |
| 1535 | ,9703 | ,0127 | 2014-06-06 21:18:19.939 |
| 1535 | ,0289 | ,9046 | 2014-06-06 21:18:19.939 |
| 1535 | ,0660 | ,9214 | 2014-06-06 21:18:19.939 |
| 1534 | ,0660 | ,9214 | 2014-06-06 21:13:22.241 |
| 1534 | 9702 | 0127 | 2014-06-06 21:13:22.241 |

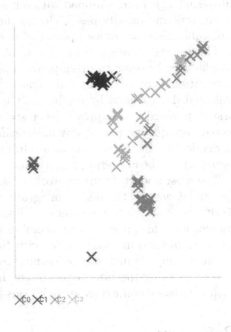

**Fig. 8.** Table representation of clusters centroids stored in a database

**Fig. 9.** Chart representation of latest clusters from the table in figure 8

The data was collected over one week, using only the network provider except for approximately one hour, when the GPS module was turned on for navigational purposes. This can be found on the chart as a trail to the north-eastern corner. Even though GPS navigation can also be thought of as part of everyday use, in this case it caused the relatively well formed green cluster to "stretch" and was not correctly assigned to the grey cluster representing the "road" *domain*. A possible reason for such behaviour would be the sudden "spike" in data quality which upset the previous balance. Although the overall clustering quality is not satisfactory, the algorithm actually managed to learn a correct number of clusters – the red cluster to the west is a correct separate *domain*, although the point to the south should ideally be assigned to the cluster representing the "road" *domain*. Integer parts of decimal degrees representing longitude and latitude from Figure 8 and axes tick labels from Figures 4, 5, 6, 7 and 9 were removed to preserve author's privacy.

# 5   Summary and Future Work

In this paper we presented and evaluated a method that allows for automatic clusters extraction from user location traces with modified version of K-means clustering algorithm equipped with a module for automatic discovery of number of clusters and density-based cluster merging. This method allows for online, adaptable discovery of user points of interests, and transportation routines.

The results obtained from the proof of concept application were relatively satisfactory, however an attempt to implement the method in a more practical application were not. The main reason for this was the insufficient quality of collected data, caused by relying only on the network provider. Therefore, the first step in order to improve the clustering quality would be improving the collected data quality, perhaps by integrating the data collection method described in Section 4.1 in the context-aware framework or by introducing more features (sensors) for the clustering algorithm.

The most important future work is labelling the clusters to actually represent specific *domains*. Thanks to integrating the solution with a AWARE framework, the application has access to all kinds of contextual data gathered by the framework, which may be very useful in inferring correct *domains*. Developing a labelling method in combination with the automated clustering method would create a complete method for learning concrete routine user's locations. We are also considering the integration of the here described localisation applications with rule-based context aware solutions [18].

# References

1. Alvares, L.O., Bogorny, V., Kuijpers, B., de Macedo, J.A.F., Moelans, B., Vaisman, A.: A model for enriching trajectories with semantic geographical information. In: Proceedings of the 15th Annual ACM International Symposium on Advances in Geographic Information Systems, GIS 2007, pp. 22:1–22:8. ACM, New York (2007), http://doi.acm.org/10.1145/1341012.1341041
2. Ashbrook, D., Starner, T.: Using gps to learn significant locations and predict movement across multiple users. Personal Ubiquitous Comput. 7(5), 275–286 (2003), http://dx.doi.org/10.1007/s00779-003-0240-0
3. Bobek, S., Porzycki, K., Nalepa, G.J.: Learning sensors usage patterns in mobile context-aware systems. In: Proceedings of the FedCSIS 2013 Conference, Krakow, pp. 993–998. IEEE (September 2013)
4. Debatty, T., Michiardi, P., Thonnard, O., Mees, W.: Determining the k in k-means with MapReduce. In: ICDT 2014, 17th International Conference on Database Theory, in conjunction with EDBT/ICDT 2014, Athens, Greece, March 24-28 (2014), http://www.eurecom.fr/publication/4366
5. Dey, A.K., Mankoff, J.: Designing mediation for context-aware applications. ACM Trans. Comput.-Hum. Interact. 12(1), 53–80 (2005), http://doi.acm.org/10.1145/1057237.1057241
6. Ester, M., Peter Kriegel, H., Sander, J., Xu, X.: A density-based algorithm for discovering clusters in large spatial databases with noise, pp. 226–231. AAAI Press (1996)
7. Ferreira, D.: AWARE: A mobile context instrumentation middleware to collaboratively understand human behavior. Ph.D. thesis (2013)

8. Flach, P.: Machine Learning: The art and science of algorithms that make sense of data. Cambridge University Press (September 2012)
9. Foundation, A.S.: Apache Mahout, https://mahout.apache.org/
10. Hamerly, G., Elkan, C.: Learning the k in k-means. In: Neural Information Processing Systems, p. 2003. MIT Press (2003)
11. Hartigan, J.A., Wong, M.A.: Algorithm AS 136: A K-Means Clustering Algorithm. Applied Statistics 28(1), 100–108 (1979), http://dx.doi.org/10.2307/2346830
12. Kang, J.H., Welbourne, W., Stewart, B., Borriello, G.: Extracting places from traces of locations. In: Proceedings of the 2nd ACM International Workshop on Wireless Mobile Applications and Services on WLAN Hotspots, WMASH 2004, pp. 110–118. ACM, New York (2004), http://doi.acm.org/10.1145/1024733.1024748
13. Leung, K.W.T., Lee, D.L., Lee, W.C.: Clr: A collaborative location recommendation framework based on co-clustering. In: Proceedings of the 34th International ACM SIGIR Conference on Research and Development in Information Retrieval, SIGIR 2011, pp. 305–314. ACM, New York (2011), http://doi.acm.org/10.1145/2009916.2009960
14. Lloyd, S.: Least squares quantization in pcm. IEEE Transactions on Information Theory 28(2), 129–137 (1982)
15. MacQueen, J.: Some methods for classification and analysis of multivariate observations. In: Proceedings of the Fifth Berkeley Symposium on Mathematical Statistics and Probability. Statistics, vol. 1, pp. 281–297. University of California Press, Berkeley (1967), http://projecteuclid.org/euclid.bsmsp/1200512992
16. Mahalanobis, P.C.: On the generalised distance in statistics. Proceedings of the National Institute of Science 2, 49–55 (1936), http://ir.isical.ac.in/dspace/handle/1/1268
17. Montoliu, R., Gatica-Perez, D.: Discovering human places of interest from multimodal mobile phone data. In: Proceedings of the 9th International Conference on Mobile and Ubiquitous Multimedia, MUM 2010, pp. 12:1–12:10. ACM, New York (2010), http://doi.acm.org/10.1145/1899475.1899487
18. Nalepa, G.J., Bobek, S., Ligęza, A., Kaczor, K.: Algorithms for rule inference in modularized rule bases. In: Bassiliades, N., Governatori, G., Paschke, A. (eds.) RuleML 2011 - Europe. LNCS, vol. 6826, pp. 305–312. Springer, Heidelberg (2011)
19. Nalepa, G.J., Bobek, S.: Rule-based solution for context-aware reasoning on mobile devices. Computer Science and Information Systems 11(1), 171–193 (2014)
20. Palma, A.T., Bogorny, V., Kuijpers, B., Alvares, L.O.: A clustering-based approach for discovering interesting places in trajectories. In: Proceedings of the 2008 ACM Symposium on Applied Computing, SAC 2008, pp. 863–868. ACM, New York (2008), http://doi.acm.org/10.1145/1363686.1363886
21. Pelleg, D., Moore, A.: X-means: Extending k-means with efficient estimation of the number of clusters. In: Proceedings of the 17th International Conf. on Machine Learning, pp. 727–734. Morgan Kaufmann (2000)
22. Shindler, M., Wong, A., Meyerson, A.: Fast and accurate k-means for large datasets. In: Shawe-Taylor, J., Zemel, R.S., Bartlett, P.L., Pereira, F.C.N., Weinberger, K.Q. (eds.) NIPS, pp. 2375–2383 (2011), http://dblp.uni-trier.de/db/conf/nips/nips2011.html#ShindlerWM11
23. Sugar, C.A., James, G.M.: Finding the number of clusters in a data set: An information theoretic approach. Journal of the American Statistical Association 98, 750–763 (2003)
24. Tibshirani, R., Walther, G., Hastie, T.: Estimating the number of clusters in a dataset via the gap statistic 63, 411–423 (2000)
25. Wang, J., Ghosh, R., Das, S.: A survey on sensor localization. Journal of Control Theory and Applications 8(1), 2–11 (2010), http://dx.doi.org/10.1007/s11768-010-9187-7

# Capturing Dynamics of Mobile Context-Aware Systems with Rules and Statistical Analysis of Historical Data

Szymon Bobek[✉], Mateusz Ślażyński, and Grzegorz J. Nalepa

AGH University of Science and Technology,
al. Mickiewicza 30, 30-059 Krakow, Poland
{szymon.bobek,mslaz,gjn}@agh.edu.pl

**Abstract.** Mobile context-aware systems gained huge popularity in recent years due to the rapid evolution of personal mobile devices. Nowadays smartphones are equipped with a variety of sensors that allow for on-line monitoring of user context and reasoning upon it. Contextual information in such systems is very dynamic. It changes rapidly and these changes may have impact on system behaviour. Although there are many machine learning methods like Markov models that allow to handle such dynamics, they do not provide intelligibility features that rule-based systems do. In this paper we propose an extension to XTT2 rule representation that allows for modelling dynamics of the mobile context-aware systems using rules and statistical analysis of historical data. This was achieved by introducing time-based operators to rule conditions and statistical operators to right hand side of the rules.

**Keywords:** Rule-based system · Mobile computing · Reasoning · Statistics

## 1 Introduction

Mobile context-aware systems make use of contextual information to infer higher-level context or trigger some pre-defined actions. In mobile environments context changes very fast and therefore has to be processed in a real time. The naive approach for handling this task is to provide fast and efficient mechanism based on simple key-value matching between current context and pre-defined patterns that triggers actions [26] or invokes further inference [5].

Although such solutions are very popular due to their simplicity, they do not take into consideration historical states of the system, treating all new incoming observations independently from the previous ones. Discarding historical data, makes the system insensitive to patterns that may be present in such data. Knowledge about such patterns can be used to predict future system state and therefore to prepare desired information in advance, before the application actually requests it. What is more, statistical analysis of historical information

This work was funded by the National Science Centre, Poland as a part of the KnowMe project (reference number 2014/13/N/ST6/01786).

L. Rutkowski et al. (Eds.): ICAISC 2015, Part II, LNAI 9120, pp. 578–590, 2015.
DOI: 10.1007/978-3-319-19369-4_51

about sensor data, allows for better understanding of the sensor characteristics which can improve system adaptability and optimize it in terms of energy consumption [3].

One of the most common formalisms that allow for time-based inference is temporal logic. It provides mechanisms for representing, and reasoning about propositions qualified in terms of time. What is more, with temporal logics it is possible to express modalities of time that allows to capture time-spanned events with simple clauses. Although temporal logic provides huge capabilities of time related reasoning, it lacks support for standard statistical operators like mean or variance.

The most widely used methods that are based on the paradigm of statistical analysis of historical data are machine learning algorithms. In contrary to other approaches, machine learning (ML) solutions do not use fixed model, but rather learn it from data discovering patterns hidden within it. The most popular ML techniques used extensively in the area of context-aware systems are probabilistic graphical models (PGM) [9], as they provide a very effective way of modelling and reasoning on dynamic and uncertain information. However, exact inference in complex probabilistic models is an NP-hard task and is not always tractable.

Intractability of the system inference, on the other hand, violates intelligibility feature, which is one of the fundamental requirements for the user-centric systems [14]. It is defined as the capability of the system for being understood. This feature is crucial in systems that require interaction with the user, like mobile context-aware systems [17]. The ability of explaining system decisions to the user makes it possible to collect user feedback about system. This on the other hand, can be used to significantly improve overall system performance by resolving ambiguous context, or prioritising rules.

In this paper we propose a solution that combines strengths of statistical analysis available in machine learning with basic time modalities and intelligibility features of rule-based system. We extended XTT2 rule notation [20] with statistical operators that allow for basic reasoning on historical data. We also provide a proof-of-concept implementation of this operators in HEARTDROID[1] inference engine [15].

The rest of the paper is organised as follows. Section 2 presents the current works in the area of exploiting historical information in context-aware systems and presents our motivation. An extension to the XTT2 rule representation was presented in Section 3, while Section 4 discusses implementation of these operators and presents a simple use-case scenarios. Summary and directions for future work were presented in Section 5.

## 2    Related Work and Motivation

Historical information about the system states is crucial for modelling dynamics of the environment. There are several approaches that incorporates such data in the model.

---

[1] HEARTDROID is a rule-based inference engine for Android mobile devices, that is based on HeaRT inference engine. See https://bitbucket.org/sbobek/heartdroid

One of the most common formalism that provides a toolset for reasoning in time-based environments is temporal logic. In [24] authors present the context model for the home domain called CAMUS, and show how it entails implicit reasoning with a combination of several different paradigms, including temporal logic for time-related events handling. Nick Palmer in [21] proposes a flexible context expression language for smartphones called Swansong. It adapts some of the temporal logic modalities like *always, never* and allows for windowed searches in previous states for minimal and maximal values.

Historical data are also the most important input for case-based reasoning systems (CBR). Such approach allows for solving new problems based on the solutions of similar past problems. In [11] a recommendation context-aware system was presented, which uses case-based reasoning for suggesting music. It exploits information about user's demographics and behavioural patterns but also his/her context at the time of making recommendation. In [10] authors propose a mobile context-aware comparative shopping system that automatically estimates user preferences to determine the best purchase. It uses case-based reasoning and negotiation mechanism for estimating the buyer's current preference for the product based on the previous purchases. The survey on the usage of CBR in ambient intelligent systems is presented in [22].

Probabilistic approaches are most widely used in the area of context-aware systems to model human activities [8], transportation routines [12], and other aspects that are characterized by high uncertainty of data. Time-dependant dynamics of the system can be modelled in such approach with and usage of dynamic Bayesian networks or Markov models [23]. Bui *et al* [4] incorporates historical information to the model by using a multi-layer Bayesian dynamic structure, called an Abstract Hidden Markov Model, to track an object and predict its future trajectory.

An interesting approach was proposed by Jaroucheh *et al* in [7]. Authors presents there a solution that uses processes to model user context. According to Jaroucheh, it is crucial to denote user current, past and possible future context in determining full context. For example, user is in the room – has he just came in, or is he about to leave? This was achieved by the authors with an usage of Petri nets and process mining techniques.

## 2.1   Motivation

Although there exist methods that allow for modelling dynamics of the system, like Markov models, or dynamic Bayesian networks, they do not provide intelligibility features. Such models are not understandable for the user and cannot be changed, or adjusted easily. This on the other hand can be efficiently done with rule-based knowledge representation. Case-based reasoning methods make use of historical data to solve similar new problems. However, this approach does not allow for analysing previous states of the system individually (e.g.. asking what was user activity an hour ago). This is crucial in mobile context-aware systems, as the knowledge about previous system state can determine context of the current situation. Such capabilities of referring to the past states are available in temporal logics. These however do not allow for more sophisticated statistical analysis like calculating variance, standard deviation, means and other factors that allow to capture dynamics of the past states in an aggregated manner.

Therefore, the primary motivation for the work presented in this paper was a need for methods that would combine statistical analysis of historical data with rule-based inference capabilities. Such methods would allow for better modelling of the dynamics of the mobile context-aware systems that are immersed in dynamic environment. What is more, rule-based model will provide intelligibility capabilities, which can be further used to obtain user feedback and improve overall system performance. We decided to use XTT2 rule representation method [20] as the starting point for the work, as it is used by the HEARTDROID inference engine, dedicated for the mobile platforms. The following sections describe in details results of our work.

## 3 Time-based Operations in XTT2

### 3.1 Extended Tabular Trees

XTT2 is a visual knowledge representation method for rule-based systems software [13,18,19] where rules are stored in tables connected with each other creating a graph. Figure 1 represents a simple XTT2 model that was used in a mobile context-aware application for online threat monitoring in urban environment [1]

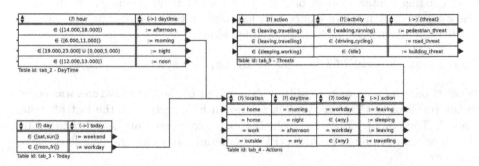

**Fig. 1.** Example of the model for a mobile threat monitor [1]

The XTT2 has a textual representation called HMR that is used by the HEARTDROID inference engine. An example of a rule written in HMR language is presented below. The rule is referenced in Figure 1, in table *Today*.

```
xrule Today/1: [day in [sat,sun]] ==> [today set weekend].
```

Every HMR rule consists of two elements: conditional part (LHS) and decision part (RHS). LHS of the rule is encoded with Attribute Logic with Set Values over Finite Domains (ALSV(FD) for short). The basic elements of the language of ALSV(FD) are attribute names and attribute values. There are two attributes types: *simple* which allows the attribute to take a single value at a time, and *generalized* that allows the attribute to take set values. The values that every attribute can take are limited by their domains. For the purpose of further discussion let's assume that: $A_i$ represents some arbitrarily chosen attribute, $D_i$ is a domain of this attribute, and $V_i$ represents a subset of values from domain $D_i$, where $d_i \in V_i$. Therefore we can define a valid ALSV(FD) formula as $A_i \propto d_i$ for simple attributes, where $\propto$ is one of the operators from set $=, \neq, \in, \notin$ and $A_i \propto V_i$ for generalized attributes, where $\propto$ is one of the operators from set $=, \neq, \sim, \not\sim, \subset, \supset$.

The operators for both *simple* and *generalized* attributes do not assume existence of time. They are evaluated only for the current values of the attributes. Thus, it is not possible to model dynamics of the environment in a compact way, without defining additional attributes that store historical data.

In order to provide high-level declarative way to handle time in HEART-DROID, the syntax of the HMR notation had to be extended. In general there can be distinguished two major types of syntactic novelties: 1.) parameterization of the existing ALSF(FD) operators introduced in previous section, 2.) family of so-called statistical operators for ALSV(FD) attribtues. Both of them are investigated in the following sections.

## 3.2   Parametrized Operators

The motivation behind adding the parameters to the operators lies in generalizing existing syntax instead of adding the brand new structures. In our case every conditional operator can be now followed by the temporal parameters put inside the curly braces, as in the example below:

```
ExpressionA eq{min 50% in -50 to 0} ExpressionB
```

What should be read as a condition: "the result of the `ExpressionA` was equal to the result of the `ExpressionB` in minimum fifty percent of the last fifty one states". The equality operator from the example above can be substituted by any operators available in ALSV(FD). Generally, parameters consist of three elements:

1. quantitative relationship — how is the amount of the states satisfying the condition related to the specified number of states. There are three possible relationships:
   (a) `min` (at least as many as . . . );
   (b) `max` (at most as many as . . . );
   (c) `exact` (exactly as many as . . . ).
2. amount — the second argument of the quantitative relation can be specified in two ways:
   (a) simply as a number (for example `min 5` means "at least 5 states");
   (b) as a fraction of the total number of states (for example `exact 50%` means "exactly the half of the states").

**Table 1.** Statistical operators supporting only numeric types

| Syntax | Description |
|---|---|
| max(Attr, Period) | Returns the biggest value of an attribute from specified period of time. |
| min(Attr, Period) | Returns the smallest value of an attribute from specified period of time. |
| mean(Attr, Period) | Returns mean of the attribute's values from specified period of time. |
| med(Attr, Period) | Returns median of the attribute's values from specified period of time. |
| stddev(Attr, Period) | Returns standard deviation of the attribute's values from specified period of time. |
| trend(Attr, Period) | Returns slope of the trend line fitted to attribute's values using the least–squares fit. |

3. vector of past states, which also can be written twofold:
   (a) as a range of non–positive numbers which should be regarded as indices of time samples relative to the current state designated by 0). For example -15 to 0 means last sixteen states including the current state.
   (b) using time units and Octave–like notation[2]. For example -2h:1min:0 means last two hours of states sampled once per minute (121 samples including the current one).

Using this notation it is possible to create rules which are fired only when the certain amount of past states satisfies the specified condition. It is a simple generalization allowing to capture basic dynamic features of the user context.

### 3.3 Statistical Operators

All of the proposed statistical operators are simply binary operators corresponding directly to the common statistical operations like mean or standard deviation. The first argument of the operator designates the attribute, while second contains the vector of past states, written exactly the same way as in the parameters. There is only one exception of this rule — in order to simplify the notation, there is a special operator valat (value at) which takes only a single index of time (for example -1 for the previous state) as the second argument. Therefore in HMR expression A could be treated as an abbreviation of the valat(A, 0) statement. Unlike the parameters, statistical operators evaluate in the same way as the normal operators — the result is not different from other values, so it can be used both in the LHS and RHS part of the rule.

On the other hand, restrictions applicable to other operators apply also in context of statistics, particularly statistical operators are susceptible to the domain constraints. While HMR supports both numerical and symbolic types, most

---

[2] GNU Octave is a high-level interpreted language, primarily intended for numerical computations. See http://www.gnu.org/software/octave/

operators support only numeric domains — Table 1 contains their complete list. In order to enable limited tracking of dynamics in symbolic domains the variance operator has two implementations and in symbolic domains works like the roughly equivalent entropy measure [6]. All the statistical operators supporting both types are listed in Table 2.

**Table 2.** Statistical operators supporting both numeric and symbolic types of attribute

| Syntax | Description |
|---|---|
| valat(Attr, Time) | Returns value of an attribute at the given moment of time. |
| var(Attr, Period) | In case of numeric attribute, returns variance of the attribute's values from specified period of time. In case of symbolic type, variance is replaced with entropy. |
| mode(Attr, Period) | Returns set of the most frequent attribute's values from specified period of time |

## 4   Implementation and Use Case Scenarios

### 4.1   Time Handling in HEARTDROID Inference Engine

HEARTDROID is a rule-based inference engine for Android mobile devices, that is distributed under the GNU General Public License. It is implemented in Java and therefore it can be easily integrated with native Android applications. It provides callbacks mechanism based on Java reflection, that allows for easy integration with other systems. HEARTDROID provides also basic mechanism for handling uncertainty that is based on modified certainty factors algebra [2].

The architecture of the HEARTDROID inference engine is presented in Figure 2. The engine consists of three main elements:

- reasoner – which is responsible for executing inference tasks,
- model manager – which stores different models and allow for switching between them and reasoning on them,
- working memory middleware – common memory for all the models, where current and historical states are stored.

The state of the system in HEARTDROID is understood as a snapshot of all attributes values registered in working memory. Each state contains timestamp, which represents time in milliseconds indicating when the snapshot was made. Besides that every value within a state contains a timestamp indicating time in milliseconds when the value was assigned to the attribute (i.e. when a sensor delivered some measurement). Due to possible large grow of such state history, only a finite number of states is stored in a FILO queue. When the limit of stored states is exceeded, the older state is removed from the queue.

The state of the system is saved every time the inference is invoked. This is represented in Figure 3 by bold vertical lines labelled $S_1, S_2, S_3$. The inference can be invoked by many different causes like new sensor reading, expired

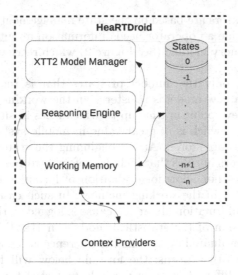

**Fig. 2.** Architecture of HEARTDROID inference engine

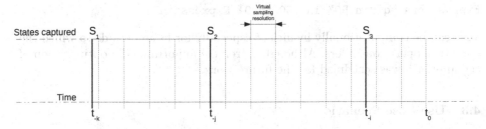

**Fig. 3.** State interpretation in HEARTDROID inference engine

attribute value, or on user demand. Therefore snapshots are taken in indeterministic time intervals. To allow statistical operations on attributes virtual sampling frequency is assumed – this is denotes as vertical dotted lines in Figure 3. Even though there is no actual snapshot at samples between $S_1$ and $S_2$, all of the virtual samples will refer to last available state, in this case $S_1$. Such approach allows for reliable statistical analysis of samples taken in variable intervals. The following section describes in details implementation of the time-based operators in HEARTDROID.

## 4.2  Implementation of Time-related Operators

Section 3 describes two types of statistical operators available in HEARTDROID:

1. statistical functions that allows for statistical analysis of attributes values,
2. parametrized operators that allows for using ALSV(FD) logic operators for time-related formulae.

Both of these operators are based on the state management system presented in Section 4.1. Any time an operator needs information about historical data it contacts working memory module (See Figure 2) which retrieves such data from state registry.

The system stores only the number of states that is required to evaluate models. Every time a new model is registered in the working memory module, it is analysed to retrieve point in time up to which rules in such model refer. In order to save memory, which is of great value in mobile systems [25], only the states up to this point are stored. At the beginning the state registry is empty which may lead to errors in rules that includes referrals to the non existing data. Thus, the system does not allow for evaluation of formulae that refer to data older than these stored in the working memory. In such case, the inference is interrupted and the information about the cause is logged to the debug channel.

In the current version of the statistical module in HEARTDROID inference engine, formulae are evaluated every time the inference is triggered for the every state individually. In other words, the formula below will have to be evaluated at worst for 50 different states separately to test if the equality between ExpressionA and ExpressionB was true in at least 50% percent cases.

```
ExpressionA eq{min 50% in -50 to 0} ExpressionB
```

This can be computationally inefficient especially for large periods to which the statistical operations refers. Although extremely important, the optimization of the approach was scheduled for the future work.

### 4.3  Use Case Scenario

The model presented in Figure 1 does not use historical information to determine current state of the user. This is especially visible in XTT2 table called *Actions* (the bottom right table in the Figure). The table was used to determine user action based on three attributes like *location*, *daytime* and *day*. Such approach assumes existence of a strong expert knowledge about user habits that cannot be violated by any exceptional circumstances. For example not going to work because of holiday, or going to work on weekend will not be handled by the model appropriately as such actions does not fit the model.

Our extension to the XTT2 notation allows including parametrized operators that allow for evaluation formulae that contains time-aggregated values. The example of the possible modification of table *Actions* with such operators is presented in Figure 4.

Rule number (1) from the table should be read as: *If the user was at home for most of the time during last hour and now is outside, he or she has left the home* and can be represented using following HMR notation:

```
xrule Actions/1 [
       location eq{MIN 80% in -1h to 0} home,
       location eq outside ]
  ==> [action set leaving_home].
```

| No. | (?) location | (->) action |
|-----|--------------|-------------|
| 1 | location **eq** {MIN 80% in -1h to 0} home,<br>location **eq** outside | action = leaving_home |
| 2 | location **eq** {MIN 80% in -1h to 0} work,<br>location **eq** outside | action = leaving_work |
| 3 | location **eq** {EXACTLY 100% in -1h to 0} work | action = working |
| 4 | location **eq** {EXACTLY 100% in -1h to 0} outside | action = travelling |
| 5 | location **eq** {EXACTLY 100% in -1h to 0} home | action = resting |

**Fig. 4.** *Actions* XTT2 table from Figure 1 enhanced with parametrized statistical operators

Such notation allows to use less attributes to model the same (or even more) than in model from Figure 1. It also allows for handling unexpected situations, as it is based on the on-line analysis of the data rather than purely expert knowledge.

The other possible application of statistical functions could be adjusting sensor sampling rates to the system dynamic. In [3] we proposed the solution based on machine learning approach. It requires a lot of data to learn and time to update in case the user habits changed. In [2] we proposed expiration time functions that could be used to better adjust sampling rates of context providers. Such approach required separate module that will monitor all the attributes values. When the expiration period of the attribute value passed the module has to to query the sensor for new data. Statistical functions allow for online monitoring of sensor dynamics without a need of an external mechanism. The fragment of a model that adjusts sampling rate of the accelerometer is presented in the Figure 5. For the brevity it was presented only for one accelerometer axis.

The model assumes that the accelerometer is used to detect user activity like walking, running, sitting, etc. In every of such cases the sampling rate could be different to keep the balance between energy consumption of the sensor and the reliable resolution of data. It takes 100 historical values of accelerometer data to calculate variance and adjust sampling rate appropriately. The lower the variance, the more constant readings provided by the sensor; thus, the lower sampling rate for the sensor can be applied.

## 5   Summary and Future Work

In this paper we presented a toolset for building a mobile context-aware applications that are immersed in highly dynamic environments. The approach is

| No. | (?) acc_x | (->) sampling |
|---|---|---|
| 1 | var(acc_x, -100 to 0) lt 0.3 | sampling = lowest |
| 2 | var(acc_x, -100 to 0) in [0.3 to 0.5] | sampling = normal |
| 3 | var(acc_x, -100 to 0) ge 0.5 | sampling = fastest |

**Fig. 5.** Fragment of the XTT2 model that controls accelerometer sampling rate based on the dynamic of the sensor

based on a rule representation called XTT2, which is used by the HEARTDROID engine that offers inference [15] and verification capabilities [16]. We extended the rule-representation language with statistical functions that allow for on-line statistical analysis of historical data and parameterized operators which introduce simple time modalities into the system, allowing compact evaluation of rules conditions in a time domain.

Such a solution combines strengths of statistical analysis available in machine learning with intelligibility features of rule-based system. The intelligibility is one of the most important features in systems that require interaction with users, as it gives an opportunity for explaining system decisions to them. When users understand how the system works it is possible to collect feedback from them and improve overall system performance by resolving ambiguous contexts, prioritizing or modifying rules, adapting the system to user needs and preferences, etc. Therefore combining intelligibility with mediation techniques is one of the primary focuses for the future work. The other important future tasks include practical evaluation of the methods presented in the paper on a real-life example. This in particular will include performance analysis and optimization for a high load data (high frequency of data, and large history).

Further work includes also introducing uncertainty to statistical analysis. HEARTDROID allows basic modelling of uncertain knowledge with certainty factors algebra [2]. Such formalisms assume that not all the data that are provided by the context providers should be treated evenly in the statistical equations (i.e. very uncertain data should have less impact that the certain one). Future work assumes also including statistical analysis for the certainty factors themselves. This will allow to monitor how the certainty of some values (sensors) change and perform appropriate actions if it decreases rapidly.

# References

1. Bobek, S., Nalepa, G.J., Ligęza, A., Adrian, W.T., Kaczor, K.: Mobile context-based framework for threat monitoring in urban environment with social threat monitor. Multimedia Tools and Applications (2014), http://dx.doi.org/10.1007/s11042-014-2060-9

2. Bobek, S., Nalepa, G.J.: Incomplete and uncertain data handling in context-aware rule-based systems with modified certainty factors algebra. In: Bikakis, A., Fodor, P., Roman, D. (eds.) RuleML 2014. LNCS, vol. 8620, pp. 157–167. Springer, Heidelberg (2014), http://dx.doi.org/10.1007/978-3-319-09870-8_11

3. Bobek, S., Porzycki, K., Nalepa, G.J.: Learning sensors usage patterns in mobile context-aware systems. In: Proceedings of the FedCSIS 2013 Conference, Krakow, pp. 993–998. IEEE (September 2013)

4. Bui, H.H., Venkatesh, S., West, G.: Tracking and surveillance in wide-area spatial environments using the abstract hidden markov model. Intl. J. of Pattern Rec. and AI 15 (2001)

5. Dey, A.K.: Providing architectural support for building context-aware applications. Ph.D. thesis, Atlanta, GA, USA (2000), aAI9994400

6. Domingo-Ferrer, J., Solanas, A.: A measure of variance for hierarchical nominal attributes. Inf. Sci. 178(24), 4644–4655 (2008), http://dx.doi.org/10.1016/j.ins.2008.08.003

7. Jaroucheh, Z., Liu, X., Smith, S.: Recognize contextual situation in pervasive environments using process mining techniques. J. Ambient Intelligence and Humanized Computing 2(1), 53–69 (2011)

8. van Kasteren, T., Kröse, B.: Bayesian activity recognition in residence for elders. In: 3rd IET International Conference on Intelligent Environments, IE 2007, pp. 209–212 (2007)

9. Koller, D., Friedman, N.: Probabilistic Graphical Models: Principles and Techniques. MIT Press (2009)

10. Kwon, O.B., Sadeh, N.: Applying case-based reasoning and multi-agent intelligent system to context-aware comparative shopping. Decis. Support Syst. 37(2), 199–213 (2004), http://dx.doi.org/10.1016/S0167-92360300007-1

11. Lee, J.S., Lee, J.C.: Context awareness by case-based reasoning in a music recommendation system. In: Ichikawa, H., Cho, W.-D., Satoh, I., Youn, H.Y. (eds.) UCS 2007. LNCS, vol. 4836, pp. 45–58. Springer, Heidelberg (2007), http://dblp.uni-trier.de/db/conf/ucs/ucs2007.html#LeeL07

12. Liao, L., Patterson, D.J., Fox, D., Kautz, H.: Learning and inferring transportation routines. Artif. Intell. 171(5-6), 311–331 (2007)

13. Ligęza, A., Nalepa, G.J.: A study of methodological issues in design and development of rule-based systems: proposal of a new approach. Wiley Interdisciplinary Reviews: Data Mining and Knowledge Discovery 1(2), 117–137 (2011)

14. Lim, B.Y., Dey, A.K., Avrahami, D.: Why and why not explanations improve the intelligibility of context-aware intelligent systems. In: Proceedings of the SIGCHI Conference on Human Factors in Computing Systems, CHI 2009, pp. 2119–2128. ACM, New York (2009), http://doi.acm.org/10.1145/1518701.1519023

15. Nalepa, G.J., Bobek, S., Ligęza, A., Kaczor, K.: Algorithms for rule inference in modularized rule bases. In: Bassiliades, N., Governatori, G., Paschke, A. (eds.) RuleML 2011 - Europe. LNCS, vol. 6826, pp. 305–312. Springer, Heidelberg (2011)

16. Nalepa, G.J., Bobek, S., Ligęza, A., Kaczor, K.: HalVA - rule analysis framework for XTT2 rules. In: Bassiliades, N., Governatori, G., Paschke, A. (eds.) RuleML 2011 - Europe. LNCS, vol. 6826, pp. 337–344. Springer, Heidelberg (2011), http://www.springerlink.com/content/c276374nh9682jm6/

17. Nalepa, G.J., Bobek, S.: Rule-based solution for context-aware reasoning on mobile devices. Computer Science and Information Systems 11(1), 171–193 (2014)

18. Nalepa, G.J., Kluza, K.: UML representation for rule-based application models with XTT2-based business rules. International Journal of Software Engineering and Knowledge Engineering (IJSEKE) 22(4), 485–524 (2012), http://www.worldscientific.com/doi/abs/10.1142/S021819401250012X

19. Nalepa, G.J., Ligęza, A.: Designing reliable Web security systems using rule-based systems approach. In: Menasalvas, E., Segovia, J., Szczepaniak, P.S. (eds.) AWIC 2003. LNCS (LNAI), vol. 2663, pp. 124–133. Springer, Heidelberg (2003)

20. Nalepa, G.J., Ligęza, A., Kaczor, K.: Formalization and modeling of rules using the XTT2 method. International Journal on Artificial Intelligence Tools 20(6), 1107–1125 (2011)

21. Palmer, N., Kemp, R., Kielmann, T., Bal, H.: Swan-song: A flexible context expression language for smartphones. In: Proceedings of the Third International Workshop on Sensing Applications on Mobile Phones, PhoneSense 2012, pp. 12:1–12:5. ACM, New York (2012), http://doi.acm.org/10.1145/2389148.2389160, doi:10.1145/2389148.2389160

22. Petersen, A.K.: Challenges in Case-Based Reasoning for Context Awareness in Ambient Intelligent Systems. In: Minor, M. (ed.) 8th European Conference on Case-Based Reasoning, Workshop Proceedings, pp. 287–299. Ölüdeniz/Fethiye, Turkey (2006)

23. Rabiner, L., Juang, B.H.: An introduction to hidden markov models. IEEE ASSP Magazine 3(1), 4–16 (1986)

24. Shehzad, A., Ngo, H.Q., Pham, K.A., Lee, S.Y.: Formal modeling in context aware systems. In: Proceedings of the 1st International Workshop on Modeling and Retrieval of Context, MRC 2004 (2004)

25. Bobek, S., Nalepa, G.J., Ślażyński, M.: Challenges for migration of rule-based reasoning engine to a mobile platform. In: Dziech, A., Czyżewski, A. (eds.) MCSS 2014. CCIS, vol. 429, pp. 43–57. Springer, Heidelberg (2014)

26. Want, R., Falcao, V., Gibbons, J.: The active badge location system. ACM Transactions on Information Systems 10, 91–102 (1992)

# Reasoning over Vague Concepts

Mustapha Bourahla[✉]

Computer Science Department, University of M'sila,
Laboratory of Pure and Applied Mathematics (LMPA),
BP 166 Ichebilia, M'sila 28000, Algeria
mbourahla@hotmail.com

**Abstract.** Ontologies representing knowledge, are expressed in well-defined formal languages for example, Ontology Web Language (OWL2), which are based on expressive description logics (as SROIQ(D) for OWL2). The ontology concepts are language adjectives referring the meaning of classes of objects. If the meaning is deficient (imprecise) then we will face the problem of vague concepts. In this paper we propose a vagueness theory based on the definition of truth gaps to express the vague concepts in OWL2 and an extension of the Tableau algorithm for reasoning over vague ontologies.

**Keywords:** Vagueness · Ontology · OWL2 · Description Logics · Automatic Reasoning

## 1 Introduction

Formalisms for dealing with vagueness have started to play an important role in research related to the Web and the Semantic Web [9,15]. Ontologies are the definition of domain concepts (extensions) and the relations between them. Formal ontologies are expressed in well-defined formal languages (for example, OWL2) [5,8] that are based on expressive description logics (for example, SROIQ(D)) [2,17,6]. We say ontology is vague if it has at least a vague definition of a concept. A concept (an extension) is vague if it defines a meaning gap with which we cannot decide the membership of certain objects (vague intension).

We state the problem with the following example. Assume an ontology defining a concept called *Expensive* in a domain about cars. The meaning of the concept is vague. This vagueness is pervasive in natural language, but until now is avoided in ontologies definitions. For the concept *Expensive*, we can define three sub-extensions, definitely expensive extension (there are some car prices that we regard as definitely expensive), definitely cheap extension (others we regard as definitely cheap cars) and a vagueness extension, average car prices are neither expensive nor cheap. The source of this indecision is the imprecise definition of concepts that is caused by lack of rigorous knowledge.

**Related Works:** The rising popularity of description logics and their use, and the need to deal with vagueness, especially in the Semantic Web, is increasingly attracting the attention of many researchers and practitioners towards description logics able to cope with vagueness. There are many works in literature

© Springer International Publishing Switzerland 2015
L. Rutkowski et al. (Eds.): ICAISC 2015, Part II, LNAI 9120, pp. 591–602, 2015.
DOI: 10.1007/978-3-319-19369-4_52

for dealing with vagueness and most of them express it as a concept property as those based on fuzzy logics [15,3,10,14]. In this case, any concept instance will have a degree of membership that is determined by a defined fuzzy function. The vagueness under fuzzy theory is treated by extended fuzzy description logics that are supported by fuzzy semantics and fuzzy reasoning. The fuzzy description logics are applied in many domains.

In our work, the concepts are treated as having a fixed meaning (not a balanced meaning), shared by all users of the ontology; we propose instead that the meaning of a vague concept evolves during the ontology evolution, from more vague meaning to less vague meaning until it reaches if possible, a situation where it becomes non-vague concept. This meaning instability is the base of our vagueness theory that is used for reasoning over vague ontologies. The closest work to ours is the work in [12] which presents a framework for adjusting numerical restrictions defining vague concepts. An inconsistency problem can happen when aligning the original ontology to another source of ontological information or when ontology evolves by adding learned axioms. This adjustment is used to repair the original ontology for avoiding the inconsistency problem by modifying restrictions parameters called adaptors specified as concept annotations. The idea of this work is close to ours in the sense that we reduce the truth gaps when adding new assertions as learned knowledge to the ontology to guide the reasoning process which will play the same role as adjusting the vague concept restrictions. However, this work differs from our approach by the repair (modification) process applied on the original ontology to avoid introduced inconsistency. In our approach, we define the vague concepts as super concepts over restriction definitions. So, we dont have the problem of inconsistency to repair the ontology.

This paper is organized as follows. We begin in Section 2, by presenting Ontology Web Language (OWL2) and its correspondent description logic (SROIQ(D)). In Section 3, a vagueness theory is presented to show how to express vague concepts and to describe the characteristics of vague ontologies; also a brief comparison with vagueness under fuzzy description logics is given. Section 4 presents the extended version of Tableau algorithm, to reason over vague ontologies. At the end, we conclude this paper by conclusions and perspectives.

## 2   OWL and Description Logics

Ontologies are definitions of concepts and the relationships between them. They can be represented formally using formal languages. These formal description languages are based on well-defined description logics (DLs) [2,1], a family of knowledge representation formalisms. OWL2 DL is a variant of SROIQ(D) [6], which consists of an alphabet composed of three sets of names. The set $\mathcal{C}$ of atomic concepts corresponding to classes interpreted as sets of objects, the set $\mathcal{R}$ of atomic roles corresponding to relationships interpreted as binary relations on objects and the set $\mathcal{I}$ of individuals (objects). It consists also of a set of constructors used to build complex concepts and complex roles from the atomic ones.

The formal semantics of DLs is given in terms of interpretations. A SROIQ(D) interpretation is a pair $I = (\Delta^I, (.)^I)$ where $\Delta^I$ is a non-empty set called the domain of $I$, and $(.)^I$ is the interpretation function which assigns for every $A \in \mathcal{C}$ a subset $(A)^I \subseteq \Delta^I$, for every $o \in \mathcal{R}$ a relation $(o)^I \subseteq \Delta^I \times \Delta^I$, called object role, for every $c \in \mathcal{R}$ a relation $(c)^I \subseteq \Delta^I \times \mathcal{D}$, called concrete role ($\mathcal{D}$ is a data type as integer and string) and for every $a \in \mathcal{I}$, an element $(a)^I \in \Delta^I$. The roles (object or concrete) are called properties; if their range values are individuals (relation between individuals) then they are called object properties. If their range values are concrete data (relation between individual and a concrete data) then they are called concrete (data) properties. The set of SROIQ(D) complex concepts can be expressed using the following grammar:

$$C ::= \top \mid \bot \mid A \mid \{a\} \mid \neg C \mid C \sqcap D \mid C \sqcup D \mid \exists o.Self \mid \forall o.Self \mid \exists o.C \mid \quad (1)$$
$$\exists c.P \mid \forall o.C \mid \forall c.P \mid \geq n\, s.C \mid \leq n\, s.C \mid \geq n\, c.P \mid \leq n\, c.P$$

Where $\top$ is the universal concept, $\bot$ is the empty concept, $A$ is an atomic concept, $a$ an individual, $C$ and $D$ are concepts, $o$ an object role, $c$ a concrete role, $s$ a simple role w.r.t. $\mathcal{R}$, and $n$ a non-negative integer. $P$ is a predicate over a concrete domain that can have the form

$$P ::= DataType\,[\sim value] \mid P \sqcap P \mid P \sqcup P, \sim \in \{<, \leq, >, \geq\} \quad (2)$$

The data type can be any recognized data type as integer, real, etc. The interpretation function is extended to complex concepts and roles according to their syntactic structure. $(\top)^I = \Delta^I$, $(\bot)^I = \emptyset$, $(\{a\})^I = (a)^I$, $(\neg C)^I = \Delta^I \setminus (C)^I$, $(C \sqcap D)^I = (C)^I \cap (D)^I$, $(C \sqcup D)^I = (C)^I \cup (D)^I$, $(\exists o.Self)^I = \{a \in \Delta^I | \exists (a, b) \in (o)^I \wedge a = b\}$, $(\forall o.Self)^I = \{a \in \Delta^I | \forall (a, b) \in (o)^I \implies a = b\}$, $(\exists o.C)^I = \{a \in \Delta^I | \exists (a, b) \in (o)^I \wedge b \in (C)^I\}$, $(\forall o.C)^I = \{a \in \Delta^I | \forall (a, b) \in (o)^I \implies b \in (C)^I\}$, $(\exists c.P)^I = \{a \in \Delta^I | \exists (a, d) \in (c)^I \wedge P(d)\}$, $(\forall c.P)^I = \{a \in \Delta^I | \forall (a, d) \in (c)^I \implies P(d)\}$, $(\geq n\, s.C)^I = \{a \in \Delta^I | \, |\{b \in \Delta^I | (a, b) \in (s)^I \wedge b \in (C)^I\}| \geq n\}$ (same for $(\leq n\, s.C)^I$), and $(\geq n\, c.P)^I = \{a \in \Delta^I | \, |\{a | (a, d) \in (c)^I \wedge P(d)\}| \geq n\}$ (same for $(\leq n\, c.P)^I$), where $P(d)$ means the value $d$ verifies the predicate $P$.

We have seen how to build complex concept and role expressions, which allow one to denote concepts and roles with a complex structure. However, in order to represent real world domains, one needs the ability to assert properties of concepts and relationships between them. The assertion of properties is done in DLs by means of an ontology (or knowledge base). A SROIQ(D) ontology is a pair $\mathcal{O} = \langle \mathcal{T}, \mathcal{A} \rangle$, where $\mathcal{T}$ is called a terminological box and $\mathcal{A}$ is called an assertional box. The terminological box consists of a finite set of assertions on concepts and roles. There are inclusion assertions on concepts, object and concrete roles to define a hierarchy (taxonomy) on the names of concepts and roles, (we write $C \sqsubseteq D$ to denote inclusion assertions on concepts, where $C$ and $D$ are concepts, $C \equiv D$ as an abbreviation for $C \sqsubseteq D \wedge D \sqsubseteq C$ and $r_1 \sqsubseteq r_2$ for role inclusion, where $r_1$ and $r_2$ are object (concrete) roles, the same equivalence abbreviation can be applied on roles). The assertional box consists of a finite set of assertions on individuals. There are membership assertions for concepts

$(C(a)$ means the object (individual) $a$ is member of $C)$, membership assertions for roles $(o(a, b)$ means the objects $a$ and $b$ are related by the object property $o$ and $c(a, d)$ means the object $a$ has the data property (concrete role) $c$ with a value equals $d)$. We say the interpretation $I$ is a model of a SROIQ(D) ontology $\mathcal{O} = \langle \mathcal{T}, \mathcal{A} \rangle$, if it satisfies all the assertions in $\mathcal{T}$ and $\mathcal{A}$. In addition, it is a model of any satisfied assertion by the ontology $\mathcal{O}$.

Thus, the assertional box $\mathcal{A}$ of a knowledge base, provides a description of a world. It introduces individuals by specifying their names, the concepts to which they belong, and their relations with other individuals. The semantics of the language uses either the closed world assumption or the open world assumption. With the closed world assumption, we consider that the world is limited to what is stated. It is this assumption that is normally adopted in databases. In description logics, it is rather the assumption of the open world which prevails. This open world assumption has an impact in the way of making inferences in description logics. The inference is more complex with the assumption of the open world; it is often called to consider several alternative situations for the proof. Another important aspect of description logic is that it does not presuppose the uniqueness of names (the standard names). That is, two different names do not necessarily mean that there is case to two separate entities in the described world. To be sure that two different entities $a$ and $b$ are represented, should be added the assertion according to the assertional box $\mathcal{A}$: $a \neq b$.

# 3    Proposed Vagueness Theory

We define a concept $C$ as vague if it has a deficiency of meaning. Thus, the source of vagueness is the capability of meaning (it has borderline cases). Thus, for example the concept $YoungPerson$ is extensionally vague and it remains intentionally vague in a world of young and non-young persons. This means that there are truth-value gaps where a vague concept is extensionally (intensionally) definitely true $(t\!t)$, definitely false $(f\!f)$ and true or false $(t\!f)$. Let us consider the following ontology.

$$\mathcal{O} = \left\langle \begin{array}{l} \mathcal{T} = \left\{ \begin{array}{l} Young \equiv Person \ \sqcap \exists age.\,(\mathrm{int}\,[\geq 20] \sqcap \mathrm{int}\,[\leq 30])\,, \\ NonYoung \equiv Person \ \sqcap \exists age.\,(\mathrm{int}\,[\leq 10] \sqcup \mathrm{int}\,[\geq 40])\,, \\ Young \sqsubseteq YoungPerson, NonYoung \sqsubseteq \neg YoungPerson \end{array} \right\}, \\[4mm] \mathcal{A} = \left\{ \begin{array}{l} Person(a), Person(b), Person(c), \\ age(a, 25), age(b, 45), age(c, 18) \end{array} \right\} \end{array} \right\rangle \quad (3)$$

In this knowledge base (ontology), we assume (the reader may not agree on this) the age of a definitely young person $(Young)$ is between twenty and thirty years, and a definitely no-young person $(NonYoung)$ has an age less than or equal to ten years (a minor person) or greater than or equal to forty years (an old person). The concept $YoungPerson$ and its complement are subsuming two complex concept expressions $(Young$ and $NonYoung)$. Each concept expression contains a sub-expression that is defined as quantified (universal or existential) restriction on a concrete role (for example, the concrete role is $age$ and the restricted sub-expressions are $\exists age.$ (int $[\geq 20] \sqcap$ int $[\leq 30]$) for *Young* and $\exists age.$ (int $[\leq 10] \sqcup$ int $[\geq 40]$) for *NonYoung*).

We have taken advantage of the open world assumption in description logics to define vague concepts. Thus, this ontology satisfies the assertions $YoungPerson(a)$ and $\neg YoungPerson(b)$ but the assertions $YoungPerson(c)$ and $\neg YoungPerson(c)$ are both not satisfied. With this knowledge base (ontology), we assign *tt* to *Young Person(a)*, *ff* to *YoungPerson(b)*, and *tf* to *YoungPerson(c)*). This means, there is a deficiency of meaning (truth value gaps) between *YoungPerson* and $\neg Young$ *Person*. Consequently, the concept *YoungPerson* is considered vague.

Thus, the satisfaction of a membership assertion to a vague concept depends on the concrete property value and the truth gaps. The vagueness definition of a concept will create one or more truth gaps. These are convex intervals (or ordered sequences) of values from a concrete domain with which the satisfaction of a membership assertion to the vague concept cannot be decided. There are two borderline values for each interval (or sequence). They are the lower ($l$) and the upper ($u$) bounds of a truth gap. Thus, we associate with each vague concept $C$ a set of truth gap assertions according to a concrete role $r$.

$$C_r(\{\langle x_1(l_1), y_1(u_1)\rangle, \langle x_2(l_2), y_2(u_2)\rangle, \cdots, \langle x_n(l_n), y_n(u_n)\rangle\}) \qquad (4)$$

Where $n$ is the number of truth gaps. For $1 \leq i \leq n : x_i, y_i \in \{tt, ff\}$, $x_i \neq y_i$, and $l_i, u_i$ are the lower and upper borderlines, respectively.

**Lemma 1.** *(Acceptability condition). The truth gaps set defined in (4) of any vague concept $C$ associated with a role $r$ should verify the condition of acceptability, this means $\forall i = 1, \cdots, n - 1 : y_i = x_{i+1} \wedge l_i < u_i < l_{i+1} < u_{i+1}$. A non-vague (crisp) concept $C$ will have an empty set of truth gaps according to any concrete role $r$ $(C_r(\emptyset))$.*

These truth gaps assertions defined in (4) can be formulated using the description logic SROIQ(D) as a result of ontology description pre-processing. This will augment the ontology $\mathcal{O} = \langle \mathcal{T}, \mathcal{A} \rangle$ by the membership and property assertions to be $\mathcal{O} = \langle \mathcal{T}, \mathcal{A} \cup \{C(tt), \neg C(ff), r(x_i, l_i), r(y_i, u_i)\} \rangle$ if $C$ is checked to be a vague concept according to a concrete role $r$, for $1 \leq i \leq n$, where $n$ is the number of the truth gaps, *tt* and *ff* are considered as two additional dummy individuals. The individuals $x_i, y_i$ are either *tt* or *ff* with the conditions $x_i \neq y_i \wedge x_{i+1} = y_i$, $l_i$ and $u_i$ are numerical values from the range of the concrete role $r$ with $l_i < u_i < l_{i+1}$ (the acceptance condition). Also, this description should verify the vagueness consistency which is stated by the formula.

$$(\{C(tt), r(tt, d_1), r(tt, d_2), \neg C(ff), r(ff, d)\} \subseteq \mathcal{A} \Rightarrow d \notin [d_1, d_2]) \wedge$$
$$(\{\neg C(ff), r(ff, d_1), r(ff, d_2), C(tt), r(tt, d)\} \subseteq \mathcal{A} \Rightarrow d \notin [d_1, d_2]) \qquad (5)$$

The intuition for this vagueness theory is as follows. Ontology is considered the knowledge base of an intelligent agent; if the ontology (knowledge base) $\mathcal{O}$ contains a vague concept $C$ with respect to a concrete role $r$ and one of its truth gaps has the distance $dist = u - l$, where $r(tt, u), r(ff, l)$ with $u > l$, are in $\mathcal{O}$. The agent cannot decide if an individual (object) $a$ with $r$-property value within the distance $dist$ if it belongs to $C$ or to its complement (we say that the knowledge base is incomplete). We assume that at a moment, assertions like $C(a), r(a, d)$ are added to the ontology $\mathcal{O}$, where $l < d < u$. These new information will change the ontology agent beliefs by reducing the truth gap distance to be $dist' = d - l$. Now, if we add the assertions $\neg C(b), r(b, d')$ with $u > d' > d$, this will produce a vagueness inconsistency according to this vagueness theory because the agent has change its beliefs so that every property assertion of an individual with respect to the concrete role $r$ where its range is greater than $d$ should be member of the concept $C$. This vagueness theory is used to adjust the truth intervals (or the truth gaps) described in the original ontology by acquired new information.

## 3.1  Generating Truth Gaps Assertions

The truth gaps assertions for each concept $C$ in ontology $\mathcal{O} = \langle \mathcal{T}, \mathcal{A} \rangle$, can be generated using the rules defined below. The objective is to produce truth gaps between the two evidences true ($tt$) and false ($ff$). These rules use the notations $C[C_i]$ and $\neg C[D_i]$ to express that the concept $C_i$ (or $D_i$) is a concept sub-expression of the concept expression subsumed by $C$ or $\neg C$ described in $\mathcal{T}$. The notation $C_r^x[P]$ denotes that $P$ is a data type predicate used for describing a quantifiably (existentially or universally) restricted concept over the concrete role $r$, and $C_r[x(d)]$ is used to denote that $d$ is a truth gap borderline, where $x \in \{tt, ff\}$. The symbol $d$ can be any numerical value.

$$R_1 : \frac{\langle \{C\left[(\exists \text{ or } \forall)r.P_{tt}\right], \neg C\left[(\exists \text{ or } \forall)r.P_{ff}\right]\} \subseteq \mathcal{T}, \mathcal{A} \rangle}{\left\langle \mathcal{T} \cup \left\{C_r^{tt}\left[P_{tt}\right], C_r^{ff}\left[P_{ff}\right]\right\}, \mathcal{A} \right\rangle}$$

$$R_2 : \frac{\langle \{C_r^x\left[P_1(\sqcap \text{ or } \sqcup)P_2\right]\} \subseteq \mathcal{T}, \mathcal{A} \rangle}{\langle \mathcal{T} \cup \{C_r^x\left[P_1\right], C_r^x\left[P_2\right]\}, \mathcal{A} \rangle} x \in \{tt, ff\}$$

$$R_3 : \frac{\langle \{C_r^x\left[dataType\left[\sim d\right]\right]\} \subseteq \mathcal{T}, \mathcal{A} \rangle}{\langle \mathcal{T} \cup \{C_r\left[x(d)\right]\}, \mathcal{A} \rangle} \sim \in \{<, \leq, >, \geq\}$$

$$R_4 : \frac{\langle \{C_r\left[x_i(d_i)\right]_{i=1}^n\} \subseteq \mathcal{T}, \mathcal{A} \rangle}{\langle \mathcal{T}, \mathcal{A} \cup C_r(\{\langle x_j(d_j), x_{j+1}(d_{j+1})\rangle \mid x_j \neq x_{j+1} \wedge d_j < d_{j+1}\}_{j=1}^{n-1}) \rangle}$$

The notation $C_r\left[x_i(d_i)\right]_{i=1}^n$ is the abbreviation of $C_r\left[x_1(d_1)\right], \cdots, C_r\left[x_i(d_i)\right], \cdots, C_r\left[x_n(d_n)\right]$, $1 \leq i \leq n$ (and the same for $C_r(\{\langle x_j(d_j), x_{j+1}(d_{j+1})\rangle \mid x_j \neq x_{j+1} \wedge d_j < d_{j+1}\}_{j=1}^{n-1})$). The first rule is used to identify possible vague concepts from a normalized $\mathcal{T}$ (Section 4). The other rules expand concept expressions from $\mathcal{T}$ until they generate at the end assertions over sets of truth gaps for each vague concept. For example, the set of truth gaps for the concept $YoungPerson$ can be computed using these rules. First, the result of normalization will add $YoungPerson\left[\exists age.(\text{int}\left[\geq 20\right] \sqcap \text{int}\left[\leq 30\right]\right]$ and $\neg YoungPerson[\exists age.(\text{int}\left[\leq 10\right] \sqcup \text{int}\left[\geq 40\right]]\}$ to $\mathcal{T}$. The results of generation process are:

$$R_1 \Rightarrow \left\langle \mathcal{T} = \mathcal{T} \cup \left\{ \begin{array}{l} YoungPerson_{age}^{tt}[(\text{int}[\geq 20] \sqcap \text{int}[\leq 30])], \\ YoungPerson_{age}^{ff}[(\text{int}[\leq 10] \sqcup \text{int}[\geq 40])] \end{array} \right\}, \mathcal{A} \right\rangle$$

$$R_2 \Rightarrow \left\langle \mathcal{T}=\mathcal{T} \cup \left\{ \begin{array}{l} YoungPerson_{age}^{tt}\,[(\text{int}\,[\geq 20])]\,, YoungPerson_{age}^{tt}\,[(\text{int}\,[\leq 30])]\,, \\ YoungPerson_{age}^{ff}\,[(\text{int}\,[\leq 10])]\,, YoungPerson_{age}^{ff}\,[(\text{int}\,[\geq 40])] \end{array} \right\}, \mathcal{A} \right\rangle$$

$$R_3 \Rightarrow \left\langle \mathcal{T}=\mathcal{T} \cup \left\{ \begin{array}{l} YoungPerson_{age}\,[tt(20)]\,, YoungPerson_{age}\,[tt(30)]\,, \\ YoungPerson_{age}\,[ff(10)]\,, YoungPerson_{age}\,[ff(40)] \end{array} \right\}, \mathcal{A} \right\rangle$$

$$R_4 \Rightarrow \langle \mathcal{T}, \mathcal{A} = \mathcal{A} \cup YoungPerson_{age}(\{\langle ff(10), tt(20)\rangle, \langle tt(30), ff(40)\rangle\})\rangle$$

The new ontology after generation of truth gap assertions on the original ontology $\mathcal{O} = \langle \mathcal{T}, \mathcal{A}\rangle$ is $\mathcal{O}^{new} = \langle \mathcal{T}^{new}, \mathcal{A}^{new}\rangle$ where, $\mathcal{T}^{new} = \mathcal{T}$ and $\mathcal{A}^{new} = \mathcal{A} \cup YoungPerson_{age}(\{\ \langle ff(10), tt(20)\rangle, \ \langle tt(30), ff(40)\rangle\}$. Using the syntax of SROIQ(D), $\mathcal{A}^{new} = \mathcal{A} \cup \{YoungPerson(tt), \neg YoungPerson(ff), age(ff, 10), age(tt, 20), age(tt, 30), age(ff, 40)\}$. This new ontology containing concept truth gaps is considered vague and then it is incomplete for reasoning.

**Definition 1.** *(Complete ontologies). An ontology is complete if we can assign only the definite truth values (tt and ff) to assertions. A vague (incomplete) ontology is an ontology that has at least one vague concept and then it is possible to assign the value tf to certain assertions. In addition, a vague ontology should be acceptable (Lemma 1), which means all the truth gap sets should be acceptable.*

We define a partial order between ontologies that is noted by $\langle \mathfrak{D}, \leq\rangle$, where $\mathfrak{D}$ is a non-empty set of ontologies describing a domain. If $\mathcal{O}_1$ and $\mathcal{O}_2$ are two ontologies from $\mathfrak{D}$ we write $\mathcal{O}_1 \leq \mathcal{O}_2$, if $\mathcal{O}_1$ is less complete than $\mathcal{O}_2$ (we say also that $\mathcal{O}_2$ extends $\mathcal{O}_1$). The relation $\leq$ (we call it also the extension relation) is based on comparison of truth gaps and it is transitive and antisymmetric. By this partial order definition, there is a canonical normal ontology $\mathcal{O}_n$ that is the least complete ontology, which can be extended by other complete ontologies.

The set $\mathfrak{D}$ has a base ontology that corresponds to description of which all other descriptions are extensions. This base ontology is composed of the terminological assertions and eventually some membership assertions. A condition that can be imposed on domain ontology is its completeability. It states that any intermediate ontology can be extended to a complete ontology. We suppose that ontology $\mathcal{O}$ has a vague concept $C$, with an acceptable set of truth gaps defined by the assertion $C_r(\{\langle x_1(l_1), y_1(u_1)\rangle, \langle x_2(l_2), y_2(u_2)\rangle, \cdots, \langle x_n(l_n), y_n(u_n)\rangle\})$, then we define the ontology extension by the assertions $\{C(a), r(a, d)\}$ as follows.

$$extend(\langle \mathcal{T}, \mathcal{A}\,[C(a), r(a, d), C_r(\{\cdots \langle x_i(l_i), y_i(u_i)\rangle, \cdots\})]\rangle\,|\,l_i < d < u_i) = $$
$$\left\langle \mathcal{T}, \mathcal{A} \cup \left\{ \begin{array}{l} \{C_r(\{\cdots, \langle x_i(d), y_i(u_i)\rangle, \cdots\})\} \ \text{if}\ x_i = tt \\ \{C_r(\{\cdots, \langle x_i(l_i), y_i(d)\rangle, \cdots\})\} \ \text{if}\ y_i = tt \end{array} \right. \right\rangle$$

$$extend(\langle \mathcal{T}, \mathcal{A}\,[\neg C(a), r(a, d), C_r(\{\cdots \langle x_i(l_i), y_i(u_i)\rangle, \cdots\})]\rangle\,|\,l_i < d < u_i) = $$
$$\left\langle \mathcal{T}, \mathcal{A} \cup \left\{ \begin{array}{l} \{C_r(\{\cdots, \langle x_i(d), y_i(u_i)\rangle, \cdots\})\} \ \text{if}\ x_i = ff \\ \{C_r(\{\cdots, \langle x_i(l_i), y_i(d)\rangle, \cdots\})\} \ \text{if}\ y_i = ff \end{array} \right. \right\rangle$$

The membership assertions will update the truth gaps sets. For example, if we extend the example ontology by the membership assertions $\mathcal{O} = \langle \mathcal{T}, \mathcal{A} \cup \{YoungPerson(a), \neg YoungPerson(b), age(a, 16), age(b, 18)\}\rangle$ then the extension is $extend(\mathcal{O}) = \langle \mathcal{T}, \mathcal{A} \cup \{YoungPerson_{age}(\{\langle ff(18), tt(16)\rangle, \langle tt(30), ff(40)\rangle\})\}\rangle$. Using the DL syntax, the extended ontology is $\mathcal{A}^{new} = \mathcal{A} \cup \{YoungPerson(tt), \neg YoungPerson(ff), age(ff, 10), age(tt, 16), age(ff, 18), age(tt, 20), age(tt, 30), age(ff, 40)\}$. The new set of truth gaps of the concept $YoungPerson$ as shown is not acceptable (Lemma 1).

**Lemma 2.** *(stability property of $\langle \mathfrak{O}, \leq \rangle$). Let $\alpha$ be an assertion, we say $\langle \mathfrak{O}, \leq \rangle$ is stable if*

$$\forall \mathcal{O}_1, \mathcal{O}_2 \in \mathfrak{O}, \mathcal{O}_1 \leq \mathcal{O}_2 : \mathcal{O}_1 \models \alpha \Rightarrow \mathcal{O}_2 \models \alpha \text{ and } \mathcal{O}_2 \not\models \alpha \Rightarrow \mathcal{O}_1 \not\models \alpha$$

The complete ontology may not be available to remove completely the vagueness, thus it is necessary to work with the most extended ontology. This means, the truth-valuation is based upon the most extended ontology. Ontology can be extended to complete ontology by learned assertions as a process of ontology evolution when using an intelligent agent or inferred assertions. The learned assertions can be imported from other domain ontologies, RDF databases or simply added by the user.

## 3.2   Comparison with Fuzzy Description Logics

Almost all concepts we are using in natural language are vague (imprecise). Therefore common sense reasoning based on natural language must be based on vague concepts and not on classical logic. The notion of a fuzzy set proposed by Lotfi Zadeh [18] is the first very successful approach to vagueness. Fuzzy description logics (FDLs) are the logics underlying modes of reasoning which are approximate rather than exact. The fuzzy knowledge base is interpreted as a collection of constraints on assertions. Thus, the inference is viewed as a process of propagation of these constraints. In FDLs, assertions are true to some degree [10,15]. Assertions in fuzzy description logic, rather being satisfied (true) or unsatisfied (false) in an interpretation, are associated with a degree of truth using semantic operators, where the membership of an individual to the union and intersection of concepts is uniquely determined by its membership to constituent concepts. This is a very nice property and allows very simple operations on fuzzy concepts. In addition to the standard problems of deciding the satisfiability of fuzzy ontologies and logical consequences of fuzzy assertions from fuzzy ontologies, two other important reasoning problems are the best truth value bound problem and the best satisfiability bound problem.

Truth gap theory is still another approach to vagueness. With every vague concept we associate two crisp sub-concepts, the first sub-concept consists of all individuals that surely belong to the concept, whereas the second sub-concept (called boundary region) constitutes of all individuals that possibly belong to the concept. It consists of all individuals that cannot be classified uniquely to the concept or its complement, by employing available knowledge. Thus any vague concept, in contrast to a crisp concept, has a non-empty boundary region. In this vagueness theory based on truth gaps, which can be considered as a dynamic epistemic logic, we describe the static knowledge and beliefs of agents and we offer dynamic features to revise the agent beliefs as a result of new acquired information. Thus, the facts describing the ontology remain the same. In the fuzzy theory, the facts change (ontic change), and the resulting consequences of such factual changes for the beliefs update of the agents. So, we have many views on the vagueness which depend on the way we model our problem, it can be an incomplete (abstract) static model and the beliefs are revised (from $tf$ to $tt$ or $ff$ as result of previous ignorance (this is called epistemic view) when new information arrived (this is the view we adopted). On the other hand, the ontic view supposes that the model (description) is complete and the beliefs are updated as information is changed (this is the view adopted by the fuzzy logic).

Both theories represent two different approaches to vagueness. Fuzzy theory addresses gradualness of knowledge, expressed by the fuzzy membership, whereas truth gap theory addresses granularity of knowledge, expressed by the indiscernibility relation. The result of reasoning over vague ontology using truth gap theory is the posterior description that represents a revision of the prior description on the light of the evidence provided by acquired information. This property can be used to draw conclusions from prior knowledge and its revision if new evidence is available. In the following, we propose an extension of reasoning that can take into account the proposed vagueness theory.

## 4    Reasoning Over Vague Ontologies

An interpretation $I$ is a model of an ontology $\mathcal{O} = \langle \mathcal{T}, \mathcal{A} \rangle$ denoted by $I \models \mathcal{O}$ if $I$ satisfies all the assertions in $\mathcal{T}$ and all the assertions in $\mathcal{A}$. The reasoning is for checking concept and role instances and for query answering over a satisfiable ontology [11,19,4,13]. Ontology satisfiability is to verify whether ontology $\mathcal{O}$ admits at least one model where consistency properties should be verified. Concept instance checking is to verify whether an individual $a$ is an instance of a concept $C$ in every model of $\mathcal{O}$, i.e., whether $\mathcal{O} \models C(a)$. Role instance checking is to verify whether a pair $(a, b)$ of individuals is an instance of a role $r$ in every model of $\mathcal{O}$, i.e., whether $\mathcal{O} \models r(a, b)$.

The satisfaction properties will be extended to deal with the vagueness in ontologies. A vague ontology is satisfiable if it generates acceptable truth gaps for all its concepts (note that an empty set of truth gaps is acceptable). For example, if we modify the concept $YoungPerson$ in the vague ontology of the previous example to be $Person \sqcap \exists age. (\text{int} [\leq 10] \sqcap \text{int} [\geq 27]) \sqsubseteq \neg YoungPerson$, this will change the set of truth gaps assertion associated with the vague concept $YoungPerson$ to be $YoungPerson_{age}(\{ \langle ff(10), tt(20) \rangle, \langle tt(30), ff(27) \rangle \})$. This set of truth gaps is not acceptable because it is a false assertion. Nevertheless, the vague ontology is satisfiable by using the traditional reasoning techniques. However, if we add the assertions $\{ Person(d), age(d, 28) \}$ to the assertional box, the vague ontology becomes inconsistent because $d$ is now at the same time young person and no-young person, although the ontology was initially satisfiable. In the following, we will extend the reasoning Tableau algorithm to cope with the problem of vague ontologies using this proposed vagueness theory.

The principle of this reasoning algorithm is the expansion a finite configuration $(T = \{A_1, \cdots, A_n\})$ of assertions that is represented as a set of subsets, each subset is composed of assertions on individuals, using well defined rules until no rule can be applied on at least one subset (satisfaction) or contradictions (clashes) are observed within all subsets (unsatisfaction). We will have a clash in a subset $A_i$ when a contradiction happens in it. There are three types of contradictions: $\perp(a) \in A_i$, $C(a) \in A_i \wedge \neg C(a) \in A_i$, or unacceptable truth gaps assertion. If no expansion rule can be applied in $A_i$ we say that $A_i$ is open. The terminological box should be normalized to apply the expansion rules. It is necessary to begin the inference with formulas that are independent from any terminology. This means elimination of the definitions (equivalence assertions) and subsumptions (inclusion assertions) in the terminological box. If it contains no cycle in the definitions (which will be the case most of the time), it will happen simply by replacing all the terms in the formula by their definitions in the terminology. Obviously, if a term of formula has no definition in terminology, it remains unchanged. We repeat this process until the resulting formula contains no term which has a definition in the terminology.

For reasoning over vague ontologies using the proposed vagueness theory, we have added the following two expansion rules that should be applied after every expansion by a classical Tableau rule (the reader can be referred to [6,7,11] for the classical Tableau rules). We will get a clash (contradiction) if any new set of truth gaps is not acceptable (Lemma 1 and Equation 5). The configuration length depends on ontology description and property being checked. Using the DL syntax of SROIQ(D), these two rules can be formulated as

$$V - Rule^+(DL) : \frac{A_i \in T \wedge \{C(a), r(a,d), C(t\!t)\} \subseteq A_i}{(T \setminus A_i) \cup (A_i \cup \{r(t\!t, d)\})} r(t\!t, d) \notin A_i$$

$$V - Rule^-(DL) : \frac{A_i \in T \wedge \{\neg C(a), r(a,d), \neg C(f\!f)\} \subseteq A_i}{(T \setminus A_i) \cup (A_i \cup \{r(f\!f, d)\})} r(f\!f, d) \notin A_i$$

These two rules will augment the assertions subset $A_i$ by the property assertion $r(t\!t, d)$ if $A_i$ contains the assertion $C(a) \wedge r(a,d) \wedge C(t\!t)$ (the rule $V - Rule^+(DL)$) or by the property assertion $r(f\!f, d)$ if $A_i$ contains the assertion $\neg C(a) \wedge r(a,d) \wedge \neg C(f\!f)$ (the rule $V - Rule^-(DL)$). We explain this algorithm extension on a simple example. The vague ontology has a vague concept expensive (any price greater than or equal to 100 units is expensive) and it is not expensive if is lower than or equal to 50 units. The ontology description is

$$\mathcal{O} = \left\langle \begin{array}{l} \mathcal{T} = \{ \exists price. \text{int} [\geq 100] \sqsubseteq Expensive, \exists price. \text{int} [\leq 50] \sqsubseteq \neg Expensive \quad \}, \\ \mathcal{A} = \{price(a, 80), Expensive(a), price(b, 90)\} \end{array} \right\rangle$$

The truth gaps assertion associated with the vague concept based on the concrete role $price$ as it can be generated by rules described in Section 3, is

$Expensive_{price}(\{\langle f\!f(50), t\!t(100)\rangle\})$. Thus, this vague ontology containing the vague concept $Expensive$, is satisfiable and acceptable. We want to check the membership of the individual $b$ to the class $Expensive$ ($\mathcal{O} \models Expensive(b)$). This means that we want to prove that $\neg Expensive(b)$ is inconsistent with the ontology description. After elimination of terminological assertions and normalization as preliminary steps before applying Tableau Rules, we have:

$$T^0 = \left\{ A_0^0 = \left\{ \begin{array}{l} ((\forall price.(\text{int }[< 100]) \sqcup Expensive) \sqcap \\ (\forall price.(\text{int }[> 50]) \sqcup \neg Expensive))(b), \\ price(a, 80), Expensive(a), price(b, 90), \neg Expensive(b) \\ Expensive(t\!t), price(t\!t, 100), \neg Expensive(f\!f), price(f\!f, 50) \end{array} \right\} \right\}$$

By applying the rule $V - Rule^+(DL)$, because $A_0^0$ contains the assertions $\{price(a, 80), Expensive(a)\}$, we get: $T^1 = \left\{ A_0^1 = \left\{ A_0^0 \cup \{price(t\!t, 80)\} \right\} \right\}$. As $A_0^1$ contains the assertions $\{price(b, 90), \neg Expensive(b)\}$) the rule $V - Rule^-(DL)$ can be applied to get: $T^2 = \left\{ A_0^2 = \left\{ A_0^1 \cup \{price(f\!f, 90)\} \right\} \right\}$. It is clear, the subset $A_0^2$ of assertions contains unacceptable truth gaps assertions (the implication $\{Expensive(t\!t), price(t\!t, 80), price(t\!t, 100), \neg Expensive(f\!f),$ $price(f\!f, 90)\}$ $\in A_0^2 \Rightarrow 90 \notin [80, 100]$ is false) which makes $b$ a member of $Expensive$.

The principle of this approach is as follows. Without this vagueness theory, $b$ which has the price of 90 (greater than 50 and less than 100) cannot be decided by the classical reasoners, as $Expensive$ or $\neg Expensive$ because the definition of $Expensive$ is vague. However, the ontology contains an assertion indicating that the price 80 of $a$ is an expensive price ($Expensive(a)$); this information can help the reasoner to decide that 90 (the price of $b$) is also an expensive price.

## 5  Conclusion

In this paper, we have presented a vagueness theory to deal with the problem of ontologies containing vague concepts. The vague property (characteristic) of a concept is based in general, on certain concept data properties that may generate truth gaps. With the traditional reasoning methods, it is not possible to decide the membership of an individual (object) to a vague concept (class) if its data property is in the truth gap. Ontologies could have extension (evolution), where assertions may be added, intentionally or as result of inferences. This ontology evolution can reduce the truth gaps and then logically it will be possible to infer on previously undecided assertions. This proposed vagueness theory is used to extend the current reasoning method to take into account these vagueness notions. In this vagueness theory, it is not necessary to add syntax and semantics to the logic SROIQ(D), for specifying the truth gaps assertions. Implementation of this approach as an extension of Fact++ [16] is one of our perspectives.

## References

1. Baader, F., Horrocks, I., Sattler, U.: Description logics. In: van Harmelen, F., Lifschitz, V., Porter, B. (eds.) Handbook of Knowledge Representation, pp. 135–179. Elsevier (2007)

2. Baader, F.: What's new in description logics. Informatik-Spektrum 34(5), 434–442 (2011)
3. Bobillo, F., Delgado, M., Gomez-Romero, J., Straccia, U.: Joining gödel and zadeh fuzzy logics in fuzzy description logics. International Journal of Uncertainty, Fuzziness and Knowledge-Based Systems 20(4), 475–508 (2012)
4. Glimm, B., Lutz, C., Horrocks, I., Sattler, U.: Answering conjunctive queries in the $\mathcal{SHIQ}$ description logic. In: Veloso, M. (ed.) Proceedings of the Twentieth International Joint Conference on Artificial Intelligence (IJCAI 2007), pp. 299–404. AAAI Press (2007)
5. Hitzler, P., Krötzsch, M., Parsia, B., Patel-Schneider, P.F., Rudolph, S. (eds.): OWL 2 Web Ontology Language: Primer. W3C (2009)
6. Horrocks, I., Kutz, O., Sattler, U.: The even more irresistible SROIQ. In: Proc. of the 10th Int. Conf. on Principles of Knowledge Representation and Reasoning (KR 2006), pp. 57–67. AAAI Press (2006)
7. Horrocks, I., Sattler, U.: A tableau decision procedure for SHOIQ. Journal of Automated Reasoning 39(39-3), 249–276 (2007)
8. Krötzsch, M.: OWL 2 profiles: An introduction to lightweight ontology languages. In: Eiter, T., Krennwallner, T. (eds.) Reasoning Web 2012. LNCS, vol. 7487, pp. 112–183. Springer, Heidelberg (2012)
9. Lukasiewicz, T., Straccia, U.: Managing uncertainty and vagueness in description logics for the semantic web. J. Web Sem. 6(4), 291–308 (2007)
10. Lukasiewicz, T., Straccia, U.: Description logic programs under probabilistic uncertainty and fuzzy vagueness. Int. J. Approx. Reasoning 50(6), 837–853 (2009)
11. Lutz, C., Milicic, M.: A tableau algorithm for DLs with concrete domains and GCIs. Journal of Automated Reasoning 38(1-3), 227–259 (2007)
12. Pareti, P., Klein, E.: Learning vague concepts for the semantic web. In: Proc. Joint WS on Knowledge Evolution and Ontology Dynamics. In conj. with ISWC 2011. CEUR workshop proceedings, vol. 784 (2011)
13. Pérez-Urbina, H., Horrocks, I., Motik, B.: Efficient query answering for OWL 2. In: Bernstein, A., Karger, D.R., Heath, T., Feigenbaum, L., Maynard, D., Motta, E., Thirunarayan, K. (eds.) ISWC 2009. LNCS, vol. 5823, pp. 489–504. Springer, Heidelberg (2009)
14. Stefan, B., Peñaloza, R.: Consistency reasoning in lattice-based fuzzy description logics. Int. J. Approx. Reason. (2013)
15. Straccia, U.: Foundations of Fuzzy Logic and Semantic Web Languages. CRC Studies in Informatics Series. Chapman & Hall (2013)
16. Tsarkov, D., Horrocks, I.: faCT++ description logic reasoner: System description. In: Furbach, U., Shankar, N. (eds.) IJCAR 2006. LNCS (LNAI), vol. 4130, pp. 292–297. Springer, Heidelberg (2006)
17. Turhan, A.-Y.: Introductions to description logics – A guided tour. In: Rudolph, S., Gottlob, G., Horrocks, I., van Harmelen, F. (eds.) Reasoning Weg 2013. LNCS, vol. 8067, pp. 150–161. Springer, Heidelberg (2013)
18. Zadeh, L.A.: Knowledge representation in fuzzy logic. IEEE Transactions on Knowledge and Data Engineering 1(1), 89–100 (1989)
19. Zhou, Y., Grau, B.C., Horrocks, I., Wu, Z., Banerjee, J.: Making the most of your triple store: Query answering in owl 2 using an rl reasoner. In: Proc. of the Twentysecond International World Wide Web Conference (WWW 2013). ACM (2013)

# Parallel Simulated Annealing Algorithm for Cyclic Flexible Job Shop Scheduling Problem

Wojciech Bożejko[1(✉)], Jarosław Pempera[1],
and Mieczysław Wodecki[2]

[1] Department of Automatics, Mechatronics and Control Systems,
Faculty of Electronics, Wrocław University of Technology,
Wyb. Wyspiańskiego 27, 50-370 Wrocław, Poland
{wojciech.bozejko,jaroslaw.pempera}@pwr.edu.pl
[2] Institute of Computer Science, University of Wrocław,
Joliot-Curie 15, 50-383 Wrocław, Poland
mieczyslaw.wodecki@ii.uni.wroc.pl

**Abstract.** This paper deals with scheduling of tasks in cyclic flexible job shop scheduling problem (CFJSSP). We have proposed a new method of computing cyclic time for CFJSSP. This method is based on the known properties of the job shop problem as well as new properties of cyclic scheduling. We have developed two versions of proposed method: sequential and parallel. The parallel version is dedicated to the computing devices supporting vector processing. Finally, we have developed double paralyzed simulated annealing algorithms: fine grained - vector processing, multiple walk - multi core processing. Computation results, provided on market multicore processors, are presented for a set of benchmark instances from the literature.[1]

## 1 Introduction

Currently, in the vast majority of production systems there are multifunctional machines used that are configured and controlled remotely not only by industrial information systems but also by electronic drivers. Machines versatility helps in the implementation of a number of stages in the process of products manufacturing on the same machine or with the use of multiple machines which perform the most time-consuming production steps. This type of feature is called flexibility of manufacturing systems. The high flexibility of production systems supported by electronic exchange of information enables the use of advanced methods of production systems management (kanban, lean manufacturing) which adjust the schedule of the tasks execution to the needs of customers while reducing storage costs and work in progress.

Due to the high complexity of flexible manufacturing systems the efficient scheduling at the operational levels has significant importance. Operational planning guarantees conflict-free production and not only enables reduction of production costs but also increases the efficiency of the production system due to

---

[1] The work was supported by the OPUS grant DEC-2012/05/B/ST7/00102 of Polish National Centre of Science.

© Springer International Publishing Switzerland 2015
L. Rutkowski et al. (Eds.): ICAISC 2015, Part II, LNAI 9120, pp. 603–612, 2015.
DOI: 10.1007/978-3-319-19369-4_53

the application of optimization algorithms. Both of these features enhance the economic efficiency of enterprises because the production of computer support systems, in particular, optimizing the operational level are subjects of interest of many practitioners.

Even the simplest flexible manufacturing systems generate NP-hard optimization problems. For this reason, researchers focused attention on the development of heuristic algorithms based on local search methods. Among a wide variety of algorithms for flexible job shop systems, the best algorithms are based on tabu search methods: Hurink, Jurish and Thole [9], Mastrolilli and Gambardella [14]. Due to the current tendency of boosting performance by increasing the number of processing units, population algorithms, that can be in a relatively simple way parallelized, are gaining importance. Examples of such algorithms are: genetic algorithm (Yang Kacem and Borne [11]), particle swarm algorithm with simulated annealing search method (Xia and Wu [16]), genetic algorithm combined with the search algorithm with a variable environment (Jie Linyan oraz Mitsuo [10]). Dedicated parallel algorithms were proposed by Bożejko [4] and Bożejko et al. [2, 3].

In many real manufacturing systems, there is a cyclic production strategy used. Cyclic manufacturing simplifies the logistics chain management for the production supplying distribution process with finished products. Scheduling of operations in such systems is still a challenge for researchers. This challenge particularly concerns the development of computational models and optimization algorithms.

The most general models of cyclic systems and detailed models for selected production systems were collected by Kampmeyer [12]. Kampmeyer and Brucker [6] used an algorithm based on tabu search method for cyclic job shop problem with no storage constraints, whereas neural networks which optimize the cycle time in job shop problem were used by Kechadi et al. [13].

## 2    Cyclic Flexible Job Shop Scheduling Problem CFJSP

A flexible job shop production system consists of $m$ multifunction machines from the set of $M = \{1, ..., m\}$. In the production system the set of $n$ tasks from the set $J = \{J_1, ..., J_n\}$ must be performed infinite number of times. Task $J_i \in J$ consists of $n_i$ operations from the set of $O_i = \{(i, 1), (i, 2), ..., (i, n_i)\}$. The set $J$ consists of $o = \sum_{J_i \in J} n_i$ technological operations. For each operation $(i, k) \in O_i$, $i = 1, ..., n$, $k = 1, ..., n_i$ there is assigned a set of machines $M_{ik} \subseteq M$ on which it may be executed. If $M_i = M$ for every $J_i \in J$, then the production system is called fully flexible. Operation $(i, k)$ is performed on the machine $l \in M_{ik}$ in $p_{ikl} > 0$ time. Each machine can perform only one operation at a time. At any given time only one operation from the task can be executed. Operations are performed on the machines continuously without interruptions.

In the cyclic production systems tasks are performed in the so-called production cycles. In one cycle, all tasks from the set of tasks $J$ are performed. The order of operations execution on the machines in the first production cycle is reproduced in subsequent cycles.

Let $\pi_l = ((j_l(1), k_l(1)), ..., (j_l(n_l), k_l(n_l)))$ be a permutation of determining the order of operations on the machine $l \in M$, where $n_l$ denotes the number of operations executed on machines. The set $\pi = (\pi_1, ..., \pi_{n_l})$ describes the sequence of operations for all machines in the production system. Note that $\pi$ unambiguously describes the assignment of operations to machines. Let $S_{ik}^x$ ($C_{ik}^x$) be the moment of starting (completion) of the performance of the $k$-th operation of $J_i$ task in $x$-th $x = 0, 1, ....$ production cycle. The schedule of execution of operations in each production cycle must comply with the requirements arising from technological route and the order of operations on the machines $\pi$. Technological requirements for the tasks performed in $x$-th $x = 0, 1, ...$ production cycle can be formally described with the inequality:

$$S_{i,k}^x \geq C_{i,k-1}^x, J_i \in J, \ k = 2, ..., n_l, \tag{1}$$

whereas executing of operations in the cycle, in the order of $\pi$ require the fulfilment of inequality:

$$S_{j_l(s),k_l(s)}^x \geq C_{j_l(s-1),k_l(s-1)}^x, \ l \in M, \ s = 2, ..., n_l, \tag{2}$$

which means that the start of execution of $s$-th, in the order of $\pi_l$, operation $(j_l(s), k_l(s))$ can only take place after the end of the previous operation $(j_l(s-1), k_l(s-1))$ performed on the machine $l$.

In addition, the schedule of operations execution for two consecutive production cycles $x - 1$ and $x$, $x = 1, 2, ...$ must fulfill the following conditions:

$$S_{j_l(1),k_l(1)}^x \geq C_{j_l(n_l),k_l(n_l)}^{x-1}, \ l \in M. \tag{3}$$

Due to the fact that operations are executed in a production system without interruptions the starting and completion of operations have the following relationship:

$$C_{ik}^x \geq S_{ik}^x + p_{ik,\mu_{ik}}, \ J_i \in J, \ k = 1, ..., n_i, \tag{4}$$

where $\mu_{ik}$ denotes, resulting from $\pi$, the machine assigned to operation $(i, k)$, $\mu_{ik} = l$ dla $(j_l(s), k_l(s))$, $s = 1, ..., n_l, l \in M$.

The schedule of operations execution in the production system is called *cyclic* if the following condition is met:

$$S_{ik}^x = S_{ik}^0 + \tau \cdot x \quad J_i \in J, \ k = 1, ..., n_i, \ x = 1, 2, ..., \tag{5}$$

where $\tau$ is a period called cycle time.

The order of operations execution in a cyclical system $\pi$ is feasible if there is a solution to the inequality (1–5).

Let us denote by $\tau(\pi)$ the smallest value of the cycle time for the feasible order of $\pi$. The problem to be found is a sequence of operations execution on the machines $\pi^*$ such that

$$\tau(\pi^*) = \min_{\pi \in \Pi} \tau(\pi), \tag{6}$$

where $\Pi$ is the set of all allocations of operations to machines and all permissible order of operations for these assignations.

The problem of designation of a cyclic schedule for flexible job shop problem with a minimum cycle time belongs to a class of sequencing problems. Sequencing problems embrace scheduling problems in which the solution can be uniquely represented in the form of the order of operations on the machines as for the given order the value of the objective function is defined unambiguously. There is a wide range of methods for constructing algorithms for sequencing problems in which the most effective use of problem properties are being solved in order to increase the efficiency. However, the most time consuming part of these algorithms is determination of the objective function value or its estimation.

## 3    Determination of the Cycle Time for the Sequence $\pi$

In the section we propose an original method of determining the cycle time for a given order $\pi$. Considerations begin by analyzing the performance of left shifted schedule for execution of operations in cyclic systems. At this stage, it is required to fulfil the constraints (1–4), whereas the constraints (5) do not have to be met. The earliest completion moments of operations on the machines can be calculated on the following recursive formula:

$$C^x_{j_l(s),k_l(s)} = \max\{C^x_{j_l(s-1),k_l(s-1)}, C^x_{j_l(s),k_l(s)-1}\} + p_{j_l(s),k_l(s)}, \qquad (7)$$

where $C^x_{j_l(s),0} = 0$, $C^x_{j_l(0),k_l(0)} = 0$ for $x = 0$ and $C^x_{j_l(0),k_l(0)} = C^{x-1}_{j_l(n_l),k_l(n_l)}$ for $x = 1, 2, \ldots$.

It can be easily seen that the execution of the calculations in accordance with the order $Q$ for subsequent cycles (see Section 2) enables determination of the completion times for the operation in a sequential way because at the time of designation of the value of expression(7) the completion times of machine and technological predecessor are known, i.e. have been designated earlier.

For the operation $(i, k)$ performed in the production cycle $x$ there is a sequence $u^x_{i,k} = (u^0_1, \ldots, u^{x_s}_s, \ldots, u^{x_{n_u}}_{n_u})$, $u^{x_s}_s = (i_s, k_s)$, $u^{x_{n_u}}_{n_u} = (i, k)$ defined, such that $S^{x_s}_{i_s,k_s} = C^{x_s-1}_{i_{s-1},k_{s-1}}$. Obviously, the predecessor operation $(i_s, k_s)$ in a sequence $u^x_{i,k}$ is its machine or technological predecessor. Operation $u^0_1 = (i_1, k_1)$ performed in 0 cycle will be called a source of schedule for the operation $(i, k)$ executed in a cycle $x$. By $L(u^x_{i,k}) = \sum_{s=1}^{n_u} p_{i_s k_s}$ let us designate the sum of operations' execution times belonging to a sequence $u^x_{i,k}$. It is easy to observe that $C^x_{i,k} = S^0_{i_1,k_1} + L(u^x_{i,k})$.

Let us consider the sequence $u^x_{i,k}$, $J_i \in J$, $k = 1, \ldots, n_k$, $x = 1, \ldots$ with the source $u^0_{i,k}$. We have $C^x_{i,k} = S^0_{i,k} + L(u^x_{i,k}) = C^0_{i,k} - p_{i,k} + L(u^x_{i,k})$, thus, the cycle time $\tau(\pi)$ must meet the following condition:

$$\tau(\pi) \geq (L(u^x_{i,k}) - p_{ik})/x \; for \; J_i \in J, \; k = 1, \ldots, n_k, \; x = 1, \ldots. \qquad (8)$$

**Property 1** *For a given order of operations execution in a cyclic flexible job shop system* $\pi = (\pi_1, ..., \pi_m)$, *where* $\pi_l = ((j_l(1), k_l(1)), ..., (j_l(n_l), k_l(n_l)))$, $l \in M$, *the cycle time is:*

$$\tau(\pi) = \max\{(L(u^x_{j_l(1),k_l(1)}) - p_{j_l(1),k_l(1)})/x | l \in M, \, x = 1, ..., m-1\}, \qquad (9)$$

where $L(u^x_{j_l(1),k_l(1)})$ is a sum of times assigned to elements of a sequence $u^x_{j_l(1),k_l(1)}$ with source $u^0_{j_l(1),k_l(1)}$. Property 1 is given without a proof.

Arbitrarily selected sequence $u^{x^*}_{j_{l*}(1),k_{l*}(1)}$ such that $\tau(\pi) = (L(u^{x^*}_{j_{l*}(1),k_{l*}(1)}) - p_{j_{l*}(1),k_{l*}(1)})/x^*$, $l^* \in M$, $x^* \in \{1, ..., m-1\}$ will be called *a critical sequence.*

Algorithm 1 describes, in a precise manner, the proposed method for the determination of cycle time $\tau(\pi)$ for a given order $\pi$. In the commentary the discussion of the algorithm will be limited only to steps 2 and 3.1, since the rest of the steps are obvious. In Step 2 in positions 0 in the permutation $\pi_l$ there is fictional operation $-l$ inserted. Let us observe the fact that during performing the computations for the machine $l \in M$, the completion time for operation execution is initiated by a large natural number $B$. Since the operation $-l$ is the machine predecessor of operation $(j_l(1), k_l(1))$ therefore this initiation makes $(j_l(1), k_l(1))$ the source of schedule.

## Algorithm 1. Sequential Computing $\tau(\pi)$

1. Determine sequence $Q(\pi)$
2. Set $\pi_l(0) = -l$
3. For $l = 1, \ldots, m$ do
3.1 Set $C^0_{j_l(-s),k_l(-s)} = B$ for $s = l$ and $C^0_{j_l(-s),k_l(-s)} = 0$ for $s \neq l$, $s = 1, \ldots, m$
3.2 For $x = 0, \ldots, m-1$ do
3.2.1 For $s = 1, \ldots, o$ do
3.2.1.1 Compute $C^x_{j_s,k_s}$ $((i_s, k_s) = q_s)$ from (7).
4. Determine $\tau(\pi)$ from (9).

**Property 2** *The cycle time* $\tau(\pi)$ *can be determined in time* $O(om^2)$.

**Proof.** Step 3.2.1.1 requires $O(1)$ computation time. This step is executed $(m \cdot m \cdot o)$ times (loops 3.2, 3.2.1, 3.2.1.1). Step 3.1 requires $O(m)$ time and is executed $m$ times. Step 4. requires $O(m^2)$ time.

By $C^{(l)x}_{i,k}$ let us designate the completion time of execution of operation $(i, k)$ in $x$-th production cycle for the source schedule $(j_l(1), k_l(1))$. The sequence $C^x_{i,k} = (C^{(1)x}_{i,k}, C^{(2)x}_{i,k}, ..., C^{(m)x}_{i,k})$ creates vector of $m$-elements. Algorithm 2 describes the vector processing version of the proposed method for determining the cycle time.

## Algorithm 2. Vector Computing of $\tau(\pi)$

**1.** Determine sequence $Q(\pi)$
**2.** For $l = 1, ..., m$ set $\pi_l(0) = 0$, set in parallel $\boldsymbol{C}_{0,0}^0 = \boldsymbol{0}$, set $\boldsymbol{C}_{0,0}^{(l)0} = \boldsymbol{B}$.
**3.** For $x = 0, ..., m - 1$ do
**3.1** For $s = 1, ..., o$ do
**3.1.1** Compute in parallel $\boldsymbol{C}_{j_s,k_s}^x$ $((i_s, k_s) = q_s)$ from (7).
**4.** Determine $\tau(\pi)$ from (9).

**Property 3** *The cycle time $\tau(\pi)$ can be designated in time $O(om)$ on the vector processor consisting of $m$ computing cores.*

**Proof.** Step 3.2.1 requires $O(1)$ computing time on vector processor. The step is performed $(m \cdot o)$ times (loops 3. and 3.1). Other steps require much less time.

# 4   Simulated Annealing Algorithm

One of the most effective and, at the same time, easiest to implement methods of construction of local search algorithms is Simulated Annealing (SA, see Pempera et al. [15]). In each iteration of the algorithm, on the basis of the base solution $\pi$ there is a new solution $\pi'$ generated. If $T(\pi') \leq T(\pi)$, then this solution is accepted unconditionally, otherwise with probability $p = \exp(-\Delta/t)$, where $\Delta = T(\pi') - T(\pi)$, whereas $t$ is the temperature in a given iteration of the algorithm. The temperature decreases in each iteration of the algorithm according to the approved cooling scheme. The algorithm terminates computations after a predetermined number of iterations.

In the proposed algorithm, the new solution is generated by shifting a single operation. It is implemented in the three following steps:

1. randomly select operation $(i, k)$ from the critical path,
2. randomly select machine $l$ from the set $M_{ik}$,
3. designate feasible positions in which operation $(i, k)$ on machine $l$ can be inserted and insert randomly selected.

The proposed method of generating new solutions is limited to generating feasible solutions potentially better than the current one, i.e. is based on the following property:

**Property 4** *Let $\pi'$ be the order of operations on the machines resulting from the order $\pi$ such that $T(\pi') < T(\pi)$, then at least one operation from the critical path is performed on a different machine or in a different position.*

Property 4 is a simplification of a known, for a wide class of scheduling problems, block theory [7], [8].

At the same time the above operation is not time-consuming since the most time consuming is Step 3 performed in time $O(o)$ (see Property 5).

**Property 5** *Let* $(i, k)$, $J_i \in J$, $k = 1, ..., n_i$ *be any operation and* $l$, $l \in M_{ik}$ *any machine on which this operation can be performed. The range of feasible positions on machine* $l$ *in which operation* $(i, k)$ *can be inserted, can be designated in time* $O(o)$.

## 5    Results of Computational Studies

Simulated annealing algorithm described in Section 5 was implemented in 4 versions: (SA) – Single-walk Simulated Annealing,(MSA) – Multiple-walk Simulated Annealing,(PSA) – Parallel single-walk Simulated Annealing algorithms with parallel computing of the cycle time, and (MPSA) – Multiple-walk Parallel Simulated Annealing algorithms with parallel computing of the cycle time. The algorithms have been implemented in the Visual Studio 2010 environment in C++ language. The tests were conducted on an Intel I7-core 2.4GHz 4-core (Intel Hyper Threading 8-cores) computer, 4GB of RAM, managed by 32-bit Windows 7 operating system. Experimental studies were conducted on the set consisting of 21 instances proposed by Barnes and Chambers [1]. The set consists of instances containing from 10 to 15 tasks and from 11 to 18 machines with varying degrees of flexibility. In a single path of an algorithm, the simulated annealing process was carried out *rep* times. The first computations process began with the solutions generated by a construction algorithm, the remaining began with the last solutions generated by the previous process. The simulated annealing was performed with the following parameters: the initial temperature of 1000, the rate of cooling scheme $\lambda = 0.995$, the number of iterations 10000. In order to generate the initial solution there was construction algorithm used, with the priority rule: earliest completion time.

Computational study of the proposed algorithms were divided into two stages. The aim of the first phase was to examine the speedup of algorithms obtained by the use of vector processing in a real computer system, while the second assessment concerned the quality of the generated solutions, in particular the quality of the solutions generated by multipath parallel algorithms. During the computational study there were: $T(A)$ -time cycle for the best solutions found by $A$ algorithms and $CPU(A)$ - time of computations of algorithm $A$, $A \in \{SA, PSA, MSA, MPSA\}$ remembered.

### 5.1    Assessment of Vector Processing Speedup

Today's processors produced by leading manufacturers, used in stationary and mobile computers, support parallel processing on two levels: processor instructions and multi-core processing. In case of instructions level (SSE), in one cycle of calculation one identical computational activity is performed on the number of data, remembered in computer registers as a vector consisting of a certain number of elements $s$. In other words, the calculations are performed by the vector processor consisting of $s$ cores. SSE registers size is 128- bit, thus for the

**Table 1.** Time of running and sppedup of SA algorithms

| Name | $n \times m$ (o) | one path | | | 4 paths | | | 8 paths | | |
|---|---|---|---|---|---|---|---|---|---|---|
| | | SA | PSA | SU | MSA | MPSA | SU | MSA | MPSA | SU |
| mt10c1 | 10×11 (100) | 30.6 | 6.1 | 5.0 | 38.4 | 8.0 | 4.8 | 50.2 | 10.1 | 5.0 |
| mt10cc | 10×12 (100) | 36.7 | 6.7 | 5.5 | 43.6 | 8.8 | 5.0 | 60.4 | 11.2 | 5.4 |
| mt10x | 10×11 (100) | 31.6 | 5.9 | 5.3 | 37.2 | 8.2 | 4.6 | 49.8 | 9.9 | 5.0 |
| mt10xx | 10×12 (100) | 36.0 | 6.5 | 5.5 | 41.9 | 8.8 | 4.8 | 59.9 | 11.0 | 5.5 |
| mt10xxx | 10×13 (100) | 42.7 | 7.1 | 6.0 | 47.3 | 9.3 | 5.1 | 65.7 | 11.9 | 5.5 |
| mt10xy | 10×12 (100) | 35.9 | 6.6 | 5.4 | 41.7 | 8.8 | 4.8 | 59.6 | 10.8 | 5.5 |
| mt10xyz | 10×13 (100) | 42.5 | 7.1 | 6.0 | 49.1 | 8.9 | 5.5 | 70.1 | 12.1 | 5.8 |
| setb4c9 | 15×11 (150) | 46.6 | 8.6 | 5.4 | 52.8 | 10.7 | 4.9 | 74.0 | 13.4 | 5.5 |
| setb4cc | 15×12 (150) | 55.6 | 9.4 | 5.9 | 63.3 | 11.3 | 5.6 | 86.4 | 14.4 | 6.0 |
| setb4x | 15×11 (150) | 46.6 | 8.5 | 5.5 | 52.9 | 10.2 | 5.2 | 73.0 | 14.1 | 5.2 |
| setb4xx | 15×12 (150) | 54.8 | 9.0 | 6.1 | 62.1 | 10.8 | 5.8 | 85.6 | 14.5 | 5.9 |
| setb4xxx | 15×13 (150) | 64.4 | 10.0 | 6.4 | 73.2 | 11.8 | 6.2 | 100.8 | 16.0 | 6.3 |
| setb4xy | 15×12 (150) | 54.6 | 9.4 | 5.8 | 61.1 | 11.4 | 5.4 | 86.0 | 14.6 | 5.9 |
| setb4xyz | 15×13 (150) | 65.4 | 9.6 | 6.8 | 71.8 | 12.0 | 6.0 | 99.8 | 15.7 | 6.4 |
| seti5c12 | 15×16 (225) | 156.9 | 17.2 | 9.1 | 172.2 | 22.1 | 7.8 | 233.5 | 27.5 | 8.5 |
| seti5cc | 15×17 (225) | 177.1 | 19.3 | 9.2 | 195.8 | 24.2 | 8.1 | 264.4 | 31.1 | 8.5 |
| seti5x | 15×16 (225) | 157.3 | 17.0 | 9.3 | 172.2 | 21.0 | 8.2 | 234.2 | 27.8 | 8.4 |
| seti5xx | 15×17 (225) | 177.4 | 19.8 | 8.9 | 197.6 | 23.7 | 8.3 | 265.9 | 30.7 | 8.7 |
| seti5xxx | 15×18 (225) | 202.4 | 20.2 | 10.0 | 221.1 | 25.6 | 8.6 | 293.4 | 32.7 | 9.0 |
| seti5xy | 15×17 (225) | 175.8 | 19.6 | 9.0 | 193.3 | 24.1 | 8.0 | 261.0 | 30.6 | 8.5 |
| seti5xyz | 15×18 (225) | 196.5 | 20.7 | 9.5 | 217.1 | 25.7 | 8.4 | 294.3 | 32.4 | 9.1 |

data of Int16 type, used in the calculations, the size of the vector is $s = 8$. Undoubtedly, in case of vectors with sizes larger than $s$, the vector is divided into fragments of $s$-elements and then they are processed sequentially.

All algorithms were run with parameter $rep = 20$ while the multipath algorithms were started simultaneously at 4 and 8 cores (each realized a different path). Table 1 presents algorithms' execution times for all instances of the test. In addition, on the basis of the time of the algorithm running in the basic version and using the processing vector, there was designated the speedup of calculations $SU = CPU(SA)/CPU(PSA)$ ($SU = CPU(MSA)/CPU(MPSA)$).

The analysis of single-path algorithms shows that for certain instances the speedup is greater than the number of cores of vector processor $s = 8$. This stays in contrast to Ahmdal's Law. In fact, in a sequential and parallel processing participate other CPU instructions of varying execution time. What is more, the most frequently used function $max$ for SSE instruction is executed in one processor cycle, while in case of sequential x86 instruction it consists of comparison and jump instructions. The use of vector processing helps to accelerate the SA algorithm running from 5 to 10 times in single-path version. In case of multipath versions the speedup is slightly smaller. The size of the speedup depends on the number of machines. The smallest speedup is observed, e.g. for a small number of machines and distant from the multiple of $s = 8$ (mt10c).

Comparing the running time of single-path PSA algorithm and 4-path MPSA algorithm it can be seen that the MPSA running time is on average by 1.3 (minimum 1.2) times longer than the SA time. I7 processor consists of 4 identical cores, the MPSA algorithm performs exactly 4 times more computations than the SA. In case of 8-track MPSA algorithm the running time is on average 1.7 times longer than the SA. In this case, we can see the beneficial effects of Hyper Threading technology.

## 5.2  Assessment of Algorithms Efficiency

The aim of the second phase of research was to assess the quality of solutions generated by PSA (single-path), PSA4 (4-paths) and PSA8 (8-paths) algorithms. In assessing the quality the relative deviation was used for the cycle time of solution $\pi^A$ generated by the $A$ algorithm compared to the cycle time of the best know solution $\pi^*$: $Dev(A) = (\tau(\pi^A) - \tau(\pi^*))/\tau(\pi^*)$. The algorithm was executed with the parameter $rep = 20$. Reference solutions $\pi^*$ were generated by the PSA8 algorithm with $rep = 50$.

As a result of detailed analysis of the test results it was noted that for the PSA single-walk algorithm deviation was 2.1% to 8.1%, 4.7% in average, PSA4 at the same time generates solutions with the value of $Dev$ from 0% to 4.6%, in average 2.1%. Solutions of PSA8 have an average coefficient of $Dev = 1.3\%$.

In summary, the results show that the use of vector processing significantly accelerates SA algorithm. In addition, the use of multiple-walk search yields a significantly better solutions in the same time of calculations. The average value of $Dev$ for 4 and 8-path algorithms is more than 2 and almost 4 times smaller than the $Dev$ for single-walk algorithm, respectively.

## 6  Conclusions

The work is devoted to the scheduling of tasks in a cyclic flexible production system. The paper presents new properties of the problem and the properties characteristic of the cyclic manufacturing. Based on the theoretical properties, a genuine method of the cycle time determination was proposed. Sequential and parallel (based on vector processing) implementations were presented as well as the analysis of the computational complexity of the proposed methodology.

As further research, parallel processing techniques are planned to be designed for efficient calculations on modern computational units (GPU, HPC), equipped with large number of cores.

## References

1. Barnes, J.W., Chambers, J.B.: Flexible Job Shop Scheduling by tabu search, Graduate program in operations research and industrial engineering, Technical Report ORP 9609, University of Texas, Austin (1996)

2. Bożejko, W., Uchroński, M., Wodecki, M.: Parallel hybrid metaheuristics for the flexible job shop problem. Computers & Industrial Engineering 59, 323–333 (2010)
3. Bożejko, W., Uchroński, M., Wodecki, M.: The new golf neighborhood for the flexible job shop problem. In: Proceedings of the ICCS 2010. Procedia Computer Science, vol. 1, pp. 289–296. Elsevier (2010)
4. Bożejko, W.: On single-walk parallelization of the job shop problem solving algorithms. Computers & Operations Research 39, 2258–2264 (2012)
5. Bożejko, W., Pempera, J., Smutnicki, C.: Parallel Tabu Search Algorithm for the Hybrid Flow Shop Problem. Computers and Industrial Engineering 65, 466–474 (2013)
6. Brucker, P., Kampmeyer, T.: Cyclic job shop scheduling problems with blocking. Annals of Operations Research 159, 161–181 (2008)
7. Grabowski, J., Skubalska, E., Smutnicki, C.: On Flow Shop Scheduling with Release and Due Dates to Minimize Maximum Lateness. Journal of the Operational Research Society 34(7), 615–620 (1983)
8. Grabowski, J., Pempera, J.: New block properties for the permutation flow shop problem with application in tabu search. Journal of Operational Research Society 52, 210–220 (2001)
9. Hurink, E., Jurisch, B., Thole, M.: Tabu search for the job shop scheduling problem with multi-purpose machine. Operations Research Spektrum 15, 205–215 (1994)
10. Jia, H.Z., Nee, A.Y.C., Fuh, J.Y.H., Zhang, Y.F.: A modified genetic algorithm for distributed scheduling problems. International Journal of Intelligent Manufacturing 14, 351–362 (2003)
11. Kacem, I., Hammadi, S., Borne, P.: Approach by localization and multiobjective evolutionary optimization for flexible job-shop scheduling problems. IEEE Transactions on Systems, Man, and Cybernetics Part C 32(1), 1–13 (2002)
12. Kampmeyer, T.: Cyclic Scheduling Problems, Ph. D. Thesis, University Osnabrück (2006)
13. Kechadi, M., Low, K.S., Goncalves, G.: Recurrent neural network approach for cyclic job shop scheduling problem. Journal of Manufacturing Systems 32, 689–699 (2013)
14. Mastrolilli, M., Gambardella, L.M.: Effective neighborhood functions for the flexible job shop problem. Journal of Scheduling 3(1), 3–20 (2000)
15. Pempera, J., Smutnicki, C., Żelazny, D.: Optimizing bicriteria flow shop scheduling problem by simulated annealing algorithm. Procedia Computer Science 18, 936–945 (2013)
16. Xia, W., Wu, Z.: An effective hybrid optimization approach for multi-objective flexible job-shop scheduling problem. Computers and Industrial Engineering 48, 409–425 (2005)

# Transactional Forward Chaining: A Functional Approach

Konrad Grzanek[✉]

IT Institute,
University of Social Science (SAN),
Sienkiewicza 9, Lodz 90-113, Poland
kgrzanek@spoleczna.pl

**Abstract.** Forward chaining is an effective method of reasoning used in production systems. Enhancing it with a transaction support enables rollback actions in productions and opens a way to define and perform reversible reasoning schemes. We present selected implementation details of a custom transactional production system with forward chaining, based on the Rete algorithm, realized in the functional programming style. We also discuss some design issues, like operating in multi-core environment, indexing, using immutable collections, and the Software Transactional Memory in Haskell. Additionally we give a prospect of exploiting partial knowledge stored in Rete network for the purpose of performing analysis in the absence of information.

**Keywords:** Production Systems · Forward Chaining · Rete · Functional Programming

## 1  Introduction

It is assumed that expert systems are a class of intelligent software systems using knowledge and inference rules to solve problems that are so hard to solve, that it requires special "expert" knowledge (after Feigenbaum - see [4]) to be used. There is usually a strong demand for them to cope with some difficult domain problems as effectively as a human specialist in the field. Moreover, we expect them to provide an insight into their inference process, and, more generally speaking, into they way they store and use their knowledge. In other words, they are expected to provide a human readable explanation of the way they solve problems. These demands raise the knowledge representation and inference issues to the status of key concepts from the point of view of designers and implementers of these systems.

A typical architecture of an expert system consists of a base of facts (*knowledge base*), the internal representation of *(inference) rules*, and the *inference engine* that does the actual job of applying rules to facts. Usually, when a solution is found, the system undertakes some actions. These actions may be modifying the knowledge base, the rule-set, or simply informing the user about the success (solution found). An important issue here is also solving conflicts; the situations in

© Springer International Publishing Switzerland 2015
L. Rutkowski et al. (Eds.): ICAISC 2015, Part II, LNAI 9120, pp. 613–624, 2015.
DOI: 10.1007/978-3-319-19369-4_54

which more than one solution is found (e.g. see [6]). Nonetheless, the knowledge base and the inference engine are the core, and the conflict set solvers should be treated as an important but optional part.

The above paragraph is actually a description of a *rule-based* approach, one of the most transparent and robust ways of encoding expert knowledge [5]. Rules are in some sense the central concept in this approach. We call them *productions* and the software systems based on this approach are called the *production systems*. Usually a production consists of a set of *conditions* (also called *predicates*) and a set of *actions*.

The inference process in the production systems consists of iteratively applying *modus ponens* $(P \to Q, P \vdash Q)$ to the conditions (of the rules) and to the facts in the knowledge base, to find the facts matching the conditions. Matches cause a series of transitions from the current system state, through the actions (of productions) that modify the knowledge base and/or the rule-set, to the next state with an updated base of facts and rule-set, until the occurrence of inference conditions that actually stop the whole process. Then we get either a solution to some problem or a state that means the impossibility of continuing due to the lack of further matches. This process called *forward chaining* [1], [2], [3] is one of the two major mechanisms found in the rule-based inference engines[1].

In this paper we:

- Present the motivations for enhancing forward chaining with transaction support.
- Introduce an ongoing project [28] - an implementation of the above idea in Haskell.
- Discuss some decisions having an impact on design and implementation of this system, like operating in the multi-tasking environment, indexing, and using functional programming language with its ecosystem as the main implementation tool.
- Give an overview of some element of our code-base to whet an appetite of a reader wanting to participate in the project and/or use our software for his own purposes.

## 2    Motivations for the Design and Implementation of a Transactional Production System

Transactions in software and implementing the systems that provide/support them has been an area of active research since the early days of computing[2]. The core *ACID* properties of transactions make them the natural choice for building production-quality software that aims to manage data in a robust way, especially under the assumption of operating in a *multi-tasking* (mostly *concurrent* but also *parallel*) environment.

---

[1] The other one, known as *backward chaining* is the core of famous *Prolog* - the general purpose logic programming language.

[2] For an extensive set of references see [7], [8].

Production systems with forward chaining are naturally "predisposed" to be implemented with the use of transactions. Unfortunately, the accessible production systems of industrial quality do not admit to implement this feature[3]. This is why we decided to provide a custom solution supporting transactional forward chaining. Further and detailed motivations for this project are as follows.

*Rollbacks.* The ability to roll back the transaction when performing the forward chaining process opens a way to provide the users of the production system with the ability to execute roll-back actions in productions. This in turn opens the door for both defining new business rules ("break and return to the starting point", a *backtracking*-like behavior) and for performing "speculative" runs of the inference process, during which we add some new facts (possibly random ones) and observe the system behavior, making conclusions and rolling back in the end. This may be called reversible reasoning schemes.

*Robust Concurrency.* Contemporary production systems are intended to be used in concurrent, multi-core world. Transactions are the only known means to implement concurrent updates of data (facts and rule-set in this case) in a provably correct way.

*Insight into Inference.* A production system implemented from the ground up is completely transparent for us. In particular, it is possible (and expedient) to design its API in such way, that it would allow us to write routines to perform observations of how the facts are matched against the production conditions. The abilities of performing detailed analysis of the process may be highly valuable. Especially in combination with ...

*... Partial Knowledge Representation.* As it will be presented further, the system is intended to store partial matches of the facts and conditions. When one is able to dig into the internal structure of these matches (and so the information represented by them), he is also capable of deriving some conclusions out of the incomplete knowledge.

The rest of this article presents the core of the algorithm and some implementation details of our transactional production system. Selected Haskell source codes will be used for the purpose of the presentation. For a more detailed insight, please visit the full project's GitHub repository [28].

## 3   Rete/UL

The basis of forward chaining is searching for facts that match the conditions of rules. In a naive approach the production system must re-evaluate conditions of

---

[3] In particular we mean *Drools* http://www.drools.org, *Microsoft Business Rules Engine* http://msdn.microsoft.com/en-us/library/aa561216.aspx and *CLIPS* http://clipsrules.sourceforge.net/.

all rules against all facts gathered in the knowledge base after any act of manipulating facts or the rule-set. This highly ineffective process makes this approach unusable in practical scenarios due to a poor scalability. It is worth mentioning here that in large production systems a number of hundreds of thousands rules and millions of facts is not unusual [11].

Rete algorithm developed by Dr Ch. Forgy in early 1970s [10] is the established first-class algorithm that performs the matching in an effective way. Its outstanding characteristics led to its wide adoption in the expert systems domain. The mentioned Drools, CLIPS, and Microsoft Business Rules Engine (part of BizTalk) are examples of its use in a production environment. It has been a subject of research and was used in research projects (e.g. [12]). Over the years many optimizations of the algorithm were made, with some of them being published as a research papers, others of a proprietary nature. Our implementation relies on great work of R. B. Doorenbos. He is a designer of an optimization called Rete/UL and an author of a clear and comprehensive description of the algorithm [11]. We will give a brief overview of Rete and the mentioned optimization in subsequent sections.

## 3.1  Rete Algorithm Overview

The basic Rete achieves such great results by using two techniques:

1. Storing all the match results, including the partial ones, in a specified graph (this is where the name of the algorithm comes from - "Rete" in Latin means "net" or "comb"). This in turn eliminates the need to re-evaluate matching of all facts against all conditions.
2. Sharing the network structure between productions. It is a source of massive optimization in the situations when we have a large number of productions having the same or similar sets of conditions.

Facts in Rete are represented by tuples (*object, attribute, value*) called, for brevity, *Wmes* (*Working Memory Elements*). The main role of the network is to propagate Wmes starting from the working memory, through the graph nodes, down to so called *production nodes*, where the appropriate *actions* are fired. The following Fig. 1 presents a network for three productions $P1, P2, P3$ that share the structure of the graph. At the figure the production nodes are called like the productions: $P1, P2, P3$ (see the bottom of the network).

Between the working memory and the production nodes there is a non trivial network structure. Its first layer are the $\alpha$ *memory* nodes. Their role is to store the Wmes matching constant tests in productions. The $\alpha$ memories pass their Wmes to *join nodes* (symbol $\bowtie$) where the join operations are performed. The role of joins is to find wmes that match more than one condition within a production. Cross-condition variable value tests are performed here, regarding that conditions may use variables, e.g. like in ($\langle x \rangle$ *is red*), where $\langle x \rangle$ is a variable. Matching Wmes are grouped into *Tokens* and stored in $\beta$ *memories* (symbolized by a white rectangle with $\beta$ at the diagram). Tokens represent matches for the production's conditions "so far" accordingly to the network level of the join node that "produced" them. The production nodes receive complete (full) tokens from above and then fire their actions.

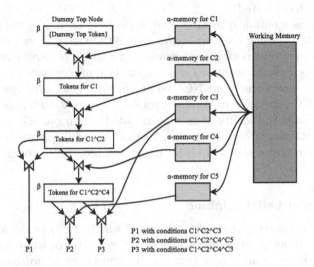

**Fig. 1.** Rete network for three productions with node sharing exposed. Source: [11] (re-edited).

Fig. 2 shows a concrete situation for one production and a group of Wmes. Tokens are symbolized by curly braces, e.g. $\{w1, w2, w3\}$ is a token with three Wmes: $w1$, $w2$, and $w3$.

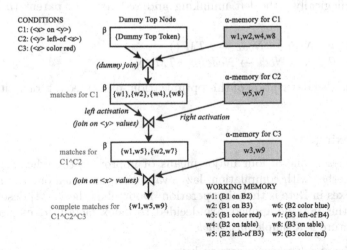

**Fig. 2.** Instantiated network for a single production. Source: [11] (re-edited).

By convention, the $\alpha$ memories are called the $\alpha$ *part* of the network, and the other nodes are the $\beta$ *part*. When an $\alpha$ memory passes a Wme to a join node, it is called a *right activation* of the node. When a $\beta$ memory passes a token into its child join node, we call it *left activation*. *beta* memories and production nodes may only be left-activated.

All conditions mentioned so far were the positive ones. Negation is also supported by Rete by using *negative nodes* and *NCC nodes*. A negative node is a node in the $\beta$ part that performs a negation of a single positive condition, while the NCC nodes perform negations of a conjunction of conditions (either positive or not). This is where the name NCC comes from; it is *negated conjunctive condition*. The NCC support is particularly useful, because $\forall_x \bullet P_x$ may be rewritten as $\neg\exists_x \bullet \neg P_x$, and the ability of nesting negated conditions allows us to define conditions containing arbitrary combinations of $\forall$ and $\exists$ quantifiers.

For an exhaustive discussion on all details of how Rete works, see [11] and [10].

## 3.2 Right and Left Unlinking

Doorenbos [11] observed, that performing right activations in the absence of tokens from the above $\beta$ memory, as well as left activations, when the $\alpha$ memory of the underlying join node is empty, heavily affects the performance. To counteract this negative phenomenon, he proposed a technique of unlinking nodes under specified conditions and re-linking them when proper data appears.

In the described implementation right unlinking and re-linking to the proper $\alpha$ memory is being performed by two complementary procedures with the following signatures:

$rightUnlink :: Node \rightarrow Amem \rightarrow STM$ ()
$relinkToAlphaMemory :: Node \rightarrow STM$ ()

And analogically - the left unlinking and re-linking to parent ($\beta$ memory) node:

$leftUnlink :: Node \rightarrow Node \rightarrow STM$ ()
$relinkToParent :: Node \rightarrow Node \rightarrow STM$ ()

For a detailed description of this optimization, please see [11] or visit our code base [28].

## 3.3 Indexing

Using indexes is one of four major means of improving the efficiency of algorithms, together with compilation, lazy evaluation, and memorization. A place to use indexes in Rete is the join operation. Doorenbos thesis [11] describes various ways this may be applied. We decided to index facts in $\alpha$ memories. The index structure is a simple *hash-table*[4]:

---

[4] We use the *unordered-containers* package
https://hackage.haskell.org/package/unordered-containers.

**type** *WmesIndex* = (*Map.HashMap Symbol* (*Set.HashSet Wme*))

that maps symbols to sets of Wmes. In every $\alpha$ memory there are the following transactional fields:

*amemWmesByObj* :: (*TVar WmesIndex*)
*amemWmesByAttr* :: (*TVar WmesIndex*)
*amemWmesByVal* :: (*TVar WmesIndex*)

By analogy, we index the Wmes stored in the global context (*Env*):

*envWmesByObj* :: (*TVar WmesIndex*)
*envWmesByAttr* :: (*TVar WmesIndex*)
*envWmesByVal* :: (*TVar WmesIndex*)

Together with the global Wmes registry defined as a type:

**type** *WmesRegistry* = (*Map.HashMap WmeKey Wme*)

and used in the Env

*envWmesRegistry* :: (*TVar WmesRegistry*)

these indexes form a working memory of our production system. While indexing the $\alpha$ memory is used to optimize joins (precisely: left activations of join nodes), the global indexes work on adding new productions.

*Discussion.* Choosing a right indexing strategy is not an easy task. The decision to index the $\alpha$ memories and leaving $\beta$ part of the network unindexed has been made relying on the observations derived from [11], that the $\alpha$ part of the network has a greater impact on the overall performance with respect to the amount the data being propagated down the network than the $\beta$ part. On the other hand, indexing $\beta$ memories in the inevitably transactional way would increase the number of accesses to the transactional variables when performing joins. This is why we decided to leave the tokens unindexed.

## 4    Functional Programming Language as the Implementation Tool

Essentially, the functional programming is a programming style in which all procedures are realizations of *computable functions* in mathematics, there are no side effects, and so the *referential transparency* is achievable with no effort [13]. Purity of functions and lack of variables means we do not have to put locks on data when doing the multi-core programming; as locks do not compose, this gets us out of serious trouble.

The lack of destructive operations on data also means that rolling the transactions back is trivial. Any "changes" may be "reversed" by simply removing them from the memory. This makes this programming style a perfect choice for implementing robust transactional systems.

Out of many functional programming languages, Haskell [15], [16] is the one that possessed features that make is especially suited for the task. It is a strongly and statically typed, purely functional language, that uses advanced notions from the type theory and from category theory [14], to make the programs written in it as close to being provably correct as possible. There are some great books on the subject worth mentioning, like [17], [18], as well as comprehensive on-line materials: [19], [20], and [21].

## 4.1  Discussion on the Data Structures

Traditional, imperative Rete implementations use arrays and doubly linked lists to make the operations on sequential data as effective as possible. The functional style demands persistent (immutable), acyclic sequential collections [22]. The work by Clayman [9] states that "[...] efficiencies of having $O(1)$ access to data structures in a rule-based system can not be overcome by using parallelism". Hughes [23] gives an explanation, why the functional concatenation ($+\!\!+$) operator on linked lists used to *append* elements to the end of a list does not exhibit an optimistic complexity. These reasons led as to depend on sequences implemented with use of *2-3 finger trees*, as described in [24]. Fortunately, these sequences are a part of standard Haskell library (*Data.Sequence* module).

Sequences offer $O(1)$ insertion into the front and at the end with the following operators:

```
(◁) :: a → Seq a → Seq a
(▷) :: Seq a → a → Seq a
```

as well as sequence concatenation of class $O(log(min(n_1, n_2)))$, where $n_1$ and $n_2$ are the sizes of arguments:

```
(⋈) :: Seq a → Seq a → Seq a
```

Creating a sequence object from a standard Haskell list is $O(n)$:

```
fromList :: [a] → Seq a
```

and similarly, conversion to a standard list is also $O(n)$ with Seq being an instance of the *Foldable type-class*:

```
toList :: Foldable t ⇒ t a → [a]
```

The use of the append operation (▷) can be seen at the following code[5]:

```
relinkToAlphaMemory :: Node → STM ()
relinkToAlphaMemory node = do
```

---

[5] Taken from https://github.com/kongra/Rete/blob/master/AI/Rete/Algo.hs.

*ancestorLookup* ← *relinkAncestor node*
**case** *ancestorLookup* **of**
   *Just ancestor* →
     *modifyTVar'*
       (*amemSuccessors* (*vprop nodeAmem node*))
       (*node* '*insertBeforeFirstOccurence*' *ancestor*)
   *Nothing* → *modifyTVar'*
       (*amemSuccessors* (*vprop nodeAmem node*))
       (▷*node*)
*writeTVar* (*vprop rightUnlinked node*) *False*

Besides the sequences, we also use hash-sets (from the *unordered-containers* package mentioned earlier) for non-sequential access and standard Haskell lists where possible.

## 4.2   Syntactic Sugar in the STM Monad

*Software Transactional Memory* as described in [27], [25], [26] is a way to simplify multi-tasking programming by grouping many state changing operations and executing them atomically [27]. In Haskell[6] it is the most effective technique that leads to implementing correct software which use shared memory (variables) to communicate threads. No wonder we decided to use STM as our transactional core.

We introduced few enhancements to the STM API. The API itself is very comprehensive and easy to use, so we developed just some tools to make our source codes more clear and succinct. First, let us present some basic types of transactional collections:

```
type TList a = TVar [a]
type TSeq a = TVar (Seq.Seq a)
type TSet a = TVar (Set.HashSet a)
```

The procedure *nullTSet* simply answers the question, whether the transactional set is empty. Its functionality boils down to reading value of a transactional variable and then passing the value (a hash-set) to a lifted *Set.null*:

```
nullTSet :: TSet a → STM Bool
nullTSet = liftM Set.null ∘ readTVar
```

Similarly, we have an STM-aware conversion of foldables to lists:

```
toListT :: Foldable f ⇒ TVar (f a) → STM [a]
toListT = toListM ∘ readTVar
```

The implementation of Rete network uses *NodeVariant*, an *algebraic data-type*, that holds the data specific to various kinds of nodes. Thus, we have a non-transactional accessor to the specific variant value of nodes:

---
[6] The package *stm*, http://hackage.haskell.org/package/stm.

$$vprop :: (NodeVariant \rightarrow a) \rightarrow Node \rightarrow a$$
$$vprop\ accessor = accessor \circ nodeVariant$$

and then, the transactional one:

$$rvprop :: (NodeVariant \rightarrow TVar\ a) \rightarrow Node \rightarrow STM\ a$$
$$rvprop\ accessor = readTVar \circ vprop\ accessor$$

And finally, there is the example use[7] of *rvprop* procedure:

$$findNccOwner :: Node \rightarrow Maybe\ Token \rightarrow Maybe\ Wme$$
$$\rightarrow STM\ (Maybe\ Token)$$
$$findNccOwner\ node\ ownersTok\ ownersWme = \textbf{do}$$
$$tokens \leftarrow rvprop\ nodeTokens\ node$$
$$return\ \$\ headMay\ (filter\ matchingTok$$
$$(Set.toList\ tokens))$$
**where**
$$matchingTok\ tok =$$
$$isJust\ ownersTok\ \wedge$$
$$tokParent\ tok \equiv fromJust\ ownersTok\ \wedge$$
$$tokWme\ tok \equiv ownersWme$$

## 5   Limitations and Future Work

While writing this paper, the presented transactional production system is a project in a stage of heavy development. Due to various design decisions and compromises its current version exhibits the following limitations:

- Lack of $\beta$ memory indexation. This characteristic is worth re-thinking, but any further decisions about indexing tokens must be delayed until some initial benchmarking.
- No predicate conditions. Implementing this feature is relatively easy and will be introduced in the future.
- The implementation has been using STM from the start. Due to the nature of STM it does not provide durability. We do not expect this characteristic to change in predictable time. Actually, introducing some kind of data persistence would require building an abstraction above STM as well as above other data storage layers (IO monad). This may be an area of promising research on its own.

Rete is famous for its complexity. It would be excellent to use some techniques like *dependent types* or *type families* in Haskell to improve the ability of checking some semantic dependencies between parts of the algorithm on the compile time. This surely will be a subject of future research.

---

[7] Again from https://github.com/kongra/Rete/blob/master/AI/Rete/Algo.hs.

# References

1. Bacchus, F.: Yee Whye Teh: Making Forward Chaining Relevant. In: Proc. 4th Intl. Conf. AI Planning Systems (1998)
2. Ugur, K., Nau, D.: Forward-Chaining Planning in Nondeterministic Domains. In: (AAAI 2004) Nineteenth National Conference on Artificial Intelligence (2004)
3. Siler, W., Buckley, J.J.: Fuzzy Expert Systems and Fuzzy Reasoning. John Wiley & Sons, Inc. (2005)
4. Sasikumar, M., Ramani, S., Muthu Raman, S., Anjaneyulu, K.S.R., Chandrasekar, R.: A Practical Introduction to Rule Based Expert Systems. Narosa Publishing House, New Delhi (2007)
5. Polach, P., Valenta, J., Jirsik, V.: Knowledge coding methods for rule-based expert systems. WSEAS Transactions on Information Science and Applications 7(8), 1101–1114 (2010)
6. Pakiarajah, V., Crowther, P., Hartnett, J.: Conflict Resolution Techniques for Expert Systems Used to Classify Remotely Sensed Satellite Images. GeoComputation (2000), http://www.geocomputation.org/2000/GC025/Gc025.htm
7. Weikum, G., Vossen, G.: Transactional Information Systems Theory - Algorithms, and the Practice of Concurrency Control and Recovery. The Morgan Kaufmann Series in Data Management Systems. Morgan Kaufmann Publishers (2002)
8. Bernstein, P.A., Newcomer, E.: Principles of Transaction Processing, 2nd edn. Morgan Kaufmann Publishers (2009)
9. Clayman, S.: Developing and Measuring Parallel Rule-Based Systems in a Functional Programming Environment. PhD Thesis. University College London, Department of Computer Science (1993)
10. Forgy, C.: On the efficient implementation of production systems. Department of Computer Science, Carnegie-Mellon University (1979)
11. Doorenbos, R.B.: Production Matching for Large Learning Systems. PhD Thesis. Computer Science Department, Carnegie Mellon University Pittsburgh, PA (1995)
12. Veera Narayana, M., Sunil Kumar, A., Suneel Kumar, B., Samkishan, N., Jogeswara Rao, B.: Implementation of RETE Algorithm Using Lemon Expert System. International Journal of Emerging Research in Management & Technology 2(7) (2013) ISSN: 2278-9359
13. Bird, R., Wadler, R.: Introduction to Functional Programming. Series in Computer Science (Hoare, C.A.R. (ed.)). Prentice Hall International (UK) Ltd. (1988)
14. Awodey, S.: Category Theory, 2nd edn. Oxford University Press (2010)
15. Peyton Jones, S.: The Implementation of Functional Programming Languages. Prentice-Hall International Series in Computer Science. Prentice Hall International (UK) Ltd. (1987)
16. Hudak, P.: The Haskell School of Expression, Learning Functional Programming by Multimedia. Cambridge University Press (2000)
17. Lipovaca, M.: Learn You a Haskell for Great Good!: A Beginner's Guide, 1st edn. No Starch Press (April 21, 2011)
18. Doets, K., van Eijck, J.: The Haskell Road to Logic. Math and Programming. College Publications (2004) ISBN-10: 0954300696, ISBN-13: 978-0954300692
19. Haskell Wikibook, http://en.wikibooks.org/wiki/Haskell
20. Haskell Programming Guidelines - HaskellWiki, http://www.haskell.org/haskellwiki/Programming_guidelines
21. Haskell Programming Tips - HaskellWiki, http://www.haskell.org/haskellwiki/Things_to_avoid

22. Allison, L.: Circular Programs and SelfReferential Structures. Software Practice and Experience 19(2), 99–109 (1989)
23. Hughes, J.R.: A Novel Representation of Lists and Its Application to the Function "Reverse". Information Processing Letters 22, 141–144 (1986)
24. Hinze, R., Paterson, R.: Finger trees: a simple general-purpose data structure. Journal of Functional Programming 16(2), 197–217 (2006)
25. Discolo, A., Harris, T., Marlow, S., Peyton Jones, S., Singh, S.: Lock-Free Data Structures using STM in Haskell. In: Hagiya, M. (ed.) FLOPS 2006. LNCS, vol. 3945, pp. 65–80. Springer, Heidelberg (2006)
26. Harris, T., Peyton Jones, S.: Transactional memory with data invariants. In: First ACM SIGPLAN Workshop on Languages, Compilers, and Hardware Support for Transactional Computing, Ottawa, Canada (June 11, 2006)
27. Marlow, S.: Parallel and Concurrent Programming in Haskell. OReilly Media, Inc., Sebastopol (2013) ISBN: 978-1-449-33594-6
28. Rete GitHub Repository, https://github.com/kongra/Rete

# Metasets and Opinion Mining
# in New Decision Support System

Magdalena Kacprzak[1], Bartłomiej Starosta[2(✉)],
and Katarzyna Węgrzyn-Wolska[3]

[1] Bialystok University of Technology, Bialystok, Poland
m.kacprzak@pb.edu.pl
[2] Polish-Japanese Academy of Information Technology, Warsaw, Poland
barstar@pjwstk.edu.pl
[3] ESIGETEL, Villejuif, France
katarzyna.wegrzyn@esigetel.fr

**Abstract.** The paper is devoted to the problem of modeling human attitudes towards imprecise ideas. A metaset is used for representing an imprecise concept and Opinion Mining techniques are applied to build a preference function which reflects someone's attitude towards the idea. The preferences are then evaluated as real numbers for the sake of comparison and selection of the best matching instance. The core of the idea of representing any imprecise concept with a metaset lies in splitting it into a tree-like hierarchy of related sub-concepts. The nodes of the tree determine the membership degrees for metaset members and they are natural language terms which also describe reasons for some particular member to satisfy the represented idea. The Opinion Mining allows for automatic gathering and evaluation of opinions from the Internet. The proposed mechanism is applied to solve the problem of selecting the car best matching the imprecise idea of *a good car for a lady*. This approach can be applied in a decision support systems that helps both marketers and customers.

**Keywords:** Metaset · Partial membership · Opinion mining

## 1 Introduction

In the contemporary marketing two issues play an important role: to identify customer preferences and desires, and to select the product that fits the customer's needs. On the one hand, sellers and manufacturers want to know what might appeal to a potential client, who are potential customers for their products and how to select the product which meets customers' expectations. On the other hand, in the age of rapidly evolving technologies, a producer is the one who awakens in the client the need to have a new model of a smartphone or other kind of mobile devices. Product advertising needs to hit the preferences of users to be effective. This is why it is very important to recognize the opinions of various people about the product. The aim of our research is to design a system that can help in making decisions for both the customer and the manufacturer. More specifically, we are working on a system that will: (a) collect people's opinions about the product and select the features of the product which are the most

© Springer International Publishing Switzerland 2015
L. Rutkowski et al. (Eds.): ICAISC 2015, Part II, LNAI 9120, pp. 625–636, 2015.
DOI: 10.1007/978-3-319-19369-4_55

important for them; (b) create a profile of a customer or a group of customers; (c) calculate (evaluate) how much the selected product matches the customer profile. In our approach we do not focus on commonly shared opinions only. We rather put emphasis on the individual needs of users, especially if they are unusual. The aim of the analysis is to determine how much the chosen product fits the selected user. The obtained result is described with numerical values.

In the paper [7] we showed how to use the idea of metasets to model and solve the problem of evaluation of the attractiveness of tourist destinations. In this case, the imprecise idea of *a perfect holiday destination* is represented as a metaset of places whose membership degrees in the metaset are interpreted as their qualities. Client preferences are functions which enable real-number evaluation of the subjective rating of a given destination. The input in this problem is a list of sites with the location and a brief description of each. The output has to be a numeric score assigned to each location that allows us to compare them and ultimately select the best one. Such an approach can be used in automated personalized tour-planning devices. In particular, it can be used in solving Tourist Trip Design Problems, TTDP (see e.g. [15]).

Metasets are the perfect tool for representation and processing of vague, imprecise data, similarly to fuzzy sets [17] or rough sets [9]. Metasets admit partial membership, partial equality and other set-theoretic relations [11] which may be evaluated in a Boolean algebra. The certainty values for metaset relations or even compound sentences [14,13] may also be represented as natural language terms, what is especially important in applications. The general idea of metaset is inspired by the method of forcing [1] in the classical set theory [8,6]. Despite these abstract origins, the definitions of metaset and related notions (i.e. set-theoretic relations or algebraic operations) are directed towards efficient computer implementations [12] and applications [10,7].

In the current paper we develop another application of metaset concept. We use a metaset for representing the imprecise term of *a good car for a lady*. For this metaset we acquire data which are used for building the preference function for a sample client. This function is a slight modification of membership evaluation function for metasets. The data are acquired using the methods and techniques of Opinion Mining. They involve building a system to collect and categorize opinions about a product. This consists in examining natural language conversations happening around a certain product for tracking the mood of the public. The analysis is performed on large collections of texts, including web pages, on-line news, Internet discussion groups, on-line reviews, web blogs, and social media. Opinion Mining aims to determine polarity and intensity of a given text, i.e., whether it is positive, negative, or neutral and to what extent. To classify the intensity of opinions, we use methods introduced in [2,3,4].

The paper is structured as follows. In Sec. 2 we briefly recall the main definitions and lemmas concerning metasets. Section 3 is devoted to issues of Opinion Mining. Section 4 presents the problem of detection of users' preferences. Section 5 gives the solution to the problem in terms of metasets. Conclusions are given in Sec. 6.

## 2  Metasets

Metaset is a new approach to partial membership, similarly to fuzzy sets [17] and rough sets [9]. Metasets allow for representing imprecise notions. In this paper we focus on the vague idea of a *good car for a lady*. Members of this metaset are cars which match this idea to various degrees.

A metaset is a classical crisp set with a specific internal structure which encodes the membership degrees of its members. The membership degrees are expressed as nodes of the binary tree $\mathbb{T}$. All the possible membership values make up a Boolean algebra. They can be evaluated as real numbers. In applications we may use natural language terms for expressing the degrees.

### 2.1  Basic Definitions

A first-order metaset[1] is a relation between a set and a set of nodes of the binary tree $\mathbb{T}$.

**Definition 1.** *A set which is either the empty set $\emptyset$ or which has the form:*

$$\tau = \{ \langle \sigma, p \rangle : \sigma \text{ is a set}, p \in \mathbb{T} \}$$

*is called a first-order metaset.*

Thus, the structure we use to encode the degrees of membership is based on ordered pairs. The first element of each pair is the member and the second element is a node of the binary tree which contributes to the membership degree of the first element.

The binary tree $\mathbb{T}$ is the set of all finite binary sequences, ordered by the reverse prefix relation: if $p, q \in \mathbb{T}$ and $p$ is a prefix of $q$, then $q \leq p$ (see Fig. 1). The root $\mathbb{1}$ being the empty sequence is the largest element of $\mathbb{T}$ in this ordering.

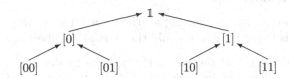

**Fig. 1.** The levels $\mathbb{T}_0$–$\mathbb{T}_2$ of the binary tree $\mathbb{T}$ and the ordering of nodes. Arrows point at the larger element.

We denote binary sequences which are elements of $\mathbb{T}$ using square brackets, for example: [00], [101]. If $p \in \mathbb{T}$, then we denote its children with $p \cdot 0$ and $p \cdot 1$. A *level* $\mathbb{T}_n$ in $\mathbb{T}$ is the set of all finite binary sequences with the same length $n$. The level 0 consists of the empty sequence $\mathbb{1}$ only. A *branch* in $\mathbb{T}$ is an infinite binary sequence. Abusing the notation we write $p \in \mathcal{C}$ to denote that the binary sequence $p \in \mathbb{T}$ is a prefix of the branch $\mathcal{C}$.

---

[1] For simplicity, in this paper we deal only with finite first-order metasets. See [11,12] for the introduction to metasets in general.

## 2.2  Interpretations

An interpretation of a first-order metaset is a crisp set. It is produced out of a
given metaset using a branch of the binary tree. Different branches determine
different interpretations of the metaset. All of them taken together make up a
collection of sets with specific internal dependencies, which represents the source
metaset by means of its crisp views. Properties of crisp sets which are interpretations of the given first-order metaset determine the properties of the metaset
itself. In particular we use interpretations to define set-theoretic relations for
metasets.

**Definition 2.** *Let $\tau$ be a first-order metaset and let $C$ be a branch. The set*

$$\tau_C = \{\, \sigma \in \mathrm{dom}(\tau)\colon \langle \sigma, p \rangle \in \tau \wedge p \in C \,\}$$

*is called the interpretation of the first-order metaset $\tau$ given by the branch $C$.*

In the above definition $\mathrm{dom}(\tau) = \{\, \sigma\colon \exists_{p \in \mathbb{T}} \ \langle \sigma, p \rangle \in \tau \,\}$ is the domain of $\tau$.

The process of producing an interpretation of a first-order metaset consists
in two stages. In the first stage we remove all the ordered pairs whose second
elements are nodes which do not belong to the branch $C$. The second stage
replaces the remaining pairs – whose second elements lie on the branch $C$ – with
their first elements. As the result we obtain a crisp set contained in the domain
of the metaset.

As we see, a first-order metaset may have multiple different interpretations
– each branch in the tree determines one. Usually, most of them are pairwise
equal, so the number of different interpretations is much less than the number
of branches. Finite first-order metasets always have a finite number of different
interpretations.

## 2.3  Partial Membership

We use interpretations for transferring set-theoretic relations from crisp sets onto
metasets.[2] In this paper we discuss only the partial membership.

**Definition 3.** *We say that the metaset $\sigma$ belongs to the metaset $\tau$ under the
condition $p \in \mathbb{T}$, whenever for each branch $C$ containing $p$ holds $\sigma_C \in \tau_C$. We
use the notation $\sigma \,\epsilon_p\, \tau$.*

Formally, we define an infinite number of membership relations: each $p \in \mathbb{T}$
specifies another relation $\epsilon_p$. Any two metasets may be simultaneously in multiple
membership relations qualified by different nodes: $\sigma \,\epsilon_p\, \tau \wedge \sigma \,\epsilon_q\, \tau$. Membership
under the root condition $\mathbb{1}$ resembles the full, unconditional membership of crisp
sets, since it is independent of branches.

The conditional membership reflects the idea that an element $\sigma$ belongs to a
metaset $\tau$ whenever some conditions are fulfilled. The conditions are represented
by nodes of $\mathbb{T}$.

---

[2] For the detailed discussion of the relations or their evaluation the reader is referred
to [12] or [14].

*Example 1.* Recall, that the ordinal number 1 is the set $\{0\}$ and 0 is just the empty set $\emptyset$. Let $\tau = \{\langle 0, [0]\rangle, \langle 1, [1]\rangle\}$ and let $\sigma = \{\langle 0, [1]\rangle\}$. Let $\mathcal{C}^0 \ni [0]$ and $\mathcal{C}^1 \ni [1]$ be arbitrary branches containing $[0]$ and $[1]$, respectively. Interpretations are: $\tau_{\mathcal{C}^0} = \{0\}$, $\tau_{\mathcal{C}^1} = \{1\}$, $\sigma_{\mathcal{C}^0} = 0$ and $\sigma_{\mathcal{C}^1} = \{0\} = 1$. We see that $\sigma \; \epsilon_{[0]} \; \tau$ and $\sigma \; \epsilon_{[1]} \; \tau$. Also, $\sigma \; \epsilon_1 \; \tau$ holds.

Note, that even though interpretations of $\tau$ and $\sigma$ vary depending on the branch, the metaset membership relation is preserved.

## 2.4   Evaluating Membership

Membership degrees for metasets are expressed as nodes of $\mathbb{T}$. In fact, these nodes determine the basis of the Boolean Algebra of closed-open sets in the Cantor space $2^\omega$. Indeed, a $p \in \mathbb{T}$ is just a prefix for all infinite binary sequences which form a clopen subset of $2^\omega$. Thus, the membership relation for metasets is valued in the Boolean algebra. Nonetheless, for the sake of simplicity and in applications we usually refer to the binary tree when talking about membership.

In applications we frequently need a numerical evaluation of membership degrees. In order to define it, we first consider the smallest subset of $\mathbb{T}$ consisting of elements which determine the membership.

**Definition 4.** *Let $\sigma$, $\tau$ be first-order metasets. The set*

$$\|\sigma \in \tau\| = \max\{p \in \mathbb{T}: \sigma \; \epsilon_p \; \tau\}$$

*is called the certainty grade for membership of $\sigma$ in $\tau$.*

Here, $\max\{p \in \mathbb{T}: \sigma \; \epsilon_p \; \tau\}$ denotes the set of maximum elements (in the tree ordering) of the set of nodes in $\mathbb{T}$, for which the relation $\sigma \; \epsilon_p \; \tau$ holds. Note, that by the definition 3, $\|\sigma \in \tau\| = \max\{p \in \mathbb{T}: \forall_{\mathcal{C} \ni p} \; \sigma_{\mathcal{C}} \in \tau_{\mathcal{C}}\}$. In other words, if $p \in \|\sigma \in \tau\|$, then for each branch $\mathcal{C}$ containing $p$ holds $\sigma_{\mathcal{C}} \in \tau_{\mathcal{C}}$.

We define the numerical evaluation of membership taking the following assumptions. All nodes within a level contribute equally to the membership value – none of them is distinguished. For the given $p \in \mathbb{T}$, its direct descendants $p \cdot 0$ and $p \cdot 1$ add half of the contribution of the parent $p$, each. Therefore, the contribution of a $p \in \mathbb{T}$ must be equal to $\dfrac{1}{2^{|p|}}$, where $|p|$ is the length of the sequence $p$.

**Definition 5.** *Let $\sigma$, $\tau$ be first-order metasets. The following value is called the certainty value of membership of $\sigma$ in $\tau$:*

$$|\sigma \in \tau| = \sum_{p \in \|\sigma \in \tau\|} \frac{1}{2^{|p|}} .$$

One may easily see that $|\sigma \in \tau| \in [0,1]$. If $\|\sigma \in \tau\| = \{\mathbb{1}\}$, i.e., $\sigma \; \epsilon_1$ holds, then $|\sigma \in \tau| = 1$. And if $\|\sigma \in \tau\| = \emptyset$ ($\sigma \; \epsilon_p$ holds for no $p$), then $|\sigma \in \tau| = 0$.

For the sake of the main topic of the discussion it is worth stressing that in the above definition we treat all the nodes within the same level uniformly, without distinguishing one from another. This will not be the case for the problem of evaluation of client preferences, where we modify the above function to reflect interests in particular properties which compose an imprecise idea.

## 2.5  Representing Imprecise Ideas with Metasets

Just like a set represents a collection of objects which satisfy a property given by a formula, a metaset represents a "fuzzy" collection of objects which satisfy some imprecise idea. In this paper we use a metaset to represent the imprecise term of a *good car for a lady*. Its members are particular cars which match the given idea to a variety of degrees, usually different than the complete truth.

The core of the idea of representing any imprecise concept with a metaset lies in splitting it into a tree-like hierarchy of related sub-concepts. For instance, a good car must have good *looks* and be *comfortable*. But what does it mean to have good *looks*? For us, it means to have a nice *color* and *shape*. Similarly, we split the meaning of *comfortable* into sub-ideas. A *comfortable* car must have a friendly *user-interface* and must be fully *automated*. We might proceed splitting for arbitrary many steps. For the sake of simplicity we stop at the second step.

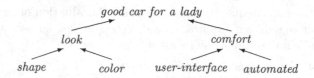

**Fig. 2.**  The binary tree of the features describing a *good car for a lady*

The binary tree in the Fig. 2 is used throughout the paper to represent the discussed idea of a good car by means of the metaset $\Delta$. Note, that the nodes of the tree which determine the membership degrees are natural language terms, which also describe reasons for some particular car to satisfy the discussed idea.

# 3  Opinion Mining

Opinion Mining consists in identifying orientation or intensity of opinion in pieces of texts (blogs, forums, user comments, review websites, community websites, etc.). It enables determining whether a sentence or a document expresses positive, negative or neutral sentiment towards some object ($O$) or more. Also, it allows for classification of opinions according to intensity degrees.

**Definition 6.** *An opinion is a quadruple (O, F, H, S), where O is a target object, $F = \{f_1, f_2, \ldots, f_n\}$ is a set of features of the object O, H is a set of opinion's holders, S is the set of sentiment/opinion values of the opinion's holder on the feature $f_i$ of the object O.*

An object $O$ is represented with a finite set of features, $F = \{f_1, f_2, \ldots, f_n\}$. Each feature $f_i \in F$ can be expressed with a finite set of words or phrases $W_i$, where $W_i$ is a set of corresponding synonym sets $W_i = \{W_{i1}, W_{i2}, \ldots, W_{in}\}$ for the features.

Thus, an object $O$ is represented as a tree or taxonomy of components $F$ (or parts), sub-components, and so on. Each node represents a component and is associated with a set of attributes. $O$ is the root node, which also has a set of attributes. An opinion can be expressed on any node or attribute of the node.

An opinion holder $j \in H$ makes comments concerning a subset of the features $S_j \subseteq F$ of an object $O$. For each feature $f_j \in Sj$ that the holder $j$ comments on, the holder $j$ chooses a word or phrase from $W_k$ to describe the feature $f_k$, and expresses a positive, negative or neutral opinion on $f_k$.

In general, the first step of such a process is to retrieve the information from the Web [16] (tweets, blogs, forums, etc.) related to the object ($O$: *a good car for a lady* in our case, presented in Example 2), to extract the opinions about the selected features ($F$) and then to classify this information according to their emotional value.

Opinion Mining is a complex technique. Opinions can be expressed in a subtle manner which creates difficulty in the identification of their emotional values. Moreover, opinions are highly sensitive to the context and dependent of the field in which they are used: the same string might be positive in one context and negative in another. In addition, on the Internet, everyone uses his own style and vocabulary, that adds extra difficulty to the task. It is not yet possible to find out an ideal case to marking the opinion in a text written by different users, because the text does not follow the rules. Therefore, it is impossible to schedule every possible case. Moreover, very often the same phrase can be considered as positive for one person and negative for another one.

There are many methods used in Opinion Mining. We can divide the existing approaches in two categories: supervised and unsupervised methods. The most applied supervised learning techniques are Support Vector Machines and Naïve Bayes. These techniques give better results but at the same time they are very sensible to over-training and dependent on the quality, size and domain of the training data. The unsupervised approaches are based on external resources (dictionaries such as WordNet Affect or SentiWordNet, General Inquirer). The most painful disadvantages of these approaches are sensibility to the domain and dependence of the dictionary construction.

The classification of the opinion polarity consists in the decision between positive and negative status. A value called semantic orientation is created in order to demonstrate words' polarity. It varies between two values: positive and negative and it can have different intensity levels. There are several calculation methods of the words semantic orientation (SO). The most often used method is called SO-A (Semantic Orientation from Association):

$$\text{SO-A}(word) = \Sigma_{p \in P} \text{A}(word, p) - \Sigma_{n \in N} \text{A}(word, n) \tag{1}$$

where:

- $A(word, p)$ is the association of studied word with the positive word,
- $A(word, n)$ is equivalent negative,
- $A(word)$ is a measure of association.

If the sum is positive, the word is oriented positively, and if the sum is negative, the orientation is negative. The absolute value of the sum indicates the orientation intensity.

To classify intensity of opinions concerning cars' buyers, we use the engine of our system [2,3,4].

## 4   Users' Profile Detection

Customer feedback is now targeted not only at companies directly, but also broadcast on the Net via weblogs, Twitter, Facebook, and comments at retailers' websites. This feedback can be very rich. It may consist of the evaluations of specific aspects of the product, information about the author/reviewer, and feedback from readers about the review, etc.

The objective of this section is to describe the framework to analyze the typical profile of a car buyer. The steps we take to achieve the goal are: selection of the features for the car, evaluation of their importance, retrieval and evaluation of the opinions for individual users, and finally – construction of particular user's profile. To perform these tasks we use Opinion Mining (OM) techniques.

In order to demonstrate our methodology we use the hierarchy of conditions depicted in the Fig. 2, which comprise the notion of a *good car for a lady*. The purpose is to find the opinions related to this topic. Particularly, for each holder $j \in H$ we want to find his/her opinions about the selected features $F$ of cars and the intensities of these features, particularly, when the opinion holder buys the car. We consider that the opinions of both negative and positive polarity in the same way declare that the feature is important for the user. Therefore, the polarity of opinion (negative, positive) is not relevant, only the intensity of the opinion's value matters and it is considered to be the significant contribution to values of parameters. To calculate the intensity (SI – Semantic Intensity from Association) we use modified SO-A method:

$$\text{SI-A}(word) \quad = \quad \Sigma_{p \in P}\text{A}(word, p) + \Sigma_{n \in N}\text{A}(word, n) . \tag{2}$$

To find the intensity of each feature, we sort these opinions from highly-rated extremal opinion (positive, negative) to the neutral one.

By Def. 6, the basic components of an opinion are: object $O$ (on which an opinion is expressed, in our case it is a car), opinion's holder $j$ (a person that holds an specific opinion on a particular object), and sentiment/opinion (a view, attitude, or appraisal on an object from an opinion holder). According to the idea presented by the tree in the Fig. 2, the set $F$ is composed of 6 elements *{look, comfort, shape, color, user-interface, automated}*.

For each element $f_i$ we select manually the corresponding set $w_i$. For example,

$$w_{look} \quad = \quad \{\, appearance,\ outlook,\ aspect,\ air,\ outside, \dots \} \tag{3}$$

$$w_{comfort} \quad = \quad \{\, accommodation,\ commodious,\ convenience, \dots \} \tag{4}$$

We formalize the preferences of a sample customer in the following example.

*Example 2.* For demonstration purposes we consider here opinions of a sample user, named Ann, extracted from the Internet. Her posts included, among other pieces texts, also opinions of this sort: *"I love my new car, it's great, I can drive and call at the same time, my smartphone is connected", "... when driving, I can listen to the music from my mp3", "it had manual transmission, now I have automated one, but it didn't change a lot ...", "it is red", "its modern silhouette is very nice", "the seats are really comfortable",* and so on. Based on these we have estimated the following ratios for her preferences.

Ann prefers to have a comfortable car than a nice one. We found that her attitude is expressed by the ratio 3/2 in favor of *comfort* over *look*. She likes driving a lot, changing the transmission gears is not a problem for her. On the other hand, she likes to use her connected mobile devices a lot when she is driving, so the *user-interface* is very important feature for her. She professed a ratio of 3/1 in favor of *user-interface* over *automated*. According to her opinion some aspects of *shape* are critical for her, and therefore the discovered ratio is 4/1 over *color*.

## 5   Modeling with Metasets

We use the metaset approach to model the vague idea of a *good car for a lady*. Throughout the paper the metaset $\Delta$ represents the "fuzzy" collection of *good cars for a lady*. Potential members of $\Delta$ are the cars which match this imprecise notion more or less. Their membership degrees in $\Delta$ correspond to the levels of satisfaction of this property. When evaluating membership we assume that the capabilities of cars, represented by nodes within a level in $\mathbb{T}$, are equally important. By modifying the evaluation function so that some capabilities become more important than others, we may reflect particular clients' interests towards specific capabilities of cars which are $\Delta$ members. The real values obtained this way seem to reflect human reasoning. For instance, evaluating preference for a person interested in fast cars will result in higher value if a car has properties of a fast car indeed (acceleration, power), than when it has not.

### 5.1   Evaluating Client Preferences

Definition 5 (certainty value of membership) assumes uniform distribution of values throughout the nodes in $\mathbb{T}$: each $p \in \|\delta \in \Delta\|$ contributes the value of $\frac{1}{2^{|p|}}$ to $|\delta \in \Delta|$. In the context discussed in the paper this might be interpreted as a client's indifference as to what to choose: all possible choices represented as nodes within the same level are equally weighted. Particularly, for a $p \in \mathbb{T}$ both its children $p \cdot 0$ and $p \cdot 1$ contribute equally to the membership evaluation. In real life, however, clients have some preferences concerning choices they make. For instance, the *look* of the car might be more important than *comfort* for some clients. Such preferences, may be taken into account while evaluating client's attitude towards a particular instance of a car. We express these preferences numerically with the following function.

**Definition 7.** *We define client preference to be a function* $\mathfrak{p}\colon \mathbb{T} \mapsto [0,1]$ *such that*

$$\forall_{q\in\mathbb{T}}\ \mathfrak{p}(q\cdot 0) + \mathfrak{p}(q\cdot 1) = 1\ . \tag{5}$$

*and we take* $\mathfrak{p}(\mathbb{1}) = 1$ *for the root.*

Given the preference function $\mathfrak{p}$ we evaluate the quality of a car $\delta$ taking preferences $\mathfrak{p}$ into account to obtain the subjective value of client's attitude towards $\delta$. For this purpose we generalize the Def. 5 slightly to obtain an evaluation function which increases the impact of some nodes and decreases that of others. In applications we may (and we do in this paper) build this function based on the Opinion Mining techniques, as described in Sec. 4.

**Definition 8.** *Let* $\delta$ *be a car and let* $\Delta$ *be a metaset of good cars for a lady. The* $\mathfrak{p}$-*quality of the car* $\delta$ *is the following value:*

$$|\delta \in \Delta|_{\mathfrak{p}} = \sum_{q\in\|\delta\in\Delta\|}\ \prod_{0\le i\le |q|} \mathfrak{p}(q_{\restriction_i})\ .$$

The symbol $q_{\restriction_i}$, where $0 \le i \le |q|$, denotes the prefix of the length $i$ of the binary sequence $q$. For $i = 0$, it is the empty sequence $\mathbb{1}$, and for $i = |q|$, it is the $q$ itself.

The $\mathfrak{p}$-quality of a car reflects client's preferences. For different clients with different $\mathfrak{p}$ preference functions it may result in different ratings for the given car.

*Example 3.* Based on the ratios discovered in the Ex. 2 we build the preference function $\mathfrak{p}$ for Ann (see Fig. 3). Since Ann prefers *comfort* to *look* with the ratio of $3/2$, then we set $\mathfrak{p}(look) = 0.4$ and $\mathfrak{p}(comfort) = 0.6$. The ratio of $3/1$ in favor of *user-interface* over *automated* results in setting $\mathfrak{p}(user\text{-}interface) = 0.75$ and $\mathfrak{p}(automated) = 0.25$. And since the ratio of *shape* over *color* is $4/1$, then we have $\mathfrak{p}(shape) = 0.8$ and $\mathfrak{p}(color) = 0.2$.

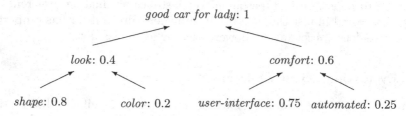

*good car for lady*: 1

*look*: 0.4                    *comfort*: 0.6

*shape*: 0.8        *color*: 0.2     *user-interface*: 0.75   *automated*: 0.25

**Fig. 3.** The $\mathfrak{p}$ function for Ann

## 5.2    Solution to the Problem

We use Ann's preferences described in the Examples 2 and 3 in order to demonstrate the mechanism of evaluating client's preferences and to show that indeed, it results in values reflecting human reasoning.

Let $\Delta$ be the metaset representing a *good car for lady*. Let $\alpha$ and $\beta$ denote cars with the following capabilities. The $\alpha$ has perfect *shape* and it has a good *user-interface*, whereas $\beta$ is fully *automated* and it has a nice *color*. Thus, we may write

$$\alpha \; \epsilon_{shape} \; \Delta \quad \wedge \quad \alpha \; \epsilon_{user-interface} \; \Delta \,, \tag{6}$$

$$\beta \; \epsilon_{automated} \; \Delta \quad \wedge \quad \beta \; \epsilon_{color} \; \Delta \,. \tag{7}$$

Therefore,

$$\|\alpha \in \Delta\| \;=\; \{\, shape, user\text{-}interface \,\} \;=\; \{\, [00], [10] \,\} \,, \tag{8}$$

$$\|\beta \in \Delta\| \;=\; \{\, color, automated \,\} \;=\; \{\, [01], [11] \,\} \,. \tag{9}$$

and

$$|\alpha \in \Delta| \;=\; \frac{1}{2^{|[00]|}} + \frac{1}{2^{|[10]|}} \;=\; \frac{1}{2^2} + \frac{1}{2^2} \;=\; 0.5 \,, \tag{10}$$

$$|\beta \in \Delta| \;=\; \frac{1}{2^{|[01]|}} + \frac{1}{2^{|[11]|}} \;=\; \frac{1}{2^2} + \frac{1}{2^2} \;=\; 0.5 \,. \tag{11}$$

We see, that both cars satisfy the requirements for the *good car for a lady* to the same degree of 0.5.

However, if we take into account the client's preferences expressed as the preference function $\mathbf{p}$, then these cars turn out to be quite different.

$$|\alpha \in \Delta|_{\mathbf{p}} \;=\; 0.4 \cdot 0.8 + 0.6 \cdot 0.75 = 0.77 \,, \tag{12}$$

$$|\beta \in \Delta|_{\mathbf{p}} \;=\; 0.4 \cdot 0.2 + 0.6 \cdot 0.25 = 0.23 \,. \tag{13}$$

We conclude, that Ann's interest in the car $\alpha$ is much greater than in car $\beta$. The values and the relation $|\alpha \in \Delta|_{\mathbf{p}} > |\beta \in \Delta|_{\mathbf{p}}$ confirm her opinions shared on the Internet, as described in the Ex. 2.

# 6   Conclusions

The aim of our research is to design a decision support system which can find its application in traditional marketing and e-marketing. In this paper we show how methods and techniques of Opinion Mining can be used for selecting from users' declarations the most important features of products as well as for building users' profiles. This data is represented as a metaset and then analyzed. In this way, the theory of metasets is applied for evaluating clients' preferences. Our approach is used in designing a software tool which supports making decisions. It can help marketers evaluate the success of an ad campaign or a new product and identify the product features which the users like or dislike.

**Acknowledgments.** Kacprzak thanks the Polish Ministry of Science and Higher Education at the Bialystok University of Technology under Grant S/W/1/2014.

# References

1. Cohen, P.: The Independence of the Continuum Hypothesis 1. Proceedings of the National Academy of Sciences of the United States of America 50, 1143–1148 (1963)
2. Dziczkowski, G., Wegrzyn-Wolska, K.: Rcss - rating critics support system purpose built for movies recommendation. In: Advances in Intelligent Web Mastering. Springer (2007)
3. Dziczkowski, G., Wegrzyn-Wolska, K.: An autonomous system designed for automatic detection and rating of film. Extraction and linguistic analysis of sentiments. In: Proceedings of WIC, Sydney (2008)
4. Dziczkowski, G., Wegrzyn-Wolska, K.: Tool of the intelligence economic : Recognition function of reviews critics. In: ICSOFT 2008 Proceedings (2008)
5. Esuli, A., Sebastiani, F.: SentiWN: A Publicly Available Lexical Resource for Opinion Mining. In: Proc. of the Fifth International Conference on Language Resources and Evaluation (LREC 2006), pp. 417–422 (2006)
6. Jech, T.: Set Theory: The Third Millennium Edition, Revised and Expanded. Springer, Heidelberg (2006)
7. Kacprzak, M., Starosta, B.: An Approach to Making Decisions with Metasets. In: Gomolinska, A., Grabowski, A., Hryniewicka, M., Kacprzak, M., Schmeidel, E. (eds.) Trends in Contemporary Computer Science, Podlasie 2014, pp. 159–172 (2014)
8. Kunen, K.: Set Theory, An Introduction to Independence Proofs. Studies in Logic and Foundations of Mathematics. North-Holland Publishing Company (1980)
9. Pawlak, Z.: Rough Sets. International Journal of Computer and Information Sciences 11, 341–356 (1982)
10. Starosta, B.: Application of Meta Sets to Character Recognition. In: Rauch, J., Raś, Z.W., Berka, P., Elomaa, T. (eds.) ISMIS 2009. LNCS(LNAI), vol. 5722, pp. 602–611. Springer, Heidelberg (2009)
11. Starosta, B.: Metasets: A New Approach to Partial Membership. In: Rutkowski, L., Korytkowski, M., Scherer, R., Tadeusiewicz, R., Zadeh, L.A., Zurada, J.M. (eds.) ICAISC 2012, Part I. LNCS, vol. 7267, pp. 325–333. Springer, Heidelberg (2012)
12. Starosta, B., Kosiński, W.: Meta Sets – Another Approach to Fuzziness. In: Seising, R. (ed.) Views on Fuzzy Sets and Systems. STUDFUZZ, vol. 243, pp. 509–532. Springer, Heidelberg (2009)
13. Starosta, B., Kosiński, W.: Metasets, Intuitionistic Fuzzy Sets and Uncertainty. In: Rutkowski, L., Korytkowski, M., Scherer, R., Tadeusiewicz, R., Zadeh, L.A., Zurada, J.M. (eds.) ICAISC 2013, Part I. LNCS(LNAI), vol. 7894, pp. 388–399. Springer, Heidelberg (2013)
14. Starosta, B., Kosiński, W.: Metasets, Certainty and Uncertainty. In: Atanassov, K.T., et al. (eds.) New Trends in Fuzzy Sets, Intuitionistic Fuzzy Sets, Generalized Nets and Related Topics. Foundations, vol. I, pp. 139–165. Systems Research Institute, Polish Academy of Sciences, Warsaw (2013)
15. Souffriau, W., Vansteenwegen, P., Vertommen, J., Vanden Berghe, G., Van Oudheusden, D.: A personalizes tourist trip design algorithm for mobile tourist guides. Applied Artificial Intelligence 22(10), 964–985 (2008)
16. Wegrzyn-Wolska, K., Bougueroua, L.: Tweets mining for French Presidential Election. In: Proc. of the 4th IEEE/WIC International Conference on Computation Aspects of Social Networks, CASoN 2012, SaO Carlos, Brazil (November 2012)
17. Zadeh, L.A.: Fuzzy Sets. Information and Control 8, 338–353 (1965)

# Practical Approach to Interoperability in Production Rule Bases with SUBITO

Krzysztof Kaczor[⊠]

AGH University of Science and Technology,
Al. Mickiewicza 30, 30-059 Kraków, Poland
kk@agh.edu.pl

**Abstract.** Knowledge interoperability is an active research area in Artificial Intelligence. Rules are one of the most successful knowledge representations that currently found application in Business Rules Management Systems. Because of the increasing number of such systems, the need for efficient rule interoperability methods is still growing. Currently many approaches providing formalized models and methods were developed. Nevertheless, many of them are very general and therefore they suffer from weak tool support. This paper provides presentation of a new interoperability tool for rule-based knowledge. The tool is called SUBITO and it supports the formalized model of production rule representation and interchange. Thanks to the well-defined scope of model expressiveness it allows for efficient translation of rule bases expressed in such representation like CLIPS, JESS, DROOLS or XTT2.

## 1 Introduction

Rule-Based Systems (RBS) [6,13] constitute a mature technology in the field of Artificial Intelligence (AI) [26]. Over the years, they were successfully applied in the Decision Support Systems (DSS) working in many domains like medicine, engineering, security systems [21], etc. Nowadays, classic RBS evolved and constitute a source of ideas and solutions for new technologies like Business Rules (BRs) [7], Semantic Web (SW) [1], context-aware systems [17], etc. Despite the maturity of the RBS, many problems are still unsolved.

The work presented in this paper is a part of the PhD thesis of the author [9] and is focused on the problem concerning efficient *rule interoperability*. This problem is related to translation of knowledge between rule bases expressed in different representations. It is assumed that the efficient interoperability method allows for preserving knowledge semantics during the translation by considering both syntax and semantics levels. In our work, *knowledge semantics* is understood as the meaning of an *entire knowledge base* and not only as the semantics of all individual knowledge elements (rules, facts, etc.). In turn, the semantics of an *entire knowledge base* corresponds to the so-called operational semantics, as

The paper is supported by the SaMURaI Project funded from NCN (National Science Centre) resources for science DEC-2011/03/N/ST6/00886.

© Springer International Publishing Switzerland 2015
L. Rutkowski et al. (Eds.): ICAISC 2015, Part II, LNAI 9120, pp. 637–648, 2015.
DOI: 10.1007/978-3-319-19369-4_56

presented in [28], and describes changes of a fact base after rules application considered from the user perspective. Therefore, it is assumed that two rule bases, expressed in different representations, have the same semantics if for a given initial state both production systems infer the same conclusion [9].

The part of the research presented in this paper aims at providing an implementation of the framework supporting an efficient interoperability for the production rules. It is assumed that the framework is based on a formalized model which takes the most important aspects of the existing rule representations into account. These aspects have already been identified in the earlier works [12], [10] and [11]. The presented framework is called SUBITO and is intended to support translation of the rule bases between such rule languages as CLIPS [25], JESS [4], DROOLS [3] and XTT2 [22]. The paper provides presentation of the tool architecture, and its practical evaluation that shows the results of translation and execution of a selected use case.

This paper is organized as follows: Section 2 elaborates on the current state of the research concerning the rule interoperability issue and addresses existing problems in this area that constitute motivation for this work. Section 3 briefly discusses features of the formalized production rule representation model that is supported by the SUBITO tool. The following Section 4 provides most important information concerning the tool like architecture, supported language, current state of the development, etc. The practical results of usage of the tool are introduced in Section 5. This section presents an exemplary translation and execution output of a selected use case. Section 6 discusses selected important challenges of the efficient rule interoperability problem that were overcome with the help of the formalized model and presented tool. The paper is concluded by short summary and description of future works provided in Section 7.

## 2   State of the Art

Nowadays, the increasing significance of rule interoperability can be observed. This is mainly due to the fact that distributed and collaborative environments for rule modeling and sharing became more common. In such environments knowledge engineers work in a collective way [19], but often use different rule representation languages which can cause severe problems [10]. The main purpose of the interoperability approaches is to provide the means for reusing, publication and translation of rules between different systems and tools.

An efficient interoperability method can find an application in many contexts. The first and the most obvious is the *knowledge translation* from one representation to another [18]. Having an efficient interoperability method, one can translate rules into another representations and use within other contexts, domains, etc. One can also apply different tools for rules processing and inference, what allow for using knowledge in a different way. What is more, this also make the knowledge sharing and deployment easier. The another application area involves *collective knowledge development*. Thanks to interoperability methods taking rule semantics into account, it is possible to create a knowledge repository, where knowledge is stored in different representations. Every knowledge engineer can design rules by using most convenient technology. Later, the knowledge is processed by an engine that translates all stored rules into one representation and performs inference [20]. This application area is important nowadays, because the collaboration between knowledge engineers becomes more common.

Over the time, many different methods and approaches to the knowledge interoperability problem were developed. Some of them are general-purpose i.e. aim at providing framework for translation between many different representations. Historically, first of such approaches was *Knowledge Interchange Framework* (KIF) [5]. Due to the difficulty of maintaining and supporting of such general approaches, there is very few technologies like this framework. This is why, modern methods providing wide support for many different representations are usually divided into so-called dialects. Each of such dialects has a well-defined semantics and thus is intended to translation of rules expressed in some well-defined representations. *Rule Interchange Framework* (RIF) [27] consists of four main dialects providing support for inter alia production rules. Apart from the methods supporting many different representations, more specialized approaches were also developed. Many of the existing interoperability methods are dedicated for a certain set of representations that share similar assumptions and thus have similar semantics. Important of examples such methods are *Rule Markup Language* (RULEML) [2] and *REWERSE Rule Markup Language* (R2ML) [24] that are dedicated for representations used mainly within Semantic Web. In turn, *Production Rule Representation* (PRR) [23] allows for expressing production rules that perform actions and thus allow for changing system state.

The mentioned methods provide complex meta-models, vague formalisms and allows for informal rule specification. Therefore, they are mostly very abstract and general what makes the practical application hard. This is why the current rule interoperability methods suffer from the lack of the supportive tools and the formalism that can be used in practical applications. Furthermore, the production system representation models provided by these methods support only flat rule bases whereas the tools like CLIPS, JESS or DROOLS allow for modeling structured ones. Therefore, they cannot be applied to such representations as the structure has a significant impact on the accessibility of knowledge during inference [15] as well as on the response of the rule-based system for a given initial state [16]. Thus, application of these methods to structured rule bases cannot assure semantics-preserving transformations that are required by e.g. RIF [8]. Moreover, the tools like CLIPS, JESS, DROOLS provide rule languages that can be considered as only programming solutions without underlying formal model providing precise definition of semantics of the language constructs. Thus, the application of formal-based interoperability methods to such rule languages is useless as they cannot assure the semantically coherent rule interoperability without unambiguous definition of rule language semantics.

Therefore, the work presented in this paper focuses on the development of the unified rule representation model supported by tools that is intended to be used not only as an intermediate representation but also as a logical model for rule languages, even for those which are only programming solutions.

## 3  Formalized Model of Production Rule Representation

The paper presents a practical application of the interoperability method that is supported by SUBITO tool. This interoperability method is based on the formalized production rule representation model based on the *Attributive Logic with Set of Values over Finite Domains* logic (ALSV(FD)) [13]. In the interoperability procedure, this model plays a role of the intermediate representation having well defined semantics. Thanks to that, the rule bases expressed in this representation have an unequivocal interpretation. Formula (1) is intended to give an intuition of the model formalization. It provides a definition of $r_{driver-age}$ rule that grants ten percents of discount for the driver between 40 and 55 years old.

$$r_{driver-age}(M, H_{\iota}) = \begin{array}{l} \text{if } \left\{ H_{\iota} \in \mathcal{P}\Big(\mathbb{F}, T_{Driver}, \big(A_{Age}(H_{\iota}) \Subset [40, 55]\big)\Big) \right. \\ \text{then } \left\{ \begin{array}{l} \mathcal{A}\Big(T_{Modifier}, (-10), \emptyset\Big) \\ M \end{array} \right. \end{array} \tag{1}$$

The model formally describes semantics of the most significant elements of the rule base from the interoperability perspective. It defines simplified type system of objects and facts, different types of formulae, rules and finally rule base structure. Moreover, the model considers a rule base as a dynamic system that has a state. This state can be changed by execution of rules that, in turn, are considered as dynamic elements [12]. Therefore, apart from the definition of rule semantics, the model also defines the logical consequence of rule application by providing operational semantics of rules.

Operational semantics plays a crucial role from the interoperability point of view. This is because, according to the assumption concerning equivalence of semantics of rule bases, the rule base translation based on an efficient interoperability method must ensure the same logical consequence of rules application (for a given initial state) in the source and target representations. Due to the fact that every separate rule execution is determined by rule base structure, the interoperability method cannot neglect this issue during translation.

In the model, the rule base structure is one of the most important issues. It involves all the elements that allow for changing default inference flow. Therefore, the definition of the rule base structure includes such elements like: modules that restrict the set of rules that can be activated and executed[1], rule properties like no-loop that prevents an inference engine from falling into infinite loop caused by mutual and self dependencies between rules, etc.

Considering formalization of the representation model it is possible to prove that the interoperability method based on the model preserves the operational

---

[1] A concept of a module corresponds to modules known from CLIPS or JESS or RuleFlowGroups known from DROOLS.

semantics of rule bases (for details see [9]). This allows for obtaining the same conclusions before and after rule base translation. Results of the executions of rules bases that were obtained with the help of model-based interoperability method are provided in this paper in Section 5.

# 4   Design Implementation of the SUBITO Tool

The model described in the previous section is supported by a proof-of-concept software environment. This environment supports a model concrete syntax called MCS that allows for expressing model-based rule bases with the help of XML-based language. Syntax of this language is defined by XML Schema (XSD)[2] that allows for model validation against several important issues like: undefined references, existence of required model elements (definitions of facts, rules and modules) as well as correctness of the formulae syntax (number of arguments, usage of operators, etc.). Furthermore, each type of formula defined within the model corresponds to separate XML element provided by XSD. Therefore, the appropriate nesting of expressions can be verified by schema validator.

The environment consists of a toolchain called SUBITO Translation that includes two elements: (1) *Samurai Translator* and (2) *SamUrai Batch Integration TOol* (SUBITO). These tools allow for rapid translation and execution of rule bases expressed with the help of supported representations.

The translator tool is responsible for reading model expressed in MCS or in one of the supported languages and generation of the corresponding model in another representation. Such a translation is performed in analogous way as in case of methods using intermediate format and consist of two steps. In the first step, the model expressed with the help of a certain language is translated to the MCS format. During the second step, the MCS-based model is translated to the target rule language[3].

This tool is implemented with the help of Qt library[4] and provides a modularized architecture designed according to the *Model-View-Controller* pattern (see Figure 1). The main goal of the *view* layer is to provide a support for the considered representations. Therefore, it is divided into *parser* and *generator* sublayers that are responsible for reading and writing knowledge bases expressed in the syntax provided by the rule languages. This layer communicates with *controller* that is responsible for mapping between representation required by *view* and the application internal representation defined by the *model* layer.

The SUBITO tool is a Bash shell script that integrates the translator tool and tools supporting the considered rule languages. It allows for performing automated translation of a given knowledge base to other representations and

---

[2] http://home.agh.edu.pl/ kk/lib/exe/fetch.php?media=others:samurai:cases:mcs.xsd cases:mcs.xsd

[3] Development of the translator is in an early stage, and therefore, it does not support a complete translation procedure. Currently, it supports only the second step of translation and provides command line user interface.

[4] See: http://qt-project.org

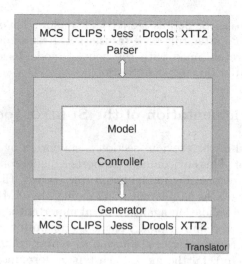

**Fig. 1.** Translator Architecture

later their execution using dedicated tools. The CLIPS and JESS models are executed with the help of native engines working in the batch mode. A DRL model is loaded and compiled by a JAVA application implemented as an integral part of the SUBITO tool. This application provides a runtime environment for DROOLS and command line user interface that allows for passing DRL model as an argument of its execution. In turn, in order to execute XTT2 model, SUBITO uses the HEART inference engine.

The next section provides a use case study that presents results the of the practical application of the model-based rule interoperability method. This study was supported by the SUBITO environment.

## 5    Use Case Study

This section provides a practical evaluation of the implemented SUBITO framework. The evaluation procedure is based on the PLI use case that is described below. In the first step, the evaluation includes translation of the MCS-based model of the use case into CLIPS, JESS, DROOLS and XTT2 languages. In the second step, the execution results of each of the obtained models are compared against inferred conclusions in order to confirm the expected theoretical results.

Polish Liability Insurance (PLI)[5] use case example presents a system of determining the price of the liability insurance, which protects against third party insurance claims. The insurance price can be determined based on data such as the driver's age, the period of holding the license, the number of accidents in the last year, and the previous class of insurance junction. Another relevant

---

[5] http://ai.ia.agh.edu.pl/wiki/student:msc2008_cbizrules_ccases:hekate_ccase_cploc

factors in calculating insurance price are data about the vehicle: the engine capacity, age, car seats, a technical examination. Moreover, in the calculation, the insurance premium can be increased or decreased because of number of payment installments, other insurances, continuity of insurance or the number of cars insured. This illustrative example consists of 49 business rules in his original version. For the compact representation, all rules are grouped within four modules that correspond to four steps of insurance price calculation. The first step consists of 5 rules and determines the value of `base rate` according to the vehicle engine capacity. The second step concerns the discounts and increases resulting from accident-free driving. Within this step 28 rules are distinguished. The third step, consisting of 16 rules, takes discounts and other increases such as the driver age, additional insurance, etc. into account. The last step contains only one rule that calculates the final price of the insurance according to the `base charge` and assigned increases/decreases.

According to the first step of the evaluation, the PLI use case was expressed using MCS format and translated into considered rule languages by using model-based interoperability method supported by SUBITO tool[6]. The following listing depicts only a part of the MCS model and contains definition of the `driver-age` rule that corresponds to the $r_{driver-age}$ rule defined by Formula (1):

```
1  <rule id="da" name="driver-age">
2    <rulevariables><rulevariable id="h1" name="h1"/></rulevariables>
3    <lhs>
4      <patternexpr factsource="allfacts" facttype="driver" rulevariableref="h1">
5        <logicalexpr operator="none">
6          <relationexpr operator="in">
7            <algebraicexpr operator="none">
8              <rulevariableref rulevariableref="h1"/>
9            </algebraicexpr>
10           <setexpr operator="none">
11             <set><range><from>40</from><to>55</to></range></set>
12           </setexpr>
13         </relationexpr>
14       </logicalexpr>
15     </patternexpr>
16   </lhs>
17   <rhs>
18     <assertexpr typeref="modifier">
19       <tuple><item><set><item>-10</item></set></item></tuple>
20     </assertexpr>
21   </rhs>
22   <scope type="none"/>
23 </rule>
```

Later, the obtained models were executed using dedicated inference engines. As a result of these executions, one can notice that each execution leads to the same result in terms of the calculated insurance price as well as in terms of the sequence of modules evaluation and fired rules. The following listing presents an output generated during the inference preformed by CLIPS[7]. Lines from 1 to 7 are the most important as they correspond to particular rules that were executed. In turn, line 13 was printed by the calculation rule and it states that the final value of the insurance price is equal to 865.95.

---

[6] The complete translations to CLIPS, JESS, DROOLS and XTT2 can be found in http://home.agh.edu.pl/~kk/doku.php?id=others:samurai:cases:ploc.

[7] The same result can be observed in case of JESS and due to the limited space of the paper it is not presented here.

```
-------------------------------------------------------
SUBITO: Execution of ploc-clips.clp using CLIPS...
-------------------------------------------------------
 1 The base charge is set to 753
 2 Driver class has been increased from 1 to 2
 3 90% of base charge because of the driver class (2)
 4 +30% because of the small driver experience (2) that is less than 3 years
 5 -10% because of the single payment
 6 -10% because driver continues the previous agreement
 7 +15% because of the car age (12) that is older than 10 years
 8 Modifying insurance value 753 by 15% of basecharge 753
 9 Modifying insurance value 865.95 by -10% of basecharge 753
10 Modifying insurance value 790.65 by 30% of basecharge 753
11 Modifying insurance value 1016.55 by -10% of basecharge 753
12 Modifying insurance value 941.25 by -10% of basecharge 753
13 The final amount to pay is equal to 865.95

real    0m0.026s
user    0m0.024s
sys 0m0.000s
-------------------------------------------------------
SUBITO: Execution of ploc-clips.clp using CLIPS...done
-------------------------------------------------------
```

Inference executed in the DROOLS rule engine gives the same value of the final price of insurance. It can be observed that the modules were executed in the same order: first the **base charge** was determined, later the new **DriverClass** and, at the end, the increases and decreases were granted. It can also be noticed that on one hand the order of rules executed within single module is different, however, it does not have any impact on the final conclusion:

```
-------------------------------------------------------
SUBITO: Execution of ploc-drools.drl using Drools...
-------------------------------------------------------
 1 The base charge is set to 753
 2 Driver class has been increased from 1 to 2
 3 -10% because of the single payment
 4 -10% because driver continues the previous agreement
 5 +15% because of the car age (12) that is older than 10 years
 6 +30% because of the small driver experience (2) that is less than 3 years
 7 90% of base charge because of the driver class (2)
 8 Modifying insurance value 753.0 by -10.0% of basecharge 753.0
 9 Modifying insurance value 677.7 by 30.0% of basecharge 753.0
10 Modifying insurance value 903.6 by 15.0% of basecharge 753.0
11 Modifying insurance value 1016.5500000000001 by -10.0% of basecharge 753.0
12 Modifying insurance value 941.2500000000001 by -10.0% of basecharge 753.0
13 The final amount to pay is equal to 865.9500000000002

real    0m2.792s
user    0m4.596s
sys 0m0.160s
-------------------------------------------------------
SUBITO: Execution of ploc-drools.drl using Drools...done
-------------------------------------------------------
```

In the case of XTT2, the order of rule evaluation is not determined by the inference engine, but by the position within a decision table. This position can be easily changed by knowledge engineer. Therefore, the representation model assumes that the knowledge base structure must be divided into modules and submodules in such a way that sequence of rule execution within any submodule does not affect final conclusion. Thus, the inference in XTT2 also gives the same value of insurance price despite the different sequence of rule execution:

```
-----------------------------------------------------------
SUBITO: Execution of ploc-xtt.pl using HeaRT...
-----------------------------------------------------------
 1 HEART: Executing decisions baseValue set 753.0
 2 HEART: Executing decisions resultValue set 753.0
 3 HEART: Executing decisions driverClass set (driverClass + 1.0)
 5 HEART: Executing decisions baseModifierValue set -10.0
 6 HEART: Executing decisions baseModifierValue set (baseModifierValue - 10.0)
 7 HEART: Executing decisions baseModifierValue set (baseModifierValue - 10.0)
 8 HEART: Executing decisions baseModifierValue set (baseModifierValue + 30.0)
 9 HEART: Executing decisions baseModifierValue set (baseModifierValue + 15.0)
10 HEART: Executing decisions resultValue set (baseValue+(baseValue*(baseModifierValue/100)))
12 Attribute baseValue = 753.0
13 Attribute driverLicage = 2.0
14 Attribute baseModifierValue = 15.0
15 Attribute resultValue = 865.95

real    0m0.546s
user    0m0.892s
sys 0m0.064s
-----------------------------------------------------------
SUBITO: Execution of ploc-xtt.pl using HeaRT...done
-----------------------------------------------------------
```

The presented examples shows that all the obtained models lead to the same conclusion (final price of insurance). It is important to emphasize that during the translation the structure of rule base is taken into account. Comparing the proposed approach to other ones that neglect the rule base structure, their executions lead to different results. The difference can be observed when the internal structure of the module determining value of the DriverClass attribute is neglected. In such a case, the inference engine executes all the rules from this module that involve value of DriverClass greater or equal than its initial value. Therefore, the final value of this attribute will always be equal to 9 what, in majority cases, constitutes incorrect result. This is caused by mutual dependencies between rules that are undesirable in this case and were not eliminated by internal structure of the module. An exemplary execution of such model may produce the following output:

```
 1 The base charge is set to 753
 2 Driver class has been increased from 1 to 2
 3 Driver class has been increased from 2 to 3
 4 Driver class has been increased from 3 to 4
 5 Driver class has been increased from 4 to 5
 6 Driver class has been increased from 5 to 6
 7 Driver class has been increased from 6 to 7
 8 Driver class has been increased from 7 to 8
 9 Driver class has been increased from 8 to 9
10 -10% because of the single payment
11 -10% because driver continues the previous agreement
12 +15% because of the car age (12) that is older than 10 years
13 +30% because of the small driver experience (2) that is less than 3 years
14 40% of base charge because of the driver class (9)
15 Modifying insurance value 753.0 by -60.0% of basecharge 753.0
16 Modifying insurance value 301.2 by 30.0% of basecharge 753.0
17 Modifying insurance value 527.1 by 15.0% of basecharge 753.0
18 Modifying insurance value 640.0500000000001 by -10.0% of basecharge 753.0
19 Modifying insurance value 564.7500000000001 by -10.0% of basecharge 753.0
20 The final amount to pay is equal to 489.4500000000001
```

The lines from 2 to 9 show that more than one rule are executed in this module despite the fact that, according to the use case specification, execution of only one of them is allowed. According to Section 2, such result can be obtained using PRR or RIF interoperability methods as they do not take rule base structure into account.

# 6    Selected Challenges

The rule interoperability problem is a very complex issue facing many challenges. The part of the work presented in this paper, tries to overcome several of them. Most important ones can be summarized in the following way:

*Trade-off between expressiveness and practical support.* Due to many significant differences between existing rule representations, an interoperability method, that is intended to be supported by tools, cannot simultaneously provide translation methods for all of them. This is because, the known rule systems fall into three broad categories: first-order, logic-programming, and action rules. These paradigms share little in the context of syntax and semantics. Moreover, there are large differences between systems even within the same paradigm [27]. Therefore, practical support for approach assuming very general model is hardly possible. Due to this fact, the presented work is restricted to production rule systems providing forward chaining inference and closed world assumption.

*Efficient translation of the knowledge semantics.* Translation of syntax is not sufficient for efficient interoperability. The translation methods must also take rule base semantics into account. Nevertheless, majority of the existing methods consider semantics of all individual elements of rule base neglecting its structure and dynamic dimension. Meanwhile, these aspects are very important in a way that is briefly clarified in Section 3.

*Support for rule languages being only programming solutions.* Rule languages like CLIPS, JESS or DROOLS are just programming solutions that do not provide any underlying formalization. Application of the formalized interoperability methods is useless when a given representation provides informal semantics. Therefore, in order to overcome this limitation, formulation of the model takes elements of these languages into account. In this way, the important aspects of these languages have formally defined semantics.

Apart from the abovementioned challenges, many others can also be identified. They are usually related to differences in semantics of corresponding representation elements as well as differences in expressiveness of language syntax.

# 7    Summary and Future Work

The paper provides an overview of implementation of the SUBITO toolchain that constitutes an environment supporting rule interoperability for CLIPS, JESS, DROOLS and XTT2 rule bases. It provides a native support for formalized model of production rule representation that is based on the ALSV(FD) attributive logic [13]. The framework uses MCS format for describing rule bases which is an XML-based language defined with the help of XML Schema. Currently the tool is on an early stage of development and allows for translation of rule bases from the MCS format to CLIPS, JESS, DROOLS and XTT2 languages. The paper also presents an exemplary translation of the PLI use case model and compares the execution results in all of the selected languages. The provided example shows that all the obtained models infer the same conclusions for corresponding inputs. Moreover, comparison of model execution obtained by application of a method that neglects rule base structure is also provided.

In the context of the presented research, several threads of future works are considered. The most important of them include completion of the framework development by implementation of the bi-directional translation and support for all important constructs of the rule languages. Moreover, the expressiveness of the formalized model is planned to be extended towards similar tools like OPENRULES[8] and other technologies like *Complex Event Processing* (CEP) [14].

# References

1. Antoniou, G., van Harmelen, F.: A Semantic Web Primer. The MIT Press (2008)
2. Boley, H., Tabet, S., Wagner, G.: Design rationale for ruleml: A markup language for semantic web rules. In: Cruz, I.F., Decker, S., Euzenat, J., McGuinness, D.L. (eds.) SWWS, pp. 381–401 (2001)
3. Browne, P.: JBoss Drools Business Rules. Packt Publishing (2009)
4. Friedman-Hill, E.: Jess in Action, Rule Based Systems in Java. Manning (2003)
5. Genesereth, M.R., Fikes, R.E.: Knowledge Interchange Format Version 3.0 Reference Manual (January 1992)
6. Giurca, A., Gašević, D., Taveter, K. (eds.): Handbook of Research on Emerging Rule-Based Languages and Technologies: Open Solutions and Approaches. Information Science Reference. Hershey, New York (2009)
7. von Halle, B.: Business Rules Applied: Building Better Systems Using the Business Rules Approach. Wiley (2001)
8. Hallmark, G., Paschke, A., de Sainte Marie, C.: RIF production rule dialect. Candidate recommendation, W3C (October 2009),
http://www.w3.org/TR/2009/CR-rif-prd-20091001/
9. Kaczor, K.: Knowledge Formalization Methods for Semantic Interoperability in Rule Bases. Ph.D. thesis, AGH University of Science and Technology, Krakow, Poland (2014)
10. Kaczor, K., Kluza, K., Nalepa, G.J.: Towards rule interoperability: Design of Drools rule bases using the XTT2 method. In: Nguyen, N.T. (ed.) Transactions on CCI XI. LNCS, vol. 8065, pp. 155–175. Springer, Heidelberg (2013)
11. Kaczor, K., Nalepa, G.J.: Critical evaluation of the XTT2 rule representation through comparison with CLIPS. In: Canadas, J., Nalepa, G.J., Baumeister, J. (eds.) 8th Workshop on Knowledge Engineering and Software Engineering (KESE 2012) at the at the biennial European Conference on Artificial Intelligence (ECAI 2012), Montpellier, France (August 28, 2012), http://ceur-ws.org/Vol-949/
12. Kaczor, K., Nalepa, G.J.: Semantically-Driven Rule Interoperability – Concept Proposal. In: Rutkowski, L., Korytkowski, M., Scherer, R., Tadeusiewicz, R., Zadeh, L.A., Zurada, J.M. (eds.) ICAISC 2013, Part II. LNCS(LNAI), vol. 7895, pp. 511–522. Springer, Heidelberg (2013),
http://www.springer.com/computer/ai/book/978-3-642-38609-1
13. Ligęza, A.: Logical Foundations for Rule-Based Systems. Springer, Heidelberg (2006)

---

[8] See: http://openrules.com

14. Luckham, D.: Complex event processing (CEP). Software Engineering Notes 25(1), 99–100 (2000), http://portal.acm.org/citation.cfm?id=341080\&coll=portal\&dl=ACM

15. Nalepa, G.J., Bobek, S., Ligęza, A., Kaczor, K.: Algorithms for rule inference in modularized rule bases. In: Bassiliades, N., Governatori, G., Paschke, A. (eds.) RuleML 2011 - Europe. LNCS, vol. 6826, pp. 305–312. Springer, Heidelberg (2011)

16. Nalepa, G.J., Bobek, S., Ligęza, A., Kaczor, K.: HalVA – Rule analysis framework for XTT2 rules. In: Bassiliades, N., Governatori, G., Paschke, A. (eds.) RuleML 2011 - Europe. LNCS, vol. 6826, pp. 337–344. Springer, Heidelberg (2011), http://www.springerlink.com/content/c276374nh9682jm6/

17. Nalepa, G.J., Bobek, S.: Rule-based solution for context-aware reasoning on mobile devices. Computer Science and Information Systems 11(1), 171–193 (2014)

18. Nalepa, G.J., Kluza, K.: UML representation for rule-based application models with XTT2-based business rules. International Journal of Software Engineering and Knowledge Engineering (IJSEKE) 22(4), 485–524 (2012), http://www.worldscientific.com/doi/abs/10.1142/S021819401250012X

19. Nalepa, G.J., Kluza, K., Ciaputa, U.: Proposal of automation of the collaborative modeling and evaluation of business processes using a semantic wiki. In: Proceedings of the 17th IEEE International Conference on Emerging Technologies and Factory Automation, ETFA 2012, Kraków, Poland (September 28, 2012)

20. Nalepa, G.J., Kluza, K., Kaczor, K.: Proposal of an inference engine architecture for business rules and processes. In: Rutkowski, L., Korytkowski, M., Scherer, R., Tadeusiewicz, R., Zadeh, L.A., Zurada, J.M. (eds.) ICAISC 2013, Part II. LNCS(LNAI), vol. 7895, pp. 453–464. Springer, Heidelberg (2013), http://www.springer.com/computer/ai/book/978-3-642-38609-1

21. Nalepa, G.J., Ligęza, A.: Designing reliable Web security systems using rule-based systems approach. In: Menasalvas, E., Segovia, J., Szczepaniak, P.S. (eds.) AWIC 2003. LNCS (LNAI), vol. 2663, pp. 124–133. Springer, Heidelberg (2003)

22. Nalepa, G.J., Ligęza, A., Kaczor, K.: Formalization and modeling of rules using the XTT2 method. International Journal on Artificial Intelligence Tools 20(6), 1107–1125 (2011)

23. OMG: Production Rule Representation (OMG PRR) version 1.0 specification. Tech. Rep. formal/2009-12-01, Object Management Group (December 2009), http://www.omg.org/spec/PRR/1.0

24. REWERSE Working Group I1: A UML-Based Rule Modeling Language (2006), http://oxygen.informatik.tu-cottbus.de/rewerse-i1/?q=URML

25. Riley, G.: CLIPS - A Tool for Building Expert Systems (January 2008), http://clipsrules.sourceforge.net

26. Russell, S., Norvig, P.: Artificial Intelligence: A Modern Approach, 3rd edn. Prentice-Hall (2009)

27. W3C Working Group: RIF Primer (December 2012), http://www.w3.org/2005/rules/wiki/Primer

28. Winskel, G.: The Formal Semantics of Programming Languages: An Introduction. MIT Press, Cambridge (1993)

# Measuring Complexity
# of Business Process Models Integrated with Rules

Krzysztof Kluza[✉]

AGH University of Science and Technology,
al. Mickiewicza 30, 30-059 Krakow, Poland
kluza@agh.edu.pl

**Abstract.** Complexity assessment is often used in software and knowledge engineering for controlling the quality and improving models. In fact, complexity is one of the main factors affecting the understability and maintainability of models. Although there are many complexity measures that can be used in order to assess the complexity of process models or rule bases, the complexity of the integrated model of processes with rules is not addressed and constitutes a challenging issue. In this paper, we consider a new metric that is suitable for measuring the integrated models and present a short evaluation based on the selected cases of different size.

## 1 Introduction

Business Process Management (BPM) [2] is a holistic approach for improving organization's workflow in order to align processes with client needs. It focuses on reengineering of processes to obtain optimization of procedures, increase efficiency and effectiveness by the constant process improvement.

In such the approach, a Business Process (BP) can be simply defined as a collection of related tasks which produces a specific service or product for a customer [3]. Models of BPs are intended to be a bridge between technical and business people. They are simple and visualizations make them much easier to understand than using a textual description. Modeling is an essential part of the BPM approach.

Although processes provide a universal method of describing operational aspects of business, detailed aspects of process logic should be described on different abstraction level. Business Rules (BR) can be successfully used to specify process low-level logic [4,5]. What is important, the BR approach supports the specification of knowledge in a declarative manner. Rules may provide declarative specification of domain knowledge, which can be encoded into a process model. On the other hand, a process can be used as a procedural specification of the workflow, including the inference control [6]. The use of BR in BP design helps to simplify complex decision modeling.

The paper is a part of the PhD thesis of the author [1]. The research presented in the paper was supported by the HiBuProBuRul Project funded from NCN (National Science Centre) resources for science (no. DEC-2011/03/N/ST6/00909).

© Springer International Publishing Switzerland 2015
L. Rutkowski et al. (Eds.): ICAISC 2015, Part II, LNAI 9120, pp. 649–659, 2015.
DOI: 10.1007/978-3-319-19369-4_57

Complexity is an important quality factor, defined in IEEE Standard Computer Dictionary as *the degree to which a system or component has a design or implementation that is difficult to understand and verify* [7]. Thus, it is considered during quality assessment in software engineering as well as in knowledge engineering, as an alternative to verification [8,9,10] There are many complexity measures that can be used in order to assess the complexity of process models or rule bases. However, in the case of the integrated model of processes with rules, it is still a challenging issue.

Complexity assessment is often used in software and knowledge engineering for controlling the quality and improving models.

The rest of this paper is organized as follows. In Section 2, the motivation for the research is presented. Section 3 describes how BPMN process model can be integrated with rules. Section 4 provides the description of the existing complexity metrics for rule bases and BPs. Section 5 introduces a new complexity measure for the integrated model of processes with rules and provides a short evaluation based on the selected benchmark cases. The paper is summarized in Section 6.

## 2    Motivation

Complexity metrics for Business Processes can be used for the better understanding and controlling the quality of process models, thus improving their quality [11]. In the case of rule bases, the complexity corresponds mainly to the maintainability of the rule base. Thus, the design of process models with rules can be improved by the availability of metrics that are transparent and easy to be interpreted by the designers.

It is important to mention that there are plethora of complexity metrics for process models. There exist also metrics for rule bases, especially for complexity assessment of expert systems. However, nowadays in business practice, process models are integrated with rules. Therefore, addressing the complexity of such integrated models is a vital issue.

Cardoso et al. distinguished four perspectives to process complexity [12]:

- activity complexity – affected by the number of activities a process has,
- control-flow complexity – affected by such elements and constructs as splits, joins, loops, start and end,
- data-flow complexity – concerns data structures, and the number of formal parameters of activities, and the mappings between data of activities [13],
- resource complexity – concerns different types of resources that have to be accessed during process execution.

In this paper, we consider mainly activity complexity and control-flow complexity. Moreover, the presented problem of the integrated model complexity can be seen as another, rule perspective to process complexity.

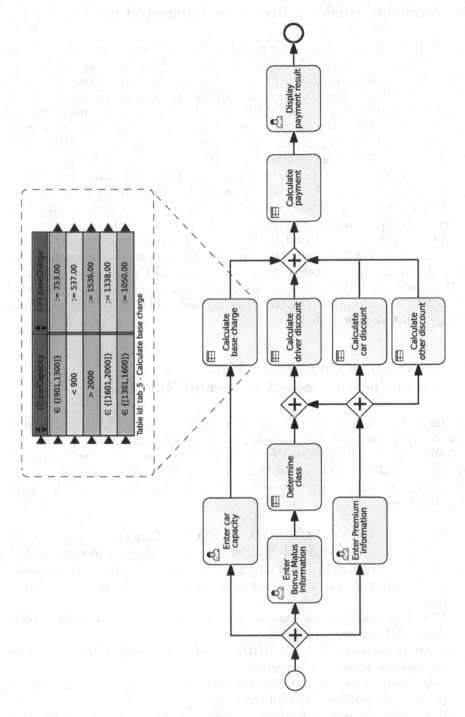

**Fig. 1.** An example of the integrated model (BPMN process model with rules)

# 3   Modeling Business Processes Integrated with Rules

BPMN [14] is a visual notation for modeling Business Processes using workflow-like diagrams. As the BPMN is used only for modeling the workflow between tasks, their low-level specification is not defined within the BP model. Recently, the Business Rules approach has been used for this purpose. Although there is a difference in abstraction levels of BP and BR, rules can be complementary to processes. Especially, they can precisely define the logic of a process task. Such a separation of BP and BR is consistent with the BPMN specification [14], which clarifies that BPMN is not suitable for modeling such concepts as rules.

The XTT2 representation [15,16] provides an expressive formal logical calculus for rules and a structured knowledge representation. Rules in the XTT2 rule base working together in a common context are grouped into a decision table that consists of columns containing conditional and decision attributes.

In this paper, we consider a BPMN process model integrated with the XTT2 rules, e.g. models obtained using the algorithm for generation of integrated models [17]. An example of such a model is presented in Figure 1 – it consists of 4 User tasks and 6 Business Rule tasks. Each Business Rule task is connected to an XTT2 decision table (an exemplary decision table for the "Calculate base charge" BR task is presented).

# 4   Overview of Complexity Metrics
# for Business Process Models and Rule Bases

In this section, a short overview of the complexity metrics used for assessing complexity of rule bases and business process models is given.

Table 1 presents the selected complexity metrics used to assess complexity of process models. According to Mendling [21], BP model complexity cannot be directly determined by only one type of metrics, as each of them has some limitations, e.g.:

- Size metrics (such as NOA, NOAC, NOCAJS or Diameter) – larger models may be more understandable than smaller ones if they are more sequential,
- Density – larger and more complex models can be less dense than smaller ones; the metric is insufficient for comparing models of different number of nodes,
- CNC – models with the same value of CNC can vary in comprehensibility due to different types of nodes,
- Gateway degree (GH, AGD, MGD) – models which differ in size can have the same value of gateway degree,
- Sequentiality – models with the same value of sequentiality can vary in complexity due to different kind of gateways,
- Concurrency – understandability of two models with the same token split can differ due to size, structuredness, etc.

**Table 1.** Simple complexity metrics for Business Process Models

| Source | Metrics | Description |
|---|---|---|
| [18] | NOA | Number of activities in a process. |
| [18] | NOAC | Number of activities and control-flow elements. |
| [18] | NOAJS | Number of activities, joins, and splits. |
| [18] | IC | Interface Complexity is measured as follows: $IC = Length*(NoI*NoO)^2$, where the length of the activity can be calculated using traditional Software Engineering metrics such as LOC (1 if the activity source code is unknown) and NoI and NoO are the number of inputs and outputs. |
| [19] | NOF | Number of control flow connections. |
| [19] | CNC | Coefficient of Network Complexity calculated as: $CNC = NOF / NOAJS$. |
| [20] | Diameter | Length of the longest path from a start node to an end node. |
| [20] | Density | Ratio of the total number of arcs to the maximum number of arcs. |
| [20] | AGD | Average Gateway Degree is the average of the number of both incoming and outgoing arcs of the gateway nodes in the process model. |
| [20] | MGD | Maximum Gateway Degree is the maximum sum of incoming and outgoing arcs of these gateway nodes. |
| [20] | Sequentiality | Degree to which the model is constructed out of pure sequences of tasks. |
| [20] | Depth | Maximum nesting of structured blocks in a process model. |
| [20] | GM | Gateway Mismatch is represented by the sum of gateway pairs that do not match with each other, e.g. when an AND-split is followed by an OR-join. |
| [20] | GH | Gateway Heterogeneity is represented by the number of different types of gateways used in a model. |
| [20] | Concurrency | Maximum number of paths in a process model that may be concurrently activate due to AND-splits and OR-splits. |
| [21] | Structuredness | Related to simple reduction rules, defined by Mendling in [22]. Metric is calculated as a one minus the number of nodes from the model after reduction, divided by the number of nodes from the original graph. If BP model is well structured, it is considered to be less complex. |
| [23] | CFC | Control-Flow Complexity borrows some ideas from McCabe's cyclomatic complexity. It uses the number of states induced by control-flow elements in a process. |
| [24] | CL | Connectivity level between activities in a process: Total Number of Activities / Number of Sequence Flows between these Activities. |
| [25] | MaxND | Maximum Nesting Depth, where the nesting depth of an action is the number of decisions in the control flow that are necessary to perform this action. |
| [25] | MeanND | Mean Nesting Depth. |

Wider overview of the current state of the art in various areas of business process metrics can be found in papers [26,27,28,29,30,31] as well as in the book [21].

Table 2 presents the selected complexity metrics for rule bases. In the case of rule bases, there are not so many simple metrics as there are various rule representations and the complexity of a rule base mainly depends on its structure.

**Table 2.** Complexity metrics for rules and rule bases

| Source | Metrics | Description |
|--------|---------|-------------|
| [32] | NOR | Number of rules. |
| [32] | NOD | Number of decision components. |
| [32] | ABSS | Average breadth of search path (breadth of the knowledge base). |
| [32] | ADSS | Average depth of search space. |
| [33] | NAC | Number of antecedents and consequents of a rule. |
| [34] | BC | Buchanan's Complexity: $ABSS^{ADSS}$. |
| [34] | RC | Rule base complexity based on the content, connectivity and size. |
| [34] | ERC | Entropy based rule base complexity. |

According to [34], there exists a positive relationship between the complexity and anomaly rate in rule bases. The higher complexity value, the higher number of anomalies (anomaly rate).

## 5  Complexity Measure for Process Models Integrated with Rules

Although there exist many metrics for measuring complexity of process models, they do not consider rules. As process models are often integrated with rules, a single complexity measure that allows to assess the complexity of such an integrated model can be useful.

In order to assess the complexity of the integrated model, the following combined metrics is introduced:

$$Complexity = \frac{NOR}{NOD} * \frac{NoA}{ALL} * Concurrency,$$

where $ALL = NOAC + NOF$ is a number of all elements in a process model (for other metrics used in the above formula see Tables 2 and 1). This measure combines the complexity of the knowledge base (an average number of rules in the decision component) and the complexity of a process model (the ratio of the number of activities to the number of all elements) with the concurrency of the model. Although it is simple, it allows for practical complexity measurement for quality assurance.

The proposed complexity measure is tested and used for complexity assessment of BPMN process models integrated with the XTT2 rules. However, as it takes advantage of simple metrics for processes and rules, it can be easily adjusted to any process model integrated with rules.

For the evaluation purposes three benchmark cases were selected: the Polish Liability Insurance case study – *PLI* (developed as a benchmark case for the SKE approach for rule-based systems [16]), EUrent Company – *EUrent* (provided as a part of SBVR specification [35]), and the UServ Financial Services case – *UServ* (a benchmark case study from Business Rules Forum[1]).

In order to compare the selected benchmark cases, in this section selected complexity metrics are calculated for them. Although the PLI and EURent cases have similar number of elements (see Table 3), they are significantly different, as it can be observed based on Diameter metrics (see Table 4). UServ, in turn, is a more complex case with more elements in the model than in two other cases.

For the three selected cases, Table 5 presents the metrics that measure the complexity of the rule base. In the case of selected cases these are related to the XTT2 components, specifically decision tables, and rules.

**Table 3.** Simple metrics – number of elements

| Metrics | PLI | EURent | UServ |
|---|---|---|---|
| Number of User tasks | 4 | 6 | 6 |
| Number of Business Rule tasks | 9 | 7 | 19 |
| Number of parallel gateways | 4 | 4 | 17 |
| Number of activities (NOA) | 13 | 13 | 25 |
| Number of activities and control flow elements (NOAC) | 19 | 18 | 44 |
| Number of activities, joins and splits (NOAJS) | 17 | 16 | 42 |
| All Elements (ALL) | 41 | 39 | 101 |

**Table 4.** Business process metrics based on number of elements

| Metrics | PLI | EURent | UServ |
|---|---|---|---|
| Coefficient of Network Complexity (CNC) | 1.29 | 1.31 | 1.35 |
| Interface Complexity (IC) | 13 | 13 | 25 |
| Diameter | 4 | 9 | 14 |
| Average Gateway Degree (AGD) | 4 | 4.6 | 3.65 |
| Maximum Gateway Degree (MGD) | 5 | 6 | 6 |
| Concurency | 4 | 5 | 11 |
| Sequentiality | 0.32 | 0.33 | 0.09 |
| Gateway Heterogenity (GH) | 1 | 1 | 1 |

**Table 5.** Rule base metrics for the selected cases

| Metrics | PLI | EURent | UServ |
|---|---|---|---|
| Number of the XTT2 decision tables (NOD) | 9 | 7 | 19 |
| Number of the XTT2 rules (NOR) | 61 | 31 | 84 |

Based on the comparison of these three cases representing various size and complexity, the following conclusions can be drawn:

---

[1] See: http://www.businessrulesforum.com

– As all the selected models have similar structure and consist of the same elements; they have the same value of Gateway Heterogenity (GH), and similar values of Coefficient of Network Complexity (CNC) and Maximum Gateway Degree (MGD).

– It is difficult to determine the complexity of such models based on only one type of metric. However, there are some metrics that can be taken into account in order to distinguish the complexity of the models, such as Average Gateway Degree (AGD) or Diameter.

– With the number of elements, especially parallel gateways, the Interface Complexity (IC) and Concurrency grows, while Sequentiality declines.

– As the number of elements in the UServ model is very high, the model should be decomposed in order to be more comprehensible.

The values of the complexity metrics for process models integrated with rules for the selected models are shown in Table 6. This single complexity metrics is comparable to the complexity metrics of the integrated model components.

**Table 6.** The complexity metrics for the integrated model

|  | PLI | EURent | UServ |
|---|---|---|---|
| *Complexity* of the integrated model | 8.60 | 7.38 | 11.89 |

For all three case studies, selected complexity metrics were calculated. It can be observed that the complexity metrics for the integrated model have similar results as separate metrics for process models and rule base. This can be treated as an element of model quality assurance, especially in model complexity management. As the UServ model is very complex one, it should be further decomposed in order to be more comprehensible.

## 6   Conclusion

In software and knowledge engineering, complexity assessment is used for controlling the quality of models. In fact, complexity is one of the main factors affecting their understability and maintainability. Although there are many complexity measures that can be used in order to assess the complexity of process models or rule bases, the complexity of the integrated model of processes with rules is not addressed and constitutes a challenging issue. In this paper, we consider a new metric that is suitable for measuring the integrated models and present a short evaluation based on the selected cases of different size. Such metric can be used for measuring complexity of integrated models [36], as well as used for continuous monitoring of model complexity in various systems, like for improving safety [37] or context-aware ones [38].

# References

1. Kluza, K.: Methods for Modeling and Integration of Business Processes with Rules. PhD thesis, AGH University of Science and Technology Supervisor: Grzegorz J. Nalepa (March 2015)
2. Dumas, M., La Rosa, M., Mendling, J., Reijers, H.A.: Fundamentals of Business Process Management. Springer, Heidelberg (2013)
3. Lindsay, A., Dawns, D., Lunn, K.: Business processes – attempts to find a definition. Information and Software Technology 45(15), 1015–1019 (2003)
4. Charfi, A., Mezini, M.: Hybrid web service composition: Business processes md,,eet business rules. In: Proceedings of the 2nd International Conference on Service-Oriented Computing, ICSOC 2004, pp. 30–38. ACM, New York (2004)
5. Knolmayer, G.F., Endl, R., Pfahrer, M.: Modeling processes and workflows by business rules. In: van der Aalst, W.M.P., Desel, J., Oberweis, A. (eds.) Business Process Management. LNCS, vol. 1806, pp. 16–29. Springer, Heidelberg (2000)
6. Kaczor, K., Nalepa, G.J., Łysik, Ł., Kluza, K.: Visual design of Drools rule bases using the XTT2 method. In: Katarzyniak, R., Chiu, T.-F., Hong, C.-F., Nguyen, N.T. (eds.) Semantic Methods. SCI, vol. 381, pp. 57–66. Springer, Heidelberg (2011), doi:10.1007/978-3-642-23418-7
7. Geraci, A.: IEEE Standard Computer Dictionary: Compilation of IEEE Standard Computer Glossaries. IEEE Press (1991)
8. Coenen, F., Bench-Capon, T., Boswell, R., Dibie-Barthélemy, J., Eaglestone, B., Gerrits, R., Grégoire, E., Ligęza, A., Laita, L., Owoc, M., Sellini, F., Spreeuwenberg, S., Vanthienen, J., Vermesan, A., Wiratunga, N.: Validation and verification of knowledge-based systems: report on eurovav99. Knowl. Eng. Rev. 15(2), 187–196 (2000)
9. Szpyrka, M., Nalepa, G.J., Ligęza, A., Kluza, K.: Proposal of formal verification of selected BPMN models with Alvis modeling language. In: Brazier, F.M.T., Nieuwenhuis, K., Pavlin, G., Warnier, M., Badica, C. (eds.) Intelligent Distributed Computing V. SCI, vol. 382, pp. 249–255. Springer, Heidelberg (2011)
10. Nalepa, G.J., Bobek, S., Ligęza, A., Kaczor, K.: HalVA – rule analysis framework for XTT2 rules. In: Bassiliades, N., Governatori, G., Paschke, A. (eds.) RuleML 2011 - Europe. LNCS, vol. 6826, pp. 337–344. Springer, Heidelberg (2011)
11. Kluza, K., Nalepa, G.J.: Proposal of square metrics for measuring business process model complexity. In: Ganzha, M., Maciaszek, L.A., Paprzycki, M. (eds.) Proceedings of the Federated Conference on Computer Science and Information Systems – FedCSIS 2012, Wroclaw, Poland, September 9-12, pp. 919–922 (2012)
12. Cardoso, J.: Control-flow complexity measurement of processes and weyuker's properties. In: 6th International Enformatika Conference. Transactions on Enformatika, Systems Sciences and Engineering, Budapest, Hungary, October 26-28, vol. 8, pp. 213–218 (2005)
13. Cardoso, J.: About the data-flow complexity of web processes. In: Proceedings from the 6th International Workshop on Business Process Modeling, Development, and Support: Business Processes and Support Systems: Design for Flexibility. The 17th Conference on Advanced Information Systems Engineering (CAiSE 2005) June 13-17, Porto, Portugal, pp. 67–74 (2005)
14. OMG: Business Process Model and Notation (BPMN): Version 2.0 specification. Technical Report formal/2011-01-03, Object Management Group (January 2011)
15. Nalepa, G.J., Ligęza, A., Kaczor, K.: Formalization and modeling of rules using the XTT2 method. International Journal on Artificial Intelligence Tools 20(6), 1107–1125 (2011)

16. Nalepa, G.J.: Semantic Knowledge Engineering. A Rule-Based Approach. Wydawnictwa AGH, Kraków (2011)

17. Kluza, K., Nalepa, G.J.: Automatic generation of business process models based on attribute relationship diagrams. In: Lohmann, N., Song, M., Wohed, P. (eds.) BPM 2013 Workshops. LNBIP, vol. 171, pp. 185–197. Springer, Heidelberg (2014)

18. Cardoso, J., Mendling, J., Neumann, G., Reijers, H.A.: A discourse on complexity of process models. In: Eder, J., Dustdar, S. (eds.) BPM Workshops 2006. LNCS, vol. 4103, pp. 117–128. Springer, Heidelberg (2006)

19. Latva-Koivisto, A.M.: Finding a complexity for business process models. Technical report, Helsinki University of Technology (February 2001)

20. Sánchez-González, L., García, F., Mendling, J., Ruiz, F., Piattini, M.: Prediction of business process model quality based on structural metrics. In: Parsons, J., Saeki, M., Shoval, P., Woo, C., Wand, Y. (eds.) ER 2010. LNCS, vol. 6412, pp. 458–463. Springer, Heidelberg (2010)

21. Mendling, J.: Metrics for business process models. In: Mendling, J. (ed.) Metrics for Process Models. LNBIP, vol. 6, pp. 103–133. Springer, Heidelberg (2009)

22. Mendling, J.: Verification of epc soundness. In: Mendling, J. (ed.) Metrics for Process Models. LNBIP, vol. 6, pp. 59–102. Springer, Heidelberg (2009)

23. Cardoso, J.: How to measure the control-flow complexity of web processes and workflows. In: Fischer, L. (ed.) Workflow Handbook 2005, pp. 199–212. Future Strategies Inc., Lighthouse Point (2005)

24. Aguilar, E.R., Ruiz, F., García, F., Piattini, M.: Applying software metrics to evaluate business process models. CLEI Electronic Journal 9(1) (June 2006)

25. Laue, R., Gruhn, V.: Complexity metrics for business process models. In: Witold Abramowicz, H.C.M. (ed.) Business Information Systems, 9th International Conference on Business Information Systems, BIS 2006, Klagenfurt, Austria, May 31-June 2, pp. 1–12 (2006)

26. Kluza, K., Nalepa, G.J., Lisiecki, J.: Square complexity metrics for business process models. In: Mach-Król, M., Pełech-Pilichowski, T. (eds.) Advances in Business ICT. AISC, vol. 257, pp. 89–107. Springer, Heidelberg (2014)

27. Thammarak, K.: Survey complexity metrics for reusable business process. In: Proceedings from 1st National Conference on Applied Computer Technology and Information System (ACTIS 2010), pp. 18–22. Bangkok Suvarnabhumi College (2010)

28. Muketha, G., Ghani, A.A.A., Selamat, M.H., Atan, R.: A survey of business process complexity metrics. Information Technology Journal 9(7), 1336–1344 (2010)

29. Becker, M., Laue, R.: A comparative survey of business process similarity measures. Computers in Industry 63(2), 148–167 (2012)

30. Dijkman, R., Dumas, M., van Dongen, B., Käärik, R., Mendling, J.: Similarity of business process models: Metrics and evaluation. Information Systems 36(2), 498–516 (2011)

31. Kunze, M., Weidlich, M., Weske, M.: Behavioral similarity – a proper metric. In: Rinderle-Ma, S., Toumani, F., Wolf, K. (eds.) BPM 2011. LNCS, vol. 6896, pp. 166–181. Springer, Heidelberg (2011)

32. Suen, C.Y., Grogono, P.D., Shinghal, R., Coallier, F.: Verifying, validating, and measuring the performance of expert systems. Expert Systems with Applications 1(2), 93–102 (1990)

33. Kaisler, S.H.: Expert system metrics. In: Proceedings of the 1986 IEEE International Conference on Systems, Man, and Cybernetics, vol. 1, pp. 114–120 (1986)

34. Chen, Z., Suen, C.Y.: Complexity metrics for rule-based expert systems. In: Proceedings of the International Conference on Software Maintenance, pp. 382–391. IEEE (1994)
35. OMG: Semantics of Business Vocabulary and Business Rules (SBVR). Technical Report dtc/06-03-02, Object Management Group (2006)
36. Kluza, K., Maślanka, T., Nalepa, G.J., Ligęza, A.: Proposal of representing BPMN diagrams with XTT2-based business rules. In: Brazier, F.M.T., Nieuwenhuis, K., Pavlin, G., Warnier, M., Badica, C. (eds.) Intelligent Distributed Computing V. SCI, vol. 382, pp. 243–248. Springer, Heidelberg (2011)
37. Adrian, W.T., Ciężkowski, P., Kaczor, K., Ligęza, A., Nalepa, G.J.: Web-based knowledge acquisition and management system supporting collaboration for improving safety in urban environment. In: Dziech, A., Czyżewski, A. (eds.) MCSS 2012. CCIS, vol. 287, pp. 1–12. Springer, Heidelberg (2012)
38. Nalepa, G.J., Bobek, S.: Rule-based solution for context-aware reasoning on mobile devices. Computer Science and Information Systems 11(1), 171–193 (2014)

# On Perturbation Measure for Binary Vectors

Maciej Krawczak[1,2](✉) and Grażyna Szkatuła[1](✉)

[1] Systems Research Institute, Polish Academy of Sciences
Newelska 6, 01–447 Warsaw, Poland
{krawczak,szkatulg}@ibspan.waw.pl
[2] Warsaw School of Information Technology
Newelska 6, 01–447 Warsaw, Poland

**Abstract.** The paper is about remoteness of objects described by the nominal-valued attributes. Nominal values of the attributes are replaced by respective binary vectors. A new measure of remoteness between sets, based on binary attributes' values, is introduced. The new measure is called *a measure of perturbation of one binary vector by another binary vector* and can be treated as a binary version of developed by the authors sets' perturbation measure. Values of the newly developed measure range between 0 and 1, and the perturbation measure of one binary vector by another is not the same as the perturbation of the second binary vector by the first one - it means that the measure is not symmetric in general.

**Keywords:** Perturbation of vectors · Sets' matching · Binary vectors

## 1 Introduction

There are problems wherein comparison of objects plays an essential role and the result of such comparison often depend on applied similarity measures between objects. Generally, we can distinguished two different kinds of methods for measuring proximity between objects. The first kind is based on a measure of distance between points described in Cartesian coordinates; in the second kind an object is described by sets of features or attributes (Tversky [8]) instead of geometric points.

For nominal-valued attributes definitions of similarity (or dissimilarity) measures of two sets, Krawczak and Szkatuła introduced concepts of *perturbation of one set by another set* (cf. Krawczak and Szkatuła [3], [4], [5]). The proposed measures identifies changes of the first set after adding the second set and/or changes of the second set after adding the first set. It is shown that this measure is not symmetric, it means that a value of the measure of perturbation of the first set by the second set can be different then a value of the measure of perturbation of the second set by the first set. Of course there are cases with symmetric perturbation measures. The proposed measure can be normalized in different ways to a value ranged from 0 to 1, where 1 is the highest value of perturbation, while 0 is the lowest value of perturbation. *The measure of perturbation type 1 of one*

© Springer International Publishing Switzerland 2015
L. Rutkowski et al. (Eds.): ICAISC 2015, Part II, LNAI 9120, pp. 660–668, 2015.
DOI: 10.1007/978-3-319-19369-4_58

*set by another set* was introduced in the papers by Krawczak and Szkatuła (cf. Krawczak and Szkatuła [3], [4], [5], [6]). The mathematical properties of this measure were studied and the authors rewrote equivalent definitions of the few selected measures based on the measure of perturbation type 1 (cf. Krawczak and Szkatuła [6]). *The measure of perturbation type 2 of one set by another set* was proposed in the paper by Krawczak and Szkatuła [7] and the mathematical properties of this measure were studied.

In this paper, we introduce a binary vector representation of a nominal-valued sets based on a procedure of *binary encoding of sets*. For the new representation of sets, namely binary vector representation we propose *the perturbation of one binary vector by another binary vector*. And next, we introduce *the measure of perturbation type 2 of one binary vector by another binary vector*. This new definition allows us to compare the newly introduced measure to other proximity measures. Next the mathematical properties of the measure are studied.

## 2   Asymmetric Matching Between Binary Vectors

Let us assume a collection of subsets $\{A_1, A_2, \ldots, A_S\}$, $A_1, A_2, \ldots, A_S \subseteq V$, where $V$ is a finite set of nominal values, and $V = \{v_1, v_2, \ldots, v_L\}$ for $v_{l+1} \neq v_l$, $\forall l \in \{1, 2, \ldots, L-1\}$, $L = card(V)$.

Attaching the first set $A_i$ to the second set $A_j$, where $A_i, A_j \subseteq V$, can be considered that the second set is perturbed by the first set, in other words the set $A_i$ perturbs the set $A_j$ with some degree. In such a way we defined a new concept of *perturbation of set $A_j$ by set $A_i$*, which is denoted by $(A_i \mapsto A_j)$, and interpreted by a set $A_i \setminus A_j$. The cardinality of the set $A_i \setminus A_j$ can be normalized to a value ranged from 0 to 1 and can be defined a measure of perturbation. *The measure of perturbation type 2 of one set by another set* was proposed in the paper by Krawczak and Szkatuła [7] in the following manner:

$$Per(A_i \mapsto A_j) = \frac{card(A_i \setminus A_j)}{card(A_i \cup A_j)} \tag{1}$$

The measure of perturbation type 2 of one set by another set (1) was developed for nominal-valued sets' representation. By application of the following binary sets encoding procedure we are able to replace nominal sets representation by binary vector sets representation. The replacement allows us comparison of the selected measures for binary data to the newly developed measure of perturbation of one binary vector by another. The selected measures taken from literature (e.g. Choi et al. [1]) describe various forms of the distance measures and similarity measures for binary cases.

Let us introduce the following procedure of *binary encoding of sets* which will be applied to change sets representation from nominal-valued into binary vector representation.

Now each subset $A_i$, $A_i \subseteq V$, $i = 1, 2 \ldots, S$, $V = \{v_1, v_2, \ldots, v_L\}$, has a binary representation as the $L-dimensional$ *binary vector* $\overline{A_i} = [w_1^i, w_2^i, \ldots, w_L^i]$, where $L = card(V)$, $w_l^i \in \{0, 1\}$, $l = 1, 2 \ldots, L$, in the following manner:

$$w_l^i = \begin{cases} 1 \text{ for } v_l \in A_i \\ 0 \text{ for } v_l \notin A_i \end{cases} \tag{2}$$

for $\forall v_l \in V$. Equipped with procedure (2) we can formulate the new representation of the nominal sets which are described by binary vectors of dimension equal to the cardinality of the set $V$. Let us illustrate the new set's representation by the following example.

*Example 1.* There are considered the following set $V=\{a,b,c,d\}$ and subsets $A_i \subseteq V$. Due to the introduced notation, for $car(V)=4$, we can describe any subset of $V$ in a form of a binary vector, where digit 1 and 0 correspond to presence and absence of a respective nominal value in each subset, see Table 1.

**Table 1.** The subsets represented as a binary vectors

| $\{a\}$ | $\{b\}$ | $\{c\}$ | $\{d\}$ | $\{a,b\}$ | $\{a,c\}$ | ... | $\{b,c,d\}$ | ... | $\{a,b,c,d\}$ |
|---|---|---|---|---|---|---|---|---|---|
| 1 | 0 | 0 | 0 | 1 | 1 | ... | 0 | ... | 1 |
| 0 | 1 | 0 | 0 | 1 | 0 | ... | 1 | ... | 1 |
| 0 | 0 | 1 | 0 | 0 | 1 | ... | 1 | ... | 1 |
| 0 | 0 | 0 | 1 | 0 | 0 | ... | 1 | ... | 1 |

Table 1 should be interpreted as follows: a first set $A_1 = \{a\}$ is represented by a binary vector $\overline{A_1} = [1,0,0,0]$, i.e., a binary vector $\overline{A_1}$ describe a set $A_1$. The last set $V=\{a,b,c,d\}$ is represented by a 4-dimensional unit vector, i.e., a 4-dimensional unit vector describe a set $V$.

In literature we can find various forms of the distance measures and similarity measures for binary cases. Considering two $L$-dimensional binary vectors $\overline{A_i} = [w_1^i, w_2^i, \ldots, w_L^i]$ and $\overline{A_j} = [w_1^j, w_2^j, \ldots, w_L^j]$ let us calculate the following numbers which help to create unified notations of proximity measures (e.g. Choi et al. [1]): $\hat{a}$ - the number of elements equal 1 in both vectors $\overline{A_i}$ and $\overline{A_j}$; $\hat{b}$ - the number of elements equal 1 for vector $\overline{A_i}$ and 0 for vector $\overline{A_j}$; $\hat{c}$ - the number of elements equal 0 for vector $\overline{A_i}$ and 1 for vector $\overline{A_j}$; $\hat{d}$ - the number of elements equal 0 in both vectors $\overline{A_i}$ and $\overline{A_j}$.

For example, for a binary vectors: $\overline{A_1} = [1,0,0,0]$ and $\overline{A_2} = [1,0,1,0]$ we obtain $\hat{a}=1$, $\hat{b}=0$, $\hat{c}=1$, $\hat{d}=2$.

This way it is interesting to notice the sum $\hat{a} + \hat{b} + \hat{c} + \hat{d}$ of all four coefficients is always equal to dimension of the binary vector. Then it can be noticed that the sum $\hat{a} + \hat{d}$ represents the total number of matches between the binary vectors $\overline{A_i}$ and $\overline{A_j}$ while the sum $\hat{b} + \hat{c}$ represent the total number of mismatches between the binary vectors $\overline{A_i}$ and $\overline{A_j}$.

Let us consider two $L$-dimensional binary vectors $\overline{A_i}$ and $\overline{A_j}$ represented as vectors $[w_1^i, w_2^i, \ldots, w_L^i]$ and $[w_1^j, w_2^j, \ldots, w_L^j]$, $w_l^j, w_l^j \in \{0,1\}$, $l = 1, 2, \ldots, L$, respectively. We will need to define the subtraction, summation and intersection of binary vectors $\overline{A_i}$ and $\overline{A_j}$, as also the $L$-dimensional binary vector $\overline{A_k}$, $A_k = [w_1^k, w_2^k, \ldots, w_L^k]$, as shown in Table 2, 3 and 4.

**Table 2.** Binary subtraction $\overline{A_i} \setminus \overline{A_j}$

| \ | 1 | 0 |
|---|---|---|
| 1 | 0 | 1 |
| 0 | 0 | 0 |

**Table 3.** Binary summation $\overline{A_i} \vee \overline{A_j}$

| ∨ | 1 | 0 |
|---|---|---|
| 1 | 1 | 1 |
| 0 | 1 | 0 |

**Table 4.** Binary intersection $\overline{A_i} \wedge \overline{A_j}$

| ∧ | 1 | 0 |
|---|---|---|
| 1 | 1 | 0 |
| 0 | 0 | 0 |

*Example 2.* Let us consider two 4-dimensional binary vectors $\overline{A_1}$ and $\overline{A_2}$, and the set $V=\{a,b,c,d\}$. A vector $\overline{A_1} = [1,0,1,0]$ describe a set $A_1=\{a,c\}$ and a vector $\overline{A_2} = [1,0,0,0]$ describe a set $A_2=\{a\}$. According to Table (2), (3) and (4) the values of the subtraction, summation and intersection are calculated in the following way: $\overline{A_3}=\overline{A_1} \setminus \overline{A_2}=[0,0,1,0]$, $\overline{A_4}=\overline{A_1} \vee \overline{A_2}=[1,0,1,0]$ and $\overline{A_5}=\overline{A_1} \wedge \overline{A_2}=[1,0,0,0]$. This way the 4-dimensional binary vector $\overline{A_3}$ describe a set $A_1 \setminus A_2=\{c\}$, vector $\overline{A_4}$ describe a set $A_1 \cup A_2=\{a,c\}$ and vector $\overline{A_5}$ describe a set $A_1 \cap A_2=\{a\}$.

Let us consider two $L$-dimensional binary vectors $\overline{A_i}$ and $\overline{A_j}$ which describe a sets $A_i$ and $A_j$, where $A_i, A_j \subseteq V$, $L = card(V)$, respectively. The following conditions are satisfied:

– the value $\hat{a}$ (i.e., the number of elements equal 1 in both binary vectors $\overline{A_i} \wedge \overline{A_j}$) is equal to the number $card(A_i \cap A_j)$;

– the value $\hat{b}$ (i.e., the number of elements equal 1 in binary vector $\overline{A_i} \setminus \overline{A_j}$) is equal to the number $card(A_i \setminus A_j)$;

– the value $\hat{c}$ (i.e., the number of elements equal 1 in binary vector $\overline{A_j} \setminus \overline{A_i}$) is equal to the number $card(A_j \setminus A_i)$;

– the value $\hat{d}$ (i.e., the number of elements equal 1 in binary vector $I \setminus (\overline{A_i} \vee \overline{A_j})$, where $I$ is $L$-dimensional unit vector) is equal to the number $card(V \setminus (A_i \cup A_j))$.

According to Eq. (1) we can define the measure of perturbation type 2 of one binary vector by another binary vector.

**Definition 1.** *Let us consider $L$-dimensional binary vectors $\overline{A_i}$ and $\overline{A_j}$. The measure of perturbation type 2 of vector $\overline{A_j}$ by vector $\overline{A_i}$ can be written as follows*

$$Per(\overline{A_i} \mapsto \overline{A_j}) = \frac{\hat{b}}{\hat{a} + \hat{b} + \hat{c}} \tag{3}$$

*In the case of the measure of perturbation type 2 of vector $\overline{A_i}$ by vector $\overline{A_j}$ the definition is written as*

$$Per(\overline{A_j} \mapsto \overline{A_i}) = \frac{\hat{c}}{\hat{a} + \hat{b} + \hat{c}}. \tag{4}$$

Introducing the measure of perturbation type 2 of the $L$-dimensional binary vectors we will discuss some its properties. It is important to notice that this measure is not symmetrical in general, by Definition 1.

It can be proved that this measure is positive and ranges between 0 and 1, where 0 is the lowest level of perturbation while 1 is interpreted as most level of perturbation, as it is shown in the Corollary 1.

**Corollary 1.** *Let us consider $L$-dimensional binary vectors $\overline{A_i}$ and $\overline{A_j}$. The measure of perturbation type 2 of vector $\overline{A_j}$ by vector $\overline{A_i}$ satisfies the following inequality*

$$0 \le Per(\overline{A_i} \mapsto \overline{A_j}) \le 1 \tag{5}$$

*In the case of the measure of perturbation type 2 of vector $\overline{A_i}$ by vector $\overline{A_j}$ the inequality is similar*

$$0 \le Per(\overline{A_j} \mapsto \overline{A_i}) \le 1 \tag{6}$$

Proof. 1) Let us prove the first inequality $0 \le Per(\overline{A_i} \mapsto \overline{A_j})$. It should be noticed that the inequality $\hat{a} \ge 0$, $\hat{b} \ge 0$ and $\hat{c} \ge 0$ are satisfied, and by Definition 1 we thus obtain $Per(\overline{A_i} \mapsto \overline{A_j}) \ge 0$.

2) Now, we will consider the second inequality $Per(\overline{A_i} \mapsto \overline{A_j}) \le 1$. Considering two $L$-dimensional binary vectors $\overline{A_i}$ and $\overline{A_j}$, it should be noticed that the inequality $\hat{b} \le \hat{b} + \hat{c} + \hat{a}$ for $\hat{a} \ge 0$ and $\hat{c} \ge 0$ is satisfied, and then we can obtain the following inequality

$$Per(\overline{A_i} \mapsto \overline{A_j}) = \frac{\hat{b}}{\hat{a} + \hat{b} + \hat{c}} \le 1$$

Proof of Eq. (6) is similar.

Additionally we can prove that a sum of measure of perturbation type 2 of the $L$-dimensional binary vectors is always positive and less than 1, as shown in the Corollary 2.

**Corollary 2.** *The sum of the measures of perturbation type 2 for $L$-dimensional binary vectors $\overline{A_i}$ and $\overline{A_j}$ satisfies the following inequality*

$$0 \le Per(\overline{A_i} \mapsto \overline{A_j}) + Per(\overline{A_j} \mapsto \overline{A_i}) \le 1 \tag{7}$$

Proof. 1) By Corollary 1, the sum $Per(\overline{A_i} \mapsto \overline{A_j}) + Per(\overline{A_j} \mapsto \overline{A_i})$ is non negative. 2) It can be noticed that the inequality $\hat{b} + \hat{c} \le \hat{b} + \hat{c} + \hat{a}$ for $\hat{a} \ge 0$ is satisfied. The right side of inequality (7) can be written as

$$Per(\overline{A_i} \mapsto \overline{A_j}) + Per(\overline{A_j} \mapsto \overline{A_i}) = \frac{\hat{b}}{\hat{a} + \hat{b} + \hat{c}} + \frac{\hat{c}}{\hat{a} + \hat{b} + \hat{c}} = \frac{\hat{b} + \hat{c}}{\hat{a} + \hat{b} + \hat{c}} \le 1.$$

Additionally we can prove an interesting property of the introduced in this paper the measures of perturbation type 2 for the $L$-dimensional binary vectors and the Jaccard's coefficient presented as Corollary 3. The Jaccard's coefficient for two binary vectors, denoted by $S_{Jaccard}(\overline{A_i}, \overline{A_j})$, is defined in the following manner (e.g. Choi et al. [1]):

$$S_{Jaccard}(\overline{A_i}, \overline{A_j}) = \frac{\hat{a}}{\hat{a} + \hat{b} + \hat{c}} \tag{8}$$

**Corollary 3.** *The sum of the measures of perturbation type 2 for L-dimensional binary vectors $\overline{A_i}$ and $\overline{A_j}$, and and Jaccard's coefficient satisfies the following inequality*

$$Per(\overline{A_i} \mapsto \overline{A_j}) + Per(\overline{A_j} \mapsto \overline{A_i}) + S_{Jaccard}(\overline{A_i}, \overline{A_j}) = 1 \tag{9}$$

Proof. 1) By Definition 1 and Eq. (8) the left side of equation (9) can be rewritten as follows

$$Per(\overline{A_i} \mapsto \overline{A_j}) + Per(\overline{A_j} \mapsto \overline{A_i}) + S_{Jaccard}(\overline{A_i}, \overline{A_j}) =$$

$$= \frac{\hat{b}}{\hat{a} + \hat{b} + \hat{c}} + \frac{\hat{c}}{\hat{a} + \hat{b} + \hat{c}} + \frac{\hat{a}}{\hat{a} + \hat{b} + \hat{c}} = 1$$

The proposed in this paper measure of perturbation type 2 of one binary vector by another binary vector can be compared with the selected measures for binary data. In literature (e.g. Choi et al. [1]) we can find various forms of the distance measures and similarity measures for binary cases, just here we would like to recall the following definitions of the selected measures given below.

– Jaccard's similarity

$$S_{Jaccard}(\overline{A_i}, \overline{A_j}) = \frac{\hat{a}}{\hat{a} + \hat{b} + \hat{c}},$$

– Dice's similarity

$$S_{Dice}(\overline{A_i}, \overline{A_j}) = \frac{2\hat{a}}{2\hat{a} + \hat{b} + \hat{c}},$$

– Nei-Li's similarity

$$S_{Nei-Li}(\overline{A_i}, \overline{A_j}) = \frac{2\hat{a}}{(\hat{a} + \hat{b}) + (\hat{a} + \hat{c})},$$

– 3W-Jaccard's similarity

$$S_{3W-Jaccard}(\overline{A_i}, \overline{A_j}) = \frac{3\hat{a}}{3\hat{a} + \hat{b} + \hat{c}},$$

– Sorgenfrei's similarity

$$S_{Sorgenfrei}(\overline{A_i}, \overline{A_j}) = \frac{\hat{a}^2}{(\hat{a} + \hat{b})(\hat{a} + \hat{c})},$$

– Tanimoto's similarity

$$S_{Tanimoto}(\overline{A_i}, \overline{A_j}) = \frac{\hat{a}}{(\hat{a} + \hat{b}) + (\hat{a} + \hat{c}) - \hat{a}},$$

– Sokal-Sneath's I similarity

$$S_{Sokal-Sneath}(\overline{A_i}, \overline{A_j}) = \frac{\hat{a}}{\hat{a} + 2\hat{b} + 2\hat{c}},$$

– Driver-Kroeber's similarity

$$S_{Driver-Kroeber}(\overline{A_i}, \overline{A_j}) = \frac{\hat{a}}{2} \left( \frac{1}{\hat{a} + \hat{b}} + \frac{1}{\hat{a} + \hat{c}} \right),$$

– Lance-Williams's distance

$$S_{Lance-Williams}(\overline{A_i}, \overline{A_j}) = \frac{\hat{b} + \hat{c}}{2\hat{a} + \hat{b} + \hat{c}},$$

– Bray-Curtis's distance

$$S_{Bray-Curtis}(\overline{A_i}, \overline{A_j}) = \frac{\hat{b} + \hat{c}}{2\hat{a} + \hat{b} + \hat{c}},$$

Let us consider the following example which illustrates the mutual relationships between the above recalled proximity measures.

*Example 3.* Let us consider two 9-dimensional binary vectors $\overline{A_1}$ and $\overline{A_2}$, where $\overline{A_1} = [1, 1, 1, 1, 0, 1, 0, 0, 0]$ and $\overline{A_2} = [1, 1, 0, 1, 1, 1, 1, 0, 0]$. The problem is to calculate degrees of proximity between these vectors. The values of the measures of perturbation type 2 and the selected measures are compared. It seems that the best way to illustrate the proximity measure relationships is the graphic illustration shown in Fig. 1.

It must be emphasized that the calculated measure values were done for these two exemplary binary vectors $\overline{A_1}$ and $\overline{A_2}$.

It is obvious that objects' proximity measures are not universal and applied for the same objects return different values (see Fig. 1). In general, the known in the literature measures of objects' proximities are developed and designed for specified data or even for considered data mining problem. The same specification is observed for binary vector representation of sets. Such approach is commonly used for nominal-valued data as well as for its binary vector representation. It seems that the proposed measure of perturbation type 2 of one vector by another vector can be considered as more general because we did not give any primary conditions for considered data set.

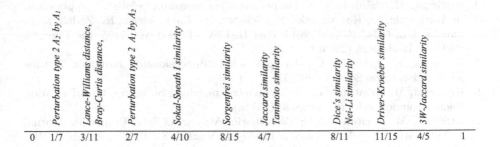

**Fig. 1.** A graphical illustration of selected proximity measures

## 3   Conclusions

In this paper we consider problem of remoteness of objects described by attributes of nominal values. In general such problems are converted to binary representation and proceed as binary vectors comparisons. Therefore we proposed a novel remoteness measure called the measure of perturbation of one binary vector by another binary vector. The proposed measure can be treated as an extension of the previously developed by the authors measure of one set by another set. The binary version of the perturbation measure causes some procedure simplification and additionally allows us to compare the developed measure to other approaches known in the literature. Some mathematical properties of the proposed in this paper *the measure of perturbation type* 2 *for the L−dimensional binary vectors* are explored. The proposed measure was compared with the selected measures for binary data. In must be emphasized that the developed measure of perturbation of one binary vector by another has some advantage compare to other methods because there are any initial assumptions on the considered data structure. Therefore the new measure can be considered as more general than others. Additionally, the measure has another advantage, namely it is not symmetric. The approach is illustrated by several examples which bring the new idea closer.

**Acknowledgment.** The research has been partially supported by the National Centre of Science under Grant No. UMO-2012/05/B/ST6/03068.

## References

1. Choi, S., Cha, S., Tappert, C.C.: A survey of binary similarity and distance measures. Systemics, Cybernetics and Informatics 8(1), 43–48 (2010)
2. Azzouzi, M., Nabney, I.T.: Étude comparative de la distribution florale dans une portion des alpes et des jura. Bulletin del la Société Vaudoise des Sciences Naturelles 37, 547–579 (1998)
3. Krawczak, M., Szkatuła, G.: A new measure of groups perturbation. In: Proceedings of the 2013 Joint IFSA World Congress NAFIPS Annual Meeting, Edmonton, Canada, pp. 1291–1296 (2013a)

4. Krawczak, M., Szkatuła, G.z.: On perturbation measure of clusters - application. In: Rutkowski, L., Korytkowski, M., Scherer, R., Tadeusiewicz, R., Zadeh, L.A., Zurada, J.M. (eds.) ICAISC 2013, Part II. LNCS(LNAI), vol. 7895, pp. 176–183. Springer, Heidelberg (2013b)
5. Krawczak, M., Szkatuła, G.: An approach to dimensionality reduction in time series. Information Sciences 260, 15–36 (2014)
6. Krawczak, M., Szkatuła, G.: On asymmetric matching between sets. Information Sciences (under reviewers' process) (2015a)
7. Krawczak, M., Szkatuła, G.: On Perturbation Measure of Sets - Properties. Journal of Automation, Mobile Robotics & Intelligent Systems 8 (2015b) (accepted 2014)
8. Tversky, A.: Features of similarity. Psychological Review 84, 327–352 (1977)

# A Quick Method for Dynamic Difficulty Adjustment of a Computer Player in Computer Games

Ewa Lach[✉]

The Silesian University of Technology, Institute of Informatics, Gliwice, Poland
Ewa.Lach@polsl.pl

**Abstract.** Games are boring when they are too easy and frustrating when they are too hard. A game in which the challenge level matches the skill of the human player has the greatest entertainment value. In this paper a simple and fast method for adjusting a difficulty level of a computer opponent is introduced. An empirical investigation of the method when playing a FPS game is conducted. Different kinds of players are analyzed. The results show that proposed method matches the difficulty level of an opponent to a player's skill level even without full information about player's abilities.

**Keywords:** Dynamic difficulty adjustment · Game AI · Computer games

## 1 Introduction

Dynamic Difficulty Adjustment (DDA) seeks to adapt the challenge a game poses to a human player. Generally, a game in which the challenge level matches the skill of the human player (called an "even game") has a greater entertainment value than a game that is either too easy or too hard. Historically, singleplayer games allow adjusting a difficulty level only at the beginning of the game by the player's choice of a game mode (easy, medium, hard and sometimes additionally very hard) but their overall level of a challenge cannot be adjusted according to the player's actual input during the game. In this situation both beginners and experts alike can become frustrated or bored . In this situation, it is desirable to automatically adjust the difficulty level as the game proceeds.

Several methods have been proposed so far to dynamically adjust a difficulty level in games: multi-layered perceptrons (MLPs) [1], dynamic scripting [2], Hamlet System [3], reinforcement learning [4], Upper Confidence bound for Trees (UCT) and neural networks [5], exponential update algorithm POSM predicting "just right" difficulty settings [6], self-organizing system [7], etc. However, the game industry looks suspiciously at new ideas proposed by academic researchers in a game AI . Most AI techniques (e.g. neural networks, evolutionary algorithms) can't guarantee a failure-free performance for every experiment, which is usually essential in commercial games. Game development companies prefer to avoid the risk with the amount of money they spend on games. Another problem with most of the AI techniques is that they are complex and time

© Springer International Publishing Switzerland 2015
L. Rutkowski et al. (Eds.): ICAISC 2015, Part II, LNAI 9120, pp. 669–678, 2015.
DOI: 10.1007/978-3-319-19369-4_59

consuming, so their application slows down games, sometimes even to the extent that they can't perform in real time. Usually players prefer less "intelligent" opponents to ones who take their time to decide their actions.

In this paper the author evaluates a simple and fast method for adjusting a computer player's behavior so its difficulty level is adequate for a human player.

The paper continues by introducing the proposed method in section 2. Sections 3 presents conducted experiments, the FPS game as the test bed for the proposed method and simulation results. Section 4 concludes the paper.

## 2    Dynamic Difficulty Adjustment for a Computer Player

The paper presents two methods: the Full Dynamic Difficulty Adjustment for a Computer Player FDDACP and the Single Feature Dynamic Difficulty Adjustment for a Computer Player SFDDACP. Both methods focus on adjusting a computer opponent, so its challenge level is compatible with the game player skills. The FDDACP is an uncomplicated method, proposed by the author, that can quickly produce an opponent for an "even game". To test its effectiveness its results are compared with the ones obtained from the SFDDACP method. This is a method similar to a traditional DDA used in current games: an opponent changes its attributes' values so they are comparable with the player's attributes. This method could produce an opponent with a skill level identical to player's if only all player's characteristics could be defined and introduced to a computer player. Unfortunately, human behavior is too complex for that. As a result others methods are researched [1]-[7], including the FDDACP.

### 2.1    General Definition

The FDDACP method uses a quantitative evaluation function $ef$ to calculate a human player and a computer opponent skills level. The evaluation function is game specific. Next, the two measures: $ef_P$ for player and $ef_O$ for opponent are compared with the help of a percentage value $p_{lim}$, that is defined as method's parameter. If $diffef = |ef_P - ef_O|$ is less or equal to $p_{lim}*ef_P$, then it is believed that opponent's and player's skills are similar, else every aspect of the computer opponent behavior is adjusted, with the use of the $diffef$ value. The greater the $diffef$ the more significant the change in an opponent's behavior. The value $p_{lim}$ defines a region without adjustment. An opponent is changed more often for smaller $p_{lim}$ values.

In the SFDDACP method each aspect of an opponent's behavior is evaluated and adjusted separately. A quantitative value for every evaluated enemy feature is obtained and compared with its player counterpart. If the absolute difference of these values ($diffefF_i$ for $i = 1, ...n$, where $n$ is a number of evaluated player features) is grater than a percentage of the player's feature value ($p_{lim}*efF_{P,i}$) then the opponent feature is changed to the player's value. Afterwards, to create diverse behaviors of computer players minor random changes are added to the analyzed feature.

The FDDACP method is more general and all opponent features are adjusted at the same time in accordance with one value defining entire computer player's skill set. This might make this method less precise but its fault tolerance should be better than the SFDDACP method. Player's rare accidental mistakes that don't influence player behavior taken as a whole shouldn't impact simulated opponent behavior in the same degree that analyzing every aspect of player behavior in the SFDDACP could. Nonetheless, the SFDDACP could behave better in situations where player has to accomplish a mixture of tasks from across the skill spectrum to finish a game.

## 2.2 Specialized Methods

In many games players are characterized with the use of various attributes (e.g. health, ammunition, lives, strength) that describe player features. Players with different skills' level have different attributes' values. Therefore if we change values of attributes we can change players behavior. For such games specializations of the FFDDACP and the SFDDACP methods were developed. In this work two types of attributes were identified: BVBP attributes for which the bigger the attribute value the better the player behavior (e.g. strength) and SVBP attributes for which the smaller the value the better the player (e.g. reaction time). Depending on the attribute's type alternative estimation functions can be defined. A subsequent evaluation function was proposed for player features:

$$efF_i = \begin{cases} \frac{Fval_i - Fmin_i}{Fmax_i - Fmin_i} & \text{for BVBP attributes} \\ \frac{Fmax_i - Fval_i}{Fmax_i - Fmin_i} & \text{for SVBP attributes} \end{cases} \quad (1)$$

where $i$ is an index of a player's attribute ($i = 1...n$, where $n$ is a number of evaluated player attributes), $efF_i$ is an estimate of a player skill for feature $i$, $Fval_i$ is a value of a player's attribute $i$ defining feature $i$, $Fmin_i$ is the minimal value of an attribute $i$ and $Fmax_i$ is the highest value of an attribute $i$.

$Fmax_i$ and $Fmin_i$ can be set on the basis of common knowledge, could be defined intuitively or obtain from practical experiments. A value $Fval_i$ is determined during or after each encounter with an enemy. For example, in games like FPS (first person shooter) and TPS (third person shooter) we can measure a reaction time of a human player (i.e. an interval from an enemy becoming visible to a player starting shooting) or his weapon spread. In car racing games we can calculate player's speed in different circumstances or evaluate player's understeering, oversteering or counter-steering. There are many possibilities.

The value $efF_i$ ranges from 0 to 1. The greater a $efF_i$ value is the more skilled in analyzed aspect the player is. If player's $efF_i$ is equal to 1 and opponent's $efF_i$ is equal to 0 then we have the easiest situation for human player in regard to the feature $i$.

In the FDDACP we can use a weighted sum of the $efF_i$ values to compute a human player and a computer opponent skills level, if more than one attribute contributes to the final value (else we use equation 1):

$$ef = \frac{\sum_{i=1}^{n} (efF_i * weight_i)}{\sum_{i=1}^{n} weight_i} \quad (2)$$

where $ef$ is an estimate of a player skill, $efF_i$ is an estimate of a player skill for a feature $i$, $weight_i$ is a weight of a feature $i$ informing how critical is that feature to the overall player behavior.

The value $ef$ ranges from 0 to 1. The greater the $ef$ value the more skilled the player. In order to simplify obtaining $ef$ value we can often try to use values, which logically define how player perform in a game. For example, in racing games we can use time a player takes to finish a race (the time of race is a SVBP attribute).

The SFDDACP method compares $efF_i$ values for a human player and a computer opponent for each player feature. The FDDACP method compares $ef$ values.

For the SFDDACP method, if $diffefF_i > (p_{lim} * efF_{P,i})$, where $efF_{P,i}$ is an estimate of a skill $i$ ($efF_i$) for a human player, value of opponent's attribute $i$ is adjusted:

$$Fval_{O,i} = Fval_{P,i} \pm (Fmax_i - Fmin_i)p_r \qquad (3)$$

where $Fval_{O,i}$ is a new value of a opponent's attribute $i$, $Fval_{P,i}$ is a value of a human player's attribute $i$, $Fmin_i$ is the minimal value of an attribute $i$. $Fmax_i$ is the highest value of an attribute $i$ and $p_r$ is a SFDDACP method's parameter, a percentage value. The greater the $p_r$, the more diversified the changes to opponent's behavior.

In the FDDACP method, if $diffef > (p_{lim} * ef_P)$, opponent's $Fval_{O,i}$ for each attribute is adjusted by the means of increasing or decreasing $Fval_{O,i}$ value. Which operation will be chosen is decided based on two factors: firstly we check which player has bigger value, secondly there are alternative functions for attributes BVBP and SVBP.

First of all we compute $adjF_i$ that will be used to adjust opponent's attributes values:

$$adjF_i = \begin{cases} \text{diffef} * (Fmax_i - Fmin_i) & \text{for BVBP attributes} \\ -\text{diffef} * (Fmax_i - Fmin_i) & \text{for SVBP attributes} \end{cases} \qquad (4)$$

where $Fmin_i$ and $Fmax_i$ are extreme values of an attribute $i$ and $diffef$ is absolute difference of players' skill estimates. In the next step of the FDDACP method, we change all opponent's attributes as follows:

$$Fval_{O,i} = \begin{cases} \text{FvalOld}_{O,i} + adjF_i & \text{for } ef_P > ef_O \\ \text{FvalOld}_{O,i} - adjF_i & \text{for } ef_p < ef_O \end{cases} \qquad (5)$$

where $Fval_{O,i}$ is a new value of a opponent's attribute $i$ and $FvalOld_{O,i}$ is a value of a opponent's attribute $i$ used during previous confrontation, $Fmin_i$ and $Fmax_i$ are extreme values of an attribute $i$. After that we check, in both methods, if new $Fval_{O,i}$ ranges from $Fmin_i$ to $Fmax_i$. If it is not the case we clamp $Fval_{O,i}$ to a valid range:

$$Fval_{O,i} = \begin{cases} Fmax_i - (Fmax_i - Fmin_i)p_{ri} & \text{for Fval}_{O,i} > \text{Fmax}_i \\ Fmin_i + (Fmax_i - Fmin_i)p_{ri} & \text{for Fval}_{O,i} < \text{Fmin}_i \end{cases} \qquad (6)$$

where $p_r$ is a method's parameter: a percentage value that includes a little diversity to opponent's behavior.

In the ideal circumstances the SFDDACP should generate a more accurate adjustment than the FDDACP, but in reality, it has an important drawback: it needs to recognize all player's features. For complex behaviors it can be impossible. In the FDDACP if we make an error while identifying essential attributes others features of a computer player can be used to mitigate that. For example in shooting game we can improve an opponent by increasing its endurance or improving its hitting aim. In the SFDDACP we improve each feature separately. Consequently if we overlook an opponent feature, its behavior as a whole might suffer. For this reason, the author presents a study on adjusting player's attributes based on the knowledge of player's overall behavior. The achieved results will be compared with those obtained from the SFDDACP method.

## 3    Experiments

To evaluate the effect of the proposed methods a FPS game "Seek&Shoot" was employed. The game was developed in the Unity 3D game engine (version 4.3.1), with the aid of several leading systems like RAIN AI (version 2.0.11.0) and Ultimate FPS (UFPS, version 1.4.7c). Unity is a cross-platform game creation system developed by Unity Technologies, including a game engine and an integrated development environment (IDE). The game's characters mechanics and characters behaviors (AI) have been created with the RAIN system. The UFPS was utilized for the implementation of shooting and the injury simulation. For the characters motion the Navigation Mesh and the Waypoint Network were used.

The aim of the human and computer player in this game is to find an enemy in a three-dimensional scene and shoot him. In order to simplify a study of methods' performance and find clear relationship between method's parameters and opponent's actions, a simple game's environment and a player's behavior were proposed. The game scenes are enclosed spaces with different number of randomly placed walls (fig. 1). Walls block players' vision of each other. A virtual player is equipped with a visual sensor that allows him to spot the enemy. An opponent's behavior is described by means of behavior tree (fig. 2) with actions: look around, move, face player (when you see him or when he hits you), shoot player.

During and after each confrontation data about player is collected: health, number of player hits, angle of weapon spread, ammunition used, reaction time (i.e. an interval from an enemy becoming visible to a player starting shooting), view range and view horizontal angle. These values are next used in DDA methods to define computer player attributes: BVBP attributes: a1-endurance (how much health decrease results in a player's death), a2-weapon damage force, a3-ammunition, a4-view range, a5 -view horizontal angle and SVBP attributes: a6-weapon spread and a7- gun reload time (i.e. an interval, when a character can't shoot). For every game there are 100 encounters (rounds). The round ends

**Fig. 1.** The game scene

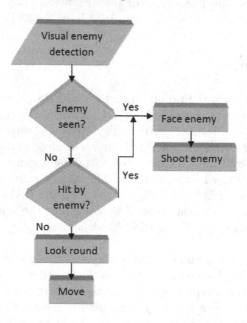

**Fig. 2.** Computer player's behavior algorithm

when one of the players dies (i.e. its health rate drops past an endurance level) . If both players die during a fight the round ends in a draw. At first an opponent gets random attributes values ranging from $Fmin_i$ to $1/3(Fmax_i\text{-}Fmin_i)$. Then after each encounter its values are adjusted according to equations (3) - (6). For a calculation of $ef$ value a player health rate registered at the end of the round is used, $p_{lim}$ is set to 10%.

To test a mechanism of the evaluated method four different computer agents were used, that could play through the rounds unaided: average player (AP), mixed beginner player (MBP), mixed expert player (MEP) and continuously improving with time player (IP). An average player is the one whose skill level for every feature is set to average value. For MBP and MEP players all attributes but a2 are set at the same level (beginner or expert). Attribute a2 is set with expert value for MBP player and with beginner value for MEP player. An IP players improve their skills during a game. Preliminary experiments showed that all methods behave the same regardless of a player skill level. As a result experiments with a beginner and an expert player were omitted.

Computer opponents try to obtain the same difficulty level as players. Their attributes are adjusted by means of five different methods: a standard SFDDACP (SFD), a standard FDDACP (FD), a short FDDACP (sdFD and saFD), a SFD-DACP without adjustment of an attribute a1 (SFDa1) and a FDDACP without adjustment of an attribute a1 (FDa1). A standard FDDCP method adjusts opponent's attributes after every round, continuously fine-tuning an opponent's behavior. A short FDDACP method stops an adjustment after obtaining results judged sufficient: in the sdFD method after four draws in succession and in the saFD after four rounds that ends successively without adjustment. The last two methods, SFDa1 and FDa1, work like standard ones, but one of the attributes (a1 - an endurance) is omitted during adjustment to test methods fault tolerance. It is an important test because identifying all significant attributes for complex games can be difficult and omissions may occur.

Each performed test has been given an identifier created from a name of a player and a used method (e.g. test AP-SFD for average player with standard SFDDACP method). Ultimately, there were twelve tests performed: AP-SFD, AP-FD, AP-sdFD, AP-saFD, IP-SFD, IP-FD, MBP-SFD, MBP-FD, MEP-SFD, MEP-FD, AP-SFDa1, AP-FDa1. Each test was repeated 100 times. The aim of the test AP-FD is determining if using a general measure, which value does not directly result from attributes' states can adjust these attributes in satisfying way. Next, results from AP-FD can be compared with ones obtained from AP-SFD. The AP-saFD test and the AP-sdFD test aim at finding how fast we can obtain adjusted values and what will be their quality. Obtained results can be compared with results from AP-FD. Next we test how proposed methods behave for players improving their skills continuously (IP-SFD, IP-FD). After that we analyse FDDACP and SFDDACP methods for players with mixed skills: experts in one aspects and beginners in others (MBP-SFD, MBP-FD, MEP-SFD, MEP-FD). These are valuable tests, as one of the aims of DDA is introducing the possibility of adjusting to players that can't be simply categorized as beginners or experts. The last experiments are test of methods' fault tolerance (AP-SFDa1, AP-FDa1).

## 3.1   Simulation Results

Table 1 shows results of the performed experiments. For every test six rates are calculated: OWR (opponent's win rate), PWR1 ( player's win rate 1), DR (draw rate), PWR2 ( player's win rate 2), HR ( health rate) and AR (adjustment rate). The sum of OWR, PWR1 and DR for each experiment is equal to 100%. These values tell us (in percentages) how many times one of three situations occurs: a player wins (PWR1), an opponent wins (OWR), there is a draw (DR). The bigger DR is the better matched a player and an opponent are. The PWR2 value defines a player's win rate calculated from rounds with the winner. Ideal PWR2 value is 50% . The health rate informs us about the percentage of health a winner of the round is able to retain averagely during the encounter. The smaller HR is the more comparable players are. The last rate AR shows how frequently a computer opponent is changed for every game. In addition to these measures for the experiments AP-saFD and AP-sdFD the medians (M) of rounds, where last adjustment for a game occurred, are calculated.

**Table 1.** The results of FPS games

| | OWR (*HR*) | PWR1 (*HR*) | DR | PWR2 | AR |
|---|---|---|---|---|---|
| AP-SFD | 7.71 (*7.08*) | 26.44 (*6.55*) | 65.86 | 75.75 | 0.81 |
| AP-FD | 20.62 (*11.93*) | 35.74 (*8.85*) | 43.63 | 63.41 | 26.21 |
| AP-sdFD | 28.87 (*12.87*) | 30.52 (*9.38*) | 40.61 | 51.39 | 14.98 |
| AP-saFD | 17.42 (*11.03*) | 37.99 (*9.02*) | 44.59 | 68.57 | 4.53 |
| IP-FD | 18.48 (*11.12*) | 31.19 (*10.69*) | 50.34 | 62.80 | 25.77 |
| IP-SFD | 2.68 (*7.19*) | 56.54 (*13.74*) | 40.77 | 95.47 | 17.32 |
| MEP-FD | 59.73 (*5.09*) | 22.00 (*9.93*) | 18.27 | 26.92 | 30.15 |
| MEP-SFD | 40.49 (*2.65*) | 36.57 (*3.81*) | 22.94 | 47.46 | 0.75 |
| MBP-FD | 20.41 (*15.97*) | 37.47 (*11.09*) | 42.13 | 64.74 | 36.55 |
| MBP-SFD | 18.50 (*5.44*) | 13.53 (*7.07*) | 67.96 | 42.24 | 0.95 |
| AP-FDa1 | 36.53 (*6.15*) | 23.83 (*10.89*) | 39.63 | 39.48 | 22.87 |
| AP-SFDa1 | 0.00 | 99.42 (*21.68*) | 0.58 | 100 | 0.98 |

Results obtained from AP-SFD indicates that the player is better than the adjusted opponent (PWR2 -76%) for the same values of identified attributes. However, based on a high DR (66%) and a low HR (6.5%) we can assume that the difference is not big. In that case by changing opponent's attributes values we should obtain similar performances from both players.

The outcomes of both methods: SFDDACP and FDDACP for average player are similar. The SFDDACP method generates more draws but there is smaller difference between the number of opponent's and player's wins in the results acquired from the FDDACP method (PWR2 - 63%). The higher adjustment rate for FDDACP (26%) suggests that the adjustment process for this method takes more time and we need more rounds to obtain the searched values.

The AP-saFD and the AP-sdFD experiments aimed at finding how fast we can obtain adjusted values with FDDACP method and what will be their quality. Two conditions for stopping an adjustment were tested: reaching four draws in succession (AP-sdFD) and reaching four rounds that ends successively without adjustment (AP-saFD). Results from AP-saFD are only minimally worse than the ones from AP-FD with a lot smaller AR (4.5%) and a median M=9. Consequently we can get with the saFD method rather fast quite good results. Interestingly, quality of results from AP-sdFD is better than those from standard SFDDACP and FDDACP with a median M equal to 28.5 and AR equal to 15%. Therefore, this method is slower than saFD but still faster than FD and the obtained opponent matches player more precisely than any other find in performed experiments. We can assume that the reason for the saFD method being better than the standard FDDACP is a fluctuation of results around player's values.

After four draws adjusted values are closer to the searched ones. The results of saFD method are better than the ones from the standard SFDDACP method presumably because FDDACP method can adjust opponent's values so they can substitute for player's attributes we can't identified.

To test this last assumption two experiments were conducted: SFDa1 and FDa1. An attribute a1 (an endurance) was chosen because of its significance to the player's behavior. Without it the SFDDACP method is not able to adjust an opponent. The player wins almost all rounds. The FDDACP method deals better with this situation. Even without such an important attribute there are 40% of draws and win rate is close to 40%. This confirms our hypothesis.

A slow improvement of player's skills does not have a negative impact on the results of the FDDACP method. There is even about 7% more draws. Again the fluctuation of opponent's values in AP-FD test can be the cause. When the opponent level of skills exceeds player's the player's values increases and the opponent's level does not have to be reduced. For the SFDDACP method, as a result of changes in the player's skill level, the number of rounds in which the player is better than an opponent significantly increases with the win rate's rise to 95% and 41% of draws.

The FDDACP method behave the worst for a player with mixed skills, in particular for an expert in all aspects except one (MEP-FD). Its win rate is 27% with 18% of draws. However, in the MBP-FD experiment we have obtained results similar to results from the AP-FD. This contradicts the conclusion that the FDDACP method is not suitable for players with mixed levels of skills. At a closer look at the MEP-FD results it can be seen that the opponent wins with a very low value of the health rate (5%). This raises the suspicion that for the lower value of $p_{lim}$ there will be smaller number of opponent's wins. Detailed analysis of the learning curve for opponent's attributes seems to indicate this as well. With this method, we cannot at the same time raise the level of one skill and lower the level of other skills. However, the FDDACP method cope with this problem by setting the beginner skills at a higher level, and the expert skills at a lower level. In the end, we are interested in the final results of the overall behavior of the player.

As expected, we did not observe worsening of the results of the SFDDACP method because of the mixing of skill levels for various attributes in a single player. We can even see some improvement due to the fact that now players are better matched.

## 4   Conclusion

In this paper we presented FDDACP method, which matches the difficulty level of an opponent to a player's skill level. The results shows that the FDDACP method is insensitive to errors in the definition of the opponent's abilities and cope well when a player has mixed levels of skills. The obtained results indicate that we can adjust opponent's behavior with the use of general quantitative measure resulting from an outcome of player's and opponent's actions. In this situation, we do not need to make a detailed classification of the player's behavior.

Analyzing the results is sufficient. This can significantly simplify construction of DDA for games. In a future work experiments with human players will be conducted. Additionally, more complex computer opponents will be investigated.

**Acknowledgment.** This work is part of the General Statutory Research Project BK266/RAU2/2014 conducted at the Institute of Informatics, the Silesian University of Technology.

# References

1. Shaker, N., Yannakakis, G., Togelius, J.: Towards automatic personalized content generation for platform games. In: Proceedings of Artificial Intelligence and Interactive Digital Entertainment (AIIDE 2010). AAAI Press (2010)
2. Spronck, P., Sprinkhuizen-Kuyper, I., Postma, E.: Difficulty scaling of game AI. In: Proceedings of the 5th International Conference on Intelligent Games and Simulation (GAME-ON 2004), p. 3337 (2004)
3. Hunicke, R., Chapman, V.: AI for dynamic difficulty adjustment in games. In: Challenges in Game Artificial Intelligence AAAI Workshop, San Jose, pp. 91–96 (2004)
4. Tan, C.H., Tan, K.C., Tan, A.T.: Dynamic game difficulty scaling using adaptive behavioural based AI. IEEE Transactions on Computational Intelligence and AI in Games 3(4), 289–301 (2011)
5. Li, X., He, S., Dong, Y., Liu, Q., Fu, Y., Shi, Z., Huang, W.: To create DDA by the Approach of ANN from UCT-Created Data. In: International Conference on Computer Application and System Modeling (ICCASM), Taiyuan (2010)
6. Missura, O., Grtner, T.: Predicting Dynamic Difficulty. In: Shawe-Taylor, J., Zemel, R.S., Bartlett, P., Pereira, F.C.N., Weinberger, K.Q. (eds.) Advances in Neural Information Processing Systems, vol. 24, pp. 2007–2015 (2011)
7. Ebrahimi, A., Akbarzadeh-T, M.-R.: Dynamic difficulty adjustment in games by using an interactive self-organizing architecture. In: Intelligent Systems (ICIS), pp. 1–6 (2014)

# UCT-Based Approach to Capacitated Vehicle Routing Problem

Jacek Mańdziuk[(✉)] and Cezary Nejman

Faculty of Mathematics and Information Science,
Warsaw University of Technology,
Koszykowa 75, 00-662 Warsaw, Poland
mandziuk@mini.pw.edu.pl, nejmanc@student.mini.pw.edu.pl

**Abstract.** Vehicle Routing Problem (VRP) is a popular combinatorial optimization problem which consists in finding an optimal set of routes for a fleet of vehicles in order to serve a specified collection of clients. Capacitated VRP (CVRP) is a version of VRP in which every vehicle has a capacity parameter assigned.

The UCT (Upper Confidence bounds applied to Trees) is a heuristic simulation-based algorithm used for learning an optimal policy in games. The algorithm is an extension of the Monte Carlo Tree Search (MCTS) method, however, unlike MCTS which makes use of uniformly distributed simulations in a game tree (in order to find the most promising move), the UCT aims at maintaining an optimal balance between exploration and exploitation, which results in more frequent visits to and deeper expansion of the most promising branches of a game tree.

The paper is the first attempt to apply the UCT algorithm to solving CVRP. The critical issue here is suitable mapping of the CVRP onto a game tree structure, which is not straightforward in this problem domain. Furthermore, in order to keep the tree size within reasonable limits the appropriate way of child nodes selection must be considered. Another pertinent issue is interpretation of game-related terms "win" and "loss" in the CVRP context.

Experimental results of several mappings of CVRP to game tree-like structure are presented for a collection of popular benchmark sets.

**Keywords:** UCT · Routing problems · Dynamic optimization

## 1 Introduction

Vehicle Routing Problem (VRP) along with its variants is a widely known combinatorial optimization task. Due to its practical relevance there is a strong interest in finding new approaches to solving this problem despite already existing heuristic and approximate methods. UCT method, in turn, is one of the most popular approaches to game playing mainly due to its adaptability and long-term efficiency. An additional asset of UCT is the lack of need for domain-specific knowledge. Taking the qualities of UCT approach and requirements of VRP problem into consideration, we conducted research on possible ways of

© Springer International Publishing Switzerland 2015
L. Rutkowski et al. (Eds.): ICAISC 2015, Part II, LNAI 9120, pp. 679–690, 2015.
DOI: 10.1007/978-3-319-19369-4_60

incorporating the UCT algorithm, in its basic form, into specific class of Capacitated Vehicle Routing Problems (CVRP). The most promising factor of such a combination is the fact that UCT proved to be very effective in solving the so-called "exploration vs. exploitation dilemma", i.e. the issue of balancing the usage of discovered best solutions vs. finding the new ones. This property seems to be very well suited to the nature of VRP/CVRP. Moreover, it is worth noting the novelty of the proposed approach as, to the best of our knowledge, it is the first time the UCT method is applied to solving the VRP/CVRP. The main issues analyzed in this piece of research are related to appropriate problem representation, interpretation of "win" and "loss" situations and finding efficient UCT parameterization. Initial experiments showed that implementation of the basic UCT method with naive problem representation leads to mediocre results. After finding weak points of this preliminary approach the baseline algorithm was modified by raising the importance of exploration as well as discretizing the solution evaluation values. These changes led to the overall improvement of results and allowed making a conclusion that the modified method with discretization factor is a promising way of incorporating UCT into CVRP.

The remainder of the paper is organized as follows: in the next section a formal definition of the CVRP is provided. Section 3 presents the UCT method and the proposed way of its application to solving CVRP. Section 4 is devoted to experimental setup, simulation results and conclusions. The last section summarizes the main contribution of the paper and points directions for future research.

## 2    CVRP Formulation

VRP was formulated in 1959 [4] and proved to be NP-hard in 1981 [11]. In its base formulation, there is a number of homogenous vehicles and a number of clients (sometimes interpreted as cities) and each client has a certain (known) demand which must be satisfied by (exactly) one of the vehicles. The goal is to deliver demanded goods to all clients while minimizing the sum of vehicles routes' costs (lengths). The delivered goods are homogenous. Each vehicle's route must start and end in the specified depot. Each client as well as the depot has a certain 2-dimensional location. It is worth noting that in the basic formulation of VRP, there is no limit on the number of clients that can be serviced by a single vehicle. In practical applications though, the capacity parameter must be added to a vehicle characteristics in order to ensure that there will be no situation of servicing clients with higher total demand than the vehicle's capacity. Such a formulation leads to CVRP. Since VRP/CVRP is NP-Hard no polynomial method of its solving is known. Thus, exact solutions can only be obtained for small-size problems. In practice, approximation algorithms must be used in order to obtain the results in acceptable time. Among the exact algorithms, there are three main approaches: full tree search, dynamic programming and integer programming. An example of the first approach would be spanning tree and shortest path relaxations method [16]. A dynamic programming method was, for instance, proposed in [6] for problems with known number of vehicles. As for the third approach, a three-index vehicle flow formulation was presented in [7]. There exist various approximation algorithms for VRP/CVRP, most of them designed to address specific problem formulations, e.g. Savings algorithm [3] which assumes that the number of vehicles is unlimited. Other well-known methods include Multi-route improvement algorithm [1], Sweep algorithm [10], Ant Colony Optimization [5] or Particle Swarm Optimization [12,18].

## 3    UCT Search Tree Method

UCT (Upper Confidence Bound applied to Trees) is an extension to Monte Carlo Tree Search (MCTS) method developed in 2006 [13]. MCTS is an optimization algorithm used in decision making processes. Its main advantage is the knowledge-free nature [14,15], i.e. the only domain knowledge required is the ability to recognize positive and negative final outcomes of decisions made. The space (problem domain) in which the algorithm operates is represented by a tree structure. The current state is located in the root of a tree. Each node represents particular state and stores information about actions (game moves) taken in this state as well as the respective scores (fractions of simulations that led to a "win" outcome) assigned to that (action, state) pair. Each path in the tree represents a particular sequence of decisions (game moves) with the final outcome being read out in the leaf.

UCT relies on massive random four-stage simulations (see Fig. 1) performed before making a decision:

- **Choice** - starting from the root, go down the tree until a leaf or unexplored node is reached;
- **Expansion** - if possible, create child nodes of previously found node;
- **Simulation/Play-out** - from one of the created nodes, perform a random simulation (game) until the final state;
- **Backpropagation** - populate the result of the above random simulation (game) up the tree, thus update all nodes visited on the path from the root to the leaf node.

The more iterations are performed the better estimations of the true min-max value of each (action, state) pair are obtained, hence the better algorithm's behavior is observed. The issue which needs further explanation is the way nodes are selected in the first stage (Choice). In UCT [13] the strategy of tree expansion is based on the previous simulation outcomes and visit counts. This way the method balances exploration and exploitation factors in order to find the most promising directions of tree growth. In each node $X$ if there exist child nodes (actions) which had not been yet chosen, one of them is selected at random. Otherwise (if all actions had been tried at least once already) the child node $k$ maximizing the following formula is selected:

$$X_j + C\sqrt{\frac{\ln n}{n_j}} \tag{1}$$

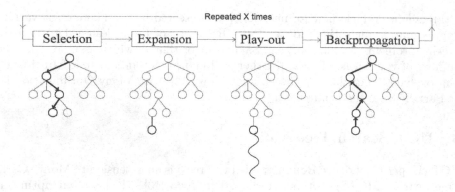

**Fig. 1.** Operational scheme of the UCT method (reproduced from [2])

where $X_j$ stands for the average score of simulations performed so far from $j$-th child node, $n_j$ is the number of times the $j$-th action (child node) was selected while visiting node $X$, $n$ is the total number of visits to node $X$ and $C$ is the exploration coefficient. In theory $C$ should be equal to $\sqrt{2}$, but experiments show that, for a given problem at hand, the best way is to test multiple values and select the most appropriate one. The most popular applications of UCT are those related to games, in particular the so-called General Game Playing [9,20] and Go [8].

While both VRP and UCT algorithm are commonly known and researched, there are no documented experiments on incorporating UCT into VRP. Thus, to the best of our knowledge, analysis made and described in this paper is very likely to be the first such attempt. Please note that it is the "capacitated" variant of the problem which is considered. Nonetheless, the presented approach may also be suitable for other formulations. In order to adapt UCT into CVRP, several key issues must be considered:

- Representation of the problem in a tree-like structure;
- A method of simulation results evaluation;
- Node selection strategy basing on simulation data.

A tree-like representation is a standard way of describing the current situation in many games, e.g. chess or checkers. As UCT was primary meant for gaming, a corresponding data structure was an obvious choice. However, for CVRP it is not straightforward and natural to translate the possible routes' configurations into tree structure. The first assumption made is that no baseline solution is used and instead routes are built from scratch, i.e. at the beginning all vehicles are located in the depot. This situation is represented by the root node. Going one level down the tree corresponds to assigning one of the clients to a (specific) vehicle. Thus, the height of the tree will be equal to the number of clients. Three methods of making such assignments were analyzed:

- **City-To-Vehicle (CTV)** - each node has $k$ child nodes, where $k$ stands for the number of vehicles. The $i$-th node corresponds to selection of the $i$-th vehicle and appending the closest client at end of its current route;

- **Vehicle-To-City (VTC)** - each node has $p$ child nodes, where $p$ stands for the number of unserved clients. The $i$-th node corresponds to the selection of the $i$-th unserved client and appending it at the end of the route of the currently closest vehicle;
- **Vehicle-To-City Optimized (VTCO)** - similar to VTC, but unserved client is not automatically assigned to the closest vehicle. Instead, all current routes (i.e. the partial routes of all vehicles) are analyzed in order to find the place minimizing the insertion cost, i.e. the increase of a total routes length due to the insertion of a new client. The client is then added at the specified place.

The first two methods are naive while the third one was created as a result of analysis of their weakness, i.e. proneness to client assignment order caused by the rule of always appending clients at the end of a specified route. VTCO became immune to this issue thanks to the best insertion place search.

Having resolved the first key issue, the next thing was to properly interpret the result of a simulation. While it is trivial in games where (in majority of them) the player can win, lose or draw, in CVRP one obtains a set of routes (one per vehicle) and their total length as a solution. In order for the UCT to expand the tree in the right directions, simulation results must be properly classified as good/poor or promising/unpromising. The problematic issue here is appropriate distinguishing of better routes from the worse ones. Assuming that an approximation of the optimal solution is known (which is the case of the benchmark problems used in this paper), the following formula of solution assessment is proposed:

$$f(x) = \begin{cases} 1 & \text{for } x < BEST \\ g(x) & \text{for } BEST \le x \le 2 \cdot BEST \\ 0 & \text{otherwise} \end{cases} \qquad (2)$$

where $x$ is the assessed solution's length, $g(x)$ is the inner evaluation function and $BEST$ is the optimal solution length or its approximation. The inner function defines the results' gradation pattern, i.e. the policy of promoting and degrading particular solutions. Three such functions

- **Hyperbolic:**

$$g(x) = \left( \frac{2 \cdot BEST}{x} - 1 \right)^2 \qquad (3)$$

- **Linear:**

$$g(x) = 2 - \frac{x}{BEST} \qquad (4)$$

- **Parabolic:**

$$g(x) = \frac{x}{BEST} \left( 2 - \frac{x}{BEST} \right) \qquad (5)$$

depicted in Fig. 2 were proposed by the authors. The hyperbolic function (3) concentrates on promoting the very best results while ignoring poor and average ones, the linear function (4) downgrades them proportionally, independent of a

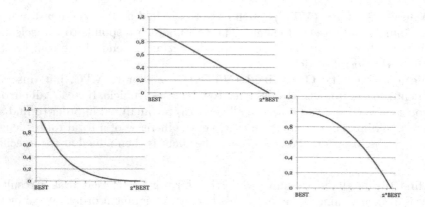

Fig. 2. Inner evaluation functions. From left: hyperbolic, linear and parabolic

distance to the optimal length and the parabolic one (5) has the widest range of solutions which are promoted (treated as promising). As will be seen in the results section the profile of the inner function has a crucial impact on the method's performance.

The last key issue is a suitable decision (node selection) strategy. After a specified number of simulations, a proper choice of the next node (client-vehicle assignment) must be made based on simulation data, i.e. fractions of won simulations in child nodes. Using those one of the child nodes is selected and added to the final solution. It also becomes a root node for the next series of simulations. Three possible strategies were analyzed: **best reward, simulations count, two-phase method**. The first two strategies are known approaches existing in game domain.

In the best reward strategy, a child with the highest ratio of won simulations to played simulations is chosen. In the simulations count strategy a child with the highest visits count is chosen.

The two-phase method was invented by the authors based on critical analysis of the usefulness of the first two node selection policies in CVRP domain. Please observe that in the game playing suboptimal moves are generally acceptable since the game can often still be won after making such a suboptimal choice. In CVRP, however, assigning a client to a wrong vehicle usually means that the optimal solution is no longer obtainable. In this respect, the best reward strategy or the simulation count policy (both basing on high averages of simulation results) will rather lead to a selection of a subtree containing many good solutions than a subtree containing the best solution and some poor ones. In effect, making wrong decision at the early stage of the algorithm will cost the loss of the optimal result. Two-phase method was designed to partially alleviate this problem. In the first phase child nodes are sorted in descending order based on their average reward values (i.e. won/played ratio). Then, P best children are taken into account in the second phase and among them the child node with the best (indivitwo) solution found during simulations is selected. This way both the most promising regions

**Table 1.** Test instances. In the instance name X-nY-kZ, X∈ {$A, B, P$} denotes type of a benchmark, Y its size, and Z the number of available vehicles

| Instance | #Clients | #Vehicles | Capacity | Best solution ($BEST$) |
|---|---|---|---|---|
| P-n19-k2 | 19 | 2 | 160 | 212.66 |
| P-n20-k2 | 20 | 2 | 160 | 220 |
| P-n21-k2 | 21 | 2 | 160 | 211 |
| P-n22-k2 | 22 | 2 | 160 | 216 |
| P-n22-k8 | 22 | 8 | 3000 | 603 |
| P-n23-k8 | 23 | 8 | 40 | 554 |
| B-n43-k6 | 43 | 6 | 100 | 747.54 |
| B-n45-k5 | 45 | 5 | 100 | 751 |
| A-n60-k9 | 60 | 9 | 100 | 1408 |
| P-n70-k10 | 70 | 10 | 135 | 834 |
| A-n80-k10 | 80 | 10 | 100 | 1764 |
| P-n101-k4 | 101 | 4 | 400 | 681 |

of a tree (in terms of average results) and the best indivitwo solution found in these regions are taken into account by the node selection policy.

# 4   Experimental Setup and Results

Experiments were conducted using selected instances of CVRP obtained from [17] whose basic parameters are presented in Table 1. The solution for one of the considered benchmark sets is presented in Fig. 3. The following algorithm parameters' settings were tested:

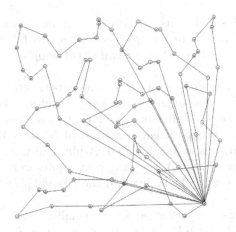

**Fig. 3.** Solution for the A-n80-k10 benchmark problem

- Assignment method: CTV, VTC, VTCO;
- Inner evaluation function $g(x)$ in (2): hyperbolic, linear, parabolic;
- Decision strategy: best reward, simulations count, two-phase method;
- Exploration factor $C$ in (1);

**Table 2.** Comparison of top-5 results (in terms of the average results of 50 tests) obtained with CTV, VTC and VTCO methods in test instance with 19 clients and 2 vehicles (P-n19-k2)

| Decision | $C$ | $AVG$ | $SD$ | $MIN$ | $MAX$ | Evaluation |
|---|---|---|---|---|---|---|
| City-To-Vehicle | | | | | | |
| Simulations | 0.5 | 294.719 | 21.752 | 248.764 | 343.572 | Hyperbolic |
| Simulations | 0.2 | 296.479 | 23.304 | 248.764 | 352.021 | Hyperbolic |
| Reward | 1 | 296.955 | 22.463 | 248.764 | 341.348 | Linear |
| Reward | 2 | 297.347 | 20.806 | 248.764 | 341.348 | Linear |
| Reward | 0.2 | 298.018 | 22.531 | 248.764 | 341.348 | Linear |
| Vehicle-To-City | | | | | | |
| Reward | 1 | 252.304 | 5.313 | 243.402 | 261.811 | Hyperbolic |
| Reward | 0.2 | 252.933 | 4.514 | 243.402 | 264.302 | Hyperbolic |
| Reward | 0.5 | 253.459 | 4.035 | 243.402 | 261.811 | Hyperbolic |
| Reward | 0.5 | 253.496 | 3.360 | 243.402 | 263.906 | Hyperbolic |
| Reward | 0.2 | 253.600 | 3.013 | 243.402 | 261.811 | Hyperbolic |
| Vehicle-To-City Optimized | | | | | | |
| Reward | 2 | 222.867 | 4.975 | 217.964 | 239.946 | Hyperbolic |
| Reward | 1.5 | 229.535 | 0 | 229.535 | 229.535 | Hyperbolic |
| Reward | 0.5 | 230.018 | 2.066 | 226.159 | 233.636 | Hyperbolic |
| Reward | 5 | 235.741 | 0 | 235.741 | 235.741 | Hyperbolic |
| Reward | 15 | 235.741 | 0 | 235.741 | 235.741 | Hyperbolic |

– Parameter $P$ in two-phase method: constant value ($P = 5$) or variable selection dependent on the number of clients ($P = 0.25 \cdot$ #Clients).

The number of UCT simulations performed on a single tree level was adaptive and equal to 50 000 on the first (top) level, then was falling linearly down to 5 000 on the penultimate level. Please recall that the number of levels equals the number of clients.

The following data was collected during the experiments: $AVG$ (the average value of results), $SD$ (the standard deviation of results), $MIN$ (the best result found), $MAX$ (the worst result found), $EFF$ (the number of times the $MIN$ result was found). Each experiment consisted of 50 tests based on which the above-mentioned statistics were calculated. Additionally, in the last experiment (summarized in Tables 4 and 5), the ranges of results were analyzed, e.g. 0.5% stands for the number of results falling into the interval $[MIN, MIN(1+0.5\%)]$.

The first set of tests was performed for the smallest (thus computationally inexpensive) benchmark P-n19-k2 and aimed at selection of appropriate ranges or exact settings of the main steering parameters. For each combination of (assignment method, $C$, inner evaluation function) 50 tests were performed for each of the three main problem mappings: CTV, VTC, VTCO. The values of $C$ belonged to the set $\{0.2, 0.5, 1.0, 1.5, 2.0, 5.0, 15.0\}$. The top-5 results for each mapping are presented in Table 2. The results show that VTCO outperforms both CTV and VTC representations. Not only the average scores are better but also stability, measured by standard deviation is clearly superior. Nevertheless obtained results are far from optimal. This led to analysis and design of two-phase method.

**Table 3.** Results of two-phase method with VTCO in test instance with 19 clients and 2 vehicles. Column EFF denotes the number of trials in which the MIN value was found in the respective 50 tests.

| Decision | $C$ | $AVG$ | $SD$ | $MIN$ | $MAX$ | Evaluation | EFF |
|---|---|---|---|---|---|---|---|
| Two-phase | 0.5 | 219.845 | 2.396 | 212.657 | 220.643 | Hyperbolic | 4 |
| Two-phase | 1.5 | 213.793 | 3.409 | 212.657 | 224.02 | Hyperbolic | 45 |
| Two-phase | 5 | 215.39 | 4.266 | 212.657 | 224.02 | Hyperbolic | 35 |
| Two-phase | 15 | 214.254 | 3.194 | 212.657 | 220.643 | Hyperbolic | 41 |
| Two-phase | 0.5 | 218.799 | 4.333 | 212.657 | 226.159 | Linear | 16 |
| Two-phase | 1.5 | 213.456 | 2.396 | 212.657 | 220.643 | Linear | 46 |
| Two-phase | 5 | 212.657 | 0 | 212.657 | 212.657 | Linear | 50 |
| Two-phase | 15 | 212.657 | 0 | 212.657 | 212.657 | Linear | 50 |

Based on these initial outcomes we decided to use the two-phase decision strategy and VTCO mapping as well as to skip parabolic inner evaluation function in further tests. We also restricted the tested values of $C$ parameter to the set $\{0.5, 1.5, 5.0, 15.0\}$. The results for each combination of ($C$, inner evaluation function) for two-phase VTCO are presented in Table 3. Two-phase method proved to be clearly the most efficient among tested approaches for the P-n19-k2 instance. The AVG values are within a few per cent points from the BEST value and in two cases (5, linear) and (15, linear) all 50 tests ended with the *BEST* score. While VTCO representation and two-phase decision strategy are clearly better than the competitive approaches, the inner evaluation functions do not have such leader. Apart from parabolic function, which gave very poor results, hyperbolic and linear functions have both their better and worse outcomes, however, more data is needed to form any firm conclusion in this matter.

Using the best configuration found, i.e. VTCO representation, two-phase method, hyperbolic and linear evaluation functions and high exploration factors (C=5, 15), the final tests were performed on an ensemble of test instances. The results are presented in Table 4.

The final experiments show that the two-phase VTCO method with proposed configuration performs well on a wide range of test instances. However, there is still room for potential improvement. First of all, it is difficult to tell the influence of P parameter on the test results. In small-size problems a difference between constant value and a calculated one ($P = 0.25 \cdot \#$Clients) is minimal. In larger sets no rule can be found as in some tests one option is clearly better while in others it is the other way round. As for the evaluation functions, the situation is similar. For both choices there exist test instances where one is visibly better than the other. Linear function seems to work better for large test instances. Generally speaking, higher exploration factor ($C$) values provide better results. On the other hand, there are still some cases where the situation is the opposite. Most probably this can be attributed to too large increase of this parameter and therefore some intermediate values of $C$ should be used instead. On a general note, the results support the claim that two-phase method can be regarded as efficient application of the UCT algorithm to solving CVRP. In order to compare

**Table 4.** Top-3 results of VTCO with two-phase method. Columns denoted $k\%$ present the numbers of results falling into the interval $[MIN, MIN(1 + k\%)]$

| Instance | C | P | Evaluation | AVG | SD | MIN | MAX | EFF | 0.5% | 1% | 2.5% | 5% |
|---|---|---|---|---|---|---|---|---|---|---|---|---|
| P-n19-k2 | 15 | 5 | Linear | 217.367 | 2.189 | 212.657 | 222.387 | 4 | 4 | 4 | 36 | 48 |
| | 15 | 4 | Linear | 217.378 | 2.735 | 212.657 | 222.627 | 7 | 7 | 7 | 38 | 48 |
| | 5 | 4 | Linear | 217.53 | 2.821 | 212.657 | 222.627 | 6 | 6 | 6 | 39 | 46 |
| P-n20-k2 | 5 | 5 | Hyperbolic | 217.416 | 0 | 217.416 | 217.416 | 50 | 50 | 50 | 50 | 50 |
| | 15 | 5 | Hyperbolic | 217.416 | 0 | 217.416 | 217.416 | 50 | 50 | 50 | 50 | 50 |
| | 5 | 5 | Linear | 217.469 | 0.212 | 217.416 | 218.309 | 50 | 50 | 50 | 50 | 50 |
| P-n21-k2 | 5 | 5 | Hyperbolic | 212.712 | 0 | 212.712 | 212.712 | 50 | 50 | 50 | 50 | 50 |
| | 5 | 5 | Linear | 212.712 | 0 | 212.712 | 212.712 | 50 | 50 | 50 | 50 | 50 |
| | 15 | 5 | Hyperbolic | 212.712 | 0 | 212.712 | 212.712 | 50 | 50 | 50 | 50 | 50 |
| | 15 | 5 | Linear | 212.712 | 0 | 212.712 | 212.712 | 50 | 50 | 50 | 50 | 50 |
| P-n22-k2 | 5 | 5 | Hyperbolic | 217.852 | 0 | 217.852 | 217.852 | 50 | 50 | 50 | 50 | 50 |
| | 5 | 5 | Linear | 217.852 | 0 | 217.852 | 217.852 | 50 | 50 | 50 | 50 | 50 |
| | 15 | 5 | Hyperbolic | 217.852 | 0 | 217.852 | 217.852 | 50 | 50 | 50 | 50 | 50 |
| | 15 | 5 | Linear | 217.852 | 0 | 217.852 | 217.852 | 50 | 50 | 50 | 50 | 50 |
| P-n22-k8 | 5 | 5 | Linear | 605.833 | 4.681 | 601.424 | 616.633 | 7 | 30 | 34 | 49 | 50 |
| | 5 | 5 | Hyperbolic | 606.441 | 4.743 | 601.424 | 616.639 | 7 | 23 | 31 | 48 | 50 |
| | 15 | 5 | Linear | 611.746 | 7.282 | 601.424 | 628.255 | 5 | 12 | 15 | 35 | 50 |
| P-n23-k8 | 5 | 5 | Hyperbolic | 534.665 | 5.033 | 531.174 | 555.088 | 17 | 33 | 38 | 47 | 50 |
| | 5 | 5 | Linear | 535.522 | 5.540 | 531.174 | 558.924 | 12 | 29 | 38 | 46 | 49 |
| | 15 | 5 | Hyperbolic | 536.290 | 7.687 | 531.174 | 575.287 | 5 | 21 | 39 | 47 | 48 |
| B-n43-k6 | 15 | 10 | Linear | 771.621 | 9.230 | 760.211 | 803.806 | 1 | 14 | 21 | 42 | 49 |
| | 5 | 10 | Linear | 771.624 | 7.843 | 756.949 | 790.680 | 1 | 4 | 9 | 39 | 50 |
| | 5 | 10 | Linear | 771.903 | 7.320 | 747.891 | 790.981 | 1 | 1 | 1 | 12 | 49 |
| B-n45-k5 | 5 | 5 | Hyperbolic | 773.888 | 6.690 | 760.315 | 790.599 | 1 | 4 | 9 | 38 | 50 |
| | 5 | 11 | Hyperbolic | 773.967 | 6.287 | 756.580 | 797.029 | 1 | 1 | 1 | 32 | 49 |
| | 5 | 11 | Linear | 775.486 | 6.262 | 763.029 | 790.939 | 1 | 4 | 11 | 42 | 50 |
| A-n60-k9 | 15 | 15 | Hyperbolic | 1460.932 | 30.257 | 1390.822 | 1533.801 | 1 | 2 | 3 | 4 | 27 |
| | 5 | 15 | Linear | 1461.015 | 30.044 | 1406.876 | 1524.494 | 1 | 2 | 7 | 13 | 34 |
| | 15 | 15 | Linear | 1465.919 | 27.417 | 1402.179 | 1526.206 | 1 | 1 | 2 | 8 | 29 |
| P-n70-k10 | 5 | 17 | Linear | 929.452 | 18.142 | 879.660 | 965.643 | 1 | 1 | 1 | 5 | 17 |
| | 5 | 17 | Hyperbolic | 933.520 | 17.375 | 898.108 | 969.764 | 1 | 2 | 3 | 11 | 37 |
| | 5 | 5 | Linear | 933.928 | 22.629 | 889.544 | 990.779 | 1 | 2 | 3 | 9 | 27 |
| A-n80-k10 | 5 | 20 | Hyperbolic | 1940.641 | 30.098 | 1889.752 | 2009.415 | 1 | 5 | 9 | 26 | 45 |
| | 15 | 20 | Hyperbolic | 1941.046 | 28.495 | 1883.619 | 2013.686 | 1 | 2 | 2 | 22 | 45 |
| | 5 | 20 | Linear | 1943.568 | 35.479 | 1882.487 | 2012.718 | 1 | 3 | 5 | 22 | 42 |
| P-n101-k4 | 5 | 5 | Hyperbolic | 730.058 | 6.899 | 712.358 | 748.911 | 1 | 1 | 2 | 26 | 49 |
| | 5 | 5 | Linear | 730.617 | 7.238 | 714.500 | 747.140 | 1 | 2 | 6 | 32 | 50 |
| | 15 | 5 | Hyperbolic | 732.697 | 6.322 | 718.433 | 748.421 | 1 | 2 | 7 | 35 | 50 |

the results with an external approach adequate tests with a simplified version of the 2-phase PSO method [18,19] were performed on same test instances. The results are presented in Table 5.

A comparison of results presented in Tables 4 and 5 shows that the overall results of 2PSO are a few percent points better than those of UCT, especially for larger problem instances. It should be noted, however, that 2PSO is a highly complex optimization approach which uses both PSO and 2-opt local optimization. Moreover, the differences are relatively small, even though only the baseline UCT implementation was tested in our approach, which did not include any enhancements, commonly used in games domain. Hence, we believe that proposed approach has potential which we plan to continue investigating in our future research.

**Table 5.** Test results of a simplified version of a 2-phase PSO approach

| Test | AVG | MIN | MAX | EFF | 0.5% | 1% | 2.5% | 5% |
|---|---|---|---|---|---|---|---|---|
| P-n19-k2 | 213.13 | 212.66 | 226.02 | 45 | 45 | 45 | 50 | 50 |
| P-n20-k2 | 219.94 | 219.94 | 219.94 | 50 | 50 | 50 | 50 | 50 |
| P-n21-k2 | 213.26 | 212.71 | 218.31 | 46 | 46 | 50 | 50 | 50 |
| P-n22-k2 | 220.05 | 217.85 | 225.68 | 38 | 38 | 49 | 49 | 50 |
| P-n22-k8 | 607.01 | 600.83 | 742.12 | 32 | 34 | 46 | 46 | 50 |
| P-n23-k8 | 531.17 | 531.17 | 531.17 | 50 | 50 | 50 | 50 | 50 |
| B-n43-k6 | 757.82 | 746.98 | 871.31 | 1 | 15 | 29 | 48 | 50 |
| B-n45-k5 | 766.72 | 754.22 | 921.59 | 3 | 13 | 20 | 43 | 50 |
| A-n60-k9 | 1415.51 | 1374.83 | 1700.44 | 1 | 3 | 11 | 42 | 49 |
| P-n70-k10 | 896.18 | 846.66 | 1132.65 | 1 | 1 | 2 | 18 | 39 |
| A-n80-k10 | 1888.69 | 1796.51 | 2272.38 | 1 | 1 | 4 | 13 | 38 |
| P-n101-k4 | 719.25 | 706.19 | 827.07 | 1 | 4 | 18 | 46 | 50 |

## 5    Conclusions and Future Work

In this paper, a novel approach to solving the NP-Hard CVRP based on the UCT method was proposed and experimentally evaluated. In order to adapt the UCT formulation to this new problem domain a two-phase node selection procedure, which breaks the classical UCT selection scheme, was proposed and experimentally verified. With larger exploration factors and appropriate choice of the internal evaluation function the results are very promising and only slightly inferior to those accomplished by a complex two-phase PSO algorithm.

In the future we plan to verify the efficiency of several UCT modifications (commonly used in games) in CVRP domain, e.g. Rapid Action Value Estimation [8] or weighted simulations [21]. We believe that application of the enhancements which proved to be efficient in games domain may lead to further improvement of the CVRP results and strengthen the claim about potential applicability of the UCT method beyond games.

**Acknowledgements.** The research was financed by the National Science Centre in Poland, based on the decision DEC-2012/07/B/ST6/01527.

## References

1. Breedam, A.V.: An analysis of the behavior of heuristics for the vehicle routing problem for a selection of problems with vehicle-related, customer-related, and time-related constraints. Ph.D. thesis, University of Antwerp, Belgium (1994)
2. Chaslot, G., Winands, M.H.M., Szita, I., van den Herik, H.J.: Cross-Entropy for Monte-Carlo Tree Search. ICGA Journal (3), 145–156 (2008)
3. Clarke, G., Wright, J.: Scheduling of vehicles from a central depot to a number of delivery points. Operations Research 12(4), 568–581 (1964)
4. Dantzig, G.B., Ramser, J.: The truck dispatching problem. Management Science 6(1), 80–91 (1959)
5. Dorigo, M.: Optimization, Learning and Natural Algorithms. Ph.D. thesis, Politecnico di Milano (1992)
6. Eilon, S., Watson-Gandy, C., Christofides, N.: Distribution Management: Mathematical Modelling and Practical Analysis, 1st edn., Griffin (January 1976)

7. Fisher, M., Jaikumar, R.: A Decomposition Algorithm for Large-scale Vehicle Routing. Paper / Department of Decision Sciences, Wharton School, University of Pennsylvania, Philadelphia, Pa. Dep. of Decision Sciences, Wharton School, Univ. of Pennsylvania (1978)

8. Gelly, S., Silver, D.: Monte-carlo tree search and rapid action value estimation in computer go. Artificial Intelligence 175(11), 1856–1875 (2011)

9. Genesereth, M.R., Love, N., Pell, B.: General game playing: Overview of the aaai competition. AI Magazine 26(2), 62–72 (2005)

10. Gillett, B., Miller, L.: A heuristic algorithm for the vehicle dispatch problem. Operations Research 22(2), 340–349 (1974)

11. Lenstra, J.K., Rinnooy Kan, A.R.K.: Complexity of vehicle routing and scheduling problems. Networks 11, 221–227 (1981)

12. Khouadjia, M.R., Alba, E., Jourdan, L., Talbi, E.-G.: Multi-Swarm Optimization for Dynamic Combinatorial Problems: A Case Study on Dynamic Vehicle Routing Problem. In: Dorigo, M., et al. (eds.) ANTS 2010. LNCS, vol. 6234, pp. 227–238. Springer, Heidelberg (2010)

13. Kocsis, L., Szepesvári, C.: Bandit based Monte-Carlo planning. In: Fürnkranz, J., Scheffer, T., Spiliopoulou, M. (eds.) ECML 2006. LNCS (LNAI), vol. 4212, pp. 282–293. Springer, Heidelberg (2006)

14. Mańdziuk, J.: Knowledge-Free and Learning-Based Methods in Intelligenet Game Playing. SCI, vol. 276. Springer, Heidelberg (2010)

15. Mańdziuk, J.: Towards cognitively-plausible game playing systems. IEEE Computational Intelligence Magazine 6(2), 38–51 (2011)

16. Christofides, N., Mingozz, A., Exact, P.T.: algorithms for the vehicle routing problem, based on spanning tree and shortest path relaxations. Mathematical Programming 20(1), 255–282 (1981)

17. Networking, N.: Emerging Optmization (2013), http://neo.lcc.uma.es/vrp/vrp-instances/capacitated-vrp-instances/

18. Okulewicz, M., Mańdziuk, J.: Application of Particle Swarm Optimization Algorithm to Dynamic Vehicle Routing Problem. In: Rutkowski, L., Korytkowski, M., Scherer, R., Tadeusiewicz, R., Zadeh, L.A., Zurada, J.M. (eds.) ICAISC 2013, Part II. LNCS(LNAI), vol. 7895, pp. 547–558. Springer, Heidelberg (2013)

19. Okulewicz, M., Mańdziuk, J.: Application of Particle Swarm Optimization Algorithm to Dynamic Vehicle Routing Problem. In: Proceedings of the 2nd IEEE Symposium on Computational Intelligence for Human-Like Intelligence, pp. 86–93. IEEE Press (2014)

20. Świechowski, M., Mańdziuk, J.: Self-adaptation of playing strategies in general game playing. IEEE Transactions on Computational Intelligence and AI in Games 6(4), 367–381 (2014)

21. Xie, F., Liur, Z.: Backpropagation modification in monte-carlo game tree search. In: IITA 2009 Proceedings of the 2009 Third International Symposium on Intelligent Information Technology Application, vol. 2, pp. 125–128 (2009)

# An Improved Magnetotactic Bacteria Moment Migration Optimization Algorithm

Hongwei Mo, Jingwen Ma, and Yanyan Zhao

Automation College, Harbin Engineering University, 150001 Harbin, China
honwei2004@126.com, {chuyanghainuo,ayanyan2011}@163.com

**Abstract.** Magnetotactic Bacteria Moment Migration Algorithm (MB-MMA) is a new bionic optimization algorithm. It is developed based on orginal MBOA, which is a new bio-inspired optimization algorithm based on a kind of polyphyletic group of prokaryotes with the characteristics of magnetotaxis that make them orient and swim along geomagnetic field lines. In the MBMMA, the moments of relative good solutions can migrate each other to enhance the diversity of the MBMMA. But it is easy to trap in local optimal for some problems. In this paper, the population is divided into two sub ones and moments can migrate between them. A moment differential mechanism is combined with the migration. It is compared with Differential Evolution and CLPSO on standard functions problems. The experiment results show that the improved MBMMA is much more effective than the MBMMA and the other compared algorithms.

**Keywords:** Magnetotactic bacteria · Nature inspired computing · Moment migration

## 1 Introduction

Optimization has been a kind of important problem in engineering for a long time. Today, many types of nature inspired algorithms(NIAs) have been proposed to solve optimization problems, including classical Genetic Algorithm, Ant Colony Optimization (ACO)[1], Particle Swarm Optimization (PSO)[2] and some new swarm intelligence optimization algorithms, such as Artificial Bee Colony (ABC)[3], Artificial Fish Swarm(AFS)[4], Bacterial Foraging Optimization algorithm(BFOA)[5], which mimics the ants, birds, bees, fish and bacteria behaviors, respectively. Although so many kinds of NIAs can be chosen to solve optimization problems, most of them have their own advantages because of different inspiration mechanisms of nature. But most of them also have similar disadvantages. So none of them can beat the other algorithms on all problems. It is always meaningful to find new ways for solving optimization problems.

In nature, magnetotactic bacteria (MTBs) is a special kind of bacteria which have many micro magnetic particles named magnetosome in their bodies. These magnetic particles can generate moments to guide the bacteria to swim along geomagnetic field lines of the earth[6][7]. Mo had proposed an optimization algorithm named Magnetotactic Bacteria Optimization Algorithm(MBOA) inspired

© Springer International Publishing Switzerland 2015
L. Rutkowski et al. (Eds.): ICAISC 2015, Part II, LNAI 9120, pp. 691–702, 2015.
DOI: 10.1007/978-3-319-19369-4_61

by the magnetotactic bacteria[8]. It has been tested on standard benchmark functions including multi-modal functions and compared with many popular and classical NIAs. MBOA shows better performance and good potential ability in solving optimization problems. It has been improved into several new variants of MBOA[9][10][11][12][13]. In [14], a new magnetotactic bacteria moment migration algorithm(MBMMA) is proposed. The moments of magnetosomes in MTBs are considered as the feature values of solutions in the MBMMA. The moments of relative good solutions can migrate to the other solutions. Such a migration strategy can enhance the diversity of solutions in the algorithm and make the algorithm be effective in solving optimization problems. Although the MBMMA has good ability on some tested problems, it still cannot solve some problems well. In this paper, we proposed an improved MBMMA in order to overcome the shortcomings of MBMMA.

## 2   Improved Magnetotactic Bacteria Moment Migration Algorithm

In the following we briefly describe the basic operators and the main steps of MBMMA. MBMMA mainly has three steps and three main operators including moment generation, moment migration, moment replacement. At the same time, we show the improvement strategies for the MBMMA.

### 2.1   Interaction Distance

In the algorithm, each solution is looked as a cell containing a magnetosome chain. Before obtaining the interaction energy of cells, the distance $d_{i,r}$ of two cells $x_i$ and $x_r$ calculated as follows:

$$d_{i,r} = x_i - x_r \tag{1}$$

Thus, we can get a distance matrix $D = [d_{1,r}, d_{2,r}, ..., d_{i,r}, ..., d_{N,r}]'$, where $r$ is a randomly chosen from $[1, N]$. $N$ is the size of cell population.

### 2.2   Moments Generation

Based on the distances among cells, the interaction energy $e_i$ between two cells is defined as:

$$e_i(t) = \left( \frac{d_{ij}(t)}{1 + c_1 * D_{i,r} + c_2 * d_{pq}(t)} \right)^3 \tag{2}$$

where $t$ is the current generation number, $c_1$ and $c_2$ are constants, $d_{ij}$ is one element of distance matrix $D$. $d_{pq}$ is a randomly selected element from $D$. $p$ and $r$ are randomly integers in $[1, N]$. $q \in [1, n]$ stands for one randomly selected dimension. $n$ is the dimensions of a cell. $D_{i,r}$ stands for the Euclidean distance between two cells $x_i, x_r$.

After obtaining interaction energy, the moments $m_i$ are generated as follows:

$$m_i(t) = \frac{e_i(t)}{B} \tag{3}$$

where $B$ is a constant.

Then the total moments of a cell is regulated as follows:

$$x_{i,j}(t) = x_{i,j}(t) + m_{r,q}(t) \tag{4}$$

where $m_{r,q}$ is randomly selected element from $m_i$.

## 2.3   Moments Migration

In MBMMA, after moments generation, the moments migration is realized as follows.

If $rand > 0.5$, the moments in the cell migrate as follows:

$$x_{i,j}(t+1) = x_{r,j}(t) \tag{5}$$

Otherwise,

$$x_{i,j}(t+1) = x_{i,j}(t) + (x_{cbest,q}(t) - x_{i,q}(t)) * rand \tag{6}$$

where $x_{cbest,q}$ is the $q$th dimension of the best individual in the current generation.

While in the improved MBMMA, the population is divided into two sub populations. One consists of the half better cells, another the half worse ones.

If $rand > 0.5$, the moments in the cell migrate as follows:

$$x_{i,j}(t+1) = x_{cbest,j}(t) \tag{7}$$

Otherwise, two cells $x_{r1}, x_{r2}$ are randomly chosen from population. $r1, r2$ are two randomly chosen integers from $[1, N/2]$. A cell is changed as follows:

$$x_{i,j}(t+1) = x_{best,j}(t) + (x_{r1,q}(t) - x_{r2,q}(t)) * rand \tag{8}$$

where $rand$ is a random number in interval (0,1).

## 2.4   Moments Replacement

After the moments migration, in the MBMMA, some cells with worse fitness are replaced as follows:

$$x_i(t+1) = m_{r,q}(t) * ((rand(1,n) - 1) * rand(1,n)) \tag{9}$$

where $m_{r,q}$ is the $q$th dimension of $m_r$. $r$ is a randomly integer in $[1, N]$. $q \in [1, n]$ stands for one randomly selected dimension. $rand(1, n)$ is a random vector with $n$ dimensions.

While, in the improved MBMMA, some cells with worse fitness are replaced as follows:

$$x_i(t+1) = x_i(t) + m_{r,q}(t) * rand(1,n) \tag{10}$$

Generally, a pseudo code of improved MBMMA is as follows:

I. Data Structures: Define the simple bounds, determination of
   algorithm parameters.
II. Initialization: Randomly create the initial population in
   the search space.
III. while stop criteria is not met
       for i=1:N
         interaction distance according to (1)
       end
       for i=1:N
         moments generation according to (2),(3) and (4)
       end
         evaluate the population according to fitness
       for i=N/2:N
         moments migration according to (7) and (8)
       end
         evaluate the population according to fitness
       for i=N/5:N
         moments MTS replacement to (10)
       end
         evaluate the population according to fitness
VI. End while

**Table 1.** Classical test functions used in experiments.(U: Unimodal, M: Multimodal, S: Separable, N: Non-Separable)

| Function | Range | D | C | Formulation |
|---|---|---|---|---|
| $f_1$ : Matyas | [-10, 10] | 2 | UN | $f(x) = 0.26(x_1^2 + x_2^2) - 0.48x_1x_2$ |
| $f_2$ : Schwefel2.22 | [-10, 10] | 30 | UN | $f(x) = \sum_{i=1}^{n} |x_i| + \prod_{i=1}^{n} |x_i|$ |
| $f_3$ : Schwefel1.2 | [-100, 100] | 30 | UN | $f(x) = \sum_{i=1}^{n}(\sum_{j=1}^{i} x_j)^2$ |
| $f_4$ : Step | [-100, 100] | 30 | US | $f(x) = \sum_{i=1}^{n}(|x_i + 0.5|)^2$ |
| $f_5$ : Quartic | [-1.28, 1.28] | 30 | US | $f(x) = \sum_{i=1}^{n} ix_i^4 + random[0, 1)$ |
| $f_6$ : Rosenbrock | [-30, 30] | 30 | UN | $f(x) = \sum_{i=1}^{n-1}[100(x_{i+1} - x_i^2)^2 + (x_i - 1)^2]$ |
| $f_7$ : Rastrigin | [-5.12, 5.12] | 30 | MS | $f(x) = \sum_{i=1}^{n}[x_i^2 - 10\cos(2\pi x_i) + 10]$ |
| $f_8$ : Generalized Schwefel | [-500, 500] | 30 | MS | $f(x) = \sum_{i=1}^{n} -x_i \sin\sqrt{|x_i|}$ |
| $f_9$ : Griewank | [-600, 600] | 30 | MN | $f(x) = \frac{1}{4000}\sum_{i=1}^{n} x_i^2 - \prod_{i=1}^{n}\cos(\frac{x_i}{\sqrt{i}}) + 1$ |
| $f_{10}$ : Ackley | [-32, 32] | 30 | MN | $f(x) = -20exp(-0.2\sqrt{\frac{1}{n}\sum_{i=1}^{n} x_i^2})$ $-exp(\frac{1}{n}\sum_{i=1}^{n}\cos(2\pi x_i)) + 20 + e$ |

In the algorithm, the value of test benchmark function is used as the fitness. one fifth of the population which has lower fitness is replaced by new generated cells.

**Table 2.** Statistical results on Unimodal Functions obtained by DE, CLPSO, MBMMA and IMBMMA

| Func. | | DE | CLPSO | MBMMA | IMBMMA |
|-------|--------|------|-------|-------|--------|
| $f_1$ | Mean | 1.2641e-204 | 6.5842e-09 | 0 | 0 |
| | Dev | 0 | 2.0931e-08 | 0 | 0 |
| | median | 5.3176e-206 | 4.1739e-13 | 0 | 0 |
| | best | 0 | 3.3867e-34 | 0 | 0 |
| | worst | 1.7784e-203 | 9.6012e-08 | 0 | 0 |
| | h | 1+ | 1+ | 0= | / |
| $f_2$ | Mean | 0.0016 | 20.9629 | 0 | 0 |
| | Dev | 0.0013 | 3.9494 | 0 | 0 |
| | median | 0.0015 | 20.2734 | 0 | 0 |
| | best | 1.0333e-04 | 12.7994 | 0 | 0 |
| | worst | 0.0064 | 30.9006 | 0 | 0 |
| | h | 1+ | 1+ | 0= | / |
| $f_3$ | Mean | 46.8152 | 2.6149e+04 | 0 | 0 |
| | Dev | 23.1241 | 7.3906e+03 | 0 | 0 |
| | median | 38.2941 | 2.4913e+04 | 0 | 0 |
| | best | 17.6039 | 1.3724e+04 | 0 | 0 |
| | worst | 119.6183 | 4.5889e+04 | 0 | 0 |
| | h | 1+ | 1+ | 0= | / |
| $f_4$ | Mean | 0 | 2.9387e+03 | 0 | 0 |
| | Dev | 0 | 949.3369 | 0 | 0 |
| | median | 0 | 2862 | 0 | 0 |
| | best | 0 | 1210 | 0 | 0 |
| | worst | 0 | 5134 | 0 | 0 |
| | h | 0= | 1+ | 0= | / |
| $f_5$ | Mean | 0.0144 | 1.3270 | 2.8279e-05 | **1.9774e-05** |
| | Dev | 0.0037 | 0.7225 | 2.6055e-05 | **2.0264e-05** |
| | median | 0.0150 | 1.0993 | 2.1164e-05 | **1.1981e-05** |
| | best | 0.0060 | 0.3309 | 3.2567e-06 | **3.0979e-07** |
| | worst | 0.0210 | 3.3995 | 1.2886e-04 | **7.3399e-05** |
| | h | 1+ | 1+ | 0= | / |
| $f_6$ | Mean | **21.1902** | 1.7652e+06 | 28.9798 | 25.4273 |
| | Dev | **0.7738** | 1.7708e+06 | 0.0507 | 0.6686 |
| | median | **21.1305** | 9.8036e+05 | 29.0000 | 25.2433 |
| | best | **19.3793** | 1.1663e+05 | 28.7962 | 24.8688 |
| | worst | **22.9060** | 7.5413e+06 | 29.0000 | 28.6371 |
| | h | 1− | 1+ | 1+ | / |
| sig-better | | 4 | 6 | 1 | |
| sig-worse | | 1 | 0 | 0 | |

"+", "=", "−"mean that IMBMMA is signicantly better, equal and signicantly worse, respectively, when compared with other algorithms.

**Table 3.** Statistical results on Unimodal Functions obtained by DE, CLPSO, MBMMA and IMBMMA

| Func. | | DE | CLPSO | MBMMA | IMBMMA |
|-------|--------|------------|-------------|--------------|----------------|
| $f_7$ | Mean | 190.0541 | 99.4707 | 0 | 0 |
| | Dev | 12.5012 | 19.8349 | 0 | 0 |
| | median | 191.1107 | 98.2333 | 0 | 0 |
| | best | 145.6027 | 59.6658 | 0 | 0 |
| | worst | 210.4773 | 138.7718 | 0 | 0 |
| | h | 1+ | 1+ | 0= | / |
| $f_8$ | Mean | -5.7955e+03 | -8.7606e+03 | -9.9582e+03 | **-1.2569e+04** |
| | Dev | 472.3437 | 659.8812 | 1.9797e+03 | **2.0267e-12** |
| | median | -5.8736e+03 | -8.7756e+03 | -1.0658e+04 | **-1.2569e+04** |
| | best | -6.8423e+03 | -1.0042e+04 | -1.1791e+04 | **-1.2569e+04** |
| | worst | -5.1008e+03 | -7.1358e+03 | -5.4177e+03 | **-1.2569e+04** |
| | h | 1+ | 1+ | 1+ | / |
| $f_9$ | Mean | 1.0341e-10 | 29.1105 | 0 | 0 |
| | Dev | 9.0362e-11 | 13.8523 | 0 | 0 |
| | median | 7.3054e-11 | 24.2522 | 0 | 0 |
| | best | 3.0156e-11 | 14.2609 | 0 | 0 |
| | worst | 4.7350e-10 | 77.8893 | 0 | 0 |
| | h | 1+ | 1+ | 0= | / |
| $f_{10}$ | Mean | 3.1034e-05 | 12.2771 | -8.8818e-1 | -8.8818e-16 |
| | Dev | 1.2140e-05 | 1.2696 | 0 | 0 |
| | median | 3.1484e-05 | 12.4802 | -8.8818e-16 | -8.8818e-16 |
| | best | 1.1829e-05 | 9.7830 | -8.8818e-16 | -8.8818e-16 |
| | worst | 7.3276e-05 | 146394 | -8.8818e-16 | -8.8818e-16 |
| | h | 1+ | 1+ | 0= | / |
| sig-better | | 4 | 4 | 1 | |
| sig-worse | | 0 | 0 | 0 | |

# 3    Simulation Results

To analyze the performance of improved MBMMA, the experiments are carried out on 10 benchmark functions. These benchmark functions are widely used in evaluating global numerical optimization algorithms. In this section, the benchmark functions are presented rstly. Secondly, the parameter settings of improved MBMMA and the algorithms chosen for comparison are presented. Finally, the simulation results obtained from different experimental studies are analyzed and discussed.

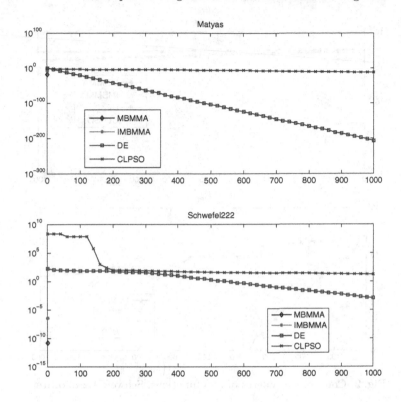

**Fig. 1.** Convergence curves of two functions: Matyas and Schwefel2.22

## 3.1   Benchmark Functions

A short description of 10 benchmark functions is shown in Tables 1. These functions can be classified into two groups. The rst six functions $f_1$–$f_6$ are unimodal functions. The unimodal functions here are used to test if improved MBMMA can maintain the fast-converging feature compared with the other methods. The next four functions $f_7$–$f_{10}$ are multimodal functions with many local optima. These functions can be used to test the global search ability of the algorithm in avoiding premature convergence.

Initial range, formulation, characteristics, the dimensions and parameters setting of these problems are listed in Tables 1. In Tables 1, characteristics of each function are given under the column titled C. In this column, M means that the function is multimodal, while U means that the function is unimodal. If the function is separable, abbreviation S is used to indicate this specification. Letter N refers that the function is non-separable. Dimensions of the problems we used can be found in Tables 1 under the column titled D.

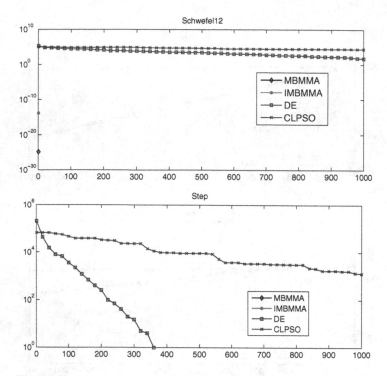

**Fig. 2.** Convergence curves of two functions: Schwefel1.2 and Step

## 3.2   Experiments Settings

In all experiments, during each run, a maximum number of 3000 generations is used. To reduce statistical errors, each test is repeated 30 times independently and the mean results are used in the comparisons. In order to make a fair comparison, the population size for the algorithms is uniformly set to 40.

The other specific parameters of the improved MBMMA and the other compared algorithms are given below:

DE Settings[12]: In DE, F is a real constant which affects the differential variation between two solutions and set to 0.5 in our experiments. Value of crossover rate, which controls the change of the diversity of the population, is chosen to be 0.9.

CLPSO Settings[13]: In our experiments, cognitive and social components are both set to 1.49445. Inertia weight, which determines how the previous velocity of the particle influences the velocity in the next iteration, is linearly from 0.9 to 0.2.

MBMMA setting: In the MBMMA, only the magnetic field $B$ needs to be set up as a parameter, $B=3$.

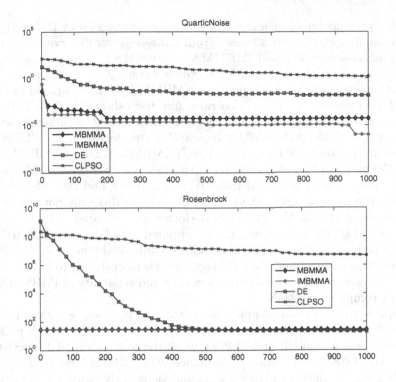

**Fig. 3.** Convergence curves of two functions: Quartic and Rosenbrock

Improved MBMMA(IMBMMA) setting: In the IMBMMA, only the magnetic field B needs to be set up as a parameter, $B=3$.

### 3.3   Experimental Results and Discussions

The compared results on test functions are listed in Tables 2-3, which are in terms of the mean, best and standard deviation of the solutions obtained in the 30 independent runs by each algorithm.

In order to determine whether the results obtained by improved MBMMA are statistically different from the results generated by other algorithms, the nonparametric Wilcoxon rank sum tests[14][15][16] are conducted between the improved MBMMA results and the best result achieved by the other three algorithms for each problem. The h values presented in the Tables 2-3 are the results of Wilcoxon rank sum tests. An h value of one indicates that the performances of the two algorithms are statistically different with 95% certainty, whereas h value of zero implies that the performances are not statistically different.

On unimodal functions $f_1$–$f_6$ , it is relatively easy to locate the global optimum. Therefore, we focus on comparing the performance of the algorithms in terms of solution accuracy.

Table 2 presents the mean and the best tness values yielded by IMBMMA and the compared methods after 30 runs. From the results, we observe that for unimodal functions, the proposed IMBMMA achieves the highest accuracy or has equal performace with the compared methods except $f_6$. In general, it clearly demonstrates the superior performance of IMBMMA to the compared methods. According to the results of Wilcoxon rank sum tests shown in Table 2, the differences between the results obtained by the IMBMMA and the other algorithms are statistically signicant. IMBMMA signicantly outperforms DE and CLPSO and has the same performance on $f_1$ to $f_3$. For $f_4$, IMBMMA, DE and MBMMA can obtain the best results and signicantly outperform CLPSO. IMBMMA has better performance on $f_5$ compared with DE and CLPSO, and the differences between the results obtained by the IMBMMA and MBMMA are not statistically signicant. For $f_6$, IMBMMA has better performance compared with CLPSO and MBMMA and shows worse performance compared with DE. Overall, IMBMMA performs better than the compared methods on unimodal functions.

On multimodal functions, the global optimum is more difcult to locate. Therefore, in the comparison, we study the accuracy and reliability of IMBMMA and the other compared methods.

Comparisons of solution accuracy on multimodal functions are given in Table 3. According to the results of Wilcoxon rank sum tests, IMBMMA performs signicantly better than DE and CLPSO on all the test multimodal functions $f_7$ to $f_{10}$. IMBMMA has the same performance with MBMMA on $f_7$, $f_9$, $f_{10}$. For $f_8$, IMBMMA can obtain the best results and signicantly outperforms the other three methods. Overall, IMBMMA performs better than the compared methods on multimodal functions.

In Figure 1, Figure 2 and Figure3, it can be seen that IMBMMA has the fastest convergence speed than all the other three algorithms.In total, as seen from the results, IMBMMA achieves better performance than compared methods in terms accuracy of global optima for unimodal as well as multimodal functions. IMBMMA produces better quality of optima and there are significant differences among IMBMMA and the compared algorithms.

## 4    Conclusions

In this paper, we propose an improved Magnetotactic Bacteria Moment Migration Algorithm (IMBMMA), which is based on the original idea of magnetotactic bacteria optimization algorithm(MBOA). IMBMMA adopts energy function to produce moments. It is compared with 3 optimization algorithms including DE, CLPSO and MBMMA. The experimental results show that it has superior performance on some optimization problems than DE,CLPSO and MBMMA. In future, IMBMMA will be improved to solve more complex problems including constrained optimization, multi-objective optimization and some real engineering problems.

**Acknowledgement.** This work is partially supported by the National Natural Science Foundation of China under Grant No.61075113, the Excellent Youth Foundation of Heilongjiang Province of China under Grant No. JC201212, the Fundamental Research Funds for the Central Universities No.HEUCFZ1209 and Harbin Excellent Discipline Leader, No. 2012RFXXG073.

# References

1. Dorigo, M., Manianiezzo, V., Colorni, A.: The ant system: optimization by a colony of cooperating agents. IEEE Trans. Sys. Man and Cybernetics 26, 1–13 (1996)
2. Kennedy, J., Eberhart, R.: Particle swarm optimization. In: IEEE Int. Conf. on Neural Networks, Piscataway, NJ, pp. 1942–1948 (1995)
3. Tereshko, V.: Reactiondiffusion model of a honeybee colonys foraging behaviour. In: Deb, K., Rudolph, G., Lutton, E., Merelo, J.J., Schoenauer, M., Schwefel, H.-P., Yao, X. (eds.) PPSN 2000. LNCS, vol. 1917, pp. 807–816. Springer, Heidelberg (2000)
4. Bastos, F., Carmelo, J.A., Lima, N., De Fernando, B.: A novel search algorithm based on fish school behavior. In: IEEE Int. Conf, on Systems, Man, and Cybernetics, Cingapura, Singapore, pp. 32–38 (2002)
5. Meller, S., Marchetto, J., Airaghi, S., Koumoutsakos, P.: Optimization based on bacterial chemotaxis. IEEE Trans. on Evolutionary Computation 6, 16–29 (2002)
6. Faivre, D., Schuler, D.: Magnetotactic bacteria and magnetosomes. Chem. Rev. 108, 4875–4898 (2008)
7. Mitchell, J.G., Kogure, K.: Bacterial motility: links to the environment and a driving force for microbial physics. FEMS Microbiol. Ecol. 55, 3–16 (2006)
8. Hongwei, M.: Research on magnetotactic bacteria optimization algorithm. In: The Fifth International Conference on Advanced Computational Intelligence (ICACI 2012), Nanjing, pp. 423–427 (2012)
9. Mo, H.W., Xu, L.F.: Magnetotactic bacteria optimization algorithm for multimodal optimization. In: IEEE Symposium on Swarm Intelligence (SIS), Sinpore, pp. 240–247 (2013)
10. Mo, H., Liu, L., Xu, L., Zhao, Y.: Performance research on magnetotactic bacteria optimization algorithm based on the best individual. In: The Sixth International Conference on Bio-Inspired Computing (BICTA 2014), Wuhan, China, pp. 318–322 (2014)
11. Mo, H., Geng, M.: Magnetotactic bacteria optimization algorithm based on best-rand scheme. In: 6th Naturei and Biologically Inspired Computing, Porto Portugal, pp. 59–64 (2014)
12. Mo, H., Liu, L.: Magnetotactic bacteria optimization algorithm based on best-target scheme. In: International Conference on Nature Computing and Fuzzy Knowledge, 2014, Xiamen, China, pp. 103–114 (2014)
13. Mo, H., Liu, L., Xu, L.: A power spectrum optimization algorithm inspired by magnetotactic bacteria. Neural Computing and Applications 25(7-8), 1823–1844 (2014)
14. Mo, H., Liu, L., Geng, M.: A new magnetotactic bacteria optimization algorithm based on moment migration. In: Tan, Y., Shi, Y., Coello, C.A.C. (eds.) ICSI 2014, Part I. LNCS, vol. 8794, pp. 103–114. Springer, Heidelberg (2014)
15. Beyer, H.G.: The Theory of Evolution Strategies. Springer, Heidelberg (2001)

16. Storn, R., Price, K.: Differential evolutuion-a simple and efficient heuristic for global optimization over continuous spaces. Journal of Global Optimization 11, 341–359 (1997)
17. Liang, J.J., Qin, A., Suganthan, K.P., Baskar, N., Comprehensive, S.: learning particle swarm optimizer for global optimization of multimodal functions. IEEE Trans. Evolut. Comput. 10, 281–295 (2006)
18. Garca, S., Fernndez, A., Luengo, J.: A study of statistical techniques and performance measures for genetics-based machine learning: accuracy and interpretability. Soft Comput. Fusion Found. Methodol. Appl. 13, 959–977 (2009)
19. Cai, Y.Q., Wang, J.H., Yin, J.: Learning-enhanced differential evolution for numerical optimization. Soft Comput. 16, 303–330 (2012)
20. Derrac, J., Garca, S., Molina, D., Herrera, F.: A practical tutorial on the use of nonparametric statistical tests as a methodology for comparing evolutionary and swarm intelligence algorithms. Swarm Evol. Comput. 1, 3–18 (2011)

# SBVRwiki a Web-Based Tool
# for Authoring of Business Rules

Grzegorz J. Nalepa[✉], Krzysztof Kluza, and Krzysztof Kaczor

AGH University of Science and Technology,
al. Mickiewicza 30, 30-059 Krakow, Poland
{gjn,kluza,kk}@agh.edu.pl

**Abstract.** In the paper, a new tool called SBVRwiki is proposed. It is an online collaborative solution that allows for distributed and incremental SBVR rule authoring for business analytics and users. It uses the Dokuwiki back-end for storage and unlimited version control, as well as user authentication. It supports creation of vocabularies, terms and rules in a transparent, user friendly fashion. Furthermore, it provides visualization and evaluation mechanisms for created rules. It is integrated with the Loki knowledge engineering platform that allows for on-the-fly conversion of the SBVR rule base and vocabularies to Prolog.

## 1 Introduction

SBVR (Semantics of Business Vocabulary and Business Rules) [19] is a mature standard for capturing expressive business rules [22]. It is also suitable to model their semantics, including vocabularies in a formalized way. Furthermore, it can be perceived as a useful tool in the communication of business analytics with business people. Finally, the set of vocabularies and rules described with the use of SBVR can be an important part of requirements specification from the classic software engineering methodologies.

However, an effective use of the SBVR notation is non trivial, as it requires certain knowledge engineering skills. Moreover, practical software tools are needed to support business analytics in the rule acquisition process. Such tools should allow for syntax checking, and automatic hinting, as well as preliminary evaluation of the resulting set of rules on the semantic level. Currently, there are only few specialized tools that offer proper SBVR authoring. In fact, this is one of the limiting factors in the wider adoption of the notation.

In order to improve this situation, in this paper, a new tool called *SBVRwiki* is discussed. It is an online collaborative solution that allows for distributed and incremental rule authoring for all participating parties. SBVRwiki uses the Dokuwiki[1] back-end for storage and unlimited version control, as well as user authentication. It supports creation of vocabularies, terms and rules in a transparent, user friendly fashion. Furthermore, it provides visualization and evaluation

---

The paper is supported from the *Prosecco* project funded by NCBR.

[1] A lightweight and opesource wiki engine, see: www.dokuwiki.org.

© Springer International Publishing Switzerland 2015
L. Rutkowski et al. (Eds.): ICAISC 2015, Part II, LNAI 9120, pp. 703–713, 2015.
DOI: 10.1007/978-3-319-19369-4_62

mechanisms for created rules. Besides basic syntax highlighting and checking, the tool allows for logical analysis. It is integrated with the Loki knowledge engineering platform [14,15] that allows for on-the-fly conversion of the SBVR rule base and vocabularies to Prolog. Use of the Prolog-based representation opens up possibilities of formalized analysis of SBVR rules on the semantic level. In this paper, the design and implementation of SBVRwiki is discussed. The preliminary version of the tool was first demonstrated in [7].

The rest of the paper is structured in the following way. In Sect. 2 available tools for SBVR are discussed, along with the motivation for our work. Then, in Sect. 3 the concept of the wiki-based collaborative knowledge engineering is discussed. In Sect. 4 the specification of the proposed SBVRwiki system is introduced, along with the main design assumptions. The main aspects of the implementation of the tool are also presented. The tool is evaluated using practical examples in Sect. 5. The paper is summarized in the final Sect. 6.

## 2  Related Work and Motivation

Among the currently existing SBVR tools one can distinguish editors that 1) support text-based creation of dictionaries and business rules providing syntax highlighting and suggestions; 2) modelers that allow for generating models based on SBVR compliant documents; as well as 3) tools that allow a user to import various models and transform them into SBVR syntax. Three representative examples of such tools are presented next.

RuleXpress[2] is a tool in which a user can define terms, facts and rules using natural language. It does not support SBVR natively but is compliant with and allows a user to import the SBVR definitions of concepts and rules. Moreover, it provides a mechanism of rule quality checking using simple lexical validation. Another advantage of the tool is the FactXpress module that allows for editing the SBVR facts. Although RuleXpress provides an additional web-based interface, it allows only for browsing the content of a knowledge base and does not support editing functionality.

SBeaVeR[3] is a plugin for the Eclipse integrated development environment. The tool supports defining terms, facts and business rules in Structured English, provides also syntax highlighting feature as well as allows for syntax verification. As it is implemented as an Eclipse IDE plugin, it is addressed rather to software engineers than to an average enterprise employee. SBeaVeR does not provide any web-based interface for collaborative content editing.

SBVR Lab 2.0[4] is a web application used to edit concepts and business rules using SBVR that provides syntax highlighting, simple verification and visualization features. However, the tool has several disadvantages, it does not support exporting of the created terms and rules to other formats or a local file. Moreover, all the specified elements are stored in one place and it is not possible to

[2] See: http://www.rulearts.com/RuleXpress.
[3] See: http://sbeaver.sourceforge.net.
[4] See: http://www.sbvr.co.

separate term glossary from facts or rules, as well as the application does not support dividing a rule set into subsets or categories. Thus, in the case of large, real world examples, rules are not transparent. Moreover, because of the online verification, the application slows down so much so that typing new rules or searching for a particular data becomes time consuming task.

Considering the limitations of the existing tools supporting SBVR, our primary motivation was to deliver a lightweight tool that would allow for easy creation of the SBVR knowledge bases even for inexperienced users. The tool should support the designer during the identification of the vocabulary and the rule creation process. It should offer syntax highlighting and hinting. Moreover, we opted for a web-based solution that would allow business users and analytics to collaborate using a familiar browser-based interface. To deliver such a solution, we decided to use our experience with Loki, a semantic wiki platform [14,15].

## 3   Collaborative Knowledge Engineering with Loki

The goal of Wiki systems is to provide a conceptually simple tool for massively collaborative online knowledge sharing and social communication. Such a system allows a user to build content in the form of the so-called wiki pages and upload media files. The structure of wikipages is simple and uses special wiki markup (e.g. for structuring content). What is important, is the fact that the pages are human readable plain text documents, making them more accessible than HTML or XML files. Another advantage of Wikis is the integrated version control mechanism, which allows for registering all subsequent versions of every page, as well as to see introduced differences. Thus, all wiki edits may be identified by user names and time stamps, and it is possible to recreate any previous state of the wiki at any given time. Moreover, for more complex application, wikis have access control mechanisms such as ACL (Access Control Lists).

Semantic wikis enrich the wiki technology by extending the content of wiki pages with semantic annotations, including relations and categories [1]. A very popular implementation is the SemanticMediaWiki [9] which enables a user to query the semantic knowledge stored in the wiki with a specific query language providing dynamic wiki pages. More complex systems allow for building an ontology of the domain to which the content of the wiki is related. In this way, semantic wikis turn regular wikis into knowledge management platforms [14]. Such systems are being used not only in knowledge engineering but also software engineering [10,3,4].

Loki [14,15] is an example of a semantic wiki that uses an expressive logic-based knowledge representation. It is based on Horn clauses for facts, relations and rules, as well as dynamic queries. It enhances both representation and inference features allowing for a complete rule framework in the wiki. PlWiki [13], the prototype implementation of Loki, uses Prolog-based representation on the knowledge base level. It allows for analyzing the knowledge stored in wiki using procedures specified in the wiki. Loki was developed as a set of independent plugins for a regular wiki engine called Dokuwiki, which is a flexible platform with low runtime requirements on the server side. It provides back-end for storage and unlimited version control, browser independent web-based operation, as well as user authentication. What makes it favorable from the developer point of view is the modular architecture in which most of the functionality of the system is implemented and integrated by a set of plugins. It allows for extending the basic functionality very easily. Moreover, Dokuwiki is distributed as free software.

Apart from the knowledge represented in the form of facts, relations and rules, companies also use procedures that can be represented as business process models. BPwiki [17] (Business Process Wiki) is a wiki plugin that allows for collaborative modeling and evaluation of business processes in BPMN [20] in a semantic wiki. It provides an architecture that supports a collaborative, gradual and evaluative design process. BPWiki is a tool integrated into Loki supporting business process design, involving not only modeling activities, but also supporting cooperation between developers, software architects and business analysts, as well as providing quality measurement tools for constant evaluation of processes in a distributed and collaborative wiki environment. Such a system combines the advantages of the semantic wiki systems with simple business process design environment. In BPwiki, business process models can be decomposed into subpages and namespaces corresponding to subtasks and subprocesses respectively, and every wiki page provides space for the discussion and comments.

Taking into account the above mentioned solutions, we decided to implement a new SBVR editor as a plugin to Loki. Such a plugin should be integrated with the base Loki system, as well as with the BPwiki plugin. In such a way complex specification of systems including both business processes and rules, along with concept vocabularies could be developed. The detailed specification and design decisions are described in the following section.

## 4    SBVRwiki Prototype

Based on the previously mentioned motivation as well as the availability of the Loki platform, the main requirements for the SBVRwiki plugin can be summarized as follows: 1) creation of a new SBVR project composed of vocabularies, facts, and rules using a set of predefined templates, 2) authoring of a project using structured vocabularies, with identified categories, 3) SBVR syntax verification and highlighting in text documents, as well as syntax hinting, 4) visualization of vocabularies and rules as UML class diagrams to boost the transparency of the knowledge base, 5) file export in the form of SBVR XMI, 6) knowledge interchange with the existing PlWiki platform, 7) integration with the BPwiki plugin for building combined specification of business rules and processes. 8) full support for the SBVR syntax, including at least binary facts, 9) ease of use including templates for creating new sets of facts and rules, and 10) constant assistance during the editing of the SBVR statements, including elimination of common errors, the use of undefined concepts, duplicated entries, etc.

In order to provide this functionality, number of design decisions for the system were taken. First of all the new tool is developed as a web-based solution for online SBVR authoring using a browser-based interface for maximum usability and accessibility. Moreover, a wiki system was selected as storage for the SBVR documents in order to provide collaborative authoring and full version control. Furthermore, we decided to adopt the Loki semantic wiki platform in order to process the SBVR description on the logical level, as well as integrate it with the BPwiki plugin. Using these requirements and assumptions, a prototype implementation of SBVRwiki was developed [23]. Here we describe an extended version of the prototype.

SBVRwiki is tightly integrated with Dokuwiki as a plugin implemented in PHP. In fact Dokuwiki offers several classes of plugins that allow for fine-grained processing of the wiki text. SBVRwiki implements two main plugin components for syntax and actions. The *SBVRwiki Action Plugin* is responsible for the file export in the XMI (XML) format. Moreover, it handles the user interface events, and extends the built-in Dokuwiki editor with number hooks that implement shortcuts for common SBVR constructs.

The process of creating a new SBVR projects is supported by a set of simple built in wizards that guide a user. The project starts with the definition of concepts, using them facts can be defined. Finally rules can be authored. Each of these categories is stored as a separate namespace in the wiki. The Lexer module in the plugin detects all the defined tokens which allows not only for proper syntax highlighting, but also for detecting the use of undefined concepts. Full interaction of the user with the plugin can be observed in Fig. 1

The *SBVRwiki Syntax Plugin* is used to enter SBVR expressions as wiki text. To make it possible, a special wiki markup `<sbvr>` is introduced. Using it a user can enter legal SBVR expressions. The plugin offers rich syntax highlighting, as presented in Fig. 4b. Moreover, vocabularies can be visualized with the dynamic translation to UML class diagrams. The diagrams are then rendered by the wiki using the PlantUML tool[5], see Fig. 2.

The use of wiki as the implementation platform has number of advantages. SBVR expressions can be stored in separate wiki pages, that can be simultaneously edited by a number of users. Moreover, these pages can contain additional information, such as comments, figures, media attachments, and hypertext links to other resources in the wiki and on the Web. The Loki engine can be programmed to select only the relevant parts of this knowledge on the fly. Such a model corresponds to a modularized rule base [11].

## 5   Use Cases and Evaluation

For evaluation purposes, several benchmark cases of SBVR knowledge bases were modeled. This includes the classic EU Rent case provided as a part of SBVR specification [19] and published as a separate document [21]. EU-Rent is a (fictional) international car rental business with operating companies in several countries. In each country it offers broadly the same kinds of cars, ranging from "economy" to "premium" although the mix of car models varies between countries. Rental

---

[5] See http://plantuml.sf.net.

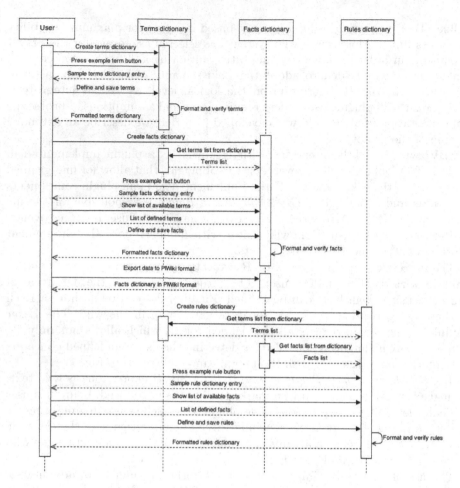

**Fig. 1.** User Interaction with SBVRwiki

prices also vary from country to country. It seeks repeat business, and positions itself to attract business customers. A rental customer may be an individual or an accredited member of a corporate customer. A car rental is a contract between EU-Rent and one person, the renter, who is responsible for payment for the rental and any other costs associated with the rental. Different models of cars are offered, organized into groups. All cars in a group are charged at the same rates within a country. A rental booking specifies: the car group required; the start and end dates/times of the rental; the EU-Rent branch from which the rental is to start. Visualization of parts of the vocabulary modeled by the wiki can be observed in Fig. 2.

Furthermore, SBVRwiki has been recently used in the Prosecco[6] research project as a tool for authoring SBVR rules. One of the objectives of the project is the development of system supporting management of SMEs using designing

---

[6] See: http://prosecco.agh.edu.pl.

**Rentals**

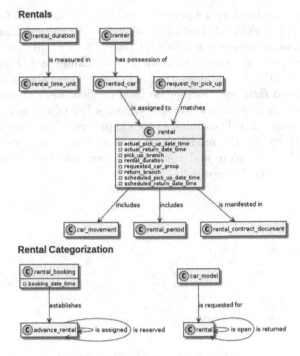

**Rental Categorization**

**Fig. 2.** EU Rent Fact Visualization

methods that will significantly improve BPM systems. Rules were selected as one of such methods and are used for precise and unequivocal specification of the decision processes. In the first phase of the project, the knowledge related to decision processes performed within the selected companies was acquired. During this phase, the first three steps of business rule systems development methodology were accomplished: *scoping*, *discovery* and *analysis*. Among those steps, the *discovery* and *analysis* steps played a crucial role. The knowledge discovery was made by a number of structured interviews with employees of the selected companies conducted by knowledge engineers and by deep analysis of the ISO documentation. Despite the fact that schema of interview was based on the proposal described in [5], the acquired knowledge required verification in order to avoid semantic mismatch. This verification was performed during the *analysis* step. For this purpose, the acquired knowledge was expressed with the help of SBVR representation and its modeling was supported by SBVRwiki. The main motivation behind SBVR was the fact that it is based on the modal logics and thus allows for clear representation in controlled natural language that can be easily readable by people without technical or mathematical skills. What is more, SBVRwiki is a web-based tool and therefore the created models may be shared on the Internet and accessed by ordinary web browser without installation of any sophisticated software. This may significantly reduce the time of knowledge verification as the analysts can work collaboratively whereas the knowledge engineers can fix the errors if they have only internet access.

The knowledge modeled in the project contains description of five companies and consists of 213 rules divided into 30 categories. All rules belonging to a certain category were defined in a single wiki page. In turn, all categories related to a single company were created in a single wiki namespace. Figure 3 depicts SBVRwiki in the editor (3a) and render (3b) modes where the facts are defined. The already defined facts may further be used for definition of rules. A built-in rule editor (see Figure 4a) allows for displaying a list of already existing facts and their quick usage in rule definitions by simple selecting them from the list. This significantly speeds the modeling process and prevents from using undefined elements. The complete and correct rules are rendered with the help of colored font as depicted in Figure 4b.

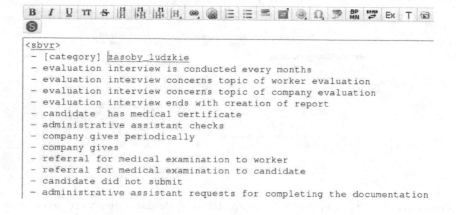

(a) Editor mode

## zasoby_ludzkie

1. evaluation interview *is conducted every* months
2. evaluation interview *concerns topic of* worker evaluation
3. evaluation interview *concerns topic of* company evaluation
4. evaluation interview *ends with creation of* report
5. candidate *has* medical certificate
6. administrative assistant *checks*
7. company *gives periodically*
8. company *gives*
9. referral for medical examination *to* worker
10. referral for medical examination *to* candidate
11. candidate *did not submit*
12. administrative assistant *requests for completing the documentation*

(b) Rendered output with syntax highlighting

**Fig. 3.** Definition of the facts in SBVRwiki

The here discussed prototype meets all the requirements identified at the beginning of Section 4. Moreover, with respect to existing tools discussed in

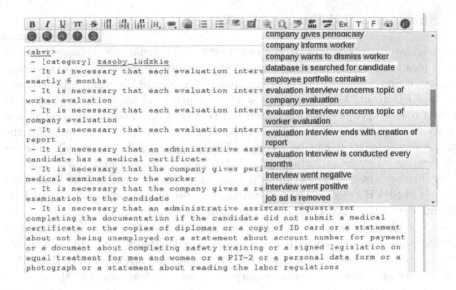

(a) Editor mode

**zasoby_ludzkie**

Create new SBVR project

[                ] ok

1. It is necessary that each evaluation interview *is conducted every* exactly **6** months
2. It is necessary that each evaluation interview *concerns topic of* the worker evaluation
3. It is necessary that each evaluation interview *concerns topic of* the company evaluation
4. It is necessary that each evaluation interview *ends with creation of* a report
5. It is necessary that an administrative assistant *checks* if the candidate *has* a medical certificate
6. It is necessary that the company *gives periodically* a referral for medical examination *to* the worker
7. It is necessary that the company *gives* a referral for medical examination *to* the candidate
8. It is necessary that an administrative assistant *requests for completing the documentation* if the candidate *did not submit* a medical certificate or the copies of diplomas or a copy of ID card or a statement about not being unemployed or a statement about account number for payment or a document about completing safety training or a signed legislation on equal treatment for men and women or a PIT-2 or a personal data form or a photograph or a statement about reading the labor regulations

(b) Rendered output

**Fig. 4.** Definition of the rules in SBVRwiki

Section 2 it can be observed that it offers fully interactive SBVR editing (unlike RuleXpress or SBVR Lab) and lightweight and fast online environment (unlike SBeaVeR). The current version of our tool does not support all aspects of the SBVR standard. However, it implements enough of its elements to allow users to create complex models of business rules in Structured English. Limitations include the lack of support for multi-argument facts, polymorphism or additional attributes for the expressions, dictionaries, facts and rules.

# 6    Summary and Future Work

The original contribution of the paper concerns SBVRwiki, a web-based collaborative tool allowing for rule-based knowledge authoring in SBVR. We presented the design and implementation of the tool and evaluated it using a benchmark use case EU Rent. Moreover, we discussed a practical application of the tool in the Prosecco project. We also discussed related work, and demonstrated how our tool is superior to the existing alternatives. As the tool is a plugin for the Loki semantic wiki, it can be integrated with the BPwiki plugin allowing for specification of systems including both business processes and rules. The use of the Prolog-based representation in Loki opens up possibilities of formalized analysis of SBVR rules on the semantic level. Our future work will also include full support of the SBVR standard and usability improvements.

We are also planning to continue our previous work on the integration of BPMN models in BPwiki with rule models in SBVRwiki, see [8,6]. When rule models are formalized, rule analysis can be performed automatically [12,2]. Ultimately we are considering more enterprise modeling features [16,18].

# References

1. Baumeister, J., Reutelshoefer, J., Puppe, F.: Knowwe: A semantic wiki for knowledge engineering. Applied Intelligence, 1–22 (2011), http://dx.doi.org/10.1007/s10489-010-0224-5, 10.1007/s10489-010-0224-5
2. Boehm, B.W.: Verifying and validating software requirements and design specifications. IEEE Software 1(1), 75–88 (1984)
3. Decker, B., Ras, E., Rech, J., Jaubert, P., Rieth, M.: Wiki-based stakeholder participation in requirements engineering. IEEE Software 24(2), 28–35 (2007)
4. Dengler, F., Vrandečič, D., Simperl, E.: Comparison of wiki-based process modeling systems. In: Proceedings of the 11th International Conference on Knowledge Management and Knowledge Technologies, i-KNOW 2011, pp. 30:1–30:4. ACM, New York (2011)
5. von Halle, B.: Business Rules Applied: Building Better Systems Using the Business Rules Approach. Wiley (2001)
6. Kluza, K., Kaczor, K., Nalepa, G.J.: Enriching business processes with rules using the Oryx BPMN editor. In: Rutkowski, L., Korytkowski, M., Scherer, R., Tadeusiewicz, R., Zadeh, L.A., Zurada, J.M. (eds.) ICAISC 2012, Part II. LNCS, vol. 7268, pp. 573–581. Springer, Heidelberg (2012), http://www.springerlink.com/content/u654r0m56882np77/
7. Kluza, K., Kutt, K., Woźniak, M.: SBVRwiki (tool presentation). In: Nalepa, G.J., Baumeister, J. (eds.) Proceedings of 10th Workshop on Knowledge Engineering and Software Engineering (KESE10) Co-located with 21st European Conference on Artificial Intelligence (ECAI 2014), Prague, Czech Republic (August 19, 2014), http://ceur-ws.org/Vol-1289/
8. Kluza, K., Maślanka, T., Nalepa, G.J., Ligęza, A.: Proposal of representing BPMN diagrams with XTT2-based business rules. In: Brazier, F.M.T., Nieuwenhuis, K., Pavlin, G., Warnier, M., Badica, C. (eds.) Intelligent Distributed Computing V. SCI, vol. 382, pp. 243–248. Springer, Heidelberg (2011), http://www.springerlink.com/content/d44n334p05772263/

9. Krötzsch, M., Vrandecic, D., Völkel, M., Haller, H., Studer, R.: Semantic wikipedia. Web Semantics 5, 251–261 (2007)
10. Liang, P., Avgeriou, P., Clerc, V.: Requirements reasoning for distributed requirements analysis using semantic wiki. In: 2009 Fourth IEEE International Conference on Global Software Engineering (ICGSE 2009), Limerick, Ireland, July 13-16, pp. 388–393. IEEE (2009)
11. Nalepa, G.J., Bobek, S., Ligęza, A., Kaczor, K.: Algorithms for rule inference in modularized rule bases. In: Bassiliades, N., Governatori, G., Paschke, A. (eds.) RuleML 2011 - Europe. LNCS, vol. 6826, pp. 305–312. Springer, Heidelberg (2011)
12. Nalepa, G.J., Bobek, S., Ligęza, A., Kaczor, K.: HalVA – rule analysis framework for XTT2 rules. In: Bassiliades, N., Governatori, G., Paschke, A. (eds.) RuleML 2011 - Europe. LNCS, vol. 6826, pp. 337–344. Springer, Heidelberg (2011), http://www.springerlink.com/content/c276374nh9682jm6/
13. Nalepa, G.J.: PlWiki – A generic semantic wiki architecture. In: Nguyen, N.T., Kowalczyk, R., Chen, S.-M. (eds.) ICCCI 2009. LNCS(LNAI), vol. 5796, pp. 345–356. Springer, Heidelberg (2009)
14. Nalepa, G.J.: Collective knowledge engineering with semantic wikis. Journal of Universal Computer Science 16(7), 1006–1023 (2010), http://www.jucs.org/jucs _16_7/collective_knowledge_engineering_with
15. Nalepa, G.J.: Loki – semantic wiki with logical knowledge representation. In: Nguyen, N.T. (ed.) Transactions on CCI III 2011. LNCS, vol. 6560, pp. 96–114. Springer, Heidelberg (2011), http://www.springerlink.com content/y91w134g03344376/
16. Nalepa, G.J., Kluza, K.: UML representation for rule-based application models with XTT2-based business rules. International Journal of Software Engineering and Knowledge Engineering (IJSEKE) 22(4), 485–524 (2012), http://www.worldscientific.com/doi/abs/10.1142/S021819401250012X
17. Nalepa, G.J., Kluza, K., Ciaputa, U.: Proposal of automation of the collaborative modeling and evaluation of business processes using a semantic wiki. In: Proceedings of the 17th IEEE International Conference on Emerging Technologies and Factory Automation, ETFA 2012, Kraków, Poland (September 28, 2012)
18. Nemuraite, L., Ceponiene, L., Vedricka, G.: Representation of business rules in UML and OCL models for developing information systems. The Practice of Enterprise Modeling 15, 182–196 (2008)
19. OMG: Semantics of Business Vocabulary and Business Rules (SBVR). Tech. Rep. dtc/06-03-02, Object Management Group (2006)
20. OMG: Business Process Model and Notation (BPMN): Version 2.0 specification. Tech. Rep. formal/2011-01-03, Object Management Group (January 2011)
21. OMG: SBVR Annex G - EU-Rent Example. Tech. rep., Object Management Group (2013)
22. Ross, R.G.: Principles of the Business Rule Approach, 1st edn. Addison-Wesley Professional (2003)
23. Woźniak, M.: Analysis of applications of rule-based tools in requirements engineering. Master's thesis, AGH UST (2013), Supervisor: G. J. Nalepa

# Classification in Sparse, High Dimensional Environments Applied to Distributed Systems Failure Prediction

José M. Navarro[✉], Hugo A. Parada G., and Juan C. Dueñas

Center for Open Middleware CTB Building, floor 1, Campus de Montegancedo,
Universidad Politécnica de Madrid, 28223, Pozuelo de Alarcón, Spain
{josemanuel.navarro,hugo.parada,
juancarlos.duenas}@centeropenmiddleware.com
http://www.centeropenmiddleware.com

**Abstract.** Network failures are still one of the main causes of distributed systems' lack of reliability. To overcome this problem we present an improvement over a failure prediction system, based on Elastic Net Logistic Regression and the application of rare events prediction techniques, able to work with sparse, high dimensional datasets. Specifically, we prove its stability, fine tune its hyperparameter and improve its industrial utility by showing that, with a slight change in dataset creation, it can also predict the location of a failure, a key asset when trying to take a proactive approach to failure management.

**Keywords:** Online failure prediction · Machine learning · System management · Automatic feature selection · Logistic regression · Multivariate prediction

## 1 Introduction

Big Data has revolutionized the way industry works. From data-driven decisions to breakthrough discoveries through the analysis of massive data, exploiting all the available data we generate is improving and broadening our capabilities in ways we hadn't thought possible. This discipline relies heavily on distributed systems, as the power of big data platforms, such as Hadoop, resides on the fact that they scale horizontally, working over a grid of commodity hardware-based nodes that are coordinated to work together. In terms of failures, a distributed system has an inherent complexity due to the sheer amount of devices it is composed of, including all the network layer to connect the different hosts. In fact, the network layer is one of the key factors in ensuring fault transparency. In its book, Tanenbaum [21] remarks how "reliable networks simply do not exist" and that is the exact point we tackle in this paper. To do so, we employ a discipline called Proactive Fault Management. And, more specifically, one part

Center for Open Middleware is a Joint Technology Center created by Universidad Politécnica de Madrid, Produban, Isban and Banco Santander.

© Springer International Publishing Switzerland 2015
L. Rutkowski et al. (Eds.): ICAISC 2015, Part II, LNAI 9120, pp. 714–726, 2015.
DOI: 10.1007/978-3-319-19369-4_63

of it called Online Failure Prediction, which deals with identifying situations that will possibly cause a failure. We improve a method we already proposed in [10], validating and expanding it, to achieve a reliable failure prediction model for a large infrastructure IT network which could be integrated in a Reliability Solution for companies. Our key contribution is showing how this model can predict not only the possible occurrence of a failure, which has already been extensively treated [4][7][8], but where it will happen. This feature is crucial in ensuring fault transparency in large scale systems, as knowing that an event will happen will often not be enough to pinpoint it and correct it before it affects service quality. At the point of writing this paper, the authors are only aware of few efforts in this direction. What sets apart our paper from them is the dataset we use and its associated method. Our data present two problems: first, data sparsity, which happens when (assuming binary data) most of the dataset matrix is composed of zeroes (event absences), instead of ones (event presences). This situation is a tricky one for most usual machine learning classification methods, such as logistic regression, where they tend to overfit or not estimate correctly the target variable [15]. The second problem in our environment is the high complexity of our data: we start with more than 1300 input variables. This situation can also affect the performance of classification methods so we are forced to select which variables are actually affecting each event in each node. Genetic Algorithms (a technique used by other works in this area) suffer an exponential increase when the number of elements to mutate is large, so we consider our approach is more valid for this kind of environment.

Apart from the main contribution we exposed before, in this paper we show several additional contributions related to the problem at hand: we test the randomness introduced by our method's preprocessing phase, fine-tune the method's hyperparameters and analyze the effect of adding resource consumption information. In the following sections we analyze the current works in Online Failure Prediction, briefly comment the methodology we used, expose the scenario we worked on, detail the experiments we carried on and the results they yielded, draw some conclusions and expose future lines of work that could span from this research.

## 2 Related Work

In terms of the industrial problem we are solving, the current state of the art [22] shows that network hardware failures are still a key aspect of distributed systems reliability, which justifies the practical aspects of our contribution. In fact, [23][24][25] independently perform an analysis of failure logs from distributed systems and conclude that network errors are often present on them, along with closely correlated failures. So we now turn to which techniques have been applied to solve similar problems as the one we deal with. Dealing with critical systems, whose correct performance must be ensured, we can not rely on reactive approaches to maintain their reliability. We, thus, turn to Online Failure Prediction, which takes a proactive approach to system reliability [1]. This discipline covers from data cleaning and preprocessing to the actual creation of the prediction model. Though most of the work has been carried out in the creation phase, there have also been efforts in the preprocessing phase, such as [16][17]. They filter and clean data to improve a prediction model's performance. There has also been a whole array of techniques applied to predicting failures in distributed system and computing clusters, where the works of Watanabe et al. [2][3], who show a method of pattern learning for the prediction of failures, Salfner et al. [6][11], who model a system using Semihidden Markov Models and add fuzzy logic to the OFP scenario, and, specially, Zheng et al. [5][7] are the main ones. The latter authors have worked for several years with the IBM Blue Gene supercomputer and have a long streak of papers related to the issue at hand. Apart from these main works, there have also been separate relevant works in the area, like the combination of time series analysis and fault trees [4], an anomaly detection approach to OFP [9], the creation of failure clusters measured by their correlation [8] and the research presented in [13] by Pitakrat et al., that proposes a full framework for OFP and tests several Machine Learning methods such as Naive Bayes or Support Vector Machines to test their performance. Compared to all these previous works, our proposal has a key feature that separates it from them and a minor one: the major one is that we include location awareness in our prediction, this is, our method not only predicts which event will happen but also indicates its node. As we stated in the introduction, the only work that also addresses this point is the one present in [12] by Zheng et al. The main advantage of our system over Zheng's work is its ability to work in a difficult environment (a high dimensional sparse one) and produce valid, sparse outputs. Additionally, the final model we train in this paper has two different data input sources: system events and system resource consumption. Most previous works only have a single kind of data source. As a side note, even though some works we have discussed do not model distributed systems' networks they are still relevant to our research, taken that, from an OFP point of view, they can be modelled using similar techniques.

The model creation algorithm we use, which we presented in [10], uses several approaches found on literature to work in the complex environment we defined before. Regarding the high dimensionality of the problem, we use a technique called Elastic Net, proposed by Zou et al. in [14], which allows the user to select the amount of two regularization types he prefers. This feature expands the capabilities of our model to use the optimal regularization amount for each event by optimizing it through a grid search. To work with sparse data we follow the advices given in [15], which suggests to trim the amount of zero (absences of the target event) instances included in the training dataset to optimize logistic regression performance. Summed up, the algorithm we use follows these steps:

1. Dataset randomized separation in training, validation and test datasets with zero-trimming to fulfill a user defined zero-to-one proportion.
2. For each event to model, train eight different logistic regression models with different regularization options (L1 and L2 proportions). Each of them is also internally cross validated to optimize model complexity and perform feature selection.

3. Test each model against the validation dataset to select the best performing one.
4. Test the best model against the test dataset to obtain its score.

Using this model we showed in [10] how we were able to successfully predict system failures in a distributed system. In this work we validate and expand it to improve its usefulness for real Big Data environments. This method also fulfills the requirements given in [20] by Trendafilov et al., as it produces a robust, sparse solution and allows the method to work over large datasets with a minimal amount of valuable data without producing a linear combination of variables as a results of the anaylisis, which allows for an easy interpretation of the output. Other interesting approaches to sparse data found in literature are the method proposed by Chickering and Heckerman in [18], which adapts standard machine learning methods to work with dense matrices instead of sparse ones and the work of Li et al. in [19], which is centered around calculating data distances from a conditional sample of the dataset. They are not directly appliable to our method, though, as we do not use distances and to modify the elastic net to work with dense matrices is out of our research scope.

## 3  Experiments and Results

### 3.1  Scenario

As in [10], the dataset we worked with was obtained from a big Spanish bank's IT network infrastructure. It was composed of two different structures, an intranet and an internet-connected section. They were a total of 36 devices, whose structure was divided in:

- Eighteen switches.
- Two DNS.
- Four routers.
- Six firewalls.
- Six load balancers.

We had system event logs from every device listed before, comprising a total of 22823 training instances. These events were categorized by their severity, the node they happened in, their timestamp and the event ID. Our key objective is to be able to forecast as many events' occurrence as possible in the distributed systems environment with the highest attainable detail. Some examples of these events were the three critical events present on our dataset: "'99% CPU usage threshold has been surpassed"', "'A single device is down or is not reachable by SNMP messages"' and "'A chassis is down or is not reachable by SNMP messages."'.

We will now describe our main contributions divided in the different experiments we carried out and their results. The first two ones are related to validating and fine tuning the model we use, and the last two experiments expand and improve the forecasting capabilities of our method, adding a new prediction dimension and testing new information sources.

## 3.2   Preprocessing Method Stability

We started by testing the preprocessing method of our algorithm in terms of its stability. As it randomizes the dataset before splitting it, it may introduce random noise in the output models' performance. To check the validity of this assertion, we ran the algorithm for every model twenty times, as we considered this number of iterations large enough to show any random behaviour that could harm the models' performance, and analyzed each created model.

The first metric we extracted was the amount of created models for each iteration. The minimum amount was 53 and the maximum one was 56, with a mean ± standard deviation of 54.15 ± 0.9333 models. So, in terms of amount of created models, the algorithm is stable. This, indeed, does not seem like a large rate, unless it affects some critical events, which could lead to not modelling a key objective. This is not the case, though, as the only one that has a slightly high standard deviation is associated with a manual change in the network, as experts confirmed us. Lastly, we checked each model's performance in terms of average F-score and its standard deviation. Fig. 1 shows the obtained results. Only six events suffer from a deviation of more than 0.1 and none of them is a critical one. On the other hand, most models have a very narrow deviation bar and keep a stable score over the whole process. We, thus, consider the stability of the preprocessing phase sufficiently justified for the environment we are working in. We strongly emphasize the fact that this approach has only been proven to be suitable for this specific dataset. The large deviation found in the six anomalous events would lead us to deduce there are separate information clusters in those data, where modelling one cluster is not enough to forecast other ones. We would have to test this assertion to confirm it. Had more models presented this behaviour, we would have had to change our preprocessing phase to a more complex one, such as k-fold cross validation. Taking into account the number of models to be created, short computation time for each model's creation is a requisite; so we prefer simpler methods whenever they perform good enough. We consider, thus, that our preprocessing phase stability has been proven.

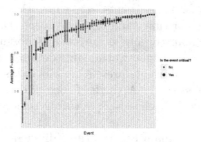

**Fig. 1.** Average F-score for 20 iterations of the algorithm for each event. Critical events and most non-critical ones have a stable performance.

## 3.3    Zero to One Proportion Study

Another step in the preprocessing phase is the pruning of excessive zeroes in the dataset, according to the advice given by King et al. in [15], where they suggest to start from a 1 to 1 proportion and start adding zeroes from there. In order to find the optimal amount of zeroes to add to our datasets, we performed a grid search over the zero proportion value, running our elastic net model for values ranging from 1 to 15. To compare its performance with a standard elastic net logistic regression approach, we also ran the algorithm without varying the zero to one proportion in the dataset. Considering that the stability of the preprocessing method was proven in the previous section, we only ran each model once. We will now compare each result in three dimensions: number of created models, computation time and average peformance for every event. We set as the main criteria for proportion selection the highest possible performance, unless the disparity in one of the other two metrics were unreasonably high.

For the first two metrics, created models with an f-score higher than zero and computation time, the distribution can be found on Table 1. In terms of created models, apart from an outlier at 1 to 1 proportion, a growing tendency is clear in the data. Assuming the second value is spurious, the optimal zero to one value would be 13, though the other ones are close to it. Regarding computation time, the total execution time we can draw two main points: the first one is that pruning zeroes has a drastic effect on computation time, reducing it by a factor of, at least, 22. The second conclusion is that, when pruning zeroes, computation time is linearly related with the zero to one proportion. As every value is, at least, 22 times less than the standard total execution time, we conclude that every zero to one proportion is equally valid for our experiment and, at the same time, justify the use of zero pruning as a time saving tool.

**Table 1.** Secondary metrics for each zero to one proportion

| Proportion amount | No | 1 | 2 | 3 | 4 | 5 | 6 | 7 | 8 | 9 | 10 | 11 | 12 | 13 | 14 | 15 |
|---|---|---|---|---|---|---|---|---|---|---|---|---|---|---|---|---|
| Created models | 36 | 44 | 37 | 37 | 37 | 38 | 40 | 41 | 40 | 42 | 42 | 41 | 42 | 43 | 41 | 42 |
| Computation time (s) | 8275 | 57 | 97 | 113 | 132 | 153 | 176 | 194 | 214 | 230 | 255 | 275 | 298 | 324 | 340 | 362 |

But the time saving that we have just studied would be completely irrelevant if performance decreased when zeroes are pruned. To study it, we plot in Fig. 2 the average F-score of models created with each proportion value. In this figure the model with a proportion of 3 to 1 of zeroes to ones is the one with best overall average performance, combined with a really low standard deviation. This settles the discussion of which proportion to use. As the amount of created models is not too low and the performance is the best one, 3 is the appropriate proportion of zeroes for our dataset.

We want to comment on the possibility of adding the optimization of this hyperparameter to the actual model training. We declined this option for two main reasons: computation time and dataset limitations. Adding another grid search over the already convoluted process of multiple cross validations would have imposed a burden on training time and would have forced us to split our dataset into even more groups. As it is not a specially big one, we preferred to obtain a suboptimal, though usually good value for the zero proportion and take that as a fixed value for every experiment.

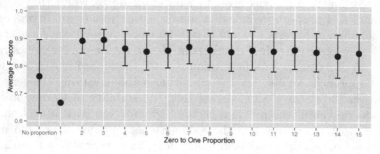

**Fig. 2.** Average F-score for each zero to one proportion

### 3.4 Locality Awareness

Now that we know that our algorithm is fine tuned and validated, we set on to improve its industrial interest by adding another prediction dimension to it. This section is divided in three different experiments, all of them related to locality and being able to predict where a failure will happen. We will compare them through the number of correctly created models, the distribution of the obtained performances and, numerically, by the average F-score and its standard deviation. We will first state the purpose of each experiment and then compare them all together. The first experiment is the most simple one and starts from the hypothesis that the occurrence of an event in a specific node is only affected by previous events on that node. To test this hypothesis, we divided our dataset in as many different datasets as nodes were in the system, and trained the elastic net model for each event on each node separately under the assumption previously stated.

The second and third experiments are, in essence, just a subtle change in the dataset preparation, but they completely alter the working environment and can enhance the practical utility of the models. This change we speak of deals with changing the input and output variables. Previously, our input features where "Event X has happened in the system" and the variable to predict was "Event Y will happen in the system". Now, when preprocessing our data, we deal with new input variables: we divide the $n$ previous features in $\beta \leq \alpha n$ variables, where $\alpha$ indicates the number of nodes in the system and $W$ the chosen observation window, where each feature now indicates "Event A has happened in Node $\psi$ in the last $W$ minutes". Inversely, our output now changes to "Event B will happen in node $\psi'$ in the next $W'$ minutes". With this subtle change, without altering the actual algorithm in any way, our problem changes (the number of variables is greatly increased), forcing our model to work in a much harder environment, but we also increase its industrial utility. The difference between these two experiments is that in the second one, both the input and the output are divided by locality, whereas in the third one, only the output is divided by node, this is, it takes as a input just what has happened in the system and tries to predict where and which event will happen.

We can see in Table 2 the amount of models that yielded a higher than zero performance (measured in F-score), their average F-score and their standard deviation for the three experiments. The first observation we can draw from the first table is the drastic decrease in the percentage of created models over the total possible amount. We see two possible reasons for this behaviour, comparing it with the high amount percentage of created models obtained in previous experiments: the first one would be to assume that more data is needed as the number of features is increased. But we must also take into account the conditions of previous and current experiments: modelling events on a system, a steady pattern in a node can make an event predictable, even if its appearances are random in other nodes. Predicting failures in a specific node only yields models for nodes that actually exhibit a certain pattern. Thus, this severe decrease in created model percentage is not, necessarily, an ominous sign, as it may just indicate that not every event in every node exhibits any kind of pattern. Apart from this remark, we can also state that events in a node are influenced by events in other nodes. This is, each node is not an isolated system. This supports the correlated error conclusion that is exposed in [24] and [25]. If we had to choose which model better predicts our environment, we would tend to choose the option that yields better models as a whole, which is the second one, the Complex Input Complex Output Node Aware Elastic Net.

**Table 2.** Performance metrics for each node-awareness experiment

|  | Single Nodes | Complex Input Complex Output | Simple Input Complex Output |
|---|---|---|---|
| Models Amount | 1140 | 1336 | 1336 |
| Correctly Created Models Amount | 420 | 601 | 564 |
| Correctly Created Models Proportion | 36.84% | 44.99% | 42.21% |
| Average F-score | 0.826 | 0.931 | 0.9254 |
| F-score Standard Deviation | 0.201 | 0.102 | 0.108 |

To further study how each different option affects the models' performance, in Fig. 3 we show the distribution of the F-scores obtained for each option, which allows us to study in finer detail each option's effect. This figure reinforces the conclusions we previously drew. Events in a certain node are affected by events in different nodes and both experiments of locality are satisfactory, though, at the expense of computation time, performance can be slightly improved (and the amount of information extracted from the model) by using a complex input, this is, using every event in every node as a single input feature.

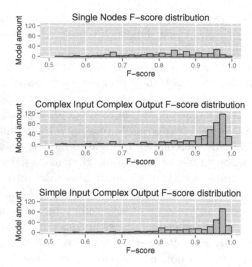

**Fig. 3.** F-score distribution for each node-awareness experiment.

## 3.5  Resource Consumption Addition

Once we have proved that the elastic net logistic regression model is able to forecast failures and their location in a much harder environment than previous experiments, we then tried to improve the node-aware model by adding resource consumption information. The information we had available was CPU, memory, hard drive and network interfaces usage, expressed in time series with a five-minute sampling frequency. For every node to forecast failures in, we add its resources consumption as new input features. We ran several experiments with different ways of creating these new variables, taking the Simple Input Complex Output Node-Aware Elastic Net model we trained in the previous section. We used this model to reduce the number of input variables, which would allow new input variables to have a greater influence on the model. The first experiments we ran added one single resource to the model, but it did not affect the model's performance in any remarkable way, so we will not include their detailed results in this work. The two experiments that provided good results were the following ones, each of them centered around different ways to transform a time series to ensure its stationarity: first, using a technique called E-Divisive with Medians proposed by James et al. in [26] to detect changes in the mean of a time series, we divided each resource information in two different time series: one with its mean value for every moment and one with the variation over the mean for each specific moment. The second experiment we ran took a different approach: instead of separating each time series, the input we fed to the algorithm was the difference of the time series, this is, for any specific moment $T$, the value of the series in $T$ substracted the value of the series in $T - 1$. This difference in input variables shows two underlying assumptions about our dataset: in the first experiment we consider that changes in the mean as well as variations over

**Table 3.** Performance metrics for each resource consumption experiment

|  | Separated Resource Usage | Differenced Resource Usage |
|---|---|---|
| *Models Amount* | 1336 | 1336 |
| *Correctly Created Models Amount* | 554 | 546 |
| *Correctly Created Models Proportion* | 41.47% | 40.87% |
| *Average F-score* | 0.946 | 0.929 |
| *F-score Standard Deviation* | 0.089 | 0.104 |

the mean are significant to the forecasting of events, whereas in the second one we only consider that the value difference after a certain moment is what holds useful information. We now present the results of these two experiments. Looking at Table 3 allows us to study in detail these models' performance. The main conclusion to draw would be that events in this system do not seem to be affected by resource consumption or that there are no examples of resource-affected events in our dataset. Actually, average F-score for the first experiment is higher than previous ones, but at the expense of less created models. We consider this variation part of the normal randomness of the model, though.

## 4  Conclusions

In this research paper we started from the basis that network errors are still an important problem in assuring distributed systems reliability. To tackle this problem we presented a series of experiments over a machine learning model that stands as a suitable algorithm for performing Online Failure Prediction in a distributed system, in order to take a proactive approach to system failures. In the first two experiment sections we validate the algorithm's preprocessing method and find, using a grid search, the optimal value of the only fixed parameter it was using. Then we present how our model can predict, not only what event will happen, but where it will do so, greatly improving the industrial utility of this model in large-scale distributed systems. We also show how just knowing which events occurred in the system is enough to predict their location with almost the same performance as the more computing-intensive option. Lastly, we analyzed whether adding resource consumption information to the model improved its performance in any significant way. Results showed that it did not and, furthermore, taking into account the storage and computational costs of using resource information, we would discourage their usage for this environment. Again, we must state that this analysis and advices are completely dataset-dependent, e.g. if most events were caused by resource consumption sudden peaks, our advice would be the complete opposite.

Summed up, we have presented a viable model for distributed systems failure prediction that could be incorporated in an Online Failure Prediction system. Additionally, we have also shown that our model is able to work in situations that are hard for standard algorithms but usual for network environments: a large number of devices and very infrequent failures.

## 5  Future Work

There are two possible lines of work that span from this research. One would be to, now that it has been tested and improved, compare our model's performance with some more complex state of the art algorithms, like Artificial Neural Networks or Semihidden Markov Models [6]. Such a change would be interesting because of the way certain models behave: modelling a system with a Semihidden Markov model, for example, would allow us to specify with more certainty when an event would happen, but we would also need an external, previous, feature selection method to filter the input. Indeed, that would be the case with most algorithms, unless we were to use one that includes feature selection in the optimization process, we would need to take two steps (feature selection and model creation) to replicate the work of our algorithm, which increases the dimensions to explore and test. The second line of work we could go for takes a more industrial approach to extending this model: after proving that our algorithm correctly models large-scale networks, we would like to apply it to higher levels of infrastructure: servers, virtual machines, application layers... to try and find correlations between errors and provide a complete solution to ensuring a distributed system's reliability.

**Acknowledgments.** The authors would like to express their gratitude to PRODUBAN who inspired and motivated this challenge as a real business case and provided all necessary assistance to carry out this work.

## References

1. Salfner, F., Lenk, M., Malek, M.: A Survey of Online Failure Prediction Methods. ACM Computing Surveys (CSUR) 42(3), 10 (2010)
2. Watanabe, Y., Otsuka, H., Sonoda, M., Kikuchi, S., Matsumoto, Y.: Online Failure Prediction in Cloud Datacenters by Real-Time Message Pattern Learning. In: 2012 IEEE 4th International Conference on Cloud Computing Technology and Science (CloudCom), pp. 504–511 (2012)
3. Sonoda, M., Watanabe, Y., Matsumoto, Y.: Prediction of Failure Occurrence Time Based on System Log Message Pattern Learning. In: 2012 IEEE Network Operations and Management Symposium (NOMS), pp. 578–581 (2012)
4. Chalermarrewong, T., Achalakul, T., See, S.C.W.: Failure Prediction of Data Centers Using Time Series and Fault Tree Analysis. In: 2012 IEEE 18th International Conference on Parallel and Distributed Systems (ICPADS), pp. 794–799 (2012)
5. Guan, Q., Zhang, Z., Fu, S.: A Failure Detection and Prediction Mechanism for Enhancing Dependability of Data Centers. International Journal of Computer Theory and Engineering 4(5) (2012)
6. Salfner, F., Malek, M.: Using Hidden Semi-Markov Models for Effective Online Failure Prediction. In: 26th IEEE International Symposium on Reliable Distributed Systems, SRDS 2007, pp. 161–174. IEEE (2007)

7. Guan, Q., Zhang, Z., Fu, S.: Proactive Failure Management by Integrated Unsupervised and Semi-Supervised Learning for Dependable Cloud Systems. In: 2011 Sixth International Conference on Availability, Reliability and Security (ARES), pp. 83–90 (2011)

8. Fu, S., Xu, C.-Z.: Exploring Event Correlation for Failure Prediction in Coalitions of Clusters. In: Proceedings of the 2007 ACM/IEEE Conference on Supercomputing, SC 2007, pp. 1–12. IEEE (2007)

9. Guan, Q., Fu, S.: Adaptive Anomaly Identification by Exploring Metric Subspace in Cloud Computing Infrastructures. In: 2013 IEEE 32nd International Symposium on Reliable Distributed Systems (SRDS). IEEE (2013)

10. Navarro, J.M., Hugo, A., Parada, G., Dueñas, J.C.: System Failure Prediction through Rare-Events Elastic-Net Logistic Regression. In: 2014 International Conference on Artificial Intelligence, Modelling and Simulation, AIMS (2014)

11. Troger, P., Becker, F., Salfner, F.: FuzzTrees-Failure Analysis with Uncertainties. In: 2013 IEEE 19th Pacific Rim International Symposium on Dependable Computing (PRDC). IEEE (2013)

12. Zheng, Z., Lan, Z., Gupta, R., Coghlan, S., Beckman, P.: A Practical Failure Prediction with Location and Lead Time for Blue Gene/p. In: 2010 International Conference on Dependable Systems and Networks Workshops (DSN-W), pp. 15–22. IEEE (2010)

13. Pitakrat, T., et al.: A Framework for System Event Classification and Prediction by Means of Machine Learning (2014)

14. Zou, H., Hastie, T.: Regularization and Variable Selection via the Elastic Net. Journal of the Royal Statistical Society: Series B (Statistical Methodology) 67(2), 301–320 (2005)

15. King, G., Zeng, L.: Logistic Regression in Rare Events Data. Political Analysis 9(2), 137–163 (2001)

16. Yu, L., Zheng, Z., Lan, Z., Jones, T., Brandt, J.M., Gentile, A.C.: Filtering Log Data: Finding the Needles in the Haystack. In: 2012 42nd Annual IEEE/IFIP International Conference on Dependable Systems and Networks (DSN), pp. 1–12 (2012)

17. Zheng, Z., Lan, Z., Park, B.H., Geist, A.: System Log Pre-Processing to Improve Failure Prediction. In: IEEE/IFIP International Conference on Dependable Systems Networks, DSN 2009, pp. 572–577 (2009)

18. Chickering, D.M., Heckerman, D.: Fast Learning from Sparse Data. In: Proceedings of the Fifteenth Conference on Uncertainty in Artificial Intelligence, pp. 109–115. Morgan Kaufmann Publishers Inc. (1999)

19. Li, P., Church, K.W., Hastie, T.J.: Conditional Random Sampling: A Sketch-Based Sampling Technique for Sparse Data. In: Advances in Neural Information Processing Systems, pp. 873–880 (2006)

20. Trendafilov, N., Kleinsteuber, M., Zou, H.: Sparse Matrices in Data Analysis. Computational Statistics 29(3–4), 403–405 (2014)

21. Tanenbaum, A.S., van Steen, M.: Distributed Systems: Principles and Paradigms. Pearson Prentice Hall, Upper Saddle River (2007)

22. Ahmed, W., Wu, Y.W.: A Survey on Reliability in Distributed Systems. Journal of Computer and System Sciences 79(8), 1243–1255 (2013)

23. Schroeder, B., Gibson, G.A.: A large-scale study of failures in high-performance computing systems. IEEE Transactions on Dependable and Secure Computing 7(4), 337–350 (2010)

24. Kondo, D., Andrzejak, A., Anderson, D.P.: On correlated availability in internet-distributed systems. In: Proceedings of the 2008 9th IEEE/ACM International Conference on Grid Computing. IEEE Computer Society (2008)
25. Gallet, M., Yigitbasi, N., Javadi, B., Kondo, D., Iosup, A., Epema, D.: A model for space-correlated failures in large-scale distributed systems. In: D'Ambra, P., Guarracino, M., Talia, D. (eds.) Euro-Par 2010, Part I. LNCS, vol. 6271, pp. 88–100. Springer, Heidelberg (2010)
26. James, N.A., Kejariwal, A., Matteson, D.S.: Leveraging Cloud Data to Mitigate User Experience from 'Breaking Bad', November 28 (2014), http://arxiv.org/pdf/1411.7955.pdf

# Balanced Support Vector Regression

Marcin Orchel[✉]

Department of Computer Science, AGH University of Science and Technology,
Al. Mickiewicza 30, 30-059 Kraków, Poland
marcin@orchel.pl

**Abstract.** We propose a novel idea of regression – balancing the distances from a regression function to all examples. We created a method, called balanced support vector regression (balanced SVR) in which we incorporated this idea to support vector regression (SVR) by adding an equality constraint to the SVR optimization problem. We implemented our method for two versions of SVR: $\varepsilon$-insensitive support vector regression ($\varepsilon$-SVR) and $\delta$ support vector regression ($\delta$-SVR). We performed preliminary tests comparing the proposed method with SVR on real world data sets and achieved the improved generalization performance for suboptimal values of $\varepsilon$ and $\delta$ with the similar overall generalization performance.

**Keywords:** Support vector machines · Regression · Prior knowledge

The most popular problems in machine learning are classification and regression. For classification, the goal is to separate data of different classes, for regression the goal is to fit the function to the data. The support vector machines (SVM) are the popular machine learning methods for solving classification and regression problems invented by Vapnik; the standard soft margin version of SVM for solving classification problems was proposed in [1]. The SVM method for solving regression problems, was proposed in [3]. It is the $\varepsilon$-SVR version, which minimizes the distances from a regression function to examples lying outside the $\varepsilon$ bands. Recently, an alternative SVR method was proposed, [12], called $\delta$-SVR, which transforms the problem of regression to classification, and solves the classification problem by using standard SVM. In the same paper, the authors find out that the $\delta$-SVR has better generalization performance related to $\delta$ than $\varepsilon$-SVR with regard to $\varepsilon$, which means that $\delta$-SVR is able to achieve better generalization performance for suboptimal values of $\delta$ than $\varepsilon$-SVR for suboptimal values of $\varepsilon$. Such characteristic could be potentially useful to speed up the training by using suboptimal values of $\varepsilon$ and $\delta$.

We propose a novel idea of balancing the distances between all examples and a regression function – the sum of distances below the regression function should be equal to the sum of distances above the regression function. The main motivation for this constraint is that it is already fulfilled for the least squares (LS) regression. So the goal is to incorporate balancing to the SVM methods by adding one constraint to the SVM optimization problems.

© Springer International Publishing Switzerland 2015
L. Rutkowski et al. (Eds.): ICAISC 2015, Part II, LNAI 9120, pp. 727–738, 2015.
DOI: 10.1007/978-3-319-19369-4_64

We use the following notation: the subscript $r$ stands for regression, while the subscript $c$ for classification, for example $y_r^i$, the *red* subscript near the vector stands for reduced and it is a vector without the last coefficient of the original vector.

The outline of the paper is as follows. First, we will show the idea of the balanced regression. Then we will present the new optimization problems for balanced SVR. Finally, we will show experiments and results.

# 1    Balanced Regression

The standard regression in the probability setting is defined for a joint distribution $X, Y$ based on the conditional mean function,

$$r(X) = E(Y|X) \ , \tag{1}$$

where $X$ is a multivariate random variable, $Y$ is a random variable. For a set of events $e_i$ for X, for $i = 1 \ldots n$ we can define random variables $Y_i - r(e_i)$, where $Y_i = (Y|e_i)$. After summing them, we can compute the expected value

$$E\left(\sum_{i=1}^{n} Y_i - r(e_i)\right) = \sum_{i=1}^{n} E(Y_i - r(e_i)) = \sum_{i=1}^{n} EY_i - r(e_i) = 0 \ . \tag{2}$$

The (2) is a necessary condition that must be met by the regression function. The idea of the proposed method is to use the (2) in the sample space as a requirement for the approximated regression function. In practice, we have only sample data, the training data $x_i$ are mapped to regression values $y_r^i$ respectively, so we do not know the expected values of $Y_i$. What we can do is to estimate the requirement (2) as

$$\sum_{i=1}^{n} y_r^i - g(x_i) = 0 \ , \tag{3}$$

where $g(\cdot)$ is the estimated regression function. The geometric interpretation of the (3) is balancing data below and above the regression function – the sum of all distances below the regression function should be equal to the sum of all distances above the regression function. We can imagine that based only on the condition (3), we can get multiple solutions, some of them not necessarily with good fitness to the data. So the new requirement alone is not enough to build a regression estimator.

We may notice that the LS regression balances the data due to the following proposition.

**Proposition 1.** *The LS regression balances the data.*

*Proof.* The solution for a LS regression for the function $w \cdot x + b$ and the sample data is normal equations in the form:

$$bn + \sum_{j=1}^{m} w_j \sum_{k=1}^{n} x_k^j = \sum_{k=1}^{n} y_i \tag{4}$$

for $i = 0$, and

$$\sum_{k=1}^{n} bx_k^i + \sum_{j=1}^{m} w_j \sum_{k=1}^{n} x_k^i x_k^j = \sum_{k=1}^{n} y_i x_k^i \qquad (5)$$

for $i = 1, \ldots, m$. We can notice that the equation (4) is equivalent to (3).    □

Others regression methods may not balance the data, for example ridge regression or SVR. For the ridge regression methods, we get the balanced solution for a big value of the $C$ parameter, when we are close to the LS solution. For the $\varepsilon$-SVR method, we get close solutions to the LS ones for the $L_2$ norm variant, and $\varepsilon = 0$. Then the $\varepsilon$-SVR method becomes the ridge regression method. For the least absolute deviations (LAD) regression, the regression line will go through some of two points in the case of unique solutions, so we might not get the balanced solutions at all (the LAD regression could be approximated by $\varepsilon$-SVR with $L_1$ norm, with $\varepsilon = 0$ and high value of the $C$). We can notice that the balanced solutions are more visually appealing – they seem to be better fitted to the data, Fig. 1. We expect that for more points the solutions will be closer to each other and to the optimal solution.

For $\varepsilon$-SVR, generally increasing value of $\varepsilon$ leads to more flat solutions with reduced number of support vectors and worse performance, finally the number of support vectors becomes 0. The $\delta$-SVR overcomes this effect. We expect the similar effect with added balancing. For $\varepsilon$-SVR, when we sum the constraints we have

$$-n\varepsilon - \sum_{i=1}^{n} \xi_r^{i*} \le \sum_{i=1}^{n} y_r^i - g\left(\boldsymbol{x}_i\right) \le n\varepsilon + \sum_{i=1}^{n} \xi_r^i \qquad (6)$$

Notice that we have better bounds for balancing when errors from outside $\varepsilon$ bands are smaller and when $\varepsilon$ is smaller.

We measure the performance of balancing by the parameter $p_b$, which we define as

$$p_b := \left| \sum_{i=1}^{n} y_r^i - g\left(\boldsymbol{x}_i\right) \right| . \qquad (7)$$

For balanced solutions, $p_b = 0$, Fig. 1.

We list some advantages of different loss functions for a regression estimation. For a joint distribution of $X, Y$ we can write that

$$Y = r\left(X\right) + h\left(X, Y\right) . \qquad (8)$$

The function $r(X) = E(Y|X)$ minimizes the mean square deviation $E\left(Y - r\left(X\right)\right)^2$. So the LS loss might be preferred. In [15], page 92, authors propose more statistically motivated reasons for the LS loss functions when the conditional distributions $P(\cdot|\boldsymbol{x})$ have finite variances. For some specific cases, for example symmetric distributions, or for data with extreme outliers, other losses might be preferred. In [14], page 80, authors state that the LS loss is preferred for the Gaussian noise due to the maximum likelihood estimation, but in practice we do not know the noise model and other losses might be good as well. They also state the disadvantage of the LS

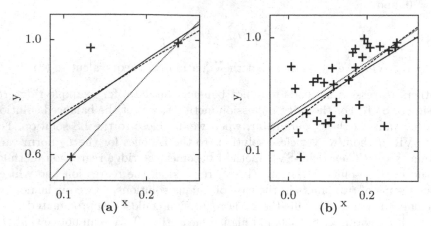

**Fig. 1.** Balanced Regression. Points—examples, solid lines—LS regression solutions, dashed lines—balanced LAD regression solutions, dotted lines—LAD regression solutions. (a) For 3 points. The balancing performance, $p_b$ is: for the LS solution, $p_b = 0$, for the balanced LAD regression, $p_b = 0$, for the LAD regression, $p_b = 0.1$. (b) For 30 points. The balancing performance, $p_b$ is: for the LS solution, $p_b = 0$, for the balanced LAD regression, $p_b = 0$, for the LAD regression, $p_b = 0.04$.

loss, that it does not lead to robust estimators. The robustness is the property of the $\varepsilon$-insensitive loss. Moreover the $\varepsilon$-insensitive loss has a property of returning sparse values. Balancing can be seen as the property of the function which minimizes the sum of loss functions values for some data.

We can notice that balancing does not change the type of mentioned loss functions, for the LS loss we have

$$L\left(\boldsymbol{x}, y, g\left(\boldsymbol{x}\right)\right) = \left(y - g\left(\boldsymbol{x}\right)\right)^2 \tag{9}$$

We have a function space of functions in the form (24), we can incorporate the balance constraint (3) to (9) by substituting $b$ and we get a form of the loss

$$L\left(\boldsymbol{x}, y, g\left(\boldsymbol{x}\right)\right) = \left(y - y' - g_r\left(\boldsymbol{x} + \boldsymbol{x}'\right)\right)^2 \tag{10}$$

where $\boldsymbol{x}'$, $y'$ are some constants, and $g_r$ belongs to a set of functions without the $b$, $g_r = \boldsymbol{w} \cdot \boldsymbol{x}$. So we get the LS loss but for different function space and with translated data. Similarly for the $\varepsilon$-insensitive loss function, we get

$$L\left(\boldsymbol{x}, y, g\left(\boldsymbol{x}\right)\right) = \max\left(0, |y - y' - g_r\left(\boldsymbol{x} + \boldsymbol{x}'\right)| - \varepsilon\right) . \tag{11}$$

The $\delta$-SVR transforms the problem from regression to classification, and uses the hinge loss for the classification which is

$$L\left(\boldsymbol{x}, y, g\left(\boldsymbol{x}\right)\right) = \max\left(0, 1 - y_c h\left(\boldsymbol{x}\right)\right) , \tag{12}$$

where $h(\boldsymbol{x})$ is defined in (30), $y_c \in \{-1, 1\}$. Motivated by the relation between $\delta$-SVR and $\varepsilon$-SVR stated in [13], we will show that this loss is equivalent to the dynamic version of the $\epsilon$-insensitive loss. For the points with class 1 the loss can be written as

$$\max\left(0, 1 - \boldsymbol{w_{c,red}} \cdot \boldsymbol{x} - w_c^{m+1}\left(y_r + \delta\right) - b_c\right) \tag{13}$$

After reformulation we have

$$\max\left(0, w_c^{m+1}\left(\frac{1}{w_c^{m+1}} - \frac{\boldsymbol{w_{c,red}}}{w_c^{m+1}} \cdot \boldsymbol{x} - y_r - \delta - \frac{b_c}{w_c^{m+1}}\right)\right) \tag{14}$$

We can write

$$\max\left(0, v\left(\frac{1}{v} + g\left(x\right) - y_r - \delta\right)\right) \tag{15}$$

where $v = w_c^{m+1}$. Similar for the $y_c = -1$

$$\max\left(0, v\left(\frac{1}{v} - g\left(x\right) + y_r - \delta\right)\right) \tag{16}$$

After merging (15) and (16) we get

$$|v| \max\left(0, |g\left(x\right) - y_r| + \text{sgn}\left(v\right)\left(\frac{1}{v} - \delta\right)\right) \tag{17}$$

So the $\delta$-SVR solves the problem with the hinge loss, which can be converted to the $\varepsilon$-insensitive loss after finding the solutions, by setting

$$\varepsilon = \text{sgn}\left(v\right)\left(\frac{1}{v} - \delta\right) . \tag{18}$$

Finally, we make a conclusion, that for $\delta$-SVR, the type of loss function which can be converted to the $\varepsilon$-insensitive remains unchanged.

## 2    Incorporating Balancing to SVR

We add the balanced property, (3) to SVR. We add the balanced property to two variants of SVR, $\varepsilon$-SVR and $\delta$-SVR. We incorporate the (3) to SVR by adding the equality constraint to the optimization problems of $\varepsilon$-SVR and $\delta$-SVR (see [13] for detailed descriptions of the optimization problems). We incorporate the (3) in a kernel space. After incorporation we still have convex optimization problems. The optimization problem for the balanced $\varepsilon$-SVR is

**Optimization problem (OP) 1.**

$$\min_{\boldsymbol{w_r}, b_r, \boldsymbol{\xi_r}, \boldsymbol{\xi_r^*}} f\left(\boldsymbol{w_r}, b_r, \boldsymbol{\xi_r}, \boldsymbol{\xi_r^*}\right) = \frac{1}{2}\left\|\boldsymbol{w_r}\right\|^2 + C_r \sum_{i=1}^{n}\left(\xi_r^i + \xi_r^{*i}\right) \tag{19}$$

subject to

$$\sum_{i=1}^{n} y_r^i - g\left(\boldsymbol{x_i}\right) = 0 , \tag{20}$$

$$y_r^i - g(\boldsymbol{x_i}) \le \varepsilon + \xi_r^i \;, \tag{21}$$

$$g(\boldsymbol{x_i}) - y_r^i \le \varepsilon + \xi_r^{i*} \;, \tag{22}$$

$$\boldsymbol{\xi_r} \ge 0 \;, \quad \boldsymbol{\xi_r^*} \ge 0 \tag{23}$$

for $i \in \{1, \ldots, n\}$, where $\varepsilon \in \mathbb{R}$,

$$g(\boldsymbol{x_i}) = \boldsymbol{w_r} \cdot \boldsymbol{x_i} + b_r \;. \tag{24}$$

The $g^*(\boldsymbol{x}) = \boldsymbol{w_r^*} \cdot \boldsymbol{x} + b_r^*$ is a regression function, $\varepsilon$ is a parameter, $\xi_r^i$, $\xi_r^{*i}$ are slack variables. The difference between OP 1 and the $\varepsilon$-SVR optimization problem, OP 6, is an additional equality constraint (20). We solve OP 1 by using a technique introduced in [13]. The technique allows to incorporate the general equalities in the form

$$\sum_{i=1}^{s} s_i g(\boldsymbol{d_i}) = e \;, \tag{25}$$

where $s_i$ are some parameters, for which $\sum_{i=1}^{s} s_i \ne 0$, $d_i$ are some points, $s$ is the number of $d_i$ points, $e$ is a parameter, $g$ is defined in (24). We apply the technique by noticing first that the (20) is a special case of (25), for $s = n$, $s_i = 1$, $\boldsymbol{d_i} = \boldsymbol{x_i}$, $e = \sum_{i=1}^{n} y_r^i$.

The optimization problem for the balanced $\delta$-SVR is

**OP 2.**

$$\min_{\boldsymbol{w_c}, b_c, \boldsymbol{\xi_c}} \quad f(\boldsymbol{w_c}, b_c, \boldsymbol{\xi_c}) = \frac{1}{2} \|\boldsymbol{w_c}\|^2 + C_c \sum_{i=1}^{2n} \xi_c^i \tag{26}$$

subject to

$$\sum_{i=1}^{n} \frac{-\boldsymbol{w_{red}} \cdot \boldsymbol{x_i} - b_c}{w_c^{m+1}} = \sum_{i=1}^{n} y_r^i \;, \tag{27}$$

$$y_c^i \left( \boldsymbol{w_{c,red}} \cdot \boldsymbol{x_i} + w_c^{m+1} \left( y_r^i + y_c^i \delta \right) + b_c \right) \ge 1 - \xi_c^i \;, \tag{28}$$

$$\boldsymbol{\xi_c} \ge 0 \tag{29}$$

for $i \in \{1, \ldots, 2n\}$.

The $C_c$ is a parameter. The $\xi_c^i$ are slack variables. We are looking for the decision boundary

$$h^*(\boldsymbol{x}) = \boldsymbol{w_c^*} \cdot \boldsymbol{x} + b_c^* = 0 \;. \tag{30}$$

The difference between OP 2 and the $\delta$-SVR optimization problem, OP 8, is an additional equality constraint (27). We solve OP 2 by using a technique introduced in [13]. We apply the technique by noticing first that the (27) is a special case of (25), for $s = n$, $s_i = 1$, $\boldsymbol{d_i} = \boldsymbol{x_i}$, $e = 0$. The solution for both optimization problems is derived for the dual forms with the dual variables $\alpha_i$ for $i = 1 \ldots n$ and the kernel function $K(x, y)$, where $x$, $y$ are vectors.

Due to the space limits, we provide only short description of all optimization problems that are used in the derivation of the solutions of OP 1 and OP 2

**OP 3.** This is a standard SVM problem for solving classification problems.

**OP 4.** Another variant of support vector classification (SVC) is the SVC without the offset $b_c$, analyzed recently in [16]. The optimization problem is the same except missing $b_c$ term.

**OP 5.** The $\varphi$ support vector classification ($\varphi$-SVC) optimization problem is the extension of the SVC optimization problem, OP 3, where the margin knowledge of an example in the form of the margin weights $\varphi_i$ is introduced. It was presented in [8, 9].

**OP 6.** This is a standard $\varepsilon$-SVR soft case optimization problem in the primal form for solving regression problems.

**OP 7.** This is a dual form of the SVC without the offset, OP 4.

**OP 8.** This is the optimization problem for $\delta$-SVR after transformation to the classification problem. The $\delta$-SVR has been first introduced in [10]. We use special kernels in $\delta$-SVR as following

$$K\left(x, y\right) = K_o\left(x_{\mathbf{red}}, y_{\mathbf{red}}\right) + x_{m+1}y_{m+1} \ , \tag{31}$$

where $x$ and $y$ are $m + 1$ dimensional vectors, $x_{\mathbf{red}} = (x_1, \ldots, x_m)$, $y_{\mathbf{red}} = (y_1, \ldots, y_m)$, $K_o\left(\cdot, \cdot\right)$ is the original kernel from which the new one was constructed.

We derive the solution for OP 1 by first defining a special version of (25) for classification problems that is

$$\sum_{i=1}^{s} s_i h\left(d_i\right) = e \ , \tag{32}$$

where $s_i$ are some parameters, for which $\sum_{i=1}^{s} s_i \neq 0$, $d_i$ are some points, $s$ is the number of $d_i$ points, $e$ is a parameter, $h$ is defined in (30). The constraint (32) is incorporated to the $\varphi$-SVC optimization problem, OP 5, for classification. The incorporation leads to the $\varphi$-SVC optimization problem without the offset, which is the SVC optimization problem without the offset, OP 4 with additional margin weights. Then we incorporate (25) to OP 6 by noticing that $\varepsilon$-SVR is a special case of $\varphi$-SVC, [11], and we have derived already the incorporation for $\varphi$-SVC. Finally, the incorporation of (25) to $\delta$-SVR leads to the SVC optimization problem without the offset OP 4.

**Table 1.** Performance of the balanced SVR for real world data per different value of $\varepsilon/\delta$, part 1. The numbers in descriptions of the columns mean the methods: 1 - $\varepsilon$-SVR, 2 - balanced $\varepsilon$-SVR, 3 - $\delta$-SVR, 4 - balanced $\delta$-SVR. Column descriptions: *id* – id of a test, *dn* – the name of a data set, *size* – the number of all examples, *dim* – the dimension of a problem, *eps/delta* – a value of the parameters $\varepsilon$ and $\delta$, *trse* – root-mean-square error (RMSE) for testing data; the best method is in bold, *tamse* – the average for the balancing parameter $p_b$ for testing data; the best method is in bold.

| id | dn | size | dim | eps/delta | trse1 | trse2 | trse3 | trse4 | tamse1 | tamse2 | tamse3 | tamse4 |
|---|---|---|---|---|---|---|---|---|---|---|---|---|
| 0 | abalone | 4177 | 8 | 0.01 | 0.087 | **0.084** | 2.782 | 0.103 | 0.027 | **0.008** | 2.22 | 0.019 |
| 1 | abalone | 4177 | 8 | 0.04 | **0.084** | 0.085 | 0.09 | 0.09 | **0.003** | 0.016 | 0.017 | 0.022 |
| 2 | abalone | 4177 | 8 | 0.16 | 0.105 | 0.097 | 0.088 | **0.088** | 0.054 | **0.006** | 0.023 | 0.008 |
| 3 | abalone | 4177 | 8 | 0.32 | 0.159 | 0.098 | **0.095** | 0.15 | 0.11 | **0.005** | 0.039 | 0.019 |
| 4 | abalone | 4177 | 8 | 0.64 | 0.147 | 0.115 | **0.092** | 0.093 | 0.092 | **0.004** | 0.007 | 0.005 |
| 5 | bodyfat | 252 | 14 | 0.01 | **0.019** | 0.02 | 0.05 | 0.043 | **0.001** | 0.005 | 0.011 | 0.001 |
| 6 | bodyfat | 252 | 14 | 0.04 | 0.043 | 0.042 | 0.033 | **0.03** | 0.007 | **0.003** | 0.009 | 0.005 |
| 7 | bodyfat | 252 | 14 | 0.16 | 0.092 | 0.106 | 0.019 | **0.018** | 0.026 | 0.008 | **0.003** | 0.006 |
| 8 | bodyfat | 252 | 14 | 0.32 | 0.151 | 0.148 | **0.033** | 0.035 | 0.041 | 0.018 | **0.007** | 0.01 |
| 9 | bodyfat | 252 | 14 | 0.64 | 0.183 | 0.165 | **0.056** | 0.056 | 0.08 | 0.005 | **0.004** | 0.004 |
| 10 | cadata | 20640 | 8 | 0.01 | **0.159** | 0.17 | 1.85 | 0.223 | **0.009** | 0.013 | 0.243 | 0.009 |
| 11 | cadata | 20640 | 8 | 0.04 | **0.154** | 0.155 | 0.154 | 0.156 | 0.027 | 0.011 | 0.014 | **0.009** |
| 12 | cadata | 20640 | 8 | 0.16 | 0.151 | 0.159 | 0.159 | **0.15** | 0.032 | 0.011 | 0.007 | **0.007** |
| 13 | cadata | 20640 | 8 | 0.32 | 0.196 | 0.162 | **0.148** | 0.149 | 0.075 | **0.006** | 0.007 | 0.009 |
| 14 | cadata | 20640 | 8 | 0.64 | 0.278 | 0.238 | **0.18** | 0.181 | 0.143 | **0.003** | 0.026 | 0.012 |
| 15 | housing | 506 | 13 | 0.01 | **0.097** | 0.099 | 0.133 | 0.147 | **0.01** | 0.014 | 0.013 | 0.018 |
| 16 | housing | 506 | 13 | 0.04 | **0.108** | 0.11 | 0.111 | 0.12 | 0.005 | 0.006 | **0.003** | 0.01 |
| 17 | housing | 506 | 13 | 0.16 | 0.142 | 0.135 | 0.095 | **0.095** | 0.006 | 0.011 | 0.009 | **0.003** |
| 18 | housing | 506 | 13 | 0.32 | 0.201 | 0.178 | 0.107 | **0.106** | 0.124 | 0.008 | 0.015 | **0.004** |
| 19 | housing | 506 | 13 | 0.64 | 0.245 | 0.204 | 0.134 | **0.129** | 0.136 | 0.005 | 0.009 | **0.005** |
| 20 | mpg | 392 | 7 | 0.01 | 0.087 | 0.086 | **0.085** | 0.154 | 0.015 | 0.01 | **0.004** | 0.014 |
| 21 | mpg | 392 | 7 | 0.04 | 0.076 | 0.075 | 0.075 | **0.073** | 0.014 | 0.008 | 0.013 | **0.003** |
| 22 | mpg | 392 | 7 | 0.16 | 0.083 | 0.082 | **0.079** | 0.081 | 0.012 | **0.0** | 0.01 | 0.006 |
| 23 | mpg | 392 | 7 | 0.32 | 0.169 | 0.115 | 0.086 | **0.085** | 0.103 | **0.007** | 0.017 | 0.012 |
| 24 | mpg | 392 | 7 | 0.64 | 0.225 | 0.211 | 0.102 | **0.099** | 0.082 | 0.024 | 0.004 | **0.001** |
| 25 | pyrim | 74 | 26 | 0.01 | **0.163** | 0.165 | 0.188 | 0.178 | **0.057** | 0.059 | 0.086 | 0.076 |
| 26 | pyrim | 74 | 26 | 0.04 | 0.065 | **0.064** | 0.075 | 0.08 | 0.004 | 0.003 | 0.016 | **0.0** |
| 27 | pyrim | 74 | 26 | 0.16 | 0.1 | 0.091 | **0.062** | 0.064 | 0.021 | **0.001** | 0.017 | 0.02 |
| 28 | pyrim | 74 | 26 | 0.32 | 0.231 | 0.217 | 0.164 | **0.162** | 0.096 | **0.053** | 0.062 | 0.06 |
| 29 | pyrim | 74 | 26 | 0.64 | 0.237 | 0.127 | 0.078 | **0.077** | 0.2 | **0.002** | 0.004 | 0.002 |
| 30 | space_ga | 3107 | 6 | 0.01 | **0.044** | 0.045 | 0.056 | 0.057 | 0.002 | 0.005 | **0.001** | 0.002 |
| 31 | space_ga | 3107 | 6 | 0.04 | 0.045 | 0.045 | **0.044** | 0.045 | **0.001** | 0.007 | 0.005 | 0.004 |
| 32 | space_ga | 3107 | 6 | 0.16 | 0.072 | 0.054 | **0.047** | 0.048 | 0.036 | **0.001** | 0.006 | 0.002 |
| 33 | space_ga | 3107 | 6 | 0.32 | 0.063 | 0.064 | 0.048 | **0.048** | 0.008 | 0.012 | 0.003 | **0.002** |
| 34 | space_ga | 3107 | 6 | 0.64 | 0.075 | 0.063 | 0.05 | **0.049** | 0.041 | 0.006 | 0.005 | **0.001** |
| 35 | triazines | 185 | 58 | 0.01 | **0.195** | 0.198 | 0.253 | 0.205 | 0.015 | **0.005** | 0.044 | 0.008 |
| 36 | triazines | 185 | 58 | 0.04 | 0.2 | 0.199 | 0.213 | **0.199** | 0.034 | 0.008 | 0.033 | **0.006** |
| 37 | triazines | 185 | 58 | 0.16 | 0.206 | 0.213 | 0.288 | **0.177** | **0.004** | 0.012 | 0.034 | 0.005 |
| 38 | triazines | 185 | 58 | 0.32 | 0.213 | 0.208 | **0.199** | 0.202 | 0.058 | 0.042 | 0.033 | **0.032** |
| 39 | triazines | 185 | 58 | 0.64 | 0.278 | 0.196 | **0.179** | 0.181 | 0.2 | 0.031 | **0.018** | 0.03 |

**Table 2.** Performance of balanced SVR for real world data per different value of $\varepsilon/\delta$, cont. of the part 1

| id | dn | size | dim | eps/delta | trse1 | trse2 | trse3 | trse4 | tamse1 | tamse2 | tamse3 | tamse4 |
|----|----|------|-----|-----------|-------|-------|-------|-------|--------|--------|--------|--------|
| 40 | rcv1 | 26173 | 39029 | 0.01 | **0.105** | 0.105 | 0.108 | 0.105 | **0.009** | 0.012 | 0.023 | 0.013 |
| 41 | rcv1 | 26173 | 39029 | 0.04 | 0.105 | 0.105 | **0.105** | 0.107 | 0.003 | 0.001 | 0.003 | **0.001** |
| 42 | rcv1 | 26173 | 39029 | 0.16 | 0.113 | 0.107 | 0.105 | **0.105** | 0.038 | 0.008 | 0.003 | **0.002** |
| 43 | rcv1 | 26173 | 39029 | 0.32 | 0.174 | 0.106 | 0.109 | **0.104** | 0.137 | 0.01 | 0.022 | **0.008** |
| 44 | rcv1 | 26173 | 39029 | 0.64 | 0.145 | 0.107 | 0.114 | **0.106** | 0.098 | **0.001** | 0.042 | 0.002 |
| 45 | year_pred | 24989 | 90 | 0.01 | 0.112 | **0.111** | 0.112 | 0.113 | 0.024 | 0.015 | 0.013 | **0.009** |
| 46 | year_pred | 24989 | 90 | 0.04 | **0.11** | 0.112 | 0.162 | 0.124 | **0.0** | 0.021 | 0.109 | 0.021 |
| 47 | year_pred | 24989 | 90 | 0.16 | 0.14 | 0.134 | 0.125 | **0.122** | 0.064 | 0.014 | 0.01 | **0.01** |
| 48 | year_pred | 24989 | 90 | 0.32 | 0.162 | 0.121 | **0.113** | 0.113 | 0.108 | **0.007** | 0.022 | 0.008 |
| 49 | year_pred | 24989 | 90 | 0.64 | 0.213 | 0.121 | **0.117** | 0.123 | 0.176 | 0.004 | 0.01 | **0.004** |
| 50 | abalone | | | var | 0.084 | **0.084** | 0.088 | 0.088 | **0.003** | 0.008 | 0.023 | 0.008 |
| 51 | bodyfat | | | var | 0.019 | 0.02 | 0.019 | **0.018** | **0.001** | 0.005 | 0.003 | 0.006 |
| 52 | cadata | | | var | 0.151 | 0.155 | **0.148** | 0.149 | 0.032 | 0.011 | **0.007** | 0.009 |
| 53 | housing | | | var | 0.097 | 0.099 | 0.095 | **0.095** | 0.01 | 0.014 | 0.009 | **0.003** |
| 54 | mpg | | | var | 0.076 | 0.075 | 0.075 | **0.073** | 0.014 | 0.008 | 0.013 | **0.003** |
| 55 | pyrim | | | var | 0.065 | 0.064 | **0.062** | 0.064 | 0.004 | **0.003** | 0.017 | 0.02 |
| 56 | space_ga | | | var | **0.044** | 0.045 | 0.044 | 0.045 | **0.002** | 0.007 | 0.005 | 0.004 |
| 57 | triazines | | | var | 0.195 | 0.196 | 0.179 | **0.177** | 0.015 | 0.031 | 0.018 | **0.005** |
| 58 | rcv1 | | | var | 0.105 | 0.105 | 0.105 | **0.104** | 0.009 | **0.001** | 0.003 | 0.008 |
| 59 | year_pred | | | var | **0.11** | 0.111 | 0.112 | 0.113 | **0.0** | 0.015 | 0.013 | 0.009 |

# 3   Experiments

We compare performance of standard SVR with balanced SVR for various real world data sets. We chose all real world data sets for regression from the LibSVM site [7] which originally come from UCI Machine Learning Repository and Statlog (the YearPredictionMSD data set is reduced to the first 25000 data vectors). Moreover, we chose rcv1v2 (topics; subsets) data set for multilabel classification, which we convert to a regression problem by predicting the number of classes. See the details about the data sets in Table 1 and Table 2. We use our own implementation of all methods. For all data sets, every feature is scaled linearly to $[0, 1]$. We performed all tests with the radial basis function (RBF) kernel. For variable parameters like the $C_r$, $\sigma$ for the RBF kernel, we use a double grid search method for finding the best values - first a coarse grid search is performed, then a finer grid search as described in [5]. The training set size is fixed, the rest of data become test data. The standard 5 fold cross validation is used for the inner loop for finding optimal values of the parameters. After finding optimal values, we run the method on training data, and we report results for a test set. We report the balancing parameter $p_b$ for SVR methods.

We use the Friedman test with the two tailed Nemenyi post hoc test for checking statistical significance of the regression error, as suggested in [2, 4, 6]. The statistical procedure is performed for the level of significance equal to 0.05. The critical values for the Friedman test are taken from the statistical table design specifically for the case with smaller number of tests or methods as suggested in [6]. The critical values for the Nemenyi test are taken from the statistical table for the Tukey test which are divided by $\sqrt{2}$.

We compare SVR with balanced SVR for various $\varepsilon$ and $\delta$, we choose the fixed size of training set in the outer loop which is 80. We report all results in Table 1, Table 2 and Table 3. The general conclusion is that the balanced SVR achieves similar overall generalization performance as SVM with better generalization performance for suboptimal values. The detail observations are as follows.

- A value of the balanced parameter $p_b$ generally increases for $\varepsilon$-SVR and $\delta$-SVR while increasing a value of $\varepsilon$ and $\delta$ (columns tamse1, tamse3 in Table 1 and columns tamse1, tamse3 in Table 3).
- A value of the balanced parameter $p_b$ is generally lower for balanced SVR than for standard SVR (columns tamse1, tamse2, tamse3, tamse4 in Table 1 and columns tamse1, tamse2, tamse3, tamse4 in Table 3).
- The generalization performance for various $\varepsilon$ and $\delta$ is generally slightly better for balanced SVR (rows 0-5, columns rs1, rs2, rs3, rs4 in Table 3), we did not achieve direct statistical significance for this result (columns tsn12 and tsn34), but we can notice that for example for $\varepsilon/\delta = 0.32$, we achieve better generalization performance for balanced $\varepsilon$-SVR than $\varepsilon$-SVR for all data sets except one (space_ga). The Nemenyi statistics are very conservative, [4] and we believe that such relations could be found with more sensible tests. What we can show is that the difference in generalization performance between $\varepsilon$-SVR and $\delta$-SVR can become statistically significant when we replace $\delta$-SVR with balanced $\delta$-SVR, for example for $\varepsilon/\delta = 0.16$ (row with id=2, columns tsn13, tsn14).
- The overall generalization performance (row 5 in Table 3) is similar for all methods, without statistical significance.

**Table 3.** Performance of balanced SVR for real world data per different value of $\varepsilon/\delta$, part 2. The numbers in descriptions of the columns mean the methods: 1 - $\varepsilon$-SVR, 2 - balanced $\varepsilon$-SVR, 3 - $\delta$-SVR, 4 - balanced $\delta$-SVR. The test with id=0 is for all the tests from Table 1 with $\varepsilon, \delta = 0.01$, with id=1 for all the tests with $\varepsilon, \delta = 0.04$, with id=2 for all the tests with $\varepsilon, \delta = 0.16$, with id=3 for all the tests with $\varepsilon, \delta = 0.32$, with id=4 for all the tests with $\varepsilon, \delta = 0.64$, and finally with id=5 for variable $\varepsilon, \delta$. Column descriptions: $rs$ – an average rank of the method for RMSE; the best method is in bold, $tsf$ – the Friedman statistic for average ranks for RMSE; the significant value is in bold, $tsn$ – the Nemenyi statistic for average ranks for RMSE, reported when the Friedman statistic is significant, the significant value is in bold, $tamse$ – the average for the balancing parameter $p_b$ for testing data; the best method is in bold.

| id | rs1 | rs2 | rs3 | rs4 | tsf | tsn12 | tsn13 | tsn23 | tsn14 | tsn24 | tsn34 | tamse1 | tamse2 | tamse3 | tamse4 |
|---|---|---|---|---|---|---|---|---|---|---|---|---|---|---|---|
| 0 | **1.5** | 1.8 | 3.3 | 3.4 | **17.64** | −0.52 | −3.12 | −2.6 | −3.29 | −2.77 | −0.17 | 0.017 | **0.015** | 0.266 | 0.017 |
| 1 | **2.2** | 2.3 | 2.6 | 2.9 | 1.8 | – | – | – | – | – | – | 0.01 | 0.008 | 0.022 | **0.008** |
| 2 | 3.5 | 3.2 | 2.0 | **1.3** | 19.08 | 0.52 | 2.6 | 2.08 | **3.81** | **3.29** | 1.21 | 0.029 | 0.007 | 0.012 | **0.007** |
| 3 | 3.9 | 2.9 | **1.6** | 1.6 | 22.44 | 1.73 | **3.98** | 2.25 | **3.98** | 2.25 | 0.0 | 0.086 | 0.017 | 0.023 | **0.016** |
| 4 | 4.0 | 2.8 | **1.6** | 1.6 | 23.76 | 2.08 | **4.16** | 2.08 | **4.16** | 2.08 | 0.0 | 0.125 | 0.009 | 0.013 | **0.006** |
| 5 | 2.56 | 3.11 | 2.33 | **2.0** | 3.53 | – | – | – | – | – | – | 0.009 | 0.011 | 0.012 | **0.007** |

# 4    Summary

In this paper, we proposed a novel regression method of balancing data, balanced SVR. We provided details on the method and performed experiments. The advantage of the proposed method is an improvement in the suboptimal performance compared to SVR. In the future, we plan to extend the theoretical analysis and to perform thorough experiments.

**Acknowledgments.** I would like to express my sincere gratitude to Professor Witold Dzwinel (AGH University of Science and Technology, Department of Computer Science) for discussion and useful suggestions. This research is supported by the Polish National Center of Science (NCN) project DEC-2013/09/B/ST6/01549 titled "Interactive Visual Text Analytics (IVTA): Development of novel user-driven text mining and visualization methods for large text corpora exploration".

# References

[1]  Cortes, C., Vapnik, V.: Support-vector networks. Machine Learning 20(3), 273–297 (1995)

[2]  Demšar, J.: Statistical comparisons of classifiers over multiple data sets. J. Mach. Learn. Res. 7, 1–30 (2006)

[3]  Drucker, H., Burges, C.J.C., Kaufman, L., Smola, A.J., Vapnik, V.: Support vector regression machines. In: Neural Information Processing Systems, pp. 155–161 (1996)

[4]  Garcia, S., Herrera, F.: An extension on "statistical comparisons of classifiers over multiple data sets" for all pairwise comparisons. J. Mach. Learn. Res. 9, 2677–2694 (2008)

[5]  Wei Hsu, C., Chung Chang, C., Jen Lin, C.: A practical guide to support vector classification (2010)

[6]  Japkowicz, N., Shah, M.: Evaluating Learning Algorithms: A Classification Perspective. Cambridge University Press, New York (2011)

[7]  Libsvm data sets (June 2011)

[8]  Orchel, M.: Incorporating detractors into svm classification. In: Cyran, K.A., Kozielski, S., Peters, J.F., Stańczyk, U., Wakulicz-Deja, A. (eds.) Man-Machine Interactions. AISC, vol. 59, pp. 361–369. Springer, Heidelberg (2009)

[9]  Orchel, M.: Incorporating a priori knowledge from detractor points into support vector classification. In: Dobnikar, A., Lotrič, U., Šter, B. (eds.) ICANNGA 2011, Part II. LNCS, vol. 6594, pp. 332–341. Springer, Heidelberg (2011)

[10]  Orchel, M.: Regression based on support vector classification. In: Dobnikar, A., Lotrič, U., Šter, B. (eds.) ICANNGA 2011, Part II. LNCS, vol. 6594, pp. 353–362. Springer, Heidelberg (2011)

[11]  Orchel, M.: Support vector regression as a classification problem with a priori knowledge in the form of detractors. In: Czachórski, T., Kozielski, S., Stańczyk, U. (eds.) Man-Machine Interactions 2. AISC, vol. 103, pp. 351–358. Springer, Heidelberg (2011)

[12]  Orchel, M.: Support vector regression based on data shifting. Neurocomputing 96, 2–11 (2012)

[13] Orchel, M.: Incorporating Prior Knowledge into SVM Algorithms in Analysis of Multidimensional Data. Ph.D. thesis, AGH University of Science and Technology (2013)

[14] Schölkopf, B., Smola, A.J.: Learning with Kernels: Support Vector Machines, Regularization, Optimization, and Beyond. MIT Press, Cambridge (2001)

[15] Steinwart, I., Christmann, A.: Support Vector Machines. Information Science and Statistics. Springer (2008)

[16] Steinwart, I., Hush, D.R., Scovel, C.: Training svms without offset. J. Mach. Learn. Res. 12, 141–202 (2011)

# Adaptation Mechanism of Feedback in Quaternion Kalman Filtering for Orientation Estimation

Przemysław Pruszowski[1], Agnieszka Szczesna[1(✉)], Andrzej Polański[2],
Janusz Słupik[3], and Konrad Wojciechowski[2]

[1] Silesian University of Technology, Institute of Informatics, Gliwice, Poland
{Przemyslaw.Pruszowski,Agnieszka.Szczesna}@polsl.pl
[2] Research Center of Polish-Japanese Academy of Information Technology,
Bytom, Poland
{APolanski,KWojciechowski}@pjwstk.edu.pl
[3] Silesian University of Technology, Institute of Mathematics, Gliwice, Poland
Janusz.Slupik@polsl.pl

**Abstract.** In this paper an adaptation mechanism of feedback in Kalman filtering is presented for orientation estimation of rigid body. This filter fuses the measurements from Inertial Measurement Unit (IMU) sensors to determine the 3D orientation. It is well known that a factor that strongly influences the orientation measurement is the existence and magnitude of the external acceleration of the IMU sensor. To show results of simulated experiments the quaternion-based Extended Kalman Filter with and without adaptation regarding accelerometers measurement mechanism were implemented.

**Keywords:** Kalman filter · Adaptation mechanism · Orientation estimation · IMU sensors · Quaternion · Motion tracking

## 1 Introduction

There are two major lines of the development of instrumentation for motion capture (MOCAP) measurement systems. The first line is based on optical measurement and tracking systems. The second class of the development involves MOCAP measurements based on sensors of different types and using fusions of their measurements for estimating motion parameters. Miniature IMU (inertial magnetic unit) sensors combining inertial, gyroscopic and magnetic measurements have attracted a lot of interest of researchers, who developed algorithms for estimating parameters of motion based on fusions of their measurements [1]. Compared to the previous class, MOCAP systems based on IMU sensors are more flexible in the sense of the possibility of scheduling record sessions in different locations. The flexibility is, however, achieved at the cost of lower accuracy of motion measurements.

In MOCAP systems based on IMU sensors the angle of rotation, necessary to determine the orientation of segment, is determined by integrating the output signal from the gyroscope, so the accuracy of determining the angle to the

© Springer International Publishing Switzerland 2015
L. Rutkowski et al. (Eds.): ICAISC 2015, Part II, LNAI 9120, pp. 739–748, 2015.
DOI: 10.1007/978-3-319-19369-4_65

greatest extent depends on the sensor stability of zero. Zero drift (for example due to changes in temperature) results in a short time of the large error values in determined angle. The integration accumulates the noise over time and turns noise into the drift, which yields unacceptable results. Besides the gyroscope, in IMU the accelerometers measure the sum of linear acceleration and gravitation acceleration. The magnetometers measure the direction of the local magnetic field. For a stationary sensor in an environment free of magnetic anomalies, it is simple to determine the orientation by measuring Earth's gravitational and magnetic fields along all three axes of the orthogonally mounted sensors. The combination of the two resulting vectors can provide complete roll, pitch and yaw (RPY) angles information. In more dynamic applications, high frequency angular rate information can be combined in a complementary manner with accelerometer and magnetometer data through the use of a sensor fusion algorithms like complementary or Kalman filters [2]-[10].

It is well known that a factor that strongly influences the orientation measurement is the existence and magnitude of the external acceleration of the IMU sensor. In the adaptive orientation estimation systems some auxiliary computations are performed in order to estimate the temporary magnitude of the external acceleration and then the weight for accelerometer channel is adaptively changed on the basis of the estimates. In this paper the comparison of results for simulated data between direct state quaternion Kalman Filters to orientation estimation with and without adaptive feedback are presented.

## 2   Notation and Relations for Measurement Vectors

The system based on IMU sensors includes inertial, gyroscopic and magnetic measurements. Modeling of the motion of a moving body involves introducing two coordinate frames. The first one is the Earth fixed coordinate system (navigation frame) pointing north $(x^N)$, east $(y^N)$ and up $(z^N)$. The second one is the coordinate system related to the moving body, denoted by $(x^B, y^B$ and $z^B)$. Consistently to our notational convention we add superscript $N$ or $B$ to indicate coordinate frames in which these vectors are expressed (measured). Consequently, $g^N$, $m^N$, $g^B$ and $m^B$ denote, respectively **gravitational** and **magnetic field** vectors measured in the navigation frame $N$ and body frame $B$. Vectors $g^N$, $m^N$ are constant and known. Their coordinates are $g^N = [0, 0, -9.81]^T$ and $m^N = [\cos(\varphi^L) - \sin(\varphi^L)]^T$, where $\varphi^L$ is the geographical latitude angle. For the geographical position of the laboratory, where measurements were done, we have $\varphi^L = 66^\circ = 1.1519$ rad. The same value was used in all simulations. **Body acceleration** vector is denoted by $a$. By $a^N$ and $a^B$ we denote this vector expressed in navigation and body coordinate systems. **Rotation velocity** vector (rotation rate vector, angular rate vector) of the moving body is denoted by $\omega$.

## 2.1 Kinetics of the Orientation Change

The relative orientation between navigation and body coordinate frames is defined by a $3 \times 3$ rotation matrix $R$. Consequently, navigation and body coordinates of a given free vector $v$ are related by

$$v^N = R v^B. \tag{1}$$

Rotation matrix $R$ can be represented/parameterized in several ways. Most common are parametrisation by using Euler angles and parametrisation by using quaternions. Because of their simplicity, mathematical elegance, and lack of any singularities, quaternions became a very popular representation for encoding the orientation of a rigid body. We also have implemented described methods with use of quaternions to represent orientation.

Due to the motion of the body, the rotation matrix $R$, the unit quaternion $q$ and Euler angles $\phi_y$, $\phi_p$, $\phi_r$ are functions of time, i.e., $R = R(t)$, $q = q(t)$ and $\phi_{ypr} = \phi_{ypr}(t)$. Mathematical models for the evolution of rigid body orientation with time can be formulated for all parametrisation of the rotation matrix in the form of differential equations.

For parametrisation of orientations defined by unit quaternions $q(t)$ the differential equation for motion is

$$\frac{d}{dt} q(t) = \frac{1}{2} \omega^N \otimes q(t) = \frac{1}{2} q(t) \otimes \omega^B \tag{2}$$

where $\otimes$ stands for quaternion multiplication.

In practical implementations, estimators of orientations are realised on the basis of digital systems. Therefore, in descriptions of algorithms in the forthcoming sections equations for kinetics of orientations changes are replaced by their discrete counterparts. Discrete time index is denoted by the subscript $k$.

# 3 Descriptions of Algorithms for Estimation of Relative Orientation

## 3.1 Problem Formulation

The problem considered here and solved by two compared algorithms concerns estimating orientation of the moving body, using of parametrisation by quaternions ($q$), on the basis of available measurements in body frame: output vector of the magnetometer $y^m$, $y^a$ the output vector of the inertial sensor (accelerometer), and $y^g$ for the output vector of the gyroscopic sensor. The discrete time is indicated by adding the subscript $k$. The notation for estimated orientations is by adding the over - hat symbol, $\hat{q}$.

Equations, which relate the true parameters of orientation and motion with the sensors outputs (sensor models) are assumed as follows. The equation for the output vector of the magnetometer is given by

$$y_k^m = K_m \cdot R(q_k) m^N + w_k^m, \tag{3}$$

the equation for the output vector of the accelerometer is

$$y_k^a = K_a \cdot (R(q_k)(g^N + a^N)) + w_k^a \tag{4}$$

and the equation for the output of the gyroscopic sensor is given by

$$y_k^g = K_g \cdot \omega^B + w_k^g. \tag{5}$$

In the above formulae (3)-(5) $K_g$, $K_a$, $K_m$ are scale factor matrices, whose entries are computed (estimated) in the process of sensors calibrations. $R(q_k)$ is a rotation matrix defined by the unit quaternion $q_k$, which describes the body orientation. Measurement noises $w^g, w^a, w^m$ are uncorrelated white Gaussian random vectors with zero mean and covariance matrices $\sigma_m^2 I_{3x3}$, $\sigma_a^2 I_{3x3}$, $\sigma_g^2 I_{3x3}$, respectively. Standard deviations $\sigma_m$, $\sigma_a$ and $\sigma_g$ can be obtained from the technical documentation from the manufacturers of sensors, or can be estimated experimentally.

## 3.2    Extended Quaternion Kalman Filter (EQKF)

The first implemented for experiments quaternion Kalman filter, was proposed in [6]. In the original design in [6] state vector (here denoted by $x^{orig}$) includes three components (blocks)

$$x^{orig} = \begin{bmatrix} q \\ b^a \\ b^m \end{bmatrix}. \tag{6}$$

The quaternion $q$ (4 - dimensional) represented the body orientation and two vectors $b^a$ and $b^m$ represented biases of sensors, accelerometers and magnetometers. This is direct-state quaternion-based formulation of the EKF, where angular velocity is considered a control input and active compensation (gyro bias and magnetic effects) is achieved by using state-augmentation techniques. Since we ignore biases $b^a$ and $b^m$, here we simplify definition of the state vector by retaining only the quaternion representing the body orientation, as $x = q$.

The discretized state equation of the orientation kinematics process corresponding to (2) is following:

$$x_{k+1} = \Phi_k x_k + w_k = \exp[\frac{1}{2} M_R(y_k^g) \Delta t] x_k + w_k. \tag{7}$$

In this equation $x_k$ is the discrete - time state vector, $x_k = q_k$, and $M_R(y_k^g)$ denotes matrix representation of the quaternion right multiplication corresponding to the pure quaternion $y_k^g$ and $\Phi$ is state transition matrix. The process noise covariance matrix $Q_k$ is following:

$$Q_k = (\Delta t/2)^2 \Xi_k (\sigma_g^2 I_{4x4}) \Xi_k^T. \tag{8}$$

where for $q_k = (a, [b, c, d])$ we define as follows

$$\Xi_k = \begin{bmatrix} a & -d & c \\ d & a & -b \\ -c & b & a \\ -b & -c & -d \end{bmatrix}$$

The measurement model is of the form:

$$z_{k+1} = \begin{bmatrix} y_{k+1}^a \\ y_{k+1}^m \end{bmatrix} = f(x_{k+1}) + \begin{bmatrix} w_k^a \\ w_k^m \end{bmatrix} = \begin{bmatrix} R(q_{k+1}) & 0 \\ 0 & R(q_{k+1}) \end{bmatrix} \begin{bmatrix} g^N \\ m^N \end{bmatrix} + \begin{bmatrix} w_k^a \\ w_k^m \end{bmatrix} \quad (9)$$

where $R(q)$ is a rotation matrix defined by quaternion $q$.

Since the above output is nonlinear, it is linearized by computing the Jacobian matrix,

$$H_{k+1} = \frac{d}{dx_{k+1}} z_{k+1} \bigg|_{x_{k+1}=x_{k+1}^-} . \quad (10)$$

According to the notation introduced above, the EQKF equations are summarised as follows:

- the a priori state estimate:

$$\hat{x}_{k+1}^- = \Phi_k \hat{x}_k, \quad (11)$$

- the a priori error covariance matrix:

$$P_{k+1}^- = \Phi_k P_k \Phi_k^T + Q_k, \quad (12)$$

- the Kalman gain:

$$K_{k+1} = P_{k+1}^- H_{k+1}^T (H_{k+1} P_{k+1}^- H_{k+1}^T + V_{k+1})^{-1}, \quad (13)$$

- the a posteriori state estimate

$$\hat{x}_{k+1} = \hat{x}_{k+1}^- + K_{k+1}[z_{k+1} - f(\hat{x}_{k+1}^-)] \quad (14)$$

- the a posteriori error covariance matrix:

$$P_{k+1} = P_{k+1}^- - K_{k+1} H_{k+1} P_{k+1}^- . \quad (15)$$

## 3.3   Adaptive Extended Quaternion Kalman Filter (AEQKF)

There are two adaptation mechanisms assumed in [6], for accelerometers and for magnetometers. Here we implement only adaptation regarding accelerometers measurement, where covariance matrix of the measurement $V_{k+1}$ in (13) depends on the deviation of the value of the gravitational acceleration $\|g^N\|$ and the measured acceleration magnitude $\|y_{k+1}^a\|$, i.e.,

$$V_{k+1} = \begin{bmatrix} \sigma_a^2 \cdot I_{3\times3} & 0_{3\times3} \\ 0_{3\times3} & \sigma_m^2 \cdot I_{3\times3} \end{bmatrix} \quad (16)$$

if $\| \|y_{k+1}^a\| - \|g^N\| \| < \epsilon$ or

$$V_{k+1} = \begin{bmatrix} \infty \cdot I_{3\times3} & 0_{3\times3} \\ 0_{3\times3} & \sigma_m^2 \cdot I_{3\times3} \end{bmatrix} \quad (17)$$

otherwise. Thus, the influence of accelerometers on the orientation estimation is reduced in the presence of the external acceleration.

## 4    Experiments

Comparisons of the above described algorithms for body orientation estimation are based on the simulated data.

### 4.1    Performance Evaluation

In simulated experimental data-sets, evaluation of performances of presented algorithms is done on the basis of average deviations between true and estimated orientations of the body. Deviation index (measure) between true and estimated orientations can be, defined in different ways [11].

Here we use the deviation index $DI$ corresponding to the geodesic distance between two quaternions - filter estimate $\hat{Q}$ and the true rotation $Q$ - on the hypersphere $S^3$

$$DI = 2 * arccos(|\hat{Q} * Q|).  \tag{18}$$

All evaluations and comparisons of performances of algorithms for orientation estimation are based on deviation index (18) averaged over the experiment time horizon.

### 4.2    Simulated Data

The algorithm for generation of artificial IMU sensor data is based on computing time functions of unit quaternion $q(t)$ and elements of body acceleration vector (expressed in the navigation frame), $a^N(t)$, as sinusoidal components.

Value $q(t)$ specify perfectly orientation of the body. By using parametric form of $q(t)$, we obtain time derivative $\frac{d}{dt}q(t)$, which allows for computing angular rate vector $\omega^B = 2 * (\bar{q} * \frac{d}{dt}q)$, where $\bar{q}$ is conjugate quaternion. On the basis of the exact values of $m^B$, $\omega^B$ and $a^B - g^B$, the discrete - time measurement signals of the accelerometers sensors $y_k^a$, the gyroscopes sensors $y_k^g$ and the magnetometers sensors $y_k^m$ are computed by adding noise (disturbance) components, as follows:

$$y_k^a = a_k^B - g_k^B + w_k^a,  \tag{19}$$

$$y_k^g = \omega_k^B + w_k^g,  \tag{20}$$

$$y_k^m = m_k^B + w_k^m.  \tag{21}$$

As already stated, we assume no distortion of the magnetometers and no bias of the gyroscope. Disturbances, $w_k^a$, $w_k^g$ and $w_k^m$ are zero mean Gaussian white noises with variances $\sigma_a^2$, $\sigma_g^2$ and $\sigma_m^2$.

### 4.3    Simulation Scenario

In each of the simulated experiments the simulation time was assumed as $T = 180$ seconds. The value of the sampling interval was taken $\Delta t = 0.01$. In experiments concerning the best performance assessment of the filters, the following parameters were designated: $\sigma_g^2 = 0.0001$, $\sigma_a^2 = 0.001$, $\sigma_m^2 = 0.00001$.

We have implemented, simulation scenarios with the different choices of amplitudes, angular frequencies and phases of the sinusoidal components defining $q(t)$ and $a^N(t)$, as well as with different choices of variances $\sigma_a^2$, $\sigma_g^2$ and $\sigma_m^2$.

At the beginning we have estimated experimentally variances of the Xsens IMU sensor used in our laboratory, as

$$\sigma_{Xsens}^2 = [\sigma_{a,Xsens}^2, \sigma_{g,Xsens}^2, \sigma_{m,Xsens}^2] = [0.089, 0.058, 0.015]. \qquad (22)$$

We have related vector of variances of disturbances in (19)-(21), as $\sigma_{sensor}^2 = [\sigma_a^2, \sigma_g^2, \sigma_m^2]$. In (22), to define low variance of disturbances we use as $\sigma_{sensor}^2 = \sigma_{Xsens}^2$ and high variance of disturbances as $\sigma_{sensor}^2 = 3 \cdot \sigma_{Xsens}^2$. To show adaptation mechanism of described filter we have chosen two scenarios with external acceleration changes modelled as sinusoidal continuous and spiky changes.

Below the scenario and results obtained for two filters are presented.

**Sinusoidal Continuous Acceleration Changes.** This scenario represents movement of simulated IMU sensor that produce continuous external acceleration with small and average amplitude. Angular velocity is $2\ rad/s$ and maximum acceleration amplitude goes from $0\ m/s^2$ in first simulation to $10\ m/s^2$ in last simulation.

In Fig. 1 quaternion error computed from (18) is presented. For simulation without external acceleration two filters EQKF and AQKF give the same results. When the maximum acceleration amplitude grows, best results are obtained with

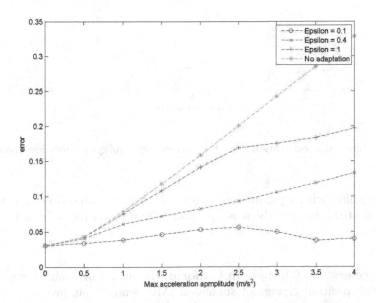

**Fig. 1.** Quaternion estimation error for scenario with sinusoidal continuous acceleration changes

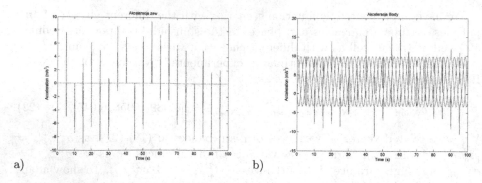

a)                                          b)

**Fig. 2.** Experiments with simulation data with external spiky acceleration changes a) external acceleration, b) body acceleration

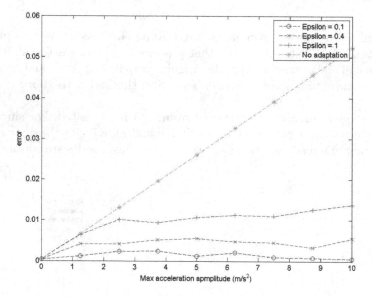

**Fig. 3.** Quaternion estimation error for scenario with spiky acceleration changes

an adaptive filter with a parameter $\epsilon = 0.1$. The highest value of error is for the application of the filter without adaptation EQKF. This result is in line with expectations.

**Spiky Acceleration Changes in Uniform Motion.** This scenario represents shorts quick position change of simulated IMU sensor that produce external acceleration with short time span by high amplitude. Acceleration spikes occurs every 5 s and continues for 0.5 s. Angular velocity is 0.5 $rad/s$. In Fig. 2a the spiky of external acceleration are presented and in Fig. 2b the result body

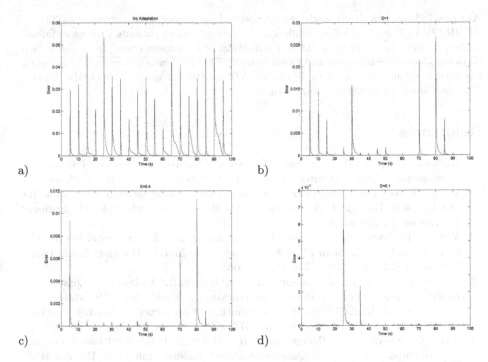

a)                                        b)

c)                                        d)

**Fig. 4.** Quaternion estimation error for scenario with spiky acceleration changes a) filter with no adaptation EQKF, b-d) filter adaptation mechanism in filter AEQKF

acceleration (uniform motion plus external spikiest) is presented. Acceleration amplitude start as 0 $m/s^2$ in first simulation up to 10 $m/s^2$ in last simulation.

The values of errors are similar to previous experiment with continuous acceleration changes. Also the best results are obtained by filter AEQKF with small value of parameter $\epsilon = 0.1$.

The Fig. 4 presents changes in value of the quaternion error in time, where you can observe the levelling of external spiky acceleration changes and quick response of the adaptation mechanism of the filter AEQKF (Fig. 4d).

## 5   Conclusions

The paper presents the experiments to verify the mechanism of adaptation that reduces the impact of external acceleration in the problem of orientation estimation. Although external acceleration is one of the main source of loss of performance in attitude estimation methods, this problem has not been sufficiently addressed in the literature. For this purpose the quaternion-based Extended Kalman filter has been implemented, with and without this mechanism. Through a series of experiments in simulation environment was also defined the parameter $\epsilon$ impact on the improvement of estimation. In both scenarios we can noticed that for lover $\epsilon$ value orientation estimation is improving. AEQKF method is successfully ignoring accelerations that are causing inaccurate estimation.

**Acknowledgments.** This work was supported by project Strategmed1/233221/3/ NCBR/2014 "The use of teletransmission of medical data in patients with heart failure for improvement of quality of life and reduction of treatment costs" from the Polish National Centre for Research and Development. This work was partly performed using the infrastructure supported by POIG.02.03.01-24-099/13 grant: "GCONiI - Upper-Silesian Center for Scientific Computation".

# References

1. Kulbacki, M., et al.: Scalable, Wearable, Unobtrusive Sensor Network for Multimodal Human Monitoring with Distributed Control. In: Lacković, I., Vasic, D. (eds.) 6th European Conference of the International Federation for Medical and Biological Engineering. IFMBE, vol. 45, pp. 914–917. Springer International Publishing, Switzerland (2015)
2. Yun, X., Bachmann, E.R.: Design, Implementation, and Experimental Results of a Quaternion-Based Kalman Filter for Human Body Motion Tracking. IEEE Transactions on Robotics 22(6), 1216–1227 (2006)
3. Yun, X., Lizarraga, M., Bachmann, E.R., McGhee, R.B.: An Improved Quaternion-Based Kalman Filter for Real-Time Tracking of Rigid Body Orientation. In: Proceedings of the 2003 IEEE/RSJ International Conference on Intelligent Robots and Systems, Las Vegas, Nevada, pp. 1074–1079 (October 2003)
4. Yun, X., Aparicio, C., Bachmann, E.R., McGhee, R.B.: Implementation and Experimental Results of a Quaternion-Based Kalman Filter for Human Body Motion Tracking. In: Proceedings of the 2005 IEEE International Conference on Robotics and Automation, ICRA 2005, pp. 317–322 (2005)
5. Shuster, M.D., Oh, S.D.: Three-Axis Attitude Determination from Vector Observations. Journal of Guidance and Control 4(1), 70–77 (1981)
6. Sabatini, A.M.: Quaternion-Based Extended Kalman Filter for Determining Orientation by Inertial and Magnetic Sensing. IEEE Tran. Biomedical Eng. 53(7), 1346–1356 (2006)
7. Sabatini, A.M.: Kalman-Filter-Based Orientation Determination Using Inertial/Magnetic Sensors: Observability Analysis and Performance Evaluation, Sensors (2011)
8. Sabatini, A.M.: Estimating three-dimensional orientation of human body parts by inertial/magnetic sensing. Sensors 11(2), 1489–1525 (2011)
9. Mahony, R., Hamel, T., Pflimlin, J.M.: Nonlinear Complementary Filters on the Special Orthogonal Group, Automatic Control. IEEE Transactions on Automatic Control 53(5), 1203–1218 (2008)
10. Słupik, J., Szczęsna, A., Polański, A.: Novel Lightweight Quaternion Filter for Determining Orientation Based on Indications of Gyroscope, Magnetometer and Accelerometer. In: Chmielewski, L.J., Kozera, R., Shin, B.-S., Wojciechowski, K. (eds.) ICCVG 2014. LNCS, vol. 8671, pp. 586–593. Springer, Heidelberg (2014)
11. Gramkow, C.: On averaging rotations. Journal of Mathematical Imaging and Vision 15(1-2), 7–16 (2001)

# Using Graph Grammar Systems with Memory in Computer Aided Design

Iwona Ryszka[✉] and Barbara Strug

Jagiellonian University, Lojasiewicza 11, Krakow, Poland
{iwona.ryszka,barbara.strug}@uj.edu.pl

**Abstract.** Any design problem can be treated as a cooperative task involving many different tasks and requirements that have to be satisfied in order to produce a final design. Each participant, which can be seen as an agent contributes its knowledge and abilities to the common goal. This paper deals with an approach based on graph grammar model of cooperation and distribution for generating designs in computer aided design domain. Each design is represented as a graph. Thus each agent is equipped with its own set of rules (a graph grammar) enabling it to add to the design. The motivation for the idea presented is given and some possible modes of application are briefly described.

## 1 Introduction

Graphs are considered to be very useful as a way of representing complex objects in different domains of computer science [15]. They are widely recognized to have the ability to represent the structure of an object as well as the relations of different types between its components makes them particularly useful in computer aided design. They can represent an artifact being designed taking into account the inter-related structure of many design objects i.e. the fact that parts of an object can be related to other parts in different ways. Designing new artifacts requires a method of generating representing them graphs.

In order to represent the cooperative nature of the design process a graph grammar system is used instead of a single grammar. This approach is based on earlier research in the domain of application of the theory of formal languages to the computer aided design [5]. In particular the graph based representation jointly with graph grammars [1,6,12], and grammar systems [2,4,17] were used as the inspiration for this research. It is also an extension of earlier research into graph grammars systems and distributed design systems [7,10,9]

It can be observed that one of the main problems of graph generation with graph grammars lies in the complexity and size (understood as the number of rules) of grammars needed in real world problems (that can be encountered in the domains of both engineering and design). As a result such grammars tend to be both difficult to define and not very intuitive, resulting in being difficult to understand. Thus the use of a number of simpler grammars cooperating together seems to be a good solution to much of the above mentioned problem.

© Springer International Publishing Switzerland 2015
L. Rutkowski et al. (Eds.): ICAISC 2015, Part II, LNAI 9120, pp. 749–759, 2015.
DOI: 10.1007/978-3-319-19369-4_66

A grammar system consists of a finite number of grammars (called components of the system) which together influence (change) an environment by applying some operations to it. At a given moment the state of the system is described by the current environment (sub-environments). The system works by changing its state.

Two main types of grammar systems are researched: parallel communicating grammar systems (PC grammar systems) [3,13] and cooperating distributed grammar systems (CD grammar systems) [2,11]. The main difference between these types of grammar systems consists in the model of environment they work on. In PC grammar systems each component operates on its own copy of the form under derivation and they only exchange information on request.

In case of CD grammar systems the grammars operate on one common form, one grammar at a time. As in computer aided design domain a single object is usually developed, the CD grammar systems seem more appropriate here. In CD grammar systems at any given time step there is only one graph being generated. Each component grammar operates on this graph according to a communication protocol called the derivation mode [2]. The protocol may allow a single component to performed a predefined number of steps or to work until no production of this component can be applied. The method of selecting which grammar should be used as the next "active" component is also important. Such cooperating grammars can be seen as independent cooperating agents solving the same problem by modifying a common environment. (often compared with the blackboard model in artificial intelligence) [8].

In this paper a modification of CD grammar systems is introduced. The formal aspects are described and the example from the computer aided design domain is presented to demonstrate the practical usage of the proposed solution.

## 2    Graph Based Design Representation

A graph is formally defined as a pair $(V, E)$, where $V$ and $E$ are sets of graph nodes and edges, respectively.

In case of a design system a node in a graph usually represents either an object or a group of objects or, more generally, it may be seen as a "container" for a part of a design that may be designed at later time. For example, in a house design system a node can represent a floor of a house that in turn will be divided into rooms. Each node of a graph is labelled by a symbol from a predefined set (alphabet) that is later used to add some semantics to the representation.

Edges represent relations between objects. They are labelled by symbols being names od the relations. Labels are assigned to nodes and edges by means of node and edge labelling functions.

Moreover, as there is a need to represent some particular features/parameters of the objects and relations between them attributing of both nodes and edges is used. Attributes represent properties of an element represented by a given node (for example size, position, colour or material) or edge (for example distance). Attributes are assigned by node and edge attributing functions. Formally, an *attribute* is a function $a : W \rightarrow D_a$, where $W$ is a domain of the attribute and $D_a$ a set of possible values of the attribute.

Let $R_V$ and $R_E$ be the sets of node and edge labels, respectively, let $\Sigma = R_V \cup R_E$. Let $A$ and $B$ be sets of node and edge attributes and $D_a$ and $D_b$ sets of possible values of attributes of nodes and edges, respectively.

**Definition 1.** *A labelled attributed graph LAG over $\Sigma$ is defined as a 6-tuple $LAG = (V, E, lab_V, lab_E, att_V, att_E)$, where*

1. *$(V, E)$ is a graph,*
2. *$lab_V : V \rightarrow R_V$ is a node labelling function,*
3. *$lab_E : E \rightarrow R_E$ is an edge labelling function,*
4. *$att_V : V \rightarrow 2^A$ is a function assigning a set of attributes to each node,*
5. *$att_E : E \rightarrow 2^B$ is an edge attributing function, i.e. it assigns a set of attributes to each edge.*

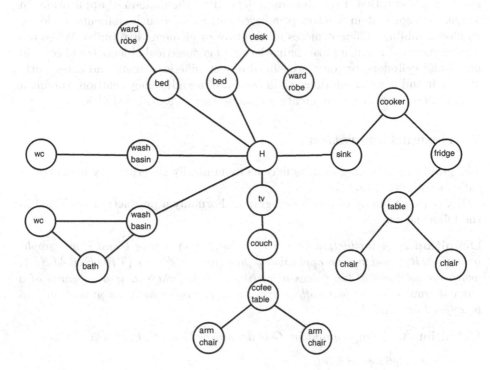

**Fig. 1.** An example of a graph representing a flat furnishing

In fig. 1 a graph representing a flat containing a hall, kitchen and several bedrooms is depicted. Nodes represent elements of house furnishing and edges represent communication possibility between them and distances or relative placement. This graph may be further developed to add more details, for example node representing a hall (H) can be replaced by nodes representing elements of hall design. Moreover door or windows can be added. For the clarity of the figure attributes are not shown, but they include sizes, position and other features specific for the elements of furnishing.

To represent an actual design we must define a graph instance, which is a labelled attributed graph in which to all attributes assigned to all nodes and edges values of these attributes are assigned. In a house design system for all rooms we have to specify its size attribute for example.

Moreover, as the graph represents the syntax of the design we also need some form of the semantics. Partially it is obtained by the use of labels in the graph, but some form of interpretation is also needed. An interpretation of a graph $G$ is defined as a pair of functions $(I_V, I_E)$, where $I_V$ assigns geometrical objects to nodes, while $I_E$ establishes a correspondence between edges and relations between these objects. The objects assigned by $I_V$ are called primitives. The primitives may be either simple geometrical objects or more complex objects. The geometry of these objects may be internally represented by means of any known representation. Primitives used depend on the domain of application. In a house design system a set of primitives can contain such elements as doors, windows, cabling, different pieces of furniture or elements like bulbs. When designing pieces of furniture like chairs the set of geometrical objects could contain boxes and cylinders, or some predefined objects like legs, seats and other parts of a chair and a set of relations could consist of an adjacency relation. Having a graph interpretation we can create a visualisation of a designed object.

## 3   Design Generation

The graphs representing designs may be dynamically generated by means of so called graph grammars [1].

Let $G_A$ be a family of attributed graphs. Formally a production is defined in the following way:

**Definition 2.** *A production is a triple $p = (l, r, \pi)$, where $l$ and $r$ are graphs over $R_V \cup R_E$, and $\pi$ is an applicability predicate $\pi : 2^{G_A} \to \{TRUE, FALSE\}$, which on the basis of the values of attributes of $L$ (where $L$ is a subgraph of a current graph $c$ isomorphic with $l$), $r$ and $c$ determines whether a production can be applied or not.*

**Definition 3.** *A graph grammar $G$ is defined as $G = (\Sigma, P, x)$ where:*

- *$\Sigma$ is an alphabet of labels,*
- *$P$ is a finite set of productions $p = \{l, r, \pi\}$, and*
- *$x$ is a labelled node over $\Sigma$ and is called the **axiom** of the grammar.*

Let $p = (l, r, \pi) \in P$ be a production in $G$. The first element of the pair $l$ and the second element $r$ are called the *left-hand-side* and the *right-hand-side* of $p$, respectively. The application of production $p$ to a graph $c$ consists in finding a subgraph $L$ of the current graph $c$ isomorphic with $l$ and substituting a graph $r$ for a subgraph $L$ of the current graph $c$ isomorphic with the graph $l$ and replacing the connections of $l$ with the connections of $r$.

Having defined a graph grammar, we can introduce a control diagram, which determines the order in which the productions should be applied.

**Definition 4.** *Let $G = (\Sigma, P, x)$ be a graph grammar. Let $\Omega = \{I, F\} \cup \{p_1, ..., p_m\}$, where $m = |P|$, be the cardinality of the set of node labels.*

*By a control diagram $CD$ **over** $\Omega$ defined for $G$ is a directed node labelled graph $D = (V_D, E_D, s, t, lb_D)$, where*

- *$s, t : E_D \mapsto V_{CD}$ are two mappings assigning to each edge $e \in E_D$ elements $s(e)$ and $t(e)$ called the source and the target, respectively.*
- *$lb_D : V_D \mapsto \Omega$, is a labelling function, and*
- *there exists exactly one node labelled $I$ and exactly one node labelled $F$,*
- *there is no edge in-coming to the initial node labelled $I$ and no edge out-coming from the final node labelled $F$.*

In many design situations there is a need to preserve or even to propagate some information throughout the generation process, that is some sort of communicating between productions is needed. In this paper we propose an approach similar to the blackboard method in artificial intelligence i.e. all the productions of a given grammar can access and/or modify a common set of variables. This set will be called *memory*.

Formally a grammar with memory is defined in the following way;

**Definition 5.** *A grammar with memory is a pair $GM = (G, M)$, where*

- *$M$ is a set of variables, $M = \{m_1, \ldots, m_n\}$, such that $\forall i = 1 \ldots n, m_i \in D_i$, where $D_i$ is a set of all possible values for $m_i$, and*
- *$G = (\Sigma, P, x)$ is a graph grammar, where $P$ is a set of productions $p = (l, r, \pi, f)$ defined as follows:*
  - *$l$ and $r$ are left and right hand sides of $p$, respectively,*
  - *$\pi$ is an applicability predicate, $\pi : 2^{G_A} \times 2^M \to \{TRUE, FALSE\}$, where $L$ is a subgraph of a current graph isomorphic with the $l$ and $M$ is a memory associated with the grammar $G$,*
  - *$f = (f_1, \ldots, f_n)$ is a set of functions responsible for changing values of memory variables, where $f_i : 2^M \times 2^{A_L} \to D_i, 1 \geq i \geq n$.*

It can be noticed here the definition of a predicate $\pi$ is extended to take into account the possibility of including memory variables while deciding whether a production can or cannot be applied. It also important that the above definition does not put any additional constraints on the type of grammar $G$, i.e. it can be a context-free or context grammar.

In this paper a modification of CD grammar systems is proposed. It can be observed that while absolutely justifiable in string grammars the requirement that only one grammar can operate on a given temporary form (called sentential form ) seems too strong in case of graph grammars. Moreover in design systems it would be useful to allow more then one grammar to operate on the same, common, sentential form. It can be seen as an equivalent of many design teams or agents working on different parts of the same design. To maintain the consistency of the design it must be ensured that no two agents work at the same time on the same part of the design, i.e no two grammars (components) operate on the same nodes of the sentential form.

Moreover, some way of activating particular components must be defined. In this paper a so called terminal derivation mode is used, i.e. each grammar works as long as it contains a production that can be applied to current graph.

**Definition 6.** *A graph grammar system is defined as $(n + 3)$-tuple $GGS = (N, T, G_1, G_2, \ldots, G_n, g_0)$, where*

- *$N$ and $T$ are the sets of non-terminal and terminal symbols, respectively,*
- *$G_i = (N_i, T_i, C_i, P_i), (i = 1 \ldots n)$ are graph grammars such that*
  - *$N_i$, $T_i$ and $C_i$ are the sets of non-terminal, terminal and communication symbols for the $i - th$ a component, respectively,*
  - *$N_i \cap T_i \cap C_i = \emptyset$,*
  - *$N = \bigcup_{i=1}^{n} N_i, T = \bigcup_{i=1}^{n} T_i$,*
  - *$\forall x \in C_i, (i = 1 \ldots n) \exists j \neq i$ such that $x \in N_j$,*
  - *$\forall x \in N_i, (i = 1 \ldots n) \exists p \in P_i$ such that its left side graph is labelled by $x$,*
  - *$P_i$ is a set of productions $G_L \Rightarrow G_R$ where $G_L$ and $G_R$, called left side and right side, respectively, are the labelled attributed graph over $N_i \cup T_i \cup C_i$ and $|V_{G_L}| = 1 \wedge lab_{G_L} \in N_i$,*
- *$g_0$ is an initial graph.*

For short nodes labelled with terminal, non-terminal and communication symbols will be called, terminal, non-terminal and communication nodes, respectively.

Similarly as in single grammar case when applying a grammar system to real life problems a need to communicate between grammars may occur. To provide for such a situation we introduce grammar system with memory.

**Definition 7.** *A grammar system with memory is a triple $SM = (S, M, F)$, where $S$ is a grammar system, $M$ is a memory and $F$ is a family of functions allowing each production of each grammar in $S$ to change the value of elements of system memory M.*

It has to be noted here that some or all grammar in the grammar system can actually be grammars with memory, thus the system may contain two different levels of memory.

Each component grammar contains productions that have at least one node on the left side labelled by a symbol from the set of non-terminals. The nodes of the graph on the right side of the production can labeled by any symbol, terminal, non-terminal or communication one.

The non-terminal nodes can be intuitively understood as representing a part of a design that is not finished but a given grammar knows how to deal with it further. Taking this intuition further a communication symbol means that a particular grammar knows that some part of design is not finished but it is not specialist in this part and thus it communicates with other grammar that knows how to deal with this part. Terminal symbols finally represent part of a design that is considered to be finished (at least by the set of available rules).

The definition of a grammar system guarantees that if any grammar introduces a communication symbol into current graph then there exists other grammar exists such which contains the same symbol in its set of non-terminals. It should be noted here that the communication symbols are in fact non-terminals symbols for some grammars.

To demonstrate advantages of the proposed graph derivation method the sample grammar graph system with memory is proposed. The purpose of this system is to design an apartment. The memory of the system is defined as $M = (p\_c, space, br\_c)$. The variable $p\_c$ is specified by the user and determines the number of residents in the flat. The next property $space$ is also defined by the user to specify the apartment. The last variable $br\_c$ has a default value and it is a counter describing the number of bedrooms.

The grammar $G1$ is responsible for generating the structure of the apartment. In fig.2a some of productions are presented. The central point is a hall represented by node labelled by $H$. There is a set of productions that are responsible for adding the other rooms, like a kitchen $K$, a living room $LR$, a bath $B$, a dinning room $BR$ and a set of bedrooms $BR$. Applying the production $P2$ results in incrementing the variable $br\_c$ from the memory. The control diagram is presented in the figure 2b. Additionally, the predicates are used for some productions to cover apartment requirements for example that there must be one bedroom for each resident or that a separate toilet can be added only when the apartment area is greater than 60 and there are more that 2 people.

The nodes representing rooms are communication symbols that trigger other grammars that are responsible for furnishing particular rooms. The grammar $G2$ shown in figure 2c generates cooking area by defining a kitchen and a dinning room. The control diagram for this grammar is presented in figure 2d. In similar way to grammar $G1$ predicates for productions are used to generate the structure suitable to requirements. Next grammar in figure 3a introduces the furniture for living room. The grammar $G4$ generates the content of the bath and if the space is suitable also for a toilet (figure 3b). The last grammar $G5$ is responsible for bedroom furniture and is presented in figure 3c. The control diagrams for these grammars make use of predicates an memory variables as shown in figures 3d-3f.

In this example by means of set of grammars operating on specific nodes a parallel method of graph derivation can be used. Introduction of the memory paradigm is a facilitation for a designer. It can be used to specify the initial requirements (like the number of residents) or to perform some operations on logical layer that could be difficult to express on syntax level (like counting bedrooms).

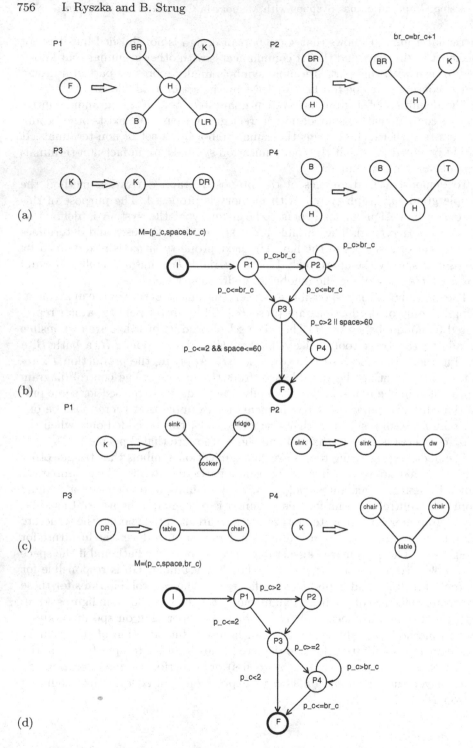

**Fig. 2.** Selected productions from grammars G1 and G2 of the design system

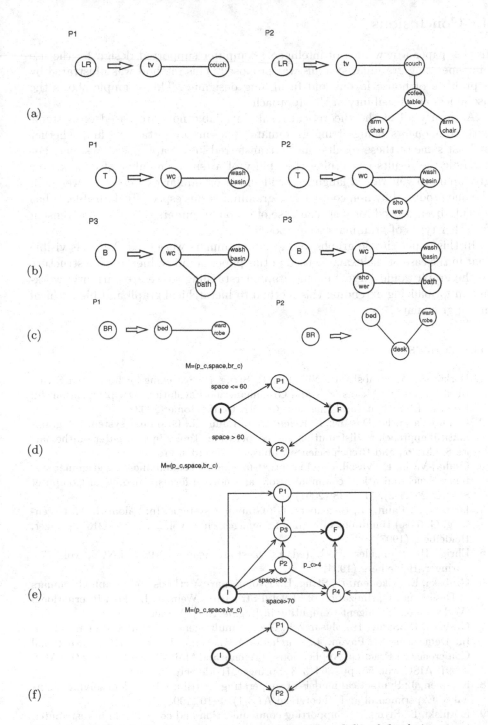

**Fig. 3.** Selected productions from grammars G3, G4 and G5 of the design system

## 4    Conclusions

In this paper a new idea of intelligent, computer supported design by the use of cooperating grammar systems was proposed. This method was illustrated by a problem of house layout and furnishing designing. This example shows the usefulness and feasibility of the approach.

As nearly all of the theoretical results available now are based on systems with components being string grammars, it seems important to find whether at least some of these results can be transferred into graph based systems. For example the results concerning the ability of a (small) number of context-free grammars to generate a language of identical or similar expressive power with the one produced by non context-free grammar seems especially desirable. It has already been proved for a special case of graph grammars [16] but an extension for other types of grammars seems possible.

In this paper simple graphs and graph grammars were used. Yet it is visible that in the case of the example used in this paper adding a hierarchical structure to the graph would largely extend its understanding so we are currently working on formalizing extending this method to hierarchical graph and hierarchical graph grammars.

## References

1. Borkowski, A., Grabska, E., Nikodem, P., Strug, B.: Searching for Innovative Structural Layouts by Means of Graph Grammars and Esvolutionary Optimization. In: Proc. 2nd Int. Structural Eng. and Constr. Conf., Rome (2003)
2. Csuhaj-Varjú, E., Dassow, J., Kelemen, J., Paun, G.: Grammar systems. A grammatical approach to distribution and cooperation. Topics in Computer Mathematics 8. Gordon and Breach Science Publishers, Yverdon (1994)
3. Csuhaj-Varjú, E., Vaszil, G.: On context-free parallel communicating grammar systems: Synchronization, communication, and normal forms. Theoretical Computer Science 255(1-2), 511–538 (2001)
4. Dassow, J., Paun, G., Rozenberg, G.: Grammar systems. In: Salomaa, A., Rozenberg, G. (eds.) Handbook of Formal Languages, ch. 4, vol. 2, pp. 155–213. Springer, Heidelberg (1997)
5. Ehrig, H., Schneider, H.-J. (eds.): Dagstuhl Seminar 1993. LNCS, vol. 776. Springer, Heidelberg (1994)
6. Grabska, E., Nikodem, P., Strug, B.: Evolutionary Methods and Graph Grammars in Design and Optimization of Skeletal Structures Weimar. In: 11th International Workshop on Intelligent Computing in Engineering, Weimar (2004)
7. Grabska, E., Strug, B., Ślusarczyk, G.z.: A multiagent distributed design system. In: Demazeau, Y., Pavón, J., Corchado, J.M., Bajo, J. (eds.) 7th International Conference on Practical Applications of Agents and Multi-Agent Systems (PAAMS 2009). AISC, vol. 55, pp. 364–373. Springer, Heidelberg (2009)
8. Kelemen, J.: Syntactical models of cooperating/distributed problem solving. Journal of Experimental and Theoretical AI 3(1), 1–10 (1991)
9. Kotulski, L., Strug, B.: Supporting communication and cooperation in distributed representation for adaptive design. Advanced Engineering Informatics 27, 220–229 (2013)

10. Kotulski, L., Strug, B.: Distributed Adaptive Design with Hierarchical Autonomous Graph Transformation Systems. In: Shi, Y., van Albada, G.D., Dongarra, J., Sloot, P.M.A. (eds.) ICCS 2007, Part II. LNCS, vol. 4488, pp. 880–887. Springer, Heidelberg (2007)
11. Martín-Vide, C., Mitrana, V.: Cooperation in contextual grammars. In: Kelemenová, A. (ed.) Proceedings of the MFCS 1998 Satellite Workshop on Grammar Systems, pp. 289–302. Silesian University, Opava (1998)
12. Nikodem, P., Strug, B.: Graph Transformations in Evolutionary Design. In: Rutkowski, L., Siekmann, J.H., Tadeusiewicz, R., Zadeh, L.A. (eds.) ICAISC 2004. LNCS (LNAI), vol. 3070, pp. 456–461. Springer, Heidelberg (2004)
13. Paun, G., Salomaa, A. (eds.): Grammatical models of multi-agent systems. Gordon and Breach, Amsterdam (1999)
14. Rozenberg, G.: Handbook of Graph Grammars and Computing by Graph Transformations, Fundations, vol. 1. World Scientific, London (1997)
15. Rozenberg, G.: Handbook of Graph Grammars and Computing by Graph Transformations, Applications, Languages and Tools, vol. 2. World Scientific, London (1999)
16. Simeoni, M., Staniszkis, M.: Cooperating graph grammar systems. In: Paun, G., Salomaa, A. (eds.) Grammatical Models of Multi-agent Systems, pp. 193–217. Gordon and Breach, Amsterdam (1999)
17. Strug, B., Paszynska, A., Paszynski, M., Grabska, E.: Using a graph grammar system in the finite element method. International Journal of Applied Mathematics and Computer Science 23(4), 839–853 (2013)

# Software Framework for Modular Machine Learning Systems

Marcin Korytkowski[1(✉)], Magdalena Scherer[2], and Sohrab Ferdowsi[3]

[1] Institute of Computational Intelligence, Częstochowa University of Technology,
al. Armii Krajowej 36, 42-200 Częstochowa, Poland
marcin.korytkowski@iisi.pcz.pl
http://iisi.pcz.pl
[2] Faculty of Management, Częstochowa University of Technology,
al. Armii Krajowej 19, 42-200 Częstochowa, Poland
mscherer@zim.pcz.pl
http://www.zim.pcz.pl/en
[3] University of Geneva, Computer Science Department,
7 Route de Drize, Geneva, Switzerland
http://sip.unige.ch

**Abstract.** Machine learning methods and algorithms can be combined into ensembles to obtain better performance than a single base learner. In the paper we present a framework for distributed system based on Common Object Request Broker Architecture for creating ensembles of learning systems. The systems are handled by the server which sends and receives learning and testing data. They can be located on different machines with various operating systems or hardware. The structures of the base learners are described by XML files.

## 1 Introduction

Machine learning algorithms [18][19] can be used to develop learning systems that can perform certain tasks after learning from data. The knowledge about the task can be known or unknown. The systems can be used for control [8][12][17], face recogition [1], medical classification [4], robotics [10] or even physics [23]. The systems ranges from multi-layer neural networks, [20] support vector machines [5], neuro-fuzzy systems [7][24], to multi-agent systems [2]. Despite a plethora of learning systems, there is sometimes a need to decompose a complex problem into smaller tasks. Usually, there is used a finite number of subsystems, trained by an additional meta-algorithm to achieve better accuracy than a single learner. The most common techniques are bootstrap aggregating (bagging), boosting, Bayesian model averaging or other, less sophisticated techniques. Implementing new algorithms is a very time-consuming task and there is a high demand in the scientific community for a flexible software systems to perform experiments. There are many software systems for machine learning, e.g. [6][9][16]. In this paper we present a framework which can be used to create and train in parallel modular structures of neural networks, neuro-fuzzy systems or any

© Springer International Publishing Switzerland 2015
L. Rutkowski et al. (Eds.): ICAISC 2015, Part II, LNAI 9120, pp. 760–767, 2015.
DOI: 10.1007/978-3-319-19369-4_67

other network structures. A method to describe network structures using the XML language was shown in [11] along with the backpropagation learning. The framework presented here uses this XML structure description and is meant to create and learn ensembles of classifiers in a distributed object environment of several learners and one server for task distribution. Bagging (Bootstrap AG-GregatING) [13][22] is an algorithm for creating an ensemble that uses the same dataset. Bagging produces replicates of the training set $\mathbf{z}$ and trains a classifier $D_k$ on each replicate $S_k$. Each classifier is applied to a test pattern $\mathbf{x}$ which is classified on a majority vote basis, ties being resolved arbitrarily. We have a set of labels $\Omega = \{\omega_1, \omega_2, \ldots, \omega_C\}$, where $C$ is the number of possible classes, labeled $\omega_i$, $i = 1, \ldots, C$. We consider the ensemble of classifiers $\mathbf{D} = [D_1, \ldots, D_J]$, where there are $J$ base classifiers $D_k$, $k = 1, \ldots, J$. We assume that the output of classifier $D_k$ is $\mathbf{d}_k(\mathbf{x}) = [d_{k,1}(\mathbf{x}), \ldots, d_{k,C}(\mathbf{x})]^T \in \{0,1\}^C$ , where $d_{k,j} = 1$ if $D_k$ determines that $\mathbf{x}$ belong to class $\omega_j$, and $d_{k,j} = 0$ otherwise. The majority vote will result in an ensemble decision for class $\omega_k$ if

$$\sum_{i=1}^{J} d_{i,k}(\mathbf{x}) = \max_{1 \leq j \leq C} \sum_{i=1}^{J} d_{i,j}(\mathbf{x}). \qquad (1)$$

The Bagging algorithm consists of the following steps

1. Initialize the parameters
   - the ensemble $\mathbf{D} = \emptyset$
   - the number of classifiers to train $J$
2. For $k = 1, \ldots, J$ repeat points 3-5
3. Take sample $S_k$ from original dataset $\mathbf{Z}$
4. Build a classifier $D_k$ using $S_k$ as the training set
5. Add the classifier to the current ensemble $\mathbf{D} = \mathbf{D} \cup D_k$
6. Return $\mathbf{D}$ as algorithm outcome
7. Run $\mathbf{x}$ on the input $D_1, \ldots, D_J$
8. The vector $\mathbf{x}$ is a member of class $\omega_k$, if condition (1) is fulfilled.

The next most popular ensembling method is the AdaBoost algorithm [3][15][21], in its basic form designed for binary classification. Let us denote the $l$-th learning vector by $\mathbf{z}^l = [x_1^l, \ldots, x_n^l, y^l]$ , $l = 1 \ldots m$ is the number of a vector in the learning sequence, $n$ is the dimension of input vector $\mathbf{x}^l$, and $y^l$ is the learning class label. Weights $D^l$ assigned to learning vectors, have to fulfill the following conditions

$$(i) \ 0 < D^l < 1 \,,$$
$$(ii) \ \sum_{l=1}^{m} D^l = 1 \,. \qquad (2)$$

The weight $D^l$ is the information how well classifiers were learned in consecutive steps of an algorithm for a given input vector $x^l$. Vector $\mathbf{D}$ for all input vectors is initialized according to the following equation

$$D_t^l = \frac{1}{m}, \quad \text{for } t = 0, \ldots, T \,, \qquad (3)$$

where $t$ is the number of a boosting iteration (and a number of a classifier in the ensemble). Let $\{h_t(\mathbf{x}) : t = 1, ..., T\}$ denotes a set of hypotheses obtained in consecutive steps $t$ of the algorithm being described. For simplicity we limit our problem to a binary classification (dichotomy) i.e. $y \in \{-1, 1\}$ or $h_t(\mathbf{x}) = \pm 1$. Similarly to learning vectors weights, we assign a weight $c_t$ for every hypothesis, such that

$$\text{(i)} \sum_{t=1}^{T} c_t = 1 \,, \tag{4}$$
$$\text{(ii)} \; c_t > 0 \,.$$

Now in the AdaBoost algorithm we repeat steps 1-4 for $t = 1, ..., T$ :

1. Create hypothesis $h_t$ and train it with a data set with respect to a distribution $d_t$ for input vectors.

2. Compute the classification error $\varepsilon_t$ of a trained classifier $h_t$ according to the formula

$$\varepsilon_t = \sum_{l=1}^{m} D_t^l(z^l) I(h_t(\mathbf{x}^l) \neq y^l) \,, \tag{5}$$

where $I$ is the indicator function

$$I(a \neq b) = \begin{cases} 1 \text{ if } a \neq b \\ 0 \text{ if } a = b \end{cases} \,. \tag{6}$$

If $\varepsilon_t = 0$ or $\varepsilon_t \geq 0.5$, stop the algorithm.

3. Compute the value

$$\alpha_t = 0.5 \ln \frac{1 - \varepsilon_t}{\varepsilon_t} \,. \tag{7}$$

4. Modify weights for learning vectors according to the formula

$$D_{t+1}(\mathbf{z}^l) = \frac{D_t(\mathbf{z}^l) \exp\{-\alpha_t \mathbf{I}(h_t(\mathbf{x}_l) = y^l)\}}{N_t} \,, \tag{8}$$

where $N_t$ is a constant such that $\sum_{l=1}^{m} D_{t+1}(\mathbf{z}^l) = 1$. To compute the overall output of the ensemble of classifiers trained by AdaBoost algorithm, the following formula is used

$$f(\mathbf{x}) = \sum_{t=1}^{T} c_t h_t(\mathbf{x}) \,, \tag{9}$$

where

$$c_t = \frac{\alpha_t}{\sum_{t=1}^{T} \alpha_t} \tag{10}$$

is classifier importance for a given training set, $h_t(\mathbf{x})$ is the response of the hypothesis $t$ on the basis of feature vector $\mathbf{x} = [x_1, ..., x_n]$. The coefficient $c_t$ value is computed on the basis of the classifier error and can be interpreted as the measure of classification accuracy of the given classifier. Moreover, the assumption (2) should be met. As we see, the AdaBoost algorithm is a meta-learning algorithm and does not determine the way of learning for classifiers in the ensemble.

## 2    System Architecture

To establish connections between the server and client applications we used the CORBA (Common Object Request Broker Architecture) standard defined by the Object Management Group (OMG). CORBA is developed for communication between various systems and is independent of operating system, platform, programming language and hardware. It is based on object-oriented programming as distributed model with encapsulation and reuse. Each of the objects in a CORBA system has a unique address of the Interoperable Object Reference (IOR). It stores the address of the computer with the type of the object, the object number, the order of bits transmission, etc., in the form of several hundred characters. Description of objects (for the exchange of information, more specifically the ability to call their component functions) is performed with the use of the Interface Definition Language (IDL). IDL is the language used to define the interface for classes used in CORBA. A developer describes what methods can be found on the individual objects, giving the program code to perform in them. Thus, when we use the IDL language, we have to create both: method names and the names and types of the input and return parameters. After we create the class skeleton, it will be translated to a code for a programming language. e.g. C#, Delphi, Java (their choice depends entirely on the developer) to create the appropriate code program for the server and the client. Interfaces of classes written in IDL can be divided into modules, and there is possibility to make the inheritance between them. IDL language has its own data types (similar to Java and C). The developer does not have to take care of the appropriate casting these types to types of the used programming language as this is handled by the IDL specification. The main benefit of using CORBA compared to .NET Remoting or Java RMI is its universality. The final program codes (client and server) can be created using any of common programming languages such as C#, Java, etc. In the case of .NET platform we have three ways to our disposal: open-source IIOP.NET project, J-Integra Espresso and VisiBroker for .NET (a part of Borland's VisiBroker CORBA). In case of Java-based solutions we have Object Request Broker (ORB), the Java CORBA ORB and Internet InterORB Protocol (IIOP).

Many meta-algorithms for creating ensembles can be designed to allow parallel execution. The example can be bagging where all subsystems can be trained independently. Of course, there are some constraints coming from large memory requirements of multiple learning structures what could be overcome by distributing the load into multiple machines.

The proposed system has two types of modules: server (ServerMS) and clients (ClientMS). Figure 1 shows the architecture of the system. In the process of creating and training modular systems, only one application of ServerMS type and many (according of used algorithm) client applications run. The main task of the ServerMS is to coordinate the work of ClientMS instances. Generally, we can distinguish two stages: the process of the construction of such a modular systems and their testing. Testing process for most algorithms is very similar, while creating a modular system is more varied depending on the meta learning

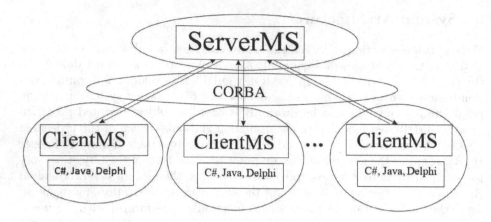

**Fig. 1.** Architecture of the presented solution

algorithm. In the case of boosting, at the learning stage, ServerMS application must submit to subsequent clients (modular system components) respectively the modified learning set. There is some extra information added, e.g. weights of samples. Boosting learning can be described as:

1. User loads a learning dataset to ServerMS program,
2. ServerMS assigns to each sample from the learning set a weight
3. The ClientMS communicates with the server application and receives its learning set,
4. After the learning process, ClientMS updates weights of samples and such a modified learning set is sent back to the ServerMS,
5. Then, the ClientMS is run and receives new samples to learn from the ServerMS.

Steps 3 to 5 are repeated until a stop condition is met.

The situation is different in the case of the bagging algorithm. Now ServerMS performs a simple task, i.e. it loads the entire learning set and then splits the dataset at random to the predetermined number of clients. Each of the clients establishes a communication with the ServerMS, and as a result receives from it another training set with which the learner selects its parameters (weights in the case of neural networks, fuzzy sets parameters in the case of neuro-fuzzy systems). Testing process is very simple and is similar in both the bagging and boosting algorithms. It can be summarized as follows:

1. ServerMS loads a testing dataset,
2. Each of the previously learned clients gets the testing dataset from the server and generates its answer,
3. The server reads the responses from individual clients and depending on the algorithm determines a definitive answer of the modular system.

Below we present an example of IDL script, used to create communication between the server and client programs.

```
// Combine
typedef sequence<double> TmyArray;
typedef sequence<TmyArray> TmyMatrix;
interface Combine {
TmyMatrix Give_SamplesToCombine(in long ClientNo,
     in double ClientEror);
  void Send_Answers(in long ClientNo,
       in TmyMatrix ResultSet); };
```

The above listing presents main components of an IDL file. Of course, developers extend them to their needs. Because we were not able to find suitable data type to declare two-dimensional array in IDL, we created our own type named *TmyMatrix*. To do that, we used the special command *typedef*. After that there is a declaration of the base interface for objects that will feature code methods for communication. As in Java, C++, and c#, each block program begins with { and finishes with a }. In addition, each line of the code is terminated with a semicolon. The name of the interface described by us is Combine. In its simplest form it should implement two methods *SamplesToCombine* and *SendAnswers*. Those methods are sufficient to create the communication between ServerMS and ClientMS programs.

## 3  Experiments

We performed an experiment on the Glass Identification dataset [14]. The goal is to classify window and non-window glass on the basis of nine features. As we can see in Table 1, boosting procedure created five classifiers, each with two fuzzy rules. The ensemble achieved 97.67% overall classification accuracy. Each classifier had its own software instance with data handled by the server and was learned by the backpropagation algorithm.

**Table 1.** Experiment results for Glass Identification dataset and boosting

|  | Classifier 1 | Classifier 2 | Classifier 3 | Classifier 4 | Classifier 5 |
|---|---|---|---|---|---|
| No of rules | 2 | 2 | 2 | 2 | 2 |
| No of epochs | 20 | 30 | 50 | 100 | 40 |
| coeff. $c_t$ | 0.13024 | 0.00601 | 0.173716 | 0.345017 | 0.345017 |
| Classification accuracy % | 88.37 | 76.74 | 90.6 | 97.67 | 97.67 |

## 4  Summary and Conclusions

We developed a software system for creating and learning various types of ensembles in a distributed, platform-independent environment. It allows to create, describe and save network machine learning structures in an XML form. The system consists of the server and learner modules. Communication between them is done by CORBA remote procedure calls. The server handles the data needed to learn the ensemble subsystems and collects the data from them. The system can operate on various platforms as the IDL language allows to exchange data between them. Currently we implemented bagging, boosting and the backpropagation algorithm for any type of base learner structures.

**Acknowledgments.** This work was supported by the Polish National Science Centre (NCN) within project number DEC-2011/01/D/ST6/06957.

# References

1. Akhtar, Z., Rattani, A., Foresti, G.L.: Temporal analysis of adaptive face recognition. Journal of Artificial Intelligence and Soft Computing Research 4(4), 243–255 (2014)
2. Boukhtouta, A., Berger, J., George, A., Powell, W.B.: An approximate dynamic programming approach for semi-cooperative multi-agent resource management. Journal of Artificial Intelligence and Soft Computing Research 2(3), 201–214 (2012)
3. Breiman, L.: Bias, variance, and arcing classifiers. Technical Report In: Technical Report 460, Statistics Department, University of California (1997)
4. Bruzdzinski, T., Krzyzak, A., Fevens, T., Jelen, L.: Web–based framework for breast cancer classification. Journal of Artificial Intelligence and Soft Computing Research 4(2), 149–162 (2014)
5. Chu, J.L., Krzyak, A.: The recognition of partially occluded objects with support vector machines and convolutional neural networks and deep belief networks. Journal of Artificial Intelligence and Soft Computing Research 4(1), 5–19 (2014)
6. Collobert, R., Bengio, S., Mariéthoz, J.: Torch: a modular machine learning software library. Technical report, IDIAP (2002)
7. Cpalka, K., Rutkowski, L.: Flexible takagi-sugeno fuzzy systems. In: Proceedings of the 2005 IEEE International Joint Conference on Neural Networks, IJCNN 2005, vol. 3, pp. 1764–1769 (July 2005)
8. Folly, K.A.: Parallel pbil applied to power system controller design. Journal of Artificial Intelligence and Soft Computing Research 3(3), 215–223 (2013)
9. Hall, M., Frank, E., Holmes, G., Pfahringer, B., Reutemann, P., Witten, I.H.: The weka data mining software: an update. ACM SIGKDD Explorations Newsletter 11(1), 10–18 (2009)
10. Kilicaslan, Y., Tuna, G.: An nlp-based approach for improving human-robot interaction. Journal of Artificial Intelligence and Soft Computing Research 3(3), 189–200 (2013)
11. Korytkowski, M., Scherer, R., Rutkowski, L., Drozda, G.: Xml-based language for connectionist structure description. In: Cader, A., Rutkowski, L., Tadeusiewicz, R., Zurada, J. (eds.) Artificial Intelligence and Soft Computing, pp. 469–474. Academic Publishing House EXIT, Warsaw (2006)
12. Koshiyama, A.S., Vellasco, M.M.B.R., Tanscheit, R.: Gpfis-control: A genetic fuzzy system for control tasks. Journal of Artificial Intelligence and Soft Computing Research 4(3), 167–179 (2014)

13. Kuncheva, L.: Combining Pattern Classifiers. STUDFUZZ. John Wiley & Sons (2004)
14. Lichman, M.: UCI machine learning repository (2013)
15. Meir, R., Rätsch, G.: An introduction to boosting and leveraging. In: Mendelson, S., Smola, A.J. (eds.) Advanced Lectures on Machine Learning. LNCS (LNAI), vol. 2600, pp. 118–183. Springer, Heidelberg (2003)
16. Pedregosa, F., Varoquaux, G., Gramfort, A., Michel, V., Thirion, B., Grisel, O., Blondel, M., Prettenhofer, P., Weiss, R., Dubourg, V., et al.: Scikit-learn: Machine learning in python. The Journal of Machine Learning Research 12, 2825–2830 (2011)
17. Rigatos, G.G., Siano, P.: Flatness-based adaptive fuzzy control of spark-ignited engines. Journal of Artificial Intelligence and Soft Computing Research 4(4), 231–242 (2014)
18. Rutkowski, L.: Flexible Neuro-Fuzzy Systems. Kluwer Academic Publishers (2004)
19. Rutkowski, L.: Computational Intelligence Methods and Techniques. Springer, Heidelberg (2008)
20. Saitoh, D., Hara, K.: Mutual learning using nonlinear perceptron. Journal of Artificial Intelligence and Soft Computing Research 5(1), 71–77 (2015)
21. Schapire, R.E.: A brief introduction to boosting. In: Conference on Artificial Intelligence, pp. 1401–1406 (1999)
22. Setness, M., Babuska, R.: Bagging predictors. Machine Learning 26(2), 123–140 (1996)
23. Tambouratzis, T., Chernikova, D., Pazsit, I.: Pulse shape discrimination of neutrons and gamma rays using kohonen artificial neural networks. Journal of Artificial Intelligence and Soft Computing Research 3(2), 77–88 (2013)
24. Theodoridis, D.C., Boutalis, Y.S., Christodoulou, M.A.: Robustifying analysis of the direct adaptive control of unknown multivariable nonlinear systems based on a new neuro-fuzzy method. Journal of Artificial Intelligence and Soft Computing Research 1(1), 59–79 (2011)

# Using Co-occurring Graph Patterns
# in Computer Aided Design Evaluation

Barbara Strug[1,2(✉)]

[1] Department of Physics, Astronomy and Applied Computer Science,
Jagiellonian University, Łojasiewicza 11, Krakow, Poland
[2] Department of Applied Computer Science,
AGH University of Science and Technology,
Al. Mickiewicza 30, 30 059 Krakow, Poland
bstrug@agh.edu.pl, barbara.strug@uj.edu.pl

**Abstract.** Different types of graphs can be used to represent designs.
Such graphs can be generated by different methods, both automatic and
interactive, as a result producing a large number of possible designs that
have to be evaluated in some way. As in many real world design problems
good designs share similar elements in this paper a method for design
evaluation based on patterns' co-occurrence is presented. It allows for
the designs to be evaluated at the level of its representation, and thus do
not require visualisation of designs. As a hypergraph-based representation is used for designs, patterns are selected by frequent graph mining
algorithm. An application of the proposed evaluation method is also presented. A floor layout design example is used to illustrate the approach.

**Keywords:** Computer aided design · Hypergraph representation · Graph
patterns

## 1 Introduction

Graphs are a proven way of representing many complex objects in different domains of computer science [15] such as engineering, system modeling and testing,
bioinformatics, chemistry and other domains of science [2].

In this paper generalization of simple graphs known as hypergraphs is used
as a design object representation [9]. Designing new artifacts requires a method
of generating hypergraphs representing them. These methods researched include
those based on formal languages [15], graph based representation jointly with
graph grammars [2,8,14], and grammar systems [16,4,6,5], but also evolutionary
computations that were used in different domains of design [2,8,14].

As a result of a generative design a large database of hypergraphs - and at the
same time designs, is produced. Then, the basic problem is how to automatically
or semi-automatically evaluate the quality of the hypergraphs (where the quality
of a hypergraph is understood as the quality of the design it represents in respect
to a given design problem). In many cases the process of evaluation is solved by
the use of a human designer who selects best solution or assigns some numerical

© Springer International Publishing Switzerland 2015
L. Rutkowski et al. (Eds.): ICAISC 2015, Part II, LNAI 9120, pp. 768–777, 2015.
DOI: 10.1007/978-3-319-19369-4_68

values to each design. The requirement of the presence of the human "evaluator" limits the number of possible solutions that can be analysed as all hypergraphs have to be visualized, what in many design problems can be complex and time-consuming.

While the total elimination of the need for a human evaluator is not the aim of this research it would be useful to eliminate as many designs as possible on the basis of their structural or spatial flaws or on incompatibility with the design task being solved. Such problems could be found at the representation level without the need of visualizing designs. One of the possible approaches of eliminating the visualization step is to use the earlier designs, and their representations in form of hypergraphs, for which a quality in respect to a given task is already known, being defined by a human "evaluator". Such a set of previous designs can be considered as corresponding to the "prior knowledge" or "experience" factor used by the human designers.

It can be observed that designs getting high quality evaluations often are similar in some way, that is. they share some common elements. Thus exploring these common elements by finding frequently recurring substructures in hypergraphs is proposed in this paper.

## 2   Hypergraph Representation of Designs

The methods used in CAD problems, like boundary representations, sweep-volume representation, surface representations or CSG (constructive solid geometry) [13,11], usually allow for the geometry of an object being designed to be coded but do not take into account the inter-related structure of many design objects i.e. the fact that parts of an object can be related to other parts in different ways. A representation taking relations into account is usually based on some type of graphs. Different types of graphs have been researched and used in this domain, for example composition graphs [7]. In this paper hypergraphs are used.

Hypergraphs (HGs) consist of nodes and hyperedges. In simple graphs edges always connect two nodes, hypergraphs, on the other hand, are composed of nodes and hyperedges with different numbers of ordered *tentacles*, each of them linked to a node. Hyperedges used in this paper can represent both design components (component hyperedges) and relations among them (relational hyperedges).

Nodes and hyperedges in hypergraphs can be labelled and attributed. Labels are assigned to nodes and hyperedges by means of node and hyperedge labelling functions, respectively, and attributes - by node and hyperedge attributing functions. Labels usually denote the type of the entity represented by a given atom or geometrical primitive used. In case of the floor layout problem the labels denote type of the area (for component hyperedges) or the relation (for relational hyperedges) Attributes, on the other hand, represent properties (for example size, position, colour or material) of a component or relation represented by a given hyperedge. An example of a floor layout and its hypergraph representation is depicted in Fig. 1a and 1b, respectively. As there is no standard way of drawing hyperedges in this figure they are drawn as rectangles (for component hyperedges) and ellipsis (for relational hyperedges). Hyperedges are connected with nodes, denoted by small filed circles, by tentacles depicted as continuous line segments. Nodes are not labelled in the figure for the clarity reasons and they represent walls of the flat.

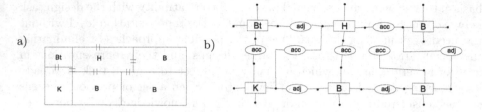

**Fig. 1.** Examples of a floor diagram and its hypergraph representation. Label B stands for a bedroom, Bt - for a bathroom, H - for a hall and K - for a kitchem, double lines in a flat diagram represent doors.

## 3   Frequent Pattern Mining in Design Evaluation

Frequent graph mining techniques are developed on the basis of a more general frequent pattern mining. Frequent pattern mining was first proposed by Agrawal et al. [1] for market basket analysis in the form of association rule mining and later extended for various kinds of applications, from scalable data mining methodologies, to handling a wide diversity of data types [12,10]. In graph mining a subgraph is considered frequent if its support, i.e. the number of graphs that contain this subgraph, is larger then some predefined threshold. The support is usually expressed as a percentage of graphs containing a given subgraph. In this paper two algorithms, FFSM and gSpan, are considered. Both algorithms can work on undirected graphs with labelled nodes and edges [24,23]. They perform the analysis of graphs in a depth-first order and can only find connected subgraphs. These algorithms are formulated for graphs. In case of hypergraphs some modifications must be introduced. Firstly both the nodes and hyperedges are treated in a way only nodes are treated in standard algorithm. Moreover the tentacles (shown as "links" joining visually hyperedges and nodes) in a hypergraph are treated as edges in the algorithm.

The approach to evaluating designs used in this paper has been implemented and tested on examples of a floor layout design. The process starts by coding a database of floor layouts, consisting of hypergraphs of size of 20 to 50 atoms, in GraphML format and importing to the GraphSearcher application [22]. Then the set of frequent patterns is generated and finally these patterns are used to evaluate new designs.

A number of experiments was carried out using different support values and both FFSM and gSpan algorithms. As the gSpan algorithm consistently generates more frequent patterns it is used as a basis for further experiments. More

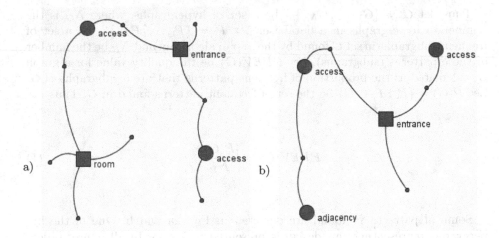

**Fig. 2.** Examples of frequent patterns representing design requirements and meaning-less rules

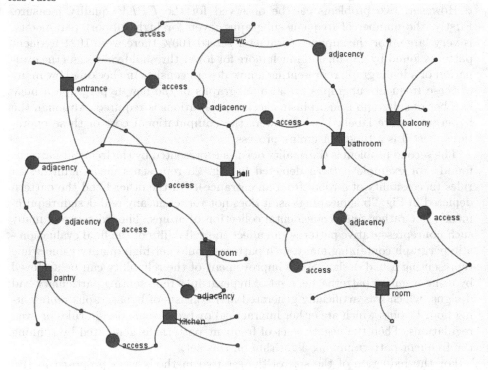

**Fig. 3.** Hypergraph representing a new design

detailed results obtained with the use of the FFSM method were presented in [17], and the results obtained with the use of the gSpan algorithm and a comparison of both results were presented in [18].

Thus, let $G = \{G_1, \ldots, G_{N_G}\}$ - be a set of hypergraphs, where $N_G$ is the number of hypergraphs in a database. Let $P = \{P_1, \ldots, P_{N_P}\}$ - be a set of frequent subgraphs in set $G$ found by the gSpan algorithm and $N_P$ be the number of these patterns (subgraphs). Let $FPEV(G)$ be the quality value for a graph $G$, calculated as the proportion of frequent patterns that are a subgraphs of $G$. Let $P(G) = \{P_i : P_i \subset G\}$ be the set of frequent patterns found in $G$. Thus

$$FPEV(G) = \frac{|P(G)|}{N_P}. \tag{1}$$

Some of patterns $P_i$ found are depicted in Fig. 2a and b. One of the hypergraphs representing new design is presented in Fig. 3. In all figures object hyperedges are depicted as squares and relational ones - as circles. For a hypergraph depicted in Fig. 3 the value $FPEV(G) = 0.91$

However, two problems can be observed for the $FPEV$ quality measure. Firstly, the number of frequent subgraphs, even for high support parameters, is very large. For the support parameter set to 100% there were 1021 frequent patterns found by gSpan, and much more for lower threshold values. As the evaluation of a hypergraph representing a new design consists in checking how many of these frequent subgraphs are also subgraphs of the new hypergraph a huge number of subgraph isomorphism checking operations is required. Although the hypergraphs are labelled, what lowers the computational cost of these operations, it still is a time consuming process.

The second problem is the quality of rules represented by the frequent patterns found. For example pattern depicted in Fig. 2a represents meaningful design rules (accessibility of a room from an entrance). On the other hand the pattern depicted in Fig. 2b is meaningless, it does not represent any real design requirements, but rather some coincidental collection of atoms. The existence of many such nonrepresentative patterns can affect the reliability of the final evaluation - a hypergraph containing many such patterns could get high quality value while representing a bad design. Some improvement of the reliability can be achieved by using negative patterns, i.e. a set of hypergraphs representing particulary bad designs, which was artificially generated and consists of hypergraphs representing floor layouts which are either impractical or break some design rules or even regulations. Then the negative set of frequent patterns is generated by running the frequent pattern mining algorithm on this set.

For the reduction of the size of the set two methods were proposed in [19] and in [20]. As for the second problem (i.e many meaningless patterns) a possible solution based on using negative patterns and frequency of occurrence was presented in [21].

In this paper another approach is taken; rather then defining different measures or reducing the set of frequent patterns a co-occurrence of patterns is analysed.

## 3.1 Using Pattern Co-Occurrence

As it was mentioned above a number of frequent patterns does not represent any meaningful design requirements. Moreover the fact that a given pattern is present in many good designs and represents a real design requirement or rule does not warrant it should positively contribute to the final evaluation of another design. In many cases a given pattern should only contribute to the final evaluation when it occurs alongside other pattern or group of patterns.

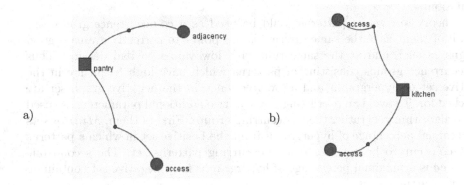

**Fig. 4.** Examples of frequent patterns mostly useful when occurring together

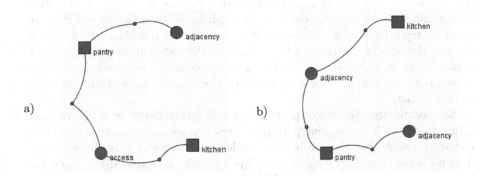

**Fig. 5.** Examples of patterns containing elements of co-occurring patterns

For example a frequent pattern depicted in Fig. 4a represent a design requirement of a pantry being accessible from some other space and also being adjacent to at least one other space. While this is a sensible requirement on its own, actually the existence of pantry makes more sense when a kitchen is also present in the same design. In typical design tasks the presence of a pantry without a kitchen can even not be permitted, thus making the same pattern depicted in Fig. 4a a negative one. As in many cases a pantry would be either accessible from the kitchen or at least adjacent to it such a design requirement would be represented by one of patterns shown in Fig. 5a and b. Yet, this pattern can not replace the co-occurring patterns from Fig. 4a and b, as the pantry can be separated from the kitchen by a hall, passageway or other spaces without it significantly lowering the evaluation for a given design. So this example demonstrates that the same frequent pattern can represent positive or negative rule depending on the context in which it occurs i.e. on other frequent patterns present (or not) in a given hyper graph.

Thus the goal is to find frequent patterns and then group them into sets of frequently co-occurring patterns that can be used as the basis for the quality evaluation.

In theory any set of patterns could be used as a co-occurrence group, but not all of them have the same discriminative power to correctly evaluate good designs as such and at the same time give low values to bad designs. Thus co-occurrence groups consisting of patterns which have high frequency in the positive set of hypergraphs and a low frequency in the negative graph set are searched for. To avoid an overfitting problem two additional parameters are used in the algorithm generating the co-occurring groups. First of them, $MinPos$ sets the minimal percentage of hypergraphs from the positive set in which a patterns must co-occur to be considered a co-occurring patterns set. The second one $MaxNeg$ is a maximal percentage of hypergraphs from negative set containing the co-occurring group.

Finding such sets requires two steps. In the first one each frequent subgraph found by the mining algorithm is assigned numbers of hypergraphs it is found in (from both positive and negative sets). This step in practice is performed at the same time as the mining for frequent patterns by small modification of the mining algorithm. For each hypergraph in a set a list is maintained, containing references to all frequent subgraphs it contains. Each time a new frequent subgraph is determined and added to the set of frequent patterns, a reference to it is added to the beginning of appropriate reference lists. Thus this step does not increase the complexity of the algorithm, as it only involves maintaining lists.

In the second step the set of groups of co-occurring patterns is determined. Starting from the first frequent pattern a largest possible group of co-occuring patterns and such that they co-occur in at least $MinPos$ positive hypergraphs and in no more then $MaxNeg$ negative hypergraphs is searched for. Then the patterns included in this group are discarded and subsequent groups are determined following the same rule. This process ends when no more frequent patterns exist or no more group satisfying threshold values can be built.

Then the groups are used to evaluate new designs. Each design is given a quality value which, similarly to using single frequent patterns, is the function of the number of groups of co-occurring patterns it contains. Moreover a contribution each group makes to the total quality value is based on its *positive discrimination factor* - $PosF$, i.e. how likely it is that the co-occurring patterns represent positive and not negative design rule. This rate is calculated as a difference between the frequency of the group in positive set and in negative set divided by 100. Thus, obviously $PosF \in [(MinPos - MaxNeg)/100, 1]$ with the value of 1 reached for groups of patterns co-occurring in all hypergraphs in positive set and in none of the negative set. Then the quality value based on the co-occurring patterns $CoEV$ is calculated in the following way:

$$CoEV(G) = \frac{\sum_{i=1}^{|C_G|} PosF_i}{MaxEV}, \tag{2}$$

where $G$ is a hypergraph being evaluated, $C_G$ is the number of co-occurring groups contained in $G$, $PosF_i$ is the positive discrimination factor for the $i - th$ group. $MaxEV$ is the maximum possible value of the evaluation i.e. $MaxEV = \sum_{i=1}^{NumG} PosF_i$ (where $NumG$ is the total number of groups of co-occuring patterns found). Thus $CoEV \in [0, 1]$.

The approach presented above was tested on a small set of new hypergraphs representing designs not present in the positive and negative sets used to generate groups of patterns. The set consisted of six hypergraphs, three of them represented good designs (denoted by G in table 1, two moderately good but still acceptable (denoted by M) and one very bad (denoted by B). Table 1 contains evaluation values calculated for all test hypergraphs with different threshold values ($MinPos$ and $MaxNeg$) as well as the values obtained by the use of single frequent patterns (equation 1).

It can be observed that increasing the $MaxNeg$ threshold increases the quality value, what most likely is caused by the higher number of negative patterns allowed. Yet, the general "ranking" of hypergraphs is preserved. In all caesa good hypergraphs receive consistently higher values then medium or bad ones. More importantly, the good hypergraphs get usually higher quality values then those assigned by single patterns, and the bad ones get usually lower quality values then when using only single patterns. Thus this approach seems better at discriminating between good and bad designs.

**Table 1.** Experimental results for some of test hypergraphs

| measure | FPEV | CoEV | | | |
|---------|------|------|------|------|------|
| MinPos  |      | 80 % | 80 % | 90 % | 90 % |
| MaxNeg  |      | 10 % | 5 %  | 10 % | 5 %  |
| G1      | 0.92 | 0.98 | 0.93 | 0.97 | 0.94 |
| G2      | 0.83 | 0.89 | 0.86 | 0.90 | 0.85 |
| G3      | 0.91 | 0.92 | 0.88 | 0.95 | 0.94 |
| M1      | 0.55 | 0.53 | 0.45 | 0.49 | 0.47 |
| M2      | 0.62 | 0.60 | 0.60 | 0.60 | 0.58 |
| B1      | 0.24 | 0.19 | 0.17 | 0.20 | 0.22 |

## 4   Concluding Remarks and Future Work

In this paper the approach based on using groups of co-occurring patterns as a tool to evaluate the quality of designs at the level of hypergraph representation.

The results obtained suggest that this approach is better at discriminating between good and bad designs then using single frequent patterns. In the approach presented in this paper neither the size of each group of frequent co-occurring patterns nor the size of frequent patterns included in these groups is taken into account. Yet, it is possible that a large pattern would bring more information then a small one so some weighting of patterns is planned to be tested. Moreover the groups are established by a greedy algorithm and use each frequent pattern only once. Establishing the groups in different way, such that would maximizes the number of hypergraphs that can be given the best (i.e. closest to a human designer) evaluation is also planned.

# References

1. Agrawal, R., Imielinski, T., Swami, A.: Mining association rules between sets of items in large databases. In: Proc. 1993 ACM-SIGMOD, pp. 207–216 (1993)
2. Borkowski, A., Grabska, E., Nikodem, P., Strug, B.: Searching for Innovative Structural Layouts by Means of Graph Grammars and Esvolutionary Optimization. In: Proc. 2nd ISEC Conf., Rome, pp. 475–480 (2003)
3. Csuhaj-Varjú, E., Dassow, J., Kelemen, J., Paun, G.: Grammar systems. A grammatical approach to distribution and cooperation. Topics in Computer Mathematics 8. Gordon and Breach Science Publishers, Yverdon (1994)
4. Csuhaj-Varjú, E.: Grammar systems: A short survey. In: Proceedings of Grammar Systems Week 2004, pp. 141–157, Budapest, Hungary (2004)
5. Csuhaj-Varjú, E., Vaszil, G.: On context-free parallel communicating grammar systems: Synchronization, communication, and normal forms. Theor. Comp. Sc. 255(1-2), 511–538 (2001)
6. Csuhaj-Varjú, E., Dassow, J., Paun, G.: Dynamically controlled cooperating/distributed grammar systems. Information Sciences 69(1-2), 1–25 (1993)
7. Grabska, E.: Graphs and designing. LNCS, vol. 776. Springer, Heidelberg (1994)
8. Grabska, E., Nikodem, P., Strug, B.: Evolutionary Methods and Graph Grammars in Design and Optimization of Skeletal Structures Weimar. In: 11th ICE 2004 (2004)
9. Habel, A., Kreowski, H.J.: Some structural aspects of hypergraph languages generated by hyperedge replacement. In: Brandenburg, F.J., Wirsing, M., Vidal-Naquet, G. (eds.) STACS 1987. LNCS, vol. 247, pp. 207–219. Springer, Heidelberg (1987)
10. Han, J., Pei, J., Yin, Y., Mao, R.: Mining Frequent Patterns without Candidate Generation: A Frequent-pattern Tree Approach. Data Mining and Knowledge Discovery 8(1), 53–87 (2004)
11. Hoffman, C.M.: Geometric and Solid Modeling: An Introduction. Morgan Kaufmann, San Francisco (1989)
12. Inokuchi, A., Washio, T., Motoda, H.A.: An Apriori-Based Algorithm for Mining Frequent Substructures from Graph Data. In: Proc. of PKDD 2000, pp. 87–92 (2000)
13. Mantyla, M.: An Introduction To Solid Modeling, vol. 87. Computer Science Press, Rockville (1988)
14. Nikodem, P., Strug, B.: Graph Transformations in Evolutionary Design. In: Rutkowski, L., Siekmann, J.H., Tadeusiewicz, R., Zadeh, L.A. (eds.) ICAISC 2004. LNCS (LNAI), vol. 3070, pp. 456–461. Springer, Heidelberg (2004)

15. Rozenberg, G.: Handbook of Graph Grammars and Computing by Graph Transformations, vol. 1-3. World Scientific, London (1997-1999)
16. Simeoni, M., Staniszkis, M.: Cooperating graph grammar systems. In: Grammatical Models of Multi-agent Systems, pp. 193–217. Gordon and Breach (1999)
17. Strug, B., Ślusarczyk, G.: Reasoning about designs through frequent patterns mining. Advanced Engineering Informatics 23, 361–369 (2009)
18. Strug, B., Ślusarczyk, G.: Frequent Pattern Mining in a Design Supporting System. Key Engineering Materials 450, 1–4 (2011); Trans. Tech. Pub.
19. Strug, B.: Using graph mining approach to automatic reasoning in design support systems. In: Burduk, R., Kurzyński, M., Woźniak, M., Żołnierek, A. (eds.) Computer Recognition Systems 4. AISC, vol. 95, pp. 489–498. Springer, Heidelberg (2011)
20. Strug, B.: Selection of Subgraphs for Automatic Reasoning in Design Systems. In: Corchado, E., Kurzyński, M., Woźniak, M. (eds.) HAIS 2011, Part I. LNCS, vol. 6678, pp. 280–287. Springer, Heidelberg (2011)
21. Strug, B.: Graph Similarity Measure in Automatic Evaluation of Designs. In: Czachórski, T., Kozielski, S., Stańczyk, U. (eds.) Man-Machine Interactions 2. AISC, vol. 103, pp. 267–275. Springer, Heidelberg (2011)
22. Tomanek, M.: Searching for graph patterns and applications. MSc thesis, Jagiellonian University (2009) (in Polish)
23. Yan, X., Yu, P.S., Han, J.: Substructure Similarity Search in Graph Databases. In: SIGMOD 2005, pp. 766–777 (2005)
24. Yan, X., Yu, P.S., Han, J.: Graph Indexing: A Frequent Structure-based Approach. In: SIGMOD 2004, pp. 335–346 (2004)

# Parallel Cost Function Determination on GPU for the Vehicle Routing Problem

Mieczysław Wodecki[1], Wojciech Bożejko[2(✉)], Szymon Jagiełło[2],
and Jarosław Pempera[2]

[1] Institute of Computer Science, University of Wrocław,
Joliot-Curie 15, 50-383 Wrocław, Poland
mieczyslaw.wodecki@ii.uni.wroc.pl
[2] Department of Automatics, Mechatronics and Control Systems,
Faculty of Electronics, Wrocław University of Technology,
Wyb. Wyspiańskiego 27, 50-370 Wrocław, Poland
{wojciech.bozejko,szymon.jagiello,jarolaw.pempera}@pwr.edu.pl

**Abstract.** The paper deals with parallel variants of optimization algorithms dedicated to solve transportation optimization issues. The problem derives from practice of logistics and vehicle routes planning. We propose parallelization method of the cost function determination dedicated to be executed on GPU architecture. The method can be used in metaheuristic algorithms as well as in exact approaches. [1]

## 1 Introduction

Vehicle Routing Problem (VRP) is an NP-hard problem, which solution constitutes a key element for effectiveness improvement in transportation. The problem, introduced by Dantzig and Ramser [8] in 1959, appears in many variants with different level of complexity. From this time literature relating to it has been expanded by thousands of items. The software used to solve VRP problems generates considerable savings of 5% – 30% for Companies which are using it [10]. Up to now, the exact methods are not able to solve in a reasonable time solutions for instances with more than 50 - 100 clients [10]. This is a very serious limit if we take into account that customer lists of large companies may contain thousands of items. Consequently, for such cases, it is necessary to use approximate methods.

In Capacitated Vehicle Routing Problem (CVRP) we consider the following scenario: we own a delivery business that sends goods to clients via vehicles. Transport begins at the base station. The time needed to travel from base station to every client (and from every client to every other client) is known. We can look at this set-up as a full weighted graph with one highlighted vertex. The goal is to deliver every package to clients in the smallest possible time according to their demands. The capacity of each vehicles is fixed. The vehicles needs to

---

[1] The work was partially supported by the OPUS grant DEC-2012/05/B/ST7/00102 of Polish National Centre of Science.

L. Rutkowski et al. (Eds.): ICAISC 2015, Part II, LNAI 9120, pp. 778–788, 2015.
DOI: 10.1007/978-3-319-19369-4_69

go back to the base station to reload when empty. A general CVRP assume that demand of every client, number of vehicles and their capacity are not bound by any assertion. The vehicle routing problems have been attracting the interest of combinatorial optimization experts for over 50 years. The motivation to study this class of problems lies in its relevance to the real world as well as in its difficulty. One of books that are worth mentioning is [17]. It is an overview of main VRP variations (including CVRP). The authors show both exact and heuristic methods of finding the solutions. Large portion of the book covers the main variations, like: VRP with time windows, backhauls, pickup and delivery. Parallel Tabu Search for multi-criteria VRP problem was proposed in [11]. Other efficient methods, for multi-criteria discrete problems, were proposed and tested. Among them simulated annealing [13], genetic algorithm with local search method [15] or GACO hybrid algorithm [16]. Our further research on the multi-criteria VRP will certainly draw from the above mentioned work.

In our variation of the CVRP we assume that every client demands exactly one package and we have only one delivery vehicle with fixed capacity. It is easy to see that with these constraints our problem transforms into a permutation problem. Furthermore, it is very similar to the classical Travelling Salesman Problem (TSP) [7] with only difference being exclusion of the base station from permutation. Therefore, only vertices that represent clients are being permutated. Next, we can evenly partition the resulting permutation into sets of size equal to the capacity of the vehicle. These sets represent paths the vehicle will make with each round of deliveries.

The main goal of the research presented in this paper is to propose a new methodology of parallelization of the cost function determination function dedicated to be executed on the GPGPU (*General-Purpose computing on Graphics Processing Units*). The paper is organized as follows: firstly, we give a specification of the CVRP variation we will be solving. Next, we introduce multi-GPU algorithm. After that we show the results of the performed experiments. The main goal is to show the scalability of the algorithm.

## 2   Problem Definition

We consider Capacity constrained VRP (CVRP) here, in which the main constraint is connected with capacity of a single vehicle. Assumptions of the *CVRP* are:

- a fixed number of identical vehicles with specific capacity,
- a fixed number of customers with a specific orders of sizes and locations
- vehicles are able to perform client orders, but the total size handled by vehicle orders cannot be larger than its carrying capacity,
- vehicles are located in a central base, in which they starts and finish its work,
- travel costs between the points are given,
- the goal of optimization is to minimize the cost of customers service.

An instance of the *CVRP* can be described with using following notions:

$$C = \{1, ..., n\} \quad - \text{set of clients},$$  (1)
$$G = (N, E) \quad - \text{graph, where}$$  (2)
$$N = \{0\} \cup C \quad - \text{base with a set of clients (set of vertexes),}$$  (3)
$$E \subseteq N \times N \quad - \text{set of edges},$$  (4)
$$D = \{d_1, ..., d_n\} \quad - \text{size of order of particular clients,}$$  (5)
$$q \geq d_i, i \in \{1, ..., n\} \quad - \text{capacity of a single vehicle,}$$  (6)
$$V = \{1, ..., K\} \quad - \text{set of vehicles,}$$  (7)
$$[A_{ij}] \quad - \text{matrix of transport costs for}$$
$$\text{elements of the set } N, i, j = 0, 1, 2, \ldots, n.$$  (8)

A solution of the *CVRP* consists of above elements and fulfills constraints presented below:

- $K$ routes(single route for each vehicle),
- beginning and end of each routes in the same base,
- total size of all order on the route $\leq q$,
- each client is served exactly one time,
- sum of costs of driving on the particular route the cost of this route,
- sum of routes costs is the cost of the solution.

The aim of the optimization can be formulated as:

*Find a solution with the smallest cost.*

An adequate formal description can be presented as:

$$\text{minimalize} \sum_{k \in V} \sum_{\substack{i = \{0,1,...,n\} \\ j = \{0,1,...,n\}}} A_{ij} x_{ij}^k,$$  (9)

$$\text{where } x_{ij}^k = \begin{cases} 1, & \text{if the vehicle } k \text{ drives from } i \text{ to } j \\ 0, & \text{otherwise.} \end{cases}$$

## 3  Parallel Algorithm

The role of parallel algorithms which solves NP-hard problems significantly increased in the last decade, in particular for vehicle routing problems.

Rego [14] proposed a parallel tabu search algorithm (see also [4,5,6]) for the VRP which uses *ejection chain* type neighborhood; four *slave* processors were used in the implementation. The SSMS (*Single Starting point Multiple Strategies*) model was used, according to the classification Vo ss and  cite Voss, i.e. slave processors receive the same starting solution, but have used different search strategies. Evaluation of the objective function also takes place concurrently.

Alba and Dorronsoro [1] proposed parallel genetic algorithm for VRP (*cellular* version), wherein crossover and mutations operators used local search procedures. The algorithm allowed oppearing if unfeasible solutions using the appropriately modified cost (penalty) function. The population is organized in mesh structure with crossover limitation to four neighbors on the mesh (see [2]).

Multi-colonial ant colony optimization (ACO) algorithm for VRP was proposed in the work of Doerner et al. [9]. Authors propose three different strategies of *master-slave* type with using standard local search operators and focusing exclusively on sequential algorithm speedup without improvement of the quality of obtained solutions. Tests were performed on 32 processors. Computational experiments show good scalability of the algorithm using up to 8 processors, for the greater number of them, as a result of increase the role of communication in parallel algorithm, the efficiency deteriorating.

On the other hand, for the problem of routing with time windows (*VRP with Time Windows*, VRPTW) Bouthillier and Crainic [12] proposed an effective procedure of parallel optimization based on four metaheuristics (two based on the tabu search method and two genetic-based approaches) and post-optimization procedure which uses *ejection chains* technique as well as local search procedures. The authors analyzed the profit resulting from co-operating nature of their algorithm by comparing the quality of obtained solutions with the approach without communication between processors.

## 4    Case Study

The huge computational complexity of the problem forces the use of more sophisticated techniques than a complete overview. No matter what technique will be used common fragments which are specific for a problem will occur. For VRP problems one of such parts is computing the cost of a solution. The following paper provides a study of scalability for computing the solution cost by using GPU units for three problems: VRP (without any limitations), Distance constrained Vehicle Routing PRoblem (DVRP) and Distance and Capacity Constrained Vehicle Routing Problem (DCVRP).

### 4.1    Generation of Test Data

Test data was generated in the initialization phase of the algorithm. In order to generate the cost (distance) matrix a pseudo-random number generator (srand function from gcc 4.4.3) was initialized with the constant value 7378342. Matrix elements were calculated as follow:

- if the element is located on the main diagonal of the matrix it takes the value 0,
- if the element is located above the main diagonal it is set to a random value in the range from 1 to 30 (computed by using rand function from gcc 4.4.3),

– if the element is located below the main diagonal then it will take the value of an element obtained by swapping its indexes. Next a pseudo-random test number is drawn. If it is even then the element value will increase by 0.20 and decrease by 0.20 otherwise.

In order to generate the capacity demands of each client a pseudo-random number generator (srand function from gcc 4.4.3) was initialized with the constant value 478 342. Each value was pseudo-randomly selected within the range from 0 to 99 (computed by using rand function from gcc 4.4.3).

The solutions were constructed in two stages. In the first stage the length of the route for a single vehicle was calculated by dividing the number of customers by the number of available vehicles (1 was added to the length of the route for the first R routes, where R is the rest of the division). Next the vehicle routes were populated with rising client numbers. In the second stage the order of solution elements was changed pseudo-randomly. For this purpose, a pseudo-random number generator was initialized with the constant value 5625 (srand function from gcc 4.4.3). Next two positions were picked pseudo-randomly and their values were swapped. The action was repeated as many times as the solution length.

## 4.2   Hardware

Studies were performed by using the following hardware:

– Intel R Core i7 CPU X 980 @ 3.33GHz (12 available cores),
– 24GB RAM memory,
– nVidia Tesla S2050 - 4 GPU units, each with 448 cores, 14 multiprocessors and 3GB RAM memory (global).

Used GPU units are equipped with the following types of memory (OpenCL names):

– global memory - the largest and slowest volume of available memory,
– constant memory - heavily buffered (an therefore much faster) read-only global memory. For Tesla S2050 GPU units its volume is limited to 64KB,
– local memory - very fast on-chip memory. For Tesla S2050 GPU units its volume is limited to 48KB per multiprocessor,
– private memory - this term usually refers to the registers.

Used GPU units provide a mechanism that can hide the global memory latency by minimising memory transactions. Unfortunately random accesses which are present in cost determination for the VRP problems make it impossible to take advantage of it.

## 4.3   Solution Methods

The maximum number of threads used was calculated by multiplying the total number of available cores with a multiplier. The resulting value is rounded up to the nearest multiple of the block size. Solutions are divided between the available devices (GPU) and threads (not necessarily the maximum number). While running the algorithm each threads calculates the costs for its set of solutions.

For the VRP problem the cost (distance) matrix and appropriate solutions were copied to the global memory of available devices. Additional global memory area is reserved for returning the calculated total cost value for each solution. The calculation is mostly associated with data reads of the first two global memory areas.

For the DVRP problem no additional data was copied to the devices but an additional global memory region was allocated for returning the maximum vehicle distance for each solution. The algorithm was slightly more complex due to the calculation of two costs but it does not involve additional reading of global memory. Computational overhead associated with parallelism remains unchanged, so the scalability of the problem DVRP should be slightly better than the VRP problem.

For the DCVRP problem additional data containing the clients capacity demands was copied to the devices. This data was read for calculating the maximum load of a single vehicle for each solution. Due to the necessity of additional cost calculation the algorithm gained complexity again but it is associated with additional global memory readings. In order to minimize the latency impact the algorithm was developed in two versions. The first version holds the additional DCVRP specific data in the global memory and the second in the constant memory. Computational overhead associated with parallelism is identical for both versions, so the scalability for the version using constant memory should be better. Fig. 1 contains the GPU code fragment which is responsible for calculating the costs for the DCVRP problem with constant memory.

## 4.4   Computational Experiments

The study was focused on the analysis of the scalability of calculating solutions costs for three problems (VRP, DVRP, DCVRP). The DCVRP problem was tested in two variants. In total four problems were tested.

The maximum number of threads was determined by multiplying the number of available cores by the multiplier. Each problem was tested with three different multiplier values (1, 2, 3).

The figures Fig.1.A., Fig.1.B, Fig.1.C, Fig.1.D. present the speed up (code executed on the GPU) for an increasing number of threads with respect to one thread for all four problems, the multiplier value set to 3, the length of a single solution set to 1099 and the total number of solutions set to 40000. The speedup is increasing even when the number of threads exceeds the number of available cores. This increase is relatively stable when the number of threads is less than about 2400.

Maximal speedups obtained for a particular problem was:

− VRP: 1098.17,

```
//This is one of the cost functions used to calculate the costs
//__global and __constant - address space used to refer to memory
//       objects allocated in the global or constant memory pool
//COST_TYPE - data type used to store track costs
//CAPA_TYPE - data type used to store vehicle capacities/client demands
//matrix, matrixRank - cost matrix and rank of the matrix
//clientCapas - demands of all clients
//solution, solLen - the solution and length of the solution
//cost, maxVehicle, maxVehicleCapa - variables used to return the calculated
//       values of cost of all tracks, maximum track cost, maximum track demand
void dcvrpCountCost(__global COST_TYPE* matrix, int matrixRank,
                __constant CAPA_TYPE * clientCapas,
                __global int * solution, int solLen,
                __global COST_TYPE * cost, __global COST_TYPE * maxVehicleCost,
                __global CAPA_TYPE * maxVehicleCapa) {

        //following 5 variables are stored in private memory (usually registers)
        //private memory is the fastest type of memory avialable
        COST_TYPE totalSolCost = 0;

        //dvrp
        COST_TYPE vehicleCost = matrix[0 + solution[0]];
        COST_TYPE tmp_maxVehicleCost = 0;

        //cvrp
        CAPA_TYPE vehicleCapa = clientCapas[solution[0]-1];
        CAPA_TYPE tmp_maxVehicleCapa = 0;

        //iterate over the elements of the solution
        for(int i=0; i<sol_len-1; i++) {
                //add travel cost between two clients or base to current track cost
                vehicleCost += matrix[solution[i]*matrixRank + solution[i+1]];
                //add client demand to current track demand
                if(solution[i] != 0) {
                        vehicleCapa += clientCapas[solution[i]-1];
                }
                //if this is true then all costs and demands of
                //the current track have been added
                if(solution[i+1]==0) {
                        //dvrp
                        //check if the current track has the biggest cost
                        if(i==0 || tmp_maxVehicleCost<vehicleCost) {
                                tmp_maxVehicleCost = vehicleCost;
                        }
                        //cvrp
                        //check if the current track has the biggest demand
                        if(i==0 || tmp_maxVehicleCapa<vehicleCapa) {
                                tmp_maxVehicleCapa = vehicleCapa;
                        }
                        //add current track cost to total cost of all tracks
                        totalSolCost += vehicleCost;
                        vehicleCost = 0;
                        vehicleCapa = 0;
                }
        }
        //following operations are used for the last track
        vehicleCost += matrix[solution[sol_len-1]*matrixRank + 0];
        vehicleCapa += clientCapas[solution[sol_len-1]-1];
        totalSolCost += vehicleCost;

        //dvrp
        if(tmp_maxVehicleCost<vehicleCost) {
                tmp_maxVehicleCost = vehicleCost;
        }
        //cvrp
        if(tmp_maxVehicleCapa<vehicleCapa) {
                tmp_maxVehicleCapa = vehicleCapa;
        }

        //copy the results to global memory
        *cost = totalSolCost;
        *maxVehicleCost = tmp_maxVehicleCost;
        *maxVehicleCapa = tmp_maxVehicleCapa;
}
```

**Fig. 1.** GPU code

- DVRP: 1419.27,
- DCVRP with global memory: 1395.84,
- DCVRP with constant memory: 1457.15.

The significant speedup improvement is very explicit between the DVRP and VRP problems which confirms previous assumptions. Increased complexity of the DCVRP algorithm was not enough to compensate the additional global memory readings. Therefore the maximal speedup obtained for DCVRP with global memory was lower than the maximal speedup for the DVRP problem. The use of constant memory has significantly increased this value so that it was even better than the speed up value obtained for the DVRP problem.

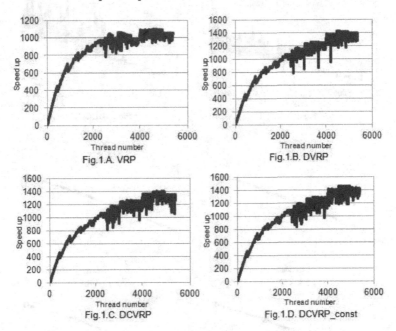

Fig.1.A. VRP     Fig.1.B. DVRP

Fig.1.C. DCVRP     Fig.1.D. DCVRP_const

The figures Fig.2.A., Fig.2.B, Fig.2.C, Fig.2.D. present the change of the optimum block size with respect to the number of threads (block size was tested in the range from 1 to 32). A relatively stable growth can be observed when the number of threads is less than about 2400. Beyond this value the optimum size of the block still does not fall below certain base levels. For example for the DCVRP with constant memory the block size base level increases after the number of threads exceeds 448, 904, 1368, 1808, 2340. The number of available multiprocessors is 4x14=56 so the number of blocks is never greater than 8-9 per multiprocessor.

The figures Fig.3.A., Fig.3.B, Fig.3.C, Fig.3.D. present the obtained speedup for different number of devices (in respect to one device) for all four problems. For four devices the speed up was never less than 3.5 times.

The figure Fig.4. presents the execution time (GPU code) for the studied problems depending the number of solutions (the solution length is 1099). Explicit

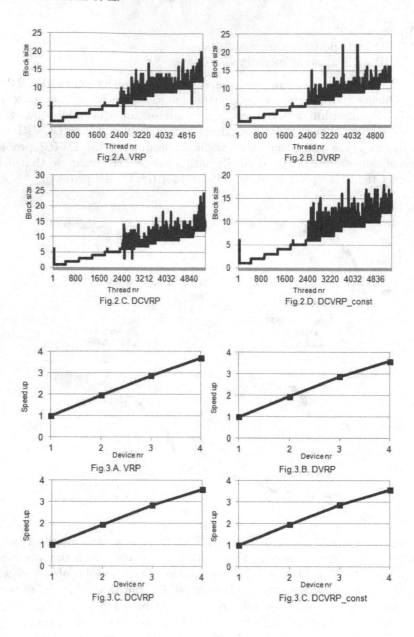

Fig.2.A. VRP

Fig.2.B. DVRP

Fig.2.C. DCVRP

Fig.2.D. DCVRP_const

Fig.3.A. VRP

Fig.3.B. DVRP

Fig.3.C. DCVRP

Fig.3.C. DCVRP_const

increase can be observed between the VRP, DVRP and DCVRP with global memory problems. For the DCVRP with constant memory problem the time has dropped so much that its chart practically overlaps with the time chart for the DVRP problem.

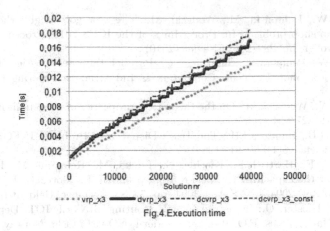

Fig.4.Execution time

## 5    Conclusions

Vehicles routes determination constitutes a major challenge for modern optimization algorithms. Most existing approaches are based on metaheuristic approach, due to the possibility of (approximate) solving of large size examples. Recently, the the role of parallel and distributed algorithms have been increasing, which further expands the range of potential applications of parallel discrete optimization methods in the field of logistics and management. Calculating the solution cost is one on of the most computationally intensive part of a local optimization algorithm of a VRP problem. In this paper we have checked the possibility to move cost calculation to the GPU in order to take advantage of the larger number of available cores. The method has been parallelized and tested against several aspects of the GPU architecture like the usage of different memory pools, different block sizes and number of threads in relation to the number of physical cores and multiprocessors.

## References

1. Alba, E., Dorronsoro, B.: Computing Nine New Best-So-Far Solutions for Capacitated VRP with a Cellular Genetic Algorithm. Information Processing Letters 98(6), 225–230 (2006)
2. Bożejko, W., Wodecki, M.: Parallel genetic algorithm for minimizing total weighted completion time. In: Rutkowski, L., Siekmann, J.H., Tadeusiewicz, R., Zadeh, L.A. (eds.) ICAISC 2004. LNCS (LNAI), vol. 3070, pp. 400–405. Springer, Heidelberg (2004)
3. Bożejko, W., Wodecki, M.: Parallel Evolutionary Algorithm for the Traveling Salesman Problem. Journal of Numerical Analysis, Industrial and Applied Mathematics 2(3-4), 129–137 (2007)
4. Bożejko, W., Wodecki, M.: Solving Permutational Routing Problems by Population-Based Metaheuristics. Computers & Industrial Engineering 57, 269–276 (2009)

5. Bożejko, W., Uchroński, M., Wodecki, M.: The new golf neighborhood for the flexible job shop problem. In: Proceedings of the ICCS 2010. Procedia Computer Science, vol. 1, pp. 289–296. Elsevier (2010)
6. Bożejko, W., Pempera, J., Smutnicki, C.: Parallel Tabu Search Algorithm for the Hybrid Flow Shop Problem. Computers & Industrial Engineering 65, 466–474 (2013)
7. Bożejko, W., Wodecki, M.: On the theoretical properties of swap multimuwes. Res. Lett. 35(2), 227–231 (2007)
8. Dantzig, G.B., Ramser, J.H.: The Truck Dispatching Problem, INFORMS. Management Science 6(1), 80–91 (1959)
9. Doerner, K.F., Hartl, R.F., Kiechle, G., Lucká, M., Reimann, M.: Parallel ant systems for the capacitated vehicle routing problem. In: Gottlieb, J., Raidl, G.R. (eds.) EvoCOP 2004. LNCS, vol. 3004, pp. 72–83. Springer, Heidelberg (2004)
10. Hasle, G., Kloster, O.: Industrial Vehicle Routing, SINTEF ICT, Department of Applied Mathematics, P.O. Box 124 Blindern, NO-0314 Oslo, Norway
11. Jagiełło, S., Żelazny, D.: Solving Multi-criteria Vehicle Routing Problem by Parallel Tabu Search on GPU. Procedia Computer Science (18), 2529–2532 (2013)
12. Le Bouthillier, A., Crainic, T.: A cooperative parallel meta-heuristic for the vehicle routing problem with time windows. Computers & Operations Research 32, 1685–1708 (2005)
13. Pempera, J., Smutnicki, C., Żelazny, D.: Optimizing bicriteria flow shop scheduling problem by simulated annealing algorithm. Procedia Computer Science (18), 936–945 (2013)
14. Rego, C.: Node-ejection chains for the vehicle routing problem: Sequential and parallel algorithms. Parallel Computing 27, 201–222 (2001)
15. Rudy, J., Żelazny, D.: Memetic algorithm approach for multi-criteria network scheduling. In: Proceeding of the International Conference on ICT Management for Global Competitiveness and Economic Growth in Emerging Economies (ICTM 2012), pp. 247–261 (2012)
16. Rudy, J., Żelazny, D.: GACO: a parallel evolutionary approach to multi-objective scheduling. In: Gaspar-Cunha, A., Henggeler Antunes, C., Coello, C.C. (eds.) EMO 2015. LNCS, vol. 9018, pp. 307–320. Springer, Heidelberg (2015)
17. Toth, P., Vigo, D.: Vehicle Routing Problem, Society for Industrial and Applied Mathematics, Philadelphia (2001)

# A DSS Based on Hybrid Meta-Heuristic ILS-VND for Solving the 1-PDTSP

Hiba Yahyaoui[(✉)] and Saoussen Krichen

LARODEC Laboratory, Higher Institute of Management,
University of Tunis, Tunis, Tunisia
hiba.yahyawi@gmail.com

**Abstract.** The one-commodity pickup-and-delivery travelling salesman problem is a well known combinatorial optimization problem applied in numerous practical situations. It consists of a set of customers dispersed on a geographical area and a vehicle with a predefined capacity that must not be exceeded. The vehicle starts from a depot, and should visit each customer only once then end at at the depot. The objective is to minimize the total length of the traveled path way. As the 1-PDTSP is known to be NP-hard, meta-heuristics perform well when generating solutions in a reasonable computation time. In this paper, we propose a hybrid-meta-heuristic Iterated Local search with Variable Neighborhood Descent (ILS-VND). In order to demonstrate the performance of the proposed approach in term of solution quality, we apply it on benchmark instances. Our approach is also applied in a real case on the city of Jendouba in the north west of Tunisia. The results are then highlighted in a cartographic format using Google Maps.

**Keywords:** Combinatorial optimization · Metaheuristics iterated local search · Pickup-and-delivery travelling salesman problem

## 1 Introduction

The one-commodity pickup-and-delivery travelling salesman problem (1-PDTSP) is a well-studied routing problem that belongs to the class NP-Hard combinatorial problems. It was introduced in [1] by Hernandez-Perez then extensively studied in the literature in various versions using alternative algorithmic approaches (see, e.g., [6], [5]) surveys was presented in [7], [8].

**Problem Description.** 1-PDTSP is a routing problem that generalizes the classical TSP. Given a set of locations and the travel distances or costs. One specific location (the starting point) is considered to be a vehicle depot, while the remaining nodes are identified as clients. Customers are divided into two groups in term of the required service. A single commodity has to be transported from some customers to the others. Customers (deliveries/pickups) supply/demand a given amount of this product. The commodity collected at pickup customers can be supplied to delivery ones. Moreover, the vehicle has a known capacity that must not be exceeded after visiting a pickup customer, must start and end

© Springer International Publishing Switzerland 2015
L. Rutkowski et al. (Eds.): ICAISC 2015, Part II, LNAI 9120, pp. 789–798, 2015.
DOI: 10.1007/978-3-319-19369-4_70

its route at the depot, and must visit each customer only once. The objective of the the 1-PDTSP consists of finding a minimum length Hamiltonian route for the vehicle that satisfies all customers' requirements. However, it is not assumed whether the vehicle leaves the depot empty or full loaded, and the initial load of the vehicle has to be determined.

Since the 1-PDTSP is NP-hard, only small size instances are solved to optimality using exact approaches. Heuristic approaches were used for solving large sized instances while generating high quality solutions. The 1-PDTSP has several real-world applications, mainly in routing a single commodity through a circular network in a graph connecting different sources and destinations. In this context we address a real case study in the city of Jendouba (Tunisia) studied by Krichen et al [9].

**Problem Statement and Notation.** We now introduce the notation used in this article. Let $G = (V, E)$ be a complete and undirected graph. The set $V = 1, 2, ..., n$ is the vertex set and $E$ is the edge set. Vertex 1 represents the depot while the other vertices from 2 to n denote customers. Each vertex is associated with demand $q_i$. Note that we have only one vehicle, that starts from the depot. The depot can be considered as a customer whose demand $q_1 = -\sum_{i=2}^{n} q_i$.

The quantity $q_1$ can represents the initial load of the vehicle if $q_1 > 0$, otherwise it represents the final load after visiting all customers.

we assume that $i$ is a pickup customer, if $q_i > 0$, otherwise, it is a delivery customer.

We denote the travel distance (or cost) between pair of locations $i, j$ by $c_{ij}$.

**Proposed Case Study.** In this paper we apply the ILS approach to a commercial firm that supplies food merchandises in the region of Jendouba located in north west of Tunisia. The results of our framework is a tour, that the vehicle should travel, is designed using a free plugin proposed by google earth: Tour Builder, in order to simplify the obtained result to the decision maker of the commercial company.

## 2    An ILS-VND Approach for the 1-PDTSP

### 2.1    Variable Neighborhood Descent

The Variable Neighborhood Descent (VND) was proposed by Hansen and Mladenovic (2003).

**Basic Concepts.** It performs as follows. Let $N_1, ..., N_n$ be the set of predefined neighborhood structures, and $N_k(s)$ be the set of solutions using the $k^{th}$ neighborhood of $s$. The local optimum $s'$ of $f$ regarding to $N_k(s)$, is a feasible solution, where no solution $s \in N_k(s')$ such that $f(s) < f(s')$. The VND is a metaheuristic that switches between neighborhoods $N_1, ..., N_n$ according to a predefined order.

Starting with the first neighborhood $N_1$, VND performs a local search until no further improvements are available. Then, from local optimum, it continues the local search with neighborhood $N_2$. If there is improvement in the current solution, VND restart with $N_1$ again; otherwise, it continues with $N_3$, and so forth.

If the last structure $N_n$ has been performed and no additional improvements are feasible, the solution corresponds to a local optimum with respect to all neighborhoods. The performance of the VND depends significantly on the choice of the neighborhoods at each iteration.[3].

## 2.2  Iterated Local Search

The fundamental idea of ILS [12] is to generate a sequence of solutions produced by an embedded heuristic. Four basic procedures are applied to operate an ILS algorithm:

- Generate Initial Solution : generate an initial solution.
- Local Search: replaces the current solution by a improvement neighbor solution.
- Perturbation: a scheme of how to perturb a solution.
- Acceptance Criterion: decide from which solution the search is continued.

The effectiveness of the ILS strongly depends on the efficiency of the four procedures so far detailed. As it is strongly influences the final solution quality ILS search procedure is the most important element [13]. Although, the perturbations mechanism aim to effectively find a local optima, avoid the disadvantages of random generation. On the other hand, the acceptance criterion and the perturbation mechanism, provides a balance among the intensification and diversification of the search.

Our proposed ILS implementation starts with an initial solution, then performs a VND implementation (in a predefined order). The perturbation mechanism performed by applying local search heuristics in sequence. The acceptance criterion is based on the improving of the incumbent solution.

## 2.3  Adaptive ILS-VND approach for 1-PDTSP

**Initialization.** For the initial solution we use a procedure from [2] since it gives good results. This method starts by a random customer $x_2$. From the set of closest customers $cl$ to the last inserted customer $x_i$, we add the next customer $x_{i+1}$ to the current sub-tour $T$. Among these $cl$ closest customers, we consider only feasible sub-tours without violating the capacity constraints with respect to the customer $x_i + 1$ to deliver or to collect the demand. Then we choose from the customers not yet been visited, the customer who can be feasibly added at the end of the tour $T$, and we select the customer with the greatest demand. Then we choose from the customers not appeared in the sub-tour $T$, the customer who can be feasibly added at the end of the tour $T$, and we select the customer with the greatest demand. If such a customer does not exist, we search for all customers not yet been visited.

---

**Algorithm 1.** *Hybrid heuristic ILS-VND for the 1-PDTSP*

---

**Input:** $cmd \leftarrow list\ of\ commands$
   $C \leftarrow capacity$
   $Matrix \leftarrow list\ of\ coordinates$
   List of neighborhoods $N_k,\ k = 1, ...., K_{max}$
1: Find the initial solution $x_0$ using a HeuristicInitSol()
2:
3: $s = x_0$
4: $k = 1$
5: **while** $k < K_{max}$ **do**
6:    $N_k$: List of neighborhoods= {Swap, Insert, Exchange, twoOpt, treeOpt, back-Insert, backThreeOpt }
7:    $s' = N_k(s)$
8:    **if** $f(s') < f(s)$ and Valid$(s)$ **then**
9:       $s = s'$
10:      $k = 1$
11:    **else**
12:      $k = k + 1$
13:    **end if**
14: **end while**
15: $x* = s$
16: **while** $t < t_{max}$ **do**
17:    $x' = $ RandubleBridge$(x*, h)$
18:    $s = x'$
19:    $k = 1$
20:    **while** $k < K_{max}$ **do**
21:      $s' = N_k(s)$
22:      **if** $f(s') < f(s)$ and Valid$(s)$ **then**
23:        $s = s'$
24:        $k = 1$
25:      **else**
26:        $k = k + 1$
27:      **end if**
28:    **end while**
29:    $x* = s$
30:    If $f(x*) <= f(x*')orf(x*) <= B$ and Valid$(s)$
31:    Accept $x* = x*'$
32:    Lower Boundary $B = B - \Delta B$
33: **end while**
**Output:** Best found tour

---

**Neighborhood Exploration and VND Order.** In our VND we used the following neighborhoods.

**Neighborhoods**

- **Swap:**The swap neighborhood leads to swapping a pairs of points location $(i, j)$. If the size of the permutation is $n$, the size of this neighborhood is $\frac{n(n-1)}{2}$.

- **Insert:** The insert neighborhood consists of removing a point location from position $i$ and reinserting it in position $j$, where $i \neq j$. The size of the INSERT neighborhood is $n(n-1)$.

- **Exchange:** [10] A classical neighborhood in permutations, is the exchange operator, where two elements $(i, j)$, $i \neq j$, are swapped. For permutation of size $n$ using the exchange operator, the cardinality of the search space is $n!$ and the maximum distance between two permutations is $n-1$ [11].

- **Back insert:** This neighborhood works in a similar way as the forward insertion, but the selected customer in the position $i$ is moved to a position $j$ such that $j < i$.

- **k-opt:** Operators drop some k edges and adds knew edges in order to reconstruct a new tour. in our work we use the 2-opt, 3-opt and 3-opt with change direction.

**Local Search and Shaking.** The shaking procedure was performed by using a neighborhood specifically designed for solving TSP named double-bridge (is a special case of 4-opt). We generate a random solution from the neighborhood by performing k double-bridge moves. The double-bridge: is a special case of 4-opt. it consist of partitioning a tour into 4 sub-tours and putting it back together in a specific and jumbled ordering. The double-bridge moves are performed on the incumbent solution, and we accept non-feasible solutions.

## 3 Experimentations

### 3.1 Experimental Design

The experiments were tried on the benchmark instances of 1-PDTSP published by Hernandez-Perez in [4] available at
http://webpages.ull.es/users/hhperez/PDsite/#XM94.

The proposed benchmark instances are randomly generated in the following way. The n-1 nodes are randomly spread in the square $[-500, 500]$ X $[-500, 500]$. Each customer has a demand $q_i (2 < i < n)$ randomly chosen and it belong to thee interval $[-10, 10]$. The depot is located in the origin $(0, 0)$, it has a demand $q_1 = -\sum_{i=2}^{n} q_i$.

The vehicle has a capacity value from the set 10, 20, 40. The randomly generated instances are denoted by (A, B, B, C, D, E, F, G, H, and I).

In our experiments, we report the minimum values obtained on those 10 problem instances provided by the studied algorithms.

### 3.2 Computations

Tables 1, 2, and 3 report experimental results by applying ILS-VND heuristic and compute the improvement where embedding the ILS with the VND heuristic.

**Table 1.** Comparison of the results on the benchmark instances; $n = 20$ and $Q = 10$

| Instance | VND | ILS-VND | Improvement (%) |
|---|---|---|---|
| A | 5141 | 4964 | 1.77 |
| B | 5238 | 4980 | 2.58 |
| C | 6523 | 6340 | 1.28 |
| D | 6557 | 6280 | 2.77 |
| E | 6600 | 6466 | 1.34 |
| F | 5150 | 4855 | 2.95 |
| G | 5395 | 5195 | 2 |
| H | 5785 | 5594 | 1.91 |
| I | 5341 | 5130 | 2.11 |
| J | 4560 | 4410 | 1.5 |

**Table 2.** Comparison of the results on the benchmark instances fol $n = 20$ and $Q = 20$

| Instance | VND | ILS-VND | Improvement (%) |
|---|---|---|---|
| A | 4107 | 3817 | 2.9 |
| B | 4394 | 4244 | 1.5 |
| C | 4797 | 4500 | 2.9 |
| D | 4820 | 4706 | 1.14 |
| E | 4750 | 4675 | 0.7 |
| F | 4250 | 4118 | 1.32 |
| G | 4473 | 4370 | 1.03 |
| H | 4230 | 4163 | 0.67 |
| I | 4218 | 4116 | 1.02 |
| J | 3820 | 3703 | 1.17 |

**Table 3.** Comparison of the results on the benchmark instances for $n = 20$ and $Q = 40$

| Instance | VND | ILS-VND | Improvement (%) |
|----------|------|---------|-----------------|
| A | 3905 | 3817 | 0.8 |
| B | 4102 | 3942 | 1.6 |
| C | 3980 | 3900 | 0.8 |
| D | 3877 | 3745 | 1.32 |
| E | 4450 | 4301 | 1.49 |
| F | 4315 | 4118 | 1.97 |
| G | 4345 | 4250 | 0.95 |
| H | 4217 | 4009 | 1.08 |
| I | 4215 | 4026 | 1.89 |
| J | 3865 | 3679 | 1.86 |

**Table 4.** Main steps of the DSS

| Initialization | Optimization | Results | Tour viewer |
|----------------|--------------|---------|-------------|

| costumer | 1 | 2 | 3 | 4 | 5 | ... |
|----------|---|---|---|---|---|-----|
| demand | -9 | 8 | 3 | 1 | 1 | ... |

We can note from these results that the perturbation mechanism of the ILS algorithm has a significant importance since it provides better results in term of solution quality for corresponding problem. It appears that at the ILS algorithm outperforms the VND approach in terms of solution quality among 70% for all instances.

This can justify the importance of the perturbation of the local optimum provided by the VND and the right parametrization of our approach with regard to the problem instances.

# 4    A DSS Design for a Transportation Firm in the City of Jendouba: Tunisia

In order to test the proposed approach, we experiment it for a commercial firm that supply merchandises in the region of Jendouba in the north west of Tunisia.

We consider a set of 30 customers' within the addressed area, knowing that the customers are divided into deliveries and pickups. We assume that the the capacity of the vehicle is 30 and the proposed customers' demands in the interval [-9,9]. Table 4 reports the geographical coordinates of the considered case study. The customers' demands are given in table 4.

**Table 5.** Geographical coordinates $n = 30$

| $i$ | Longitude | Latitude | $i$ | Longitude | Latitude |
|---|---|---|---|---|---|
| Depot | 36.493078 | 8.778076 | 16 | 36.501909 | 8.55011 |
| 1 | 36.540536 | 8.857727 | 17 | 36.487557 | 8.4375 |
| 2 | 36.602299 | 8.843994 | 18 | 36.507429 | 8.53363 |
| 3 | 36.574732 | 8.912659 | 19 | 36.546053 | 8.64624 |
| 4 | 36.677231 | 8.835754 | 20 | 36.512947 | 8.598862 |
| 5 | 36.612221 | 8.964844 | 21 | 36.620488 | 8.686066 |
| 6 | 36.520673 | 9.044495 | 22 | 36.660708 | 8.691559 |
| 7 | 36.475411 | 8.99231 | 23 | 36.673926 | 8.638 |
| 8 | 36.421282 | 8.927765 | 24 | 36.743836 | 8.681259 |
| 9 | 36.354951 | 8.956604 | 25 | 36.69375 | 8.618088 |
| 10 | 36.333934 | 8.784943 | 26 | 36.663462 | 8.690186 |
| 11 | 36.364904 | 8.692932 | 27 | 36.59403 | 8.744431 |
| 12 | 36.337253 | 8.578949 | 28 | 36.64308 | 8.831635 |
| 13 | 36.45995 | 8.633881 | 29 | 36.604504 | 8.769836 |
| 14 | 36.415757 | 8.567963 | 30 | 36.660157 | 8.55835 |
| 15 | 36.457741 | 8.467712 | | | |

**Table 6.** Customers' demands

| i | $d_i$ | C | i | $d_i$ | C | i | $d_i$ | C |
|---|---|---|---|---|---|---|---|---|
| 1 | -9 | D | 11 | 1 | P | 21 | -6 | D |
| 2 | 8 | P | 12 | 3 | P | 22 | 9 | P |
| 3 | 3 | P | 13 | -3 | D | 23 | 7 | P |
| 4 | 1 | P | 14 | -9 | D | 24 | -9 | D |
| 5 | 1 | P | 15 | -8 | D | 25 | -6 | D |
| 6 | 5 | P | 16 | 5 | P | 26 | 8 | P |
| 7 | 8 | P | 17 | -7 | D | 27 | -6 | D |
| 8 | 9 | P | 18 | -7 | D | 28 | 6 | P |
| 9 | 1 | P | 19 | -1 | D | 29 | 1 | P |
| 10 | 0 | P | 20 | -5 | D | 30 | 5 | P |

In this study we used Google Earth (plugin: Tour Builder). The tour to be traveled by the vehicle, determined by our ILS, shown in figure below and designd by Tour Builder.

## 5 Summary and Conclusions

We developed in this paper an efficient hybrid heuristic algorithm ILS-VND for solving the one-commodity pickup-and-delivery travelling talesman problem (1-PDTSP). A VND procedure with a set of neighborhood structures is integrated in the ILS local search phase. The ILS-VND provided better results, in terms of solution quality, than the VND results. Besides, our approach was applied on a real application and it showed its effectiveness in generating promising results.

## References

1. Hernandez-Perez, H., Salazar-Gonzalez, J.J.: Heuristics for the onecommodity pickup-and-delivery travelling salesman problem. Transportation Science 38, 245–255 (2004)
2. Zhao, F., Li, S., Sun, J., Mei, D.: Genetic algorithm for the one-commodity pickup-and-delivery travelling salesman problem. Computers & Industrial Engineering 56, 1642–1648 (2009)
3. Puchinger, J., Raidl, G.: Bringing order into the neighborhoods: relaxation guided variable neighborhood search. J. of Heuristics 14, 457–472 (2008)
4. Hernandez-Perez, H., Rodriguez-Martin, I., Salazar-Gonzalez, J.J.: A hybrid GRASP/VND heuristic for the one-commodity pickup-and-delivery travelling salesman problem. Computers & Operations Research 36, 1639–1645 (2009)

5. Mladenovic, N., Urosevic, D., Hanafi, S., Ilic, A.: A general variable neighborhood search for the one-commodity pickup-and-delivery travelling salesman problem. European Journal of Operational Research 220, 270–285 (2012)
6. Chalasani, P., Motwani, R.: Approximating capacitated routing and delivery problems. SIAM Journal on Computing 28, 2133–2149 (1999)
7. Parragh, S.N., Doerner, K.F., Hartl, R.F.: A survey on pickup and delivery problems. Part I: Transportation between customers and depot. Journal fur Betriebswirtschaft 58, 21–51 (2008)
8. Parragh, S.N., Doerner, K.F., Hartl, R.F.: A survey on pickup and delivery problems. Part II: Transportation between pickup and delivery locations. Journal fur Betriebswirtschaft 58, 81–117 (2008)
9. Faiz, S., Krichen, S., Inoubli, W.: A DSS based on GIS and Tabu search for solving the CVRP: The Tunisian case. The Egyptian Journal of Remote Sensing and Space Sciences 17, 105–110 (2014)
10. Geiger, M.J.: On heuristic search for the single machine total weighted tardiness problem- some theoretical insights and their empirical verification. EJOR 207(3), 1235–1243 (2010)
11. Talbi, E.-G.: Metaheuristics: From Design to Implementation
12. Lourenco, H.R., Martin, O., Stutzle, T.: Iterated Local Search, pp. 321–353. Kluwer Academic Publishers, Norwell (2002)
13. den Besten, M., Stützle, T., Dorigo, M.: Design of iterated local search algorithms: An example application to the single machine total weighted tardiness problem. In: Boers, E.J.W., et al. (eds.) EvoIASP 2001, EvoWorkshops 2001, EvoFlight 2001, EvoSTIM 2001, EvoCOP 2001, and EvoLearn 2001. LNCS, vol. 2037, pp. 441–452. Springer, Heidelberg (2001)

# On Enhancing the Label Propagation Algorithm for Sentiment Analysis Using Active Learning with an Artificial Oracle

Anis Yazidi, Hugo Lewi Hammer, Aleksander Bai, and Paal Engelstad[✉]

Department of Computer Science,
Oslo and Akershus University College of Applied Sciences, Oslo, Norway
{anis.yazidi,hugo.hammer,aleksander.bai,paal.engelstad}@hioa.no

**Abstract.** A core component of Sentiment Analysis is the generation of sentiment lists. Label propagation is equivocally one of the most used approaches for generating sentiment lists based on annotated seed words in a manual manner. Words which are situated many hops away from the seed words tend to get low sentiment values. Such inherent property of the Label Propagation algorithm poses a controversial challenge in sentiment analysis. In this paper, we propose an iterative approach based on the theory of Active Learning [1] that attempts to remedy to this problem *without* any need for additional manual labeling. Our algorithm is bootstrapped with a limited amount of seeds. Then, at each iteration, a fixed number of "informative words" are selected as new seeds for labeling according to different criteria that we will elucidate in the paper. Subsequently, the Label Propagation is retrained in the next iteration with the additional labeled seeds. A major contribution of this article is that, unlike the theory of Active Learning that prompts the user for additional labeling, we generate the additional seeds with an *Artificial Oracle*. This is radically different from the main stream of Active Learning Theory that resorts to a human (user) as oracle for labeling those additional seeds. Consequently, we relieve the user from the cumbersome task of manual annotation while still achieving a high performance. The lexicons were evaluated by classifying product and movie reviews. Most of the generated sentiment lexicons using Active learning perform better than the Label Propagation algorithm.

**Keywords:** Sentiment analysis · Label propagation · Active learning

# 1 Introduction

With the increasing amount of unstructured textual information available on the Internet, sentiment analysis and opinion mining have recently gained a groundswell of interest from the research community as well as among practitioners. In general terms, sentiment analysis attempts to automate the classification of text materials as either expressing positive sentiment or negative sentiment. Such classification is particularity interesting for making sense of huge amount

© Springer International Publishing Switzerland 2015
L. Rutkowski et al. (Eds.): ICAISC 2015, Part II, LNAI 9120, pp. 799–810, 2015.
DOI: 10.1007/978-3-319-19369-4_71

of text information and extracting the "word of mouth" from product reviews, and political discussions etc.

Possessing beforehand a sentiment lexicon is a key element in the task of applying sentimental analysis on a phrase or document level. A sentiment lexicon is merely composed of sentiment words and sentiment phrases (idioms) characterized by sentiment polarity, positive or negative, and by sentimental strength. For example, the word 'excellent' has positive polarity and high strength whereas the word 'good' is also positive but has a lower strength. Once a lexicon is built and in place, a range of different approaches can be deployed to classify the sentiment in a text as positive or negative. These approaches range from simply computing the difference between the sum of the scores of the positive lexicon and sum of the scores of the negative lexicon, and subsequently classifying the sentiment in the text according to the sign of the difference.

In order to generate a sentiment lexicon, the most obvious and naive approach involves manual generation. Nevertheless, the manual generation is tedious and time consuming rendering it an impractical task.

Due to the difficulty of manual generation, a significant amount of research has been dedicated to presenting approaches for automatically building sentiment lexicon. To alleviate the task of lexicon generation, the research community has suggested a myriad of semi-automatic schemes that falls mainly under two families: dictionary-based family and corpus-based family. Both families are semi-automatic because the underlying idea is to bootstrap the generation from a short list of words (seed words), however they differ in the methodology for iteratively building the lexicon.

The majority of dictionary-based approaches form a graph of the words in a dictionary, where the words correspond to nodes and where relations between the words (e.g. in terms of synonyms, antonyms and/or hyponyms) may form the edges. A limited number of seed words are manually assigned a positive or a negative sentiment value (or label), and an algorithm, such as the Label Propagation mechanism proposed in [2], is used to automatically assign sentiment scores to the other non-seed words in the graph.

Label propagation is one of the most used semi-automatic methods for generating sentiment lists based on seed words. A major drawback of Label Propagation in these settings resides in the fact that words which are situated many hops away from the seed words tend to get low sentiment values. Such phenomenon poses a controversial challenge in sentiment analysis as words that have high sentiment values can end up with a low score.

In this paper, we propose an iterative approach to Label Propagation that is based on the principles of Active Learning theory. Our approach boosts the propagation process and avoids having labels that get low scores only because they merely are located many hops away from a seed word. Our work presents a two-fold contribution. First, to the best of our knowledge, this is the first reported work in lexicon generation that embraces the theory of Active Learning as a tool for enhancing the Label Propagation process. Unlike Active Learning, our approach does not require prompting the user to label some "informative examples", but we will rather do it in an automatic manner using an Artificial Oracle, thus alleviating the user from the burden of annotation. In fact, the manual annotation of seeds is a cumbersome and time-consuming task that we will attempt to minimize. Furthermore, different methods will be presented for selection procedures of the seed words to be annotated.

Another latent motivation in this article is to investigate the potential of generating lexicon in an automatic manner without any human intervention or refinement. We try to achieve this by increasing the sources of information, namely three different thesauruses, instead of solely relying on a single thesaurus as commonly done in the literature. In fact, we suggest that by increasing the number of thesauruses we can increase the quality of the generated lexicon.

Finally, while most of research in the field of sentiment analysis has been centered on the English language, little work has been reported for smaller languages where there is a shortage of good sentiment lists. In this paper, we tackle the problem of building sentiment lexicon for a smaller language, and use the Norwegian language as an example.

## 1.1 Background Work

The underlying idea of a dictionary-based approach is to build the lexicon based on a dictionary containing synonyms and antonyms, and possibly hyponyms. A set of seed words is used to iteratively extend the list by resorting to the synonym and antonym structure. A word-graph is formed where a word corresponds to a node and a relationship between two words (e.g. a synonym relationship) corresponds to an edge. The intuitive idea behind the approach is that polarity of a sentiment word is preserved by a synonym relationship and inverted by an antonym relationship.

Dictionary-based approaches were introduced by Hu and Liu in their seminal work [3]. They stop the generation when no more words can be added to the list. Mohammad, Dunne and Dorr [4] used a rather subtle and elegant enhancement of Hu and Liu's work [5,3] by exploiting the antonym-generating prefixes and suffixes in order to include more words in the lexicon. In [6], the authors constructed an undirected graph based on adjectives in WordNet [7] and define distance between two words as the shortest path in WordNet. The polarity of an adjective is then defined as the sign of the difference between its distance from the word "bad" and its distance from the word "good". While the strength of the sentiment depends on the later quantity as well as the distance between words "bad" and "good".

Blair and his colleagues [8] employ a novel bootstrapping idea in order to counter the effect of neutral words in lexicon generation and thus improve the quality of the lexicon. The idea is to bootstrap the generation with neutral seed in addition to a positive and a negative seed. The neutral seeds are used to avoid positive and negative sentiment propagation through neutral words. The latter work uses a modified version of the label propagation algorithm proposed in [2]. The label propagation algorithms have an initial phase: where a score $+1$ is assigned to positive seed words and a score $-1$ to negative seed words, and 0 to the rest of words obtained through bootstrapping, then the transfer of score is performed from the seed to the rest of words using the simple idea that the sentiment of a word is the average of its neighbor. Note that the scores are updated in an iterative manner.

Rao and Ravichandran [9] used semi-supervised techniques based on two variants of the Mincut algorithm [10] in order to separate the positive words and negative words in the graph generated by means of bootstrapping. In simple words, Mincut algorithms [10] are used in graph theory in order to partition a graph into two partitions minimizing the number of nodes possessing strong similarity being placed in different partitions. Rao and Ravichandran [9] employed only the synonym relationship as a similarity metric between two nodes in the graph. The results are encouraging and show some advantages of using Mincut over label propagation.

In [11], Hassan and Radev use elements from the theory of random walks of lexicon generation. The distance between two words in the graph is defined based on the notion of hitting time. The hitting time $h(i|S)$is the average number hops it takes for a node $i$ to reach a node in the set $S$. A word $w$ is classified as positive if $h(w|S_+) > h(w|S_-)$ and vice versa, where $S_+$ denotes the set of positive seed words, and $S_-$ refers to the set of negative seed words.

Kim and Hovy [12] resorts to the Bayesian theory for assigning the most probable label (here polarity) of a bootstrapped word.

In [13], a hybrid approach was proposed that combines both elements from corpus based approaches and dictionary based approaches. In fact, the bootstrapping is done based on a dictionary while the score assigning is based on corpus.

It is worth mentioning that another research direction for building lexicon for foreign language is based on exploiting the well-developed English sentiment lexicon. A representative work of such approaches is reported in [14].

## 1.2    Active Learning Theory

The merit of Active Learning [1] manifests in situations where there is an abundant amount of data to be labeled, while the amount of available labeled data is scarce. Usually, in normal supervised learning situations, we have enough labels in order to build a classifier that has good classification performance. Thus, the theory of Active Learning attempts to solve this problem by proposing ways to intelligently choose very few informative data points to label. Then the user/human is prompted to return labels for these carefully chosen data points. In this sense, Active Learning idea identifies some data points whose labeling can present a high value for the classification and then prompts the user to label them. A lot of work in the field of Active Learning is concerned with algorithms for devising schemes for selecting the data points to be annotated. Without loss of generality, we claim that the closest Active Learning approach to our work [1] is "Query by committee" where the labels that the committee disagrees most are chosen for manual labeling.

In Active Learning, a selection procedure is used in order to select the informative examples to be labeled, and then the user is actively asked for annotation. Thus, the user plays the role of an oracle for labeling.

In this article, the oracle is not a human but rather an Artificial Oracle (i.e, algorithm). Therefore, we relieve the human user from the manual task of annotation. We use the term Artificial Oracle for describing the oracle in order to emphasize the difference between the user as oracle and an algorithm as oracle. Despite that relying on the Artificial Oracle for annotating the informative examples introduces some inaccuracy, we were still able to get good performance.

## 2   The Novel Approach

A major shortcoming of the Label Propagation algorithm [2] is that while the seed values are propagated throughout the word graph of synonyms, the algorithm does not take into account that for each edge between two synonyms, there is an introduction of inaccuracy. The source of inaccuracy is primarily that the meaning of two synonyms is typically not overlapping. A synonym of a word might carry a different and skewed meaning and sentiment compared to the meaning and sentiment of the word. Thus, the sentiment value of a word is not a 100% trustworthy indicator of the value that should be propagated to its synonyms. Problems are typically observed in the middle area between the positive and the negative seed words, i.e. typically several hops away from any seed word. While other works have introduced fixes to this problem (e.g. by introducing neutral seed words as described above), we take a different approach to the solution.

To account for this effect, we propose a novel approach that combines the ideas from Label Propagation and the Active Learning, and that focuses on the shortest path between a word and the seed words. This is described in the following section.

### 2.1   Description of the Main Algorithm

Our Active Learning base algorithm consists of four phases, which are executed iteratively for a fixed number of iterations:

- Running the label propagation
- Selecting the *Top L* lowest absolute values of the scores.
- Among the top *Top L* values, apply a *Selection Algorithm* in order to select a subset of $K$ informative words for automatic labeling
- Annotate the later subset of informative words using *Annotation Based Graph Voting Procedure*

The formal algorithm, which puts all the pieces of this puzzle together, follows in Algorithm 1.

The core elements of our algorithm are delineated in the following two sections. In section 2.2, we will describe the *Annotation Based Graph Voting* (ABGV) procedure and in section 2.3 the different variants of *Selection Procedure*.

## Algorithm 1. Main_Algorithm

**Input:**      $G = (V, E)$, is the graph built from the dictionaries.
$\mathcal{S} = \{s \in V \text{such that } s \text{ is seed}\}$
$\mathcal{W} = \{w \in V \text{such that } w \text{ is not a seed word}\}$.
Finite number of iterations $N$.

**Output:**    $Score(\mathcal{S}) = \{score(w) \text{ such that } w \in \mathcal{W}\}$.
**Method:**
 1: **for** iteration $\leq$ N **do**
 2:     Apply Label Propagation on $G$
 3:     Identify $\mathcal{Z} = \{w \in \mathcal{W} \text{ such that } |score(w)| \text{ is among the } Top\ L \text{ lowest values}\}$.
 4:     Apply a *Selection Procedure* to select a subset $\mathcal{Z}' \subset \mathcal{Z}$.
 5:     **for** each $w$ in $\mathcal{Z}'$ **do**
 6:         **if** $\mathcal{V}_p(w) \geq \mathcal{V}_N(w)$ (Annotation Based Graph Voting Procedure) **then**
 7:             $score(w) = +5$
 8:         **else**
 9:             $score(w) = -5$
10:         **end if**
11:     **end for**
12: **end for**
End Main_Algorithm

## 2.2   The Annotation Based Graph Voting Procedure

The Annotation Based Graph Voting (ABGC) Procedure is responsible for annotating a word $w$ that is selected by the *Selection Procedure*.

For a given word selected by the *Selection Procedure* to be a seed word, the oracle annotates it by considering what we define as positive and negative votes from all the seed words. To vote focuses on the shortest path between a word and a seed word and accounts for the number of antonyms along that path.

We shall now define what is meant by the term vote.

Let $\mathcal{V}(s \rightarrow w)$ be the vote of seed $s$ to a word $w$.

- $\mathcal{V}(s \rightarrow w) = +1$, i.e, positive vote from seed $s$ to word $w$, if one of the following two cases takes place:
  - if $score(s) > 0$ and number of *antonyms* along the *shortest path* from $s$ to $w$ in the graph $G$ is *even*.
  - or $score(s) < 0$ and number of *antonyms* along the shortest path is odd.
- $\mathcal{V}(s \rightarrow w) = -1$, i.e, negative vote from seed $s$ to word $w$, if one of the following two cases is valid:
  - $score(s) < 0$ and number of *antonyms* along the shortest path is even.
  - or $score(s) > 0$ and and number of *antonyms* along the shortest path is odd.

We define $\mathcal{V}_P(w)$ as the total number of positive votes to word $w$, or formally as the cardinality of the set $\{s \in \mathcal{S} \text{ such that } \mathcal{V}(s \rightarrow w) = +1\}$. Similarly, we define $\mathcal{V}_N(w)$ as the total number of negative votes to word $w$, or formally as the cardinality of the set $\{s \in \mathcal{S}$ such that $\mathcal{V}(s \to w) = -1\}$.

$\mathcal{V}_p(w) = \sum_{s \in \mathcal{S}} I(\mathcal{V}(s \to w) = -1)$

Similarly, $\mathcal{V}_N(w) = \sum_{w \in \mathcal{S}} I(\mathcal{V}(s \to w) = +1)$

Where $I(\cdot)$ is the indicator function.

The idea behind the voting procedure is that an even number of antonyms along the shortest path from a seed to a word would preserves the sentiment polarity since antonym of antonym is synonym. Similarly, an odd number of antonyms along the shortest path from a seed to a word would invert the sentiment polarity.

*Artificial Oracle:* The informed reader should note that a crucial element of our approach is that we do not prompt the user (human) to label the words returned by the *Selection Procedure*, but we rather develop a simple and intuitive method for automatically annotating these words without human intervention using an Artificial Oracle. The motivation behind the automatic annotation is based on the concept of voting.

### 2.3 The Selection Procedure

The Selection Procedure is responsible for choosing at each iteration a set of informative words to be annotated. This is achieved using a set of approaches or variants that we shall describe in this section.

At each iteration, the Selection Procedure selects $K$ words for automatic annotation from $\mathcal{Z} = \{w \in \mathcal{W}$ such that $|score(w)|$ is among the *Top L* lowest values$\}$.

However, it is difficult to judge whenever a word gets a score around 0, whether it is neutral word or just far away from the seed. In order to counter this, we develop range of different strategies to decide this, as outlined in the following.

**Purity Based Selection.** Low certainty is measured using the notion of Purity, and captures the case where the number of positive votes is significantly larger than the number negative votes or vice-versa. Let us define the entropy of a word of $w$ in the graph as:

$$H(w) = -(p_P(w) \log p_P(w) + p_N(w) \log p_N(w))$$

where $p_P(w) = \mathcal{V}_P(w)/(\mathcal{V}_P(w)+\mathcal{V}_N(w))$ and $p_N(w) = \mathcal{V}_N(w)/(\mathcal{V}_P(w)+\mathcal{V}_N(w))$. The Purity is defined as $P(w) = 1 - H(w)$.

**Centrality Based Approach.** We select the Top $K$ most *central* words for automatic annotation from $L$ lowest values based on two definition of centrality:

- *High betweenness centrality*: captures the fact that a node lies in the path of a high number of shortest pathes in the whole graph. Betweeness centrality can be useful for many algorithms in order to locate nodes that are important for vehiculating some sort of information between the different nodes in the graph, where we suppose that this information flows through the shortest path.

- *High Closeness Centrality*: captures the concept that a node might be important locally within its own cluster since it is connected to many nodes in the cluster. Thus, a node that is near to the center of local clusters will have high centrality.

**Weighted Centrality and Purity Based Approach.** We define a weighted function that is a compromise between two of the aforementioned Selection Procedures, namely high closeness centrality and high purity. At each iteration, the Selection Procedure selects $K$ words for automatic annotation from the *Top L* lowest absolute values of the scores that have the following highest score:

$$\beta_1 CC(w) + \beta_2 P(w) \tag{1}$$

where $CC(w)$ defines the closeness centrality while $P(w)$ the purity, and $\beta_1$, $\beta_2$ are normalized weights . Intuitively, we try to find a balance between choosing the locally central nodes, and the nodes that have high purity, which might indicate a strong sentiment strength.

**Other strategies.** In addition to strategies above we also consider the following two simple strategies

- We select the nodes which are closest to zero among the lowest $L$ scores around 0, thus the nodes with the lowest value in absolute value in the whole graph.
- We sample randomly a subset from the pool of the lowest $L$ scores around 0.

## 3    Linguistic Resources and Benchmark Lexicons for Evaluation

### 3.1    Building a Word Graph From Thesauruses

We built a large undirected graph of synonym and antonym relations between words from the three Norwegian thesauruses [15]. The words were nodes in the graph and synonym and antonym relations were edges. The full graph consisted of a total of 6036 nodes (words) and 16475 edges.

For all lexicons generated from the word graph, we started with a set of 109 seed words (51 positive and 57 negative). The words were manually selected where all used frequently in the Norwegian language and spanned different dimensions of positive ('happy', 'clever', 'intelligent', 'love' etc.) and negative sentiment ('lazy', 'aggressive', 'hopeless', 'chaotic' etc.).

## 3.2   Benchmark Lexicons

We generated sentiment lexicons from the word graph using the Label Propagation algorithm [2] which is the most popular method to generate sentiment lexicons.

As a complement to the graph-generated lexicons, we generated a benchmark sentiment lexicon by translating the well-known English sentiment lexicon AFINN [16] to Norwegian using machine translation (Google translate). We also generated a second lexicon by manually checking and correcting several different errors from the machine translation.

## 3.3   Text Resources for Evaluation

We tested the quality of the created sentiment lexicons using 15118 product reviews from the Norwegian online shopping sites www.komplett.no, mpx.no and 4149 movie reviews from www.filmweb.no. Each product review contained a rating from one to five, five being the best and the movie reviews a rating from one to six, six being the best.

## 4   Evaluation of Novel Approach Against Benchmark Lexicons

We generated a sentiment lexicon by applying our novel approach in Section 2 to the same word graph used for the Label Propagation benchmark lexicon, and by using the same seed words.

For each lexicon, we computed the sentiment score of a review by simply adding the score of each sentiment word in a sentiment lexicon together, which is the most common way to do it [17]. If the sentiment shifter 'not' ('ikke') was one or two words in front of a sentiment word, sentiment score was switched. E.g. 'happy' ('glad') is given sentient score 0.8, while 'not happy' ('ikke glad') is given score −0.8. Finally, the sum is divided by the number of words in the review, giving us the final sentiment score for the review. We also considered other sentiment shifter, e.g. 'never' ('aldri'), and other distance between sentiment word and shifter, but our approach seems to be the best for such lexicon approaches in Norwegian [18].

**Classification performance.** We evaluated the classification performance using average difference in absolute value between the true and predicted rating based on sentiment lexicons. For details, see [15].

## 5   Results

This section presents the results of classification performance on product and movie reviews for different sentiment lexicons. The results are shown in Tables 1

**Table 1.** Classification performance for sentiment lexicons on `komplett.no` and `mpx.no` product reviews. The number of words automatically annotated si 40. The columns from left to right show the sentiment lexicon names, the number of words in the sentiment lexicons, the mean absolute error with standard deviation and the 95% confidence intervals for mean absolute error.

|  | N | Mean (Stdev) | 95% conf.int. |
|---|---|---|---|
| AFINN | 6036 | 1.43 (1.41) | (1.4, 1.47) |
| AFINN_M | 6036 | 1.47 (1.39) | (1.44, 1.5) |
| ZERO | 6036 | 1.49 (1.38) | (1.46, 1.52) |
| BETWEENESS | 6036 | 1.51 (1.42) | (1.48, 1.54) |
| PC_0.5_0.5 | 6036 | 1.52 (1.4) | (1.49, 1.55) |
| CLOSENESS | 6036 | 1.53 (1.38) | (1.5, 1.56) |
| PC_0.7_0.3 | 6036 | 1.56 (1.41) | (1.53, 1.6) |
| PURITY | 6036 | 1.57 (1.44) | (1.54, 1.6) |
| SAMPLING | 6036 | 1.58 (1.46) | (1.55, 1.61) |
| PC_0.3_0.7 | 6036 | 1.61 (1.46) | (1.58, 1.64) |
| LABEL | 6036 | 1.69 (1.51) | (1.66, 1.72) |

and 2. AFINN and AFINN_M refer to the translated and manually adjusted AFINN sentiment lists. LABEL refers to the Label propagation algorithm. ZERO refers to closest to zero, PC refers to the weighting between purity and centrality. Further CLOSENESS and BETWEENESS, refer to closeness and betweenness centrality and finally SAMPLING refers to random sampling of nodes to be annotated. Training and test sets were created by randomly adding an equal amount of reviews to both sets. All sentiment lexicons were trained and tested on the same training and test sets, making comparisons easier. This procedure were also repeated several times and every time the results were in practice identical to the results in Tables 1 and 2, documenting that the results are independent of which reviews that were added to the training and test sets.

For both review types we observe some variations in classification performance ranging from 1.43 to 1.69 for product reviews and from 1.87 to 2.08 for movie reviews. Comparing Tables 1 and 2, we see that the classification performance is poorer for movie reviews than for product reviews. It is known from the literature that sentiment analysis of movie reviews is normally harder than product reviews [17]. E.g. movie reviews typically contain a summary of the plot of the movie that could contain many negative sentiment words (sad movie), but still the movie can get an excellent rating.

We see that most of the active learning strategies performs better than the Label propagation algorithm. Among the active learning approaches, we see that the ZERO strategy performs the best indicating that detecting nodes that are close to zero is an effective strategy to build reliable sentiment lists. The PURITY strategy seems to perform poorer than the BETWEENESS and CLOSENESS centrality strategies. The automatically generated sentiment lexicons are also competitive to the translated AFINN lists. We also considered cases where the number of automatically annotated words was 30 and 50 and the results were similar to the results above.

**Table 2.** Classification performance for sentiment lexicons on `filmweb.no` movie reviews. The number of words automatically annotated is 40. The columns from left to right show the sentiment lexicon names, the number of words in the sentiment lexicons, mean absolute error with standard deviation and 95% confidence intervals for mean absolute error.

|              | N    | Mean (Stdev) | 95% conf.int.  |
|--------------|------|--------------|----------------|
| ZERO         | 6036 | 1.87 (1.1)   | (1.82, 1.91)   |
| PC_0.7_0.3   | 6036 | 1.88 (1.14)  | (1.84, 1.93)   |
| SAMPLING     | 6036 | 1.94 (1.11)  | (1.89, 1.99)   |
| PC_0.5_0.5   | 6036 | 1.95 (1.13)  | (1.9, 2)       |
| CLOSENESS    | 6036 | 1.96 (1.1)   | (1.91, 2)      |
| AFINN        | 6036 | 2.02 (1.12)  | (1.97, 2.07)   |
| PC_0.3_0.7   | 6036 | 2.04 (1.1)   | (1.99, 2.08)   |
| AFINN_M      | 6036 | 2.04 (1.17)  | (1.99, 2.09)   |
| LABEL        | 6036 | 2.05 (1.1)   | (2, 2.1)       |
| BETWEENESS   | 6036 | 2.07 (1.12)  | (2.02, 2.11)   |
| PURITY       | 6036 | 2.08 (1.11)  | (2.04, 2.13)   |

# 6 Conclusion

In this paper, we have shown that an approach inspired by Active Learning theory offer a new promising alternative for overcoming the limitations of Label Propagation. In fact, we propose different methods for intelligently selecting seed words for labeling. In addition, we alleviate the user from manual annotation of the selected seed words by introducing an Artificial Oracle. Comprehensive simulation results demonstrate the feasibility of our approach. As a future work, we would like to compare Active Learning based on human annotation with our Artificial Oracle based approach.

# References

1. Settles, B.: Active learning. Synthesis Lectures on Artificial Intelligence and Machine Learning 6(1), 1–114 (2012)
2. Zhu, X., Ghahramani, Z.: Learning from labeled and unlabeled data with label propagation. Technical report, Technical Report CMU-CALD-02-107, Carnegie Mellon University (2002)
3. Hu, M., Liu, B.: Mining opinion features in customer reviews. In: Proceedings of AAAI, pp. 755–760 (2004)
4. Mohammad, S., Dunne, C., Dorr, B.: Generating high-coverage semantic orientation lexicons from overtly marked words and a thesaurus. In: Proceedings of the 2009 Conference on Empirical Methods in Natural Language Processing, vol. 2, pp. 599–608. Association for Computational Linguistics (2009)
5. Hu, M., Liu, B.: Mining and summarizing customer reviews. In: Proceedings of the ACM SIGKDD Conference on Knowledge Discovery and Data Mining (KDD), pp. 168–177 (2004)
6. Kamps, J., Marx, M., Mokken, R.J., De Rijke, M.: Using wordnet to measure semantic orientations of adjectives (2004)

7. Miller, G.A.: Wordnet: a lexical database for english. Communications of the ACM 38(11), 39–41 (1995)
8. Blair-Goldensohn, S., Hannan, K., McDonald, R., Neylon, T., Reis, G.A., Reynar, J.: Building a sentiment summarizer for local service reviews. In: WWW Workshop on NLP in the Information Explosion Era, p. 14 (2008)
9. Rao, D., Ravichandran, D.: Proceedings of the 12th Conference of the European Chapter of the Association for Computational Linguistics. In: Association for Computational Linguistics, pp. 675–682 (2009)
10. Blum, A., Lafferty, J., Rwebangira, M.R., Reddy, R.: Semi-supervised learning using randomized mincuts. In: Proceedings of the twenty-first International Conference on Machine Learning, p. 13. ACM (2004)
11. Hassan, A., Radev, D.: Identifying text polarity using random walks. In: Proceedings of the 48th Annual Meeting of the Association for Computational Linguistics, pp. 395–403. Association for Computational Linguistics (2010)
12. Kim, S.M., Hovy, E.: Automatic identification of pro and con reasons in online reviews. In: Proceedings of the COLING/ACL on Main Conference Poster Sessions, pp. 483–490. Association for Computational Linguistics (2006)
13. Peng, W., Park, D.H.: Generate adjective sentiment dictionary for social media sentiment analysis using constrained nonnegative matrix factorization. Urbana 51, 61801 (2004)
14. Hassan, A., Abu-Jbara, A., Jha, R., Radev, D.: Identifying the semantic orientation of foreign words. In: Proceedings of the 49th Annual Meeting of the Association for Computational Linguistics: Human Language Technologies: Short Papers-Volume 2, pp. 592–597. Association for Computational Linguistics (2011)
15. Hammer, H., Bai, A., Yazidi, A., Engelstad, P.: Building sentiment lexicons applying graph theory on information from three Norwegian thesauruses. In: Norweian Informatics Conference (2014)
16. Nielsen, F.Å.: A new ANEW: Evaluation of a word list for sentiment analysis in microblogs. CoRR abs/1103.2903 (2011)
17. Bing, L.: Web Data Mining. Exploring Hyperlinks, Contents, and Usage Data. Springer (2011)
18. Hammer, H.L., Solberg, P.E., Øvrelid, L.: Sentiment classification of online political discussions: a comparison of a word-based and dependency-based method. In: Proceedings of the 5th Workshop on Computational Approaches to Subjectivity, Sentiment and Social Media Analysis, pp. 90–96. Association for Computational Linguistics (2014)

# Author Index